Contents

PART IV: ELECTRONIC PRIVACY AND ACCESS TO INFORMATION

PART V: ELECTRONIC INFORMATION MISUSE

List of Contributors

THE EDITOR

Chris Reed is Professor of Electronic Commerce Law at the Centre for Commercial Law Studies, Queen Mary, University of London, where he was formerly Director of the Centre and subsequently Academic Dean of the Faculty of Law & Social Science. He consults to companies and law firms, having previously been Of Counsel to the City of London law firms Lawrence Graham, Tite & Lewis and Stephenson Harwood.

Chris has worked exclusively in the computing and technology law field since 1987, and teaches University of London LLM students from all over the world. He has published widely on many aspects of computer law; he is the author of *Internet Law* (2nd edn, Cambridge University Press, 2004), *Digital Information Law: electronic documents and requirements of form* (Centre for Commercial Law Studies, 1996), and *Electronic Finance Law* (Woodhead Faulkner, 1991), and the co-editor of *Cross-Border Electronic Banking* (2nd edn, Lloyd's of London Press, 2000). Research with which he was involved led to the EU directives on electronic signatures and on electronic commerce. His most recent project was funded by the Leverhulme Foundation via a Major Research Fellowship (2009–11) and investigates how best to make laws for cyberspace.

From 1997 to 2000 Chris was Joint Chairman of the Society for Computers and Law, of which he is an inaugural Honorary Fellow, and in 1997–8 he acted as Specialist Adviser to the House of Lords Select Committee on Science and Technology. Chris has acted as an Expert for the European Commission, represented the UK Government at the Hague Conference on Private International Law, and has been an invited speaker at OECD and G8 international conferences.

THE CONTRIBUTING AUTHORS

Ben Allgrove is a Partner in the London office of Baker & McKenzie. Ben's practice focuses on the cross-over space between IP and technology, including digital media issues, online IP rights enforcement, content licensing for new platforms and includes both contentious and non-contentious work. Ben is a solicitor-advocate and also teaches copyright and design law at Kings College London.

Robert Blamires is a Senior Associate with Field Fisher Waterhouse LLP. He advises both consumer and business facing enterprises on commercial and regulatory matters, with a focus on the technology, media and communications sectors. Robert has been seconded to the UK's consumer protection regulator (the OFT), where he helped establish its Internet Enforcement Team, as well as advising on specific OFT enforcement action against online traders. Robert writes and speaks regularly on issues relevant to his practice, such as: social media; online regulation and enforcement; exploitation of digital media rights; convergence; virtual worlds; and interactive and collaborative technologies, and has presented in several international jurisdictions to organizations such as: the International Trademark Association; the University of Cambridge; and the European Association of Animation Film, as well as to UK and other European regulatory authorities.

Mark Lewis, partner and leader of the Commercial law practice in Berwin Leighton Paisner, has practised exclusively in IT and outsourcing for over 26 years, during which he has acted in some of the largest ITO and BPO transactions in Europe and Asia/Asia Pacific. His outsourcing experience, first as a senior UK government lawyer, goes back to the 1980s. He has been in private practice in the City of London since 1989. Barrister (England & Wales) 1982, Solicitor (England & Wales) 1991. Mark has written extensively on outsourcing in the UK and international press and has contributed chapters on outsourcing to a number of leading texts and practitioner manuals. He served first as Non-Executive Chairman and later as a Non-Executive Director of what is now EquaTerra, a KPMG company and one of the world's top sourcing consultancies.

Christopher Millard is Professor of Privacy and Information Law at the Centre for Commercial Law Studies, Queen Mary, University of London. He is also a Senior Research Fellow at the Oxford Internet Institute, University of Oxford and is Of Counsel to the law firm Bristows. Christopher graduated from the University of Sheffield with an LLB (Hons) in 1980, and from the University of Toronto with an MA in Criminology in 1982 and an LLM (which formed the basis for one of the first international comparative computer law books) in 1983. He then spent almost 25 years in practice at Clifford Chance and Linklaters, specializing in technology and privacy law, before taking up his current appointments in 2008. He has published widely on privacy, technology, and communications law and is joint editor of the *International Journal of Law and Information Technology* and of *International Data Privacy Law* (both published by Oxford University Press). He has served as Chair of the Society for Computers and Law, as President of the International Federation of Computer Law Associations, and as Co-Chair of the Technology Committee of the International Bar Association.

David Naylor is a partner with Field Fisher Waterhouse LLP and specializes in working with technology, media, and communications businesses and investors.

Clients he advises are active in media and entertainment, internet and e-commerce, software, consumer devices and electronics, IT, and communications. He also works on technology and intellectual property matters for companies in other fields and has a busy privacy and information law practice. He speaks and writes widely on technology, new media, and privacy issues. David is regularly acknowledged as a leading technology, e-commerce, and communications lawyer in publications including *Legal 500*, PLC's *Which Lawyer?* and *Who's Who Legal*. He is on the editorial board of silicon.com and qualified as a solicitor in 1995. He has an MBA from Imperial College of Science, Technology, and Medicine.

Jeremy Newton is a Director of Technology Law Alliance, a specialist technology and outsourcing law firm based in the UK. He has over 20 years' experience of IT law and contracts, including periods in-house with Sun Microsystems (as Assistant General Counsel in EMEA) and with HM Treasury (on secondment to the PFI Taskforce). He is co-editor of *A Manager's Guide to IT Law*, published by the British Computer Society, and is actively involved with the Society as Secretary of the BCS Financial Services Specialist Group.

Peter O'Byrne is a Senior Associate in the London Intellectual Property Group of Baker & McKenzie with a practice focused on IP enforcement and litigation, and managing brand protection campaigns targeting counterfeits and parallel trade online and off. Peter is a member of MARQUES, writes regularly in journals such as *European Lawyer*, *World Trademark Review*, and *JIPLP*, and has acted before many tribunals including the EU Court of Justice, World Motor Sport Council, Federal Court of Australia, and the English High Court and Court of Appeal in disputes involving trade marks, passing off, copyright, breach of confidence, patents, and designs.

Antonis Patrikios is a Senior Associate with Field Fisher Waterhouse LLP. He specializes in complex cross-jurisdictional privacy and information, data protection and security matters, including new projects compliance, with a focus on the technology, media, entertainment, and communications sectors. Antonis has considerable experience advising on commercial transactions and agreements in those sectors. He writes and speaks widely on matters of interest. Antonis is a dual-qualified English Solicitor and Greek *Dikigoros* (Athens Bar) and holds a PhD in transnational e-business and arbitration from the Centre for Commercial Law Studies, Queen Mary, University of London.

Timothy Pitt-Payne QC is a barrister practising from 11 King's Bench Walk Chambers, where he heads the Information Law practice group. He specializes in information law, as well as in public law generally and in employment law. He regularly appears before the courts and tribunals in both freedom of information and data protection cases. He was called to the Bar in 1989, appointed QC in 2010, and has been a Visiting Professor in Information Law at Northumbria University since 2007.

Tim Press is a lecturer at Cardiff University Law School, where he teaches intellectual property on undergraduate and postgraduate courses and commercial litigation and litigation and advocacy on the Legal Practice Course. After obtaining a chemistry degree from the University of Oxford, he qualified as a solicitor and practised in London with Woodham Smith and then Taylor Joynson Garrett, latterly as a partner. His field of practice was mainly contentious and non-contentious intellectual property work. He left practice to work in higher education in 1992.

Gavin Sutter is a full-time legal academic involved in research and teaching at the Institute of Computer & Communications Law within the Centre for Commercial Law Studies at Queen Mary, University of London. His primary area of research is the regulation of media content, particularly in the online context, with, in recent years, a particular emphasis being placed upon the liability position of online intermediaries. He is the author of contributions to a range of academic journals and volumes, including the 'Defamation On The Net' chapter in *Sweet & Maxwell's Encyclopaedia of E-Commerce Law*. In his spare time he is continuing a PhD thesis on the enforcement of national content regulations over material published on the borderless internet.

Professor Ian Walden is Professor of Information and Communications Law and head of the Institute of Computer and Communications Law in the Centre for Commercial Law Studies, Queen Mary, University of London. His publications include *EDI and the Law* (1989), *Information Technology and the Law* (1990), *EDI Audit and Control* (1993), *Cross-border Electronic Banking* (2nd edn, 2000), *Telecommunications Law Handbook* (1997), *E-Commerce Law and Practice in Europe* (2001), *Telecommunications Law and Regulation* (3rd edn, 2009), *Computer Crimes and Digital Investigations* (2007), and *Media Law and Practice* (2009). Ian has been involved in law reform projects for the World Bank, the European Commission, UNCTAD, UNECE, and the EBRD, as well as for a number of individual states. Ian was a National Expert seconded to the European Commission DG-Industry (1995–6); Board Member and Trustee of the Internet Watch Foundation (2004–9). Ian is a solicitor and Of Counsel to Baker & McKenzie. He is a member of the Press Complaints Commission and, in January 2010, was asked by the Government to chair the Industry Working Group of the UK Council for Child Internet Safety.

Table of Cases

Commission Decisions

Tables of Legislation

UK Statutory Instruments

Table of Treaties and Conventions

Abbreviations

ACA	Additional Costs Allowance
ADR	alternative dispute resolution
ADSL	asymmetric digital subscriber line
ASA	Advertising Standards Authority
ASP	applications services provision
AUP	acceptable use policy
B2B	business-to-business
B2C	business-to-consumer
BBS	bulletin board system
BERR	Department for Business, Enterprise and Regulatory Reform
BIOS	basic input-output system
BIS	Department for Business Innovation and Skills
BOT	build operate transfer
BPO	business process outsourcing
BRPs 2008	Business Protection from Misleading Marketing Regulations 2008
BVerf G	Bundesverfassungsgericht
BVerf GE	Entscheidungen des Bundesverfassungsgericht
CAFC	Court of Appeals for the Federal Circuit
CBI	Confederation of British Industry
CC	Creative Commons
CCMI	Capability Maturity Model Integration
ccTLD	country code Top-Level Domain
CDPA 1988	Copyright, Design and Patents Act 1988
CD-Rom	Compact Disc Read-Only Memory
CEA 1995	Civil Evidence Act 1995
CELRE	Computer Economics Limited and Remuneration Economics
CGI	computer-generated imagery
CIO	Chief Information Officer
CISG	UN Convention on Contracts for the International Sale of Goods
CLI	caller line identification
CMMI	Capability Maturity Model Integration
CPCR 2004	Consumer Protection Cooperation Regulation 2004
CPI	Consumer Price Index
CPRs 2008	Consumer Protection from Unfair Trading Regulations 2008
CPU	Central Processing Unit
CRB	Criminal Records Bureau

CRM	Customer Relationship Management
CSP	communications service provider
CTM	Community Trade Mark
CTMR	Community Trade Mark Regulation
DA 1996	Defamation Act 1996
DCFR	Draft Common Frame of Reference
DDOS	distributed denial of service
DfES	Department for Education and Skills
DMCA 1998	Digital Millennium Copyright Act 1998 (USA)
DNS	domain name server
DOS	denial of service
DPA 1984	Data Protection Act 1984
DPA 1998	Date Protection Act 1998
DPS	dynamic purchasing systems
DSRs 2000	Consumer Protection (Distance Selling) Regulations 2000
DRS	dispute resolution service
DTI	Department of Trade and Industry
dUCTB	draft Unfair Contract Terms Bill
DVD	Digital Versatile Disc
EA 2002	Enterprise Act 2002
EBA	Enlarged Board of Appeal
ECA 2000	Electronic Communications Act 2000
ECHR	European Convention for the Protection of Human Rights and Fundamental Freedoms
ECJ	European Court of Justice
eComRs	Electronic Commerce (EC Directive) Regulations 2002
EDI	electronic data interchange
EEA	European Economic Area
EFTA	European Free Trade Association
EHTP	Electronic Hardware Technology Parks
EIR 2004	Environmental Information Regulations 2004
EPC	European Patent Convention
EPO	European Patent Office
ETO	economic, technical, or organizational
EU	European Union
EULA	End-User Licence Agreement
FEDMA	Federation of European Direct Marketing Associations
FM	facilities management
FOI	freedom of information
FOIA 2000	Freedom of Information Act 2000
FOISA 2002	Freedom of Information (Scotland) Act 2002
FOSS	free and open source software

FSA	Financial Services Authority
FTSE	Financial Times and London Stock Exchange
FTZ	Free Trade Zones
GFA	global framework agreement
gTLD	generic Top Level Domain
GUI	graphical user interface
HR	human resources
IaaS	Infrastructure as a Service
IANA	Internet Assigned Numbers Authority
ICANN	Internet Corporation for Assigned Names and Numbers
ICC	International Chamber of Commerce
ICCP	Information Computers and Communications Policy
ICPEN	International Consumer Protection and Enforcement Network
ICSTIS	Independent Committee for the Supervision of Standards of Telephone Information Services
IDN	Internationalized Domain Name
IP	intellectual property/internet protocol
IPR	intellectual property right
ISDN	integrated services digital network
ISP	Internet Service Provider
IT	information technology
ITeS	IT-enabled services
ITO	information technology outsourcing
ITT	invitation to tender
IWF	Internet Watch Foundation
JHA	Justice and Home Affairs
LEA	law enforcement agency
LGA 1972	Local Government Act 1972
LGA 2000	Local Government Act 2000
LPO	legal process outsourcing
MOU	memorandum of understanding
MSA	master service agreement
NAF	National Arbitration Forum
NASDAQ	National Association of Securities Dealers Automated Quotation (system)
NISCC	National Infrastructure Security Co-ordination Centre
NTAC	National Technical Assistance Centre
ODR	online dispute resolution
OECD	Organisation for Economic Co-operation and Development
Ofcom	Office of Communications
OFT	Office of Fair Trading
OGC	Office of Government Commerce

OIC	Office of the Information Commissioner
P2P	peer-to-peer
PaaS	Platform as a Service
PAS	problem and solution approach
PC	Personal Computer
pCRD	proposed Consumer Rights Directive
PCT	Patent Co-operation Treaty
PECRs 2003	Privacy and Electronic Communications (EC Directive) Regulations 2003
PNC	Police National Computer
POCA 1978	Protection of Children Act 1978
RAM	random access memory
RFI	request for information
RFP	request for proposals
RIPA 2000	Regulation of Investigatory Powers Act 2000
ROM	Read-Only Memory
RPI	Retail Price Index
SaaS	Software as a Service
SABAM	Société Belge des auteurs, compositeurs et éditeurs
SCGAGD	Sale of Consumer Goods and Associated Guarantees Directive
SEZ	Special Economic Zones
SGA 1893	Sale of Goods Act 1893
SGA 1979	Sale of Goods Act 1979
SGITA 1973	Supply of Goods (Implied Terms) Act 1973
SGSA 1982	Supply of Goods and Services Act 1982
SLA	service level agreement
SNS	social networking services
SPV	special purpose vehicle
SSGA 1994	Sale and Supply of Goods Act 1994
SSGCRs 2002	Sale and Supply of Goods to Consumers Regulations 2002
STPI	Software Technology Parks of India
TACD	Transatlantic Consumer Dialogue
TBA	Technical Board of Appeal
TCAD Principles	Core Consumer Protection Principles in Electronic Commerce 1999 of the Transatlantic Consumer Dialogue
TLD	Top-Level Domain
TMA 1994	Trade Marks Act 1994
TRIPs	Trade-Related Aspects of Intellectual Property Rights
TUPE 2006	Transfer of Undertakings (Protection of Employment) Regulations 2006
UCPD 2005	Unfair Commercial Practices Directive
UCTA 1977	Unfair Contract Terms Act 1977

UDRP	Uniform Domain Name Dispute Resolution Policy
UGC	user-generated content
UK	United Kingdom
UNCID Rules	Uniform Rules of Conduct for Intercharge of Trade Data by Teletransmission
US	United States
USA	United States of America
USPTO	United States Patent and Trademark Office
UTCCD	Unfair Terms in Consumer Contracts Directive
UTCCRs 1999	Unfair Terms in Consumers Contracts Regulations 1999
UWG	Gesetz gegen den unlauteren Wettbewerb
VOIP	Voice Over Internet Protocol
VPN	virtual private network
WIPO	World Intellectual Property Organization
WSIS	World Summit of Information Society
WTO	World Trade Organization
XML	extensible markup language
Y2K	Year 2000

INTRODUCTION

Chris Reed

This book, as its title suggests, is about computer law. When the first edition was published in 1990 it was quite clear what this meant.[1] In those days we could define computer law as the branch of the law which regulated the *technological* aspects of information, or to put it another way, the law which governed information *processing*. Information processing was (and still is) undertaken by computers, and thus early editions covered all the topics which one might expect: contracts to purchase computer hardware and software, the intellectual property protection of computer products, data protection, and computer crime. All these are still to be found in this edition. Chapter 1, 'System Supply Contracts', continues to track the never-ending stream of cases on the liability of systems and software suppliers and Chapter 3, 'Information Technology Outsourcing and Services Arrangements', examines this increasingly important class of contracts, focusing in particular on outsourcing by the public sector and the phenomenon of offshoring and nearshoring. The pace of change in patent and copyright law shows no sign of slowing down, and so Chapters 6 and 7 have been extensively updated to explain new decisions and legislation. Patents for business methods receive particular attention, as do the copyright problems arising from file sharing and the development of cloud computing. The fifth edition explained in Chapter 8 how the European Court of Justice judgment in *British Horseracing Board Ltd and Others v William Hill Organization Ltd* had overturned the conventional understanding of database protection, and since then case law has resolved some of the resulting uncertainties and highlighted new areas of doubt. Data protection law will not stand still, and has developed markedly in its interaction with issues of privacy and human rights, and the legal problems which arise from globalization and the increased flow of personal data cross-border. The European Union is becoming an increasingly important player in the field of computer crime, and these and other international issues are examined in Chapter 12.

---

[1] Or at least, it was quite clear to the authors and to most readers, though some commentators grumbled that computer law was not a proper field of law and would soon fade away. This is not merely the seventh edition but also the 21st anniversary of the book, so we are confident that both the field and the book have come of age.

Over the years, choices have needed to be made about whether a particular topic fell within the remit of the book. The general approach has been that *Computer Law* should not seek to cover:

(a) areas of law where the challenges posed by computing technology did not radically alter the underlying law, such as the substantive law of defamation. This is not to say that we have ignored developments in these areas entirely—Chapter 5 on the liability of online intermediaries examines defamation as part of that wider examination of liability, which also extends to copyright and issues of potentially unlawful content, such as online pornography;

(b) the law relating to technologies which have developed their own body of regulation which cannot be explained in the space available for a single chapter, or which is more concerned with the regulation of systems than with individual rights and obligations. Telecommunications law fits both these tests, and readers interested in that subject should see I Walden and J Angel, *Telecommunications Law and Practice*; or

(c) legal issues which arise from the cross-border use of computing technology—the focus of *Computer Law* has always been on the UK-based supplier or user of computing technology. This does not mean that the authors have confined themselves to discussing purely UK sources and ignoring cross-border issues which impact UK suppliers and users. Much of the development in UK computer law since 1990 has arisen from EU initiatives, and these are examined at length. Furthermore, comparison with foreign laws is a valuable way of illuminating the meaning of UK law, and most chapters make appropriate comparisons to enhance the reader's understanding.

With this in mind, the book no longer deals in detail with confidential information, competition law, or the law of evidence. In all these areas the issues arising from computing technology are adequately dealt with in standard works on the topics, such that separate treatment in this book is now not necessary.

A continual difficulty has been to decide how *Computer Law* should deal with the legal issues which have arisen from the remarkable and dramatic explosion in both the availability and use of computing technology since 1990. In that year major law firms were just starting to provide computing facilities to their lawyers, and many smaller law firms used no computers at all. Computers in the home were the province of those with a strong interest in the workings of the technology, and were used to understand the technology rather than as tools to perform useful functions for the user. 'Power users' might have had dial-up access to some form of electronic communication service, but these services normally allowed communication only between their subscribers and were not usable as a general communications tool. Now, computing technology has pervaded daily life to such an extent that most private individuals use multiple devices which have substantial processing power. A typical UK household will contain one or more personal computers, mobile phones, DVD recorders, broadband routers, and digital music players. Most of these are more powerful computers than the typical 1990 personal computer.

The greatest change, however, is the universal connectivity which has been made possible by the internet. If we were to deal with all the legal questions which the internet raises, this book would be substantially larger in scope and size and, indeed, a very different book.

Our approach has therefore been to start from the proposition that *Computer Law* primarily addresses the legal questions which face UK suppliers and users of computing technology. This has identified four areas of law which need to be explained:

(a) Modern business has responded to the spread of computing technology and the near universal availability of internet access by using these technologies to communicate and do business with customers. Electronic commerce is now a core issue for business, and the main legal issues are explained in Chapter 4, 'Electronic Commerce'.

(b) To access customers online, businesses need to use internet intermediaries and in many cases to act as intermediaries themselves. This raises important liability questions which are different in kind from those encountered by purely offline businesses. Chapter 5, 'Online Intermediaries', analyses these matters and attempts to explain the direction in which UK law is evolving.

(c) Because these technologies are now used by private individuals as well as businesses, they are also used to sell and supply goods and services to those individuals. Selling and supplying to consumers raises a number of novel legal issues, particularly as lawmakers (most saliently at EU level) have identified new consumer protection risks in B2C online trading and introduced special protective measures. These are considered in depth in Chapter 2, 'Mass Market Contracting'.

(d) When a business goes online its use of trade marks is likely to conflict with that of other businesses in very different ways from offline trading. Chapter 9, 'Online Use of Trade Marks and Domain Names', explores the legal consequences of these conflicts in depth.

The pervasiveness of computing technology has also meant that not only is a substantial amount of information about individuals collected and processed, but also that individuals can more easily be *given* information (both the information which is held about them and information about the activities of public and private organizations). The Freedom of Information Act 2000 sets out the circumstances in which that information must be disclosed, and Chapter 11, 'Access to Electronic Information', analyses the Act and the fast-growing body of case law which it has generated. Of particular note are the series of cases relating to MPs' expenses and the developments in relation to information used for the purpose of developing governmental policy.

We do not doubt that there are other topics which our readers would have hoped *Computer Law* would cover, and can only plead limitations of space for our failure to do so. We can, however, predict with some certainty that the field of computer law will continue to develop at the same, startling pace as over the last 21 years, and that future editions will cover matters which we cannot begin to predict today.

Part I

COMMERCIAL EXPLOITATION
OF INFORMATION TECHNOLOGY
PRODUCTS AND SERVICES

1

SYSTEM SUPPLY CONTRACTS

Jeremy Newton

1.1 INTRODUCTION

1.1.1 System supply contracts

1.1.1.1 *What is a 'system supply contract'?*

Expressions like 'system supply contracts' and 'computer contracts' cover a multitude of commercial transactions, ranging from the purchase of a single CD-ROM from a high street retailer through to multi-million pound systems or communications outsourcing projects. The traditional approach to examining such contracts drew a distinction between hardware and software agreements, but this distinction is becoming increasingly irrelevant. For the purposes of this chapter, then, a system supply contract is one under which the customer is to purchase or otherwise obtain the use of one or more of the following:

(a) hardware;

(b) software;

(c) other equipment (such as cabling or power supply); and

(d) services (such as consultancy, installation, support, and maintenance).

1.1.1.2 *Contract structures*

System supply contracts can be structured in numerous ways. One common structure is known as the 'turnkey' arrangement, whereby the supplier undertakes to supply all the elements of the system under one contract, or as prime contractor at the top of a chain of connected subcontracts. More complex structures are also possible, whereby the supplier acts effectively as a broker between the customer and third party suppliers. These traditional models are starting to be challenged by the growth of 'cloud computing', which enables customers to obtain the use of IT platforms or software 'as a service', without a major investment in proprietary infrastructure. Regardless of the exact contracting structure, however, there are essential features common to all kinds of system supply contract.

1.1.2 The contract process

1.1.2.1 *Function of a written contract*

In most commercial transactions, the terms of these contracts will be recorded in writing, and understanding the reasons for having a written contract can help the parties to negotiate it effectively. The function of a written contract is to record the terms governing the supply of goods and services. In the absence of a clear, express understanding between the parties, the law implies certain terms into the contract (discussed in more detail in section 1.2.1 below) which may run counter to the parties' actual intentions, so a written agreement gives certainty to the transaction.

1.1.2.2 *Significance of the negotiation process*

There is also an important function to the negotiation process that leads up to signature of a written agreement. This process should help to ensure that the parties understand each other's expectations about the deal in question, and to draw out differences in those expectations that can then be resolved before they lead to problems. Many IT projects fail precisely because the parties do not exercise sufficient care to ensure that the supplier's and the customer's expectations match. Ensuring that these do match is, in the opinion of this author, the key role of the legal adviser in the contract process.

1.1.2.3 *Use of standard terms*

It is a feature of doing business in the IT sector that most suppliers prefer to deal on their own set of standard terms. These are usually negotiable to some degree, depending on the customer's bargaining power. Probably the only negotiable term in a contract for a single PC is the price, whereas a buyer who is paying several million pounds per annum as part of a major outsourcing deal will be able to negotiate most of the terms. The danger of uncritically accepting the standard terms of even the most respectable supplier can be illustrated by *Mackenzie Patten v British*

Olivetti,[1] one of the earliest IT contract disputes to be heard by the English courts. In that case, a law firm bought an Olivetti computer system to run its accounts. They discussed their needs with the salesperson, and signed up on Olivetti's standard terms. These dealt only with the system's technical performance, but did not address certain other important issues. The system proved unsuitable for the firm's purposes; it was slow, difficult to use, and could not expand to cope with new business. None of these matters was dealt with in the contract. In the event, the court found that Olivetti was bound by the salesperson's claims that the system would be suitable for their needs, but by that stage the firm had expended time and money in the litigation, and then of course had to find a replacement system.

Put another way, 'standard' forms are only suitable for 'standard' transactions. No matter how comprehensive the standard contract, it will usually fail to cover some essential point envisaged by the particular parties to any particular deal.

1.1.2.4 *Negotiating for the long term*

There is a further reason for negotiating a detailed contract for any significant deal: unlike many sale of goods contracts, the delivery of a computer system (or the commencement of service provision) is only the beginning of the relationship, not its culmination. Further work will be necessary to install the system and get it working properly, to obtain upgrades, and to monitor service levels. So although the aim of the negotiator is to get the best possible deal for the client, this should not mean gaining at the expense of the other side. The aim is to produce a mutually satisfactory contract which will provide a comprehensive basis for the continuing relationship between them.

1.1.2.5 *Types of contractual provision*

Any well-drawn contract will have provisions relating to three broad categories of expectation:

(a) Contract mechanics: for example, who delivers what, and when?

(b) Commercial highlights: for example, what is the price, who owns resulting intellectual property rights, and what warranties are given in respect of the system?

(c) Problem management: what happens if the project goes wrong, and what remedies are available?

The objective is to ensure that no essential terms are missing from the contract. Some of these are discussed in section 1.3 of this chapter, and others relevant to the particular circumstances should come out of the negotiations themselves. However, before looking at specific contractual provisions, this chapter will discuss some of the principal legal aspects of system supply agreements.

---

[1] (1984) 1 CL&P 92, 95.

1.1.3 Terminology

As a general point on terminology, there are a number of expressions that may correctly be used to denote the different parties to any system supply contract. In the context of the software licensing elements, it is common to refer to 'licensor' and 'licensee'. Hardware sale agreements usually refer to 'buyers' and 'sellers'. Consultancy or software development contracts will tend to refer to 'consultant' and 'client'. However, as a system supply contract may comprise any combination of these various elements, the author refers generally in this chapter to 'supplier' and 'customer' unless there is a sound reason for using the narrower expressions (such as in the discussion of Sale of Goods legislation which specifically refers to buyers and sellers).

1.2 PRINCIPAL LEGAL ISSUES APPLICABLE TO SYSTEM SUPPLY CONTRACTS

1.2.1 Implied terms

1.2.1.1 *Background to the statutory implied terms*
Certain terms may be implied into contracts (both consumer and business contracts) as a matter of statute law or common law. The main statutory implied terms arise under the Sale of Goods Act 1979 ('SGA 1979') and under the Supply of Goods and Services Act 1982 ('SGSA 1982'), both as amended by the Sale and Supply of Goods Act 1994 ('SSGA 1994'). These terms are generally characterized as either conditions or warranties, the distinction being that breach of a condition entitles the innocent party to terminate the contract outright, whereas breach of a warranty entitles him to sue for damages only (but he remains committed to perform his side of the deal). The principal terms are discussed in sections 1.2.1.2 to 1.2.1.14 below.

1.2.1.2 *SGA 1979, section 12(1): the right to sell*
The SGA 1979, section 12(1), implies a term[2] into all contracts of sale that the seller has the right to sell the goods. If the seller fails to transfer ownership, then he will be in breach of this term, and the buyer can reject the goods and recover the price, plus damages if they can be proved.[3]

---

[2] In England, Wales and Northern Ireland, this term is a condition by virtue of s 12(5A), added by SSGA 1994.

[3] This is not affected by any use of the goods by the buyer. The essence of a sale of goods contract is the transfer of ownership from seller to buyer, and a failure to effect this means that there is a total failure of consideration (*Rowland v Divall* (1923) 2 KB 500).

1.2.1.3 *Implications of SGA 1979, section 12(1), for hardware sales*

In order to satisfy section 12(1), the buyer must receive full and unfettered rights of ownership (unless the contrary has been agreed under section 12(3)). This means that the seller will be in breach of the condition if the goods are subject to rights belonging to a third party. The most obvious rights which exist independent of ownership are intellectual property rights (IPRs), so hardware producers risk running into difficulty if the product infringes someone else's IPR. In that eventuality, a patentee or copyright owner might prevent the buyer using any infringing equipment (or software loaded on legitimate equipment), so an innocent buyer could be prevented from using the hardware he has purchased. This is a clear breach of section 12(1) on the seller's part, even if the IPR owner chooses not to exercise his rights.

1.2.1.4 *SGA 1979, section 12(2): quiet possession*

The seller will be in breach of section 12(1) if the third party's rights existed at the time of sale. However, some IPRs (eg, patents and trade marks) only come into existence on registration, so it is possible that such rights might only arise *after* the sale was made. In that case, the seller is not in breach of section 12(1), but is in breach of the warranty[4] in section 12(2)(b) that the buyer will have quiet possession of the goods.[5] This is in effect a promise by the seller that no person will in the future acquire rights over the goods and enforce them against the buyer. The warranty is broken only when the third party enforces its rights, at which point the buyer becomes entitled to claim damages from the seller (but not to reject the goods). However, if the third party prevents the buyer from using the goods, the buyer's damages will be assessed as the cost of buying a replacement, in effect returning the price.

1.2.1.5 *SGA 1979, section 13: correspondence with description*

The SGA 1979, section 13, provides for an implied condition that goods will correspond with their description,[6] and the question often arises whether claims made by salespeople or contained in the manufacturer's publicity material amount to a description for these purposes. The traditional test is to ask whether the words used are a term of the contract or a mere representation: this is answered by examining whether the seller intended to promise, as part of the contract, that the words were true. In practice, however, it is impossible to ascertain the seller's real intention

---

[4] In England, Wales, and Northern Ireland, this term is a warranty by virtue of s 12(5A), added by SSGA 1994.

[5] For a clear illustration of the distinction see *Microbeads AG v Vinhurst Road Markings Ltd* [1975] 1 WLR 218.

[6] In the context of an IT contract, the description of the goods will generally be the user requirements specification, which might be the supplier's standard specification, or a bespoke one specifically developed for the particular supply.

(indeed, the seller may have had none) and what the courts appear to be asking themselves is whether the buyer actually obtained that which he was led to believe he was buying. The test would thus be whether a reasonable person in the buyer's position would have been led to believe that the seller was promising a true description of the goods. As a general rule, only if the buyer examines the goods thoroughly before he buys will the court decide that descriptive words which had no influence on his decision to buy are not part of the description of the goods for the purposes of section 13.

1.2.1.6 *SGA 1979, section 14: quality and fitness for purpose*

The SGA 1979, section 14, provides for an implied condition that goods will be of satisfactory quality (s 14(2)) and reasonably fit for their purpose (s 14(3)). However, obligations of quality raise particular problems in relation to IT systems as it is often difficult to define a system's purposes with sufficient precision, let alone decide if it is reasonably fit. In this respect, the description of the goods can again be very important—in some cases, it is almost the sole determinant of the quality the buyer is entitled to expect.

1.2.1.7 *Satisfactory quality*

'Satisfactory quality' is defined in section 14(2A) and (2B) (inserted into SGA 1979 by SSGA 1994):

(2A) For the purposes of this Act, goods are of satisfactory quality if they meet the standard that a reasonable person would regard as satisfactory, taking account of any description of the goods, the price (if relevant) and all the other relevant circumstances.

(2B) For the purposes of this Act, the quality of goods includes their state and condition and the following (among others) are in appropriate cases aspects of the quality of goods:

(a) fitness for all the purposes for which goods of the kind in question are commonly supplied;

(b) appearance and finish;

(c) freedom from minor defects;

(d) safety; and

(e) durability.

It will be clear from the above definition that no hard and fast rule can ever be drawn as to whether goods fulfil the obligation of satisfactory quality. Instead, the courts will examine the circumstances of the contract in an attempt to decide whether a reasonable buyer would have been satisfied with the quality of the goods.

1.2.1.8 *Exceptions to section 14(2)*

The obligation set out in section 14(2) does not extend to defects that the seller specifically reveals, nor to those defects that should have been discovered by the inspection (if any) that was *actually made* by the buyer.[7] It should also be noted that it is not only the goods sold that must be satisfactory—any goods *supplied* under the contract (eg, manuals or magnetic media) must also be of satisfactory quality, even if they remain the seller's property and are to be returned to him.

1.2.1.9 *Implications of section 14(2) for system supply agreements*

The problem of ascertaining whether a system fulfils section 14(2) is likely to turn almost exclusively on the question whether the system is fit for all its common purposes. In this context, freedom from minor defects is probably an aspect of that fitness, unless the defects are merely cosmetic (eg, dents in computer cases). The court's task is to determine what purposes systems *of the kind in question* are commonly supplied for. This is a very difficult matter, particularly in relation to hardware, the functioning of which is determined by the software which runs upon it. Similarly, in relation to software, programs invariably contain programming errors or 'bugs', and it is likely that a court will take note of this in determining whether a program is of satisfactory quality. Indeed, in *Saphena Computing Ltd v Allied Collection Agencies Ltd*[8] the recorder acknowledged precisely this when he observed that 'even programs that are reasonably fit for their purpose may contain bugs'. So the real question to be determined is what functions the seller might reasonably foresee the buyer as requiring. Predictably, no clear answers can be given, and for this reason it is common in substantial computer contracts to agree a detailed specification, listing the functions to be performed and objective criteria for testing that performance, and then to exclude the terms implied by section 14(2) and (3). (Note that different considerations apply to the purchase of commodity items such as PCs and peripherals as individual transactions, where the contract value is too low to permit the negotiation of detailed specifications. In many such cases, it may become necessary to rely on section 14(2).)

1.2.1.10 *Fitness for the buyer's particular purpose*

If the seller sells in the course of a business and the buyer expressly or impliedly makes known a particular purpose or purposes for which he intends to use the hardware, section 14(3) implies a condition[9] that it will be reasonably fit for those purposes. This condition is imposed because the buyer relies on the seller to use his expertise to select goods suitable for the buyer's needs. If the buyer produces the user requirements specification himself, this would normally suggest that he is not relying on the seller's skill and judgement to select appropriate equipment, and that section 14(3) accordingly has no relevance. However, the seller will still be liable under that subsection in respect of matters not covered by the specification,

---

[7] Sale of Goods Act 1979, s 14(2C), as amended by the Sale and Supply of Goods Act 1994.
[8] [1995] FSR 616.
[9] In England, Wales, and Northern Ireland, this term is a condition by virtue of s 14(6), substituted by the Sale and Supply of Goods Act 1994.

as illustrated by *Cammell Laird & Co Ltd v Manganese Bronze & Brass Co Ltd*.[10] In that case, the buyer entered into a contract for the supply of a ship's propeller, to be manufactured to the buyer's specification and used on a named ship. The propeller proved unsuitable for the ship because its pitch was incorrect, a matter not provided for in the specification. The court held that as this had been left to the seller's discretion it clearly showed reliance on the buyer's part. The court also made it clear that if the defect had been in the buyer's specification the seller would not have been in breach of the condition.

In the context of IT systems, standard hardware and software are not of course designed for any particular user, and will be unlikely to meet all the requirements of any user. However, where customized hardware or bespoke software is supplied, the user may more reasonably expect to receive a warranty that it will comply with his requirements: indeed, it is far from unusual for the buyer to expect the seller to check the specification, particularly where it has been arrived at in consultation between them. In such cases, the buyer will claim to have relied on the seller's skill and judgement.

1.2.1.11 *Exceptions to section 14(3)*
The condition is not implied where it is unreasonable for the buyer to rely on the seller's expertise. This might be the case where the seller makes it clear that he cannot say whether the hardware will be suitable (eg, where it is purchased for research purposes) or where the buyer fails to give him the information he needs to exercise his judgement properly.[11]

1.2.1.12 *SGSA 1982, section 13: reasonable care and skill*
The implied terms discussed above all apply to contracts for goods. The SGSA 1982, section 13, implies a different term into contracts for services, to the effect that the services will be provided with 'reasonable care and skill'.

1.2.1.13 *Implications of SGSA 1982, section 13, for system supply contracts*
Although the SGSA 1982, section 13, may have little significance for contracts for hardware alone, the implied term is of course important to the supply of related services—for example, hardware maintenance, software development and support, consultancy, and training. There is also a possibility that the supply of software per se may be viewed by the courts as a supply of services, for the reasons set out below.

---

[10] [1934] AC 402. Followed in *Ashington Piggeries v Christopher Hill Ltd* [1972] AC 441.
[11] See *Griffiths v Peter Conway Ltd* [1939] 1 All ER 685.

1.2.1.14 *Classification of software as goods or services*

Four cases illustrate the development of judicial thinking on the classification of software as goods or services, and the statutory implied terms that apply as a result:

(a) *Eurodynamics:* In *Eurodynamics Systems plc v General Automation Ltd*,[12] Steyn J refused to decide whether software was goods, or whether the terms implied by the SGA 1979 applied to the software licence in question, as he was able to decide the case without reaching a view on these issues.

(b) *Saphena:* By contrast, in *Saphena Computing Ltd v Allied Collection Agencies Ltd*[13] the recorder decided that 'it was an implied term of each contract for the supply of software that the software would be reasonably fit for any purpose which had been communicated to the plaintiff [claimant]'. This decision is unsatisfactory, however, since the recorder did not explain the basis on which he found that the term was implied. He did find, however, that the software had been supplied on terms that the software might not be lent, sold, or hired to any third party without the licensor's consent, which might suggest a hiring rather than a sale, though this is by no means conclusive. On appeal Staughton LJ stated:

. . . it was, we are told, common ground that the law governing these contracts was precisely the same whether they were contracts for the sale of goods or the supply of services. It is therefore unnecessary to consider into which category they might come.

On the face of it that is an extraordinary statement since the law relating to goods is quite different from the law relating to services: the only term implied into a contract for services is that reasonable skill and care will be used, not that the result will be fit for any particular purpose or meet any standard of quality.

(c) *St Albans:* A clearer statement that the SGA 1979 applies to the supply of software appears in the obiter dictum of Scott Baker J in *St Albans City and District Council v International Computers Ltd*.[14] The judge concluded that although the disks or tapes on which a program is recorded certainly are goods, the program of itself is not.

(d) *Holman v Sherwood:* In the most recent reported decision on the point, *Horace Holman Group Ltd v Sherwood International Group Ltd*,[15] the court found that the computer program that a supplier had contracted to provide did not constitute 'goods' for the purposes of section 6 of UCTA 1977 (discussed below).

---

[12] 6 September 1988 (unreported).
[13] [1995] FSR 616.
[14] [1996] 4 All ER 481 (CA).
[15] (2002) 146 SJLB 35.

Against this line of cases, the Scottish decision of *Beta Computers (Europe) Ltd v Adobe Systems (Europe) Ltd*,[16] holding that a supply of 'shrink-wrapped' software was not a sale of goods, should also be noted, although the decision is only of persuasive authority in England.

To what extent are these decisions helpful in determining whether the supply of software amounts to the provision of 'goods' or of 'services'? The view of this author is that a more subtle distinction is required, and that the classification (and hence the legal rules that apply to the supply) should really depend on the circumstances in which the software is procured: the purchase of, say, a standard computer game should be regarded as a sale of goods irrespective of the medium by which the software is delivered; whereas a bespoke system written specially by the supplier for a particular customer necessarily entails the supply of services. (Whether the terms implied by section 13 of SGSA 1982 provide adequate protection for the customer in this latter case is an argument beyond the scope of this chapter.)

1.2.1.15 *Relevance of 'goods' and 'services' in cloud computing*
In the context of cloud computing, the only term that is likely to be implied into a contract is that the supplier will use reasonable skill and care under the SGSA 1982, section 13. A detailed account of the nature and merits of cloud computing is beyond the scope of this chapter, but its essence is the delivery of IT functionality 'as a service'. Cloud computing encompasses a wide range of offerings such as 'Software as a Service' (in which the use of application software is delivered as a hosted or managed service over the internet, the pioneering instance of this being the customer relationship management service provided by salesforce.com) and 'Infrastructure as a Service' (where the supplier makes available remote access to IT infrastructure like servers, storage, and local network resources as a commoditized utility, to allow the customer to run its own software on it). Given that cloud contracts are essentially contracts for services, the implied terms relating to goods are unlikely to apply.

1.2.1.16 *Additional implied terms in consumer contracts*
The terms discussed above apply to any contract for the sale of goods or provision of services, whether business-to-business or business-to-consumer. However, the law also provides for an additional layer of protection in consumer contracts, and although a detailed discussion of consumer law is beyond the scope of this chapter, readers should also be aware of the Sale and Supply of Goods to Consumers Regulations 2002 (SI 2002/3045). These Regulations implement Directive 1999/44/EC on certain aspects of the sale of consumer goods and associated guarantees, amending existing legislation on the sale and supply of goods and unfair terms in order to provide additional remedies to consumers in certain circumstances. The principal changes include the introduction of a new Part 5A into the 1979 Act, to the

---

[16] [1996] FSR 367.

effect that where goods fail to conform to the contract of sale at the time of delivery, then the buyer first has the right to require the seller to repair or replace the goods within a reasonable time and without causing significant inconvenience to the buyer. If repair or replacement is impossible or disproportionate, or if the seller fails to repair or replace the goods within a reasonable time and without significant inconvenience to the buyer, then the buyer may require the seller to reduce the purchase price of the goods by an appropriate amount, or rescind the contract. (A similar right is introduced into SGSA 1982.)

1.2.1.17 *Common law implied terms*
It should be remembered that apart from terms implied by statute, terms may also be implied from the facts and circumstances of the particular contract. Here the courts use the 'officious bystander' and 'business efficacy' tests to determine whether the implication of a term is proper, as illustrated by *Greaves & Co (Contractors) Ltd v Baynham Meikle & Partners*.[17] In a contract for the provision of engineering consultancy services, there was an implied term that the design which was the subject of the contract should be fit for certain specific purposes. Similarly, in a software contract that is a mere contract for services (eg, programming), it may be possible to imply a term that the software supplied should comply with particular criteria, over and above the statutory term that the work be carried out with reasonable skill and care.

1.2.2 Limitations and exclusions of liability

1.2.2.1 *Introduction*
It is common for system supply contracts to contain provisions excluding or limiting the supplier's liability, and in particular it is common to exclude all liability for loss consequential on a breakdown or malfunction of the equipment. Such provisions need to be carefully drafted if they are to be effective, and some exclusions are not permitted by law. There are two levels of legal control over exclusion clauses—the common law, and statutory control under the Unfair Contract Terms Act 1977 ('UCTA 1977') and the Unfair Terms in Consumer Contracts Regulations 1999 (SI 1999/2083), which implements the EC Directive on Unfair Terms in Consumer Contracts 1993. These two pieces of legislation contain inconsistent and overlapping provisions, using different language and concepts to produce similar but not identical effects, and the Law Commission has noted that the statutory controls on unfair terms would benefit considerably from consolidation and simplification—see section 1.2.2.14 below.

---

[17] [1975] 1 WLR 1095.

1.2.2.2 *Common law rules: incorporation of terms*[18]

In order for an exclusion clause to protect the supplier, it must be contractually binding on the customer. This is most easily effected if it is contained in a written contract signed by the buyer. Many contracts for goods of low value, however, are made by exchange of letters, each referring to the other's standard terms, and it may be a difficult matter to decide whether the clause in question is part of the contract.[19]

1.2.2.3 *Common law rules: construction and the* 'contra proferentem' *rule*

Even if it is duly incorporated, an exclusion clause will only protect the seller if, as a matter of construction, it covers the breach that has occurred. The rules of construction are complicated but in general the more serious the breach of contract, the more clearly worded the clause must be if it is to exclude liability for that breach: it is interpreted against the party seeking to rely on it (the *contra proferentem* rule). A good illustration of this principle at work can be found in *Pegler v Wang*,[20] in which the clause in question purported to exclude liability for 'consequential loss in connection with or arising out of the supply, functioning or use of the system'. The court interpreted this language as not excluding liability for consequential loss arising from the *failure* to supply or the *delay* in supplying the system.

Similarly, in *Tektrol v International Insurance of Hanover*,[21] the Court of Appeal considered an insurance policy that excluded liability for losses 'caused deliberately by rioters, strikers, locked-out workers, persons taking part in labour disturbances or civil commotions or malicious persons'. The claimant had unknowingly downloaded a global computer virus which deleted the source codes for its process-control systems, and had unfortunately suffered a burglary shortly afterwards as a result of which its back-up copies (both electronic and hard copy) were also lost. The Court of Appeal held that the exclusion was worded in such a way that the actions falling within the scope of the exclusion had to be actions directed against the claimant's business and premises specifically. For more general malicious actions to be covered—such as a global computer virus—they would have to be addressed in a separate provision that distinguished between the various types of interference. Liability was accordingly not excluded for either the virus or the burglary.

More recently, in *Internet Broadcasting Corp (trading as NetTV) v MAR LLC (trading as MARHedge)*,[22] the court went a step further, and introduced a rebuttable presumption that an exclusion clause should not apply to a deliberate personal repudiatory breach of contract. In that case, the wording 'neither party will be liable to the other for any damage to software, damage to or loss of data, loss of profit,

---

[18] See generally J Adams and H MacQueen, *Atiyah's Sale of Goods*, 12th edn (London: Longman, 2010) ch 14.

[19] This point is too complicated for examination here, but the rules for construing such an agreement can be found in any standard work on the law of contract.

[20] [2002] BLR 218.

[21] [2005] EWCA Civ 845.

[22] [2009] EWHC 844.

anticipated profit, revenues, anticipated savings, goodwill or business opportunity, or for any indirect or consequential loss or damage' was held not to exempt the defendant from liability for deliberate breach. Particularly clear drafting will accordingly be needed if a defendant wants to be able to persuade a court that the parties intended an exclusion clause to cover a deliberate personal repudiatory breach of contract.

1.2.2.4 *Unfair Contract Terms Directive: background*
The newest statutory control on exclusion clauses is the EC Directive on Unfair Terms in Consumer Contracts,[23] implemented in the UK by the Unfair Terms in Consumer Contracts Regulations 1999 (SI 1999/2083).[24] The Directive provides that in a contract between a seller or supplier and a consumer, unfair terms shall not be enforceable against the consumer, although the remainder of the contract remains in force so far as that is feasible.

1.2.2.5 *Unfair Contract Terms Directive: terms which may be regarded as 'unfair'*
A term is unfair for the purposes of the Directive if (a) it has not been individually negotiated, and (b) 'contrary to the requirement of good faith, it causes a significant imbalance in the parties' rights and obligations arising under the contract, to the detriment of the consumer' (Art 3(1)). The annex to the Directive contains a list of terms which 'may be regarded as unfair' (Art 3(3) and Sch 2 to the 1999 Regulations).[25] Examples from that list which are particularly relevant to computer contracts include terms:

(b) Inappropriately excluding or limiting the legal rights of the consumer . . . in the event of total or partial non-performance . . .

(f) Authorising the seller or supplier to dissolve the contract on a discretionary basis where the same facility is not granted to the consumer . . .

(h) Automatically extending a contract of fixed duration where the consumer does not indicate otherwise, when the deadline fixed for the consumer to express this desire not to extend the contract is unreasonably early.[26]

---

[23] Directive 93/13/EEC, OJ L95, 21 April 1993.

[24] The 1999 Regulations replaced the Unfair Terms in Consumer Contracts Regulations 1994 (SI 1994/3159), by which the UK had originally implemented the 1993 Directive. Most of the 1994 Regulations were in fact re-enacted in 1999, but with modifications to reflect more closely the wording of the Directive.

[25] In a consultative document, *Implementation of the EC Directive on Unfair Terms in Consumer Contracts* (London: DTI, 1993), the DTI took this wording to mean that the terms in the list may be, but are not necessarily, unfair. Other Member States may have taken a stronger position on this point, but in any event sellers should take the cautious approach that including any of the terms in the annex is likely to give rise to a presumption of unfairness.

[26] Examples (f) and (h) are particularly likely to arise in maintenance contracts.

(i) Irrevocably binding the consumer to terms with which he had no real opportunity of becoming acquainted before the conclusion of the contract.[27]

(k) Enabling the seller or supplier to alter unilaterally without a valid reason any characteristics of the product or service to be provided.

(p) Giving the seller or supplier the possibility of transferring his rights and obligations under the contract, where this may serve to reduce the guarantees for the consumer, without the latter's agreement.[28]

(q) Excluding or hindering the consumer's right to take legal action or exercise any other legal remedy, particularly by . . . unduly restricting the evidence available to him or imposing on him a burden of proof which, according to the applicable law, should lie with another party to the contract.

These examples are not exhaustive—others from the annex may be applicable to particular computer contracts, and in any case the annex is purely indicative, so that terms having a similar effect are likely also to be construed as unfair.

1.2.2.6 *UCTA 1977: background*
UCTA 1977 is of more general application than the Directive, as it applies to contracts between businesses as well as to those between businesses and consumers. Suppliers of IT systems to consumers will need to consider both forms of control, whereas suppliers only to businesses can ignore the Directive.

1.2.2.7 *UCTA 1977, section 6: exclusions of liability under the SGA 1979*
Section 6 of UCTA 1977 deals with attempts to exclude liability under the SGA 1979. In particular:

(a) Section 6(1) provides that it is not possible to exclude the condition that the seller has the right to sell the goods (see sections 1.2.1.2 to 1.2.1.4).

(b) Section 6(2) provides that where the buyer deals as a consumer, it is not possible to exclude the seller's liability for correspondence to description, quality, and fitness for purposes (see sections 1.2.1.5 to 1.2.1.11). A buyer 'deals as a consumer' if (i) he does not buy in the course of a business, (ii) the seller sells in the course of a business, and (iii) the goods are of a type normally supplied for private use or consumption—see UCTA 1977, section 12.

(c) Section 6(3) provides that, where the buyer does *not* deal as a consumer, the seller's liability for correspondence to description, quality, and fitness *may* be excluded, provided the exclusion clause satisfies the test of reasonableness.

---

[27] This is a particular problem in mail order sales, especially where the order is placed by telephone.
[28] This too is a term which may be found in a maintenance contract.

1.2.2.8 *UCTA 1977, section 3: exclusions of liability for breaches other than of the SGA 1979 implied terms*

UCTA 1977 also affects clauses that attempt to exclude liability for breaches of terms other than those imposed by the SGA 1979. The most relevant section is section 3, which provides that where the buyer deals as a consumer, or where he deals on the seller's written standard terms, the clause must satisfy the test of reasonableness to be effective. In most IT contracts, section 3 will apply as well as section 6, in which case the section that provides the best protection for the buyer will be applied.

1.2.2.9 *When does UCTA 1977 not apply?*

The only obvious case in which UCTA 1977 will be irrelevant is where the parties depart substantially from the seller's standard terms, and the breach is not of one of the implied terms. The theory is perhaps that if the parties are of such equal bargaining power that they can negotiate a non-standard contract, any exclusion clause is seen by both sides as fair. The question remains whether the entire contract needs to be in standard form, or whether it is sufficient to bring the case within section 3 if the exclusion clause alone is the seller's standard term. These issues have been examined in some depth in a line of cases in the 1990s:

(a) *Salvage Association v CAP:* In *Salvage Association v CAP Financial Services Ltd,*[29] which related to the supply of bespoke software, CAP had put forward its standard contract and had negotiated certain changes to it. In deciding whether section 3 of UCTA 1977 applied to those exclusions, the official referee set out a list of factors which would be relevant:

    (i) the degree to which the standard terms are considered by the other party;

    (ii) the degree to which the terms are imposed on the other party;

    (iii) the respective bargaining power of the parties;

    (iv) the willingness of the party putting forward the terms to negotiate them;

    (v) how far any alterations to the terms were agreed; and

    (vi) the extent and duration of the negotiations.

On the facts of the case, because the Salvage Association had considered various drafts and taken legal advice on them and persuaded CAP to agree to changes (though not, it is implicit, in the relevant exclusion terms), this was enough to show that the contract was not made on CAP's written standard terms.

---

[29] [1995] FSR 654.

(b) *St Albans v ICL:* In *St Albans City and District Council v International Computers Ltd*,[30] CA, ICL had developed a complex package (COMCIS) to calculate and administer the community charge or poll tax system of local taxation. St Albans used COMCIS to calculate the number of community charge payers in its area, and used that figure to set its community charge rate. The COMCIS software contained an error, so that although the St Albans database contained all the necessary details, the population figure reported was too high and, as a result, St Albans suffered a financial loss.

The contract contained a clause limiting ICL's liability to the price or charge payable for the item of equipment, program, or service in respect of which the liability arises or £100,000 (whichever is the lesser); and completely excluding liability for, inter alia, any indirect or consequential loss or loss of business or profits sustained by the customer. Liability turned on whether this clause was reasonable under section 11 of UCTA 1977—see sections 1.2.2.10 to 1.2.2.13—and the first question to be decided was whether UCTA 1977 applied at all.

ICL contested that UCTA 1977 did not apply at all, arguing that the contract had not been on standard terms. However, the judge held that UCTA 1977 did apply: in other words, that St Albans had contracted on ICL's written standard terms. Even though many elements of the contract were negotiated at length (eg, delivery dates, specification), ICL's General Conditions (which contained the limitation and exclusion clauses) 'remained effectively untouched in the negotiations', and indeed were referred to by ICL staff as ICL's Standard Terms and Conditions in witness statements and letters.[31]

(c) *South West Water v ICL:* In *South West Water Services Ltd v International Computers Ltd*,[32] Toulmin J followed the *St Albans* decision in finding that, even though SWW originally offered its own terms in negotiations, in the event ICL had dealt on ICL's own standard terms which had been only slightly adapted. The fact that one fairly predictable eventuality—failure to progress the project to a point where there was a system in place for SWW and capable of being tested—had not been specifically addressed in the documentation also tended to suggest that the contract should be regarded as 'standard terms'.

(d) *Pegler v Wang:* In *Pegler v Wang*,[33] the contract in question consisted of a set of standard terms with an attached schedule of variations and additional terms. One of these additional terms was a provision entitling the customer, Pegler, to

---

[30] [1996] 4 All ER 481.

[31] In the earlier case of *Flamar Interocean Ltd v Denmac Ltd* [1990] 1 Lloyd's Rep 434, the judge suggested (though did not specifically decide) that the fact that many parts of the defendant's standard terms, other than the exclusion clause, were modified in negotiations meant that s 3 did not apply. One clear difference between that case and *St Albans v ICL* is that in *St Albans* there was a clear distinction between the particular terms, which were negotiated, and the General Conditions, which were not.

[32] 29 June 1999 (unreported).

[33] [2000] EWHC Technology 137.

recover any financial loss in the event that it terminated the contract for material breach. This conflicted with an exclusion clause in the main contract which set out a broadly worded exclusion of liability.

Purely on the question of whether the contract was on 'standard terms', the court found—perhaps somewhat counter-intuitively—that the contract was on standard terms notwithstanding the schedule of variations, as the standard exclusion clause itself had been included without any material variation to its wording.

(e) *Holman v Sherwood:* A similar approach was adopted by the court in *Horace Holman Group v Sherwood International Group Ltd.*[34] In this case, as in *Pegler*, the contract had taken the form of a set of the supplier's standard terms together with an attached annex of amendments, additions, and deletions. The court took the view that the fact that some degree of negotiation had taken place was not relevant to the question of whether any particular term had ceased to be 'standard'. In fact, as the changes to the supplier's standard limitation clauses were only minor in this instance, these terms in particular were to be treated as 'standard terms', so UCTA 1977 did apply.

1.2.2.10 *The UCTA reasonableness test*

The test of reasonableness is set out in section 11 of, and Schedule 2 to, UCTA 1977. Section 11(1) provides that for a particular provision to be 'reasonable', it must have been fair and reasonable to include the clause at the time the contract was made. The court will take account of the matters mentioned in Schedule 2, including:

(a) The strength of the bargaining position of the parties.

(b) Whether the buyer received some benefit (eg, a lower price) for agreeing to the clause.

(c) How far the buyer knew or ought to have known of the existence and extent of the clause.

(d) If the exclusion is contingent on compliance with some condition (eg, regular maintenance) whether it was reasonable to expect the condition to be complied with.

(e) Whether the goods were specially made or adapted to the customer's order.

The courts have also held that the question as to which of the parties can most readily insure against the loss is a relevant consideration, and that a limitation of liability is more likely to be reasonable than a complete exclusion.[35]

---

[34] [2002] 146 SJLB 35.
[35] *George Mitchell (Chesterhall) Ltd v Finney Lock Seeds Ltd* [1983] 2 AC 803. This was a case decided under the slightly different provisions of the Supply of Goods (Implied Terms) Act 1973 as its facts occurred before the 1977 Act came into force, but it was nonetheless clearly decided with at least one eye on that Act.

The courts have been through several stages of increasing sophistication in determining how the reasonableness test should apply in practice to system supply contracts, and the main currents are discussed below.

1.2.2.11 *The reasonableness test in practice: (1) towards the high water mark*
The earlier cases in the line of decisions mentioned in section 1.2.2.9 illustrate how the reasonableness test has historically been applied:

(a) *Salvage Association v CAP:* In *Salvage Association v CAP Financial Services Ltd*,[36] the official referee found the following factors tended to support the supplier's contention that the exclusion was reasonable: first, the parties were of equal bargaining power and, secondly, the Salvage Association had taken legal advice and advice from its insurers and auditors. Against those factors, however, were the following:

  (i)   UCTA 1977 puts the burden of proof of reasonableness on CAP;
  (ii) CAP had insurance up to £5,000,000, and could thus stand a greater liability, whilst the Salvage Association could not easily obtain insurance against CAP's failure;
  (iii) the risk of CAP's failure should have been low;
  (iv) CAP assured the Salvage Association that it would succeed in constructing the software as required under the contract, and the Salvage Association had no reason to doubt this;
  (v)   CAP had already decided to increase the maximum limit of its liability from £25,000 to £1,000,000, but failed to do so in this contract for unexplained reasons;
  (vi) CAP called no evidence to justify the £25,000 limit in relation to CAP's turnover or insurance, or the contract value, or the financial risk the Salvage Association was running.

The official referee found that the factors in favour of the clause being unreasonable far outweighed those in favour of its reasonableness, and held the clause to be invalid so that CAP's liability for the breaches of contract was unlimited.

(b) *St Albans v ICL:* Similarly, the judge in *St Albans City and District Council v International Computers Ltd*[37] held that the exclusion clause was not fair and reasonable, and was thus ineffective to exclude or limit ICL's liability.

---

[36] [1995] FSR 654.
[37] [1996] 4 All ER 481.

Although St Albans knew of the limitation and had attempted to negotiate it, the following factors operated to render the clause unreasonable:

(i) ICL had substantially more resources than St Albans;

(ii) ICL held product liability insurance in an aggregate sum of £50 million worldwide;[38]

(iii) ICL called no evidence to show that the limitation to £100,000 was reasonable, either in relation to the potential risk or the actual loss;

(iv) as in *Salvage Association v CAP Financial Services Ltd*, the contract had mistakenly been made on a superseded version of the General Conditions. In the current version the limitation was £125,000;

(v) local authorities are not in the same position as private sector businesses; their operations are constrained by statute and financial restraints and they cannot necessarily be expected to insure against commercial risks;[39]

(vi) St Albans received no inducement to agree to the limitation, and there was evidence that all ICL's competitors imposed similar limitations of liability;

(vii) when St Albans tried to negotiate the limitation, albeit at the last moment, ICL in effect said that this was not possible because it would delay the provision of the software to St Albans beyond the date for implementation of the community charge.

The judge accordingly found that ICL had not discharged its burden of proving that the term was fair and reasonable, and also that financially ICL was best placed to bear a risk of this kind through insurance and thus spread it across its customer base.

(c) *South West Water v ICL:* The judge in *South West Water Services Ltd v International Computers Ltd*[40] noted further that the extent to which a party has had discussions and has freely entered into a contract on the other party's standard terms may be relevant as an important circumstance in considering whether those terms are reasonable. ICL argued that its standard limitation clause should be treated as reasonable in this case because its terms had been subject to arm's length discussion and negotiation, but this was found not to be the case on the evidence.

---

[38] It is not clear how this figure was discovered by St Albans. In *Flamar Interocean Ltd v Denmac Ltd* [1990] 1 Lloyd's Rep 434, the judge specifically held that details of the defendant's insurance cover did not have to be disclosed on discovery, as the relevant question under UCTA was not the specific cover that the defendant held but the availability of insurance cover in similar situations.

[39] The case has received substantial criticism on this ground, which appears to reflect a somewhat idealized view of the relationship between local authorities and their suppliers. It seems unlikely to survive serious argument before another court.

[40] 29 June 1999 (unreported).

1.2.2.12 The reasonableness test in practice: (2) the high water mark
Horace Holman Group v Sherwood International Group Ltd[41] probably represents the high water mark of the courts' stringent application of the *contra proferentem* rule and the reasonableness test in favour of the customer. The contract had provided that the supplier, Sherwood, would have no liability for 'indirect, special, consequential or economic loss or loss of contracts, goodwill, revenue, profits, anticipated savings or other benefits . . . or for any loss [arising from third party claims]', and that certain other losses were subject to a 'price paid' cap.

On the specific issue of reasonableness, the court made several observations which seem a little counter-intuitive. For example:

(a) the court said that whilst both parties were large and capable of negotiating on their own behalf, this was not a major consideration to the determination of the reasonableness of the limitation;

(b) the court observed that as Sherwood's system was the best on the market at that time, and the equivalent could not have been obtained elsewhere without a lot of extra work, this also tended to undermine the reasonableness of the limitation—though it is unclear to this author why a supplier's standard limitation clause should be treated particularly unfavourably just because the supplier happens to have the best product on the market;

(c) there was evidence from both parties that all the terms were commonplace in the software industry, and the court held that Holman could not have obtained a contract from a different supplier without substantially similar clauses—though again, it is not clear why this should tend to undermine the reasonableness of a clause;

(d) with regard to the price paid cap, the court observed that the potential for loss was significantly greater than the financial limits in question—but this is precisely the reason for seeking to put a financial cap on the supplier's liability in the first place;

(e) with regard to the exclusion of liability for loss of savings, the court said in a memorable phrase, 'people buy software to make savings because . . . if it works properly, one computer loaded with the right software can replace a dozen Bob Cratchits sitting at their stools with pens'. On that basis, the court emphasized again that a good reason was required to justify the exclusion and none was found, so the exclusion of lost savings failed as well.

---

[41] [2002] 146 SJLB 35.

1.2.2.13 *The reasonableness test in practice: (3) the tide turns*

As a result of that line of cases leading up to *Holman v Sherwood*, the question started to arise whether the English courts 'had it in' for the IT industry.[42] However, beginning in about 2001, the tide turned back in favour of the supplier.

(a) *Watford v Sanderson:* In *Watford Electronics v Sanderson*,[43] Watford had purchased an integrated sales accounts and warehouse package for use in its mail order business. Total software and hardware costs and licence fees were in the region of £100,000, with damages claimed in excess of £5 million.

The contract was in standard terms, and also contained an exclusion of consequential loss and a price paid limitation clause. At first instance, the judge found that these limitations taken together were unreasonable, and the supplier Sanderson appealed on this point to the Court of Appeal.

The Court of Appeal overruled the 'broad brush' approach taken by the lower court in treating the consequential loss and the price paid limitation clauses as interconnected terms. This represents good news for suppliers, as these clauses will henceforth be construed separately so that if one is found to be unenforceable, there is at least a chance of succeeding under the other.

With regard to the consequential loss exclusion specifically, the Court of Appeal went back to some first principles, and the logical argument was expressed as follows:

(i) there is significant risk that a customized software product may not perform to a customer's satisfaction;

(ii) if that happens, the customer will not make savings it has expected to make, and this risk is (or at least ought to be) in the contemplation of the parties at the outset of the contract.

(iii) in this particular case, the supplier was better able to appreciate the risk of *whether* the product might fail; but the customer was in a better position to *quantify* that risk;

(iv) the risk of loss can generally be covered by insurance, although this may be available only at a cost which will in turn be reflected in the contract price.

Given all that background, when parties of equal bargaining power negotiate a price under an agreement which provides for the risk to fall on one particular party, the Court of Appeal said that the judiciary should be 'cautious' about saying that

---

[42] 'Do the Courts have it in for the IT industry?' was the title of a discussion at the Computing Services and Software Association at the end of 2001, where the panellists included the chairman of ICL and the judge in *Watford v Sanderson*. One of the themes at that session was that the IT industry does not help itself with poorly drafted specifications and contracting processes, multiple personalities within different parts of the supplier—different individuals dealing with software, hardware, and support sales—and so on.

[43] [2001] All ER 290.

the term is not reasonable. The parties should be taken to be the best judges of the commercial fairness of the agreement, with a court not intervening unless one party has in effect taken unfair advantage of the other. In the circumstances of *Watford v Sanderson* itself, the consequential loss exclusion was upheld.

(b) *SAM v Hedley:* That approach of the Court of Appeal was followed in the following year with *SAM Business Systems v Hedley*.[44] The case concerned a Y2K upgrade project, that the customer only decided to undertake at the last minute, signing the contract in October 1999, without doing proper due diligence either on the supplier or its standard contract documentation. The software licence provided for a money-back guarantee in certain circumstances, and it also contained clauses that excluded liability for damages resulting from use of the software, and excluding warranties as to fitness for purpose.

In the Technology and Construction Court, Judge Bowsher looked at these together and concluded that he would have found the exclusions unreasonable but for the money-back guarantee. He also took into account other factors like the parties' equal bargaining power, the existence of similar clauses in contracts from SAM's competitors, Hedleys' own failure to try to negotiate terms, and also their failure to do proper due diligence.

(c) *Kingsway v Red Sky:* Although the more recent case of *Kingsway Hall Hotel v Red Sky IT (Hounslow) Ltd*[45] went against the supplier, it illustrates again that the courts will at least be willing to treat exclusions in standard IT contracts as reasonable.

Kingsway operated a chain of hotels, and bought Red Sky's reservations software. The software was licensed under Red Sky's standard terms, clause 10.1 of which purported to exclude all warranties as to performance, quality, fitness for purpose, 'except as provided in clause 10.2' of the contract. Clause 10.2 then consisted of a warranty that the software would provide the facilities and functions set out in certain 'Operating Documents' to be supplied to Kingsway. There were also exclusions of loss of profits, and a liability cap of four times the contract value.

After the software turned out to be unsuitable, Red Sky sought to rely on its standard terms, arguing that clauses 10.1 and 10.2 together excluded the SGA implied terms as to satisfactory quality and fitness for purpose. They also said that the exclusions satisfied the 'reasonableness' test because the software package was just an off-the-shelf package—it had not been customized to Kingsway's requirements (in which case the hotel company might have been entitled to a higher standard of commitment). Kingsway argued in response that the exclusions could

---

[44] [2002] All ER (D) 311.
[45] [2010] EWHC 965 (TCC).

only have applied if it had been supplied with the Operating Documents referred to in clause 10.2, which was not the case.

In the event, the court found for Kingsway. Red Sky's attempted exclusion of liability did not apply, because it was based on the assumption that customers would satisfy themselves about fitness for purpose by reading the Operating Documents. The Operating Documents were critical, and as they had not been given to Kingsway, Kingsway could not decide for itself whether the system would be suitable for its needs, and had to rely instead on Red Sky's recommendations. As a result, the clause 10.1 exclusion did not apply and the statutory implied terms therefore formed part of the contract between Red Sky and Kingsway.

It is notable, however, that the court did not express fundamental reservations about the exclusion clause itself. The court observed that it might be reasonable for the supplier to exclude the implied terms as to satisfactory quality and fitness for purpose where the customer has the means to satisfy itself and does not have to rely on the advice of the supplier. In this case, it was rather the failure of Red Sky to observe process—providing the Operating Documents—that essentially led to the failure of the exclusions.

Taking these cases together, then, it is clear that there has been a major change in the way that the courts look at liability clauses in IT contracts. This may be in part attributable to the increasing use of IT systems in everyday domestic and business life, which has 'demystified' IT for the judiciary as it has for the wider population. The parties are now considered to be the best judges of the commercial fairness of the agreement, and this means that a really detailed, critical reading of the liability provisions in any IT contract is more important now than it ever was.

1.2.2.14 *Future developments in the law relating to unfair contract terms*

In February 2005, the Law Commission published its final Report and recommendations on unfair contract terms, together with a draft Bill intended to consolidate and simplify the statutory controls under UCTA 1977 and the 1999 Regulations.

In particular, the Law Commission recommended producing a single, unified regime to cover the whole of the UK, and improving protection for small businesses, which frequently find themselves signing contracts with larger businesses that contain unfair terms (a common feature of many IT contracts). However, despite the fact that the recommendations were widely welcomed, at the time of writing there has been no further progress, and the initiative is currently on hold pending negotiations on the draft EU Consumer Rights Directive (due to finish in late 2011).

1.2.3 Remedies

1.2.3.1 *Conditions, warranties, and intermediate terms*

The remedies available to a party for a given breach of contract are determined partly by the classification of the particular obligation that has been breached.

English law distinguishes between three broad categories of contractual obligation:[46]

(a) *Conditions:* A condition is a term of the contract which, if not performed, gives the innocent party the right to terminate the contract and to claim damages for breach.

(b) *Warranties:* A warranty is a term of the contract which, if breached, gives the innocent party the right to claim damages (but not to terminate outright).

(c) *Intermediate terms:* Because the effect of a breach of a given term may not become clear until the point in time at which it happens, many obligations are not readily capable of classification as either a condition or a warranty. For these 'intermediate terms', the remedy for breach depends on the effect of the breach itself. If the effect is such as to substantially deprive the innocent party of the entire benefit of the contract, the remedies will be the same as for breach of a condition (ie, termination and a claim for damages). Otherwise, the remedy will be the same as for breach of a warranty (ie, damages only).

1.2.3.2 *Classification of contract terms in practice*

The parties are free to designate any given provision as either a condition or a warranty. Where they do so, the courts will generally aim to give effect to the stated intention when it comes to remedies, although this is subject to several caveats. First, if the parties have designated the term as a warranty, but statute or case law expressly provides that terms of that kind are to be treated as conditions, then the courts will follow the statute or case law when it comes to remedies. Secondly, if the contract expressly provides for a particular remedy as the consequence of a breach of the relevant term, and that remedy is inconsistent with the parties' own stated designation, then the court will give the contractual provision about the remedy priority over the stated designation. Thirdly, the nature of the contract itself, or the circumstances and implications of the breach, may lead the court to apply a remedy that is inconsistent with the parties' original designation.

Where the parties themselves have *not* expressly identified a term as a condition or warranty, then different principles apply. First, if statute or case law expressly provides that the term is a condition or a warranty (as is the case with many of the implied terms under the SGA 1979 or the SGSA 1982, discussed above), then the court will apply the relevant designation. Secondly, if the contract expressly provides that breach of the term would entitle the innocent party to terminate the contract, then the court will treat that term as a condition; otherwise it will be a warranty. Thirdly, if the nature of the contract, or the circumstances and implications of the breach, lead the court to the conclusion that the parties must have intended that the effect of the breach should be to entitle the innocent party both to terminate the contract and to claim damages, then the court will treat that term as a condition;

---

[46] *Chitty on Contracts*, 30th edn (London: Sweet & Maxwell, 2009) 12-019 and 12-020.

conversely, if the court decides that the parties must have intended that the breach would only entitle the innocent party to damages, then it will be a warranty.[47]

1.3 COMMERCIAL AND DRAFTING ASPECTS

1.3.1 Introduction

1.3.1.1 *The need for express contract terms*

It will be clear from the above discussion that there is no shortage of contractual terms that can be implied by law into contracts for the provision of computer systems. These implied terms will not always reflect the parties' commercial intentions, and to that extent it is preferable for the parties to set out in express terms the position they are trying to achieve. However, the contract is more than just a 'legal' document. Its function should be to record all the terms governing the supply of the system—in terms of what is being delivered, how it is paid for, what happens if the goods or services supplied are unsatisfactory, and so on. The function of the negotiation process that leads to a written contract is to ensure that the parties understand each other's expectations (and their own) about the deal in question, and to draw out differences in understanding that can then be addressed before they lead to problems. Many projects go wrong precisely because, for whatever reason—time pressure, pushy salesmen, deliberate misrepresentation—the parties do not exercise sufficient care to ensure that the supplier's and the customer's expectations match.

1.3.1.2 *The need for proper due diligence*

Both parties should undertake a proper due diligence exercise as part of the preparation for a major system procurement. Although there is no standard template for what should be covered in this kind of investigation, prudent purchasers of IT systems and services will perform a thorough investigation into the technical feasibility of the engagement, the achievability of the development and implementation timetable, the accuracy of the financial modelling, the resources to be committed on each side, and any other important areas of risk or commercial exposure. The most carefully crafted contract is no substitute for critical thinking about risks and mitigation in the early stages of the procurement exercise.

The case of *BSkyB Ltd v HP Enterprise Services UK Ltd (formerly Electronic Data Systems Ltd)*[48] was the biggest IT dispute ever to come before the English courts, with the broadcaster claiming more than £700 million from the supplier, and it illustrates the risks of relying uncritically on ill-considered plans and timetables.

BSkyB made an announcement in February 2000 that they were going to implement a new CRM system within 12 months. It was known to be an ambitious

---

[47] Ibid 24-038 to 24-040.
[48] [2010] EWHC 86 (TCC).

timetable for such a major project, but having committed itself publicly to that goal, BSkyB conducted a tender process and signed a letter of intent with EDS. The parties initially agreed that they would aim for a go-live date of November 2001, but—under pressure from senior people at BSkyB—EDS subsequently represented that the go-live date could be brought forward by several months to July 2001.

The only way that EDS could make the timetable work on paper was to cut the contingencies that had been built into the original plan, which of course increased significantly the risk of failure. There were major disagreements about this approach within EDS, and indeed there were internal emails that suggested that the project manager had 'artificially manipulated' the timetable for the sake of acceding to the client's demands.

The project encountered extensive delays, and BSkyB dismissed EDS before the engagement was complete. The new CRM system was originally supposed to go live in July 2001 at a budget of £48 million, but was finally completed in March 2006 at a cost of £265 million—nearly five years late and more than five times over budget. BSkyB claimed damages totalling £700 million for a range of matters, including consequential losses and damage to reputation.

From the purely legal point of view, the principal issue in the case was the relationship between the contractual exclusion clauses and BSkyB's claim for fraudulent misrepresentation. EDS was found to have misrepresented the feasibility of the implementation timetable, and as a result was exposed to an unlimited claim for damages because none of the contractual liability caps operated to limit liability for fraudulent misrepresentation.

However, the case also illustrates the practical necessity of conducting a proper analysis of the major risks before committing to a contract. The court found that EDS's statement that they would be able to achieve go live by the July date carried an implication that they had done proper analysis and had reasonable grounds to believe that it was achievable. However, there was also evidence that BSkyB itself could and should have taken a more critical approach to the assurances from EDS: there had actually been strong reservations expressed within the broadcaster about the feasibility of the shortened timetable, and BSkyB's own Chief Technology Officer had suggested that the project was heading for disaster if EDS had not done sufficient analysis. A more thorough, open, and critical approach to the identification of these concerns might not have prevented the failure of the project altogether, but it could certainly have helped to mitigate the risk.

1.3.1.3 *The role of the legal adviser*

As noted at section 1.1.2 above, a well-drawn system supply contract will record all the parties' principal expectations about the procurement in question. Ensuring that these expectations match, and that they are properly documented in the contract paperwork, is the key role of the legal adviser in the contract process.

There is a common misconception in the IT industry that contract documentation is purely a matter for lawyers, and is somehow separate from the commercial realities of a transaction. As a result, the legal adviser is often left out of the early stages of negotiation, and frequently has to raise key issues such as limitations of liability at a very late stage in the process. Putting together the right team for the procurement or sale should mean involving the legal team at the outset, and using their expertise to help draft and structure the documentation generally.

1.3.2 Specification

1.3.2.1 *Need for a written specification*

A clear specification is the foundation stone of a successful system supply contract. It defines what the supplier will provide, sets out the quality standards to be achieved, and forces both sides to think seriously about what is really wanted, and what is achievable. In every case, the specification should address:

(a) Functionality (ie, what the system is to do).

(b) Performance (ie, how well it is supposed to do it).

(c) Compatibility (ie, any software and hardware with which the system is likely to be used).

The importance of including a suitably detailed specification can be illustrated by two cases:

(a) *Micron v Wang:* In *Micron Computer Systems Ltd v Wang (UK) Ltd*,[49] one of Micron's complaints was that the system bought from Wang did not provide 'transaction logging'. The judge observed that

the acknowledged absence of a transaction logging facility is not in reality a fault in the system which was sold. Micron can only complain about its absence if Micron can establish a contractual term, express or implied, or an actionable representation, to the effect that the system included such a facility. In order to make good its case on transaction logging, Micron must therefore establish that they made known to Wang that they required such a facility.

In the event, the judge found on the evidence that Micron had not made its requirement for transaction logging clear to Wang, and accordingly that part of Micron's case failed.

(b) *St Albans v ICL:* By contrast, in *St Albans City and District Council v International Computers Ltd*,[50] the local authority had made its requirements clear in its invitation to tender which had itself been expressly incorporated into the contract. When the system supplied failed to meet those requirements, the authority claimed successfully against the supplier on the basis of breach of an express term.

---

[49] 9 May 1990, QBD (unreported).
[50] [1996] 4 All ER 481.

1.3.3 Delivery and acceptance arrangements

1.3.3.1 *Delivery*

The arrangements for delivery should always be dealt with by express provisions in the supply contract. The contract should set out the date (or dates) on which delivery is to be made, whether all the elements of the system are to be delivered at one time or whether it is to arrive in instalments, and who has responsibility for installation and testing. From the point of view of contractual certainty, the ideal situation is for the contract to set out specific delivery dates. This may not be possible if, say, there is a lengthy development project prior to delivery, but even in that eventuality the contract should set out a timetable or project plan showing roughly how long each phase is likely to take. If no clear date is identified or identifiable, then as a matter of law the system will have to be delivered within 'a reasonable time': a position of contractual uncertainty that is unlikely to provide significant advantage to either party in the event of a dispute.

Consequences of late delivery and non-delivery   What commonly happens if delivery is late is that the buyer waives the seller's obligation to achieve that date, and so loses the right to reject: for example, by continuing to request delivery after the contractual date has passed. This means that there is now *no* contractual date for delivery, and at best the seller is obliged to deliver within a reasonable time. In order to regain the right to reject, the buyer must reimpose a date by giving the seller reasonable notice that the buyer will refuse to accept that part of the system after a particular date.[51] Such notice is normally express, but it may be given impliedly (eg, by service of a writ[52]). As an additional protection for the buyer, the contract should ideally contain an express provision permitting cancellation of the contract, with or without compensation to the buyer, if the goods are not delivered by some cut-off date. Alternatively, if the supplier does not agree to a clear target date for delivery, the contract may provide for a notice period after which the buyer can withdraw, with an appeal against the notice to a third party.[53]

1.3.3.2 *Acceptance arrangements*

Formal acceptance procedures are a crucial aspect of any successful system procurement. Systems are acquired in order to perform a specified set of functions, within particular performance requirements. Until the system has been tested, the buyer will not be able to assess whether what has been delivered accords with the contract.

---

[51] *Charles Rickards Ltd v Oppenhaim* [1950] 1 KB 616.

[52] *Tool Metal Manufacturing Co Ltd v Tungsten Electric Co Ltd* [1955] 1 WLR 761.

[53] eg, an arbitrator, the engineer in construction contracts, etc.

Defining acceptance criteria The nature of acceptance tests varies widely between projects. Where a major piece of development work is involved, the parties may negotiate and document detailed testing arrangements as part of the contract document. At the other extreme, the acceptance procedure may simply be that if the buyer uses the system 'live' for, say, 30 days without rejecting it, then it is deemed to have been accepted. The vital features of any acceptance procedure, however, are:

(a) That it provides for an objective and measurable 'yardstick' as to the standards of performance and functionality to be demonstrated.

(b) From the buyer's point of view, that this yardstick will demonstrate to its full satisfaction that the system meets its requirements.

(c) That the procedure is clear as to the consequences of both the passing and failing of the acceptance test.

Consequences of acceptance On successful completion of the testing, the system will be deemed to have been accepted. Acceptance will generally trigger payment of the whole or the final instalment of any lump sum charges, or the commencement of periodic charges, and following acceptance the buyer's remedies will be limited to a claim under the warranty provision. The contract should also provide expressly for the consequences of failure to achieve acceptance. Typically, there will be a period during which the supplier may rectify problems and then retest; but further failure will signal the premature end of the contract, with the buyer able to return the hardware and software in exchange for a refund of any moneys paid.

1.3.4 Timetable

1.3.4.1 *Need for the timetable*
The preparation of the specification should enable the parties to assess the likely timescale for the project and so to prepare a project plan setting out key deliverables (or 'milestones') and their expected dates. In almost all major systems implementations, staged payments will be triggered by the achievement of individual milestones. It is accordingly essential that these are identified with as much precision as possible, and reflect the terminology of the contract generally. The buyer will generally have in mind a timescale within which it wants the system provided, although the sophistication of the timetable will vary according to:

(a) The complexity of the project in question—a major development contract may include target dates for numerous stages, each of which may be divided up into smaller phases such as functional specification, systems specification, program specification, development, program testing, systems testing, debugging, retesting, and acceptance.

(b) Payment arrangements—in particular, whether the price and payment arrangements are tied in to specified milestones, and the implications for both parties of any failure to meet target deadlines.

1.3.5 Pricing and payment

1.3.5.1 *Pricing and payment structures generally*
From the supplier's point of view, the heart of the contract is ensuring that he gets paid for the goods or services he provides. There are as many pricing and payment structures as there are types of IT deal. For example:

(a) a single charge for the entire development and implementation project;

(b) periodic charges for ongoing maintenance and support;

(c) separate purchase and licence fees in respect of hardware and software elements of the system (which licence fees may themselves be periodic or a single lump sum);

(d) 'utility' pricing for cloud computing services, based on utilization and payable according to the supplier's published tariff.

As a result, there is little to be gained from making generalizations about pricing and payment terms. The one point worth making is that, where payments are tied into specific targets (such as system acceptance), the terminology and structure of the payment schedule should accurately reflect that of the timetable.

1.3.5.2 *Timing of payments*
The time of payment will generally not be of the essence unless it is expressed as such. However, for the sake of contractual certainty, it is of course desirable to specify precisely when sums become due. This links in with delivery dates. A common practice in systems contracts is to pay by instalments as the various parts of the system are delivered, retaining a proportion of the price until the complete system has been tested. This arrangement will incentivize the supplier to perform these obligations in accordance with the contractual timetable, while the retention of a significant proportion of the fee until acceptance will give the buyer some security for performance. Suppliers will also often seek an express right to payment of interest on overdue amounts.

In respect of periodic fees specifically, the buyer will be concerned about the supplier's rights to increase the fee, and may seek to circumscribe these in some way. For example, only one increase a year may be permitted or rises may be limited by reference to an appropriate index. The buyer may also seek to delay the first payment until after the system has been accepted.

1.3.5.3 *Retention of title*
Where the seller gives credit to the buyer, there is always some doubt whether the seller will be paid. (Even substantial banks and law firms have been known to

default on debts.) For this reason, it is common for hardware suppliers to retain title in the goods they supply as security for payment. A retention of title clause is a provision in the contract that although the buyer is to be given possession of the goods, ownership is to remain with the seller until certain conditions (normally payment in full) are complied with. If the buyer fails to comply with the conditions, the seller is entitled to repossess the goods, and can then sell them to recoup its losses.

Retention of title clauses are permitted under section 19 of the SGA 1979. It is important that the seller retains title, property, or legal ownership (all these terms are equivalent).[54] As risk normally passes with property, a retention of title clause will also provide that the goods are at the buyer's risk from the moment of delivery. It should contain a clear statement of when the seller is entitled to repossess the goods, normally if payment is not made within the credit period, or if the buyer commits an act of insolvency or a receiver is appointed. It is also common to include a provision that the seller has the right to enter the buyer's premises to repossess the goods.

1.3.6 Intellectual property rights (IPRs)

1.3.6.1 *The need for express treatment of IPR issues*
System supply contracts generally involve the transfer of information, in some form, from one party to another: for example, program specifications (in a consultancy agreement), software (in a software licence), data for processing (in a bureau services agreement), or confidential business information (in a development agreement). The lawful use of such information is dependent on compliance with the laws relating to copyright, confidentiality, database rights, and other forms of intellectual property. In addition, the use of certain computer equipment may constitute an infringement of patent or similar rights if it is undertaken without the consent of the rights owner. As a result, it is essential that any system supply contract deals comprehensively with IPR issues, and in particular addresses:

(a) ownership; and

(b) IPR warranties and indemnities.

1.3.6.2 *Ownership*
The contract should specify what IPRs are to be created or used, and precisely who owns them. This is particularly important in contracts for software development or consultancy work because of section 11 of the Copyright Designs and Patents Act 1988, which contains a common trap for the unwary: work done under a consultancy contract will normally vest in the supplier, not the customer, so a formal written assignment of copyright is needed if the aim is for the customer to own the work product outright.

---

[54] Note that any drafting which amounts to a retention of equitable ownership will result in the creation of a charge which must be registered under the Companies Act 2006 or the Bills of Sale Act 1878.

1.3.6.3 *Treatment of third party software*

For similar reasons, where the system incorporates any third party software, the prudent customer will want an express assurance that the supplier has authority to grant the licence or sub-licence in respect of those third party rights. As a practical matter, it is essential to ensure that there is no 'hiatus' between the scope of the third party licence and the uses envisaged in respect of all other aspects of the system.

1.3.6.4 *IPR warranties and indemnities*

Although section 12 of the SGA 1979 provides a remedy for the customer if the seller should turn out not to have the right to sell the products in question,[55] in practical terms, the parties are unlikely to be happy to rely on this general law position:

(a) The customer will often impose a formal obligation to take curative action to deal with any allegations of third party IPR infringement: this is particularly so if the system is a critical part of the customer's business and merely rejecting it and claiming back the purchase price would leave the customer in a difficult position.

(b) Equally, the supplier may wish to reserve the right to dispute the existence or extent of the third party's claims, in order to preserve its reputation and position in the market.

As a result, most system supply contracts will contain a warranty in favour of the customer that use of the system will not infringe third party rights, and an indemnity in respect of any claims that may arise. (Similar provisions are commonplace in distribution and agency contracts, to protect the distributor/agent and its end-user customers against IPR claims brought in respect of products supplied by the principal.) The contract should set out any express warranties as to the supplier's ownership or entitlement in respect of the IPRs comprised in the system, together with a process for addressing any breach of those warranties. A clause which incorporates the following procedural points should assist in removing some of the potential complications:

(a) A right on the supplier's part to take over and litigate (in the customer's name) any such action by a third party, and to settle the action.

(b) A right for the supplier to modify the system so that it does not infringe the alleged right, provided that it still conforms with the specification.[56]

(c) An indemnity given by the supplier against the customer's losses in the event of a successful third party claim.

---

[55] See section 1.2.1.2 above.

[56] It must be noted that a seller cannot exclude or restrict the condition in the SGA 1979, s 12(1)—see sections 1.2.1.2–1.2.13. However, until the third party has established that the right has in fact been infringed, the seller is arguably not in breach of that condition. In any event, most buyers should be satisfied with effective cure.

1.3.6.5 *Confidentiality*
A further feature of the transfer of information between suppliers and customers is that provision needs to be made to ensure that the information is treated in confidence. In the context of a consultancy agreement or a bureau services contract, for example, the consultant may have access to all kinds of commercially sensitive information about the customer's business and systems. The customer will want to ensure that this information is only used for the express, permitted purposes. Similarly, where a software house is licensing programs for use by its customer, the supplier will want to ensure that its proprietary software is not disclosed to third parties.

1.3.6.6 *Access to source code*
Software elements of the system will usually be delivered to the customer in object code form, with the source code being retained by the supplier. The practical consequence of this will be that, whilst the buyer is able to use the software, he will not be able to modify or maintain it. He is dependent on the supplier for software maintenance, although he may be able to protect himself against the more dire consequences of such dependence by reason of the error correction rights conferred in section 50C of the Copyright Designs and Patents Act 1988. Again, however, the prudent customer would be unwise to rely on this general law provision, for which reason the contract should expressly provide for either:

(a) An express right to call for and to use the source code for development or maintenance purposes (a requirement which will often be vigorously resisted by suppliers), perhaps subject to confidentiality conditions, in order to protect the supplier's legitimate interests in the secrecy of this material.

(b) An escrow arrangement, whereby the supplier agrees to deposit a copy of the source code with an independent third party (the escrow agent) and then the supplier, customer, and escrow agent enter into a tripartite agreement to govern its release. The escrow agreement will provide for the initial deposit of the source code, and for its updating with error corrections and new releases. On the occurrence of certain specified events (eg, such as the supplier going into liquidation, or failing to provide maintenance services as contracted for), the escrow agent will release the source code to the customer for the purposes of maintaining the software. Organizations providing escrow services in the UK include industry bodies like the National Computing Centre and Intellect, and commercial operators like Iron Mountain. So far it would seem that the arrangements work successfully.

1.3.7 Other express warranties

1.3.7.1 *The need for express warranties*
The existence or otherwise of implied terms in system supply contracts is, as we have seen, a matter of some uncertainty. Indeed, such terms are seldom of much

assistance to the parties because of the very generalized way in which they are expressed. Concepts like 'satisfactory quality' or 'reasonable skill and care' are inevitably open to a high degree of judicial interpretation.

Furthermore, in the real world, the majority of IT contracts (whether on the supplier's standard terms or specially negotiated between the parties) will specifically exclude or limit the operation of all implied conditions and warranties. (The efficacy of such exclusions and limitations is examined at section 1.2.2 above.) As a result, it is in the interests of both the supplier and the customer to ensure that their agreement accurately documents all the assurances that the parties regard as important.

1.3.7.2 *Basic forms of warranty*

Express warranties given by suppliers are accordingly of considerable importance. Such express warranties normally take one of two basic forms:

(a) The warranty may state that the system will comply with its functional specification or user manual, or the service will conform with a documented service description, or meet certain specified performance criteria, or the like: such a warranty has the advantage that compliance or breach can be objectively measured, and is usually the best form of express warranty that a customer can obtain.

(b) The warranty may provide that defects or service failures will be corrected by the supplier, though the disadvantage here is that it begs the question of what constitutes a defect: for example, in the event of failure to perform a particular function, there may be a dispute about whether the lack of the particular function in fact amounts to a defect (which was precisely the issue in *Micron*—see section 1.3.2.1(a) above).

1.3.7.3 *Restrictions on warranties*

Whatever the form of warranty, it is likely to be subject to a number of restrictions:

(a) It will generally be limited to a fairly short period of time, probably between three and 12 months. After this time the system may be covered by the maintenance and support arrangements: in other words, ongoing maintenance after expiry of the warranty period has a separate price attached to it.

(b) Some warranty clauses also state that the supplier's only liability is to correct the non-compliance or the defect. The purpose would seem to be to exclude any liability for damages. To the extent that the supplier complies with the warranty this would seem to be effective, but if he fails to remedy the non-compliance or defect, an action for damages would lie for that failure.

(c) Warranties often state that they cease to apply if the customer makes any additions or modifications to the system. Customers would be well advised to limit the qualification to errors or defects in the system that are actually caused by the addition or modification.

1.3.8 Limitations and exclusions of liability

1.3.8.1 *Drafting effective exclusion clauses*
IT suppliers generally seek to restrict their potential exposure to users resulting from breach of contract or defects in the system. This is treated by some as purely a 'legal' issue, but in fact is a major question of commercial risk assessment and allocation. This type of provision is commonplace in system supply contracts, particularly where the contract is based on the supplier's standard terms, which typically contain a limitation clause along the following lines:

(a) The supplier does not exclude liability for death or personal injury caused by negligence, or for fraudulent misrepresentation.

(b) The supplier seeks to exclude liability altogether for 'special', 'indirect', or 'consequential' losses.

(c) The supplier accepts a limited degree of liability for certain other classes of 'direct' loss.

The general legal issues as to the enforceability of limitation and exclusion clauses are discussed at section 1.2.2 above. The first point in (a) above requires little further discussion: liability for death or personal injury caused by negligence, and liability for fraud, *cannot* be limited, as a matter of law.[57] The second and third points in (b) and (c) are discussed below.

1.3.8.2 *Consequential loss: general principles*
The parties need to consider what kinds of loss might result from a system failure, and who takes the risk. The basis of the supplier's argument to exclude liability for consequential loss or loss of profits is essentially that the nature of IT products means that their uses (and thus the potential consequential losses) are not easily foreseeable at the time the contract is made, and that the potential exposure is in any case disproportionate to the contract value. Whether this is an acceptable commercial stance depends on the nature of the system and the extent of the customer's dependence on it.

1.3.8.3 *Consequential loss: drafting issues*
However, turning that commercial position into effective (and commercially acceptable) drafting can be more problematic. There is no consensus as to the meaning of the expressions 'special', 'indirect', and 'consequential' in the context of contractual claims, and there is often a resulting lack of certainty as to the precise effect of the intended exclusion. It is not the purpose of this chapter to try to offer a definitive interpretation of these terms, but it may be helpful to summarize the semantic and

---

[57] UCTA 1977, s 2(1).

philosophical problems encountered by judges and academics in trying to pin down their meanings.

1.3.8.4 *Consequential loss:* Hadley v Baxendale

The starting point for any discussion of consequential damages is *Hadley v Baxendale*,[58] which distinguished two classes of loss recoverable for breach of contract. These are:

(a) 'such [damages] as may fairly and reasonably be considered either as arising naturally, i.e., according to the usual course of things . . . or such as may reasonably be supposed to have been in the contemplation of both parties at the time they made the contract as the probable result of the breach of it'; and

(b) if the parties were aware of 'special circumstances' at the time the contract was made, the damages 'which they would reasonably contemplate would be the amount of injury which would ordinarily flow from a breach under these special circumstances'.

1.3.8.5 *Consequential loss: the semantic labyrinth*

That basic distinction drawn in *Hadley v Baxendale* has been recast on numerous occasions over the last 150 years. However, the difficulty for the draftsman is that the terminology in common usage—'indirect' or 'consequential' loss, or 'special' damages—does not fit neatly into the *Hadley v Baxendale* rules, nor is it used in a consistent fashion.

For example, the expression 'consequential loss' is taken by some to mean pecuniary loss consequent on physical damage. However, when used in an exclusion clause, 'consequential' means losses arising under the second rule in *Hadley v Baxendale*, and so does *not* preclude recovery of pecuniary losses under the first rule.[59]

A more recent discussion of 'consequential loss' is *British Sugar plc v NEI Power Projects Ltd*.[60] It is also a good example of the confusion that can be caused by trying to use *Hadley v Baxendale* terminology to define concepts like 'direct', 'indirect', or 'consequential' loss. NEI supplied some defective power equipment to British Sugar, under a contract that expressly limited the seller's liability for 'consequential loss'. As a result of breakdowns, British Sugar claimed for increased production costs and resulting loss of profits. British Sugar argued for the narrowest construction of the term 'consequential loss', interpreting it to mean 'loss not resulting directly and naturally from breach of contract'; whereas NEI argued that the term meant 'all loss other than the normal loss which might be suffered as a result of the breach of contract, negligence or other breach of duty'. The courts found for the

---

[58] (1854) 9 Exch 341.
[59] See *Saint Line Ltd v Richardsons, Westgarth & Co* [1940] 2 KB 99.
[60] [1997] EWCA Civ 2438.

claimant, and approved earlier authorities that 'consequential damages' means the damages recoverable under the second limb of *Hadley v Baxendale*.

By this analysis, where loss of profits or loss of business (commonly regarded as typical examples of 'consequential loss') arise naturally from the breach of contract, they should be recoverable by the user. This is a result that may surprise many IT suppliers, but which was clearly followed in *Simkins Partnership v Reeves & Co Ltd*.[61] Reeves & Co had agreed to supply a telephone system at Simkins' offices. As a result of some modification work, various voicemail ports were left unsecured, with the result that an unknown third party obtained access to the system and used it to make international calls, for which Simkins was billed some £17,200. Simkins in turn claimed that amount from Reeves on the basis of breach of the implied terms of reasonable care and skill. Reeves sought to rely on a contractual exclusion of 'consequential loss', but the court held that the £17,200 claim was a *direct* loss; the unauthorized charges were (or should reasonably have been) in the contemplation of the parties at the time the contract was made, as a possible consequence of failing to secure the system adequately. The case clearly fell into the first limb of *Hadley v Baxendale*.

Similar confusion is often encountered in the interpretation of other commonly used terms, where the courts have sometimes struggled to express in a clear fashion their approach to the intertwined concepts of causation, foreseeability, and remoteness. For example:

(a) In relation to 'indirect loss', it used to be the case that the courts would hold a defendant liable (particularly in negligence) for all 'direct consequences' whether foreseeable or not, but they have long since ceased to try to define issues of remoteness and quantum in terms of 'direct', 'natural', or 'ordinary'. Instead, following the *Wagon Mound*[62] cases in the 1960s, the test of liability (in tort at least) is analysed simply in terms of foreseeability.

(b) To complicate matters further, the term 'consequential' has at one point been defined simply to mean 'not direct'—see *Millar's Machinery v David Way*[63]—but there is also an argument, following certain observations of Lord Diplock in *P&M Kaye v Hosier*[64] that the expression 'direct' could include 'consequential' losses provided these were not too remote.

(c) The term 'special damages' has at least four possible meanings, including (i) past (pecuniary) loss calculable as at the trial date—as opposed to all other items of unliquidated 'general damages'; and (ii) losses falling under the second rule in

---

[61] 18 July 2003, QB (unreported).

[62] *Overseas Tankship (UK) v Morts Dock and Engineering Co (The Wagon Mound)* [1961] AC 388, [1961] 2 WLR 126; and *Overseas Tankship (UK) v Miller Steamship C Pty (The Wagon Mound (No 2))* [1967] 1 AC 617, [1966] 3 WLR 498.

[63] (1935) 40 Com Cas 204.

[64] [1972] 1 All ER 121.

Hadley v Baxendale—as opposed to 'general damages' being losses recoverable under the first rule.

1.3.8.6 *Towards an 'assumption of responsibility' test*

In summary, the meanings of the terms 'indirect', 'consequential', and 'special' are at best unclear in the context of IT contracts, and it is surprising that they should continue routinely to be used. The inclusion of such imprecise terminology inevitably delays the contract process, creates uncertainty for users and suppliers alike, and reflects badly on the IT industry and its legal advisers. However, a line of recent cases in the higher courts shows a shift in judicial thinking, and one that will be welcomed by many IT contract specialists.

(a) *Transfield:* In *Transfield Shipping Inc v Mercator Shipping Inc*,[65] the charterers of a ship returned the vessel nine days late, which meant that the owners had to re-negotiate a follow-on charter on much less favourable terms than they had originally agreed. The owners sought damages for their loss of profit amounting to $1.3 million. The charterers argued, however, that the loss should be limited to the difference between the normal market rate for the follow-on charter and the rate that the original charterers had paid for the nine-day over-run, which came to just $158,000. In the House of Lords, their lordships held that the higher level of loss claimed by the owners was too remote to recover. Unfortunately, as often happens, they came to their various decisions for different reasons, but certain comments of Lord Hoffmann were of particular interest.

What Lord Hoffmann said was that the test of remoteness—that is to say, the test of whether a particular heading of loss is recoverable, or whether it was too far removed from the breach of contract—does not just depend solely on foreseeability, which is the conventional *Hadley v Baxendale* test. Rather, he said, the proper question to ask was whether in all the circumstances the loss was a type of loss which the defaulting party could reasonably be regarded as having assumed responsibility for at the time the contract was made.

If that is not the case—if the defaulting party cannot be regarded as having assumed responsibility for the particular kinds of loss—the innocent party will not be able to recover losses that may occur in the usual course of things. In effect, the remoteness test in *Hadley v Baxendale* is therefore a prima facie presumption about what the parties may be taken to have intended, which works fine in most cases, but is nevertheless capable of rebuttal where the commercial context or general understanding of market practice shows that a party would not reasonably have been regarded as assuming responsibility for those losses.

(b) *Supershield:* There was some initial doubt about whether *Transfield* was of wider application than just the shipping business (and indeed whether Lord

---

[65] [2008] UKHL 48.

Hoffmann had intended to create a new test of recoverability), but this was resolved within months by the Court of Appeal decision in *Supershield v Siemens*.[66] The case concerned a faulty water valve that led to flooding in the basement of an office block in the City of London, and the background involved a chain of sub-contracts for a water tank sprinkler system. At the heart of that system was a valve provided by Supershield, and it was this valve that failed. The flooding that resulted was exacerbated because the drains were blocked. Supershield claimed that in the normal course of things (ie the first limb of *Hadley v Baxendale*) the water should have just run away, and the damage would accordingly have been much less. The additional damage caused by the flooding should not, they said, be Supershield's responsibility.

Lord Justice Toulson took the opportunity to talk about the 'policy' rationale that underlies the rules about remoteness. The law on remoteness is based on the idea that the loss recoverable by the innocent party should be limited to the loss which the defaulting party may reasonably be taken to have assumed responsibility for, to protect the innocent party against those losses. The question of remoteness therefore cannot be considered in isolation from the overall purpose of the contract and the scope of the contractual obligations. Here the purpose of the valve was to protect from flooding, and thus Supershield had assumed contractual responsibility for the valve to work so as to prevent that loss even though the probability of simultaneous failure of the drains as a backup system was low.

These comments seem to confirm the approach of Lord Hoffmann in *Transfield*, that the question of assumption of responsibility is the proper question to ask.

(c) *Centrica*: The *Transfield* approach appears also to have been followed in a major IT case, *GB Gas Holdings Ltd v Accenture (UK) Ltd*.[67] GB Gas Holdings, a subsidiary of the energy group Centrica, engaged Accenture to supply a new IT system, which included a billing system for residential customers. Each party's liability was subject to a number of financial caps, according to different headings of potential loss or damage, and the contract excluded loss of profits; loss of business or revenue and any losses or damages to the extent that they were 'indirect', 'consequential', or 'punitive'.

There were problems with the system, and large numbers of customer accounts went unbilled. BG would then issue late bills, which led to major issues with customer satisfaction. Customer satisfaction was exactly what the new billing system was supposed to improve. Centrica claimed several heads of damage in the proceedings, and in particular, as far as this discussion of 'indirect' and 'consequential' loss is concerned, they claimed that the backlog of unresolved 'exceptions' had caused loss because they had had to pay out compensation to customers; pay increased gas

---

[66] [2010] EWCA Civ 7.
[67] [2009] EWCA Civ 912.

distribution charges; employ large numbers of additional staff to try to resolve the problems and to deal with the volume of customer complaints; and they also had had to write off millions of pounds for unbilled or late-billed supply of gas and/or electricity. Predictably, Accenture disputed that these losses were recoverable, arguing that many of these headings were 'indirect' or 'consequential'.

In the event, the first instance court found—and the Court of Appeal upheld—that many of the headings were in fact 'direct' and therefore recoverable. In particular:

(i) The £18 million paid out as additional gas distribution charges was recoverable, because the gas company's inability to provide its wholesale suppliers with complete and correct information about consumption had led to it being overcharged. Accenture had argued that these were 'indirect' losses as they were the result of contracts that were totally outside Accenture's knowledge, but the court decided that this was a direct loss as it arose naturally from the breach of contract.

(ii) Compensation paid out by Centrica to customers, totalling £8 million, was also recoverable. This was a direct loss because the context of the Agreement made it clear that one of its key purposes was to improve customer relations and services—this was actually stated in the recitals. Applying the *Transfield* concept of the 'assumption of responsibility', the court found that Accenture had assumed responsibility for losses in terms of customer compensation if the billing system failed to perform as intended.

(iii) Centrica recovered charges of £2 million for additional borrowing which had been incurred in order to make up for lost revenue through the period of late billing or non-billing of customers. The court held that these were direct losses, and 'the very likely consequence' of the breach by Accenture.

(iv) Centrica also recovered various other customer service charges, like stationery and correspondence costs arising from keeping customers up to date: the court held that all of these were direct losses as well.

1.3.8.7 *Drafting issues: reliance on standard terms and blanket exclusions*
What all these cases tell us is that the concepts of 'direct', 'indirect', or 'consequential' loss are very fluid, and they should be treated with extreme caution. In the context of IT and outsourcing contracts, though, companies routinely agree to use these terms in their liability clauses, with very little consideration about what they might actually mean in the context of any particular contract. This cannot be the best approach to this difficult but important aspect of the parties' relationship, and two

cases illustrate the risks for suppliers of simply trying to rely on blanket exclusions of liability.

(a) In *Regus (UK) Ltd v Epcot Solutions Ltd*,[68] a dispute over the failure to provide air conditioning at a serviced office, the supplier's standard terms contained an exclusion clause which purported to exclude liability for 'loss of business, loss of profits, loss of anticipated savings, loss of or damage to data, third party claims or any consequential loss'. At first instance, the court found that the term did not satisfy the UCTA reasonableness test because it effectively deprived the customer of any remedy for the supplier's failure to provide what was, in the overall commercial context, a basic element of the service. On appeal, the Court of Appeal[69] held that the first instance judge had been wrong, as the exclusion clause had not purported to exclude the 'prima facie' measure of contract damages, which in this case was the diminution in value of the services—a decision that was met with relief by many IT companies who routinely rely on this kind of provision—but the case nevertheless illustrates the importance of thinking critically about the types of loss.

(b) Similarly, in *Internet Broadcasting Corp Ltd (t/a NetTV) and NetTV Hedge Funds Ltd (formerly MARHedge TV Ltd) v MAR LLC (t/a MARHedge)*,[70] the deputy judge found it significant that the effect of the exclusion clause was effectively to deprive NetTV of any realistic remedy for default by MARHedge. The clause had provided that 'neither party will be liable to the other for any damage to software, damage to or loss of data, loss of profit, anticipated profit, revenues, anticipated savings, goodwill or business opportunity, or for any indirect or consequential loss or damage.' The court recognized that, ultimately, any loss suffered by a company can be characterized as financial or economic loss, so a clause that purports to exclude all liability for financial loss incurred by a company is more likely to be considered unreasonable by the courts.

There are of course sound reasons why companies may make a commercial decision to rely on standard exclusion clauses, including the simple practicality of using standard form contracts. However, where the engagement is of a nature that permits them to do so, it is surely preferable that both suppliers and customers should focus on the specific risks associated with the particular procurement. The customer will generally accept that the supplier has a legitimate concern about exposure to unspecified types of liability; but the kinds of loss that will flow from a breach of an IT supply contract *can* be classified, at least in general terms.

1.3.8.8 *Drafting issues: drafting for the allocation of specific risks*
In this respect, the hearing on assessment of damages in *Holman v Sherwood* provides some helpful headings for consideration. Once the limitation clauses

---

[68] [2007] EWHC 938 (Comm).
[69] [2008] EWCA Civ 361.
[70] [2009] EWHC 844 (Ch).

had been overturned, the parties went back to court to determine the heads of damage for which Sherwood would be liable. Holman had claimed under six heads of damage:

(a) third party costs (including disaster recovery, maintenance, contractors' fees, and the costs of upgrading its PCs to cope with the replacement system);

(b) other costs savings (which included savings which Holman had expected to make by bringing its insurance policy preparation work in-house, but which it was unable to achieve until three years after the original target date);

(c) audit savings, which it was unable to achieve for the same reason;

(d) the costs of employing staff who *would* have been made redundant if the system had gone live when promised;

(e) time wasted by directors and staff in attempting to implement the Sherwood system; and

(f) lost revenue opportunities—the work which the company might have won had it been administratively geared up to have handled the extra volume that the system was supposed to be able to manage—together with interest that might have been earned on those revenue opportunities.

These categories of loss are not intended to be definitive: there is no 'definitive list' as such, and each customer and supplier will have its own specific concerns. However, the starting point for constructing an effective provision must be to identify what categories of loss are foreseeable and how the parties intend to allocate these risks between themselves. The aim is to avoid the (ultimately futile) job of trying to *define* 'direct' or 'consequential' loss, and instead—having regard to all the commercial circumstances of the particular transaction—to try to allocate responsibility for those *specific* types of loss that the parties might have in mind: up front, and without resorting to semantic contortions. This approach, which has been advocated by many IT contract lawyers for years, now appears to have judicial backing by reason of the 'assumption of responsibility' test described in *Transfield*. Perhaps the trend over time will be away from traditional *exclusion* clauses, which describe the categories of loss for which a party will not be liable, and towards *inclusion* clauses which set out clearly the particular types of foreseeable loss that might arise from given breaches of contract.

1.3.8.9 *Financial caps on liability*

The recovery of potential loss is often limited to an agreed financial cap. It is common to place a financial cap on the supplier's liability, both for any one breach and also as a global limit (eg, £100,000 for any breach, £500,000 in total). Other than contracts on standard terms, it is likely that such figures will be subject to negotiation, and it is clear from the limited case law under UCTA 1977 that where the parties have genuinely negotiated a limitation the court will be likely to find that limitation to be reasonable.[71] Some sellers limit liability to the contract price, though this seems to set the limits rather too low.

1.3.9 Contractual remedies

1.3.9.1 *Introduction*
Consideration needs to be given to the question of what happens if a contract does not go according to plan—for example, if the supplier fails to deliver a working system within the contracted time frames. The general law principles as to the remedies available for breaches of contract are set out in section 1.2.3 above. However, for the reasons discussed in that section, it is often desirable for the contract documentation to provide for specific remedies in particular situations.

1.3.9.2 *Customer remedies: liquidated damages*
One typical solution to the common problem of failure to adhere to a planned timetable is to provide for payment of liquidated damages to the customer for each day or week that final acceptance is overdue. This will involve a good faith attempt to estimate the cost to the customer of such delay; and if the delay persists for a specified length of time, the customer may also want a right to terminate. The liquidated damages clause sets in advance the precise sum to be paid as compensation for certain breaches (eg, late delivery at £X per day). Provided that sum is a *genuine pre-estimate* of the likely losses, and not a *penalty* to force the supplier to perform, the clause will be enforceable. This is so even if the customer's loss is in fact less than the agreed sum.

1.3.9.3 *Customer remedies: service credits*
Even if the project phase runs to plan, it may be the case that once use of the system has moved into its 'business as usual' phase, the supplier underperforms against its ongoing service obligations. It is common for contracts to include a service level agreement (or SLA) that sets out the targets that the supplier has to meet in terms of matters like system availability and performance. That statement of targets is then backed up by a remedy known as service credits, which provide for amounts to be deducted from the payments due under the contract, if actual performance fails to meet the target standards. As with liquidated damages, the aim is not so much to penalize the supplier for under-performance, as to incentivize effective delivery of the services. Service credits are a particularly important feature of outsourcing contracts—see section 3.2.2.10.

---

[71] *Phillips Products Ltd v Hyland* [1987] 1 WLR 659. See also the discussions of *Salvage Association v CAP Financial Services Ltd* [1995] FSR 645; *St Albans City and District Council v International Computers Ltd* [1996] 4 All ER 481 (CA); *South West Water Services Ltd v International Computers Ltd*, 29 June 1999 (unreported), at section 1.2.2.9 above, as illustrations of the consequences of failure properly to negotiate such limits.

1.3.9.4 *Supplier remedies: interest on late payment*

Similarly, on the supplier's side, the supplier may want an express right to withhold its services or to charge interest in the event of late payment, and in the last resort to terminate the contract altogether.

1.3.10 Change control

1.3.10.1 *The need for change control provisions*

The successful implementation of a complex IT system imposes responsibilities not just on the supplier, but also on the customer. Unlike the supply of a simple package, a bespoke contract is more of a joint effort and, whilst the primary obligation will be on the supplier to write any software and to deliver the system, the supplier will depend on the customer providing information about its business, testing the software, providing employees to be trained, and so on. Crucially, since the customer's requirements may change as the project progresses, the contract should provide a procedure for specifying and agreeing changes to the scope of work. These will involve adjustments to the functional specification, the price, and probably also the timing of the project.

1.3.10.2 *Documenting change procedures*

The proper documentation of these changes will avoid disputes later about what the supplier's obligations actually were. The contract should accordingly include a formal 'change control' clause, setting out a mechanism whereby the customer can request (and the supplier can recommend) changes to the specification, the project plan, or any other aspect of the deal. Any such change would need to be considered from the point of view of technical feasibility and its impact on timing and pricing generally, and no change should take effect unless it has been formally agreed by both parties and documented in the manner envisaged by the change control clause.

1.3.11 Termination

Provision has to be made for termination of the contract, setting out the circumstances in which the contract may be brought to an end and the consequences of that action. These provisions will vary according to the nature of the contract and the deliverables. Apart from a general right to terminate the contract in the event of material breach or the insolvency of the other party, the following points should be considered:

(a) Hardware procurement—the customer may wish to cancel/terminate the contract before the delivery date, and in that event the contract should set out the compensation payable to the supplier.

(b) Software development—contracts for development services are typically terminable by the customer if specific time-critical milestones are significantly overdue. Provision should be made for treatment of the developed software on termination, including delivery up of all copies (and source code) and certification that no copies have been retained.

(c) Contracts for continuing services—consultancy, support, and maintenance services, and bureau services should in any event be terminable on notice. The length of the notice, and the earliest dates on which it may be effective, are matters of negotiation in each case.

1.4 ADDITIONAL CONSIDERATIONS FOR SPECIFIC CONTRACTS

1.4.1 Introduction

The general legal and drafting issues discussed in sections 1.1 to 1.3 of this chapter will apply to the full range of system supply contracts. However, there are additional specific considerations that may apply to particular agreements, and these are discussed in this section.

1.4.2 Software licences

1.4.2.1 *Why is software different?*
Software comprises the instructions which cause hardware to work in a particular way: for example, to process a company's payroll. Looked at in this way, software is intangible, and difficult to classify in legal terms. Some of the relevant case law, as to whether the supply of software comprises 'goods' or 'services', is discussed at section 1.2.1 above. Equally important from the contractual point of view is the fact that software is primarily protected by the law of copyright, as a consequence of which the use of software generally requires a licence from the rights owner.

1.4.2.2 *Types of software*
There are various distinctions that need to be kept in mind when discussing software contracts:

(a) *Standard, bespoke, and customized software:* 'Standard' (or package) software is marketed as an off-the-shelf product to meet the requirements of a large number of users: commonly used business applications for example, such as Word or Excel. By contrast, 'bespoke' software is specially written to meet the requirements of the particular customer. 'Customized' software falls somewhere in between, involving the supplier altering its standard package so that it fits the customer's needs more closely. Predictably, standard software will tend to be cheaper than bespoke, but may not reflect the way the customer's business operates, while bespoke will be more expensive but should be exactly tailored to the customer's requirements.

(b) *System software and application software:* System software organizes the way in which the hardware operates, whereas application software performs the functions actually required by the user (word processing, accounts, or whatever). System software is generally supplied by the manufacturer of the hardware, as a standard package, while application software might be standard, bespoke, or customized.

(c) *Source code and object code:* A final distinction to be aware of is that between source code and object code. This distinction is discussed at greater length in Chapter 7, but for the purposes of this chapter, 'source code' may be defined as a version of a program, using alpha-numeric symbols, which cannot be processed directly by a computer without first being 'translated' (or 'compiled') into a machine-readable form. 'Object code' is the machine-readable form of that program, which essentially comprises long series of ones and zeroes, corresponding to the complex 'on-off' instructions used to process data. (The significance of the distinction in the context of this chapter is that it is difficult for a person to read object code, and hence access to source code is needed in order to enable a person to support or modify a computer program.)

1.4.2.3 *Types of software contract*
Standard software is often supplied by retailers or distributors, without the customer entering into any direct contract with the software owner. The technique of 'shrink-wrap' licensing (discussed in section 1.4.2.6 below) is commonly used to try to establish this kind of direct contractual relationship. Contracts for bespoke software tend to be entered into on a more formal basis, because of the need to agree a specification and to address other issues arising out of the development process.

1.4.2.4 *Why is software licensed?*
Copyright subsists in computer software, so the use of software requires the grant of a licence. Apart from legitimizing the customer's use, however, the licence also enables the software owner to impose restrictions on the use of the software. For this reason, even where a copy of the software is sold without a direct agreement between the software owner and the customer, software owners still seek to impose shrink-wrap licence terms. The efficacy of such licences is discussed at section 1.4.2.6 below. A further discussion of the requirement for a licence, and the extent of implied and statutory rights in relation to acts such as decompilation and error correction, appears in Chapter 7, section 7.5.

1.4.2.5 *The main licence clause*

There is a broad range of possible licensing structures for computer software. These include, by way of illustration:

(a) the right to use the software on a single computer (sometimes identified by reference to a specific CPU number) at a single location;

(b) the right to use the software on any number of networked or clustered computers at different sites; or any combination of numbers and sites.

Limitations on use The use permitted is often restricted to the 'internal purposes' of the customer. This restriction is justified by the supplier on the basis that using the software for other purposes, particularly by using it to provide a bureau service for third parties, might adversely affect the supplier's ability to charge licence fees that it might otherwise receive from those third parties. The licence terms may also restrict the customer from transferring the software to any third party, again on the basis that the supplier has a right to know precisely who is using its software. Although these concerns appear reasonable, however, customers should be aware that these provisions have a number of serious implications:

(a) Companies which are members of a corporate group may find that such wording restricts their ability to process data for their associated companies.

(b) The restriction on assignment may be invoked by the supplier as an opportunity to charge increased fees in the event that the system has to be transferred, whether between companies in the same group (as part of a group restructuring, say) or to a third party (perhaps in the context of a business sale).

(c) Such restrictions are also sometimes invoked by the supplier as a means to prevent the customer getting a third party in to manage the system, or as a bar to outsourcing the system to third parties. (Outsourcing is discussed in more detail in Chapter 3.)

It is accordingly vital that the customer considers the business effect of licence restrictions at the very outset of its relationship with the supplier (and does so in the context of its long-term plans for its IT function and the business as a whole), and where necessary negotiates appropriate changes to the contract documentation. Failure to do so may leave the customer exposed to a claim for copyright infringement if it exceeds the scope of the permitted use, or to being charged additional licence fees for the right to do so.

Licence duration The licence will often be expressed as perpetual, or for a long fixed term (say, 99 years). In the absence of any express contractual provision, the normal rule is that an intellectual property licence is determinable by 'reasonable notice'. However, in determining what *is* reasonable (and indeed whether the licence should in fact be treated as unlimited as to duration), the court might have regard to the consequences of termination for the licensee: these consequences might be severe in the context of business-critical systems or software.

1.4.2.6 *Shrink-wrap licensing*

Background   Software is often mass-marketed through a distribution chain (or by mail order), in a similar manner to CDs or cassettes, with the result that there is no opportunity for the customer to enter into a formal licence agreement with the software owner. Many software owners have accordingly adopted the technique of the 'shrink-wrap licence': a licence agreement the terms of which are set out on the outside of the packaging, visible through clear plastic film, and are deemed to be accepted if the packaging is opened. The shrink-wrap licence purports to be a direct contract between the software owner and the customer (quite separate from the contract of sale by which the customer acquired the software) which takes effect when the customer breaks the shrink-wrap seal in order to remove the disk.

Enforceability   Although the 'headline' terms of shrink-wrap licences are broadly the same as can be found in other forms of software licence (scope of use, duration, restrictions, and so on), there is a question as to whether shrink-wrap licences are actually enforceable as a matter of law, for two reasons:

(a) *Can a shrink-wrap licence embody all the elements of a contract?* Any valid contract requires three basic elements—offer, acceptance, and consideration—but the shrink-wrap structure does not 'map' cleanly onto these formal legal require-ments. The visible display of the licence terms clearly constitutes an offer, and consideration is given by the licensee by virtue of the promises set out in the licence. However, it is unclear whether the licensee validly accepts the offer by breaking the seal, as the usual rule is that acceptance of an offer must be communicated to the offeror.

It is of course open to the offeror to waive that requirement for communication, and a court anxious to enforce the licence against the licensor may well find that the wording on the licence constitutes such a waiver. However, when considering enforcement against the licensee, the same considerations do not apply: an offeror cannot unilaterally declare that silence will constitute consent, nor can a party impose a contract by ultimatum. In the absence of clear acceptance by words (such as by signing a user registration card) or conduct (such as returning a defective CD for replacement), the enforceability of the licence by the licensor is uncertain.

(b) *Does the doctrine of privity of contract operate to prevent enforcement of the shrink-wrap licence?* The doctrine of privity provides that a person cannot take the benefit of a contract unless he is also a party to it. This principle has historically posed problems for suppliers of shrink-wrap software in England and Wales, as it has been open to question whether they are legally entitled to enforce such licence terms in the absence of a direct contract with the customer.

Beta v Adobe The Scottish case of *Beta Computers (Europe) Ltd v Adobe Systems (Europe) Ltd*[72] illustrates the difficulties that these legal issues can cause in practice. The customer (Adobe) had placed a telephone order with its supplier (Beta) to provide a standard package produced by a third party software house (Informix). Beta delivered a copy of the program to Adobe, which came in shrink-wrap packaging which included the statement: 'Opening the Informix software package indicates your acceptance of these conditions'. Adobe did not use the software, and sought to return the package (unopened) to Beta. Beta refused to accept it back, and sued for the price. In its defence, Adobe argued that its transaction with Beta was conditional on Adobe seeing and approving the licence terms: in other words, that there was no effective contract until Adobe had accepted the terms of the shrink-wrap licence by breaking the seal. Lord Penrose found that:

(a) A contract for the supply of a standard package made over the telephone was not completed until the customer had seen and accepted the shrink-wrap licence terms—and since Adobe had not in fact accepted the terms and had rejected the software, there was accordingly no contract.

(b) If the customer *had* accepted the licence terms by opening the package, then the licensor would have been able to enforce those terms under the Scottish doctrine of *ius quaesitum tertio* (ie, as a third party beneficiary).

(c) The licence terms were not in themselves capable of constituting a contract between Informix and Adobe that was discrete from the main transaction between Adobe and Beta.

However, as already noted in section 1.2.1.14, this decision is heavily dependent upon a Scots law doctrine for which there was no English equivalent, and so is of dubious value as an authority in England.

In England and Wales, the position was clarified by the Contracts (Rights of Third Parties) Act 1999, which applies to all contracts entered into after 10 May 2000. A non-party to a contract will henceforth be entitled to enforce a term in it where:

(a) the contract expressly provides that he may (s 1(1)(a)); or

(b) the term purports to confer a benefit on him (and it does not appear from the contract that the parties did *not* intend it to be enforceable by him) (s 1(1)(b)).

As a result, the English law concerns as to enforceability have largely evaporated. The Act applies to contracts entered into after May 2000 and it seems unlikely that we will now see any legal challenge to the basic concept of a shrink-wrap licence.

---

[72] [1996] FSR 367.

1.4.2.7 *Specific issues applicable to bespoke software*
Contracts for bespoke software development work have many similarities to licences
of standard software, but there are also important differences that arise from the fact
that the bespoke software does not exist at the time the contract is made. The main
differences are summarized below.

Unique specification   The essence of a bespoke software contract is that the software is written, or a package is to be tailored, to the requirements of the user. This
means that the functional specification is of critical importance, just as in other
system supply contracts (see sections 1.2.1 and 1.3.2 above). In the context of software development, the functional specification is best prepared by the user alone
(possibly with the help of outside independent consultants) or by a combination of
the user and the software house, with the user maintaining ultimate control of its
contents. Indeed, where a large and complex system is proposed there may be a
contract with the software house or a consultant, for the production of the specification, quite separate from the contract from the writing of the software.

Acceptance testing   Acceptance testing will also occupy a more important role in
relation to bespoke software than it does in relation to a standard package.[73] If package software has been seen working at other users' sites or has been used on a trial
basis by the user, the requirement for a formal acceptance test of the package may
not be so important. However, in the case of completely new software, acceptance
testing is clearly crucial, to determine whether the software house has delivered
software conforming with the contract and to determine whether it is entitled to
be paid.

IPR ownership   By contrast with contracts for the supply of standard packages, the
intellectual property rights in which necessarily remain with the software supplier, a
bespoke contract may vest the intellectual property rights to the software in the user.
The property rights that are relevant are primarily copyright and (to a lesser extent)
confidential information, although patent rights cannot be totally ignored. The
general rule of English copyright law is that where a person commissions another to
produce a copyright work, the copyright in that work vests in the author, and not in
the commissioning party.[74] If there is no express provision as to ownership it would
be open to the court to imply that notwithstanding the general rule, in equity the
copyright belongs to the user, but to reach such a conclusion there would have to be
some evidence that this was the intention of the parties.
    All these matters should be explicitly addressed in any bespoke software
contract.

---

[73] See S Charlton, 'Product Testing: Liability, Acceptance, Contract Terms', *Computer Law and
Security Report*, January–February 1989, p 23.
[74] See section 7.3.1.

1.4.3 Maintenance and support contracts

1.4.3.1 *Introduction*
Almost all new systems are supplied with a warranty as to functionality and performance, though this warranty will generally be of limited duration. It is quite common for the supplier, in addition to this warranty, to offer a maintenance contract which covers part or all of the expected lifetime of the system, subject to payment of additional periodic charges.

1.4.3.2 *General maintenance obligations*
The extent of the maintenance offered will vary according to the particular contract. It may be:

(a) Regular preventative maintenance.

(b) Repair on a time-plus-parts cost basis.

(c) Remote diagnostics with on-site attendance where required (primarily in respect of hardware).

(d) Full maintenance service with every fault attended to within a certain number of hours of its reporting, in accordance with a set SLA.

The precise service will depend on the customer's requirements, the supplier's ability to provide maintenance, and the charges agreed between the parties. Some important points that should be covered by any maintenance agreement are:

(a) *Response time:* The supplier should guarantee that problems will be attended to within a specified time, with 'target' times for activities such as responding to initial calls, provision of telephone assistance, attendance on site, and time to actually fix. The shorter the response time required, the more expensive the contract. While it is not possible to guarantee in advance how long any actual repair will take, the contract should be clear as to the consequences of failing to meet these target times, which may include liquidated damages in the event of late response or delayed repair.

A related point on time limits is that contractual response times to calls for assistance are often less stringent in software maintenance contracts than in hardware maintenance contracts. This is curious, since the consequences of faulty software are at least as serious as those of faulty hardware, if not more so.

(b) *Fault classification:* Faults vary in importance, depending upon the extent to which the functionality and performance of the system are affected, and the supplier may agree to respond more quickly to more important faults. For example, a 'Level 1' fault might be one that effectively stops the customer doing business and to which an urgent fix is required; whereas a 'Level 3' fault may be some defect in the system that is trivial or annoying, but not directly harmful. There are no universally recognized classifications of fault severity, and the classifications are a frequent sticking point in contract negotiations. However, it is essential that there is a clear and effective mechanism for classifying faults quickly: leaving classification 'to be agreed at the time' is just as risky as providing that either party has the unilateral right to classify faults in its sole discretion.

(c) *Replacement:* The contract should make it clear what is to happen if part of the system (particularly any hardware element) needs to be removed for repair or replacement, and in particular whether the supplier will provide temporary replacement equipment and within what period of time.

(d) *Duration, increase of charges, and renewal:* As the system ages, maintenance charges will necessarily increase. The contract should set out a minimum period of time for which the supplier will provide maintenance, and some way of assessing the charges that will be made in future years, for example by reference to indexation. Phrases like 'the supplier's current charges as amended from time to time' should not be acceptable, as there is no ceiling on what he might decide to charge. The agreement should also, from the customer's point of view at least, contain a right of renewal.

(e) *Transferability:* If the customer wishes to resell the system at some later date, or to transfer it intra-group, he will also need to transfer the benefit of the maintenance agreement. The contract should therefore contain a provision to this effect. The supplier might also wish to transfer the burden of the contract to another organization, but a provision permitting this should be resisted by the customer: there is no guarantee that the new supplier will have sufficient expertise or experience of the system in question.

1.4.3.3 *Specific issues relating to software maintenance: source code*

Software maintenance usually comprises two elements:

(a) the correction of software errors (or 'bugs'); and

(b) the provision of enhancements and updates to the software.

Software maintenance—sometimes also called 'support'—has up to now normally been provided by the supplier of the software because of the necessity to have access to the program source code. However, as noted in Chapter 7, section 7.5.7, the customer has a limited right to decompile the object code to produce source code for the purpose of error correction (though not any other form of maintenance such as the development of enhancements or updates).[75] The source code may in any case be made available to the customer, either because it is the policy of the supplier to do so,[76] or because the intellectual property rights vest in the customer (eg, under a

---

[75] However, the right can be excluded by contract, at least as implemented in the UK: s 50C of the Copyright Designs and Patents Act 1988.

[76] In *Andersen Consulting v CHP Consulting Ltd*, 26 July 1991, Ch D (unreported), the judge described the standard licence agreement of the claimants relating to the program in question, under which the

bespoke contract), or because the customer has obtained access to the source code pursuant to an escrow agreement. In such cases the customer should be able to maintain the software on its own account (or appoint a third party to do so).

1.4.3.4 *Specific issues relating to software maintenance: upgrades*

Apart from error correction, the supplier will usually agree to supply a copy of all enhancements and updates developed by him during the term of the maintenance agreement. These fall into a number of categories:

    (a) Corrections of previously reported errors.

    (b) Updates necessitated by changes in the law.

    (c) Variations necessitated by changes in the system software that runs on the hardware in question.

    (d) Improvements or new functions.

The customer will often be obliged to accept and install the enhancements and updates, so that the whole of the maintenance company's customer base is using the same version of the software. For this reason, it will often be a requirement of the software licence that the licensee enters into a software maintenance agreement in the first place.

1.4.3.5 *Warranties and liability*

Maintenance agreements are contracts for the provision of services and accordingly, by virtue of section 13 of the SGSA 1982, there will be an implied term that the maintenance company will use reasonable skill and care in carrying out the service. It is fairly unusual to find express warranties as to the *quality* of the maintenance services, although ideally the supplier should agree to maintain system functionality and performance to the standards set out in the original system supply agreement. Suppliers will often seek to impose liability limitations similar to those in other system supply contracts, and the observations already made in that regard apply equally in this context.

1.4.4 Cloud computing

1.4.4.1 *Introduction*

Cloud computing involves the delivery of computing facilities as a service over the internet, with access to shared resources (like computers and data centres) located in different locations, and perhaps ultimately controlled by different entities. It is intended to be a kind of 'utility' model of computing, where the user can buy

---

program source code was supplied to licensees for a fee of £125,000. The judge noted that 'the result is that the plain intent of the contract was that the licensee should have the ability, the material and the right to alter and amend the programme [sic] by persons other than those who had written it'.

computing capacity as he needs it, without the infrastructure costs of purchasing and implementing a system specifically for himself.

At the heart of the model is the idea that hardware and software will be provided remotely as a service, on an as-needed basis. Cloud services can also be accessed by users regardless of their location, and regardless of device—a PC, laptop, or a mobile phone. There have been cloud services aimed at consumers for some time, such as Gmail, Hotmail, and Facebook. Businesses have been slower to take up cloud services, but that is increasingly happening, with the way being led by sales-force.com which provides a CRM solution where all the information about a client's customers is likewise stored and processed somewhere out there 'in the cloud'.

1.4.4.2 *Categories of cloud service*

There are several broad categories of cloud service. Almost any computing resource can be offered 'as a service', but the most common classifications are as follows:

(a) *Infrastructure as a Service (IaaS):* Providing 'infrastructure as a service' means making available IT infrastructure (eg server and storage capacity and associated local network resources) on an 'on-demand' basis, such as Amazon.com's Elastic Compute Cloud (also known as EC2). The service provider supplies to the customer a generic hardware 'foundation' on which the customer can install and run its own operating system and applications. The customer's staff can then just access the resources via the internet when they need them. The service is normally charged for according to usage (eg x pence per hour of server time), so the customer does not have to make any upfront investment in its server and storage infrastructure. On top of that, maintaining and upgrading the basic infrastructure should be the job of the service provider, which means that the customer should always have access to the latest technology without having to do its own technology refresh project.

(b) *Platform as a Service (PaaS):* 'Platform as a Service' is a level above that. Here the customer has access to a full 'platform'—that is to say, the basic infrastructure overlaid with the relevant operating systems and tools to create a full 'runtime' environment—in which to develop and deploy applications. This approach is often used by developers to get access to the substantial computing power that may be needed to create and host new applications. Users can store their code and data in the cloud, paying only for the storage space and processing time that they actually need, and then using the cloud as a large-scale channel for distributing their software to consumers. Examples include Microsoft's Azure platform, which specifically targets developers.

(c) *Software as a Service (SaaS):* At the highest level, there is 'Software as a Service'. This is the cloud offering that has most penetrated the business world, probably because it was already familiar from earlier models of remote computing like bureau services or ASP. In this case, application software is delivered as a hosted or managed service over the internet. Users can then access that software as required, and the best-known instance is the CRM service provided by salesforce.com.

Charging is usually based on a 'per seat per month' subscription, with additional fees based on usage. Apart from the purely financial implications, though, the service provider takes responsibility for ongoing support, patches, and upgrades, which takes a major administrative burden off the in-house IT department.

1.4.4.3 *Cloud models*

In order to understand the special legal issues arising from cloud computing it is also important to understand the various models through which cloud services can be delivered. These are commonly referred to as 'private', 'public', 'hybrid', and 'community' cloud. What differentiates these models is the degree of control that the user has over the infrastructure, which in turn informs the privacy and contractual implications of buying cloud computing.

(a) *Private cloud:* The private cloud is the simplest and most easily understood model. When people talk about a 'private' cloud, they are referring to a dedicated, customized cloud service under which multiple organizations (maybe different companies within the same corporate group, or different locations within a single company) share computing resources within a single organization. That 'private cloud' might be proprietary to the user—so, for example, a big Wall Street bank might set up data centres in two or three time zones around the world, which can be used by all its affiliates, and which is managed internally: that is, effectively building its own cloud model. Equally, though, the bank could use an outsourced service, with a third party supplier housing and managing all the computing resources, but again in private data centres, and on physical infrastructure which is dedicated only to that bank.

It will be self-evident that pursuing this highly bespoke route erases some of the perceived benefits of cloud computing. It is bespoke, it is not shared with other companies, and it is more expensive. This model is not fundamentally different from having proprietary data centres—the customer is just using them more efficiently. On the other hand, it means that the customer has a high degree of visibility and control over matters like performance and security, and can still take advantage of certain other benefits of cloud computing, like optimizing usage and maximizing resilience against outages.

(b) *Public cloud:* At the other end of the scale, there is the 'public' cloud, consisting of a completely outsourced service provided by a third party, where all the infrastructure is shared for maximum economies of scale. So in this case the customer gets the financial benefit, but with little customization and little control over matters like security. Amazon EC2, Google AppEngine, and the Windows Azure are all examples of a public cloud: the user can sit at a desk, click through to one of those services, enter a few credit card details, and begin using the service. (It really is as simple as that.)

Predictably, use of the public cloud gives rise to security and privacy issues. Depending on what the user is actually doing in the public cloud, he may be handing substantial volumes of data over to the service provider, which is then processed in half a dozen different data centres across the world. Companies are rightly cautious about giving data to a service provider in circumstances in which they cannot say with certainty where the data is stored or how to get it back if the service provider goes out of business.

(c) *Hybrid cloud:* As the result of these concerns, an intermediate model has developed, called the 'hybrid' cloud, which as the name suggests combines elements of both the private and public model. In this kind of arrangement, a company provides and manages some resources in-house and has others provided externally. For example, a company might use a public cloud service like Amazon's Simple Storage Service (Amazon S3) for archiving, but still maintain in-house data storage for operational customer data that is needed from day to day.

The hybrid model is supposed to allow a business to take advantage of the scalability and cost-effectiveness of the public cloud, whilst still keeping its arms firmly around essential applications and data that are critical to its business.

(d) *Community cloud:* Finally, the 'community cloud' consists of the sharing of private clouds among entities with similar interests. For example, computing resources could be shared across organizations like the military or government, or across companies operating in the same sector. The UK Government proposes to create a 'G-Cloud' for use across public sector organizations.[77]

Because of the issues of privacy and security, many businesses are cautious about the public cloud, and contracts lawyers are most likely to be asked to consider documentation for the other models. The key contractual implications are discussed below.

1.4.4.4 *Key legal and contractual issues*[78]
At one level, a cloud computing contract is just another contract for IT services. The customer should undertake proper due diligence into the supplier and its track record, and ensure that the contract documentation contains a suitable description of the services to be provided, warranties, and service level commitments. The current practice among the major public cloud providers is to try and keep performance assurances to a minimum: they generally currently offer their services only on an 'as is' basis, with many excluding warranties as far as they legally can. Note that any such exclusions will of course be subject to UCTA 1977, as the public cloud offerings are by their very nature contracted for on the supplier's standard terms.

---

[77] UK Cabinet Office, *Government ICT Strategy* (March 2011).

[78] For a comparative analysis of leading cloud computing service terms see S Bradshaw, C Millard, and I Walden, 'Contracts for Clouds: Comparison and Analysis of the Terms and Conditions of Cloud Computing Services', 1 September 2010, Queen Mary School of Law Legal Studies Research Paper No 63/2010, available at <http://ssrn.com/abstract=1662374> (1 September 2010).

This often pushes corporate customers in the direction of a private or community cloud, where these issues can be negotiated properly and the customer can get some firmer commitments about service availability and security, for example. The degree of negotiability is of course linked, inextricably, to the degree of customization of the required cloud solution and the price that the customer is paying for it.

The nature of the cloud means that special consideration needs to be given to the treatment of data, and the key issues are set out below.

(a) *Control of data and confidentiality:* One of the major obstacles to the universal take-up of cloud computing is that service providers are basically asking consumers and businesses to rely on their reputations as a security policy. In the public cloud at least, where many contracts are simple 'click through' standard terms on a computer screen, the service providers currently purport to disclaim almost any liability for loss or corruption of data. It is essential that customers review the terms of any cloud computing contract critically, to ensure that they fully understand what is being promised (or more likely, excluded) in terms of assurances about data security.

Having said that, there is also a valid alternative viewpoint, that cloud computing offers much greater security than traditional methods of storing and transferring data. Most of the data security incidents that come in front of the Information Commissioner's Office in England have been to do with individuals taking work home and then losing an unencrypted laptop or memory stick. IT security at the largest cloud vendors is very good—companies like Amazon.com and Google employ extremely smart people—so if data is held in the cloud and users can access that from their PCs at home, that is arguably a much better way of dealing with home working than allowing people to copy data onto USB sticks which then get lost or stolen.

(b) *Data protection and privacy:* Data protection is predictably a major issue if personal data is going to be put into the cloud. A detailed discussion is beyond the scope of this chapter,[79] but in terms of legal analysis, it is the customer who will be the data controller under the Data Protection Act 1998 ('DPA'), because it is the customer who is responsible for deciding the purposes and manner in which the personal data is processed. Customers accordingly need to ensure that the processing of personal data by the cloud service provider is done under a written agreement; and that the service provider undertakes to do so only in accordance with the data controller's instructions and to ensure that appropriate technical and organizational measures are taken to keep the personal data secure.

---

[79] The Information Commissioner's online code of practice, published in 2010, sets out some specific questions that users should ask of cloud service providers before committing any personal data to the cloud. See further W K Hon, C Millard, and I Walden, 'Who is Responsible for "Personal Data" in Cloud Computing? The Cloud of Unknowing, Part 2', 21 March 2011, Queen Mary School of Law Legal Studies Research Paper No 77/2011, available at <http://ssrn.com/abstract=1794130>.

As noted above, few of the standard terms that are offered online by public cloud service providers include any such provisions; or, if they do, they undermine the effect by purporting to exclude any liability for loss or corruption of, or unauthorized access to, personal data. For that reason, it seems unlikely that most current public cloud offerings are going to satisfy the requirements of the DPA.

(c) *Ensuring access to data:* Customers need to consider what measures they should be putting in place internally to ensure that they can get hold of their data if there are problems with the cloud service. Should customers make their own back-ups, say, so that they can readily reconstitute data if the service provider has a catastrophic failure? If so, does that actually undermine the very value proposition that the cloud provider is offering?

(d) *Business continuity and disaster recovery:* Associated with the question of data security generally, customers will want to be sure that the service provider has adequate business continuity and disaster recovery plans in place. Here, the private cloud model permits a high degree of customization, so customers can adopt a more traditional and tailored approach in terms of specifying what the service provider should be doing by way of business continuity. Conversely, in the public cloud there will be a limited degree to which customers can influence the service provider's business continuity and disaster recovery, but it would nevertheless be sensible to investigate this as part of due diligence.

1.5 CONCLUSION

The delivery of a working system which meets the customer's needs is a difficult enough task, but it is even more difficult to achieve in a contractual vacuum. In summary, there are three main advantages to a properly negotiated and well-drawn contract:

(a) Identification of the issues.

(b) Clarity as to the obligations of each party.

(c) Agreement in advance on how disagreements are to be resolved.

The overall aim is a good working relationship, leading to successful performance of the contract and the installation of an effective system. While it is tempting to use standard form contracts, particularly given the time and cost that can be involved in negotiating individual agreements, for any major system procurement the preferred approach must always be to try to ensure that the contract documentation specifically addresses the risks of the particular engagement and the implications of failure.

2

MASS MARKET CONTRACTING

David Naylor, Antonis Patrikios, and Robert Blamires

2.1 INTRODUCTION

This chapter examines the principal laws and issues relevant to businesses engaging in, or seeking to engage in, mass market contracting with consumers in Europe. For consistency with the core theme of this book, many of the topics and examples of regulatory intervention discussed relate to online and e-commerce contracting[1] and/ or to contracts for technology goods or services (concluded online and/or offline). However, many of the issues discussed will be relevant to any enterprise doing business with consumers in Europe.

The size, population, and economic significance of the European Union continue to grow. The 27 countries that currently make up the EU now have a combined population of over 500 million[2] and the EU is by far the world's largest economy.

---

[1] The term 'e-commerce' is used in this chapter to refer to all forms of electronic contracting, whether taking place using a PC connected to the internet, using a mobile phone ('m-commerce') or otherwise.

[2] See statistics produced by Eurostat, the statistical office of the European Union, at: <http://epp. eurostat.ec.europa.eu/tgm/table.do?tab=table&language=en&pcode=tps00001&tableSelection=1& footnotes=yes&labeling=labels&plugin=1>.

Traditionally, Europe has been at the forefront of consumer protection policy development and lawmaking and, in many significant respects, is now also the driving force for global developments in this area. The pace of change has also accelerated in recent years; since 1997, there have been well over 20 EU legislative measures in the field of consumer protection, in the form of regulations, directives, and recommendations, as well as a multitude of soft law initiatives.

Failure to comply with applicable consumer protection law can have serious consequences, including: investigation by a regulator; payment of damages and fines; having to alter trading and contracting practices; and reputational and brand damage. Regulatory scrutiny of contractual terms and commercial practices is common practice in the UK, in all sectors, including the IT sector,[3] and this chapter discusses many examples of such scrutiny.

Although the majority of the examples in this chapter are UK cases investigated by a UK regulator on the basis of UK law, most of the UK's consumer law is derived from European instruments, which are also implemented into the national laws of other EU Member States. As a result, these cases also reflect the risk that many standard terms commonly used by businesses dealing with consumers in one EU Member State may be void and unenforceable in other Member States (with the seriousness of the consequences of failing to comply varying in different states). For instance, in France, AOL found itself in the unenviable position of having its standard online terms ruled unfair by the French courts,[4] on grounds which arguably would have applied in the UK, as well as in other EU Member States.[5] The consequences for AOL were not insignificant and included requirements to: pay damages of €30,000; remove the offending terms within a month (with a fine of €1,000 per day for failure to do so); notify customers of the resulting changes to the online terms; and publish the substantive parts of the judgment on its website and in three national daily newspapers.

Perhaps more importantly from a business-compliance perspective, not only has the volume and scope of EU consumer protection law increased, but since 2006,

---

[3] eg, in 2003, 12 companies in the IT sector were investigated by the OFT and gave undertakings in respect of their consumer terms and conditions, see: <http://www.oft.gov.uk/news-and-updates/press/2003/pn_77-03> (accessed 3 August 2011).

[4] Prospectively as well as retrospectively, so that AOL could not rely on provisions in its existing contracts with French consumers.

[5] *Union Fédérale des Consommateurs 'Que Choisir?' v SNG AOL France*, TGI Nanterre, 2 June 2004; see further D Naylor and C Ritter, 'French Judgement Condemning AOL Illustrates EU Consumer Protection Issues Facing US Businesses Operating in Europe' [2005] 1(3) NYU Journal of Law & Business 881. The decision of the court of first instance was upheld on appeal, see *Union Fédérale des Consommateurs 'Que Choisir?' v SNG AOL France*, CA Versailles, 15 September 2005, <http://www.juriscom.net/documents/caversailles20050915.pdf> (accessed 3 August 2011).

the EU has turned its attention to ensuring more effective enforcement.[6] This is now one of the fundamental components of current EU consumer protection policy.[7]

The EU has also strengthened its consumer protection framework through the adoption of the Consumer Protection Cooperation Regulation 2004 ('CPCR 2004'), which establishes a formalized network of European public authorities with enforcement powers; the Unfair Commercial Practices Directive 2005 ('UCPD 2005'), a maximum harmonization measure[8] intended to protect consumers against perceived gaps and weaknesses in other EU consumer protection instruments and set the standards against which unfair commercial practices will be tested; and the Directive on Injunctions for the Protection of Consumer Interests 2009, which sets out a common procedure to allow a qualified body from one country (usually a consumer representative body) to seek an injunction in another for the cessation of infringements of consumer rights.[9]

In addition, the Commission is currently considering a proposal for a Directive on Consumer Rights[10] aimed at further strengthening and streamlining the high level

---

[6] In addition to the existing instruments discussed in this chapter, the European Commission is currently working on consumer collective redress. In 2008 and 2009, it published consultation papers on the subject (see <http://ec.europa.eu/consumers/redress_cons/greenpaper_en.pdf> (accessed 3 August 2011), and <http://ec.europa.eu/consumers/redress_cons/docs/consultation_paper2009.pdf> (accessed 3 August 2011)) and in March 2010 the European Parliament approved a resolution which, among other things, called on the Commission for further feedback on the Green Paper, see <http://www.europarl. europa.eu/sides/getDoc.do?type=REPORT&reference=A7-2010-0024&language=EN> (accessed 3 August 2011). In February 2011, the Commission launched a consultation on identifying common legal principles relating to collective redress in order to develop a coherent European approach, see Commission Staff Working Document, Public Consultation: Towards a Coherent European Approach to Collective Redress, SEC(2011)173 final, 4 February 2011, <http://ec.europa.eu/justice/news/consulting_public/0054/ ConsultationpaperCollectiveredress4February2011.pdf> (accessed 3 August 2011), identifying six general principles that should guide possible future EU initiatives on collective redress in all areas.

[7] Current EU consumer policy is enshrined in the consumer policy strategy adopted by the Commission for the period 2007–13, see n 1 above. The overall objectives of the consumer policy strategy are to empower consumers, to enhance their welfare, and to protect them effectively. The Commission's vision is to achieve by 2013 a single, simple set of rules for the benefit of consumers and suppliers alike. The priorities of the strategy are: increasing consumer confidence in the internal market; strengthening the position of consumers in the marketplace; ensuring that consumer concerns are taken into account in EU policies; complementing the consumer policies of Member States; and collecting consumer-related data to support the development of legislation and other initiatives.

[8] In other words, Member States are not allowed to introduce or maintain differentiated provisions, even if they set forth more stringent protective measures. However, UCPD 2005, Art 3(3) provides that at least until 12 July 2013, Member States may continue to apply national provisions within the field approximated by the Directive which are more restrictive or prescriptive, provided that such measures are essential to ensuring that consumers are adequately protected against unfair commercial practices and are proportionate to the attainment of this objective.

[9] Directive 2009/22/EC of the European Parliament and of the Council of 23 April 2009 on injunctions for the protection of consumers' interests (Codified version), text with EEA relevance (OJ L110/30, 1 May 2009). This is a codifying directive, necessary in the light of the substantial amendments made to its predecessor Directive 98/27/EC of the European Parliament and of the Council of 19 May 1998 on injunctions for the protection of consumers' interests (OJ L166/51, 11 June 1998). The new Directive repeals and replaces Directive 98/27/EC and its amending legislation, but fully preserves their content. It was due to be implemented into national law by Member States by 29 December 2009.

[10] See section 2.1.3.

of protection by consolidating the four EU Directives on Sale of Consumer Contracts and Guarantees,[11] Unfair Contract Terms,[12] Distance Selling,[13] and Doorstep Selling.[14] Other elements of the complex legal framework for mass market online and technology contracting are also under review at present or have been reviewed recently. For instance, the EU has embarked on an overhaul of privacy and data protection law: the e-Privacy Directive was recently amended[15] and the Data Protection Directive is undergoing a fundamental review.[16] Furthermore, in 2010, the Commission consulted with stakeholders on whether there is a need to review the e-Commerce Directive.[17]

Finally, the EU has encouraged the proliferation of 'soft law' instruments, such as industry codes of conduct, and alternative dispute resolution ('ADR') methods for consumer disputes.[18]

In short, it is becoming increasingly important for businesses that trade in European markets to understand the extent and impact of the EU consumer protection regime, and how to comply with it.

---

[11] Directive 1999/44/EC of the European Parliament and of the Council of 25 May 1999 on certain aspects of the sale of consumer goods and associated guarantees (OJ L171/12, 7 July 1999).

[12] Council Directive 93/13/EEC of 5 April 1993 on unfair terms in consumer contracts (OJ L095/29, 21 April 1993).

[13] Directive 97/7/EC of the European Parliament and of the Council of 20 May 1997 on the protection of consumers in respect of distance contracts—Statement by the Council and the Parliament re Article 6(1)—Statement by the Commission re Article 3(1), first indent (OJ L144/19, 4 June 1997).

[14] Council Directive 85/577/EEC of 20 December 1985 to protect the consumer in respect of contracts negotiated away from business premises (OJ L372/31, 31 December 1985).

[15] Directive 2002/58/EC of the European Parliament and of the Council of 12 July 2002 concerning the processing of personal data and the protection of privacy in the electronic communications sector (Directive on privacy and electronic communications) (OJ L201/37, 31 July 2002).

[16] Directive 95/46/EC of the European Parliament and of the Council of 24 October 1995 on the protection of individuals with regard to the processing of personal data and on the free movement of such data (OJ L281/31, 23 November 1995).

[17] Directive of the European Parliament and of the Council of 8 June 2000 on certain legal aspects of information society services, in particular electronic commerce, in the Internal Market (Directive on electronic commerce) (OJ L178/1, 17 July 2000) as now amended by Directive 2009/136 EC of the European Parliament and of the Council of 25 November 2009 amending Directive 2002/22/EC on universal service and users' rights relating to electronic communications networks and services, Directive 2002/58/EC concerning the processing of personal data and the protection of privacy in the electronic communications sector and Regulation (EC) No 2006/2004 on cooperation between national authorities responsible for the enforcement of consumer protection laws (Text with EEA relevance) (OJ L337/11, 18 December 2009). The Commission is expected to publish a Communication on electronic commerce in 2011.

[18] eg, among other EU instruments the e-Commerce Directive promotes the development and uptake of soft law instruments and ADR, including Online Dispute Resolution ('ODR'), schemes, see e-Commerce Directive, Arts 16 and 17 and recitals 49 and 52. From January to March 2011, the European Commission consulted on the use of ADR as a means to resolve disputes related to commercial transactions and practices in the EU, see <http://ec.europa.eu/dgs/health_consumer/dgs_consultations/ca/docs/adr_consultation_paper_18012011_en.pdf> (accessed 9 April 2011). The consultation was aimed specifically at cross-border mediations, and sought views on how some specific difficulties might be resolved so as to improve the use of ADR within the EU.

The purpose of this chapter is to examine that regime, from a business perspective, in the context of mass market consumer contracting. By this we mean contracting with consumers for the sale or supply of goods and/or services, using standard form terms and conditions, in whatever medium, whether offline or online.[19]

Since the advent of e-commerce, the distinction between offline and online contracting has often served as the starting point for legal analysis of consumer contracts, and remains appropriate in many instances. However, it is worth noting that, in relation particularly to certain products, the contractual process itself has now changed so that transactions which would traditionally have been conducted entirely offline now also include increasingly significant online elements. So, for example, offline sales of technology hardware and software products now frequently involve a request that the consumer, after the initial (offline) purchase, go online to: register and activate the product; accept necessary software licences; and/or provide personal and other details. This online element enables the consumer to receive services (such as applications, content, and/or software updates/upgrades) which may be helpful or even fundamental to the consumer's initial and ongoing ability to use the product, or which may constitute associated or value-added services. This hybrid transactional model inevitably raises the question of whether transactions that businesses currently assume are 'offline' could be subject to the additional layer of consumer protection legislation governing offline contracts (although a detailed discussion of this interesting issue is outside the scope of this chapter).

In recent years we have also witnessed further important developments including: a substantial increase in broadband penetration; the significant lowering of the cost of consumer hardware (coupled with a further increase of computing capacity); technology and media convergence; the proliferation of mobile phones and other handheld devices; and the increasing functionality, network access, and cost-effectiveness of accessing the internet and online services using such devices. As a result, the way in which consumers are using the internet and the services available to them online have evolved.

Two good examples of online consumer services exemplify this evolution. The first is the evolution, during the early years of the new millennium, in the use of the internet, from a means for users to access static content, over which only the service provider had control (so-called 'Web 1.0'), to services which allow users to control and manipulate the information they receive, as well as to submit content themselves (user-generated content or 'UGC') and to engage, interact, and collaborate with the service provider and other users (conveniently referred to in this chapter as 'Web 2.0'[20]). Paradigmatic examples of Web 2.0 services are social networking

---

[19] The examples in this chapter typically relate to online contracting, as websites (and often e-commerce websites) are now, for most consumer-facing businesses, an invaluable, if not essential, route-to-market, without which they would be unlikely to flourish, or even survive.

[20] However, with commentators already using the expressions 'Web 3.0' and even 'Web 4.0', and with the internet being fundamentally based on concepts of information sharing and collaboration the limitations of the expression 'Web 2.0' should not be forgotten.

services, wikis, and communication tools that enable users to share content and collaborate online.

The second example is cloud computing, which essentially consists in the provision of commoditized IT services such as applications, back-up, storage, and processing capacity as a utility (as US analysts Gartner put it, 'a style of Computing where scalable and elastic IT capabilities are provided as a service to multiple customers using Internet technologies'). Many services of course involve both Web 2.0 and cloud computing.

When targeted at consumers, contracts relating to Web 2.0 and cloud computing services are subject to the same legal regimes which apply to other types of mass market consumer contracts. However, it can be argued that the application of certain central legal concepts that form the cornerstone of mass market contracting regulation may not be straightforward in the context of Web 2.0 and cloud computing, because of the operational and economic realities of these services. These concepts include the notion of 'consumer' under consumer protection legislation and the standards of 'reasonableness' or 'fairness' under unfair contract terms legislation. Although this chapter is not the place to engage in an exhaustive discussion of these stimulating issues, we do outline them and offer our high-level thoughts in the relevant sections below.

Inevitably, the limitations of a single chapter of a book necessitate narrowing the scope of our analysis. We therefore focus on the legal regime governing mass market contracts in the UK (sections 2.1 to 2.4), as the reference point for our discussion of certain key contractual terms and legal issues that commonly arise in regulatory investigations (section 2.5). The principles governing the consumer protection regimes of the UK and other EU Member States are similar. This is largely the result of the EU's harmonization programme for integrating the European market, which has gathered particular momentum in the areas of consumer protection and e-commerce. As a result, this chapter may also offer useful insights into the consumer protection regimes of other national European markets and the EU market generally.

Before we embark on our analysis, we first address two preliminary questions: what is a consumer and what are the grounds for the differentiated treatment of consumers and businesses?

The EU instruments relevant to this chapter define a consumer as a *natural* person acting for purposes outside,[21] or not directly related to,[22] his trade, business, or profession. The pertinent UK Regulations adopt definitions that are either

---

[21] UTCCD, Art 2(b); Distance Selling Directive, Art 2(2); Unfair Commercial Practices Directive, Art 2(a), defining a consumer as any natural person acting for purposes outside his trade, business, craft, or profession. This position is confirmed by decisions of the European Court of Justice ('ECJ'), see, eg, the judgment in Joined Cases C-541/99 *Cape SNC v Idealservice SRL* and C-542/99 *Idealservice MN RE SAS v OMAI* [2001] All ER (EC) 657, holding that the term 'consumer' in the UTCCD relates only to natural persons.

[22] Sale of Consumer Goods and Associated Guarantees Directive, Art 1(2)(a); for the practical impact of the difference between 'outside' and 'not directly related to', see R Bradgate and C Twigg-Flesner,

identical[23] or similar in that they define a consumer as any *natural* person acting outside his business.[24] Hence, the position of the EU instruments and the UK Regulations implementing them is that only a natural person can be a consumer.

However, under other UK legislation, including the Unfair Contract Terms Act 1977 ('UCTA 1977') as amended by the Sale and Supply of Goods to Consumers Regulations 2002 ('SSGCRs 2002'), a consumer does not necessarily have to be a *natural* person.[25] In *R&B Customs Brokers Co Ltd v United Dominions Trust Ltd*,[26] the court held that the implied terms in the Sale of Goods Act 1979 ('SGA 1979'), which are subject to UCTA 1977, section 6, may apply to businesses in certain circumstances.[27] However, a legal person would not be treated as a consumer for the purposes of the Unfair Terms in Consumer Contracts Regulations 1999 ('UTCCRs 1999') or the Consumer Protection (Distance Selling) Regulations 2000 ('DSRs 2000'), nor would it be able to seek treatment as a consumer in the context of services as opposed to sales, since UCTA 1977, section 6(2) only applies to the

Blackstone's Guide to Consumer Sale and Associated Guarantees (Oxford: Oxford University Press, 2003) 20.

[23] Unfair Terms in Consumer Contracts Regulations 1999 (SI 1999/2083) as amended by the Unfair Terms in Consumer Contracts (Amendment) Regulations 2001 (SI 2001/1186), reg 3—see also *Barclays Bank plc v Alfons Kufner* [2008] EWHC 2319 (Comm), where the High Court held that an experienced businessman purchasing a yacht through a company was not acting as a consumer for the purposes of the UTCCRs 1999; Consumer Protection from Unfair Trading Regulations 2008 (SI 2008/1277), reg 2(1); Sale and Supply of Goods to Consumers Regulations 2002 (SI 2002/3045), reg 2. With regard to the latter Regulations it is noteworthy that they adopt two distinct standards as to the status of the buyer as a 'consumer': regs 3–5 amending the Sale of Goods Act 1979 apply when the buyer *deals as a consumer*, a term of art that has been held by the courts also to include a business or even a company, see further discussion below; on the contrary, reg 15 dealing with consumer guarantees is applicable only where goods are sold or otherwise supplied *to a consumer*. The Enterprise Act 2002, s 210 also adopts a dual definition: in relation to domestic infringements, a consumer is an *individual* who receives, or seeks to receive, goods or services other than in the course of his business, or with a view to setting up a business, from a person who supplies them in the course of business, thereby excluding partnerships and corporate bodies from the definition of consumer; it is irrelevant whether the supplier of the goods or services has a place of business in the UK. In relation to community infringements, it is any *person* who is a consumer for the purposes of the Injunctions Directive and the relevant directives listed therein; the exact definition will therefore depend upon the directive being enforced, but broadly speaking it will be a person not exercising a commercial, industrial, craft, or professional activity. On another note, bizarrely enough, several UK consumer protection instruments, including the Consumer Protection Act 1987, do not provide a definition of the term 'consumer'.

[24] Distance Selling Regulations 2000 (SI 2000/2334), reg 3.

[25] UCTA, ss 12(1), 12(1A), 12(2), and 25(1): the requirement is that, first, a party does not enter into contract in the course of a business, nor holds itself out as doing so; and, secondly, that the counterparty does enter into contract in the course of a business; and, unless the party is an individual, thirdly, that in the case of a contract governed by the law of the sale of goods or hire purchase, or by UCTA, s 7, the goods passed under or in pursuance of the contract are of a type ordinarily supplied for private use or consumption.

[26] [1988] 1 All ER 847.

[27] The idea here is that a business can be acting as a consumer when it is purchasing products 'like' a consumer, eg, a law firm purchasing stationery. Although the business will not be acting as a consumer if the contract for the goods is an integral part of its business or, if incidental to the business, is entered into on a regular basis.

SGA 1979. Nevertheless, *R&B Customs Brokers* is an important case that has not been overturned to date. It was applied in *Feldaroll Foundry plc v Hermes Leasing (London) Ltd and Others*,[28] where the court held that it is settled law that a company could deal as a consumer in respect of the purchase of a car.[29] Therefore, in the UK, a consumer may, according to the legislation in question, include or exclude legal persons.

From a different angle, an interesting question arises in the context of Web 2.0, where the use of a platform usually has, broadly, two elements. The first consists in the user's consumption of the service and content available through the platform (eg, a social networking site or a virtual world) which are provided by the supplier (and other users). The second element entails the supply of content *by the user* who will, for example, create and/or upload content onto the platform (eg, uploading photographs on a social networking site or creating a building in a virtual world). This second element therefore appears to be turning the supplier–consumer model on its head with the user supplying content for use by others and/or the platform provider, rather than consuming content supplied by the platform provider. Perhaps, then, it is possible to argue that a user generating the content is no longer a 'consumer' under European and UK law. Furthermore, for certain B2C Web 2.0 transactions the black-and-white distinction between supplier and consumer does not cover all scenarios so that, in the context of UGC, there is a grey area of user activity that does not fit squarely with the behaviour and activities normally expected by a 'consumer', but is rather a hybrid of 'supply' and 'consumption' activities that the law has not recognized yet. If so, the consumer protection rights discussed in the remainder of this chapter may not always apply, or may not apply in full, to such hybrid activities.

These are truly stimulating questions. One can think of scenarios where this line of argument could be relied on to argue that because for some aspects of the service the users are not consumers, European consumer protection legislation does not extend to those aspects and, therefore, it is possible, for instance, effectively to exclude the user's right to cancel the service where this would not be otherwise possible under the law, or subject future disputes to arbitration in the USA, or limit or even exclude the supplier's liability to the user beyond what is normally acceptable in consumer contracts. Unfortunately, the limitations of a chapter do not allow an

---

[28] [2004] All ER (D) 138 (May).

[29] cf *Stevenson v Rogers* [1999] 1 All ER 613, where the Court of Appeal held that for the purposes of SGA 1979, s 14 concerning the implied term of quality and fitness of the goods, any sale by a business is in the course of a business. The court distinguished *R & B Customs Brokers* on the grounds that the case concerned a different statute, UCTA as opposed to the SGA 1979, and the status of a buyer as opposed to that of a seller. *Stevenson v Rogers* has been applied in several cases, see most recently *Titan Steel Wheels v Royal Bank of Scotland plc* [2010] EWHC 211 (Comm).

exhaustive discussion of this topic. At a high level, this line of argument would need to overcome some difficult hurdles, including:

(a) the definitions of 'consumer' in the main EU and UK legal instruments do not lend support to this line of argument. The material criterion is the context in which the user's activities are undertaken and not the nature of the actual activities themselves. In other words, the law does not distinguish between consumption and supply;[30] the test is whether the user acts for purposes outside his business, trade, or profession. So long as the user is acting in a non-professional capacity, for European law purposes he will be a consumer;

(b) in any event, even where the consumer 'supplies' UGC, there is always an underlying service consumption element. In order to be able to generate the content, the user has to use the underlying service or platform that enables him to upload the UGC; in this regard, he remains a consumer;

(c) the public policy purpose that underpins EU consumer protection legislation is, precisely, to protect individuals. Even if there is indeed a grey area, it is highly likely that in deciding such cases under the current legal regime, national and European regulators and courts would be inclined to err on the side of caution: if in doubt, they would be likely to give precedence to the outcome that ensures that the consumer's rights are protected. It is telling in this regard that the European Court of Justice recently held that, in light of the principle of consumer protection in the Unfair Terms in Consumer Contracts Directive[31] ('UTCCD') and the weakness of the consumer's position, a national court was under a duty, as opposed to just a right, to assess the fairness of a term on its own initiative even where its fairness had not been challenged by the consumer.[32]

Legislative grounds for granting privileged status to consumers have historically been based essentially on notions of fairness and the perceived weakness in the position of the average consumer[33] as against the professional trader.[34] European legislators and the courts have repeatedly recognized that consumers are in an

---

[30] Albeit one of the elements of the definition of consumer under the Enterprise Act for Community infringements purposes is that in respect of the individual 'goods or services are or are sought to be *supplied*' and the individual receives or seeks to receive goods or services, see n 23.

[31] Council Directive 93/13/EEC.

[32] Case C-243/08 *Pannon GSM Zrt v Erzsébet Sustikné Győrfi.*

[33] The term 'average consumer' is used here in order to denote a 'reasonably well-informed and reasonably observant and circumspect' consumer, a concept developed as a benchmark in ECJ jurisprudence, see C Twigg-Flesner et al, 'An Analysis of the Application and Scope of the Unfair Commercial Practices Directive', A Report for the Department of Trade and Industry, 18 May 2005, <http://www.dti. gov.uk/files/file32095.pdf> (accessed 3 August 2011), 2.41–2.59. The ECJ has also developed the concept of the 'vulnerable consumer', see ibid, 2.59–2.69. The distinction between average and vulnerable consumers is also one of the fundamental concepts of the UCPD 2005 discussed in section 2.2.1.4 below.

[34] On the historical, economic, and philosophical background to the UK and EU consumer protection regime, see, eg, G Howells and S Weatherill, *Consumer Protection Law*, 2nd edn (Aldershot: Ashgate, 2005) 1–144.

inherently weaker position than sellers, both in terms of bargaining power and their knowledge of the product.[35] Additional concerns, which have also generally been regarded as putting the consumer at a material disadvantage, include the use of standard terms (small print), distance selling, doorstep selling, and generally the use of aggressive marketing and sales techniques, particularly those directed at classes of individuals considered to be vulnerable or unusually susceptible to high-pressure selling.

Consumers may also face problems of access to justice when seeking redress and compensation, because the costs and complexity of litigation are usually disproportionate to the value of the goods or services purchased by them.[36] As other commentators have noted, individual actions by the consumer against the trader are inadequate in the context of modern economies of mass production and extended distribution and marketing chains.[37] In addition, consumer protection policies are considered to benefit not only consumers, but also honest traders exposed to dishonest competition and, generally, the public interest in an efficient market system.[38]

Over the last several decades it has become the accepted position in Europe that state regulation of consumer transactions is the appropriate response to redress the economic imbalance between the parties.[39] In the context of transactional models that transcend or defy national borders such as e-commerce, there is an increasing realization at the political and legislative level of the need to address consumer protection policy and issues regionally or even globally, as exemplified by the EU harmonization programme and the international initiatives concerning consumer protection in e-commerce discussed below. However, it is disappointing, but not surprising, that little progress has been made at the global level in the last five years.

Beyond these generic considerations, specific business practices often raise consumer protection issues that need to be addressed by particular measures. Thus, attempts by suppliers to exclude liability in sales and hire-purchase contracts were addressed by UCTA 1977, which mostly deals with exclusion clauses in particular types of contracts. The proliferation of small print standard terms not individually negotiated with consumers and often used as a hiding place for unfair terms led to the adoption of the UTCCD and the Unfair Terms in Consumer Contracts Regulations 1994 and the UTCCRs 1999. A perceived need to modernize the

---

[35] Thus, eg, the system of protection introduced by the UTCCD is based on the idea that consumers are in a weak position vis-à-vis the seller or supplier as regards both their bargaining power and their level of knowledge, see Cases C-240–244/98 *Oceano Grupo Editorial SA v Rocio Murciano Quintero* [2000] ECR I-4941.

[36] For an enlightening exposition of the problem see generally H Genn, *Paths to Justice* (Oxford: Hart, 1999). A possible scenario is offered by the creation of a 'Consumer Advocate', see brief discussion in 2.4.2 below.

[37] Howells and Weatherhill, n 34, 49–51.

[38] Ibid. See further the Unfair Commercial Practices Directive 2005, recital 8.

[39] Howells and Weatherhill, n 34, 31.

consumer rights enforcement regime led to the Injunctions Directive[40] that was initially implemented in the UK by the Stop Now Orders (EC Directive) Regulations 2001,[41] now replaced by the Enterprise Act 2002 ('EA 2002'), Part 8. The SSGCRs 2002 implemented the Sale of Consumer Goods and Associated Guarantees Directive ('SCGAGD') and modernized provisions on implied terms, consumer rights and remedies, and consumer guarantees. The need to coordinate the enforcement of consumer protection laws across the EU led to the adoption of the CPCR 2004. Aggressive and misleading business practices and a perceived need to plug gaps and generally update EU consumer protection led to the adoption of the UCPD 2005. The proliferation of distance selling, the advent of e-commerce, and the specific issues they each raise for consumers resulted in the Distance Selling Directive and the e-Commerce Directive, the principal provisions of which were implemented in the UK by the DSRs 2000 and the Electronic Commerce (EC Directive) Regulations 2002 ('eComRs 2002').[42] The need to further ramp-up the efficiency and effectiveness of European consumer protection law is the driver behind the current review and consolidation of the European framework. Web 2.0, in particular social networking, and cloud computing and the additional issues they create for the protection of EU consumers have contributed, to a significant extent, to the launch of yet more initiatives to strengthen EU consumer protection, such as the currently ongoing review of the Data Protection Directive and the possible review of the e-Commerce Directive in the near future.

Further, the truly international nature of e-commerce and the consumer protection issues it raises point to the need for approximation or harmonization of national consumer protection standards for e-commerce and have triggered initiatives such as the Guidelines for Consumer Protection in the Context of Electronic Commerce 1999 of the Organisation for Economic Co-operation and Development ('OECD Guidelines')[43] and the Core Consumer Protection Principles in Electronic Commerce 1999 of the Transatlantic Consumer Dialogue ('TACD Principles').[44]

The rationale, purpose, and most important provisions of these core instruments, in relation to technology and e-commerce consumer contracts, are discussed below.

---

[40] Directive 98/27/EC of the European Parliament and of the Council of 19 May 1998 on injunctions for the protection of consumers' interests (OJ L166/51, 11 June 1998).

[41] SI 2001/1422.

[42] SI 2002 /2013. In relation to the implementation of the two directives in the UK, see further section 2.2.1.5 below.

[43] (Paris: OECD Publications, 2000), <http://www.oecd.org/dataoecd/18/13/34023235.pdf> (accessed 3 August 2011).

[44] DOC NO Ecom 10-99, September 1999, <http://www.tacd.org/index2.php?option=com_docman &task=doc_view&gid=135&Itemid=> (accessed 3 August 2011).

2.2 GOVERNING RULES OF LAW

Before we turn (in section 2.5) to a discussion of some of the key contractual terms and legal issues in mass market contracting, a review of the main sources of applicable hard and soft law is essential.

2.2.1 Legislation

Those legal provisions with immediate and extensive relevance to technology and e-commerce consumer contracts in the UK are found in legislation on the sale and supply of goods; unfair terms and commercial practices; distance selling and e-commerce contracts; and the enforcement of the collective interests of consumers. Accordingly, the main instruments considered here are those which apply to the majority of mass market contracts: the SGA 1979, the Supply of Goods and Services Act 1982 ('SGSA 1982') and the SSGCRs 2002; UCTA 1977, the UTCCRs 1999; the Consumer Protection from Unfair Trading Regulations 2008 ('CPRs 2008') and current developments affecting the law of unfair contract terms; finally, the DSRs 2000 and the eComRs 2002. Legislation concerning the enforcement of consumer rights is discussed separately in sections 2.3 and 2.4. Although directly relevant, privacy and data protection legislation is not discussed here, as it is examined in depth elsewhere in this book.[45]

As discussed in detail in section 2.3, most of the legislation described below, in addition to, in some cases, itself granting duties and/or powers to applicable enforcement authorities (typically the Office of Fair Trading, 'OFT'), is also, provided that certain conditions are met, enforceable under the regime created by the EA 2002.[46]

2.2.1.1 Sale and supply of goods legislation
Implied terms are the cornerstone of private law consumer protection.[47] They can be categorized into terms implied by statute and terms implied under the common law, and the relationship between the parties may be of profound importance in determining whether a term is implied.

It is entirely possible in the context of technology contracting, as it is generally, that the common law may imply terms that a particular product or service must comply with standards over and above or in addition to the statutory implied terms. In this regard, it is worth noting the statement of Sir Iain Glidewell in the judgment

---

[45] See Chapter 10. Similarly, several pieces of legislation that may be relevant in particular instances of mass market technology contracting are not discussed further here for reasons of space. Eg, in relation to Web 2.0 we do not examine the legal issues of UGC concerning copyright infringement, defamation, or obscenity.

[46] See section 2.3.2 below.

[47] Bradgate and Twigg-Flesner, n 22, 46 and 44–54 generally on the historical development and importance of implied terms.

of the court in *St Albans City & DC v International Computers Ltd*,[48] who, after considering the nature of software, accepted that a computer program is not goods under the definitions of either the SGA 1979, section 61 or the SGSA 1982, section 18.[49] In other words, computer disks containing computer programs constitute goods, but a computer program supplied purely in intangible form does not. However, if a program has been encoded onto a disk that is sold or hired but the program is defective, so that it will not instruct or enable the computer to achieve the intended purpose, the disk as a whole is defective and thus the seller or hirer of the disk will be in breach of the terms about quality or fitness implied by the SGA 1979, section 14 and the SGSA 1982, section 9. Interestingly, Sir Iain submitted that even where a computer program is not sold or hired in tangible form, the common law might still imply a term that the program itself is reasonably fit for purpose. This approach would have the result of affording equal protection to purchasers of software, irrespective of whether it is supplied physically or digitally, and seems wholly sensible. However, Sir Iain's discussion of the status of software is *obiter* (and was not conclusive in any event), and the courts have not subsequently ruled definitively on whether software constitutes goods, services, or some other *sui generis* chose in action. As will be seen below, this has potentially problematic implications in a number of areas.

Despite the relevance of terms implied by the common law, for reasons of conciseness and focus the remainder of this section deals only with statutory implied terms.

The SGA 1979 and the SGSA 1982 were both amended by the Sale and Supply of Goods Act 1994 ('SSGA 1994'). The SGA 1979, the SGSA 1982, and the SSGCRs 2002 are the main sources of statutory implied terms concerning both consumer and business contracts, although implied terms are also introduced for hire-purchase contracts by the Supply of Goods (Implied Terms) Act 1973 ('SGITA 1973'). The SGA 1979 and SGSA 1982 are discussed elsewhere in this book;[50] for the sake of brevity and to avoid duplication we provide here only a brief review of the two Acts and the key implied terms they introduce in the context of mass market contracting. The SSGCRs 2002 deserve more extensive consideration because of the extent of their impact and their particular significance in respect of consumer contracts.

---

[48] [1996] 4 All ER 481.

[49] See also *Horace Holman Group Ltd v Sherwood International Group Ltd* (2002) 146 SJLB 35, where the court found that the computer program did not constitute goods for the purposes of UCTA, s 6; the Scottish decision (with only persuasive force in England) in *Beta Computers (Europe) Ltd v Adobe Systems (Europe) Ltd* [1996] FSR 367, finding that the supply of shrink-wrapped software was not a sale of goods, and stating that the sale of software was a unique form of contract; *Saphena Computing Ltd v Allied Collection Agencies Ltd* [1995] FSR 616, where, however, the basis for the conclusion that the term was implied was not explained.

[50] Chapter 1, section 1.2. For the additional layer of consumer protection introduced by the SSGCRs 2002, see below.

Sale of Goods Act 1979   The SGA 1979 as amended[51] remains by far the most important source of UK domestic law on the sale of goods.[52] Remarkably, the SGA 1979 has not substantially changed from the original Sale of Goods Act 1893 ('SGA 1893'), as it essentially consolidates, with additional amendments, the SGA 1893 and some changes made to it prior to 1979. The SGA 1979 sets out the law governing contracts for the sale of goods and regulates a wide range of matters, including formation of contract;[53] transfer of title;[54] performance of the contract;[55] buyer's rights;[56] and actions for breach of contract.[57] Crucially, the SGA 1979 introduces several implied terms,[58] generally characterized as either conditions or warranties;[59] the difference being that in the former case a breach gives the non-breaching party a right to terminate the contract, whereas in the latter, the contract remains in force and the aggrieved party remains bound by its contractual obligations, but may bring an action for damages against the breaching party. The main implied terms introduced by the SGA 1979 are the condition of the right to sell;[60] the warranty of

---

[51] Beyond the SSGA 1994, the DSRs 2000, and the SSGCRs 2002 discussed below, the SGA 1979 has also been amended by the Sale of Goods (Amendment) Act 1994, and the Sale of Goods (Amendment) Act 1995.

[52] The remaining sources being the numerous other statutory provisions of varying importance including, eg, UCTA 1977 and the UTCCRs 1999, and of course the growing body of case law of the UK courts and the ECJ. In 2009, the Draft Common Frame of Reference was published, see <http://ec.europa.eu/justice/policies/civil/docs/dcfr_outline_edition_en.pdf> (accessed 3 August 2011). The DCFR is an academic document which essentially constitutes a draft of the main components of a European Civil Code and covers principles, definitions, and model rules of civil law including contract and tort law for both commercial and consumer contracts. In relation to the sale of goods, it derives extensively from the UN Convention on Contracts for the International Sale of Goods ('CISG'), Vienna, 11 April 1980 (which has not been signed by the UK)—see further JN Adams and H MacQueen, *Atiyah's Sale of Goods*, 12th edn (Harlow: Pearson, 2010) 3–6. See also European Commission, Green Paper from the Commission on policy options for progress towards a European Contract Law for consumers and businesses, COM(2010)348 final, 1 July 2010, setting out the Commission's view that differences between the contract laws of Member States impede cross-border trade and proposing seven alternative harmonizing measures ranging from light touch to a mandatory EU-wide civil code. Among other options, the Commission's favourite measure is a '2nd regime', ie, a set of optional, self-contained contract rules which contracting parties would be free to choose as the law regulating their contract in place of a Member State's national law, and based on those parts of the DCFR which are directly or indirectly relevant to contract law—see pp 9–10 of the Green Paper. The Committee on Legal Affairs of the European Parliament endorsed the approach of setting up an optional instrument for European Contract Law by virtue of a regulation in its Draft Report on policy options for progress towards a European Contract Law for consumers and businesses (Rapporteur: Diana Wallis), 20011/2013 (INI), 25 January 2011.

[53] SGA 1979, Pt II.

[54] Ibid ss 21–25.

[55] Ibid Pt IV.

[56] Ibid Pts V and 5(A), the latter enshrining the additional rights of consumers introduced by the SSGCRs 2002.

[57] SGA 1979, Pt VI.

[58] Ibid ss 10–15.

[59] Ibid s 11.

[60] Ibid s 12(1), and 12(5) added by the SSGA 1994 (not applicable in Scotland).

quiet possession;[61] the condition of correspondence with description;[62] and the conditions of satisfactory quality[63] and fitness for purpose,[64] both of which are subject to exceptions.[65] Given the particular relevance of the last two conditions to technology contracts, we offer some comments on them below.

First, the SGA 1979 provides no bright-line rule for the determination of whether the quality of goods is satisfactory. Instead, the test is whether, on the basis of any description of the goods, the price, and all other relevant circumstances, a reasonable person would regard the quality as satisfactory.[66] Secondly, qualitative considerations may be particularly problematic in relation to technology equipment. It is not always easy to delineate the exact purpose, let alone to specify fitness for such purpose, of both software, prone to bugs and errors even when fit for purpose,[67] and hardware, the proper functioning of which is dependent upon software. In the business context this can be resolved by a contractual commitment that the hardware and/or software will comply with defined specifications.[68] However, this is rarely a solution in the consumer context where, normally, either the transaction will be of relatively low value and the supplier will not offer or agree to negotiate any material specifications, or the consumer may provide a broad indication of the purpose for which the equipment is needed at the time the sale is negotiated without keeping a record of any discussions with the vendor. As a result, the vendor's description of the product is likely to be the most material factor for the determination of the reasonable standard of quality that can be expected for most consumer technology sales. Under the amendment introduced by the SSGCRs 2002 discussed below, such descriptions include public statements made by the seller, producer, or his representative, including in particular advertising and labelling.[69] Thirdly, the requirement of satisfactory quality not only covers the goods sold but also extends to other goods supplied under the contract such as manuals, drivers, or

---

[61] SGA 1979, s 12(2), and 12(5) added by the SSGA 1994 (not applicable in Scotland).

[62] Ibid 1979, s 13(1), and 13(1A) added by the SSGA 1994 (not applicable in Scotland).

[63] Ibid 1979, s 14(2) and (6). The SSGCRs 2002 introduced additional provisions concerning consumer contracts, see below.

[64] SGA 1979, s 14(3).

[65] Ibid ss 14(2C)(a) concerning unsatisfactory quality drawn to the attention of the buyer before the sale; 14(2C)(b) concerning unsatisfactory quality that ought to have been revealed by the examination of the goods by the buyer prior to the sale, if such examination took place; and 14(3)(b) concerning unfitness for purpose where the circumstances show that the buyer did not rely, or it was unreasonable for him to rely, on the skill and judgement of the seller or, if relevant, of the credit-broker.

[66] Ibid s 14(2A). Further, s 14(2B) provides an indicative non-exhaustive list of aspects of the quality of goods, namely their condition and state; fitness for all purposes for which goods of the particular kind are commonly supplied; appearance and finish; freedom from minor defects; safety; and durability. In most cases, fitness for common purposes of goods of the particular kind is likely to emerge as the crucial factor in the determination of the sufficiency of quality.

[67] *Saphena Computing*, n 49.

[68] See Chapter 1, section 1.3.2. The agreed testing procedures will also be relevant in determining fitness for purpose.

[69] SGA 1979, s 14(2D) subject to the exceptions in s 14(2E).

CD-ROMs. This will remain the case even when such accompanying products remain the property of the seller.[70]

Supply of Goods and Services Act 1982   The SGSA 1982 codified the dated and disparate common law rules relating to the supply of services and transfer of goods in the numerous instances not covered by the SGA 1979 or the SGITA 1973.[71] It amended the law in relation to implied terms concerning certain contracts for the hire of goods,[72] certain contracts for the supply of a service,[73] and certain contracts for the transfer of property in goods other than by a contract of sale as defined under the SGA 1979,[74] for instance work and materials contracts including the installation of goods. Certain of its provisions are also applicable to sale of goods contracts that also involve the supply of services.[75] The implied terms introduced in relation to services concern the requirements for the supplier to exercise reasonable skill and care[76] and to carry out the service within a reasonable time;[77] and, if not fixed by the contract, the price for the provision of the services must be reasonable.[78]

Prior to the SGSA 1982 it was necessary to distinguish between pure contracts of sale governed by the SGA 1979 and work and materials contracts, including contracts to manufacture and supply goods and contracts to supply and install goods. Following the implementation of the SGSA 1982, however, in the context of implied terms, the distinction is far less important because the SGSA 1982 implies into contracts for services the term that they will be provided with reasonable skill and care, irrespective of whether the contract is solely for services or for services and the transfer of goods. In contracts for both,[79] it also implies terms similar to those implied by the SGA 1979 in respect of contracts involving the transfer of goods. As a result, the SGSA 1982 ensures that, in respect of mixed contracts for work and materials, the supply of goods is in accordance with the contractual description and that the goods are of satisfactory quality and reasonable fitness, and that the supply of services is carried out with reasonable skill and care.

Sale and Supply of Goods to Consumers Regulations 2002   Both the SGA 1979 and the SGSA 1982 were amended by the SSGCRs 2002, which also amended the

---

[70] Chapter 1, section 1.2.1.8.

[71] Generally speaking, both the SGITA 1973 and the SGSA 1982 seek to a considerable extent to assimilate the rules of law applicable to the contracts they govern with those applicable to contracts for the sale of goods, see Bradgate and Twigg-Flesner, n 22, 26.

[72] SGSA 1982, ss 6–10.

[73] Ibid ss 12–15. The perennial discussion on whether software is goods or services remains relevant, see section 2.2.1.1 above.

[74] SGSA 1982, ss 1–5.

[75] Ibid ss 12–15.

[76] Ibid s 13.

[77] Ibid s 14.

[78] Ibid s 15.

[79] Ibid s 1(3) concerning England, Wales, and Northern Ireland.

SGITA 1973 and UCTA 1977. The SSGCRs 2002 implemented the SCGAGD,[80] which is a minimum harmonization measure permitting Member States to adopt or maintain more stringent provisions in order to achieve a higher standard of consumer protection, provided that this is not incompatible with the EC Treaty and particularly Article 28 on the free movement of goods.[81] A report compiled for the DTI (the predecessor of BIS, the Department for Business Innovation and Skills) in 2006 concluded that arguably the SSGCRs 2002 go further than required in several respects,[82] including that:

(a) the SCGAGD's remedial scheme is applied to contracts for the supply of goods other than sales, covered by the SGSA 1982;

(b) the definition of 'consumer' in the implementation allows a business to qualify as a consumer and claim protection of the rights derived from the SCGAGD;

(c) retention of the right to reject goods for breach of condition under the SGA 1979 gives consumers an additional right to escape the contract, not available under the SCGAGD; and

(d) under domestic law, the consumer is entitled to invoke the rights derived from the SCGAGD for up to six years, rather than for two as under the SCGAGD.[83]

---

[80] In summary, the SCGAGD deals mainly with three topics: implied terms of conformity of products in consumer contracts creating liability for the seller, Art 2; consumer rights and remedies in the event of lack of conformity of products, Art 3; and certain requirements relating to consumer guarantees and their legal enforceability, Art 6. The primary objective of the SCGAGD is the removal of barriers distorting the operation of the internal market caused by the differentiation of national consumer protection laws; although the elevation of consumer protection is sought, it is a secondary objective, see recitals 2–5. It is noteworthy that despite its focus on consumer sales, the SCGAGD derives from the CISG which has not been signed by the UK.

[81] SCGAGD, Art 8(2); cf, eg, the UCPD 2005 which is a maximum harmonization measure, see section 2.2.1.4 below.

[82] On the other hand, several provisions of the SCGAGD do not have an equivalent provision in the SSGCRs 2002, including two situations deemed not to constitute lack of conformity of the goods with the contract set forth in SCGAGD, Art 2(3); the right of redress of a final or retail seller when held liable to a consumer for non-conformity of the goods set forth in SCGAGD, Art 4; certain time limits pursuant to SCGAGD, Art 5; the establishment of the binding nature of the SCGAGD set forth in Art 7(1) and (2); and, a provision of general interest enshrined in SCGAGD, Art 12 requiring the Commission to report on the application of the SCGAGD.

[83] R Bradgate, A Nordhausen, and C Twigg-Flesner, 'Review of the Eight EU Consumer *Acquis* Minimum Harmonisation Directives and their Implementation in the UK and Analysis of the Scope for Simplification', Report Compiled for the Department of Trade and Industry, Consumer and Competition Policy Directorate, URN 05/1951, February 2006, <http://www.dti.gov.uk/files/file27199.pdf> (accessed 3 August 2011), para 49. The report concludes in para 52 that in a number of respects the SCGAGD has not been properly implemented in the UK, especially with regard to contracts to manufacture and supply goods and contracts to supply and install goods.

The SSGCRs 2002 are important and far-reaching, affecting both the law of the sale and supply of goods and the law of unfair contract terms.[84] They provide a further layer of consumer protection by introducing additional implied terms into consumer contracts and provisions on consumer guarantees concerning in particular the time when the guarantee takes effect, the form, language, wording, and contents of the guarantee, and the remedy for non-compliance. Note that neither the SCGAGD nor the SSGCRs 2002 require the provision of such guarantees. Rather, they stipulate that, if given, any such guarantees will have binding force as a contractual obligation, and they empower enforcement authorities to apply for an injunction or, in Scotland, an order of specific implement, in order to ensure compliance.[85]

In relation to the sale of goods, the main amendments introduced by the SSGCRs 2002 concern the statutory implied terms of satisfactory quality and reasonable fitness for purpose; provisions on the transfer of risk and delivery of goods; and the rights and remedies of the consumer, including the right to have goods that do not conform with the contract repaired or replaced, their price reduced, or the contract rescinded.

SSGCRs 2002, regulation 3 amended the SGA 1979, section 14 concerning the implied condition as to satisfactory quality, in order to include public statements (particularly in advertising and on labelling)[86] in the description of the goods, as a circumstance relevant to the determination of whether their quality is satisfactory.[87] The rule is subject to exceptions when the seller demonstrates that at the time the contract was made the seller was not, and could not reasonably have been, aware of the statement, or that before the contract was made the statement had been withdrawn or corrected in public, or that the decision to buy the goods could not have been influenced by the statement.[88]

SSGCRs 2002, regulation 4 introduces amendments concerning the passing of risk and the acceptance of goods: the amended SGA 1979, section 20(4) now provides that in the case of buyers dealing as consumers,[89] the goods remain at the seller's risk until they are delivered to the buyer, irrespective of when the property in them is transferred to the buyer,[90] or which party is at fault for delay in the delivery.[91] Further, the SGA 1979, section 32(4) as amended by the SSGCRs 2002

---

[84] For a detailed discussion of the SCGAGD and the SSGCRs 2002 including their background and adoption process as well as discussion of their provisions, see generally Bradgate and Twigg-Flesner, n 22.

[85] SSGCRs 2002, reg 15.

[86] SGA 1979, s 14(2D).

[87] Ibid s 14(2A).

[88] Ibid s 14(2E). However, a public statement will not be prevented from being a relevant circumstance, if the statement would have been a relevant circumstance irrespective of these provisions—s 14(2F).

[89] Or in Scotland, where there is a consumer contract in which the buyer is a consumer—references below to buyers dealing as a consumer should incorporate this difference for Scotland.

[90] Ibid s 20(4) excluding the application of s 20(1).

[91] Ibid s 20(4) excluding the application of s 20(2).

provides that where the buyer acts as a consumer, delivery of the goods to a carrier does not constitute delivery of the goods to the buyer.

More importantly, SSGCRs 2002, regulation 5 introduced a new Part 5A[92] to the SGA 1979 concerning additional rights of buyers acting as consumers, and providing a hierarchical array of new remedies[93] for cases of non-conformity of the goods with the contract at the time of delivery[94] owing to breach of either an express term or a term implied by any of the SGA 1979, sections 13, 14, and 15.[95] Furthermore, for the purposes of Part 5A remedies, any lack of conformity that manifests itself within six months of the delivery of the goods is presumed to have existed at the time of delivery,[96] unless such presumption is incompatible with either the nature of the goods or the nature of the lack of conformity.[97] The presumption is rebutted if the seller establishes that the goods did in fact conform at the day of delivery.

If non-conformity exists, the buyer dealing as a consumer, may choose to require that the seller either repairs[98] or replaces the goods within a reasonable time and without causing significant inconvenience to the buyer.[99] Any costs must be borne by the seller, including in particular any costs for labour, materials, or postage.[100] The right of the buyer to request the replacement or repair of goods is restricted in that neither remedy may be required if it is impossible or disproportionate in comparison either with the other remedy, or with the remedies of reduction of price or rescission of contract.[101] The latter two remedies[102] are only available if repair or replacement are impossible or disproportionate, or, even if available in principle, if the seller has failed to repair or replace the goods within a reasonable time and without significant inconvenience to the buyer.[103] In support of these remedies the courts are empowered to make an order for specific performance[104] or a conditional or unconditional order for damages.[105] Finally,[106] it should be noted that the amended

---

[92] SGA 1979, ss 48A–48F.

[93] Ibid ss 48B–48E.

[94] Ibid s 48A(1)(b).

[95] Ibid s 48F.

[96] Ibid s 48A(3).

[97] Ibid s 48A(4).

[98] The term repair is defined by SGA 1979, s 61(1) pursuant to SSGCRs 2002, reg 6(2) as meaning the bringing of the goods into conformity with the contract.

[99] SGA 1979, ss 48A(2)(a), 48B(1), and (2)(a).

[100] Ibid s 48(2)(b).

[101] Ibid s 48B(3). The test of proportionality is to be carried out primarily by reference to the costs imposed on the seller taking into account the value of the goods, the significance of the lack of conformity, and whether an alternative remedy would satisfy the buyer without causing him significant inconvenience, s 48B(4).

[102] Ibid s 48C(1).

[103] Ibid s 48C(2).

[104] Ibid s 48E(2).

[105] Ibid s 48E(6).

[106] A further amendment of the SGA 1979 was introduced indirectly by the SSGCRs 2002, reg 14 amending, as we see below, UCTA 1977, s 12 concerning the definition of consumer, because pursuant

Act implicitly recognizes that the traditional remedies of the common law and the SGA 1979 remain available.[107]

Similar amendments relating to the supply of goods were introduced by the SSGCRs 2002 to the SGSA 1982. In this context, the SSGCRs 2002 added provisions making public statements of the transferor relevant to the determination of the quality to be reasonably expected from the goods[108] and included a similar scheme of rights and remedies as described above in relation to the amendments made by the SSGCRs 2002 to the SGA 1979.[109] In relation to the hire of goods, the provisions on the relevance of public statements for the determination of the quality that can be reasonably expected from the goods were introduced.[110] Finally, definitions of the terms 'producer' and 'repair' were introduced.[111] Similarly, the SSGCRs 2002 amended the SGITA 1973 in order to introduce the provisions on the relevance of public statements.[112]

Finally, the SSGCRs 2002 amend the definition of the term 'dealing as consumer' in UCTA 1977:[113] the condition that in order for a party to a contract to be considered as dealing as a consumer, the goods passing under or in pursuance of the contract must be of a type ordinarily supplied for private use or consumption[114] is not applicable where the consumer is an individual.[115] Further changes were introduced in relation to auctions.[116]

2.2.1.2 Unfair terms legislation

The question that logically follows concerns the extent to which the statutory implied terms discussed above can be excluded by contract. Broadly speaking, legislation on unfair contractual terms restricts the use of exclusion or limitation clauses and, in the consumer context, generally prohibits unfair contractual terms that are not individually negotiated and are detrimental to the consumer. Of course, the

---

to the amendment introduced by SSGA 1994, s 7, Sch 2 para 5(9)(c), SGA 1979, s 61(5A) stipulates that references to 'dealing as a consumer' are to be construed in accordance with UCTA 1977, Pt I.

[107] SGA 1979, s 48D. In brief, these remedies include the rejection of the goods and/or the termination of the contract for breach, and the diminution or extinction of the price for breach of warranty of quality, see further M Bridge et al (eds), *Benjamin's Sale of Goods*, 8th edn (London: Sweet & Maxwell, 2010) chs 12, 14-102–14-111, and 17.

[108] SGSA 1982, s 4(2B)–(2D) pursuant to SSGCRs 2002, reg 7; see also reg 8 in relation to Scotland.

[109] SGSA 1982, Pt 1B pursuant to SSGCRs 2002, reg 9.

[110] SGSA 1982, s 9(2B)–(2D) pursuant to SSGCRs 2002, reg 10; see also reg 11 in relation to Scotland.

[111] SGSA 1982, s 18(1) pursuant to SSGCRs 2002, reg 12, also clarifying the meaning of the term 'consumer contract' in this context by reference to SGSA 1982, s 11F(3).

[112] SGITA 1973, s 10(2D)–(2F) pursuant to SSGCRs 2002, reg 13, also clarifying the meaning of the term 'consumer contract' in relation to Scotland, and setting forth the definition of 'producer' in SGITA 1973, s 15(1).

[113] SSGCRs 2002, reg 14.

[114] UCTA 1977, s 12(1)(c).

[115] Ibid s 12(1A).

[116] Ibid s 12(2).

determination of whether the terms can be excluded by contract will be preceded by the common law consideration of whether the terms were part of the contract in the first place. The application of the common law rules precedes the application of statutory rules. Thus, indirect methods of controlling unfair terms under the common law retain their relevance, because an unincorporated term will not be binding irrespective of whether it is fair or not. Since the adoption of UCTA 1977, however, English law pursues a direct statutory control of unfair terms: UCTA 1977 poses a direct challenge to unfair terms that are undisputedly part of the contract and subjects their enforceability to the decision of the courts.[117] Accordingly, the power of the courts directly to challenge unfair terms has reduced their motivation to pursue indirect routes in order to attack unfair clauses.[118]

In the UK,[119] the main sources of direct statutory control over unfair terms are UCTA 1977 and the UTCCRs 1999. There exist several differences between the two instruments concerning the types of contracts covered, the types of terms covered, and the control tests applied,[120] the most notable being that whereas UCTA 1977 regulates only exclusion and limitation of liability clauses in both consumer and business contracts, as well as indemnity clauses in consumer contracts, the UTCCRs 1999 regulate unfair terms generally, but only in consumer contracts. UCTA 1977 sets forth a test of 'reasonableness', while the UTCCRs 1999 set forth a different test of 'fairness', albeit the results will usually be the same.[121] UCTA 1977 is also applicable to individually negotiated terms, while the UTCCRs 1999 apply only to terms that have not been individually negotiated with the consumer; UCTA 1977 also addresses exclusion clauses contained in notices, while the UTCCRs 1999 do not; and UCTA 1977 has effect only between the immediate parties, while the UTCCRs 1999 empower various bodies, including the OFT, to take action to prevent the use of unfair terms. Hence, in some respects UCTA 1977 provides more extensive coverage, and in other respects the UTCCRs 1999 are more comprehensive.

As to the scope of application of the two instruments, in some cases only UCTA 1977 will be applicable; in others, only the UTCCRs 1999; and in some, the validity of a disputed clause will have to be determined against both UCTA 1977 and the

---

[117] Similarly Adams and MacQueen, n 52, 226 et seq; Howells and Weatherhill, n 34, 267.

[118] Ibid.

[119] For the historical development of unfair terms legislation see Law Commission and Scottish Law Commission, 'Unfair Terms in Contracts: A Joint Consultation Paper' (Law Com Consultation Paper No 166, Scots Law Com Discussion Paper No 119, August 2002), <http://www.lawcom.gov.uk/docs/cp166.pdf> (accessed 8 April 2011), 2.10–2.16.

[120] For a more detailed illustration of the principal differences between the two instruments, see Law Commission and Scottish Law Commission, 'Unfair Terms in Contracts: Report on a Reference under section 3(1)(e) of the Law Commissions Act 1965' (Law Com No 292, Scots Law Com No 199, Cm 6464 SE/2005/13), <http://www.lawcom.gov.uk/docs/lc292(1).pdf> (accessed 8 April 2011), 2.6–2.7.

[121] Consider in this regard that the notion of 'fairness' is also an element of the UCTA reasonableness test: UCTA 1977, s 11 states that the requirement for reasonableness is 'that the term shall be fair and reasonable'. In *Director General of Fair Trading v First National Bank plc* [2001] 3WLR 1297, HL, the House of Lords stated, at 1305, that some similarity of approach in applying the two tests may be appropriate. However, until there is a case in which both tests are applied, the point will remain uncertain.

UTCCRs 1999, in a double barrier situation reminiscent of EU competition law.[122]
In such cases, more stringent or extensive provisions under UCTA 1977 will apply
because the UTCCD is a minimum harmonization measure allowing Member States
to maintain or adopt more stringent provisions.[123] Thus, for instance, UCTA 1977
can be invoked in order to achieve control over unfair exclusion clauses in individually negotiated consumer contracts.

Unfair Contract Terms Act 1977   UCTA 1977 was the result of the first EU
consumer protection programme. The title of the Act is a misnomer, because it does
not apply to unfair terms generally, but only to exclusion and limitation of liability
clauses in particular types of contract,[124] and to indemnity clauses in consumer
contracts. Although it is not concerned exclusively with consumer protection, in
many respects it offers a higher level of protection for consumers than the more recent
UTCCRs 1999. For example, UCTA 1977, section 2(1) provides that liability for
death and injury resulting from negligence cannot generally be limited or excluded.[125]
In the case of other loss or damage, any exclusion or restriction of liability for negligence will generally be valid only to the extent that it is reasonable.[126] One party's
agreement to or awareness of an exclusion or limitation of liability clause or notice
is not of itself an indication of voluntary acceptance of any risk.[127] Further, in respect
of contracts where one party deals as a consumer or on the other party's standard
terms, UCTA 1977, section 3 subjects to a reasonableness test all terms that seek to
exclude or limit the liability of the other party if it is in breach of contract;[128] or by
reference to which that party claims to be entitled not to perform its contractual
obligation or to render a contractual performance substantially different from that
which was reasonably expected by the other party.[129] UCTA 1977 also renders some
types of exclusion clauses null and void without applying the test of reasonableness.[130] Furthermore, as noted above, not only do these provisions apply to protect

---

[122] *Wilhelm v Bundeskartellamt* [1969] CMLR 100; *Boehringer Mannheim GmbH v Commission*
[1973] CMLR 864.
[123] UTCCD, Art 8.
[124] UCTA 1977, Sch 1 and ss 26, 27(1), and 29(1) exclude from the application of the Act certain types
of contract or certain specific provisions in any type of contract, see further below.
[125] Although death and personal injury are generally unlikely in the context of IT contracts, they are
not inconceivable. For instance, in 2006 two major computer companies had to recall over 4,800,000
batteries of a major manufacturer costing £90–136m, because they caused their computers to overheat
and in certain instances explode into flames, reportedly causing minor injuries to a few users, see
Financial Times, 25 August 2006, p 1.
[126] UCTA 1977, s 2(2).
[127] Ibid s 2(3).
[128] Ibid s 3(1).
[129] Ibid s 3(2).
[130] Ibid s 6 concerning contracts of sale and hire purchase; s 7 concerning goods passing under a
contract other than a contract of sale or hire purchase; and s 2(1) concerning death or personal injury
discussed above.

businesses when dealing as consumers,[131] but certain of them are applicable even when neither party deals as a consumer.[132]

For a provision to be reasonable under UCTA 1977, it must have been reasonable at the time of conclusion of the contract, having regard to the circumstances that were, or ought reasonably to have been, known to, or in the contemplation of, the parties.[133] Where a supplier seeks to restrict liability to a specified sum of money, in determining the reasonableness of the limitation regard shall be had in particular to the resources which the supplier could expect to be available to him for the purposes of meeting the liability and how far it was open to him to cover himself by insurance.[134] UCTA 1977, Schedule 2 sets out a non-exhaustive list of the matters that a court should consider in determining whether a contractual term satisfies the reasonableness test. These are the relative bargaining power of the parties; whether the customer received any inducement in order to accept the term; whether the customer knew, or ought reasonably to have known, of the existence and extent of the term; in the case of a term excluding or limiting liability for non-compliance with a condition, whether it was reasonable at the time of conclusion of the contract to expect that compliance with the condition would be practicable; and whether the goods were manufactured, processed, or adapted in accordance to a special order.

It is often thought that these factors are relevant to all questions of reasonableness under the Act. In fact, section 11(2) provides that the matters set out in Schedule 2 are relevant to the determination of reasonableness in respect only of those contractual terms that seek to limit liability for breach of the undertakings as to title, conformity with description, and fitness for purpose implied in respect of contracts for the sale of goods under the SGA 1979;[135] the equivalent undertakings implied in respect of hire-purchase contracts under the SGITA 1973;[136] and similar undertakings implied in respect of other contracts under which possession or ownership of

---

[131] See nn 25 and 26 above and accompanying text.

[132] See, eg, *Kingsway Hall Hotel Ltd v Red Sky IT (Hounslow) Ltd* [2010] EWHC 965 (TCC), May 2010, where Toulmin J found that a software supplier's standard exclusion clause, which attempted to exclude the statutory implied terms as to satisfactory quality and fitness for purpose, was not enforceable. The basis for the exclusion clause was that before the customer would enter into the contract, it would receive certain operating documents which would enable it to make an informed decision about the software's suitability for its business. The customer was not provided with the relevant documents, and had therefore not been able to make its own assessment; instead, it had to rely on the supplier's advice that the software was suitable. The judge found that, as a result, the exclusion did not apply, the implied terms were not excluded and, even if the exclusion clause applied, it would have been unreasonable under UCTA 1977 in these circumstances. The judge, therefore, concluded that the software was neither fit for purpose nor of satisfactory quality and awarded damages to the customer. Toulmin J observed that it might be reasonable for the supplier to exclude the implied terms as to satisfactory quality and fitness for purpose where the customer has the means to satisfy itself as to these factors and does not rely on the supplier's advice.

[133] UCTA 1977, s 11(1).

[134] Ibid s 11(4).

[135] Ibid s 6.

[136] Ibid.

goods pass, such as quasi-sale and simple hiring contracts.[137] However, although the Schedule 2 guidelines technically do not apply to all contractual terms governed by UCTA 1977, it has been suggested that this makes little practical difference.[138]

The UCTA reasonableness test is discussed extensively elsewhere.[139] For our purposes, in addition to our observations above, it is sufficient to note that, first, when the reasonableness test is applicable, UCTA 1977 does not itself distinguish between its applicability to business or consumer contracts. In practice, however, because of the nature of the factors that UCTA 1977 requires to be taken into account by a court when determining the reasonableness of any particular provision, it is generally less likely that the test will be satisfied if the disputed term is part of a consumer contract. Secondly, the application of the test by the courts in practice indicates that the established business practice of using standard exclusion clauses across multiple transactions without adaptation to the particular circumstances is likely from time to time to be considered unreasonable, a fact that should be regarded as the downside of the overall benefits of standard contracting for businesses.[140] As discussed in the following section, the negative aspects of standard contracting may be aggravated in the consumer context, because of the additional restrictions imposed by the UTCCD and the UTCCRs 1999 specifically on terms that have not been individually negotiated with the consumer.

The UCTA 1977 provisions most likely to be applicable in the majority of consumer transactions (including technology transactions) will be section 3, which is discussed above, and applies to contracts where one of the parties acts as consumer or on the other party's written standard terms;[141] and section 6, concerning exclusion or limitation of liability for breach of the implied undertakings under the SGA 1979 and the SGITA 1973 in respect of sale and hire-purchase contracts.[142] Section 6(1) provides that liability for breach of the seller's obligations under the SGA 1979 in relation to the implied obligations as to title, freedom from encumbrances, and quiet possession, cannot be excluded or restricted by reference to any term; the same

---

[137] UCTA 1977, s 7.

[138] *Danka Rentals Ltd v Xi Software* [1998] 7 Tr LR 74.

[139] eg, Adams and MacQueen, n 52, 235 et seq; Howells and Weatherhill, n 34, 5.6.1, comparing the reasonableness test with the fairness test of the UTCCRs 1999; C Christou, *Drafting Commercial Agreements*, 4th edn (London: Sweet & Maxwell, 2009), pp 4 et seq.

[140] Chapter 1, section 1.2.2.13.

[141] UCTA 1977, s 3(1).

[142] Further, UCTA 1977, s 4 regulates unreasonable indemnity clauses imposed on persons dealing as consumers; s 5 concerns the guarantee of consumer goods; s 8 deals with misrepresentation and substitutes the Misrepresentation Act 1967, s 3; s 9 states the effect of breach; s 10 proscribes the evasion of liability by means of a secondary contract; and s 7 concerns other contracts under which goods pass, such as quasi-sale and simple hiring contracts, which in the context of our subject matter will be applicable only in a minority of cases. Additionally, an attempt to exclude or limit liability as to description, fitness for purpose, or satisfactory quality against a consumer in the context of a sale or hire-purchase contract may constitute a criminal offence under the Consumer Transactions (Restrictions on Statements) Order 1976 (SI 1976/1813 as amended by SI 1978/127), though contracts for the supply of services or for goods and services fall outside the scope of the Order.

applies to obligations under the SGITA 1973 in relation to hire purchase. Furthermore, with regard to implied undertakings as to the conformity of goods with description or sample, or as to quality or fitness for a particular purpose, liability for breach cannot be limited or excluded when the other party deals as a consumer or, when the other party does not deal as a consumer, can be limited or excluded only to the extent that this is reasonable.[143] Often, both section 3 and section 6 will be simultaneously applicable and, ultimately, the section that affords more effective protection to the consumer will be enforced.[144]

UCTA 1977 excludes from its ambit certain types of contract and certain provisions in any type of contract, in particular any contract so far as it relates to the creation, transfer, or termination of a right or interest in intellectual property ('IP'). Furthermore, as discussed below, international supply contracts (which, essentially, are contracts involving both a material cross-border element and the sale or transfer of possession or ownership of goods) are expressly excluded from the UCTA 1977 regime.[145] Finally, in the case of contracts governed by the law of any part of the UK by virtue only of the parties' choice of law, but the law of another country would otherwise apply, the substantive provisions of UCTA 1977 are disapplied.[146] In the context of mass market contracting, the UCTA 1977 international supply contracts and IP rights-related exemptions need to be addressed in more detail.

The international supply contracts exception raises an issue concerning the application of UCTA 1977 to cross-border technology contracting. In the light of the courts' current position with regard to whether software (and, by extension, other digital content) constitutes goods or services or is *sui generis*,[147] the determination of whether UCTA 1977 applies to an international contract for the supply of software (and, we submit, digital content) currently appears likely to depend on whether it is supplied on a tangible medium. If it is supplied on a tangible medium, for example a CD, which is also sold or whose possession or ownership also passes under the contract, the contract will be exempted from the application of UCTA 1977. If, on the other hand, the software is not supplied on a tangible medium, because, for example, it is downloaded from the supplier's website, the courts would probably consider that the supply of the software or other content did not involve the sale or

---

[143] UCTA 1977, s 6(2) and (3).

[144] The issue of which provision takes precedence was raised but not decided in *Sovereign Finance v Silver Crest Furniture* [1997] CCLR 76. The correct position seems to be that the claimant can rely on both provisions.

[145] UCTA 1977, s 26. Of course, an exclusion clause in a cross-border consumer contract may constitute an unfair term in the meaning of the Unfair Terms Directive and the UTCCRs 1999, see generally the discussion on unfair exclusion clauses in section 2.5 below, eg section 2.5.13.

[146] UCTA 1977, s 27(1). However, where a term applies or purports to apply the law of another country, UCTA will nevertheless be applicable if the term appears to a court or arbitrator or arbiter to have been imposed wholly or mainly in order to avoid the application of UCTA, s 27(2)(a), or one party is a consumer resident in the UK and the essential steps for the making of the contract were taken in the UK either by the consumer or by others on the consumer's behalf, s 27(2)(b).

[147] Section 2.2.1.1 above.

transfer of possession or ownership of goods and consequently UCTA 1977 will not be excluded. If this analysis is correct, it leads to the conclusion that a consumer's rights against a foreign supplier will depend upon the mode of delivery of the content. The anomaly of this position is driven home by the example of the consumer who does not receive the content ordered (either because physical items are not shipped or they do not reach their destination, or because an electronic download does not take place). Despite the fact that in each case, the consumer ends up with nothing, the effectiveness of a supplier's exclusion clause for non-delivery may well depend on how the non-delivered content should have been delivered.

As noted above, UCTA 1977 also does not apply to any contract insofar as it relates to the creation, transfer, or termination of a right or interest in IP. At first glance, the exemption appears extremely broad, potentially excluding from the ambit of the Act the sale or supply of copyright protected digital content (whether in tangible or intangible form)—essentially, most music and video download content transactions. In *Salvage Association v CAP Financial Services Ltd*[148] concerning the installation of computer software, it was suggested that because all the issues of the case concerned IP matters, the action was within the excluding provisions of UCTA 1977, Schedule 1. The official referee, however, referred to *Micklefield v SAC Technology*[149] and rejected this argument, on the basis that the provisions of UCTA 1977, Schedule 1 are applicable only to the specific provisions of a contract that deal with the creation or transfer of a right or interest in the relevant IP. The referee ruled that:

It does not extend generally to all the terms of a contract simply because the contract is concerned overall with the provision of a service, performance of which will result in a product to which the law affords the protection of one or more of the specified intellectual property rights.

The referee concluded that although UCTA 1977, Schedule 1 applies to any term concerned with the creation or transfer of a right or interest in IP, it will not apply to a term that is concerned with other aspects of the contract. In reaching this conclusion, the referee emphasized the difference in the wording between the UCTA 1977 exclusion provisions concerning IP referring to any contract 'so far as it relates' to IP, and those concerning insurance contracts, which simply refer to 'any contract of insurance', which necessitates the exclusion of the entire contract as opposed to just the exclusion of individual terms. The decision in *Salvage Association* is consistent with the general thrust of UCTA 1977, and it would have been difficult for the referee to interpret the scope of the exception in question any more narrowly.

---

[148] [1995] FSR 654.

[149] [1991] 1 All ER 275, concerning an employment contract that included provisions concerning an interest in securities. In examining the issue of whether the terms of the share option scheme that excluded or limited the liability of the company were within UCTA 1977, the court found that the wording of the exclusion in UCTA referring to any contract so far as it relates to the creation or transfer of an interest in securities was enough to bring the relevant term within the exclusion.

Nevertheless, although this decision means that entire contracts should not generally now be excluded by the exception from the application of the Act, its potential impact remains substantial, even if its application is limited to provisions relating to IP. For example, it is difficult on the face of it to see how a provision disclaiming supplier liability for third party IP infringement claims in respect of rights licensed to a consumer (eg, to listen to downloaded music, or watch movies) would be caught by UCTA 1977 at least. From a business perspective, the exception may appear to be one concession in an otherwise heavily regulated environment: however, it is our submission that such an assessment would be ill-conceived and dangerous. While there may indeed be good policy grounds for exempting certain IP transactions from the application of UCTA 1977, allowing suppliers to exclude liability for IP-related liability in mass market transactions in the modern, multi-media environment, would run entirely counter to current consumer protection policy, principles, and law. We therefore consider that courts and regulators would not hesitate to challenge such exclusions under other consumer protection measures.[150]

As noted, the international supply and IP exemptions discussed above potentially exclude many technology contracts from the ambit of UCTA 1977. On the face of it, UCTA 1977 does not apply to cross-border online or offline transactions involving the supply of physical goods, and limitation and exclusion clauses relating to IP rights in, for example, electronic content like music and movie downloads, and software, are also excluded from its ambit. Nevertheless, save perhaps in a few limited circumstances, it seems unlikely that regulators will be willing to stand idly by if consumers are perceived to be disadvantaged in these areas, particularly given the weight of policy, legislative, and regulatory initiatives aimed at encouraging consumer confidence in e-commerce in Europe. We expect that rather than see this happen, it is likely that other consumer protection measures would be drafted in by regulatory authorities to plug the gaps, though when and in what circumstances remains unclear. The current developments discussed at section 2.2.3 below could offer a platform for reform.

Unfair Terms in Consumer Contracts Regulations 1999 The UTCCRs 1999 implement, almost verbatim, the UTCCD. They create a distinct regime from that of UCTA 1977. The UTCCRs 1999 apply to unfair terms in any contract between a seller or supplier and a consumer.[151] This is also the case where a contract term applies or purports to apply the law of a non-Member State, if the contract has a close connection with the territory of the Member States.[152] The broad scope is

---

[150] See further section 2.5.15 below for examples of common issues concerning IP rights.

[151] UTCCD, Art 1(1); UTCCRs 1999, reg 4(1).

[152] UTCCD, Art 6(2); UTCCRs 1999, reg 9. A Member State is defined in reg 3(1) as including the contracting parties to the European Economic Area (EEA), ie the 27 EU Member States, Iceland, Norway, and Liechtenstein.

subject to relatively few exceptions.[153] These are that the UTCCRs 1999 do not apply to contractual terms that reflect mandatory statutory or regulatory provisions, including provisions under the law of any Member State or in Community legislation having effect in the UK without further enactment; or provisions or principles of international conventions to which the Member States or the Community are party. Furthermore, as seen below, the UTCCRs 1999 do not apply to core contractual terms concerning the description of the subject matter of the contract and the price, provided that they meet the requirement for plain and intelligible language. Nor do they apply to terms that have been individually negotiated.[154] It is worth noting here that, in some cases, a term which involves a breach of other legislative provisions is also capable of being an unfair term under the UTCCRs 1999, for example a term which purports to deny a consumer his or her rights to cancel a distance contact is likely both to fall foul of the DSRs 2000[155] and to be an unfair term under the UTCCRs 1999.

A contractual term that has not been individually negotiated with the consumer will be regarded as unfair,[156] if contrary to the requirements of good faith[157] it causes a significant imbalance[158] in the parties' rights and obligations arising under the contract to the detriment of the consumer.[159] The OFT takes the view that the imbalance must be significant in practical terms, meaning that taken together with the rest of the contract the term should be capable of causing detriment to the consumer; however, this does not mean that the term must be proven to have caused actual harm.[160] No definition of what constitutes a term not individually negotiated is provided. However, a term will always be regarded as not having been individually negotiated where it has been drafted in advance and the consumer has therefore not

---

[153] UTCCD, Art 1(2); UTCCRs 1999, reg 4(2).

[154] UTCCD, Art 3; UTCCRs 1999, reg 5(1) and (3).

[155] See section 2.2.1.5 below.

[156] UTCCD, Art 3(1); UTCCRs 1999, reg 5(1).

[157] The requirement of good faith is not defined in the UTCCRs 1999, but is explained in Directive recital 16: in assessing good faith, attention must be paid to the strength of the bargaining positions of the parties; to whether the consumer had an inducement to agree to the term; and, to whether the goods or services were sold or supplied to the special order of the consumer. Further, the requirement of good faith may be satisfied by the seller or supplier where he deals fairly and equitably. In the UK, good faith has been held to mean that suppliers must deal fairly, equitably and openly with consumers, see *Director-General of Fair Trading v First National Bank plc* [2002] All ER 97 (decided under the UTCCRs 1999).

[158] According to the OFT, contractual imbalance may arise when a term gives to the seller or supplier powers or safeguards which could put the consumer at a disadvantage, whether or not actual harm is caused, see OFT, 'IT Consumer Contracts Made at a Distance: Guidance on Compliance with the Distance Selling and Unfair Terms in Consumer Contracts Regulations', OFT 672, December 2005, <http://www.oft.gov.uk/shared_oft/reports/consumer_protection/oft672.pdf> (accessed 3 August 2011), 66 ('OFT 672').

[159] *First National Bank*, n 157.

[160] The OFT takes the view that such terms may be unfair if they have the effect of reducing the consumer's rights under the ordinary rules of contract or the general law, see OFT, 'Unfair Standard Terms', OFT 143 (edn 09/08, 2008), <http://www.oft.gov.uk/shared_oft/business_leaflets/unfair_contract_terms/oft143.pdf> (accessed 3 August 2011), p 2.

been able to influence the substance of the term.[161] Notwithstanding that a specific contractual term (or part of a term) has been individually negotiated, the UTCCRs 1999 apply to the rest of the contract if an overall assessment of it indicates that it is a pre-formulated standard contract.[162] The seller or supplier who claims that a term was individually negotiated bears the burden of proof.[163]

Furthermore, the seller or supplier must ensure that written contract terms are expressed in plain intelligible language.[164] The UTCCD and the UTCCRs 1999 adopt the *contra proferentem* rule, specifically stating that in proceedings brought by consumers, in case of doubt as to the meaning of a term, the interpretation which is most favourable to the consumer shall prevail; however, this rule does not apply in injunctive proceedings brought by qualifying bodies[165] against the seller.[166]

The effect of establishing a term as being unfair is that the term is not binding on the consumer, though the remainder of the contract will continue to be binding on both parties if it is capable of existence without the unfair term.[167] Schedule 2 to the UTCCRs 1999 contains an indicative and non-exhaustive list of the terms that may be regarded as unfair.[168] The terms in the list are not necessarily unfair, in other

---

[161] UTCCD, Art 3(2); UTCCRs 1999, reg 5(2), with slight differentiation in the wording in that the Regulations do not include the sentence 'particularly in the context of pre-formulated contracts'. The differentiation appears to be innocuous, since the essence of the provision remains the same. Where a consumer has the choice whether to contract on standard terms, it can be argued that he actually had the opportunity to influence the terms, which, therefore, do not constitute non-negotiated terms in the meaning of UTCCRs 1999, reg 5(1): in *Bryen and Langley Ltd v Boston* [2004] All ER (D) 61 (Nov), where the form of contract had been selected by the advisers of the employer, ie the consumer, under a building contract, Judge Seymour's *obiter dictum* accepted that 'it is at least arguable that where the "consumer" has been able to influence the substance of the relevant term because he chose to use the standard form of contract in which it is contained, the term does not fall to be regarded as not having been individually negotiated'. On appeal, [2005] All ER (D) 507 (Jul), the court declined to express a specific opinion, however it remarked that despite the fact that the consumer did not make use of the opportunity to influence the term, the availability of this opportunity itself allows at least an argument that the term is not within the scope of UTCCRs 1999, reg 5(1).

[162] UTCCD, Art 3(2); UTCCRs 1999, reg 5(3).

[163] UTCCD, Art 3(2); UTCCRs 1999, reg 5(4).

[164] UTCCD, Art 5; UTCCRs 1999, reg 7(1). See also *Office of Fair Trading v Foxtons* discussed at n 172.

[165] The qualifying bodies are specified in Annex A and most have also enforcement powers under the EA 2002, Pt 8 to take action against unfair terms that harm the collective interests of consumers. They include the pubic qualifying bodies listed in UTCCRs 1999, Sch 1 Pt 1, ie statutory regulators and trading standards departments such as the Information Commissioner's Office, the Office of Communications (Ofcom), the Financial Services Authority (FSA), as well as the Consumers' Association, aka Which? The OFT and the qualifying bodies cooperate and coordinate their action, see, eg, OFT and FSA, 'Unfair Terms in Consumer Contracts Regulations 1999 (UTCCRs) & Enterprise Act 2002 (EA02): A Concordat between the Office of Fair Trading (OFT), and the Financial Services Authority (FSA)', 31 July 2006, <http://www.oft.gov.uk/shared_oft/general_policy/oft860.pdf> (accessed 3 August 2011), concerning the coordination of enforcement action and cooperation 'in all ways permitted by law to ensure effective and consistent delivery of consumer protection'.

[166] UTCCD, Arts 5 and 7(2); UTCCRs 1999, regs 7(2) and 12. On the powers of the qualifying bodies see below.

[167] UTCCD, Art 6(1); UTCCRs 1999, reg 8(1) and (2).

[168] UTCCD, Art 3(3); UTCCRs 1999, reg 5(5).

words this is a grey list, not a black list. The list includes terms that cause one or more of certain common unfair results: they mislead consumers about the contract or their legal rights; they deny consumers full redress; they unfairly tie the consumer to the contract; they relieve the business of its contractual obligations; they unfairly compel consumers to lose pre-payments if the contract is cancelled; they allow the business to vary the terms of the contract after they have been agreed; and they subject consumers to unfair penalties. This list, along with the recitals of the UTCCD, can be used as guidance for the application of the fairness test.

The fairness test requires that the unfairness of a contractual term is assessed taking into account the nature of the goods or services for which the contract was concluded and by referring, at the time of conclusion of the contract, to all the circumstances attending the conclusion of the contract and to all the other terms of the contract or of another contract on which it is dependent.[169]

The fairness test is subject to an important qualification concerning the so-called 'core terms' of the contract: so far as they are in plain intelligible language, terms relating to either the definition of the main subject matter of the contract, or to the adequacy of the price or remuneration as against the goods or services provided in exchange, are exempted from assessment as to their fairness.[170] The exemption aims at allowing freedom of contract in relation to terms that are genuinely central to the bargain. The OFT has taken the view that the core term exemption is conditional upon the expression and presentation of the terms being such that they ensure that the terms 'are, or at least are capable of being, at the forefront of the consumer's mind in deciding whether to enter the contract'.[171]

It is not unusual for enforcement authorities to have concerns with the fairness of terms that are commonly used by suppliers in consumer contracts and the courts

---

[169] UTCCD, Art 4(1); UTCCRs 1999, reg 6(1).

[170] UTCCD, Art 4(2); UTCCRs 1999, reg 6(2). See further *Office of Fair Trading v Abbey National plc and Others* [2009] UKSC 6, where the Supreme Court allowed the appeal brought by the banks and overturned the judgments of the Court of Appeal and High Court, which ruled that the unfairness rules of the UTCCRs 1999 could be applied to assess unarranged overdraft charges in personal current accounts. The Supreme Court decided that the relevant charges were part of the price or remuneration paid by customers in exchange for the package of services which make up a current account. Therefore, the OFT was precluded, by UTCCRs 1999, reg 6(2)(b), from making any assessment of the fairness of the charges which relates to their appropriateness as against the services supplied in exchange. Following the judgment, the OFT announced that it would review it carefully and decide whether to continue its investigation into unarranged overdraft charging terms and stated that it would be seeking discussions with banks, consumer organizations, the FSA, and the Government in the light of this judgment. On 22 December 2009, the OFT announced that after detailed consideration of the judgment and of the various options available to it, it concluded that any investigation it were to continue into the fairness of the then current unarranged overdraft charging terms under the UTCCRs 1999 would have a very limited scope and low prospects of success. Consequently, the OFT decided against taking forward such an investigation, see the OFT press release at <http://www.oft.gov.uk/news-and-updates/press/2009/144-09> (accessed 3 August 2011).

[171] OFT 672, p 67.

have also found such terms to be unfair in certain circumstances.[172] Often, widely used but potentially unenforceable terms can be found in terms and conditions for the supply of novel products where, on the one hand, suppliers are (understandably) attempting to limit their exposure to the extent possible and, on the other, the regulators have not yet had the reasons or the opportunity to turn their attention to the issue.

At present, a good example is the terms and conditions of many cloud computing service providers: in the current state of play, consumer contracts for cloud services often include terms of questionable enforceability under EU and UK consumer protection legislation. Typical examples include terms aimed at: (a) limiting liability at a very low level (typically ranging from one month's to 12 months' fees); or even (b) totally excluding the liability of the cloud services provider, including for the integrity and availability of data, which is often the main purpose of the cloud services contract; (c) enabling the provider unilaterally to amend the terms at any time, without notice to the consumer; and (d) subjecting the contract to the law and courts of, or an arbitral tribunal sitting in, a jurisdiction other than the consumer's home country (typically a US state).[173] As we will see later, such terms may fall foul of unfair contract terms legislation; the OFT's guidance clearly states that in many cases such terms are likely to be unfair, and therefore unenforceable, under the UTCCRs 1999 (albeit the OFT has not examined such terms in the cloud computing context).[174] Furthermore, it appears that cloud service suppliers would also face difficulties if such wide exclusion and limitation of liability terms were scrutinized under UCTA 1977. The question of the fairness and enforceability of such terms in the cloud computing context is particularly complex and a detailed analysis would necessitate much more space than that available here.[175] Nevertheless, we offer some high-level thoughts below.

---

[172] See, eg, *Office of Fair Trading v Foxtons* [2009] EWHC 1681 (Ch), 10 July 2009, where Mann J held that some of the charges that estate agent Foxtons imposed on landlords were unfair under the UTCCRs 1999. The case was brought by the OFT, which said clauses in the small print of Foxtons' contracts for managing tenanted properties were a trap. Foxtons required a renewal commission if a tenant stayed beyond the initial one-year tenancy and 2.5% of the value of the property if the tenant went on to buy it. Unlike the court's conclusion in *Office of Fair Trading v Abbey National plc and Others*, see n 170, Mann J in *OFT v Foxtons* held that the renewal commission term did not form part of the core bargain between the parties; therefore, it was subject to review for fairness under the UTCCRs 1999. In considering the actual fairness of the terms, the judge found that some were not in plain language, that they were not sufficiently brought to the attention of landlords, and that they became increasingly disproportionate as the years went by, without Foxtons having to provide any commensurate services.

[173] See S Bradshaw, C Millard, and I Walden, 'Watching Cloud Services Contracts Take Shape' (2011) 21(6) *Computers & Law*, February–March 7; and S Bradshaw, C Millard, and I Walden, 'Contracts for Clouds: Comparison and Analysis of the Terms and Conditions of Cloud Computing Services', Queen Mary School of Law Legal Studies Research Paper No 63/2010, 1 October 2010, also available at <http://ssrn.com/abstract=1662374> (accessed 3 August 2011), for further analysis.

[174] See generally section 2.5 below.

[175] The Queen Mary University of London Cloud Legal Project is expected to publish a dedicated research paper on this topic, see Bradshaw et al, 'Contracts for Clouds', n 173, 16.

In order to assess whether these terms are likely to be binding and enforceable in the UK, the terms must withstand scrutiny under the UTCCRs 1999 fairness test and the UCTA reasonableness test. The same or similar considerations will be applied by regulators and courts in other EU jurisdictions. Drilling down in more detail, the key questions are:

(a) In light of the provisions of the UTCCRs 1999 and the OFT's approach to such terms, is there a material factor that potentially distinguishes cloud computing from other types of service investigated by the OFT that might justify a different treatment of such terms under the UTCCRs 1999 in the cloud computing context? An interesting issue here is whether the nature of cloud computing services as commoditized services, where each individual contract has low economic value to the supplier, is a material factor in assessing the fairness of terms, bearing in mind that the low value of the contract to the supplier will in most cases not correspond with the value of the data to the consumer and, therefore, limiting the liability of the supplier to, for example, the value or a small multiple of the value of the contract is in many cases unlikely adequately to compensate the consumer for, for example, loss or unavailability or accidental disclosure of the data.

(b) If the exclusion and limitation of liability clauses can be said to be likely to pass the UTCCRs 1999 fairness test, the next step is to examine whether they are likely also to withstand the reasonableness test under UCTA 1977 when it may apply to cloud computing services, that is, to exclusion of liability for damage caused by negligent performance (s 2(2)) or failure to perform (s 3(2)).

It is convenient to address the second question first. As a preliminary point, although it was expected that case law would develop precedents that sufficiently flesh out the few guidelines provided by UCTA 1977 in relation to the application of the reasonableness test, the cases are not always particularly helpful, especially in the consumer context. This is because, first, the majority of the UCTA 1977 cases concern business-to-business scenarios and, secondly, these cases generally turn on their actual facts. For this reason, it has been suggested that (both in relation to UCTA 1977 and, for that matter, the UTCCRs 1999) the 'good sense' of the court comes closest to the mark.[176]

In determining the reasonableness of a term under UCTA 1977, the court must have regard to the circumstances that were or ought to have been known to the parties and in particular (per section 11(4)) to the resources available to the supplier to meet the liability should it arise and how far it is possible to cover this liability off by insurance. The latter consideration includes an assessment not only of the availability of relevant insurance in the market, but also of the insurance that the supplier

---

[176] Christou, n 139, at 8 regarding reasonableness under UCTA 1977 and 58 regarding fairness under the UTCCRs 1999.

has actually been able to obtain.[177] The term 'resources' clearly refers in this context to financial resources, so it seems that the economic value of services is one of the considerations to be taken into account. Furthermore, although UCTA 1977 does not, when assessing the reasonableness of terms in contracts for services, require the application of the Schedule 2 guidelines, the guidelines have inevitably influenced courts in their assessment of reasonableness in the context of all types of contracts.[178] The guidelines include, among other factors: (a) the relative bargaining power of the parties; (b) whether the customer knew or ought reasonably to have known of the term; and (c) whether the customer could have found another party who could have contracted without the exemption clause—a relevant consideration at present in cloud computing, since most suppliers tend to limit or exclude their liability. Some further broad guidelines can be derived from reports of the Law Commission and case law,[179] which include that: consumers are more likely than businesses to succeed in assertions that a clause is unreasonable; the greater the imbalance in bargaining power the less likely the courts are to find that a term is reasonable; the courts are more favourably disposed to clauses that limit, as opposed to excluding altogether, liability; and force majeure clauses are prima facie likely to be reasonable. Furthermore, it should be remembered that a failure to notify consumers of their statutory rights is a criminal offence.[180]

On the basis of these guidelines, it seems clear that: an exclusion of all liability by the cloud supplier for failure to perform the contract because of wilful default is likely to be unreasonable in most cases; whereas an exclusion of all liability for reasons outside the supplier's reasonable control will be reasonable in most circumstances. In between these two extremes is the case where the supplier fails to perform because of acts or omissions (other than wilful default) within its control; again, an exclusion of all liability in such cases is unlikely to be reasonable. In this latter case, the more serious the type of breach, for example complete failure to apply appropriate technical and organizational security measures, the more unlikely the exclusion of liability is to be reasonable.

When it comes to limitation of liability by way of excluding liability for economic loss (eg, loss of profit or business), such clauses are probably unlikely to be fair in the consumer context because the amount of loss suffered by the consumer could be disproportionate compared to his financial resources, while probably not as serious for the supplier, who probably could also insure against such liability (at least for inadvertent default) since it is likely to be low level.[181] The problem in the cloud computing context is that where data are lost for one customer, they are also likely to

---

[177] See *St Albans City v International Computers*, n 48; *Britvic Soft Drinks Ltd v Northern Security Solutions Ltd* [2002] EWHC 2147.

[178] See, eg, *Watford Electronics v Sanderson CFL Ltd* [2002] FSR 19; and *Granville Oil & Chemicals Ltd v Davis Turner & Co Ltd* [2003] 2 Lloyd's Rep 356.

[179] See generally Christou, n 139, 7–11 and 23–34.

[180] Ibid 11.

[181] See ibid 32, citing *Harris v Wyre Forest DC* [1988] 1 All ER 691.

be lost for hundreds or thousands of other customers as well. It follows that, if the supplier were to accept liability that is unlimited or limited to a relatively high percentage of such economic loss, the financial impact of a single breach could obviously be disproportionate to the economic value of the service to the supplier and could, conceivably, have catastrophic consequences. Does this mean, then, that unlike other consumer contexts, for cloud computing it is possible to argue that such limitations of liability are reasonable in principle? In the absence of clear guidelines, this appears to be a potentially plausible argument. There are two paramount considerations: first, on the reasonable assumption that a convincing argument about the economic viability of cloud services can be made, in assessing its impact on the reasonableness of the limitation of liability, the courts would be likely to examine whether the supplier could effectively cover this risk by insurance, and the exclusion of liability for financial loss would be likely to be unreasonable if the supplier can obtain insurance coverage at a proportionate cost. In principle, insurance for loss or corruption of customer data will be available as part of the supplier's professional indemnity insurance; furthermore, insurance companies are at present also developing standalone insurance products specifically covering loss of data by data processors. If, however, cloud suppliers can show that it is not possible to obtain insurance coverage at proportional cost, then such limitations of liability may be reasonable. Secondly, much will depend on careful drafting of the clause, both in terms of the substance and the structure of the limitation of liability provisions: UCTA 1977 relates to unfair terms, not unfair contracts, and if drafted properly, even if a part of a limitation of liability clause fails the test, others may survive and provide at least partial coverage.

In relation to limitation of liability by reference to a monetary figure, either a fixed sum or a percentage of the fees payable under the contract (where the percentage is greater than 100 per cent), the question to be asked is whether the amount is reasonable having regard to the financial resources of the supplier, the extent to which the supplier can take out insurance to cover the risk, and what insurance the supplier has actually been able to take out to cover this risk. The same considerations apply concerning insurance coverage and drafting discussed above. Such limitations of liability might be found to be reasonable under UCTA 1977, provided that the cap is not a trivial one—although even trivial liability caps have been held to be enforceable in the business-to-business context; in the consumer context it appears unlikely that a liability cap that does not allow the consumer to recover (a) the amounts paid as fees for the services plus (b) at least some compensation for other loss suffered, would be reasonable, not least because of the inequality in the parties' bargaining power.[182] Fixing the cap at a fixed sum or the total value of the contract, whichever

---

[182] In *Frans Maas (UK) Ltd v Samsung Electronics (UK) Ltd* [2004] EWHC 1502, a limitation of liability clause was upheld despite the trivial cap, in particular because there was no inequality of bargaining power, the cap was industry standard, and the customer could have negotiated a different cap. In our context, however, even if liability caps were in principle negotiable, it is clear that the consumer does not have the bargaining power effectively to negotiate them.

is the higher, may also be reasonable, however fixing the cap to a fixed sum or total value, whichever is the lower, is unlikely to be reasonable.

To summarize, it appears that under UCTA 1977 the economic reality of the services is a factor that will be taken into consideration in certain instances and that, on the basis of the guidelines available in UCTA 1977 itself, Law Commission Reports, and case law it appears likely that in most circumstances: total exclusions of liability will be unreasonable except in relation to breaches caused by reasons outside the control of the cloud supplier; exclusions of economic loss may, in principle, be reasonable if the supplier can show that it is not possible to obtain insurance coverage at a reasonable cost; and limitations of liability by reference to a cap are also likely to be reasonable in principle, provided the cap allows the consumer to recover the amounts paid as fees for the services plus at least some compensation for other loss suffered, especially if insurance is not available to the supplier at a reasonable cost. Careful drafting of the clause is of paramount importance in ensuring that the clause covers the relevant breaches; in assessing the reasonableness of the clause; and in ensuring that at least certain parameters of the limitation of liability will remain effective even if others fail.

Of course, the fact that such limitation of liability clauses may be reasonable under UCTA 1977 becomes redundant if they fail to pass the fairness test under the UTCCRs 1999. As seen above, it appears likely that the two tests will normally provide similar results; however, in the absence of cases where both tests have been applied to the same facts, the point remains uncertain. Under the UTCCRs 1999, the fairness test is applicable not only to the exclusion and limitation of liability clauses, but also to any other term that has not been individually negotiated, including the variation of terms and choice of law and forum clauses. In applying the UTCCRs 1999 fairness test, three questions must be asked about a term that has not been individually negotiated:[183] first, does the term cause a significant imbalance in the rights and obligations of the parties? Secondly, is this imbalance to the detriment of the consumer? And thirdly, is this imbalance to the detriment of the consumer contrary to the requirements of good faith? At a very high level, it seems straightforward that such clauses do cause an imbalance to the rights and obligations of the parties, which may be significant, and that such imbalance is to the detriment of the consumer. The key question, therefore, seems to be whether the imbalance is contrary to good faith. In answering these questions, suppliers should look at the text of the UTCCRs 1999, the OFT's guidance and practice in the area, and the relevant court cases.

As mentioned above, the UTCCRs 1999 set out an indicative list according to which contract terms are likely to be unfair if they, inter alia: (a) inappropriately exclude the legal rights of the consumer in the event of total or partial non-performance or inadequate performance by the supplier of any contractual obligations;

---

[183] See also *Director General of Fair Trading v First National Bank plc*, n 157, at 1307.

(b) enable the supplier to alter the terms of the contract unilaterally without a valid reason which is specified in the contract, except when this right is reserved for contracts of indeterminate duration, provided that the supplier is required to inform consumers with reasonable notice and the consumer is given the right to dissolve the contract; and (c) exclude or hinder the consumer's right to take legal action or exercise any other legal remedy, particularly by requiring the consumer to take disputes exclusively to arbitration not covered by legal provisions.

Furthermore, the OFT[184] has issued guidance specifically addressing these types of terms.[185] In relation to exclusion and limitation of liability clauses, the OFT takes the view that any term which undermines the value of the contractual obligations of the supplier by preventing or hindering the consumer from seeking redress when the supplier does not comply with them falls under suspicion of unfairness. Any term which can have the effect of allowing the supplier to act unreasonably or negligently without consequences is particularly likely to be considered unfair. In particular in relation to exclusion of liability for poor service, the OFT suggests that a clause that excludes liability only for losses for which the supplier is not at fault or which were not foreseeable when the contract was entered into may be fair; however, a term that intentionally or unintentionally serves to relieve a supplier of the obligation to provide services at a reasonable standard or exercise reasonable care is likely to be unfair, even where the services are provided free of charge to the consumer.[186] In relation to limitations of liability, the OFT takes the view that clauses that limit liability are open to the same objections as clauses that exclude it, because the consumer should be entitled to full compensation where the supplier fails to honour its obligations.[187] Furthermore, in relation to limitations of liability by excluding consequential loss, the OFT considers that they can stop consumers from seeking redress in certain circumstances where it ought to be available; however, excluding liability for losses that were not foreseeable to both parties when the contract was formed or losses that were not caused by a breach of the supplier, are unlikely to be considered unfair.[188] Finally, terms which allow the supplier to exclude liability for failure to perform contractual obligations have clear potential to be unfair, but may be unobjectionable in limited circumstances, including where they enable the supplier to deal with technical problems or other circumstances outside its control.[189]

---

[184] For a discussion of the powers and duties in relation to breaches of the UTCCRs 1999 conferred on the OFT (and other enforcers): under the EA 2002, see section 2.3.2, and under the UTCCRs 1999 themselves, see section 2.3.3.1.

[185] 'Unfair Contract Terms Guidance—Guidance for the Unfair Terms in Consumer Contracts Regulations 1999', September 2008, OFT 311, <http://www.oft.gov.uk/shared_oft/reports/unfair_contract_terms/oft311.pdf> (accessed 3 August 11) ('OFT 311').

[186] Ibid 21–2.

[187] Ibid 23.

[188] Ibid 24–5.

[189] Ibid 33.

In relation to the supplier's right unilaterally to vary the terms of the contract, the OFT takes the view that such terms are under great suspicion of unfairness.[190] A variation clause can upset the legal balance of the contract, and therefore be unfair, even if it is intended solely to facilitate minor adjustments, if its wording means it could be used to impose more substantial changes, for example changes concerning costs, penalties, new requirements, or reduced benefits. Variation terms are more likely to be fair if: (a) they are narrow in effect so that they cannot be used to change the balance of advantage under the contract; (b) they can be exercised only for clear and specific reasons stated in the contract; and (c) the supplier is under a duty to give notice and the consumer has a right to cancel the contract before being affected by the variation, without penalty or otherwise being worse off for having entered the contract.

Finally, in relation to choice of law and forum clauses, the OFT takes the view that consumers should not be prevented from starting legal proceedings in their local courts; even requiring consumers to travel to a different part of the UK with its own laws and courts is likely to be unfair; the same is true for terms which seek to subject the contract to the law of a country where consumers have significantly less protection (eg, a non-EU country).[191] Furthermore, in the UK, compulsory arbitration clauses are automatically unfair under section 91 of the Arbitration Act 1996 if they relate to claims of £5,000 or less. According to the OFT, such a clause would be both legally ineffective and open to regulatory action in all cases.[192]

It follows that in accordance with the UTCCRs 1999 and the OFT's guidance, it is clear that widely drafted variation of terms clauses, foreign choice of law and forum clauses, and compulsory arbitration clauses are unlikely to be binding on consumers. These terms clearly cause a significant imbalance to the detriment of the consumer and it appears that it would be difficult to argue that the supplier deals with the issues 'fairly and equitably with the other party whose legitimate interests he has to take into account', the key element of the requirement of good faith per recital 16 of the UTCCD. However, the position may be different in relation to exclusion and limitation of liability clauses.

Although exclusion and limitation of liability clauses are mentioned in the list of indicative terms that may be unfair, the determination of whether in a particular set of circumstances they are indeed unfair is subject to the fairness test. The test requires the assessment of the unfairness of a contractual term taking into account, among other factors, the nature of the goods or services for which the contract was concluded. It is not clear from the text of the UTCCRs 1999 and the Directive

---

[190] Ibid 52–3.
[191] Ibid 68.
[192] Ibid 67. See also, eg, *Mylcrist Builders Ltd v Buck* [2008] EWHC 2172 (TCC), where the court found that the effect of an arbitration clause was to prevent the defendant from having access to the courts, caused an imbalance to the rights and obligations of the parties under the contract and was, therefore, unfair.

(including its recitals) whether the 'nature of the services' also includes their economic characteristics, in particular their value to the supplier, but it appears reasonable to assume that this is the case. Furthermore, as seen above, out of the three questions to be asked in assessing the fairness of the terms, the question of whether a significant imbalance is contrary to the requirements of good faith appears to be the key question for our purposes. According to recital 16 of the UCTTD 'the requirement of good faith may be satisfied by the seller or supplier where he deals fairly and equitably with the other party whose legitimate interests he has to take into account'.

In *Director General of Fair Trading*, the House of Lords elaborated further: Lord Bingham stated that the element of good faith amounts to fair and open dealing.[193] Openness requires that 'the terms should be expressed fully, clearly and legibly, containing no concealed pitfalls or traps' with appropriate prominence given to terms which may operate disadvantageously to the consumer. Fair dealing requires

that a supplier should not, whether deliberately or unconsciously, take advantage of the consumer's necessity, indigence, lack of experience, unfamiliarity with the subject matter of the contract, weak bargaining position or any other factor listed in or analogous to those listed in Schedule 2 to the Regulations.

Good faith 'looks to good standards of commercial morality and practice'. Furthermore, Lord Millet stated that:[194]

It may also be necessary to consider the effect of the inclusion of the term on the substance or core of the transaction; whether if it were drawn to his attention the consumer would be likely to be surprised by it; whether the term is a standard term, not merely in similar non-negotiable consumer contracts, but in commercial contracts freely negotiated between parties acting on level terms and at arms' length; and whether, in such cases, the party adversely affected by the inclusion of the term or his lawyer might reasonably be expected to object to its inclusion and press for its deletion.

Furthermore, Lord Bingham stated that the test of unfairness 'is a composite test, covering both the making and the substance of the contract'.[195] In other words, in determining fairness regard is to be had not only to the substance of the term (ie, is the term fair) but also to the process by which it was imposed and whether both the substantive and procedural elements are contrary to the requirement of good faith.

In the cloud computing context, some of the criteria formulated in *Director General of Fair Trading* would support the fairness of the exclusion and limitation of liability clauses. Others would operate against a conclusion that such terms are fair; for instance, when the purpose of a contract is the back up of and ability to

---

[193] *Director General of Fair Trading v First National Bank plc*, n 157, at 1308.
[194] Ibid 1318.
[195] Ibid 1308.

retrieve data, a consumer would be likely to be 'surprised' if he realized that the supplier would have no liability for unavailability of data for reasons within the supplier's control. Nevertheless, it appears that for cloud computing it can be logically argued that clauses limiting liability at a relatively low level are standard in the current state of play of cloud computing; they are justified on the grounds that assuming higher levels of liability would jeopardize the commercial viability of this innovative service, which would ultimately be to the detriment of society; and that these clauses are not intended to take advantage of the weak position of the consumer contrary to the requirements of good faith, but rather are necessary for the supplier acting in good faith to ensure the commercial viability of the service. Much would also depend on how the terms and conditions are drafted and presented to the consumer in order also to satisfy the requirement for openness. On that basis, limitation of liability clauses that put a reasonable cap on the supplier's liability (eg, along the lines discussed in relation to UCTA 1977 above) and exclusion of liability clauses for reasons outside the supplier's control, which are 'expressed fully, clearly and legibly, containing no concealed pitfalls or traps', may stand a good chance of being found to be fair by UK courts. Suppliers could argue (probably convincingly, especially if the risk cannot be insured against at reasonable cost) that such limitation and exclusion of liability clauses can be said to be industry standard not only in the consumer, but also in the business-to-business, context and that, therefore, consumers would be unlikely to be surprised by them and their lawyers could not reasonably be expected to press for their deletion. The reason for such clauses is not a malevolent plan to take advantage of weak consumers, but rather a genuine necessity, resorted to by the supplier acting in good faith in an effort to shield itself from disproportionate exposure. Requiring the supplier to assume disproportionate risk would threaten the commercial viability of the service and the supplier's ability to provide it. From a public policy point of view, this would have a chilling effect on innovation, contrary to the interests of consumers and the economy. However, it would be difficult to rely on this line of argument in relation to total exclusions of liability for wilful or negligent default or for limitations of liability that do not allow the consumer to recover the amounts paid as fees and at least some compensation for other loss suffered. As under the UCTA 1977, careful drafting of the clause is important.

2.2.1.3 The draft Unfair Contract Terms Bill ('dUCTB'), the proposed Consumer Rights Bill, and the proposed Consumer Rights Directive ('pCRD')

It is widely acknowledged in the UK that the existence of two statutory sources of control over unfair terms, that is, UCTA 1977 and the UTCCRs 1999, with different scope, and inconsistent and overlapping provisions that use different wording and concepts in order to produce similar but not identical results, causes confusion and uncertainty and is increasing the cost of legal compliance. As a result, in 2001 the DTI (the predecessor of BIS) asked the Law Commission and the Scottish Law Commission to redraft the law of unfair contract terms as a single instrument setting

forth a unified regime. Following a joint consultation paper in 2002,[196] the Law
Commissions produced a comprehensive final report[197] and the dUCTB, which
rewrites the law of unfair contract terms for the whole of the UK in a comparatively
clearer way, and plugs some gaps in protection.[198] Broadly speaking, the dUCTB
preserves the existing level of consumer protection with certain minor exceptions
and recommends improved protection for small businesses employing nine or fewer
staff. It therefore envisages three regimes of protection: first, unified protection for
consumer contracts;[199] secondly, protection for business contracts;[200] and, thirdly,
specific protection for small businesses contracts.[201] In July 2006, the government
announced that it had in principle accepted the recommendations for reform, subject
to further consideration of the detail of the issues and to further work to identify
potential cost impacts; the proposed legislation would be subject to full public consultation.[202] However, following the European Commission's proposal for a new
CRD, the dUCTB has been put on hold, as the pCRD contains provisions on unfair
contract terms, which the dUCTB will need to reflect.[203]

In July 2009, the government also released a White Paper on consumer law
reform, in which it announced its intention to modernize and simplify consumer
sales law and implement the pCRD once it becomes law.[204] This would include
developing rules on digital products to ensure that the core principles of consumer
protection apply. In the longer term, the intention is to promulgate a new Consumer
Rights Bill. At the time this chapter was written, there was no clear information
concerning the relationship between the dUCTB and the proposed Consumer Rights
Bill. However, it seems logical that the proposal for a Consumer Rights Bill has
supplanted the dUCTB.

The pCRD is intended to create a uniform set of consumer rights across the EU
in relation to business-to-consumer contracts and to replace and enhance four existing consumer protection directives.[205] In effect, this would allow suppliers to sell to

---

[196] See n 119.

[197] See n 120.

[198] Law Commission and Scottish Law Commission, 'Unfair Terms in Contracts: Summary'
(Law Com No 298, Scots Law Com No 199, 24 February 2005), <http://www.lawcom.gov.uk/docs/
lc292sum.pdf> (accessed 3 August 2011), 5.

[199] The Law Commissions' Report on Unfair Terms in Contracts 2005, n 120, pt 3.

[200] Ibid pt 4.

[201] Ibid pt 5.

[202] Statement by the Minister of Trade, Hansard HC vol 449 pt 190 col 108WS (25 July 2006 WA),
<http://www.publications.parliament.uk/pa/cm200506/cmhansrd/cm060725/wmstext/60725m0174.htm>
(accessed 3 August 2011).

[203] See Ministry of Justice, 'Report on the Implementation of the Law Commission Proposals', 24
January 2011, <http://www.justice.gov.uk/publications/docs/report-implementation-law-commission-
proposals.pdf> (accessed 3 August 2011), p 7.

[204] See Secretary of State for Business Innovation and Skills, 'A Better Deal for Consumers, Delivering
Real Help Now and Change for the Future', July 2009, <http://www.berr.gov.uk/files/file52072.pdf>
(accessed 3 August 2011).

[205] See nn 11–14 and accompanying text.

consumers in 27 Member States with, for example, the same standard contract terms and the same information materials, thereby reducing compliance costs for suppliers while at the same time increasing consumer protection. At the time of writing the pCRD was still being debated by the EU institutions[206] and it seemed that agreement whether it should be a maximum or minimum harmonization measure was still some way off. When the pCRD comes into force, it will cover all sales to consumers whether online, in a shop, or on the doorstep and all suppliers who sell via distance channels such as the internet, telesales, or tele-shopping will be affected. The pCRD is likely to include a fully harmonized 'cooling off' period during which consumers can cancel the contract with the supplier, and more stringent information requirements. It may fully harmonize information requirements, delivery deadlines, and withdrawal rights for distance and off-premises sales and provide for minimum consumer protection in other areas, including lack of conformity of goods with contract, with these to apply to all contracts whether concluded at a distance, on a doorstep, in shops or otherwise.

2.2.1.4 Unfair trading legislation

The UCPD 2005 is a maximum harmonization measure.[207] It was adopted in order to harmonize unfair trading laws in the EU Member States and introduce a general prohibition of the unfair treatment of consumers by traders. It contains:

(a) a prohibition on unfair commercial practices generally[208] (which are defined as any commercial practices that are contrary to the requirements of professional diligence and materially distort or are likely materially to distort consumers' economic behaviour[209]);

(b) two specific categories of unfair commercial practice, misleading actions and omissions[210] and aggressive commercial practices[211]; and

(c) 31 commercial practices which are unfair in all cases.[212]

The UCPD 2005 introduces several key concepts, some of which are novel, including professional diligence; honest market practice; material distortion of consumers'

---

[206] The authors would like to thank their colleague Emily Parris, Senior Associate (PSL) at Field Fisher Waterhouse, for her contribution to this section.

[207] In other words, Member States are not allowed to introduce or maintain differentiated provisions, even if they set forth more stringent protective measures. However, UCPD 2005, Art 3(3) provides that at least until 12 July 2013, Member States are able to continue to apply national provisions within the field approximated by the UCPD 2005 which are more restrictive or prescriptive and which implement directives containing minimum harmonization clauses, provided that such measures are essential to ensuring that consumers are adequately protected against unfair commercial practices and are proportionate to the attainment of this objective.

[208] Ibid Art 5(1).

[209] Ibid Art 5(2).

[210] Ibid Arts 6 and 7.

[211] Ibid Arts 8 and 9.

[212] Ibid Annex I.

economic behaviour; average consumers and vulnerable consumers; and transactional decisions.[213]

The CPRs 2008[214] implemented the UCPD 2005 and Article 6(2) of the Sale of Goods Directive[215] and consolidated the UK's fair trading regime. In its place, the CPRs 2008 implemented a regime (reflecting the UCPD 2005) which bans unfair commercial practices which are: unfair in general;[216] misleading actions or omissions;[217] aggressive; and/or one of a list of 31 commercial practices which are automatically deemed to be unfair, as explained in detail below.

The CPRs 2008 apply to 'traders'[218] engaged in 'commercial practices', which is defined broadly as: 'any act, omission, course of conduct, representation or commercial communication (including advertising and marketing) by a trader, which is directly connected with the promotion, sale or supply of a product to or from consumers, whether occurring before, during or after a commercial transaction (if any) in relation to a product'[219] (where 'product' means 'any goods or service and includes immovable property, rights and obligations'[220]). The key factor is the direct connection with the promotion, sale, or supply of a product, however this does not mean that a trader must sell or supply directly to consumers to be caught; traders at other points in the supply chain may find that their activities are also in scope.

Therefore, all of the following are potentially commercial practices: information supplied with a product (eg, user documentation/information on a product's packaging); a website (including, eg, a price-comparison website); all forms of advertising and marketing; oral and written communications between sales staff and the consumer; and after-sales activities, such as customer support or complaints handling.

Unfair commercial practices fall into three categories: (a) those that will be unfair if they materially distort or are likely materially to distort the economic behaviour[221]

---

[213] For a discussion of these concepts see C Twigg-Flesner et al, 'An Analysis of the Application and Scope of the Unfair Commercial Practices Directive', A Report for the Department of Trade and Industry, 18 May 2005, <http://www.dti.gov.uk/files/file32095.pdf> (accessed 3 August 2011), 2.1–2.40.

[214] See also the Business Protection from Misleading Marketing Regulations 2008, which came into force on the same day as the CPRs 2008 and implement into UK law Directive 2006/114/EC of the European Parliament and of the Council concerning misleading and comparative advertising (OJ L376/21, 27 December 2006).

[215] n 11.

[216] ie, a contravention of the requirements of professional diligence which materially distorts or is likely materially to distort the economic behaviour of the average consumer with regard to a product, CPRs 2008, reg 3(3).

[217] CPRs 2008, regs 5 and 6.

[218] Defined as 'any person who in relation to a commercial practice is acting for purposes relating to his business, and anyone acting in the name of or on behalf of a trader', CPRs 2008, reg 2(1).

[219] Ibid reg 2(1).

[220] Ibid reg 2(1), so software, digital content licensed to the consumer, financial products, land, club memberships, and tangible goods are all examples of products.

[221] 'Materially distort the economic behaviour' means in relation to an average consumer, appreciably to impair the average consumer's ability to make an informed decision thereby causing him to take a transactional decision that he would not have taken otherwise, see CPRs 2008, reg 2(1).

of the average consumer[222] with regard to the product (generally unfair commercial practices[223]); (b) those that will be unfair if they cause or are likely to cause the average consumer to take a transactional decision[224] he would not have taken otherwise (misleading actions and[225] omissions[226] and aggressive practices[227]); and (c) those that will in all circumstances be unfair (so-called 'banned practices').[228]

For the purposes of commercial practises in categories (a) and (b) above, there are two tests before the legislation is breached: one relating to the trader's conduct (the trader must have, in general terms, contravened the requirements of professional diligence,[229] or more specifically, behaved misleadingly or aggressively); and the other relating to the effect of such conduct on the consumer (in the case of a breach of professional diligence, such conduct must distort or be likely to distort the average consumer's economic behaviour, and, in the case of misleading or aggressive behaviour, such conduct must cause or be likely to cause the average consumer to take a different transactional decision). Material distortion to economic behaviour and taking a different transactional decision are treated as broadly similar concepts and might include: whether to buy a product; how to buy it and on what terms; how much to pay for it; and/or the consumer's contractual rights.

---

[222] The 'average consumer' is considered to be 'reasonably well informed, reasonably observant and circumspect' (CPRs 2008, reg 2(2)). Where a commercial practice is directed to a particular group of consumers: the average consumer is the average member of that group (CPRs, reg 2(4)) and the CPRs clearly seek to protect vulnerable consumers by explicitly providing that, where a clearly identifiable group of consumers is particularly vulnerable to the practice or the underlying product because of their mental or physical infirmity, age, or credulity in a way which the trader could reasonably be expected to foresee, and the commercial practice is likely materially to distort the economic behaviour only of that group, the average consumer is the average member of that group—see CPRs, reg 2(5), albeit subject to 'the common and legitimate advertising practice of making exaggerated statements which are not meant to be taken literally'—see CPRs, reg 2(6).

[223] CPRs 2008, reg 3(3).

[224] 'Transactional decision' means any decision taken by a consumer, whether it is to act or to refrain from acting, concerning: (a) whether, how, and on what terms to purchase, make payment in whole or in part for, retain or dispose of a product; or (b) whether, how, and on what terms to exercise a contractual right in relation to a product—see CPRs 2008, reg 2(1).

[225] Ibid reg 5.

[226] Ibid reg 6.

[227] Ibid reg 7.

[228] Ibid Sch 1.

[229] 'Professional diligence' means the standard of special skill and care which a trader may reasonably be expected to exercise towards consumers which is commensurate with either: honest market practice in the trader's field of activity; or the general principle of good faith in the trader's field of activity, ibid reg 3(3). The test is an objective one. It is possible, of course, that actual market practice may fall short of honest practice, and in that case, actual market practice will not be an appropriate benchmark. In its Guidance, the OFT and the Department for Business, Enterprise and Regulatory Reform ('BERR') advise traders to approach transactions professionally and fairly as judged by a reasonable person: OFT and BERR, Guidance on the Consumer Protection from Unfair Trading Regulations 2008, OFT 1008 (Edition 08/08), August 2008, <http://www.oft.gov.uk/shared_oft/business_leaflets/cpregs/oft1008.pdf> (accessed 3 August 2011), 48. Simply falling short of the professional diligence standard is not enough to trigger criminal liability.

Commercial practices in category (c) are far simpler. Schedule 1 to the CPRs 2008 contains a list of some 31 commercial practices that are regarded as inherently unfair, without the need to show an effect on the average consumer. Examples include: 'bait advertising' (advertising products at low price without making clear that only a limited number of products are available at that price and for an unreasonably short period—considering the scale of the advertising and the price of the product);[230] 'bait and switch' advertising ('luring' customers in by offering them a low price on a product with the intention of supplying them a different product);[231] 'advertorials' (advertising presented as editorial content[232]); and pretending to be a consumer, for example to promote a product.[233]

In relation to advertorials, the European Commission has specifically identified as unfair the practice of companies paying bloggers to promote and advertise their products without informing other users about the fact that they are paid to do this.[234] The OFT has also taken action against traders in this regard.[235]

These practices are of particular significance in the Web 2.0 context, as businesses are increasingly harnessing Web 2.0 technologies and social networks for word-of-mouth or 'buzz' marketing. The CPRs 2008 do not explicitly prohibit buzz marketing, but, as demonstrated by paragraphs 11 and 22 of Schedule 1, they do require transparency, without which relevant commercial practices will be unfair.

One of the aims of the CPRs 2008 is to prevent aggressive commercial practices, which significantly impair or are likely significantly to impair the average consumer's freedom of choice or conduct in relation to the product concerned through the use of harassment, coercion, or undue influence.[236] Another is to ensure that consumers are not misled by poor quality (or a lack of) information, which is reflected by:

(a) explicitly requiring the truthfulness and accurate presentation of certain information (price, availability, specification, characteristics, and sponsorship of the product; the identity, assets, qualifications, and affiliations of the trader; the motives

---

[230] CPRs 2008, Sch 1 para 5. An example of a trader which fell foul of this paragraph is Markco Media, which, in March 2011, was subject to an investigation by, and gave undertakings to, the OFT as a result of heavily promoting Apple iPhone 4s for sale at £99 (normal retail price was £499), when it only had eight handsets available, see <http://www.oft.gov.uk/news-and-updates/press/2011/30-11> (accessed 3 August 2011).

[231] CPRs 2008, Sch 1 para 6.

[232] Ibid Sch 1 para 11.

[233] Ibid Sch 1 para 22. Markco Media, see n 230, also gave undertakings in relation to this paragraph.

[234] Commission Staff Working Document, Guidance on the Implementation/Application of Directive 2005/29/EC on Unfair Commercial Practices, SEC(2009)1666, 3 December 2009, p 8.

[235] Notably Handpicked Media Ltd, from which the OFT obtained undertakings in relation to 'commercial blogging' activities, see <http://www.oft.gov.uk/news-and-updates/press/2010/134-10> (accessed 3 August 2011).

[236] CPRs 2008, reg 7.

for the commercial practice; and after-sales issues, such as customer assistance and complaints handling);[237]

(b) prohibiting marketing that creates confusion with a competitor's products, trade marks, or trade names; and

(c) prescribing certain information that must be made available to consumers in relation to invitations to purchase,[238] which can include interactive TV advertisements, webpages, text messages, and radio advertisements, where those invitations invite/enable consumers to respond with an order for a product.[239]

Given this emphasis on ensuring that consumers have proper information, the CPRs 2008 are particularly pertinent to businesses whose principal function is providing information to consumers about third party products, such as aggregator websites, which are coming under increasing scrutiny.[240]

In most cases, as well as being a civil breach enforceable by 'enforcement authorities',[241] a breach of the CPRs 2008 is also a criminal offence, for which any trader, including a corporate entity, its employees,[242] and its officers,[243] can be liable, with penalties ranging from a fine to up to two years' imprisonment.[244]

---

[237] It should be noted that there is some overlap between the information requirements under the CPRs 2008 and the requirements under the DSRs 2000 (discussed in section 2.2.1.5 below). The latter apply to businesses that enter into contracts with consumers via distance methods (eg, interactive television, text messaging, telephone, or a website) and remain in force in parallel with the CPRs 2008. However, as we see below the requirements are not identical and in-scope businesses need to comply with both sets of rules. Eg, under the DSRs 2000, the supplier need only provide details of its address where payment is required in advance, whereas under the CPRs 2008, the trader must always provide its address details in the context of an invitation to purchase.

[238] A commercial communication which indicates characteristics of the product and the price in a way appropriate to the means of that commercial communication and thereby enables the consumer to make a purchase, ibid reg 2(1).

[239] See p 36 of the OFT and BERR Guidance, n 229.

[240] Research groups have pointed to a lack of transparency over affiliations and sponsorships of some sites, particularly where the sponsor's products are featured. In 2008, the FSA, prompted by the British Insurers Brokers Association, carried out a study in relation to insurance price-comparison sites, see <http://www.fsa.gov.uk/pages/Doing/Regulated/Promo/thematic/gi_comparison.shtml> (accessed 3 August 2011). The results of that study suggested that current practice falls far short of the standards required under the CPRs 2008: the FSA found instances of comparison websites providing incorrect or out-of-date information on featured products; failing to provide the same level of information for comparable products with the result that consumers could be misled into believing that certain features were available under some policies and not others; and providing consumers with quotes that differed from the amount actually charged by the broker or insurer.

[241] CPRs 2008, reg 19. 'Enforcement authority' means the OFT, every local weights and measures authority in Great Britain (within the meaning of s 69 of the Weights and Measures Act 1985) and the Department of Enterprise, Trade and Investment in Northern Ireland, CPRs, reg 2(1).

[242] By virtue of the definition of 'trader' which includes 'anyone acting in the name of or on behalf of a trader'—see CPRs, reg 2(1).

[243] CPRs 2008, reg 15. See eg *Office of Fair Trading v Purely Creative Ltd and Others* discussed at n 245, where the defendants included the directors and one former director of the companies.

[244] CPRs 2008, reg 13.

The lead enforcer of the CPRs is the OFT,[245] which has issued specific guidance on the CPRs 2008.[246] In addition, established self-regulatory regimes such as the CAP broadcast and non-broadcast advertising codes administered by the Advertising Standards Authority run in parallel with the CPRs 2008,[247] although a detailed discussion of the ASA and its remit is beyond the scope of this chapter.

As a final point on the CPRs 2008, it is worth noting that, in some cases, a breach of other legislative provisions is also capable of constituting a breach of the CPRs 2008. So, for example:

(a) 'material information' for the purposes of assessing whether a trader has committed a misleading omission under the CPRs 2008 includes[248] 'any information requirement which applies in relation to a commercial communication as a result of a Community obligation', which could include information required under the DSRs and the eComRs;[249]

(b) a term which is unfair under the UTCCRs 1999 could also constitute a misleading action under the CPRs 2008;[250] and

---

[245] In February 2011, the High Court ruled on the first substantive case brought by the OFT under the CPRs 2008, see *Office of Fair Trading v Purely Creative Ltd and Others* [2011] All ER (D) 47 (Feb), which concerned various promotions encouraging recipients to claim prizes using premium-rate numbers, distributed as inserts in magazines and newspapers as well as by direct mailing. The parties had failed to agree upon satisfactory undertakings and therefore the OFT sought an enforcement order under the EA 2002, against five companies and four directors or former directors of the companies involved, on the grounds that the promotions breached the CPRs 2008. Mr Justice Briggs held that there had been 'a wholesale engagement in conduct altogether prohibited [by the CPRs 2008] and, save in certain very limited respects, the aggregate effect of the misleading acts or omissions which [he had] found to be proved has been such as to satisfy the relatively stringent test for causation laid down by the Regulations'. The court found that the defendants' promotions constituted misleading actions (per reg 5) and omissions (per reg 6) as well as one of the commercial practices which, under the CPRs 2008, Sch 1, are considered unfair in all circumstances, namely 'creating the false impression that the consumer has already won, will win, or will on doing a particular act win, a prize or other equivalent benefit, when in fact either— (a) there is no prize or other equivalent benefit, or (b) taking any action in relation to claiming the prize or other equivalent benefit is subject to the consumer paying money or incurring a cost' (per Sch 1 para 31). Given, in particular, evidence that the promotions amounted in the aggregate to almost 11.5 million and therefore that (even allowing for substantial overlap and unsold publications into which inserts had been placed) the promotions reached a substantial section of the public, Mr Justice Briggs was able to find that the breaches had caused harm to the collective interests of consumers therefore constituted Community infringements under the EA 2002.

[246] See n 229. For a discussion of the powers and duties in relation to breaches of the CPRs 2008 conferred on the OFT (and other enforcers): under the EA 2002, see section 2.3.2 below, and under the CPRs 2008 themselves, see section 2.3.3.1 below.

[247] The CPRs 2008 themselves acknowledge that enforcement through established regimes may be desirable, CPRs 2008, reg 19(4).

[248] Ibid reg 6(3)(b).

[249] See section 2.2.1.5 below.

[250] Per CPRs 2008, reg 5. This is also the view of the OFT, see OFT 311, n 185, p 12, 'Certain kinds of unfair term can have that distorting effect, for instance through misleading consumers about their rights. The use of such terms could give rise to enforcement action under the CPRs as well as, or instead of, the [UTCCRs 1999]' and furthermore at para 1.4, 'the fact that a term is void under other legislation— and thus, if it comes before a court, cannot have the harmful effect intended—is not something that the

(c) it is easy to see how a breach of other legislation could be considered a breach of the (broadly defined) 'professional diligence' standard.

2.2.1.5 Distance selling and e-commerce legislation

Businesses that sell or supply goods or services at a distance, including electronically, must also comply with the EU and UK instruments governing distance selling and electronic contracting. The main UK instruments are the DSRs 2000,[251] which implement the Distance Selling Directive[252] and are generally applicable to contracts concluded with consumers at a distance; and, in respect of the provision of online services, the eComRs 2002,[253] which implement the majority of the provisions[254] of the e-Commerce Directive. Where a contract for the sale or supply of goods or services is concluded with a consumer at a distance by use of electronic communication, it must meet the requirements of both the DSRs 2000 and the eComRs 2002. Failure to comply can lead to both civil liability and regulatory intervention: the OFT and other enforcers are empowered to pursue injunctive action under the DSRs 2000.[255]

There exists some overlap between the two sets of Regulations. For example, they each impose information disclosure requirements on traders.[256] In this respect,

---

consumer may be aware of and so not only is such a term pointless, it is also potentially misleading. This is liable to make it actionable as an unfair commercial practice.'

[251] As amended by the Consumer Protection (Distance Selling) (Amendment) Regulations 2005 (SI 2005/689) introduced changes to the information requirements when supplying services and to the cancellation periods for the supply of services.

[252] With the exception of Art 10 concerning restrictions on the use by the supplier of automatic calling machines and faxes, which are covered by the Privacy and Electronic Communications (EC Directive) Regulations 2003 (SI 2003/2426) ('PECRs 2003') implementing in part the e-Privacy Directive, see n 15. The DSRs 2000 are more detailed than the Directive, but on the whole the additional detail constitutes gap filling contemplated by the Directive, see DTI 05/1951, n 83 above, para 35.

[253] As extended by the Electronic Commerce (EC Directive) (Extension) Regulations 2003 (SI 2003/115) extending the application of the eComRs 2002 to cover the Copyright (Visually Impaired Persons) Act 2002 and the Tobacco Advertising and Promotion Act 2002; the Electronic Commerce (EC Directive) (Extension) (No 2) Regulations 2003 (SI 2003/2500) extending the application of the eComRs 2002 to cover enactments amended by the Copyright and Related Rights Regulations 2003 (SI 2003/2498), as well as the Performances (Reciprocal Protection) (Convention Countries and Isle of Man) Order 2003 (SI 2003/773), and the Copyright (Application to Other Countries) (Amendment) Order 2003 (SI 2003/774); and the Electronic Commerce (EC Directive) (Extension) Regulations 2004 (SI 2004/1178) extending the application of the eComRs 2002 to cover the Sexual Offences Act 2003.

[254] The remaining four statutory instruments implementing the Directive concern financial services and are not examined here.

[255] DSRs 2000, regs 26–29; eComRs 2002, reg 16. For the purposes of the EA 2002, the Distance Selling Directive and the e-Commerce Directive are listed directives.

[256] There is also an overlap with the information provision requirements of the CPRs 2008, see n 214 and accompanying text. Furthermore, the Provision of Services Regulations 2009 (SI 2009/2999) impose a number of obligations on service providers in relation to their interactions with actual or prospective customers which focus on the provision of basic information, the handling of complaints, and the prohibition of discrimination. As far as the information provision obligations are concerned, service providers operating in the UK are required to make certain information available to their customers in accordance with the requirements in Pt 2 of the Regulations. This obligation applies irrespective of where the service

the eComRs 2002 are generally broader in scope because their application is not restricted to either the consumer or the contractual context. There is further differentiation in relation to the nature of the required information, in that the eComRs 2002 require disclosure of general information relating to the trader (whether or not any contract between the parties is contemplated), as well as contract specific information and disclosure of information about the contracting process, if indeed a contract is to be entered into. In addition, the eComRs 2002 impose obligations with regard to the trader's implementation of the online contracting process. However, while the eComRs 2002 are in some respects broader than the DSRs 2000, the DSRs 2000 alone establish a limited statutory 'cooling off' period, during which consumers may cancel a contract that they have entered into with a trader, effectively without penalty.

Distance Selling Regulations 2000   The DSRs 2000 ensure that businesses supplying goods and services at a distance in the normal course of their business comply with certain basic requirements. They provide additional rights to consumers in relation to most goods and services, in order to compensate for the inability of the consumer to inspect the goods or services prior to their delivery. They apply to most contracts for the supply of goods or services to consumers,[257] provided that they have been concluded exclusively by means of distance communication,[258] under an organized distance sales or services provision scheme run by the supplier,[259] who for the purpose of the contract makes exclusive use of one or more means of

provider is based or established. However, the information provision obligations of the Regulations are likely to have a minimal impact on most UK service providers, especially those already engaging in mass market technology contracting, as they will already fulfil them as a result of their compliance with the information provision requirements of the DSRs 2000 and the eComRs 2002 (or other legislation such as the Companies (Trading Disclosures) Obligations Regulations 2008 (SI 2008/495)). The Provision of Services Regulations implement into UK law the Directive 2006/123/EC of the European Parliament and of the Council of 12 December 2006 on services in the internal market (OJ L376/36, 27 December 2006) ('the Services Directive'), which aims at encouraging the provision of services between Member States by simplifying the process for providing those services.

[257] See DSRs 2000, reg 5(1) for exemptions, most of which are not relevant to mass market technology contracts. Contracts concluded at an auction are excluded, in relation to which the OFT takes the view that some activities described as auctions may not necessarily result in sales at auction, in which case the DSRs 2000 provisions will apply, see OFT, 'A Guide for Businesses on Distance Selling', OFT 698 (edn 09/06), September 2006, <http://www.oft.gov.uk/NR/rdonlyres/1E6F3C94-8BB0-4374-A65B-6281E030C3C9/0/oft698.pdf> (accessed 10 April 2011) ('OFT 698'), pp 6 and 8. Case C-336/03 *easy-Car (UK) v Office of Fair Trading* [2005] ECR I-1947 has held that contracts for the provision of car hire services constitute contracts for transport services and are, therefore, partially exempted from the DSRs 2000.

[258] That is means that do not necessitate the simultaneous physical presence of the consumer and the supplier, see DSRs 2000, reg 3(1) and, further, the indicative list of distance communication means in DSRs 2000, Sch 1.

[259] That is any person acting in a commercial or professional capacity, DSRs 2000, reg 3(1).

distance communication up to and including the moment at which the contract is concluded.[260]

Suppliers must provide certain pre-contractual information by any method appropriate to the form of distance communication employed for the conclusion of the contract, so long as it is clear, comprehensible, and made with due regard to the principles of good faith and the principles governing the protection of persons unable to give their consent (eg, minors).[261] The commercial purpose of the communication must be made clear.[262] The supplier is required to provide specified pre-contractual information that enables the consumer to identify the supplier and, where payment in advance is required, the supplier's geographic address; a description of the main characteristics of the goods and services on offer; the price, including all taxes; delivery costs; the arrangements for payment, delivery, or performance; and, where applicable, the existence of a right of cancellation.[263] Further, where the cost of using the distance means of communication is calculated other than at the basic rate, information on the cost, including VAT, and advice on the possibility of variation of charges depending on the consumer's network provider; the period for which the offer of the price remains valid; and the minimum duration of the contract where goods and services are to be provided permanently or recurrently.[264] Finally, the supplier must inform the consumer, if he so proposes, that in the event of unavailability of the goods or services ordered, substitute goods or services of equivalent quality and price will be provided; and that, in the event of cancellation by the consumer, the cost of returning such substitute products will be met by the supplier.[265]

DSRs 2000, regulation 8 requires certain information to be confirmed in writing or in another durable medium available and accessible to the consumer[266] if this was not done at the time the information was originally provided.[267] The information subject to this requirement is the pre-contractual information required by DSRs

---

[260] DSRs 2000, reg 3(1).
[261] Ibid reg 7(2).
[262] Ibid reg 7(3)–(4).
[263] Ibid reg 7(1)(a)(i)–(vi).
[264] Ibid reg 7(1)(a)(vii)–(ix).
[265] Ibid reg 7(1)(b)–(c).
[266] Ibid reg 8(1) and (2)(a).
[267] With regard to the obligation to provide a copy of the terms, the OFT's current position is that information on a website may not be amenable to being stored or reproduced by the consumer, see OFT 698, pp 3 and 14. It is debatable whether this is a correct approach, since information on a website can be saved or printed out and can be specifically displayed and formatted for such purpose. Obviously, the website itself is not a durable medium—eg, it may be frequently edited by the supplier. However, the saved version of the website or the print-out are available to the consumer for storing and reproducing, and cannot be edited by the supplier, and arguably, therefore, constitute durable media. It is another matter whether the solution of requiring the consumer to save or print out the webpage is practicable. For this reason and in the light of the position of the OFT, the status of information provided on a webpage available to the consumer for saving and printing out remains uncertain and, therefore, a confirmatory email is advisable.

2000, regulation 7(1)(a)(i)–(vi) (concerning the supplier's identity and address, the description of the goods, the price and the arrangements for payment, delivery, or performance, and the right of cancellation) as well as information on: the procedures and conditions of exercising the cancellation right, including notification of any requirement for the consumer to return the goods and how to do so; who bears the cost of returning the goods to the supplier or of the supplier recovering the goods, and the consequences of agreeing to a service starting before the end of the usual seven-working-day cancellation period;[268] the geographic address of the business to which the consumer may address complaints; any guarantees or after-sales services; and the conditions for exercising any contractual right to cancel, if the contract is of an unspecified duration or of a duration exceeding one year.[269] As seen below, the time at which this information is provided affects the duration of the cooling-off period. Confirmation of the required information must be made either prior to the conclusion of the contract, or in good time thereafter,[270] and in any event during performance in the case of a contract for services, and at the latest upon delivery of the goods where goods not for delivery to third parties are concerned.[271]

The contract must be carried out within the time limits agreed as stated in the supplier's terms and conditions. In the absence of an agreement, the DSRs 2000 impose a statutory time limit of 30 days beginning with the day after the day that the consumer sent the order to the supplier.[272] In case of inability to perform the contract within the agreed or statutory time limit because the goods or services are not available, the supplier must notify the consumer[273] before the expiry of the deadline and reimburse, within 30 days beginning with the day following the day on which the period for performance expired,[274] any sum paid by or on behalf of the consumer to the person by whom it was paid.[275] A contract that has not been performed within the period for performance is treated as if it had not been made, save for any rights or remedies available to the consumer under the contract or as a result of the non-performance.[276] If the supplier is unable to supply the goods or services ordered by the consumer, it is possible to perform the contract by providing substitute goods or

---

[268] The requirement for information on the consequences of cancellation of services is set forth in DSRs 2000, reg 8(2)(b)(iii) inserted by the Consumer Protection (Distance Selling) (Amendment) Regulations 2005.

[269] DSRs 2000, reg 8(2)(b)–(e). According to reg 9, the provisions on written and additional information of reg 8 do not apply to services supplied on only one occasion and invoiced by the operator of the means of distance communication; in such a case, the supplier must take all necessary steps to ensure that the consumer is able to obtain the supplier's geographic address and the place of business to which complaints may be addressed.

[270] OFT 698, p 15, suggests that the 'good time' requirement is satisfied if consumers have sufficient time to act on the information when they receive it, eg to enable them to exercise the cancellation right.

[271] DSRs 2000, reg 8(1).

[272] Ibid reg 19(1).

[273] Ibid reg 19(2)(a).

[274] Ibid reg 19(4).

[275] Ibid reg 19(2)(b).

[276] Ibid reg 19(5).

services of equivalent quality and price, if this possibility was provided for in the prescribed manner[277] in the pre-contractual information, and in the contract.

The cancellation right of consumers is unconditional (although it is subject to certain exceptions—see below) and begins from the moment the contract is concluded.[278] Unless provided otherwise by the DSRs 2000, the effect of a notice of cancellation is that the contract is treated as if it had not been made,[279] and the consumer is entitled to full reimbursement of any sum paid under or in relation to the contract, including any costs of delivering goods to the consumer,[280] within 30 days from the day on which the notice of cancellation was given.[281] The giving of a notice of cancellation that has the effect of cancelling the contract also has the effect of cancelling any related credit agreement.[282] The notice should be provided in writing or in a durable medium available and accessible to the person to whom it is addressed, and should be given in person, by post, by facsimile, or by email.[283] However expressed, the notice should indicate the intention of the consumer to cancel the contract.[284]

Unless the parties agree otherwise, the cancellation right will not be available to the consumer in respect of contracts for: services if, prior to the conclusion of the contract, the supplier has informed the consumer in writing or in another durable medium which is available and accessible to the consumer that he will not be able to cancel the contract; goods or services the price of which depends on fluctuations in the financial markets that cannot be controlled by the supplier; the supply of goods made to the consumer's specifications[285] or clearly personalized or which by reason of their nature cannot be returned or are liable to deteriorate or expire rapidly; audio or video recordings or computer software that the consumer has unsealed;[286] newspapers, periodicals, and magazines; and gaming, betting, and lottery services.[287]

---

[277] DSRs 2000, reg 19(7).

[278] Ibid regs 11(1) and 12(1).

[279] Ibid reg 10(2).

[280] Case C-511/08 *Handelsgesellschaft Heinrich Heine GmbH v Verbraucherzentrale Nordrhein-Westfalen eV*.

[281] DSRs 2000, reg 14(1) and (3).

[282] Ibid reg 15(1), and further regs 15(2)–(6) and 16 on other aspects of the cancellation of a related agreement and the repayment of credit and interest after cancellation.

[283] Ibid reg 10(3)–(4), the latter further prescribing the proper giving of the notice in relation to the address or number where it should be given or sent; the point in time in which it is considered to have been given in each case; and, in relation to bodies corporate or partnerships, the persons to whom the proper notice must be given. OFT 698, p 20, suggests that cancellation by phone suffices, but only if the supplier accepts such cancellation in its terms and conditions.

[284] DSRs 2000, reg 10(3).

[285] According to OFT 698, p 23, this exception does not apply to upgrade options, eg, opting for add-on memory or choosing a combination of standard off-the-shelf components when ordering a PC.

[286] On this particular topic see further discussion below.

[287] DSRs 2000, reg 13.

In relation to goods, the cancellation period[288] ends on the expiry of seven working days beginning with the day after the day on which the consumer receives the
goods, so long as the supplier provides the written information required by regulation 8 no later than at the time of delivery of the goods. If the information is provided
after the goods are delivered, but within three months from the day after the day that
the consumer receives the goods, the consumer's cancellation right ends after seven
working days from the day after the day on which the consumer received the information. In all other circumstances (ie, if the information is provided later than three
months from the day after the day that the consumer receives the goods or is not
provided at all), the cancellation right expires three months and seven working days
from the day after the day that the consumer receives the goods.[289]

In relation to services, the cancellation period ends on the expiry of seven working days beginning with the day after the day on which the contract is concluded, so
long as the supplier provides the written information required by regulation 8 no
later than the day the contract is concluded. If the information is provided after the
contract was concluded, but within three months beginning the day after the day the
contract was concluded, the consumer's cancellation right ends after seven days
from the day after the day that the information is provided. In all other circumstances
(ie, if the information is provided later than three months from the day after the day
that the contract is concluded or is not provided at all), the cancellation rights expire
three months and seven working days from the day after the day that the contract
was concluded.[290] However, different rules apply if the consumer agrees that performance of the services may begin before the usual cancellation period expires:[291]
if the supplier provides the information required under regulation 8 before performance begins, the consumer has no right to cancel;[292] if the supplier provides the
information in good time during the performance of the services, the cooling-off
period begins when the consumer receives the information and ends seven working
days later or when performance is completed, whichever is sooner.[293] At the time of
writing the pCRD,[294] if implemented in its current form, would increase the statutory
cancellation period to 14 days.

In the event of cancellation after the consumer has acquired possession of the
goods, the consumer is under a duty to retain possession and take reasonable care of
the goods until he restores them to the supplier.[295] Unless provided otherwise in the

---

[288] The DSRs 2000 do not affect the consumer's rights under other legislation, eg the SGA 1979 or the
SGSA 1982, which can, of course, be exercised irrespective of the expiration of the time limits for the
cancellation right of the DSRs 2000.

[289] DSRs 2000, reg 11.

[290] Ibid reg 12(1)–(3) and (4).

[291] Consumer Protection (Distance Selling) (Amendment) Regulations 2005.

[292] DSRs 2000, reg 13(1)(a).

[293] Ibid reg 12(3A).

[294] See s 2.2.1.3.

[295] DSRs 2000, reg 17(1)–(3), and further paras (4)–(9) on the modalities of the restoration of the
goods.

contract and the required written information,[296] the consumer is not under a duty to deliver the goods except at his own premises and following a request in writing or other durable medium available and accessible to the consumer given before or at the time when the goods are collected.[297] Breach of the duties imposed on the consumer is actionable as a breach of a statutory duty.[298]

The DSRs 2000 also introduced a range of other consumer protection measures. For example, in addition to providing for the automatic cancellation of related credit transactions on the cancellation of any contract under regulation 15, they further protect consumers using credit cards, charge cards, debit cards, and store cards in connection with distance selling contracts, by providing that a consumer is entitled to cancel a card payment in the event of fraudulent use of the card.[299] With regard to inertia selling, the DSRs 2000 provide that unsolicited goods may be treated as gifts, which consumers have the right to retain or dispose of as they see fit.[300] Furthermore, the DSRs 2000 also provide that contractual terms that are inconsistent with the consumer protection provisions of the DSRs 2000 are void, and that they will apply even to a contract which applies or purports to apply the law of a non-Member State, if the contract has a close connection with the territory of a Member State.[301]

The drafting of the DSRs 2000 raises questions in connection with mass market contracting. The first is that, for the purposes of determining when a consumer's right to cancel a contract commences and expires, the DSRs 2000 categorize contracts as being either for the supply of goods[302] or for the supply of services.[303] In this specific context, they do not acknowledge or provide for the cancellation of mixed contracts. This raises the question of whether the DSRs 2000 actually apply to such contracts. This is potentially a critical question in relation to many common types of mass market consumer contracts that involve the supply of both goods and services; for example, satellite or cable TV services (which also involve the supply of set-top boxes), mobile phone services (if, as is fairly typical, they involve the supply of a phone or SIM card), and broadband internet access services (if they also involve the supply of broadband modems). Our view is that if the question were to come before the courts, they would conclude that the DSRs 2000 do apply to such contracts. However, even if this is correct, the failure of the DSRs 2000 to address the issue still leaves unresolved the question of whether a mixed contract should be

---

[296] DSRs 2000, reg 8(2)(b).

[297] Ibid reg 17(4).

[298] Ibid reg 17(10). For a discussion of the powers and duties in relation to breaches of the DSRs 2000 conferred on the OFT (and other enforcers): under the EA 2002, see section 2.3.2 below, and under the DSRs 2000 themselves, see section 2.3.3.1 below.

[299] DSRs 2000, reg 22.

[300] Ibid reg 24.

[301] Ibid reg 25.

[302] Ibid reg 11.

[303] Ibid reg 12.

treated either as two separate contracts with potentially two different sets of cancellation rights, or as a single contract with an overarching cancellation right in respect of both the goods and services elements of the contract (with a court or the OFT having to decide which cancellation provisions apply, presumably basing such a decision on the perceived primary purpose of the agreement). One can envisage several problematic results under either scenario. The OFT's approach appears to be that a mixed contract should be treated for these purposes as two separate contracts, with potentially two different cancellation periods, which leaves unclear the rights and obligations of both parties if only one element of the mixed contract is cancelled.

The second question (which is related to the first) is that the law remains unclear on whether software and digital content constitute goods, services, or something *sui generis*. The categorization of contracts by the DSRs 2000 as being for the supply of either goods or services only, means that the DSRs 2000 do not effectively provide for the possibility that such content might actually be found to constitute neither.

A third problem is caused by the provisions that disapply the consumer's cancellation rights in respect of contracts for the supply of audio and video recordings and computer software. Regulation 13(1)(d) provides that, unless the parties have agreed otherwise, a consumer will not have a cancellation right in relation to such media, if they have been 'unsealed by the consumer'. The provision is therefore clearly directed at physical supplies. Of course, it is possible that a court might choose to interpret this provision purposively, equating the act of downloading a digital copy with the act of unsealing, and hence treat the consumer's cancellation right as having been lost in either scenario. Furthermore, the OFT takes the view that software can be sealed either through the use of a physical seal on the inner packaging or electronically.[304] However, the OFT's approach at least appears to maintain the continuing common law distinction between software (and, we assume, by analogy) audio and visual content delivered on physical media, and the digital delivery of the same content, which it considers constitutes a service.[305] As a result, there appears to be the potential for anomalous treatment of these contracts, depending on whether the supply is digital or physical. Interestingly, providers of digital content will be better off than their physical supplier counterparts if they structure their contracts and cancellation notification procedures effectively (assuming that they can show that the provision of the services began immediately with the agreement of the consumer), or worse off if they either attempt but fail to bring the service within the exception, or simply do not know about it. Of course, it might also be open to suppliers of pure digital content in certain circumstances to assert that the content

---

[304] OFT 672, p 41.
[305] Note that, according to OFT 698, p 23, digital products such as electronic books, downloadable music, screen savers, and ringtones for mobile phones are likely to constitute services as opposed to goods.

provided by them constituted neither goods nor services, and hence the DSRs 2000 cancellation provisions would not apply to them at all.

A further interesting issue arises in relation to DSRs 2000, regulation 14(1) requiring that, in the event of cancellation, the supplier must reimburse any sum paid by or on behalf of the consumer under or in relation to the contract during the cancellation period. The logical consequence of this provision is that if, for instance, the consumer cancels an internet connection or airtime contract, the supplier must also refund any charges incurred under the contract during this period, including call charges or internet connection charges. This view is adopted by the OFT in its guidance for business on distance selling.[306]

It may be possible for suppliers to avoid this risk if the contracting process is properly structured and the contract effectively drafted. Thus provided that the supplier notifies the consumer that the services will begin on commencement of the contract and the consumer will consequently have no cancellation right under the DSRs 2000, and the consumer agrees to this, the consumer's cancellation right under the DSRs 2000 will be disapplied. Of course, this option will only be available to those suppliers whose operations are structured such that they do, in fact, commence delivery of their services upon the commencement of the contract.

Electronic Commerce Regulations 2002 Businesses concluding contracts electronically must also comply with the eComRs 2002, which govern the provision of most[307] information society services, that is, any services normally provided upon request, for payment, at a distance and by use of electronic communication means.[308] They therefore cover, for example: the sale and supply of goods and services to consumers and businesses over the internet, via interactive TV, by email, or mobile phone text message (irrespective of whether the goods and services themselves are provided electronically); advertising over such communication means;[309] and the conveyance or storage of electronic information for customers or the provision of access to a communications network. By contrast, the eComRs 2002 do not apply to online activities not 'normally provided for remuneration';[310] to the goods

---

[306] OFT 698, p 21. However, the position may change under the pCRD (see section 2.2.1.3), the current draft of which provides that suppliers will be able to charge (a proportionate amount) for any part of the services which the consumer has received before cancellation.

[307] See eComRs 2002, reg 3(1)(d) for the exclusions.

[308] e-Commerce Directive, Art 2 and recitals 17 and 18 which refer to the definition of the term in Directive 98/34/EC of the European Parliament and of the Council of 22 June 1998 laying down a procedure for the provision of information in the field of technical standards and regulations and of rules on information society services and in Directive 98/84/EC of the European Parliament and of the Council of 20 November 1998 on the legal protection of services based on, or consisting of, conditional access.

[309] The Privacy and Electronic Communications Regulations 2003 also apply to marketing over such communications means.

[310] An interesting question arises here in relation (in particular) to business models which involve providing a 'free' consumer service which is funded by advertising (and whether such a service is 'normally provided for remuneration').

themselves; or to the delivery of goods and services that are not provided online; or to the offline elements of an online transaction.

The eComRs 2002 address issues of jurisdiction and applicable law[311] and set forth information requirements (applicable in addition to the information requirements of the DSRs 2000)[312] concerning:

(a) general information that online businesses must provide;[313]

(b) clarifying the commercial nature of communications;[314] and

(c) concerning the electronic conclusion of contracts.[315]

They also: regulate the contractual process;[316] determine the individual remedies available to aggrieved parties when the e-supplier does not comply;[317] and limit the liability of intermediary service providers, that is, online businesses engaging in mere conduit, caching, or hosting activities.[318]

With regard to the electronic conclusion of contracts, the eComRs 2002 provide[319] that, unless agreed otherwise between parties that are not consumers, the service provider must prior to the placement of an order provide the following information in a clear, comprehensible, and unambiguous manner: the different technical steps to conclude the contract; whether the concluded contract will be filed by the service provider and whether it will be accessible; the technical means to identify and correct input errors prior to placing an order; the languages offered for the conclusion of the contract; and the relevant codes of conduct to which the service provider subscribes (with information on how these can be consulted electronically). In any case where the service provider provides terms and conditions applicable to the contract, they must be made available in a way that the recipient can store and reproduce them (including when the contract is concluded by exchange of emails or other individual communication).

Further, in relation to placing orders, subject to any contrary agreement between parties that are not consumers, the service provider must: acknowledge the receipt of the order without undue delay and by electronic means;[320] and make available

---

[311] eComRs 2002, regs 4–5; see further Chapter 4, section 4.6.2.

[312] eComRs 2002, reg 10.

[313] Ibid reg 6; see further Chapter 4, section 4.2.3.2.

[314] eComRs 2002, regs 7–8.

[315] eComRs 2002, reg 9, see further Chapter 4, section 4.2.1.

[316] eComRs 2000, regs 11–12.

[317] Ibid regs 13–15.

[318] Ibid regs 17–22. The issue of liability of intermediary service providers is not further discussed here.

[319] Ibid reg 9(1)–(2). Note, however, that the requirements of reg 9(1) and (2) are disapplied by reg 9(4) in respect of contracts concluded exclusively by exchange of electronic mail or by equivalent individual communications.

[320] Ibid reg 11(1). Note, however, that the requirements of reg 11(1) are disapplied by reg 11(3) in respect of contracts concluded exclusively by exchange of electronic mail or by equivalent individual communications.

effective and accessible technical means allowing the recipient of the service to identify and correct input errors prior to the placing of the order. Deemed receipt of the order and acknowledgement takes place when the parties to whom they are addressed are able to access them (and acknowledgement may take the form of the provision of the service itself).

Service providers will be liable for breach of statutory duty if they fail to comply with their obligations to provide the information required by the eComRs 2002 or to acknowledge receipt of customer orders.[321] If a service provider fails to comply with the requirement to make its terms and conditions available in a way that permits them to be stored and reproduced by the recipient of the service, the recipient may seek an order from the courts requiring the service provider to comply. Finally, if a provider fails to provide recipients with the means to identify and correct input errors, any recipient that has entered into a contract with the provider may rescind the contract, unless a court orders otherwise following an application by the service provider.

2.2.2 Rules of soft law

Most forms of commercial activity are not only governed by law, but they are also frequently regulated by so-called soft law instruments.[322] This section discusses very briefly some of the principal soft law instruments relevant to mass market contracting.[323]

Soft law instruments have diverse origins and are usually adopted by national, regional, or transnational industry organizations or associations and consumer protection organizations; international governmental and non-governmental organizations; regional executive bodies; and national governments and regulators. Soft law instruments usually take the form of principles, guidelines, and codes of conduct. They are not binding and enforceable of themselves, at least not in the strict sense that legislation is. Unlike legislation, the application of soft law instruments is founded directly on the consent of the governed. Often, soft law instruments are associated with a private enforcement regime, which determines the consequences and imposes sanctions when the guidelines or code of conduct have not been respected. For instance, a common arrangement is to condition membership of a trade association and the right to display the association's trustmark on the trader's

---

[321] As seen below, the service provider may also be faced with actions undertaken by enforcement authorities pursuant to the EA 2002. Furthermore, failure to provide information may amount to an unfair commercial practice for failure to comply with the information provision requirements of the CPR.

[322] By 'soft law instrument' we mean any instrument that, first, does not constitute law in the strict sense, and therefore, secondly, is binding on, or between, parties only because they expressly or impliedly adopt it. An additional criterion applicable at the international level could be that the instrument reflects internationally accepted standards.

[323] This is a broad subject that offers insights into the regulatory reality and future of globalizing high-tech markets, a detailed discussion of which is beyond the scope of this chapter.

website with acceptance of the association's code or guidelines; failure to comply with them can lead to removal of the trustmark and suspension or termination of membership.[324]

Soft law instruments promulgated in particular by private sector industry associations tend to be effective because those who adopt them generally wish to abide by them. As a result, they are central to the concepts of self-regulation or co-regulation of industries, markets, and professions. Such concepts are especially attractive in the field of e-commerce for a number of additional reasons. These include the creation or enhancement of consumer confidence in the trader and the transaction; the rapid pace of technological change, which frequently outpaces legislative and regulatory development in the area; the instantaneous and low-cost nature of e-commerce transactions; and the inherent weakness of jurisdictionally specific legal systems in dealing with the legal issues posed by the international, cross-border medium that is the internet, a state of affairs that is generally capable of producing inadequate or inconclusive results or no results at all.[325]

Several influential legislative instruments and initiatives, such as the e-Commerce Directive,[326] the OECD Guidelines,[327] and deliberations in the context of the World Summit on Information Society ('WSIS') process,[328] acknowledge the instrumental role of soft law, especially in relation to consumer protection, and promote its use, in conjunction with extra-judicial, including online, dispute-resolution mechanisms. From another perspective, initiatives such as the OECD Guidelines and the TACD Principles[329] constitute, in essence, transnational statements of widely accepted principles of consumer protection in e-commerce. In summary, from a business perspective at least, regulation largely based on standards adopted by, as opposed to being imposed upon, the participants themselves, and applied efficiently and effectively by appropriate bodies, appears to be ideally suited to e-commerce.

The main transnational consumer protection instruments are the OECD Guidelines and the TACD Principles. The OECD Guidelines are designed to help to ensure that consumers are equally protected online as they are offline.[330] They reflect existing

---

[324] Further, false claims that a supplier is a signatory of a code of conduct or that a code of conduct has endorsement, and display of a trustmark or equivalent without authorization are capable of constituting misleading commercial practices under the CPRs 2008, discussed in section 2.2.1.1 above.

[325] See C Reed, *Internet Law*, 2nd edn (Cambridge: Cambridge University Press, 2004) ch 7.

[326] See n 7 above.

[327] OECD Guidelines, guideline IV.

[328] See, eg, the Working Group on Internet Governance (WGIG Report), Château de Bossey, June 2005, <http://www.wgig.org/docs/WGIGREPORT.pdf> (accessed 3 August 2011), para 84.

[329] Core Consumer Protection Principles in Electronic Commerce, Doc No Ecom 10-99, September 1999, <http://tacd.org/index2.php?option=com_docman&task=doc_view&gid=135&Itemid=> (accessed 3 August 2011). The Transatlantic Consumer Dialogue ('TACD') is a forum of US and EU consumer organizations that develops and agrees joint consumer policy recommendations to the US Government and EU in connection with EU and US policy-making.

[330] The Guidelines were followed up by reviews of their effect in 2001 and 2003, and by a 2001 first report on government and private sector initiatives to promote their implementation <http://www.oecd. org/document/51/0,2340,en_2649_34267_1824435_1_1_1_1,00.html> (accessed 3 August 2011).

legal protections available for more traditional forms of commerce and aim at encouraging fair business, advertising, and market practices; the provision of clear information about the identity of online businesses, the goods and services they offer, and the terms and conditions of transactions; a transparent process for confirmation of transactions; secure payment mechanisms; fair, timely, and affordable dispute resolution and redress; privacy protection; and consumer and business education. The Guidelines adopt the principle of technological neutrality. Finally, they adopt a co-regulatory approach by encouraging private sector initiatives that embrace the participation of consumer organizations and by emphasizing the need for cooperation between governments, businesses, and consumers. The same principles are enshrined in the TACD Principles, which were published prior to, and actually encouraged, the development of the OECD Guidelines. The OECD Guidelines are followed by most OECD member countries and have been used as a model for many national laws and other codes and guidelines. They are accompanied by a best practices document.[331] The OECD has also produced Guidelines for Consumer Protection from Fraudulent and Deceptive Practices Across Borders.[332]

In a recent OECD conference, the impact of the 1999 OECD Guidelines was considered and the conclusion was that they are still seen as continuing to provide an effective framework for consumer protection. They have been used extensively by governments and business to develop laws, regulations, and practices to ensure that markets are transparent and fair and that consumer rights are preserved. There was however general agreement that in order for e-commerce to reach its full potential, in particular across borders, consumer confidence would need to be strengthened. This might require further elaboration or modification of the principles in the 1999 Guidelines—see 'OECD Conference on Empowering E-consumers: Strengthening Consumer Protection in the Internet Economy, Summary of Key Points and Conclusions', DSTI/CP(2010)2/FINAL, 23 April 2010, <http://www.oecd.org/dataoecd/32/10/45061590.pdf> (accessed 3 August 2011). Further, the International Consumer Protection and Enforcement Network ('ICPEN'), <https://icpen.org/> (accessed 3 August 2011), is an organization composed by consumer protection authorities from almost 40 countries that aims to protect consumer; economic interests around the world; share information about cross-border commercial activities that may affect consumer welfare; and encourage global cooperation among law enforcement agencies. See also <http://www.econsumer. gov> (accessed 3 August 2011), an initiative of consumer protection agencies from 26 countries with the aim to respond to the challenges of multinational internet fraud and working to enhance consumer protection and confidence in e-commerce. The project has two components: a multilingual public website, and a government, password-protected website The public site allows consumers to lodge cross-border complaints, and to try to resolve their complaints through ADR. Using the Consumer Sentinel network (a database of consumer complaint data and other investigative information operated by the US Federal Trade Commission), the incoming complaints are shared with participating consumer protection law enforcers.

[331] OECD, Directorate for Science, Technology and Industry, Committee on Consumer Policy, 'Best Practices Examples Under the OECD Guidelines on Consumer Protection in the Context of Electronic Commerce', DSTI/CP(2002)2/FINAL, 17 May 2002, <http://www.oecd-ilibrary.org/science-and-technology/best-practice-examples-under-the-oecd-guidelines-on-consumer-protection-in-the-context-of-electronic-commerce_233574467655> (accessed 11 April 2011).

[332] (Paris: OECD Publications, 2003), <http://www.oecd.org/dataoecd/24/33/2956464.pdf> (accessed 3 August 2011).

In the UK, the OFT, as part of its mandate under the EA 2002,[333] is required to provide guidance on the rights of consumers[334] and the obligations of businesses[335] under the consumer protection legislation reviewed in the previous section.[336] In relation to the UTCCRs 1999, the OFT has provided comprehensive guidance on standard terms that are, in the OFT's view, potentially unfair under those Regulations.[337] It is complemented by several other guidance documents with a focus on particular contracts or agreements, legislation, or types of terms, such as the OFT Guidance on IT Consumer Contracts Concluded at a Distance,[338] the OFT Guidance on Unfair Standard Terms,[339] and the OFT and BERR Guidance on Unfair Commercial Practices.[340] Typically, such guidance includes general information, a discussion of the OFT's position on the provisions of applicable legislation, and an indicative list of terms considered to be unenforceable. For instance, the OFT Guidance on Unfair Contract Terms is a comprehensive guidance document setting forth the position of the OFT in relation to standard terms that are potentially unfair under the UTCCRs 1999.[341]

Although the purpose of regulatory guidance is to facilitate and encourage compliance with black letter law, we have included it within this section on soft law for the following reason: while it is fully to be expected that a court would give due weight to relevant regulatory guidance in any case before it, such guidance does not supplant the court's function as the proper interpreter and arbiter of issues of law (as also recognized by the OFT itself); however, such guidance often appears to be gathering a dynamic of its own[342] and, arguably, is in practice effectively supplementing or even supplanting the law which it was initially intended to serve, as the standard against which compliance should be measured.

It is also worth noting the growing body of published OFT enforcement action and guidance in this area, with detailed information on clauses with which the OFT has had concerns, its investigations, and any undertakings provided by suppliers. If the supplier undertakes to cease using certain clauses, and this alleviates the OFT's concerns, the OFT is unlikely to pursue court proceedings. This is essentially a negotiation process in which two prospective litigants settle a dispute, usually by the

---

[333] See section 2.3.1 below.

[334] <http://www.oft.gov.uk/consumer-advice/> (accessed 3 August 2011), including information on, eg, unfair terms, online shopping, and online auctions.

[335] <http://www.oft.gov.uk/business-advice/;jsessionid=90F52A4E270802A6A5BE841B0AA0273F> (accessed 3 August 2011).

[336] See the various OFT guidance documents discussed in the previous subsection.

[337] OFT 311, n 185.

[338] OFT 672. See detailed discussions in section 2.5 below.

[339] OFT 143, n 160.

[340] n 229.

[341] OFT 311, n 185.

[342] In a function that could have autopoietic properties, on which see further G Teubner, *Law as an Autopoietic System* (Oxford: Blackwell, 1993); G Teubner (ed), *Global Law Without a State* (Aldershot: Dartmouth, 1996).

supplier undertaking to cease the potentially infringing conduct. The results of these negotiations inevitably guide future negotiations by other suppliers, and thus become, in effect, a form of regulation in practice.

2.3 INTERVENTION BY REGULATORY AUTHORITIES

While the majority of the provisions discussed in this chapter give consumers rights at an individual level, certain legislation, including the EA 2002 and several of the instruments mentioned above, enables regulatory authorities[343] to intervene to protect consumer rights.

2.3.1 The EA 2002

The EA 2002, which implements the CPCR 2004, provides a regime for regulatory enforcement where a breach of those provisions harms the collective interests of consumers. Further, the EA 2002 strengthens the position of consumers in relation to business practices that prevent, restrict, or distort competition.

The EA 2002 has wide-ranging implications for businesses and consumers. It established the OFT as an independent statutory body with a board and a greater role in ensuring the proper functioning of markets.[344] The OFT's mission is to 'make markets work well for consumers' so that they 'have as much choice as possible across all the different sectors of the marketplace'. This happens when 'businesses are in open, fair and vigorous competition with each other for the consumer's custom'.[345]

The OFT pursues its mission by:

(a) encouraging compliance with competition and consumer regulation through self-regulation (eg consumer codes);[346]

(b) enforcement action;

(c) studying markets and recommending action; and

(d) empowering consumers with the knowledge and skills to make informed choices and get the best value from markets (and helping them resolve problems).[347]

---

[343] Primarily the OFT but also, in relation to specific statutes, other authorities such as the FSA, Ofcom, the Information Commissioner, etc.

[344] EA 2002, Pt 1 and, further, Sch 24.

[345] See 'What we do' on the OFT website, <http://www.oft.gov.uk/about-the-oft/what/> (accessed 3 August 2011).

[346] EA 2002, s 8.

[347] See 'What we do' on the OFT website, <http://www.oft.gov.uk/about-the-oft/what/> (accessed 3 August 2011).

2.3.2 EA 2002, Part 8

2.3.2.1 Introduction

Part 8 of the EA 2002 ('Part 8') provides a regime under which the OFT (and other 'enforcers') can enforce breaches of consumer protection law and regulation. It gives the OFT a lead enforcement role as well as making the OFT the central coordinator, ensuring that enforcement action is taken by the most appropriate body.[348] Under Part 8 the OFT is required to publish advice and information (which may be subsequently revised or replaced) explaining the provisions of Part 8 to those likely to be affected by them and how the OFT expects those provisions to operate.[349]

2.3.2.2 Infringements

Introduction The enforcement regime under Part 8 enables enforcers, such as the OFT, to take certain enforcement measures (where applicable conditions are satisfied) in relation to breaches of other specified UK legislation. The specific UK legislation is nominated by the Secretary of State and includes most of the principal legislation mentioned so far in this chapter. For the purposes of Part 8, breaches of this legislation are categorized as 'domestic infringements' or 'Community infringements'. Full definitions are set out below but, as a general point, both types of infringement require harm to the collective interests of consumers (for a domestic infringement, the harm must be to 'consumers in the United Kingdom') and a domestic infringement can only be committed by a person 'in the course of a business'.[350]

The OFT's enforcement history demonstrates preferences for enforcement under certain statutes during certain periods. For example, during the first few years of the new millennium the OFT's 'weapon of choice' was clearly the UTCCRs 1999,[351] whereas, since their implementation, the CPRs 2008 have taken precedence.[352]

---

[348] See, eg, EA 2002, s 216, which allows the OFT to direct that an application for an enforcement order in relation to a particular infringement, can only be made by the OFT itself or by another enforcer directed by the OFT.

[349] See EA 2002, s 229. For an example of such advice and information, see <http://www.oft.gov.uk/shared_oft/business_leaflets/enterprise_act/oft512.pdf> (accessed 3 August 2011).

[350] See EA 2002, s 211(1)(a).

[351] eg, between 1 April 2005 and 31 March 2006, the OFT obtained changes to over 1,000 unfair contract terms in consumer contracts, Annexe A to the OFT Annual Report 2005–6, <http://www.oft.gov.uk/shared_oft/annual_report/2005/annexea.pdf> (accessed 3 August 2011).

[352] This is partly explicable by the 'catch-all' and wide-ranging general prohibition in CPRs, reg 3(3) against unfair commercial practices which contravene the requirements of professional diligence; and materially distort or are likely materially to distort the economic behaviour of the average consumer with regard to a product. See section 2.2.1.4 above.

Community and domestic infringements A domestic infringement is defined as an act or omission which is 'done or made by a person in the course of a business'[353] that 'harms the collective interests of consumers in the United Kingdom' and falls within EA 2002, section 211(2).[354] Section 211(2) provides that acts and omissions fall within the subsection if they are of a description specified by order of the Secretary of State and consist of:

(a) a contravention of an enactment which imposes a duty, prohibition, or restriction enforceable by criminal proceedings;

(b) an act done or omission made in breach of contract;

(c) an act done or omission made in breach of a non-contractual duty owed to a person by virtue of an enactment or rule of law and enforceable by civil proceedings;

(d) an act or omission in respect of which an enactment provides for a remedy or sanction enforceable by civil proceedings;

(e) an act done or omission made by a person supplying or seeking to supply goods or services as a result of which an agreement or security relating to the supply is void or unenforceable to any extent;

(f) an act or omission by which a person supplying or seeking to supply goods or services purports or attempts to exercise a right or remedy relating to the supply in circumstances where the exercise of the right or remedy is restricted or excluded under or by virtue of an enactment; or

(g) an act or omission by which a person supplying or seeking to supply goods or services purports or attempts to avoid (to any extent) liability relating to the supply in circumstances where such avoidance is restricted or prevented under an enactment.

The legislation breach of which can constitute a domestic infringement includes:

(a) the Consumer Credit Act 1974;

(b) the SGA 1979;

(c) the SGITA 1973;

(d) the SGSA 1982;

(e) the Trade Descriptions Act 1968;

(f) UCTA 1977; and

---

[353] Under EA 2002, s 210(8), a 'business' includes a professional practice; any other undertaking carried on for gain or reward; and any undertaking in the course of which goods or services are supplied otherwise than free of charge.

[354] EA 2002, s 211(1).

(g) certain sections of the Copyright Designs and Patents Act 1988, ss 107 (making or dealing with infringing articles etc), 198 (making, dealing with, or using illicit recordings), and 297A (making and dealing with unauthorized decoders).[355]

A Community infringement is defined as an act or omission that 'harms the collective interests of consumers' and contravenes: (a) a listed Directive[356] as given effect by the laws, regulations, or administrative provisions of an EEA state; (b) such laws, regulations, or administrative provisions which provide additional permitted protections;[357] (c) a listed Regulation;[358] or (d) any laws, regulations, or administrative provisions of an EEA state which give effect to a listed Regulation.[359] The Secretary of State may specify by order the UK law that gives effect to the listed directives, provides additional permitted protections, or gives effect to a listed Regulation.[360]

The legislation breach of which can constitute a Community infringement includes:

(a) the CPRs 2008;

(b) the UTCCRs 1999;

(c) the DSRs 2000;

(d) the eComRs 2002, regulations 6–9 and 11 (requirements as to information and orders);

(e) the Financial Services (Distance Marketing) Regulations 2004;

(f) the SGITA 1973, sections 9–11, the SGA 1979, sections 13–15 and 15B, the SGSA 1982, sections 3–5, 11C–11E, and 13, as well as any rule of law in Scotland

---

[355] Enterprise Act 2002 (Part 8 Domestic Infringements) Order 2003 (SI 2003/1593). Pts I and II specify certain UK and Northern Irish legislation and Pt III specifies two rules of law; an act done or omission made in breach of a contract for the supply of goods or services to a consumer; or a duty of care owed to a consumer under the law of tort or delict of negligence.

[356] Under EA 2002, ss 212(4) and 210(7), a directive is a listed directive if it is a Directive of the Council of the European Communities or of the European Parliament and of the Council, and if it is specified in EA 2002, Sch 13 or to the extent that any of its provisions is so specified. EA 2002, Sch 13 lists several directives and provisions of directives including Council Directive 85/577/EEC of 20 December 1985 to protect the consumer in respect of contracts negotiated away from business premises (OJ L372/31, 31 December 1985); the UTCCD; the Distance Selling Directive; the Sale of Goods and Associated Guarantees Directive; the e-Commerce Directive; and the UCPD 2005.

[357] Under EA 2002, s 212(2) such instruments provide additional permitted protection if they provide protection for consumers that is in addition to the minimum protection required by the directive concerned, and such additional protection is permitted by that directive.

[358] Under EA 2002, ss 212(4) and 210(7A), a regulation is a listed regulation if it is a regulation of the Council of the European Communities or of the European Parliament and of the Council, and if it is specified in EA 2002, Sch 13 or to the extent that any of its provisions is so specified. Currently, EA 2002, Sch 13 only includes one set of regulations, Regulation (EC) No 261/2004 of the European Parliament and of the Council of 11 February 2004 establishing common rules on compensation and assistance to air passengers in the event of denied boarding and of cancellation or long delay of flights.

[359] EA 2002, s 212(1). The definition of a Community infringement in s 212 corresponds with the definition of an infringement in Art 1(2) of the Injunctions Directive.

[360] EA 2002, s 212(3).

providing protection comparable to that of the SGSA 1982, section 13 (implied terms as to quality and fitness), the SGA 1979, sections 20 and 32 (passing of risk and delivery of goods), the SGA 1979, sections 48A–48F, and the SGSA 1982, sections 11M, 11N, and 11P–11S (additional remedies for consumers); the SSGCRs 2002, regulation 15, UCTA 1977, sections 6(2), 7(1), 7(2), 20(2), 21, and 27(2), the Consumer Transactions (Restrictions on Statements) Order 1976 (anti-avoidance measures), article 3; and

(g) the Privacy and Electronic Communications (EC Directive) Regulations 2003 (SI 2003/2426), regulations 19–24, in their application to consumers (use of telecommunications services for direct marketing purposes).[361]

Legislation which is enforceable as a Community infringement is not usually also enforceable as a domestic infringement. However, there are instances in which legislation is specified twice to 'ensure that legislation can be effectively or coherently enforced'.[362]

Consumers Part 8 includes, at section 210, its own provision for construing references to consumers, as used in relation to a domestic or a Community infringement. In relation to a domestic infringement a consumer is an individual:

(a) in respect of whom goods or services are or are sought to be supplied (whether by way of sale or otherwise) in the course of a business carried on by the person supplying or seeking to supply them;[363] and

(b) who receives or seeks to receive the goods or services otherwise than in the course of a business carried on by him, or who receives or seeks to receive the goods or services with a view to carrying on a business but not in the course of a business carried on by him.[364]

In relation to a Community infringement, a consumer is a person who is a consumer for the purposes of the Injunctions Directive,[365] and the listed Directive or Regulation concerned.[366]

---

[361] Enterprise Act 2002 (Part 8 Community Infringements Specified UK Laws) Order 2003 (SI 2003/1374), Enterprise Act 2002 (Part 8 Community Infringements Specified UK Laws) (Amendment) Order 2005 (SI 2005/2418), and Enterprise Act 2002 (Part 8 Community Infringements Specified UK Laws) Order 2006 (SI 2006/3372). These Orders specify the UK laws giving effect to EC directives, and provisions of directives, listed in EA 2002, Sch 13 together with additional protections permitted under the directives.

[362] See para 3.24 of the OFT's Guidance on Part 8 'Enforcement of Consumer Protection Legislation' OFT 512 June 2003, <http://www.oft.gov.uk/shared_oft/business_leaflets/enterprise_act/oft512.pdf> (accessed 3 August 2011).

[363] Whether or not that person has a place of business in the UK, EA 2002, s 210(5).

[364] EA 2002, s 210(2)–(4).

[365] See n 9 and accompanying text.

[366] EA 2002, s 210(6).

Collective interests of consumers Part 8 is 'not a means of pursuing individual redress';[367] and therefore does not give additional individual rights to consumers (who still need to seek redress in court or through ADR). Domestic and Community infringements only take place if the breach of the applicable legislation causes harm to the 'collective interests of consumers'.[368] 'Collective interests of consumers' is not defined in either the EA 2002 or the Injunctions Directive, but recital 2 of the Injunctions Directive specifies that 'collective interests mean interests which do not include the cumulation of interests of individuals who have been harmed by an infringement'[369] and the test, according to the DTI (the predecessor of BIS), 'is intended to produce the consequence that the procedure is not available to provide redress for individual consumers who may have been harmed by an infringement'.[370]

The DTI considered (in the Explanatory Notes to EA 2002) that harm to the collective interests of consumers does not mean that a large number of consumers must already have been harmed, but rather that simply the continuation or repetition of an act or omission constituting a domestic or Community infringement could harm the collective interests of consumers, since the interests of future customers of the trader are actually or will potentially be affected. The DTI gives an example of a trader not complying with the requirement to inform consumers of their right to cancellation under the DSRs 2000 when they purchase at a distance, in which case the court would be expected to find that the repetition of the omission by the trader would be harmful to the collective interests of consumers.[371]

The 'harm to the collective interests of consumers' test does not require harm (or potential harm) to consumers generally, providing harm to a group of consumers who are likely to buy or considering buying the products in question is established. The DTI considered that the test would be satisfied where the conduct concerns goods or services purchased only by a very small minority of the community (eg, expensive luxury goods).[372]

In *OFT v MB Designs (Scotland) Ltd*,[373] the Scottish Court of Session held that 'harm to the collective interests' means that the EA 2002 is not concerned with individual breaches by traders of contract or statutory provisions, but rather 'with general trading standards, and in particular with the general standard of goods or services supplied by a particular trader'. However, the court was of the opinion that harm to the collective interests of consumers would normally be inferred from a

---

[367] Para 3.8 of the OFT's Guidance on Part 8 'Enforcement of Consumer Protection Legislation' OFT 512 June 2003, <http://www.oft.gov.uk/shared_oft/business_leaflets/enterprise_act/oft512.pdf> (accessed 3 August 2011).
[368] EA 2002, ss 211(1)(c) and 212(1); Directive, Art 1.
[369] The term is defined by the CPCR 2004, see section 2.3.5 below.
[370] Explanatory Notes to EA 2002, 488.
[371] Ibid 486.
[372] Ibid 487.
[373] [2005] SCLR 894.

number of individual breaches of contract (or other relevant defaults), providing it was also possible to conclude that something more existed. The extra element was harm to the public generally, in their capacity as consumers, or, more precisely, to the section of the public who were likely to buy or consider buying the defendant's goods and services.[374] This approach was approved, in part, in *OFT v Miller*,[375] where it was held that while the concept requires it to be shown that harm is caused to a section of the public, rather than to an individual consumer, such harm may be inferred from an accumulation of individual instances of infringement.[376]

Finally, the OFT considers that the breach 'must affect, or have the potential to affect, consumers generally or a group of consumers' and that the 'evidence must demonstrate how a particular infringement has, or may in the future have, an adverse effect upon consumers'.[377]

Investigation and enforcement   Part 8 gives enforcers[378] various powers of investigation and enforcement in relation to domestic and Community infringements. These include powers:

(a) to require any person (not just the target of the investigation) to provide information[379] (and to make an application to court for enforcement of notice requesting such information, where the recipient has failed to comply[380]);

(b) in relation to a person the enforcer believes has engaged and/or is engaging in conduct which constitutes an infringement, and/or is likely to engage in conduct which constitutes a Community infringement:

(i)   to accept undertakings not to continue or repeat the conduct, not to engage in such conduct in the course of his business or another business, and/or not to consent to or connive in the carrying out of such conduct by a body corporate with which he has a special relationship;[381]

---

[374] Ibid per Lord Drummond Young, paras 13 to 14. In the case itself, the contractual breaches were sufficiently extensive and sufficiently serious to enable the court to infer that there was indeed harm to the section of the public likely to buy the defendant's products.

[375] [2009] EWCA Civ 34.

[376] Ibid per Lord Justice Arden, paras 44–46.

[377] See para 3.8 of the OFT's Guidance on Part 8 'Enforcement of Consumer Protection Legislation' OFT 512 June 2003, <http://www.oft.gov.uk/shared_oft/business_leaflets/enterprise_act/oft512.pdf> (accessed 3 August 2011).

[378] EA 2002, s 213 distinguishes between three categories of enforcers: general enforcers such as the OFT; designated enforcers, ie independent UK public bodies and private consumer organizations that have as one of their purposes the protection of the collective interests of consumers and are vested with enforcement powers by order of the Secretary of State; and Community enforcers, ie entities from other EEA states listed in the Official Journal of the European Communities pursuant to Injunctions Directive, Art 4(3).

[379] EA 2002, ss 224 (OFT) and 225 (other enforcers).

[380] Ibid s 227.

[381] Ibid s 219, under EA 2002, s 222(3), a person has a special relationship with a body corporate if he is a controller of the body corporate, or a director, manager, secretary, or other similar officer of the body corporate or a person purporting to act in such a capacity. Undertakings are usually given in lieu of court

   (ii)   to apply for an enforcement order[382] (which will be granted if the court finds that the person has engaged in conduct which constitutes the infringement and/or that the person named in the application is likely to engage in conduct which constitutes a Community infringement[383]); and/or

   (iii) to make an application for an interim enforcement order (which will be granted if: an application for an enforcement order would be likely to be granted; it is expedient that the conduct is prohibited or prevented (as the case may be) immediately; and where no notice has been given to the alleged infringer, it is appropriate to make an interim enforcement order without notice).[384]

In relation to enforcement orders, Part 8 revoked and replaced the Stop Now Orders (EC Directive) Regulations 2001[385] and the Fair Trading Act 1973, Part III, and implemented the Injunctions Directive. An application for an enforcement order can only be made after the enforcer has engaged in appropriate consultation[386] with the person against whom the enforcement order is sought (and the OFT, if it is not the enforcer[387]) and generally constitutes the culmination of the enforcer's investigative and enforcement proceedings against an alleged infringer.

An enforcement order will indicate the nature of the conduct concerned and direct the person not to continue or repeat the conduct (other than where the infringer is alleged only to be likely to engage in conduct which constitutes a Community infringement), not to engage in such conduct in the course of his business or another business, and not to consent or connive in the carrying out of such conduct by a body corporate with which he has a special relationship.[388] An enforcement order may also require the subject of the order to publish (in a form and manner and to the extent that the court thinks appropriate) the order itself and/or a corrective statement.[389]

---

proceedings and, if complied with, court action is usually not pursued. However, if undertakings are given but not complied with, the next step for the enforcer is usually to commence court proceedings.

[382] EA 2002, s 215. General enforcers may make applications for any infringement; designated enforcers only for infringements to which their designation relates; and Community enforcers only in relation to Community infringements.

[383] EA 2002, s 217.

[384] Ibid s 218.

[385] SI 2001/1422. EA 2002, Pt 8 extended the scope of the Stop Now Orders enforcement regime to include a wider range of domestic consumer protection legislation.

[386] EA 2002, s 212(2). See further Enterprise Act 2002 (Part 8 Request for Consultation) Order 2003 (SI 2003/1375).

[387] EA 2002, s 214.

[388] EA 2002, s 217(5)–(7), under EA 2002, s 222(3) a person has a special relationship with a body corporate if he is (a) a controller of the body corporate, or (b) a director, manager, secretary, or other similar officer of the body corporate or a person purporting to act in such a capacity.

[389] EA 2002, s 217(8).

Where the court could make an enforcement order, it can instead accept an equivalent undertaking by the person concerned not to continue or repeat the conduct, not to engage in such conduct in the course of his business or another business, and/or not to consent to or connive in the carrying out of such conduct by a body corporate with which he has a special relationship or to take steps which the court believes will secure that he does not do so (which may also include a further undertaking to publish the terms of the undertaking and/or a corrective statement[390]).

Where a court has made an enforcement order or an interim enforcement order, or has accepted an undertaking, the OFT has the same right as the enforcer that made the application for the order (if this was not the OFT) to apply to the court in relation to a failure to comply.[391] An application concerning failure to comply with an undertaking may include an application for an enforcement order or an interim enforcement order. If the court finds that the undertaking is not being complied with, it may make an enforcement order or interim enforcement order instead of making any other order within its power,[392] for example that the defendant is in contempt of court, in which case the court can impose a fine and/or, if the defendant is an individual, a term of imprisonment of up to two years. If another enforcer makes an application concerning failure to comply,[393] it must notify the OFT of the application and any subsequent order.

In relation to bodies corporate,[394] if the conduct takes place with the consent or connivance of a person, an accessory, who has a special relationship with the body corporate, that consent or connivance is also conduct that constitutes the infringement. An enforcement order or interim enforcement order can be made against an accessory whether or not such an order is made against the body corporate, and a court or enforcer may accept an undertaking from an accessory whether or not it accepts such an undertaking from the body corporate. Furthermore, if an enforcement order or interim enforcement order is made against a body corporate which at the time the order is made is a member of a group of interconnected bodies corporate, or at any time after the order is in force becomes a member of such a group or such a group of which the body corporate is a member is increased by the addition of further members, the court may direct that the order is binding upon all the members of the group as if each of them were the body corporate against which the order was made.

The OFT, other general enforcers, and designated enforcers which are public bodies have the power to take proceedings for the cessation or prohibition of Community infringements against traders based in other EEA countries, either

---

[390] EA 2002, s 217(9)–(11).
[391] Ibid s 220(2).
[392] Ibid s 220(3)–(4).
[393] Ibid s 220(6). The OFT must also be notified if a local trading standards department in England and Wales intends to start proceedings for an offence under an instrument that the Secretary of State has specified for the purposes of s 230.
[394] EA 2002, ss 222–3.

unilaterally or in cooperation with a Community enforcer in the country in question.[395]

Enforcers typically publish information about their investigations and enforcement action. For example the OFT publishes information about (some of) its current cases,[396] its completed cases,[397] and undertakings obtained and enforcement orders issued both by the OFT and local Trading Standards.[398] It is clear from these publications that the effect of Part 8 on consumer enforcement has been substantial and that undertakings given by traders are now a fairly common occurrence.

2.3.3 Direct enforcement of other legislation

In addition to the powers to enforce Community and domestic infringements under the EA 2002, regulatory authorities are also able to take enforcement action directly under certain legislation. In some cases the legislation in question gives certain regulatory authorities express powers to take enforcement action in relation to breaches of it, as well as imposing certain duties to enforce, and in others the authority has a general power to act in furtherance of its functions and it is arguable that enforcing the legislation in question would further such functions.

2.3.3.1 Express powers and duties

In addition to infringements under Part 8, which may arise from breaches of legislation such as the CPRs 2008, the DSRs 2000, and the UTCCRs 1999 and which entitle enforcers to bring civil proceedings under the EA 2002 regime, such legislation (and in some cases other legislation) also itself gives regulatory authorities express investigative and enforcement powers in relation to breaches and imposes related duties on those authorities.

---

[395] EA 2002, s 221. In December 2004, in the first ever cross-border court action taken in Europe to stop a trader in one country deceiving consumers in another, the OFT obtained a successful ruling by the Commercial Court in Brussels preventing Belgian company D Duchesne SA sending misleading mailings to UK consumers, see <http://www.oft.gov.uk/news-and-updates/press/2004/208-04> (accessed 3 August 2011). The decision was subsequently upheld by the Brussels Court of Appeal, see <http://www.oft.gov. uk/news-and-updates/press/2005/234-05> (accessed 3 August 2011). In July 2008, the OFT obtained its second ever cross-border injunction, and its first court order in the Netherlands, against the Dutch company Best Sales BV trading as Best Of and Oliveal for sending mailings, which the OFT believed were misleading, to UK consumers, see <http://www.oft.gov.uk/news-and-updates/press/2008/86-08> (accessed 3 August 2011).

[396] See <http://www.oft.gov.uk/OFTwork/consumer-enforcement/consumer-enforcement-current/> (accessed 3 August 2011).

[397] See <http://www.oft.gov.uk/OFTwork/consumer-enforcement/consumer-enforcement-completed/> (accessed 3 August 2011).

[398] See   <http://www.oft.gov.uk/OFTwork/consumer-enforcement/undertakings-court-action/> (accessed 3 August 2011). See further section 2.5 below, where several undertakings are discussed in detail in relation to specific infringements.

The BPRs 2008 and the CPRs 2008   The Business Protection from Misleading Marketing Regulations 2008 ('BPRs 2008'), which replaced large parts of the Control of Misleading Advertisements Regulations 1988,[399] prohibit businesses from advertising products in a way that misleads traders (as well as setting out conditions under which comparative advertising, to consumers and business, is permitted). Although a detailed discussion of the BPRs 2008 is outside the scope of this chapter (as they relate to relationships between businesses, rather than between businesses and consumers), they are mentioned here as one example of legislation giving direct enforcement powers.

In addition to breach of the CPRs 2008 being potentially a Community infringement,[400] the CPRs 2008 and the BPRs 2008 create a number of criminal offences[401] and give enforcers, primarily the OFT, various investigation and enforcement powers, several of which are similar to their powers under Part 8.

In addition, the CPRs 2008 and the BPRs 2008 contain almost identical provisions placing enforcement authorities[402] under a duty to enforce them.[403] In determining how to comply with their enforcement duties, each enforcement authority is obliged to have regard to the desirability of encouraging control, by such established means as it considers appropriate having regard to all the circumstances of the particular case, of:

(a) unfair commercial practices (in the case of the CPRs 2008);[404] and

(b) advertising which is misleading[405] and comparative advertising which is not permitted[406] (in the case of the BPRs 2008).[407]

The DSRs 2000 and UTCCRs 1999   While there are no criminal offences under the UTCCRs 1999, in addition to being potentially a Community infringement under Part 8, the UTCCRs 1999 also give the OFT and any 'qualifying body'[408]

---

[399] And which were repealed by the CPRs 2008.

[400] But, notably, a breach of the BPRs 2008 is not a Community infringement (as the concern advertisements by traders to other traders, rather than to consumers).

[401] As a consequence of which a breach of the CPRs 2008 is capable of being both a (civil) Community infringement under Pt 8 and a criminal offence under the CPRs 2008 themselves.

[402] The definition of 'enforcement authority' is identical for both the BPRs 2008 and the CPRs 2008, namely: 'the OFT, every local weights and measures authority in Great Britain (within the meaning of section 69 of the Weights and Measure Act 1985) and', reg 2(1), CPRs 2008 and reg 2(1), BPRs 2008. The OFT is under a general duty to enforce the relevant regulations, while each local weights and measures authority is under a duty to enforce in its area and the Department of Enterprise, Trade and Investment in Northern Ireland is under a duty to enforce in Northern Ireland.

[403] See BPRs 2008, reg 13 and CPRs 2008, reg 19.

[404] See reg 19(4).

[405] Under BPRs 2008, reg 3.

[406] Ibid reg 4.

[407] See ibid reg 13(4).

[408] Under UTCCRs 1999, reg 3(1) and Sch 1: The Information Commissioner; The Gas and Electricity Markets Authority; The Director General of Electricity Supply for Northern Ireland; The Director General of Gas for Northern Ireland; The Office of Communications; The Water Services Regulation

a direct right[409] to apply for an injunction,[410] including an interim injunction, against persons who appear to be using or recommending the use of terms, in general contracts with consumers, which are unfair under the UTCCRs 1999. Further, the UTCCRs 1999 clearly envisage that undertakings will be given to the OFT and qualifying bodies (in relation to the continued use of unfair terms in consumers contracts)[411] as several regulations refer to the possibility of such undertakings.[412] Finally, the OFT and qualifying bodies are empowered to require the production of standard contracts, and information about their use, to facilitate the investigation of complaints and compliance with undertakings or court orders.[413]

While there are similarly no criminal offences under the DSRs 2000, in addition to being potentially a Community infringement under Part 8, the DSRs 2000 also give the OFT and any other 'enforcement authority'[414] a direct right[415] to apply for an injunction (including an interim injunction) against any person who appears to be responsible for a breach,[416] by following a similar procedure to the EA 2002.[417] Further, while there is no explicit right to seek undertakings under the DSRs 2000, they too (like the UTCCRs 1999) envisage that undertakings will be given to

---

Authority; The Office of Rail Regulation; every weights and measures authority in Great Britain; The Department of Enterprise, Trade and Investment in Northern Ireland; and The Financial Services Authority. Qualifying bodies are obliged, under UTCCRs 1999, reg 12(2), to notify the OFT if they apply for an injunction.

[409] Under UTCCRs 1999 reg 12.

[410] Or, in Scotland, an interdict.

[411] See, eg, the undertaking given by the On-Line Partnership Ltd to the FSA, published on 22 January 2009, <http://www.fsa.gov.uk/pubs/other/undertaking_online.pdf> (accessed 12 March 2011). Also, as breach of the UTCCRs 1999 is capable of being a Community infringement under Pt 8, the OFT can seek undertakings in respect of such a Community infringement under via Pt 8 (providing the additional requirements for such an infringement are met).

[412] UTCCRs 1999, reg 10(3) gives the OFT the option, 'if it considers it appropriate to do so' to 'have regard to any undertakings given to it by or on behalf of any person as to the continued use of [an unfair] term in contracts concluded with consumers', when deciding whether to apply for an injunction; regs 13(1) and 13(2) allow the OFT and qualifying bodies to exercise powers to obtain documents and information for the purpose of (amongst other things) ascertaining whether a person has complied with an undertaking; reg 14(a) requires qualifying bodies to notify the OFT of any undertaking given to them and of the terms of any undertaking given to the court; reg 15(1) requires the OFT to publish any undertakings given to it and notified to it by qualifying bodies; reg 15(2) requires the OFT to inform any person on request whether a particular term to which the UTCCRs 1999 apply has been the subject of an undertaking given or notified to the OFT (and give them details of such undertaking, together with a copy of any amendments which the person giving the undertaking has agreed to make to the term in question).

[413] UTCCRs 1999, reg 13.

[414] Under DSRs 2000, reg 3(1), 'enforcement authority' means the OFT, every weights and measures authority in Great Britain, and the Department of Enterprise, Trade and Investment in Northern Ireland. Other enforcement authorities have to notify the OFT of their intention to apply for an injunction, reg 27(2), as well as about any undertakings and orders that they have obtained, reg 28.

[415] Under DSRs 2000, reg 21.

[416] Where, under DSRs 2000, reg 3(1), 'breach' means contravention by a supplier of a prohibition in, or failure to comply with a requirement of, the DSRs 2000 and 'supplier' means any person who, in contracts to which the DSRs 2000 apply, is acting in his commercial or professional capacity.

[417] Of course the EA 2002 has further requirements, see section 2.3.2 below. See further Howells and Weatherhill, n 34, 381.

enforcement authorities[418] as regulation 26(4) provides that enforcement authorities may, if they consider it appropriate to do so, have regard to any undertaking given to them by or on behalf of any person as to compliance with the DSRs 2000.

In addition, the UTCCRs 1999 and the DSRs 2000 contain similar provisions placing the OFT and qualifying bodies[419] (in the case of the UTCCRs 1999) and enforcement authorities (in the case of the DSRs 2000) under a duty to consider any complaints made to them about breaches unless the complaint appears to be frivolous or vexatious or the complaint is already being considered by: a qualifying body (in the case of the UTCCRs 1999); or another enforcement authority (in the case of the DSRs 2000).[420] Both provisions also include an obligation to give reasons for a decision to apply or not to apply, as the case may be, for an injunction, in relation to any such complaint.[421]

Finally, both the UTCCRs 1999 and the DSRs 2000 allow enforcers to make available to the public not just relevant advice and information, but also undertakings and court applications and orders themselves.[422]

2.3.3.2 Implied powers

Where a regulatory authority has a general power to act (eg in furtherance of its functions) it is arguable that enforcing certain legislation would further such functions and therefore the regulatory authority has the power to enforce such legislation (even if the legislation does not confer express powers on the regulatory authority and is not covered by, eg, Part 8).

For example, paragraph 13 of Schedule 1[423] to the EA 2002 provides that: 'The OFT has power to do anything which is calculated to facilitate, or is conducive or incidental to, the performance of its functions'. 'Anything' would include commencing proceedings but such proceedings would have to be connected (however incidentally) to the OFT's functions. The OFT's general functions are set out in sections 5–8 of the EA 2002 and include the function of: 'promoting good practice in the carrying out of activities which may affect the economic interests of consumers in the United Kingdom'.[424] Therefore, for the purposes of this example, it is arguable that the OFT could commence proceedings under legislation which did not confer

---

[418] In any event, as breach of the DSRs 2000 is capable of being a Community infringement under Pt 8, the OFT can seek undertakings in respect of such a Community infringement via Pt 8.

[419] If such qualifying body has notified the OFT that it agrees to consider such a complaint, see UTCCRs 1999, reg 11(1).

[420] See UTCCRs 1999, regs 10 and 11 and DSRs 2000, reg 26.

[421] See UTCCRs 1999, reg 10(3) and DSRs 2000, reg 26(3). In addition, OFT guidance provides (in relation to the UTCCRs) that those with a legitimate interest in the outcome of a complaint are entitled to be given reasons for decisions by the OFT as to whether an injunction against the use of a term will or will not be sought and that suppliers are given an explanation as to why a particular challenged term is considered potentially unfair. OFT 143, n 160, p 5.

[422] DSRs 2000, reg 29 and UTCCRs 1999, reg 15.

[423] Sch 1 is given effect by EA 2002, s 1(3).

[424] EA 2002, s 8(1).

express powers for it do so and was not covered by Part 8, where commencing such proceedings was linked to promoting good practice in activities which may affect UK consumers' economic interests.[425]

Examples in the online context might be the Computer Misuse Act 1990 and the Fraud Act 2006. It is easy to envisage scenarios where proceedings by the OFT for offences under either of those statutes would promote (or at least be linked to the promotion of) 'good practice in activities which may affect UK consumers' economic interests'.[426]

2.3.4 Financial penalties

Typically, breach of consumer protection legislation invites injunctive-style remedies (which seek to prevent further breaches) and, in some cases, criminal prosecution, rather than monetary fines.[427] However, the Regulatory Enforcement and Sanctions Act 2008 has paved the way for regulatory authorities to be granted new powers to impose fixed and variable monetary penalties of up to £500,000 as an alternative to criminal prosecution.[428] At the time of writing a pilot scheme is being implemented which will give the OFT powers to impose such penalties in relation to breaches of the CPRs 2008. Although the enforcement authority must consider beyond a reasonable doubt that the offence in question has been committed, the powers will avoid recourse to the court system and therefore are likely to have a significant impact on consumer enforcement. Other potential sanctions include enforcement undertakings, which may include action that the trader will take to restore the position to what it would have been had the offence not been committed, and action that the trader will take to benefit those affected by the offence, which can include compensation payments.

---

[425] There is case law to support such an argument, eg, in *R v Security Industry Authority, ex p Securiplan plc* [2008] EWHC 1762 (Admin), the Divisional Court rejected the claimant's contention that the Security Industry Authority had no power to prosecute for the offence of using unlicensed security operatives under the Private Security Industry Act 2001, s 5, because the statute was silent on the question of prosecution, on the grounds that 'a consistent legislative practice [has not been established] to grant overt and unambiguous powers of prosecution to a regulator whenever this was intended', per Blake J (at para 32).

[426] The Computer Misuse Act 1990 and the Fraud Act 2008 are particularly pertinent to the OFT as the 1997–2010 Labour Government was considering whether expressly to empower the OFT to prosecute online offences under these two statutes, see para 3.3.5 of Government White Paper (Command Paper 7669) 'A Better Deal for Consumers—Delivering Real Help Now and Change for the Future', published July 2009 and available at <http://www.bis.gov.uk/files/file52072.pdf> (accessed 12 March 2011).

[427] Although it is worth noting that breach of an enforcement order can constitute contempt of court which is punishable by an unlimited fine (or imprisonment of up to two years) and that persons found guilty of breaches that constitute criminal offences are liable to fines (see, eg, CPRs 2008, reg 13).

[428] The fines are intended to ensure that, where businesses have saved costs through non-compliance, they do not gain an unfair advantage over those businesses which have complied.

2.3.5 Regulation on consumer protection cooperation

The CPCR 2004[429] coordinates consumer enforcement policy at the European level.[430] It is intended to enable individual Member States to enforce consumer protection legislation against traders targeting consumers in their Member State, but located in another Member State, by establishing a framework and general conditions for cooperation between Member States under which authorities can call on other members of the network for assistance in investigating possible breaches of consumer laws.[431] The CPCR 2004 does not contain any new substantive consumer protection measures, but rather seeks to improve the effectiveness of and protection offered by existing measures across Europe.

Like EA 2002 Part 8, the CPCR 2004 is intended to protect the collective interest of consumers, and therefore refers to 'the interests of a number of consumers that have been harmed or are likely to be harmed by an infringement',[432] rather than to individual consumers. The CPCR 2004 is also intended to strengthen consumer and business confidence in cross-border trading, by enhancing the intra-Community enforcement structure.[433] It provides an enhanced role for the European Commission in the facilitation of administrative cooperation and common projects aiming at the information, education, and empowerment of consumers.

The CPCR 2004 created a formal pan-European network of competent authorities[434] with similar investigation and enforcement powers, which, while designed not to cut across existing cooperation networks or practices,[435] is empowered to cooperate and share information for the purpose of enforcing specific European laws. A competent authority is defined as 'any public authority established either at national, regional or local level with specific responsibilities to enforce the laws that protect consumers' interests'.[436] These laws consist of 'the Directives as transposed into the internal legal order of the Member States and the Regulations listed in the Annex'

---

[429] Regulation (EC) No 2006/2004.

[430] For information about the UK's implementation of the CPCR 2004, see the DTI Consultation document, 'Implementing the EU Regulation on Consumer Protection Co-operation: Consultation', URN 05/1361, 5 July 2005 <http://www.bis.gov.uk/files/file15246.pdf> (accessed 3 August 2011).

[431] eg, unfair practices should be dealt with (under the UCPD 2005) by enforcers in the jurisdiction where the trader responsible for the practice is situated. The CPCR 2004 allows Member States to share information and to request enforcement action to be taken to stop breaches of the legislation implementing the UCPD 2005 (eg, the CPRs 2008 in the UK) and other Community consumer protection rules, see para 11.23 of the OFT's Guidance 'Consumer Protection from Unfair Trading—Guidance on the UK Regulations (May 2008) Implementing the Unfair Commercial Practices Directive' OFT 1008, <http://www.oft.gov.uk/shared_oft/business_leaflets/cpregs/oft1008.pdf> (accessed 3 August 2011).

[432] CPCR 2004, Art 3(k).

[433] Ibid recitals 2–3 and 6–8.

[434] Ibid Art 4.

[435] Ibid Art 2(2)–(7).

[436] Ibid Art 3(c).

to the CPCR 2004[437] and include: the UTCCD;[438] the Distance Selling Directive;[439] the Sale of Goods and Associated Guarantees Directive;[440] and the UCPD 2005.

There are no restrictions on the number of competent authorities in a Member State. The CPCR 2004 also requires Member States to designate a single liaison office, which is responsible for coordinating the application of the CPCR 2004 within each Member State.[441] In the UK, the OFT is both the single liaison office[442] and the OFT and three sectoral regulators[443] are the UK's competent authority, together with three other competent authorities.[444]

Each competent authority must have the investigation and enforcement powers necessary to fulfil its obligations under the CPCR 2004 and must exercise those powers in conformity with national law.[445] Those powers may be exercised either directly under its own authority or under the supervision of the judicial authorities,[446] or by application to competent courts to grant the necessary decision.[447] The powers may be exercised where there is reasonable suspicion of an intra-Community infringement and include the right to have access to any document; to require relevant information from any person; to carry out on-site inspections; to request in writing the cessation of infringement; to obtain undertakings as to the cessation of infringement and to publish the undertakings; to require the cessation or prohibition of infringements and to publish resulting decisions; and to require losing defendants to make payments to the public purse or any designated beneficiary in the event of failure to comply with the decision.[448]

The CPCR 2004, Chapter II sets out provisions for mutual assistance between Member States, such as: the exchange of information among competent authorities on or without request;[449] the coordination of market surveillance and enforcement activities;[450] and requests for enforcement measures from one authority to another (in which case the requested authority must take all necessary measures to bring about the cessation or prohibition of the intra-Community infringement

---

[437] CPCR 2004, Art 3(a),
[438] Directive 93/13/EEC.
[439] Directive 2002/65/EC.
[440] Directive 1999/44/EC.
[441] CPCR 2004, Arts 3(d) and 4(1).
[442] See <http://www.oft.gov.uk/news-and-updates/press/2006/07-06> (accessed 3 August 2011).
[443] The Civil Aviation Authority, the Medicines and Healthcare products Regulatory Agency, and the Ministry of Trade and Industry (Gibraltar).
[444] See <http://www.bis.gov.uk/files/file33886.pdf> (accessed 3 August 2011).
[445] CPCR 2004, Art 4(3).
[446] Ibid Art 4(4)(a).
[447] Ibid Art 4(4)(b).
[448] Ibid Art 4(6).
[449] Ibid Arts 6 and 7.
[450] Ibid Art 9.

without delay).[451] The CPCR 2004, Chapter III[452] sets out the conditions governing such mutual assistance. The European Commission maintains an electronic database, in which the information it receives in relation to exchanges of information, requests for enforcement, and coordinated market surveillance and enforcement activities will be stored and processed.[453]

Finally, the CPCR 2004[454] acknowledges the essential role of consumer organizations in terms of consumer information and education and in the protection of consumer interests, including in the settlement of disputes, and the importance of Member States encouraging such organizations to cooperate with competent authorities to enhance the application of the CPCR 2004.[455]

2.4 INTERVENTION BY OTHER INTERESTED/ AFFECTED PARTIES

The enforcement powers described in section 2.3 do not give enforcers the ability to take action on behalf of individual consumers (or to give advice to individual consumers about the best way to seek compensation or other redress in private disputes).[456] This section considers options for direct representation of affected consumers by specific bodies.

2.4.1 Super-complaints

The EA 2002, section 11 introduced super-complaints and allows complaints to be submitted to the OFT by consumer bodies, representing consumers, which have been designated by the Secretary of State,[457] concerning a goods or services market feature, or a combination of market features, such as the structure of a market or the

---

[451] Ibid Art 8(1), although, under Art 8(3), the requested authority can fulfil its obligations by instructing a body designated in accordance with the second sentence of Art 4(2) as having a legitimate interest in the cessation or prohibition of intra-Community infringements to take all necessary enforcement measures available to it under national law to bring about the cessation or prohibition of the intra-Community infringement on behalf of the requested authority. The UK has designated PhonePayPlus (formerly ICSTIS), the regulator of premium rate telephone numbers in the UK.

[452] CPCR 2004, Arts 11–15.

[453] Ibid Art 10.

[454] At recital 14.

[455] For more information on the CPCR 2004, see <http://ec.europa.eu/consumers/prot_rules/admin_coop/index_en.htm> (accessed 4 August 2011) and <http://europa.eu/legislation_summaries/consumers/protection_of_consumers/l32047_en.htm> (accessed 12 March 2011).

[456] See, eg, OFT 143, n 160, p 5.

[457] Current designated bodies include: the Campaign for Real Ale Ltd; the Consumer Council for Water; the Consumers' Association (trading as 'Which?'); the General Consumer Council for Northern Ireland; the National Association of Citizens Advice Bureaux; the National Consumer Council (trading as 'Consumer Focus'); and the Scottish Association of Citizens Advice Bureaux ('trading as Citizens Advice Scotland').

conduct of those operating within it, that is or appears to be significantly harming the interests of consumers. The OFT considers the evidence submitted and undertakes whatever work is necessary to establish the extent, if any, of the alleged problems. It must then publish a response within 90 days from the day after which the super-complaint was received stating what action, if any, it proposes to take in response to the complaint and giving the reasons behind its decision,[458] accompanied by remedies, if possible within the 90-day period, or proposals for further work in more complex cases.

Possible action by the OFT following a super-complaint includes: improving the quality and accessibility of information for consumers; encouraging businesses in the market to self-regulate; making recommendations to government to change regulations or public policy; taking competition or consumer enforcement action; making a market investigation reference to the Competition Commission; or a clean bill of health.[459]

2.4.2 Collective actions

In 2006, the DTI undertook a consultation concerning the possible introduction of representative actions undertaken by appropriate interested bodies that would represent groups of consumers in recovering damages for similar individual losses caused by the same company.[460] Despite the support of a number of consumer organizations, the consultation concluded that there was a lack of clear evidence for introducing representative actions. Therefore the government commissioned further research,[461] which suggested that a gap exists between successful enforcement action and adequate consumer compensation and proposed, as one solution, an independent publicly funded figure to bring representative actions (alongside the delivery compensation though public enforcement).

The government has subsequently consulted on the role of a 'Consumer Advocate'. It is proposed that the Consumer Advocate would have powers: to take collective actions on behalf of consumers to obtain compensation (when other routes have failed); to facilitate the return of funds that have been identified as belonging to or due to UK consumers which have been secured by overseas enforcement agencies; and to tackle unfairness in consumer credit agreements.[462]

---

[458] See EA 2002, s 11(2) and (3).

[459] For further information on super-complaints, see <http://www.oft.gov.uk/OFTwork/markets-work/super-complaints/> (accessed 8 August 2011).

[460] See <http://www.berr.gov.uk/consultations/page30259.html> (accessed 8 August 2011).

[461] From the Lincoln Law School, see <http://www.berr.gov.uk/files/file51559.pdf> (accessed 8 August 2011).

[462] <http://www.bis.gov.uk/Consultations/role-powers-consumer-advocate?cat=closedawaiting response> (accessed 8 August 2011).

2.5 COMMON TERMS AND KEY ISSUES IN MASS MARKET CONTRACTING

We now turn to an examination of a number of categories of contractual term often found in consumer contracts and the key issues that typically arise in actual regulatory practice in relation to such terms.

2.5.1 Pre-contractual representations and statements

2.5.1.1 Statements in advertising, brochures, and on websites
The CPRs 2008 provide a detailed regime prohibiting unfair commercial practices which are misleading actions or omissions[463] and which are largely concerned with advertisements and other pre-contractual information given to consumers. For example:

(a) a commercial practice will (providing other conditions are satisfied[464]) be a misleading action if (amongst other things), it 'concerns any marketing of a product (including comparative advertising) which creates confusion with any products, trade marks, trade names or other distinguishing marks of a competitor';[465]

(b) a commercial practice will (providing other conditions are satisfied[466]) be a misleading omission if, in its factual context, taking account of certain matters,[467] it (amongst other things) omits, hides, or provides in a manner which is unintelligible, ambiguous, or untimely, material information[468] (where certain specific information, in addition to any other information which is within the definition of material

---

[463] CPRs 2008, regs 3(1), 3(4)(a), 3(4)(b), 5, and 6.

[464] Namely that the commercial practice 'causes or is likely to cause the average consumer to take a transactional decision he would not have taken otherwise, taking account of its factual context and of all its features and circumstances', CPRs 2008, reg 5(3).

[465] Ibid reg 5(3)(a).

[466] Namely that it 'causes or is likely to cause the average consumer to take a transactional decision he would not have taken otherwise', ibid reg 6(1).

[467] Namely: all the features and circumstances of the commercial practice; the limitations of the medium used to communicate the commercial practice (including limitations of space or time); and where the medium used to communicate the commercial practice imposes limitations of space or time, any measures taken by the trader to make the information available to consumers by other means, ibid reg 6(2).

[468] Ibid regs 6(1)(a), 6(1)(b), and 6(1)(c). 'Material information' means: the information which the average consumer needs, according to the context, to take an informed transactional decision; and, notably, any information requirement which applies in relation to a commercial communication as a result of a Community obligation, which, information required 'under other Community law provisions', see para 7.3.3 and examples at para 7.34 of the OFT's Guidance 'Consumer Protection from Unfair Trading—Guidance on the UK Regulations (May 2008) implementing the Unfair Commercial Practices Directive' OFT 1008, <http://www.oft.gov.uk/shared_oft/business_leaflets/cpregs/oft1008.pdf> (accessed 8 August 2011). This means that a trader's failure to provide information required by Community law, such the e-Commerce Directive and the Distance Selling Directive, will, in addition to breaching the Community

information, will be material—if not already apparent from the context) in relation to commercial practices which are invitations to purchase;[469] and

(c) Schedule 1 to the CPRs 2008 (which is a list of commercial practices which will in all circumstances[470] be considered unfair) includes a number of commercial practices which are forms of advertising, such as bait advertising, bait and switch advertising, and advertorials.[471]

In addition, public statements concerning the specific characteristics of a product, especially in advertising or on labelling, may form part of the contract.[472] This is true for both statements made by the supplier and for statements made by the manufacturer, in the latter case if the supplier could reasonably have been aware of the manufacturer's statements at the time of conclusion of the contract. According to the OFT, where the terms of the supplier exclude liability for public statements, such as descriptions in sales literature and price list details, there exists a clear risk of unfairness.[473] In addition, advertisers should take care to ensure that advertisements comply with applicable advertising codes. For example, the CAP (Non-broadcast) Code[474] applies to non-broadcast internet advertising.[475]

---

law in question, also constitute a misleading omission under (and therefore be capable of constituting a breach of) the CPRs 2008. See also section 2.2.1.4.

[469] CPRs 2008, reg 6(4). It is submitted that an 'invitation to purchase' would cover most forms of advertising, although it is worth noting that the concept is not the same as the UK contract law concept of 'invitation to treat'. For more information about invitations to purchase, see paras 7.20–7.34 of the OFT's Guidance 'Consumer Protection from Unfair Trading—Guidance on the UK Regulations (May 2008) implementing the Unfair Commercial Practices Directive' OFT 1008, <http://www.oft.gov.uk/shared_oft/business_leaflets/cpregs/oft1008.pdf> (accessed 8 August 2011).

[470] ie, without evidence of an effect on the averages consumer's transactional decision.

[471] See nn 231–233 and accompanying text. For further information about the Schedule 1 'Banned Practices', see Ch 6 of the OFT's Guidance 'Consumer Protection from Unfair Trading—Guidance on the UK Regulations (May 2008) implementing the Unfair Commercial Practices Directive' OFT 1008, <http://www.oft.gov.uk/shared_oft/business_leaflets/cpregs/oft1008.pdf> (accessed 8 August 2011).

[472] See section 2.2.1.1 above on the SGA 1979 and the SSGCRs 2002.

[473] See para 3.5 of OFT 672.

[474] The 12th edition of the UK Code of Non-Broadcast Advertising, Sales Promotion and Direct Marketing (CAP Code), which came into force on 1 September 2010, <http://www.cap.org.uk/The-Codes/CAP-Code.aspx> (accessed 8 August 2011).

[475] The CAP Code applies to (amongst other things): advertisements in emails, text transmissions (including SMS and MMS), and other electronic material; advertisements in non-broadcast electronic media such as online advertisements in paid-for space (including banner or pop-up advertisements and online video advertisements), paid-for search listings, preferential listings on price-comparison sites, viral advertisements, advertisements transmitted by Bluetooth, advertisements distributed through web widgets and online sales promotions and prize promotions; and advertisements and other marketing communications by or from companies, organizations, or sole traders on their own websites, or in other non-paid-for space online under their control, that are directly connected with the supply or transfer of goods, services, opportunities, and gifts, or which consist of direct solicitations of donations as part of their own fund-raising activities.

2.5.1.2 *Oral representations and statements*

Although it is always advisable to include, in the written contract, all representations and statements made during negotiations, which help to secure the agreement, in practice such representations and statements are often made orally by the supplier or the supplier's representative to the consumer, but not included in the written document itself. However, this does not necessarily prevent the parties being bound by such representations and statements and standard terms (however drafted[476]) which purport to exclude from the contract, and therefore the supplier's liability for, such representations and statements, are likely to be unenforceable.

Schedule 2 to the UTCCRs 1999 includes terms which have the object or effect of 'limiting the seller's or supplier's obligation to respect commitments undertaken by his agents or making his commitments subject to compliance with a particular formality'.[477]

Therefore contractual terms which attempt to limit the supplier's liability for oral representations and statements (whether made by the supplier or by the supplier's agents) are potentially unfair. The OFT considers this is especially likely where such terms:

(a) say that all terms and conditions are contained in the written contract and that these replace oral statements or representations;

(b) only allow changes to be made in writing;

(c) require that consumer changes have to be approved by a director of the company;

(d) state that no employee has authority to change terms of the contract; or

(e) exclude the supplier's liability for any promises made that are not written in the contract.[478]

---

[476] There are several types of wording which have the same effect, such as clauses providing: that employees or agents have no authority to make binding statements or amendments to the contract; that contract changes may only be made in writing; or that they must be signed by a director. See Group 14(a), pp 61–2, (a), pp 95–9 of OFT 311.

[477] UTCCRs 1999, Sch 2 para 1(n).

[478] See paras 3.6 and 3.7 of OFT 672.

The following are examples from cases where the OFT had objections under the UTCCRs 1999 with terms limiting liability for oral statements, on the grounds of potential unfairness under paragraph 1(n) of Schedule 2 to the UTCCRs 1999:

Original term[479]	New term/Other result[480]
The placing of the order with the company will be deemed to bind the customer to the following terms and conditions and no oral representation shall bind the company. Any variation or alteration in the following terms and conditions shall only be binding upon the company if made in writing and signed by a director of the company.	To protect your own interests please read the conditions carefully before signing them. . . . If you are uncertain as to your rights under them or you want any explanation about them please write to or telephone our customer queries department, at the address and telephone number set out above.
Vacation 2000 (Holiday Club Anglian) Limited takes no responsibility for any verbal claims, or other offers made in conjunction with this offer by its distributors, agents which are not included in this promotion.	Vacation 2000 accepts responsibility under these Terms and Conditions for its commitments to you. It also accepts responsibility by its duly authorised agents.
All the terms of the Contract between the Company and the Customer are contained in the Contract and in these conditions and no oral or written arrangements between the Customer and any agent or representative of the company not contained in the Contract shall be in any way binding upon the Company.	The Company intends to rely upon the written terms set out here and on the other side of this document. If you require any changes, please make sure you ask for these to be put in writing. In that way, we can avoid any problems surrounding what the Company and you the Customer is expected to do.
The agreement is the entire agreement between the parties and supersedes all prior understandings and representations of the parties.	Neither Calortex nor you may alter the terms of this agreement . . . without the agreement of the other.
The following terms and conditions alone are the basis of the contract.	Term deleted.

---

[479] In this and the remainder of the tables in section 2.5, 'Original term' represents the term with which the OFT had concerns and 'New term/Other result' represents the replacement term or other result obtained by the OFT.

[480] See para 3.7 of OFT 672, and Group 14(a), pp 95–9, of the Annexes to OFT 311.

An example of a trader from which the OFT obtained an undertaking (in relation to an exclusion of liability for oral representations that had not been confirmed in writing) is Dell Corp Ltd whose standard terms included a provision that 'any variations to this Agreement must be confirmed by Dell in writing. Any other Terms and Conditions are excluded.' The OFT had concerns with this term in relation to paragraph 1(n) of Schedule 2 to the UTCCRs 1999 (as well as having concerns with several other provisions of Dell's standard terms). As a result, Dell agreed to revise the term to provide that variations to the terms must be documented in the contract in writing, and gave a corresponding undertaking.[481]

The OFT observes that there is no objection to wording which warns the consumer that the law favours written terms,[482] so long as it does not undermine the court's power to consider other statements where necessary. Such a warning can, in fact, strengthen the effect of written terms, provided consumers are genuinely likely to see it and understand and act on it.[483]

2.5.1.3 Provision of pre-contractual information by the supplier[484]

As discussed above,[485] prior to the conclusion of the contract the supplier must make available certain information, as required by the DSRs 2000 and the eComRs 2002,[486] in a clear and comprehensible manner that is appropriate to the means of distance communication used and, where the distance communication means are electronic, in an easily and permanently available form. Because websites can be difficult to navigate, the OFT suggests[487] that the best practice for suppliers to ensure that pre-contractual information is provided in a clear and comprehensible manner is to include an 'About Us' page that contains the company details and a 'Terms and Conditions' page, both with a direct link from the supplier's home page, and to provide the terms and conditions as a single printable document in order to help to ensure that customers do not overlook important terms.

---

[481] <http://www.oft.gov.uk/OFTwork/consumer-enforcement/traders/2244/1/> (accessed 8 August 2011).

[482] eg, the contract may include an explanatory statement that it is a binding document, and advising consumers to read it carefully and ensure it contains everything they want and nothing they are not prepared to agree to.

[483] See paras 14.1.6–1.4.1.7 of OFT 311.

[484] See also Chapter 4, section 4.2.3.2.

[485] See section 2.2.1.5 above.

[486] There is some overlap in the categories of information required.

[487] OFT 672, para 3.10.

2.5.2 Contract formation

2.5.2.1 Introduction

A contract is an agreement between two or more parties that will be enforced by the courts.[488] Under UK law, and for that matter under the laws of most jurisdictions,[489] a valid contract presupposes the following essential elements:

   (a) the parties must be legally capable of entering into a contract;

   (b) there must exist an offer by one of the parties;

   (c) the acceptance of the offer must be communicated by the other party;

   (d) consideration, such as the payment of money, must flow between the parties; and

   (e) the parties must intend to be legally bound.

It follows that there must be a meeting of minds between the parties, who must be aware of and accept the terms of the contract they are entering into. Therefore, to be binding on the customer, the supplier's terms must be brought to the customer's attention sufficiently before the customer enters into the contract.

In this regard, the OFT takes the view that terms that attempt to bind consumers to other terms they have not seen are open to objection.[490] The successful incorporation of the supplier's terms into the contract is subject to: the effect of any terms implied by the courts or by statute; the reasonableness of such terms under UCTA 1977 (where the terms in question are covered by UCTA 1977); and the fairness of such terms under the UTCCRs 1999 (where the terms in question are covered by the UTCCRs 1999). In addition, terms which purport to allow the supplier unilaterally to alter the contract, to the detriment of the consumer, are unlikely to be enforceable against the consumer.[491]

Terms and conditions should be clearly drafted, in plain, comprehensible, and intelligible language and be understandable to consumers without the need for legal advice and consumers must get an adequate opportunity to read them before agreeing to them. The OFT advises suppliers as far as possible to use:

   (a) ordinary words;

   (b) short sentences;

   (c) subheadings to group similar issues;

---

[488] For a detailed discussion of online contracting see Chapter 4, section 4.2.

[489] Although certain jurisdictions impose additional requirements on certain contracts, eg, formalities concerning writing.

[490] OFT 672, para 3.12.

[491] See further section 2.5.3 below.

and to avoid

(d) technical language or legal jargon, such as references to 'indemnity' or copying out legislation;

(e) extensive cross-referencing.[492]

Further, the OFT considers terms to be open to objection if they:

(a) give the supplier a right to cancel a concluded contract regardless of whether the consumer is at fault; or

(b) give the supplier discretion to change without a valid reason what is being supplied, particularly if this relates to a price or product specification.[493]

2.5.2.2 'Electronic' contract formation

Although essentially electronic contracting is governed by the ordinary rules of contract law,[494] as seen in the first part of this chapter,[495] the e-Commerce Directive (as implemented in the UK by the eComRs 2002) and the Distance Selling Directive (as implemented in the UK by the DSRs 2000) impose additional requirements including:

(a) information on commercial communications;

(b) the provision of information by the supplier (including whether the contract will be filed by the supplier or a third party except where the contract is concluded by email exchanges or other form of individual communication);

(c) the explanation by the supplier of the various technical steps that must be followed in order for the contract to be concluded (except where the contract is concluded by email exchanges or other form of individual communication);

(d) the availability of the terms and conditions of the contract in a way that they can be stored and reproduced;

(e) the description of the technical means for identifying and correcting input errors prior to the placement of the order; and

(f) the acknowledgement of orders and the time when these two communications will be effective.

---

[492] OFT 672, para 3.11.

[493] Ibid para 3.19.

[494] However, the specifics of online contracting necessitate an exploration of the online contract formation process, especially with regard to offer and acceptance and in the light of the involvement of numerous intermediaries; formal requirements of writing and signatures; the specific regulation of commercial communications and supplier information imposed by the e-Commerce Directive and the eComRs 2002; and, the impact of the online element in the determination of applicable law and jurisdiction in cross-border online contracts. These issues are examined in Chapter 4.

[495] Section 2.2.1.5 above.

Thus, three principal issues must be considered by suppliers, with a view to ensuring that their contracts are effective. First, suppliers need to structure their contracts carefully so that they create a binding contract at the appropriate time (and do not inadvertently become contractually bound earlier—or later—than they intend to or fail to bind the consumer at the appropriate time—or at all). This leads directly to the second issue, which is isolating (and making clear to the consumer) the point in time when the contract is actually concluded. Thirdly, suppliers need to employ contract mechanics that ensure that, subject to any implied terms, the supplier's express terms and conditions are effectively incorporated into the contract and are enforceable.

However, there is normally a tension between, on the one hand, the legal need to comply with applicable informational and procedural requirements (to ensure contractual certainty) and, on the other, the business imperative of creating a transactional experience for the customer that is as 'friction' free as possible. Broadly speaking, the more invasive the supplier's contracting process, the more it is likely to deter customers and encourage them to take their business to other traders with less onerous contracting processes in place. As a result, suppliers may in practice conclude that they have no option but to engage in a cost/risk/benefit analysis exercise in order to establish the approach that optimally serves their interests.

The first and second issues identified above (ie, ensuring contracts are formed at the appropriate time), essentially concern the questions of: what constitutes an offer and what constitutes an acceptance; the point in time at which they take place; and how the use of electronic communication affects the determination of these issues. These questions are addressed in more detail elsewhere in this book in to the context of online contracting.[496]

It is important to note, however, that several jurisdictions (including Australia, Canada, Germany, Sweden, the UK, and the USA) draw a fundamental distinction between an offer and an invitation to treat. While an offer is capable, if accepted, of binding the supplier, an invitation to treat is regarded as an invitation to make an offer or to engage in negotiations. In particular, in relation to online contracting, there are no reported UK cases dealing with whether the advertisement of goods or services on a website constitutes an offer or an invitation to treat, nor do the eComRs 2002 clarify the issue.[497] However, the display of goods in a shop is considered an invitation to treat.[498] It is therefore generally accepted that by analogy an advertisement on a website should also be treated as an invitation to treat.

In jurisdictions that adopt the distinction between an offer and an invitation to treat, it is vital (in the absence of any case law on this issue) for suppliers to ensure that the advertising of goods and services for sale functions as an invitation to treat,

---

[496] Chapter 4, section 4.2.

[497] e-ComRs, s 12 provides that the term 'order', as used in the eComRs 2002, will be the contractual offer in certain circumstances and in others it may be, but need not be.

[498] *Pharmaceutical Society of Great Britain v Boots Cash Chemists (Southern) Ltd* [1953] 1 QB 410.

as opposed to an offer, and that the process by which customers place an order online, functions as an offer, as opposed to acceptance of an offer by the supplier. Otherwise, suppliers may find themselves in the untenable position of being bound by contractual obligations that they cannot or are not willing to fulfil and, therefore, being potentially vulnerable to unpredictable numbers of claims for breach of contract. This risk is particularly significant in the context of online orders, because of the speed at which news about inventory or pricing errors that benefit consumers can be shared online, and the scope for very large numbers of orders to be placed on a website in a very short space of time.[499]

Suppliers can significantly reduce the likelihood and impact of such a situation by taking certain practical steps:

(a) notify customers on the website and in the online terms and conditions: that the information available on the website (concerning products for sale) does not constitute an offer to sell such products; that the customer's completion of an order constitutes an offer to buy such products; that the supplier will not be bound unless it accepts such an offer (with an explanation of how such acceptance will be communicated, eg, by confirming that the product has been dispatched[500]); and that all purchases are subject to availability;

(b) implement an effective pricing error checking mechanism (and, if appropriate, notify customers in the online terms and conditions: of the consequences of erroneous pricing (eg, that the supplier will not be bound to supply goods or

---

[499] There are numerous examples of online retailers making pricing mistakes on their websites, such as:

- Kodak, which, in 2002 misstated the price of a digital camera on its site at £100 instead of £329, and, following legal action by disgruntled customers (arguing that the company had entered into a contract from which it could not withdraw) coupled with weeks of bad publicity, ultimately honoured around 2,000 sales, see <http://www.computerweekly.com/Articles/2002/03/21/185858/What-is-an-invitation-to-treat.htm> (accessed 8 August 2011);
- Amazon, which, in March 2003, accidentally priced a handheld computer at £7.32 instead of £275, but which was able to cancel orders (although not without negative publicity), thanks to its terms and conditions, which provide that no contract is formed until it sends an email confirming it has dispatched an order, see <http://news.bbc.co.uk/1/hi/business/2864461.stm> (accessed 8 August 2011); and
- Apple, which, in January 2006, mistakenly advertised for sale digital cameras at less than one-sixth of their normal price) but, following the placement of several orders and the receipt of a confirmatory email by at least one shopper, cancelled the orders on the ground that the camera was no longer available (the question of whether legally binding contracts had been entered to had a negative answer, precisely because the advertisement was considered an invitation to treat as opposed to an offer, see C Arthur, 'Can I Buy a £600 Camera for £100?', *The Guardian*, 12 January 2006, <http://technology.guardian.co.uk/weekly/story/0,1683936,00.html> (accessed 8 August 2011)).

See also section 2.5.4 below.

[500] See, eg, Amazon.co.uk's Conditions of Use & Sale, which provide, at para 14, that 'Your order represents an offer to us to purchase a product which is accepted by us when we send e-mail confirmation to you that we've dispatched that product to you (the "Dispatch Confirmation E-mail"). That acceptance will be complete at the time we send the Dispatch Confirmation E-mail to you': <http://www.amazon.co.uk/gp/help/customer/display.html/ref=footer_cou?ie=UTF8&nodeId=1040616> (accessed 8 August 2011).

services)[501] and/or that any liability of the supplier for errors in the description or pricing of goods is limited or excluded[502]);

(c) implement an effective contract acceptance notification mechanism;

(d) ensure that the online ordering form incorporates the supplier's standard terms and conditions and that the customer is unable to purchase unless the standard terms and conditions have been accepted.

In relation to the timing of conclusion of the contract, the OFT guidance is that suppliers have a right to decide at what stage, or in what circumstances, they accept a consumer's order. However, both parties should be clear about when the contract has been entered into. Terms that effectively give the supplier discretion to decide whether the contract has been formed are vulnerable to challenge. Fairness is more likely to be achieved if there is clarity over when the parties become bound by the contract.[503]

In relation to online contracting in particular, there is a broad spectrum of approaches that range from the certainly unenforceable to the clearly enforceable. For example, methods that essentially deny the customer the ability to review the terms and conditions prior to entering the contract will be unenforceable; methods that assist the customer through the terms in a way that enables the customer to review them and express acceptance (or decline acceptance and be taken outside the transactional process) before concluding the contract are much more likely to be enforceable. Between these two models lie a countless number of variations which, depending on their proximity to either end of the spectrum, will be more or less likely to be capable of enforcement. For example:

(a) at one extreme, a website with no terms at all; the business will not be able to enforce its terms and conditions;

(b) a business which only includes its standard terms and conditions via a link at the bottom of the splash page of its website; such a model will rarely create a binding relationship between the parties;

(c) a business which provides a link on its website to its standard terms and conditions, independently, requires users to click on a separate button (in a different place from the link to the terms) to indicate that the user has understood and accepts

---

[501] Amazon.com's Conditions of Use & Sale, eg, provide, at para 16, that 'Despite our efforts, a small number of the millions of products in our catalogue are mispriced. Rest assured, however, that we verify prices as part of our dispatch procedures. If a product's correct price is lower than our stated price, we charge the lower amount and send you the product. If a product's correct price is higher than our stated price, we will, at our discretion, either contact you for instructions before dispatch or cancel your order and notify you of such cancellation': <http://www.amazon.co.uk/gp/help/customer/display.html/ref=footer_cou?ie=UTF8&nodeId=1040616> (accessed 8 August 2011).

[502] However, for the regulatory treatment of such provisions, see generally discussion below, eg, sections 2.5.3, 2.5.4, 2.5.5, and 2.5.13.

[503] OFT 672, paras 3.18 and 3.19.

the site's terms; for reasons discussed below, it is unlikely that such terms will be binding on the user.

And, further along the spectrum:

(d) a business that presents the terms and conditions on the website to the user, enabling him to scroll through them and, at the end of the terms, click one button to confirm that he has read the terms and understands and accepts them (with another button to indicate that he does not accept them and 'click-away' from the page)—this model is quite likely to produce a binding relationship with users;

(e) finally, at the other extreme, a website that fits the description immediately above, but also requires the user to confirm their acceptance by using tick boxes against any potentially onerous terms and conditions, as well as a mechanism enabling the user to click a button to confirm that he has read the terms and accepts them (with another button to indicate that he does not accept them and 'click-away' from the page), and a mechanism that records the date of acceptance and the identity of the user; this method is most likely to create an enforceable relationship with the user, though of course the enforceability of particular terms will still be subject to applicable law.

It is worth noting that the same contract principles, requirements, and issues arise in connection with mechanisms for seeking user acceptance for subsequent modifications to the terms of the terms and conditions. For example, it is common practice to state that the website operator is entitled to change the terms at any time; that it is the customer/user's responsibility to check regularly for changes; and that by continuing to use the website the customer/user accepts the new terms.[504] However, this approach to modification of a contractual agreement between the parties is rarely likely to be enforceable.

2.5.2.3 *'Shrink-wrap', 'browse-wrap', and 'click-wrap' contracts*
The incorporation of the supplier's terms and conditions is therefore a matter of contract mechanics. In most jurisdictions the terms will only be incorporated effectively, and therefore binding on the customer, if the customer actually knows, or has sufficient notice, before the point in time when the contract is concluded, that the transaction is subject to such terms and conditions. This requirement raises the question of enforceability in relation to certain online and offline contractual methods commonly employed in the context of mass market contracting, namely: shrink-wrap, click-wrap, and browse-wrap contracts.

Before we briefly discuss the enforceability of such contracts, some general observations are essential. First, as noted above, the supplier may have to balance its

---

[504] See, eg, <http://www.lotuscars.com/about/en/terms>; <http://www.bfi.org.uk/help/terms.html>; <http://www.ralphlauren.co.uk/helpdesk/index.jsp?display=corp&subdisplay=terms>; <http://www.unileverus.com/terms/termsofuse.html> (all accessed 8 August 2011).

desire for certainty of enforceability against its need for 'user-friendliness' in the contracting process. Secondly, a distinction may usefully be made between the risks from the supplier's perspective of non-enforceability in respect of, say, a pure informational website and the risks of non-enforceability in respect of a transactional website. Operators with websites with both types of functionality may be prepared to take a relatively relaxed view with regard to the contracting process for use of the basic informational portions of the site, and then migrate users wishing to use the transactional portions of the site through a more robust and reliable process.[505]

'Shrink-wrap', 'click-wrap', and 'browse-wrap' are software industry terms for contractual methods commonly employed in mass market contracting. The shrink-wrap model was originally devised by the software industry because as the market for software grew it became impractical to negotiate individual licence agreements with every end-user, and the distribution of software 'off the shelf' through intermediary retailers rendered it very difficult, if not impossible, to establish a direct contractual relationship between the software developer and the end-user. These concerns were addressed through the contractual method of shrink-wrap and, following the advent of e-commerce, click-wrap and browse-wrap licensing. Nevertheless, all three types of contracting face issues of enforceability.

'Shrink-wrap' contracts   As the name suggests, shrink-wrap licence agreements typically provide that the customer accepts the terms of the licence by opening the software packaging or unsealing it. However, by definition, the customer only becomes aware of the terms and conditions after he has opened the package (and thereby become, assuming such arrangements are enforceable, bound by such terms and conditions). The problem with the shrink-wrap approach is that it is generally very difficult to show any meeting of minds in relation to the conclusion of the contract. Software companies have come up with several ways to enhance the enforceability of shrink-wrap licences, such as the repetition of the terms and conditions on the initial pages of the software's installation screens, and requiring the user to confirm acceptance electronically, but none of these solutions is always watertight. Nevertheless, there is support in case law for the validity of shrink-wrap agreements, provided that the customer has been offered the opportunity to read and accept or reject the terms by returning the software within a reasonable period.[506]

---

[505] Therefore, such operators often have two sets of terms and conditions, one set governing use of the website (which the user is deemed to accept, both initially and in any subsequent modified form, by his continued use of the website) and a second set governing transactions (which the user accepts during the transaction process, by reading, scrolling through, checking a box etc, and any modifications to which are sent to the user, with a right for the user to accept such mortifications or cancel the contract).

[506] eg, the Scottish decision in *Beta Computers (Europe) Ltd v Adobe Systems (Europe) Ltd* [1996] FSR 367; see further in the US *ProCD Inc v Zeidenberg*, 86 F 3d 1447 (7th Cir CA 1996), although the *ProCD* case has received some judicial criticism and featured in several dissenting opinions (see, eg, *Wrench LLC v Taco Bell Corp*, 51 F Supp 2d 840 and *Lexmark Int'l, Inc v Static Control Components, Inc*, 387 F3d 522.

'Browse-wrap' contracts   In the online environment, browse-wrap contracts have perennially suffered from issues with enforceability. They gained their name from the contracting approach of seeking to bind users by providing, in web terms (that users may or may not have seen, generally the latter) that use (or 'browsing') of the website itself constituted the user's acceptance of the terms (and, typically, that continued use of the website constituted the user's ongoing acceptance of the terms, as modified from time to time). While the browse-wrap approach is procedurally unintrusive it is rarely likely to be contractually effective because, like the shrink-wrap approach, users will generally be unaware of the terms before they are purportedly bound by them. For instance, in the US case of *Specht v Netscape Communications Corp*,[507] the court considered that a user was unlikely to have had the opportunity to discover the existence of and view a software licence made available via a link, posted underneath the link to download the software itself, and held that when the provisions do not appear to be contract terms and such terms are not brought to the attention of the user, no contract can be formed in respect of such terms. The court also held that, where consumers are urged to download free software at the immediate click of a button, reference to the existence of terms on a submerged screen does not suffice to enable the consumer to inquire or notice the terms.[508] However, in the US case of *Hubbert v Dell Corp*,[509] it was held that a statement that the sale was subject to the seller's terms and conditions combined with the availability of the terms and conditions of sale via blue hyperlinks was sufficient notice to the customer that purchasing computers online would result in the customer being bound by the seller's terms and conditions.

'Click-wrap' contracts   If structured effectively, click-wrap agreements are more likely to be contractually effective. Click-wrap refers to the method of obtaining user acceptance of terms and conditions by clicking on an 'I accept' button. Provided that the user is given the opportunity to review the terms and conditions before confirming acceptance, the approach should generally be effective. For this reason, there exists considerable support in several jurisdictions (including the USA,

---

[507] 306 F3d 17, 30 (2d Cir 2002).

[508] See however *Register.com, Inc v Verio, Inc*, 356 F3d 393, 401–403 (2d Cir 2004), holding that terms not displayed until after the website user had received the benefit sought, would nevertheless apply where the user visited on a daily basis with full knowledge of the terms. *Register.com*, although explained, distinguished, and referenced in dissenting opinions in subsequent cases (see, eg, *The Guard Publishing Co d/b/a The Register-Guard v Eugene Newspaper Guild, CWA Local 37194*, 351 NLRB 1110 at 1126), was cited in *Cairo, Inc v Crossmedia Services Inc*, 2005 WL 756610 (ND Cal, 1 April 2005), which proposed that knowledge of a website's terms can be imputed to a party using a software robot or crawler to visit the website repeatedly.

[509] 835 NE2d 113, 122 (Ill App 2005). There exists a growing body of case law concerning shrink-wrap, click-wrap, and browse-wrap, the elaborate consideration of which falls outside the scope of this chapter. For a discussion of such cases, including more elaborate discussion of the cases cited above, see TJ Smedinghoff, 'Online Transactions: The Rules of Ensuring Enforceability in a Global Environment' [2006] The Computer & Internet Lawyer, April, 6; RG Kunkell, 'Recent Developments in Shrink-wrap, Click-wrap and Browse-wrap Licenses in the United States' [2002] Mur U EJL 34.

Australia, and Canada) that click-wrap agreements are considered valid and enforceable.[510] The downside of the approach is that it is procedurally more invasive and therefore potentially less user-friendly.

2.5.2.4 The consumer's declaration of acceptance

The OFT considers that declarations that the consumer has read and/or understood an agreement give rise to special concerns. The UTCCRs 1999 implement the UTCCD, which provides that terms must be clear and intelligible and that consumers must have a proper opportunity to read all of them. According to the OFT, including a declaration of this kind effectively requires consumers to say these conditions have been met, whether they have or not, and therefore tends to defeat the purpose of the Directive.[511]

Further, the OFT observes that, in practice, consumers often do not read, and rarely understand fully, any but the shortest and simplest contracts and that, while it might be better if they tried to do so, that does not justify requiring them to say they have done so if they have not.[512]

The OFT suggests that much more likely to be fair and acceptable is a clear and prominent warning that the consumer should read and understand the terms before agreeing to them or placing an order.[513] Alternatively, suppliers may ask consumers to check a box to indicate simply that they accept the terms and conditions.[514]

The following examples are from cases where the OFT had objections under the UTCCRs 1999 with standard declarations to be made by consumers:

Original term	New term/Other result[515]
I have read and understood the terms and conditions.	It is important that you read and understand the terms and conditions that will apply to this contract before signing. If there are any terms that you do not understand or do not wish to agree to please discuss it with us before signing. Only sign this agreement if you wish to be bound by the terms and conditions . . .

---

[510] eg, *Hotmail v Money Pie, Inc*, 47 USPQ2d (BNA) 1020 (ND Cal 1998); *iLan Sustems, Inc v Netscout Service level Corp*, 2002 WL 15592 (D Mass 2002), adopting the *ProCD* decision, n 506 above, and submitting that since in *ProCD* a shrink-wrap agreement was enforced where any assent was implicit, it is also correct to enforce a click-wrap agreement where assent is explicit; *Hughes v AOL, Inc*, USDC, D Mass, summary judgment, civil action no 2001-10981-RBC, upholding a click-wrap agreement and the forum selection clause contained therein.

[511] See OFT 672, para 18.5.5.

[512] Ibid para 18.5.6.

[513] See OFT 311, paras 18.5.7 and 14.1.6–14.1.7.

[514] See OFT 672, paras 3.2.5–3.2.7 and 18.5.

[515] See ibid para 3.27 and Group 18(e), pp 120–1, of the Annexes to OFT 311.

Original term	New term/Other result
I/We have read the Conditions of Sale overleaf and agree to be bound by them.	Before signing this order, the customer should carefully read the terms and conditions set out on the other side of this agreement.
I/we the undersigned hereby agree to enter this Airtime Agreement upon the terms and conditions set out overleaf which I/we acknowledge have been drawn to my/our attention and which I/we have read . . .	New term: It is important that you read and understand the terms and conditions that will apply to this contract before signing. If there is any term that you do not understand or do not wish to agree to, then please discuss it with Intercell's representative before signing.

The Office of Communications (Ofcom) formally investigated O2 (UK) Ltd's mobile pre-pay terms and conditions in 2004[516] and its mobile pay monthly terms and conditions in 2005,[517] both as a result of consumer complaints. O2's pre-pay terms and conditions included a term allowing O2 to modify them at any time, such amendments taking effect immediately on notification to the customer, with the means of notification reserved to O2's discretion. Ofcom regarded the ability of O2 to determine the means of notification as potentially unfair where O2 chooses a means of notification which does not give customers a reasonable opportunity of becoming acquainted with any amendments, therefore O2 agreed to amend the relevant provisions to provide that O2 could amend the terms but with notification to the consumer: in advance (by text message) in the case of increased charges; and by posting on the website (and, in some cases by voicemail, text, or media message) or national advertising campaign, in the case of changes to service terms and conditions. O2's pay monthly terms and conditions purported to allow it to apply, at its discretion, a usage limit (and to alter it simply by advising the customer) with corresponding rights to impose changes and suspend the service if the limit was exceeded. Ofcom considered the lack of clarity about the notification of a change of usage to be potentially unfair under paragraph 1(i) since it was analogous to binding consumers to terms with which they had no real chance of becoming acquainted prior to contractual conclusion. Therefore O2 agreed to a replacement term which provided that, although O2 could not set usage limits, O2 would monitor usage and

---

[516] See <http://stakeholders.ofcom.org.uk/enforcement/competition-bulletins/closed-cases/all-closed-cases/cw_778/> (accessed 8 August 2011).

[517] See <http://stakeholders.ofcom.org.uk/enforcement/competition-bulletins/closed-cases/all-closed-cases/cw_820/> (accessed 8 August 2011).

attempt to contact customers whose usage gave O2 cause for concern, and, if unable to do so, O2 might restrict and/or bar service.

2.5.3 Unilateral changes

Paragraph 1(j) of Schedule 2 to the UTCCRs 1999 provides that terms may be regarded as unfair which have the object or effect of 'enabling the seller or supplier to alter the terms of the contract unilaterally without a valid reason which is specified in the contract'.

There the OFT considers that a term will be 'under strong suspicion of unfairness' and 'open to strong objection' if it gives a right for one party to alter the terms of the contract after it has been agreed, regardless of the consent of the other party, without a valid reason.[518] Of particular concern are terms which could be used to force consumers to accept (amongst other things) new requirements or reduced benefits, whether or not meant to be used in that way, and even terms intended solely to facilitate minor adjustments will be problematic if their wording means they could be used to impose more substantial changes.[519]

The OFT's practical guidance is that such a term is more likely to be fair if:

(a) it is narrowed in effect, so that it cannot be used to change the balance of advantage under the contract—for example, allowing variations to reflect changes in the law, to meet regulatory requirements, or to reflect new industry guidance and codes of practice which are likely to raise standards of consumer protection;

(b) it can be exercised only for reasons stated in the contract which are clear and specific enough to ensure the power to vary cannot be used at will to suit the interests of the supplier, or unexpectedly to consumers; and

(c) there is a duty on the supplier to give notice of any variation, and a right for the consumer to cancel before being affected by it, without penalty or otherwise being worse off for having entered the contract.[520]

---

[518] OFT 311, para 10.1 and OFT 672, para 3.46.
[519] Ibid para 10.2.
[520] Ibid para 10.2.

The following are examples from cases where the OFT had objections to standard terms purporting to allow suppliers to vary contractual terms:

Original term	New term/Other result[521]
We reserve the right to alter hours of business if found necessary and change the annual membership system and/or price structure.	Term deleted.
Sky may at any time vary or add to these Conditions as it deems necessary.	[Sky may] change or add to Conditions . . . for security, legal or regulatory reasons . . . We will give you at least one month's notice of any changes or additions. We will not use this right to vary the terms of any special offer which applies to you . . . you may end this contract at any time . . . by giving one month's notice, if we tell you . . . we are going to change these conditions.[522]
Any typographical, clerical or other error or omission in any sales literature, quotation, price list, acceptance of offer, invoice or other document or information issued by the seller shall be subject to correction without any liability on the part of the Seller.	Any error or omission in any information, or document issued by us shall be subject to correction provided that the correction does not materially affect the contract.[523]

Examples of suppliers which regulatory authorities have formally investigated, under paragraph 1(j) of Schedule 2 to the UTCCRs 1999, in respect of clauses purporting to enable the supplier to vary the contract include:

(a) Namesco Ltd, whose terms and conditions were investigated by Ofcom in 2005 and included a clause purporting to reserve Namesco the right to add, delete, or modify any provisions of the terms and conditions at any time without notice, which Namesco agreed to delete;[524] and

---

[521] Group 10, pp 77–9 the Annexes to OFT 311.
[522] Ibid pp 77–9 the Annexes to OFT 311.
[523] Ibid.
[524] See <http://stakeholders.ofcom.org.uk/enforcement/competition-bulletins/closed-cases/all-closed-cases/CW822/> (accessed 8 August 2011).

(b) Hutchison 3G (UK) Ltd, a number of whose terms Ofcom had concerns with including a term which purported to require consumers to agree to terms in all documents produced by 3, including those 3 might publish in future and which therefore could allow 3 to bind the consumer to any changes 3 chose to make to the terms, which 3 agreed to amend so as not to refer to terms to be published in future.[525]

2.5.4 Prices

Terms that set the price are so-called 'core terms' and therefore exempt from the general test of fairness under the UTCCRs 1999 providing they are in plain and intelligible language.[526]

However, price terms will be open to objection if:

(a) they are unclear or uncertain about what will be charged[527] (ie, they are not in plain and intelligible language);

(b) they allow unilateral variation of the price once an agreement has been concluded;[528]

(c) they attempt to make customers responsible for the direct costs of recovering goods when exercising their statutory cancellation rights,[529] unless specifically stated in the contract;[530]

(d) they attempt to charge customers for the return of faulty or unsatisfactory goods;[531]

(e) they attempt to charge unreasonable interest on overdue accounts (an interest rate of 3 per cent above clearings banks' base rate is unlikely to be challenged, while a rate excessively above the base rates is likely to be).[532]

Furthermore, the DSRs 2000 require that before the contract is concluded the consumer is made aware of the full price including taxes and any additional charges concerning delivery and additional services, as well as for how long the offer or price remains valid.[533]

---

[525] <http://stakeholders.ofcom.org.uk/enforcement/competition-bulletins/closed-cases/all-closed-cases/cw_888/> (accessed 8 August 2011). Ofcom also had concerns with this term under para 1(i) of para 2 to the UTCCRs, see section 2.5.2.4 above.

[526] UTCCRs 1999, reg 6(2). For further discussion of core terms, see section 2.2.1.2 above.

[527] See OFT 672, para 3.29.

[528] See section 2.5.5 below.

[529] Under the DSRs 2000.

[530] See OFT 672, para 3.31.

[531] See ibid para 3.32.

[532] See ibid para 3.35. For more on charging consumers who failed to fulfil their contractual obligations, see section 2.5.14.

[533] Section 2.2.1.5 above.

2.5.5 Pricing errors and variations

In addition to the risks associated with pricing errors in pre-contractual materials,[534] there is also a risk of contracts being concluded which contain pricing errors. Therefore, suppliers often purport to give themselves the right either to change the price as a result of such errors or, more commonly, to cancel a contract concluded in relation to such an erroneous price. In addition, as both another means to deal with pricing errors, and a mechanism to allow them to vary prices, suppliers often attempt to reserve the right to change prices unilaterally or to fix prices after the contract has been concluded.

Among the terms which may be regarded as unfair in Schedule 2 to the UTCCRs 1999 are terms which have the object or effect of 'allowing a seller of goods or supplier of services to increase their price without . . . giving the consumer the corresponding right to cancel the contract if the final price is too high in relation to the price agreed when the contract was concluded'.[535] The OFT's position is that price terms are open to objection if they allow unilateral variation of the price once an agreement has been concluded[536] and that 'a clause allowing the supplier to increase the price—varying the most important of all of the consumer's contractual obligations—has clear potential for unfairness'.[537]

However, while any purely discretionary right to set or vary a price after the consumer has become bound to pay 'is obviously objectionable', including rights to increase payments under continuing contracts where consumers have no penalty-free right to cancel,[538] the OFT acknowledges that a degree of flexibility may be achieved by: specifying the level and timing of any increases within narrow limits and drawing them to the customer's attention; linking any increases to published price indexes, such as the Retail Price Index; and/or allowing consumers to exit the contract before the variation takes effect (providing the consumers are not left worse off for having entered the contract, whether by experiencing financial loss—eg, forfeiture of a pre-payment—or serious inconvenience, or any other adverse consequences).[539]

---

[534] See discussion at section 2.5.2.2 above.
[535] See UTCCRs 1999, Sch 2 para 1(l).
[536] See OFT 672, para 3.2.9.
[537] See OFT 311, para 12.1.
[538] See ibid para 12.2.
[539] See ibid para 12.4.

The following are examples from cases where the OFT objected to terms of this kind under paragraph 1(l) of Schedule 2 to the UTCCRs 1999, as well as, in some cases, inconsistency with regulation 7 of the DSRs 2000:

Original term	New term/Other result [540]
The vendor reserves the right to vary the quoted price of the goods by upward additions in accordance with the market conditions at the date of actual supply . . .	Wherever it is not possible to accept your order to buy goods of the specification and description at the price indicated, we will advise you by email, offer to sell you the goods of the specification and description at the price stated in the email and will state the period for which the offer or the price remains valid.
Prices of the Goods shall include delivery of the Goods to the Buyer's premises. Provided, however, that the Seller reserves the right to impose a delivery charge where the Seller sees fit. Any charge for delivery will be at the Seller's rates from time to time in force.	Term deleted.
Discounts may apply from time to time . . . The Company reserve the right to withdraw a discount at any time or instance of actuality [sic].	Term deleted.
Any additional work requested which is not specified in writing within this contract shall be charged at current rate.	Any additional work requested . . . which is not specified in writing within this contract will only be carried out if a new contract is entered into with the company.

Terms revised by the introduction of cancellation rights

The Company may increase the Service charges at any time after a period of one year from the installation date by giving notice in writing stating the increase and the date it shall become effective. The Subscriber may within one month after the service of any notice of increase give three month's notice in writing terminating this Agreement.	The Company may increase the Service charges at any time after a period of one year from the installation date by giving notice in writing stating the increase and the date it shall be effective. The Subscriber may within one month after the service of any notice of increase give one week's notice in writing terminating this Agreement.

---

[540] See OFT 672, para 3.29 and Group 12, pp 143–7, of the Annexes to OFT 311.

Original term	New term/Other result
The Goods are sold at the Seller's ruling price at the time of delivery to the Purchaser. If prior to delivery there is any increase in the quoted price of the Goods the Purchaser may within seven days of receiving notice of such increase cancel this Contract and recover from the Seller any deposit paid. The Seller shall be under no further liability.	If a Confirmed Purchase Price is shown overleaf: this is the price you will pay. If a Provisional Purchase Price is shown: the price of the vehicle on the Date of Sale may be higher or lower, but only if its list price is altered by the manufacturer or importer or applicable tax legislation is revised. . . . You will be entitled to withdraw from this agreement if there is a price increase which you consider excessive.

Terms revised to become price indexation clauses

The Company may increase the service charge at any time after 12 months from the Agreement date by giving notice in writing to the Customer stating the new Service Charge and the date (not being earlier than the date of the notice) on and after which the new Service Charge shall become effective.	We can change our service or monitoring at any time after 12 months from the date of this agreement . . . . . . Our new charges will be index-linked. The index we use is the latest monthly BEAMA index (electrical engineering) published before the date we send you the invoice . . .
The maintenance charge is reviewable annually but will not normally over time be increased by more than the Retail Price Index.	Price increases year by year will generally be in line with increases in the Retail Price Index, but in any three-year period will not in total exceed the Retail Price Index by more than 5 per cent.

Examples of traders from which the OFT has obtained undertakings in respect of price variation clauses include:

(a) Micro Anvika Ltd, an IT retailer, which provided undertakings to the OFT in June 2003 in relation to several of its terms and conditions of business, including: a clause excluding liability for errors in descriptions of contract goods and in contract goods pricing advertised on Micro Anvika's website; and clauses allowing variation of the goods or the prices of the goods following contract formation. The terms were revised to prevent Micro Anvika varying prices or product specifications once the order was accepted and the contract formed.[541]

---

[541] <http://www.oft.gov.uk/news-and-updates/press/2003/pn_77-03> (accessed 09 April 2011).

(b) Hosiery Corporation International which, in March 2006, gave an undertaking to the OFT that several standard terms with which the OFT had concerns under the UTCCRs 1999 would be revised, including a term (which was deleted) that bound the consumer to a price of which they would be unaware when they entered into the contract.[542]

2.5.6 Performance: delivery and acceptance

The timing for performance of a contract by the supplier should take place in accordance with the terms agreed in the contract, in the absence of which, the general position is that performance should take place within a reasonable time.[543] However, under the DSRs 2000:

(a) where there is no agreement on timing, the supplier must perform the contract within 30 days from the day after the consumer sent the order to the supplier;[544]

(b) if the supplier cannot perform within the agreed or deemed period, the consumer must be notified[545] and agree to any later performance (which will not affect the consumer's cancellation rights[546]);

(c) if the consumer does not agree to any such alteration, the supplier must treat the contract as if it had not been made (except for any rights or remedies that the consumer has as a result of non-performance) and all moneys must be refunded within 30 days of the day after the date on which the performance period expires.[547]

Paragraph 1(b) of Schedule 2 to the UTCCRs 1999 provides that terms may be unfair if they have the object or effect of

inappropriately excluding or limiting the legal rights of the consumer vis-à-vis the seller or supplier or another party in the event of total or partial non-performance or inadequate performance by the seller or supplier of any of the contractual obligations, including the option of offsetting a debt owed to the seller or supplier against any claim which the consumer may have against him.

---

[542] <http://www.oft.gov.uk/OFTwork/consumer-enforcement/traders/1213/1/>.

[543] According to numerous authorities, including: SGA 1979, s 29(3); *Postlethwaite v Freeland* (1880) 5 App Cas 599; *Castlegate Shipping Co Ltd v Dempsey* [1892] 1 QB 854; *Hick v Raymond* [1893] AC 22; *Carlton SS Co Ltd v Castle Mail Packet Co Ltd* [1898] AC 486; *Lyle Shipping Co Ltd v Cardiff Corp* [1900] 2 QB 638; *Hulthen v Stewart & Co* [1903] AC 389; *Barque Quilpué Ltd v Brown* [1904] 2 KB 264; *Monkland v Jack Barclay Ltd* [1951] 2 KB 252; *Re Longlands Farm* [1968] 3 All ER 552; *Jolley v Carmel Ltd* [2000] 2 EGLR 153, 160; *National Car Parks Ltd v Baird (Valuation Officer)* [2004] EWCA Civ 967, [2005] 1 All ER 53 at [58].

[544] DSRs 2000, reg 19(1).

[545] Ibid reg 19(2)(a).

[546] See further section 2.2.1.5 above and section 2.5.8 below.

[547] DSRs 2000, regs 19(2)(b), 19(4), and 19(5).

Standard terms which are open to objection under paragraph 1(b) include those which attempt to: exclude liability for delay; allow unduly long periods for delivery or completion of work (or excessive margins of delay after an agreed date); or reserve the right to amend the timing of performance (eg, the delivery date) unilaterally.

According to the OFT, terms likely to be challenged in relation to late delivery include those which:

(a) exclude the supplier's liability for delayed delivery, regardless of the cause;

(b) try to prevent consumers cancelling if delivery is not at the agreed time;

(c) exclude the supplier's liability to refund the consumer in full where there has been delay;

(d) exclude the supplier's liability for the consumer's reasonably foreseeable loss caused by the late delivery.[548]

Furthermore, if suppliers cannot deliver a whole order on time, terms giving the consumers the choice of either terminating the whole contract without penalty or deferring payment under the contract are more likely to be acceptable[549] while terms are likely to be unfair if they:

(a) prevent the consumer from cancelling a contract for goods where some of the goods have already been delivered but the supplier has failed to deliver a subsequent instalment;

(b) are so widely drafted as to leave consumers with no remedy for breaches of delivery terms;

(c) give the supplier a wide discretion to deliver and/or install goods in as many stages as the supplier sees fit.[550]

Terms excluding the supplier's liability for delay may be acceptable if they are limited in scope to delays caused by factors which are genuinely outside the supplier's control (bearing in mind that situations such as shortage of stock, labour problems, etc can be the fault of the supplier).[551] See section 2.5.16 below for further discussion.

---

[548] See OFT 672, para 3.41.
[549] See ibid para 3.43.
[550] See ibid para 3.42.
[551] See OFT 311, para 2.6.5.

The following are examples of OFT objections to standard terms relating to delay in the supplier's performance:

Original term	New term/Other result
The Company will do its best to meet the installation date, but will only accept this contract on the strict understanding that no guarantee whatsoever can be given regarding the delivery dates. The Company shall be entitled to make delivery of the goods by instalments.	The Company will do all it reasonably can to meet the dates given for delivery and/ or installation. In the case of unforeseen circumstances, beyond the reasonable control of the Company, the Company will contact the Consumer and give an alternative date.[552] Delivery of any goods will be on a mutually agreed date.[553]
Whilst the Company may quote a delivery period . . . time for delivery shall not be of the essence of this contract and in the event of supplies or labour being adversely affected by strikes, lock outs or any other disruptions or contingencies beyond the company's control, the company shall not be held responsible for . . . loss or liability incurred by the customer.	We will make every effort to complete the work on time (or, if no date has been agreed, within a reasonable time from the date of your order) but we cannot be held responsible for delays due to weather or other circumstances beyond our control. In this case we will complete the work as soon as reasonably possible.
The Seller shall not be liable to the Purchaser for any loss or damage howsoever caused resulting from non delivery or delayed delivery but in the event that the Seller is unable to deliver the Goods for any reason whatsoever either the Seller or the Purchaser may terminate this Contract by seven days notice in writing and in this event the Seller shall be under no further liability.	If a confirmed Date of Sale is shown overleaf: we guarantee that the vehicle will be available on this date. If a Provisional Date of Sale is shown: we guarantee that the vehicle will be available within 10 days of this date unless an unforeseen increase in demand for the model of vehicle you require prevents its manufacturer fulfilling the order. In the unlikely event that we do not supply a suitable vehicle within 60 days of the Provisional Date of Sale you will have the option of cancelling . . . If we fail to meet either of the above supply guarantees due to our own negligence, we will compensate you for any costs which you incur.

---

[552] OFT 672, para 3.41.
[553] Ibid para 3.43.

Original term	New term/Other result
Times quoted are estimated times only and shall not be binding on the Company and the Company shall not accept any loss or liability whatsoever arising out of any failure to adhere to the times and dates quoted and nor shall any failure be deemed to be a breach of this contract.	The Company will (subject to the Company's duty to take reasonable care) install the units as efficiently and as quickly as is possible . . .

Examples of traders from which enforcement authorities have obtained undertakings in respect of standard terms relating to delay in the supplier's performance include Micro Anvika Ltd, see section 2.5.5 above, and Dell Corporation, see section 2.5.1.2 above. Other include:

(a) Tecaz Ltd, which, in February 2007, gave an undertaking to the OFT as a result of several standard terms with which the OFT had concerns under the UTCCRs 1999, including a term which purported to allow Tecaz to ignore the convenience of consumers and even verbal commitments in respect of delivery deadlines (the term was revised so that where delivery is delayed by circumstances under Tecaz's control, an alternative expected date of delivery will be arranged and under such circumstances Tecaz undertakes that delivery will still be within a reasonable period of time).[554]

(b) UK Online Ltd, whose terms and conditions were referred to Ofcom by a member of the public. Ofcom found several of the terms and conditions to be problematic under the UTCCRs 1999, including a term stating that UK Online would endeavour to provide the service within given timescales, but if these timescales were not met, UK Online would not be liable. Ofcom regarded this term as potentially unfair because it sought to eliminate liability for delay in providing the service and therefore UK Online agreed to amend it to a commitment to endeavour to provide the service within the timescales communicated to the consumer.[555]

It is worth noting at this point that, as seen below,[556] clauses attempting to limit statutory rights in respect of defective goods are likely to be unfair and therefore that suppliers should be careful concerning acceptance procedures and, in particular,

---

[554] See <http://www.oft.gov.uk/OFTwork/consumer-enforcement/traders/2826/1/> (accessed 8 August 2011).

[555] See <http://stakeholders.ofcom.org.uk/enforcement/competition-bulletins/closed-cases/all-closed-cases/cw_887/> (accessed 8 August 2011).

[556] Section 2.5.9 below.

deemed acceptance, to ensure that they do not give rise to unfairness, for example by providing too short a time for evaluation of the goods or setting out a restrictive procedure for notifying faults and returning goods. The OFT also had concerns with the Tecaz Ltd terms (see above), which allowed the consumer only three days to report shortages or defects in products ordered (this time limit was increased to five days and limited to shortages and faults that are visible to the consumer).[557]

2.5.7 Substitutions/variations of in goods/services supplied

Among the terms 'which may be regarded as unfair' in Schedule 2, UTCCRs 1999 are terms which have the object or effect of 'enabling the seller or supplier to alter unilaterally without a valid reason any characteristics of the product or service to be provided'.[558]

The main characteristics of the goods and/or services to be provided to consumers need to be clear under any consumer contract, including distance selling and electronic contracts.[559] Consumers have a right not only to receive goods which are of satisfactory quality[560] and services delivered with reasonable skill and care,[561] but also to receive what in all significant respects they agreed to buy, not merely something similar or equivalent. Terms which allow a supplier unilaterally to substitute something different for what it has actually agreed to supply are unlikely to be fair to the consumer and, according to the OFT, are open to 'strong objection', if they allow the supplier to do so without a valid reason.[562]

Reasons which the OFT considers may be valid[563] are restricted to certain, limited, circumstances:

(a) changes which are clearly minor technical adjustments which can be of no real significance to the consumer, or changes required by law;[564]

---

[557] See <http://www.oft.gov.uk/OFTwork/consumer-enforcement/traders/2826/1/> (accessed 8 August 2011). Note that, although it considered that further action in this case was not warranted, the OFT remained concerned about any term requiring the consumer to bring defects to the attention of the supplier within a certain period of time on the grounds that such a term might reduce the time which the consumer has by law to notify the supplier of defects and that, under the SGA 1979, the burden of proof is on the supplier to show that the product was not damaged or defective at the time of sale.

[558] See UTCCRs 1999, Sch 2 para 1(k).

[559] See further sections 2.2.15, 2.5.1, and 2.5.2 above.

[560] SGA 1979, s 14(2) and (6). See section 2.2.1.1 above.

[561] SGSA 1982, s 13. See section 2.2.1.1 above.

[562] See OFT 672, para 3.46. Note that unilateral changes to pricing (see section 2.5.5 above) or other terms (see section 2.5.3 above) can be equally problematic.

[563] According to the OFT a reason can be considered 'valid' only if its inclusion in the contract offers real protection to the consumer against encountering unexpected and unacceptable changes in his position. Vague or unclear reasons are unlikely to be considered valid. In any case, no statement of reasons can justify making consumers pay for a product substantially different from what they agreed to buy, see OFT 311, para 11.5.

[564] See OFT 311, para 11.3.

(b) changes which are more significant, but still only limited in scope, where the consumer fully understands and agrees to the change in advance;[565]

(c) changes as a result of reasons genuinely beyond the supplier's control[566] (which are more likely to be acceptable if they are made clear to the consumer at the outset and if, in addition to cancellation rights under the DSRs 2000, the consumer is given the unconditional right to cancel the contract without penalty if not satisfied with the change and to receive a full refund);[567]

(d) other circumstances that could prevent the supply of the goods or services agreed (or a version of them that the consumer has indicated is acceptable) accompanied by a right for the consumer to cancel the contract, and receive a refund of pre-payments. However where it is known that, for example, a chosen item could be unavailable from the manufacturer, that risk should be drawn to the consumer's attention.[568]

While a right of cancellation and refund may, in some cases, render fair a clause allowing the supplier to vary what is supplied, this will not, for example, render fair a clause allowing the supplier to vary what is supplied at will (rather than because of bona fide external circumstances).[569]

If the original goods or services are unavailable and the supplier wishes to substitute goods or services of equivalent quality and price, then the OFT takes the view that in order to reserve the right to do so the supplier must:

(a) inform the consumer of this in good time before the conclusion of the contract;

(b) tell the consumer at the outset that the supplier will meet the costs of returning any substitute goods;

(c) not charge the consumer the direct costs of recovering any substitute goods delivered if the consumer wants to cancel under the DSRs 2000 or otherwise;

(d) confirm in a written or durable medium, on delivery at the latest, that the supplier will pay the cost of returning substitute goods.[570]

---

[565] See OFT 311, para 11.4.
[566] See also section 2.5.6 above and further section 2.5.16 below.
[567] See OFT 672, para 3.46.
[568] See OFT 311, para 11.6.
[569] 'The consumer should never have to choose between accepting a product that is not what was agreed, or suffering the inconvenience of unexpectedly not getting, for example, goods for which he or she may have an immediate need, or a long-planned holiday, just because it suits the supplier not to supply what was promised', see OFT 311, para 11.7.
[570] OFT 672, paras 3.47 and 3.48.

The following are examples from cases where the OFT had objections under the UTCCRs 1999 with clauses allowing suppliers to vary what they supplied under consumer contracts:

Original term	New term/Other result[571]

Clauses claiming the right to vary goods/materials

. . . the vendor is not responsible for minor variations in specification in colour or other design features, and no such minor variation shall entitle the purchaser to rescind the contracts or shall be the subject of any claim against the vendor . . .	Wherever it is not possible to accept your order to buy the goods of the specification and description . . . we will advise you by email and offer to sell you the goods of the specification and description . . . in the email and will state the period for which the offer or the price remains valid.
If, for any reason, the Company is unable to supply a particular item of furniture or a particular appliance, the Company will notify the Customer. The Company will normally replace it with an item of equivalent or superior standard and value.	If, for any reason beyond the Company's reasonable control, the Company is unable to supply a particular item of furniture or a particular appliance, the Company will notify the Customer. With the agreement of the Customer the Company will replace it with an item of superior standard and value.
The Company reserves the right to vary design and/or specification of any installation and/or product used without prior notice to the customer.	As it is our policy to continually improve products, methods and materials, we reserve the right to change specifications from time to time, we will not make any significant variations without your agreement.

Clauses claiming the right to vary service

Stena Sealink accepts no liability for any inaccuracy in the information contained in this publication, which may be altered at any time without prior notice, and also reserves the right to alter, amend or cancel any of the arrangements shown in this publication.	New term: We reserve the right, before you book, to vary the services described in our brochures, including prices and departure dates and times and to designate a different ferry for a particular journey.

---

[571] See OFT 672, para 3.46 and Group 11, pp 80–4 of the Annexes to OFT 311.

Original term	New term/Other result
. . . a reduction or other variation in the number or identity of the channels included in the Sky Multi-Channels Package will not vary the Subscription Payments payable by the Subscriber . . . bonus Channels will be supplied to Subscribers at no additional cost . . . Sky may at any time without notice vary the terms on which these Channels are supplied including but . . . not limited to introducing or otherwise making a charge . . .	New term: You may end this contract at any time . . . if we . . . withdraw any Sky Premium Channel or reduce significantly the level of service of the Sky Multi-Channels Package.

Examples of traders from which the OFT has obtained undertakings in respect of standard terms allowing suppliers to vary what they supplied under consumer contracts include Anchor Trust, which, in February 2007, gave an undertaking to the OFT as a result of several standard terms with which the OFT had concerns under the UTCCRs 1999, including a term which provided that services to be provided under the contract (a 24-hour on-site emergency response service) could 'be varied by Anchor from time to time'. In what is perhaps a rather lenient response by the OFT, the term was amended so as to require Anchor to 'act reasonably'.[572] See also Hosiery Corporation International (section 2.5.5 above) and Micro Anvika Ltd (sections 2.5.5 and 2.5.6 above).

2.5.8 Cooling off and cancellation

The consumer and the supplier will both have general rights to terminate the contract after it has been entered into (eg, for breach), not just under common law but also, in all probability, under the contract itself (and such contractual rights must comply with the UTCCRs 1999). These rights are discussed elsewhere.[573] In addition, under the DSRs 2000 consumers have a specific right, to cancel (ie, treat as if they had not been made) most contracts concluded at a distance, during a specified period (often referred to as the 'cooling off' period).[574]

---

[572] <http://www.oft.gov.uk/OFTwork/consumer-enforcement/traders/2674/1/> (accessed 8 August 2011).
[573] See section 2.2.1.2 above. See also 2.5.17 below.
[574] See section 2.2.1.5 above.

This cancellation right does not apply in respect of software that has been unsealed.[575] The OFT takes the view that fairness can only be achieved if software terms and conditions are made available to consumers before they have accepted the software, that is before they have broken its seal.[576]

It is relatively easy for a supplier's cancellation terms to fall foul of the DSRs 2000. The OFT makes it clear that terms are likely to be inconsistent with the DSRs 2000 (and thus challengeable not only under the DSRs 2000 themselves but also under the UTCCRs 1999 and the CPRs 2008[577]) if in relation to the consumer's statutory cancellation rights they:

(a) demand that the consumer uses a particular form of wording or method of communication in order to exercise his cancellation rights;

(b) insist that the supplier receives the notice within the cancellation period (the contract is cancelled on the day the consumer sends the cancellation notice by post, email, or fax, or leaves it at the supplier's last known address);

(c) require consumers to give reasons why the goods are being returned;

(d) require that the goods are returned as new;

(e) require that goods be returned in their original packaging;

(f) make cancellation and any refund conditional on the consumer returning the goods (the terms can require the consumer to return the goods but cancellation rights cannot be conditional on compliance with such terms);

(g) only allow cancellation where there has been breach of contract by the supplier;

(h) make all cancellations subject to part payment;

(i) stipulate that a consumer will always be liable to pay the supplier compensation if he cancels.[578]

Several of the examples relating to the supplier's formalities for returns, may also be unfair under paragraph 1(n) of Schedule 2 to the UTCCRs 1999 which provides that terms may be regarded as unfair which have the object or effect of 'limiting the seller's or supplier's obligation to respect commitments undertaken by his agents or *making his commitments subject to compliance with a particular formality*'. A business cannot opt out of important obligations where the consumer fails to comply with a minor or procedural requirement,[579] particularly in the case of the consumer's statutory cancellation rights.

---

[575] Amongst other exceptions, see DSRs 2000, reg 13.

[576] See OFT 672, para 3.92.

[577] For a discussion of this overlap in relation to the UTCCRs 1999, see section 2.2.1.2 and in relation to the CPRs 2008, see section 2.2.1.4.

[578] OFT 672, paras 3.65–3.68.

[579] See OFT 311, para 14.2.2.

It is now settled that suppliers cannot require consumers to bear the original delivery costs on cancellation,[580] although suppliers can require consumers, following cancellation, to return goods at their own costs (and for the supplier to charge the consumer the direct costs of recovering goods that are not so returned). However, consumer cannot be held responsible for the cost of returning defective or substitute goods supplied where ordered goods are unavailable.

In any event, the cancellation rights cannot be limited (contractually or otherwise)[581] and any attempt, in a consumer contract, to limit or exclude such rights is likely not only to be void and unenforceable under the DSRs 2000 but also to breach the CPRs 2008 and be unfair under paragraph 1(b), and possibly paragraph 1(n) of Schedule 2 to the UTCCRs 1999.[582]

Under regulation 17 of the DSRs 2000, consumers who have cancelled a contract for goods under the DSRs 2000 are under a duty to: retain possession of those goods and take reasonable care of them; and, on receipt of written notice, make them available for collection at their own premises. However, terms will be challengeable if they:

(a) require the consumer to send returned goods by registered or recorded mail;

(b) require the consumer to use a registered courier;

(c) require the consumer to use some other specific method of return that involves unnecessary additional cost or difficulty.[583]

The DSRs 2000[584] require the supplier to reimburse the consumer as soon as possible and in any case within 30 days from the day on which the notice of cancellation was given. Terms will be inconsistent with this obligation if they:

(a) make a refund conditional on the consumer returning the goods;

(b) fail to refund the whole amount, including deposit, advance payment, and outbound delivery charges;

---

[580] By Case C-511/08 *Handelsgesellschaft Heinrich Heine GmbH v Verbraucherzentrale Nordrhein-Westfalen eV*, in which the ECJ held that attempts to refuse to refund consumers the initial delivery costs on cancellation is incompatible with Distance Selling Directive, Arts 6(1) and 6(2). Both Arts 6(1) and 6(2) provide that '. . . The only charge that may be made to the consumer because of the exercise of his right of withdrawal is the direct cost of returning the goods.' Similarly DSRs 2000, reg 14(1) provides that '. . . the supplier shall reimburse any sum paid by or on behalf of the consumer under or in relation to the contract to the person by whom it was made free of any charge, less any charge made in accordance with paragraph (5).' Reg 14(5) provides, broadly, that the supplier may charge for the direct costs of recovering goods if the consumer fails to comply with a contract term providing that the consumer must return goods on cancellation (unless that contract term breaches the UTCCRs 1999 or the consumer has a contractual or statutory right to reject the goods).

[581] See, eg, Consumer Protection Act 1987, s 7.

[582] For a discussion of overlaps in relation to the UTCCRs 1999, see section 2.2.1.2 and in relation to the CPRs 2008, see section 2.2.1.4.

[583] OFT 672, para 3.77.

[584] Reg 14(3).

(c) require a consumer to accept a credit note;

(d) deduct a restocking fee.[585]

The following are examples from cases where the OFT had objections under the DSRs 2000 and the UTCCRs 1999 to a term restricting cancellation rights:

Original term	New term/Other result[586]
The vendor will not accept goods [returned on cancellation] unless . . . [the] return has been authorised by a director, and the goods are received by the vendor in stock condition, with original packaging, software . . .	You have a right to cancel the agreement at any time before the expiry of a period of 7 working days beginning with the day after the day on which you receive the goods. You may cancel by giving us notice in any of the following ways . . .
Returns will not be accepted unless accompanied by: ON ALL PRODUCTS—NO MANUAL—NO RETURN The Invoice, Full and complete packaging inc Disks, Manuals etc.	Term deleted.
. . . during the cooling off period . . . any postal cancellations must be by recorded delivery or registered post and receipt of post will be required should there be doubt as to when the contract was cancelled.	. . . during the cooling off period . . . any cancellation must be given by written notice by either party.

Examples of traders from which the OFT or local enforcement authorities have obtained undertakings in respect of standard terms relating to cancellation rights include:

(a) dabs.com which, in May 2007, gave an undertaking to the OFT as a result of numerous standard terms with which the OFT had concerns under both the DSRs 2000 and the UTCCRs 1999, including terms which:

   (i) required consumers to follow the supplier's returns merchandise authorization procedure (including logging into their dabs.com account, having a returns merchandise authorization number, etc) when returning goods (the revised term requests the consumer to follow the supplier's procedure when returning goods),

---

[585] OFT 672, para 3.79.
[586] Ibid para 3.69 and Group 2(a), pp 12–15, and Group 14(b), pp 100–1, of the Annexes to OFT 311.

    (ii)   made a refund conditional upon return of cancelled goods (the revised term obliges the supplier to make an unconditional refund within 30 days of cancellation under the DSRs 2000),

    (iii)   purported to exclude used stock from the DSRs 2000 (the term was deleted),

    (iv)   required consumers to return goods in an unopened state (the term was replaced with requirements to take reasonable care of the goods);[587]

  (b) Micro Anvika Ltd (see sections 2.5.5, 2.5.6, and 2.5.7 above);

  (c) Supercom Ltd, t/a Looking4DVDs which, in October 2006, gave an undertaking to Stockport Metropolitan Borough Council in relation to, amongst other things, failing, on cancellation, to give a refund within 30 days;[588]

  (d) Tecaz Ltd (see section 2.5.6 above).

2.5.9 Defective goods and product liability

Suppliers are required to ensure that the goods they provide are: of satisfactory quality in relation to appearance, finish, safety, and durability; fit for the purpose for which they are supplied, including any purpose made known to the supplier by the recipient; and are provided as described.[589] To the extent that defective goods cause damage, the supplier of such goods (amongst others) is likely to be liable for such damage.[590]

These statutory rights given to consumers cannot be limited (contractually or otherwise)[591] and any attempt, in a consumer contract, to limit or exclude such rights is likely not only to be void and unenforceable under the applicable statutes[592] but also to breach the CPRs 2008[593] and be unfair under paragraph 1(b) of Schedule 2 to the UTCCRs 1999, as well as, where relevant, under paragraph 1(n) of Schedule 2 to the UTCCRs 1999.[594]

---

[587] <http://www.oft.gov.uk/OFTwork/consumer-enforcement/traders/2669/1/> (accessed 8 August 2011).

[588] <http://www.oft.gov.uk/OFTwork/consumer-enforcement/traders/2075/1/> (accessed 8 August 2011).

[589] See section 2.2.1.1 above.

[590] Consumer Protection Act 1987, s 2.

[591] See, eg, ibid s 7.

[592] It is also important to note that a statement that statutory rights are not affected, without explanation, cannot make such a term acceptable, see OFT 311, para 2.1.3.

[593] For a discussion of overlaps in relation to the UTCCRs 1999, see section 2.2.1.1 and in relation to the CPRs 2008, see section 2.2.1.4.

[594] Para 1(n) provides that terms may be regarded as unfair which have the object or effect of 'limiting the seller's or supplier's obligation to respect commitments undertaken by his agents or making his commitments subject to compliance with a particular formality'.

The OFT's examples of terms which might have the effect of unfairly excluding liability for unsatisfactory goods include the following:

Term	Rationale
Terms that require the goods to be accepted as satisfactory on delivery, fail to allow a reasonable time (which will depend on the nature of the goods), for examination and/or impose unreasonably strict, complex or onerous conditions on their return and corresponding refund, such as:	Consumers cannot be deprived of their right to a reasonable opportunity to examine (which, in the case of complex goods, a chance to try out) goods and reject them if faulty.
• requiring original packaging	
• requiring permission to return goods (for example, an authorisation by the supplier)	
• requiring the customer to call a premium rate phone number or pay postage for returning goods	
• making the customer pay unreasonably high call-out charges before defective goods will be inspected, and/or making such charges non-refundable even if the goods are proven to be defective	
• allowing the supplier to restrict or refuse a full cash refund (eg, by retaining deposits), or requiring the customer to accept a free repair, replacement or credit note	
Terms that say the goods must be (or that they have been) examined or give the supplier sole discretion to determine whether the goods are defective, and/or restrict or prevent independent testing	Consumers cannot be deprived of redress for faults in goods (except obvious faults) other than faults that are specifically drawn to their attention before purchase.
Terms saying that goods only have the description and/or purpose stated on the invoice	Consumers cannot legally be deprived of redress where goods do not meet the description under which they were actually sold, nor if they are not reasonably fit for all the purposes for which goods of the kind are commonly supplied.

Term	Rationale
Terms that seek to pass on the risk of damage or loss before the goods are actually delivered—for example, from when the seller notifies their availability[595]	Consumers cannot have no recourse where goods are destroyed, stolen, or damaged while in the care of the supplier. The fact that such terms apply when the consumer fails to collect or take delivery as agreed does not make them fair. Depriving consumers of redress for negligence—as opposed to (say) making them liable for reasonable storage and insurance charges—is not an appropriate sanction with which to encourage punctuality.
Terms that attempt to transfer liability to the goods manufacturer.	These statutory obligations fall on the supplier in its relationship the consumer and cannot (contractually or otherwise) be transferred to any third party.[596]
Terms that limit or exclude liability unreasonably, for example by saying denying reasonably foreseeable losses	Consumers have a right to seek compensation for loss or damage caused by faulty goods (even if they are no longer entitled to reject the goods, or choose not to do so). Compensation is generally awarded for loss or damage that the parties could have reasonably foreseen at the time of entering the contract (even if others could not have foreseen it).
Terms that disclaim liability for sale goods or saying that sale goods cannot be returned	Consumers have the same rights whether or not they buy goods at a reduced price.[597]
Terms that end consumer rights to redress after the consumer has dealt with the goods in a particular way.	If, even after being legally 'accepted' and used repeatedly or modified in some way, goods subsequently prove to have been defective when sold, the supplier will still be liable to provide redress.[598]

---

[595] See also section 2.5.10 below.

[596] It is of course open to the supplier to insure against its losses arising as a result of such liability, but that does not alter the supplier's liability to the consumers themselves.

[597] Further, in relation to second-quality or damaged goods, disclaimers are just as likely to be considered unfair, eg, using the phrase 'sold as seen'. It is appropriate to warn the consumer when the standard of quality that can reasonably be expected is lower, but the law forbids use of terms which disclaim responsibility for failure to meet any reasonable standard. See OFT 311, para 2.1.5.

[598] See OFT 311, para 2.1.4 and OFT 672, para 3.83.

The following are examples from cases where the OFT objected to a term relating to the consumers' rights in respect of faulty goods:

Original term	New term[599]
The Seller will not be liable to the Buyer at any time . . . for . . . economic-loss, or consequential loss (including loss or damage suffered by the Buyer as a result of an action brought by a third party) caused by defects in the goods even if such loss is reasonably foreseeable.	The Buyer and the Seller shall only be liable under this contract for losses which are a reasonably foreseeable consequence of the relevant breach of contract.
. . . the company will issue a credit note to the buyer for any goods found to be defective by reason of faulty materials or by poor workmanship	The term was deleted.
All goods returned as faulty must be tested in our workshop by our technicians before replacement or refund.	. . . Each party will agree that only a qualified person in Computers . . . performs an inspection [of goods returned as faulty].
The Seller will assume no responsibility that the Goods concerned herein are fit for any particular purpose for which they are bought other than for the purpose set forth and specified in the User manual supplied therewith.	All hardware is sold in accordance with the manufacturer's specification subject to any qualification or representation contained in the brochures, advertisements, or other documentation.
All conditions and warranties whatsoever (whether expressed or implied and whether arising at common law or statute) . . . are hereby excluded to the extent permitted by law.	The term was deleted.
Please keep this invoice in a safe place as it will be required should a need for after sales service arise in the future too.	Please keep the invoice in a safe place as it will assist should a need arise in future for after sales service.[600]

---

[599] See OFT 672, paras 3.83–3.89 and Group 2(a), pp 12–18, and Group 14(b), pp 100–1, of the Annexes to OFT 311.
[600] See Group 14(b), pp 100–1, of the Annexes to OFT 311.

Original term	New term
You shall be responsible for any loss or damage to the equipment however caused . . . except by fair wear and tear.	You are responsible for any loss or damage to the equipment except if such loss or damage is: (i) caused by us or our employees, (ii) due to a manufacturing design or design fault, or (iii) due to fair wear and tear.

Clauses dealing with 'sale' goods

No claims whatsoever will be entertained and no liability attaches to the Company in any event for goods sold at discount prices as remnants or as sub-standard stock.	Goods sold at discount prices, as remnants or as substandard stock will be identified and will be stated to be sold as such.
Goods . . . which for any reason whatsoever are sold at less the manufacturer's recommended list price . . . shall be delivered to the purchaser in the condition as seen and approved by the Purchaser and without any . . . condition or warranty . . . implied by statute, common law or otherwise.	The term was deleted.

Clauses requiring consumers to examine goods

Upon taking possession of the goods the Buyer shall . . . notify the Seller if the goods are damages or defective . . . In any case such notification must take place within 3 working days and in writing.	If the Buyer seeks to reject the goods as defective within a reasonable period of time then the Buyer will . . . notify the Seller.
It is the customer's responsibility to make sure they have tried the goods before delivery and that they are fit for the purpose for which they are intended.	The term was deleted.[601]
Your signature constitutes acceptance that all merchandise and indicates 100 per cent satisfaction as per order.	The term was deleted.

---

[601] See Group 2(a), pp 12–18, of the Annexes to OFT 311.

Examples of traders from which enforcement authorities have obtained undertakings in respect of standard terms relating to faulty products include:

(a) Bulldog Communications Ltd, which was referred by a member of the public to Ofcom in respect of its terms and conditions, of which Ofcom found the following to be potentially unfair under paragraph 1(b) of Schedule 2 to the UTCCRs 1999:[602]

    (i)   a clause excluding all representations, warranties, terms, and undertakings, express or implied, statutory or otherwise, other than those set out in one clause, which was seen as potentially excluding Bulldog's liability for implied and statutory rights of consumers,

    (ii)   clauses limiting rights to reject equipment purchased by consumers from Bulldog to the limited rights set out in the equipment manufacturer's warranty, and excluding Bulldog's liability for representations or warranties in relation to the quality, fitness, or interoperability of the equipment, which Ofcom considered would exclude the consumer's statutory rights against Bulldog, and might also exclude Bulldog's liability for its or its agent's representations,

    (iii)   a clause providing that the consumer shall not be entitled to any right of credit, set-off, or counterclaim against any amounts due to Bulldog, which was seen as inappropriately excluding or limiting the consumer's rights against Bulldog (eg, to off-set a debt owed to Bulldog against a claim against Bulldog),

    (iv)   various clauses excluding or limiting Bulldog's liability in circumstances where Ofcom considered a blanket exclusion or limitation was potentially unfair (eg, because it excluded liability even when the fault or incident may have been due to the fault of Bulldog);[603]

(b) Micro Anvika Ltd (see sections 2.5.5, 2.5.6, 2.5.7, and 2.5.8 above), dabs. com (see section 2.5.8 above) and Tecaz Ltd (see sections 2.5.6 and 2.5.8 above).

It is worth considering software in the context of defective goods. The statutory obligations are implied in relation to goods, but not in relation to intangible items. Therefore, in the context of software, while the obligations would apply to the physical media on which software is supplied (and potentially to the software programs encoded on that media), there is some doubt about whether they apply to software delivered online (although it is possible that the common law would imply

---

[602] As a result of which Bulldog amended its terms and conditions, not just substantively but to alter the format of the contract and the numbering of the clauses.

[603] See <http://stakeholders.ofcom.org.uk/enforcement/competition-bulletins/closed-cases/all-closed-cases/cw_793/> (accessed 8 August 2011).

a requirement for software to be fit for purpose in this case[604]). While cancellation rights under the DSRs 2000 cease to apply if software is unsealed,[605] the consumer's other statutory rights will apply whether or not they are unsealed (in many cases defects would not be detectable without unsealing, not to mention installing, the software) and thus the consumer's right to reject faulty software will not cease because he opens the software packaging. Therefore, although the OFT does not object to requiring or encouraging consumers to contact a helpline in order to resolve any installation or interoperability problems (so long as this is not a condition of returning faulty software[606]), terms that deny the right of the consumer to reject software that is faulty are open to challenge by the OFT.

See for example the following, from cases where the OFT had objections under paragraph 1(b) of Schedule 2 to the UTCCRs 1999 with a term relating to the consumers' rights in respect of faulty software:

Original term	New term/other result[607]
The support provided hereunder shall be substantially as described. This warranty is exclusive and is in lieu of all other warranties and Microsoft disclaims all other warranties, express or implied, including but not limited to warranties of merchantability and fitness for a particular purpose.	Microsoft warrants that it will provide Support with reasonable care and skill, within a reasonable time, and substantially as described in this Agreement. Microsoft does not make any other promises or warranties about Support service.
. . . defects in the Software . . . do not give rise to a liability on the part of the Seller.	The Seller will replace any faulty disks if the defect is notified to them within a reasonable period of time after delivery . . .

In addition, pursuant to the cancellation rights under the DSRs 2000, consumers may also return software even if it conforms with the contract, provided that the software has not been unsealed. The supplier must inform the consumer of this right and the OFT's guidance indicates that it, at least, has taken the view that a seal can be either a physical security seal on the inner packaging or an electronic seal.[608] While this leads to a logical and consistent approach with regard to the treatment of cancellation rights in software whether it is physically supplied or digitally downloaded,

---

[604] *St Albans* case discussed in section 2.1.1 above.
[605] See sections 2.2.1.5 and 2.5.8 above.
[606] OFT 672, para 3.97.
[607] See Group 2(a), pp 12–18, of the Annexes to OFT 311 and OFT 672, para 3.97.
[608] See OFT 672, para 3.95.

it should be noted that, as discussed in 2.1.5.1 above, the DSRs 2000 as drafted simply exclude the cancellation right if the software is 'unsealed by the consumer'—a phrase which does not readily suggest that the intention was to cover both physical and electronic 'opening' or 'activation' of the software itself.

2.5.10 Risk

Risk allocation is one of the basic objectives of any technology contract and is often hotly negotiated in B2B dealings. The position of two equally matched parties negotiating a bespoke contract in a business context offers flexibility in relation to risk allocation, but when contracting with a consumer there is much less room for manoeuvre. Any term that attempts to restrict a right that the consumer has at law will be subject to statutory allocations of risk, such as under regulation 5 of the UTCCRs 1999 and the DSRs 2000.

The OFT has indicated that the following terms will be considered unfair:

(a) terms placing risk on the consumer where it is more appropriate for the supplier to bear the risk, for example where the risk is within the supplier's control, is one which the consumer cannot be expected to be aware of or insure against, and/ or is one which the supplier can insure against more cheaply than the consumer[609] or where the risk is outside both parties' control, for example weather damage (the consumer should not be made to insure the supplier);[610]

(b) terms attempting to place the risk of goods upon the consumer before the consumer has received them (the consumer's right to cancel under the DSRs 2000 is unconditional and cannot be circumvented by passing the risk of loss or damage in transit to the consumer; if consumers do not receive the goods they have ordered, they can cancel and the total price, including delivery charges, must be refunded[611]);

(c) terms that increase the consumer's responsibilities when returning goods beyond an obligation to take reasonable care to ensure they are received and are not damaged during transit, for example, by making the consumer absolutely liable for damage in return transit;[612]

(d) terms which make the consumer bear a risk that the supplier could remove or at least reduce by taking reasonable care are subject to 'particular suspicion',[613] for example damage to equipment that the supplier operates, or the risk of encountering

---

[609] OFT 672, para 3.101 and OFT 311, para 18.2.1.

[610] The OFT has little sympathy for the argument that allocating risk in this way enables prices to be kept down (unless suitable insurance is easily available to the consumer at reasonable cost) on the basis that the end result is that the consumer pays more overall (or goes unprotected against the risk in question). See OFT 311, para 18.2.3.

[611] See section 2.2.1.5 above and see OFT 672, para 3.9.

[612] OFT 672, para 3.11.

[613] Such an exclusion would probably fall within the categories of unfair exclusion described in UTCCRs 1999, Sch 2 para 1(a) or (b).

foreseeable structural problems in installation work (otherwise the consumer could effectively be negligent with impunity).[614]

The OFT takes the view that often terms can be made more fair if they:

(a) allocate responsibility to the consumer only for losses caused by the consumer's actions; and

(b) are narrow in scope, so as to relate only to risks against which a consumer is likely to, or can easily, insure, for example loss or damage while the goods are in the consumer's home (in which case consumers need to be made aware of their obligations through, eg, effective highlighting, bold print (if the contract is short and simple) or separate warnings away from the main body of the contract).[615]

Some specific types of risk allocation which may be problematic are:

(a) terms which effectively pass on the risk of the supplier's insolvency to the consumer, for example by requiring payment of most or all of the purchase price substantially earlier than is needed to cover the supplier's costs (which is liable to be lost by the consumer if the business is wound up before the corresponding goods/services are delivered);

(b) terms requiring the consumer to indemnify the supplier for costs which could arise through no fault of the consumer (particularly where the supplier could itself be at fault) on top of which the word 'indemnify', like 'force majeure'[616] is itself is legal jargon which should be avoided, or at least explained carefully.[617]

See for example the following, from cases where the OFT had concerns with certain clauses relating to allocation of risk being potentially inconsistent with regulation 17(6) of the DSRs 2000, and/or unfair exclusions under regulation 5 of the UTCCRs 1999:

Original term	New term/Other result[618]
The purchaser shall . . . be responsible for the cost of . . . insurance of all goods returned . . . to the vendor. Goods shall be at the risk of the purchaser until actual receipt of the goods by the vendor. The onus of proof of safe delivery shall rest with the purchaser . . .	The term was deleted.

---

[614] OFT 311, para 18.2.2.

[615] OFT 672, para 3.101 and OFT 311, paras 18.2.4 and 18.2.5.

[616] See section 2.5.6 above and section 2.5.16 below.

[617] OFT 311, paras 18.2.6 and 18.2.7.

[618] OFT 672, para 3.100 and Group 2(a), pp 12–18, and Group 18(b), pp 110–12 of the Annexes to OFT 311.

Original term	New term/Other result
Risk of damage to or loss of the Goods shall pass to the Buyer . . . at the time when the Seller notifies the Buyer that the Goods are available for collection.	The term was deleted.
You will be still be liable for the minimum charge and all call charges [if] you . . . lose . . . the apparatus or it is stolen.	You will still be liable to pay these sums if the apparatus is lost or stolen. When we receive notice from you confirming the genuine loss or theft and that matter has been reported to the police, you will not be liable for call charges from that date.

Indemnities

The Advertiser shall indemnify the Publisher in respect of any claim, cost or expenses resulting from libellous or malicious matter or untrue statement in any advertisement published for the Advertiser or from any infringement of copyright, patent, or design therein.	. . . the Customer shall be responsible for any losses, expenses, or other costs incurred by Auto Trader which are caused by an untrue statement made deliberately by the Customer.
You must indemnify us against any claims or legal proceedings arising from use of BT Cable which are brought or threatened against us by another person.	If you use the service for business purposes you must also indemnify us against any claims made against us by third parties because the service is faulty or cannot be used.

Examples of suppliers which have been subject to formal investigation in respect of standard terms relating to faulty products include Nexus Data Systems Ltd trading as KT Hosting whose web hosting terms and conditions were investigated by Ofcom in May 2005 as a result of a complaint by a member of the public. Ofcom concluded that a number of the terms and conditions were potentially unfair under the UTCCRs 1999 including a term requiring the consumer to provide some security for KT Hosting and its directors against any action arising from the registration or use of domain names. Ofcom considered this created an imbalance between the consumer and supplier because it imposed a risk on the consumer of which he was unlikely to be aware and which the supplier was better able to bear.[619]

---

[619] See <http://stakeholders.ofcom.org.uk/enforcement/competition-bulletins/closed-cases/all-closed-cases/cw_829/> (accessed 8 August 2011).

2.5.11 Services

Where a mass market contract concerns the provision of services, consumers can expect that the services will be performed to a reasonable standard in relation to the skill and care exercised by the supplier, the time for the provision of the service, and the price.[620] This applies not only to the main task that the supplier undertakes to perform but to any other task that is performed, or should be performed pursuant to the contract.[621]

Any term which could, whether intentionally or not, serve to relieve the supplier of services of the obligation to exercise reasonable skill and care in any of its dealings with consumers, including by inappropriately excluding or limiting liability for poor service,[622] is particularly likely to be considered unfair (and a mere statement that the term does not affect the statutory rights of the consumer will not remedy its unfairness[623]). However, a narrow exclusion of liability, covering only losses where the supplier is not at fault or for losses that were not foreseeable, may have more success.[624] Terms which disclaim liability for loss or damage (eg, to the consumer's property) which is the consumer's own fault may also be acceptable, but this does not mean that a disclaimer which operates whenever the consumer is in breach of contract is necessarily fair (this is unlikely to be acceptable if it could deprive the consumer of all redress in the event of a trivial or technical breach, or where the supplier may be partly responsible for loss or harm suffered by the consumer).[625]

Software and hardware contracts will often include installation, support, or maintenance services aspects, which (providing they are more than a product warranty) are likely to constitute separate contracts in their own right, which must have separate prices and will be subject to the DSRs 2000[626] information requirements and cancellation rights. Even services provided for free alongside the main goods or services being supplied (eg, advice and guidance on the use of the product or help with installation) should not be protected by a disclaimer that could cover negligence.[627]

As part of the DSRs 2000 information requirements, suppliers need to make clear to consumers their practice in relation to the provision of services including support services. For instance, if the supplier's practice is first to provide support by telephone or an online helpdesk and then, if required, through an on-site visit, this must be made clear to the consumer.[628]

---

[620] See section 2.2.1.1 above.
[621] See OFT 311, para 2.2.1.
[622] Exclusion and limitation of liability is discussed below in 2.5.11.
[623] OFT 311, para 2.2.2.
[624] Ibid para 2.2.4.
[625] Ibid paras 2.2.6–2.2.7.
[626] OFT 672, para 3.104.
[627] See OFT 322, para 2.2.8.
[628] OFT 672, para 3.107.

Terms relating to such services are, according to the OFT, open to challenge if they give the supplier the right to decide not to attend on-site, when the service is described as 'on-site', or require consumers to make a premium rate call to reject services that do not conform to the contract.[629]

See for example the following, from cases where the OFT had concerns with certain clauses relating to the provision of services as being potentially unfair exclusions under paragraph 1(b) of the UTCCRs 1999, or in one case under legislation which was replaced by the UTCCRs 1999:

Original term	New term/Other result[630]
All conditions, warranties, and representations, whether express or implied, relating to the quality of Service whether arising by reason of statute, common law or otherwise, are hereby expressly excluded. This clause does not affect the terms implied by statute in favour of the Customer by the Sale of Goods Act 1979.	This term was deleted.
DAMAGE—The subscriber shall pay for the cost of all work required to be carried out to the installation and materials therefore due to damage for whatever cause.	DAMAGE—The subscriber shall pay for the cost of all work required to be carried out to the installation and materials thereof due to damage resulting from misuse or negligence by the subscriber.
Where British Gas Services needs to connect new equipment to your existing central heating system it shall not be liable for any breakdown or poor performance of or damage caused to your existing system as a result of faulty pipework or some other defect or malfunction of your central heating system.	Where we need to connect new equipment to your existing central heating, we will not accept liability for the cost of repairing or replacing parts of your existing system which occurs due to faults in that system unless we have been negligent in not realising that such damage may occur or in the way we did the work.

Examples of suppliers which have been subject to formal investigation in respect of standard terms relating to faulty products which were potentially unfair include

---

[629] OFT 672, para 3.108.
[630] See Group 2(b), pp 19–22, of the Annexes to OFT 311.

Bulldog Communications Ltd (see section 2.5.9 above) and O2 (UK) Ltd (see section 2.5.2.4 and 2.5.3).

2.5.12 Warranties and guarantees

The statutory requirements for guarantees are that they must: be in plain, intelligible language; include the essential particulars necessary for making a claim under the guarantee; say how long the guarantee lasts; indicate the territorial scope of the guarantee; give the name and address of the guarantor; be made available within a reasonable time to the consumer on request in writing or some other durable medium; and be written in English where the goods are offered within the UK.[631] The OFT's 'Best practice tip' for compliance and to help to make consumers fully aware of suppliers' guarantee arrangements is to highlight these through prominent headings in suppliers' terms and conditions.[632]

Suppliers often give consumers guarantees or warranties (which terms are frequently used interchangeably in the consumer context) that are intended to give consumers additional protection over and above their statutory rights. Where a guarantee offers no more protection than is available to the consumer under statute, this should be marketed with caution (or not at all), as presenting rights given to consumers in law as a distinctive feature of the supplier's offer is likely to fall foul of the CPRs 2008.[633]

Further, guarantees can also operate to reduce the legal protection available to consumers, in which case they are likely to be considered unfair (on the same grounds as exclusion or limitation clause can).[634] Therefore, as well as ensuring they can comply with any guarantees they do provide, it is important for suppliers to avoid providing guarantees that in fact offer more limited rights than are available under the law (either because the benefits are less, or because their availability is made subject to special conditions or restrictions).[635] Adding a statement that statutory rights are not affected is not enough to render an otherwise unfair guarantee fair and in fact might itself breach the requirement to use plain and intelligible language, under regulation 7 of the UTCCRs 1999.[636]

According to the OFT, guarantee/warranty terms may be considered unfair if they:

(a) exclude liability for any loss incurred by the consumer for, or purport or appear to deny customers their rights to reject, defects in the goods or goods which do not match their description;

---

[631] OFT 672, para 3.110, see section 2.2.1.1. above, and further section 2.5.18 below.

[632] Ibid para 3.115.

[633] CPRs 2008, Sch 1 para 10.

[634] See OFT 672, para 3.113 and OFT 311, para 2.8.1. See section 2.5.13 below.

[635] See OFT 311, para 2.8.2.

[636] For a guarantee to be made fair by adding a statement of this kind, the words used need to have some practical meaning for the ordinary consumer (eg, by giving an indication as to what sort of protection is involved and/or indicating where advice on it can be obtained). See OFT 311, paras 2.8.4–2.8.5.

(b) rely on an additional qualifying statement such as 'this does not affect your statutory rights' after a more explicit statement that appears to restrict those statutory rights;

(c) impose unjustified formality requirements on the consumer such as following specified procedures or completing specific forms, as a precondition of claiming warranty cover;

(d) allow the supplier to opt out of important obligations if consumers commit a minor breach of their obligations;

(e) purport to charge consumers for returning goods rejected because they do not conform to contract;

(f) impose an unreasonably short time limit on claims;

(g) are buried in the small print;

(h) try to limit the customer to claiming against the manufacturer and attempt to exclude the supplier's statutory liability.[637]

The OFT has specifically addressed printer warranties, observing that terms that invalidate printer warranties if the consumer makes use of third party ink cartridges are at clear risk of being unfair if they purport to exclude liability for failures and defects in the printer that are not caused by the cartridges themselves. Concerns would also be raised by any other printer warranty terms that potentially exclude or limit liability for faulty or misdescribed goods (see also section 2.5.9 above).[638]

The following are examples from cases where the OFT had concerns with certain guarantee clauses as being potentially unfair exclusions under paragraph 1(b) of the UTCCRs 1999, or in one case under legislation which was replaced by the UTCCRs 1999:

Original term	New term/Other result[639]
All hardware sold by the Seller is guaranteed only to the extent of the original manufacturer's warranty.	The term was deleted.
All repair items under guarantee must be brought to the shop and collected by the consumer.	The term was deleted.

Examples of suppliers which have been subject to formal investigation in respect of standard terms relating to guarantee or warranty terms which were potentially unfair,

---

[637] OFT 672, paras 3.114, 3.119, 3.101.
[638] Ibid para 3.112.
[639] See Group 2(h), pp 49–50, of the Annexes to OFT 311.

under paragraph 1(b) of Schedule 2 to the UTCCRs 1999 include Dell (see sections 2.5.1.2 and 2.5.6 above), dabs.com (see sections 2.5.8 and 2.5.9 above), and Bulldog Communications Ltd (see sections 2.5.9 and 2.5.11 above).

2.5.13 Limitation and exclusion of liability[640]

When providing goods and services to consumers, certain contractual obligations will be imposed on suppliers as a matter of law, for instance the satisfactory quality of goods or the exercise of reasonable skill and care in the provision of services. Terms that have the object or effect of excluding or limiting the liability of the supplier in relation to these legal obligations are highly likely to be considered unfair, particularly those seeking to limit or exclude liability for death or personal injury[641] and the consumer's right to set-off.

The OFT takes the view that terms that are likely to be unfair include those that:

(a) exclude or limit the supplier's liability for damages caused by faulty goods or poor service, for example a term denying responsibility for loss of data if the consumer has not made back-ups;

(b) seek to transfer all liability for any defect to the manufacturer;

(c) limit the kind of loss for which compensation is paid, including the consumer's claim to consequential losses (a more promising way to achieve fairness is to exclude liability for losses that were not reasonably foreseeable by both parties at the time the contract was entered into);

(d) limit the supplier's liability where the goods have been physically damaged before or during delivery;

(e) limit the supplier's liability to the value of the goods sold;

(f) exclude or limit liability if the consumer has not yet paid;

(g) limit the supplier's liability to the amount that the supplier can claim against the manufacturer in any given case;

(h) require consumers to go to unjustifiable lengths when returning goods.[642]

Many of the examples of terms in other categories discussed elsewhere in this chapter constitute exclusion or limitation clauses which have been considered potentially unfair under the UTCCRs 1999. The following are additional specific examples, from cases where the OFT had concerns with certain exclusion and/or limitation

---

[640] Limitation and exclusion of liability provisions are also considered in section 2.2.1.2 and several other subsections of section 2.5 of this chapter. See, eg, section 2.5.9 above concerning faulty goods; section 2.5.3 concerning unilateral variations of contract; or section 2.5.10 concerning risk.

[641] Which are always void under UCTA 1977, s 2.

[642] OFT 672, para 3.124.

clauses as being potentially unfair exclusions under paragraph 1(a) or 1(b) of the UTCCRs 1999:

Original term	New term/Other result
No responsibility is accepted by [the supplier] for any . . .injury . . . even when such . . . injury . . . is attributed to any negligence on the part of [the supplier] or its servants.	In the absence of any negligence or other breach of duty by [the supplier] or its servants and agents, you will be responsible for any . . . injury . . .[643]
The Customer will pay all amounts due to the Company free from all deductions and without set-off. The Customer shall not be entitled by reason of any claim against the Company to withhold payment for the Goods.	The term was deleted.[644]

Many of the examples previously discussed involve suppliers whose terms and conditions have been subject to formal investigation in relation to exclusions or limitations of liability which were potentially unfair under paragraph 1(b) of Schedule 2 to the UTCCRs 1999. One additional example is Wanadoo UK plc whose terms were investigated by Ofcom in October 2004 and included, among others, the following provisions which Ofcom considered were unfair as they inappropriately excluded or limited the legal rights of the consumer vis-à-vis Wanadoo in the event of total or partial non-performance or inadequate performance by Wanadoo of its contractual obligations:

(a) excluding all liability for errors, inaccuracies, or omissions in relation to all information provided by Wanadoo in connection with the services;

(b) excluding Wanadoo's liability in contract, tort (including negligence), or otherwise for any damage or loss arising from the consequence of viruses received by the consumer via the Wanadoo services or of its failure to provide the services in accordance with the terms of use;

(c) limiting to £500 Wanadoo's liability for any loss or damage suffered by the consumer in relation to the provision of the service in any 12-month period.[645]

---

[643] OFT 672, para 3.125.
[644] Ibid para 3.126.
[645] <http://stakeholders.ofcom.org.uk/enforcement/competition-bulletins/closed-cases/all-closed-cases/cw_779/> (accessed 8 August 2011).

2.5.14 Breach by the consumer

The issues here are twofold, namely: whether the consumer is in breach; and the validity of contractual sanctions where the consumer is in breach.

2.5.14.1 Determining whether the consumer is in breach

Terms which give the supplier excessive power to determine whether the consumer is in breach (and ought to be subject to a penalty, obliged to make reparation of any kind, or deprived of any benefits under the contract), especially if the relevant criteria are left unstated or are vaguely defined, are likely to attract a suspicion of unfairness.[646] Such terms are more likely to be fair if there is a clear procedure under which the consumer, if unhappy with the decision that he is in breach, can refer the matter to an independent expert or arbitrator.[647]

Terms will be invalid where they purport to treat the consumer as in breach in circumstances where the supplier cannot do so, for example where the consumer is exercising his statutory rights. So, for example, a consumer cannot be in breach of contract where he exercises his right to cancel under the DSRs 2000 (and, eg, refuses to accept delivery of goods)[648] or to reject goods that are fault or misdescribed under the SGA 1979.[649]

2.5.14.2 Sanctions on breach

Suppliers inevitably seek to protect their position and avoid incurring loss as a result of a breach of contract by the consumer. However, the imposition on the consumer of disproportionate sanctions for the consumer's breach of contract is likely to be unfair.

Payments While the consumer can be required to compensate the supplier commensurate with the supplier's loss (or with the loss the supplier could have expected to incur), such compensation must be no more than a reasonable pre-estimate of the supplier's loss and not a penalty.[650] This accords not only with common law principles of contract generally, but also with the UTCCRs 1999, which include, among the terms 'which may be regarded as unfair' in Schedule 2, terms which have the object or effect of 'requiring any consumer who fails to fulfil his obligation to pay a disproportionately high sum in compensation'.[651]

---

[646] OFT 322, para 18.7.4.

[647] Note, however, that compulsory arbitration clauses are likely to be unfair (see section 2.5.19 below)—OFT 311, para 18.7.5.

[648] See section 2.2.1.5.

[649] See section 2.2.1.1.

[650] See section 2.2.1.2 above.

[651] See UTCCRs 1999, Sch 2 para 1(e).

Terms which are likely to be unfair in this context include terms which, on a consumer's breach of contract:

(a) allow the supplier to claim a fixed or minimum sum, which would be too high in some cases;

(b) allow the supplier excessive discretion to decide the sum to be paid by the consumer, or could have that effect through being vague, or unclear, or misleading;

(c) allow the supplier to claim all costs and expenses, not just net (and reasonable) costs;

(d) allow the supplier to claim both costs and loss of profit where this would lead to being compensated twice over for the same loss ('double counting');

(e) allow the supplier to charge unreasonable interest[652] on outstanding payments due from the consumer;

(f) allow the supplier to charge excessive storage or similar charges where the consumer fails to take delivery as agreed;

(g) allow the supplier to pass on legal costs to the consumer, on an indemnity basis[653] or when it is unreasonable to do so;

(h) transfer responsibility for all claims to the consumer, even where the consumer is not at fault;

(i) seek to make consumers responsible for all costs which could arise, even when the consumer is not at fault, or to cover third party IP claims (eg, under an indemnity);

(j) allow the supplier to terminate the contract and require immediate payment of the balance, or a large part of the balance of the charges due under the contract (or loss of a substantial pre-payment);

(k) do not take account of the supplier's duty to keep its losses to a minimum (ie, to mitigate).[654]

---

[652] eg, at a rate excessively above the clearing banks' base rates.

[653] The term 'indemnity' is also legal jargon which is likely to fall foul of the 'plain and intelligible language' requirement of UTCCRs 1999, reg 7, and therefore should be avoided in any event (see also sections 2.2.1.2 and 2.5.2.1).

[654] See OFT 311, paras 5.2–5.6 and OFT 672, paras 3.129, 3.131, and 3.133.

The following are examples where the OFT had objections on the grounds of potential unfairness under regulation 5 of the UTCCRs 1999, with a term concerning consequences of consumers' breach:

Original term	New term/Other result[655]
All items returned to the vendor by pre-arrangement and found to contain no fault, will be subjected to a 25% restocking charge, provided the goods are in original condition.	Your right to cancellation [ie under the DSRs 2000] . . . We will reimburse any sum paid by you or on your behalf under or in relation to the agreement including the costs of carriage and any insurance which you directed us to incur.
	[The restocking fee was deleted.]
In the event of legal action . . . for breach of payment, the customer shall be responsible for all costs and disbursements incurred by A&S on a full indemnity basis.	In the event of legal action . . . for breach of payment, the customer shall be responsible for all costs allowable by the courts if an award is made in A&S's favour.
Late payment penalties	
Failure to comply with the payment of the balance on the due date . . . will entitle the company to charge interest on the balance at the rate of 7% compound interest [ie per annum] above bank base rate.	Failure to pay the balance outstanding will entitle the company to charge interest on the balance at the rate of 3% interest [p.a.] above the [name of bank] base rate.
Interest will be charged at the rate of 10 per cent per month or part thereof on any sum outstanding for more than seven days following the delivery and installation of the goods . . .	Term deleted.
Uncertain and discretionary penalties	
The Company reserve the right to suspend provision of service for the duration of any non-payment period and the customer may be liable (at the Company's discretion) to pay a reconnection fee to the Company to recommence subscription services.	Term deleted.

---

[655] See OFT 672, para 3.34 and Group 5, pp 55–8 of the Annexes to OFT 311.

Original term	New term/Other result
If the Purchaser shall fail . . . to perform any of his obligations . . . the Purchaser shall become liable to the seller for the loss of profit upon this agreement, and such other losses as the Seller may have suffered. A written statement of the amount of such damages prepared and signed by or on behalf of the Seller shall be conclusive proof of such loss.	Term deleted.

Examples of suppliers which have been subject to formal investigation in respect of standard terms relating to breach by the consumer which were potentially unfair under paragraph 1(e) of Schedule 2 to the UTCCRs 1999 include:

(a) J Furneval (a sole trader trading under the names Ventura, Ventural, and Ventura hotweeks), which, in September 2009, gave undertakings to Bournemouth Trading Standards not to use standard terms which impose financial penalties on consumers for breach;[656]

(b) McCarthy & Stone plc, which, in September 2008, gave undertakings to Bournemouth Trading Standards in relation to numerous standard terms with which the authority had concerns, including a term requiring consumers to keep the supplier fully indemnified from all costs and claims arising from any breach or non-performance, which was revised to acknowledge that consumers would only have to pay the supplier's reasonable costs, reasonably incurred.[657]

Other terms which, on the consumer's breach, purport to give the supplier rights to impose sanctions on consumers (other than to make payments), which are disproportionate are also likely to be unenforceable. Examples of such terms are those purporting to grant suppliers a right which can only normally and properly only be authorized by court order such as a right of entry without consent to private property, for example to repossess goods for which consumers have not paid (or paid on time),[658] to take other direct action to secure redress, for example to sell goods belonging to the consumer which the supplier has in its possession.[659]

---

[656] See <http://www.oft.gov.uk/OFTwork/consumer-enforcement/traders/3453/1/> (accessed 16 April 2011).

[657] See <http://www.oft.gov.uk/OFTwork/consumer-enforcement/traders/3197/1/> (accessed 16 April 2011).

[658] A term which purports to exclude liability for causing property damage in the course of exercising such rights is even less justifiable.

[659] OFT 311, paras 18.3.2–18.3.5 and OFT 672, para 3.140.

The following are examples where the OFT had objections on the grounds of potential unfairness under regulation 5 of the UTCCRs 1999, with a term purporting to give the supplier certain rights, in the event of breach by the consumer:

Original term	New term/Other result[660]
At any time the company may recover from the buyer the goods remaining in the buyer's possession and for the purposes thereof may enter upon any premises . . . occupied by the buyer . . .	The term was deleted.
The Seller shall have no liability . . . under the Contract unless the Purchaser shall have complied with the terms of payment agreed with him and all other terms binding on him . . .	Term deleted.
If the Customer shall commit any breach of this Agreement . . . the Company shall be at liberty to treat this Agreement as repudiated and accordingly may terminate it forthwith by notice in writing to the Customer and shall be entitled to recover possession of the Company's Equipment together with the costs for so doing.	If the Customer shall commit and continue to commit a serious breach of this Agreement for 21 days or more after notice from the Company of the breach, the Company shall be at liberty to treat this Agreement as repudiated and accordingly may terminate it forthwith by notice in writing to recover possession of the system together with the costs for doing so.

2.5.15 Intellectual property rights

Protection of IP rights is crucial to most suppliers of technology products and therefore terms relating to ownership and licensing of IP rights are usually a key feature of technology contracts and drafted heavily in favour of (as well as strongly defended by) suppliers. Therefore, clauses in consumer contracts governing IP rights are often very imbalanced, which gives them the potential to be unfair in several respects.

Terms which seek, at a basic level, to prevent a supplier's IP rights from being misused or misappropriated are likely to be unproblematic, such as terms which seek to protect software from being copied or downloaded for free (provided they do not deny redress to consumers who find that the software is defective after they have

---

[660] OFT 672, para 3.139 and Group 18(c), pp 113–15 of the Annexes to OFT 311.

opened or downloaded it).[661] This is of particular relevance to providers of social networking and other sites that allow the submission of user-generated content, as such providers seek maximum rights from users to content they submit, while at the same time requiring users to give broad warranties and indemnities in relation to such content.

Terms relating to IP that might be open to challenge include terms that:

(a) exclude or limit liability or otherwise restrict remedies for any IP infringement inappropriately;

(b) purport to require consumers to provide indemnity protection for liabilities arising from third party or other claims of IP infringement;[662]

(c) use technical terms or jargon in breach of the 'plain, intelligible language' requirement of regulation 7 of the UTCCRs 1999.[663]

Examples of suppliers which have been subject to formal investigation in respect of standard terms relating to IP rights which were potentially unfair under the UTCCRs 1999 include Dell Corporation Ltd (see sections 2.5.1.2, 2.5.6, and 2.5.12 above), whose standard terms included a clause requiring consumers to indemnify the supplier against action by a third party for infringement of third party IP, which the OFT had concerns with under regulation 5 of the UTCCRs 1999 as an unfair transfer of risk (as a result of which Dell amended the term so that the consumer is only responsible for indemnifying the supplier where claims for infringing third party IP rights arise due to the consumer's default and of which the supplier is not aware).[664]

2.5.16 Force majeure

Force majeure is not a legal term of art (and thus needs defining in any contract), but is generally understood to refer to provisions where parties are exempted from delays or failures to perform contractual obligations due to events outside their control (eg, a terrorist explosion at a supplier's factory, which renders the supplier unable to supply goods ordered). In consumer contracts it is advisable to avoid use of the term 'force majeure' itself, particularly without detailed explanation, as it may fall foul of the requirement for 'plain, intelligible language' in regulation 7 of the UTCCRs 1999.[665]

---

[661] OFT 672, para 3.94.

[662] Ibid para 3.131.

[663] There are numerous examples of terminology that OFT considers likely to breach this requirement, including 'indemnity' and 'indemnify', 'force majeure', 'lien', 'merchantable quality', and 'liquidated damages' (see Group 19(b), pp 128–40 of the Annexes to OFT 311) and it is easy to envisage detailed and technical IP provisions covering issues such as: types of IP protected, extent of rights granted, extent of rights reserved, etc falling foul of this requirement.

[664] See <http://www.oft.gov.uk/OFTwork/consumer-enforcement/traders/2244/1/> (accessed 16 April 2011).

[665] OFT 311, para 2.6.7.

In relation to consumers, while clauses excluding liability for delay may be acceptable where they are restricted in scope to delays unavoidably caused by factors beyond the supplier's control, a supplier must be careful to ensure that a force majeure clause does not also cover matters within the supplier's control (such as shortage of stock, strikes, etc).[666] The contract must be performed in time or the consumer must be informed why this is not possible, and a consumer must have the right to accept or refuse an alternative delivery date. If the consumer does not agree to this, his money must be refunded.

Further, while liability for delay for reasons outside the supplier's control can be excluded, terms should not contain a right to delay at will, or exclude liability where the supplier has not, for example, taken reasonable steps to minimize delay. In addition, a right for the consumer to cancel without penalty in the event of substantial delay may help to achieve fairness.[667] See section 2.5.6 above for further discussions of the supplier's liability for delay and examples of relevant terms with which the OFT had concerns under the UTCCRs 1999.

2.5.17 Termination

Aside from cancellation rights under the DSRs 2000, contracts usually allow for termination for certain types of breach (in addition to common law rights to terminate for serious—'repudiatory'—breaches), and often for termination at will, especially in long-running contracts.

Schedule 2 to the UTCCRs 1999 provides that terms may be regarded as unfair which have the object or effect of (amongst other things):

(a) 'authorising the seller or supplier to dissolve the contract on a discretionary basis where the same facility is not granted to the consumer, or permitting the seller or supplier to retain the sums paid for services not yet supplied by him where it is the seller or supplier himself who dissolves the contract';[668]

(b) 'enabling the seller or supplier to terminate a contract of indeterminate duration without reasonable notice except where there are serious grounds for doing so';[669]

(c) automatically extending a contract of fixed duration where the consumer does not indicate otherwise, when the deadline fixed for the consumer to express his desire not to extend the contract is unreasonably early.[670]

---

[666] OFT 311, para 2.6.5.
[667] Ibid para 2.6.6.
[668] Para 1(f).
[669] Para 1(g).
[670] Para 1(h).

Cancellation clauses risk being unfair under the above provisions if they:

(a) give the supplier wide rights to terminate and/or the consumer few or none;

(b) make consumers pay for goods and services they have not received;

(c) allow the supplier to cancel without acknowledging the customer's right to a refund (where the supplier is obliged to return pre-payments, but without further liability, this is unlikely to be sufficient[671]);

(d) seek to deny or limit the supplier's liability for breach of contract;

(e) allow the supplier to cancel the contract for vague reasons or for a trivial breach by the consumer, particularly when the consumer cannot cancel in similar circumstances;

(f) allow the supplier to terminate suddenly and/or unexpectedly;[672]

(g) allow the supplier to justify cancellation by citing external circumstances which may be within the supplier's control;

(h) purport to rule out all possibility of cancellation by the consumer;

(i) require the consumer to cancel a long way ahead of time, in relation to a contract: of fixed period with automatic renewal; or which continues indefinitely.[673]

Terms which are likely to be unproblematic include:

(a) terms which merely reflect the ordinary law (eg, prohibiting consumer cancellation where the supplier is not in breach of the contract, and alert the consumer to his liability in damages for wrongful cancellation);

(b) terms which clearly explain that circumstances (outside the supplier's control) in which a supplier could cancel the contract.[674]

---

[671] A right to cancel at will, with liability only to return prepayments, may be acceptable if it operates exclusively where circumstances make it impossible or impractical to complete the contract, providing: attention is drawn to the risk of cancellation if it is a real possibility; the circumstances are clearly and specifically described; there is no listing of matters that could be within the supplier's control (eg, strikes by the supplier's own workforce, equipment breakdown, or transportation difficulties); and the supplier is required to find out and inform the consumer as soon as possible if such circumstances do apply, explaining the reasons for the proposed cancellation (if they are not obvious).

[672] A right for the supplier to cancel a contract without notice may be fair if it is effectively restricted to situations in which there are 'serious grounds' for immediate termination (eg, circumstances in which there is a real risk of loss or harm to the supplier or others if the contract continues for even a short period, such as a reasonable suspicion of fraud or other abuse). However, fairness is likely to require some clear indication of the nature of any 'serious grounds' for cancellation without notice. If the consumer will be unaware whether an immediate cancellation is or is not contractually justified, he is in no position to seek redress if it is not, and the term will in practice be open to abuse.

[673] OFT 672, para 3.52 and OFT 311, paras 6.1.2–6.1.6, 6.2.1, 7.2.1–7.2.4, and 8.2–8.3.

[674] OFT 311, para 6.1.7 and OFT 672, para 3.5.

The following are examples where the OFT had objections on the grounds of potential unfairness under paragraphs 1(f), 1(g), and/or 1(h) of Schedule 2 to the UTCCRs 1999, with a cancellation clause:

Original term	New term/Other result[675]
. . . if [goods are not available] the seller shall be at liberty to determine the contract . . . by giving [the buyer] notice in writing . . .	If we are unable to deliver the goods within 30 days beginning with the day after the day of the agreement: we shall inform you by email . . . we will reimburse any sum, paid by you or on your behalf under . . . the agreement within a period of 30 days beginning with the day after the day on which the time for delivery expired.
This Contract is not subject to cancellation by the Customer . . . the Company reserves the right to cancel or refuse acceptance of any order at any time by refunding all monies paid less an administrative charge.	Either party shall have the right to terminate this Contract without penalty within seven days . . . In the event of such termination by either party the Company shall refund to the Customer all sums paid by the Customer.
. . . this agreement shall remain in force for a minimum period of 12 months ... Sky may terminate the Agreement at any time.	You may end this contract at any time during the Minimum Term by giving us one month's notice if we [exercise variation rights in various ways—see details in terms listed under Groups 10 and 11] . . . Except where you break the Conditions of this Contract we will not terminate this Contract during the Minimum Term.
This Agreement shall following the completion of the installation and the payment of the cost of this installation in full by the customer to the Company terminate: (a) at the expiration of 12 months written notice given by either party to the other to such effect . . .	This Agreement shall commence on the commencement date and shall continue in force for the term unless either party gives twenty one days written notice to the other party of its intention to terminate this Agreement, or if this Agreement is terminated by either party pursuant to clause 14.

---

[675] See OFT 672, para 3.53 and Group 6(a), pp 62–7 and Group 8, pp 73–4 of the Annexes to OFT 311.

2.5.18 Assignment

In principle, the parties to a contract are, generally, free to assign the benefit of a contact to a third party. In practice, the contract will usually provide for whether it can be assigned and, if so, by whom and in what circumstances.

Terms in consumer contracts risk unfairness where they, without good reason, restrict the consumer's right to assign, or give the supplier broad rights to transfer at will both its rights and obligations under the contract to a third party. Paragraph 1(p) of Schedule 2 to the UTCCRs 1999 provides that a term may be regarded as unfair which has the object or effect of 'giving the seller or supplier the possibility of transferring his rights and obligations under the contract, where this may serve to reduce the guarantees for the consumer, without the latter's agreement'.

Therefore, while suppliers will often wish to retain flexibility in their business (eg, to enable them to sell parts of it) by providing for a right to assign their rights and obligations under consumer contracts, consumers' legal positions should be protected in the event of such 'assignment'. Similarly, while suppliers may want to restrict the ability of consumers to assign (eg, a guarantee in relation to goods),[676] such restrictions should be used with caution.

In relation to consumer assignment, terms limiting the circumstances in which the consumer can assign, for example a guarantee, are unlikely to raise concerns if they simply require:

(a) the new purchaser to demonstrate that the guarantee was properly assigned, provided the procedures for this are straightforward;

(b) the supplier's consent to the transfer of the guarantee, provided this cannot be withheld unreasonably.[677]

In relation to supplier assignment, the issue is protection of the consumer's legal position, which can be achieved by:

(a) giving the consumer a right to be consulted and assignment to be permitted only if he consents (with a penalty-free right of exit if he does not);

(b) allowing the supplier to assign only in circumstances which ensure that the consumer's rights under the contract will not be prejudiced.[678]

A particularly striking term to which the OFT objected stated: 'The goods ordered by the customers are for the customer's own requirements and as such cannot be resold by the customer to any other party.' Following the OFT objection the term was deleted.[679]

---

[676] OFT 672, para 3.116.
[677] Ibid para 3.117.
[678] OFT 311, para 16.2.
[679] Group 18(d), pp 118–19 of the OFT 311.

Examples of suppliers which have been subject to formal investigation in respect of standard terms relating to assignment which were potentially unfair under regulation 5 of, and, in some cases, paragraph 1(p) of Schedule 2 to the UTCCRs 1999 include Wanadoo (see sections 2.5.13 above), O2 (UK) Ltd (see section 2.5.2.4), Bulldog Communications (see sections 2.5.9, 2.5.11, and 2.5.12 above) and UK Online (see section 2.5.6).

2.5.19 Choice of law, jurisdiction, and dispute resolution

The advantages to a supplier of restricting any disputes to a law or jurisdiction of its choosing are clear in terms of both convenience and cost. However, terms which prevent consumers from being able to pursue legal proceedings in their local courts (eg, requiring a customer in Edinburgh to claim via the English courts and English law only) are likely to be considered unfair. It is not fair for the aggrieved consumer to be forced to travel long distances and use unfamiliar procedures. International conventions lay down rules on this issue,[680] which are part of UK law. Terms which conflict with those conventions are likely to be unenforceable for that reason, too.[681]

A fixed procedure for resolving disputes can be advantageous in avoiding the unfairness which can arise when the supplier is the sole judge of disputes as to, for example, what constitutes a breach. However, clauses requiring the consumer to go to arbitration can also cause problems. Paragraph 1(q) of Schedule 2 to the UTCCRs 1999 provides that terms may be unfair if they have the object or effect of

excluding or hindering the consumer's right to take legal action or exercise any other legal remedy, particularly by requiring the consumer to take disputes exclusively to arbitration not covered by legal provisions, unduly restricting the evidence available to him or imposing on him a burden of proof which, according to applicable law, should lie with another party to the contract.

Further, section 91 of the Arbitration Act 1996 provides that compulsory arbitration clauses for claims of £5,000 or less are always unfair, and therefore always invalid under the UTCCRs 1999.

According to the OFT, compulsory arbitration clauses are problematic if they could be used to prevent or hinder consumers from seeking legal redress when the supplier is in default, make arbitration compulsory, or fail to make clear that the consumer can choose whether or not to go to arbitration.[682]

Examples of suppliers which have been subject to formal investigation in respect of standard terms relating to choice of law/jurisdiction which were potentially unfair

---

[680] See further Chapter 4, section 4.6.2.
[681] OFT 311, para 17.4.
[682] OFT 672, para 3.136.

under paragraph 1(q) of Schedule 2 to the UTCCRs 1999 include Hutchison 3G (UK) Ltd (see section 2.5.3), and UK Online (see sections 2.5.6 and 2.5.18).

2.6 CONCLUSION

The task of synthesizing EU and UK unfair contract terms and practices, consumer protection, distance selling, and e-commerce law and soft law, as well as the law concerning intervention from regulators and other interested bodies, and applying it to mass market contracting has been substantial and frequently challenging. We hope that the extent of the challenges faced by even compliance-focused businesses operating in Europe, and the scope and pace of change in the regulatory environment in which they operate is now apparent. To help those facing such challenges, we conclude this chapter with some final thoughts on what we consider the principal current issues in mass market contracting.

First, businesses that wish to penetrate European mass markets and trade with European consumers must contend with a highly complex legal framework affecting not only their contractual terms and conditions, but also, as a result of the UCPD 2005 implemented in the UK by the CPRs 2008, their commercial practices in general, including advertising material, all communications with consumers, order and sales processes, and website content. There are multiple, frequently overlapping, applicable legal instruments, a growing body of case law, and a proliferation of soft law instruments and measures coupled with a growing body of regulatory action. Some of the latter are actually or effectively legally binding (such as regulatory decisions and trade association terms and conditions), others compelling (such as self-regulatory standards and codes of practice), some influential (eg, proposed legislative initiatives), and the remainder non-binding and wholly voluntary. The sheer volume of applicable and potentially applicable law and the significant lack of coordination in its implementation creates an unnecessarily complex and burdensome compliance regime. At the same time, lack of clarity in and across key measures, and in their national implementations, compounds the problem. For example, as we have already noted, there is not even an essential, unifying definition of the term 'consumer', a surprising (or, more accurately, perhaps not surprising, but certainly disappointing) fact in light of more than three decades of legislation at the European level in this area. Technological and market developments, such as Web 2.0 and cloud computing, may further complicate the issues; for instance, the consumption of Web 2.0 services is of a hybrid nature which also entails a 'supply' element, but the law has not recognized this.

Secondly, the problems described above have been exacerbated in the area of mass market contracting, particularly in the area of e-commerce where there has been frequent, if perhaps inevitable, failure to draft or make laws that keep up with (let alone anticipate) developments in the sector. For example, although the UK courts began seriously addressing the question more than ten years ago, there is still no answer to the question whether software (and now, digital content generally) should be regarded as goods, services, or something *sui generis*. UCTA 1977 does not appear to apply to cross-border online or offline transactions involving the supply of physical goods, and limitation and exclusion clauses relating to IP rights in, for example, electronic content, also appear to be excluded from its ambit; it seems eminently possible that other consumer protection measures may well be drafted in by legislators and/or regulatory authorities to plug the gaps, though when and in what circumstances exactly remains unclear. Possible platforms for reform of the law include review of the e-Commerce Directive, the proposed pCRD, or perhaps market-specific consultations, such as the European Commission's consultation on cloud computing (planned for 2011). And the DSRs 2000, measures specifically implemented to address issues of consumer protection in the context of e-commerce and other contracts concluded at a distance, appear to ignore the possibility of digital content downloads and the existence of hybrid contracts for goods and services, despite the fact that such contracts are increasingly the model for many forms of technology transactions. The fact that the law still leaves unanswered the question of whether software and other digital content actually constitute goods or services or something else makes the application of cancellation rights uncertain.

Thirdly, the law's failure to keep up with technology and rapidly globalizing technology contracting models also leads to increasingly unexpected results. For example, it is unclear whether certain clauses in free software and open source software licences would be enforceable in the UK under UCTA 1977 or applicable consumer protection law, in either consumer contracts or, potentially, business-to-business contracts on standard terms. The same is true in relation to the exact impact of the nature and economic reality of commoditized technology services (such as cloud computing) in assessing the reasonableness and fairness, and therefore the binding nature and enforceability, of commonly used terms such as clauses excluding or limiting the supplier's liability at a relatively low level. A detailed analysis of these issues is outside the scope of this chapter, but we believe that they are important ones that merit further analysis.

Fourthly, enthusiasm for continuing action at the policy-making and legislative levels remains unabated. In fact, it appears to have increased. However, enthusiasm is not always coupled with effectiveness: although steps have recently been taken towards reform, notably in the form of the UCPD 2005 and CPCR 2004, and further steps are likely to be taken in the near future, such as the pCRD and, at the UK level, the dUCTB or, perhaps, the proposed Consumer Rights Bill, these measures appear destined to leave significant issues unresolved and are likely to create new areas of confusion. At the same time, most recent policy and legislative activity has been directed at enhancing regulatory enforcement powers rather than at rationalization. While most honest and responsible traders should be able to see some benefit in a consistently applied, predictable, and meaningful consumer protection regime, the case for beefing-up enforcement powers in a relatively unpredictable and confusing environment is less clear. Nevertheless, the enhancement and prioritization of consumer protection enforcement throughout the EU is now a fact of life, and businesses that ignore this do so at their peril.

Fifthly, the prospect of customer dissatisfaction, reputational damage, potential regulatory sanctions, and civil and, in exceptional circumstances, possibly criminal liability for consumer protection compliance failures might seem a sufficiently potent threat to deter most businesses from engaging in activities that are substantially damaging to consumers. However, such failures may have wider ramifications. These include, for example, potential disclosure obligations that may arise under financing arrangements in connection with mergers and acquisition activity, public offerings or generally for publicly quoted companies as a result of their status as such. It is also possible that companies that are quoted on a US national exchange or NASDAQ (and hence subject, irrespective of where they headquartered, to the disclosure obligations under the US Sarbanes-Oxley Act of 2002) could be potentially obliged to disclose breaches of European consumer law to the US Securities and Exchange Commission. If compliance failures give rise to any of these potential disclosure obligations, they may have additional significant and negative economic consequences for the disclosing company, and in certain circumstances could also trigger actions for breach of contract, and even contract termination, if commitments regarding general compliance with law (which are often broadly drafted) have been made in the contract.

Effectively addressing these challenges will be a major and continuing task for mass market businesses, particularly those with presence in multiple jurisdictions. The developing legal environment, changes in technology and in contracting practice, and the cross-border nature and exposure of such businesses also mean that there are no 'out of the box' compliance solutions. However, experience shows that there are certain common steps that businesses should consider taking to assess and manage their regulatory and transactional exposure.

These include identifying at the outset an appropriate individual with sufficient authority to be able to design, implement, and promote a corporate compliance strategy and programme. Businesses should then design and implement an audit process that will enable them to assess both the legal and regulatory environment in the jurisdictions in which they have exposure, and the scope and nature of their operations and strategic objectives in those jurisdictions. Without this information, it is impossible to determine where compliance exposure exists, and the steps needed effectively to reduce and manage that exposure. Before implementing any compliance programme, businesses with presence in multiple jurisdictions will also face at least one further strategic compliance issue. This is whether they should adopt a highly jurisdiction-specific approach, tailoring their compliance activities to take advantage of all features of each jurisdiction's regime, or whether, instead, to take a 'highest common denominator' approach, trading local flexibility and advantages in more liberal regimes for relative uniformity of approach and ease of administration across the board. Of course, most businesses will select, or end up with, a hybrid approach, but the fundamental question and decision on the appropriate approach is important and may have significant costs or savings consequences for the business. Finally, businesses will need to focus on implementation, and ensuring that compliance assessment and management remains a continuing process: if it is not, the compliance function will effectively have failed.

Compliance is a reactive exercise. In our view businesses should also be proactive in trying to shape tomorrow's legal and regulatory framework: they should monitor current and forthcoming developments with the aim to proactively engage in the consultations in order to explain their concerns and interests and propose solutions. Businesses should therefore target their lobbying and advocacy at educating legislators and regulators about justified business concerns and legitimate interests concerning the law and how it should be adapted or interpreted in a changing environment in order to provide effective consumer protection without stifling innovation. Often, businesses will be able to make practical recommendations about how consumer protection can be achieved in a business friendly manner. Consider that recently, for example, the European Commission and national governments, legislators, and regulators essentially turned to the industry for a practical solution to the issue of obtaining valid consent for online behavioural advertising purposes; and to browser manufacturers for a practical solution to the problem of compliance with the new requirement under the amended e-Privacy Directive for obtaining the user's consent before using cookies.

In conclusion, we have shown that ensuring effective compliance with the laws affecting mass market contracting in Europe is a formidable and challenging task. A raft of new legal and regulatory measures is making its way onto the statute books and the scale of the task is rapidly increasing. Dynamically changing technologies and contracting practices add to the challenge. As a result of progressive strengthening of the enforcement regime, the stakes for businesses that fail to comply are therefore rising exponentially. Both legislators and regulators have publicly confirmed this. At the same time, mass market businesses are complex, resource-intensive operations that cannot change the way they do business overnight. We believe that these are powerful warning signs. Responsibly run companies with mass market contracting exposure should not delay in seeking to address and manage their risk: waiting until competitors come under fire to confirm whether the time has come to act inevitably means that things have been left too late, and a risk reduction project that could have been conducted without regulatory or public scrutiny may have just become a far more costly, public, crisis management exercise with potentially serious reputational and brand damage implications. Instead, such companies should heed the admonition of influential American business consultant, W Edwards Deming:

It is not necessary to change. Survival is not mandatory.

3

INFORMATION TECHNOLOGY OUTSOURCING AND SERVICES ARRANGEMENTS

Mark Lewis

3.1 INTRODUCTION

3.1.1 What is an information technology and services outsourcing contract?

An information technology (referred to below in this chapter as 'IT') and services outsourcing contract usually involves the transfer of all, part, or parts[1] of the IT and

---

[1] The references to 'parts' and to 'one or more third party service providers' reflects the trend of 'multi-sourcing', in which the customer outsources different services or 'service stacks' to different providers. Multi-sourcing adds additional risks for the customer. Managing more than one provider is not only a challenge to the (usually) smaller function retained by the customer after the outsourcing to manage the outsourcing relationship. It also adds the new risk of ensuring that the different services or service stacks supplied by different providers work properly together. And there is the further risk that, by outsourcing IT functions to more than one provider, it is more difficult for the customer to attribute to any one provider the responsibility—and therefore for the customer to retain legal recourse—for defects in the outsourced services.

related services functions of a customer's undertaking to one or more third party service providers. Often, an IT outsourcing arrangement will therefore involve the transfer of assets and, frequently, staff (either employed by the customer or now, more commonly, by an incumbent third party provider) that were previously used to support the activity or operation, to the provider. Where assets are transferred, they may for a time then be used to provide IT and related services back to the customer, to agreed levels of service. These contracts are referred to most commonly as 'information technology outsourcing' contracts (often abbreviated in the outsourcing and consulting industries to 'ITO' to distinguish them from business process outsourcing or 'BPO' contracts). More recently, the trend is to refer to them by their specific, functionally based, descriptions, for example 'applications development and maintenance outsourcing' contract or 'desktop outsourcing' contract. In other cases, the term 'outsourcing' is dropped altogether, such as in relation to managed services contracts or UK public sector 'externalization' or 'commercialization' services contracts. The reasons for such nomenclature vary: in the case of managed services, there is—or was—perhaps a functional distinction between outsourcing and providing or managing a single service or related services, the best example of which is desktop outsourcing. In the case of public sector outsourcing and even private sector outsourcing in the economic climate prevailing at the time of this edition, there are undoubtedly presentational reasons for wishing to describe outsourcing contracts euphemistically as something else. The point worth making, which is repeated in different contexts and ways below in this chapter, is that you need to understand *what* services are being provided and the other basic commercial, operational, technological, and other relevant terms of the transaction: what the transaction is *actually* called is irrelevant, in both the commercial and legal senses.

IT outsourcing has been around for many years now, although IT outsourcing in its modern form has developed from the introduction of the early time-sharing, facilities management, and service bureau arrangements from the 1960s and 1970s. The nature of these facilities management and service bureau arrangements is described below.[2] Although facilities management and service bureau contracts are different in nature to a 'pure' IT outsourcing, they heavily influenced its development.

It is generally agreed that the first landmark IT outsourcing contract was the contract entered into in 1989 between Eastman Kodak and an IBM subsidiary, Integrated Systems Solutions Corporation. Under the terms of that agreement Integrated Systems Solutions Corporation built and operated a computer centre for Kodak, taking on some 300 Kodak staff in the process.[3] Since then the global IT

---

[2] See section 3.1.2.
[3] See TR Mylott, *Computer Outsourcing Managing the Transfer of Information Technology* (Englewood Cliffs, NJ: Prentice Hall, 1995) 15 and R Klepper and WO Jones, *Outsourcing Information Technology Systems and Services* (Upper Saddle River, NJ: Prentice Hall, 1998) xxii.

outsourcing market has expanded rapidly as a growing number of corporate (now increasingly including outsourcing providers themselves) and governmental entities have rushed to jump on the outsourcing bandwagon and take advantage of the perceived benefits that an outsourced function could bring.

IT functions that are now outsourced typically include one or more of the following:

(a) data centre and systems infrastructure;

(b) voice and data networks;[4]

(c) telecommunications;

(d) applications development;

(e) applications support and maintenance;

(f) server and desktop environments;

(g) project management;

(h) multi-vendor management;

(i) contract management;

(j) support, help desk, and call centre;

(k) IT training;

(l) disaster recovery and business continuity;

(m) research & development;

(n) auditing;

(o) software testing; and

(p) IT procurement.

IT outsourcing contracts will frequently include a bundle of functions that are transferred to a provider, especially given the natural dependencies that exist between many different IT functions.[5]

Although most IT functions are capable of being outsourced, the crucial decision for any undertaking will be: which elements of our IT function should, in practice, be outsourced? Generally, where an IT function is critical to the business (such as where a particular system enables the business to distinguish itself from its competitors) a degree of caution should be exercised before the running of that function is entrusted to a third party.

---

[4] With the move to Voice Over Internet Protocol ('VOIP') communications, the distinction is blurring.

[5] See n 1 above for a short discussion of the trend to multi-sourcing and the attendant risks because of the dependencies that exist between different IT functions.

3.1.2 IT outsourcing contracts distinguished from other computing services, facilities management, and managed services contracts

The early time-sharing and bureaux-based contracts from which the modern IT outsourcing contract has evolved were more limited in their scope of service and seldom involved the transfer of assets to the provider. Instead, under time-sharing arrangements the customer would be given a connection to enable it to access the provider's systems at the provider's site. The customer remained responsible for the use to which he put those systems. Similarly with service bureau arrangements, the provider would process an application, such as payroll, using its mainframe computers to provide similar processes for a number of customers.[6]

Under facilities management ('FM')[7] or (sometimes) managed services contracts, it is generally the customer's IT systems (whether they are owned by the customer or licensed to it by third parties) that are used by the provider to deliver one or more 'bundled' services to the customer. Again, there may be no change of ownership in the assets, which usually remain under the customer's ownership or are licensed to it and which remain located at the customer's premises. The provider is merely granted access to use those IT systems necessary in order to provide the outsourced, or managed, services.

The term 'managed services' as it relates to IT services is, at the time of writing, more prevalent than previously. As with most, if not all, terms to describe functional (as opposed to technological) and economic terms in the IT services sector, there is no one compelling definition. It has for some time been used synonymously with the term 'outsourcing'. As in other cases,[8] use of the term 'managed services' was sometimes seen either as a way of distinguishing the particular service offering from others (notably in the case of IT desktop outsourcing) or avoiding the unpalatable reality (eg, for trades unions and works councils, whose members were likely to be made redundant or transfer to the service provider under the Acquired Rights Directive or TUPE Regulations[9]) that the transaction concerned was in all but name an outsourcing arrangement. Now, 'managed services' has in the context of IT services come to mean that a provider assumes responsibility to the customer for an end-to-end service, including the management of IT assets and networks and sub-contractors.[10]

---

[6] The similarity to the cloud computing functional and economic models is striking: see section 3.1.3.1 below.

[7] The usage of the term 'FM' as it has come to be applied in the IT services sector should be distinguished from current usage of the term as it applies to the management of various services relating to the occupancy of premises, eg cleaning, building maintenance, hygiene services, security services, and so on. By the next edition of this work, it is almost certain that the term will no longer apply to IT services.

[8] See p 207 below in relation to UK public sector outsourcing.

[9] See section 3.4 below.

[10] The author is grateful to Dr Julia Kotlarsky, Associate Professor of Information Systems and Management Group, Warwick Business School, The University of Warwick, for this suggestion.

The question of whether a particular arrangement is an IT outsourcing contract is really a question of scope and degree. For example, many long-term services arrangements entered into by UK central and local government are outsourcing contracts in all but name. Although it may have been official policy *not* to refer to these deals as 'outsourcing' they typically involve a provider building or supplying, taking over the management of, or owning and operating information technology and then providing services to the public sector entity concerned using those systems.

Even where the transaction is not a 'pure' IT outsourcing, involving the transfer of assets and the related activity, and instead falls under the guise of, for example, cloud computing or a managed services contract, many of the considerations covered in this chapter will still be relevant to that transaction.

Nomenclature is, however, much less important than having, in relation to any proposed IT services arrangement, as precise an understanding as possible of the following:

(a) what services are going to be provided;

(b) whether one or more service provider will be engaged to provide those services;

(c) what functions in the customer organization will be affected;

(d) the duration of the proposed arrangements;

(e) from where the IT services will be provided, that is, onshore, nearshore, offshore, or a combination of some or all such locations;

(f) what quality or levels of service will apply to those services;

(g) whether there are any people who will transfer to the provider and, if so, who is within the scope of the transfer;

(h) whether there are any assets that will transfer to the provider and what they are;

(i) the implications for any incumbent third party providers;

(j) any dependencies in the provision of the proposed outsourced services on the responsibilities of the customer or other third party providers and, if so, what those dependencies are; and

(k) the timing of the proposed outsourcing project.[11]

---

[11] This is clearly not intended to be an exhaustive checklist for creating any outsourcing contract—it is a list of the basic questions that will determine whether to approach the transaction as an outsourcing and, if so, how to reflect the arrangements in a contractual structure.

3.1.3 Recent trends

3.1.3.1 *Cloud computing*

Disconcerting though it may be for those who argue that cloud computing is a disruptive new technology,[12] or at the very least a new development in the functional or economic model of computing—in fact that cloud computing is *the* future of computing—there are striking similarities between the early time-sharing, bureaux-based, and later applications services provision ('ASP') computing models and the cloud computing model. Customers do not need to own expensive IT estates.[13] They access with other customers the provider's IT infrastructure and applications environment as a utility service. Granted, newer technologies have emerged that are deployed in the cloud, notably virtualization, and the utility computing model has been further developed in the cloud computing model.

12

> The interesting thing about Cloud Computing is that we've redefined Cloud Computing to include everything that we already do. I can't think of anything that isn't Cloud Computing with all of these announcements. The computer industry is the only industry that is more fashion-driven than women's fashion. Maybe I'm an idiot, but I have no idea what anyone is talking about. What is it? It's complete gibberish. It's insane. When is this idiocy going to stop? . . . We'll make Cloud Computing announcements. I'm not going to fight this thing. But I don't understand what we would do differently in the light of cloud.

(Larry Ellison, Chief Executive Officer of Oracle, in an address to Oracle OpenWorld on 26 September 2008, quoted in <http://news.cnet.com/8301-13953_3-10052188-80.html> (accessed 8 August 2011).) See also the much publicized statement from Vineet Nayar, Chief Executive Officer of Indian offshore IT and outsourcing provider HCL Technologies:

> Cloud is bullshit . . . My view on Cloud is that I always look for disruptive technologies that redefine the way the business gets run. If there is a disruptive technology out there that redefines business I am for it. If there is no underlying technology there, and it is just repackaging of a commercial solution, then I do not call it a business trend. I call it hype . . . So, whatever we have seen on the Cloud—whether it is virtualization, if it's available to . . . now before I go there, and the reason I believe what I'm saying is right, is because you have now a new vocabulary which has come in Cloud, which is called Private Cloud. So now it is very difficult, so what everybody is saying is 'yes, it is private Cloud and public Cloud'. So, in my vocabulary Private Cloud is typically data center and when I say Cloud it is about Public Cloud. So let's be very clear about it . . . So my view is that I have not seen anything from a technology point of view which is not available for the enterprise for usage for me to get very excited and saying, 'Hey all of this is going to move to the Cloud.' And that's the reason I'm not as bullish about the Cloud as somebody else is . . .

(Address to HCL Analyst Conference, Boston, USA, December 2010, quoted in <http://www.enterpriseirregulars.com/30118/%E2%80%9Ccloud-is-bullsht%E2%80%9D-%E2%80%93-hcl%E2%80%99s-ceo-vineet-nayar-explains-why-he-said-just-that/> (accessed 8 August 2011).)

While both statements were—and remain—striking, what both Larry Ellison and Vineet Nayar are saying is that cloud computing—at least in its current form—is not a new and disruptive information technology or 'killer application': it is a functional and economic computing solution that has been repackaged. And the new economic models and technologies that are emerging are doing so in 'public' cloud computing models.

[13] See section 3.1.2 above. Interestingly, the first use of the term 'cloud computing' is attributed to Dr Ramnath K Chellappa, Associate Professor, Infosystems and Operations Management, Goizueta Business School, Emory University, USA, as long ago as 1997. Professor Chellappa presented a paper entitled 'Intermediaries in Cloud-Computing' at INFORMS in Dallas, Texas. He then suggested that cloud computing would be a 'new computing paradigm where the boundaries of computing would be determined by economic rationale rather than technical limits'. Note the emphasis on economics not technologies. And quite prescient, too. In 2002 Professor Chellappa produced a research paper in which he proposed pricing models specifically for active intranets.

At the time of writing, it is commonly implied that cloud computing is an alternative to IT outsourcing and moreover that it will in the medium term replace IT outsourcing.[14] Undoubtedly, there are features of the current 'public' and 'hybrid' cloud computing models[15] that resemble those of IT outsourcing, essentially (at the highest level of definition) the engagement of a third party supplier to provide services that might otherwise have been provided by an in-house IT function or another third party services provider. For the purposes of this chapter, this writer will take 'public' cloud computing as the representative cloud computing comparator of IT outsourcing.

There are various IT functions that are now provided as cloud computing services. These are evolving, but at the time of writing include:

(a) Storage-as-a-Service;

(b) Database-as-a-Service;

(c) Information-as-a-Service;

(d) Process-as-a-Service;

(e) Application-as-a-Service;

(f) Platform-as-a-Service;

(g) Integration-as-a-Service;

(h) Security-as-a-Service;

(i) Management-as-a-Service/Governance-as-a-Service;

---

[14] 'In the next five years, outsourcing as we know it will have disappeared . . . New players, which have yet to enter the market, will soon rule the industry' (Arjun Sethi, Head of Outsourcing, AT Kearney, quoted in <http://www.cio.com/article/603075/The_End_of_IT_Outsourcing_As_We_Know_It> (accessed 8 August 2011), August 2010). The interview with Arjun Sethi continues:

> At the heart of Sethi's prediction of a 'massive reconfiguration of the outsourcing industry' is the rise of cloud computing. Most existing providers simply won't adapt quickly enough. As a result, Sethi says, Amazon, Google . . . or a vendor we've not yet heard of will become the market leaders. Meanwhile, traditional infrastructure providers like HP . . ., Dell . . . and Xerox . . . may struggle to keep up, and many Indian providers will disappear completely.

This is a bold statement. For a more measured pronouncement, see <http://www.computerworlduk.com/in-depth/outsourcing/3240266/cloud-computing-spells-the-end-for-traditional-it-outsourcing/> (accessed 8 August 2011), quoting Kevin Campbell, Group CEO Technology, Accenture, and former head of Outsourcing at Accenture, on 17 September 2010, as saying: 'The Cloud is still emerging and all its related implications haven't been thought through.' He is further quoted as saying that cloud computing is already displacing traditional outsourcing, though (by implication) not replacing it. He explained that one of the inhibitors to the development of cloud computing is that global companies tend (at least at the time of writing) not to run their business critical systems in the cloud. Service availability/outage is a concern, he says, as is security—the risk most often raised by Chief Information Officers ('CIOs').

[15] See Chapter 1, section 1.4.4.2. The 'private' cloud computing model seems less like an outsourced service, as its most common features appear to be the use of virtualization technologies within the customer's firewall. Admittedly, the 'private' cloud computing model could be provided by a third party systems or services integrator and hosted by a third party cloud computing provider for the customer organization, in which case it, too, will resemble IT outsourcing.

   (j) Testing-as-a-Service; and

   (k) Infrastructure-as-a-Service.

New providers have emerged to provide cloud computing services. Some of them are long-established IT and outsourcing service providers,[16] some have moved into the area from other parts of the digital economy[17] and others are new entrants.[18] The emergence of new provider communities indicates that there is a difference between IT outsourcing as we have come to know it and the new model that is cloud computing; although it is also clear that established IT and outsourcing providers, including the offshore providers, have adapted their service offerings to include cloud computing.

   Cloud computing contracts reflect another difference with IT sourcing: the former are designed to cover commoditized, shared, utility computing services at a fraction of the cost of most outsourced IT services arrangements. While outsource providers still aspire to greater commoditization in both service provision and contracting and there is a growing level of commoditization in IT outsourcing contracts, the latter still tend to be heavily customized for particular projects, even if the outsourced IT services and related processes may in themselves be commoditized. Cloud computing contracts designed for corporate users on a commercial basis[19] are closer to hosting services and other online services contracts than IT outsourcing contracts, providing as they generally do for:

   (a) standardized shared services using a common platform;

   (b) restrictions on service availability;

   (c) limited service levels, if any;

   (d) limited legal recourse for breaches of service provision and contract;

   (e) relatively wide exclusions of provider liability and relatively low quantum limitations on the liability of the provider;

   (f) acceptable use policy (also known as an 'AUP');

   (g) the provider's freedom to process data from anywhere in the world;

   (h) the removal of customer's data on termination of the contract; and

   (i) the provider's ability to vary the standard terms of contract.[20]

---

[16] Like Dell, Sun, HP, and IBM.

[17] Like Google, Amazon, and Facebook.

[18] Like 3Tera, Salesforce, Joyent, ElasticHosts, Rackspace, and Skytap.

[19] In contrast, eg, to social networking cloud computing offerings from, say, Facebook.

[20] For an excellent analysis of 31 US and European cloud computing provider contracts, see S Bradshaw, C Millard, and I Walden, 'Contracts for Clouds: Comparison and Analysis of the Terms and Conditions of Cloud Computing Services', Queen Mary School of Law Legal Studies Research Paper N .63/2010, 1 September 2010, available for downloading from <http://ssrn.com/abstract=1662374> (accessed 8 August 2011).

While corporate users of cloud computing services will benefit from standardized services provided at lower cost as a utility service, there are residual concerns about cloud computing services and contract terms. Some of the main concerns include:

(a) for how long a cloud computing provider will continue to provide the offered service at the stated supported levels of service;[21]

(b) how easy it would be to migrate from one cloud computing service to another;[22]

(c) the integrity and security of data held in the cloud;[23]

(d) data sovereignty and compliance;[24] and

(e) the provider's right to remove the customer's data on termination, or shortly after termination, of the cloud computing contract.[25]

In this writer's view, the essential difference between IT outsourcing and cloud computing services is currently not one of great substance, but of degree. Cloud computing models, services, and contracts are still evolving. It is too soon to say what the true impact of cloud computing on IT outsourcing will be. However, at the time of writing there are some real and substantial concerns about cloud computing, the most often-cited being security of data processed in the cloud. It appears that, until the security issue is satisfactorily resolved, it will inhibit the growth of cloud computing in the large corporate sector. Even for small and medium-sized business customers, while cloud computing is an attractive solution to IT needs, security remains an issue. Finally, as with any form of IT outsourcing,

---

[21] There is also concern about the financial viability of some cloud computing providers. Some have already disappeared, eg, the rather aptly named G.ho.st.

[22] Switching between cloud computing providers will depend on their use of common standards and sharing similar characteristics and features, together with data porting facilities. So far, there are no common standards. This remains a serious concern.

[23] The security of information stored, processed, and transmitted through the cloud and on cloud computing servers is of paramount importance to customers, but at the time of writing there is no industry-wide security standard for cloud computing solutions. Co-location and segmentation of cloud servers raises questions about the integrity of sensitive corporate data. The Cloud Security Alliance has been founded to address this concern. Its mission statement is 'to promote the use of best practices for providing security assurance within Cloud Computing, and provide education on the uses of Cloud Computing to help secure all other forms of computing': <http://www.cloudsecurityalliance.org/> (accessed 8 August 2011). Security concerns are most often cited as the reason for larger companies being reluctant to adopt the 'public' and 'hybrid' cloud computing models.

[24] In this sense, 'data sovereignty' means where the data will be stored and which government or foreign agency will have control over the data or the ability as a sovereign to intervene in the transmission into, and the storage, processing, and transmission out of, their countries. Of course, one of the main features of cloud computing is that it is not 'location dependent', ie, the IT infrastructure used for cloud computing service may be anywhere in the world. Some cloud computing providers do offer to process data in certain areas, sometimes called 'availability zones' to meet EU data protection compliance and avoid data transfers outside the EEA. Eg, Amazon offers customers 'regional zones' in which it undertakes to process data, and not to transfer data outside those zones. For customers of cloud computing services subject to regulation, this will remain an important issue.

[25] See generally on this issue Bradshaw, Millard, and Walden, n 20 above.

nomenclature and form are not as important as substance: see the last paragraph of section 3.1.2 above.

3.1.3.2   *Global framework and master services arrangements*

One thing that is certain is that the IT outsourcing market is not a static one: the outsourcing industry tends to reinvent or refine itself every few years. A number of new variants on the traditional structure have surfaced. The increasingly global nature of business is driving a shift towards more complex, flexible outsourcing contracts. Organizations are frequently looking to outsource their IT operations not necessarily on a country-by-country basis, but under a global relationship with one or more providers. These global transactions raise important structural, commercial, contractual, and legal issues.

The contract itself can be structured in a number of ways. Frequently, a relationship agreement is adopted at the highest corporate level. This prescribes a framework of master terms under which subsequent or local agreements can be entered into by the contracting parties or other group or local entities, both on the customer and the provider side. Standard templates for local agreements are often then provided in order to reduce the scope for negotiation at a local level and to ensure that services are provided on as uniform a basis as possible. Nevertheless, some amendment of those local agreements may be required, for example to reflect local law requirements in relation to employee, data protection, or competition issues.

As well as the move towards global contracts, flexibility is seen as an important goal to ensure that the contract can develop to mirror changes to the needs of the customer undertaking—this in addition to the more customary change management provisions seen in IT outsourcing contracts.[26] In addition, some customers have in mind the scope of IT services to be outsourced initially, but are concerned to conduct a test or 'pilot' project before committing to further outsourcing. Also, customers may have a strategic plan for the outsourcing over the course of a period of, say, three years of significant parts of their IT functions, but they are simply not ready to specify the scope of the services to be outsourced or commit to a course that would result in IT staff transferring to the provider at the point of contract.

A further driver for such global framework or master services arrangements is the increasing move to nearshore or offshore outsourcing, especially the customer's need to take advantage immediately or in the short term of the cost savings that can be achieved by such outsourcing. This induces the customer to enter into a global framework or master services arrangement to get the benefit of the nearshore or offshore cost arbitrage available instantly or over the short term. Even if there is no exclusivity or minimum volume commitment by the customer, providers can recognize initial revenues and (realistically) take the view that, once a customer

---

[26] See section 3.2.2.7 below.

has committed to the first local agreement, it is not likely in the medium term either to engage another external provider to outsource, or 'insource' future IT services.

Finally, there is the clear need in the case of IT to set up a contract that takes into account the need for technical changes over a relatively short-term period (such as the introduction of new technology or the refresh of existing systems), business change (such as the need to absorb a newly acquired subsidiary into a business structure or, conversely, to allow for partial termination of a contract where a particular service is no longer required), or regulatory change (such as IT modifications or re-platforming needed to accommodate a number of the recent changes in EU financial services regulation).

Accordingly, many IT outsourcing contracts are now structured as global framework agreements ('GFAs') or master services agreements ('MSAs').[27] The main body and certain schedules of such an agreement typically prescribe the default legal terms that are intended to apply to all subsequent local agreements—called variously 'call-offs', 'work orders', 'statements of work', or 'orders' (for the sake of neutrality, called a 'local agreement' in this section, whether or not they are geographically local). The detailed template for each such local agreement will be set out as a schedule to the main body of the GFA or MSA. It is important and therefore common in GFAs or MSAs to provide for situations in which there may be conflicts or inconsistencies between the terms of the main body of the GFA or MSA and those of the local agreements, with an order of precedence in the event of such conflicts or inconsistencies.

As indicated above, one of the perceived advantages of GFAs and MSAs is that the parties will have purported to legislate for all the legal and contractual terms to apply to the outsourcing. However, reality is mostly otherwise. Apart from the obvious need, as outlined above, to vary the terms of the GFA or MSA for local regulatory environments, there are often operational, technological, or commercial needs at a local agreement level that are particular to that local agreement— whatever has previously been agreed at the GFA or MSA level. Care needs to be taken that these are properly reflected in the local agreement and so as to ensure that the general terms of the GFA or MSA do not override the specific terms of the local agreement to the extent that there is any conflict or inconsistency between them. With the additional driver to move IT functions offshore as quickly as possible (see above in this section) there is an understandable tendency for the parties to defer difficult contractual positions to the local agreement. The result is that, increasingly, local agreements actually call for virtually the same level of contractual and legal

---

[27] For the purposes of this chapter, these terms are used interchangeably, as the author's experience is that this remains common practice. Purists might argue that there is or should be a distinction between a GFA and a MSA to reflect the multi-jurisdictional or cross-border nature of the GFA. Again, nomenclature is less important than the substance of the transaction and the need for the contract to reflect that substance.

care and attention as the GFA or MSA, but there is a natural resistance to recognize this. The result is that a number of such local agreements are inadequate.

3.1.3.3 *Business process outsourcing*

It would now be wrong to describe BPO as a trend: it is well established as one of the two main generic forms of outsourcing, ITO being the other.[28] BPO continues to grow rapidly. One of the leading industry research and consulting organizations, Gartner, Inc, defines BPO as 'the delegation of one or more IT-intensive business processes to an external provider that, in turn, owns administers and manages the selected processes based on defined and measurable performance metrics'.[29]

The four main forms of BPO globally are: supply chain management; finance and accounting; human resources; and sales, marketing, and customer care.[30] More commonly, call or contact centre operations fall within BPO; although the distinction in this submarket is generally between the relative content and scope of voice and data operations. With the rapid growth in nearshore and offshore outsourcing, knowledge-based processes, such as research, analysis, and financial modelling are developing under the generic title of knowledge process outsourcing (inevitably, 'KPO' or 'knowledge services'). Professional services like accounting and legal services have been identified as BPO/KPO[31] areas highly suitable for offshore delivery.

One of the more recent trends that is set to grow is that providers are increasingly focusing on vertical industries. The financial services sector remains one of richest sources of business process for BPO, but it is now being seen as a number of 'sub vertical' markets, such as life and pensions, general insurance, reinsurance, investment management, the administration of special investment funds,[32] retail banking, mortgages. The government and manufacturing sectors are also significant for outsourcing generally, including BPO.

The BPO providers' drive to ever-more specialist industry verticals and sub verticals, with other drivers (such as the move 'up the value chain' to more complex BPO and the need to be closer to their onshore customer base), has made BPO providers avid acquirers of complementary, specialist competitors. Accordingly, the BPO market is now—and is likely to continue to be—as much about mergers and acquisition and other corporate finance activity by providers and service providers

---

[28] Indeed, some industry analysts and commentators would argue that BPO is just another element of IT services. BPO is often described as 'IT-enabled services' ('ITeS') as opposed to 'IT' services, which, in many ways, is or should be, accurate: see, eg, Research Paper No G00131095, *Gartner on Outsourcing, 2005*, Gartner, Inc (14 December 2005), in which they state that 'BPO is one of the fastest-growing segments of the IT services market', p 17.

[29] Ibid para 5.1, p 17.

[30] Ibid para 5.1, p 17.

[31] Inevitably, legal services outsourcing has been allocated its own three letter acronym, 'LPO' or legal process outsourcing.

[32] See, eg, Case C-169/04 *Abbey National plc and Inscape Investment Fund v Commissioners of Customs & Excise* [2006] ECJ (Third Chamber), 4 May 2006.

(sometimes, in joint ventures with their customers) as the underlying assets of their businesses—the BPO or IT outsourcing contracts themselves.

As the definitions cited above and in the footnotes show, BPO often comes hand in hand with the outsourcing of the IT infrastructure and applications that support the business processes. It is therefore right to see much of BPO as IT-enabled services and hence an element of IT outsourcing.

Whether as a separate form of outsourcing or as an element of IT outsourcing, BPO deserves more detailed treatment than a work of this kind permits. Since the publication of the last edition of this book, one trend that is now integral to IT outsourcing and BPO is that of migrating services from developed to developing economies—the nearshore and offshore revolution, which now merits a separate section in this chapter.

3.1.4 Nearshore and offshore IT and services outsourcing[33]

The concept of moving industrial or commercial activities from higher to lower cost bases is, of course, not new. What has been remarkable is the impact and acceleration of such moves on the IT industry in general, and on IT outsourcing in particular. As with BPO, it is not feasible in a work of this kind to do justice to such a vast and growing subject, even if the author were to restrict himself to nearshore and offshore issues in the context of IT outsourcing alone. This section can therefore offer no more than an outline of the main legal and contractual implications of nearshore and offshore operations for IT outsourcing contracts.

There are no precise definitions of 'nearshore' and 'offshore' in this context.[34] In industry usage and practice, a 'nearshore' destination is one closer to home than one 'offshore'. So, at the time of writing, continental European outsourcing destinations, including localities in the Czech Republic, Hungary, Ireland, Latvia, Lithuania, Poland, Romania, Russia, Slovakia, and Spain have all been written about as 'nearshore' outsourcing destinations from the UK, while India,[35] China, the Philippines,

---

[33] The literature and volume of other material on this subject is vast. Readers are referred to Gartner, Inc publications of the kind quoted in this chapter: see <http://www.gartner.com/> (accessed 8 August 2011). See also <http://www.forrester.com/> (accessed 8 August 2011) and the website of the UK's National Outsourcing Association at <http://www.noa.co.uk> (accessed 8 August 2011). There is also a large and growing number of books on the subject of globalization and offshore outsourcing. Readers are referred to TL Friedman, *The World is Flat, A Brief History if The Globalized World in the 21st Century* (London: Allen Lane, 2005), which is considered required reading by many senior executives in the offshore outsourcing industry, especially in India. For the wider implications of offshore and nearshore outsourcing, see HS Kehal and VP Singh, *Outsourcing and Offshoring in the 21st Century: A Socio-economic Perspective* (Hershey, PA: Idea Group, 2006) and S Nadeem, *Dead Ringers: How Outsourcing is Changing the Way Indians Understand Themselves* (Princeton, NJ: Princeton University Press, 2011). And it has been said that, with cloud computing, 'offshore' becomes 'noshore'.

[34] Gartner, Inc is content with the following definition: '. . . "nearshore" (in a neighbouring country) or "offshore" (halfway around the world)': see *Gartner on Outsourcing, 2005*, n 28, para 2.1, p 5.

[35] India is still considered to be the country of choice for substantial offshore outsourcing. It is now becoming common for offshore IT companies to set up facilities in other, lower cost, offshore centres.

Brazil, Mexico, and South Africa (to name but a few from an ever-growing list) are considered to be 'offshore'. Where that leaves Belfast (at the time of writing, an increasingly popular destination for call centre and certain back office business process outsourcing) or, indeed, those parts of lower-cost mainland Britain to which IT and back office operations are moved, is difficult to gauge.

As the nearshore and offshore IT outsourcing model is maturing, it has become more common for customers and providers to adopt and agree a blend of onshore, nearshore, and offshore service provision in relation to the same transaction. For example, in an applications development and maintenance outsourcing with a provider having a number of facilities in different countries, it is becoming common for business analysts and similar consultants to base themselves onshore while they are learning about the customer's business and its needs, for first level support to be based onshore (sometimes at the customer's sites), with the basic development work itself being sourced from an offshore base (to achieve the lowest possible labour cost saving) and the more complex work being sourced from a facility in a nearshore location, along with second level support functions. Similarly, customers and providers are willing to deploy a combination of structures for the IT outsourcing, such as an onshore joint venture between the parties, with an outsourcing contract (or contracts) with nearshore and offshore facilities providing designated services. This is sometimes referred to as the 'blended model'.

It is suggested that these definitions are in themselves sterile, especially in relation to the blended model. Leaving aside the purely financial, socio-economic, geopolitical, operational, technological, or other strategic drivers for moving IT services to a particular nearshore or offshore destination (or a blend of both together with an onshore component) the main legal and contractual concerns specific to offshore or nearshore IT outsourcing will be:[36]

(a) from which locations and facilities within those locations specific IT services will be provided, whether onshore, nearshore, offshore, or a combination of some or all such locations;

(b) whether there are any regulatory prohibitions or restrictions on moving those services to any of the proposed destinations;[37]

So, eg, the Indian Tier 1 IT outsourcers Tata Consultancy Services Ltd and Infosys Technologies Ltd each have, at the time of writing, facilities in China.

[36] This is not intended to be an exhaustive checklist, rather an indicative list of some of the main considerations specific to offshore outsourcing contracts and legal issues.

[37] eg, if the customer is a UK-based, regulated financial services institution, it will need to confirm that the proposed offshore outsourcing meets the rules and requirements of the UK Financial Services Authority ('FSA') and it should also take into account the guidelines issued by the FSA from time to time. See, eg, in the context of offshore outsourcing in the UK financial services sector, the FSA report on their findings following a fact-finding mission to India in 2005, *Offshore Operations: Industry Feedback*, April 2005, <http://www.fsa.gov.uk/pubs/other/offshore_ops.pdf> (accessed 8 August 2011). Another example is the restriction on the ability of organizations in the EEA to transfer personal data to offshore destinations, say, for processing in the course of outsourcing, that do not offer through the applicable

(c) whether there are any such prohibitions or restrictions on the provision of those services to the customer's undertaking or any such prohibitions or restrictions that could expose the organization to greater regulatory risk in its home jurisdiction;[38]

(d) the nature of the structure that will be deployed to provide the services—a 'captive' (typically a facility that the customer will itself own), a 'hybrid' (typically one that the customer will require the provider to set up, own, operate, and perhaps transfer to the customer at a pre-agreed point),[39] a 'simple' outsourcing or some other structure (at the time of writing the most common being a corporate joint venture);

(e) the tax and regulatory conditions applying to the customer's presence in the chosen location(s)[40] and to the structure(s) proposed to deploy for the outsourcing, for example whether having a small management presence and servers in the location concerned would give rise to a permanent establishment and liability to corporation and other taxes in the jurisdiction concerned, whether there would be restrictions on the ability of the entity to remit funds to the customer's home jurisdiction, or whether there would be restrictions on acquiring the shares or underlying assets of a hybrid structure and any chosen staff;

(f) the particular service risks that need to be addressed contractually or otherwise because they will be provided from a distant location and often reliant on data communications;

(g) the direct and indirect taxation implications of the transaction and the extent to which it may need to be structured so as to avoid or mitigate the application of tax;[41]

---

legal systems the same level of protection for personal data as are required within the EEA: see section 3.2.2.13 below and Chapter 10.

[38] eg, note the FSA offshore guidelines (FSA Handbook SYSC 3A, explained in more detail in FSA, *Operational Risk Systems and Controls* (CP142 2002) and FSA, *Organisational Systems and Controls: Common Platform for Firms* (CP06/9 2006) that apply to processes and systems operated in more than one country, ie, offshore. Financial services institutions are expected to consider: the local business operating environment, including the likelihood and impact of political disruption or cultural differences; the application of UK and EU data protection legislation to, and restrictions on, the transfer of personal data across borders, especially outside the EEA; and the extent to which local law and regulation may restrict the UK institution in meeting its UK regulatory obligations, eg customer confidentiality, access to information by the FSA, internal audit.

[39] Often called a 'Build Operate Transfer' or 'BOT' structure. At the time of writing, there are various models, the main ones being corporate or contractual. See below in this section.

[40] eg, see a small sample of a list of Indian laws and regulations that may apply to IT outsourcing in that country—admittedly in the context of BPO, but many of which will also apply to IT outsourcing: Pavan Duggal, *Law of Business Process Outsourcing* (New Delhi: Saakshar Law Publications, 2004) chs 3, 4, and 10.

[41] For any organization considering establishing a presence of any kind in a foreign jurisdiction, the first question will be whether the presence would create a permanent establishment or other connection with that jurisdiction that would result in the organization having to pay corporation or other direct taxes to the revenue authorities concerned. VAT, sales, and other indirect taxes are also an issue.

(h) the effects of, and implications for, the proposed offshore or nearshore outsourcing on the customer's local (ie, onshore) staff; and

(i) social, cultural, linguistic, or other similar issues in the provider's offshore or nearshore organization that could affect the reliability and quality of the IT services.[42]

Except for the considerations such as those outlined above that distinguish an offshore or nearshore IT outsourcing from the onshore variety, the provisions of most offshore and nearshore IT outsourcing contracts are usually substantially the same as their onshore equivalents. Some of the differences are outlined below.

One of the first considerations in any offshore or nearshore IT outsourcing is that outlined in paragraph (d), namely the structure of the transaction. Creating captive operations in a foreign jurisdiction can be complex and time-consuming. It will also require a detailed knowledge of local regulations, especially those concerning the establishment by a foreign company of a branch, subsidiary, or other form of presence in the territory concerned.

The captive is, essentially, a wholly-owned branch or, more usually, subsidiary of, the customer operation. It may be set up by the customer itself (often with the help of consultants and other advisers) or by an outsourcing provider—usually under a local agreement under the terms of a GFA or MSA. Either the customer will actually own and itself provide service to its onshore operations from the captive, or it will contract with a third party provider to provide some or all of those services.

One of the alternatives to the captive offshore or nearshore operation is the hybrid, or BOT model described above. This structure is most commonly used where the customer is not sure that, in the medium to long term, it will need or wish to have a captive offshore or nearshore presence and recognizes that it has neither the resource, nor the expertise, nor the time to build an operation in the chosen country. The BOT structure usually takes two forms: corporate and contractual.

The corporate BOT structure involves the provider setting up a special purpose vehicle, or SPV (almost invariably, a company), which may be wholly owned by the provider or owned jointly with the customer. All the necessary IT and other infrastructure, contracts and other assets are therefore in the SPV and the key staff are employed by the SPV. The customer is granted a call option in relation to the

---

Since 1 January 2010, and the change in the 'place of supply' rules for UK and EU VAT, VAT will be imposed on services provided from offshore locations, as it will apply in relation to the place of consumption of the supplied service, ie the customer's location, not in relation to the location of provision of the service, ie the offshore provider's location.

[42] This is clearly not intended to be an exhaustive checklist for creating any outsourcing contract—it is a list of the basic questions that will determine whether to approach the transaction as an outsourcing and, if so, how to reflect the arrangements in a contractual structure.

shares owned by the provider. At an agreed point, either specified by reference to a time or times, or level of maturity of the operations (eg, the point at which the SPV employs 1,500 staff) or some other trigger, the customer may exercise the call option, so acquiring total or a majority ownership of the SPV. The parties need to agree a means of valuing the company at the time the option is exercised. Issues that need to be confirmed in setting up the structure will, as indicated above, include the ability of the foreign customer to step in as owner of the SPV and enjoy all the benefits of ownership held by the local provider, such as the ability to retain special regulatory, infrastructure, customs, and fiscal incentives often made available by developing countries to those setting up in specially designated zones.[43] Planning for, negotiating, and documenting a corporate BOT structure will add a significant layer of complexity to the IT outsourcing and those entering into such transactions will therefore need to allow considerably more time than that usually allotted to an offshore or nearshore IT outsourcing. As BOT structures are relatively new in the context of offshore and nearshore outsourcing, it is too soon to say whether they have been judged by customers and providers to have been successful.[44]

The contractual BOT may take a number of forms, but essentially involves the parties identifying at the start or through the life of the IT outsourcing contract the infrastructure, processes, assets, and staff to be transferred at the agreed trigger point.[45] The provider agrees in the outsourcing of a specific BOT contract to transfer the physical and intangible assets to the customer on the exercise of the option and to enable the customer to solicit the employees—often key employees—of the provider at that time. In addition, the provider may agree to ring-fence the infrastructure, assets, and staff in a separate division or company. The parties will have to agree a mechanism to ascertain the price of the assets and the costs of the transfer, as for the corporate BOT.

While the point at (h) above concerning staff implications is common both to onshore, nearshore, and offshore outsourcing, it is commonly overlooked in the

---

[43] eg, in India the Software Technology Parks of India (STPI) and Special Economic Zones (SEZ), Free Trade Zones (FTZ), and Electronic Hardware Technology Parks (EHTP) initiatives. The STPI initiative is due to end in March 2011.

[44] At the time of writing, this author is aware of a small number of BOT operations in respect of which the call option has been exercised at various times and one such operation in which, after some 24 months' successful operation, the UK customer dispensed with the call option entirely and converted the BOT into a straight outsourcing relationship. The nature of these transactions is such that it is difficult to obtain reliable information from public sources or, in the case of the author as a specialist practitioner in this area, to disclose information, about the transactions concerned. A number of providers, especially in India, have at the time of writing expressed their concern to the author about the unnecessary (as they see it) complexity of BOT structures, whether corporate or contractual.

[45] At the time of writing, in the author's experience, there is a tendency for customers to focus on the specific infrastructure, assets, processes, or staff they will need on exercising the option. Eg, in some situations, customers focus only on the key staff necessary to manage what will become their captive operation, relying on freely available and relatively low-cost real estate, infrastructure, and set up costs to enable them to create the captive that will employ the staff. In such cases, the BOT contractual option is reflected in personnel-centric provisions in the IT outsourcing contract.

context of nearshore and offshore outsourcing, because it is (wrongly) assumed that the TUPE Regulations[46] do not apply to such outsourcing. While TUPE will be dealt with in section 3.4 below, it is worth clarifying here that they *do* apply in the context of nearshore and offshore outsourcing and their application has therefore to be provided for, along with the statutory processes that are required under the Regulations or related procedures, such as selection for redundancy. It is especially important that the parties allocate the obligations, costs, and liabilities between them.

Finally, there are other, regulatory and operational issues that must be taken into account specifically in any offshore or nearshore IT outsourcing contract. These include compliance with data protection laws (where personal data is being processed as part of the IT outsourcing), applying home-based or international IT security standards and the availability of local intellectual property protection for applications or data developed or processed by the offshore or nearshore provider.

3.1.5 The partnership myth

One of the common myths in outsourcing is—and remains—that the relationship between the customer and provider can be likened to a partnership. Whilst commendable on a commercial level, the legal reality is somewhat different. A true partnership involves the equal sharing of risk and reward. Providers may be keen to reap the benefits of the outsourcing relationship although, even then, there is no making of a 'common profit' from the outsourcing relationship—a concept at the heart of the legal definition of a partnership. Indeed, the converse is true. The provider uses its service provision to the customer at a carefully calculated charge to make a profit from the customer. It is also virtually unheard of for the risks to be divided equally. This is evidenced most clearly in the detailed limitation of liability clauses that providers will seek to impose to control their risk exposure.

References to the relationship being a true partnership should therefore be avoided by the provider and treated with a healthy dose of cynicism from the customer.[47]

The term 'partnership' is also sometimes used in a slightly different context to refer to the creation of an ongoing relationship where it is envisaged that a number of contracts will be awarded over time to the provider. In these circumstances, the provider is effectively an exclusive or preferred provider for any future

---

[46] The Transfer of Undertakings (Protection of Employment) Regulations 2006 (SI 2006/246), implementing Council Directive (EC) 2001/23 on the approximation of the laws of the Member States relating to the safeguarding of employees' rights in the event of transfers of undertakings, businesses or parts of undertakings or businesses [2001] OJ L82, referred to in this chapter as 'TUPE' or the 'TUPE Regulations'. See section 3.4 below.

[47] This is not intended to belittle the outsourcing relationship. A high degree of trust and a solid working relationship will be vital to maximize the benefits that can be achieved by both parties.

IT outsourcing. For example, a GFA or MSA may be entered into governing the overall business relationship and acknowledging the intention that the provider is a preferred one and providing certain key terms (such as pricing for any outsourced service).

However, the overriding concern is that this so-called partnership approach often masks a situation in which the customer is treated as being jointly responsible for the services it receives and pays for, with the lessening of contractual recourse if things go wrong. As said above, this is not and it should not be the commercial reality.

3.1.6 Reasons for outsourcing

The reasons for outsourcing are varied. The most frequently quoted incentives in the private sector are the added value that third party expertise and experience can bring and costs savings. The added value is evidenced through the enhanced levels of service that a provider will usually offer which, because of the experience and economies of scale available to the provider, are often provided at a cheaper cost than that achievable in-house. Whether the first wave of outsourcing contracts entered into in the early 1990s brought the anticipated costs savings and improved service is unclear. It is apparent that at least in some cases this was not the result.[48] With the move to offshore and nearshore outsourcing, there is from the customer's perspective only one real, overriding, driver to outsource IT: cost savings. Since the downturn in the developed world markets, cost saving is and will for the foreseeable future remain the predominant driver. The other drivers, such as the added value through enhanced expertise and advanced IT accreditations that the Tier 1 Indian IT outsourcers offer,[49] are certainly present, but are almost always secondary.

The technology industry is highly competitive and continues to grow at a rapid rate as the modern economy becomes increasingly reliant on IT. Consequently, over recent years staff costs in this sector have spiralled upwards, including in the cost

---

[48] Rudy Hirschheim, who with Mary Lacity researched IT outsourcing over a nine-year period, has commented that

> many companies that have gone through large scale outsourcing exercises are finding that their flexibility is not as enhanced as they thought it would be with outsourcing, and that service levels they thought would improve have actually dropped . . . They're beginning to find that outsourcing is not the panacea they hoped for when they initially outsourced.

(See *Backsourcing: An Emerging Trend?* in Outsourcing-Academics.com at <http://www.outsourcing-academics.com/html/acad1.html> (accessed 8 August 2011).) Accordingly, some companies are beginning to take back in-house functions that they had previously outsourced as a result of this dissatisfaction. What this chapter should assist to establish is that a well-drafted contract can protect many of the customer's expectations as to the level of service and costs.

[49] Such as Capability Maturity Model Integration ('CMMI') Level 5: see the Carnegie Mellon University and Software Engineering Institute website at <http://www.sei.cmu.edu/cmmi/index.cfm> (accessed 8 August 2011).

arbitrage, offshore centres. Outsourcing obviates the need to recruit and, crucially, to retain IT staff and enables the business to focus on its core business competencies. Provided a good contract manager is appointed by the customer to oversee the operation of the contract, management will generally need to spend considerably less time in overseeing the IT function. The role required will be that of strategic input and direction, rather than managing day-to-day operational issues.

The outsourcing of an IT function or functions may necessitate the transfer of the assets used to support and run that function to the provider. Accordingly, responsibility for maintaining and updating those systems will also pass. The financial burden for the customer is translated from that of the costs of resources to provide an in-house service and the fluctuating costs of improving the existing, and acquiring any new, technology to a more stable regular service charge. Not only do the costs of receiving the service become more certain but the use of a third party provider should improve access to new technology. Providers can acquire such technology more quickly, being able to spread the cost over a number of customers. In addition, the provider will have the resources and skill available to evaluate and implement that new technology more rapidly than the typical corporate or government entity. The larger-scale provider will also often be able to negotiate substantial discounts from the price of any new software or hardware. This rapid access to, and potentially lower cost of, new technology can make IT outsourcing a very attractive proposition.

These are some of the more common reasons for outsourcing. With any corporate or government customer, the business case will differ and a careful evaluation of the advantages and disadvantages of outsourcing any IT function should always be undertaken.

3.1.7 Disadvantages of outsourcing

One of the distinctions between the typical IT outsourcing contract and other computer contracts (such as software and hardware procurement or maintenance contracts) is the ongoing cooperation that will be required from the parties over the life of the contract. Without a close working relationship and an understanding of the parties obligations and responsibilities (in both the strict contractual sense and more generally) the IT outsourcing relationship may be doomed to failure.[50]

As with any business proposition, there are potential downsides to be considered. As noted above, although costs reduction is often cited as a primary motivator the much sought after savings do not always happen in practice. Indeed, with some contracts the cost to the customer has increased as a result of the contract. This is particularly the case where the service requirements are ill-defined in the initial

---

[50] Interestingly, a cultural 'mismatch' is often referred to as being the cause of many breakdowns in the IT outsourship relationship.

contract, enabling the provider to demand additional charges through any contract change mechanism as the scope of the contract is formally increased to cover service requirements of the customer which, although always intended by the customer to form part of the outsourced function, fall outside the strict wording of the service schedule.[51]

The transfer of staff to the provider as part of the outsourcing process[52] could result in the loss of specialist skill and expertise within the business. This can be a particular problem if the business is left without any person with the technical skills required to oversee the running of the contract. Obviously, the more of the IT functions of any business which are outsourced the more likely this will be an issue. This problem can also effectively lock a customer into a relationship with a provider. If the business lacks the technical skills required to bring the service back in-house, it may be easier to leave the service provision with an under-performing provider rather than to expend the necessary time and management resource to locate an alternative vendor.

A decision to outsource should be treated with some sensitivity within an organization, particularly as regards the dissemination of information to employees. Staff are not always receptive to the prospect of outsourcing and to the transfer of their employment to a third party IT provider, although the manner in which the proposal to outsource is communicated to employees can reduce some of this negativity. An effective communications process will therefore be required to avoid negative publicity and potential strike or other employee action.[53]

Outsourcing invariably involves the transfer of a number of assets to the provider. This may result in a lack of control over the nature of the IT infrastructure used to deliver the services—which may be a particular problem when the infrastructure is returned to the customer on the expiry or termination of the contract and the customer is left with an outdated system and with little or no knowledge as to its detailed operation. Although the essence of the IT outsourcing contract is the delivery of services to a stated level it is nevertheless therefore advisable to include provisions requiring technology refreshment on a regular basis to ensure an acceptable standard of infrastructure is maintained. An adequate flow of information throughout the duration of the contract regarding the composition of the technology architecture used by the provider will also be essential.

One of the consequences of having part of a business function run by a third party is the security risk. In particular, there is an increased risk that others may access, and misuse, information which is confidential to the business and that the staff of the

---

[51] The importance of the service description cannot be overstated. See section 3.2.2 (in particular section 3.2.2.1) below.

[52] The TUPE Regulations will usually apply to transfer staff associated with the function that is outsourced to the provider. See section 3.4.

[53] In addition to the commercial necessity of such an effective communications process, where the TUPE Regulations apply there are legal requirements about the consultation process that must take place. See section 3.4.

provider may unintentionally or otherwise misuse the customer's intellectual property. Detailed provisions regarding the use of, and access to, confidential information and intellectual property are the norm in IT outsourcing contracts. Providers should also be compelled to comply with the customer's security policies and procedures.

Rigid contracts may also prevent future expansion and growth of the customer's business. One of the inevitable consequences of the outsourcing relationship will be that the provider's consent must be obtained before any changes can be made to the scope of the service. Contract change provisions will therefore play an important role in any contract.[54]

The constant expansion of the IT outsourcing market is testament to its popularity. The disadvantages and risks of IT outsourcing seem rarely, in practice, to outweigh the perceived benefits. For those contemplating an outsourcing contract, it will therefore be comforting to know that many of the risks outlined above can be controlled or minimized through appropriate contractual provisions.

3.1.8 The outsourcing contract

The essence of an IT outsourcing contract is a commitment by the provider to deliver services to predefined service levels. The contract will then go on to define what happens in the event these service levels are not met. A failure to meet a particular service level will often result in the payment of service credits, a specified sum of money which becomes payable automatically in the event of a breach. Without service credits being stipulated, the customer would need to prove on each occasion that any failure to meet the service levels is a breach of contract and that it is entitled to damages from the provider accordingly. To specify the service credits that will become payable in this way therefore gives certainty to both parties and helps to avoid protracted disputes as to whether any contract breach has occurred and, if so, whether it has caused any loss and damage to the customer which should be recoverable from the provider. These service credit regimes differentiate the IT outsourcing contract from other IT contracts, such as system supply contracts, where such schemes are found more rarely.

The contract will contain other provisions that are key to the effective management of the ongoing relationship between the parties. IT outsourcing contracts are usually long in nature, with contracts for seven- to ten-year periods being relatively standard industry market practice. Flexibility will therefore be crucial, in terms of adapting the contract to reflect the customer's changing business requirements and to introduce new forms of technology and other service improvements.

Section 3.2 below examines some of the key features of the IT outsourcing contract.

---

[54] See section 3.2.2.7 below.

3.1.9 The outsourcing process

3.1.9.1 *Board/business decision*

The process will begin with an evaluation by the customer of the business case for outsourcing. The evaluation process will review both the benefits and any disadvantages of outsourcing the particular IT function in question.

The evaluation team should ideally be comprised of those who will be involved in the entire outsourcing process to ensure continuity in approach and full accountability for the outsourcing decision. The team should include those with appropriate IT technical skills and suitable management or board representation. Finance and HR managers may also need to play an important role, depending on the size and scope of the outsourcing in question. Increasingly, both private and public sector undertakings are resorting to consultants to assist in this process.

With the main driver in outsourcing now being the need to achieve targeted cost reduction, the board will often revisit the outsourcing business case more than once in the process. It is no longer a foregone conclusion that the board will 'rubber stamp' the decision to outsource.

3.1.9.2 *Specifying requirements/service levels*

Assuming a decision to outsource is made, the customer will initially need to put together a statement of its requirements for the outsourced function. The importance of this exercise cannot be underestimated. A detailed requirements specification that clearly specifies the business need will help to attract the correct providers competent to provide the relevant services and avoid (or, at least, minimize) later disagreements about the scope (and consequent cost) of the service that providers are tendering for. Cost will be an important factor for any customer and the evaluation process should undertake a thorough review of the cost that is currently incurred in providing the service in-house and an assessment of the likely costs savings that can be achieved through outsourcing.

As well as identifying the particular function that is to be outsourced, due consideration must be given to associated issues. For example, which of the assets that are currently used by the customer to deliver the service in-house are to be transferred to the provider? Who owns those assets and where are they located? Are there staff who are to transfer? What dependencies are there between the function to be outsourced and other functions that are to be retained in-house by the customer or with third party providers? Should assets used to provide the service be returned to the customer at the termination or expiry of the outsourcing arrangement? Once these, and other, questions have been considered, the customer will be in a position to go out to the marketplace and tender for a provider.

Putting together the tender documentation is a skilled and time-consuming process and one in relation to which external consultants are also often employed. Such consultants help to draft the tender documentation, evaluate the responses, sit on the negotiation team, and generally steer the client through the outsourcing process.

External specialist IT outsourcing lawyers are also usually engaged from the early stages. They will define the contract requirements to be included in the tender, together with advising on associated legal issues (such as confidentiality agreements). Lawyers will also play a key role in the negotiation process, reducing the client's requirements to contractual form.

3.1.9.3 *Going out to tender or RFP*
The tender documentation needs to include a detailed description of the services required and the service levels to which they should be delivered. This information is contained in either an invitation to tender ('ITT') or request for proposal ('RFP').[55] The ITT or RFP will need to be sufficiently detailed to enable the provider to provide a detailed costing. This means information regarding assets and staff to transfer, contract duration, reporting requirements, and any business processes the provider must adhere to should be included.

Whether the contract should be attached to the ITT is often a subject of debate. This can take the form of either the entire contract or an outline of key terms only. It enables the customer to specify the terms on which it wishes to do business and compels the provider to indicate at an early stage which of those terms are acceptable (or otherwise) to it. The provider will therefore be reviewing and commenting on those contractual terms when its negotiating power is at its weakest and the desire to win an attractive contract may force it into making more concessions than it would otherwise do so.

In some circumstances, time constraints may mean that it is simply not feasible to include contract terms at the ITT stage, especially where the customer is new to outsourcing and has no standard contract terms in place. In any event it must also be accepted that a certain amount of negotiation will be inevitable, even where the contract was included as part of the ITT and a provider has indicated its acceptance of its terms in its tender response.

3.1.9.4 *Choosing a preferred provider*
Essentially, there are two methods that can be adopted in selecting a provider. The first is to produce a shortlist with a number of preferred providers and to run negotiations in tandem with each of them. The disadvantage of such an approach is that it is very costly in terms of the management time required to participate in several negotiations at once and the associated expense of external advisers evaluating and negotiating a number of draft contracts. This acts as a considerable deterrent in smaller value contracts. However, the advantages can be considerable. Providers who know they are in competition with others will adopt a far more flexible approach in negotiations than they would if they were the sole preferred provider. Providers will inevitably end up in a 'contract race' with the first to agree acceptable

---

[55] The RFP may be preceded, especially in public sector IT outsourcing procurement, by a Request for Information ('RFI').

terms and price winning the contract. This can assist to speed up the contract negotiation process (although this must be balanced against the management resource required to undertake negotiations with several providers).

An objective set of assessment criteria should be adopted against which any potential provider is assessed, with a review of all aspects of the tender response. In addition to the obvious considerations, such as capability to provide the service and price, other factors may be relevant. The relationship between the parties will usually be a long one and it is important to ensure that there is a 'cultural' fit between the two entities. Without this, the parties may simply be unable to work together effectively.

Visits to other customer sites may also be beneficial to assess the provider's performance in practice compared to any assurances given as part of its tender response. It also enables the customer to gain a valuable insight into the day-to-day working methods of the provider.

3.1.9.5 *Due diligence*

Due diligence plays an important role, enabling the provider to verify that information provided regarding the IT infrastructure and other systems, service levels, assets, and employees is correct, to ascertain the condition of any assets that are to be transferred, and to consider whether the provider believes the desired service levels can be achieved using them. Due diligence is also used to investigate any other matters which may impact on the provider's costs model. This process helps to flush out any potential issues and, more importantly, for them to be dealt with prior to contract signature. Due diligence also helps to foster an early working relationship between the parties.

One of the aspects that will be investigated will be software and databases licensed to the customer where the provider needs to use that software or database to continue providing the service. Many licences are drafted so as to prevent access to, or use of, that software or database by anyone other than the customer, such as in terms providing for confidentiality, a prohibition on the customer transferring, or giving access to, the software to any third party and, in more recent times, prohibitions on the licensed software being used other than for the customer's own internal business purposes or by an outsourcing provider. To allow access and use by the IT outsourcing provider without obtaining the third party provider's consent would therefore place the customer in breach of its licence terms, with the risk of that licence being terminated and a damages claim made against it.[56] In addition, the provider may itself be making copies of such software or databases in the course

---

[56] There is a long history of litigation, or out-of-court settlements achieved after litigation has been threatened or started, mainly in the USA, by third party software vendors against customers and outsourcing providers for copyright infringement and breach of contract. This is not, therefore, a purely theoretical issue and could result in a proposed outsourcing transaction being aborted or severely delayed, with (in either event) significant additional costs to both the customer and outsourcing provider.

of the service provision and thereby infringing the intellectual property rights of the third party owner. Restrictions of this kind might in theory be challenged, in appropriate cases, as infringements of competition law,[57] but in practice the need to complete the negotiations to a tight timetable means that the restrictions must be assumed to be enforceable.

Due diligence is usually carried out prior to contract signature following selection of the preferred provider. This is most desirable for both parties enabling certainty to be achieved before the contractual relationship is commenced. This is particularly the case where software is licensed to the customer and third party consent must be obtained to allow for the service provider to gain access to that software or for a new licence to be granted direct to the service provider. Identifying licences where consents must be obtained and the procedure to obtain this consent can take many months.

The alternative is for due diligence to take place in a period after the contract is entered into with an adjustment to the contract charges to take into account any inaccuracies in the information provided to the provider which impact on the cost of providing the services. This approach can lead to disputes as to whether correct information was or was not provided initially which can sour relations between the parties at a very early stage in the relationship. For this reason, it is best avoided.

3.1.9.6 *Negotiating the contract*

There will usually be much negotiation of the detailed terms of an IT outsourcing contract. These contracts are complex in nature providing a well-defined service requirement whilst allowing for future change and flexibility in terms of the customer's changing business requirements and the rapid developments in the technology market.

Even where the draft contract forms part of the tender documentation, it is common to find considerable negotiation over its terms, especially where the provider's tender indicates that the terms are acceptable in principle but subject to detailed negotiation (a commonplace, and understandable, response). This sort of response allows a 'get out' enabling the provider to defer lengthy negotiation until after its selection as the preferred provider. However, the most time-consuming part of such negotiations is often the development, documentation, and subsequent negotiation of the IT service definitions or specifications and service levels to be applied. It appears that relatively few customer organizations have developed such specifications or service levels—after all, in the case of a first outsourcing, the services have been provided by the internal IT function to other business functions. Accordingly, where such specifications or service levels do not exist or are not adequately documented, the parties need in the project timetable to provide for a lengthy period during which both sides understand, develop, document, and then

---

[57] See generally R Whish, *Competition Law*, 6th edn (London: Butterworths, 2008).

negotiate the service specifications and service levels to be applied. As stated above, without such specifications and service levels, there is no sense in entering an outsourcing relationship.

In consequence, it can take many months to finalize the detailed contract terms and a suitable amount of time should be scheduled accordingly for this process to take place.

3.1.9.7 Public sector outsourcing

The UK public sector has historically embraced IT outsourcing with as much zeal as the UK private sector. With the need to reduce the financial deficit in the UK, the scale of outsourcing in both central and local government and the National Health Service is set to grow exponentially.

There is a developing library of standard form IT service contracts developed for particular situations or for certain parts of central and local government, mainly under Office of Government Commerce ('OGC') initiatives.[58]

An entity within the public sector will approach the outsourcing process in a very different manner from that of a private sector business. There are a number of laws and regulations that have an impact on the public sector procurement process, including the manner in which a tender is carried out, the negotiation process, and contract award.

In 2004 the EU adopted a consolidated directive on the procurement of works, supplies, and services[59] by the European public sector which was implemented under English law in 2006 by the Public Contracts Regulations 2006.[60] Apart from consolidating the three regulated areas of public sector procurement, the Directive and Regulations also reflect the jurisprudence of the European Court of Justice in the years since the adoption of the earlier public procurement directives. As readers of this work will now be more generally familiar with the public procurement regime, it is proposed to do no more than outline here those changes reflected in the new Regulations that are most relevant to IT outsourcing and substantial IT services contracts in the UK public sector.[61]

---

[58] See generally <http://www.ogc.gov.uk/index.asp> (accessed 8 August 2011).

[59] Council Directive (EC) 2004/18 on the coordination of procedures for the award of public works contracts, public supply contracts and public service contracts [2004] OJ L351/44, 26 November 2004.

[60] Public Contracts Regulations 2006 (SI 2006/5), which came into force on 31 January 2006 for England, Wales, and Northern Ireland. See also the Public Contracts (Scotland) Regulations 2006 (SSI 2006/1). For the utilities sector, there are separate consolidated Regulations: the Utilities Contracts Regulations 2006 (SI 2006/6) for England, Wales, and Northern Ireland and the Utilities Contracts (Scotland) Regulations 2006 (SSI 2006/2). The focus in this section of the chapter is on the mainstream public sector, rather than the utilities sector. For the sake of brevity only, references are to the regs as applied in England, Wales, and Northern Ireland.

[61] The new rules have introduced detailed provisions for e-procurement, including electronic purchasing, such as dynamic purchasing systems ('DPS') and electronic auctions. These are unlikely to appear in IT outsourcing and larger IT services contracts, so they are not outlined here: see, eg, reg 20 (dynamic purchasing systems) and reg 21 (electronic auctions).

Since the *Alcatel*[62] case, it has been clear that public authorities are, in effect, required to allow enough time between the announcement of a decision to award a public sector contract subject to the EU public procurement rules and the award of any resulting contract to enable national courts in EU Member States to review and set aside contract awards in cases of irregularity. The Regulations now provide that contracting authorities should allow a 'standstill' period of at least ten calendar days between the date of notifying tenderers of an award of contract and the date proposed to enter into the contract. There is also a debriefing requirement built into the timetable, so that aggrieved tenderers should have enough time after their debriefing to decide whether to challenge the award decision.[63]

Framework contracts have been much used by the UK public sector (mainly by central government and other non-departmental public bodies), but the European Commission has over the years questioned their use. They are now strictly regulated under regulation 19. Under the new rules, framework agreements cannot usually exceed a term of four years. Also, all the main terms of a framework arrangement must be agreed from the start. Having let a framework contract, either the contracting authority may award subsequent contracts, or 'call-offs', without any further competition under the terms of the framework agreement (assuming they are precise enough for the purpose) or they must convene a 'mini-competition' of all the providers within the framework capable of meeting the particular need.[64]

Finally, the Regulations introduce the 'competitive dialogue' procedure, alongside the more familiar open, restricted, and negotiated procedures, for 'particularly complex contracts'.[65] It is likely that a number of IT outsourcing and substantial IT services contracts will fall within the ambit of this new procedure.[66] The main features of the competitive dialogue are that:

(a) dialogue is permitted with selected tenderers to identify and define the solutions required by the contracting authority;

(b) the contract is awarded only on the basis of most economically advantageous tender;

(c) the dialogue may be held over a number of stages, to reduce the number of tenderers or solutions potentially on offer; and

(d) post-tender negotiation is allowed, but within the strict confines of the rules.

---

[62] Case C-81/98 *Alcatel Austria v Bundesministerium für Wissenschaft und Verkehr* [1999] ECR I-7671.

[63] See reg 32 of the Public Contracts Regulations 2006.

[64] For a helpful summary and guidance on the use of frameworks, see the OGC guidelines at <http://www.ogc.gov.uk/documents/guide_framework_agreements.pdf> (accessed 8 August 2011).

[65] See reg 18.

[66] Indeed, the OGC has stated in its guidance on competitive dialogue that they envisage it being used in relation to 'complex IT projects': see generally <http://www.ogc.gov.uk//documents/competitive_dialogue.pdf> (accessed 8 August 2011) and in particular, para 2.

The main differences between the new competitive dialogue procedure and the competitive negotiated procedure are that there are now structured tendering procedures in place of informal procedures in such situations and, even more importantly, that post-tender negotiations—previously forbidden—are possible in the cases in which this new procedure can be used.

3.2 THE IT OUTSOURCING CONTRACT

3.2.1 The services agreement and related documents

The central document in any outsourcing relationship will be the services agreement. This documents the services to be provided by the provider and the service levels to which those services must be provided. It also includes other provisions relating to the ongoing management of the outsourcing relationship. There are, however, other contractual documents which may be entered into leading up to, and in the course of, the outsourcing contract.

Heads of agreement (also known as memoranda of understanding, or 'MOUs') are sometimes used to reflect the early commercial agreement reached between the parties prior to entering into the detailed outsourcing contract. For the most part, these heads of agreement simply reflect the commercial intent of the parties and are sometimes little more than an agreement to agree future detailed contract terms. As agreements to agree, they are unenforceable under English law. The exceptions to this are terms such as confidentiality and exclusivity undertakings (ie, that during a fixed time period negotiations will not be conducted with any other third parties) which will be legally binding. Their value is therefore for the most part in the commercial comfort that they give to each party that there is a mutual understanding that an outsourcing relationship will be embarked on and, very broadly, what the scope of any contract will be.

Frequently, providers may be asked to commence work, or may themselves suggest that certain activities should be performed, before the services agreement itself is signed. This is a reflection of the time that is usually required in order to complete the due diligence process and contract negotiations. Once a provider has been selected as the preferred provider it may make business sense for certain investments to be made prior to contract signature in order to minimize any period of delay once the contract is up and running. This sort of investment may include acquiring new technology or employees in order to provide the services. Providers will seek to cover their risk exposure during this period leading up to contract signature by obtaining from the customer its written consent to specified activities being carried out by the provider on behalf of the customer (ie, the acquisition of a specific piece of hardware or software) and an indemnity in favour of the provider in respect of the costs relating to those activities (such as the price of that piece of hardware or software). Relatively informal letter agreements are frequently used to record the parties' understanding in relation to any such arrangements. The letter agreement can also formally acknowledge the customer's intention to enter into a contract with the provider, on the assumption that suitable contract terms can be agreed.

Providers may seek to expand the scope of these undertakings by the customer to cover other activities and costs prior to contract signature. It should be accepted that any provider must invest a certain amount of time and resource in order to achieve a successful contract. However, where there are activities which should genuinely be rewarded on a time and materials basis, the provider should not be left out of pocket if the contract negotiations later fail. Any recovery under these sorts of arrangements should be on the basis of specified fee rates. In order to avoid rapidly escalating costs of which the customer is unaware, the provider should be required to obtain the prior consent of the customer before incurring the costs. It will be in neither party's best interests for these sorts of informal arrangements to continue on an indefinite basis and it is therefore common to find time limits imposed on the expiry of which the letter agreement terminates if no outsourcing contract has been entered into by the specified date.

A consequence of the detailed discussion and disclosure process which takes place prior to contract signature is that the provider inevitably has access to a large amount of confidential information of the customer. It will therefore be important to ensure that the provider is required to enter into a confidentiality (or non-disclosure) agreement. This will govern the use that can be made of the confidential information (essentially, to evaluate whether a contract should be entered into) and will prevent the disclosure of that information to third parties. The provider should also be restricted in the internal disclosures it can make of the confidential information within its own organization—disclosure should be limited to those who are part of the bid team. This agreement should be put in place before any information or documentation, which is confidential in nature, is disclosed to the provider. Where a letter (or other agreement) is used to cover any pre-contract investments or activities (as referred to above) these obligations can be incorporated into that letter agreement. Otherwise, a separate confidentiality agreement can be used.

As part of the outsourcing arrangement there may be a transfer of assets and third party contracts from the customer to the provider. These are likely to include third party computer programs, hardware, related contracts (such as hardware and support arrangements), software which has been developed and is owned by the customer, buildings and land and other assets, items, contracts, and arrangements. The transfer of these assets can take place either within the principal services agreement or alternatively as a separate contract. In any event, the terms regarding the asset transfer will be the same.[67]

---

[67] See section 3.3 for a discussion of the main elements of an asset transfer agreement.

In some of the more sophisticated outsourcing arrangements, two established entities may join together in order to provide a combined service to a particular customer. This can be done by establishing a joint venture vehicle into which each of the two entities contributes staff and assets. In such circumstances, a joint venture agreement will therefore be required to record the establishment and operation of the joint venture vehicle. The customer will need to be satisfied that the joint venture company is not merely a shell company but is a substantive entity backed up by sufficient value and assets.[68] In any event, it may be appropriate to seek a financial and performance guarantee by the original parent entity or entities in the event of any failure to perform by the joint venture company. A joint venture created in this way may, in addition, require merger clearance from the relevant European or national competition authorities, as the compulsory merger control regimes mostly have triggers based on group turnover size. A merger authorization is particularly likely to be required if the joint venture is expected to be able to operate independently and to be able to sell similar outsourced services to other customers in its own right within a fairly short time.

3.2.2 The services agreement

As noted above, the services agreement is the principal contract between the parties governing the delivery of the services to the customer. Contracts are usually medium to long term, that is, five to ten years in duration, reflecting the complex nature of the relationship and the need for the service provider to have a relatively long period in order to achieve the promised costs savings. Contracts for seven- to ten-year periods are still relatively common in the industry, although there is now a movement to shorter five-year contracts. The negotiation of the contract terms will often take many months and in light of the very commercial nature of their subject context, they will usually be highly tailored to meet any particular customer's requirements.

This section outlines some of the key provisions that will appear in any IT outsourcing contract. There will, of course, be many other terms regarding the ongoing service provision and outsourcing relationship.

3.2.2.1 *Definition of the services*
The description of the services (and the service levels that must be attained) lies at the very heart of the outsourcing contract. It is essential to ensure that the service description captures all of the IT services to be provided by the provider under the outsourcing arrangements. For example, where data centre operations are to be outsourced to a provider it will not be sufficient simply to give a description of the data

---

[68] Not least so that the customer can effectively pursue that company for damages claims or for service credits in the event of any failure to provide the services.

centre operations themselves. Other questions which should be considered by the customer will include the following:

(a) What other ancillary services are to be provided by the provider?

(b) Who will be providing the disaster recovery service and/or business continuity arrangements?

(b) Who is providing the service that links the data centre to desktop and other IT environments?

(d) How is the provider to interact with the customer's in-house IT function and other third party service providers?

(e) What additional services or duties should the main outsourcing provider have, recognizing the need that it should work effectively with the customer's in-house and external IT providers?

(f) Are there any other services that the customer is likely to need in the future that should be covered within the scope of the services agreement?

Similar sorts of issues will be relevant to any other type of IT function to be outsourced. The answers to these and other questions should result in the outsourcing contract listing, in addition to the core IT services to be outsourced, a number of related and ancillary services and obligations.

The value of a well-defined service description cannot be underestimated. It will avoid, or at least minimize, subsequent disputes as to what is included within the contract scope. Hastily drawn up service schedules frequently lead to a large number of contract change requests being entered into after the contract has been commenced to add in elements which have been simply overlooked during the negotiation phase, with the attendant cost increases for the customer. All too often, it is inadequately drafted service schedules that provoke the disputes that can fundamentally damage the outsourcing relationship. The service schedule should include as much detail as possible regarding the exact scope of any activity to be performed by the provider and should be intelligible to someone who was not involved in its negotiation. Although it may be tempting to reduce the schedule to a fairly high-level set of obligations it should always be borne in mind that, at a later date, a court, or some other third party expert or mediator, may be called on to interpret the terms of that schedule.

A distinction is sometimes drawn between services provided during an initial transition period and those fully developed services to be provided afterwards. This is usually to reflect the fact that those services provided during the initial transitional phase might be very different—in scope, duration, level of service, and possibly even in the charges—than the services to be provided after that phase. Where an exception is to be made in respect of transitional services, the contract should specify very clearly which of the contract provisions they are subject to.

In some circumstances, it is not always possible for the customer to list in detail at the outset of any contract all of the services it would like to see provided in the future. It may be appropriate to include a section of additional services which the customer is entitled to require the provider to provide at a later date on the terms of the services agreement. One advantage of such an approach will be to set out a clear fees structure which will apply to these additional services.

The services agreement will obviously need to identify the entities who are to benefit from the services provided. In a simple outsourcing arrangement there will simply be one corporate entity that will constitute the customer. In more complex arrangements, there may be an entire customer group which is to benefit and the contract therefore needs to be very clear as to whom the customer group comprises. Where there are group companies involved, it may be the case that not all of the corporate entities are to receive the services as of the commencement date. As noted earlier in this chapter, there is an increasing trend for companies to instead put in place framework contracts with outsourcing providers under which the centralized outsourced or 'shared' services are provided to the holding company or principal operating vehicle, with provision to roll out the outsourced services to other group companies as and when they decide to take those services.

Clauses that restrict the customer's ability to purchase services from other third parties or that restrict the provider's ability to deliver services of a similar nature to other customers may infringe national or EU competition regulation and therefore need careful consideration.

3.2.2.2 *Service levels*
Service levels are at the core of the IT outsourcing contract, as they define the quality of the service to be provided by the provider. Specifically, the customer will want to be assured, as a minimum, that:

(a) the services will be available when the customer needs them (ie, with limited 'down time' or 'outage');

(b) the services will be responsive and speedy;

(c) they will be effective in supporting the customer's business operations; and

(d) above all, they will deliver the cost savings and other benefits promised by the provider, as reflected in the services agreement.

Service levels therefore play a very important role. However, as indicated earlier in this chapter, producing a defined set of service levels to be attached to the contract can often be a difficult and time-consuming process. For many customers, there will simply be no documented records as to the level of service which has been provided in-house prior to the outsourcing contract being entered into. It may be tempting to adopt the commonly used process of entering into a contract without any service levels attached, merely incorporating a contractual provision that the service levels will be reviewed and agreed during an initial stated time period. To follow this approach simply defers discussion regarding the required service levels to a stage when the customer is in a very unfavourable negotiating position which, from the customer's perspective, is a recipe for disaster.

If this approach is adopted then the contract must also deal with the issue of what should happen if the parties still cannot agree service levels even after the contract has been signed and the initial review period has passed. In these circumstances, it would be sensible to allow the customer to terminate the agreement in respect of those services for which no service levels have been agreed with the resulting changes to be made to other provisions of the agreement through the contract change mechanism, such as a reduction in charges.

Service levels may not be attached to every type of service to be provided by the provider as part of the services agreement. For example, there may be certain categories of service that are not seen as being a crucial part of the agreement or activities to which no objectively measurable service level can be set.

Importantly, the service level schedule needs to set out not only the service level to be attained but also how that service level will be measured (in terms of both method and frequency). In the event of any failure to achieve the service levels, service credits will usually be payable to the customer by the provider.[69]

3.2.2.3 *Customer obligations*

Performance by the provider of its obligations will, by varying degrees, depend on the customer or other third parties providing related services to the customer meeting their own obligations. As a result, many contracts specify certain obligations which the customer must perform in order for the provider to provide the services or other service dependencies. For example, any failure to transfer assets that have been agreed by the parties to be transferred, or any defects discovered in those assets which were not disclosed previously, will obviously have an impact on the services that can be provided. Any obligations that are imposed on the customer should be specified clearly within the contract to avoid any later disputes.

Where the provider will need access to the customer's premises to provide the services, standard provisions should be incorporated regarding the access to and use of those premises and other facilities.

3.2.2.4 *Performance improvement*

Although a customer may be prepared to accept that the contract duration should span, typically, five to ten years to allow the provider to achieve the promised costs savings, in return the customer will want to ensure that they continue to receive a cost effective and high-quality service for the duration of that contract. This is one of the primary reasons for the inclusion of such provisions in a typical contract.

---

[69] See section 3.2.2.10 for a description of how service credit regimes operate. Service credits are a valuable remedy and the 'teeth' by which the agreement is enforced.

Under performance improvement mechanisms, reviews of the service provision will be carried out by either the provider itself or by external third party consultants. For example, providers are often required to carry out annual reviews of the services to identify areas for development or improvement and to identify ways in which the services can exploit falling technology costs within the marketplace. Any changes which the parties agree should be made are then implemented through the contract change control mechanism.

In order to bring a degree of independence to the contractual arrangements, third party review procedures can be incorporated. Under such procedures external third party consultants conduct an assessment of the services to see if services of an equivalent nature and quality can be obtained more cheaply or at increased service levels from elsewhere. These procedures are known as benchmarking procedures. Benchmarking reviews can be costly and absorb much time on both sides of an outsourcing contract, not to mention the time of the benchmarking consultants appointed under appropriate contractual mechanisms. Because contract pricing and service levels (where they are documented at the point of contract) are usually favourable to the customer, it has become the norm not to benchmark pricing, service levels, or other agreed contractual aspects until after a suitable period following commencement of the services. At the time of writing, the norm would seem to be two to three years. After that period has expired, benchmarking may take place annually, less frequently, or at the instance of the customer (but usually not more than once a year).

To facilitate the benchmarking process, the provider will need to agree to allow the third party consultant access to its systems data, software, hardware, networks, and financial and operational data that are used in, or in relation to, providing the services. Such third parties will, as a matter of course, be required to sign up to stringent confidentiality undertakings regarding the information and assets to which they have access.

Such performance mechanisms provide a useful function in ensuring that the services and pricing are continually assessed and improved. However, they should not replace regular detailed reporting and meeting requirements which provide for the day-to-day review and discussion of the provider's performance under the contract.

The main difficulty with benchmarking is what follows from a finding that services and/or prices are not within the agreed bands of competitiveness when compared with similar, 'comparator' outsourcing transactions. The customer would usually seek an automatic adjustment of the prices and/or service levels to meet those bands, followed by a contract amendment to reflect the adjustment. The provider usually seeks to have a discussion with the customer, at which the parties will try to agree suitably balanced changes. The more vexed question is what is to happen if the parties cannot agree on a suitable adjustment. Should the customer be entitled to terminate without cause, or at least be in a position to threaten to do so? The consequences of benchmarking remain a thorny issue in IT outsourcing contracts.

3.2.2.5 *Relationship management*

Any IT outsourcing relationship necessitates a cooperative working relationship between the parties and an open exchange of information. The contract should formalize the discussion and reporting process without creating an unnecessary administrative burden for the provider. With a trend towards more complex, high value, and global transactions, the importance of relationship management increases.

Typically, contracts will stipulate regular meetings at two levels. First, regular (such as monthly) meetings between the respective project managers of the parties to discuss day-to-day operational issues, resolve any disagreements, and generally oversee the running of the contract. Secondly, meetings of representatives at a more senior level (such as a Chief Information Officer or Chief Financial Officer). These need to occur less frequently (eg, on a quarterly basis) and their purpose should be to review the overall strategic direction of the contract and the outsourcing relationship, to build the relationship at an executive level, to resolve any disputes or issues submitted to them, and review any annual benchmarking survey results.

Meetings should be supplemented by a detailed reporting process. Regular reports should be submitted by the provider regarding the performance of the services, any failures to achieve the service levels (and why this occurred), and any service credits that are paid. Reports should also be tailored to meet the specific requirements of a particular customer, for example detailing any security breaches that have occurred or on specific aspects of the services provided. These reports will provide an invaluable tool to track performance, display any trends in over or under-performance, and generally to monitor the performance of the contract.

3.2.2.6 *Acceptance testing*

In some circumstances, the provider is required to build and supply or integrate new systems before starting to provide the outsourced services. Where the provider is to own such a system then traditional acceptance testing is likely to be inappropriate. This is because of the nature of an IT outsourcing contract, that is, an obligation on the provider to deliver services to an agreed service level. How these service levels are achieved (ie, whether or not the system conforms to any particular detailed design build and specification) is irrelevant. In this scenario, evaluation testing is only likely to be appropriate where it enables the customer to check that the system is capable of delivering the output required to support the outsourced services.

In the event that the customer is to own the system from which the outsourced services are to be provided then it will be more appropriate to impose traditional acceptance testing. Contractual procedures will need to specify the process by which such acceptance testing is to be carried out, provide detailed obligations on the provider to remedy or fix any defects that are located during the testing period, specify details of the tests that are to take place, and provide the consequences of a failure to pass the acceptance testing procedure.

In addition, if further deliverables are to be provided by the provider during the course of the outsourcing contract, such as new items of software or hardware, it may be appropriate to include a general acceptance testing provision governing the procedure to apply which is to be used on the delivery of any such items.

3.2.2.7 *Contract change mechanisms*

Contract change provisions will have a particular role to play in an IT outsourcing contract. The purpose of these provisions is to allow the contract to change over its life as the scope of existing services is changed, as new services are introduced, and as new forms of technology are utilized.

Contracts need to incorporate a formal process by which any changes to the contract scope will be discussed and implemented. Any changes to the scope of the contract or the services to be provided, however small, should be subjected to this procedure to enable a proper evaluation to take place. It is important to ensure that a detailed assessment is carried out by the provider to review the impact of the change on the terms of the contract and the provision of the existing services. This then enables the customer to make an informed decision as to whether, and the basis on which, to proceed with any change. Any consequent amendments to the charges will be agreed through this procedure.

Mutual agreement is always at the core of any change control procedure, although in some contracts where the negotiating power of the customer is particularly strong, the ultimate decision as to whether to accept or reject the proposal for the change may lie with the customer.

3.2.2.8 *The charges*

As in any contract, the charging structure that is to be adopted will very much be a matter of negotiation for the parties. The charges can either be fixed or variable or a combination of the two. One of the prime concerns of a customer will be how to predict and control costs over the life of the contract, in particular to ensure that the opportunity for the provider to introduce any increases to the charges is limited. The contract should therefore state those circumstances in which the charges may be changed.

Providers will naturally seek to ensure that the charges are linked to indexation with changes being made on an annual basis to reflect any change in an appropriate inflationary index. A matter which is frequently debated is the appropriate index to apply in these circumstances. The Retail Price Index ('RPI'), or Consumer Price Index ('CPI'), as published by the Office for National Statistics is used in many contracts, both within the IT industry and otherwise, to govern future price increases. However, this index reflects the more general rates of inflation in the economy and is based on the prices of household goods and services or supplies that are not particularly relevant to the cost of IT or labour in the IT industry. Both parties may therefore look to other indices specific to the IT industry as the basis on which charges should be increased.[70] Any other changes to the charges should only be made if agreed through the contract change control mechanism.

As with any contract, provisions regarding the mechanism for payment will need to be included. Issues such as the timing of payments (ie, whether charges are paid in arrears or in advance) and the frequency of payments must be stipulated, together with the mechanism by which any penalties under the contract, such as service credits, are to be paid. Service credits can be paid direct to the customer from the provider or they may be deducted from invoices for the charges. Providers invariably favour the latter approach, not least because of the reluctance to incur costs as opposed to a loss of revenue.

As noted above, contracts will often be put in place with a certain degree of flexibility, enabling the customer to require the provider to provide certain additional services as and when required. Ideally, the costs for any additional services which can be predicted as being a likely future requirement should be agreed at the outset and specified in the services agreement. This will not always be possible. For services that cannot be foreseen at the outset it may nevertheless be possible to specify a price formula within the contract by which the charges for any additional service will be calculated. This may be a cost-plus basis with the provider being able to recover the cost of the new element of the services, together with an additional fixed profit element.

At the time of writing, there is a trend developing of payment under outsourcing contracts by achieved results. This is currently being led by the UK public sector. For example, the UK Department for Work and Pensions is running a procurement programme for its welfare-to-work programme. Successful bidders will be paid according to their success in getting jobless people back into employment. It remains to be seen how far this approach will be applied to IT outsourcing, both in the public and private sectors. With the increasing alignment of IT to business objectives in many organizations, there is no reason why this approach should not apply more widely to IT outsourcing and related services in both the public and private sectors.

3.2.2.9 *Contract duration*

At first sight, this may appear to be a straightforward issue. In reality, the position will be more complex. The length of the contract term will be determined by a

---

[70] eg, the Xpert HR Salary Surveys used to show the movement in employment costs in the IT industry: see <http://www.xperthr.co.uk/salary-surveys/home> (accessed 8 August 2011). For offshore IT outsourcing and services contracts, the Hewitt Associates surveys are frequently used. See <http://www.hewittassociates.com/Intl/NA/en-US/Default.aspx> (accessed 8 August 2011).

number of factors, most of which are operational, financial, and strategic in nature. The key factor is whether the customer and provider will realize their respective financial returns and other benefits from the IT outsourcing over the proposed term.

A view widely held by both customers and providers is that, because IT outsourcing contracts are difficult to enter into and exit costs need to be amortized, such contracts must necessarily be medium to long term. For this reason, there are still many IT outsourcing contracts that are entered into for five-, seven-, or ten-year periods. However, there are a number of other factors that should also be borne in mind that may favour a shorter contract period. These include the fact that the customer's business changes over time and long-term contracts may often be inflexible and also that it may not always be in the customer's best interests to enter into an outsourcing contract that will run beyond the life expectancy of the customer's technology. For these and other reasons, many advisers now tend to recommend shorter contract durations, such as a three- to five-year term. But, as explained, much will depend on the complexity of the IT outsourcing concerned.

A more recent trend that affects the duration of the contract is the offer by certain outsource providers or a requirement by customer organizations to pay a premium or 'golden hello' for longer term outsourcing contracts—typically ten years—or for the extension beyond ten years of existing contracts. For cash-strapped customers (or those owned by private equity funds), this can be an attractive proposition, but it can also deflect them from the primary purpose of the outsourcing: to achieve short- or medium-term cost savings and greater efficiencies, with the option to move to another provider if the outsourcing becomes less effective after an initial three- to five-year term.

Contract renewal can be another contentious issue. Many customers will seek the right to extend the basic contract term for a certain time period without having to renegotiate the contract. This will be particularly important if the contract is for a shorter duration, such as a three-year period. In practice, providers will often be happy to extend the contract term provided that an acceptable charging basis for that extension period can be agreed. The exercise of an option to extend the contract term may also be used by the provider to renegotiate other terms which it sees as being less than favourable, such as service levels or exit arrangements. Attempts to renegotiate any terms other than those that are directly impacted by the contract extension should be firmly resisted.

3.2.2.10 *Service credits and debits*

If the essence of the services agreement is a commitment by the provider to deliver services to a stated service level, then the contract must define any consequences of a failure to achieve those service levels. Traditionally, service credit regimes have been adopted. Service credits are a stated monetary amount (or formula from which such an amount is derived) that becomes payable by the provider to the customer on a failure to achieve a service level to which those service credits apply. They are often expressed as being a certain percentage of the monthly charges. At the time of writing, the industry norm appears to be in the range of 10 to 20 per cent of the charges.

The advantage of such a service credit regime is that it provides the customer with an automatic financial remedy in the event of a service failure, thereby avoiding the customer being required to pursue formal legal claims for damages against the provider. It also removes the potential for disputes between the parties as to the amount of loss and damage that has occurred in practice as a result of any service level failure and whether that loss and damage is of a type which should be recoverable from the provider.

The imposition of service credits therefore incentivizes the provider to ensure the service levels are achieved and, in the event that they are not, provides an effective form of financial recourse to the customer.

It usually takes some time to calculate and negotiate the monetary amount that would constitute a service credit. Contracts will typically set service credits either at a relatively nominal level or at a much higher level which aims to provide true compensation for the breach of the particular service level that has occurred.

Under English law, an amount stated in a contract that operates as a penalty is not enforceable. Accordingly, service credits that are set at unrealistic levels (in other words, not reflecting a genuine pre-estimate of the likely losses to the customer caused by service failures) run the risk of being legally unenforceable. It will therefore be important to ensure that any service credits reflect a reasonably genuine pre-estimate of the likely loss and damage that will be suffered in the event of a service failure. In practice, however, this is hardly ever achievable, and the reality is that most, if not all, service credit regimes are legally unenforceable. While the point has not, at least to this author's knowledge, ever been litigated in the UK, that is only a reflection of acceptance by the IT and outsourcing industries that it is better to be exposed to relatively low-level service credits, even if they are penalties, than face more formal legal claims. Another compensating feature for providers is that service credits are very often treated as exclusive remedies for the breaches concerned. There is accordingly a settlement of the matter by an administrative contractual remedy. Nevertheless, those involved in calculating service credits should retain records from the time of contract negotiations in the event of any later disputes as to the validity of the amounts specified.

The imposition of service credits will usually provoke a response from a provider that the converse should also apply, that is, that in the event that the service levels are exceeded the provider should receive some form of compensation. For many, the idea that a provider should be compensated for performing in excess of a level required and whilst the customer is still paying for that service is counter-intuitive. If it is accepted that some form of service debit should be payable then the most frequent way of incorporating them into the contractual framework is to set up a service credit/debit bank. This requires an account, either real or notional, to be established. Service credits are then paid into the account as they are triggered. The provider is then given the opportunity to reduce the amounts of credits payable by performing in excess of the service levels. On any over-performance, service debits will be paid into the account having the effect of reducing the balance of credits in that account. The account should then be settled on a regular basis with an appropriate payment to the customer, either direct or by a reduction against the charges which are invoiced for. Where such mechanisms are used, it is usual to ensure that service debits can only reduce the amount of credits that are payable to a zero amount and that service debits never become an amount which the customer is actually liable to pay direct to the provider.

Service credit regimes are, of course, only one method of compensating for service level failures. Other remedies include termination rights and damages claims where service credits are not an exclusive remedy.[71] On a more practical note, providers are also usually contractually required to provide such additional resources as may be necessary to remedy the service level failure with, occasionally, the right for the customer to call on a third party to provide that failing service where the provider has failed to remedy the situation within a specified time period.

3.2.2.11 *Liability*

Providers will inevitably seek to limit as far as possible their risk exposure under any IT outsourcing contract through the imposition of detailed exclusions and limitations of liability clauses. Such clauses will usually impose a limit on the amount of any loss or damage, whether arising from a breach of contract, tort, or otherwise, to a stated amount. Customers should also limit their own liability to the customer in the same way.

Under English law, liability for certain types of loss and damage cannot be excluded. These include, most notably, exclusions or limitations for death or personal injury caused by a party's negligence,[72] and, where the IT outsourcing contract involves the sale of goods (such as the sale of hardware from the customer to the provider as part of the initial asset transfer), the term that the seller has the right to sell those goods.[73]

English law also provides that certain exclusions and limitations of liability must be subject to the test of reasonableness. For example, where the parties contract on the basis of one party's standard terms of business, the exclusions and limitations of liability for loss and damage in respect of any contract breach must be reasonable.[74] Although it is likely that many IT outsourcing and complex services contracts

---

[71] See section 3.2.2.11 below regarding the relationship between service credits and damages claims.

[72] Unfair Contract Terms Act 1977, s 3.

[73] Sale of Goods Act 1979, s 12; Supply of Goods and Services Act 1982, s 7.

[74] Unfair Contract Terms 1977, s 3. Whether or not the exclusion/limitation is 'reasonable' will be assessed in light of a number of factors specified in Sch 2 to that Act.

will be the subject of extensive and detailed negotiations so that the negotiated transaction can no longer be said to be on one party's standard terms of business, those negotiating and drafting contracts should be aware of this principle.[75]

Providers generally seek to exclude their liability totally for indirect or consequential loss and damage. It was—and unfortunately at the time of writing still is—assumed (mainly by providers and their advisers) that loss of revenues, loss of profits, loss of anticipated savings, loss and corruption of data, and the remedial costs of restoring data, third party claims, and so on, are all *of themselves* 'indirect' or 'consequential' loss.[76] This was part of the tradition and lore of the IT and outsourcing industry as a result of advice received over the years in relation to specific contracts. This advice was probably based partly on prevailing case law and partly on wishful thinking. The fact is that, since the *British Sugar* case and a line of cases since *British Sugar*, that view is untenable at law.[77] Certainly, all are categories of loss that providers are anxious to exclude altogether. But whether as a matter of contract such losses *should* be excluded altogether is another matter. Customers, either because they are not properly advised, or they feel cowed by the inflexible line taken by the provider,[78] or through their inability or unwillingness

---

[75] Especially given the willingness of courts recently to strike out liability clauses which were in breach of the Unfair Contract Terms Act 1977, s 3. See in particular *St Albans City and DC v International Computers Ltd* [1995] FSR 686 and *South West Water Services Ltd v International Computers Ltd* (Technology & Construction Court, 29 June 1999), although both of these cases involved rather specific facts which may well enable courts later to distinguish from them in future judgments. However, since then, the Court of Appeal has upheld a provider's contractual position in excluding consequential loss and limiting liability: see *Watford Electronics Ltd v Sanderson CFL Ltd* [2001] 1 All ER (Comm) 696, which was followed by the Technology and Construction Court in *SAM Business Systems Ltd v Hedley & Co* [2002] All ER (D) 311. More recent case law includes *Regus (UK) Ltd v Epcot Solutions Ltd* [2008] EWCA Civ 361 and *Lobster Group Ltd v Heidelberg Graphic Equipment Ltd & Close Asset Finance Ltd* [2009] EWHC 1919 (TCC).

[76] See *British Sugar v NEI Power Projects Ltd* (1998) 87 BLR 42, in which the Court of Appeal held that the meaning of the word 'consequential' was loss that flows from special circumstances and therefore within the second limb of the *Hadley v Baxendale* (1854) 9 Exch 341 damages test. If loss of profit and increased production costs (both items claimed by British Sugar from NEI) flowed directly and naturally, without further intervention, from NEI's breach, they were direct and not consequential loss (consequential losses being limited to the contract(s) value and direct losses being unlimited under the terms of the contract). Since *British Sugar*, the courts have adopted a similar line, in that they have found that, eg, loss of profit may well be a direct loss and therefore recoverable from the provider if the exclusion of liability is merely of 'indirect' or 'consequential' loss: see *Deepak Fertilisers & Petrochemical Corp v Davy McKee (UK) London Ltd* [2002] All ER (D) 208 (Jul); *Hotel Services Ltd v Hilton International Hotels (UK) Ltd* [2000] 1 All ER (Comm) 750; *Simkins Partnership (a firm) v Reeves Lund & Co Ltd* [2003] All ER (D) 325 (Jul); and *University of Keele v Price Waterhouse (a firm)* [2004] All ER (D) 264. See now also *Supershield Ltd v Siemens Building Technologies FE Ltd* [2010] EWCA Civ 7, [2010] 1 Lloyd's Rep 349; *Sylvia Shipping Co Ltd v Progress Bulk Carriers Ltd* [2010] EWHC 542 (Comm), [2010] 2 Lloyd's Rep 81; *Pindell Ltd v AirAsia Berhad* [2010] All ER (D) 133; *The Amer Energy* [2009] 1 Lloyd's Rep 293; *Classic Maritime v Lion Diversified Holdings* [2009] EWHC 1142 (Comm), [2010] 1 Lloyd's Rep 59; and *Borealis AB v Geogas Trading SA* [2010] EWHC 2789 (Comm).

[77] See the cases cited in preceding note.

[78] Often taking the line that expecting the provider to bear such losses will add disproportionately to the costs under the contract to be met by the customer, or that, in any event, such losses are uninsurable at any cost.

to analyse and quantify such loss and damage, tend to give in and agree to such exclusions.

However, there are signs that the trend is changing: customers are beginning to realize, especially with the outsourcing of strategic or mission-critical IT systems, that they need to hold the provider accountable for some of the losses that had previously been totally excluded, in the main including loss of profits, loss of anticipated savings, and loss arising from third party claims. Similarly, where the provider is engaged in the course of an IT outsourcing to operate on systems and (directly or indirectly) on the data that are processed by those systems, there is no logic to a blanket exclusion of loss and damage caused by loss and corruption of data, or the costs of restoring or repairing such data.

A growing body of case law in the area now supports the view outlined in the preceding paragraph. Accordingly, providers who do wish to exclude their liability for indirect or consequential loss will need to draft appropriate exclusions and limitations with increasing care.[79]

The services agreement will include a number of provisions regarding the provider's liability in specific circumstances. Common examples include liability in the event of an infringement of a third party's intellectual property rights, specific indemnities (eg, regarding employee transfers and the application of the TUPE Regulations), and in the event of a failure to achieve general or specific service levels. The services agreement must bring together all of these forms of the provider's liability under the contract and detail how these specific liabilities are linked to the general caps on the provider's liability for contract breaches, if at all.

The relationship between the liability provisions and the provider's liability to pay service credits in the event of a failure to achieve a service level to which service credits relate will merit special consideration. The liability for such service credits may fall within the general cap, be subject to a separate cap, or be unlimited. The services agreement will need to find a balance between ensuring that the customer can recover appropriately in the event of a service failure (bearing in mind that including service credits within a general liability cap of, say, the total contract price, may not provide adequate compensation to the customer or incentive to the provider to avoid breaches) against the provider's understandable desire to limit its total liability exposure.

The services agreement will, typically, include some specific remedies that are available to the customer in the event of a contract breach. A good example comes

---

[79] See Chapter 1, section 1.2.2 for a detailed discussion of liability generally and the effectiveness of exclusion clauses. See also *British Sugar v NEI Power Projects Ltd* (1998) 87 BLR 42; *Deepak Fertilisers & Petrochemical Corp v Davy McKee (UK) London Ltd* [2002] All ER (D) 208 (Jul); *Hotel Services Ltd v Hilton International Hotels (UK) Ltd* [2000] 1 All ER (Comm) 750; *Simkins Partnership (a firm) v Reeves Lund & Co Ltd* [2003] All ER (D) 325 (Jul); and *University of Keele v Price Waterhouse (a firm)* [2004] All ER (D) 264.

from provisions stipulating what will happen in the event that any of the customer's data is lost or corrupted. This loss of data is a category of loss for which typically (as noted above) the provider will seek to exclude its liability. However, to leave a customer with no remedy in these circumstances where the potential for damage to the customer's business as a result of that loss is so great, would be unacceptable. Services agreements therefore often require the provider to restore or procure the restoration of any data that has been lost or corrupted to the last transaction processed. This data recovery is carried out at the provider's cost.

In any event proper consideration should be given not only to what liability provisions can be negotiated but also as to the likely ability of the provider to pay out under any claims. This is particularly important where the provider is either one of the smaller, newer, entrants to the market or where services are provided though a particular subsidiary (with limited assets) of a more well-known market player. In these circumstances, obtaining contractual assurances as to insurance cover or seeking parent company guarantees would be worth considering.

It has long been settled law that it is not open to a party who has made a fraudulent misrepresentation or behaved otherwise fraudulently to exclude or limit its liability for that misrepresentation or conduct. It has also been known, through not until last year widely and publicly acknowledged, that there has been—and unfortunately probably still is—a tendency for sales teams in the IT sector to oversell the capabilities, resources, and commitments of their employers.[80] These circumstances converged in the recent case *of BSkyB Ltd and Another v HP Enterprise Services UK Ltd and Electronic Data Systems Ltd.*[81] Though understandably much has been made of the case, it is less significant legally than it is for the amount ultimately awarded against EDS/HP Enterprise Services (£318m) and for its practical implications for the sales teams, senior management, and internal governance processes of IT outsourcing and services providers.

3.2.2.12 *Warranties*

The services agreement will need to incorporate a number of warranties to deal both with the status and performance of the provider generally and then to cover a number of specific issues arising in relation to IT outsourcing contracts.

English law will imply certain terms into any contract for the supply of goods and services (see section 1.2.1). In relation to a contract for the provision of services, as an IT outsourcing contract will be, the provider will be required to use reasonable

---

[80] See *DSL Group Ltd v Unisys International Services Ltd* (unreported, 4 May 1995). Unisys had supplied a defective computer system to DSL who in turn had supplied it to a third party. The third party sued DSL for breach of contract and the action was settled. DSL sued Unisys to recover its loss. The judgment in this unreported case concerns the nature and effect of misrepresentations by Unisys employees (fraud and deceit were claimed) and to what extent DSL's losses under the settlement were recoverable from Unisys.

[81] See Chapter 1, section 1.3.1.2 for a fuller discussion of the case.

care in the provision of the services.[82] In practice, this implied warranty will usually be replaced by detailed contractual assurances regarding the nature of the services to be provided. Accordingly, the application of implied terms is often expressly excluded.[83]

Assuming that the contract will therefore replace warranties implied by law with express warranties, general warranties to be included regarding service performance will include those regarding the performance by the provider of its obligations in accordance with all applicable laws, the use of skilled and experienced personnel, and performance of obligations in accordance with good industry practice. Warranties are also included regarding the general standing of the provider at the time the contract is entered into, such as warranties that the provider has full capacity and all necessary consents and licences to enter into the contract, that it is not subject to insolvency (or similar) proceedings, and that there is no material litigation pending to which the provider is a party.

Equivalent warranties may also be sought regarding the general standing of the customer at the time the contract is entered into.

Specific issues to be covered include euro compliance and the absence of any viruses, software locks, and similar code in systems provided or used.

Assurances should be obtained regarding euro compliance where any IT system provided or used by the provider needs to recognize and deal in euros.

As noted above, the position regarding viruses should also be considered. Where software is provided by a provider, contractual assurances may be obtained acknowledging that the software does not contain any virus or lock or any other device which enables the provider to prevent its continued operation. For example, if the customer fails to make payment the software is then disabled by the provider activating such a device. Such locks and time bombs will be illegal under the terms of the Computer Misuse Act 1990—see section 12.4.2.2—unless the provider has notified the customer in advance of its intention to use such devices in the software and their effect.

3.2.2.13 Data and data protection[84]

Most IT outsourcing contracts are likely to involve the provider handling the customer's data, either where the provider generates data using systems which are utilized by the provider as part of the services or data which the provider itself directly generates in the course of performing the services.

---

[82] Supply of Goods and Services Act 1982, s 13. Where goods are supplied, the Sale of Goods Act 1979, ss 14, 15 requires them to be of satisfactory quality and fit for their purpose.

[83] As with any exclusion or limitation of liability, caution must be exercised to ensure the Unfair Contract Terms Act 1977 (and, in particular, s 2) is adhered to.

[84] See, further, Chapter 10, and in particular section 10.3.8.

Customers should therefore ensure that they own all of the rights in their data and that appropriate assignments are obtained from the provider of the intellectual property rights in the data.

Data protection law, in particular the Data Protection Act 1998 if data processing is to take place in the UK, will also have a considerable impact on outsourcing activities.[85] Both the customer and provider must ensure that they comply with the Act and the contract should allocate responsibilities and liabilities accordingly.

For the most part in any IT outsourcing or services contract, the customer will be the data controller, being the party that is most likely to determine the purposes for which, and the manner in which, personal data are to be processed in the course of an outsourcing[86] or provision of services. It follows that the provider is most likely to be the data processor, that is, it will be carrying out the processing of personal data on behalf of the customer. However, the factual and technical background should be analysed to confirm that this will be the position.

The Data Protection Act 1998 requires that a data controller should impose certain obligations on any data processor that it appoints. Data processors must be appointed under a written contract and must carry out any processing activities only on the instructions of the data controller. Importantly, the data controller must choose a data processor with sufficient guarantees in respect of the security measures they take to protect the data processed against unlawful or accidental loss or destruction.

With the growth of offshore and nearshore outsourcing, the much-publicized eighth principle under Schedule 1 to the Act has become very important in IT outsourcing. Schedule 1 lists a number of principles with which a data controller must comply. The eighth principle states that personal data cannot be transferred to a country outside the EEA unless that third country offers an adequate level of protection for the data concerned. Unfortunately, most offshore outsourcing destinations[87] are not countries that, under the terms of the eighth principle, offer an adequate level of protection. Businesses therefore need to be aware of the eighth principle and that further steps may need to be taken to ensure compliance with it.[88]

---

[85] See the Information Commissioner's website for useful guidance on the Act and its implications for business: <http://www.ico.gov.uk/for-organisations/data-protection/the-guide.aspx> (accessed 8 August 2011). In particular, the Information Commissioner has issued guidelines on data protection issues in outsourcing, aimed at small and medium-sized businesses: <http://www.ico.gov.uk/upload/documents/library/data_protection/detailed_specialist_guides/outsourcing_-_a_guide_for_small_and_medium_businesses.pdf>.

[86] Data Protection Act 1998, s 1(1).

[87] However, a number of nearshore destinations are now within the EEA, which means that they can be assumed to offer an adequate level of protection in the processing of personal data.

[88] See the Information Commissioner's guidance at <http://www.ico.gov.uk/upload/documents/library/data_protection/practical_application/the_eighth_data_prtection_principle_and_transborder_dataflows.pdf>.

The most common approach is to provide in the outsourcing contract for each party's obligations with regard to the processing of personal data, with suitable mutual warranties and indemnities. The object of such provisions should be to ensure that both parties undertake to comply with their respective obligations as data controller and data processor, that neither does anything or omits to do anything that would impose liability on the other with regard to personal data, that the data processor—usually the provider—will comply with the lawful and reasonable instructions and requests of the data controller to enable the controller to meet its obligations with regard to personal data,[89] and that the provider will comply with certain technical standards to ensure the integrity and confidentiality of the personal data. Where it is not envisaged in the contract that personal data will be transferred outside the UK or the EEA, there will usually be an absolute prohibition on such a transfer of personal data, with an obligation on the provider to obtain the prior written consent of the customer to any such transfer. Often, breach of this provision will be treated as a material breach of contract. Where, however, the parties intend that personal data will be processed outside the EEA, they will, in addition to the operational provisions outlined above, provide for each of them to enter into a separate data transfer agreement to comply with the Data Protection Directive[90] and the 1998 Act. Such an agreement will usually be in the form of the 'model clauses' approved by the European Commission for transfers from data controllers in the EEA to those outside.[91]

3.2.2.14 *Termination*

As with any IT contract, a number of standard termination rights should be incorporated. These should include rights of termination in the event that the other party to the contract breaches one of its terms or becomes insolvent.

More specific termination rights should then be catered for. These will often include defining a minimum service level and providing that if the service drops below this minimum level then the customer has a right of immediate termination. Defining a minimum service level in this way effectively defines what the parties consider amounts to a material breach and avoids protracted disputes about whether any particular service level failure is of sufficient impact to otherwise entitle the customer to terminate under standard material breach provisions.

---

[89] eg, if the customer receives a request from a data subject claiming that data concerning the subject is incorrect and requiring the customer as data controller to correct that information, the provider as processor should be obliged to take the steps necessary to carry out that correction, as it will be storing and processing the data on behalf of the customer.

[90] Council Directive (EC) 95/46 on the protection of individuals with regard to the processing of personal data and on the free movement of such data [1995] OJ L281.

[91] Pursuant to Art 26(4) of the Data Protection Directive, the European Commission has approved model clauses in a number of decisions to cover various data transfer situations: see *Data Protection Act 1998, The Eighth Data Protection Principle and international data transfers* (v 2.0, Office of the Information Commissioner, 30 June 2006) at <http://www.ico.gov.uk/upload/documents/library/data_protection/practical_application/the_eighth_data_prtection_principle_and_transborder_dataflows.pdf>.

It is not only one-off breaches of the service levels that should be considered for specific treatment within the termination provisions but also persistent, albeit more minor, breaches of service levels. It may be unacceptable for the parties to be locked into a contract indefinitely where there are repeated minor breaches (even where this triggers service credits) and it may therefore be useful to define further termination rights as existing after there have been a specified number of these more minor breaches within any fixed time period.

Under many IT outsourcing contracts there is a mix of a different number of services that are provided by the providers. For this reason, rights to partial termination may be appropriate, and highly desirable, enabling the customer to retain a high degree of flexibility as to how its business develops in the future. In each circumstance, those drafting a contract will need to consider the extent to which the services are bundled together and whether they can be easily separated. If it is possible to separate the services, or part of a service, partial termination rights may be appropriate. In practice, any partial termination rights are likely to be resisted heavily by the provider. Where the services are partially terminated there will inevitably be an impact on the remaining provisions of the contract (such as the other services being provided, the service levels, and the charges). Accordingly, any necessary changes to the remaining contract terms should be made through the contract change provisions.

'Break options' (or rights to terminate for convenience, as opposed to cause) are also a popular remedy, entitling the customer to terminate a contract at will after a number of years. The customer therefore does not need to prove any breach by the provider or any other cause entitling them to terminate. Many providers will calculate their cost models on the basis of recovery of various investment costs over a relatively long period and to allow termination in this way would potentially leave a provider seriously out of pocket or at least having failed to realize its margin on the transaction. For this reason, break options are usually accompanied by significant financial penalties under which the provider seeks to recoup this type of investment cost.

As has been seen, IT outsourcing contracts require a close working relationship to be established between the parties and a number of the customer's assets will have transferred to the provider at the beginning of that relationship. The exercise of termination rights can therefore pose difficult issues for the customer.[92] It is not a relationship from which the customer is likely to be able to extricate itself in a number of weeks. Assets will need to be transferred back to the customer or to a replacement service provider to enable the customer to continue to receive the service. There will need to be a flow of information and assistance between the parties. Consequently, exit provisions dealing with the handover of assets and information and ensuring ongoing service provision whilst the customer or its

---

[92] Where the customer is a regulated financial services institution, it will in any event be required by FSA rules to have appropriate exit management provisions in place.

replacement service provider take over the service provision will be vital to ensure a seamless transition of the services. The importance and nature of exit provisions are discussed in more detail at section 3.5 below.

3.2.2.15 *Dispute resolution*

It is increasingly common to formalize escalation procedures within a contract providing for stated levels within each entity to which any dispute will be escalated (within fixed timescales) before the matter can be referred to the courts—if it is to be referred to the courts at all. For example, project managers may initially be required to resolve any dispute and, on their failing to do so within a specified time, the issue is referred to the finance directors of each organization. The purpose of these provisions is to encourage settlement of any dispute at an early stage.[93]

There are a number of matters which should be excluded from the scope of these escalation procedures as there are some circumstances in which it will not be appropriate to follow this type of process before being free to pursue legal action. For example, where one party has committed a material breach of the contract the other party will want the immediate right to terminate and to pursue any other legal remedies (such as a damages claim) without being required to first discuss the dispute with the other party. Also, if one party suspects that its intellectual property rights have been, or are about to be, infringed or if it thinks that its confidential information has been, or is or is about to be, disclosed then immediate action will be required (eg, through seeking an injunction) to protect the rights of that party.

Contracts may also provide, in addition to the internal escalation procedures referred to above, for other forms of dispute resolution in the event that the internal escalation process does not resolve the matter. This is a reflection of an increasing reluctance to refer matters to court because of costs and time to trial and judgment. In addition, disputes arising out of IT outsourcing contracts can often be of a highly technical nature meaning that it may be more appropriate to refer the issue to an expert with suitable knowledge and understanding rather than to the courts.

Third party experts may therefore be used for disputes of a technical nature. The contract will need to specify the processes the expert will adhere to and how

---

[93] There is increased formal pressure on the parties to any dispute to have tried to resolve their differences by mediation or alternative dispute resolution ('ADR') before starting formal judicial proceedings. See the UK Civil Procedure Rules 1998, particularly the Practice Direction on Pre-Action Conduct in the Civil Procedure Rules 1998. There is also case law supporting this point: see, for a recent example, *Darren Egan v Motor Services (Bath) Ltd* [2007] EWCA Civ 1002. See also the Jackson Report, *Review of Civil Litigation Costs—Final Report*, December 2009, at <http://www.judiciary.gov.uk> (accessed 8 August 2011). Finally, the importance of ADR has been recognized at EU level: see Directive 2008/52/EC on certain aspects of mediation in civil and commercial matters. It applies to mediation in cross-border disputes and must be implemented in Member States before 21 May 2011.

that expert is appointed. Experts' decisions are usually expressed as being binding. Mediation is often used to resolve other disputes (ie, those of a non-technical nature) and the contract will need to specify a body which, in the event of a failure by the parties to agree on the identity of a mediator, will be required to appoint one. The Centre for Dispute Resolution is often used in this context. Again, the contract will need to specify the process which will be adopted where mediation is used.

Finally, it is becoming increasingly common to refer matters to arbitration and there is a growing body of local and international arbitrators with experience of IT disputes.

3.3 SALE AGREEMENTS

3.3.1 Purpose of sale agreement

One of the features of an IT outsourcing contract may be the transfer of assets from the customer to the provider. A formal document of transfer will be required to identify those assets that are to be transferred, the mechanism by which they are to be transferred, and the price which the provider is to pay for them.

Provisions can be incorporated into the principal services agreement dealing with the assets transfer. It may, however, be easier to use a separate sale agreement to document the provisions regarding the one-off transfer of assets. This is particularly likely to be the case where there are a considerable number of assets to be transferred.

3.3.2 Identification of assets

Early in the outsourcing process the customer should identify the assets which are currently used by it to deliver the service in-house. This should include a listing of the assets themselves and any related contracts. Ultimately, this information will need to be attached as a schedule to the sale agreement. It is important not to underestimate the length of time that will be required to compile this listing. Unfortunately, it is often found to be the case that customers have poorly documented the systems that are used in providing services in-house, especially regarding pieces of software which are developed on a fairly ad hoc basis for use by the company. It can therefore be a difficult and time-consuming task to piece together the relevant information.

The types of assets which are likely to have been used by the customer and which the provider may require will include software and hardware and their related support arrangements, together with other items such as premises, equipment, and other items and contracts. In respect of items of software, hardware, or other equipment which is owned by the customer, the position will be relatively straight-forward. A decision will need to be taken whether these assets are to be transferred to the provider for an appropriate payment or whether a lease or licence for them will be provided and, if so, the terms of that lease or licence.

Items of software or hardware that are owned by third parties and leased or licensed to the business may cause more difficulties. Often the terms of those contracts will prevent the use of that item by a third party, even where the third party is acting on behalf of the customer, let alone an outright transfer of it to the provider. Any use by a provider of those items will therefore be in breach of the contract provisions exposing the customer to a damages claim and to termination of the contract for material breach of its terms. In addition, such unauthorized use will infringe the intellectual property rights (usually copyright) of the third party and the provider may therefore be liable accordingly.

The third parties who provide those items of software, hardware, or other equipment will therefore need to be approached to give their consent to the transfer of the relevant item by the third party provider. If this consent cannot be obtained then the primary alternative will be to seek a licence in favour of the provider from the third party owner of the item involved. Obviously, the consequences of either of these two methods is the sum of money which the third party imposes on the provider to provide its consent or provide the licence. Traditionally, the customer is forced to bear the costs associated with obtaining any necessary consents from third parties. This will, however, very much depend on the negotiating power of the parties. Also, it should be noted that the process for approaching those third parties and obtaining consents from them can be a lengthy one and it should therefore be started well in advance of the anticipated contract commencement date.

The contract should also specify the consequences if relevant third party consents cannot be procured. It may be that an alternative item can be found or that the customer continues to operate the item of software or hardware that cannot be transferred. This is discussed in more detail in section 3.3.3 below.

3.3.3 The sale agreement

The sale agreement will thus identify all of the assets that are to transfer to the provider and will specify the date on which this is to take effect. As the provider will usually take over the obligations and liabilities in relation to third party items after the transfer date, the customer will usually warrant that it has fulfilled all of those obligations and liabilities up to that date.

The provider will be in control of those third party items after the transfer date, so the customer will want to have assurance that, if there are any problems that arise after that date, the provider will be legally responsible for them. It is therefore usual for the customer to seek an indemnity from the provider in respect of any claims and expenses arising after the transfer date. Often, the provider then seeks a counter-indemnity from the customer in respect of the fulfilment of the customer's obligations in relation to the third party items prior to the transfer date.

The provider may seek warranties from the customer regarding the performance and quality of assets which are to be transferred to it. Whether these warranties are ultimately incorporated into the sale agreement will be a question of the respective bargaining power of the parties. Where, as is usually the case, the provider undertakes a detailed due diligence process prior to entering into the contract,[94] then one of the primary purposes of this due diligence exercise will have been for the provider to ascertain the quality and condition of the assets and for this to be reflected in the purchase price accordingly. On this basis, warranties should be resisted. Where no, or little, due diligence has taken place prior to entering into the contract it may be necessary to incorporate some limited warranties for the benefit of the provider.

A great deal of cooperation will be required between the customer and the provider to ensure the smooth transition of the assets to the provider. As mentioned above, it should be accepted that there may be some items where consent simply cannot be obtained from the relevant third party prior to the commencement of the services agreement. In this circumstance, it will be necessary to consider other options in order to ensure that the services can nevertheless still be provided by the provider. Contracts may therefore need to build in a mechanism to deal with this scenario, including, for example, removing those third party items from the scope of the outsourcing or for the third party vendor to simply manage those contracts on behalf of the customer until such time as the third party consents to the transfer.[95]

In relation to any particular IT function that is being outsourced, there may well be assets which, although related to the function, are not to be transferred and will be retained by the customer. For the sake of clarity, contracts may also need to identify the assets and contracts which are to be retained by the customer in this way and which are therefore outside the scope of the sale agreement.

As far as the transfer of third party contracts is concerned, the most effective form of legal transfer will be novation. The legal effect of novating a contract is to terminate the existing legal arrangement between the customer and third party and to create a new legal arrangement (on the same terms as the previous contract) between the provider and the third party. The other method of transfer which may be referred to is an assignment. However, generally, an assignment can only transfer benefits and not burdens.[96]

Where real property is involved, the provider may need to be sold or leased premises, or a sublease may need to be granted. Where the customer is granting a

---

[94] See section 3.1.9.5.

[95] Note that these arrangements, too, can be problematic as many third party contracts will contain standard provisions preventing or restricting the customer's ability to assign, transfer, or otherwise dispose of its rights under that contract. Also, there are often confidentiality obligations imposed on the parties to such contracts which will effectively prevent the access to, and use of, that item by a third party. The management option may therefore not always be a viable option.

[96] So, where the customer has obligations to perform, as in a standard software licence, novation is the more effective and complete way of transferring that licence.

sublease of property, it will need to get the owner's consent. As with other third party assets that are transferred, there are likely to be costs implications in obtaining these consents and other conditions may be imposed. The sale or leasing of property will also raise issues of property law (which are beyond the scope of this publication) and specialist advice should be obtained in this regard.

Staff may also transfer to the provider, together with the valuable body of knowledge that each staff member will have built up regarding the IT systems and, generally, in relation to the business operations of the customer.

3.4 STAFF AND TRANSFERS OF UNDERTAKINGS

The Transfer of Undertakings (Protection of Employment) Regulations 2006 (SI 2006/246), implementing the EU Acquired Rights Directive,[97] came into effect on 6 April 2006.[98] Assuming that the operation and impact of the TUPE Regulations are now more widely known and understood, the purpose of this section is to highlight the changes made by the new TUPE Regulations, insofar as those changes are likely to be applicable to IT outsourcing arrangements.

Since the enactment of the original Regulations in 1981, there had been a high level of uncertainty about their application to outsourcing arrangements. It became clearer over the years, mainly with the development of case law in the UK and in the jurisprudence of the European Court of Justice, that the 1981 Regulations were likely to apply to many outsourcing transactions, including IT outsourcing. The reason for this was the realization by many companies and, increasingly, public sector organizations, that IT or certain IT processes, while critical, were not core operations in their undertakings. For reasons given elsewhere in this chapter, with high employment costs and even higher wage inflation, there was an additional reason to seek cost savings and operational efficiencies by transferring those functions to IT outsourcing providers, whose core business it was (and remains) to undertake such functions. It became more common for the functions of an entire IT department, or a substantial part of it in the course of 'selective' outsourcing, to be outsourced to external providers. With that development and the application of the case law and jurisprudence as mentioned, it became increasingly more difficult to argue that the 1981 Regulations did *not* apply to proposed IT outsourcing arrangements. By the time the new TUPE Regulations were enacted, this position was well understood by customers, providers, and their advisers. Against that

---

[97] Council Directive (EC) 2001/23 on the approximation of the laws of the Member States relating to the safeguarding of employees' rights in the event of transfers of undertakings, businesses or parts of undertakings or businesses [2001] OJ L82.

[98] The new TUPE Regulations replace the 1981 Regulations completely, but many of the provisions of the 1981 Regulations have been carried into the new Regulations and much of the case law decided before April 2006 will remain relevant.

background, it can be seen that the new TUPE Regulations do not radically change existing law. However, they put beyond much doubt when they apply and make certain procedural changes that will affect both customer and provider in an outsourcing arrangement.

The TUPE Regulations (to avoid any uncertainty, meaning below in this section the new Regulations) apply to relevant transfers, which now expressly include a 'service provision change'.[99] A service provision change occurs where:

(a) activities cease to be undertaken by a client on its own behalf and are undertaken instead by a contractor on the customer's behalf;

(b) activities cease to be undertaken by a contractor on a client's behalf (whether or not those activities have previously been undertaken by the client on its own behalf) and are carried out instead by a subsequent contractor on the client's behalf; or

(c) activities cease to be undertaken by a contractor or subsequent contractor on a client's behalf (whether or not those activities have previously been undertaken by the client on its own behalf) and are undertaken instead by the client on its own behalf.

From this additional condition for the application of the TUPE Regulations, it is clear that these provisions will apply to an initial outsourcing, a change of outsourcing provider (or a succession of them), and any 'insourcing' by the customer. It will remain the case, however, that a good many IT outsourcing transactions will still meet the current test of 'transfer of an economic entity'. In addition to there being a service provision change, for the TUPE Regulations to apply there are three additional sub-conditions:

(a) that, immediately before the service provision change, there is an organized grouping of employees in Great Britain whose main purpose is the undertaking of the activities concerned (ie, the services) on behalf of the client;[100]

(b) that the client intends that, following the service provision change, the activities concerned will be undertaken by the transferee (ie, new contractor) other than in connection with a single, specific event or task of short-term duration;[101] and

(c) that the activities concerned do not consist wholly or mainly of the supply of goods for the client's use.[102]

One of the purposes of introducing the above sub-conditions is to limit the scope for customer and provider to avoid the TUPE Regulations by structuring the contract in such a way that the services appear to be delivered in a very different way from that

---

[99] Reg 3(1).
[100] Reg 3(3)(a)(i).
[101] Reg 3(3)(a)(ii).
[102] Reg 3(3)(b).

of the previous services—the so-called 'innovative bid':[103] another major difference between the old 'economic entity' and the 'service provision change' tests is that, under the latter, it is no longer relevant that assets of the economic entity have transferred.[104]

One of the more vexed questions in recent times is about the application of the old and new TUPE Regulations to offshore or nearshore outsourcing. There is no direct decision on the point, though it was decided *obiter* in a recent case that the TUPE Regulations *are* capable of applying to offshore outsourcing.[105] However, it is clear that the TUPE Regulations apply to an organized grouping of employees situated in Great Britain. The location of the provider, say, for the purposes of an IT outsourcing or service contract, is irrelevant for the purposes of determining whether there has been a TUPE transfer. Applying the governing laws of another country (eg, those of the offshore outsourcing destination) to the outsourcing contract will not avoid the application of the TUPE Regulations. Accordingly, however counter-intuitive it may be, where a UK-based customer enters into an IT outsourcing contract with a Bangalore-based provider and the 'economic entity' or 'service provision change' test is met, there is a TUPE transfer by operation of law. The most obvious question is: does that mean the transferring staff have to move from the UK to work in Bangalore? It is becoming more common for offshore outsourcers to employ onshore local staff in IT and BPO service provision, either in a subsidiary or, for the most part currently, in a branch. In such cases, UK staff are transferred under TUPE to the subsidiary or branch.[106] In those cases where all UK functions are to transfer offshore, the route adopted by customers is to make staff redundant before the transfer offshore for economic, technical, or organizational ('ETO') reasons, in which case the dismissal will not be unfair, provided it complies with all other relevant law.[107] And it is by no means inconceivable that some UK employees may positively welcome the prospect of living and working in Bangalore, especially on UK terms!

So far as TUPE processes are concerned, the TUPE Regulations have made some changes of significance for IT outsourcing.

---

[103] Under the old Regulations, part of the test threshold test of 'an economic entity' involved determining whether it had retained its identity after the transfer. In innovative bid situations, the parties would seek to argue that, with the change in service provider, there was no TUPE transfer, because the way the services were to be, or were being, provided after the transfer was so drastically different, ie the economic entity had not retained its pre-transfer character.

[104] It follows that, in this respect, *Suzen v Zehnacker Gebaudereinigung GmbH* [1977] IRLR 255 and *Spijkers v Gebroeders Benedik Abbatoir CV* [1986] ECR 1119 no longer apply.

[105] *Holis Metal Industries Ltd v (1) GMB (2) Newel Ltd* [2008] IRLR 187.

[106] In other cases, the provider and customer may create a joint venture, which employs the staff: see, for an example from the BPO world, the Tata Consultancy Services and Pearl outsourcing: <http://www.ovum.com/go/content/c,64433> and <http://www.telegraph.co.uk/money/main.jhtml?xml=/money/2006/05/15/cnindia15.xml> (both accessed 8 August 2011).

[107] Reg 7(2) and (3), but this is without prejudice to the application of s 98(4) of the Employment Rights Act 1996 (reasonableness requirement) and the statutory dismissal procedures under the Employment Act 2002.

There is now a specific obligation on transferring employers to provide 'employee liability information' to transferee employers.[108] This change is aimed at second, third, and subsequent outgoing providers. It has been a feature of reletting or terminating outsourcing contracts that incumbent, outgoing providers were extremely reluctant to pass meaningful (or any) employee information to replacement, incoming providers. This defeated due diligence and caused great difficulty to the replacement, incoming provider in submitting a realistic bid. The effect was to give the economic advantage to the incumbent. The provision of employee liability information is now a statutory obligation, and so is in addition to any due diligence provisions that may apply in the outsourcing services contract.[109]

Employee liability information (to be provided in writing or some other 'readily accessible form' at least 14 days before the transfer) comprises:

(a) age and identity;

(b) written particulars under section 1 of the Employment Rights Act 1996;

(c) details of collective agreement that will have effect in relation to that employee after the TUPE transfer;

(d) details of any disciplinary procedure taken against, and of any grievance procedure taken by, the transferring employee in the previous two years; and

(e) details of any litigation or legal claim brought or made by the employee against the transferring employer in the previous two years, and details of any litigation or legal claim that the transferring employer has reasonable grounds to believe that the employee may bring or make against the transferring employer.

The penalty for failure to provide such information in accordance with the TUPE Regulations is at least £500 per employee in relation to whom such information is not provided, and is payable to the transferee employer.[110]

Under the old TUPE Regulations, when employees transferred under TUPE to the transferee employer, the transferring employer ceased to be liable in relation to the transferred employees, even (except for criminal liability) for its own defaults regarding those employees. The new TUPE Regulations impose joint and several liability on both the transferring and transferee employers where, amongst other things, the transferring employer has failed to inform and consult the

---

[108] Reg 11.

[109] It is in any case prudent for a customer to require its providers to provide such information to the customer or a replacement provider on a service provision change.

[110] It is open to an employment tribunal, which has jurisdiction in such cases, to make an award to the transferee employer of such compensation as the tribunal thinks just and equitable. The £500 amount is therefore a minimum award in each case.

employee representatives.[111] The employee may therefore make a claim against either or both of the employers. Where there is a contractual relationship between the employers (eg, in the case of a first outsourcing), it will still be open to the parties to allocate the responsibilities and liabilities for pre- and post-transfer defaults.

One of the inviolable principles upon which the original Acquired Rights Directive,[112] and current Directive,[113] and jurisprudence of the European Court of Justice is based is that the protection under the Directive, and therefore under local law implementing the Directive, is mandatory and that employees cannot contract out of such protection, even if they wish to.[114] In the context of outsourcing, this has created real difficulties for transferee employers in seeking reasonably to harmonize the terms of transferred employees with those of the general workforce soon after the TUPE transfer. The new TUPE Regulations now allow limited opportunities for transferee employers to make changes to employment terms by making any change in the terms of employment void if the reason for the change is either the TUPE transfer itself or a reason connected with the TUPE transfer, unless (in the case of the latter) the sole reason for the change is an 'economic, technical or organisational reason entailing changes in the workforce'.[115] The precise effect of this derogation from the strict 'automatic transfer principle' of the old TUPE law is as yet unclear and is thought to be likely to have little impact in practice. This is mainly because the phrase 'entailing changes in the workforce' has been interpreted by the UK courts as requiring changes in the overall numbers in the workforce or in the numbers or levels of employees,[116] and not a wish or need to harmonize the terms to be enjoyed by all staff, unless there is also a substantial change in the nature of roles undertaken or in the number of employees. So what otherwise might have been a useful opportunity to enable reasonable harmonization of terms of employment after a TUPE transfer appears to have been lost.

---

[111] Reg 15(9). Under reg 17(2), the 'joint and several liability' allocation will apply where the transferring employer is exempted from carrying employer's liability insurance under s 3 of the Employers' Liability (Compulsory Insurance) Act 1969.

[112] Council Directive (EC) 77/187 on the approximation of the laws of the Member States relating to the safeguarding of employees' rights in the event of transfers of undertakings, businesses or parts of businesses [1977] OJ L61.

[113] Council Directive (EC) 2001/23 on the approximation of the laws of the Member States relating to the safeguarding of employees' rights in the event of transfers of undertakings, businesses or parts of undertakings or businesses [2001] OJ L82.

[114] See *Foreningen af Arbejdsledere I Danmark v Daddy's Dance Hall* [1988] IRLR 315 and, in the UK, *Wilson v St Helens BC* [1998] IRLR 706.

[115] Reg 4(4) and (5).

[116] See *Wheeler v Patel & Golding Group* [1987] IRLR 211 and *Delabole Slate v Berriman* [1985] IRLR 305.

3.5 EXIT ISSUES

3.5.1 Importance of service continuity

Many customers find it difficult to tackle the issue of exit provisions with the provider during negotiation for the services agreement. To contemplate the end of the relationship before it has begun can seem at best like being overly detailed and, at worst, a damning indictment of the future partnership between customer and provider. However, detailed provisions which specify the rights and obligations of the parties on any termination or expiry of the contract will be important to ensure that the customer is able to exit from the relationship without undue disruption to its business and to ensure a seamless transition of the services either back in-house to the customer or to a replacement third party service provider.

Just as the services agreement (or, in some cases, the sales agreement) incorporates detailed provisions regarding the transfer of assets from the customer to the provider on the commencement of the contract, the contractual documentation should also specify how relevant assets will be transferred to the customer or the replacement service provider on the termination or expiry of the relationship. Obviously, the customer will be in a far better position to negotiate favourable exit provisions prior to entering into the original outsourcing contract when the provider is anxious to win the business rather than at the time of termination when the relationship has broken down and any goodwill between the parties may be limited or non-existent.

Typically, these provisions will be incorporated into a separate schedule of the services agreement specifying the consequences of any termination or expiry.

3.5.2 Exit provisions

The contract will need to deal with a number of issues relating to the transfer of information and assets from the provider to the customer. Some of the principal provisions are outlined below in this section. There will, of course, be other ancillary obligations with which any contract will need to deal.

3.5.2.1 *Assets register*

In order for the customer to continue to provide the service or to engage a third party to do so on its behalf, it will need to have knowledge of the assets used by the provider during the term of the services agreement. Many customers seek the option to choose the particular assets they wish to have transferred from the provider rather than being under any general obligation to take over all the relevant assets used.

The provider should therefore be required to maintain on a regular basis an inventory record which lists all of the assets used by the provider to provide the services, such as any software, hardware, data, documentation, manuals, and details of licenses, leases, or other arrangements relating to the services provided. A customer should have access to or receive copies of this inventory on a regular basis and should be provided with a copy of it on any expiry or termination. The customer will then be able to select which items it wishes to acquire from the provider on the expiry or termination of the contract. The issues regarding the transfer of such assets are discussed in more detail below.

3.5.2.2 Ongoing service provision

The typical IT outsourcing contract will take many months from selection of a preferred provider to the commencement date from which services are provided. This should serve as an indication of the complexity of exiting from an existing outsourcing relationship. For the services to be discontinued immediately by the provider on the service of a notice of termination will be unacceptable to the customer as it will find itself without crucial services for a potentially significant time period until it is able to identify a replacement service provider and enter into a suitable contract with it for the new service provision. It is therefore typical to include provisions which require the provider to continue providing the services, at the customer's option, for specified blocks of time. For example, it may be that a customer has a right to buy services from the provider for three-month periods up to a total period of one year.

During the period for which such run-off services are provided, services should be delivered in accordance with all the existing terms of the contractual arrangements, including as to the charges and to service levels. The provider may wish to exclude certain provisions which are not to apply, such as the performance improvement provisions.

3.5.2.3 Assets transfer

Provisions should be incorporated regarding the transfer of assets from the provider back to the customer.

The provider should return copies of any of the customer's proprietary software, including copies of any modifications that are to be made to that software.

In relation to third party items, such as software, hardware, and related support arrangements, the provider should novate such licences and other agreements to the customer.

It is also quite likely that the provider may have used some of its own proprietary software for the purpose of providing the services. Customers may therefore also seek a licence to use this proprietary software at a minimum during the exit period for which any ongoing services are provided and, quite possibly, beyond the expiry of that time. Licence fees will obviously need to be negotiated for any ongoing licences which are granted.

Where the provider has used its own premises to provide the services which the customer requires further access to on termination, it may be possible to obtain a lease to use part (or all) of those premises from the provider. Where the premises are leased to the provider from a third party, this will usually be done by granting a sublease to the customer for the appropriate areas of the premises. The terms of the sublease will generally need to mirror those of the head lease. Consents may well be required from the original head lessor to any sublease and, in addition, the head lease may stipulate terms which must be incorporated into a sublease.

In addition to the tangible and intangible assets that may be required by the customer, there will also be a considerable amount of knowledge obtained by the provider's personnel regarding the operation and use of any IT systems and other procedures involved. Exit provisions should therefore also provide for a transfer of knowledge from the technical staff of the provider to the customer through the provision of general information and assistance, as required by the customer. Access should also be given to the provider's premises and equipment used to provide the services and to staff deployed in the provision of the services.

The TUPE Regulations may well apply on the expiry of the IT outsourcing contract to transfer the staff of the provider who have been substantially employed in providing the services to the customer and the outsourcing agreement will usually provide for the application of the Regulations on 'exit'.

3.5.2.4 *Exit plans*

Although the contractual provisions should specify as much detail as possible regarding the respective rights and obligations of the parties, it will be impossible to stipulate every act that should take place on termination at the time that the services agreement is entered into. It is therefore common to include general provisions requiring the provider to draw up an exit plan on any exit or termination. The exit plan will then specify in detail how all of the exit obligations are to be carried out.

The overall purpose of the exit plan is to ensure the smooth transition of services from the provider either back in-house to the customer or to its replacement third party service provider. Contractual assurances should be obtained so that the exit plan will achieve this if it is followed by both parties.

3.5.2.5 *Costs issues*

There will always be a considerable amount of negotiation over the extent to which the provider is permitted to charge in respect of performing its obligations under the exit provisions. As part of the exit provisions and as noted above, the customer should have the right to buy further periods of service provision up to a maximum specified time period. Obviously, the charging provisions will continue to apply and the provider will therefore be paid in respect of the base service provision. There are, however, likely to be a number of additional costs arising as a result of the exit provisions, including the costs of obtaining any necessary third party consents and the additional resource costs of drawing up and implementing the exit plan. Providers are therefore likely to seek payment on a time and materials basis for any assistance provided under the exit provisions. Ultimately, the contract should specify which types of obligations the provider is entitled to recover additional amounts for and those which the provider is expected to bear as part of its internal costs.

3.6 CONCLUSION

The outsourcing concept has evolved from a relatively simple service relationship in the days of the early time-sharing, facilities management, and bureaux agreements into a complex arrangement between provider and customer that is often compared to a partnership. Now, and even more in the future, it will span not just towns, but continents. Outsourcing has, in Thomas Friedman's words, 'flattened the earth'.[117] The impact of cloud computing on IT outsourcing and IT services in general has yet to be seen: it is too soon to evaluate, though it is somewhat ironic that the utility computing model takes us back to the days of time-sharing and bureaux agreements. (Of course, virtualization was not invented then.)

In earlier editions of this work, it seemed necessary to cite statistics to show how fast IT outsourcing and IT-enabled services (essentially BPO) were growing and how far they would be likely to grow. It is no longer necessary to cite those statistics. Readers of this work need no such evidence. IT outsourcing has grown, not just in complexity, but also in the volume and value of transactions around the world. Ever since its infancy, BPO has been tipped as the 'next big thing', but IT outsourcing remains the predominant form of outsourcing wherever it is practised. Undoubtedly, BPO will develop. But even within BPO, IT is an integral—and integrated—core element of transactional processes. In any case, all forms of outsourcing seem to have a way of changing subtly and ultimately transforming themselves.

From this chapter's (necessarily) short outline of the typical legal and contractual issues arising in an IT outsourcing transaction, it should be clear that the contract performs a number of critical functions. Unlike most other services contracts, it needs to document many seemingly non-legal, sometimes bureaucratic, processes. In defining service categories and service levels, the outsourcing contract seems to be more the preserve of information technologists and systems analysts than lawyers. In specifying service credits and complex charging structures, it may seem to be in the domain of accountants and financial officers. The contract now has an even more vital role: it needs to capture the anticipated cost savings and efficiencies that are and will continue to be the main driver in all outsourcing in the developed world since 2008.

Yet the IT and outsourcing lawyer has to understand, advise on, and document all of these—and many more—issues in the context of an IT outsourcing. It is hoped that this chapter helps in that respect.

---

[117] T Friedman, *The World is Flat, A Brief History if the Globalized World in the 21st Century* (London: Allen Lane, 2005).

As outlined elsewhere in this chapter, the trend in outsourcing is to ever-greater commercial, technological, operational, regulatory, and legal complexity. While acknowledging the importance of regulatory compliance, non-lawyers in the outsourcing world tend to underestimate the importance of the outsourcing contract. The time invested in the contract and related issues will reap rewards, providing a clear definition of the services to be provided and the cost savings and performance levels expected, facilitating the relationship between the parties with clear information flows and reporting obligations, and with adequate exit provisions striking a sufficient balance between the competing interests of provider and customer on any termination or expiry of the contract—and all between continents. And although the contract alone cannot always guarantee the ultimate success of the outsourcing relationship, it can and should play a major role in doing so.

Part II

ONLINE COMMERCE

4

ELECTRONIC COMMERCE

Chris Reed

4.1 INTRODUCTION—WHAT IS ELECTRONIC COMMERCE?

The term 'electronic commerce' or 'e-commerce' is often seen as equivalent to internet commerce, but it has a far longer history. For over 40 years technologies based on private or closed electronic networks have been used to facilitate electronic communications between commercial entities, initially to help perform obligations under pre-existing contracts[1] and later to enter into binding agreements or contracts.

Electronic Data Interchange ('EDI'), a system of business-to-business electronic communications between commercial parties over a closed system, governed by a set of previously agreed rules for contracting, was perhaps the most commonly used pre-internet technology. Other closed communications systems were developed within particular industries, and these too constitute a form of electronic commerce. Quite aside from these closed networks, new techniques and protocols are continually being developed to allow users to create virtual private networks ('VPNs') across the internet, which form a new class of closed networks.

---

[1] eg, funds transfers via interbank networks.

The internet, by contrast, is an open network which permits communication without the need for both parties to subscribe to the same closed network. Over the last 15 years it has pervaded UK businesses and households, making it an attractive medium for both business-to-business ('B2B') and business-to-consumer ('B2C') e-commerce. The wide reach of the internet presents an attractive medium through which commercial entities can advertise and sell their wares.

So what is electronic commerce? Though the question is easy to ask it is very hard to answer, or at least to answer in a definite manner, because the technology is so flexible that a wide variety of commercial activities are possible. Much depends on one's view as to what is and what is not commerce or commercial activity.[2] In its most generic sense electronic commerce could be said to comprise commercial communications, whether between private individuals or commercial entities, which take place in or over electronic networks. The communications could involve any part of the commercial process, from initial marketing to the placing of orders through to delivery of information products and background transaction processing.[3] The subject matter of these transactions might be tangible products to be delivered offline, such as books and DVDs for B2C e-commerce or chemicals for B2B e-commerce, or intangibles such as information products which might be delivered either offline or online.[4] The common factor is that some or all of the various communications which make up these transactions take place over an electronic medium, usually with a high degree of automated processing as opposed to human-to-human communication. Whether these communications take place via closed or open networks, or indeed a combination of these systems, is irrelevant. All that matters is that the commercial transactions utilize some form of electronic communication. Much of the discussion in this chapter will relate to online electronic commerce via the internet, but the legal principles involved will apply equally to closed, proprietary network e-commerce.

The law relating to electronic commerce is, by definition, all the laws worldwide which might apply to a particular online transaction. It is thus impossible in a single chapter to produce an exhaustive treatment. This chapter therefore concentrates on three issues which are core to all e-commerce activities: making

---

[2] See the discussion in *Defying Definition* (Washington DC: US Department of Commerce, 2000).

[3] The *Sacher Report* (OECD, 1997), p 20 gives a generic yet comprehensive definition which forms a good starting point from which to proceed:

> Definitions of electronic commerce vary considerably, but generally, electronic commerce refers to all forms of commercial transactions involving organizations and individuals that are based upon the processing and transmission of digitized data, including text, sound, and visual images. It also refers to the effects that the electronic exchange of commercial information may have on the institutions and processes that support and govern commercial activities. These include organizational management, commercial negotiations and contracts, legal and regulatory frameworks, financial settlement arrangements, and taxation among many others.

[4] Information products are often combinations of both the tangible and the intangible, eg a CD which records software or games or contains a database.

contracts online, using records of online communications as evidence of those trans-actions, and how to determine which foreign laws are potentially applicable. A brief explanation of the UK regulation of e-commerce is included for completeness, and some of the issues raised are explored further in Chapter 2. Intermediaries play a vital role in making electronic commerce possible, and the question of how far they should be liable for the actions of others has been subject to sufficient extensive legislative and judicial activity to justify a separate discussion in Chapter 5.

4.2 ONLINE CONTRACTS

Because the internet is fundamentally no more than a means of communication, one might expect there to be no difference between online contracts and those made by offline communication. Indeed, this is essentially true—online contracts are still contracts, and all the rules of contract law apply.

However, there are four issues relating to online contracts which need to be explored:

(a) The online contract formation process uses a communications technology which involves numerous intermediaries such as ISPs. Internet communications do not fit easily within the contract formation rules which were developed for the exchange of physical documents (see section 4.2.1 below).

(b) Some agreements will only be legally binding contracts if they are in writing and/or signed, and thus it is necessary to understand whether electronic communica-tions can amount to writing and how an electronic communication can be signed (see section 4.2.2 below).

(c) There are specific regulations which apply to those who sell goods or services online, regulating commercial communications and requiring particular information to be provided to the other contracting party (see section 4.2.3 below).

(d) Where the contract has a cross-border element then it is necessary to deter-mine the applicable law and jurisdiction, which may not be the same as for an analogous transaction made offline (see section 4.6.2 below).

4.2.1 Contract formation

The basic principles of contract formation are the same online as offline. A contract requires offer and acceptance to demonstrate agreement, consideration to support the promises made in the agreement, and an intention to create legal relations. Only the first of these is potentially different online.

Even where contracts are entered into by exchanging written, physical documents it may be hard to identify which of those communications amounted to an offer and its acceptance.[5] This problem can be even more difficult to solve online, particularly as we need to apply the existing legal rules to those online communications, even though they were designed only for offline agreements.

4.2.1.1 Offer and acceptance[6]

Unless particular formalities such as writing are specifically required (see section 4.2.2 below), the general rule of English law and of most other jurisdictions is that a contract is formed when the parties reach an agreement on its terms—this can be done orally, as our everyday experience in shops demonstrates. There is thus no theoretical objection to using electronic messages for this purpose. In English law the process of formation is analysed into two stages: the offer, when one party sets out the terms on which he is prepared to contract, either in one document or by express or implied reference to a preceding course of negotiations; and the acceptance, when the other party agrees to these terms without attempting to amend them in any way. If both parties perform their side of the bargain there is no need to involve the law to resolve contract formation questions. However, there are three types of dispute which might arise, and which can be resolved by examining the formation process:

(a) One party believes a contract to have been concluded, but the other disputes it.

(b) Both agree that a contract has been formed, but disagree as to its terms.

(c) The parties disagree as to when and where the contract was formed.

In order to understand how English law will deal with these disputes, a number of basic principles of contract law must be borne in mind:

(a) Unless otherwise stated, an offer remains open for a reasonable time or until it is accepted or rejected by the other party.

(b) An offer may be withdrawn (unless there has been some consideration for the promise to keep it open, eg an option) at any time before it is accepted, but this withdrawal is only effective when it reaches the other party.[7]

(c) A counter offer, that is, the suggestion of different terms, brings the original offer to an end, and no contract is formed until the new offer is accepted.[8] If the parties engage in a so-called 'battle of the forms' where each purports to contract on

---

[5] See, eg, the 'battle of the forms' cases such as *Butler Machine Tool Co v Ex-Cell-O Corp* [1979] 1 WLR 401.

[6] For a more extensive discussion of offer and acceptance in online contracts, see AD Murray, 'Entering into Contracts Electronically: The Real WWW' in L Edwards and C Waelde (eds), *Law and the Internet: A Framework for Electronic Commerce*, 2nd edn (Oxford: Hart, 2000).

[7] *Byrne v Van Tienhoven* (1880) 5 CPD 344.

[8] *Hyde v Wrench* (1840) 3 Beav 334.

its own terms, the set of terms that applies will be those contained in the last offer made before acceptance.[9]

(d) The contract is formed when, and where, acceptance takes place.

In applying these principles to electronic communications, we need to understand when the messages sent by each party take legal effect.[10] Whilst offers and withdrawals of offers must actually be communicated to the other party[11] the rules governing acceptances can be quite different. Where acceptance is made by some instantaneous means such as face-to-face communication or telephone, the acceptance message must actually reach the offeror. It has been held that telex communications are instantaneous, and thus contracts made by telex are made where the telex is received.[12] This rule is certain to apply to electronic communications where there is a direct online communication link between the parties, for example where all communications take place via website pages.

The position may, however, be different if a third party stores the acceptance message for an appreciable period before it is delivered to the offeror. If the message is sent by email, the third party would be the ISP which hosts the recipient's mailbox. As common law lawyers learn at an early stage, if an acceptance is made in written form the postal rule applies. This provides that the acceptance takes place *when the letter is posted*, whether or not it ever arrives.[13] Might the postal rule apply to such an electronic message of acceptance?

There are two justifications suggested for the postal rule. The first is that it is an ad hoc method for solving what is inevitably a difficult question (if the rule were that the letter had to be received, would it be relevant that it arrived but was never read, or not read before withdrawal of the offer?). If this justification is the correct one, the dictum of Lord Brandon in *Brinkibon Ltd v Stahag Stahl und Stahlwarenhandelgesellschaft mbH* suggests that the postal rule might apply to electronic acceptances:

The cases on acceptance by letter and telegram constitute an exception to the general principle of the law of contract [on grounds of expediency]. . . . That reason of commercial expediency applies to cases where there is bound to be a substantial interval between the time when the acceptance is sent and the time when it is received. In such cases the exception to the general rule is more convenient, and makes on the whole for greater fairness, than the rule itself would do.[14]

---

[9] *Butler Machine Tool Co v Ex-Cell-O Corp* [1979] 1 WLR 401.

[10] The discussion here concentrates on English law. The contract formation law of other jurisdictions will differ in detail. All these issues are normally addressed in national laws, and most jurisdictions adopt roughly similar principles (except for the postal rule discussed below).

[11] *Byrne v Van Tienhoven* (1880) 5 CPD 344.

[12] *Entores Ltd v Miles Far East Corp* [1955] 2 QB 327.

[13] *Adams v Lindsell* (1818) 1 B & Ald 681; *Household Fire Insurance v Grant* (1879) 4 Ex D 216.

[14] [1982] 1 All ER 293, 300.

The nature of email technology means that there is inevitably some delay (although usually only a few seconds) between the sending of an email and its arrival at the recipient's mail server. Further delay occurs between receipt at the mail server and actual receipt by the recipient when the email is downloaded to the mail client and read. Even 'always on' devices such as BlackBerries and iPhones have their mailboxes updated at set intervals, rather than immediately a message arrives at the mail server.

The second justification is that the offeror has impliedly agreed that the accepting party may entrust the transmission of his acceptance to an independent third party, the postal authorities, and that therefore the offeree has done all that the offeror requires for acceptance when he posts his letter. This would suggest that acceptance is complete when the message is received at the recipient's mail server, rather than when it is read. The clearest analogy to using a store and forward messaging system like email is with acceptance by telegram; it is necessary for the message actually to be communicated to the telegram service, normally by telephone (an instantaneous method of communication), but once it has been received by the service acceptance is complete.[15]

The postal rule is not unique to Anglo-American law. For example, in Spain the postal rule applies to acceptances in commercial transactions,[16] although in non-commercial transactions an acceptance is not effective until it is received.[17] However, most civil law jurisdictions apply the requirement of receipt to all types of contract formation message.[18]

If the postal rule applies, the time of acceptance is the time the electronic message was received by the ISP's network, and the place of acceptance will therefore be that node of the network which received the message. In most cases this is likely to be in the same jurisdiction as the acceptor, but not inevitably—it is easy to conceive a Scottish seller accepting an offer from a US buyer where the message of acceptance is sent to a computer in England. The contract would be formed in England, which is clearly an unexpected result. Furthermore, it may not always be possible to determine precisely which computer in a network was the first to receive a message.

The place of formation is not normally important so far as the obligations in the contract are concerned, which will be governed by the applicable law (see section 4.6.2). However, it might have regulatory consequences if, for example,

---

[15] *Re London & Northern Bank* [1900] 1 Ch 200.
[16] Spanish Commercial Code, art 54.
[17] Spanish Civil Code, art 1262(2).
[18] See, eg, Swiss Code of Obligations, art 35; Italian Civil Code, art 1335. The Italian Code adopts a further refinement, that it is sufficient for the acceptance to reach the offeror's premises provided he is then likely to receive it.

the making of such a contract is unlawful in the jurisdiction[19] or if one party requires regulatory authorization to make such contracts in the jurisdiction.[20]

One way of solving this problem is to establish legal presumptions as to when and where electronic messages were received. Both the Australian Electronic Transactions Act 1999[21] and the US Uniform Electronic Transactions Act 1999[22] set out such presumptions. Time of receipt is normally the entry of the communication into the system denoted by the recipient.[23] However, the *place* of sending and receipt is based on presumptions as to the sender's and recipient's locations. The message is presumed to have been sent from the sender's physical business address, and received at the recipient's business address. This can have the result, where a network crosses national boundaries, that although we need to identify the actual place where the message was received in order to decide *when* it was received, that place is not (for legal purposes) *where* it was received. This oddness is intentional because the questions when and where an electronic communication is received are somewhat metaphysical. Thus, these laws set out bright-line rules which have no necessary connection with the actual message path. This point is specifically acknowledged by section 15(c) of the US Uniform Electronic Transactions Act 1999 which states: 'Subsection (b) applies even if the place the information processing system is located is different from the place the electronic record is deemed to be received under subsection (d)'.

An alternative is to allow the parties to agree in advance when and where their messages will take legal effect. The English courts have accepted that it is permissible for the parties to stipulate what acts will constitute acceptance,[24] so it is possible for an e-commerce trader to spell out on its website precisely how and when a customer will be contractually bound. For B2B e-commerce there appears to be a general practice that all contractually relevant communications only have operative effect when they are received.[25] B2C e-commerce is much more diverse in its approach; some websites do not define the contracting process at all, others specify that the contract only comes into effect when goods are shipped, and the remainder adopt positions in between these extremes.

---

[19] This might be particularly relevant for gambling contracts—see J Hörnle and B Zamitt, *Cross-border Online Gambling Law and Policy* (Cheltenham: Edward Elgar, 2010).

[20] eg, a contract relating to financial services.

[21] s 14.

[22] s 15.

[23] For communications by email this would be the recipient's email host, which is the portion of his email address after the @ sign, and for completed web forms it would be the IP address of the web server designated in the script (part of the web form's HTML code) which runs when the 'Buy' or 'Place Order' button is clicked.

[24] *Holwell Securities Ltd v Hughes* [1974] 1 WLR 155.

[25] This follows on from standard EDI practice—see, eg, UNCID Rules, art 7(a); TEDIS, *The Legal Position of the Member States with respect to Electronic Data Interchange* (Brussels: EC Commission, 1991).

English law's contract formation rules were developed in the context of contracts individually negotiated between the parties, which can be done online really only by exchange of emails. However, most online B2C contracts, and many B2B contracts, are concluded via a website operated either by the supplier or by a third party marketplace. Here the exchange of contract formation messages is an automated process, controlled by the website software.

The most common method of B2C contracting is via a web form, where the customer completes an order form and clicks a button or link to place that order. The online supplier's website determines whether the order can be accepted, and then transmits a webpage which confirms that the order has been placed. In the absence of any contrary indications, the contract is likely to be formed at the moment this page is displayed to the customer or a confirmatory email is sent to the customer.[26]

This may not be the result that the supplier wants—for example, it is common to find B2C websites whose terms provide that no contract is concluded until the supplier has shipped the product. A carefully designed website will thus contain contrary indications, often by incorporating terms and conditions, which specify a different moment of contract formation.

Where Article 10 of the Electronic Commerce Directive[27] applies, as it will in these circumstances, a supplier is obliged to explain the technical steps which will result in conclusion of the contract.[28] The directive does not attempt to define the formation process, but Article 10(1) requires the supplier to explain to the customer the steps which will give rise to a contract and make its terms available, while Article 11(1) requires orders to be acknowledged and provides that both these communications are only effective when received. A side effect of Article 11(1) is thus that the postal rule cannot normally apply to an acknowledgement which is also an acceptance of the customer's offer.[29]

Because the supplier determines the contracting process, by designing the website and the ordering process, the practical effect is that in many cases where the supplier complies with this obligation the contract will simply be formed in accordance with that explanation. *Holwell Securities Ltd v Hughes*[30] established that where an offer sets out the conditions for its acceptance, it will be only accepted if those conditions are fulfilled. If the supplier complies with Article 10 and provides the explanation before the contract is concluded, the offer will be made on the basis that this is the formation process to be followed, and therefore the acceptance will be the relevant communication described in the explanation.

---

[26] J Nugent and L Rodger, 'Consumer and Regulatory Law' in R Carolina and S Stokes (eds), *Encyclopedia of E-commerce Law* (London: Sweet & Maxwell, 2005) ch 4, 4–34.

[27] Council Directive (EC) 2000/31 on electronic commerce [2000] OJ L178/1, 17 July 2000.

[28] Art 10 is implemented in the UK by the Electronic Commerce (EC Directive) Regulations 2002 (SI 2002/2013), reg 9(1)(a).

[29] The exception is where, in a B2B contract, the parties have agreed that these rules do not apply.

[30] [1974] 1 WLR 155.

Under common law the question of what amounts to offer and acceptance depends on the intention of the parties, as manifested to an objective observer.[31] In other words, the question to be asked is whether the reasonable customer would have taken the supplier's conduct (eg an email acknowledging the customer's order) as an acceptance. Since the supplier is *de facto* in control of the process, if the supplier *clearly* explains the contracting process on the website, this explanation given by the supplier may well serve as *evidence* of the parties' intention.

However, Article 10 does not change the common law, by allowing the supplier unilaterally to decide when the contract is concluded.[32] Therefore, a term contained in standard terms and conditions may not be effective to define the contract forma-tion process as, taking into account the web-ordering process as a whole, a court may well determine that the contract has been concluded earlier.[33] This depends on the facts in each case and in particular, an assessment of the web-ordering process and all statements given to the buyer and how the objective, reasonable buyer would understand them.[34] If the contract is, as a matter of fact, formed before the time stated in the terms and conditions, then either that term is meaningless and to be ignored, or it is potentially void as an unfair term.[35] Hence if the supplier wishes to avoid a contract being formed before the goods are sent out and payment has been taken, it should make it clear to the customer that the acknowledgement (whether by email or by an 'acknowledgement of order' webpage) is merely an acknowledge-ment of order and that the offer will only be accepted by that later event.[36]

4.2.1.2 *Other communications*

It is important to remember that pre-contractual negotiations and post-contractual performance will also involve electronic messages. Some of these will have legal consequences. Although a number of attempts have been made to classify electronic

---

[31] GH Treitel, *The Law of Contract*, 11th edn (London: Sweet & Maxwell, 2003) 8–9, 16.

[32] See recital 55 of the Electronic Commerce Directive.

[33] AC Brock, 'Amazon and Pricing' (2003) 5(5) Electronic Business Law 16.

[34] Treitel also states:

an 'acknowledgement' may be its express terms or, in a particular context by implication, contain a statement that the sender agreed to the terms of the offer and that he was therefore accepting it: this might be, for example the effect of an "acknowledgement" of a customer's order in website trading.

(GH Treitel, *The Law of Contract*, 11th edn (London: Sweet & Maxwell, 2003) 16–17.)

[35] Such a standard term may well be seen as unfair under reg 5(1) of the Unfair Terms in Consumer Contracts Regulations 1999 (SI 1999/2083), as it creates an imbalance in the parties' rights and obliga-tions, where the consumer has prepaid for the goods or services and the supplier effectively keeps its options open. It may also be an unfair term under the Unfair Contracts Terms Act 1977, s 3(2)(b) since the supplier claims to be entitled to render no contractual performance at all. However, whether the term is unfair will depend on whether it is unreasonable. It may well be reasonable for the seller to reserve the right not to be bound, eg in the case of goods which are difficult to procure, especially, if this has been explained to the consumer.

[36] J Nugent and L Rodger, 'Consumer and Regulatory Law' in R Carolina and S Stokes (eds), *Encyclopedia of E-commerce Law* (London: Sweet & Maxwell, 2005) ch 4, 4–34.

messages according to the different legal problems raised,[37] for our purposes it is sufficient to note two broad categories, set out below.

First, some messages merely transmit information from one party to the other. Generally, the sender does not intend a message of this type to have legal consequences. Examples might range from the trivial:

Our Chairman will arrive on the 15.20 flight

to the vital:

Maximum safe operating temperature 150 degrees C.

This type of message may give rise to potential liability where the sender owes a duty[38] to the recipient to take care to ensure that the information is correct, and as a result of his carelessness the recipient suffers loss.[39]

Secondly, it is common for notices relating to online contracts to be given online.[40] This type of communication will be intended to have a legal effect and will in most cases be made in performing an existing contract. Typical examples of this category might be invoices, which are often a prerequisite for payment, or a purchase order under a contract for delivery of goods as requested.

The sort of legal questions that this type of communication will raise are threefold:

(a) Is it effective as a notice? This will often depend on whether the notice is required to be in writing, or if a signature is required.

(b) When (and possibly where) does it take effect, that is, is the sending or receipt the legally significant point?

(c) If its sending or contents are disputed, can these facts be proved?

One important unilateral notice is the Customs declaration. The penalties for false or non-declaration are severe, so the legal effect of such a notice is easily apparent. The required form and contents of Customs declarations are set out in national

---

[37] eg, Goode and Bergsten identify five types of communication:

    (a) communications having no legal significance;
    (b) communications having legal significance;
    (c) communications operative to transfer ownership, control, or contract rights;
    (d) communications required by law; and
    (e) communications requiring legal authority or licence.

(R Goode and E Bergsten, 'Legal Questions and Problems to be Overcome' in H Thomsen and B Wheble (eds), *Trading with EDI: The Legal Issues* (London: IBC, 1989) 131–3.)

[38] Under the contract's express or implied terms, or in tort.

[39] *Hedley Byrne v Heller & Partners* [1963] 2 All ER 575.

[40] This is not universal however, particularly where the notice has a fundamental effect on performance such as notice of an alleged breach of contract or a termination notice. Contracts often prescribe that notices of this kind must be given in writing or by fax, thus ensuring that the seriousness of the notice is appreciated by imposing some formality on it.

legislation, which will thus answer the question of whether it is possible to replace the paper documents with an electronic transmission. Over recent years many jurisdictions have introduced systems for electronic customs declarations which are designed to produce the necessary evidence and authentication for these documents.[41]

4.2.2 Formalities

Certain types of contract require particular formalities to be observed if they are to be enforceable. The most common of these are that the contract must be made or evidenced in writing or in a document, and that it must be signed. For example, in the UK a contract of marine insurance must be embodied in a marine insurance policy signed by the insurer,[42] and in the USA a contract for the sale of goods for a price of $500 or more must be evidenced in writing and signed by the party against whom it is to be enforced.[43]

Requirements of this kind are unusual in common law jurisdictions, but quite common in civil law jurisdictions. In deciding whether a valid contract has been formed during a cross-border e-commerce transaction, it is therefore essential to be able to identify the applicable law (see section 4.6.2 below).

Within the EU there should be no barriers which are unique to e-commerce contracts, as Article 9(1) of the Electronic Commerce Directive provides:

Member States shall ensure that their legal system allows contracts to be concluded by electronic means. Member States shall in particular ensure that the legal requirements applicable to the contractual process neither create obstacles for the use of electronic contracts nor result in such contracts being deprived of legal effectiveness and validity on account of their having been made by electronic means.

However, if *all* contracts of a particular type (eg, contracts of guarantee) require formalities such as signed writing, the question will still arise whether the e-commerce technology used has in fact complied with those formalities.

4.2.2.1 *Writing*
Unless there is legislation which specifically provides to the contrary,[44] 'writing' under English law requires the communication to be in some visible form.[45]

---

[41] eg, UK HM Revenue & Customs <http://www.hmrc.gov.uk> (accessed 8 August 2011) offer a number of online import/export services including CHIEF, eBTI, NCTS, and NES.

[42] Marine Insurance Act 1906, s 24.

[43] Uniform Commercial Code, s 201(1).

[44] eg, the Unidroit Convention on International Factoring 1988, Art 1(4)(b), defines notice in writing to include 'any other telecommunication capable of being reproduced in tangible form'.

[45] Interpretation Act 1978, Sch 1.

However, if all that is required is a 'document'[46] then, unless there is specific legislation or case law which requires visible form, a document can be produced electronically.[47] Most other countries' laws also require certain types of transaction to be made in writing and signed. This is often limited to sales of real property, but in Greece a wider range of commercial transactions require written and signed documents. France has a particular problem in that transactions carried out by persons other than *traders* need written proof if their value exceeds €800.[48] This presents a problem for B2C e-commerce, which can be overcome by the use of electronic signatures,[49] and can also affect commercial use because professionals such as architects are not classified as traders.

One way to deal with problems of formalities is to include a provision in the online contract which provides that:

(a) all communications between the parties are deemed to be in writing; and

(b) use of the prescribed authentication procedures is deemed to be the signature of the appropriate party.

Whether the first provision is legally effective must be open to doubt—where a national law is adamant that 'writing' demands visible marks on a physical carrier it might seem to be equivalent to providing that 'for the purposes of this contract, night shall be deemed to be day'. However, in the common law jurisdictions at least, a provision of this type may raise an estoppel between the parties to the contract, and thus prevent either of them from denying the validity of an electronic transaction on the ground that the law requires the transaction to have been made in writing. This would be the case even though both parties know that under their law the electronic messages do *not* amount to writing.[50] It should be noted, though, that:

(a) the estoppel will not bind a third party, who will be able to plead the lack of writing as a defence and, as a corollary, will not be able to found his own action on the estoppel; and

---

[46] In civil proceedings this is defined as 'anything in which information of any description is recorded': Civil Evidence Act 1995, s 13.

[47] C Reed, *Digital Information Law: Electronic Documents and Requirements of Form* (London: CCLS, 1996); Law Commission, *Electronic Commerce: Formal Requirements in Commercial Transactions* (December 2001).

[48] French Civil Code, art 1341.

[49] French Civil Code, art 1316.

[50]

> The full facts may be known to both parties; but if, even knowing those facts to the full, they are clearly enough shown to have assumed a different state of facts *as between themselves* for the purposes of a particular transaction, then their assumption will be treated, as between them, as true, in proceedings arising out of the transaction. The claim of the party raising the estoppel is, not that he believed the assumed version of the facts was true, but that he believed (and agreed) that it should be *treated as true*.

> (G Spencer-Bower and AK Turner, *The Law Relating to Estoppel by Representation*, 3rd edn (London: Butterworths, 1977) 60, citing *Newis v General Accident Fire & Life Assurance Corp* (1910) 11 CLR 620 at 636 per Isaacs J (High Court of Australia).)

(b) the estoppel will not be effective if the result would be to declare valid a transaction which is in fact *void* according to the law for lack of formalities.[51] This will not be so, however, if the requirement for writing is imposed by the law solely to protect the parties to the transaction, as opposed to the public interest.[52]

By contrast, the second provision stands a good chance of being effective if national law does not specifically demand that signatures be in manuscript form. For example, because English law permits signatures to be typewritten or made via a stamp,[53] there seems no reason to insist on a handwritten signature. Because the function of a signature is to authenticate the message as originating from the purported sender and demonstrate that he agreed to its contents,[54] cryptography offers the possibility of producing electronic signatures that are more difficult to forge than handwriting (see sections 4.2.2.2 and 4.3.2.4 below).

4.2.2.2 *Electronic signatures*

The authentication of e-commerce communications is vital for two reasons. Parties who wish to engage in electronic commerce and enter into an online contract will not usually have any means of verifying the other's identity.[55] As a separate issue, the parties must have some way of evidencing that they reached an agreement and intended it to be legally binding.

It is, however, important to remember that the vast majority of B2C, and even B2B, transactions do not require a signature as a condition of legal validity. There are thus two questions which need to be considered:

(a) Is a signature required for legal validity or enforceability? If so, an appropriate electronic signature technology will need to be used.

(b) If not, are there other advantages to requiring an electronic signature which outweigh the disadvantages of using the technology? The most obvious disadvantage is that the business's customers may not already possess the necessary technology, so that the need to acquire it acts as a disincentive to doing business. Where signatures are not required as a matter of law, the main advantage of demanding an electronic signature from customers is the evidence it produces of

---

[51] See, eg, *Swallow & Pearson v Middlesex CC* [1953] 1 All ER 580.

[52] Spencer-Bower and Turner, n 50, 142–4.

[53] See, eg, *Chapman v Smethurst* [1909] 1 KB 927.

[54] Law Commission, n 47; C Reed, 'What *is* a Signature' (2000) 3 Journal of Information, Law and Technology (JILT) <http://www2.warwick.ac.uk/fac/soc/law/elj/jilt/2000_3/reed/> (accessed 8 August 2011).

[55] See C Reed, *Internet Law: Text and Materials*, 2nd edn (Cambridge: Cambridge University Press, 2004) ch 5.

the customer's identity and intention to be bound, and its evidential role in authenticating communications from the customer.

To be valid and effective a signature must provide evidence of three things:

(a) the identity of the signatory;
(b) his intention to sign; and
(c) his intention to adopt the contents of the document as his own.

Manuscript signatures meet these functional requirements in a number of ways. Identity is established by comparing the signature on the document with other signatures which can be proved, by extrinsic evidence, to have been written by the signatory. The assumption is that manuscript signatures are unique, and that therefore such a comparison is all that is necessary to provide evidence of identity. In practice, manuscript signatures are usually acknowledged by the signatory once they are shown to him, and extrinsic evidence is only required where it is alleged that the signature has been forged.

Electronic signatures meet the law's functional requirements in rather different ways. To begin with, the signature itself does not provide sufficient evidence of the signatory's identity. This is because electronic signatures work by encrypting some function of the message content with a key which is known only to the sender (see section 4.3.2.4 below). This proves that the possessor of the key sent the message, but it does not prove the identity of that person. To establish this, further evidence is required which links the signature key or other signature device used to the signatory himself. There is no theoretical reason why this should not be proved by extrinsic evidence of the kind used to establish identity for manuscript signatures.[56]

However, in practice the recipient of an electronically signed document wishes to be able to rely on the signature without further checking, and so a number of organizations known as Certification Authorities have been set up.[57] These bodies take traditional evidence of identity, for example by examining passports, and (in the

---

[56] In the case of electronic signatures, the extrinsic evidence required would be that:

(a) the signature key or its equivalent was in the possession of the alleged signatory or his authorized agent;

(b) the use of that signature key produces the electronic signature affixed to the document in question; and

(c) the mathematical probability that some alternative key in the possession of a third party could have created the same signature is sufficiently low to convince the court that the signature was in fact affixed by the signatory.

In the case of the public key encryption systems discussed in section 4.3.2.4 below, proof that the signature decrypts with the signatory's public key should be sufficient if that public key can reliably be attributed to the signatory.

[57] One of the longest-established Certification Authorities is Verisign Inc, <http://www.verisign. com/> (accessed 8 August 2011).

case of public key encryption[58] signatures) check that signatures effected with the signatory's secret key are verifiable using the public key. Once the Certification Authority is satisfied as to the signatory's identity it issues an electronic certificate which includes, inter alia, a certification of the signatory's identity and of his public key.[59] This certificate may be used by the recipient to prove the signatory's identity.

Once identity has been proved, the very fact that an electronic signature has been affixed to a document should raise the same presumptions as for manuscript signatures. However, unlike a manuscript signature where the signatory has to be present in person and must have the document to be signed in front of him, electronic signature technology uses a stored signature key, either on the computer in question or on a physical token such as a smart card. Thus a third party who had access to the computer or to the storage device would be able to make the signature. For this reason, an electronic signature is more closely analogous to a rubber stamp signature.[60] The party who is seeking to rely on the validity of the signature may need to adduce extrinsic evidence that the signature was applied with the authority of the signatory[61] until the use of electronic signatures becomes so common that the courts are prepared to presume that a third party who is given access to the signature technology has been authorized by the signatory to sign on his behalf. In many cases, where an electronic signature key which has previously been

---

[58] See section 4.3.2.4 below.

[59] Of course, to operate effectively this certificate must be processable automatically without human intervention. Thus the certificate is authenticated not in a traditional paper-based way but by the Certification Authority's electronic signature. This signature will be certified by a different Certification Authority, and that certificate will also be signed electronically. The theoretical circularity of this process is obviated in practice because a recipient will have identified some Certification Authority (eg, his bank) whose electronic signature has been authenticated by some other means, and which is therefore trustworthy. Any other Certification Authority certified by *that* Certification Authority is also trustworthy, at least as to its identity, and so on. The user gradually builds up a database of authenticated electronic signatures, which reduces the amount of checking required.

The concept of authentication by a train of trusted messages was accepted by the UK courts in *Standard Bank London Ltd v The Bank of Tokyo Ltd* [1995] 2 Lloyd's Rep 169. In that case the defendant communicated with the plaintiff by trusted telexes (telex messages containing secret codes known only to sender and recipient). Because the parties did not have a trusted telex relationship between themselves, the defendant sent its messages to a correspondent with whom it did have such a relationship, and that correspondent forwarded them to another intermediary who passed them on to the plaintiff. The case was decided on the basis that these messages were properly authenticated as originating from the plaintiff, and the expert evidence (which was accepted by the court) stated that trusted telex messages were treated by banks as if they were signed.

[60] Rubber stamps create legally valid signatures if they are affixed to a document under the authority of the person on whose behalf the signature is made—*Lazarus Estates, Ltd v Beasley* [1956] 1 QB 702; *London CC v Vitamins, Ltd, London CC v Agricultural Food Products, Ltd* [1955] 2 QB 218.

[61] *Jenkins v Gaisford & Thring, In the Goods of Jenkins* (1863) 3 Sw & Tr 93; *London CC v Vitamins, Ltd, London CC v Agricultural Food Products, Ltd* [1955] 2 QB 218.

acknowledged by the signatory is used by an unauthorized third party, the apparent signatory will be estopped from denying that it was his signature.[62]

The objection that an electronic signature fails to meet the evidential requirements because a successful forgery cannot be detected is easily dismissed by pointing out that no such requirement is imposed for manuscript signatures.[63] In fact, all but the simplest electronic signatures are many orders of magnitude harder to forge than manuscript signatures.

Parties can agree between themselves whether they will accept an electronic signature as evidence of intent. In effect they can agree between themselves on the validity of an electronic signature. However, their agreement will not bind a third party unless that third party agrees to be so bound. Additionally, it is cumbersome and often impractical to enter into an agreement about signatures before beginning e-commerce communications. For this reason most developed countries have introduced laws to clarify the legal and evidential value of electronic signatures.

The starting point for electronic signature laws is Article 7(1) of the UNCITRAL Model Law on Electronic Commerce 1996, which provides:

Where the law requires a signature of a person, that requirement is met in relation to a data message if:

(a) a method is used to identify that person and to indicate that person's approval of the information contained in the data message; and

(b) that method is as reliable as was appropriate for the purpose for which the data message was generated or communicated, in the light of all the circumstances, including any relevant agreement.

Following on from this, the UNCITRAL Model Law on Electronic Signatures 2001 Article 2(a) continues the functional definition approach:

'Electronic signature' means data in electronic form in, affixed to or logically associated with, a data message, which may be used to identify the signatory in relation to the data message and to indicate the signatory's approval of the information contained in the data message.

Those jurisdictions which have introduced legislation on electronic signatures fall into two groups. The first merely define the functional requirements for an electronic signature and leave it to the courts to determine whether those requirements are met on a case-by-case basis.[64] The second group takes a two-tier approach to this issue; electronic signatures which meet the law's functional requirements are validated, but the law also makes provision for a greater level of legal acceptability for those signatures which are based on some form of third party identity certification. The UK

---

[62] *Brown v Westminster Bank Ltd* [1964] 2 Lloyd's Rep 187.

[63] eg, signatures in pencil have been held valid for such important commercial documents as bills of exchange (*Geary v Physic* (1826) 5 B&C 234) and guarantees (*Lucas v James* (1849) 7 Hare 410).

[64] See, eg, Australian Electronic Transactions Act 1999, s 10(1); US Federal Electronic Signatures in Global and National Commerce Act 2000, 15 USC 7001 §106(5).

has followed this approach, and section 7 of the Electronic Communications Act 2000 ('ECA 2000') provides:

(2) For the purposes of this section an electronic signature is so much of anything in electronic form as—

(a) is incorporated into or otherwise logically associated with any electronic communication or electronic data; and

(b) purports to be so incorporated or associated for the purpose of being used in establishing the authenticity of the communication or data, the integrity of the communication or data, or both.

An important element of such an electronic signature is that it should provide evidence that the signatory intended to sign the communication. In *Nilesh Mehta v J Pereira Fernandes SA*,[65] the sender's email address appeared in the header of an email, but there was no other element of the email which might amount to a signature. The question was whether the email had been signed so as to satisfy section 4 of the Statute of Frauds 1677 and thus create an enforceable guarantee. Because the email address was included automatically,[66] Pelling J concluded that it did not show intention to sign and was thus not Mr Mehta's signature. However he suggested *obiter* that if a party typed his name into the body of an email, that would be sufficient to create a signature for the purposes of section 4.

The UK Act implements (prospectively and in part[67]) the EU Electronic Signatures Directive.[68] Electronic signatures are defined by Article 2 of the Directive as follows:

1. 'electronic signature' means data in electronic form which are attached to or logically associated with other electronic data and which serve as a method of authentication;

2. 'advanced electronic signature' means an electronic signature which meets the following requirements:

(a) it is uniquely linked to the signatory;

(b) it is capable of identifying the signatory;

(c) it is created using means that the signatory can maintain under his sole control; and

---

[65] [2006] EWHC 813 (Ch).

[66] The judge was uncertain whether the address was incorporated by Mr Mehta's ISP or by his email software, but it is likely that it was added by the mail server software running on the ISP's servers. It is irrelevant whether the server software settings were entered by Mr Mehta, or automatically by his ISP when the mail account was set up, because most email systems require the inclusion of the sender's email address. There is thus no conscious decision to include it in any particular communication, which was the deciding point in the judgment.

[67] The other parts of the Directive are transposed into UK law by the Electronic Signatures Regulations 2002 (SI 2002/318), which deal with the supervision and liability of Certification Authorities.

[68] Council Directive (EC) 1999/93 on a Community framework for electronic signatures [2000] OJ L13/12, 19 January 2000.

(d) it is linked to the data to which it relates in such a manner that any subsequent change of the data is detectable.

This produces two types of electronic signature:

(a) simple electronic signatures, which have merely to meet the definition in Article 2(1); and

(b) advanced electronic signatures, where the identity of the signatory is confirmed by a certificate issued by an appropriate third party[69] and complying with other provisions of the Directive (a 'qualified certificate')[70] and the certificate is created by means of a secure-signature-creation device.[71]

Article 5 lays down the circumstances in which electronic signatures are to be valid, enforceable, and legally effective. For simple electronic signatures its provisions are entirely negative—Member States are to ensure that signatures of this type are not denied validity, enforceability, and effectiveness solely on the grounds that they are in electronic form or are not certified.[72] However, Member States are free to refuse to recognize electronic signatures for any other reason. Advanced electronic signatures receive more favourable treatment, and Article 5(1) provides that such signatures:

(a) satisfy the legal requirements of a signature in relation to data in electronic form in the same manner as a handwritten signature satisfies those requirements in relation to paper-based data; and

(b) are admissible as evidence in legal proceedings.

It is interesting to note that UK law has not needed to make this distinction between the legal validity of the two types of electronic signature. Section 7 of the ECA 2000 simply states that such a signature is admissible in evidence as to the authenticity or integrity of a communication. The reason for this is that a signature under English law is primarily an evidential matter,[73] and thus this purely evidential drafting makes an electronic signature de facto equivalent to a manuscript signature.

A further reason for the distinction is that the purpose of the Directive is not only to make provision for the validity of electronic signatures, but also to ensure that national laws do not impose barriers to the free flow of certification services in the European Community. Thus, Article 4 prevents Member States from granting

---

[69] A 'certification-service-provider', defined in Art 2(11), ie a Certification Authority (see Chapter 5).

[70] Art 2(10). The certificate must fulfil the requirements of Annex I, and it must be issued by a certification-service-provider who meets the requirements of Annex II.

[71] Under Art 2(6) such a device must meet the requirements of Annex III.

[72] Art 5(2).

[73] See Reed, n 54.

legal validity only to advanced signatures which use a domestic Certification Authority.

Although many Member States operate licensing schemes for Certification Authorities, the Directive is specifically drafted in such a way that certificates from unlicensed Certification Authorities can still be capable of producing a certificated signature. Under Article 5(1) an electronic signature will receive the benefit of a higher level of validity if it is based on a qualified certificate which was created using a secure-signature-creation device. To be a qualified certificate, the certificate must link the signature verification data[74] used to the signatory and confirm his identity,[75] and be issued by a certification-service-provider who meets the requirements of Annex II.[76] Additionally, the certificate itself must comply with Annex I.[77]

To fulfil the requirements of Annex II, the certification-service-provider must, in essence, be a fit and proper person to provide such services.[78] In practice, compliance with Annex II is likely to be demonstrated by acquiring a licence from a European accreditation authority or one recognized[79] by the relevant EU body, but there is no theoretical reason why it should not be proved by specific evidence in each case rather than relying on licences or accreditation.

4.2.3 Commercial communications and supplier information

4.2.3.1 *Commercial communications*

Online advertising by e-commerce businesses is subject to exactly the same advertising regulations as any other business advertising, and so those rules are not

---

[74] Defined in Art 2(7). This definition would encompass any of the electronic signature methods discussed in this chapter.

[75] Art 2(9).

[76] Art 2(10).

[77] Which states:

> Qualified certificates must contain: (a) an indication that the certificate is issued as a qualified certificate; (b) the identification of the certification-service-provider and the State in which it is established; (c) the name of the signatory or a pseudonym, which shall be identified as such; (d) provision for a specific attribute of the signatory to be included if relevant, depending on the purpose for which the certificate is intended; (e) signature-verification data which correspond to signature-creation data under the control of the signatory; (f) an indication of the beginning and end of the period of validity of the certificate; (g) the identity code of the certificate; (h) the advanced electronic signature of the certification-service-provider issuing it; (i) limitations on the scope of use of the certificate, if applicable; and (j) limits on the value of transactions for which the certificate can be used, if applicable.

[78] The criteria in Annex II are that the provider should operate a secure, efficient, and properly run business; take appropriate steps to identify signatories to whom a certificate is issued; employ suitably qualified personnel and use trustworthy computer systems and products; take measures against forgery and to preserve the confidentiality of signature keys; have sufficient financial resources; maintain proper records; not store the signatory's signature-creation data; provide proper information about the terms and conditions on which certificates are issued; and use trustworthy systems to store certificates.

[79] The principles and procedures for recognition are set out in Council Directive (EC) 1999/93 on a Community framework for electronic signatures [2000] OJ L13/12, 19 January 2000, Art 7.

examined here. However, where an e-commerce business is established in the UK, its advertising is not subject to the laws of the other EU Member States, even though its online adverts will be visible there, because of the 'country of origin' rule of the Electronic Commerce Directive (see section 4.6.1 below). The country of origin rule does not apply to non-EU Member States, and thus online businesses will need to consider whether there are any non-EU jurisdictions which might seek to apply their laws to that advertising. As a matter of practice it is unlikely that a state will do this unless it considers that the advertising targets its own citizens,[80] but this is not something which can always be relied on.

In addition to general advertising regulation, Article 6 of the Electronic Commerce Directive sets out rules which apply specifically to online commercial communications.[81] 'Commercial communication' is defined in Article 2(f) as

> any form of communication designed to promote, directly or indirectly, the goods, services or image of a company, organisation or person pursuing a commercial, industrial or craft activity or exercising a regulated profession.

Under Article 6(a) the supplier must:

(a) identify online commercial communications clearly as such;

(b) make clear the identity of the person on whose behalf the communication is made; and

(c) identify promotional offers, competitions, and games as such, and make the conditions for eligibility or entry easily available and present them clearly and unambiguously.

These provisions are clearly aimed primarily at 'spam' emails, which usually attempt to disguise both the fact that they are commercial communications and the identity of the sender. However, they can be infringed unintentionally by reputable online businesses if website design is poor, so that the identity of the business or the rules for participating in a game are not easily apparent.

4.2.3.2 *Supplier information*

The Electronic Commerce Directive also takes the, not unreasonable, position that customers have a right to know who they are proposing to deal with online. For this reason, Article 5 requires an online service provider (which includes online sellers) to make the following information 'easily, directly and permanently accessible':

(a) the identity and geographic address of the service provider;

---

[80] See, eg, the recommendation in IOSCO, *Report on Securities Activity on the Internet* (1998) pp 34–6 that states should apply their securities advertising regulation only to websites which target that jurisdiction.

[81] Implemented in the UK by Electronic Commerce (EC Directive) Regulations 2002 (SI 2002/2013), reg 7.

(b) effective contact details;

(c) if the provider is registered in a trade register or authorized by a supervisory authority or the regulator of a profession, information about that registration or authorization;

(d) the service provider's VAT number, if VAT-registered.

Additionally, where prices are given on a website they must be clear and unambiguous and indicate whether they include taxes and delivery.

Article 10(3) provides that contract terms and general conditions must be provided in a way which allows the customer to store and reproduce them. This raises questions about whether it is sufficient to make these terms and conditions available via a webpage, or whether they must be emailed to the customer—see further the discussion at section 4.5 below.

4.3 ELECTRONIC RECORDS AS EVIDENCE

4.3.1 Admissibility

There are three reasons why a record produced by a computer might be inadmissible as evidence:

(a) because it is not an original;

(b) because it is hearsay; or

(c) because some rule of law prevents the evidence from being adduced.

The Civil Evidence Act 1995 ('CEA 1995') removed all of these potential problems, so far as English law is concerned. Section 1 of the Act simply abolishes the hearsay rule, and section 8 provides that where a statement in a document is admissible, it may be proved by producing a copy of the document (even if the original is still in existence) and that the number of removes between a copy and the original is irrelevant (ie, it may be an nth generation copy). Furthermore, under section 9, documents which form part of the records[82] of a business (defined very widely) are automatically admissible[83] and the absence of an entry in those records can be

---

[82] Note that not all business documents are 'records'. *H v Schering Chemicals* [1983] 1 All ER 849, the leading case on the meaning of 'record', indicates that a document, irrespective of its form, will only be a record if:

(a) it effects a transaction or is a contemporaneous compilation of information derived from primary sources which is intended to serve as a record of events; and

(b) it is a comprehensive compilation, rather than a selection of source information.

If a document is not a comprehensive record of what has occurred, or, even if comprehensive, was not intended to serve as a primary source of information on that matter, it will not be a record. Thus, the majority of computer records will fall under s 8 rather than the more favourable provisions of s 9.

[83] A certificate signed by an officer of the business is required under s 9(2) so as to demonstrate that the document forms part of its records.

proved by an appropriately signed certificate.[84] The focus of evidential disputes will thus be on the authentication of the relevant records.

Other jurisdictions treat the question of admissibility differently, although it is now rare for a court to refuse to admit a computer record as evidence. Many common law jurisdictions have specific rules, either statutory or derived from case law, which permit the admission of computer records as exceptions to the hearsay rule. Thus, the US law business records exception to its hearsay rule allows the computer evidence to be admitted if:

(a) The computer equipment used was standard equipment, or if modified, was reliable.

(b) The data were entered in the regular course of business at or near the time of the events recorded by persons having personal knowledge of the events recorded.

(c) Adequate measures were taken to ensure the accuracy of the data during entry, storage, and processing.

(d) The printouts were prepared in such a manner as to ensure their accuracy.[85]

The Australian courts have taken a robust approach, holding that 'Courts should . . . be prepared to facilitate proof of business transactions generated by computers',[86] and South Africa's Electronic Communications and Transactions Act 2002 allows the admission of computer records as evidence without imposing any special technical conditions, the court deciding what weight is appropriate to be given to the evidence.

In civil law jurisdictions the general rule is one of freedom of proof, so that electronic records are admissible in most legal proceedings. However, in some cases national record-keeping laws make detailed provisions as to the form and content of documents, and occasionally that country's law of evidence may also give those documents a particular evidential status.[87] Loss of this status can be a disincentive to using methods of electronic messaging for contractual purposes.

4.3.2 Authentication

4.3.2.1 *Basic principles*
Authentication means satisfying the court that:

(a) the contents of the record have remained unchanged;

(b) the information in the record does in fact originate from its purported source, whether human or machine; and

---

[84] s 9(3).
[85] 85 MD Scott, *Computer Law* (New York: Wiley, 1984) 10.20.
[86] *ANZ Banking Group v Griffiths* (1990) 53 SASR 256.
[87] Provisions of this kind are increasingly being abolished to facilitate e-commerce and so no examples are given here, in case they too are repealed before this book is published!

(c) extraneous information such as the apparent date of the record is accurate.

As with paper records, the necessary degree of authentication may be proved through oral and circumstantial evidence, if available, or via technological features of the system or the record. Non-technical evidence will include a wide variety of matters:

> In an ideal world, the attorney would recommend that the client obtain and record countless bits of evidence for each message so that it could later be authenticated in court—autographs, fingerprints, photographic identification cards, attestations from witnesses, acknowledgements before notaries, letters of introduction, signature guarantees from banks, postmarks on envelopes, records of the return of acknowledgements and so forth. . . . [These] observations on conventional messages should apply equally to electronic messages.[88]

Technical evidence might come from system logs and audit trails, particularly if they are specifically designed with this end in mind, or through embedded features of the record itself such as electronic signatures.[89]

Where records are kept on paper there is normally little difficulty in convincing the court that the document produced as evidence is the same document as was originally stored. If the document is signed, it can be produced to prove the fact of sending and the contents of the message. The sender's physical signature will prove that he is responsible for it, and any alteration to its contents should be apparent on its face. The problem with electronically stored communications, however, is that alteration is simple and leaves no traces. Unless these records can be as well authenticated as physically signed documents, their value as evidence of the communication may be low.

This is because electronic records consist of a stream of numbers (normally in ASCII or some proprietary code[90]) representing the letters of the message (plus, possibly, control characters that define format, emphasis, etc). When a record is edited, the new version is saved to disk and replaces the old version. The change in the stream of numbers cannot normally be discovered by examining the record itself.

The problems occur when the apparent sender of a communication denies that he was responsible for it or where the parties' records differ. There is nothing in the record itself that authenticates it, and so the court will be forced to assess its authenticity solely by reference to any oral and circumstantial evidence that

---

[88] B Wright, 'Authenticating EDI: The Location of a Trusted Recordkeeper' (1990) 6 CL&P 80.
[89] See section 4.2.2.2 above.
[90] The American Standard Code for Information Interchange is used for most microcomputer communication. Each 8-bit binary word represents a letter of the alphabet or some control or graphics character. Eg, in ASCII code A=decimal 65, a=decimal 97, carriage return=decimal 13, etc. ASCII's 8 bits have proved insufficient for modern applications and have therefore been variously extended—the most common extension is Unicode, which allows a much wider range of characters.

may be available. It must also be remembered that most electronic records will be copies, and there is thus a need to prove that each is an *authentic* copy of the original communication. The simplest way of so doing is to give oral evidence to that effect, and failure to do so may render the copy inadmissible under English law.[91]

4.3.2.2 *Authentication provisions in contracts between the parties*
Practising lawyers seem generally to agree that it is worth including a provision in all electronic commerce agreements (eg, in a rulebook or interchange agreement—see section 4.4.4 below) which states that messages which comply with the archiving and authentication procedures of the agreement (and where appropriate, of any communications network's rulebook) are deemed to be accurate.[92] The efficacy of the provision as to authentication is inevitably uncertain, but although the courts may be unwilling to allow the parties to devise their own law of evidence in a contract, a provision of this type might be effective to raise an estoppel preventing the parties from disputing admissibility and accuracy (see section 4.2.2.1 above).

4.3.2.3 *Authentication through third party records*
If communications are monitored by an independent third party, as might occur for EDI transactions, the log of this monitoring can provide a useful level of authentica-tion. For these purposes the monitoring system should ideally record (a) the identity of sender and recipient of the message, and (b) the message contents. So far as (b) is concerned, it should not be necessary to record the entire text of the message, so long as sufficient information is retained so that any alterations can be detected. The strongest authentication evidence would come from such monitoring by an independent third party. The Bolero system[93] for online international trade is a sophisticated example of a system which provides authentication via an intermedi-ary's records.

It is quite feasible to set up such a system on a less specialized intermediary system, or to use any features of the system which have evidential value, even if they were not designed with authentication in mind.[94] However, a log would only be useful as evidence if it contained evidence of the message's contents; otherwise it could only prove that *some* message was sent by one party and received by the other, and where there has been a series of messages it will not be much help in proving

---

[91] *R v Collins* (1960) 44 Cr App R 170.

[92] See G Rowbotham, 'EDI: The Practitioner's View' [1988] International Financial Law Review, August, 32.

[93] See <http://www.bolero.net> (accessed 8 August 2011).

[94] It is possible to compel the production of information in the hands of a third party by serving a *subpoena duces tecum*, but this can only be done on notice and the court has jurisdiction to refuse the order if it would be unreasonable, oppressive, or otherwise not proper. In any event it will ensure that the third party is properly reimbursed by the parties for his expenses, which in such a case might be substantial—see *Senior v Holdsworth, ex p ITN* [1976] QB 23.

that the one in question was sent and received. The technology which would enable providers of communications networks to retain this information already exists, but the volume of communications over open networks such as the internet makes it economically unviable to offer such a service to all users.

Where the third party is unable to provide authentication evidence, for example in internet communications, the necessary authentication evidence needs to be found in the document itself and in the record-keeping logs of the person adducing the document. Electronic signatures, as discussed at section 4.2.2.2 above, can provide such evidence. All methods of authenticating e-commerce communications independent of third party evidence rely on cryptographic techniques.

4.3.2.4 *Cryptography for authentication*

The fact that electronic messages are transmitted as a stream of digital information makes it possible to use cryptographic techniques to authenticate a message. This is achieved by performing a mathematical function on the message content, or part of it, which could only have been effected by the sender. The evidential value of cryptography is based on the concept of computational infeasibility, which means that although the encryption can in theory be decoded and thus the record altered, the amount of time this would take is so great that for practical purposes the encryption can be regarded as secure. To be effective, the encrypted version must be producible by the sender alone, and any attempt to change the content of the message and re-encrypt it must in practical terms be impossible. Encryption techniques are a fundamental part of the technology of electronic signatures.

'Public key' cryptosystems such as RSA[95] were devised so as to enable secret communications without the two parties having to agree on an encryption method and exchange keys. They are thus well suited to e-commerce transactions where the parties have not agreed authentication protocols in advance, and are the basis for most electronic signature technologies.

The RSA cipher requires three numbers: N, K_p (the public key, used for encryption), and K_s (the secret key, used for decryption). The numbers N and K_p are published to form the recipient's public key, but K_s is kept secret. The sender of a message encrypts it by raising the digital form of the message to the power K_p and then calculating the result modulus N (ie, the remainder when (message) raised to the power of K_p is successively divided by N until it will no longer divide). The recipient decrypts the message using the formula (encrypted message) to the power K_s modulus N. Because of the way K_p, K_s, and N are derived it is computationally infeasible to calculate K_s knowing only K_p and N.

Because the encryption formula is symmetrical it is possible to encrypt a message using the sender's private key K_s and decrypt it with K_p, and thus effect an

---

[95] Named after its inventors—see RL Rivest, A Shamir, and L Adleman, 'A Method of Obtaining Digital Signatures and Public Key Cryptosystems' (1978) 21 Communications of the ACM 120.

electronic signature. The sender encrypts his message using K_s. When it is received, the recipient decrypts the message using the sender's public key, K_p and N. As only the sender could have encrypted the message, if both encrypted and plaintext versions are produced in court the judge can check the identity of the sender by decrypting the message and checking it against the plaintext version. This also authenticates the contents of the message, as if the recipient alters the plaintext contents he will not be able to re-encrypt the message so that it decrypts with K_p and N.

In the present state of cryptological knowledge, provided the sender's secret key is sufficiently large it is harder to forge an electronic signature than a written one. In civil cases the burden of proof is merely the balance of probabilities, and the mathematical basis of such ciphers is more than strong enough to discharge that burden.[96]

4.3.2.5 *Authentication in practice*
Authentication in practice may be easier than this discussion suggests. English criminal law imposes a high standard of proof[97] and yet in *R v Spiby*[98] the English Court of Appeal was prepared to presume that a computer was recording evidence accurately when its operator (a hotel manager) testified that he was unaware of any problems in operation, and in the absence of any evidence by the defendant that there was any question of malfunction. This approach was approved by the House of Lords in *R v Shephard*.[99] It is likely, therefore, that authenticity will be presumed by the courts if:

(a) the user can produce a human witness to testify that the system was operating properly at the relevant time; and

(b) the other party to the litigation is unable to adduce evidence to counter this presumption.

In order to ensure that an appropriate audit trail exists, and to produce evidence which will tend to authenticate records of electronic messages, it is common to agree what records the parties will keep, and whether particular categories of message are to be acknowledged by the receiving party (including provisions on what that acknowledgement should consist of). These records will assist in resolving disputes over the existence or content of electronic messages.

---

[96] If N is greater than 200 bits in length it is calculated that, using a computer which eliminated one potential factor of N every microsecond, ie 1,000 keys per second, the task would on average take longer than the expected lifetime of the universe—see B Beckett, *Introduction to Cryptology* (Oxford: Blackwell, 1988) ch 9. Note, though, that it is possible to check keys at a much faster rate than this, but that increases in computing power can be countered by increasing the key length. An increase of one bit in key length doubles the effective time required to break the encryption of that message.

[97] ie, proof beyond a reasonable doubt, as opposed to proof on the balance of probabilities as required in civil cases.

[98] (1990) 91 Cr App R 186.

[99] [1993] AC 380.

4.4 B2B E-COMMERCE

B2B electronic commerce was, until comparatively recently, undertaken solely via proprietary networks via EDI. Open networks, and in particular the internet, are increasingly becoming the communications medium of choice for business, and the term EDI is likely to fall gradually into disuse. This has not yet occurred, however, and so in this section the term EDI is used for convenience of expression.

EDI is, at the simplest level, nothing more than a technology for exchanging structured[100] information. One computer is linked to another and a stream of data is sent across the link. At this level, the only distinction from, say, a fax message is that the recipient can easily edit his copy.

Where EDI becomes interesting, both commercially and legally, is if the messages are structured in such a way that they can be processed automatically by the recipient.[101] The most common use of such messages is to carry out trade, particularly international trade, and it is in this sense that the term EDI is most commonly used. This also gives rise to the alternative term 'paperless trading', which was particularly common in the USA.[102]

Structured EDI messages offer their users two potential benefits, benefits which can be of immense commercial value:

(a) The abolition (or near abolition) of the physical, paper documents which previously effected the transaction. Estimates of the costs involved in producing and processing this paper range as high as 10 per cent of the value of the goods.

(b) The complete automation of the ordering/delivery/payment cycle.

4.4.1 Replacing paper

To take an example, suppose a motor manufacturer needs to purchase parts from a supplier. In a paper-based system a human being examines the stock inventory, decides which parts are needed, and informs the purchasing department. The purchasing department issues an order to the supplier. Payment may need to be

---

[100] Structured information is necessary to permit automated processing at both ends of the transaction, and this is perhaps the most obvious distinction between EDI and other forms of electronic commerce. In B2C e-commerce the automated processing takes place only at the supplier's end, and the information supplied by the customer is structured by the supplier's website to permit it to be processed automatically.

[101] This is somewhat different to networking methods, such as the internet where a large proportion of messages are meant to be processed by the human mind. However, the technologies exist that can easily be put into use to allow messages to be structured in such a way that they too can be processed automatically. Not only is this increasingly being used by interactive sites on the internet, but it is possible to create a virtual private network across the internet that behaves in a manner similar to EDI.

[102] See, eg, B Wright, *The Law of Electronic Commerce* (Boston, MA: Little, Brown & Co, 1991).

effected through a documentary credit, necessitating further communications between the manufacturer, one or more banks, and the supplier. Once the supplier has the parts ready to ship he must engage a carrier, thus generating further documentation which must be processed by all the parties involved in the transaction.

The EDI model is quite different. Here the manufacturer's stock control system automatically generates the order when stocks of any part are low. The order is sent without any human intervention to the supplier's computer, which accepts the order and commences manufacture. The payment mechanism is set up in a similar way, again with little or no human intervention, as is the contract of carriage. To perform the contract the only physical movement is that of the goods from the supplier's premises to those of the manufacturer. All of the messages which would have been placed on paper and circulated along the chain of banks to the manufacturer are replaced by structured EDI messages which are processed automatically, the relevant portions being copied to accounting and other computer systems. The time saved in the ordering process makes 'Just in Time' operation possible, cutting stocks held to the bare minimum. It also offers the flexibility of production seen in the modern motor industry where a production line can be switched from one model to another in a very short space of time. The manpower savings are potentially large, as EDI avoids the redundant manual processing of information in stock control, purchasing, and accounts departments.

To achieve this aim, the legal relationships set up by lawyers must make it possible to carry out the transaction without needing to generate any paper. Whether this is possible will depend very much on the legal barriers which are posed by the national laws involved, and whether those barriers can be surmounted by provisions in the rulebook or interchange agreement (see section 4.4.4 below). If the provisions of national laws make it necessary to document discrete parts of the transaction on paper or, worst of all, require duplication of, for example, invoices by generating them as both EDI messages and hard copy, the use of EDI for that transaction is likely to be inappropriate.

4.4.2 Third party networks

Whilst it is possible to set up dedicated EDI links with each of one's trading partners, this rarely makes sense in practice. The volume of communications is likely to be too small to be economical. For this reason many EDI users communicate via a third party network, which might be either a proprietary network where the communications lines and equipment are controlled by the network operator, or a VPN which uses encryption technology across the internet to create a functional equivalent to a proprietary network. B2B e-commerce across the open internet is becoming increasingly common for one-off transactions, but where both supplier and customer are using automated trading systems there are still advantages to communicating via a third party network, most particularly a guaranteed level of network availability and enhanced communications security.

Rather than communicating directly with the intended recipient, each user's computer system sends messages to the network. The network's computer systems ensure, using the address information which is part of the message structure,[103] that the message is delivered to the addressee's computer. The delivery may be near instantaneous or may take some time, depending on the number of time zones which separate the parties and the level of service contracted for. In most cases there will be an element of 'store and forward' which, as we have seen, raises potential problems when forming contracts online—these problems are usually resolved via a rulebook or interchange agreement—see section 4.4.4 below.

Sometimes there may be more than one network involved, as network providers can agree to interoperate via a 'gateway' between their networks. The address segment of the message contains the information required to route the message to the gateway, and thence to the addressee across his own network. Linking networks in this way raises interesting liability questions, as the nature of the legal relationship between the sender and the addressee's network is unclear.

4.4.3 Network access agreements

The relationship between a user and his network provider is primarily contractual. Mosteshar identifies four main responsibilities of the network provider:

(a) Conveyance of the message in the correct format and protocol.
(b) Safeguarding against corruption of the message.
(c) Securing that the message is conveyed to the recipient.
(d) Preserving the confidentiality and security of the message.[104]

The method by which these responsibilities are to be carried out will largely be covered by the user handbook, the technical manual for connecting to the network. It is most likely that the contract between user and network provider will contain an obligation that the user's communications with other users of the network should comply with the technical and operational requirements of the user handbook, but even if this is not expressly stated it is likely that the users will be contractually bound to each other under the principle in *Clarke v Dunraven*.[105] The effect of the network access agreement will be to create a contract between each user and all the other users, either because entering into the agreement amounts to a standing offer to future users to be bound which is accepted by joining the system, or perhaps more logically, by impliedly giving the system provider authority to contract as agent on behalf of the user. Alternatively, the agreement may expressly confer rights on other users under the Contracts (Rights of Third Parties) Act 1999.

---

[103] See I Walden (ed), *EDI and the Law* (London: Blenheim OnLine, 1989) App E for examples of message structures for proprietary networks.
[104] Scott, n 85, 10.20.
[105] [1897] AC 59.

The network access agreement may also make express provision for the level and quality of service to be provided, though in most cases network operators will seek to exclude much, if not all, of their liability for breach of these obligations.[106] These exclusions will be subject to the Unfair Contract Terms Act 1977 ('UCTA 1977'), and may also be limited in scope by the terms of the network operator's telecommunications licence.

The network operator's contractual liability to the user will primarily be based on the Supply of Goods and Services Act 1982 ('SGSA 1982'), section 13 which will imply into the contract an obligation to take reasonable care in supplying the service contracted for. This obligation may be breached in a number of ways:

(a) if the system goes down;
(b) if a message is not transmitted;
(c) if it is sent to the wrong person;
(d) if it is intercepted or copied by an unauthorized person; or
(e) if it is garbled in transmission.

In each case, however, the system provider will only be liable for breach of the implied term if the problem was caused by a lack of care. Commercial network users normally require a higher level of service than this, and so a network access agreement will usually contain express terms about the availability and quality of the service to be provided.

As between network users their contractual liability to each other is probably limited to compliance with the user handbook and the rulebook (if any).

4.4.4 Interchange agreements and rulebooks

The purpose of an interchange agreement is to set out the terms on which the communicating parties agree to undertake e-commerce. It is important to make a distinction between an interchange agreement, which deals only with the details of the communication process, and the underlying commercial transaction such as a sale of goods, which is entered into and performed using that communication process. Although in the USA it is not uncommon for both to be dealt with in the same agreement, this practice arose from the way EDI has developed there, through large customers forcing their suppliers to trade with them via EDI. In Europe the practice has been rather different. Industry groupings such as ODETTE[107] or TRADACOMS[108] have developed protocols for EDI, and this has focused attention

---

[106] One of the few exceptions to this practice is Swift, the Society for Worldwide Interbank Financial Telecommunications. Swift is a closed network for electronic funds transfer, used only by the banks which own it or organizations sponsored by a member. Swift limits its liability to 3,000 million Belgian francs per loss or series of losses caused by Swift's negligence, error or omission—see M Petre, 'Network Providers' (1990) 7 Computer Law & Practice 8, note 18.

[107] The European motor industry.

[108] The UK retail sector.

on the communications aspect of EDI rather than the underlying transaction. This separation makes theoretical and practical sense, as the parties can enter into different types of underlying transaction without changing the agreement on interchange.

A rulebook is, effectively, an interchange agreement whose terms are set in advance by the operator of an e-commerce system, rather than negotiated between the communicating parties. Rulebooks are used where all members of a particular e-commerce system are conducting similar types of transaction with each other, and where it is in the interests of the system provider to prevent disputes about the legal effect of their communications. All participants in the system agree to comply with the rulebook in their communications.[109]

As the purpose of the interchange agreement is to bind the parties to a particular, structured form of communication, there are a number of issues which it must address. Because different industry sectors will inevitably have different specific requirements, no universal standard is achievable. However, a number of organizations have produced model interchange agreements which provide a useful starting point for negotiations, and on an international level the International Chamber of Commerce has produced the *Uniform Rules of Conduct for Interchange of Trade Data by Teletransmission* (the UNCID Rules). Within the EC, DG XIII initiated the TEDIS[110] project which examined the technical and legal issues involved in EDI. As part of its work, TEDIS produced a model interchange agreement whose suggested provisions reflect best practice among the EDI community.[111]

The main areas covered by interchange agreements and rulebooks are:

(a) A requirement to adhere to the technical procedures of the chosen communication link. This is normally done by reference to the network user handbook.

(b) Agreement on a particular protocol for the message format, such as EDIFACT standards.[112]

(c) Agreement on acknowledgements of messages and any confirmations of their content that are required.

(d) Agreement on which of the parties takes responsibility for the completeness and accuracy of the communication. As we have already seen, it is likely that the parties will wish the received version of a message to be operative, rather than that transmitted. For this reason it will be important that the technical safeguards listed in (a) to (c) above are incorporated to ensure that transmission takes place and that errors are immediately detected. Whilst message corruption is almost certain not to

---

[109] One of the most complex examples is the Bolero rulebook, available online at <http://www.boleroassociation.org/downloads/rulebook1.pdf> (accessed 15 August 2011).

[110] *Trade Electronic Data Interchange Systems*, OJ L285, 8 October 1987.

[111] European Commission Recommendation (EC) 94/820 of 19 October 1994 relating to the legal aspects of electronic data interchange [1994] OJ L338.

[112] <http://www.unece.org/trade/untdid/welcome.htm> (accessed 8 August 2011).

produce an apparently sensible message with an entirely different meaning, it is quite conceivable that a currency field could be altered or that an entire message could be lost. As, in general, it is the received version which is operative, the onus to ensure correct transmission must be on the sender.

(e) Agreement on security and confidentiality.

(f) Agreement on data logs and the storage of messages.

(g) Agreement on which country's law is to apply to the communications process.

4.5 B2C E-COMMERCE

One of the biggest differences between B2B and B2C e-commerce is that in B2C e-commerce there is little or no scope for the individual negotiation of contracts. This means that the terms of the transaction, both in respect of online communications and the underlying transaction, are set by the supplier and must be accepted by the consumer in order to purchase from that supplier.

However, largely as a result of EU legislation, an online supplier does not have unfettered freedom to contract in whatever way he wishes. B2C e-commerce is, by definition, subject to the Distance Selling Directive.[113] That Directive needs to be read together with the information requirements in the Electronic Commerce Directive (see section 4.2.3.2 above). The Electronic Commerce Directive requirements apply to all online sales, whether B2B or B2C, whereas the Distance Selling Directive applies to all B2C sales, whether online or offline. This is unnecessarily confusing.

Article 4(1) of the Distance Selling Directive, which applies to both offline and online sales, sets out a list of information which a supplier must provide to consumers:

(a) the supplier's name and, in the case of advance payment, address;[114]

(b) the main characteristics of the goods or services to be supplied;

(c) the price including all taxes and delivery charges;

(d) the arrangements for payment, delivery of goods, or performance of services;

(e) unless the sale is exempted, that the consumer has a right of withdrawal;

---

[113] Council Directive (EC) 97/7 on the protection of consumers in respect of distance contracts [1997] OJ L144/19, 4 June 1997, implemented in the UK by the Consumer Protection (Distance Selling) Regulations 2000 (SI 2000/2334) as amended by the Consumer Protection (Distance Selling) (Amendment) Regulations 2005 (SI 2005/689). See Chapter 2 for more detailed discussion.

[114] Note that for online sales this address information must always be provided—see section 4.2.3.2 above.

(f) how long the offer or the price remains valid; and

(g) the minimum duration of the contract if there is to be a continuous or recurring supply (eg a subscription service, mobile phone contract, etc).

Under Article 5, some parts of this information must be confirmed in writing or via 'another durable medium available and accessible to [the consumer]', and further information[115] must be supplied in the same way where applicable.

The difficulty with Article 5 for online businesses is in deciding how best to provide this information. Forcing a printout of the relevant parts of the website is clearly impracticable. It seems generally to be accepted than a confirmatory email will suffice if it contains the required information,[116] but the status of a confirmatory webpage which the consumer is requested to print or store is still uncertain. The OFT has issued guidance to businesses on this matter which states:

> Our view is that [durable medium] means a form in which information can be retained and reproduced but cannot be edited, such as an email that can be printed or a letter, fax or brochure that can be kept for future reference. We do not consider that information on a website is durable as it can be changed at any time after the consumer has accessed it. Technological advances may change what we regard as durable in the future.[117]

How the Directive is to be complied with if the customer does not have (or will not give) an email address, for example for the purchase of a music download, remains a mystery, and online businesses can only hope that no enforcement action will be taken if they have done all that is possible to make the required information available to consumers.

4.6 CROSS-BORDER ISSUES

4.6.1 Foreign regulation

In theory there is no limit on the circumstances in which a jurisdiction might claim to apply its laws to regulate the electronic commerce activities of a supplier from a different jurisdiction, although in practice enforcement of those laws against a foreign enterprise may be difficult. However, governments usually attempt to limit the extraterritorial effect of their laws through the principle of comity, which requires

---

[115] How to exercise the right of withdrawal, the geographical address for complaints, information on after-sales service, and any guarantees, and how to cancel contracts which are not one year or less in duration.

[116] See DTI, *New Regulations for Business to Consumer Distance Selling—A Guide for Business* (October 2000) p 17; J Hörnle, G Sutter, and I Walden, 'Directive 97/7/EC on the Protection of Consumers in respect of Distance Contracts' in A Lodder and H Kaspersen (eds), *eDirectives: Guide to European Union Law on E-commerce* (The Hague: Kluwer, 2002).

[117] OFT, *A Guide for Businesses on Distance Selling* (OFT 698, 2006) p 3.

that a state should not claim to apply its legislation to persons within another state unless it is reasonable to do so.

The standard approach to maintaining comity is to apply a state's laws only to *activities* undertaken within the state, or the *effects* which those activities have within the state. This generally works quite well offline. However, determining the location where electronic commerce activities take place or have effects is extremely difficult. Traditional tests for localization of commercial activities look for particular trigger events, the most common of which include:

(a) the place of delivery of products sold;

(b) the place where services were performed;

(c) the place where advertising is viewed;

(d) the place where a purchaser took steps towards concluding a contract; and

(e) whether the supplier 'targeted' the jurisdiction in question.

All of these are largely metaphysical concepts where products and services are supplied online, or where products are advertised and contracts concluded via a website.

Increasingly, there is a recognition that attempts to localize electronic commerce activities are inappropriate, and that some alternative basis for maintaining comity must be found. The most promising alternative seems to be that of accepting 'country of origin' regulation, coupled with an appropriate degree of harmonization or convergence of national laws.

The most striking example of country of origin regulation is found in Articles 3 and 4 of the Electronic Commerce Directive,[118] which provide:

Article 3

1. Each Member State shall ensure that the Information Society services provided by a service provider established on its territory comply with the national provisions applicable in the Member State in question which fall within the coordinated field.

2. Member States may not, for reasons falling within the coordinated field, restrict the freedom to provide Information Society services from another Member State . . .

Article 4

1. Member States shall ensure that the taking up and pursuit of the activity of an Information Society service provider may not be made subject to prior authorisation or any other requirement having equivalent effect . . .

A number of exceptions to this principle are set out in the Annex to the Directive, but its general effect can be expressed quite simply. An electronic commerce business in one Member State is free to do business with residents of every other

---

[118] Council Directive (EC) 2000/31 on Electronic Commerce.

Member State provided that it complies with its own national laws, even if its activities would contravene the laws of the purchaser's Member State. Thus, for example, a UK electronic commerce business cannot be subject to action for breach of Germany's unfair competition law[119] simply on the ground that its website is visible to German customers and it does business with German consumers.

This adoption of the country of origin principle is only possible because of the large degree of harmonization which has already taken place in fields such as consumer protection, and because the Directive's other provisions on commercial communications (Arts 6 and 7) and the provision of information about the business (Art 5) introduce common controls on the potentially controversial aspects of these activities. How far the principle will be adopted on a global scale depends very much on the degree to which the economic pressures exerted by electronic commerce result in convergence of these aspects of other jurisdictions' laws.

4.6.2 e-Commerce contracts—applicable law and jurisdiction

The general rule of contract law is that parties are free to contract as they wish, including the freedom to agree the law and the jurisdiction[120] which they wish to govern the contract. They do this to ensure not only that they know the laws which govern the contract but also that they know the rules and procedure of the courts which may have to determine any dispute that arises as a consequence of the contract. However, the fact that the parties can choose the law or jurisdiction does not necessarily mean that the choice is valid or enforceable. In some cases the choice itself will be ineffective. In others, the choice will be effective but certain provisions of a different law (which would have applied had there been no choice of law or jurisdiction) will continue to apply.[121]

In the absence of a choice of law and/or jurisdiction clause, the UK courts will apply the Rome I Regulation[122] and the Brussels Regulation[123] to determine these matters. The explanation below covers only the rules which might apply to the most common kinds of B2C e-commerce contract, and thus omits rules which can only apply to offline dealings. Additionally, these instruments contain special rules

---

[119] *Gesetz gegen den unlauteren Wettbewerb* (UWG) of 3 July 2004.(BGBl I 2004 32/1414).

[120] These are two separate issues. Parties can choose a jurisdiction without choosing a law or choose a law without choosing a jurisdiction. However, failure to specify both law and jurisdiction is likely to lead to substantial uncertainty.

[121] See, eg, Unfair Terms in Consumer Contracts Regulations 1999 (SI 1999/2083), reg 9, which provides:

> These Regulations shall apply notwithstanding any contract term which applies or purports to apply the law of a non-Member State, if the contract has a close connection with the territory of the Member States.

[122] Regulation (EC) No 593/2008 of the European Parliament and of the Council of 17 June 2008 on the law applicable to contractual obligations (Rome I), OJ L177/6, 4 July 2008.

[123] Council Regulation (EC) 44/2001 on jurisdiction and the recognition and enforcement of judgments in civil and commercial matters, OJ L12/1, 16 January 2001.

for particular types of contract, such as sales by instalment on credit and sales of package holidays, which are also not discussed. Readers should therefore be aware that the full legal position is rather more complex.

The basic rules for e-commerce contracts for the sale of goods or the supply of services contracts are as follows, in the absence of any valid choice of law or jurisdiction:

(a) The applicable law is that of the country where the seller of goods, or the supplier of services, is habitually resident.[124] If, though, the contract is 'manifestly' more closely connected with another country, that country's law will apply.[125] If the default rules in Article 4(1) of the Rome I Regulation do not give an unambiguous answer, the applicable law is that of the country where the contracting party who is to make the characteristic performance of the contract is habitually resident[126]—for sales of goods or supplies of services, this will usually be the seller's or supplier's country.

(b) The courts which have jurisdiction to hear claims arising out of that contract are the courts of the country where the defendant is domiciled,[127] the courts of the country where the contractual obligation in issue was to be performed,[128] and, if the litigation relates to the operations of a branch, agency, or other establishment, the courts of the country where that branch, agency, or other establishment is domiciled.[129]

It is important to note that there can only be one law applicable to a contract,[130] but by contrast a claimant is often given a choice of jurisdictions in which to sue.

However, for B2C contracts the rules are different:

(a) The applicable law will be that of the consumer's country of habitual residence if the business conducts its activities in that country or 'by any means, directs such activities to that country',[131] except where the contract is for services to be supplied to the consumer in a different country.[132] A choice of law is allowed, but this may not 'have the result of depriving the consumer of the protection afforded to him by provisions that cannot be derogated from by agreement by virtue of the law which, in the absence of choice, would have been applicable'.[133] This means that the

---

[124] Rome I Regulation, Art 4(1)(a) and (b).
[125] Rome I Regulation, Art 4(3).
[126] Rome I Regulation, Art 4(2).
[127] Brussels Regulation, Art 2.
[128] Brussels Regulation, Art 5(1).
[129] Brussels Regulation, Art 5(5).
[130] Unless the contract is severable into parts to which different laws should be applied, Rome I Regulation, Art 4(1).
[131] Rome I Regulation, Art 6(1).
[132] Rome I Regulation, Art 6(4)(a).
[133] Rome I Regulation, Art 6(2).

'mandatory' rules of the law of the consumer's country of habitual residence will continue to apply.

(b) Where 'the contract has been concluded with a person who pursues commercial or professional activities in the Member State of the consumer's domicile or, by any means, directs such activities to that Member State or to several States including that Member State, and the contract falls within the scope of such activities',[134] then the consumer may sue either in his jurisdiction of domicile or that of the supplier, but can only be sued in his home domicile.[135] Any advance choice of jurisdiction clause is normally invalid, though an enforceable agreement about jurisdiction may be entered into after the dispute has arisen.[136]

Because it is extremely rare to encounter a B2B e-commerce contract which does not contain a choice of both law and jurisdiction, the provisions relating to B2C contracts are generally of most concern for electronic commerce activities. The fundamental test is now largely the same for both law and jurisdiction—did the online supplier 'direct' its activities to the consumer's country of residence?

This immediately raises the question whether a website, which by definition can be accessed worldwide, amounts to activities directed to those jurisdictions in which the website is accessible. The US courts apply the 'minimum contacts' doctrine[137] to decide questions of jurisdiction, which is functionally very similar to the 'directed activities' test under the Brussels Regulation and the Rome I Regulation. They have answered this question by making a distinction between an 'active' website, which solicits those outside the jurisdiction to undertake a commercial transaction with the website owner, and a 'passive' website which merely provides information. The former is sufficient to satisfy the minimum contacts doctrine,[138] whereas the latter is not.[139]

The Brussels Regulation drafting has been criticized on the ground that Article 15 is based on an unrealistic view of electronic commerce, that websites can easily be classified into 'active' and 'passive'. In practice, an electronic commerce supplier will wish to sell to customers in some jurisdictions, but not others, and to do this from the same website. The breadth of the wording is likely to produce the result that *all* jurisdictions are deemed to be targeted, unless the supplier takes complicated and costly steps to partition the website into purely national elements. A simple disclaimer that the site is not open to dealings with consumers in a

---

[134] Brussels Regulation, Art 15(1)(c).
[135] Brussels Regulation, Art 16.
[136] Brussels Regulation, Art 17.
[137] Derived from *International Shoe Co v Washington*, 326 US 310 (1945).
[138] *Maritz Inc v Cybergold Inc*, 947 F Supp 1328 (ED Mo, 1996); *Zippo Mfg Co v Zippo Dot Com Inc*, 952 F Supp 1119.
[139] *Bensusan Restaurant Corp v King*, 937 F Supp 295 (SDNY, 1996) aff'd 126 F3d 25 (2d Cir, 1997).

particular country will probably be insufficient.[140] It is probably also unsafe for a supplier to rely solely on a consumer's self-certification of place of residence as a means to avoid targeting a particular country, and other checks (such as the IP address from which the consumer is accessing the website and the country in which the consumer's payment instrument was issued) would be sensible as ways to avoid targeting unwanted jurisdictions.

---

[140] See M Pullen, 'On The Proposals To Adopt The Amended Brussels Convention and the Draft Rome II Convention As EU Regulations Pursuant to Article 65 of the Amsterdam Treaty', *EU Version—* Position Paper prepared for the Advertising Association <http://www.ilpf.org/events/jurisdiction/ presentations/pullen_posit.htm> (accessesd 8 August 2011) paras 1.9–1.12.

5

ONLINE INTERMEDIARIES

Gavin Sutter

5.1 INTRODUCTION—WHAT IS AN ONLINE INTERMEDIARY?

There are two distinct types of online intermediary prevalent in the modern online environment. The first is the Internet Service Provider, or ISP. Online dictionary *Webopaedia* defines ISP as:

a company that provides access to the Internet. For a monthly fee, the service provider gives you a software package, username, password and access phone number. Equipped with a modem, you can then log on to the Internet and browse the world wide web and USENET, and send and receive email.

In addition to serving individuals, ISPs also serve large companies, providing a direct connection from the company's networks to the Internet. ISPs themselves are connected to one another through Network Access Points.[1]

While this certainly covers one ISP business model which is still common at the time of writing, it does not offer an all-embracing definition, and already looks somewhat dated (not least in its capitalization of the initial letter of 'Internet'). Home internet

---

[1] <http://www.webopaedia.com/TERM/I/ISP.html> A more comprehensive picture of a modern ISP is provided by Wikipedia, at <http://en.wikipedia.org/wiki/Internet_Service_Provider> (both accessed 8 August 2011).

access really became a common thing in the UK with the arrival of non-subscription, 'pay per minute' ISPs, most notably Freeserve, in the late 1990s.[2] Recent years have seen great advances in the technology used for the typical home internet connection, and today the average user in Western Europe and the USA is most likely to be connected via a high speed 'always-on' broadband cable network,[3] ADSL modem,[4] ISDN Terminal Adapters,[5] or even wirelessly via a mobile internet dongle. High street coffee chains and even fast food restaurants commonly provide free WiFi internet connections for patrons, and a plethora of mobile internet devices are now available on the consumer market, from small, ultra-portable netbooks to touch-screen tablets, and in particular internet-accessible smartphones running Apple, Google Android, or Windows based software. It has even been estimated at the time of writing that by 2013 mobile telephones will overtake conventional personal computers as the most common web access device.[6] By 2010, according to the Office for National Statistics, 60 per cent of all adults in the UK, an estimated 30.1 million people, used the internet on a daily or near daily basis—approaching double the relevant figure for 2006.[7] Further, as the access technology has evolved, so too have the business models of most of the big players in the internet access provision market, as each seeks to find a competitive advantage over the rest by providing added-value services to the consumer. They may, for example, provide a bundle of communications services including telecommunications[8] and television.[9] Technical innovations are appearing apace, and developments such as Hotline[10] mean that even the 'standard' software set ups provided by ISPs, usually based around a

---

[2] The Freeserve brand no longer exists; the business having gone through several changes in ownership, at time of writing it is now operating as part of Orange telecommunications: <http://www.orange.co.uk>.

[3] eg, the iHome network and its franchises (<http://www.home.com/>), Virgin Media (<http://Virginmedia.com>) (both accessed 15 August 2011).

[4] Asymmetric Digital Subscriber Line.

Asymmetric Digital Subscriber Lines (ADSL) are used to deliver high-rate digital data over existing ordinary phone-lines. A new modulation technology called Discrete Multitone (DMT) allows the transmission of high speed data. ADSL facilitates the simultaneous use of normal telephone services, ISDN, and high speed data transmission, eg, video.

(Kimmo K Saarela, *ADSL* <http://www.cs.tut.fi/tlt/stuff/ads1/pt–adsl.html>.)

[5] Integrated Services Digital Network.

ISDN allows multiple digital channels to be operated simultaneously through the same regular phone wiring used for analog lines. The change comes about when the telephone company's switches can support digital connections. Therefore, the same physical wiring can be used, but a digital signal, instead of an analog signal, is transmitted across the line. This scheme permits a much higher data transfer rate than analog lines.

(Ralph Becker, *ISDN Tutorial* <http://www.ralphb.net/ISDN/index.html> at <http://www.ralphb.net/ISDN/advs.html> (both accessed 8 August 2011).)

[6] <http://www.gartner.com/it/page.jsp?id=1278413> (accessed 8 August 2011).

[7] <http://www.statistics.gov.uk/pdfdir/iahi0810.pdf> (accessed 8 August 2011).

[8] eg, British Telecom (<http://www.bt net>) and AT&T (<http://www.att.net>) (accessed 8 August 2011).

[9] eg, Virgin Media (<http://www.virginmedia.com>) (accessed 15 August 2011).

[10] See Hotline Communications Ltd (<http://www.BigRedH.com/index2.html>) (accessed 8 August 2011).

WWW browser, may be far from a permanent fixture. The typical contemporary ISP package will include basic internet access, email services, and commonly some limited free webspace for hosting the consumer's own private webpage.

As already noted, ISPs are not the only form of online service provider to whom the liability issues under discussion in this chapter may attach. The second major category of online service provider comprises those who do not provide basic access to the internet, but nevertheless provide certain other online services, whether on payment of a subscription fee or 'free'[11] to the end-user. These include web-based email providers,[12] bulletin board discussion systems (BBS),[13] and companies who provide online storage space for user-uploaded content, often with the additional ability to share that content with other users or the online public in general.[14] Since circa 2000, there has been a huge growth online in the number of 'blogs'. A blog, a term derived from 'web-log', is a form of online diary which provides the individual user with a potential international audience of millions.[15] Blogging has developed as an activity undertaken by a very wide range of individuals and entities. Of course these include the stereotypical gloomy, bedroom-dwelling teenagers, but there are also many organizations which use these services to update their membership and the public, independent artists and unsigned musicians using blogs and related networking facilities to publicize their work,[16] and political journalists using them as a dissemination tool for the very latest information on party policies and significant events.[17] Blogs are frequently used by campaigning politicians themselves, and during the US Presidential election campaign of 2008 some commentators noted that Barack Obama's greater command of internet resources as a promotional tool was a

---

[11] ie, advertising revenue-funded; commonly the contractual terms of use of such services will involve the end-user consenting to the onward sale of their contact details—subject, of course, to the restrictions set out in data protection law—see further Chapter 10: Privacy and Data Protection.

[12] eg, Hotmail (<http://www.hotmail.com>) or Yahoo Mail (<http://www.mail.yahoo.com>) (both accessed 8 August 2011).

[13] eg, the discussion forums on Harmony Central (<http://www.harmonycentral.com>) (accessed 8 August 2011), an online resource for musicians, or the Fedora Lounge (<http://.thefedoralounge.com>) (accessed 8 August 2011) for those interested in culture and style, particularly clothing, of the mid-twentieth century.

[14] eg, Photobucket (<http://www.photobucket.com>), which allows the user to upload digital photographs to a virtual photo album allocated to a registered account. Once uploaded, photos may be displayed elsewhere online via direct HTML link, and other individuals may be invited to view virtual photo albums by means of an email, containing an HTML link and a read-only password for the folder in question, sent via the Photobucket system.

[15] eg, Live Journal (<http://www.livejournal.com>), or Xanga (<http://www.xanga.com>) (accessed 8 August 2011).

[16] eg, English alternative rock band the Arctic Monkeys, whose 2005 'overnight-success', bringing them a number one chart position for their debut album on the week of release despite a general avoidance of television and other traditional media appearances, was widely attributed to fan networking via MySpace (<http://www.myspace.com>) (accessed 8 August 2011).

[17] eg, *The Guardian's Comment is Free* (<http://commentisfree.guardian.co.uk/index.html>) (accessed 8 August 2011).

key part of securing his victory.[18] Despite the success of newer, more flexible social networking services, traditional blogs continue to appear in their hundreds of thousands, one of the biggest platforms being Blogger, which was launched in 1999 by a small, independent company before being bought by its current owner, Google, in 2003.[19]

Social Networking Services (SNS) are rather more sophisticated operations than traditional blogs, offering all sorts of additional communication tools, photo-tagging, games, and applications. Such has been the success of some of these platforms in recent years that many people conduct a distinct proportion of their online interaction via an account with, for instance, Facebook,[20] often in preference to maintaining a traditional web-based email account for these purposes. Launched in 2003, the first of the contemporary SNS websites to enjoy mass success was MySpace,[21] which at its peak had more than 89 million registered accounts. In July 2005, Rupert Murdoch's News Corporation paid a reported $580 million for Myspace.[22] More recently Myspace has lost out in the popularity wars with its rival, Facebook, which launched in 2004. As of the beginning of 2011 Facebook is estimated to have over 600 million users worldwide,[23] while rival Myspace has halved its workforce.[24]

Also of growing significance is the 'micro-blogging' service Twitter,[25] a stripped-down service which allows users to post 'tweets' of up to 140 characters which can then be viewed by anyone who wishes to 'follow' the poster. Photographs can also be posted, and the system facilitates private messages. Twitter has proven especially popular among celebrities and their followers, although it is also increasingly being used as a communication and publicity tool by pressure groups, academics, and many others. It has also had an impact upon the activity of the courts, as in the furore over the super injunction granted in what has become known as the 'Trafigura affair' where the defiance that ultimately led to the setting aside of the order began in earnest via the medium of the tweet.[26]

---

[18] 'How Obama's Internet Campaign Changed Politics', *New York Times*, 7 November 2008 <http://bits.blogs.nytimes.com/2008/11/07/how-obamas-internet-campaign-changed-politics/> (accessed 8 August 2011).

[19] See <http://www.blogger.com/about> (accessed 8 August 2011).

[20] <http://www.facebook.com>.

[21] <http://www.myspace.com>.

[22] 'News Corp in $580m internet buy', BBC Online, 19 July 2005 <http://news.bbc.co.uk/1/hi/business/4695495.stm> (accessed 8 August 2011).

[23] 'Facebook Has More Than 600 Million Users, Goldman Tells Clients', *Business Insider*, 5 January 2011 <http://www.businessinsider.com/facebook-has-more-than-600-million-users-goldman-tells-clients-2011-1> (accessed 8 August 2011).

[24] 'Myspace cutting global workforce by half', BBC Online, 11 January 2011 <http://www.bbc.co.uk/news/business-12166637> (accessed 8 August 2011).

[25] <http://twitter.com> (accessed 8 August 2011).

[26] 'Twitter can't be gagged: online outcry over Guardian/Trafigura order', Guardian Online, 13 October 2009 <http://www.guardian.co.uk/media/pda/2009/oct/13/twitter-online-outcry-guardian-trafigura> (accessed 8 August 2011); 'Trafigura and Carter-Ruck end attempt to gag press freedom after Twitter uprising', *Daily Telegraph*, 13 October 2009 <http://www.telegraph.co.uk/news/politics/6316512/

The success of the online social networking phenomenon raised issues specific to child protection: it was estimated in 2006 that 61 per cent of children between the ages of 13 and 17 in the UK maintain personal profiles on such websites.[27] More recently it has been suggested that these sites are attracting an older demographic, particularly persons in their late twenties and early thirties.[28] Just as in the offline world, internet fashion is a fickle mistress; it is to be anticipated that the online social networking landscape will have changed markedly again by the time of the eighth edition of this volume.

Yet another online phenomenon of the past decade is the growth in popularity of the wiki. As defined by the most well-known of contemporary wikis, Wikipedia,[29] a wiki:

is a type of website that allows users to add, remove, or otherwise edit and change most content very quickly and easily, sometimes without the need for registration. This ease of interaction and operation makes a wiki an effective tool for collaborative writing. The term wiki can also refer to the collaborative software itself (wiki engine) that facilitates the operation of such a website . . . or to certain specific wiki sites, including the computer science site (and original wiki), WikiWikiWeb, and the online encyclopaedias such as Wikipedia.[30]

As its largest edition, the English language *Wikiapedia* has in excess of 3.6 million articles; the next largest editions, in German and French, have over 1.2 million and over 1 million entries respectively. These figures represent an effective trebling of content since the previous edition of *Computer Law* went to press.

The key common factors that link all these services is that they involve dealing with other persons and, more significantly, dealing with a wide range of content which is provided by third parties. This chapter is concerned with legal liabilities which may arise in relation to both of these factors. The contractual liability that an online intermediary may face in relation to the provision of a service will be considered, before moving on to discuss the much more complex issues arising out of liability questions in relation to dealing with third party provided content, both in general and under the qualified immunities provided by the Electronic Commerce Directive[31] as enacted in UK law by the Electronic Commerce (EC Directive) Regulations 2002.

Trafigura-and-Carter-Ruck-end-attempt-to-gag-press-freedom-after-Twitter-uprising.html> (accessed 8 August 2011).

[27] 'Teen network websites face anti-paedophile investigation', *The Guardian*, 3 July 2006, p 3.

[28] 'It's SO over: cool kids abandon social networking websites', *The Guardian*, 6 August 2009 <http://www.guardian.co.uk/media/2009/aug/06/young-abandon-social-networking-sites> (accessed 8 August 2011).

[29] See <http://en.wikipedia.org> (accessed 8 August 2011).

[30] See <http://en.wikipedia.org/wiki/Wiki> (accessed 8 August 2011).

[31] 00/31/EC.

5.2 ONLINE INTERMEDIARIES AND LIABILITY

5.2.1 Contractual liability

In their most basic form, ISPs are the 'glue' that binds the internet together, via their supply of TCP/IP packet switching services, which allow third parties to communicate data packets across the 'network of networks'. To facilitate such information transactions, these intermediaries will provide services to one or more of the parties, including fundamental communications services such as access and information storage. ISPs, and indeed other online intermediaries of all varieties discussed above, may also provide additional services to facilitate transactions between end-users, such as the provision of search facilities and indexes. Where these basic or additional services are found to be defective, liability will normally be based on the established legal principles of contract and tort, although it may not be immediately apparent how best to apply existing principles to forms of service previously unconsidered by legislators and the courts. Indeed, in the case of certain types of enhanced service, such as those involving provision of software, the courts may struggle to determine whether the service provided is in fact legally to be considered a 'service'.[32]

Any intermediary which provides internet transaction services is faced with the risk that its actions or inaction may result in the failure of the transaction. In such circumstances, it may be that it will be forced to compensate one or other of the parties to that transaction for any resulting losses. For ISPs that risk is twofold: first, there may simply be a communications failure which prevents the transaction from ever taking place. This may be considered a failure of 'basic service provision'. For a compensation claim in respect of such a failure to succeed, it will need to identify a duty on the part of the intermediary to ensure that such failures could not occur. In the absence of specific legislative provision for imposing such liability on internet intermediaries, such a duty could only arise in contract or in tort. While many types of intermediary may operate in the absence of any contractual agreement between them and communicating parties,[33] commercial ISPs are highly likely to have express terms delineating the extent of their liability. Where such terms attempt to limit an ISP's liability, this is likely to be to the bare minimum that the company's lawyers think will pass muster before the courts. Where either express terms relating

---

[32] Consider the difficulties faced by the court in *St Albans City and DC v International Computers Ltd* [1996] 4 All ER 481. See further Chapter 1, section 1.2.1.14.

[33] Not all parties offering ISP services will necessarily have a clear contractual arrangement covering communications sent by their end-users. Eg, a university offering such services to staff and students may well not have a contract for service between university and network users. Notably, however, many university regulations and guidelines now contain statements such as 'Whilst every reasonable endeavour is made to ensure that the computing systems are available as scheduled and function correctly, no liability whatsoever can be accepted by Academic Services computing for any loss or delay as a result of any system malfunction, howsoever caused.'

to liability are included or they are ruled void, contract law in most jurisdictions will imply a term that the ISP must take *reasonable* care in the provision of services to its user.[34] The mere fact of a failure alone will not generally be enough for an action to lie against an ISP unless a competent ISP could reasonably have been expected not to fail.

Secondly, there may be a failure of some additional service. As already noted, with the growth and development of the internet industry ISPs, in a bid to gain a competitive edge, have increasingly offered additional services beyond mere service provision. Such enhanced services are sometimes available to all-comers via the WWW, but can be restricted to the ISPs clients.[35] They may include the provision of:

(a) Customized software for accessing internet services, including parental controls, dedicated chat rooms, roaming capabilities, and instant messaging.

(b) Space on the ISP's servers for client webpages, and data storage.

(c) Information services such as news, weather, and financial data.

Generally these enhanced services will be governed by express contract terms, normally incorporated into a click-wrap licence which appears prior to downloading of software or each new session using a specific service. In the absence of express terms, the situation becomes more complex. Where the ISP is providing a non-contractual service, or the service is being delivered by other Internet Intermediaries who have no express contract with an end-user, there are only limited circumstances in which a contractual duty might be owed. In some cases the courts may be prepared to imply a contract between the intermediary and the end-user. This is rare, but not unknown, at least in the common law jurisdictions, even where the parties have had no previous dealings.[36] Much would turn on the closeness of the relationship between the intermediary and end-user.

For example, where the intermediary was an internet host supplying the ISP with transmission facilities, and its sole connection with an end-user of the ISP was the

---

[34] eg, UK Supply of Goods and Services Act 1982, s 13. Some ISPs explicitly spell this out. Eg, BT Internet Terms & Conditions (<http://guest.btinternet.com/html/termsconditions.html>) (accessed 8 August 2011):

> 11.3 In performing any obligation under this Contract, our duty is only to exercise the reasonable care and skill of a competent Internet service provider.

[35] AOL, eg, offers a range of pricing packages for its services. A client can purchase:

> (a) Four pricing variants on basic access to AOL's services, plus internet access.
> (b) Additional premium services, on top of one of the four basic variants.
> (c) Access to AOL's services and premium services, via another ISP.

A range of informational services are also available for free from AOL's webpage, to anyone with internet access.

[36] In the UK see *Clarke v Dunraven* [1897] AC 59 (a yacht owner's act of entering for a sailing race created an implied contract between him and all the other entrants in which they agreed to abide by the rules of the race).

reception of information packets for onward transmission, it seems unlikely that a court would be prepared to imply a contract between the intermediary and that end-user in the event of a loss of information. That would involve the implication of contracts between every internet host and all users whose packets arrive at their servers. Taken to its logical conclusion, this would potentially produce millions of individual contracts, none of whose terms could easily be identified as they would all need to be implied by the courts.

Additionally, in jurisdictions where the applicable law recognizes the concept of enforceable contractual obligations for the benefit of a third party, this might create a contractual duty owed by a host to the customers of those ISPs with which it has an express interconnection agreement (eg, if it provides the ISP with a connection to the internet on a chargeable basis).[37] However, even if such a contractual duty were found to exist, again it would be at most a duty to take reasonable care in the forwarding of packets. Proof of breach would always be extremely difficult.

If bringing a successful case against our internet host intermediary would be difficult in contract, it would be even less likely in tort, due to the extreme difficulty of demonstrating that the intermediary owed the user a tortious duty of care. This is because losses resulting from an information transaction are highly likely to be pure financial losses, and many jurisdictions will not impose a duty of care to avoid pure financial losses unless there is some clear pre-existing non-contractual relationship between the parties. The fact that the internet operates using a packet-switching protocol (TCP/IP) allowing individual information packets from the same communications to be routed via a multiplicity of different routes and hosts to ensure the best chance of delivery means that a user cannot predict with any certainty which intermediaries will be involved in the transaction, other than his ISP and that of the party with whom he is communicating, as such there can be no duty of care to him on the part of the other hosts involved. Even if the failure or malfunction of internet communication at issue were to have the capacity to cause physical injury or property damage, it would not be foreseeable that a failure on their part might cause such loss. This is because the intermediaries involved in transporting the communication would have no knowledge of the nature of the transaction, as it would appear as just a set of not necessarily related packets to them. Foreseeability of this kind is normally a prerequisite for a duty to arise. Even if, by some means it could be proven that a particular intermediary did owe a duty to one or other of the communicating parties, the fault-tolerant nature of the internet would tend to militate against any breach of that duty causing loss. In the common law jurisdictions at least, this will mean that there is insufficient causal link between the breach and the loss, which will be unrecoverable as being too remote.

---

[37] For the UK, see now the Contracts (Rights of Third Parties) Act 1999, discussed in Chapter 3, section 3.3.

In addition to provision of service liability, an ISP may owe other legal obligations to a party availing itself of its services, not least in the area of consumer protection. Another obligation that has received much media and industry attention in recent years, not least because of its importance to the development of e-commerce, is that of informational privacy. This may be granted by law, as in the case of the EU Data Protection Directive and attendant national legislation,[38] or may be incorporated or implied into the contract between ISP and user.[39] Chapter 10 explores in depth the implications of this Directive in the context of information technology and the internet.

5.2.2 Liability for third party provided content

More complex issues arise when we come to consider the potential liability of online intermediaries in relation to content which passes across or is stored on their servers. Online intermediaries usually operate using software which processes information automatically. As such, they are usually transferring the information without obtaining, or seeking to obtain, knowledge of either its content, or the nature of the transaction of which it is a part. This lack of knowledge, however, does not necessarily render them immune to legal action where the third party information content infringes another third party's rights. During the past decade, a general global consensus has been reached that while intermediaries should not have imposed upon them the same strict-liability standards to which real-world publishers are commonly held, some limited level of liability in respect of the information carried is appropriate. The exact standard to which intermediaries will be held will vary between jurisdictions, however, as a general rule liability will only arise where a certain level of knowledge (whether actual or constructive) is present. There may also in some circumstances be a further condition along the lines that the intermediary stands to gain some material benefit from the possession or transmission of the unlawful material in question.

Where a person has a legal grievance in relation to online content, or indeed where such content proves to be criminal, why sue the intermediary rather than the source of the content? There are several good reasons for this approach:

(a) Information intermediaries are often seen as potentially more lucrative targets for litigation than the originators of the offending information content. This perception may be based on the unofficial first rule of litigation 'Never sue poor people' or, in the case of large intermediaries, because the claimants suspect that it will be cheaper for the intermediary to pay them to drop the case than to fight it.

---

[38] European Union Council Directive 95/46/EC on the Protection of Individuals with regard to the Processing of Personal Data and on the Free Movement of Such Data, [1995] OJ L281/31, 23 November 1995. See Chapter 10.

[39] eg, BT's Resedential Standard Terms (available from <http:\\www.bt.com>) undertake that customer information will be protected and kept secure in accordance with BT's privacy policy.

(b) The question of jurisdiction may play a role, for example if the originator of the offending information is in a foreign jurisdiction while the intermediary is in the claimant's home jurisdiction, or if the intermediary is in a jurisdiction that has a reputation for favourable outcomes in cases similar to that brought by the claimant.[40]

(c) The outcome the claimant desires may be more effectively obtained by action against the intermediary. For example, where the desired outcome is the prevention of further access to the offending information, taking action against one originator may have minimal effect, whereas action against the intermediary may result in complete or partial blocking of all potential originators.[41] Action against an intermediary may also be part of a wider strategy by a claimant to 'chill' the willingness of other intermediaries to carry the same information.[42]

Prior to 2002, the liability position of online intermediaries under UK law was dictated piecemeal by application of a range of legal provisions, some of them created with internet technology in mind,[43] others not.[44] These specific legal provisions which have an impact upon online intermediaries are still in force, however their application must now also be considered alongside the general qualified immunities granted by the Electronic Commerce (EC Directive) Regulations 2002.[45] As will be discussed below, the core policy approach to liability under each of the relevant legal provisions should be broadly similar, even if it is not always as clear as might have been first thought that the Regulations override the prior status quo.

5.2.2.1 *General liability*
The intermediary liability provisions formulated in the Electronic Commerce Directive and incorporated into UK law by the Regulations apply to anyone operating as a 'service provider'. A service provider is defined as 'any person providing an information society service'.[46] An 'information society service' is given the same

---

[40] Consider, eg, the well-publicized possibility of jurisdiction or forum shopping in libel cases. See F Auburn, 'Usenet News And The Law' [1995] 1 Web JCLI at <http://webjcli.ncl.ac.uk/articles1/auburn1.html> (accessed 8 August 2011).

[41] This was the aim of the Bavarian Länder government when it took action against CompuServe officials in 1995 attempting to stop CompuServe providing access from within Germany to neo-Nazi newsgroups (mainly in the USA). This achieved some limited measure of success, as CompuServe was initially forced to suspend worldwide access to those newsgroups. See U Sieber, 'Criminal Liability for the Transfer of Data in International Networks—New Challenges for the Internet (part I)' (1997) 13 Computer Law and Security Report 151. However, given the distributed nature of the internet, the wide array of intermediary options for accessing information on it, and the perception of many governments that allowing such cases to be brought might damage internet growth, such apparent victories are all too likely to be transitory, as indeed was the victory here. CompuServe Ex-Official's Porn-Case Conviction Reversed, Associated Press, 17 November 1999.

[42] See *Religious Technology Center v Netcom* (1995) 33 IPR 132.

[43] eg, Defamation Act 1996, s 1.

[44] eg, Obscene Publications Act 1959, s 2.

[45] SI 2013/2002.

[46] Electronic Commerce (EC Directive) Regulations 2002, reg 2(1).

definition in the Regulations[47] as that in Article 1(2) of the Technical Standards and Regulations Directive:[48]

'service': any Information Society service, that is to say, any service normally provided for remuneration, at a distance, by electronic means and at the individual request of a recipient of services.

For the purposes of this definition:

– 'at a distance' means that this services is provided without the parties being simultaneously present,
– 'by electronic means' means that the service is sent initially and received at its destination by means of electronic equipment for the processing (including digital compression) and storage of data, and entirely transmitted, conveyed and received by wire, by radio, by optical means or by other electromagnetic means,
– 'at the individual request of a recipient of services' means that the service is provided through the transmission of data on individual request.'

It is clear that a very wide range of services will fall within this definition, including all those discussed above.[49]

The key provisions in relation to the liability of intermediary service providers are to be found in the Electronic Commerce Directive, under section 4. This section of the Directive comprises four key articles which place certain limitations upon the level of liability which may be faced by an online intermediary in relation to content provided by third parties. Three different categories of dealing with the material are set out, with greater likelihood of liability as the level of potential control over the material increases. The first category of dealing with information is set out in Article 12 of the Directive. This is concerned with the situation in which the intermediary service provider is a 'mere conduit', providing only a two-way channel by means of which information may be transferred. The intermediary here exercises no control over the sending of transmissions, the recipients, or their content. Additionally, the information is not to be stored for any greater length of time than that strictly necessary to facilitate transmission. Where these conditions are met, the service provider will have a complete immunity from liability in respect of any unlawful content so distributed by the end-user. This immunity is subject to a proviso that at the national level an intermediary may be required to block or otherwise place certain limitations upon a particular subscriber account, although as this would be done subject to court order and would include actual and official notification of specific breach(es) of the law, the situation will be very different to liability being imposed upon an intermediary in respect of unlawful content over which it exercised no control and of which it cannot be expected to have been aware.

---

[47] Ibid.
[48] Directive 98/34/EC, as amended by Directive 98/48/EC.
[49] See section 5.1.

Article 13 of the Directive is concerned with third party provided content stored in a cache on an intermediary's servers. Caching is defined so as to include 'automatic, intermediate and temporary storage . . . performed for the sole purpose of making more efficient the information's onward transmission to other recipients of the service upon their request . . .' Significantly, there is a pronounced difference between the Directive's definition of caching and caching in practice. While the Directive defines caching as a temporary function, in practice many servers which are designed to retain third party content in a cache will do so for long periods of time. This longer term storage will, under the terms of the Directive and national laws enacting it, be categorized not as caching, but hosting, and consequently subject to a greater risk of liability arising for the intermediary service provider. This different use of the terminology between law and practice may be the cause of some confusion for intermediaries in future. The availability of the Article 13 immunity from liability for third party provided content is conditional upon the absence of actual knowledge of the presence of the unlawful information on the servers. As soon as actual knowledge of the unlawful nature of cached information is received, the intermediary is obligated to remove or delete the information with all due haste. Again, at the national level the Directive permits that a national court may order an intermediary to cooperate in the termination or removal of specific unlawful material, such as that cached originating from an identified IP address.

The most qualified of the immunities provided in the Directive is that pertaining to intermediary liability for unlawful material hosted on its servers, the greater likelihood of liability arising reflecting the greater potential for control over that information. Article 14 requires that in order to be able to take advantage of the immunity, not only must the intermediary have received no actual notice of the existence of the unlawful information hosted on its servers, but further there must be no facts or circumstances from which the intermediary might reasonably be expected to have been aware of the material in question. The Directive requires that 'Upon obtaining knowledge or awareness [the intermediary must act] expeditiously to remove or disable access to the information'. This knowledge requirement is especially significant in the area of defamation, where unless the intermediary is aware of related facts other than the statement itself, there will often be no indication as to its defamatory nature. For instance, in *Godfrey v Demon*,[50] there was no reason, other than a misspelling of the claimant's name, to suspect that a racist posting attributed to the claimant was in fact made by someone else, and therefore apparently defamatory.

Article 15 of the Directive clarifies that, in relation to the intermediary services referred to by the preceding three articles, EU Member States are not to impose upon intermediaries any general obligation to monitor the information which passes through or is stored on their servers. The article does make clear that this prohibition

---

[50] [1999] EMLR 542.

does not encompass the imposition of a duty of care in relation to the material that is made available. It is also explicitly provided that a national government may put in place a legal duty to inform the relevant authorities when either notice of unlawful material is received or such content itself is discovered on servers. In such circumstances, the intermediary would be expected promptly to disable access to or delete (subject to any legal requirements on retention of evidence) the unlawful material. The Directive also leaves to Member States' discretion any introduction of an obligation to hand over details identifying individual subscribers to their services who have been implicated in dealing with unlawful content. Potential for conflict exists between the Article 15 limitation and the discretion granted to national courts under Article 14(3):

> The limitations of the liability of intermediary service providers established in this directive do not affect the possibility of injunctions of different kinds; such injunctions can in particular consist of orders by courts or administrative authorities requiring the termination or prevention of any infringement, including the removal of illegal information or the disabling of access to it.

In the German case of *Rolex v Ebay/Ricardo (Internet Auction I)*,[51] the Federal Court of Justice was asked by the claimant to find eBay liable for the sale by a subscriber of counterfeit Rolex-branded wristwatches, in breach of the claimant's registered trade mark. Further, the claimant also wished to oblige eBay to prevent future such abuse of its mark. The court ruled that under the German domestic equivalent of Article 14, eBay could not be held liable in respect of the auctions for counterfeit goods as it was entitled to rely upon the notice-based, qualified immunity provided. But eBay was not to be excused liability completely. Article 14(3) rendered this further question a matter for domestic German law. Under article 1004 of the German Civil Code, the rightholder retains a right of permanent injunctive relief against any person who has caused the property to be interfered with, insofar as the burden thus imposed is reasonable. In this case, the court held, not only must eBay take down the specific auctions complained of, but also monitor and remove any and all future auctions for infringing goods providing that it was economically reasonable for them so to do. On the facts it was found reasonable to expect eBay to police its auctions for counterfeit Rolexes via, for example, installing software which would detect such auctions.[52]

By contrast, in *L'Oreal v eBay*,[53] Arnold J was minded to find that, under European and English law, 'eBay ... are under no legal duty or obligation to prevent

---

[51] BGH 11.03.2004, I ZR 304/01, JurPC Web-Dok.

[52] In the light of the decision of the European Court in Case C-324/09, *L'Oreal v eBay* (see discussion below), such an injunction will still be permissible providing that it is fair, proportionate, not excessively costly and in compliance with the Ecommerce Directive Article 15 bar on requiring a service provider to undertake general monitoring of the data on its systems.

[53] [2009] EWHC 1094 (Ch) .

infringement of third parties' registered trade marks'.[54] He further considered that eBay should not be liable to prevent future infringements simply on the basis that such infringement had previously happened and might happen again.[55]

In substantially similar circumstances, a French court simply declined to recognize eBay as being entitled to the protection of Article 14, ruling that eBay's level of interaction with its users, services provided such as dispute resolution, and so on rendered its activities far beyond mere passive hosting.[56]

It would appear that this French approach is likely to become the standard across the EU. The *L'Oreal* case was referred to the European Court of Justice by the English courts for clarification of the law on a number of points, including the matter of 'whether the service provided by the operator of an online marketplace is covered by Article 14(1) of Directive 2000/31'.[57] In the judgement of the Grand Chamber:

> . . . the fact that the service provided by the operator of an online marketplace includes the storage of information transmitted to it by its customer-sellers is not in itself a sufficient ground for concluding that that service falls, in all situations, within the scope of Article 14(1) . . . In that regard, the Court has already stated that, in order for an internet service provider to fall within the scope of Article 14 of Directive 2000/31, it is essential that the provider be an intermediary provider within the meaning intended by the legislature in the context of Section 4 of Chapter II of that directive . . . That is not the case where the service provider, instead of confining itself to providing that service neutrally by a merely technical and automatic processing of the data provided by its customers, plays an active role of such a kind as to give it knowledge of, or control over, those data . . . It is clear . . . that eBay processes the data entered by its customer-sellers. The sales in which the offers may result take place in accordance with terms set by eBay. In some cases, eBay also provides assistance intended to optimise or promote certain offers for sale. As the United Kingdom Government has rightly observed, the mere fact that the operator of an online marketplace stores offers for sale on its server, sets the terms of its service, is remunerated for that service and provides general information to its customers cannot have the effect of denying it the exemptions from liability provided for by Directive 2000/31. . . . Where, by contrast, the operator has provided assistance which entails, in particular, optimising the presentation of the offers for sale in question or promoting those offers, it must be considered not to have taken a neutral position between the customer-seller concerned and potential buyers but to have played an active role of such a kind as to give it knowledge of, or control over, the data relating to those offers for sale. It cannot then rely, in the case of those data, on the exemption from liability referred to in Article 14(1) of Directive 2000/31.[58]

---

[54] [2009] EWHC 1094 (Ch) at 375.

[55] Ibid 381.

[56] *SA Louis Vuitton Malletier v eBay, Inc*, Tribunal de Commerce de Paris, Première Chamber B (Paris Commercial Court), Case No 200677799 (30 June 2008).

[57] Case C-324/09, *L'Oreal v eBay*, para 106.

[58] Ibid, paras 111–116.

The question of whether eBay's use of the relevant data amounted to an active role sufficient to deprive it of the protection of Article 14(1) was referred back to the UK courts to make a decision on the facts of the case. Should the referring court decide that eBay's role was sufficiently passive as to fall within the remit of Article 14(1), a further decision will have to be made by the same court as to whether eBay had sufficient awareness of the unlawful activity of some sellers for liability to arise.

In other, recent cases Spanish data protection regulators have demanded that Google actively remove from its systems links to articles (hosted elsewhere) which apparently breach the privacy of identifiable individuals.[59] Google has also been ordered by courts in both France and Italy to edit the auto-complete facility of its search engine after finding that terms such as 'conman' and 'fraud',[60] or 'rapist' and 'Satanist',[61] being associated with named individuals amounted to libel. In both the judgments, Google's argument that these terms were automatic and predicted by algorithms based on previous user search terms rather than Google itself were dismissed as irrelevant.

In the UK, the Department of Trade and Industry (DTI) first launched a public consultation on the Directive during August 2001. The responses to this consultation included criticisms of several elements of the Directive which were perceived as lacking in clarity. Certain technical issues were raised here, including the delineation made by the Directive between caching and hosting, which as noted above varies from that commonly understood by those involved in the computer industry. The internet industry was also critical of the Directive's effective imposition upon the intermediary of the burden of deciding pursuant to a complaint or upon discovery of something questionable whether material is actually unlawful and should be removed. Concerns were raised that rather than risk making an incorrect decision and suffering the legal consequences, the average intermediary would be more likely simply to treat anything over which there was any doubt as if unlawful, and delete it. According to those who put this scenario as the likely consequences of enacting the Directive, this would be likely to lead to a chill on freedom of expression— already a perceived threat in some quarters in the wake of the *Godfrey v Demon*[62] decision on intermediary liability for a defamation uploaded by a third party. A proposed solution to this potential problem commonly suggested by respondents to the consultation was the introduction of an industry code of practice, perhaps with

---

[59] 'Google to fight Spanish privacy battle', Guardian Online, 16 January 2011 <http://www.guardian. co.uk/technology/2011/jan/16/google-court-spain-privacy> (accessed 8 August 2011).

[60] 'Google Autocomplete is libellous, rules Italian Court', *TG Daily* <http://www.tgdaily.com/ business-and-law-features/55210-google-autocomplete-is-libelous-rules-italian-court> (accessed 8 August 2011).

[61] 'Google guilty of libel for satanist rape suggestions', RFI English <http://www.english.rfi.fr/ france/20100926-google-guilty-libel-satanist-rape-suggestions> (accessed 8 August 2011); 'French Court orders Google Inc to pay libel damages: report', Reuters <http://www.reuters.com/article/2010/09/25/ us-france-google-idUSTRE68O14020100925> (accessed 8 August 2011).

[62] [1999] EMLR 542; see discussion below at section 5.2.2.2 'Defamation'.

statutory backing. Such a code would set out clear notice and take down procedures for internet intermediaries to follow—were it to be followed in good faith, the intermediary should be excused liability in respect of any material taken down unfairly, or not taken down when it should have been. The Directive certainly envisaged the use of codes of practice, although they are not a requirement and no suggestion is made which would indicate that the drafters of the Directive necessarily envisaged the use of codes rooted in statute as opposed to voluntary regulation at an industry level.[63] A significant issue also raised was the lack in the Directive of any definition as to exactly what constitutes actual knowledge. This is a less important issue in relation to hosting (where constructive knowledge is sufficient, and anything falling just shy of a set requirement for actual knowledge is likely then still to be enough for liability to arise), but crucial in relation to liability for caching unlawful content, where only actual knowledge can defeat the intermediary's immunity from liability. Again, various suggestions were made as to how this might be addressed, mainly focusing again upon codes of practice upon which those intermediaries who followed them in good faith would be permitted to rely in court.[64]

A second consultation document was issued by the DTI in early 2002. Accompanying this paper was a draft of the proposed Electronic Commerce (EC Directive) Regulations. Further criticisms were made of the draft regulations, but nevertheless they were passed unaltered.[65] Regulations 17, 18, and 19 are lifted almost verbatim from, respectively, the Directive Articles 12, 13, and 14. A notable variation is that the Regulations make clear that the qualified immunity regime laid out for online intermediaries applies in respect of third party material which is unlawful at both civil and criminal law. Another important addition is that regulation 22 offers a degree of guidance as to what may constitute the 'actual knowledge' referred to in regulations 18 and 19. This guidance amounts to a non-exhaustive list of factors which a court may consider when deciding whether an intermediary has received, via any means of contact that it has made available in compliance with regulation 6(1)(c), actual notice of unlawful third party material present on its servers. Regulation 6(1) makes it obligatory for intermediaries to provide certain information to the end user 'in a form . . . which is easily, directly and permanently accessible'. Regulation 6(1)(c) refers to contact details which facilitate rapid and direct communication with the intermediary, such as email addresses, telephone numbers, and other contact details. This obligation is easily fulfilled by placing such contact details in a prominent place on an organization's homepage, or now more commonly linked to via an obvious 'contact us' hot link which is available on all pages and leads directly to a page of contact details. A dedicated (and frequently

---

[63] See in particular Art 16; see also Arts 1(2), 8(2)–(3), 10(2), and recitals 32 and 49.

[64] A summary of these responses to the DTI consultation may be found at *Consultation on Implementation of the Directive on Electronic Commerce (2000/31/EC): Summary of Responses* <http://www.dti.gov.uk> (accessed 8 March 2011).

[65] SI 2013/2002.

checked) email address for complaints of any sort is the most usual (and probably most useful) option here. Regulation 22 also lists several other factors which a court may consider:

the extent to which any notice includes—

(i) the full name and address of the sender of the notice;

(ii) details of the location of the information in question; and

(iii) details of the unlawful nature of the activity or information in question.

Although regulation 22 offers some clarification of 'actual notice', many intermediaries remain sceptical, arguing that the position is still too uncertain in the absence of a clear court decision on the issue—and following the heavy losses suffered by the defendant ISP in *Godfrey v Demon*,[66] no intermediary wishes to find itself involved in a test case. It also remains of concern to many that there is no clear delineation of the time frame in which action is expected to be taken following receipt of notice. The Regulations repeat the Directive's requirement that intermediaries act 'expeditiously', but this is not expanded upon any further. It seems likely that action being taken within a 24-hour period would be considered reasonable, but what about weekends or public holidays when the intermediary's offices are not open? Is 24 *working* hours sufficient? Or must there always be someone on duty over weekends, bank holidays, Christmas Day . . . and so on? Industry codes of practice might provide some level of clarity here too; in the absence of a clear standard of practice which intermediaries are entitled to rely upon in court if followed in good faith, intermediaries are likely to stick with an approach which entails removal of any and all material about which complaint is received,[67] within as short a time frame as possible. Some indication of what might be a reasonable time limit for deliberation by an intermediary has been given by Parliament in respect of only very limited circumstances. For instance, where terrorist content is concerned, section 3(2)(b) of the Terrorism Act 2006 refers to 'two working days'. The Defamation Bill 2010, a private member's bill introduced to the Lords by Liberal Democrat peer Lord Lester, would have allowed a very generous 14 days[68] within the context of a statutory 'notice and take down' approach. The government-sponsored draft Defamation Bill attached to a public consultation, ongoing at time of writing, does not include any such provision. It is anticipated that if something along these lines is included in the final Act (currently projected to be delivered for Royal Assent by 2013 at the earliest), it is rather more likely to tend towards a shorter grace period as required in respect of terrorist-related information. Where the

---

[66] [1999] EMLR 542; see discussion below.

[67] Unless the complaint is very obviously vexatious or otherwise has no merit, eg a television company which owns the rights to a successful comedy programme automatically issuing a notice of copyright infringement against a bulletin board which turns out merely to contain discussions about the programme, rather than infringing copy such as scripts, pictures, or video clips.

[68] Cl 9(4)(a).

standard of liability for third party material applies equally to all forms of unlawful material, there is a compelling argument for a common legal standard of what constitutes 'acting expeditiously', as opposed to piecemeal identification of different time limits for differing content.

In March 2006, the first UK court judgment referring to the Electronic Commerce Regulations was given by Eady J in *Bunt v Tilley and Others*.[69] The claimant, Bunt, was suing six different parties for defamation of him and his business. Bunt claimed that he had notified the defendants via email of some defamatory allegations, before later bringing an action in respect of both those and further allegations made by the same persons. Three of the six defendants in this case were companies who offered internet services—AOL, Tiscali, and BT. These ISP defendants applied to have the case against them struck out, and the application was heard by Eady J in the Queen's Bench Division. Significantly, Bunt's action was not brought in respect of anything which these defendants were alleged to be hosting. Instead, Bunt claimed that they should face liability for publication of the defamations on the basis that they could be accessed 'via the services provided by the ISPs'.[70] Eady J stated that the question to be considered by the court was whether the ISPs could be liable for material 'which is simply communicated via the services which they provide'.[71] Although deciding that on the basis of defamation law there was no case for the ISPs to answer,[72] Eady J did consider *obiter* the application of the immunities provided in regulations 17 and 18 of the Electronic Commerce Regulations. Unfortunately, this provides only a straightforward retelling of the Regulations as set out with no real development or clarification of concepts such as 'actual notice'.[73] On the facts it was decided that the defendant ISPs had not received any information in Bunt's emails which should have caused them to believe that they were contributing to or causing the publication of the alleged defamatory statements.[74] The claimant put forward the contention that an ISP acts as a 'gatekeeper' to information; an internet access package offered to the end-user is not limited to mere provision of a communications conduit, rather the ISP by its very nature as an access provider can in a sense be argued to be in control of the information that the user is able to access online, and offers much more than mere connection to the internet. Eady J dismissed this line of reasoning, stating that there is no such concept within the legislation, and that the Regulations would apply to ISPs in the manner already mentioned.[75] Eady J also commented that while under the Regulations an intermediary can be issued with an injunction to block certain identified users, on the facts of this case, one of the

---

[69] [2006] EWHC 407.

[70] *Bunt v Tilley*, para 5.

[71] Ibid.

[72] Ibid paras 10–37—see especially paras 15, 22, 36–7; see discussion below.

[73] Ibid paras 70–2; of course, this part of the judgment being *obiter*, had Eady J done so it would not have formed a binding precedent, however it would still have been helpful to have some further guidance than has so far been available.

[74] Ibid para 72.

[75] Ibid paras 54–5.

defendants had already done so, and to issue such an injunction would in any case be disproportionate and would not deliver the aim sought as the blocked user could easily find the same service as provided elsewhere. It turned out that although this was not the basis of the claimant's case, some level of hosting appeared to have been undertaken by one of the ISPs; the availability of any defence here under regulation 19 would stand or fall on the issue of whether sufficient notification had been given by the claimant for the immunity to be defeated, there being on the facts no reasonable expectation of awareness on the part of the ISP concerned absent actual knowledge. The much-debated regulation 22 was mentioned in Eady J's judgment, but this was limited to a mere repetition of the list of factors given in the Regulation and the comment 'none of this information was included'.[76]

A significant omission in the provisions of both the Electronic Commerce Directive and the subsequent UK Regulations is that of linking. The liability position of an intermediary which hosts a hypertext link to a page stored elsewhere which contains unlawful material is unclear. It might be assumed in the absence of case law on the matter that the Article 14/regulation 19 immunity would apply such that an intermediary which hosts an obvious link that clearly points towards unlawful material is likely to face liability, but if the link is obscure and buried among hundreds of thousands of links on the intermediary's servers, no liability will arise.[77]

5.2.2.2 *Other laws regulating online intermediary liability*
Prior to the enactment of the Electronic Commerce (EC Directive) Regulations 2002, intermediary liability for third party provided content fell to be decided upon the basis of a range of laws relevant to specific types of unlawful material. These laws are still in force, and while in the absence of case law to state otherwise it is often assumed by commentators that the Regulations will simply supersede application of these older laws to determining online intermediary liability, it remains important to consider their potential implications in this context. The most significant issues here arise under copyright and defamation, on the civil side, and in criminal law obscenity and indecency.

Copyright It is a core rule of most copyright laws that there will be a copyright infringement when an individual copies a work held in electronic format without the authority of the copyright holder.[78] The obvious difficulty which this presents is that

---

[76] *Bunt v Tilley*, para 72.
[77] See also discussion of *Godfrey v Demon* 1999] EMLR 542 below.
[78] Berne Convention, Art 9(1):

> Authors of literary and artistic works . . . shall have the exclusive right of authorising reproduction of these works, in any manner or form.

UK Copyright, Designs and Patents Act 1988, s 16(1):

> The owner of the copyright in a work has . . . the exclusive right . . . (a) to copy the work . . .

17 USC § 106:

> the owner of copyright under this title has the exclusive rights . . . (1) to reproduce the copyrighted work . . .

the very nature of computer and online technology flies in the face of such regulation, relying as it does extensively, if not entirely, upon the ability to make copies of
information. An intermediary which is merely part of the communication chain,
providing only access to the internet, will at least be copying received information
packets into memory and sending fresh packets on to the next host in the chain. This
temporary hosting was still enough to constitute a technical breach of traditional
copyright whenever the material being copied was subject to copyright protection.
Similarly, infringements may occur in the course of other standard operations on an
intermediary's servers, such as caching, or automated back-up services.

In addition to primary copyright infringement, under UK law it was also potentially possible for an intermediary to be liable for secondary copyright infringement
if it was in possession of infringing copies in the course of a business. Secondary
copyright infringement is rooted in section 23 of the Copyright, Designs and Patents
Act 1988 ('CDPA 1988'), which provides that there will be an infringement where
the possession is in the course of a business, and the defendant knows or has reason
to believe that the material held is an infringing copy. Where an intermediary offers
hosting facilities, for example, such as personal website or blogging facilities, there
is a high chance that end-users will upload photographs of musicians or other celebrities copied from other websites, or MP3 files containing infringing copies of
popular songs. Most intermediaries clearly operate on a commercial basis, and will
thus fall within the definition of a business under the first leg of the section 23 test.[79]
However, the question of possession remains uncertain. If an intermediary is merely
routing information packets constituting infringing material, it is unclear whether the
transient possession will suffice for section 23 liability, or whether more long-term
possession is necessary. Certainly, even if possession could be proven, it would be
extremely difficult for the rightholder to prove that an intermediary had specific
knowledge about the copyright status of individual packets. An intermediary's liability arising from possession is therefore likely to be limited by practical constraints
to circumstances where it hosts resources, such as webpages and Usenet postings, or
where it provides caching services.

The question of knowledge is less certain. Copyright infringement has long been
endemic on the internet,[80] either because users are unaware of the restrictions
imposed by copyright, or because they are aware of the limited likelihood of their
being held to account for infringement. As a result, very many intermediaries, and
especially those which host third party websites, carry Usenet newsgroups, and
cache resources will inevitably have a certain number of infringing copies on its
servers. Yet the fact that there is a high likelihood of infringing copies, does not
mean that an ISP can be automatically held to have sufficient knowledge of any

---

[79] Copyright, Designs and Patents Act 1988, s 178.

[80] Indeed, on the more exotic Usenet hierarchies, such as alt.binaries.pictures.erotica.* and alt.binaries.
warez.* the scale of infringement is such that over 90 per cent of postings are likely to involve infringing
material.

particular infringement to give rise to liability under section 23. The cases under the legislation prior to the CDPA 1988[81] give strong support to the theory that actual knowledge of the infringement in question is required,[82] and that a general constructive knowledge that some copies may be infringing will not be sufficient.[83] This can make determining the liability of an intermediary, in circumstances where the rightholder claims that the intermediary was given notice of infringing material, difficult to determine. If the notice identifies specific infringing material, such as a .jpg or .gif picture file on a webpage, or a computer program on a 'warez' FTP site, the matter is easy to resolve, as the intermediary can either delete or block access to the resource, reducing the likelihood of the rightholder bringing legal action. If the intermediary were to refuse to delete or block access to the resource the rightholder would have no difficulty proving continued possession with actual knowledge. However, this circumstance is probably the exception rather than the rule, as with many infringements the rightholder may only be able to determine that the infringing material is being distributed via a particular newsgroup or third party website, and its notice can only indicate that if an intermediary carries that newsgroup or caches resources requested from the website, it will come into possession of infringing copies.[84] In those circumstances, it would seem that the UK courts would be unwilling to accept that a notice couched in such general terms would be sufficient to fix a person with knowledge such that any infringing copies which appeared on their systems would be capable of leading to liability.[85]

A number of the difficulties associated with the interface between traditional copyright law and online technology have been remedied within the European Union by the Copyright in the Information Society Directive.[86] This Directive, and within the UK the subsequent Copyright and Related Rights Regulations 2003,[87] provide for a range of exclusive rights to copyright holders in respect of the use of their material online. These include the 'reproduction right',[88] the 'right of communication to the public',[89] and the 'distribution right'.[90] Such exclusive rights could well place intermediaries in a difficult position. Furthering the general trend towards

---

[81] Copyright Act 1956, s 5—infringement by importation, sale etc of copies known to be infringing.

[82] *Hoover plc v George Hulme Ltd* [1982] FSR 565.

[83] *Columbia Picture Industries v Robinson* [1987] Ch 38.

[84] For an example of an even vaguer notice, consider the form letter sent by Lucasfilm to hundreds of ISPs regarding infringing materials from the film *Star Wars: Episode I—The Phantom Menace*, discussed in D Goodin, 'Star Wars rekindles Net debate', CNETNews.com, 2 May 1999, <http://news.cnet.com/Star-Wars-rekindles-Net-debate/2100-1023-3-225266.html (accessed 15 August 2011).

[85] *Hoover plc v George Hulme Ltd* [1982] FSR 565 (under the Copyright Act 1956).

[86] 2001/29/EC.

[87] SI 2003/2498.

[88] 'the exclusive right to authorise or prohibit direct or indirect, temporary or permanent reproduction by any means and in any form, in whole or in part . . .' (Art 2).

[89] 'the exclusive right to authorise or prohibit any communication to the public of their works in such a way that members of the public may access them from a place and at a time individually chosen by them . . .' (Art 3).

[90] 'the exclusive right to authorise or prohibit any form of distribution to the public by sale or otherwise . . .' (Art 4).

limiting liability for intermediaries, however, that same Directive also provides a range of exceptions and limitations, including:

Temporary acts of reproduction . . . which are transient or incidental, which are an integral and essential part of a technological process whose sole purpose is to enable . . . a transmission in a network between third parties by an intermediary . . . shall be exempted from the reproduction right . . .[91]

The general provisions limiting intermediary liability in respect of transmission, caching, and hosting of third party provided content found in the e-Commerce Directive (and the UK implementing legislation) will also apply equally to infringing copies as to other unlawful material. These provisions have been discussed in detail above.

The Digital Economy Act 2010 introduced, inter alia, protective measures for intellectual property on the internet, in particular by placing new obligations, designed to combat illegal peer-to-peer file-sharing, upon online intermediaries.[92] These duties include the obligation to notify a subscriber that a complaint of copyright infringement regarding their online activity has been received,[93] and to provide to copyright holders information linking specific infringements with identified subscribers.[94] Most controversially, this legislation also obliges intermediary service providers to assist copyright enforcement by facilitating the suspension of identified, persistent offenders from access to the internet for a set period.[95] Compliance with the Act is to be overseen by Ofcom,[96] and intermediaries who do not meet requirements are liable to be fined up to £250,000.[97] Notably, however, Ofcom announced that only larger fixed-line service providers, those with more than 400,000 subscribers, will face obligations under these provisions in the Digital Economy Act. This has, predictably, led to suggestions that smaller intermediaries, as well as mobile broadband providers, will become 'piracy havens'.[98]

---

[91] Art 5; for UK implementation see Copyright and Related Rights Regulations 2003, regs 8–23 (Permitted Acts).

[92] See Chapter 7, section 7.4.4.

[93] Digital Economy Act 2010, s 3, inserting new s 124A 'Obligation to notify subscribers of copyright infringement reports' into the Communications Act 2003.

[94] Digital Economy Act 2010, s 4, inserting new s 124B 'Obligation to provide copyright infringement lists to copyright owners' into the Communications Act 2003.

[95] Digital Economy Act 2010, ss 9 and 10, inserting, respectively, new ss 124G 'Obligations to limit internet access: assessment and preparation' and 124H 'Obligations to limit internet access' into the Communications Act 2003.

[96] Digital Economy Act 2010, ss 11 and 12, inserting, respectively, new ss 124I 'Code by OFCOM about obligations to limit internet access' and 124J 'Content of code about obligations to limit internet access' into the Communications Act 2003.

[97] Digital Economy Act 2010, s 14, inserting new s 124L 'Enforcement of obligations' into the Communications Act 2003.

[98] 'Ofcom creates piracy havens at small ISPs', The Register, 18 May 2010 <http://www.theregister.co.uk/2010/05/18/small_iss_dea/> (accessed 8 August 2011).

The Digital Economy Act was pushed through Parliament in a hurry during the final few days of activity in the House prior to the 2010 general election. Opponents from within the intermediary community, headed by BT and TalkTalk, sought judiciary review of the Act's passage on grounds that it received 'insufficient scrutiny before being rushed through into law', and that it is in key respects incompatible with the Electronic Commerce Directive, the e-Privacy Directive and Article 10 of the European Convention on Human Rights.[99] This challenge, broadly speaking, failed, Parker J finding the Act to be acceptable within the framework of European rights.[100] The one area in which the High Court upheld the service providers' challenge is, however, far from insignificant. The Authorisation Directive[101] requires that any administrative charges imposed upon a service provider shall:

cover only the administrative costs which will be incurred in the management, control and enforcement of the general authorisation scheme and of rights of use and of specific obligations . . . which may include costs for international cooperation, harmonisation and standardisation, market analysis, monitoring compliance and other market control, as well as regulatory work involving preparation and enforcement of secondary legislation and administrative decisions, such as decisions on access and interconnection.[102]

The draft Online Infringement of Copyright (Initial Obligations) (Sharing of Costs) Order 2011[103] included 'qualifying costs' which Parker J held amounted to administrative charges which service providers would be obliged to pay to Ofcom in order for the latter and the appeals body to operate the functions delegated to them by the Act. Such charges are clearly prohibited by the Authorisation Directive, and thus are unlawful. As the Order in its draft form envisages that the service provider would pay 25 per cent of the total cost of dealing with each copyright infringement report,[104] this is a positive gain for the service providers who otherwise would have been facing a significant bill each time one of their subscribers was investigated over a claimed infringement of copyright. The other obligations still stand, although developments elsewhere in Europe may call them into question.

Developments elsewhere seem to call into question the validity of the Act under European law. In the Belgian case of *Scarlet v SABAM*, the Société Belge des

---

[99] 'BT and TalkTalk in legal challenge to Digital Economy Act', BT Press Release, 8 July 2010 <http://www.btplc.com/news/Articles/ShowArticle.cfm?ArticleID=98284B3F-B538-4A54-A44F-6B496AF1F11F> (accessed 8 August 2011).

[100] *R (BT Telecommunications plc & Another) v Secretary of State for Business, Innovation and Skills* [2011] EWHC 1021 (Admin), available online at <http://www.bailii.org/ew/cases/EWHC/Admin/2011/1021.html> (accessed 8 August 2011).

[101] Directive 2002/02/EC.

[102] Ibid Art 12(a).

[103] Available at <http://www.culture.gov.uk/images/publications/10-1199-Draft-SI-online-infringement-of-costs-order.pdf> (accessed 15 August 2011).

[104] See Draft Online Infringement of Copyright (Initial Obligations) (Sharing of Costs) Order 2011, cl 1(6)(b).

auteurs, compositeurs et éditeurs (SABAM), a royalty-collection body representing copyright holders, persuaded a court to issue an injunction against the defendant ISP ordering it to monitor its servers for any sign of unlawful file-sharing which infringed the rights of SABAM members, to identify the culprits, and to filter out and block these activities. This injunction was perpetual, and all costs of compliance with its terms fell to be borne by the service provider. Unsurprisingly, the service provider appealed against the order. The Brussels Court of Appeal referred the matter to the European Court of Justice, specifically on the question of whether such an injunction could be issued compliant with Article 8(3) of the Copyright in the Information Society Directive[105] and Article 11 of the Intellectual Property Enforcement Directive,[106] both of which require Member States to make provision for injunctive relief to protect copyright holders from online infringement. Under the Directives, such injunctions may be granted not only against the infringing parties, but also their service providers. In turn, these provisions must be enacted in a manner compliant with both the Article 8 (privacy) and Article 10 (freedom of expression) rights as set out in the European Convention on Human Rights.

The opinion of Advocate General Cruz Villalón on this matter, as provided to the European Court,[107] notes that the injunction in question is an extraordinary measure, and one which is rather arbitrary when considering both how difficult it is for a service provider to foresee whether its activities will achieve compliance and the serious cost to the service provider of attempting to comply. While the service provider has been ordered to completely block the unlawful activity, the Advocate General notes that this is not something which has been achieved before. It would indeed be a significant technological step were a service provider to manage to block an identified category of material with a 100 per cent success rate. Further, the Advocate General has identified significant problems in terms of human rights compliance in that there is no guarantee given that the terms of the injunction will respect the privacy of individual subscribers, nor has any right of appeal been provided for a subscriber who unexpectedly finds his or her internet service terminated.

---

[105] Directive 2001/39/EC. Art 8(3) states: 'Member States shall ensure that rightholders are in a position to apply for an injunction against intermediaries whose services are used by a third party to infringe a copyright or related right.'

[106] Directive 2004/48. Art 11 states:

> Member States shall ensure that, where a judicial decision is taken finding an infringement of an intellectual property right, the judicial authorities may issue against the infringer an injunction aimed at prohibiting the continuation of the infringement. Where provided for by national law, non-compliance with an injunction shall, where appropriate, be subject to a recurring penalty payment, with a view to ensuring compliance. Member States shall also ensure that rightholders are in a position to apply for an injunction against intermediaries whose services are used by a third party to infringe an intellectual property right, without prejudice to Article 8(3) of Directive 2001/29/EC.

[107] Available at <http://curia.europa.eu/jurisp/cgi-bin/form.pl?lang=EN&Submit=rechercher&numaff =C-70/10> (accessed 8 August 2011).

In the judgement of the European Court in *L'Oreal v eBay*,[108] the court specifically addressed the issue of how Article 11 of the Intellectual Property Enforcement Directive should be applied in relation to the operator of an online marketplace. In a ruling broadly in agreement with the Advocate General's opinion, the court gave consideration to the specific wording of Article 11. In particular, attention was drawn to the third sentence of this provision, which requires Member States to ensure:

that rightsholders are in a position to apply for an injunction against intermediaries whose services are used by a third party to infringe an intellectual property right . . .

The court drew a distinction between the use of the word 'injunction' in this context, and in that of the opening sentence of Article 11, which refers to an 'injunction aimed at prohibiting the continuation of the infringement'.

The court found these usages of the word 'injunction' to have separate and distinctly different meanings, ruling that while logic dictates that an injunction against the actual infringer of intellectual property rights includes a bar on continued infringement, the position of a service provider is somewhat different. Nonetheless, it was also held that 'if justified by the circumstances', the Directive permits national laws to oblige service providers to act to prevent further infringements.[109] In the absence of any such statutory provision, national courts must interpret and apply Article 11 in line with the judgement of the European Court.[110] While such injunctions against future infringement may be legitimate, the court explicitly noted that they must comply with, inter alia, Article 15(1) of the e-Commerce Directive, which would invalidate any injunction which would require a service provider to actively monitor all information on its system in order to prevent future injunctions. Such an order would also be incompatible with Article 3 of the Intellectual Property Enforcement Directive, which requires that injunctive relief for infringement of intellectual property must be proportionate, fair, and compliance should not require unreasonable expense to the service provider. Article 3 further requires that in regards to such injunctions, national courts must 'avoid the creation of barriers to legitimate trade'. The court noted that this should apply to an online marketplace such that no injunction against the operator of such a business venture can be obliged to prevent the use of a trademark in such a way as would prohibit the sale via its systems of goods carrying that mark. Subject to these limitations, the court approved the opinion of the Advocate-General that it would be legitimate for an injunction issued against the operator of an online marketplace to both withdraw service from an individual user responsible for an infringement of intellectual property and to make all users more readily identifiable.[111]

---

[108] Case C-324/09, 12 July 2011.
[109] *L'Oreal v eBay*, para 134.
[110] Ibid para 137.
[111] Ibid paras 139–142.

It seems reasonable to consider that this decision will require some degree of a rethink in Westminster as to the Digital Economy Act. The key problem with this legislation from a human rights perspective, one which was particularly raised by the Joint Committee on Human Rights, is that the degree of detail which has been left to secondary legislation makes it 'impossible [to] assess fully whether [the Act] will operate in a compatible manner in practice'.[112] Jeremy Hunt, the Culture Secretary of the coalition government returned by the general election of May 2010, in February 2011 ordered Ofcom to review the Act, accepting that 'it is not clear whether the site blocking provisions in the Act could work in practice'. The government also initiated a dialogue with the service provider community in order to explore whether it might be possible to bypass the Act with a system of voluntary blocking by service providers. It remains to be seen how the situation will be resolved.

In the USA, a similar evolution of copyright law has taken place. The first US decision in which the issue of intermediary liability for infringing copies provided by a third party was discussed concerned the uploading to an online bulletin board of images the copyright in which was owned by Playboy, the most globally famous brand associated with the publication of photographs of young women in the nude. The court in *Playboy Enterprises v Frena*[113] ruled that the operator of the BBS, which encouraged users to use the board to upload and download images in which Playboy owned copyright, had infringed Playboy's copyright by the direct copying the system undertook when storing and transmitting images. The problem with this particular interpretation of what precisely is taking place when information is being uploaded or downloaded from internet hosts is that although, as a matter of technical fact, the host is copying or reproducing the work, via its software, the commands that are being sent to that software instructing it to make the copies are in fact given by a third party. In other words, a third party is operating the host's computer system remotely. Thus, when instructions to make an infringing copy of information are sent to an internet host by a third party, the owner of the host will very likely have neither knowledge of the infringement relating to that information, nor any intent to infringe that information.[114]

This lack of knowledge, or lack of intent, was often emphasized by the interme-diaries in the early case law. However, they were soon to discover that it did not necessarily mean that they would escape liability for the infringement. The judiciar-ies in the UK and the USA, for example, have long tended towards a position that lack of intention to infringe is not a defence in copyright actions. In some of the

---

[112] House of Lords, House of Commons Joint Committee on Human Rights, *Legislative Scrutiny: Digital Economy Bill Fifth Report of Session* 2009–2010, para 1.39.
[113] 839 F Supp 1552 (MD Fla, 1993).
[114] See *Marobie-FL Inc d/b/a Galactic Software v National Association of Fire Equipment Distributors and Northwest Nexus Inc*, 983 F Supp 1167 (ND Ill, 13 November 1997) (defendant not guilty of direct infringement because it did not initiate the copying of claimants work, its systems were merely used to create a copy by a third party).

intermediary cases, it appears that that rigid position may have shifted slightly, with the courts recognizing that there might be a minimal mental element in copyright infringement—the intention to make a copy. This position was exemplified by the case of *Religious Technology Centre v Netcom On-Line Communications Services Inc*.[115] Here, an infringement action was brought by representatives of the Church of Scientology (CoS) against Netcom, an ISP, which hosted a newsgroup—alt.religion.scientology—to which a customer had posted verbatim extracts of material in which the CoS claimed copyright. The judge expressly rejected the allegation that the ISP had infringed directly and refused to follow *Playboy Enterprises v Frena*, on the ground that Netcom could only be guilty of direct infringement if it had caused the infringing copies to be made:

the mere fact that Netcom's system incidentally makes temporary copies of plaintiffs works does not mean Netcom has caused the copying.[116]

In *Playboy Enterprises, Inc v Webbworld*,[117] however, the judge noted the principle raised in the *Netcom* case that an ISP or Internet Intermediary might not have any control over the information to which it gave access, but concluded that:

Even the absence of the ability to exercise such control, however, is no defense to liability. If a business cannot be operated within the bounds of the Copyright Act, then perhaps the question of its legitimate existence needs to be addressed.

Whilst this might perhaps be true of the website that the defendants in *Webbworld* ran, as it provided subscription access to images obtained from adult newsgroups, which are notorious for egregious copyright infringements,[118] it was a harsh approach to the copyright liability position of the average intermediary. However, even if the trend in these early US cases tended to suggest that intermediaries should escape direct liability, it was clear that they might still be held to be contributory or vicarious infringers where they are vicariously liable for the users' acts or have authorized or contributed to the copying.[119]

---

[115] 907 F Supp 1361 (ND Cal, 1995).

[116] *Religious Technology Centre v Netcom On-Line Communications Services Inc*, 907 F Supp 1361 (ND Cal, 1995) at 1368. See further on contributory infringement, EA Burcher and AM Hughes, Casenote, '*Religious Tech Ctr v Netcom On-Line Communications, Inc*: Internet Service Providers: The Knowledge Standard for Contributory Copyright Infringement and The Fair Use Defense' (1997) 3 Rich JL Tech 5 <http://www.jolt.richmond.edu/jolt/v3il/burhugh.html>.

[117] 968 F Supp 1171 (ND Tex, 1997).

[118] See also *Playboy Enterprises, Inc v Russ Hardenburgh, and Others* 982 F Supp 503 (ND Ohio, 25 November 1997) (a bulletin board service operator was held liable for infringement of the copyright in Playboy's images, on the basis of his executive position, and his authority to control the BBS's content—there was no evidence that he personally approved the uploading of the images. He was also liable for contributory infringement as he had at least constructive knowledge that infringing activity was likely to be occurring on the BBS).

[119] See *Sega Enterprises Ltd v Sabella*, 1996 WL 780560 (ND Cal 1996); *Sega Enterprises Ltd v MAPHIA*, 948 F Supp 923 (ND Cal 1996) (BBS operators knew their boards were being used to copy Sega's games and actively participated in that use by soliciting users to upload games and selling copiers

Vicarious liability is predicated upon a pre-existing relationship between the defendant and the direct infringer, and not on the defendant's involvement in the infringing activity—the link essentially being that the defendant potentially benefits from the infringer's activities.[120] If someone has the 'right and ability' to supervise the infringing action of another, and that right and ability 'coalesce with an obvious and direct financial interest in the exploitation of copyrighted materials—even in the absence of actual knowledge' that the infringement is taking place—the 'supervisor' may be held vicariously liable for the infringement. Vicarious liability is based on a connection to the direct infringer (not necessarily to the infringing activity).[121] Yet in the case of online intermediaries, it is unlikely that a court will find sufficient relationship between a user and a transmission host to ground such liability.[122] Equally, even though a defendant may appear to authorize infringement by providing the necessary facilities for copying knowing that some users of that service will use it to make infringing copies,[123] this will probably not be sufficient to persuade a court that authorization is intended, in circumstances where the equipment might also be used for non-infringing purposes and where the provider cannot control the use made by the copier.[124]

The US doctrine of contributory infringement is based on 'the basic common law doctrine that one who knowingly participates or furthers a tortious act is jointly and severally liable with the prime tortfeasor . . .'[125] and thus the defendant must

---

to assist in the making of copies). Also *Marobie-FL Inc*, n 114 (defendant not vicariously liable for copyright infringement unless it has the right and ability to supervise the infringing activity and also has a direct financial interest in such activities). See further K Tickle, 'The Vicarious Liability of Electronic Bulletin Board Operators for the Copyright Infringement Occurring on Their Bulletin Boards' (1995) 80 Iowa Law Review 391.

[120] The most common example would be that of employer and employee, but any relationship in which the defendant expects to benefit from the infringer's acts might give rise to vicarious liability, thus, eg, vicarious liability could arise from an independent contract or via a licence, eg, *PRS v Bradford Corp* [1917–23] Mac CC 309; *Australasian PRA v Miles* [1962] NSWR 405 (liability of an organizer of an entertainment for infringement of performance rights by musicians); *Shapiro, Bernstein & Co v HL Green Co*, 316 F2d 304, 307 (2d Cir, 1963) (a company leasing floor space to a record department was liable for the record department's sales of 'bootleg' records despite absence of actual knowledge of infringement, because of company's beneficial relationship to the sales). See also the 'dance hall cases', *Dreamland Ball Room, Inc v Shapiro, Bernstein & Co*, 36 F2d 354 (7th Cir, 1929); *Famous Music Corp v Bay State Harness Horse Racing & Breeding Ass'n, Inc*, 554 F2d 1213 (1st Cir, 1977); *KECA Music, Inc v Dingus McGee's Co*, 432 F Supp 72 (WD Mo, 1977).

[121] Information Infrastructure Task Force, Working Group on Intellectual Property Rights, 'Intellectual Property and the National Information Infrastructure: The Report of the Working Group on Intellectual Property Rights', Bruce A Lehman (Chair) (ISBN 0-9648716-0-1).

[122] *Cubby Inc v CompuServe Inc*, 776 F Supp 135 (SDNY, 1991).

[123] *Moorhouse v University of NSW* [1976] RPC 157.

[124] *CBS Songs UK Ltd v Amstrad* [1988] RPC 567; *Sony Corp of America v Universal Studios, Inc*, 464 US 417 (1984). See, however, the contrary argument voiced in F Macmillan et al, 'Copyright Liability of Communications Carriers' (1997) 3 Journal of Information, Law and Technology (JILT) <http://www2.warwick.ac.uk/fac/soc/law/elj/jilt/1997_3/macmillan/> (accessed 15 August 2011).

[125] *Screen Gems-Columbia Music, Inc v Mark Pi Records Inc*, 256 F Supp 399 (SDNY, 1966), cited in KA Walton, 'Is a Website like a Flea Market Stall? How *Fonovisa v Cherry Auction* Increases the Risk

(a) have knowledge of the infringement, and (b) have induced, caused, or materially contributed to the third party's infringing conduct.[126] This was a key point raised by the court in the *Netcom* case. Here it was held that if Netcom had knowledge that infringing material was passing through its servers and failed to take action to prevent the dissemination of that material, it might be liable as a contributory infringer. The deciding factor would be the host's actual knowledge of the infringement:

[If the host] cannot reasonably verify a claim of infringement, either because of a possible fair use defense, the lack of copyright notices on the copies, or the copyright holder's failure to provide the necessary documentation to show that there is a likely infringement, the opera-tor's lack of knowledge will be found reasonable and there will be no liability for contributory infringement for allowing the continued distribution of the works on its system.[127]

The uncertain state of affairs that was developing out of the case law in the USA led intermediaries to hope that the Working Group on Intellectual Property Rights, set up in 1994 as part of the Department of Commerce's Information Infrastructure Task Force, would support their assertion that online service providers should not be held liable for copyright infringement, since they had no way of policing what was transmitted on their networks. The intermediaries argued that:

(a) The volume of material on any ISP's system was too great to monitor or screen.

(b) Even if an ISP was willing and able to monitor the material on its system, it would not be able reliably to identify infringing material.

(c) Failure to shield ISPs would impair communication and availability of information.

(d) Exposure to liability for infringement would drive ISPs out of business, causing the Net to fail.

(e) The law should impose liability only on those ISPs who assumed responsibility for the online activities of their subscribers.

However, when that Working Group reported in 1995,[128] intermediaries were dismayed to discover that the concerns of a more powerful lobby group, that of the copyright owners, had prevailed. The Working Group decided that it would be

---

of Third-Party Copyright Infringement liability for Online Service Providers' (1997) 19 Hastings Comm Ent LJ 921 at 926.

[126] *Gershwin Publishing Corp v Columbia Artists Management, Inc*, 443 F2d 1159, 1162 (2d Cir, 1971); *Sega Enterprises Inc v MAPHIA*, 857 F Supp 679 (ND Cal, 1994).

[127] *Religious Technology Centre v Netcom On-Line Communications Services Inc*, 907 F Supp 1361, 1374 (ND Cal, 1995). For a detailed analysis of the potential liability of intermediaries as contributory infringers, see Burcher and Hughes, n 116.

[128] Information Infrastructure Task Force, n 121.

undesirable to reduce the copyright liability of intermediaries as this might prematurely halt the development of marketplace tools that could be used to lessen their risk of liability and the risk to copyright owners, although they suggested that circumstances under which service providers should have reduced liability might be identified in the future. The Working Group noted that:

(a) Millions of files travel through a network in a given day, but believed that other industries were faced with similar situations and coped without reduced liability.[129]

(b) Online service providers could take appropriate action when notified of the existence of infringing material on their systems and therefore limit their liability for damages to those for innocent infringement.

(c) Online service providers were in the best position to know the identity and activities of their subscribers and to stop unlawful activities.

(d) Other businesses with similar risk factors had been able to take appropriate precautions to minimize their risk of liability through indemnification agreements and insurance.

In the event, the legislative response to the recommendations of the Working Group on Intellectual Property Rights and their proposed amendments to the Copyright Act was muted,[130] not least because of the protests that some of the other proposed measures provoked.[131] It was not until the passage of the Digital Millennium Copyright Act of 1998 ('DMCA 1998') that the issue of ISP liability for copying was addressed by the US legislature to the satisfaction of US ISPs. The DMCA 1998 introduced a new section 512 into the US Copyright Act, providing a series of qualified immunities for internet intermediaries in respect of infringing copies provided by third parties. These immunities, for providers of 'transitory digital network communications', caching and hosting services, although much narrower in terms of the unlawful information to which they apply, mirror those in the Electronic Commerce Directive and Regulations sufficiently as not to require further repetition here. An important distinction, between the US and European approaches is the so-called 'reposting provision' contained in section 512(g) of the DMCA 1998. Under this subsection, an intermediary will face 'no liability for taking down generally' towards any aggrieved party where material has been removed in good faith

---

[129] eg, the position of photo processing laboratories.

[130] Although the NII Copyright Protection Act of 1995 was considered by the both the Senate and House of Representatives in the 104th Congress, it was not passed by either House and was not reintroduced in the 105th Congress. See for criticism of the Act, WM Melone, 'Contributory Liability for Access Providers: Solving the Conundrum Digitalization Has Placed on Copyright Laws' (1997) 49(2) Federal Communications LJ 491.

[131] For a brief overview of other criticisms, see P Samuelson, *The Copyright Grab*, Wired 4.01, January 1996.

pursuant to a notice of infringement. An exception to this general rule applies in respect of:

material residing at the direction of a subscriber of the service provider on a system or network controlled or operated by or for the service provider that is removed, or to which access is disabled by the service provider, pursuant to a notice.

In order to take advantage of the immunity in respect of such third party provided material, the intermediary must take reasonable steps to ensure that the subscriber is promptly notified that the material has been removed and comply fully with the steps laid out in section 512(g). Effectively, this subsection provides a right of appeal for the subscriber whose material has been taken down pursuant to a complaint that it infringes copyright. If the subscriber, once notified, follows the correct procedure, the material can be reinstated by the intermediary who is then able to sidestep any further involvement in the dispute. The subscriber, in making the application for reposting, agrees to meet the full cost of any action taken by another party for breach of copyright where it is found that the subscriber has indeed infringed that right. Such an approach would be an attractive addition to the Electronic Commerce Regulations in the eyes of those who fear that intermediaries will increasingly remove material at any complaint rather than risk liability, potentially removing much which is not unlawful in the process. It is possible that some variation of this approach respecting 'freedom of expression' in a broad sense could certainly be adopted in relation to defamation, although inevitably where obscene materials or indecent images involving children are involved, a more cautious response would seem appropriate.

Defamation[132] Under English law, liability for defamation arises with the publication of a statement which is:

(a) likely to damage the reputation of the claimant by exposing him to hatred, contempt, or ridicule;[133] or

(b) likely to cause the claimant to be shunned or avoided by others;[134] or

(c) likely to lower the claimant's standing 'in the estimation of right thinking members of society generally . . .'[135]

If an action in defamation is to succeed, publication of the defamatory statement is an essential element. 'The material part of the cause of an action in libel is not the writing, but the publication of the libel.'[136] Publication for defamation purposes

---

[132] For a detailed discussion of English libel law, see D Goldberg, G Sutter, and I Walden, *Media Law and Practice* (Oxford: Oxford University Press, 2009) ch 10.
[133] *Parmiter v Coupland* (1840) 6 M&W 105.
[134] *Youssoupoff v MGM Studios* (1934) 50 TLR 581.
[135] *Sim v Stretch* [1936] 2 All ER 1237.
[136] *Hebditch v MacIlwaine* [1894] 2 QB 58 at 61 per Lord Esher MR.

entails communication of the statement in question to a third party, with no minimum circulation requirement.[137] Communicating the defamatory statement only to
the subject will not constitute publication,[138] although it may do so where the subject
is under a duty to pass that communication on to a third party or parties,[139] or where
it would otherwise be standard procedure for the subject to pass the statement on to
others and therefore reasonably foreseeable that this would occur.[140] Publication of
a defamation need not be deliberate: the standard is strict liability.[141] If the person
circulating the defamatory statement is merely a distributor rather than a publisher—a newsagent, for example, or a wholesaler selling copies of a newspaper containing a defamatory article as opposed to the newspaper's publisher or editor, or the
journalist who wrote the piece—then there may be an awareness-based defence.
Known as the 'defence of innocent dissemination', this was available at common
law where the following requirements were satisfied:

(a) the distributor has no knowledge that the publication distributed contains a
defamation;

(b) the distributor has no knowledge that the publication distributed is by its
nature *likely* to contain a defamation;

(c) the absence of such knowledge is not due to negligence on the part of the
distributor.[142]

The common law defence could potentially be open to online intermediaries as distributors of third party provided content which turns out to be defamatory, although
in practice it has been superseded by section 1 of the Defamation Act 1996. When
this Act was passed through Parliament, the internet in the guise of the world wide
web was becoming increasingly a part of the average person's everyday life, and the
government of the day was keen to encourage commercial exploitation of this then
relatively new medium. Concerns were raised as to the liability position in defamation for online service providers offering hosting services. The consideration was
that online service providers should not face the same level of liability as offline,
print publishers. Whereas a print publisher has complete control over everything it

---

[137] Obviously, however, the larger the audience to whom a defamation is published, the larger any
sum awarded in damages is likely to be. Note also that where the circulation is extremely negligible
a court may exercise its discretion to decline to hear the case on the basis of abuse of process—see, eg,
Jameel v Dow Jones [2005] EMLR 16.

[138] There are very limited exceptions to this general rule where publication of the defamation only to
the subject of it will be sufficient. These include cases involving criminal libel, and defamation under
Scots law. See, respectively, *Gleaves v Deaken* [1980] AC 477 and *MacKay v M'Cankie* (1883) 10 R 537;
note, however, that in the absence of communication to a third party damages for actual economic loss
will not be recoverable—only damages for insult will be available. M Collins, *The Law of Defamation
and the Internet* (Oxford: Oxford University Press, 2001) 56, 5.02.

[139] eg, if the subject is the secretary of an organization's executive body and is defamed in documents
sent to him and which he is under a duty to circulate to other executive members.

[140] *Theaker v Richardson* [1962] 1 All ER 229.

[141] *Hulton v Jones* [1910] AC 20.

[142] *Emmens v Pottle* (1885) 16 QBD 354.

makes available, having the opportunity to read and edit prior to publication, an online intermediary providing hosting services has little or no control over what is uploaded to those servers. Material made available online is ultimately not fixed—change can be constant—and in any case the sheer volume of material which most intermediaries host renders awareness of everything on their servers impossible. Section 1 effectively places the old common law defence on a statutory footing, and was included in the 1996 Act with online intermediaries particularly in mind. Under this section, there is a defence where a party which has published a defamation, for instance a service provider which hosts a popular blog on which a well-known local politician has been defamed, can meet the following criteria:

(a) It is not the author, editor, or publisher of the material.[143]

(b) It can demonstrate that it did not know and had no reason to believe that the statement in question was defamatory.[144]

(c) It can show that it took reasonable care in relation to the publication of the statement.[145]

The first question to arise, then, is whether an intermediary which is responsible for publishing a defamation by hosting it and thus making it available is a publisher for the purposes of section 1. Per section 1(3):

A person shall not be considered the author, editor or publisher . . . if he is only involved . . .

(c) in processing, making copies of, distributing or selling any electronic medium in or on which the statement is recorded, or in operating or providing any equipment, system or service by means of which the statement is retrieved, copied, distributed or made available in electronic form;

. . .

(e) as the operator or provider of access to a communications system by means of which the statement is transmitted, or made available, by a person over whom he has no effective control.

These provisions have clearly been drafted so as to encompass online intermediaries from being automatically and inequitably classified as publishers and exposed to strict liability for defamatory material made available via their servers. An intermediary must exercise caution, however, in fulfilling the section 1(1) requirement to take reasonable care in relation to what is made available via their servers—should it, in doing so, step over the boundary by assuming a level of editorial control over the material on its website, it can fall outside the parameters of section 1(3) and end up subject to the same strict liability standard as a print publisher.

---

[143] Defamation Act 1996, s 1(1)(a).
[144] Ibid s 1(1)(b).
[145] Ibid s 1(1)(c).

Section 1 was first applied to online intermediaries in *Godfrey v Demon*.[146] The court hearing was a preliminary session, held in order to determine whether the defendant ISP could avail itself of the section 1 defence. The facts of the case were that the claimant had been defamed in a posting to a Usenet newsgroup, hosted but not edited or in any way actively monitored by the defendants. The claimant contacted the ISP, notifying them of the defamation, however, the ISP failed to act to remove the material from its servers, instead waiting until it was automatically deleted some ten days later. The claimant then proceeded to bring an action in defamation against the ISP. On the facts, the court found that while the ISP was not to be classified as an author, editor, or publisher and so the defence was in theory available, on the facts the conditions set for the defence had not been met. Prior to the point at which the claimant had notified the ISP of the posting in question, it was held that no liability would lie as the ISP could not reasonably have been expected to be aware of any facts or circumstances that would indicate the presence of a defamation. Following the claimant's notice, Demon had actual knowledge of the apparent defamation, and liability for failure to delete or disable the posting arose from that point in time. The case later settled out of court for a reported £500,000. On the basis of this decision it can be presumed that in future cases where actual knowledge is absent, in seeking to establish whether there is sufficient constructive knowledge (awareness of facts or circumstances) to establish liability, the courts will look to the context of the posting. In a case surrounding a single posting on an otherwise innocuous bulletin board discussing guitars, cars, or, as was the case in *Godfrey*, Thai culture, it might well be considered unreasonable to expect the intermediary to be aware of the defamation. If, on the other hand, it is posted to a bulletin board on a website such as the notorious Popbitch,[147] known for celebrity gossip and the source of many 'wicked whisper' type stories in daily tabloid newspapers, the court might adopt the attitude that the service provider hosting this website could reasonably have been expected to be aware that it was likely to contain defamatory postings.

The *Godfrey* decision was also later confirmed in *Totalise plc v Motley Fool Ltd*,[148] in which the court additionally required handover of any details held by the service provider which might help to identify the source of a defamation as a condition of evading liability. While *Godfrey* was prima facie a straightforward application of section 1 of the Defamation Act 1996 to the internet context, it did at the time raise a number of concerns relating to civil liberties. Specifically, a number of commentators expressed concerns that freedom of expression would be limited as rather than risk liability by making its own judgement on the complaint, online intermediaries would simply remove the material without question. In this

---

[146] [1999] EMLR 542.
[147] <http://www.popbitch.com> (accessed 8 August 2011).
[148] 2001 WL 1479825, [2002] EMLR 20.

way, it was feared, genuine and fair comment could be crushed simply by the threat of a lawsuit.

This fear was, as discussed above,[149] raised again in relation to the Electronic Commerce Regulations, although to date it has not been addressed by the courts. It would appear that in practice it has not been a significant enough problem to require any alteration to the law, although it remains a theoretical risk at least, albeit one that can be said to have been somewhat mitigated by the judgment of Parkes QC, sitting as a deputy judge of the Queen's Bench Division in the case of *Sheffield Wednesday Football Club & Others v Neil Hargreaves*.[150] This case involved a fan-run bulletin board, on which there had been a large number of postings which were defamatory of the board of directors and others responsible for running the football club in a way which displeased its followers. The claimants sought a court order obliging those responsible for running the bulletin board to hand over any details in their possession which could help to discover the real-world identities of those screen-names which had posted the defamatory comments. In a move very favourable to defendants the court agreed to issue an order for the handover of information relating to some, but crucially not all, of those responsible for the defamatory postings. The court specifically declined to order the handover of details relating to a number of postings which, while technically defamatory, were only minor defamations. In these specific instances, it was held that the protection of these individuals' privacy should be paramount over the claimants' interest in bringing a libel suit. If this line of reasoning is followed by the courts in future, it will be very attractive from the point of view of the defendant online discussion forum provider, an environment in which so-called 'flame wars' are rife, and every abusive posting may be a libel case in waiting. It can also reasonable be said that such an approach is also less likely to occasion a 'chill' on freedom of expression.

Although *Godfrey* was decided squarely within the context of defamation law and thus only affords a precedent in that specific context, given the degree of similarity between the section 1 defence and that provided in respect of hosting unlawful material more generally by regulation 19 of the Electronic Commerce Regulations, it can be speculated that in future the reasoning in *Godfrey* might be applied by analogy to cases involving other forms of unlawful material. In essence, both are concerned with a form of notice and take-down, the intermediary, upon receipt of sufficient notice (actual or constructive), being obligated to act expeditiously take down or delete the material in question.

The interaction between the Electronic Commerce Regulations, section 1 of the Defamation Act 1996, and traditional defamation law was given some consideration by Eady J in *Bunt v Tilley*.[151] As discussed above,[152] the claimant in this case was

---

[149] See section 5.2.2.1 'General liability'.
[150] [2007] EWHC 2375 (QB).
[151] [2006] EMLR 18.
[152] See section 5.2.2.1 'General liability'.

suing several defendants whom he claimed to be responsible for publishing defamations about both himself and his business. Three of the defendants were ISPs whom the claimant did not accuse of actually hosting the material, but of making it available by providing online access, the material thus being provided via the ISPs' services. The ISPs applied to the court for the case against them to be struck out.[153] Eady J considered that the question before the court was whether the ISPs could be liable in respect of material 'which is simply communicated via the services which they provide'.[154] Comparing the ISPs to the postal service, Eady J stated '[t]hey provide a means of transmitting communications without in any way participating in that process'.[155] The view of commentators who had discussed the application of *CBS v Amstrad*[156] was also considered by way of analogy, the general principle being that it may be possible to facilitate an unlawful transmission without authorizing or approving it in any way.[157] The claimant's case against the ISPs relied upon *Godfrey v Demon*, arguing that an ISP can be liable for material which is made available through its systems, with liability depending upon whether a defence can successfully be raised. The ISPs, conversely, claimed that they faced no liability at common law, distinguishing *Godfrey* on the facts. Eady J ruled that despite the strict liability standard for publishing a defamation at common law, in order to qualify as a publisher at common law a party must have a certain level of awareness that a publication is being made, or have assumed a general level of responsibility such as an editorial role. In making this ruling, Eady J cited old case law, *McLeod v St Aubyn*,[158] in which a person handing over an unread copy of a newspaper to be returned on the following day was found to have had an insufficient degree of awareness or intention to publish for liability for publication to arise. Therefore, in Eady J's judgment, in order for the strict liability standard for a defamation to stick, there must be knowing involvement in the process of publication. On the facts, the defendant ISPs in the immediate case did not have the appropriate knowledge and were therefore not publishers:

Persons who truly fulfil no more than the role of a passive medium for communication cannot be characterised as publishers: thus they do not need a defence.[159]

It followed that as there was no case to answer, the ISPs did not have any need to raise a defence. Nevertheless, Eady J did go on to discuss the application of regulations 17 and 18 of the Electronic Commerce Regulations, as well as section 1

---

[153] [2006] EMLR 18 at para 2.
[154] *Bunt v Tilley*, para 5.
[155] Ibid para 9.
[156] [1988] AC 1013.
[157] The defendant in this case was cleared of authorizing copyright infringement by selling double-deck cassette recorders as the devices could be used for legitimate, non-infringing copying and also once sold the defendant was not in a position to exercise any control over the use made of the devices by the purchaser.
[158] [1899] AC 549.
[159] [2006] EMLR 18 at para 37.

of the Defamation Act 1996 'for the sake of completeness'.[160] Eady J's comments on the Regulations have already been discussed above.[161] The application of the section 1 defence was a simple matter on the facts. What is perhaps significant is that Eady J discussed both the Regulations and the section 1 defence alongside each other, without any reference to the one having prominence over the other. Since the enactment of the Regulations in 2002, commentators have generally assumed that the provisions therein, applying as they do to all unlawful material at both civil and criminal law, would supersede the section 1 defence. Eady J in considering them both in the course of his *obiter* comments in this case does not indicate that this will necessarily be so; the question thus remains open. Certainly it still seems likely that in the long run section 1 will fall into disuse for online intermediaries, with regulations 17 to 19 being used as a catch-all to cover any situation in which an intermediary faces potential liability in respect of third party provided unlawful content. Ironically, as this seventh edition of *Computer Law* is being compiled, it seems that the e-Commerce Regulations, despite replacing section 1 for online intermediaries, also act to ensure its survival in English law. A strident Libel Reform Campaign comprised of various interest groups including Indexs on Censorship and English Pen[162] has, since 2009, called for extensive reform of English libel laws. This has at one time and another included calls for radical reform to the section 1 defence along the lines of the US Communications Decency Act, section 230 and its complete immunity from civil liability for third party provided content.[163] Their inadvisability aside, such demands cannot be met without the UK being in breach of its obligations under section 4 of the Electronic Commerce Directive, with the curious result that section 1 is destined to remain on the statute book by virtue of the very European provision which is set, in practice, to replace it. Of course, it should also be borne in mind that section 1's application is broader than only to online service providers, as it provides an effective defence also to traditional, real-world distributors such as newspaper wholesalers and newsagents.

Another open question is whether in relation to defamatory material originating from a third party source, Eady J's judgment that the ISPs involved in transmission and caching only could not be liable at common law on the basis of lack of awareness of the publication might, if upheld by the higher courts, effectively render regulations 17 and 18 redundant insofar as defamation proceedings are concerned. Ruling that no defence was necessary as there was no case to answer in this situation, it seems at least arguable that this is exactly what Eady J did in this case, although of course the scope of the Regulations being so broad, even if this line of argument were to be pursued in later cases, these immunities will still be applicable in a wide variety of circumstances.

---

[160] Ibid para 38.
[161] See section 5.2.2.1 'General liability'.
[162] <http://www.libelreform.org> (accessed 8 August 2011).
[163] See <http://www.libelreform.org/our-report> (accessed 8 August 2011).

The liability position of an intermediary hosting a link to a defamatory article has not yet been commented upon by the courts, but it would seem likely that this would be enough to constitute publication of a defamation. Where the ISP has taken reasonable care and has the requisite lack of awareness, section 1 of the Defamation Act 1996 would provide a defence, and as discussed above[164] there will be a defence available under the Electronic Commerce Regulations.

The USA has steered a very different course in the area of intermediary liability at civil law. Outside certain specific exemptions, a very wide immunity from liability for third party provided material uploaded to their servers is provided to online intermediaries.[165] In practice, the case law regarding this immunity has been dominated by defamation actions. The basis of this immunity lies in what is left of the Communications Decency Act 1996. This Act was originally drafted and passed by Congress with the explicit purpose of dealing with what was perceived as the looming threat of 'cyberporn'. The Act imposed criminal liability (with penalties incorporating both fines and imprisonment for periods of up to two years) upon any persons who made available to a minor material which was not only obscene but also indecent, or who knowingly provided 'any telecommunications facility' for such use.[166] A wide lobby of freedom of speech activists and internet industry players, led by the American Civil Liberties Union challenged the constitutionality of these provisions, contending that even though speech be indecent, it is still entitled to First Amendment protection. In the landmark case of *Reno v ACLU*,[167] a 7:2 majority found these specific provisions to be in breach of the First Amendment, and they were thus struck out as unconstitutional.[168] Only the specifically unconstitutional provisions were excised, with section 230 remaining in force. Section 230 provides, inter alia:

(c) Protection for 'Good Samaritan' blocking and screening of offensive material

(1) Treatment of publisher or speaker

No provider or user of an interactive computer service shall be treated as the publisher or speaker of any information provided by another information content provider.

---

[164] See section 5.2.2.1 'General liability'.

[165] Communications Decency Act 1996, s 230 explicitly excludes from its ambit matters of criminal law (with specific mention being made of child pornography and obscene materials) and matters of intellectual property law. See respectively ss 230(e)(1) and 230(e)(2). Also exempted is communications privacy law (s 230(e)(4)). See also *Gucci America, Inc v Hall & Associates*, 135 F Supp 2d 409 (SDNY, 2001) in which the defendant was denied s 230 immunity in respect of trade mark infringement, and *Perfect 10, Inc v CCBill LLC* (No CV 02-7624 LGB) (CD Cal, 22 June 2004), in which it was ruled that a right of publicity claim was not covered by s 230.

[166] USCA S223 (Supp 1997) as was.

[167] No 96-511 (1997) (USSC).

[168] For further discussion of *Reno v ACLU* and the Communications Decency Act see Sutter, '"Nothing New Under the Sun": Old Fears and New Media' (2000) 8(3) International Journal of Law and Information Technology esp 354–8.

(2) Civil liability

No provider or user of an interactive computer service shall be held liable on account of—

(A) any action voluntarily taken in good faith to restrict access to or availability of material that the provider or user considers to be obscene, lewd, lascivious, filthy, excessively violent, harassing, or otherwise objectionable, whether or not such material is constitutionally protected; or

(B) any action taken to enable or make available to information content providers or others the technical means to restrict access to material described in paragraph (1).

The leading case on interpretation of section 230 is *Zeran v AOL*,[169] in which it was held that the defendant ISP was not in any way liable for hosting material which allegedly defamed the plaintiff in spite of the fact that the ISP had been in receipt of clear actual notice of the material in question and yet had failed to remove it. The court in *Zeran* referred to the fact that Congress in passing section 230 had intended to encourage intermediaries to take active steps, including the introduction of technological filtering and blocking mechanisms, to edit content on their servers without fear of setting themselves up for liability as a result. In this way section 230 represented a distinct shift in legal policy from the previous position under *Stratton Oakmount v Prodigy*,[170] in which an ISP was found to be liable for publishing a defamation uploaded to its servers by a third party as a result of the ISP having advertised itself as a 'family friendly' service provider and taking active steps to monitor content on its servers, thereby assuming editorial responsibility for all material made available via them. It does appear that the drafters of the Communications Decency Act were somewhat naïve in their belief that commercial online service providers would fall into place as moral guardians of society, but that is quite another matter.

Zeran was followed in a range of later cases, including *Blumenthal v Drudge*,[171] in which the section 230 immunity was held to excuse the defendant ISP from any liability in respect of a gossip column which it hosted, despite the fact that the ISP exercised editorial control over the column. The immunity was held to apply even where an ISP plays an active, aggressive role in making the defamatory material available to the public.[172] In *Ben Ezra, Wenstein & Co v AOL*,[173] erroneous stock values attributed to the plaintiff did not give rise to liability on the part of the intermediary, as the information had been provided by a third party.

In *Schneider v Amazon.com*,[174] the plaintiff, an author, brought an action in defamation against the defendant online retailer in respect of comments posted in the user-review section of the website pertaining to books he had written. Rejecting the

---

[169] 129 F3d 327 (4th Cir, 1997).
[170] 23 Med LR 1794 (SC Nassau County 1995).
[171] 992 F Supp 44.
[172] Ibid 51–2.
[173] (1999) No CIV 97-485 LG/LFG US DC, New Mexico.
[174] Case No 46791-3-I, 31 P3d 37 (Washington Court of Appeal, 17 September 2001).

plaintiff's argument that section 230 should not apply in this case, the court ruled that the immunity was available to the defendant, and the plaintiff's case failed.[175]

In 2003, US courts applied the section 230 immunity to a non-commercial publisher for the first time in *Batzel v Smith, Cremers & Museum Society Network*.[176] In this case, the first named defendant, Smith, claimed to have been present when the plaintiff remarked to another person that she was related to Gestapo chief, Heinrich Himmler. Smith, who had also viewed Batzel's collection of European paintings which were on display in her home, jumped to the conclusion that as she was related to a high-ranking Nazi, the artworks must have been stolen by the Nazis during the Second World War, and later inherited by Batzel. Subsequently, Smith sent an email outlining this to Cremers, the editor of the Museum Society Network, a non-commercial organization which publishes details of stolen paintings. Although Cremers did not inform Smith that the email would be published, he did indeed forward it to 1,000 Museum Society Network emailing list subscribers, having made only minor edits. Batzel became aware of this publication, and commenced defamation proceedings against Smith, Cremers, and the Museum Society Network. Overruling the decision of the court of first instance, the Ninth Circuit Appeals Court found that the minor amendments which had been made by Cremers to Smith's email were insufficient to render it a separate piece of expression, thus the email that Cremers forwarded to the 1,000 subscribers was still the same content provided by Smith. The appeal court ruled that whether the section 230 immunity could be applied in these circumstances hinged upon whether Cremers had a reasonable belief that Smith's email was intended for publication, and the matter was referred back to the lower court for a decision on the facts.[177]

The section 230 immunity, then, by 2003 had been shown to be very broad, but yet it has not been without its critics. During 2005, much publicity was given in the USA to an incident involving Wikipedia. A colleague of John Seigenthaler, a well-known writer and journalist in the USA, anonymously altered Seigenthaler's biography on Wikipedia in order to suggest that he may have been involved in the Kennedy assassinations. This alteration was not detected and corrected until over four months had passed. In interviews about the story, Seigenthaler (who chose not to pursue legal action against the identified culprit of the prank) criticized the

---

[175] A similar application was made by the Illinois Court of Appeal in *Barrett v Fonorow*, 343 Ill App 3d 1184, 799 NE 2d 916, 279 Ill Dec 113, in which the court held that an internet website was indeed a 'provider or user of an interactive computer service' within the meaning of the Communications Decency Act definition of 'interactive computer service' as 'any information service, system or access software provider that provides or enables computer access by multiple users to a computer server, including specifically a service or system that provides access to the internet.' See also Communications Decency Act 1996, s 230(f)(2).

[176] No 01-56380 DC No CV-00-09590-SVW, 24 June 2003.

[177] A Federal trial court in Los Angeles has since granted Smith's application for summary dismissal on a procedural issue. See *Batzel v Smith*, CV 00-9590 SVW (AJWx) USDC Central District of California, 8 March 2005 <http://www.politechbot.com/docs/museum.security.news.decision.031705. tiff> (accessed 9 August 2011).

section 230 immunity, while other commentators also called for it to be revised, regarding it as a disincentive for intermediaries such as Wikipedia from taking care with respect to the accuracy of information that they distribute.[178] Another critic, law professor Anita Ramasastry, was among those who suggested that section 230 should be altered such that an intermediary 'would lose that immunity if its personnel were to discover that it included a false or defamatory entry, and fail to take action'.[179]

At the time of writing the previous edition of this book, the Californian courts had issued a challenge to the established case law interpreting the section 230 immunity. The appellants in *Barret v Rosenthal*[180] were both doctors who together ran a 'quackwatch' website which provided information about various questionable 'alternative' medical practices which they considered to be 'health frauds and quackery'. In particular the site targeted for exposure products and services which were believed to be being marketed fraudulently or even illegally. Rosenthal, the respondent, was a highly active participant in a number of online forums dedicated to discussing medical treatments. Rosenthal had, in the course of these bulletin board style discussions, reposted a number of statements made by third parties which apparently defamed the appellants. At first instance, the court considered Rosenthal's entitlement to raise the section 230 defence. As mentioned above, section 230 states that:

No provider or user of an interactive computer service shall be treated as the publisher or speaker of any information provided by another information content provider.

The court therefore concluded that Rosenthal, as an individual user of an online bulletin board, was entitled to rely upon this immunity and could therefore not be successfully sued for publication of any defamation contained in the third party comments which had been reposted in his replies. This decision was of major significance, as it marked the first time in which section 230 had been applied to an individual internet user as opposed to a service provider. The Californian Court of Appeal, however, overturned this decision. The appeal court considered in its ruling that US common law has traditionally provided differing degrees of liability for primary publishers and those who merely distributed a libellous statement. Both sides in this case agreed that the defendant was indeed a 'user of an interactive computer service', and therefore entitled under section 230 to immunity from primary liability as a publisher of the third party comments. The point of difference lay in the appellants' argument that section 230 does not prevent users (or indeed

---

[178] See <http://en.wikipedia.org/wiki/John_Seigenthaler_Sr._Wikipedia_biography_controversy> (accessed 9 August 2011).

[179] A Ramasastry, 'Is an Online Encyclopedia, Such as Wikipedia, Immune From Libel Suits? Under Current Law, the Answer Is Most Likely Yes, But that Law Should Change', 12 December 2005 <http://writ.news.findlaw.com/ramasastry/20051212.html> (accessed 9 August 2011).

[180] (2003) 112 Cal App 4th 749; 5 Cal Rptr 3d 416 Cal App 1 Dist, 2003.

service providers) from being treated as *distributors* and therefore being subject to awareness-based liability (as distinct from the strict liability standard to which publishers are held). The appeal case contended that the lower court's interpretation of section 230 would shield even intermediaries who had *intentionally* distributed injurious third party provided content, a result contrary to the original aims behind the statute. It was also argued that a 'clever libeler' [sic] could escape liability by inciting another user who could not be sued in the US courts[181] to publish the material initially, then other users and intermediaries would be free to republish the material at will with no fear of liability being incurred.[182]

The Court of Appeal concurred with the appellants' arguments, and ruled that section 230 could not be interpreted in such a way as to override the common law principle that the republisher of a defamation will be liable if he knows or has reason to believe that the article in question is indeed defamatory. It therefore followed that section 230 should not be construed as an absolute immunity, and the lower court—as well as *Zeran* and the whole slew of cases following *Zeran*—were flawed in their analysis, which created a much broader immunity than that intended by Congress. The court in *Zeran* had interpreted the term 'publisher' to mean both the primary publisher of a defamation and subordinate distributors. The Communication Decency Act referred only to the generic 'publisher', however, the Court of Appeal made clear its belief that Congress had not intended this to be interpreted as a catch-all, umbrella term. A distinction has traditionally been made between primary publisher and subsequent distributor on the basis of level of control over and awareness of the nature of the material; in the Court of Appeal's view, if Congress had intended the section 230 protection also to extend to distributors, this would have been made explicit in the wording of the legislation. Referring back to the pre-Communications Decency Act *Stratton Oakmont Inc v Prodigy Services Co*[183] decision, the court in *Barrett* concurred with the *Zeran* analysis that section 230 was designed to avoid the unfair imposition of liability, but the defendant ISP in *Stratton Oakmount* was subjected to a publisher's strict liability standard in respect of all of the information held on its servers, not the lower awareness-based standard associated with a distributor. In the earlier *Cubby v Compuserve*[184] case, held to have been implicitly approved by Congress, the defendant, also an ISP, had been held to the lower, awareness-based standard of liability as a distributor. Had the ruling of the Court of Appeal been upheld by the State Supreme Court, it is certain that the case would have ended up before the Federal Supreme Court of the United States, in Washington DC. Approval of such a radical re-interpretation of section 230 at that level would have represented a sea-change in the liability regime for US

---

[181] eg, one who could not be made subject to the jurisdiction of the US courts, or someone who was untraceable.

[182] 5 Cal Rptr 3d 416 Cal App 1 Dist, 2003 at 426.

[183] 1995 WL 323710 (NY Sup Ct, 1995).

[184] 776 F Supp 135, 29 October 1991.

intermediaries as regards third party provided content, and a significant move towards the European model. This, however, was not to be, as the Supreme Court of California dismissed the Court of Appeal's ruling, finding it to be completely incorrect.[185] Delivering the majority opinion, Corrigan J confirmed that 'Congress did not intend for an internet user to be treated differently than an internet provider'. The court emphasized that the imposition of liability for defamation in respect of third party content upon either service providers *or* users would have an unacceptable tendency to chill free speech, expounding further:

> The congressional intent of fostering free speech on the internet supported the extension of Section 230 immunity to active individual users. It is they who provide much of the 'diversity of political discourse,' the pursuit of 'opportunities for cultural development,' and the exploration of 'myriad avenues for intellectual activity' that the statute was meant to protect.

In his concurring opinion, Moreno J even went so far as to suggest that section 230 would project a user who had conspired with the content provider to defame another. The majority opinion, in its conclusion, did recognize that 'the prospect of blanket immunity for those who intentionally redistribute defamatory statement on the internet has disturbing implications', but nonetheless it considered that '[a]ny further expansion of liability [beyond the limits imposed by section 230] must await Congressional action'. While not a radical reinterpretation of section 230, then, this case still represents a significant development in that it at once emphasizes the sheer breadth of the immunity, applying it for the first time in practice to a *user* rather than a service provider, while also sounding a note of caution as to the dangers of such an arrangement.

Two recent defamation judgments concerning the same website show that confusion as to the correct application of section 230 may still arise. These suits related to 'Ripoff Report',[186] a website which provides, in its own words, 'a worldwide consumer reporting Web site and publication, by consumers, for consumers, to file and document complaints about companies or individuals'. The website carries well over half a million entries in its database. Ripoff Report offers its own dispute-resolution system (at a cost to the client of $2,000) via which the subject of any of the reports it publishes can challenge statements made about it. Where any such statements is found to be false, it will be removed from the website. The Terms of Service for the website are clear that unless a subject participates in this process, Ripoff Report will refuse to take down content. In *Blockowicz v Williams*,[187] the Seventh Circuit Court of Appeals held that the defendant operators of this website could not be ordered by a court to remove allegedly defamatory postings uploaded by third parties.

---

[185] *Barrett v Rosenthal*, 40 Cal 4th 33, 146 P3d 510, 51 Cal Rptr 3d 55 (Cal Sup Ct, 20 November 2006), available online at <http://www.casp.net/cases/Barrett%20v.%20Rosenthal.html> (accessed 9 August 2011).

[186] <http://www.ripoffreport.com> (accessed 9 August 2011).

[187] 2010 WL 5262726 (7th Cir, 27 December 2010) available online at <http://www.ca7.uscourts.gov/fdocs/docs.fwx?dname=opinion> (accessed 15 August 2011).

At first instance, the District Court in Northern Illinois had ordered the individuals who had made the postings at issue to remove them from the website. They failed to do so, and so the claimants proceeded to petition the court for an order obliging the website operators to ensure their removal. The District Court declined to do so, and this decision was approved by the Court of Appeal, which found that a simple failure to remove defamatory postings did not amount to actively aiding and abetting the content providers. Despite having the technical ability to control the website in this way, there was no legal obligation imposed upon its operators to do so. Conversely, only a day later in *Giordano v Romeo*,[188] a Florida Circuit Court judge, ruling in an unrelated case against the same defendants, ordered the website operators to remove defamatory content or face proceedings in contempt. The judge had dismissed the website operators from the case, finding that they were entitled to enjoy the section 230 immunity, but the court later issued an order which obliged them to remove the disputed content. Drawing a clear distinction between liability for third party content and obligation to comply with a court order, the Florida court, referring to section 230(e)(3) (which preserves judicial authority to enforce state laws which are 'consistent' with the Communications Decency Act), professed that it '[did] not believe that Congress intended to provide immunity from an equitable injunction in such a situation'. In the circumstances, the court was prepared to interpret a refusal to remove specific content as an assumption of the role of publisher in relation to that material. Nevertheless, even if the website operators were not found to be the publishers of this content, the court held that section 230 still would not immunize them from the consequences of refusing to comply with a court order. Somewhat inevitably, Ripoff Reports have at the time of writing commenced appeal proceedings. Should this decision be approved by higher courts, it may well help to curb the worst excesses of section 230, which to date has allowed website operators to continue to make available even blatantly defamatory content with impunity. Concerns about a chilling effect on freedom of expression typically arise where intermediaries are put in a position of having to make a judgement call on the legality of material which they make available, with the risk of liability if they make a wrong call. Having a court rule on the legality of the material before making an order for its removal creates no danger of such a situation arising, yet it would also provide a means of limiting outright abuse of the immunity.

Of course, the application of section 230 is not limited to liability for defamatory content alone. It has been successfully used in order to evade liability for hosting unlawful third party content in a whole range of situations, including a sexual assault upon a minor arising from a MySpace profile which falsely identified a 13-year-old

---

[188] No 09-68539-CA-25 4 (Fla 11th Cir Ct, 28 December 2010) available online at <http://www.scribd.com/doc/46015195/Giordano-v-Romeo-Injunction-Against-Ripoff-Report> (accessed 9 August 2011).

girl as an adult,[189] financial loss occasioned by clicking on fraudulent advertisements on Google,[190] and fraudulent advertisements on an online ticket reseller website.[191]

Whatever the nature of the unlawful information, it is extremely important that a person wanting to take advantage of section 230 maintains a sufficient distinction between third party content and content which becomes its own. In *Fair Housing Council of San Fernando Valley v Roommates.com*,[192] the court was asked to consider the liability position of a website which provided a searchable database designed to allow users to advertise for a 'roommate' to share rented living quarters. The defendants drafted and posted questionnaires designed to build user profiles to the website. These questionnaires included questions about roommate preferences, including a question about the preferred sexual orientation of potential roommates. The defendants, if liable in respect of the profiles thus posted to their website, would face liability under the Fair Housing Act as this required members to answer questions that potentially enabled other members to discriminate against them, and these questionnaires were distributed via the website. The court of first instance ruled that the defendants enjoyed the protection of section 230. Due to the way in which the website was set up, the flow of information was controlled in such a way that answers to questionnaires were used to determine whether an individual should be notified of rooms available, or be allowed to view a particular profile. For instance, a person who was listed as having children would not be shown the listing of someone who did not wish to let to anyone with children. The Court of Appeal ruled that this involvement in the distribution of the material was sufficient involvement in the creation of the online content that the material was no longer wholly third party content, and thus the site was not entitled to enjoy the section 230 immunity. The plaintiffs were therefore entitled to bring a case for violation of the Fair Housing Act, which prevents discrimination in residential property lettings. Section 230 protection *was* however available in relation to an open-ended question which allowed users to post a paragraph describing what they were looking for in a roommate; most potentially discriminatory responses were found here. Users were permitted to formulate their own responses, with no set 'tick-box' type answers given. The defendants' involvement in this voluntarily supplied content was not sufficient to make then a content provider: no specific answers were suggested, and they did not prompt any of the discriminatory comments made. Further, these comments were not used in order to restrict or channel access to profiles by other members. Contrary to some commentators' views, this decision does not represent a limit on the extent of the section 230 immunity, but rather a distinction on the facts of the case between what is and is not third party content in relation to the availability of the immunity.

---

[189] *Doe v Myspace*, 528 F3d 413 (5th Cir, 2008).
[190] *Goddard v Google, Inc*, 640 F Supp 2d 1193 (ND Cal, 30 July 2009).
[191] *Milgram v Orbitz Worldwide, LLC*, ESX-C-142-09 (NJ Super Ct, 26 August 2010) available online at <http://www.scribd.com/doc/37008339/Milgram-v-Orbitz> (accessed 9 August 2011).
[192] CV-03-09386-PA (9th Cir, 15 May 2007).

Clearly those running such websites in future will have to be careful as to how they solicit and treat information if they wish it to remain third party content.

Obscenity and Indecency If one were to take media reports about internet information content at face value, one might be justified in believing that the primary activity on the internet is the provision, distribution, and downloading of obscene and indecent materials, notably pictorial pornography.[193] Whilst it is certainly possible to locate such material with relative ease,[194] media statements as to its prevalence usually considerably overstate its role and status on the internet. Despite this, the result of the extensive coverage that the topic has received has placed the question of intermediary liability for its possession and transmission firmly on the political agenda. There are, however, a number of difficult issues to address when considering the issue of liability. To begin with, there is no international understanding or definition of the type of material that would be considered 'obscene', 'indecent', or even 'pornographic'.

In the USA, 'obscenity' is limited to sexual material, and requires the material to appeal to the prurient interest, as defined by reference to the standards of the local community, and to depict sexual conduct defined by the applicable state law.[195] This classification is not based on the potential effects of the material, but on whether it contravenes locally determined standards of acceptable sexual depiction. This leads to the somewhat unfortunate result that material which is unobjectionable in one US state may be viewed as obscene in another, with potentially deleterious effects for the publishers. In the traditional media, publishers can largely avoid falling foul of locally determined standards, by adjusting their distribution networks accordingly. For an ISP, this distribution control approach may simply be untenable, as those using or accessing a potentially objectionable internet service might be based anywhere in the USA.[196]

In the UK, by contrast, the term is not limited to sexual material, but applies to any material the effect of which:

---

[193] And not just the media, see M Rimm, 'Marketing Pornography on the Information Superhighway' (1995) 83 Georgetown LJ (June) 1849–934). This study caused immense controversy when first published, making the cover of TIME magazine and being widely quoted during the passage of the ill-fated US Communications Decency Act. However, it was rapidly exposed as, at best, methodologically flawed. See <http://web.archive.org/web/200012061513/http://www2000.ogsm.vanderbilt.edu/cyberporn.debate.html> for more details.

[194] Yahoo, the popular US former web-indexing site, once contained a number of index pages to such material.

[195] See *Miller v California*, 413 US 15 (1973).

[196] This problem is clearly demonstrated by the case of *United States v Thomas*, 74 F3d 701 (6th Cir), cert denied, 117 S Ct 74 (1996), where a bulletin board operator was extradited from California to Tennessee to face criminal charges. It was stated in argument that the material, which was stored on a computer in California, was not obscene by Californian community standards, but the court determined that the appropriate standards by which to test for obscenity were the standards of Tennessee, the place in which the material was received and viewed.

is, if taken as a whole, such as to tend to deprave and corrupt persons who are likely . . . to read, see or hear the matter contained or embodied in it.[197]

Thus, while the depiction of sexual acts in pictorial or textual form is the most obvious form of potentially obscene material, UK case law demonstrates that action can also be taken against pamphlets and books about the use of drugs,[198] and material showing scenes of violence.[199]

Equally, the question of the standard that one might use to establish whether material is, or is not, 'pornography' is a highly contentious one and one that over the years has created some unusual alliances.[200] An example of the type of definition that may be used is 'offensive, degrading, and threatening material of an explicitly sexual or violent nature'. However, it is clear from the debates and the case law over the years that one person's 'offensive, degrading, and threatening material' may well be another's great work of literature,[201] great work of art,[202] protected social, political, or sexual statement, or holiday snaps.[203]

Where child pornography is concerned, despite some vast differences in the age of consent, it is now fairly common in many countries that for the purposes of pornographic images, the person depicted must be aged 18 or over. In the UK, a person of the age of 16 or over can consent to sexual activity, although for the purposes of the distribution of indecent photographs an individual is considered a child up to the age of 18.[204] Under articles 176 and 177 of the Japanese Penal Code the national age of consent in Japan is just 13, but under the Law for Punishing Acts Related to Child Prostitution and Child Pornography, and for Protecting Children 1999 a 'child', for the purposes of the offences relating to the distribution of child pornography,[205] is

---

[197] Obscene Publications Act 1959, s 1(1).

[198] *John Calder (Publications) Ltd v Powell* [1965] 1 All ER 159 (book concerning the life of a junkie in New York held to be obscene); *R v Skirving and Another* [1985] 2 All ER 705 (book concerned with the use and abuse of the drug cocaine and contained detailed explanations, instructions, and recipes for obtaining the maximum effect from ingesting cocaine held to be obscene).

[199] *DPP v A & BC Chewing Gum Ltd* [1967] 2 All ER 504 (depiction of violent activity on chewing gum cards held liable to tend to deprave or corrupt children, and thus to be obscene).

[200] cg, on this issue, but one would suspect few others, US feminist writers Catherine McKinnon (author of *Only Words* (Cambridge, MA: Harvard University Press, 1994)), and Andrea Dworkin (author of *Pornography: Men Possessing Women* (London: The Women's Press, 1981)), agree with US Christian fundamentalist groups that certain materials are pornographic, although for very different reasons.

[201] eg, *Lady Chatterley's Lover*: *R v Penguin Books* [1961] Crim LR 176; *Last Exit to Brooklyn*: *R v Calder & Boyars Ltd* [1969] 1 QB 151.

[202] In June 1998, British police seized a book, *Mapplethorpe*, from the library at the University of Central England. It contained photographs of homosexual activity and bondage scenes taken by the internationally renowned photographer and artist Robert Mapplethorpe. Despite the fact that the book was widely acknowledged as serious artistic work, the police told the university that its contents might contravene the Obscene Publications Act 1959. In the event, no charges were brought.

[203] There have been a number of reports of film processors reporting to the police pictures of nude children taken by family members on holiday. These reports are however difficult to substantiate.

[204] See s 1 of the Protection of Children Act 1978, as amended by the Sexual Offences Act 2003.

[205] Art 7.

'a person under the age of eighteen years'.[206] Since 3 July 1995, all producers of pornographic content in the USA have been required to guarantee that the performers appearing in their work are all aged 18 or over.[207] Countries in which no concept of an age of consent exists, such as Oman, tend also to be those in which pornography will be illegal both under obscenity laws and by default, as in Oman sexual intercourse cannot lawfully take place outside marriage.[208]

As ever, the devil is in the detail. While there may be some agreement internationally about the age at which minors become adult in relation to the pornography industry, the concept of what exactly constitutes an image of a child remains far from consistent across international boundaries. In the UK, for instance, 'child pornography' includes not only images of actual sexual abuse of children, but also, as noted above, digitized images which appear to be realistic depictions of actual children.[209] It is an offence not only to distribute such material or to possess with intent to distribute, but even merely to possess for an individual's own private use. In 2009, the UK took this one step further with the creation of several possession offences relating to certain types of images of children which are not the sort of adapted images that the provisions relating to 'pseudo-photographs' entail, but are in fact wholly fabricated.[210] The scope of the new offence includes material which depicts sexual acts 'with or in the presence of a child', and which include interaction with either other humans or 'an animal (whether dead, alive or imaginary)'.[211] There is no requirement that these be realistic images, although it can reasonably be presumed that prosecutions will be more likely to be pursued against CGI-type material, or even some types of Japanese *Hentai*,[212] rather than very basic stick-figure drawings. Such laws are by no means global. The Japanese Law for Punishing Acts Related to Child Prostitution and Child Pornography, and for Protecting Children as passed in 1998 referred only to offences relating to distribution and possession with intent to distribute;[213] this law was, however, updated in 2003 to include a mere possession offence. By 2010, however, Japanese law still places no restrictions upon simulated or cartoon pornography involving minors. The USA has adopted a position somewhere in the middle. Since 1978, the US Supreme Court has backed

---

[206] Art 2.

[207] 18 USC 2257.

[208] See <http://www.interpol.int/Public/Children/SexualAbuse/NationalLaws/> (accessed 9 August 2011).

[209] See treatment of 'pseudo-photographs' in s 1 of the Protection of Children Act 1978, as amended by the Criminal Justice and Public Order Act 1994.

[210] Coroners and Justice Act 2009, s 62.

[211] Ibid s 62.

[212] 'Hentai' is a form of Japanese Manga comic, or anime film, which concentrates upon the depiction of sexual activity. Often this can feature characters who appear to be minors, eg young females in school uniforms or similar. The subgenre of hentai which focuses upon sexual activity involving minors is known as 'lolicon'.

[213] Law for Punishing Acts Related to Child Prostitution and Child Pornography, and for Protecting Children, art 7.

the constitutionality of a ban on child pornography. While it is speech within the meaning of the First Amendment, the Court has ruled it may be banned as not only are children inevitably abused during its production, but it also provides a permanent record of that abuse which causes ongoing psychological harm to the victims.[214] This decision applied only to 'real' child pornography, however. The Child Pornography Prevention Act attempted to introduce into US law the concept of pseudo images of child pornography, and required that they be treated as equivalent to actual images. This was struck down by the courts. In 1999, a Ninth Circuit Appeals Court ruled that these provisions violated the First Amendment on the basis that no actual children were harmed in their production, and that:

Any victimisation of children that may arise from paedophiles' sexual responses to pornography apparently depicting children engaged in explicit sexual activity is not a sufficiently compelling justification for the CPPA's speech restrictions.[215]

In 2002 the US Supreme Court reached the same conclusion.[216] Congress responded with the Prosecutorial Remedies and Other Tools to end the Exploitation of Children Today ('PROTECT') Act 2003, which criminalized such images if, and only if, they would qualify as being obscene (and therefore fall without the ambit of First Amendment speech) without there being a child depicted in the image.

With regard to simple possession of actual child pornography offences, the UK, Japan, and the USA all criminalize such activity, but this too is not universal. Of the 94 Interpol countries which had laws specifically addressing child pornography[217] by 2008, only 58 made it an offence merely to possess without intention to distribute.[218]

Clearly, then, even in an area of criminal law relating to a form of content seemingly universally regarded as 'unacceptable', it is possible for national laws to vary greatly, to the point where online content uploaded within one jurisdiction might be perfectly legal, yet, due to being internationally available the same content will almost inevitably be available in a jurisdiction where it is wholly illegal.

This plethora of laws and approaches to obscene and indecent material can place online intermediaries in a difficult position with regard to its possession and transmission, particularly where those intermediaries have an international presence, such as AOL and CompuServe. They may find themselves being held liable in one

---

[214] *New York v Ferber*, 458 US 761 (1978); *Osborne v Ohio*, 495 US 103 (1990) extended this logic to permit the criminalization of simple possession of child pornography.

[215] *Free Speech Coalition v Reno*, 198 F3d 1083, 1102 (CA9, 1999).

[216] *Ashcroft v Free Speech Coalition*, 535 US 234 (2002).

[217] This figure does not include those countries which outlaw child pornography under more general obscenity provisions, only those which have specific child pornography laws.

[218] See International Centre for Missing and Exploited Children (2008) *Child Pornography: Model Legislation & Global Review*, 5th edn, available online at <http://www.missingkids.com/en_US/documents/CP_Legislation_Report.pdf> (accessed 9 August 2011).

jurisdiction in which they operate, for activities that are perfectly legal in their other jurisdictions of operation.

In principle, in most jurisdictions, mere possession of an obscene article will not constitute an offence. That having been said, some jurisdictions, such as the UK, have in the past made a distinction between child pornography and other obscene or indecent material, with the possession of child pornography constituting an offence in and of itself.[219] Since the publication of the previous edition of this volume, this distinction has begun to erode, notably with the passage of new offences relating to the possession of what has been termed 'extreme pornography'.

Recent years have seen specific concerns raised about the proportion of children who have been exposed to online pornography, with statistics being cited which suggest that this is as high as 57 per cent of all 9- to 19-year-olds who use the internet on a regular basis.[220] Impetus for regulation also came from high-profile cases such as *R v Coutts*,[221] in which a young woman was brutally murdered by a regular user of extreme pornographic websites, in a manner reminiscent of such material.[222] Another key factor driving the case for criminalization of mere possession of such material was the 'global nature of the internet' itself.[223] This is certainly a strong argument in favour of regulation: whereas in the print era, the means of distribution could be easily traced and dealt with at source, in the online context frequently the material is being distributed from outside the UK, often from an untraceable source, or one which cannot be extradited to face prosecution as the material is perfectly legal at point of origin.

The offence of possession of extreme pornographic images was introduced by section 63 of the Criminal Justice and Immigration Act 2008. Under this provision, it is a criminal offence punishable by fines and/or imprisonment for up to two years[224] to possess an image with is both pornographic and extreme. An image is 'pornographic' if it can 'reasonably be presumed to have been produced solely or principally for the purposes of sexual arousal'.[225] In order to be 'extreme', it must be both 'grossly offensive, disgusting or otherwise of an obscene character'[226] and fall within one of the following categories:

(a) an act which threatens a person's life,

(b) an act which results, or is likely to result, in serious injury to a person's anus, breasts or genitals,

---

[219] See the UK Criminal Justice Act 1988, s 160 as amended by Criminal Justice and Public Order Act 1994, s 84(4) to cover 'pseudo photographs', California Penal Code § 311.11(a).

[220] Home Office, *Consultation on the possession of extreme pornographic material*, August 2005, p 12; The research cited in particular is S Livingstone and M Bober, April 2005, *UK Children Go Online* <http://www.children-go-online.net>.

[221] [2005] EWCA Crim 52.

[222] Home Office, n 220, p 12, para 10.

[223] Ibid at p 8.

[224] Criminal Justice and Immigration Act 2008, s 67.

[225] Ibid s 63(3).

[226] Ibid s 63(6)(b).

(c) an act which involves sexual interference with a human corpse, or

(d) a person performing an act of intercourse or oral sex with an animal (whether dead or alive), and a reasonable person looking at the image would think that any such person or animal was real.[227]

Images are, as one would expect, defined so as to include 'data (stored by any means) which is capable of conversion into an [extreme pornographic] image'.[228] Films classified by the British Board of Film Classification are excluded,[229] while available defences include legitimate possession,[230] lack of awareness of the nature of the material,[231] and participation in consensual acts.[232] The first reported conviction under section 63 occurred in June 2010, when Andrew Charles Dymond pleaded guilty to, inter alia, the possession of ten extreme pornographic images which included realistic depictions of acts likely to result in serious injury to people's breasts or genitals, and people engaging in sexual activity with animals including horses, dogs, and what appeared to be a dead squid or octopus.[233] Online intermediaries are specifically addressed by the Act;[234] Schedule 14 makes clear that both 'domestic' and 'non-UK' service providers are subject to the section 63 offence, however, a range of gradated, qualified immunities from liability for service providers offering mere conduit, caching, and hosting services is also set out. These are, as might be expected, a reiteration of the equivalent provisions to be found in the Electronic Commerce (EC Directive) Regulations 2002.[235]

Where mere possession is not criminalized, prosecutors must usually show that some further element of intent is involved, this usually being an intent to distribute or exhibit the article. Sometimes that intent alone is sufficient to ground a criminal action,[236] whereas in some jurisdictions a more specific intent, that of distribution for gain must be proven.[237] Where child pornography is at issue, possession with intent to distribute is normally regarded as a more serious offence than mere possession.[238] Under UK Government plans to introduce a possession offence for extreme pornography, this model will be repeated in respect of other material in addition to child pornography.

---

[227] Ibid s 63(7).

[228] Ibid s 63(8)(b).

[229] Ibid s 64.

[230] Ibid s 65.

[231] Ibid s 65.

[232] Ibid s 66.

[233] 'Porn pix showed sex act with squid', *This is South Wales*, 15 June 2010 <http://www.thisissouth-wales.co.uk/news/Porn-pix-showed-sex-act-squid/article-2300582-detail/article.html> (accessed 9 August 2011).

[234] Criminal Justice and Immigration Act 2008, s 68 and Sch 14.

[235] See section 5.2.2.1.

[236] See, eg, California Penal Code § 311.2(a); under § 311.2(b) possession with intent to distribute for gain, where the subject is a minor, is a more serious offence.

[237] See, eg, the UK Obscene Publications Act 1964, s 1(2).

[238] See the California Penal Code, § 311.1(a) (possession with intent to distribute), § 311.2(b) (intent to distribute for commercial consideration).

In circumstances where the basis of liability is possession, intermediaries will only run the risk of liability for third party content if they host or cache the offending material on their servers. In this situation, the act of possession will be committed in the jurisdiction where the server is physically located. It is possible that there may be a further risk involved where the intermediary controls a server from a different jurisdiction, if the determination as to the jurisdiction in which the material is held is made by reference to the place of control, rather than the physical location of the data. As yet, however, this type of issue does not appear to have arisen in any legal proceedings.

If an intermediary is found to be in possession of obscene or indecent material, a prosecutor may also then additionally have to prove that that service provider knew that the file held on its server was unlawful.[239] Proving this with regard to an intermediary's hosted and cached resources might very well prove difficult as it would, in most circumstances, almost certainly be uneconomic for an ISP to check all its files for obscene content. Under the UK Obscene Publications Act 1964 it is a defence for the accused to show that he has not examined the article and thus has no reasonable grounds for suspicion that his possession of it amounted to an offence.[240] Whether this suggests that UK intermediaries should simply abdicate any responsibility for checking of content is a moot point, for a criminal court might take the view that a deliberate policy of not undertaking any scrutiny of content negated the defence of lack of reasonable grounds for suspicion. The question of intermediary liability in respect of criminal liability for third party provided content has been clarified to a fair degree by the provisions of the Electronic Commerce (EC Directive) Regulations in relation to caching and hosting.[241] While the Directive to which they give force deals only with civil liability,[242] the UK Regulations also apply the same qualified immunities to criminal liability.

An alternative approach, and one seemingly favoured by UK ISPs, has been a combination of hotlines for individuals to report illegal materials, and other self-regulatory mechanisms such as codes of conduct for their clients, with coordination through a UK self-regulatory body for ISPs, the Internet Watch Foundation ('IWF').[243] Whilst this approach almost certainly cannot totally prevent the storage and transmission of illegal material via an intermediary's servers, it would appear to have reduced the amount of such material on UK ISPs to a level with which the authorities and law enforcement agencies are willing to live, whilst not imposing too rigorous an economic burden on the ISPs themselves.

---

[239] See, eg, the California Penal Code, § 311.11(a).

[240] It is anticipated that this defence will be replicated in respect of possession of extreme pornography in any future legislation. See Home Office, n 220, p 12, para 49.

[241] See above section 5.2.2.1, General liability and UK Electronic Commerce (EC Directive) Regulations 2002 (SI 2002/2013), regs 18–19.

[242] Criminal law matters are beyond the remit of the European Parliament.

[243] See <http://www.iwf.org.uk/> (accessed 9 August 2011), especially <http://www.iwf.org.uk/resources/trends> (accessed 15 August 2011).

Nonetheless, such industry self-regulation is not without controversy. In December 2008, a 32–year-old album cover caused a stir when a picture of the album caused several Wikipedia pages to be temporarily added to the IWF blacklist. The picture in question depicted a naked, prepubescent girl striking an open-legged pose, her crotch obscured by an overlaid image of a cracked-glass effect; the album's title: *Virgin Killer*.[244] Following negotiations with the Wiki Foundation, the IWF issued a statement that 'in light of the length of time the image has existed and its wide availability, the decision has been taken to remove this webpage from our list'.[245] The image was reinstated by Wikipedia,[246] and no prosecution has been brought. It is, however, tempting to dismiss this handful of cases as the exceptions that prove the rule: surely, for the most part, it will be obvious whether material found online is contrary to law on sexualized depictions of children? Any content regulation law is apt to provide hard cases where material is 'near the knuckle' but not quite illegal. Nevertheless, there remains an academic, at least, concern with respect to material that, however distasteful it may be, is technically lawful. At present, the IWF blacklist is limited to child sexual abuse images, but the remit of material in which the organization takes an active interest and will, pursuant to a complaint from a member of the public, investigate, notifying both the relevant service provider host and the police, is broader, including criminally obscene material, a broad category indeed.[247] Here there is probably more scope for mistakes to be made. Should the IWF in future expand its blacklist to incorporate such material, there may be stronger concerns raised with regards to the accountability of an extra-legal body effectively censoring online content which has not been pronounced unlawful by the proper authorities.[248]

Where intent to distribute is required for liability, the issue of whether an intermediary, whose primary role is the transmission of data packets, has the requisite intention by virtue of possessing a copy of the file arises. This issue was handled in UK law by amendments to the Obscene Publications Act 1964, section 1(2).[249] However, because the section 1(2) offence is only committed if the intention is to distribute for gain, a website host will only be criminally liable under this section if it has paid subscribers, and possibly only if access to the offending website requires a separate subscription.

---

[244] BBC 6 Music News, 'Scorpions Censored', 8 December 2008 <http://www.bbc.co.uk/6music/news/20081208_scorpians.shtml> (accessed 8 August 2011).

[245] 'IWF statement regarding Wikipedia webpage' <http://www.iwf.org.uk/media/news.archive-2008.251.htm> (accessed 8 August 2011).

[246] See Wikipedia Page <http://en.wikipedia.org/wiki/Virgin_Killer#cite_ref-bbc_6_music_2-0> (accessed 8 August 2011).

[247] IWF Role and Remit <http://www.iwf.org.uk/public/page.35.htm> (accessed 17 May 2010).

[248] See further TJ McIntyre and C Scott, 'Internet Filtering: Rhetoric, Legitimacy, Accountability and Responsibility' in R Brownsword and K Yeung (eds), *Regulating Technologies* (Oxford: Hart Publishing, 2008).

[249] See s 168 and Sch 9 para 3, Criminal Justice and Public Order Act 1994.

Transmission without possession (other than temporary possession) raises different issues. It is clear that the primary purpose of most obscenity laws is to prevent the distribution of pornographic material, presumably on the ground that if individuals are prevented from distributing it, at least some of the motivation for producing it in the first place will be lost. As such the laws clearly target distributors over possessors. This is where the aims of the legislators and courts clash most obviously with the role of many intermediaries, as the primary purpose of intermediaries who provide online access and certain other services is the paid transmission of information. From the intermediaries' point of view, and depending upon their particular business model, the more people sending and receiving information, or the more information that is sent, the better, regardless of the content of that information. Legal measures that slow the flow of information, dissuade people from using the medium, or impose higher costs on the service are all undesirable. From the lawmakers' point of view, for national content laws to have any meaning, they must be applied to all media, or the distributors of undesirable content will simply shift their focus to the weakly regulated medium. The difficulty lies in determining what constitutes reasonable regulation within a new medium, and in ensuring that the financial burden of any regulation does not destroy the growth of that medium.[250]

Three different approaches to that dilemma can be ascertained from existing laws. The first approach criminalizes the knowing distribution of obscene material.[251] This approach allows intermediaries to plead ignorance of the content of the material that they host or re-transmit, providing that they do not monitor the contents of their servers. Problems may arise, however, if the relevant law defines knowledge to include constructive knowledge.[252] Hosting Usenet newsgroups such as those in the alt.binaries.pictures.erotica.* hierarchy, or alt.sex.bestiality, or webpages with names such as *.supersex.com/cumming.html and *.gang-bang.com/hardcoreXXX/Ebony would suggest, fairly strongly, constructive knowledge. The second approach criminalizes distribution of obscene material for gain, subject to a defence of lack of knowledge or reasonable suspicion of contents.[253] This would potentially catch intermediaries who carried the Usenet newsgroups and websites listed above, but would seem to permit intermediaries not to have to filter all the files, on and transmissions to and from, their systems. The third approach criminalizes

---

[250] For an interesting, if unconventional, assessment of this balance see Johnson, 'Pornography Drives Technology: Why Not to Censor the Internet', (1996) (49(1) Federal Communications LJ 217.

[251] See, eg, the Tennessee Code, § 39-17-902(a) of which provides:

> It is unlawful to knowingly . . . prepare for distribution, publish, print, exhibit, distribute, or offer to distribute, or to possess with intent to distribute or to exhibit or offer to distribute any obscene matter. . .

[252] See the Tennessee Code, § 39-17-901(1):

> 'Actual or constructive knowledge': a person is deemed to have constructive knowledge of the contents of material who has knowledge of facts which would put a reasonable and prudent person on notice as to the suspect nature of the material.

[253] See, eg, the UK Obscene Publications Act 1959, s 2(1).

knowing distribution of obscene material, but provides a specific exemption from liability for intermediaries who merely provide access to other servers without participating actively in the production or distribution of the material.[254] This model is gradually becoming more prevalent, one example being the German Federal Law to Regulate the Conditions for Information and Communications Services 1997 ('the Multimedia Law'). Under article 5(3) of the Multimedia Law, intermediaries are provided with a blanket immunity from liability except insofar as they are aware that certain material is unlawful and fail to comply with a legal duty to block access to it.[255] Intermediaries who host material, however, are liable under article 5(2) for unlawful content if (a) they know that the content is unlawful, and (b) it is technically possible for the intermediary to block access and it is reasonable to expect such blocking to be effected.[256] Liability for material distributed from the intermediary's own servers, for example from a hosted website, remains based on knowledge of the intermediary. The effect of this approach is to provide criminal sanctions against an intermediary who knowingly hosts or caches obscene material, but removes the danger of liability from those intermediaries who merely act as transmitters of third party originated packets, whatever the intermediary's state of knowledge. This degree of immunity, however, may be predicated on a fairly simple intermediary business model, where the intermediary simply provides internet access. Providing more sophisticated services may still leave an intermediary open to more stringent rules.[257]

Some jurisdictions impose criminal liability for the transmission of obscene, indecent, or other unlawful material through their national telecommunications laws. Since internet communications are often carried across telecommunications networks, these laws will also potentially be applicable. Examples of such laws are 18

---

[254] See, eg, the California Penal Code, § 312.6(a):

> It does not constitute a violation of this chapter for a person or entity solely to provide access or connection to or from a facility, system, or network over which that person or entity has no control, including related capabilities that are incidental to providing access or connection. This subdivision does not apply to an individual or entity that is owned or controlled by, or a conspirator with, an entity actively involved in the creation, editing, or knowing distribution of communications that violate this chapter.

[255] German Multimedia Law 1997, art 5(4):

> any duties to block the use of illegal content according to the general laws remain unaffected, insofar as the service provider gains knowledge of such content . . .

[256] See FW Bulst, 'Hear No Evil, See No Evil, Answer for No Evil: Internet Service Providers and Intellectual Property—The New German Teleservices Act' [1997] European Intellectual Property Law Review 32.

[257] This appears to be the situation in France, where the French Telecommunications Law of July 1996 provides those supplying basic ISP services with a limited immunity for content liability. In the situation where an intermediary hosts webpages for third parties, an increasingly common option for ISPs, a recent court ruling has held that in providing file storage and transfer facilities at the disposal of the public the intermediary is no longer a mere access provider, and becomes responsible for the content of its site even in the absence of knowledge: Tribunal de grande instance de Paris, référé, 9 June 1998 and Cour d'appel de Paris, 14th Chamber, section A, 10 February 1999, *Affaire Estelle Hallyday v Altern* (France) (<http://www.legalis.net/legalnet/judiciaire/decisions/ca–100299.htm>) (accessed 9 August 2011).

USC § 1465[258] and the UK Telecommunications Act 1994, section 43.[259] Such offences are usually only committed by the sender of the material, which suggests that an intermediary, which merely transmits packets originating outside its systems, cannot be liable.[260] Matters become less certain when the intermediary hosts a website—it may be perceived that the intermediary does send the material, in that its software responds to requests for the obscene resource by transmitting it to the requesting user,[261] although it would seem more logical to decide that the true sender is in fact the controller of the resource. Certainly, the UK Electronic Commerce (EC Directive) Regulations 2002 provide a complete immunity from liability for third party provided content intermediaries which merely provide a transmission conduit, storing data packets only for so long as is necessary to facilitate onward transmission.[262]

Contempt of Court Another information content area where the potential criminal liability of ISPs remains uncertain, due largely to a lack of decided case law, is that of criminal contempt of court.[263] Criminal contempt essentially falls into five categories:

(a) The publication of materials prejudicial to a fair criminal trial.

(b) The publication of materials prejudicial to fair civil proceedings.

(c) The publication of materials interfering with the course of justice as a continuing process.

---

[258] Offence of using a means of interstate commerce for the purpose of transporting obscene material.

[259] Offence of using a public telecommunications system to send grossly offensive, threatening, or obscene material. See T Gibbons, 'Computer Generated Pornography' (1995) 9 International Yearbook of Law Computers and Technology 83.

[260] This supposition is supported by reg 17 of the UK Electronic Commerce (EC Directive) Regulations 2002 (SI 2002/2013) which provides an immunity for intermediaries acting as a 'mere conduit', transmitting content provided by a third party from one place to another at the request of the third party and without exercising any form of control over the material or selection of its recipient.

[261] This may be the correct interpretation of the UK Indecent Displays (Control) Act 1981, s 1(1), which creates an offence of publicly displaying indecent matter in public or in a manner which permits it to be visible from any public place (s 1(2)). Although s 1(3) exempts places which exclude those under 18 and make a charge for admission, this does not apply to the s 1(1) offence. It has been suggested that this might impose liability for websites, on the grounds that they can be accessed from terminals in public places: see G Smith (ed), *Internet Law and Regulation*, 4th edn (London: Sweet & Maxwell, 2007) 12-084.

[262] See above section 5.2.2.1 'General liability'.

[263] In England and Wales, a distinction is drawn between 'civil' and 'criminal' contempts. In broad terms, civil contempt relates to circumstances where parties breach an order of court made in civil proceedings, eg injunctions or undertakings, and as such are not relevant here. Criminal contempt, in contrast, is aimed at various types of conduct that might interfere with the administration of justice, and is designed to have both a punitive and deterrent effect. See Smith, n 261, Chapter 12, section 5; and A Charlesworth, 'Criminal Liability' in C Armstrong (ed), *Electronic Law and the Information Society* (London: Library Association, 1999) 120–49.

(d) Contempt in the face of the court.

(e) Acts which interfere with the course of justice.

Whilst the law of contempt of court has been largely developed by the judiciary through the common law, it has been modified to some extent by the Contempt of Court Act 1981.[264] This makes it an offence of strict liability to publish a publication which:

includes any speech, writing, broadcast, cable programme or other communication in whatever form, which is addressed to the public at large, or any section of the public[265]

where such a publication:

creates a substantial risk that the course of justice in the proceedings in question will be seriously impeded or prejudiced.[266]

The fact that it is a 'strict liability' offence means that an offence occurs even where the person making the publication did not intend to interfere with the course of justice. The broad definition of 'publication' would cover Usenet messages, e-mail messages sent to mailing lists, and webpages. The publication of material relating to a case will only be an offence where it occurs when the case is still *sub judice*. The statutory 'strict liability' rule is only applied during the period that the case is 'active' and the definition of 'active' is laid down in the Act. However, in circumstances where an individual knows, or has good reason to believe, that proceedings are imminent, and publishes material which is likely or calculated to impede or prejudice the course of justice before the point laid down in the Act as the time when the case is 'active', may still constitute a common law contempt.

Defences to the 'strict liability' offence are:

(a) A person will not be guilty of contempt of court under the strict liability rule as the publisher of any matter to which that rule applies if at the time of publication (having taken all reasonable care) he does not know and has no reason to suspect that the relevant proceedings are active.[267]

(b) A person will not be guilty of contempt of court under the strict liability rule as the distributor of a publication containing any such matter if at the time of publication (having taken all reasonable care) he does not know that it contains such matter and has no reason to suspect that it is likely to do so.[268]

---

[264] However, the Contempt of Court Act 1981 does not codify or replace entirely the common law. It does, however, apply to Scotland (s 15).

[265] Contempt of Court Act 1981, s 2(1).

[266] Ibid s 2(2).

[267] Ibid s 3(1).

[268] Ibid s 3(2).

(c) A person is not guilty of contempt of court under the strict liability rule in respect of a fair and accurate report of legal proceedings held in public, published contemporaneously and in good faith.[269]

The enforcement of the law of contempt has been rendered more difficult in modern times, by the ability of individuals to publish material, in both traditional[270] and digital media, in countries outside the court's jurisdiction. The internet has in many ways exacerbated this situation. A prime example of this concerns the 1993 murder trials in Ontario, Canada, of Karla Homolka and Paul Bernado. During the trial of Karla Homolka for the murders of two teenage girls, Kristen French and Leslie Muhaffy, the court ordered a publication ban on reports of the trial in Ontario, in order to ensure a fair trial for Homolka's husband Paul Bernado (aka Paul Teale), also charged with the murders.[271] Despite the ban, however, information was widely available due to coverage by US newspapers, cable and TV stations, and at least one website based at a US university.[272] A Usenet newsgroup set up to disseminate and discuss information about the trial—alt.fan.karla-homolka—was censored by many Canadian universities, which were concerned about their liability to contempt proceedings.[273]

Whilst denying access to webpages is more difficult than cutting off newsgroups, it has been suggested with regard to the internet that where the court cannot bring contempt proceedings against the original publisher, it may seek to do so against the intermediary that distributed the material within the court's jurisdiction. Some clarification on the position of intermediaries in UK law with regard to hosting third party provided information which is in contempt of a court order forbidding publication may be found in the case of *John Venables and Robert Thompson v Newsgroup Newspapers Ltd, Associated Newspapers Ltd, MGN Ltd*.[274] The background to the case involved the murder in February 1993 by Thompson and Venables, then both 10 years old, of 2-year-old Jamie Bulger. The case caused considerable public outcry at the time, and was revived in 2001 when it emerged that, having served eight years each in a secure local authority institution, Thompson and Venables were to be

---

[269] Ibid s 4(1).

[270] Consider, eg, the *Spycatcher* saga, where the book in question was freely available outside the UK, but could not be published or excerpted in the UK. The judicial ban was imposed by preliminary injunction to ensure that the main trial, where the UK government sought to prevent publication of the allegations made in the book, was not rendered meaningless by prior publication in the UK. It is likely that a similar UK publication ban today would be rendered ineffective by web publication within hours. See, eg, the events surrounding the case *Nottinghamshire CC v Gwatkin* (High Court of Justice, Chancery Division, 3 June 1997) and *Cyber-Rights & Cyber-Liberties (UK) Newsletter* Issue Number 2, June 1997 at <http://www.cyber-rights.org/policy> (accessed 15 August 2011).

[271] See Action No 125/93, *R v Bernardo* [1993] OJ 2047. Also C Walker, 'Cybercontempt: Fair Trials and the Internet' (1997–8) 3 Oxford Yearbook of Media and Entertainment Law 1.

[272] Information from <http://www.web.archive.org/web/20000303081858/http://www.cs.indiana.edu/canada/karla.html> (accessed 15 August 2011).

[273] Information from <http://web.archive.org/web/20001004210637/http://www.cs.indiana.edu/canada/BannedinCanada.txt> (accessed 15 August 2011).

[274] Case No HQ 0004737 and HQ 0004986, 10 July 2001.

released rather than transferred to adult prisons. Eventually they were paroled in June 2001, with new identities. The High Court, with Dame Elizabeth Butler-Sloss presiding, issued an injunction forbidding the media to publish any information which might lead to the revelation of the new identities. This was felt to be a necessary step in the wake of public outcry over the case, in particular as a result of Bulger's mother Denise Fergus' 'Justice for James' media campaign, which demanded variously that the killers be 'locked up for life', or should serve at least a minimum of 15 years prior to being eligible for parole. Fear of vigilante action against the pair, whipped up by public comments made by Fergus herself, such as 'No matter where they go, someone out there is waiting', was high, and Fergus claimed to know the new identities and locations of the killers. The terms of the injunction expressly barred publication 'in any newspaper or broadcasting in any sound or television broadcast or by means of any cable or satellite programme service or public computer network' any information 'likely to lead to the identification of [Thompson and Venables]' or their 'past, present or future whereabouts'. Internet Service Provider Demon, seeking to avoid further liability problems after the expense of the *Godfrey* decision against them, petitioned the High Court to exempt ISPs from liability for breach of the injunction where this was occasioned by the uploading to their servers of material by third parties. The argument here was very much in the same terms as the rationale behind the defence in section 1 of the Defamation Act 1996, namely that an intermediary does not and cannot reasonably be expected to have the same level of awareness of the material it makes available as a publisher of a traditional newspaper. The rapid changeability and sheer quantity of subscriber-uploaded information available on an intermediary such as Demon's servers renders the prospect of any meaningful level of direct control a practical impossibility. Dame Butler-Sloss agreed to amend the terms of the injunction such that an intermediary's potential liability will be limited where the intermediary in question:

or any of its employees or agents:

(i) knew that the material had been placed on its servers or could be accessible via its service;

(ii) or knew that the material was likely to be placed on its servers, or was likely to be accessed via its service;

and in either case

(iii) failed to take all reasonable steps to prevent the publication.[275]

Employees or agents of an ISP who are in possession of such knowledge will similarly be in breach of the injunction if they:

failed to take all reasonable steps to prevent the publication and to induce the ISP to prevent the publication.[276]

---

[275] Proviso to para (1), (a).
[276] Proviso to para (1), (b)iii.

'Knowledge' may be actual or constructive:

an ISP, employee or agent shall be considered to know anything which he or it would have known if he or it had taken reasonable steps to find out.[277]

'Taking all reasonable steps to prevent the publication' is defined to include:

the taking of all reasonable steps to remove the material from the ISP's servers or to block access to the material.

Demon had also asked the court to outline the specific steps that would be considered reasonable for ISPs to take in order to prevent online publication, however, Dame Butler-Sloss declined this request, ruling that to do so risked rendering the injunction time-bound and vulnerable to future technological advances. As it now sits, the terms of the injunction are consistent with the principles outlined for intermediary liability in respect of third party provided content in general in the Electronic Commerce (EC Directive) Regulations 2002.[278]

5.3 CONCLUSION

As readers familiar with previous editions of this volume will be aware, the past several years have seen much development in the field of law regulating online intermediary liability. Contractual liability for service provision to customers seems unlikely to change much in coming years, but there is still room for much development in the area of liability in respect of third party provided content. In the UK, there remain a number of unanswered questions with respect to the application of the Electronic Commerce (EC Directive) Regulations 2002. The major innovation of the Regulations, which for the most part as concerns intermediaries simply repeat the text of the English version of the Directive with little alteration, is the introduction in regulation 22 of some form of guidance as to the meaning of 'actual notice' in regulations 18 (caching) and 19 (hosting). As discussed, there remains much scope for development of this in practice. Although it adds nothing to the interpretation of regulation 22, Eady J's judgment in *Bunt v Tilley* may yet be influential. While it can offer no binding precedent, Eady J's discussion of the Regulations being *obiter*, this is still the judgment of a respected, senior libel judge whose words may carry persuasive weight in later cases. His straightforward reading of regulations 17 (mere conduit) and 18 is likely to match that taken by the courts in future cases. It will be interesting to see whether other members of the judiciary will deal with provisions such as the defence in section 1 of the Defamation Act 1996 alongside the qualified immunities provided in the Regulations, or whether they will go

---

[277] Proviso to para (1), (c).
[278] See above section 5.2.2.1 'General liability'.

further and agree with those commentators who have assumed that the latter should in practice supersede the former. In the USA, section 230 seems almost unassailable, although should the reasoning of the Florida Circuit Court in *Giordano v Romeo* succeed in persuading higher courts, some limitation will be brought to bear upon those who have to date been able to provide defamatory and otherwise unlawful third party content with reckless abandon. In Europe, the liability regime remains largely unchanged, but as service providers and their business models evolve we are likely to see the courts redefining our understanding of a service provider. It remains to be seen whether this will evolve a common European position, absent to date as individual Member State jurisdictions have come to differing conclusions as regards the entitlement of eBay, to rely upon the protections of the e-Commerce Directive. A dozen years on from *Godfrey v Demon*, and two decades since *Cubby v Compuserve*, there is no sign of a definitive end to the evolution of regulation of online intermediary liabilities.

Part III

INTELLECTUAL PROPERTY AND RELATED RIGHTS IN INFORMATION TECHNOLOGY

6

PATENT PROTECTION FOR COMPUTER-RELATED INVENTIONS

Tim Press

6.1 AN OVERVIEW OF THE PATENT SYSTEM

6.1.1 The UK and European legal framework

Patent protection in the UK is governed by the Patents Act 1977 and rules made under it relating to the procedure for obtaining patents.

The Patents Act 1977 was passed in order to implement the European Patent Convention ('EPC'), to which the UK and most major European countries, including all the then members of the EEC, were signatories.[1] The Convention provides for harmonization of all major aspects of domestic patent law of the signatory states and also provides for the setting up of the European Patent Office ('EPO') to grant European patents. The national systems of granting patents via national patent offices remain in force, although patents granted at the national level are subject to the newly harmonized patent laws. On 13 December 2007 a revised version of the EPC came into force. This streamlined aspects of patent application and reduced

---

[1] The current EPC states are the EU states plus Turkey, San Marino, Serbia, Norway, Former Yugoslav Republic of Macedonia, Monaco, Liechtenstein, Iceland, Croatia, Switzerland, and Albania.

costs as well as dealing with some issues of substantive patent law. This revised version is known as EPC 2000.

The EPO is concerned solely with the granting of patents. An applicant makes an application to the EPO and EPO examiners decide whether a patent should issue. But any patent that is eventually granted takes effect as if it were a bundle of national patents granted by the domestic patent offices of each of the designated states.[2] So proceedings to restrain acts of infringement would be commenced before the German courts if the acts were committed in Bonn and the English courts if the acts were committed in Liverpool. Any remedy would only cover the territory of that court, so the English injunction would only operate within the UK and any enquiry as to damages ordered by the UK court would only cover acts of infringement carried out within the UK.[3]

The UK part of a patent granted by the EPO and designating the UK is referred to as a European Patent (UK). After grant, subject to a nine-month opposition period, all influence of the EPO over a patent ceases. This also applies to challenges to the validity of or applications to amend patents after grant, as well as to issues of infringement, which are decided by national courts or patent offices just as they would be for domestically granted patents. It is possible for the UK part of a European patent to be revoked whilst the Swedish or Spanish parts remain in force and perfectly enforceable in those jurisdictions. Of course, the basis for granting and revoking the domestic patents will be the same as that applied by the EPO because the provisions of the Treaty provide for harmonization of the key principles.

Thus, in theory, when matters relating to the validity or infringement of the German part of a European patent are considered by the German courts, the same considerations will be applied as when the same matters are considered in relation to the UK part of the same European patent by the English (or Northern Irish or Scottish) courts or the UK Patent Office. In practice there is not as much consistency as might be desired. The procedures whereby validity and infringement are considered (eg, rules relating to evidence and disclosure of documents) are very different in the different states. Also, in difficult or borderline cases, complete consistency in findings of fact would be surprising. And when it comes to matters of doctrine, the respective histories of national patent law against which the Treaty-inspired current domestic legal provisions are construed are quite different, so divergent approaches to interpretation are likely.

In the case of issues of validity, there is a source of moderation between the EPC states in the decisions arising from appeals within the EPO. Appeals from an

---

[2] The significance of 'designating' which states protection is required in is now greatly reduced as the same fee is payable regardless, and all states are automatically designated when an application is made.

[3] This is an oversimplification. There are situations when issues relating to one part of a European Patent can be litigated in another EU state and when patent litigation in different states can collide. This is beyond the scope of this chapter, and readers are directed to practitioner works on the conflict of laws within Europe or patent law generally.

examiner go to one of the Technical Boards of Appeal[4] ('TBAs'), and issues can be referred further to the Enlarged Board of Appeal ('EBA'). However, in the case of issues of infringement, although the EPC lays down a general definition there is no supranational body with jurisdiction to decide issues of infringement and develop a consistent doctrinal approach to the interpretation of the general provisions of the EPC.

It must be stressed that the EPO is not a creature of the EU and decisions of the TBAs and the EBA do not have the same force as decisions of the European Court of Justice. The EU Member States have now agreed a way forward for implementing a single EU-wide patent to be granted by the EPO.[5]

6.1.2 International considerations

Beyond the European system noted above, there is a system of international conventions in the field of patents covering essentially all the industrialized countries of the world.

(a) The Paris Convention[6] allows for the nationals of one Convention country to be granted patent protection in any other. Most importantly, it provides for an application filed in one Convention country to give priority to subsequent applications, based on that first filing, made in any Convention country provided the subsequent applications are made within one year from the first.

(b) The Patent Co-operation Treaty ('PCT') allows for an 'international application' to be made at a 'receiving office' which will generally be the applicant's national patent office. An applicant can ask for an 'international search' to be carried out in respect of an application, the results of which will be used in subsequent prosecution proceedings in the various jurisdictions.

(c) The TRIPs Agreement[7] contains some provisions harmonizing patent law.

The Paris Convention and the PCT are of immense importance in enabling effective worldwide protection to be obtained without excessive costs having to be incurred at an early stage when an invention's true value may not be apparent. Patent applications will still ultimately have to be prosecuted in all states (or supranational granting bodies such as the EPO) where protection is required, but the inventor has a year to decide whether the invention is of value and where protection should be sought, and search fees may be reduced.

---

[4] There are boards for different areas of technology and for procedural issues.
[5] See section 6.5 below.
[6] The International Convention for the Protection of Industrial Property.
[7] Agreement on Trade-Related Aspects of Intellectual Property Rights, Annex 1C of the Marrakesh Agreement Establishing the World Trade Organization, signed in Marrakesh, Morocco on 15 April 1994.

This chapter will also consider aspects of the law relating specifically to computer-related inventions from the USA. The US and European practices represent two different approaches, and other patent laws often tend to follow one or other model. It should further be noted that, whilst differences within the problem areas (and computer-related inventions are a problem area) between patent laws are interesting, patent law is an area where there is considerable congruence at the level of general principles between the laws of the countries of the world.

6.1.3 The nature of patentable inventions

Patents granted by most countries or bodies now follow a similar form. First, they set out information about the inventor, the owner, and the history of applications and dates leading up to the grant of the patent. There will then be a descriptive part forming the bulk of the patent in which the invention is explained. Lastly, there will be the numbered claims where the inventor sets out precisely what the monopoly covers. In deciding whether a patent is infringed, one looks at the claims and asks the question 'does what is complained of fall within the scope of what is described in the claims'. The description can be used to provide definition to or resolve ambiguities in the claims. The precise latitude allowed in interpreting the scope of the claims varies from jurisdiction to jurisdiction.

The claims and their precise wording are thus central to the patent system. In many cases where an inventor disagrees with the decision of a patent office, the disagreement is not about whether a patent should be granted but about the precise scope of the claims that should be allowed. Patent examiners are naturally concerned that the monopoly granted should not be wider than the law permits, whereas from the inventor's point of view, the broader the claims the better.

Claims may describe machines, articles, materials, or processes for doing or making things. The claims to patents are arranged in series (normally only one or two of them), each headed by an 'independent claim'. All non-independent claims in a series incorporate by reference the description of a product, process. or whatever from an earlier claim in the series and add further elements which serve to narrow down the scope of the claim. Thus, for example, claim 2 of a (hypothetical) patent might be worded thus: 'A method according to claim 1 in which the process is implemented by means of a programmed computer.'

The purpose of the explanatory part of a patent is to enable the invention (as claimed in the claims) to be carried out by any person reasonably skilled in the area of technology in question—to teach how to do it. This teaching is considered part of the quid pro quo for the granting of the patent monopoly: an inventor can either try to keep his technology secret or apply for a patent, but if the latter course is adopted the invention must be explained. The explanation is assumed to be of benefit to society by advancing the general corpus of knowledge available to other researchers who may use it to make further advances. It appears beyond doubt that the pace of technological development is hastened in some instances by the publication of matter in patent specifications. Whether the public benefit in each case justifies the monopoly granted is of course another matter.

The need for teaching in a patent is enforced by virtue of a rule in most jurisdictions (including Europe and the USA) that any claim in a patent that is not sufficiently well taught is invalid. Lack of adequate teaching is a not uncommon ground for objection to a patent. Apart from this issue of 'internal validity', for a patent to be granted in Europe the invention claimed in the claims has to be:

(a) an invention that is capable of industrial application and not excluded from patentability;

(b) new; and

(c) not obvious, that is containing an inventive step.

These concepts will be discussed below, particularly the concept of patentable inventions, in which area the status of computer-related inventions has been a cause of much debate.

6.2 PATENTS FOR COMPUTER-RELATED INVENTIONS IN DETAIL

6.2.1 An overview of the problem

The precise scope of what is a patentable invention is an important issue because, traditionally, patents have been granted for industrially useful things such as new machines, chemical compounds, and materials and processes for making such things or otherwise achieving a useful result. A computer program of itself is not, to many minds, such a thing. We tend to use the term 'computer program' to describe a sequence of instructions to a computer in the abstract sense, much as we talk of a novel or play as an abstract entity which is separate from the book (disk) it is recorded on or any particular performance (reading, running) of it. The example below illustrates a computer-related invention, and the distinction between that and a computer program.

In 1970 Albert and John Carter invented the 'nudge' feature on fruit machines.[8] Claim 1 of their patent reads:

A coin-operated . . . gaming machine . . ., wherein at least one drum . . . displays at least two symbols and this or each such drum has associated therewith . . . an adjustment button or mechanism the operation of which after the machine has been played, causes the respective drum . . . to be indexed to display on the combination line another symbol which was previously visible to the player but not on the combination line and which thereby completes or contributes to a winning combination.

---

[8] UK patent 1,292,712.

Note that this claim specifies a machine with reference to what it does rather than how it does it. The body of the patent sets out a method of achieving this using electromechanical means (switches, relays, and so on). By the time the patent expired, fruit machines operated under microprocessor control. In such machines the nudge was achieved by the nudge button sending a message to the microprocessor which arranged for signals to be sent to the stepping electric motor for the relevant reel which turned so as to rotate the reel by exactly one position. Such computerized machines still infringed the patent and their manufacturers paid royalties under it.

The nudge feature is an example of an invention that can be achieved by computer or mechanical means. Apart from the provision of a nudge button and suitable information on the machine, in modern machines the nudge feature is contained solely in the program that runs on the microprocessor, whereas at the time of its invention it was hard-wired by the use of conventional electromechanical components. This patent also provides a good example of the importance of careful claim drafting in ensuring that economically useful protection will last for the legal duration of the patent.

There is generally no problem with claims of the above type, that is claims to machines or processes that happen to be implemented with the aid of a suitably programmed computer. The important point to such inventions is generally not the development of the program but the realization that a better (more useful, cheaper to make, etc) machine results from making the machine behave in that particular way. All the program does is take a series of inputs (numbers), operate upon them in a certain way, and produce an output (different numbers). Consider a program used to control, say, a welding arc by relating the voltage to various measured parameters of the arc. If the method of controlling the arc was new, a patent would be granted. The same program could be used to operate a food processor or toy car if the same mathematical relationship between input and output was useful in those areas, but the patent would not cover those uses nor would previous uses in food processors or toy cars invalidate the welding equipment patent.

In fact a program on its own is nothing more than a representation, in the form of instructions how to carry it out, of a mathematical formula or relationship[9]—which could be applied in any number of ways. Such descriptions of processes are also referred to as 'algorithms' and this term has formed a central feature of discussions of patentability of computer-related inventions. Prior to the invention of computers it had always been held that scientific discoveries, laws of nature, mathematical formulae, and the like were not suitable subject matter for patents—the formula or discovery had to be applied and only the particular application developed could be patented.

---

[9] It must be understood that this term is used in a broad sense to cover matters of logic as well as arithmetic. Many modern programs are far too complex for a precise mathematical description of their operation to be written down, but at least in theory one does exist.

Broadly speaking it is still the position that mathematical formulae and so on are not patentable, but great difficulties have been experienced in applying this apparently simple concept in the field of many computer-related inventions. In the examples given above the distinction between the program/algorithm and its application is quite clear. But cases arise where the distinctions are more blurred and this is particularly so where the subject matter of the invention is not an obvious industrial process such as welding but is itself of a more abstract nature, such as methods of analysing electronic data, or an aspect of computer design, architecture, or organization. The distinction between a fruit machine and the mathematical relationships underpinning its operation is clear. The distinction between a computer and the logical and mathematical rules by which it operates is altogether more tricky. What is a computer other than an assembly of things obeying logical (mathematical) relationships? Yet patents are granted for developments in computer technology.

Another area that has caused acute problems more recently is where the subject matter of the computer-related invention is a method of doing business. In such cases the problem lies in disentangling the technological (and therefore potentially patentable) aspects of the invention from those aspects which represent developments in fields such as finance, commerce, and marketing which do not normally attract patent protection.

In terms of international law, the most relevant provision to this area is Article 27.1 of the TRIPs Agreement, which states that patents shall be granted 'in all fields of technology'. The position developed by the EPO on the issue of patentability set out below, that inventions are only patentable if they are of a technical nature, is broadly consistent with this.

6.2.2 The EPO doctrine on patentable inventions

6.2.2.1 *The basic provisions of the EPC*
The fundamental provisions of the EPC are found in Article 52(1) which states that:

European patents shall be granted for any inventions, *in all fields of technology*, provided that they are new, involve an inventive step and are susceptible of industrial application.

Article 57 further states that:

An invention shall be considered as susceptible of industrial application if it can be made or used in any kind of industry, including agriculture.

The italicized words are the only substantive change introduced by EPC 2000 in order to comply with the TRIPs Agreement. But as is explained below, the requirement for technical content is a long-standing aspect of the EPO doctrine, on which the change in wording has not had much effect. Many key cases discussed below pre-date the implementation of EPC 2000.

Article 52(2) provides exclusions to patentability:

The following in particular shall not be regarded as inventions within the meaning of paragraph 1:

    (a) discoveries, scientific theories and mathematical methods;

    (b) aesthetic creations;

    (c) schemes, rules and methods for performing mental acts, playing games or doing business, and programs for computers;

    (d) presentations of information.

The scope of the exclusions is explained (not as helpfully as might have been hoped) by Article 52(3):

The provisions of paragraph 2 shall exclude patentability of the subject-matter or activities referred to in that provision only to the extent to which a European patent application or a European patent relates to such subject-matter or activities as such.

The EPC does not elaborate on what a claim for a computer program is or indeed define a 'computer program' at all. It can be seen, however, that the restriction applies only to programs, not software or computers in the more general sense. As will be seen, the specific 'computer program as such' exclusion is by no means the only hurdle in the way of protection for computer-related inventions.

6.2.2.2 *The requirement for technical content*

The issue of patentable subject matter, including patents for computer-related inventions, before the EPO has largely concentrated on the concept that patentable inventions must be 'technical'. This concept is difficult to explain, and has developed considerably over the years. The first clear explanation of the legal basis for the requirement for technical content was given in *IBM/Document abstracting and retrieving*:[10]

Whatever their differences [they being the things excluded under Article 52(2) EPC] these exclusions have in common that they refer to activities which do not aim at any direct technical result but are rather of an abstract and intellectual character.

The decision goes on to point out that the Implementing Regulations of the EPC required a claim to have 'technical features' and therefore that the EPC requires inventions to have a 'technical character'. Reference to the patent law histories of the contracting states is made.

    Thus, it has been possible for the EPO to demonstrate compliance with the TRIPs Agreement. Notwithstanding the list of excluded things (on the face of it lists of

---

[10] Case T 22/85.

excluded things are prohibited by TRIPs) all the excluded things are not technology, and so it is permissible not to grant patents in respect of them.[11]

Having established that technical content is needed, two questions are raised:

(a) Where and how to look for the technical content.

(b) What exactly does 'technical' mean?

The EPO has developed two doctrines to deal with the first. In relation to the second, the EPO has developed a body of decisions which give examples, but has consistently avoided any exposition of a general theory or doctrine.

6.2.2.3 *Where and how the EPO looks for technical content*

Initially, the EPO developed the doctrine now known as the 'contribution approach'. The contribution approach required the 'real contribution to the art' of the invention as claimed to be determined: only if that contribution lay in a technical field would the application be held to be for an invention which fell outside the exclusions from patentability set out in Article 52(2). The UK courts still cleave to the contribution approach, and it is discussed in greater detail in relation to UK law at section 6.2.3 below.

An often-cited example of how this approach works is the case of *Koch & Sterzel/ X-ray apparatus*.[12] The invention was for an X-ray machine which controlled the power delivered to the X-ray tube in a particular way that extended the life of the (expensive) tube. The only difference between the claimed machine and a prior machine was in the software which controlled the operation of the machine. On a narrow interpretation of the claim, the only novelty lay in a computer program. The TBA held that the contribution to the art of the invention was a new type of X-ray machine, and X-ray machines were not excluded. The key to the contribution approach was to look beyond the literal nature of the claim to the practical use to which the invention could be put, viewed in the context of the existing art. The invention in *Koch & Sterzel* was not a new way of programming a known method of controlling the X-ray tube (where the contribution would be a program); rather, it was a new way of controlling the tube that happened to be implemented in software.

For many years the contribution approach was applied, but in *PBS Partnership/ controlling pension benefits system*[13] (*'Pensions'*) the TBA decided to change its approach.[14] The concept of a 'technical contribution to the art' had proved

---

[11] In fact some early EPO decisions wavered on this point in relation to computer programs, but recent decisions have made it clear that all the excluded things are non-technical.

[12] Case T 26/86 [1988] EPOR 72.

[13] Case T 931/95.

[14] The Boards are not bound by precedent, only by the Convention, and their approach to case law is more akin to that used in civil law countries. They try to be consistent, but changes of doctrine are easier for them than for a common law court.

difficult to nail down, and in *Pensions* it was pointed out that the test inevitably required a comparison between the invention claimed and the prior art. This was illogical; the enquiry under Article 52 should be capable of being carried out without any reference to the prior art or the state of general knowledge.

Thus, in *Pensions* a claim to an apparatus (a programmed computer) for carrying out a non-technical activity (determining pension benefits) was held to be an invention under Article 52(1) and not to be excluded under Article 52(2)—the apparatus was a physical thing of a technical nature. There was no further enquiry into what the thing actually did, as would have happened under the contribution approach. This approach to Article 52 has become known as the 'any hardware' approach. However, the Board went on to consider the question of obviousness/lack of inventive step. It held that the step from the prior art to the invention, if it was inventive at all, involved invention in a non-technical field of activity (calculating pension benefits). To the extent that there was a development in a technical field (computerization) it was not inventive, the task of computerizing the process being achieved using standard methods. The Board itself threw out the claims on the ground of lack of inventive step, rather than adopting the more normal approach of sending the matter back to the examining division to consider this issue.

It has always been an aspect of European patent law that the inventive step must lie in a technical field (see section 6.3.2 below). But prior to *Pensions* the approach was that the requirement for technical subject matter was a separate (and not necessarily identical) issue relating to patentability. *Pensions* thus represented a major shift from a doctrinal perspective, with only a superficial enquiry into technical subject matter taking place at the patentability stage, the in-depth enquiry taking place when novelty and inventive step are considered. It is unclear whether *Pensions* has had any effect on the substantive patentability of claimed inventions. Is the same question being asked but under a different heading, or has the question changed? Certainly in *Pensions* itself, the end result was the same as if the contribution approach had been applied.

The change in doctrine is well summarized in the following quote from the subsequent *Hitachi* case:

The Board is aware that its comparatively broad interpretation of the term 'invention' in Article 52(1) EPC will include activities which are so familiar that their technical character tends to be overlooked, such as the act of writing using pen and paper. Needless to say, however, this does not imply that all methods involving the use of technical means are patentable. They still have to be new, represent a non-obvious technical solution to a technical problem, and be susceptible of industrial application.[15]

The application and development of the *Pensions* doctrine was not uniform across all the Technical Boards, but a clear doctrinal approach has now emerged.

---

[15] Case T 258/03 [2004] EPOR 55, concerning an online auction system.

The *Duns*[16] case is now regarded by the EPO as summarizing the current position following *Hitachi* and another key case *Comvik*.[17] *Duns* concerned a method of gathering sales data from some sales outlets and estimating sales performance at other 'non-reporting' outlets using that and other (eg geographical) data. Claim 1 as originally filed was to a method including a database but not mentioning any particular way (paper, digital) of implementing it. A further version of claim 1 filed in an auxiliary request was similar, but included also reference to a processor to carry out aspects of the method. The following passage from *Duns* illustrates the dividing line between a claim that will be excluded under Article 52(2) and one that will not.

21. Determining sales data and geographical distances between outlets and using this data to estimate sales at specific outlets by means of the statistical method claimed and disclosed in the application do not solve any technical problem in a technical field. The definitions in claim 1 do not imply the use of any technical system or means. The term 'database', in particular, may be construed to designate any collection of data so that claim 1 encompasses methods which may be performed without using any technical means at all. The method of claim 1 is hence excluded from patentability under Article 52(1), (2)(c) and (3) EPC.

Auxiliary request 1

22. Auxiliary request 1 explicitly claims technical means (processor) to perform individual steps of the method. From the HITACHI decision T 258/03 (supra), Reasons Nos. 4.1 to 4.7, it follows that the claimed method is an invention in terms of Article 52(1) EPC.

The Board rejected arguments that gathering and storing data necessarily involved interaction with the physical world and thus claim 1 in its broad form was not to technical things or processes, but the narrower version of the Auxiliary request was. It went on to hold the invention obvious because the 'contribution to the prior art' was a new algorithm for estimating sales at a non-reporting outlet, which was excluded as part of a business research method. Development of this algorithm could not contribute to an inventive step. The means of implementing the algorithm (using a computer system) were technical but obvious.

It is thus clear that some earlier cases allowing patent claims of the general form 'a computer program which . . .' are not good law.[18] Under the current doctrine, such claims will be refused under Article 52(2) regardless of whether or not the invention is in fact directed to technical subject matter unless the claim mentions a technical apparatus or processes. Of course, it will be easy to re-cast the claims so that they are addressed to a computer which carries out the process, whereupon the technical nature (or lack of it) of the underlying process will be investigated at the stage of the enquiry into novelty and obviousness. This was confirmed in *Programs for*

---

[16] Case T 154/04 [2007] EPOR 38.
[17] *COMVIK/Two identities* (T 641/00) [2004] EPOR 10.
[18] Cases T 0953/97 and T 1173/97. The former is reported as *IBM's Application* [1999] RPC 563.

computers,[19] a decision of the EBA. The Board also confirmed that claims to 'a computer-readable storage medium storing computer program X' will not be excluded under Article 52(2).[20] This distinction in claim drafting will not have a great effect on the scope of the patent monopoly because of the principle of 'contributory infringement', whereby supplying the program alone is likely to amount to infringement of a claim drawn to specific hardware implementing the program.[21]

Hitachi clarified the position regarding inventions concerning both technical and non-technical matter. They should not be rejected under Article 52, but proceed to a consideration of a technical inventive step. However, in that case the use of non-technical means (changing the rules of an auction process that could just as easily be carried out face-to-face) to work around a technical problem (timing discrepancies in online auctions) did not amount to a technical inventive step.

6.2.3 EPO decisions on technical subject matter

The EPO cases that are referred to under this heading should be read with the above change in doctrine in mind, as some of them pre-date it. The patent claims involved may not have mentioned technical devices or processes, and technical content may have been decided using the 'contribution approach' or following an unclear post-*Pensions* but pre-*Comvik/Hitachi/Duns* doctrine. But these cases are nevertheless useful in helping to develop an understanding of what is and is not regarded as technical subject matter. The Technical Boards and the Enlarged Board have not, in recent cases, sought to upset the detailed development of EPO thinking in this area. As noted above, this has happened on a case-by-case basis. The cases are organized under loose headings, with the focus on topics related to computer technology and its application.

6.2.3.1 *The internal operation of computers*

In *IBM/Data processor network*,[22] the claim concerned a data processing system comprising a number of data processors forming the nodes of a communications network. In the invention claimed the processors are so arranged that a transaction request originating at one node may be split up and part or parts of the transaction carried out at another node. The claims specified in general terms a method of carrying this out but did not give any detail of the computer programming structures used to achieve the method. The TBA decided that 'the coordination and control of the internal communication between programs and data files held at different processors in a data processing system . . . is to be regarded as solving a problem

---

[19] Case G 3/08, discussed further in relation to the UK position at section 6.2.4 below.
[20] Following the decision in *Microsoft/Clipboard formats* I Case T 424/03 [2006] EPOR 39.
[21] See section 6.3.4 below.
[22] Case T 06/83.

which is essentially technical'. No attempt was made in the decision to state any general rule defining what is and is not 'technical', which was treated as simply a matter of fact to be decided in each instance.

In *Bosch/Electronic Computer Components*,[23] the claims covered a 'device for monitoring computer components' which was capable of re-setting the computer's processor. The contents of the computer's volatile memories were compared with a pattern contained in non-volatile memory to establish whether, when the computer's processor had been re-set, it was the result of the device or an operation of the manual re-set circuit. On the basis of this decision, the re-set procedure could be made significantly shorter than would otherwise be possible because it would not be necessary to re-load all programs into memory. This process was held to have the necessary technical content because it affected the efficient operation of computers, following the reasoning of *Vicom* (section 6.2.3.2 below).[24]

It is comparatively easy to understand why the Board was prepared to classify both of the above inventions as having a technical character, although difficult to define a clear dividing line between such 'hardware' inventions and programs as such which effect the operation of a computer. In *IBM/Computer-related invention*,[25] the claim was for a method of displaying one of a set of predetermined messages in response to events occurring to or within the computer. The method is achieved on a known computer, and involves using tables containing words used in the messages from which each message is built up by a 'message build program'. The problem of extracting any theoretical basis from EPO decisions is illustrated by quoting from the Board's reasons:

Generally the Board takes the view that giving visual indications automatically about conditions prevailing in an apparatus or system is basically a technical problem.

It was held that IBM's claim, in describing one way of overcoming such a technical problem, was not to a computer program as such even though the basic idea resides in a computer program.[26]

Microsoft Corp/Data transfer with expanded clipboard formats[27] concerned an improved method of transferring data between applications. The Board considered

---

[23] Case T 164/92.

[24] In *Bosch* it was also held that notwithstanding the provisions of the PCT which relieve the requirement to search in the field of computer programs, if an office was equipped (ie, had the necessary personnel) to search or examine against computer programs then it should do so. This illustrates an acceptance that computer programs can lie at the heart of inventions that are nevertheless potentially patentable.

[25] Case T 115/85.

[26] Application of the modern doctrine is interesting here: the process is essentially the computerization of a mental act—compiling a readable message from elements that may vary, so any inventiveness would reside in non-patentable areas. However, in this early case there may have been some technical considerations in realizing that the method was useful in the field of computer operation. We now take error messages for granted.

[27] Case T 0469/03.

that solving the problem of making data available across different applications was a technical matter.

6.2.3.2 *Data processing and data structures*

Here also the approach has been to cast around for some real-world, non-digital analogies in looking for technical content.

In *Vicom/Computer-related invention*,[28] the claim dealt with the manipulation of digital images to smooth edges. Although the Board talks of an image as a 'physical entity' and as a 'real world object', it is made clear that an image stored in any form, hard copy or electronic, will be regarded as a physical entity. The crux of the decision was the finding that images could be used in the design field, which was an industrial area. It was this point which enabled the Board to find the necessary technical content. It appears that the fact that images could be used in the *industrial* design field was important to this finding, although of course the invention would be equally applicable to images whose sole purpose was aesthetic.

In the light of subsequent cases, the 'real world' test needs elucidating. The reference to the 'real world' is in the context of distinguishing between digital data which represent numbers with no meaning (clearly not technical things) and data which represent numbers which represent something more, something outside the confines of the purely mathematical. It is clear that real-world content is not enough: in addition the real-world impact of the invention must have a technical (as opposed to a purely aesthetic, for example) character.

In *Philips/Data structure product*,[29] the claims concerned a data carrier for carrying picture data in accordance with a specified structure, and a retrieval device for recovering the pictures. The examiner had concluded that the claim to the data carrier alone 'had no unambiguous technical function' and objected to it as a mere presentation of information excluded by Article 52(2)(d). The Board overturned this finding and held that:

On a proper construction of this phrase the record carrier of claim 4 has technical functional features—line numbers, coded picture lines and addresses and synchronisations—which are adapted to cooperate with corresponding means in the read device to provide a picture retrieval system.

The Board also stressed a distinction between the digital *representation* of data and the *presentation* of data. The former is not excluded by Article 52(2)(d) as that exclusion is limited to presentation to humans, it does not extend to the digital encoding of data in ways which might make it more understandable to machines.

More recently, patents have been granted for methods of compressing types of data and compressed data formats. Whilst such methods will involve mathematical algorithms, technical content will come from choosing an algorithm to achieve a

---

[28] Case T 208/84.
[29] Case T 1194/97.

practical objective such as (in the case of compression of sounds and images) achieving a balance between compression efficiency, perceived quality of the decompressed result (eg, involving application of the science of psychoacoustics), and compression/decompression speed. Although the end product is in digital form, such inventions are analogous with claims to new machines where the novelty happens to be implemented in software. The MP3 music compression format and the DVD disc format are some well-known technologies with underlying computer-related patents.[30]

6.2.3.3 *Business data and business methods*
The increased use of computer networks to join up all areas of business operation has resulted in a string of cases on data processing claims where the underlying data are business data, rather than data encoding pictures and so on. Claims to such inventions are as likely to give rise to objection on the 'method of doing business' ground as the 'computer program' or 'mental act' grounds. It is claims in this area that have largely driven the development of the broad doctrine of patentable subject matter.

Some early cases in this area need to be viewed with caution as the fact that the invention could be used in a technical field was regarded as important. Under current doctrine, this would not be relevant unless the inventive step also involved technical considerations (as distinct from business considerations or programming skill).

Thus, in *Pensions*,[31] the claim was to a method of calculating pensions benefits, in *Hitachi* to methods of organizing auctions, and in *Duns* to a method of predicting sales. None of these was a technical area according to the Board. In all of these cases computers were used and thus the inventions were not excluded under Article 52(2), but any invention in devising the methods was held to be non-technical as it involved using known programming techniques to solve a non-technical problem. Of course had new methods of computer operation, data storage, manipulation, or communication been used, those methods may have been patentable.

6.2.3.4 *Text processing decisions*
Some early cases in this area illustrate that understanding and manipulating language is a mental act and not technical. In *IBM/Document abstracting and retrieving*,[32] the claim was for a system for automatically abstracting a document and storing the resulting abstract. The system involves comparing the words used in

---

[30] Currently consortia of companies claim ownership of patents related to both MP3 and DVD technology. Each consortium provides a single point from which to obtain licensing and patent information. See <http://www.mp3licensing.com/> (accessed 9 August 2011) (for MP3) and <http://www.dvdfllc.co.jp/index.html> (accessed 9 August 2011) for the DVD format/logo licensing corporation.

[31] See section 6.2.2.3 above.

[32] Case T 22/85. See section 6.2.2.2 above.

a document with a dictionary held on a computer, thereby noting proper names and the occurrence of other words which would be of assistance in characterizing the document, and incorporating these words in the abstract. This information is used to assist in identifying documents in response to enquiries. This system was held to fall into the 'mental acts' category. The Board also held that the documents had not been changed as 'technical entities', in contrast with the images in *Vicom*.

Similar IBM applications refused for essentially the same reasons were *IBM/Text clarity processing*[33] and *IBM/Semantically-related expressions*,[34] which involved editing text to make it clearer, and generating expressions that related to input expressions. Matters of language were mental acts.

In contrast to these decisions where the text processing application was rejected, the application in *IBM/Editable document form*[35] succeeded before the Technical Board. The application claimed a method of transforming text stored in one editable form to another (basically, translating word processing formats). On appeal the claim was amended to restrict its scope to documents stored as digital data and was allowed. The technical features of text processing were said to include 'printer control items' (the printer control codes which would be used to direct a line or character type of printer) and so transforming these from one system to another was a method having a technical character. The objection overcome had been that the method for transforming the documents was no more than a mental act.

This may appear to make a fine distinction with the earlier cases, but in *Editable document form* the properties of the document that were being changed were not related to the meaning of the text, so were outside the non-technical field of semantics. An example in this area according to the modern doctrine is in *SYSTRAN/Translating natural languages*.[36] The claims involved automatic language translation including methods of looking up and comparing words, against a background of prior art which include automated translation methods involving look-up techniques. The Board acknowledged the line of cases in which linguistics had been found to be non-technical:

32 Applying the principles laid down by the Board in its COMVIK decision cited above (see headnote II), the decision for one or the other matching principle does not seem to solve any technical problem and hence does not fall within the responsibility of a technically skilled person. It is rather a non-technical constraint determined by the linguistic expert and given to the skilled person as part of the framework of his task, namely implementing the known low frequency dictionary look-up process by applying the 'longest match principle'.

33 Choosing to apply the one or the other principle has clearly consequences for the technical implementation of the translation process since the computer routines have to work differently

---

[33] Case T 38/86.
[34] Case T 52/85.
[35] Case T 110/90.
[36] T 1177/97 [2005] EPOR 13

and the automated translation process will produce objectively different results, technical differences which establish novelty. These technical differences, nevertheless, are not inventive since they originate from a non-technical constraint to the technical problem, the implementation of which is obvious.

34 It follows that the method of claim 1 lacks inventive step (article 56 EPC) and hence is not patentable under article 52(1) EPC.

Thus, it is clear that if the choice of look-up process had been dictated by technical considerations (eg, greater speed of computation or more efficient use of memory when using a standard computer) then that would have been a technical consideration that would have counted towards an inventive step. The changes in the precise manner of operation of the computer were technical (as they would be when any new computer program is run), but that was not enough. This case illustrates clearly the importance of the inventive step having to be of a technical nature.[37]

6.2.3.5 *Inventions relating to programming itself*

In the decisions noted so far, the fact that the computer program might, when run on a computer, have a technical effect in the outside world or on the operation of the computer itself was important. This begs the question of whether developments in the field of computer programming itself can be patented.

In *ATT/System for generating software source code*,[38] the Board held that inventions which did not go outside the field of computer programming were claims to mental acts which lacked any technical character. In that case the patent was to a system of generating source code and the Board has this to say:

It is fully agreed that this is exactly what the claimed invention is about. But no technical improvement of the efficiency of the computer as a machine, be it the computer when generating a program in accordance with the features of Claim 1 or a computer when eventually making use of the program so generated by executing it, can be recognised therefrom. It is not disputed that the claimed invention will improve the efficiency of the programmer as submitted by the appellant but this does not mean that the computer, when generating a program or executing the generated program, would work in an essentially new way from a technical point of view.

This does not mean that claims to all aspects of programming will be unpatentable. As in *Bosch/Electronic Computer Components*,[39] programs which enhance the operation of a computer in a technical way are patentable. Inventions which

---

[37] Under the 'contribution approach' the same result would have been likely, on the basis that although there may be novelty, the contribution to the art was not technical (eg, faster way of translating by machine) but non-technical (a different way of translating that happens to be implemented by machine).

[38] *AT&T/Computer system* Case T 204/93 [2001] EPOR 39—the precise doctrine applicable has changed twice since this decision, but the finding on technical content remains valid.

[39] See section 6.2.3.1.

apparently concern programming may be patentable if some technical content can be found for them. But 'improving the efficiency of the programmer' does not count as technical content.

6.2.3.6 *Analysis of the EPO cases on technical content*

It can be seen that the Technical Boards have developed a more sophisticated means for finding 'technical content' (or perhaps seeking out the lack of it) than that used in *Vicom/Computer-related invention*.[40] In *Vicom* the usefulness of the images in a technical area (industrial design) appeared determinative. Documents are of course useful in all technical and non-technical industries, as are images, but that has not been sufficient.

Since *Pensions* the technical content must be evident in the inventive step that led to it. But whichever test is adopted, the search for technical subject matter is not superficial, but involves an enquiry that goes to the fundamental nature of the under-lying invention.

It is difficult to derive from the cases any satisfying general test for what is and is not technical content or effect. Following the text processing decisions noted above and *Vicom*, it can be seen that developments based on the meaning (to humans) of text or an image are unlikely to be patentable, but developments which make the data more intelligible, or more easily processed by, a computer may be. So, for example, developments in artificial intelligence will involve consideration of non-patentable areas (mental acts, linguistics), but also no doubt developments in rendering such problems amenable to operation by machines. The latter may well provide the technical content that was not present in *SYSTRAN*, for example (because standard programming techniques were used).

The reasoning discussed above remains difficult to apply in the field of computer technology, where no connection can be made with the outside world other than that of providing a general-purpose computer. The result of the invention will clearly be a computer, a technical thing. But the problem of identifying a technical change in it, or technical means in its achievement, remains peculiarly difficult since comput-ers run on logic (algorithms) which is either hard-wired in or contained in programs. The most that can be said is that it appears that the problem addressed has to be a low level one, close to the hardware. Thus, the method of generating messages in response to events of *IBM/Computer related invention*[41] would be of general useful-ness, yet its patentability was based on its use to monitor hardware-related events. (It has been noted that on its facts this decision might well go the other way if decided in recent times.) By contrast the method of generating a data file of abstract-ing information (a high-level concept in the software domain and related to mental acts) in *IBM/Document abstracting and retrieving*[42] was not technical.

---

[40] See section 6.2.3.2.
[41] See section 6.2.3.1.
[42] See section 6.2.2.2.

This does not rest that happily with the notion that technical content can come from software implemented inventions that result in a faster computer (as in *Bosch*). It is possible to conceive general programming techniques that result in generally faster programs, or ones that run better on small devices, or enable large teams to write complex programs so that the different parts work together without too many bugs.[43] Such considerations are at the heart of writing good computer code. Yet these general techniques, being no more than the art of programming, are by definition non-technical.

To give further examples not specifically related to computers, the following have been held to represent non-technical subject matter: methods of directing traffic flow ('economic activity' according to the French text of the EPC);[44] methods of marking sound recording carriers and their packaging to avoid counterfeiting (business method);[45] a marker for facilitating the reading and playing of music (teaching method which was a method for performing mental acts);[46] a coloured jacket for flexible disks which was claimed to be writeable on, easily distinguished, and to resist fingerprints (aesthetic creation and a presentation of information);[47] an automatic self-service machine in which the user could use any machine-readable card he possessed once that card had been recognized by the machine (method of doing business).[48] By way of contrast, a television signal has been held to constitute technical subject matter,[49] as has a system (incidentally, computer controlled) for controlling a queue sequence for serving customers at a number of service points.[50]

6.2.4 UK doctrine on patentable subject matter

The terms of the EPC are reflected, so far as patentable inventions are concerned, in the Patents Act 1977. Section 1(2) of the Act sets out, essentially verbatim, the exclusions of Article 52(2) EPC and the 'as such' caveat of Article 52(3). However, when EPC 2000 came into effect, the words 'in all areas of technology' were not inserted into section 1 although other amendments to reflect EPC 2000 were implemented. The most directly relevant authorities on the interpretation of the Act are decisions from the UK courts. The Patents Act, section 78 requires the UK courts to interpret its provisions in accordance with the provisions of the EPC, and the Court

---

[43] Such as Object-Oriented Programming.

[44] *Christian Franceries/Traffic Regulation* Case T 16/83, agreed with by Aldous J in *Lux Traffic Controls Ltd v Pike Signals Ltd* [1993] RPC 107.

[45] *Stockburger/Coded distinctive mark* Case T 51/84.

[46] *Beattie/Marker* Case T 603/89.

[47] *Fuji/Coloured disk jacket* Case T 199/88.

[48] *IBM/Card reader* Case T 854/90.

[49] *BBC/Colour television signal* Case T 163/85.

[50] *Pettersson/Queuing system* Case T 1002/82, where the ground of objection considered was 'scheme, rule or method of doing business'.

of Appeal has held that it should, where possible and even to the extent of overturning a previous Court of Appeal decision, interpret the law to be consistent with the doctrines of the TBAs and particularly the EBA.[51]

There are a number of situations when UK tribunals are required to decide issues of the validity of patents and interpret the legislation:

(a) The validity of a patent can be put in issue in infringement proceedings.

(b) Petitions to revoke patents can be made to the courts after grant.

(c) Appeals lie to the courts from decisions of the Patent Office made during the prosecution of UK patents.

(d) The UK Patent Office can hear applications to revoke UK patents and European patents (UK), from which appeals lie through the UK court system.

The UK legislative tradition in the field of patents is somewhat different from that of most other EPC countries, and in particular the concept of 'technical content' is alien to UK patent lawyers and judges. A certain difficulty in understanding and applying this concept is often expressed in the judgments. Thus, although the UK courts have sought to reach decisions in conformity with those from the EPO in relation to what does and does not amount to patentable subject matter, they have done so on the principle that there is a list of excluded things rather than adopting the overarching unifying theory of subject matter having to be 'technical'. Indeed, the view has been expressed that computer programming is (or can be) a technical activity.

More seriously from a doctrinal point of view, there is currently a divergence of doctrine in relation to how, where, and when to look for technical content. The UK courts still apply a version of the 'contribution approach' and have so far not embraced the 'any hardware' approach.[52]

In *Merrill Lynch's Application*,[53] the claim was for a computerized method of setting up a trading market in securities, using a known computer which could be suitably programmed by known techniques. It was held by the Court of Appeal that an invention was not excluded simply because the novelty lay in an excluded thing (namely a computer program) and that the claim had to be looked at as a whole. However, because *Vicom/Computer-related invention*[54] was followed the Court of Appeal also held that the contribution to the prior art must not itself be excluded, and in this case the result of the claimed invention was a method for doing business. Fox LJ postulated that a 'technical advance on the prior art' could nevertheless be

---

[51] *Generics (UK) Ltd v H Lundbeck A/S* [2009] UKHL 12, [2009] RPC 13 at para 46, although this does not extend to findings of fact on the same or a similar issue relating to a particular invention—*Eli Lilly and Co v Human Genome Sciences, Inc* [2010] EWCA Civ 33, [2010] RPC 14 at paras 38–41.

[52] See section 6.2.2.4 above.

[53] [1989] RPC 561.

[54] See section 6.2.3.2.

excluded as a business method. This last comment indicates a divergence from the EPO 'technical content' doctrine.

In *Gale's Application*,[55] Aldous J held that a computer program held on a ROM chip was patentable although the program itself did nothing more than provide the computer in which it was installed with a new method of calculating square roots. The Court of Appeal reversed this, holding that differences in the physical structures holding the program were not material and that the program did not produce a novel technical effect. The approach of *IBM/Document abstracting and retrieving*[56] was followed and it was held that the instructions embodied in the program did not represent a technical process outside the computer or a solution to a technical problem inside the computer. It was accepted that a new method for finding square roots had been discovered.

In *Wang Laboratories Inc's Application*,[57] the approach of the EPO was also approved of and followed, albeit in a characteristically English way. There the claim was for an 'expert system' program, but was phrased to include programming a conventional computer with the program. It was held that the contribution made to the art was by the program and nothing more. In this case Aldous J complained that the meaning to be attributed to the word technical in all the various ways it was used in the EPO decisions was unclear. In his judgment he therefore avoids reliance on this concept:

The machine, the computer, remains the same even when programmed. The computer and the program do not combine together to produce a 'new computer'. They remain separate and amount to a collocation rather than a combination making a different whole. The contribution is, to my mind, made by the program and nothing more.

This attempt to Anglicize the EPO's formula was not entirely successful, the concept of a 'new computer' being every bit as intractable as that of a 'technical alteration of behaviour'. Whenever a computer is operating a unique program it exists in a unique electrical configuration that could in theory be measured with physical apparatus. Yet the distinction cannot be between permanent and temporary changes because that would be contrary to the sensible and necessary *Gale* test. The problem is to distinguish those aspects of computer configuration (whether permanent or temporary, 'hardware' or 'software') in which developments are deemed patentable from those that are not.

Fujitsu Ltd's Application[58] saw a continued divergence of interpretation between the UK Court of Appeal and the TBAs. The invention was for a method of generating and manipulating graphical representations of the crystal structures of known chemicals on a computer monitor to assist chemical engineers in developing new

---

[55] [1991] RPC 305.
[56] See section 6.2.2.2 above.
[57] [1991] RPC 463.
[58] [1997] RPC 608.

compounds with a desired functionality. The claims were refused, and this demanded comparison with *Vicom*. Whilst it is unclear what the *Vicom* board would have made of the *Fujitsu* claim, it is arguable that the EPO would now also refuse it. The somewhat unsophisticated finding in *Vicom* that 'manipulating images is technical' is not binding as a general principle and the EPO interpretation of technical content has progressed since that case.[59]

Aldous LJ sought to explain *Vicom* by saying that the technical contribution there was the way that the image was reproduced and that it did not mean that anything to do with image manipulation was patentable. At first instance Laddie J had stated that whether the claims were refused as being for a 'computer program' or a 'method for performing a mental act' was a matter of mere semantics. Aldous LJ effectively approved this view by identifying the key question as 'whether the application consists of a program for a computer as such or whether it is a program for a computer with a technical contribution' (implicitly, that a technical contribution will always mean patentability—here we see the overarching need for technical content being embraced).

Aldous LJ also considered the 'method for performing a mental act' exclusion, and in this respect he was at one with the Technical Boards in finding that 'Methods for performing mental acts, which means methods of the type performed mentally, are unpatentable unless some concept of technical contribution is present'.[60] In the same passage Aldous LJ rejected arguments that the mental acts exclusion should only apply to acts which were actually carried out by human minds: 'A claim to a method of carrying out a calculation (a method of performing a mental act) is no more patentable when claimed as being done by a computer than when done on a piece of paper.'

The UK courts had problems digesting the change in EPO doctrine of *Pensions* as a result of the doctrine of precedent and the fact that *Merrill Lynch* had adopted the contribution approach.[61] In *CFPH LLC's Application*,[62] Peter Prescott QC expressed the view that the end result of most cases would not differ as a result of the change of doctrine, and applied both approaches. *CFPH* concerned an online betting system, and it was found that (as in *Pensions*) the technical features were not new and the new features were business methods. However, this did not signal a move towards a rapprochement with the Boards of the EPO. In a series of Court of

---

[59] The argument would be that, assuming no technical contribution in the basic fields of crystal structure generation and image production and manipulation, what is left is the mental process of manipulating and comparing shapes one with another, which could in theory be carried out with physical models or by manual calculation. This can be seen as a higher level of processing of information derived from images than that addressed by Vicom—see section 6.2.3.2 above.

[60] [1997] RPC 608 at 621.

[61] *Hutchin's Application* [2002] RPC 8.

[62] *CFPH LLC's Patent Applications* [2005] EWHC 1598, [2006] RPC 5 and *Halliburton Energy Services Inc v Smith International (North Sea) Ltd* [2005] EWHC 1623, [2005] Info TLR. A further case, *Shopalotto.com Ltd's Patent Application* [2005] EWHC 2416, [2006] RPC 7, follows along similar lines.

Appeal cases a clear divergence of doctrine has been confirmed. The court in the *Symbian*[63] case approved the approach of Jacob LJ in the *Aerotel*[64] case, which was as follows:

(a) properly construe the claim;

(b) identify the actual contribution;

(c) ask whether it falls solely within the excluded subject matter;

(d) check whether the contribution is actually technical in nature.

The court observed that the final stage is required to be consistent with *Merrill Lynch*. In comparing the doctrine of the EPO as set out in *Duns* to its own approach the court concentrated on the issue of non-patentability under Article 52(2) of the EPC. It did not engage in a broader consideration of the overall effect of the requirements for patentable subject matter and novelty/obviousness, although that is required for an accurate analysis of how the EPO enforces the legislative intent behind the exclusions of Article 52. The court again expressed unease at the way that the EPO lumps all the excluded areas under the 'technical' heading, and rejected the elevation of the concept of technical content to the level of a doctrine, preferring to stick with the list of excluded things as the benchmark against which patentable subject matter should be judged. The court decided that the situation was not one in which it would be appropriate to depart from its established doctrine in order to achieve consistency with the EPO decisions, and proceeded to apply the contribution approach.

The claims in *Symbian* concerned a method of indexing the routines available in a library of computer code known as a 'dynamic link library'.[65] The invention involved a programming solution to a programming problem—how to ensure that programs that reference a function within the library continue to be provided with the correct part of the library after the library is be updated. Yet a more efficiently running computer system results. The Court of Appeal held the invention not to be excluded. The court noted that the invention would be of use in cameras and other devices with embedded processors, as well as general-purpose programmable computers, and concluded:

Putting it another way, a computer with this program operates better than a similar prior art computer. To say 'oh but that is only because it is a better program—the computer itself is

---

[63] *Symbian Ltd v Comptroller-General of Patents* [2008] EWCA Civ 1066, [2009] RPC 1.

[64] *Aerotel Ltd v Telco Ltd; Macrossan's Application* [2006] EWCA Civ 1371, [2007] RPC 7.

[65] It is common in modern computer systems for basic functions to be made available in libraries and for those functions to be used by other programs that may have no commercial or authorship connection with the library. Obviously, a system is needed to ensure that the correct snippet of code from the library is used when the function is called and this would be reflected in the internal structure of the library—which is what the *Symbian* claims addressed. With some programming systems, updating a library would require all programs that referenced code within it to be updated or re-compiled, the *Symbian* system does not require that.

unchanged' gives no credit to the practical reality of what is achieved by the program. As a matter of such reality there is more than just a 'better program', there is a faster and more reliable computer.

An EPO examiner would most likely also have allowed the claims in *Symbian* on the basis that the invention enabled the different programs running on a computer to share code, just as the invention in *Microsoft Corp/Data transfer with expanded clipboard formats*[66] enabled them to share data. One reason why the court had decided not to follow *Duns* was that it perceived an inconsistency and lack of clarity in the approach of the TBAs over recent decisions including *Duns*. A point of particular importance to the court was that there was no decision of the EBA to clarify the issues—this had been suggested in *Aerotel* but the then president of the EPO had declined to make a reference. Shortly after the judgment in *Symbian* the new President of the EPO[67] referred a number of questions to the EBA.[68] The EBA need only answer such a reference if the case law of the Boards of Appeal is contradictory. The EBA found[69] that the case law was not contradictory, but decided nevertheless to set out exactly what the position was, and why it was not contradictory.[70] This is the position set out in section 6.2.2.2 above. In a paragraph clearly directed towards the supporters of the contribution approach (that is to say, the English Court of Appeal and the UK Patent Office) the Board comments:

The present position of the case law is thus that (phrasing the conclusion to match Question 2 of the referral) a claim in the area of computer programs can avoid exclusion under arts 52(2)(c) and (3) EPC merely by explicitly mentioning the use of a computer or a computer-readable storage medium. But no exposition of this position would be complete without the remark that it is also quite clear from the case law of the Boards of Appeal since T1173/97 MICROSOFT that if a claim to program X falls under the exclusion of arts 52(2) and (3) EPC, a claim which specifies no more than 'Program X on a computer-readable storage medium,' or 'A method of operating a computer according to program X,' will always still fail to be patentable for lack of an inventive step under arts 52(1) and 56 EPC. Merely the EPC article applied is different. While the Enlarged Board is aware that this rejection for lack of an inventive step rather than exclusion under art. 52(2) EPC is in some way distasteful to many people, it is the approach which has been consistently developed since T1173/97 MICROSOFT and since no divergences from that development have been identified in the referral we consider it not to be the function of the Enlarged Board in this Opinion to overturn it, for the reasons given above (see point 7.3.8).

---

[66] See section 6.2.3.1.

[67] Alison Brimelow, formerly Comptroller General of the UK Patent Office, who became the President of the EPO on 1 July 2007.

[68] *PRESIDENT'S REFERENCE/Computer program exclusion* Case G 3/08 [2009] EPOR 9.

[69] *Programs for computers* Case G 3/08 [2010] EPOR 36.

[70] Whilst the EBA acknowledged some divergent early cases following *Pensions* there is an element of hindsight in its finding that the position had been clear for a number of years—this was not clear to many commentators, as is apparent from the previous edition of this book.

Some annoyance at the Court of Appeal's avoidance of any mention of the role of the requirement for an inventive step in the EPO case law is evident here.

Given the Court of Appeal's stated ideal of following EPO jurisprudence, particularly that of the EBA, and its reasons for not doing so in *Symbian*, it is clearly open for the Court of Appeal to bring its doctrines into line with the EPO when a suitable case next comes before it. As it is clear that the EPO is not moving on this issue, the only way to achieve a harmonious position is for the Court of Appeal to do so. This may well happen in due course—though, as has been noted already, the actual effect of such a change of doctrine on any particular case is likely to be minimal.

The position under the 1949 Patents Act had developed along different lines. Claims for computers when programmed to perform specified functions were allowed on the basis that a computer programmed to perform a task was a machine and if that machine was novel and inventive then a patent should be granted.[71] The 1949 Act contained no specific exclusions so the courts based their reasoning upon general considerations of what an invention was. In some respects it can be seen that this approach persisted in decisions under the 1977 Act.[72] In the USA the statutory framework remains more similar to the 1949 Act and, as is explained below, the US Patent and Trademark Office and Federal courts have in effect continued to develop (not always in the same direction) this type of approach.

6.2.5 The US position

6.2.5.1 *The statutory provisions*
The US Constitution grants Congress the power 'to promote the progress of . . . useful arts, by securing for limited times to . . . inventors the exclusive right to their respective . . . discoveries'. Cases have interpreted 'the useful arts' to mean 'the technological arts', but not in a limiting way. Indeed, anything useful (as opposed to only of artistic or intellectual value) is considered part of the 'technological arts'.[73] This power is currently exercised by Congress in the form of the Patent Act of 1952, Title 35 USC, as amended. The section of particular interest from the point of view of computer-related inventions is section 101 which states:

Whoever invents or discovers any new and useful process, machine, manufacture, or composition of matter, or any new and useful improvement thereof, may obtain a patent therefor, subject to the conditions and requirements of this title.

---

[71] See, eg, *IBM Corp's Application* [1980] FSR 564.

[72] Which Act applies depends broadly upon when the patent was applied for, the provisions of the 1977 Act applying to applications made on or after 1 January 1978.

[73] In *Re Musgrave* 431 F2d 882 (1970), where the claims essentially related to a method of analysing seismic data and were held to form part of the technological arts.

There is no list of excluded things comparable to that contained in Article 52(2) of the EPC. The approach to computer programs taken by the United States Patent and Trademark Office ('USPTO') and the US Federal courts has fluctuated over the years, but has generally been to exclude fewer computer-related inventions than would be excluded under the EPC. The position in the USA recently swung back somewhat from one where only a narrow range of claims were excluded from patentability. It is worth considering how this position was arrived at because the arguments are of general relevance and cast an interesting sidelight on the European position.

The words of section 101 are taken to limit what may be patented to:

(a) processes;

(b) machines;

(c) manufactures; and

(d) compositions of matter,

provided they are new and useful. In decided cases, judges and examiners do not always trouble to identify clearly which of the four headings an invention falls under, preferring instead to concentrate on whether the invention falls into a general category of things outside those allowed. This judge-defined excluded category includes ideas, mental steps, and discoveries of physical phenomena or laws of nature. By reason of arguments that should now be familiar, this may exclude some computer-related inventions.

6.2.5.2 Early case law—the Freeman-Walter-Abele test

After some celebrated early cases in which the approach swung between more and less liberal ones,[74] an approach was developed in which the non-patentability of mental acts was the founding principle. From this came a doctrine based on the fact that a patent must not claim an algorithm, nor must it 'pre-empt' an algorithm. The two parts of the test were set out in *In Re Abele*[75] as:

1. *(first part)*

do the claims directly or indirectly recite an algorithm, if so

2. *(second part)*

2.1 is the algorithm applied in any manner to physical elements or process steps; and

2.2 is this application circumscribed by more than a field of use limitation or non-essential post-solution activity?

---

[74] The still influential trilogy of Supreme Court cases *Gottschalk v Benson* (1972) 409 US 63, *Parker v Flook* (1978) 437 US 584, and *Diamond v Diehr* (1981) 450 US 175.
[75] (1982) 684 F2d 902.

It can be seen that claims to processes are particularly liable to objection on the 'algorithm' ground in a way that claims to physical things ('machines' or 'manufactures' in the language of section 101) are not. But many claims relating to computer-related inventions are addressed to 'machines' but delimited solely or mainly with reference to the processes carried out by the machine (for machine read computer). This contrasts with ways of claiming machines which describe the physical nature of the elements of the machine and their interconnections. A claim to a computer-related invention in the former form would be largely hardware and software independent, whereas a claim in the latter form would be limited in its scope to only certain hardware and/or software configurations. Concerns were raised at the prospect of claims to machines being drawn which did no more than implement otherwise unpatentable processes.

Prompted by such concerns, 'means plus function'[76] (also known as 'means for') claims were included within the ambit of the test. This led to many computer-related inventions being refused protection because they were considered to amount to no more than mathematical processes notwithstanding that the claims were directed generally to apparatus involving computers.

In *Abele* itself the invention involved a system of computerized tomography (CAT scanning). Claim 5 (which was rejected) claimed simply a method of manipulating data followed by the display of that data. Claim 6 (accepted) was in essence claim 5 when the data concerned were X-ray attenuation data. The Court of Customs and Patent Appeals held that: 'The improvement in either case resides in the application of a mathematical formula within the context of a process which encompasses significantly more than the algorithm alone.'

In a series of cases, Judge Rich of the Court of Appeals for the Federal Circuit[77] ('CAFC') sought to limit the restrictive effect of *Freeman-Walter-Abele*. In *In Re Iwahashi*,[78] he overturned the rule that 'means for' claims should be interpreted widely for the purposes of examination. The result was that a claim addressed to an 'autocorrelation unit' for use in pattern recognition (eg, speech recognition) was allowable, despite the fact that the invention could have been achieved purely by programming a general-purpose computer. However the claims, whilst containing a

---

[76] *In Re Walter* (1980) 618 F2d 758. Section 112 para 6 of the US Patent Act deals expressly with such claims. For the purpose of infringement, such claims only cover the actual means taught in the body of the patent and its 'reasonable equivalents', not any means that achieve the desired function, even though the wording of the claim contains no such limitation. *In Re Walter* held that this claim interpretation rule did not apply when considering claims for validity, thus widening the scope of claims and rendering them more likely to a s 101 objection. Such claims are frequently used when claiming computer-related inventions. The EPC contains no such interpretative provision, and 'means for' claims will be interpreted as including any means suitable for the specified function. Widely-drawn claims may be held not to be 'supported by' the specification under Art 84 EPC: see, eg, *General Electric/Disclosure of computer-related apparatus* Case T 784/99.

[77] The CAFC has heard all patent appeals since 1982.

[78] (1989) 888 F2d 1370.

large number of 'means for' elements, also contained reference to specific hardware elements, namely ROM and RAM, in which the program was stored.

Iwahashi was viewed as allowing great freedom in patenting computer-based processes and machines for carrying them out, but there was still the question of the extent to which it was necessary to specify physical hardware elements as part of the claims, which had been done in that case.

6.2.5.3 In Re Alappat—*Judge Rich removes the restrictions*
In Re Alappat[79] can be viewed in part as a return to earlier case law. The claim involved a scheme for displaying a smooth waveform on a digital oscilloscope.[80] In a digital oscilloscope, the input signal is sampled and digitized. The numerical values are then portrayed by illuminating the pixels at the appropriate position on the screen in accordance with the value of the signal and its position in the waveform. A problem was experienced with this type of machine in the form of momentary aberrant signal values which made rapidly rising or falling sections of the waveform appear discontinuous. The invention used an anti-aliasing system to illuminate each pixel along the waveform differently so as to give the appearance of smoothness.

The majority opinion of Rich J in *Alappat* amounted to a direct attack on the *Freeman-Walter-Abele* test[81] as applied by the USPTO and a complete re-evaluation of section 101. Among his conclusions were:

(a) When considering a 'means plus function' claim for patentability, the same rule of interpretation should be used as when considering 'means plus function' claims for infringement, that is, the claim should be taken to be limited to the actual 'means' taught in the patent and its 'reasonable equivalents'. Construing the claim in issue in this way, the claim was held to cover patentable material, that is, a 'machine'. The USPTO in this case had ignored Judge Rich's comments to this effect in *In Re Iwahashi* as being *obiter dicta*. Rich J approved the findings in *Abele* and other cases but sought to distinguish them by pointing out that in those cases there had been no specific teaching of how to achieve the means in the specification.

(b) A machine must perform a function that the laws were designed to protect (eg, transforming or reducing an article to a different state or thing). But in the instant case the invention claimed calculations to transform digitized waveforms into anti-aliased pixel illumination data and that was sufficient.[82]

---

[79] (1994) 33 F3d 1526.

[80] An oscilloscope displays a signal representing something that fluctuates regularly with time, such as the sound pressure in the vicinity of a musical instrument or the electrical signal given off by a human heart, as a static waveform on a television screen.

[81] See section 6.2.5.2.

[82] The comparison between this case and the European case *Vicom/Computer-related invention* [1987] EPOR 74 (discussed at section 6.2.3.2) is instructive. In *Alappat* the waveform display is held to be a

(c) It was accepted that the 'mathematical algorithm' exception could apply to genuine machine claims, but section 101 should be given its widest interpretation. Thus, if a machine produced a 'useful, concrete and tangible result' it was patentable and to be contrasted with a disembodied mathematical concept.

(d) A general-purpose computer when programmed in a particular way amounted to a 'machine' which would be patentable if the other requirements for patentability were met.[83]

Apart from reversing the claim interpretation rule of *Freeman-Walter-Abele* and effectively confining the application of the rule to genuine process claims, the important contribution of this decision is in the approach adopted in analysing a claim. The focus shifted back to looking at the claim as a whole to see whether it is for a patentable thing (machine, manufacture, process, etc) rather than on searching out algorithms in the claim and then seeing if the claim goes beyond that (the *Freeman-Walter-Abele* approach).

6.2.5.4 *Post* Alappat—*programmed computers are 'machines' and data structures in a memory are 'manufactures'*

Whilst many computer-related inventions are apt to be claimed as processes or the means for carrying them out, things such as computer memories or disks can also form the basis of claims. In *In Re Lowry*,[84] the claim was for a computer memory organized in accordance with the 'attributive data model'. This comprised a way of organizing data into primitive data objects which were arranged in a hierarchy whilst also providing links between objects separate from the hierarchy. Improved data access when such structures were used in combination with programs running on the computer was claimed. The USPTO Appeals Board had allowed the claims under section 101, holding that a computer memory was an 'article of manufacture' (and this was confirmed by the Federal Circuit). However, the Appeals Board had held the claims not novel, relying on a line of cases relating to printed matter and holding that the only novelty rested in the information content and so did not count.

---

thing forming suitable subject matter for an invention in a very similar fashion to the way images were held to be 'real world objects' in *Vicom*. *Alappat* talks in more down to earth terms of electrical signals, no doubt influenced by the need to read the facts on to the well-established definition of a 'process' (see section 6.2.5.2), but the basic reasoning is similar. The important difference between the two cases is that in *Alappat* the transformation had merely to be found 'useful' to found patentability. In *Vicom* it was necessary to find 'technical content'. It seems likely that a suitable claim to the invention of *Alappat* would issue in the EPO without problems over the patentable nature of the invention because of the clear technical nature of the subject matter—an illustration that whilst the European approach may be overall more restrictive, the different approaches can operate in favour of inventors as well as against them.

[83] It can be seen that this position is now the same as that which the UK courts were working towards under the 1949 Patents Act (see the discussion at section 6.2.4).

[84] (1994) 32 F3d 1579.

The Federal Circuit cautioned against overzealous use of the printed matter exception and held that the proper test was simply, 'is the article [ie, the computer memory] useful [in the technological sense identified above]'. On this basis the claim defined a functional thing with new attributes. These were not simply the data themselves, but the organization of those data. The fact that the claims specified no particular physical organization for the data structure, only a set of logical relationships, was not material; the data structure was represented by physical (electrical or magnetic) structures. The Federal Circuit were careful to point out that the attributive data model was not being patented in the abstract.

In Re Warmerdam[85] concerned an improved method for navigating robotic machines which avoided collisions by using 'bubbles', imaginary spherical objects encompassing real objects to be avoided. The basic bubble idea was known, but the invention added a layer of sophistication by using a 'bubble hierarchy' whereby once a bubble was violated it was replaced with a set of smaller bubbles and so on. A technique of collision avoidance known as 'bubble bursting' is provided. Claims 1–4 were for 'A method for generating a data structure which represents the shape of physical object [sic] . . .'. Claim 5 was for a machine but did not use any 'means for' language. In fact the function of the machine was not referred to in any way and the only features claimed for the machine were the presence and contents of memory. It read: 'A machine having a memory which contains data representing a bubble hierarchy generated by . . . the method of claims 1–4.' Claim 6 was for a data structure generated by the method of claims 1–6. The Board of Appeals rejected claims 1–4 and 6 under section 101 and claim 5 for indefiniteness under section 112.

In *Warmerdam* the USPTO had applied *Freeman-Walter-Abele* to claims 1–6. When the case came before the court *In Re Alappat*[86] had recently been decided and the court did not feel constrained to follow the two-part test precisely. It held that in this case the crucial question in relation to section 101 was whether the claim went beyond simply manipulating 'abstract ideas' or 'natural phenomena'. The court affirmed the rejection of claims 1–4 and rejected the applicant's arguments that one first had to measure real objects to apply the process because the claims themselves did not require this, nor would such a limitation be implied into them. The court also upheld the rejection of claim 6. This was on the basis that the structure as described 'is nothing more than another way of describing the manipulation of ideas contained in claims 1–4' and so had to stand or fall with them.

However, claim 5 was allowed by the court as sufficiently claiming a 'machine'. It was held that a person skilled in the art would have no problems identifying whether a machine fell within the claims because 'the ideas expressed in claims 1–4 are well-known mathematical constructs'. It should be pointed out as a note of caution that the question of the utility of the invention of claim 5 was not in issue in

---

[85] (1994) 33 F3d 1361.
[86] (1994) 33 F3d 152s 6.

the appeal. The USPTO had not applied *Freeman-Walter-Abele* to claim 5 (it had not rejected under section 101) and the court did not apply it either. Although considering the claim under section 101 and acknowledging that it contained process elements, the court did not look at the claim from the point of view of the underlying process to be carried out by the machine.

In *State Street v Signature*,[87] the court re-examined the 'mathematical algorithm' exclusion and explained the effect of its earlier decisions in cases such as *Alappat* and *In Re Iwahashi*. Rich J again delivered the judgment, and some of his comments are worthy of note:

the mere fact that a claimed invention involves inputting numbers, calculating numbers, outputting numbers, and storing numbers, in and of itself, would not render it nonstatutory subject matter unless, of course, its operation does not produce a useful, concrete and tangible result.

. . . The question of whether a claim encompasses statutory subject matter should not focus on *which* of the four categories of subject matter a claim is directed to—process, machine, manufacture, or composition of matter—but rather on the essential characteristics of the subject matter, in particular, its practical utility.

Rich J also pointed out that every step-by-step process involves an algorithm in the broad sense of the term, and discouraged any use of *Freeman-Walter-Abele*. In *State Street* the claim was essentially for a general-purpose programmable computer programmed with so-called 'hub and spoke' software for use in assisting the management of State Street's business of an administrator and accounting agent for mutual funds. Such claims were allowed, and in allowing them Rich J buried the 'Business Method Exception' so far as the USA was concerned: 'Whether the claims are directed to subject matter within s 101 should not turn on whether the claimed subject matter does "business" instead of something else.'

Thus, after *State Street* a claim to any process (including a business method) was patentable so long as it was drafted in terms of a computer programmed to carry out the method. It appeared that some hardware elements had to be included, and that pure process claims to business methods might still be refused as the process did not involve the physical world in any way. Following *Warmerdam* and *Lowry*, claims to programs or data structures will not be held non-patentable provided they are claimed as records on media or as programmed computers.

6.2.5.5 *The current position*—Bilski *retreats from* State Street, *but to where?*

The breadth of the scope of patentable subject matter resulting from *State Street* was controversial, particularly in relation to claims to computer-implemented business methods. Indeed, partly in response to such concerns, the US Patent Act was

---

[87] (1998) 149 F3d 1368.

amended by the American Inventors Protection Act of 1999. This provides a defence to infringement of a patent for a business method where the defendant reduced the claimed business method to practice at least one year prior to the effective date of filing the application and used the method in good faith. *Bilski v Kappos*[88] was a case where the claims were directed to a method of operating in the energy market (essentially, hedging risk), claimed as a method not as a programmed computer. By now Judge Rich had ended his long and distinguished career on the bench of the CAFC, and the court departed significantly from the *State Street* approach in an *en banc* decision.

The majority of the CAFC held that *State Street* had in some respects gone too far and proposed the 'machine or transformation test':

A claimed process is surely patent-eligible under § 101 if: (1) it is tied to a particular machine or apparatus, or (2) it transforms a particular article into a different state or thing.

The second limb was relevant to the invention, and the CAFC held that the invention did not transform an article. They distinguished the financial data in that case from the X-ray data in *Alappat* on the basis that the data in *Alappat* represented tangible physical objects. The majority stated that, to the extent that the 'useful, concrete and tangible result' test of *State Street* went further than this, those aspects 'should not be relied on'. The court explicitly rejected the idea of having a 'business method exclusion' and of adopting a test for technical subject matter (on the ground that the definition of 'technology' was too uncertain[89]).

What if the claim in *Bilski* had been to a computer programmed to carry out the method? The CAFC declined to explore the 'machine' arm of their proposed test in detail:

We leave to future cases the elaboration of the precise contours of machine implementation, as well as the answers to particular questions, such as whether or when recitation of a computer suffices to tie a process claim to a particular machine.

However, in addressing the issue of process claims, they did uphold some principles from earlier Supreme Court cases: merely directing a claim to a particular activity will not necessarily prevent it from 'pre-empting' its underlying algorithm; irrelevant 'post-solution activity' will not render a claim to a principle patentable. They added that under the latter rule, irrelevant activity before or during the application of the principle would not render a claim patentable. One can infer from this that according to the CAFC, merely drawing a claim to a non-patentable process as a claim to a computer programmed to carry out that process will not result in a machine that passes the 'machine or transformation test'. What types of

---

[88] *Bilski v Kappos*, 561 US (2010), known at the Federal Appeal stage as *In re Bilski* 545 F3d 943.

[89] As set out in the previous section, the EPO has never been troubled by the lack of any general definition of 'technology' in this respect.

computerized machine claims would be patentable is, however, left to further exploration.

Bilski was appealed to the Supreme Court. All the Justices upheld the appeal, and thus the CAFC's finding that the elements of the claims that applied the principles of hedging to real-world transactions in a particular market did not make them patentable. In their reasoning, the Justices differed. The majority rejected the 'machine or transformation test' as the only test for a patentable invention, but at the same time affirmed that the claim should be refused as being a claim to an abstract idea. As the CAFC had, they looked back to the words of their earlier decisions in *Diehr*, *Gottschalk*, and *Parker*,[90] but found that those early decisions did not support such limitations on patentable subject matter.[91] However, neither did they adopt a completely liberal approach:

this Court by no means desires to preclude the Federal Circuit's development of other limiting criteria that further the Patent Act's purposes and are not inconsistent with its text.

It should be noted that the Supreme Court did not address the question of claims to machines at all. This means that the CAFC is free to develop its thinking on how and whether adding a machine to a method claim results in something patentable. Given the Supreme Court's rejection of the *Bilski* claims despite their references to real-world activity in the energy market, it appears consistent with the underlying principles for claims to general-purpose computers, programmed using known techniques to carry out unpatentable processes, to be refused. It is likely that, if the claims in *State Street* were before the CAFC today, it would refuse them and the Supreme Court would not overturn that.[92] Guidelines for the examination of method claims issued by the USPTO after the Supreme Court decision (amended from similar guidance following the CAFC decision)[93] support a more rigorous view of method claims:

The following guidance presents factors that are to be considered when evaluating patent-eligibility of method claims. The factors include inquiries from the machine-or-transformation test, which remains a useful investigative tool, and inquiries gleaned from Supreme Court precedent. While the Supreme Court in Bilski did not set forth detailed guidance, there are many factors to be considered when determining whether there is sufficient evidence to support a determination that a method claim is directed to an abstract idea.

The 'useful investigative tool' phrase is a direct quote from the majority judgment. The Guidelines also state that general principles are likely (not certain—that would

---

[90] n 74 above.

[91] Some of the majority were more explicit in their reasoning, expressing concerns at closing off opportunities for patents in areas of digital technology. The two minority judgments would have explicitly excluded business methods and related claims from patentability.

[92] Although it might argue with the precise doctrine used.

[93] 'Interim Guidance for Determining Subject Matter Eligibility for Process Claims in View of Bilski v. Kappos', published in the Federal Register, vol 75, No 143, 27 July 2010.

be contrary to the Supreme Court's decision) to be unpatentable regardless of whether they are limited to a particular field or involve other activity, and list some examples of general principles:

- Basic economic practices or theories (eg, hedging, insurance, financial transactions, marketing);
- Basic legal theories (eg, contracts, dispute resolution, rules of law);
- Mathematical concepts (eg, algorithms, spatial relationships, geometry);
- Mental activity (eg, forming a judgment, observation, evaluation, or opinion);
- Interpersonal interactions or relationships (eg, conversing, dating);
- Teaching concepts (eg, memorization, repetition);
- Human behavior (eg, exercising, wearing clothing, following rules or instructions);
- Instructing 'how business should be conducted'.

The Guidelines extend to claims to machines embodying methods. They give factors to be taken into account in deciding whether a machine or article embodying the method is general (eg, a general programmable computer) or specific. They also list factors to be taken into account in deciding whether a pure method claim is excluded or not, including whether or not a transformation of matter is involved (and if so, is it general or particular), if there is no transformation whether or not an application of a law of nature is involved and, if so, whether it is broad or narrow in its applicability.

Thus, although the Supreme Court rejected the machine or transformation test, things have not been put back as they were after *State Street*. The general tenor of the judgments is to indicate that a more rigorous investigation into the true subject matter and its patentability than undertaken in *State Street* might be appropriate. The revised USPTO Guidelines (above) indicate this, and the CAFC will presumably not regard itself as having been completely overruled and not revert to the *State Street* approach, whilst respecting the nuances of the Supreme Court decision in *Bilski*.

It should also be noted that although *Bilski* related to a business method, the principles (based on the non-patentability of abstract ideas and algorithms) are equally applicable to computer-related inventions that are not directed to business methods but to other areas, such as data processing or the internal operation of a computer. It is clear that claims that are addressed essentially to computerized methods or processes for dealing with information may escape being held unpatentable by being limited to particular machinery or confined to particular applications. Claims concerning computer operation (eg, making a computer faster or more easy to use) are likely to be held patentable.[94] On the other hand, a claim to a purely

---

[94] The absence of any exclusion of programs or programming per se in US law makes arriving at this conclusion a simpler task than under the European Patent Convention.

mental activity such as a strategy for playing poker will not be patentable, whether claimed as such, as a program, as a programmed computer, or as a data carrier containing the program.

The uncertainty that currently exists is in what criteria will be applied to the machinery or application in order to decide if the (unpatentable) underlying abstract idea (or algorithm) has been applied in a patentable way. The certainty of the very literal way such claims would have been dealt with following *State Street* (it's a machine so it's patentable) has evaporated. This will have to be worked out on a case-by-case basis.

6.2.5.6 *US computer-related patents—inventive step*

It must be stressed that non-patentable subject matter is only one reason a US patent may be refused. Particularly as the question of non-patentable subject matter is engaged in the EU at the stage of the enquiry into inventive step, an overview of US law in this area is necessary. In the example given above, any application for a patent for a strategy for playing poker would likely fail for lack of novelty in any event.

The USPTO has issued special guidance to patent examiners as to how to deal with business method applications in relation to obviousness.[95] These address the problem of the computerization, or implementation via the internet, of a known process. They indicate through a number of worked examples that, for example, if the method of implementation is obvious, then the invention claimed will be obvious. In addition it has implemented a revised system of quality control for examination procedures and a programme of training examiners in developments in computerization and business methods.

The current USPTO Manual of Patent Examining Procedure, which reflects case law interpreting 35 USC 103, summarizes the general test of obviousness as follows:

To establish a prima facie case of obviousness, three basic criteria must be met. First, there must be some suggestion or motivation, either in the [prior art] references themselves or in the knowledge generally available to one of ordinary skill in the art, to modify the reference or to combine reference teachings. Second, there must be a reasonable expectation of success. Finally, the prior art reference (or references when combined) must teach or suggest all the claim limitations. The teaching or suggestion to make the claimed combination and the reasonable expectation of success must both be found in the prior art, and not based on applicant's disclosure.[96]

---

[95] 'Formulating and Communicating Rejections Under 35 USC 103 for Applications Directed to Computer-Implemented Business Method Inventions', part of the 'Training and Implementation Guide' issued pursuant to the American Inventors Protection Act. Given the decision in State Street, lack of patentable subject matter will not form a ground of objection to such claims.

[96] USPTO Manual of Patent Examining Procedure, section 2142.

If the examiner finds a prima facie case of obviousness, the applicant can respond with evidence supporting inventive step. Unlike in Europe, there is no stress on the area of invention being technical (to put it another way, that the reason why the skilled man would not have got to the invention were not technical ones). To give a striking example, in the utility patent case of *In Re Dembiczak*[97] the patent was for orange-coloured plastic trash bags with markings which expanded when the bag was filled to show a pumpkin-lantern style of face. The prior art included similar but undecorated gusseted bags, the inventor's own prior design patent for bags with similar designs and references to the design in children's craft books. The Board of Patent Appeals and Interferences rejected the application for obviousness, but this was reversed by the CAFC. In their reasoning the CAFC stressed the need to guard against hindsight in combining prior art references, and held it was not obvious to combine the children's art references with known trash bags. There was no 'suggestion, teaching or motivation' in the prior art to combine the references in that way.[98] The technical (or non-technical) nature of the inventive step played no part in the decision.

Following *State Street* a number of business method patents of breadth and simplicity have been issued. In *Amazon.com Inc v Barnesandnoble.com Inc*,[99] Amazon were (on appeal) refused interim injunctive relief on a claim for 'one-click' internet shopping, on the basis that the defendants had mounted a substantial challenge to validity on the basis of obviousness. Proprietors of such patents are likely to be more reticent about enforcing them following *Bilski*.

6.2.6 A comparison and discussion of the two approaches

Although patent examiners in the EPO can point to computer programming and business methods as being non-patentable per se, such activities could also be categorized as having mental acts or abstract ideas (non-patentable under US law) at their core. It is submitted that there is not in fact a great deal of practical difference between the USA and the EPO over what is and is not appropriate subject matter for a patent. Rather, the difference, both in terms of the doctrine applied and the outcome, is in where and how patentable and non-patentable subject matter is looked for in the invention.

Either pre- or post-*Pensions*, the key feature of the European approach is the way that non-patentable subject matter is sought out in claims. Whether looking for the contribution to the art or the inventive step, the enquiry demands looking behind the form of the claims to the inventive concept underlying the invention. It is in this deeper view of what the invention is that technical content must be found.

---

[97] (1999) 175 F3d 994.

[98] If the distinction over the prior art had been purely decorative, that would not have been patentable.

[99] (2001) 239 F3d 1343.

By contrast, the US approach prior to *Bilski* was to look less deeply at what the invention was, with the result that the enquiry stopped at the stage of identifying an item of hardware. After *Bilski*, it is clear that a somewhat deeper enquiry will be undertaken, with irrelevant activity surrounding a process or mere computerization in the case of a machine claim not turning non-patentable abstract ideas into patentable subject matter. It seems unlikely, however, that this deeper enquiry will exclude as many claims as the European search for technical content.

The difference between the two approaches can be illustrated by considering *In Re Warmerdam*.[100] Here, a claim was allowed essentially for a computer carrying data in a particular structure (claims to the process of generating the structure were refused as mental acts). The claims were not limited to any particular use for such a computer or memory. It seems unlikely that any such general claims would succeed in the EPO. The inventive step would be a matter of mathematics only. Once this is proposed, the programming and hardware means for putting it into effect as a computer or memory (which might well have a 'technical' character) will be obvious. To comply with the requirement for technical content, any claims to the *Warmerdam* invention would have to be directed to a machine with an identifiable real-world use, such as a robot. Furthermore, the idea of using that mathematical method to navigate a robot (as opposed to the task of coming up with the mathematical idea) would have to be inventive from a technical point of view over previous ways of robotic navigation. In Europe such claims would have to be addressed to a computer or a data structure on a carrier. But they would only cover such a program or data structure to the extent that it was adapted to operate in a computer so as to achieve robotic navigation. Claims in the form upheld in the USA will afford significantly greater protection to the patentee, which might well be of economic value.

Would the claims in *Warmerdam* be granted following *Bilski*? The interim USPTO Guidelines indicate that the claims would have to be amended to specify more robot-specific hardware elements to defeat an 'abstract idea' objection. However, a crucial difference remains between the US and EPO approaches: once a specific machine, article, or process is found US law does not look for patentable subject matter in the difference from the prior art—there is no requirement for the inventive step to be of a technical nature. The EPO approach to *Warmerdam* (even with more specific claims) would almost certainly be to exclude it for lack of inventive step on the basis that the journey from prior methods of robotic navigation to the patented method involved a combination of the inventive but non-technical (mental steps) and the technically obvious (standard hardware and software).

---

[100] Section 6.2.3.5 above.

6.3 OTHER ASPECTS OF PATENT LAW

Under this heading an outline of the UK interpretation of the position under the EPC (in the form of the Patents Act 1977 as interpreted by the courts) will be given. A detailed treatment of these matters, which are largely independent of the nature of the subject matter of the invention, is beyond the scope of this chapter and readers should consult relevant works on patent law.[101] The position in other EPC jurisdictions is likely to be broadly similar as to the general principles concerned, although differing in matters of detail.

6.3.1 Novelty

Article 54 EPC (Patents Act 1977, s 1(1)) states that an invention is novel if it 'does not form part of the state of the art'. The state of the art is defined in Article 54(2) (s 1(2)) as 'comprising everything made available to the public by means of a written or oral description, by use, or in any other way'. The date on which the state of the art is considered is the priority date of the claim in question, which will be the date of the application for the patent or a date within one year prior to that on which another document was filed from which priority is claimed. US readers should note this (the 'first to file' system) most particularly. The US system of 'first to invent' means that a disclosure by the inventor of their invention cannot invalidate any patent that is subsequently duly applied for within a year of the date the invention was made. In Europe and many other jurisdictions it can, and frequently does (and US inventors are often the culprits).

It is established law that the phrase 'made available to the public' means that any disclosure will only contribute to the art that which it 'enables'. In respect of any particular invention, an enabling disclosure is one which would direct the skilled man, using only his general knowledge in his field and not having to exercise any inventive capacity, to achieve the invention, that is make the product or carry out the process claimed. There are several important points that follow from this:

(a) The skilled man is a hypothetical person who was skilled in the relevant areas of technology as at the priority date. The relevant areas are those which are relevant to a particular claim of a patent the novelty of which might be under consideration. It is thus not strictly relevant to consider a disclosure in a vacuum—there has to be an invention in mind to focus attention on a particular recipient of the information and what that recipient is enabled to do.

(b) 'Mosaicing' is not allowed. That is, different disclosures cannot be combined to add up to an enabling disclosure; each disclosure must be looked at separately.[102]

---

[101] See, eg, Thorley et al, *Terrell on the Law of Patents*, 17th edn (London: Sweet & Maxwell, 2010).
[102] There are exceptions where, eg, two documents cross-refer.

A combination of disclosures might render the patent obvious, but that is a separate ground of invalidity.

(c) Disclosures made under conditions whereby all recipients of information were under duties of confidence make nothing available to the public and are disregarded. In English legal terms, the recipient has to be 'free in law and equity' to do what they will with whatever is gleaned from the disclosure. There are savings for information published in breach of duties of confidence.

(d) The fact that nothing actually was disclosed to anyone is irrelevant, what matters is availability. If no one ever read an article in a journal that was published, matter would still be available to the public. (And since this is a work on computer law, it should be pointed out that publication by placing information on a computer to which there is unrestricted access, eg because is on a webpage, makes matter available to the public.)

(e) In the case of public demonstrations, the use of machines in public places and the distribution to the public of objects or substances, the scope of disclosure is determined by considering what the skilled man could have gleaned by inspecting the material had he got his hands on it (again it is irrelevant that no recipient of the object actually had the relevant skill).

(f) There are complex rules governing the situations that arise when a patent application anticipating a later application is not actually published (made available to the public) before the priority date of the later application.

Thus, where the use on a public road of traffic control apparatus would have revealed the claimed manner of operation to a passing skilled man had he simply observed the operation of the system, the claim was held to lack novelty.[103] In the case of computer-related inventions it will normally be the case that public distribution of computers or disks containing all the relevant software will make available all relevant matter to the skilled man (a complete decompilation and understanding of the code may not be necessary to understand the alleged invention sufficiently to reproduce it). If development products are to be distributed, this must either be done after any patent filing or conditions of confidence must be imposed on all recipients so that they are not free to communicate to the world anything they find out about the product by investigating it. The copyright issues surrounding investigating the technical functioning of software should also be borne in mind here—see Chapter 7, section 7.5.7.

Generally novelty can reside in a new thing or a new process, which can include a new use for an old thing. The case of *Mobil/Friction reducing additive*[104] represents a high point in this area. Mobil found that a certain chemical additive to engine oil reduced friction in the engine. The identical compound had been known and used

---

[103] *Lux Traffic Controls Ltd v Pike Signals Ltd* [1993] RPC 107.
[104] Case T 59/87.

as a wear-reducing agent in engine oil but it had not been realized that it reduced friction. The enlarged TBA held that a claim to use of the additive 'as a friction reducing additive' was novel. This has been criticized as effectively allowing claims to old uses of old products for new purposes, although the Board held that the use was new.[105] Subsequent patentees do not appear to have sought claims in precisely these circumstances and generally it will be possible to find some physical distinction in the product or the use over the prior art.

Whilst searching among published patents in the computer-related field is easy for patent offices, searching software that may have been sold (and thus 'made available to the public') but where no patent application has been made is more difficult. Patent offices are coming to terms with this, but the free and open source software ('FOSS') movement has established the Open Invention Network as a means for the open-source community to secure mutual protection from threats of patent infringement (both for providers and users).[106] The basic idea is that patents and technical resources are pooled and made freely available (sometimes by free licence), thereby denying such protection to proprietary providers and also making available a repository of 'prior art' which may provide means to attack the validity of patents that are asserted against the community.[107]

6.3.2 Obviousness

The requirement for an inventive step is set out in Article 52(1) EPC (Patents Act 1977, s 1(1)). Article 56 (s 3) defines an invention as having an 'inventive step' if the invention would not have been obvious to a person skilled in the art having regard to the state of the art. Whilst the basic idea of obviousness is clear and similar across the jurisdictions, as a practical matter it is the most difficult fact to address in any judicial process and a number of principles and approaches have emerged from courts and patent offices around the world. It is generally thought that the UK courts are more ready to find a patent obvious than the EPO or some European courts. This may be related to the different procedures, particularly the reliance on live expert evidence in the UK compared with a more paper-based approach elsewhere.

---

[105] The Board held that since the friction-reducing properties were not known to the public the invention was not made available. But the friction-reducing properties were available in the practical sense in every motor car using the prior additive. In the English courts at least, the claim appears unenforceable because the only difference between the prior use of the additive (which, it is axiomatic, the public can carry out as well after the patent as before) and the claim is effectively the purpose for which the additive is used, a wholly mental distinction. To find infringement one would have to postulate a mental element to the tort of patent infringement. The 'Gillette' defence which may be paraphrased as 'I am only doing what is disclosed in the prior art so either the claim doesn't cover what I am doing or it is not novel (and I don't care which)' would appear to be applicable in all cases unless a mental element is postulated.

[106] The issue of infringement by distribution and use of free and open-source software is discussed at section 6.3.4 below.

[107] See generally <http://www.openinventionnetwork.com/> and, in relation to FOSS, <http://www.gnu.org> (both accessed 9 August 2011).

It should also be pointed out that it is difficult for patent offices to deal with the issue of obviousness at the examination stage in the same way as a civil court would do on hearing an opposition to the patent. Many successful post-grant oppositions are based on obviousness.

The basic principles applied in Europe are that the skilled man is assumed to possess common general knowledge and is also assumed to know of each piece of prior art (but no subsequent disclosure). He is therefore a highly theoretical construction. Commonly, expert testimony is led on this issue and the expert is asked to put herself in the position of the hypothetical skilled man. An example of an obvious invention is the English 'sausage machine case'.[108] It was held that there was no inventiveness in combining a known machine for making sausage filling with a known machine for filling sausages since there was no difficulty in making the connection and it was obvious that the elements could be combined to produce an all-in-one machine if such was desired.

The approach of the EPO has been to identify the technical problem to be overcome and consider the possibility of moving to a solution from the 'closest' piece of prior art, known as the 'problem and solution' approach or 'PAS'. However, the TBA has recognized that this approach is not appropriate in all cases, especially where there is no obvious closest piece of prior art, and that the EPC does not specify any method of finding obviousness (which is ultimately a question of fact). In *Alcan/Aluminium alloys*,[109] it was pointed out that the problem and solution approach led to a step-by-step analysis that was based on hindsight and unreliable, although most the EPO examiners and boards still use it most of the time.

The approach of the UK courts has differed from the EPO approach somewhat. The Court of Appeal in *Actavis UK Ltd v Novartis AG*[110] has held that the question of obviousness is a 'multi-factorial' one and that no single process of steps is likely to be appropriate in all cases. Thus PAS does not work well unless the problem is clear and the closest piece of prior art can be easily identified. The Court of Appeal also pointed out that PAS is more suited to patent offices than courts hearing contested issues of obviousness. The court favoured the four-stage approach in the earlier *Pozzoli* decision:[111]

(1) (a) Identify the notional 'person skilled in the art';

  (b) Identify the relevant common general knowledge of that person;

(2) Identify the inventive concept of the claim in question or if that cannot readily be done, construe it;

---

[108] *Williams v Nye* (1890) 7 RPC 62.
[109] Case T 465/92.
[110] [2010] EWCA Civ 82, [2010] FSR 8.
[111] *Pozzoli SpA v BDMO SA* [2007] EWCA Civ 588, [2007] FSR 37.

(3) Identify what, if any, differences exist between the matter cited as forming part of the 'state of the art' and the inventive concept of the claim or the claim as construed;

(4) Viewed without any knowledge of the alleged invention as claimed, do those differences constitute steps which would have been obvious to the person skilled in the art or do they require any degree of invention?

The court recognized that this approach would not always be the correct approach, for example where there was a dispute as to what the 'inventive concept' was. Sometimes the problem-and-solution approach would be appropriate. The Patents Act and the EPC both have the single test of obviousness and the court has to find the most appropriate way to assess that. Cases on obviousness are strewn with admonitions about the care that must be taken to avoid hindsight and rejections of step-by-step arguments whereby each step on the road to the invention is painted as obvious whilst losing sight of the overall inventive contribution. Obviousness is and will remain a difficult question of fact to decide whatever theoretical frameworks it is placed into. In contested proceedings it will turn on the expert evidence.

In *Bosch/Electronic computer components*,[112] the audacious claim was made by an applicant that since prior documents cited against the application were written partly in program code and not 'ordinary language', the code listings therein should be ignored when considering obviousness. Thankfully for the sanity of commentators, this claim was rejected on the basis that the skilled man in that case would have been or have had access to a sufficiently skilled programmer to understand the prior citations. It was also held that the skilled man could in fact comprise a team of mixed skills.

The test is objective, and is sometimes stated as looking at what *could* the skilled man have done rather than *would* he have decided to do.[113]

It is the test of obviousness that ensures that mere clever programming will not found an invention. The skilled man is deemed to be a clever programmer, he is just not inventive—a different matter. This is why the patent claims discussed in this chapter have been addressed to principles of operation and organization of computers and data structures and have not recited detailed code. In a trivial sense many original programs are likely to be new, in that nothing identical has been written before, but few will be inventive.

And as we have seen, in Europe inventiveness that resides solely in the field of computer programming will not count. But inventiveness in other non-patentable areas is also ignored. Where the inventor spotted a previously unfulfilled market

---

[112] See section 6.2.3.1 above.

[113] Unless the inventive step lay in identifying the problem to be solved, ie it was not obvious to try and there was not a fair expectation of success—*Conor Medsystems Inc v Angiotech Pharmaceuticals Inc* [2008] UKHL 49, [2008] RPC 28.

need for an improved corkscrew but, given the task of developing such a product, it would have been obvious how to achieve it from a technical point of view, the invention was obvious.[114]

In general, applications written by software houses for clients or for general sale are unlikely to involve anything patentable for reasons of obviousness. Inventive data structures or modes of operation may be involved in the programming tools used to create the products (eg, database 'engines' or image-manipulation tools), but any patents to those will belong to the owner of the tools not the writer of the end product. For most software developers, therefore, limiting access to source code and enforcement of copyright are likely to be the main avenues for protection of their investment in production.

6.3.3 The need for disclosure

In return for the monopoly granted by the patent (see section 6.3.4 below), the applicant is required to disclose how the invention works. The specification must describe the invention claimed clearly and completely enough to enable the skilled man to put it into effect (Art 83 EPC; Patents Act 1977, s 14(3)). It does not have to do more, so detailed design issues need not be addressed. One reason why the drawings to patent specifications can appear old-fashioned and unworkable is because they are there to teach principles, not to give away detailed designs.

In the case of computer-related inventions, what this means is that full code listings for programs may not need to be given. Schematics or flow diagrams may suffice to teach the principles involved. The comments made about what is assumed of the relevant skilled man in relation to obviousness apply equally here—a competent programmer will not need the actual code in order to be able to implement an invention that is otherwise adequately explained.

6.3.4 The rights granted by a patent

Article 64 EPC states that holders of European patents should have the same rights as holders of national patents. A patent grants the exclusive rights to the commercial exploitation of the invention claimed. Thus the manufacture, importation, sale, or use in the course of trade of products falling within the claims of a patent may be prevented by the patent owner.[115] In the case of patents for processes, it is an infringement to use the process or to dispose of, use, or import any product obtained

---

[114] *Hallen Co and Another v Brabantia (UK) Ltd, Financial Times,* 24 October 1990, CA, approving first instance judgment of Aldous J reported at [1989] RPC 307. This approach was also taken in *Esswein/ Automatic programmer* Case T 579/88, where the 'invention' consisted of the appreciation that many consumers only required three programmes on their washing machines!

[115] Patents Act 1977, s 60(1).

directly by means of the process. A detailed description of the various ways of infringing a UK patent is set out in section 60 of the Patents Act 1977.

Two immediate contrasts can be drawn with the remedy for breach of copyright:

(a) Copying is irrelevant, as is knowledge of the patent (although absence of the latter can provide a seller with a defence to a claim for damages): the monopoly is in this sense absolute.

(b) Private and experimental use is permitted[116] so end-users of products who do not use them in the course of a trade (ie, consumers) cannot infringe patents—not even when purchasing the product from a retailer (who would be an infringer). But note that where there is dual purpose use, that will infringe.

It is necessary to provide a word of warning concerning use in the course of trade versus private or experimental use. It has been held[117] that experiments may have an ultimate commercial end in view and still fall within the exception, but that experiments to obtain regulatory approval or to demonstrate to a third party that a product works are not covered by the exception. It is clear from this that if a product or software forming part of an invention is investigated to find out how it works, for example by disassembling program code, that will not infringe any patent (compare the position under copyright law—see Chapter 7, section 7.5, and in particular section 7.5.7). But as steps are made towards a commercial product, infringement is likely to occur prior to launch or Beta-testing.

It is also an infringement for a person to supply or offer to supply

any of the means, relating to an essential element of the invention, for putting the invention into effect when he knows, or it is obvious to a reasonable person in the circumstances, that those means are suitable for putting, and are intended to put, the invention into effect in the United Kingdom.[118]

This is known as 'indirect infringement' and may be of considerable relevance to computer-related inventions. If a patent does not cover a program as such, or its material form such as a recording on a disk, suppliers of program code or data may nevertheless be liable if the code or data on the disk forms an essential element of the invention, when they know or ought to know that the means are suitable for putting the invention into effect. A possible let-out is that if the means supplied is a 'staple commercial product' then for there to be infringement the supply must be for the purpose of inducing the person supplied to do an infringing act.[119] 'Staple commercial product' is not defined, but it is submitted that whereas it would include a

---

[116] Ibid s 60(5).
[117] *Monsanto Co v Stauffer Chemical Co* [1985] RPC 515.
[118] Patents Act 1977, s 60(2).
[119] Ibid s 60(3).

blank disk or ROM, it would not include one on which a particular program or data had been recorded.

An issue that raises some questions in this regard is the provision of free and open-source software. Many such programs are available by means of download from the internet in source code and ready-compiled form, for users of open-source operating systems such as Gnu/Linux and in some cases for proprietary operating systems such as Microsoft Windows. Some of these programs potentially include, when run, technology that is covered by patented inventions, for example in the field of compression formats. Home users of such programs will not infringe as their use is both private and non-commercial. Business users should use licensed software, or patent-free codecs and so on, if they are concerned. Providers of the software for download will arguably infringe because their provision of the software can hardly be called private (although it may be non-commercial), and the users will be 'putting the invention into effect', albeit those users will have a defence. It does not appear to be relevant that the program may be provided by source code that the user can compile rather than a ready-compiled binary. The position may be different in jurisdictions other than the UK, and there is an assumption within the open-source community that whilst the use of software *may* infringe a patent, the provision of source code will not.

This still leaves the question of how to decide when a product or process falls within the scope of a claim of a patent. This is the problem of construing the claims of a patent. Two extreme points of view are possible: construe the claim literally and only things that fall within that literal interpretation infringe; or look at the claims as a mere guide and construe the patent as a whole to identify the correct scope of the monopoly. Article 69 EPC and the Protocol thereto state that the course to be adopted lies in between the two. EPC 2000 added a paragraph to the Protocol stating that elements that were technically equivalent to elements in a claim should be considered (the 'doctrine of equivalents'). The UK courts still use the doctrine of 'purposive construction' in which the meaning of the claim wording is interpreted according to how the skilled person would have interpreted it at the time of publication of the patent application, but they have recognized that Article 69 and its Protocol is what, ultimately, the courts must follow.[120] Whatever test is adopted, it does not alter the fact that careful claim drafting is the key to obtaining a commercially useful, easily enforceable patent.

The remedies for infringement of patents are similar to those available for other intellectual property rights, that is damages (based on lost profits) or an account of profits earned by the infringer, an injunction to restrain further infringement, and delivery up of infringing items. The full range of pre-emptive interlocutory remedies (early injunctions, search orders, and so on) are available in patent actions

---

[120] *Kirin-Amgen v Transkaryotic Therapies* [2004] UKHL 46, [2005] RPC 9.

in accordance with the normal principles. A detailed consideration of these is beyond the scope of this chapter.

6.3.5 Duration, revocation, and amendment

Under the EPC patents last for 20 years from the date of the full application, although priority can be claimed from a filing made up to a year prior to that. In the case of US patents filed prior to 8 June 1995 the term ran from the date of issue of the patent but was for 17 years. For subsequently filed applications the position is the same as the European position. This was necessary to take account of the TRIPS Agreement[121] which provides for a degree of uniformity between patent laws.

The validity of patents can generally be challenged after grant in the course of infringement proceedings or upon application by an opponent. In the UK the court hears such applications in the course of infringement proceedings, although in some jurisdictions matters of validity are considered by the Patent Office in separate proceedings. In the UK a patentee can apply to amend a patent after grant subject to certain safeguards. This is generally undertaken so as to narrow down the patent to give it a better chance of survival in the face of an opposition to validity.

6.3.6 Ownership, transmission, and employee inventions

The EPC states that the inventor should be the first owner of any patent, but leaves the ownership of employee inventions up to the laws of the EPC state in which the invention is made. In the UK the basic rule is that inventions made in the course of employment belong to the employer,[122] although there are provisions for compensation to be provided to employee inventors.[123]

UK employers should note the following potential pitfalls:

(a) If an employee whose normal duties do not include programming or computer-related developments and who has not been specifically assigned a computer-related task makes a computer-related invention, the employer may not own it.

(b) Workers who are on contract, not employees in the employment law sense, will own any inventions they make pursuant to a contract unless the contract specifically provides, by express or implied term, for ownership of inventions (which of course it should!).

Patents can be assigned and licensed like any other right, but assignments are only effective if in writing. The national patent offices of the EPC states have systems for

---

[121] See section 6.1.2 above.
[122] Patents Act 1977, s 39.
[123] Ibid ss 40–43.

the registration of transfers of ownership and generally registration is necessary for an assignment to be fully effective. After grant, a European patent is no different from a portfolio of national patents and the administrative requirements of each national system must be complied with. The separate national patents can be disposed of or licensed separately.

6.4 WHY EXCLUDE ANYTHING FROM PATENTABILITY?

A great deal of intellectual effort has been expended in addressing the more theoretical aspects of the issue of intellectual property protection for computer software. Some of the main arguments that are put forward in relation to patentability are discussed below.

6.4.1 Which form of protection?

It has been questioned whether patent protection (as opposed to copyright protection, some other protection, or no protection at all) is the right form of protection for computer programs or computer software.

It will be noted that this chapter has tended to use the rather cumbersome expression 'computer-related inventions'. The reason for this is that by their nature patents tend to protect matters of fundamental structure and functional features rather than the details of how those things are implemented, and thus will only protect some aspects of software.[124] By contrast, copyright tends to protect the actual way a program is written and the actual data recorded in a data structure (as well as only preventing copying). This is not to say that there can be no overlap. There is no rule which says that a description of the function of a program that is sufficiently brief and general to form the substance of a patent claim would not amount to a substantial part of that program for the purposes of copyright infringement.[125] But if there is overlap it will be at the margins.

The distinction between patent and copyright protection is easily illustrated by the following example. A document setting out a novel chemical process would attract copyright protection, but that protection would protect the document against copying, not the process from being carried out. A patent for the process would prevent it from being carried out but not from being written about or broadcast. Here there is no difficulty in separating the creative literary content from the inventive technical content. In general, prior to the introduction of computers and digital methods of recording data, literary and artistic works were easily identifiable, as were

---

[124] Because, as we have seen, the detailed working out of the principles may be difficult or time-consuming, but is unlikely to be inventive.
[125] See further Chapter 7, section 7.4.2.1.

technical inventions, and problems in classifying something as one or the other were rare (although they did arise).

The work of the programmer or computer technologist can fall into both the 'technical' and 'creative' camps. Whilst the chemist of the preceding paragraph clearly utilized literary skill to write out the instructions and technical skill to develop the process, in programming the separation of the two is more problematical (indeed it is a similar problem to that addressed by the EPO when it looks for 'technical content'). Programming clearly involves an understanding of numbers and logic and some sympathy with the technical restraints imposed by the physical apparatus on which the program is to run, which are abilities we associate with the technologist. Yet it may also require the creation of things whose performance cannot be accurately measured and an understanding of the psychology and reactions, likes and dislikes of the user of the computer on which the program will eventually run. It will certainly require close attention to the inter-relationships, syntax, and possibly layout of the code. These are abilities we associate with people in the creative literary trades such as copy-writing, design, and publishing.

Separating the 'technical' aspects of a piece of program code from its 'literary' elements may not be an easy or even meaningful process. Nevertheless, the patent system allows for principles to be extracted and afforded one form of protection whereas the copyright system gives protection to other aspects of the programmer's work. It is not sensible to take any area of human creative endeavour and arbitrarily say 'this should be protected by patents not copyright' or vice versa. In appropriate circumstances both a patent and copyright will protect different aspects of a computer programmer's work.

6.4.2 Scientific consistency

Against a restrictive approach can be ranged arguments based upon considerations of the technical reality of the situation. According to these, the problem with trying to exclude programs from patentability is that a sharp dividing line is sought where none exists. Most people involved in the computer industry would say they knew what was a program and what was not, but a computer program is a disembodied concept, whereas a patent claim must define the scope of an industrially useful monopoly. Knowing what a program is doesn't help in defining the limits of patentability.

When a computer runs a program, all or parts of the program code are copied from the computer's hard disk and stored in the computer's temporary memory. As the program runs, instructions are fetched from the memory and executed by the processor, and the computer then goes on to execute further instructions. Execution of instructions may involve the creation or transposition of data in the computer's memory or the performance of input/output operations to the screen, a printer, or a hard disk. All these operations occur inside the computer's integrated circuits as changes in the electrical values at various points. Data pathways are physically opened and closed and electrical circuits re-configured by the act of running the program.

Instead of being loaded into temporary memory from a disk, some programs are permanently held in ROM chips on the computer's circuit boards. They stay in place and are readable even when the computer is turned off. These programs are often low-level routines dealing with matters of the internal operation of the computer. Some program routines may be stored on the processor chip itself and built into it at the time of manufacture, so that they are embodied in the way the circuit elements of the chip are arranged and interconnected. These would deal with complex arithmetical instructions such as division and so on. The distinction between 'hardware' and 'software' is not sharp, there is a continuum. And however a program is executed, it results in a computer that is physically, electrically configured in a special way so as to operate that program.[126] So, the argument goes, there is no scientific basis for distinguishing computer-related inventions from those relating to bits of bent metal and plastic.

But it can also be argued that a solely scientifically driven view misses the point about patents. Patents are about monopolies for inventions that are useful to people. It is generally recognized that running a computer program produces a physical change in a computer. We have seen that both in the USA and in Europe, questions of patentability of computer-related inventions are dealt with by applying general principles that apply equally to non-computer applications. It is difficult to argue that computer-related inventions are being discriminated against in any way.

6.4.3 Upholding the basic principles of patent law

The 'bargain' theory of patent protection has already been mentioned. The purpose of patent protection in accordance with this theory is to grant a monopoly which will be commercially useful to the patentee whilst making available practically useful things and processes to society at large. Theories, scientific discoveries, mathematical formulae, and artistic works are not useful in this practical sense although their consideration might affect our quality of life in the spiritual or intellectual sense.

The notion that the scope of patent protection granted should in some way reflect the scope of what the patent teaches people to do (referred to above) satisfies a basic consideration of fairness yet is inconsistent with allowing patent protection for mere discoveries. If a discovery or mathematical relationship were to be patentable in

---

[126] It is interesting to note that this congruity between program and circuit is mirrored in the field of UK copyright law, where electrical circuit diagrams have been viewed as literary works (*Anacon Corp Ltd v Environmental Research Technology Ltd* [1994] FSR 659), just as programs are. But this does not suggest that excluding 'electrical circuits' from patentability would provide an answer to the problems discussed. Indeed one can see that precisely the same problems of what amounts to an electric circuit 'as such', and whether in any event the claim really relates to a mental process, will present themselves.

some way, then all industrial developments building on it (whether foreseen by the original 'inventor' or totally unexpected) would be covered by the scope of the claim. There are obvious moral and economic arguments to be mounted against the grant of excessively wide monopolies of this type. The general rule has emerged therefore that a principle or discovery must be applied to a practical purpose in some way for patent protection to be possible, and reasonable protection will be given to that particular application. Thus useful things, machines, or processes designed to exploit scientific discoveries or mathematical relationships are patentable provided they satisfy the various other tests for patentability.

It is not clear that the above principle is violated by excluding or not excluding particular things since, as we have seen, any exclusionary rule will have to be applied to a patent claim and the question 'what is this claim actually for?' asked. At this stage, questions of the fundamental nature of patents come into play. It is here that differences of approach between the USA and the countries that follow it and Europe become apparent. The convergence (in some respects) between the approaches adopted in the two jurisdictions over the past decade has served only to highlight the key difference: the European principle that patent protection should only cover technical advances and the absence of such a principle in the USA. The issue is of a more fundamental nature than the question 'should computer programs be patentable?'.[127]

It can be pointed out that the requirements of novelty, unobviousness, and sufficiency of teaching will be adequate to ensure that unwarranted and restrictive monopolies are not granted and that exclusions from patentability are not necessary. But as we have seen in Europe, since fundamental issues of what should be patented inform decisions on those topics as well as on questions of patentable subject matter per se, this approach cannot help to resolve those very same fundamental issues. It is submitted that questions as to the scope of what may be patented are matters of policy and recourse to legal doctrine should not be made when answering them. Thus, the US position stems from the absence of restrictive words in the relevant provisions of the US Constitution, whereas the European position derives from the identification of a requirement for technical content as an underlying principle behind the EPC. The legal doctrines have developed from those principles.

6.4.4 Economic and social expedience

Perhaps the most sensible basis for deciding these issues is simply to ask 'what do we actually want?'. There is a body of opinion that all software should be free from intellectual property restraints (understandably, many computer users subscribe to this view). Yet the software industry is an industry like any other and if intellectual

---

[127] The answer to that question, from both a US or European standpoint, is 'yes, sometimes', or perhaps 'that's not the relevant question'.

property rights are deemed desirable to reward invention and protect creative skill and labour in other industries, why make exceptions?

Having said that, it is not clear to what extent patents are a real commercial force in the computer industry (other than in relation to definite hardware elements) in the way that they are in some other industries. The pace of technological development will clearly affect the commercial lifetime of many computer-related inventions and the time involved in obtaining a patent may make it commercially pointless to apply. It is also worth repeating that patent protection will not be relevant to most new computer programs regardless of which patent system protection is sought under.

As noted below, considerations of competitiveness between trade areas can also influence intellectual property policy. The perception of such pressures is often that they dictate strong IP rights, although in some areas of business and industry a loose regime is more conducive to innovation and wealth creation. As with other intellectual property rights, there has to be a balance: make the rights too strong and development is stifled; make them too weak and it will not be promoted. The fact that Congress passed the American Inventors Protection Act perhaps indicated unease at the possibly stifling effect of the post-*Alappat* regime of patentability in the US (since modified by the Supreme Court decisions in *Bilski v Kappos*).[128] In addition, the tenor of the EU draft Directive on the Patentability of Computer-Related Inventions[129] takes a more balanced view than earlier papers where the 'strong IP good, weak IP bad' assumption prevailed. The policy pendulum may have reached the end of its swing.

6.5 THE FUTURE

The US Supreme Court will not, presumably, be considering patentable subject matter for a while, now that it has delivered the *Bilski* decision. It will take time and a few appeal decisions for a clear post-*Bilski* doctrine to emerge, but it is reasonably clear that whatever it is, it will be more restrictive in at least some respects than the previous position following cases such as *Alappat* and *State Street*.

The difference of approach in Europe from the pre-*Bilski* US position caused concern amongst European commentators and legislators. In 1997 the European Commission published its 'Green Paper on the Community patent and the patent system in Europe'.[130] This sought wide-ranging comment, including on how or whether to proceed with a Community Patent and on the issue of patent protection for computer-related inventions.

---

[128] See section 6.2.5.5 above.
[129] See section 6.5 below.
[130] COM(97)314 final.

Following the consultation period, the Commission issued a Communication[131] indicating its intended follow-up measures. These included that the then position concerning legal protection for computer programs 'did not provide sufficient transparency', and that there were national differences in interpretation within the EPC area. The Commission concluded that the difficulties in obtaining protection for some computer-related inventions in Europe when compared to the USA was damaging to European economic interests, and a more liberal regime should be put in place. It also concluded that Europeans' perception is that European patent protection for computer-related inventions is less widely available than is actually the case. According to their statistics, the bulk of what they refer to as 'software patents' in Europe were held by non-Europeans.

The Commission then published a draft Directive on the patentability of computer-related inventions, essentially followed the *Pensions*[132] approach in focusing on the nature of the inventive step in enforcing the requirement for technical content. Its passage through the EU legislative process was tortuous and, ultimately, the Commission and the Parliament were unable to agree on a text.[133] The progress of the debate illustrated clearly how the issue of the patentability of computer-related inventions had become a topic of general interest. On the one hand, advocates of free software argued vehemently that the prohibition on patenting computer programs should remain. On the other, voices from the industry argued that protection was essential to maintain investment and international competitiveness. Of course, as we have seen, the exclusion from patentability of 'computer programs as such' in the EPC, if read without reference to the case law of the EPO, is liable to give a very misleading impression in that a considerable array of computer-related inventions are nevertheless patentable. The final positions of both the Parliament and the Commission involved specific provisions that might have raised issues over their compatibility with the TRIPs Agreement.[134] The current position, where the EPC reflects the TRIPs Agreement and the additional material on non-patentability in Article 52 can be dealt with by a bit of doctrinal footwork (the principle that all the excluded things are, by definition, 'non-technical') is a good way of complying with international obligations whilst achieving a general slant against the patentability of pure programs, which appears to be a generally accepted policy objective.

---

[131] 'Communication from the Commission dated 5 February 1999 to the Council, the European Parliament and the Economic and Social Committee—Promoting innovation through patents—the follow-up to the Green Paper on the Community Patent and the Patent System in Europe', COM(99)42, also published at EPO 01 4/1999 201.

[132] See section 6.2.2.3.

[133] Fortunately for a writer of a work such as this, meaning that a detailed discussion of the final text discussed by the Parliament is not required.

[134] The Common position of the Council is no 20/2005, OJ 2005/C 144 E(02), the position of the Parliament prior to the debate is set out in the Parliament's Draft Legislative Resolution contained in their Recommendation for a second reading of 21/06/2005, A6-0207/2005.

The other area of patent law that still exercises the EU is the area of further harmonization of the European patent system. To put it bluntly, the current system, an uneasy compromise between providing some kind of centralized patent-granting system whilst preserving national sovereignty and national patent offices, is unwieldy and expensive. Under the current system patents are more expensive to maintain and vastly more expensive to enforce or challenge than would be the case with a genuinely unitary system. This does not further the aims of a single market for technology and its products within the EU. Agreement of sorts has now been reached at EU level for the EU to operate as a single state for the purposes of the EPC, and for a system of patent litigation within the EU.[135] The EPO has indicated its support in principle for this, but noted that implementing the proposals will not be a quick process.

---

[135] EU press release no IP/090/1880 dated 4 December 2009, 'Patents: EU achieves political breakthrough on an enhanced patent system'; the EPO comment on this is at <http://www.epo.org/law-practice/legislative-initiatives/eu-patent.html>; Press Release dated 15 February 2011 from the European Parliament, 'EU patent: Parliament gives go-ahead for enhanced cooperation' at <http://www.europarl.europa.eu/en/pressroom/content/20110215IPR13680/html/EU-patent-Parliament-gives-go-ahead-for-enhanced-cooperation> (both accessed 9 August 2011).
Unanimous agreement on the precise way ahead within the EU Member States was not possible, so a sub-set of the states is proceeding with it under the enhanced cooperation procedure.

7

COPYRIGHT IN INFORMATION TECHNOLOGY AND DATA

Christopher Millard[1]

7.1 INTRODUCTION

7.1.1 The nature of copyright

Notwithstanding its considerable and ever-increasing significance to business, intellectual property continues to be one of the law's more obscure and esoteric fields. In popular parlance, confusion often reigns and talk of copyrighting an invention or patenting a trade mark is not uncommon. Such misunderstandings are, perhaps, not surprising given the highly technical nature of much of the law in this area and the scope for overlaps and conflicts between the various rights.

Nevertheless, the effective protection and exploitation of intellectual property rights is crucial to the success, and in some cases the survival, of a growing number

---

[1] The author would like to thank Gaetano Dimita for his assistance with updating this chapter for the current edition.

of businesses. Nowhere is this more strikingly the case than in the computer industry. For example, the right to manufacture, sell, buy, or use a complex product such
as a computer system comprising hardware and software may depend on licences of
any or all of patents, copyrights, design rights, know-how, and trade marks.
Similarly, the primary assets of a software house will usually be its copyright works.
The focus of this chapter will be on copyright. Other intellectual property rights are
covered elsewhere in this book.

What then is copyright? Copyright is, in essence, a right given to authors or
creators of 'works', such as books, films, or computer programs, to control the
copying or other exploitation of such works. In marked contrast to patent rights,
copyright begins automatically on the creation of a 'work' without the need for
compliance with any formalities. The only prerequisites for protection, which apply
to all works, are that the work must be of a type in which copyright can subsist, and
that either the author is a 'qualifying person', or the work has been published or
broadcast in an appropriate manner. In the case of certain types of works, including
literary works such as books and computer programs, the work must also be
'original' and it must be 'recorded' in some form (eg, written down or stored in
computer memory).

In addition to controlling the making of copies, the owner of copyright in a work
has the exclusive right to control publication, performance, broadcasting, and
the making of adaptations of the work. In certain cases, the author, director, or
commissioner of a work may be entitled to exercise certain 'moral rights' which
may include the right to be identified with a work and to object to distortion or
unjustified treatment of the work.

Where any of the various exclusive rights that collectively make up copyright in
a work have been exercised without permission, civil remedies may be available to
the owner or author. In certain cases criminal sanctions may also be brought to bear,
principally where copyright is being infringed with a view to commercial gain.
Most of these concepts and terms are discussed in more detail in the rest of this
chapter.

7.1.2 Evolution of UK copyright law

English copyright law has a history going back five centuries and has been regulated
by statute for almost three.[2] The first modern copyright law, the Copyright Act 1709,
was an attempt to balance the interests of authors and publishers in the case of the
leading-edge technology of the day, the printing press. Technology has since moved
on and so has the law. The two have not, however, always been in step.
Notwithstanding regular piecemeal amendment of the law, the gap between

---

[2] For an interesting historical review, see S Breyer, 'The Uneasy Case for Copyright: A Study of
Copyright in Books, Photocopies and Computer Programs' (1970) 84 Harv L Rev 281.

copyright law and new media has periodically had to be closed, or at least narrowed, by means of a radical overhaul of the law. Increased sophistication in the means for commercial exploitation of the economic value of copyright has been a particularly powerful catalyst for change. Cable and satellite broadcasting of films and other works, and the distribution of computer programs and other works in digital form are examples.

A major realignment occurred with the enactment of the Copyright, Designs and Patents Act 1988 ('the CDPA 1988').[3] Its predecessor in the copyright field, the Copyright Act 1956 ('the 1956 Act'), had been the subject both of detailed reform discussions[4] and temporary piecemeal amendments[5] for half of its time on the statute book. The CDPA 1988, most of the provisions of which came into force on 1 August 1989,[6] represented an attempt to start again with a clean slate. On this slate were written both a restatement of the general principles of copyright, and also various sets of rules to deal with specific types of copyright work and their commercial exploitation. Although there was considerable scope for criticizing the CDPA 1988 at a detailed level, on the whole it was a far more coherent, comprehensive, and accessible statement of the law than the statutes that it replaced.

Since then, the CDPA 1988 has been repeatedly, and on occasions heavily, amended almost entirely in response to a series of EU Directives. Perhaps not surprisingly many of the changes have been, directly or indirectly, related to technology issues. As a result, some two decades on from its creation, the CDPA 1988 is starting to look, at least from the perspective of a technology lawyer and user, less like a seamless tapestry and more like a patchwork quilt. This is a great pity since many of its provisions, for example relating to fair use of everyday items such as books, films, sound recordings, and computer software, are of extremely broad application to the general public.

7.1.3 The Copyright, Designs and Patents Act 1988

The Copyright, Designs and Patents Act 1988, as its name suggests, does not deal solely with copyright. It established a significant new property right, known as

---

[3] Royal assent, 15 November 1988. Unless otherwise indicated, references to sections in this chapter are to those of the CDPA 1988.

[4] A committee set up in 1973 under the chairmanship of Mr Justice Whitford reported in 1977 that the time had come for a general revision of the 1956 Act: see *Copyright and Designs Law: Report of the Committee to Consider the Law on Copyright and Designs* (Cmnd 6732, 1977) (London: HMSO). This was followed by two Green Papers which did little to advance the reform process: *Reform of the Law Relating to Copyright, Designs and Performers' Protection* (Cmnd 8302, 1981) (London: HMSO) and *Intellectual Property Rights and Innovation* (Cmnd 9117, 1983) (London: HMSO). The publication in 1986 of a White Paper entitled *Intellectual Property and Innovation* (Cmnd 9712, 1986) (London: HMSO) set the stage for a general overhaul of the law.

[5] Design Copyright Act 1968; Copyright Act 1956 (Amendment) Act 1982; Copyright (Amendment) Act 1983; Cable and Broadcasting Act 1984; Copyright (Computer Software) Amendment Act 1985.

[6] The Copyright, Designs and Patents Act 1988 (Commencement No 1) Order 1989 (SI 1989/816).

'design right'; the law relating to registered designs was changed; changes were made to patent and trade mark law; and the law relating to performers' protection was reformed and restated.[7]

Although judges have provided some guidance on interpreting the CDPA 1988, there remain many areas that have not yet been considered by the courts. In the meantime, some pointers can be obtained from court decisions based on the 1956 Act (as amended), and indeed on earlier statutes, such as the Copyright Act 1911. The extent to which reliance can be placed on such old decisions is, unfortunately, not at all clear. This is because section 172 of the CDPA 1988, given the marginal note 'General provisions as to construction', provides:

(1) This Part restates and amends the law of copyright, that is, the provisions of the Copyright Act 1956, as amended.

(2) A provision of this Part which corresponds to a provision of the previous law shall not be construed as departing from the previous law merely because of a change of expression.

(3) Decisions under the previous law may be referred to for the purpose of establishing whether a provision of this Part departs from the previous law, or otherwise for establishing the true construction of this Part.

Each part of this section seems to introduce a layer of confusion. The first subsection states that the CDPA 1988 is both a restatement and an amendment of the old law. The second provides that a change in language does not necessarily indicate a change in meaning although, by implication, it may do. The third suggests that we look to court decisions based on the 1956 Act to see whether there has in fact been a change in meaning and generally to assist in understanding the new Act. Thus, even if it can be shown that a particular provision of the CDPA 1988 'corresponds' to a provision of the 1956 Act, the fact that the provision has been redrafted in different language may or may not indicate anything about its meaning. It is particularly difficult to see how cases decided under the 1956 Act could illuminate Parliament's intentions in 1988 in including, excluding, or substituting specific words in the CDPA 1988. There is no reference to the status, if any, of cases decided under older statutes such as the Copyright Act 1911. Taken as a whole, section 172 gives advocates plenty of scope for argument over semantics, and leaves courts with considerable discretion as to whether to rely on or disregard particular precedents as they seek to interpret and apply the new law.

---

[7] For a helpful introduction to the CDPA 1988 as a whole, which incorporates the full text of the statute, see G Dworkin and RD Taylor, *Blackstone's Guide to the Copyright, Designs and Patents Act 1988* (London: Blackstone Press, 1998). For a more detailed analysis see H Laddie, P Prescott, and M Vitoria, *The Modern Law of Copyright and Designs*, 4th edn (London: Butterworths, 2007).

7.1.4 EU Directives and their implementation in the UK

Differences in the nature and scope of the intellectual property rights available in the 25 EU Member States have frequently given rise to trade barriers. In seeking to limit the effects of such restrictions, the European Commission and the European Court have drawn distinctions between the existence and the exercise of intellectual property rights. Ownership of an intellectual property right is not inherently anti-competitive, indeed the Treaty of Rome sanctions import and export restrictions that can be justified as being 'for the protection of industrial or commercial property'.[8] However, attempts to use intellectual property rights as a means of carving up the internal market are vulnerable to challenge under the Treaty. According to the 'exhaustion of rights' doctrine developed by the European Court, goods that have been put on the market lawfully in one of the Member States by or with the consent of the owner, must be permitted to circulate freely throughout the European Union. Of particular significance to the computer industry is the availability and scope of copyright protection for software products. In June 1988 the Commission published a Green Paper entitled *Copyright and the Challenge of Technology*.[9] In that discussion document the Commission inclined towards the view that copyright is the most appropriate form of protection for computer programs and should provide the foundation for a Directive on software protection. Comments were, however, invited on a number of issues relating to the precise nature and scope of the exclusive rights that Member States should be required to grant software owners.

Following a period of consultation that ended in December 1988, a Directive on the Legal Protection of Computer Programs ('the Software Directive') was adopted by the Council of Ministers on 14 May 1991.[10] Legislation to implement the Software Directive in the UK, the Copyright (Computer Programs) Regulations 1992,[11] was enacted in time for the implementation deadline of 1 January 1993. Specific aspects of the Software Directive and UK implementing legislation are discussed later in this chapter.

The EU has also adopted a Directive on the Legal Protection of Databases.[12] The copyright provisions in the Directive only deal with the structure of databases (recital 15 and Art 5) and not the contents of databases.[13] The contents of databases remain governed by national copyright laws and a novel and separate property right introduced by the Directive, the so-called *sui generis* or database right, which exists independent of any copyright (Art 7(4)) (see Chapter 8). The Directive effectively creates three tiers of protection; databases may contain contents that are copyrighted,

---

[8] Treaty of Rome, Art 30.

[9] COM(88)172 final.

[10] Council Directive (EEC) 91/250 on the Legal Protection of Computer Programs [1991] OJ L122/42, 17 May 1991.

[11] SI 1992/3233.

[12] Council Directive (EC) 96/9 on the Legal Protection of Databases [1996] OJ L77, 27 March 1996.

[13] See the Berne Convention, Art 2(5).

the contents may also attract the *sui generis* protection, and the database itself may also be protected. The Copyright and Rights in Databases Regulations 1997[14] implemented the Directive in the UK by amending the CDPA 1988 to include a new test of originality for copyright databases[15] and introducing the *sui generis* database right.

The 'Conditional Access' Directive,[16] which was implemented in the UK on 28 May 2000[17] by the inclusion of a new section 297A in the CDPA 1988, requires Member States to prohibit the supply of devices (including software) for circumventing technical means for limiting entry to protected, and other conditional access, services.

A Directive on the harmonization of certain aspects of copyright and related rights in the information society[18] came into force on 22 June 2001 (the 'Information Society Directive'). The objectives of this Directive are to: ensure that copyright-protected works enjoy adequate protection across the Member States thereby responding to the challenges of new technology and the Information Society; facilitate cross-border trade in copyrighted goods and services relevant to the Information Society, including online and physical carriers (eg, CDs); protect technological systems for identification and protection of works; and ratify international treaties on the protection of authors, performers, and phonogram producers, agreed in December 1996 by the World Intellectual Property Organization ('WIPO') (see section 7.1.5 below).

The Information Society Directive was implemented in the UK by the Copyright and Related Rights Regulations 2003 which came into force on 31 October 2003.[19] Of particular relevance to the computer industry and to users of information technology are:

(a) provisions amending the rules relating to circumvention of copy-protection measures;[20]

(b) a new provision relating to electronic rights management information;[21]

(c) reinforcement of certain sanctions and remedies, including the introduction of a new offence of communicating a work to the public with the knowledge that by so doing copyright in the work will be infringed;[22]

---

[14] SI 1997/3032, entry into force 1 January 1998.

[15] By reason of the selection or arrangement it must be its author's 'own intellectual creation' (reg 6 inserting s 3A(1)). See, further, section 7.2.1.3 below.

[16] Council Directive (EC) 98/84 on the legal protection of services based on, or consisting of, conditional access [1998] OJ L320, adopted 20 November 1998.

[17] SI 2000/1175.

[18] Council Directive (EC) 2001/29 on the harmonization of certain aspects of copyright and related rights in the information society [2001] OJ L167.

[19] SI 2003/2498.

[20] SI 2003/2498, reg 24, discussed in section 7.4.3.4 below.

[21] SI 2003/2498, reg 25, discussed in section 7.4.3.4 below.

[22] SI 2003/2498, reg 26(1), discussed in section 7.7.2 below.

(d) new provisions relating to injunctions against service providers who have actual knowledge that another person is using their service to infringe copyright.[23]

7.1.5 International copyright conventions

International copyright conventions have had significant effects upon the development of copyright law. The Universal Copyright Convention[24] and the Berne Convention for the Protection of Literary and Artistic Works[25] oblige Member States to provide the same rights to nationals of another Member State as they provide to their own authors (the so-called 'national treatment' rule). The TRIPs Agreement[26] provides for national treatment[27] and most-favoured-nation treatment. The latter requires Member States to apply immediately and unconditionally any advantage, favour, privilege, or immunity granted by a Member State to nationals of any other country.

The TRIPs Agreement provides that, under the Berne Convention, the object and source codes of a computer program are to be protected as literary works (TRIPs, Art 10). Specific rights are provided for under TRIPs, such as the author's right to authorize and prohibit the commercial rental of a computer program, except where the computer program is not the 'essential object' of the rental (TRIPs, Art 11). The TRIPs Agreement provides that, in accordance with the Washington Treaty (1989) on the protection of integrated circuits, semiconductor chips are to be protected (TRIPs, Art 36). Infringement of integrated circuits, the term of copyright protection, compulsory licensing, and the treatment of innocent infringers are also addressed (TRIPs, Arts 37 and 38). In relation to databases, the compilation of these works is to be protected by copyright provided that it constitutes an 'intellectual creation' (TRIPs, Art 10(2)).[28] This contrasts with the position in the UK up to 31 December 1997 (prior to the Copyright and Rights in Databases Regulations 1997), in that 'originality' was sufficient to establish copyright protection (see section 7.2.1.3 below).

---

[23] SI 2003/2498, reg 27, discussed in section 7.4.4 below.

[24] 6 September 1952, 6 UST 2713 (1955), TIAS No 3324, 216 UNTS 132 (effective 16 September 1955) ('Geneva Act'); revised 24 July 1971, 25 UST 1341 (1974), TIAS No 7868, 943 UNTS 178 (effective 10 July 1971) ('Paris Act'); which requires contracting states to give adequate and effective protection to the rights of authors and other copyright proprietors of literary, scientific, and artistic work (Art 1).

[25] 9 September 1886; Paris Act of 24 July 1971, as amended on 28 September 1979.

[26] Trade Related Aspects of Intellectual Property Rights, concluded under the Uruguay Round of the General Agreement on Tariffs and Trade, Final Act Embodying the Results of the Uruguay Round of Trade Negotiations, Marrakech, 15 April 1994.

[27] Subject to the exceptions under the Paris Convention (1967) on industrial property, the Berne Convention (1971), the Rome Convention (1961) on sound recordings, producers and performers, and the Washington Treaty (1989) on integrated circuits.

[28] See further E-J Louwers and CEJ Prins (eds), *International Computer Law* (New York: Matthew-Bender, 1999) ch 8.

The WIPO Copyright Treaty supplements the Berne Convention (see Art 1) and applies the following 'traditional' copyright rules to the digital environment:

(a) the reproduction right (as set out in Art 9 of the Berne Convention),[29] particularly in the context of the use and storage of works in digital form;

(b) the fair use principle for online communications, whereby the making of a limited number of copies of a protected work is permitted provided the 'legitimate interests' of the copyright owner are not harmed (which is generally limited to use of a non-commercial nature);[30] and

(c) the right of making available to the public, which rests with the rightholder.

The WIPO Copyright Treaty provides for protection against the circumvention of technological protection devices for controlled access to copyrighted material (Art 11) and against the removal of electronic rights management information without authorization (Art 12). The following provisions of the TRIPs Agreement are restated: computer programs are to be protected as literary works within the meaning of Article 2 of the Berne Convention;[31] and compilations of data or other material may be protected by copyright where they are intellectual creations[32] (but the protection does not extend to the material contained in the database[33]).

The Treaty on intellectual property in databases initially proposed as part of the WIPO Diplomatic Conference of 20 December 1996, which was to include the *sui generis* right for data contained in databases, was not adopted. However, Article 5 of the WIPO Copyright Treaty seems to allow for the possibility of such a right in providing that:

Compilations of data or other material, in any form, which by reason of the selection or arrangement of their contents constitute intellectual creations, are protected as such. This protection does not extend to the data or the material itself and is without prejudice to any copyright subsisting in the data or material in the compilation.

The database right created by the EU Database Directive appears to be consistent with Article 5 of the WIPO Copyright Treaty. The question of adopting a *sui generis* right, similar to that of the Database Directive, was again discussed by WIPO at a meeting on database protection between 17 and 19 September 1997, but any action at an international level seems to have been postponed indefinitely.[34]

---

[29] This is by way of an 'Agreed Statement' in the Treaty.
[30] Art 10(2).
[31] The Agreed Statement to Art 4 notes this restatement of the TRIPs Agreement.
[32] The Agreed Statement to Art 5 notes this restatement of the TRIPs Agreement.
[33] Compare the EU Database Directive, n 12 above and Chapter 8.
[34] For further discussion of international copyright conventions, see C Rees and S Chalton, *Database Law* (Bristol: Jordans, 1998).

7.2 IN WHAT CAN COPYRIGHT SUBSIST?

7.2.1 General criteria for protection

7.2.1.1 *Works*
Section 1 of the CDPA 1988 provides that:

(1) Copyright is a property right which subsists in accordance with this Part in the following descriptions of work—
   (a) original literary, dramatic, musical or artistic works,
   (b) sound recordings, films, broadcasts or cable programmes, and
   (c) the typographical arrangement of published editions.
(2) In this Part 'copyright work' means a work of any of those descriptions in which copyright subsists.

Many products that are protected by copyright do not fit neatly into any single category from this list. On the contrary, by the time they are brought to market, most films, books, software packages, multimedia products, and other composite works comprise a complex bundle of discrete copyright works. Most of the categories of work listed above are of relevance in the computer context. For example, a software product such as a word processing package could be analysed as a collection of copyright works as follows:

(a) The program code which, when run on a computer system, provides word processing functions would be a literary work: section 3(1) of the CDPA 1988 defines 'literary work' as including 'a computer program' (s 3(1)(b)).

(b) The preparatory design material for the computer program would itself be a literary work (s 3(1)(c)).[35]

(c) Any documentation or other written materials supplied with the package would be one or more conventional literary works.

(d) Any built-in dictionary, thesaurus, or help-screen files would be literary works, but would probably not be computer programs.

(e) Artwork included on packaging or in documentation would be one or more artistic works (s 4).

(f) Graphic works or photographs used to produce screen images would be artistic works (s 4(1)(a)).

(g) Copyright would subsist in the typographical arrangement of the documentation supplied with the package: section 1(1) defines 'the typographical arrangement of published editions' as a separate category of copyright work (s 1(1)(c)).

---

[35] Inserted by Copyright (Computer Programs) Regulations 1992 (SI 1992/3233), reg 3, in force 1 January 1993.

In addition to these seven categories of work, three other types of work may be embodied in an audiovisual product such as a video game:

(h) The sounds which are produced when the game is run or played might include a recording of one or more musical works: section 3(1) defines 'musical work' as 'a work consisting of music, exclusive of any words or action intended to be sung, spoken or performed with the music'.

(i) The code producing the sounds would itself be a sound recording: section 5A(1)[36] defines 'sound recording' as '(a) a recording of sounds, from which the sounds may be reproduced, or (b) a recording of the whole or any part of a literary, dramatic or musical work, from which sounds reproducing the work or part may be produced, regardless of the medium on which the recording is made or the method by which the sounds are reproduced or produced'.

(j) Any set sequence of images that is produced when the program is run would be a film: section 5B(1)[37] defines 'film' as meaning 'a recording on any medium from which a moving image may by any means be produced'.

A further four bases for protection may be relevant in relation to a database[38] or multimedia product:

(k) A database itself may attract copyright protection: section 3(1) defines 'literary work' as including a database (s 3(1)(d))[39] (see, further, Chapter 8). A database will fall within the scope of the CDPA 1988, as amended, if it consists of a collection of independent works, data, or other materials arranged in a systematic or methodical way and individually accessible by electronic or other means.[40] Databases are to be protected by copyright only so far as they are original by reason of their 'selection or arrangement' and if they constitute the 'author's own intellectual creation'.[41] Therefore, a computer-generated database would not be protected by copyright as a database.

(l) A computer program used in the making or operation of a database would be a literary work (s 3(1)(b))[42] and may also comprise preparatory design material (s 3(1)(c)).

---

[36] Substituted by the Duration of Copyright and Rights in Performances Regulations 1995 (SI 1995/3297), reg 9, subject to transitional and savings provisions specified in regs 12–35.

[37] Ibid.

[38] Note that the contents of a database may also attract a *sui generis* right, which protects the investment made by database makers rather than the author's creativity in the selection or arrangement of the contents of databases, as is the case with copyright.

[39] Inserted by the Copyright and Rights in Databases Regulations 1997 (SI 1997/3032), reg 5, in force 1 January 1998.

[40] s 3A(1), inserted by the Copyright and Rights in Databases Regulations 1997 (SI 1997/3032). Presumably databases where the contents are automatically calculated using other data in the database, eg, would be excluded.

[41] s 3A(2), inserted by the Copyright and Rights in Databases Regulations 1997 (SI 1997/3032).

[42] Such programs are excluded from protection as a database (see the Directive on the legal protection of databases, Art 1(3)).

(m) Some or all of the items comprised in the product may be protected separately as literary, dramatic, musical, or artistic works or as sound recordings or films.

(n) If made available to subscribers to a broadcast videotext or cable service, the product would be a broadcast or cable programme: see definitions of 'broadcast' in section 6(1) and of 'cable programme service' in section 7(1).

While it is clear that compilations attract copyright protection,[43] the fact that, for example, a software product is not a single work for copyright purposes has a number of significant consequences. First, many different authors, graphic designers, programmers, publishers, etc may be involved in the production and marketing of the product and, as individual authors, may have separate claims to copyright in their respective contributions (see section 7.3.1 below). Secondly, copyright protection will expire at different times in respect of different component parts of the product (see section 7.3.3 below). Thirdly, the scope of copyright protection will not be the same for all of the works that make up a package. For example, unauthorized adaptation of the program code would infringe copyright, whereas there would be no copyright restriction on adaptation of the various artistic works, provided it did not amount to copying or some other restricted act (see sections 7.4.2.1 and 7.5.2 below). Fourthly, an author of the text or designer of artwork included in the documentation might be able to exercise moral rights in respect of the works he or she contributed, whereas a programmer would have no such rights in respect of the program code (see section 7.6 below).

7.2.1.2 Recording

There can be no copyright in a literary, dramatic, or musical work 'unless and until it is recorded, in writing or otherwise'. The term of copyright starts to run from the time of such recording (CDPA 1988, s 3(2)). 'Writing' is given an expansive definition in the CDPA 1988 as including 'any form of notation or code, whether by hand or otherwise and regardless of the method by which, or medium in or on which, it is recorded, and "written" shall be construed accordingly' (CDPA 1988, s 178). Storage in any form of machine-readable media would thus appear to qualify as 'writing'. The words 'or otherwise' would cover fixation in the form of, for example, an analog recording of sounds or spoken words.

The CDPA 1988 does not contain a definition of 'recording' as such. It is not clear whether a degree of permanence is implied. By analogy with 'sound recording', which is defined, the essence of the concept of recording of a work is probably that there is something from which the work, or part of it, can be reproduced. Presumably, once a work has been fixed in such a form, copyright will continue to

---

[43] See, eg, *Exchange Telegraph v Gregory* [1896] 1 QB 147, concerning the unauthorized dissemination of lists of London Stock Exchange price data; and *Waterlow Directories Ltd v Reed Information Services Ltd* [1992] FSR 409, concerning a compilation of practising solicitors in the UK.

subsist in the work notwithstanding the subsequent destruction of the original recording of the work, even where no copy has ever been made in a material form. This issue might be significant if a substantial part of a program, or other work, were to be reproduced from human memory after the author had accidentally or deliberately deleted the original from the memory of the computer on which it was created.

7.2.1.3 Originality

Literary, dramatic, musical, or artistic works are only protected under the CDPA 1988 if they are original (CDPA 1988, s 1(1)(a)). There is no definition or explanation of the concept of originality. However, the word 'original' was used in both the 1911 and 1956 Copyright Acts and, almost invariably, was interpreted by the courts as relating essentially to origin rather than to substantive considerations such as novelty. Thus, a work will usually be original provided merely that it originates with the author or creator and has not been copied. In many cases originality has been found to exist where the work was created either independently or by the exercise of the author's own skill, knowledge, mental labour, or judgement. While one (or more) of these attributes is usually required in order to secure copyright protection, courts have tended to resist arguments that the originality requirement should be interpreted as importing connotations of aesthetic quality or innovation.[44]

In *Infopaq* the European Court of Justice held that 11 words may be considered protected by copyright provided they are original, in the sense that they are 'the expression of the intellectual creation of their author'.[45] The full implications of this decision are not yet clear and whether *Infopaq* will be eventually interpreted by courts in the UK as a modification of the originality test for literary works is difficult to predict.[46]

The low level at which the originality threshold has tended to be fixed by the courts means that even relatively simple and utterly mundane works can be protected by copyright. This is very important in the computer context where programs and other functional works may lack aesthetic appeal and display little apparent creativity yet be of tremendous commercial value. Were a higher threshold to be set for the originality test, it is probable that much computer software and data would fall completely outside copyright.[47] The one area where, under the 1956 Act, the originality

---

[44] See, eg, *Victoria Park Racing & Recreation Grounds Co Ltd v Taylor* (1937) 58 CLR 479; *Football League Ltd v Littlewoods Pools Ltd* [1959] Ch 637; *Ladbroke (Football) Ltd v William Hill (Football) Ltd* [1964] 1 WLR 273; applied *John Richardson Computers Ltd v Flanders* [1993] FSR 497 (Ferris J).

[45] Case C-5/08 *Infopaq International A/S v Danske Dagblades Forening* [2009] ECDR 16 at [47].

[46] See, eg, *The Newspaper Licensing Agency Ltd and Others v Meltwater Holdings BV and Others* [2010] EWHC 3099 at [81] and *SAS Institute Inc v World Programming Ltd* [2010] EWHC 1829 (Ch).

[47] As was the case, eg, in West Germany prior to implementation of the Software Directive. See M Rottinger, 'The Legal Protection of Computer Programs in Germany: Renunciation of Copyrights?' (1987) 4 CL&P 34.

criterion was a particular cause for concern for the UK computer industry, computer-generated works, was specifically addressed in the CDPA 1988 and is discussed in section 7.2.2.2 below.

Since 1 January 1998, subject to transitional provisions, a collection within the definition of a 'database' (ie, a literary work consisting of a database) will not qualify for copyright protection unless it achieves a certain level of originality. The requisite standard is that, by reason of the selection or arrangement of the contents of the database, the database constitutes the author's own intellectual creation.[48] The standard of originality for a literary work consisting of a database remains, at this stage, untested before the English courts. It could be argued that the standard is higher than that required for other literary, dramatic, musical, or artistic works, because of the inherent difficulties associated with gauging intellect and/or requisite mental effort. Note, however, that while the 'own intellectual creation' test was contained in the Software Directive,[49] the implementing legislation for that Directive did not alter the basic 'originality' test, which suggests that the new standard was not seen to be significantly different from the old. Irrespective, this will not prevent such a database from being protected by the Database Directive's *sui generis* right (the database right under the Database Regulations), provided sufficiently substantial investment in the obtaining, verification, or presentation of the database's contents can be demonstrated (Art 7 and reg 13(1)). The database right will be infringed by the extraction or re-utilization of all or a substantial part of the contents of the data-base (see Chapter 8).

7.2.1.4 *Qualification*

Copyright will not subsist in any work unless certain 'qualification requirements' are met. The rules, which are set out in Part IX of the CDPA 1988 (ss 153–62), are complex. For most types of work, however, the general rule is that either the author must be a 'qualifying person' at the time the work is made or, alternatively, the work must be first published in the UK or some other country to which the Act extends. An author will be a qualifying person if he or she is a citizen of, or domiciled or resident in, the UK or some other country to which the Act extends. The qualification requirements will also be satisfied if the author is a citizen of, or domiciled or resident in, or first publication is in, a country to which the Act has been 'applied'.

By virtue of a statutory instrument that came into force along with most of the provisions of the CDPA 1988 on 1 August 1989, Part I of the Act has been applied to works of different types originating in over 100 specified countries.[50]

---

[48] CDPA 1988, s 3A(2), inserted by the Copyright and Rights in Databases Regulations 1997 (SI 1997/3032).

[49] Council Directive (EEC) 91/250 [1991] OJ L122/42, 17 May 1991.

[50] The Copyright (Application to Other Countries) (No 2) Order 1989 (SI 1989/1293). This was replaced by a statutory instrument in similar terms, which came into force on 4 May 1993, entitled the Copyright (Application to Other Countries) Order 1993 (SI 1993/942) and this was in turn replaced by

Special rules apply to certain countries which are not members of either the Berne Copyright Convention or the Universal Copyright Convention but in which the UK Government is satisfied that there exists adequate protection for copyright. An order has also been made applying Part I of the Act to works made by officers or employees of the United Nations and certain other international organizations that would otherwise not qualify for protection.[51]

7.2.2 Protection of programs, computer-generated works, and Web 2.0

7.2.2.1 *Computer programs*

Whereas, in its original form, the 1956 Act contained no reference whatsoever to computers or computing, in the CDPA 1988 computers make their first appearance in section 3. Further direct and indirect references are scattered throughout the Act. Section 3(1) of the CDPA 1988 defines 'literary work' as including:

(a) a table or compilation other than a database;

(b) a computer program;

(c) preparatory design material for a computer program; and

(d) a database.

This form of words has made it completely clear that programs are literary works and not merely to be protected as though they were literary works.[52]

What remains unclear is the scope of the term 'computer program', which has still not been defined. Foreign legislatures and international organizations that have defined the term have tended to characterize programs in terms of their information-processing capabilities, with specific emphasis on their ability to cause hardware to perform functions.[53] We have already seen that a software package such as a video game is in fact a complex collection of separate copyright works. Only some of the works will be computer programs. To take another example, most of the material supplied in printed or electronic form in a word processing package will not be 'programs' in the sense of computer code that will cause a computer to process information. The printed materials will be conventional literary and other works.

---

the Copyright (Application to Other Countries) Order 1999 (SI 1999/1751), which came into force on 22 July 1999.

[51] The Copyright (International Organisations) Order 1989 (SI 1989/989). In force, 1 August 1989.

[52] As was the case under the 1956 Act, as amended by the Copyright (Computer Software) Amendment Act 1985, s 1.

[53] eg, 'A "computer program" is a set of statements or instructions to be used directly or indirectly in a computer in order to bring about a certain result' (US Copyright Act 1976, 17 USC § 101); 'A "computer program" is a set of instructions expressed in words, codes, schemes or in any other form, which is capable, when incorporated in a machine-readable medium, of causing a "computer"—an electronic or similar device having information-processing capabilities—to perform or achieve a particular task or result' (WIPO, Model Provisions on the Protection of Computer Software, 1978, restated in Memorandum on a Possible Protocol to the Berne Convention, 1991).

Moreover, a great deal of the material supplied in electronic form will be digital versions of a dictionary, a thesaurus, and help-screen information, all of which, again, will be conventional literary and possibly artistic works.

The existence of special provisions in the CDPA 1988 that apply to computer programs but not to literary works in general means that the two terms are certainly not coextensive. Moreover, the inclusion in the Act of many provisions that deal with the use and distribution of conventional works in electronic form makes it clear that a work is not a program just because it is stored digitally.

Neither the Software Directive nor the Copyright (Computer Programs) Regulations 1992 shed much light on the definitional issue. The preamble (recitals) to the Directive merely includes a statement that 'the function of a computer program is to communicate and work together with other components of a computer system'. Article 1(1) is a little more explicit in stating that 'for the purpose of this Directive, the term "computer programs" shall include their preparatory design material'. The Copyright (Computer Programs) Regulations 1992 contain no reference to the meaning of the term 'computer program' except to restate that 'preparatory design material for a computer program' shall be protected (see also s 3(1)(c) of the CDPA 1988 as amended).

7.2.2.2 Computer-generated works

As already noted (see section 7.2.1.4 above) for copyright to subsist in a work, certain qualification requirements must be met. In most cases, the criterion will be whether the author of a work was 'a qualifying person' at the time the work was made. With the widespread use of programming 'tools' and automated processes for collecting, processing, and compiling data, it is likely that an increasing number of works, including computer programs and databases, will have no identifiable human author or authors. Prior to the CDPA 1988, there was considerable doubt as to whether such works were eligible for copyright protection.[54]

To ensure that substantial categories of works did not gradually fall out of the realm of copyright, provisions were included in the CDPA 1988 to enable copyright to subsist in a literary, dramatic, musical, or artistic work 'generated by a computer in circumstances such that there is no human author of the work' (ss 9(3) and 178). The author of such a 'computer-generated' work 'shall be taken to be the person by whom the arrangements necessary for the creation of the work are undertaken' (s 9(3)). Whilst providing a welcome safety net for useful and valuable works that would otherwise fall outside copyright law, determining whether these provisions apply to a particular work will still require a careful analysis of the facts.

In particular, care should be taken to distinguish between 'computer-generated' and 'computer-assisted' (or 'computer-aided') works. The latter type of work does

---

[54] See CJ Millard, *Legal Protection of Computer Programs and Data* (London: Sweet & Maxwell, 1985) 25–30.

not receive special treatment under the CDPA 1988. The availability of copyright protection for such works was in effect recognized in a decision under the 1956 Act. In pre-trial proceedings in *Express Newspapers plc v Liverpool Daily Post & Echo plc*,[55] the court ruled that grids of letters produced with the aid of a computer for use in prize draws were authored by the programmer who wrote the relevant software. Rejecting an argument to the contrary advanced by counsel for the defendants, Whitford J stated:

> I reject this submission. The computer was no more than the tool by which the varying grids of five-letter sequences were produced to the instructions, via the computer, of Mr Ertel. It is as unrealistic as it would be to suggest that, if you write your work with a pen, it is the pen which is the author of the work rather than the person who drives the pen.[56]

It was perhaps convenient for the court in the *Express Newspapers* case that the programmer was also the person who ran the program on the particular occasion in question and checked the results. The nexus between one person and the finished work was thus very close. It is not clear how the court would have resolved conflicting claims between several programmers, data providers, system operators, and so on.

In cases where the association between any individual or individuals and a finished work is so remote that it can fairly be said the work has been created without a human author, there is now the possibility that it will qualify for copyright as a computer-generated work. However, it is unlikely that the CDPA 1988 provisions will be dispositive of all doubts as to the subsistence and ownership of copyright in computer output. In theory at least, disputes may still arise where a number of competing individuals claim to have made the 'arrangements necessary for the creation of the work'. Would, for example, a person using a mass-marketed program generator be entitled to copyright in all such output? Would the author of the underlying software have any claim to copyright in the output? Would two or more identical works produced by different individuals using the same program generator all qualify for protection as original literary works?[57]

In practice, the provisions on computer-generated works have not yet proved particularly contentious. An illustration of how the rules work in practice occurred in *Nova Productions Ltd v Mazooma Games Ltd and Others and Nova Productions Ltd v Bell Fruit Games Ltd*.[58] That case, which is discussed in more detail in section 7.5.6 below, concerned alleged infringement of copyright in an arcade video game. A peripheral issue concerned authorship of the graphic works comprised in various

---

[55] [1985] FSR 306.

[56] Ibid 310. This passage echoes a statement in para 514 of the Whitford Committee Report (see n 4 above) in which it was stated that a computer used in the creation of a copyright work was a 'mere tool in much the same way as a slide-rule or even, in a simple sense, a paintbrush'.

[57] For further discussion, see JAL Sterling, 'The Copyright, Designs and Patents Bill 1987' (1988) 3(5) CLSR 2.

[58] [2006] EWHC 24.

composite video images that were created when the games were played. Mr Justice Kitchen considered section 9(3) and the definition of 'computer-generated' in section 178, together with the role of the programmer who wrote the game, a Mr Jones, and concluded:

In so far as each composite frame is a computer generated work then the arrangements necessary for the creation of the work were undertaken by Mr Jones because he devised the appearance of the various elements of the game and the rules and logic by which each frame is generated and he wrote the relevant computer program. In these circumstances I am satisfied that Mr Jones is the person by whom the arrangements necessary for the creation of the works were undertaken and therefore is deemed to be the author by virtue of s. 9(3).[59]

7.2.2.3 Web 2.0

The rapid development of collaborative online environments for creating, hosting, and disseminating material such as text, photographs, audio, and video, has resulted in an enormous growth in new copyright material and the widespread sharing and aggregation of both new and existing works. This development, often known as Web 2.0,[60] has led to complex copyright issues. In particular, three elements of Web 2.0 tend to give rise to questions regarding subsistence of copyright and related issues of authorship and ownership. These are the semantic web (entailing the use of software to analyse and index material on websites in an attempt to provide meaning-based computing);[61] user-generated content (eg, wikis,[62] content-sharing sites,[63] and social networks),[64] and virtual worlds (eg, Second Life and World of Warcraft).

In relation to the semantic web, both the techniques used to analyse websites and the resulting automated compilations and indexes can be contentious.

---

[59] *Nova Productions*, para 105.

[60] To distinguish it from the generally passive content that was made available in the earlier days of the world wide web.

[61] Common semantic web applications include 'crawlers' and other software tools used by search engines to provide a compilation of reference items concerning particular subjects, with links to corresponding webpages.

[62] A well-known example is Wikipedia, an online encyclopaedia which allows users to access, amend, and contribute to, entries. It is the most popular general reference work currently available, All texts were covered originally by GNU Free Documentation License until January 2009, now by Creative commons. <http://en.wikipedia.org/wiki/Wikipedia:Copyrights> (accessed 8 August 2011).

[63] Generally, such sites allow users to upload content, and to provide storage and other facilities. The most popular example is YouTube, a video-sharing site.

[64] Social networking sites allow users to create a personal page where they can post content, as well as send other users messages, and write or post content on other users' pages. The issue is that this content may be protected and that, owing to social interaction, an unauthorized copy posted immediately creates an infinitive number of unauthorized reproductions. The most popular social networking sites include Facebook and MySpace. Finally, Flickr should also be mentioned, which is the most popular photo management and sharing website.

As regards user-generated content, or 'UGC', it is important to distinguish between: (a) works created by users, which might be protected when original; (b) mash-ups (ie, works recombining and modifying existing works), which might be protected as new composite works; and (c) unauthorized use of existing protected works.

Virtual Worlds, perhaps more appropriately termed 'networked virtual environments',[65] are computer-based simulations typically 'inhabited' by avatars (ie, textual, two- or three-dimensional graphical representations of people, animals, etc) whereby users interact with each other.[66] The legal issues posed by virtual worlds are numerous. In particular, the issues associated with copyright law include determining authorship, publication, infringement, limitation, exceptions, defences, and applicable law. Virtual worlds incorporate and rely upon individual contributions, which may be protected by copyright, related rights or, in the EU, by the database *sui generis* right. Examples of protectable items include: the platform's software, website showing the virtual world presentations, characters ('avatars'), places (plots of land), objects (houses, vehicles, shops, clothing, sounds, images, films, cartoons, machinimas),[67] texts created by the platform provider or by the users, and rights in software providers' databases. Issues related to authorship and ownership are generally dealt with in an End-User Licence Agreement ('EULA'), with options ranging from the platform provider retaining all rights in virtual world creations[68] to the users retaining all rights in their creations.[69] Where users are permitted to own works created 'in-world' they may be required to grant non-exclusive, royalty-free licences to the virtual world operator and possibly also to other users.

7.3 OWNERSHIP AND DURATION OF COPYRIGHT

7.3.1 First ownership

The first owner of copyright in a work is usually the author of the work (CDPA 1988, s 11(1)). This is the case regardless of whose ideas underlie the work and of who commissions or pays for the work. This general rule is, however, subject to several significant exceptions. Of widest importance is the special rule that, subject

---

[65] See BT Duranske, *Virtual Law* (Chicago, IL: ABA Publishing, 2008) 4.

[66] Popular sites include Second Life, World of Warcraft, and Ultima Online, respectively 14, 11, and 3 million users. <http://secondlife.com> (accessed 9 August 2011), <http://eu.battle.net/wow/en> (accessed 9 August 2011), and <http://www.uoherald.com> (accessed 9 August 2011). Such worlds may mimic the real world or depict fantasy worlds. Many are videogames, generally defined as 'massively multiplayer online games'.

[67] Machinima is a form of film-making using videogame technology to shoot virtual reality films.

[68] See, eg, World of Warcraft's EULA. <http://us.blizzard.com/en-us/company/legal/wow_tou.html> (accessed 9 August 2011).

[69] See, eg, Second Life's Term of Services. <http://secondlife.com/corporate/tos.php> (accessed 9 August 2011).

to contrary agreement, the first owner of copyright in a work created by an employee during the course of his or her employment is the employer, not the employee (s 11(2)).[70] Whilst this rule seems straightforward in principle, in practice its consequences are frequently overlooked.

The most common difficulty arises where a software house or freelance programmer is commissioned to write software under a contract for services (as distinct from a contract of service, ie, an employment agreement). Such scenarios are often complicated where contributions to the program development process are made by employees of the company that has commissioned the work and possibly also by independent consultants. The automatic operation of the rules as to first ownership may produce results that are contrary to the reasonable commercial expectations of one or more of the parties. For example, the commissioning party may contribute a brilliant original concept and pay all the costs of its subsequent development and implementation, yet end up with no legal rights of ownership in the final product. Even if it had been understood from the start, and possibly even agreed orally, that the commissioner would in all respects 'own' the product, this will not be sufficient to alter the operation of the first ownership rules. This is because, as will be discussed below, assignments of copyright and agreements as to future ownership of copyright will only be enforceable if they are evidenced in writing (CDPA 1988, ss 90(3) and 91(1); see section 7.3.2 below). It is possible in such a case that the commissioner will be able to persuade a court of equity to order the developer to execute an assignment of copyright. This might be justified on the basis that such an assignment was an implied term of an agreement between the parties.[71] The mere fact that the commissioner paid for the work would not normally be sufficient grounds for inferring such a term, although such an arrangement may well be evidence of an implied licence to use the work for the purpose for which it was commissioned.[72]

Further potential for dispute arises where there is joint authorship and/or joint ownership of copyright. In the computer industry it is common for several people, sometimes a large number, to be involved in the initial development of a software package. Thereafter, still more people may be involved in the preparation of revised versions and updates. Multiple authorship and divided ownership are, however, by no means uncommon in the copyright field. Section 10(1) of the CDPA 1988 defines a 'work of joint authorship' as 'a work produced by the collaboration of two or more distinct authors in which the contribution of each author is not distinct from that of the other author or authors'. Thus, where the development of a program really is

---

[70] The other exceptions to the rule relate to Crown and parliamentary copyright, and the copyright of certain international organizations (CDPA 1988, s 11(3)).

[71] See, eg, *Merchant Adventurers Ltd v M Grew & Co Ltd* [1973] RPC 1. The ruling is probably limited to the special facts of that case, however. Where ownership is disputed, courts will be unlikely to upset the automatic operation of the statutory ownership rules.

[72] For judicial discussion on this point see *John Richardson Computers Ltd v Flanders* [1993] FSR 497 at 516 and *Ibcos Computers Ltd v Barclays Mercantile Highland Finance Ltd* [1994] FSR 275 at 293.

a joint effort copyright will, subject to the rules governing employee works just discussed, vest in the various contributors jointly. This scenario must be distinguished, however, from that in which a number of people have made separate contributions to a software development project each of which can be identified as such. It may well be that in the latter case there will be a number of quite distinct copyrights in a program or package.

An example of the potential problems associated with divided ownership is where a software house or contractor writes software code for a specific customer. In such an instance, there is often a great deal of collaboration between the parties with resulting issues of joint authorship or implied licence to exploit the software. The degree and kind of collaboration necessary to support a claim of joint authorship or warrant an implied licence to exploit the software was dealt with by the Chancery Division of the High Court in *Flyde Microsystems v Key Radio Systems Ltd*.[73] Laddie J found that while the defendant, who cooperated in the design of software to be used in a new generation of radios to be sold by the defendant, did in fact improve the software by ironing out 'bugs' this was more akin to the skill exhibited by a proofreader not an author. As a result, it was held that the level of 'creative' skill was not sufficient to evidence copyright ownership or give rise to an implied licence to exploit the software. In *Robin Ray v Classic FM plc*,[74] Lightman J found that, to establish joint authorship, it was necessary to show that: there was a direct responsibility for the work by providing a creative contribution that was not distinct from that of the author (CDPA 1988, ss 9 and 10); there was more than a mere contribution of ideas to the author or some division of labour in the creation of the copyright work; and there was no employment contract whereby copyright would be legally owned by the defendant. Further, if joint authorship did in fact exist, the consent of the other joint author to the exploitation of the work would need to be obtained (ss 16 and 173). It was also found that an implied licence to exploit copyright material would only arise where strictly necessary to make sense of the relevant commercial arrangements.[75]

A more recent demonstration of the scope for arguments over first ownership of copyright in software can be seen in the case of *Clearsprings Management Ltd v Businesslinx Ltd and Mark Hargreaves*.[76] In that case, Clearsprings claimed that Businesslinx, a software house that had developed a package for it, had either an equitable obligation to assign the copyright in the software or at least that a term should be implied into the development contract that Clearsprings should have exclusivity in relation to exploiting the software. Christopher Floyd QC, sitting as a Deputy High Court Judge, rejected both assertions and was only prepared to find that Clearsprings had a non-exclusive licence with no right to sub-license. This is entirely consistent both with the straightforward operation of the statutory

---

[73] [1998] FSR 449. Applied in *Pierce v Promco SA* [1998] All ER (D) 780.
[74] [1998] FSR 622.
[75] See further J Warchus, 'CSLR Briefing', 14(6) CLSR 424.
[76] [2005] EWHC 1487 (Ch).

ownership rules and with the guidance set out in *Robin Ray v Classic FM plc*[77] (from which the judge quoted extensively).

Serious difficulties may arise at the exploitation stage where a software package either has a number of joint owners, or is made up of a number of programs or modules each separately owned. In either case, infringement of copyright will occur if any of the owners seeks to exploit the package as a whole without the consent of all the others. Where the various owners have quite distinct copyrights and one owner refuses to cooperate with the rest, the others may choose to rewrite the relevant part of the package and proceed to market the software without the objecting contributor being involved. This solution will not, however, be available in the case of a single work if various people are joint owners of the whole of it. Unless the rights of the uncooperative party or parties can somehow be severed, attempts to exploit the package may be thwarted permanently.

There are thus many circumstances in which there is a possibility of more than one party claiming copyright and of disagreements about how multiple owners should exercise their rights. Such issues may arise where there is a misunderstanding about ownership of a work that has been commissioned; where a work has been or is likely to be computer-generated; where there are multiple authors; and where ownership is divided. In all such cases, the most satisfactory arrangement for all concerned will usually be for agreement about ownership and exploitation of any rights to be reached in advance and be evidenced in writing. Where the potential for disputes has not been successfully pre-empted, assignments or confirmatory assignments of copyright may be appropriate to resolve doubts about rights in existing works.

7.3.2 Assignments and licences

A copyright can be given away, be bought and sold, or be left as an inheritance under a will as personal or movable property (CDPA 1988, s 90(1)). An assignment, or other transfer, of copyright may be outright or may relate only to certain of the exclusive rights enjoyed by the owner. Thus, for example, an assignee may be given the right solely to translate a software package into a particular language. A transfer may also be limited to any part of the remaining term of the copyright (CDPA 1988, s 90(2)). In practice, limited rights, such as to convert a program for use with a particular operating system or for foreign language users, are more often granted by way of licence than by partial assignment. Where such a licence is 'exclusive', the licensee will in effect be treated as the owner in terms of rights and remedies and the distinction between such a licence and a corresponding assignment will, for most purposes, be academic.[78] Assignments of copyright and of 'future copyright'

---

[77] [1998] FSR 622.
[78] s 101(1) of the CDPA 1988 provides that: 'An exclusive licensee has, except against the copyright owner, the same rights and remedies in respect of matters occurring after the grant of the licence as if the licence had been an assignment.'

(ie, copyright which will or may come into existence in the future, eg in a commis-sioned work) will only be effective if made in writing and signed by or on behalf of the assignor (CDPA 1988, ss 90(3) and 91(1)).

Licences other than exclusive licences can be made informally without being evidenced in writing. Indeed, they may even be inferred from the circumstances of a transaction or the general or specific conduct of the parties. Licences relating to the use of software are generally recorded in a written statement of terms, although frequently there is no signed agreement or contract as such.[79] The CDPA 1988 pro-vides, in limited circumstances, for deemed licences to use second-hand copies of programs and other works distributed in electronic form (see section 7.5.9 below).

The circumstances in which a copyright owner has the right to refuse to grant a licence were at issue in the European Court of Justice case of *Radio Telefis Eireann v Commission*.[80] The case concerned the attempted production of a weekly television guide by Magill TV Guide Ltd covering programmes broadcast by the BBC, ITV, and the Irish network RTE. The networks obtained an injunction against Magill on the basis that they were entitled to refuse to grant licences of copyright. The case was then taken to the Commission where it was decided that each of the networks had abused a dominant position contrary to Article 86 of the EC Treaty.[81] This deci-sion was later upheld in the Court of First Instance.[82] Despite an opinion of the Advocate General proposing that the Court of Justice set aside the judgments of the Court of First Instance, the final judgment of the Court upheld the first instance judgment. This ruling has left considerable uncertainty amongst copyright owners as to the circumstances in which they are entitled to refuse to grant licences. Although the case only impacts upon copyright owners in a dominant position, the ability of Community authorities to invoke competition principles to curtail the rights of copyright owners may in future have significant consequences for the computer industry.

7.3.2.1 *Open source*

The term 'open source' is generally used to describe a number of loosely connected models for software development and distribution which involve sharing source code, licensing users to develop it further and, sometimes, to distribute it. However, 'open source' is not limited to simply granting access to the source code. The main difference between open source and traditional proprietary software licences lies in the terms of use of the software and the underlying business models. In the case of proprietary software, the focus tends to be on restricting access to the source code

---

[79] See CJ Millard, 'Shrink-wrap Licensing' (1987) 4 CLSR 8.

[80] Cases C-241 and 242/91 [1995] ECR I-743.

[81] *Magill TV Guide/ITP* [1989] OJ L78/43. Note that the relevant article of the EC Treaty is now Art 82.

[82] Case T-69/89 *Radio Telefis Eireann v Commission* [1991] ECR II-485 and Case T-76/89 *Independent Television Publications Ltd v Commission* [1991] ECR II-575.

while granting to users the right to run the software. Open source revenue models depend mainly on support services (eg, Linux Red Hat) with basic use of the software normally permitted without charge.

According to the Open Source Initiative,[83] in order for a licence to qualify as open source it must comply with ten criteria:[84] free redistribution; availability of the source code; permission to modify the software, create a derivative work, and to distribute it under the same terms of the original software; integrity of the author's source code; no discrimination against licensees; no restrictions based on fields of endeavour; application of rights attached to a program to all to whom the program is redistributed without the need for an additional licence; the licence must not be product-specific; must not restrict the use of other software; and must be technology-neutral.

Notwithstanding early opposition and questions regarding their validity, open source licences have become quite common. The Open Source Initiative provides a list of licences which have passed their 'approval process'.[85]

The Open Source Movement should not be confused with the Free Software Movement. They differ fundamentally from a philosophical perspective. According to R Stalman:[86]

Free software is a matter of the users' freedom to run, copy, distribute, study, change and improve the software. More precisely, it means that the program's users have the four essential freedoms . . .

These are the freedom to run the program, for any purpose (freedom 0); the freedom to study how it works, and modify it (freedom 1); the freedom to redistribute copies of the program (freedom 2); and the freedom to distribute copies of the modified versions of the program (freedom 3). An example is the GNU General Public License.[87] Despite these philosophical differences, however:

nearly all free software is open source, and nearly all open source software is free.[88]

7.3.2.2 *Creative Commons*

The Creative Commons Movement began in 2001 with the goal to find a way to free digital content from the restriction imposed by a copyright system designed for the physical world.[89] Creative Commons ('CC') licences are copyright licences that

---

[83] An organization dedicated to promoting open source software.
[84] Open Source Initiative <http://opensource.org/docs/osd> (accessed 9 August 2011).
[85] <http://www.opensource.org/licenses/index.html> (accessed 9 August 2011).
[86] <http://www.gnu.org/philosophy/free-sw.html> (accessed 9 August 2011).
[87] <http://www.gnu.org/copyleft/gpl.html> (accessed 9 August 2011).
[88] Free Software Foundation <http://www.gnu.org/philosophy/categories.htm>.
[89] See L Lessig, 'The Creative Common', 65 Montana Law Review 1 (2004); and J Boyle, 'Public Domain: Enclosing the Commons of the Mind', <http://www.thepublicdomain.org> (accessed 9 August 2011).

allow the distribution of protected works worldwide, without changes, at no charge under a number of different combinations of the following four conditions:[90]

(a) Attibution (by)—licensees may copy, distribute, display, and perform the work and make derivative works based on it only if they give the author or licensor the credits in the manner specified by these;

(b) Non-commercial (nc)—licensees may copy, distribute, display, and perform the work and make derivative works based on it only for non-commercial purposes;

(c) No Derivative Works (nd)—licensees may copy, distribute, display, and perform only verbatim copies of the work, not derivative works based on it;

(d) Share-alike (sa)—licensees may distribute derivative works only under a licence identical to the licence that governs the original work.

As a result there are 16 possible combinations, but of these only the following six are currently recommended by Creative Commons:[91]

(a) Attribution alone (by);

(b) Attribution + Noncommercial (by-nc);

(c) Attribution + NoDerivatives (by-nd);

(d) Attribution + ShareAlike (by-sa);

(e) Attribution + Noncommercial + NoDerivatives (by-nc-nd); and

(f) Attribution + Noncommercial + ShareAlike (by-nc-sa).

In addition, Creative Commons can also be CC0 (no right reserved)—a method to release material into the public domain.

Any author can obtain a CC licence from the Creative Commons websites. The licences are tailor-made for difference jurisdictions in order to comply to the relevant copyright systems. The licence comprises three documents: the commons deed (a summary of the term used in the licence); the legal code (the actual licence); and CC metadata to apply to the desired work to make it searchable by CC engines.

7.3.3 Term of protection

The term of protection afforded to various forms of copyright has been modified by the Duration of Copyright and Rights in Performances Regulations 1995[92] and the Copyright and Related Rights Regulations 1996.[93] These Regulations implemented

---

[90] <http://www.creativecommons.org> (accessed 9 August 2011).
[91] <http://creativecommons.org/licenses/> (accessed 9 August 2011).
[92] SI 1995/3297, which came into force on 1 January 1996.
[93] SI 1996/2967, which came into force on 1 December 1996.

an EU Directive on the subject, which aimed to make copyright coterminous in all Member States.[94] The CDPA 1988 originally stipulated, subject to certain exceptions, a period of 50 years from the end of the year in which the author dies for literary, dramatic, musical, or artistic works (s 12(1)). This was extended for those works to a period of 70 years from the author's death by the 1995 Regulations.[95] In the case of films, the duration of copyright was extended by the 1995 Regulations from 50 years from the making or release of the film to a period of 70 years from the death of the last to die of the principal director and the author of the screenplay, dialogue, or music. The 1996 Regulations[96] introduced an innovative new right, known as the 'publication right'. Regulation 16 provides that a person who publishes a previously unpublished work after the expiry of copyright protection will be entitled to a period of 25 years of protection from the end of the year of first publication. This right is described as a property right equivalent to copyright and is intended to cover, for example, the publication of freshly discovered works of well-known authors. The CDPA 1988 provides, unamended by the 1995 Regulations and 1996 Regulations, that, in the case of a computer-generated work, copyright expires after 50 years from the end of the year in which the work was made (CDPA 1988, s 12(3)). This latter rule is similar to the rules applying to sound recordings, broadcasts, and cable programmes (ss 13 and 14). The typographical arrangement of a published edition, which is itself a work for copyright purposes, is protected for 25 years from the end of the year of first publication (s 15). Thus, in the case of a product such as a software package comprising multiple works, copyright in the various component parts will run out on a number of different dates. Duration of copyright may depend, for example, on the life expectancy of various human contributors, the year in which any computer-generated works were made, and the year of first publication of the documentation.

The lengthening of the term of protection of various forms of copyright has two consequences, which further complicate matters in relation to those types of works. One is the extension of copyright in works whose protection in the UK would have expired under the provisions of the CDPA 1988 and the other is the revival of copyright in works whose protection has expired in the UK within the last 20 years. In respect of copyright extension, regulation 21 of the 1995 Regulations provides that copyright licences which subsisted immediately before 1 January 1996 and were not to expire before the end of the copyright period as it was under the CDPA 1988 shall continue to have effect during the period of any extended copyright. In cases of copyright revival, regulation 22 provides that any waiver or assertion of moral rights, which subsisted immediately before the expiry of copyright, shall continue to have effect during the period of revived copyright. In addition, by regulation 23,

---

[94] Council Directive (EEC) 93/98 harmonising the term of protection of copyright and certain related rights [1993] OJ L290, 24 November 1993.
[95] SI 1995/3297.
[96] SI 1996/2967.

no act done before 1 January 1996 shall be regarded as infringing revived copyright in a work and, by regulation 24, where revived copyright subsists, any acts restricted by copyright shall be treated as licensed by the copyright owner, subject to the payment of a reasonable royalty, to be determined, in case of dispute, by the Copyright Tribunal. By regulation 16, the revival provisions will apply to works in which copyright has expired, but which were, on 1 July 1995, protected in another EEA state.

The provisions of the CDPA 1988 dealing with the duration of copyright (ss 12–14, which apply respectively to literary, dramatic, musical, or artistic works, to sound recordings, to films, and to broadcasts or cable programmes) require that, in circumstances where the country of origin or the nationality of an author is not an EEA state, the duration of copyright is that to which the work is entitled in the country of origin, provided the period does not exceed that provided for under the CDPA 1988. Section 15A of the CDPA 1988[97] provides that in respect of the duration of copyright protection, the country of origin is: the country of first publication if it is a Berne Convention country (s 15A(2)); a Berne Convention country if the work is simultaneously published in a non-Berne Convention country (s 15A(3)); or an EEA state or otherwise the Berne Convention country that grants the shortest period of protection (s 15A(4)).

7.4 INFRINGEMENT OF COPYRIGHT

7.4.1 Types of infringing acts

Space does not permit a full discussion of all of the acts that can constitute infringement of the copyright in a work. Instead, the focus will be on the principal acts of so-called 'primary infringement' with reference also being made to the various acts of 'secondary infringement'. A primary infringement occurs where a person directly commits an infringing act or authorizes someone else to do so. Secondary infringers, as their name suggests, are generally one stage removed from the relevant primary infringing acts, but may be implicated by, for example, importing or distributing infringing copies without the consent of the copyright owner. A crucial distinction between primary infringers and secondary infringers is that those in the former category can be liable for infringing copyright whether or not they realize they are doing so, whereas those in the latter category are only liable if they know, or have reason to believe, that they are committing an act of secondary infringement. Three of the most relevant primary infringing acts (copying, adaptation, and issuing copies to the public) are discussed in section 7.4.2 and the various acts of secondary infringement are outlined in section 7.4.3 below.

---

[97] Inserted by the Duration of Copyright and Rights in Performances Regulations 1995 (SI 1995/3297), reg 8(1), which came into force on 1 January 1996.

7.4.2 Primary infringement

7.4.2.1 *Copying*

Whereas the 1956 Act gave the owner of copyright in a work control over the act of 'reproducing the work in any material form' (s 2(5)(a)), the CDPA 1988 contains the much simpler statement that a copyright owner has the exclusive right 'to copy the work' and to authorize anyone else to do so (s 16(1)(a) and (2)). The CDPA 1988 provides that control over copying applies in relation to the whole or any substantial part of a work, and regardless of whether copying occurs directly or indirectly (s 16(3)). As will be seen in section 7.5 below, it may be difficult to establish whether the reproduction of certain structural or other characteristics of a computer program will constitute either direct or indirect copying of a substantial part of the program.

Section 17(2) of the CDPA 1988 defines copying, in relation to a literary, dramatic, musical, or artistic work, as 'reproducing the work in a material form' including 'storing the work in any medium by electronic means'. This provision is reinforced by section 17(6) which provides that 'Copying in relation to any description of work includes the making of copies which are transient or are incidental to some other use of the work'.

This should be read in conjunction with the limitation of section 28A of the CDPA[98] which provides that copyright in a literary work is not infringed by the making of a temporary copy which is transient or incidental, which is an integral and essential part of a technological process and the sole purpose of which is to enable a transmission of the work in a network between third parties by an intermediary; or a lawful use of the work; and which has no independent economic significance.

In *Infopaq*, the European Court of Justice clarified that an act can be held to be 'transient' under Article 5.1:

> only if its duration is limited to what is necessary for the proper completion of the techno-logical process in question, it being understood that that process must be automated so that it deletes that act automatically, without human intervention, once its function of enabling the completion of such a process has come to an end.[99]

This approach has since been adopted in other UK cases.[100]

As will be seen in section 7.5.2 below, these provisions have significant consequences when applied to computer programs and other works distributed in electronic form.

---

[98] Reflecting Art 5.1 of the Information Soc Directive (2001/29/EC).

[99] Case C-5/08 *Infopaq International A/S v Danske Dagblades Forening* [2009] ECDR 16 at [64].

[100] *SAS Institute Inc v World Programming Ltd* [2010] EWHC 1829 (Ch), *The Newspaper Licensing Agency Ltd and Others v Meltwater Holding BV and Others* [2010] EWHC 3099 (Ch), 26 November 2010.

7.4.2.2 *Making adaptations*

Section 21(1) of the CDPA 1988 restricts the making of an adaptation of a literary, dramatic, or musical work. 'Adaptation' means, amongst other things, making a translation of a literary work, and 'in relation to a computer program a "translation" includes a version of the program in which it is converted into or out of a computer language or code or into a different computer language or code' (s 21(3) and (4) as amended by the Copyright (Computer Programs) Regulations 1992, reg 5). In relation to a computer program 'adaptation' means an arrangement or altered version of the program or a translation of it (s 21(3)(ab))[101] and in relation to a database 'adaptation' means an arrangement or altered version of the database or a translation of it (s 21(3)(ac)).[102] The possible implications of section 21 for the scope of a program copyright owner's control over simple 'use' of software are discussed in section 7.5.2 below.

7.4.2.3 *Issuing copies to the public*

Section 18(1) of the CDPA 1988 provides that 'the issue to the public of copies of the work is an act restricted by copyright in every description of copyright work'. The issuing of copies of a work includes the issue of the original (s 18(4)).[103] The act of issuing copies of a work to the public is defined in terms of 'putting into circulation in the EEA copies not previously put into circulation in the EEA by or with the consent of the copyright owner' (s 18(2)(a)) or 'putting into circulation outside the EEA copies not previously put into circulation in the EEA or elsewhere' (s 18(2)(b)). Broadly speaking, this gives the owner of copyright in a work control over publication of the work. Specifically excluded, however, from the ambit of section 18 are distribution, sale, hiring, loan, or importation into the UK of copies that have lawfully been issued to the public anywhere in the world (s 18(3)). Previously this exclusion was, in turn, qualified in a most significant respect with the words 'except that in relation to sound recordings, films and computer programs the restricted act of issuing copies to the public includes any rental of copies to the public'.

This restriction on the rental of copies of certain categories of works, including computer programs, was an innovative feature of the CDPA 1988. Prior to the CDPA 1988 no such automatic restriction existed. Copyright owners were, of course, able to restrict rental of their works by agreement and, in addition, the absence of a restriction on rental did not give a person who rented a copy any right to make a further copy. In practice, however, copies of works are often distributed in circumstances such that it is not feasible for appropriate restrictions to be imposed

---

[101] Inserted by the Copyright (Computer Programs) Regulations 1992 (SI 1992/3233), reg 5(2), which came into force on 1 January 1993.

[102] Inserted by the Copyright and Rights in Databases Regulations 1997 (SI 1997/3032), reg 7(b), which came into force on 1 January 1998.

[103] Inserted by the Copyright and Related Rights Regulations 1996 (SI 1996/2967), reg 9(3), which came into force 1 December 1996.

in that way. An obvious example is mass-market distribution of 'shrink-wrapped' software packages.[104] Moreover, a theoretical right to restrict the making of further copies from a rented copy is of limited efficacy in the face of widespread private copying of works such as compact discs, DVDs, and software packages. Of far greater use to copyright owners was the new right to prevent, or regulate at source, the rental of copies of such works to the public.

In response to an EU Directive on rental and lending rights adopted in 1992 ('the Rental Directive')[105] and one concerning satellite broadcasting and cable retransmission in 1993 ('the Satellite Directive'),[106] the Copyright and Related Rights Regulations 1996[107] were issued. The regulations amended the definition of 'rental' in the CDPA 1988[108] and added a new definition of 'lending'.[109] Section 18A(2) of the CDPA 1988 defines 'rental' as 'making a copy of the work available for use, on terms that it will or may be returned, for direct or indirect commercial advantage' (s 18A(2)(a)) and 'lending' as 'making a copy of the work available for use, on terms that it will or may be returned, otherwise than for direct or indirect economic or commercial advantage' by means accessible to the public (s 18A(2)(b)). These definitions exclude any arrangement by which copies are made available for the purpose of public performance, exhibition, or for on-the-spot referencing (s 18A(3)). The Regulations also provide for an extension of rental rights to all literary, musical, and dramatic works and most artistic ones.[110] The rental right is the right of the owner of copyright to authorize or prohibit the rental or copies of the work, which are deemed to be restricted acts under section 18A (s 179). As a result of the changes brought about by the Regulations, performers are accorded some additional rights, including rental, lending, and distribution rights, and rights to income for performances in films and sound recordings. The Rental Directive provides that Member States must implement a right to authorize or prohibit the rental and lending of originals and copies of copyright works,[111] but derogations may be made in respect of the grant of exclusive lending rights provided authors, at least, are remunerated for lending. A derogation is made to cover films and sound recordings in the Regulations. In addition, certain exemptions apply to libraries and educational establishments.

---

[104] See CJ Millard, 'Shrink-wrap Licensing' (1987) 4 CLSR 8.

[105] Council Directive (EEC) 92/100 on rental right and lending right and certain rights related to copyright in the field of intellectual property [1992] OJ L346, 27 November 1992.

[106] Council Directive (EEC) 93/83 on the coordination of certain rules concerning copyright and rights related to copyright applicable to satellite broadcasting and cable retransmission [1993] OJ L248, 6 October 1993.

[107] SI 1996/2967, entry into force 1 December 1996.

[108] Substituted by the Copyright and Related Rights Regulations 1996 (SI 1996/2967), reg 10(4), in force 1 December 1996. See ss 179 and 18A(2)–(6).

[109] Inserted by the Copyright and Related Rights Regulations 1996 (SI 1996/2967), reg 10(4), in force 1 December 1996. See ss 179 and 18A(2)–(6).

[110] Inserted by the Copyright and Related Rights Regulations 1996 (SI 1996/2967), reg 10(4), in force 1 December 1996. See s 178.

[111] Art 1(1). By Art 2(1) the right is granted, in special circumstances, to authors, performers, and phonogram and film producers. See s 18A(1) and (6).

The Regulations also cover the requirements of the Satellite Directive and contain provisions to determine applicable law where broadcasts are made within or outside the EEA and received in more than one Member State. They also address cable retransmission, requiring the exercise of rights by persons other than broadcasting organizations to be exercised through a licensing body.

7.4.2.4 *Communication to the public (including making available)*
This right has traditionally included a wide range of activities but it has needed to be re-shaped in the light of online activities.[112] Article 8 of the WIPO Copyright Treaty, along with the WIPO Performances and Phonograms Treaty, introduced the on-demand 'making available' right[113] as an attempt to terminate the debate concerning whether making a work available over the internet constituted a restricted act. This right forms part of a copyright owner's right to communicate the work to the public.[114] The Copyright Directive requires Member States to:

provide authors with the exclusive right to authorise or prohibit any communication to the public of their works, by wire or wireless means, including the making available to the public of their works in such a way that members of the public may access them from a place and at a time individually chosen by them.[115]

In recital 27, the Directive specifies that:

the mere provision of physical facilities for enabling or making a communication does not itself amount to communication within the meaning of this Directive.[116]

Thus, the new right appears not to be aimed directly towards the services of intermediaries, for example internet access providers and/or, arguably, online service providers, who simply provide the 'physical facilities'. There is, however, no consensus, even within the EU, concerning the scope and application of the on-demand making available right. Unresolved issues include: which acts are involved in making available, how do materials have to be placed online in order to be made

---

[112] International conventions do not define the terms 'communication' and 'public' and the debate on their interpretation is on-going. In particular, it is difficult to determine what constitutes 'public'. See JAL Sterling, *World Copyright Law* (London: Sweet & Maxwell, 2008) 9.09. For a detailed history and analysis of the communication right, see FM Makeen, *Copyright in a Global Information Society: The Scope of Copyright Protection under International, United States, United Kingdom and French Law* (Arnhem: Kluwer, 2000).

[113] The exclusive right to authorize 'any communication to the public of a work'.

[114] However, the situation differs for performers and phonogram producers, since Arts 10 and 14 WIPO Performances and Phonograms Treaty do not directly refer to any general right of communication to the public.

[115] Art 3(1). Art 3(2) mandates a similar right for performers and phonogram and film producers.

[116] Recital 27 should be read in the light of *Sociedad General de Autories y Editores de Espana (SGAE) v Rafael Hoteles SA* (ECJ, 7 December 2006).

available, and who makes available, when, and where? Litigation against infringers may fail for want of adequate answers to these basis questions.[117]

In the UK, the scope of section 20(2)(b) has been tested by courts in *Polydor*[118] and *Newzbin*[119] (discussed in 7.4.4 below).

7.4.2.5 *Authorization*

Copyright is infringed when a person without authority 'authorises another to do any of the acts restricted by the copyright'.[120] The House of Lords in *Amstrad*[121] held that 'authorize' for the purposes of the Copyright Act meant 'grant or purported grant, which may be express or implied, of the right to do the act complained of'.[122] In order to determine whether authorization is implied all the circumstances should be taken in account including

the nature of the relationship between the alleged authoriser and the primary infringer, whether the equipment or other material supplied constitutes the means used to infringe, whether it is inevitable it will be used to infringe, the degree of control which the supplier retains and whether he has taken any steps to prevent infringement.[123]

The court also specified that to grant the 'power' to copy is not 'authorisation', as it is different from 'to grant or purport to grant the right to copy'. Amstrad did not sanction, approve, or countenance an infringing use. The court substantiated this reasoning by approving a passage from the earlier decision of *CBS Inc v Ames Records & Tapes Ltd*,[124] where it was held that:

an authorisation can only come from somebody having or purporting to have authority and [that] an act is not authorised by somebody who merely enables or possibly assists or even

---

[117] eg, determining where making available takes place is important to determine jurisdiction and damages. See *Football Dataco Ltd and Others v Sportradar GmbH and Another* [2010] EWHC 2911 (Ch), [2010] WLR (D) 293, Ch D (Floyd J), 17 November 2010. The judge, determining whether a German website was making a work available in the UK, held:

I have come to the conclusion that the better view is that the act of making available to the public by online transmission is committed and committed only where the transmission takes place. It is true that the placing of data on a server in one state can make the data available to the public *of* another state but that does not mean that the party who has made the data available has committed the act of making available by transmission in the State of reception. I consider that the better construction of the provisions is that the act only occurs in the state of transmission. (para 74)

Although Floyd J favoured this interpretation he did not consider the point beyond doubt. When asked to decide the issue, the Court of Appeal concluded that the question was 'very important and difficult' and referred it to the ECJ ([2011] EWCA Civ 330, 45).

[118] *Polydor Ltd & Others v Brown & Others*, Court of Appeal (Ch), 28 November 2005, [2005] EWHC 3191 (Ch).

[119] *Twentieth Century Fox Film Corp & Another v Newzbin Ltd* [2010] EWHC 608 (Ch) (29 March 2010).

[120] CDPA, s 16(2).

[121] *CBS Songs Ltd & Others v Amstrad Consumer Electronics plc & Another* [1988] AC 1013.

[122] Ibid.

[123] Ibid.

[124] [1981] RPC 307.

encourages another to do that act, but does not purport to have any authority which he can grant to justify the doing of the act.

The High Court has since confirmed that mere distribution of a product, irrespective of whether or not it could be used to infringe copyright, is not deemed to be authorization when there is no 'further control over the use of the product'.[125]

Recently, the use of file-sharing software has raised questions concerning potential liability for 'authorising' the infringing acts of end-users. Notwithstanding the analogies between *Amstrad* and peer-to-peer file-sharing software providers, in Australia, Kazaa has been found liable for authorizing copyright infringement,[126] and in the UK Newzbin, an indexing website, was similarly found to be liable.[127] Nonetheless legal uncertainties in this field remain, as will be discussed in section 7.4.4.

7.4.3 Secondary infringement

7.4.3.1 *Dealing in infringing copies*

Secondary infringement occurs where, without the consent of the copyright owner, a person 'imports into the UK, otherwise than for his own private and domestic use, an article which is, and which he knows or has reason to believe is, an infringing copy of the work' (CDPA 1988, s 22). Infringement also occurs where a person, again without consent, 'possesses in the course of a business' or deals in articles which he knows or has reason to believe are infringing copies. Relevant dealings are selling, hiring, offering for sale or hire, commercial exhibition or distribution of copies of the work, and any other distribution 'otherwise than in the course of business to such an extent as to affect prejudicially the owner of the copyright' (s 23).

7.4.3.2 *Providing articles for making infringing copies*

Copyright in a work is infringed where, without the consent of the copyright owner, 'an article specifically designed or adapted for making copies of that work' is manufactured, imported, or commercially dealt in by a person who knows or has reason to believe that it will be used for that purpose (CDPA 1988, s 24(1)). The scope of this infringing act is not clear. It is not necessary that an article be intended specifically for use in making *infringing* copies, merely that the article is 'specifically designed or adapted' for making copies and that such copies may infringe copyright.

---

[125] eg, *Philips Domestic Appliances & Personal Care BV v Salton Europe Ltd, Salton Hong Kong Ltd and Electrical & Electronics Ltd* [2004] EWHC 2092 (Ch).

[126] See *Universal Music Australia v Sharman* [2005] FC Australia 1242 (Wilcox J), *Universal Music Australia v Cooper* [2006] FCAFC 187, and *Roadshow Films Pty Ltd & Others v iiNet Ltd* [2010] FCA 24 (4 February 2010), [2011] FCAFC 23 (24 February 2011). Compare the US concept of 'Inducement': eg, *MGM Studios Inc, and Others v Grokster, Ltd* 545 US 913, 380 F3d 1154 (2005).

[127] *Twentieth Century Fox Films Corp & Others v Newzbin Ltd* [2010] EWHC 608 (Ch), 29 March 2010.

Thus, at its broadest, the provision arguably could be construed as covering commonplace articles such as photocopiers and personal computers which every importer, manufacturer, or dealer should suspect may be used to make infringing copies of works. Such a construction of the section would, however, be absurd. An extremely limited interpretation would probably be nearer the mark. The basis for a narrow construction is the reference to the making of copies of *that* work, meaning that the device in question must have been specifically designed or adapted to make copies of a particular work owned by a particular person, and not merely for making copies of works generally.

7.4.3.3 *Facilitating infringement by transmission*

As where a copy of a work is rented out and copied by the renter, where a copy of a work is made available by transmission over a telecommunications system, there may in theory be a cause of action against each recipient who stores, and thus copies, the work on reception. However, the practical difficulties inherent in enforcing this right to sue each ultimate infringer render it of little practical use to copyright owners. Section 24(2) of the CDPA 1988 provides copyright owners with a basis for regulating such dissemination of a work at source, as follows:

Copyright in a work is infringed by a person who without the licence of the copyright owner transmits the work by means of a telecommunications system (otherwise than by broadcasting or inclusion in a cable programme service), knowing or having reason to believe that infringing copies of the work will be made by means of the reception of the transmission in the UK or elsewhere.

Accordingly, a supply down a telephone line of software, data, or any other work protected by copyright, may be an act of secondary infringement if done without an appropriate licence.

7.4.3.4 *Circumvention of protection measures*

A further area in which the CDPA 1988 strengthened the rights of owners of works distributed in electronic form relates to devices or information intended to facilitate the circumvention of copy-protection measures. As originally enacted, section 296 provided that a copyright owner who issued a work in copy-protected electronic form had the same rights against a person who, with intent, made available any device or means designed or adapted to circumvent the copy-protection as would be available against a copyright infringer. In response to the Information Society Directive,[128] the original section 296 was replaced in the Copyright and Related Rights Regulations 2003 by new provisions dealing separately with computer programs and other copyright works.

---

[128] Council Directive (EC) 2001/29.

The new section 296 is entitled 'Circumvention of technical devices applied to computer programs'. The section applies where a technical device has been applied to a computer program and provides a cause of action against a person who, with relevant intent, 'manufactures for sale or hire, imports, distributes, sells or lets for hire, offers or exposes for sale or hire, advertises for sale or hire or has in his possession for commercial purposes any means the sole intended purpose of which is to facilitate the unauthorised removal or circumvention of the technical device'. It also applies where information is published to facilitate removal or circumvention of the technical device.[129] New sections 296ZA–ZF cover circumvention of effective technological measures that have been applied to other devices and services.

A new section 296ZG was introduced to cover removal or alteration without authority of electronic 'rights management information' where a person knows or has reason to believe that an infringement of copyright will thereby be induced, enabled, facilitated, or concealed.[130] 'Rights management information' is defined as 'any information provided by the copyright owner or the holder of any right under copyright which identified the work, the author, the copyright owner or the holder of any intellectual property rights, or information about the terms and conditions of use of the work, and any numbers or codes that represent such information'.[131] This section also applies where a person distributes, imports for distribution, or communicates to the public copies of a work from which rights management information has been removed or altered where a person knows or has reason to believe that an infringement of copyright will thereby be induced, enabled, facilitated, or concealed.[132]

As with the discussion of the restriction on providing articles to be used for making infringing copies (see section 7.4.3.2 above), it is not clear how broadly the circumvention of technical devices provision will be interpreted by the courts. In *Sony Computer Entertainment v Owen*,[133] the defendants imported a 'Messiah' chip which could be inserted into a Sony PlayStation 2 in order to bypass codes embedded into CDs or DVDs which were intended to prevent copying of Sony games. Sony brought an action under the old section 296. The court considered the defendants' argument that the chip also had lawful uses because once the code was circumvented the machine could read material that was not protected by copyright. Jacob J concluded that the Messiah chip was specifically designed or adapted to circumvent the copy-protection code and therefore 'it does not matter that once circumvented the machine may read non-infringing material'. In the *Sony* case, the chip did not have any use other than to circumvent the protective code. The court may well have come to a different conclusion if the device had multiple uses, at least some of which

---

[129] CDPA 1988, s 296(1).
[130] Ibid s 296ZG(1).
[131] Ibid s 296ZG(7)(b).
[132] Ibid s 296ZG(2).
[133] [2002] EWHC 45.

were legitimate. It seems unlikely that section 296 would be applicable in cases where an article also has legitimate uses.[134]

In relation to the offence under section 296ZB, it must be established that there has been copying of the whole or a substantial part of a copyright work, but it is not necessary to consider a computer game as a whole since copyright might also subsist separately, in the form of artistic works, in the images displayed when the game is played.[135]

7.4.4 Copyright infringement via the internet[136]

The law of copyright, as has been seen, has sometimes been hard pressed to keep pace with the legal implications of technological advances. Probably the most difficult challenge to legislators and courts to date has been regulating the use and abuse of copyright material accessed via the internet.

Three of the most fundamental questions are these. First, who may be liable for copyright infringement? Secondly, what is the appropriate law and jurisdiction? Thirdly, what acts of infringement may have been committed under the relevant law? Possible infringers fall into three main categories: originators of material, recipients of it, and network operators or others who provide software or facilities for making copies. Some of the ways in which they could find themselves liable under English law are as follows.

An originator who transmits infringing material via the internet may, by the act of transmission, be infringing copyright. The originator may also infringe if he or she is regarded variously as performing, displaying, showing, playing, or broadcasting[137] the material. This is because the act of sending a message containing infringing material in the knowledge that it will necessarily be copied along the way may constitute infringement of copyright by transmission. It may also be the case that the originator will be liable for merely making material available on his or her computer to be browsed or copied by means of an instruction by another computer to send the material to it (eg, via the World Wide Web or File Transfer Protocol). However, in the case of piracy at least, the greatest problem may not be in identifying whether or not an originator of material has infringed copyright, but

---

[134] This interpretation was endorsed in *Nintendo Co Ltd v Playables Ltd* [2010] EWHC 1932 (Ch), 28 July 2010.

[135] *Christopher Paul Gilham v the Queen* [2009] EWCA Crim 2293. In *R v Higgs* [2009] 1 WLR 73 a similar prosecution failed because the prosecution did not prove that during the playing of a game, data had been copied onto the Random Access Memory of a games console.

[136] See also Chapter 5, section 5.2.2.2 in relation to the liability of internet service providers ('ISPs') for third party activities which infringe copyright.

[137] See, eg, *Shetland Times Ltd v Dr Jonathan Wills* [1998] Masons CLR 159, where, in finding that the balance of convenience fell in favour of awarding an interim injunction against the use of a website containing headlines of the pursuer, Lord Hamilton accepted the argument that there was a prima facie case of infringement of a cable broadcast service in that the information was conveyed to the user's site, and that constituted sending within the meaning of s 20 of the CDPA 1988.

in identifying who and where the originator is. Sophisticated techniques exist for ensuring the anonymity of persons making material available via the internet.[138]

Likewise, the recipient of material may be infringing copyright if he or she receives material which infringed copyright at the time of sending,[139] and someone who browses material on a website, or accesses it by instructing the originator's computer to send the material, may infringe copyright. Material may be downloaded deliberately or a copy of part or all of a file held on a remote website may be made automatically by a process known as 'caching' whereby material is copied on to a user's PC to speed up future access to a website.

On a strict application of copyright principles, network operators that carry packets of data containing infringing material, and there may be several such operators in different jurisdictions along the route of transmission, may be liable for infringement of copyright by the fact of having copied the material en route, even though copying may be automatic and although the network operator may never 'see' the material in question. The Electronic Commerce (EC Directive) Regulations 2002[140] introduced three exemptions from liability for network operators relating to mere conduit, caching, and hosting. The 'mere conduit' exemption[141] applies where a network operator is transmitting information, provided that the network operator:

(a) did not initiate the transmission;

(b) did not select the receiver of the transmission; and

(c) did not select or modify the information contained in the transmission.

If these conditions are fulfilled the network operator will not be liable for 'damages or for any other pecuniary remedy or for any criminal sanction as a result of that transmission'.

The second exemption relates to 'caching'[142] and is relevant in circumstances where a network operator is storing information solely for the purpose of making more efficient onward transmission of the information to other recipients of the transmission service. Certain conditions must be fulfilled before this exemption will apply. The network operator must:

(a) not modify the information;

(b) comply with conditions on access to the information;

---

[138] eg, 'spoofing', which involves obtaining a false internet protocol address, or the use of anonymous remailers.

[139] This would be the case if the recipient were in possession of the infringing copies in the course of a business and had the requisite mens rea.

[140] SI 2002/2013, implementing Council Directive (EC) 2000/31 on certain legal aspects of information society services, in particular electronic commerce, in the Internal Market [2000] OJ L178.

[141] Electronic Commerce (EC Directive) Regulations 2002 (SI 2002/2013), reg 17.

[142] Ibid reg 18.

(c) comply with rules regarding updating of the information; not interfere with the lawful use of technology, widely recognized and used by industry, to obtain data on the use of the information; and

(d) act expeditiously to remove or disable access to the information upon obtaining actual knowledge that the information at the initial source of the transmission has been removed from the network, or access to it has been disabled, or that a court or an administrative authority has ordered such removal or disablement. In determining whether a network operator has 'actual knowledge' for these purposes a court shall take account of all matters which appear to it to be relevant.[143]

The third exemption relates to hosting[144] and will apply when a network operator stores information without actual knowledge of unlawful activity or where upon obtaining such knowledge, the network operator expeditiously removes or disables access to the information. The same test of actual knowledge applies as for the caching exemption.

The question is what degree of knowledge is necessary to constitute 'actual knowledge' for these purposes? Would it be sufficient for a software house to issue a letter to, say, a public network operator, stating that, in all probability, that operator's network was being used for the purpose of creating infringing copies? Would it be sufficient to produce evidence that a specific customer was using the network in this manner? Would it be sufficient that the network operator knew that the material being stored was sourced from a copy of the material on a neighbouring network, which was unlikely to have received explicit permission to copy the work? In many jurisdictions the answers to such questions are unknown at this point, but network operators would probably not be held to have the requisite knowledge unless they had received very specific and detailed information concerning the activities of a specific customer.[145] In the UK, a new section 97A, which was inserted into the CDPA 1988 by the Copyright and Related Rights Regulations 2003, provides that in determining whether a service provider has actual knowledge that someone is using their service to infringe copyright:

. . . a court shall take into account all matters which appear to it in the particular circumstances to be relevant and, amongst other things, shall have regard to—

(a) whether a service provider has received a notice through a means of contact made available in accordance with . . . the Electronic Commerce (EC Directive) Regulations 2002 . . .; and

---

[143] Electronic Commerce (EC Directive) Regulations 2002, reg 22.
[144] Ibid reg 19.
[145] For a more detailed discussion of the position of network operators in relation to copyright infringement issues, see C Millard and R Carolina, 'Commercial Transactions on The Global Information Infrastructure: A European Perspective' (1996) 14(2) John Marshall Journal of Computer and Information Law 269.

(b) the extent to which any notice includes—

(i) the full name and address of the sender of the notice;

(ii) details of the infringement in question.

As yet, there has been no English court decision concerning the potential liability of network operators for copyright infringement via the internet. In the USA, however, there have been several cases already, of which we shall look briefly at two. In *Playboy Enterprises Inc v Frena*,[146] it was held that there had been infringement of the claimant's right publicly to distribute and display copyrighted photographs by the defendant, on whose bulletin board the photographs had been posted by some of the defendant's subscribers without his knowledge. A different conclusion was reached in the more recent case of *Religious Technology Center v Netcom Online Communications Services*,[147] which signalled a move away from the imposition of liability for direct infringement upon service providers despite strict liability under the Copyright Act 1976 (17 USC § 501). In the *Netcom* case the District Court of the Northern District of California held that 'it does not make sense to adopt a rule that could lead to the liability of countless parties whose role in the infringement is nothing more than setting up and operating a system that is necessary for the functioning of the internet'.[148]

The Digital Millennium Copyright Act 1998 ('DMCA 1998') came into force in the USA on 28 October 1998. The DMCA 1998 codifies the result of the *Netcom* case and distinguishes between direct infringement and secondary liability of ISPs. In *ALS Scan Inc v RemarQ Communities Inc*,[149] the US Court of Appeals for the Fourth Circuit held that the DMCA 1998 overrules the *Playboy* case, insofar as it suggests that acts by service providers could constitute direct infringement.[150] Unless ISPs have actual or constructive knowledge of infringement they will be immune from liability under the DMCA 1998.

Moreover, in June 2010, a summary judgment was granted for Google in the *Viacom* and *Football Premier League* cases.[151] Having reviewed the DCMA's legislative history in some detail, the judge concluded that general knowledge of infringements of copyright will not in itself remove an ISP's immunity. Rather, in order to be disqualified from the safe harbor, a service provider must have: 'knowledge of specific and identifiable infringements of particular individual items. Mere knowledge of prevalence of such activity in general is not enough'. In addition, it is

---

[146] 839 F Supp 1552 (MD Fla, 1993).

[147] 907 F Supp 1361 (ND Cal, 1995).

[148] Ibid.

[149] 57 USPQ 2d 1996 (2001).

[150] The District Court of Maryland in *CoStar Group Inc v LoopNet Inc*, 164 F Supp 2d 688 (2001) applied the *RemarQ* ratio and confirmed the rejection of the *Playboy* ratio.

[151] *Viacom International Inc v YouTube Inc*, 07-Civ-2103, and *The Football Association Premier League v YouTube, Inc*, 07-Civ-582 (SDNY, 23 June 2010, LLS).

clear from these cases that monitoring for infringements is a matter for the copyright owner, not the service provider.[152]

How far Web 2.0 service providers benefit from the immunity granted to intermediaries, such as 'information society service providers' under EU law, is debatable. Their liability status will depend on the services provided, on their modus operandi,[153] and on the precise immunity rules of the jurisdiction. To protect themselves, at least in part, providers usually obtain warranties and indemnities from users.

In various jurisdictions there has been litigation regarding the provision of software or facilities for making infringing copies of material via the internet. In the US case *A&M Records Inc v Napster DC*,[154] A&M Records were successful in suing Napster for contributory and vicarious copyright infringement. Napster used a central server through which users linked to files on the PCs of other users. Users' files were catalogued on the central server and users could search for specific files and then copy them. Even though Napster was not itself hosting the material that was being copied, Napster was ordered to take reasonable steps to prevent distribution of works of which it had been notified of copyright ownership. This court order effectively disabled Napster because of the huge logistical task of identifying which materials could lawfully be swapped.

The *Napster* judgment accelerated the development and deployment of systems which do not rely on a central server. Kazaa.com is one such company which distributes programs that enable file swapping over the internet. The Dutch music licensing body Burma/Stemra brought an action against Kazaa.com for copyright infringement by users of its downloadable software. At first instance the Amsterdam District Court ordered Kazaa.com to stop offering its free software online because it encouraged copyright infringement. However, the Court of Appeals in Amsterdam overturned this judgment on the basis that Kazaa.com was not responsible for its users' actions and because the software was also being used for non-infringing purposes.[155]

Globally, however, the fight was far from over. In 2002 Sharman Networks, a business incorporated in Vanuatu, purchased the Kazaa software from the Dutch

---

[152] In December 2010, Viacom filed an opening brief to the US Court of Appeals for the Second Circuit requesting a summary judgment on these issues: <http://news.viacom.com/pdf/Final_Viacom_Brief.pdf> (accessed 9 August 2011).

[153] In *Kaschke v Gray & Hilton* [2010] EWHC 690 (QB), Stadlen J held that the question of whether the defendant met the requirements of hosting immunity under Art 14 of the Electronic Commerce Directive (see Chapter 5, section 5.2.2) was to be decided solely in relation to the particular information at issue, and not by examining all the information made available from the defendant's site (para 75). It seems likely that this approach will be followed when deciding on the question of copyright immunities for hosting or transmission—if not, those immunities would become meaningless, as most service providers make their own information available in addition to the information they merely host or transmit.

[154] No CV-99-05783MHP.

[155] KG 01/2264 OdC.

company Kazaa BV. In February 2004 an action was commenced against Sharman in Australia by various record companies (eventually 30 joined the proceedings in the Federal Court of Australia). In September 2005 Mr Justice Wilcox in the Federal Court ruled in *Universal Music Australia Pty Ltd v Sharman License Holdings Ltd* that Sharman (and various other defendants) had authorized users of their software to infringe the applicants' copyright in their sound recordings.[156] The court reached this conclusion notwithstanding that the Kazaa website contained warnings against the sharing of copyright material and an end-user licence under which users agreed not to infringe copyright. For Mr Justice Wilcox these apparently mitigating factors appeared to be more than eclipsed by various other factors such as the fact that the respondents had failed to implement various filtering techniques which would have curtailed significantly the sharing of copyright material. Moreover, it was probably unhelpful to the defence that the Kazaa website contained a page entitled 'Join the Revolution' which criticized record companies for opposing file-sharing. The court gave the respondents two months (subsequently extended to 5 December 2005) to modify the Kazaa system by adopting compulsory copyright-filtering technology using lists of works supplied by the applicants. The deadline came and went and a warning notice appeared on Kazaa.com announcing that, pending an appeal in the *Universal Music v Sharman* case, the Kazaa Media Desktop should no longer be downloaded or used by persons in Australia.[157]

Similarly in *Cooper*,[158] the Federal Court of Australia ruled that online service providers are liable under the authorization theory when they provide links to infringing files. The finding of authorization was based on knowledge of infringing activity and acquiescence in its occurrence: Cooper permitted or approved and thereby authorized the users' infringing activities.[159] The fact that Cooper could not control the presence of infringing files on his website was not considered to be the relevant test for determining whether he had authorized infringements by internet users.[160] Cooper had sufficient control of his website to take actions to prevent the infringement.[161]

In contrast in *iiNet*,[162] an internet access provider was alleged to have authorized its users to infringe copyright by downloading and sharing files using peer-to-peer ('P2P') software, in particular BitTorrent. The plaintiffs claimed breach of copyright by failing to take steps to prevent account holders from engaging in unlawful file-sharing and by refusing to forward the plaintiff's complaints to the relevant users.

---

[156] [2005] FCA 1242.
[157] 'Aussie Kazaa users told to stop using Kazaa' <http://www.theregister.co.uk/2005/12/06/kazaa_pulls_p2p_code/print.html> (accessed 9 August 2011). Kazaa has subsequently been relaunched as a licensed music download service.
[158] *Universal Music Pty Ltd v Cooper* [2005] FCA 972 (14 July 2005).
[159] Ibid 84.
[160] Ibid 86.
[161] Ibid 86.
[162] *Roadshow Films Pty Ltd & Others v iiNet Ltd* [2010] FCA 24.

The judge recognized that users were infringing copyright on a wide scale, but ultimately dismissed the claim because the internet access provider did not control, nor was it responsible for, the BitTorrent system, and consequently it could not prevent the infringements. Moreover, the internet access provider merely provided users with internet and did not 'sanction, approve or countenance copyright infringements'.[163]

Meanwhile, in the USA, the Supreme Court handed down its ruling in another high-profile P2P case, *Metro-Goldwyn-Mayer Studios Inc and Others v Grokster Ltd and Others* (*'Grokster'*).[164] The Court decided unanimously that the defendants Grokster and Streamcast (maker of Morpheus) could be sued for inducing copyright infringement in distributing and promoting the use of their P2P software. In so ruling, the Supreme Court disagreed with both the District Court and the Ninth Circuit Court of Appeals, both of which had applied *Sony Corp of America v Universal City Studios Inc* (*'Sony'*)[165] as authority for the proposition that 'distribution of a commercial product capable of substantial non-infringing uses could not give rise to contributory liability for infringement unless the distributor had actual knowledge of specific instances of infringement and failed to act on that knowledge'.[166] In *Grokster*, the Supreme Court distinguished the *Sony* case on the basis that in the former case there was evidence that VCRs were used primarily for time-shifting and that this was a substantially lawful activity as it was justified as fair use under copyright law. Moreover, there was no evidence that Sony promoted infringement of copyright or sought to increase its profits from unlawful taping.

Grokster therefore arguably introduced a third claim for secondary infringement (in addition to contributory and vicarious liability): active inducement.[167]

Before moving on from internet-specific issues, it is worth mentioning two English judgments relating to P2P file-sharing. An interesting feature of *Polydor Ltd v Brown*[168] was that the court heard an application for summary judgment against one of the defendants, a Mr Bowles, in relation to infringing activities that had been carried out without his knowledge by his children. The act of placing the infringing files in a shared directory on a computer running P2P software that was connected to the internet was held to be an act of primary infringement and Mr Bowles was ordered to pay damages. Many parents worry about their children's online activities for rather different reasons. It is likely that few have ever considered that they as

---

[163] An appeal by the copyright owners was dismissed by the full bench of the Federal Court of Australia: *Roadshow Films Pty Ltd v iiNet Ltd* [2011] FCAFC 23 (24 February 2011).

[164] 545 US 913 (2005).

[165] 464 US 417 (1984).

[166] 545 US 913 (2005).

[167] eg, in *LimeWire*, the court granted a summary judgment and found LimeWire liable for inducing copyright infringement, common law copyright infringement, and unfair competition, but not for contributory and vicarious infringement. *Arista Records LLC and Others v LimeWire LLC* 2010 WL 1914816 (SDNY, 11 May 2010).

[168] [2005] EWHC 3191.

parents might personally be liable for acts of copyright infringement resulting from online sharing of music and other files by family members![169]

More recently, in *Newzbin*,[170] the operator of a website providing to its users an index and other facilities to simplify the downloading of films from Usenet servers was found liable for authorizing, making available, procuring infringement, and participating with its users in a common design to infringe. Regarding authorization, the court held that a reasonable member of the public would deduce that Newzbin purported to possess the authority to grant permission to its users to download and that it had sanctioned, approved, and countenanced the infringements. *Newzbin* suggests the circumstances that courts are likely to consider in determining whether there is authorization include encouragement, control over, and ease of, prevention, and public perception.

As regards making available/communication to the public, Kitchin J determined that Newzbin had 'made available' the films and TV programmes accessed by users of the site because it had intervened in a 'highly material' way by providing a 'sophisticated technical and editorial system' to make the content available to a new 'public' on a subscription basis. Infringements were thus encouraged in full knowledge of the consequences. These criteria are non-exhaustive but the principle appears to be that a service provider may be liable for 'making available' protected material even when the material is not hosted or disseminated by the service provider, if the service provided goes beyond providing technical facilities and the provider is not 'merely passive'.

Finally, a high-profile Swedish case is interesting in this context. In *Pirate Bay*,[171] the defendants' website provided a catalogue of .torrent files and a tracker. The plaintiffs claimed complicity in breach of the §2 of the Swedish Author's Right Act ('making available to the public'), and under Chapter 23, §4 of the Swedish Criminal Code (Act of Complicity). The defendants presented an argument based on 'mere conduit'.[172] The court concluded that Pirate Bay's users infringed authors' right. Pirate Bay was an accomplice and facilitated the execution of the principal offence, regardless of any knowledge concerning the infringements. The defendants' failure to take action prevented them from benefiting from the protection provided by the Swedish implementation of the e-Commerce Directive. The court found the defendants guilty of being accessories to a crime under the authors' rights law, notably because of the commercial and organized nature of the activity.[173]

---

[169] See R Welch, 'A Watchful Eye, P2P file sharing: ignorance is no defence' (2006) 159 Copyright World (April) 22.

[170] *Twentieth Century Fox Film Corp v Newzbin Ltd* [2010] EWHC 608 (Ch); [2010] ECC 13 (Ch D).

[171] Verdict B 13301-06, 17 April 2009, Stockholm District Court, Division 5, Unit 52.

[172] Art 12 of the e-Commerce Directive.

[173] An English translation (commissioned by IFPI, but not endorsed by the Stockholm District Court) is available at <http://www.ifpi.org/content/library/Pirate-Bay-verdict-English-translation.pdf>

Nevertheless, Pirate Bay is still online, notwithstanding attempts by copyright owners to obtain injunctions against ISPs to block access to the website.

7.5 SCOPE OF PROTECTION FOR COMPUTER PROGRAMS AND DATA

7.5.1 Idea and expression, symbolism, and functionality

In the UK there is no statutory rule that bars ideas from copyright protection.[174] However, the Software Directive[175] provides in Article 1.2 that 'Ideas and principles which underlie any element of a computer program, including those which underlie its interfaces, are not protected by copyright under this Directive'. The Copyright (Computer Programs) Regulations 1992 are silent on this point.[176] However, a number of English, and other Commonwealth, precedents appear to exclude ideas *per se* from copyright protection.[177] The apparent logic behind the rule was illustrated by the Supreme Court of Canada in *Cuisenaire v South West Imports Ltd*[178] with the observation that 'were the law otherwise . . . everybody who made a rabbit pie in accordance with the recipe of Mrs Beeton's cookery book would infringe the literary copyright in that book'.[179]

The claimed distinction then is between an idea that cannot be protected by copyright, such as the procedure for making a rabbit pie, and an expression of that idea, such as a written recipe describing the rabbit pie-making process, which can be protected by copyright. In the case of a computer program, however, such a tidy analysis is not possible. Indeed, it may be that the statement that ideas can never be protected by copyright is a misleading oversimplification.[180] Take, for example, ideas such as the algorithms on which a program is based, or perhaps the methods

---

(accessed 9 August 2011). On the 26 of November 2010, the Swedish Court of Appeal upheld the Stockholm District Court, Division 5, Unit 52 Decision (Verdict B 13301-06, 17 April 2009).

[174] Cf, eg, the position in the USA, where § 102(b) of Title 17 USC provides 'in no case does copyright protection . . . extend to any idea, procedure, process, system, method of operation, concept, principle, or discovery, regardless of the form in which it is described, explained, illustrated, or embodied in such work'.

[175] Council Directive (EEC) 91/250 on the legal protection of computer programs [1991] OJ L122.

[176] Although it is interesting to note that the Copyright and Related Rights Regulations 2003 (SI 2003/2498), rather belatedly introduced a new s 50BA into the CDPA 1988 which provides that:

It is not an infringement of copyright for a lawful user of a copy of a computer program to observe, study or test the functioning of the program in order to determine the ideas and principles which underlie any element of the program if he does so while performing any of the acts of loading, displaying, running, transmitting or storing the program which he is entitled to do.

[177] eg, in *Donoghue v Allied Newspapers Ltd* [1938] Ch 106, 109, Farwell J stated unequivocally that 'there is no copyright in an idea, or in ideas'.

[178] [1969] SCR 208.

[179] Ibid 212, citing Pape J in *Cuisenaire v Reed* [1963] VR 719.

[180] This theme is developed in more detail in section 7.5.6 below.

or processes that the program implements. Because of the nature of the interaction between software and hardware, a program, unlike a page from a recipe book, can simultaneously be symbolic (ie, a representation of instructions to be given to the computer) and functional (ie, the means by which the computer is actually instructed to carry out operations). Lines of code that describe an operation or procedure can also be used to implement it. It is as though by putting the relevant pages from Mrs Beeton's cookery book into an oven one could produce a rabbit pie. This special characteristic of computer programs has a number of significant consequences in copyright law. One is that use of a program is almost impossible without copying and/or adaptation occurring (see section 7.5.2 below). Another is that there may be no way to achieve functional compatibility between two or more items of hardware or software without reproducing a substantial amount of code to effect the desired interface or communication (see section 7.5.3 below).

7.5.2 Infringement of program copyright by use of a program

In relation to conventional works, the 'use' of a legitimate copy of a work is not generally restricted by copyright. For example, the simple act of reading a book is not controlled by copyright. It is only on the occurrence of one of the specifically restricted acts, for example the copying or adaptation of a substantial part of the book, that a question of infringement can arise. However, because computer programs in machine-code form are both symbolic and functional, normal use may necessitate such copying or adaptation. Loading or running a computer program typically entails the copying of part or all of the program from a disk (or other permanent storage medium) to the computer's random access memory ('RAM') and central processing unit ('CPU'). Section 17(6) of the CDPA 1988 makes it clear that such copying of a work, even though it may be 'transient' or 'incidental to some other use of the work', is nevertheless an infringement of copyright if done without authorization. Even screen displays generated during the running of a program may constitute infringing copies of copyright material. Because the restriction on copying applies even to simple use of a program, legitimate use can normally only take place pursuant to a licence or permission of some kind. Such a licence may be express or implied. Typically, a software house will seek to attach various conditions to a licence to use. A special provision in the CDPA 1988 dealing with transfers of second-hand copies of programs is dealt with in section 7.5.9 below.

Hence, UK copyright law appears to give indirect protection to the ideas underlying a program by making the literal copying inherent in simple use of the program an infringing act. Thus, unlike the ideas and procedures described in a cookery recipe which can be used without infringing copyright in the recipe book, the ideas and procedures embodied in a computer program are regulated by copyright along with the code which implements them whenever the program is used. It is interesting to note, by way of comparison, that under US copyright law the owner of a copy of a program does not need a licence to make or authorize the making of another copy or adaptation if doing so is 'an essential step in the utilisation of the computer program in conjunction with a machine'.[181]

A similar approach was adopted in the EU Software Directive,[182] although the deemed right to make copies or adaptations necessary for use seems to be subject to agreement to the contrary. Article 5.1 provides that 'In the absence of specific contractual provisions', copying and adaptation 'shall not require authorization by the rightholder where they are necessary for the use of the computer program by the lawful acquirer in accordance with its intended purpose, including for error correction'. The words 'in the absence of specific contractual provisions' seem to make it clear that it remains open to a copyright owner to restrict by contract these acts of copying and adaptation necessary for use.[183] This is the interpretation adopted by the UK Government in the implementing regulations. Whether copyright can also be used to prevent non-literal copying, for example where a person analyses or reverse engineers a program and writes new but functionally equivalent code, is a rather more complex issue.

7.5.3 Copying, compatibility, and reverse engineering

There may be a limited number of ways, in extreme cases possibly only one, of achieving a particular functional result using a specific configuration of hardware and/or software. Sometimes a single manufacturer can establish an almost universal standard or set of standards for carrying out particular operations, perhaps by being there first, by skilful marketing, by dominance in the industry, or sometimes by being truly innovative. Where, for whatever reason, a de facto industry standard has emerged, such as the BIOS ('basic input-output system') for IBM-compatible personal computers, the possibility of copyright being used to monopolize the specification of interfaces between hardware and hardware, hardware and software, software and software, and humans and software, has enormous policy implications. Much of the rapid growth and diversity that has characterized the computer industry in the past three decades has resulted from the widespread development of hardware and software products that are 'compatible' with those most popular in the market. Such compatible products frequently improve substantially on the products offered by the company that initiated the standard both in terms of price and performance, and often also in terms of innovation. A user who has invested in a particular 'environment' in terms of hardware, software, or training, will often wish to build on that

---

[181] Title 17 USC § 117. This derogation from the copyright owner's normal rights to prevent the making of copies and adaptations does not seem to apply where title to the physical copy does not pass to the software user.

[182] Council Directive (EC) 91/250.

[183] Confusingly, the relevant recital is inconsistent with Art 5 and provides that 'the acts of loading and running necessary for the use of a copy of a program that has been lawfully acquired, and the act of correction of its errors, may not be prohibited by contract'. Presumably, Art 5 will prevail.

investment without being tied into a particular supplier or suppliers for all future development purposes.

The development of compatible products can, of course, be effected in a number of ways with varying consequences in copyright terms. At one end of the spectrum, a clone may consist of or contain crude copies of key parts, or indeed the whole, of an established product. The maker of such a clone will be vulnerable to be sued for infringement of copyright and a number of other intellectual property rights. Certainly, the literal copying of the whole or a substantial part of an existing program will almost invariably infringe copyright. At the other end of the spectrum, a developer of a compatible product may invest substantial resources in achieving functional compatibility by independent development without making a verbatim or literal copy of any part of the product that is being emulated. To ensure that it can be proved that the competing product is the result of such original labour and skill, a manufacturer may resort to a rigorous and exhaustively documented 'clean-room' procedure. Such a procedure would normally necessitate independent work being undertaken by two discrete groups of software engineers, the first analysing the product to be emulated and producing a functional specification, the second writing code to implement that specification.[184] In between these extremes of crude copying and sophisticated reverse engineering, there are various ways in which software may be developed using particular ideas or functions derived from pre-existing software products without any substantial literal copying taking place.

Various tests have been suggested for determining whether products developed using either of the latter two approaches will infringe copyright and a certain amount of judicial consideration has been given to these issues in the UK. However, most reported cases and current litigation in the area are concentrated in the USA. Much of the argument there has concerned the extent to which copyright law can provide protection against copying of either the 'structure, sequence and organisation' of a program, or of its 'look and feel'. The former concerns the internal structure and workings of a program, the latter its external appearance and user interfaces. Underlying both issues is the fundamental dichotomy in US law between ideas, which cannot be protected by copyright, and expressions of those ideas, which can. Before looking briefly at some of the US cases, one other general issue should be noted.

7.5.4 Difficulties of proving non-literal infringement

A further consequence of the simultaneously symbolic and functional nature of software is that the traditional tests for establishing that copying of a work has occurred may be wholly inappropriate. It is by no means always the case that functional

---

[184] For an interesting discussion of the issues, inherent in duplication of the functionality of the IBM BIOS, see G Gervaise Davis III, 'IBM PC Software and Hardware Compatibility' [1984] EIPR 273.

similarity between two programs is indicative of similarity in the underlying symbolic codes. To extend the rabbit pie analogy one final stage further, just because a rabbit pie looks, smells, and tastes very similar to one made by Mrs Beeton is not in itself proof that both have been made from the same recipe. As Megarry V-C put it in *Thrustcode Ltd v WW Computing Ltd*:

> . . . where, as here, the claim is to copyright in the program itself, the results produced by operating the program must not be confused with the program in which copyright is claimed. If I may take an absurdly simple example, 2 and 2 make 4. But so does 2 times 2, or 6 minus 2, or 2 per cent of 200, or 6 squared divided by 9, or many other things. Many different processes may produce the same answer and yet remain different processes that have not been copied one from another.[185]

On the facts before it, the court was at a loss to see 'any real evidence of copying'[186] and accordingly dismissed the claimant's case. In *LB (Plastics) Ltd v Swish Products Ltd*, Lord Wilberforce observed:

> The protection given by the law of copyright is against copying, the basis of protection being that one man must not be permitted to appropriate the result of another's labour. That copying has taken place, is for the plaintiff [claimant] to establish and prove as a matter of fact. The beginning of the necessary proof normally lies in the establishment of similarity combined with proof of access to the plaintiff's [claimant's] productions.[187]

In *Cantor Fitzgerald International v Tradition (UK) Ltd*,[188] Pumfrey J held, in finding that copyright infringement had occurred where 3,000 out of 77,000 lines of the claimant's code were copied by the defendant, that it is the function of copyright to protect the relevant skill and labour expended by the author of the work and that it follows that a copyist infringes if he appropriates a part of the work upon which a substantial part of the author's skill and labour was expended. It is not determined by whether the system would work without the copied code or the amount of use the system makes of the code.

This issue is of fundamental importance in the context of software copyright infringement. It is not enough for a claimant to allege that program code has been copied merely on the basis that a later program is similar to an earlier one in terms of its functionality or its appearance to a user. Actual copying of a substantial part is the key to copyright infringement under UK law.[189] In this case, Pumfrey J accepted that the general architecture of a computer program was capable of protection provided a substantial part of the programmer's skill and labour was used.

---

[185] [1983] FSR 502 at 505.
[186] Ibid 507.
[187] [1979] FSR 145 at 149.
[188] [2000] RPC 95.
[189] See *Catnic Components v Hill & Smith* [1982] RPC 182 at 223; followed *Ibcos Computers Ltd v Barclays Mercantile Highland Finance Ltd* [1994] FSR 275; *Cantor Fitzgerald International v Tradition (UK) Ltd* [2000] RPC 95.

Therefore, it was possible for specific software modules to be infringed, even though only a small proportion of the code had been copied.[190]

7.5.5 Infringement by non-literal copying under US law

A full discussion of the many reported and pending US cases in the field of software copyright is well beyond the scope of this chapter. However, a brief consideration of some of the issues that have been raised in the USA may assist, sometimes by analogy, sometimes by way of contrast, in evaluating the position under UK copyright law.

In its landmark ruling in *Apple Computer Inc v Franklin Computer Corp*,[191] the US Court of Appeals for the Third Circuit confirmed unequivocally that computer programs in both source and object code are capable of protection as 'literary works' and that such protection extends to programs in machine code embedded in integrated circuit chips. The court then considered whether program copyright extended to operating systems, and in particular whether a merger of idea and expression would prevent Apple from claiming protection for various operating programs supplied with the Apple II microcomputer. The court ruled that: 'If other programs can be written or created which perform the same function as an Apple's operating system program, then that program is an expression of the idea and hence copyrightable.'[192] In response to claims by the defendants that there was only a limited number of ways of writing a compatible operating system:

Franklin may wish to achieve total compatibility with independently developed application programs written for Apple II, but that is a commercial and competitive objective which does not enter into the somewhat metaphysical issue of whether particular ideas and expressions have merged.[193]

The court concluded that operating system programs are not per se excluded from copyright protection.

Three years later, a different panel of judges in the same Third Circuit Court of Appeals addressed in rather more detail the application to computer programs of the idea–expression dichotomy. In *Whelan Associates Inc v Jaslow Dental Laboratory Inc*,[194] the claimants alleged that a program developed by the defendant in the PC language BASIC infringed their copyright in a similar program written in the minicomputer language EDL. It was accepted that no literal copying had occurred yet the Third Circuit ruled that substantial similarities between the BASIC and EDL programs in terms of their 'structure, sequence and organisation' provided

---

[190] See the comments of Colin Tapper at [1999] Masons CLR 265–6.
[191] 714 F2d 1240 (1983).
[192] Ibid 1253.
[193] Ibid.
[194] [1987] FSR 1.

sufficient grounds for a finding of infringement. As regards drawing a line between idea and expression, the court ruled that 'the line between idea and expression may be drawn by reference to the end sought to be achieved by the work in question'.[195] Where the desired purpose can be achieved in more than one way, then any particular means of achieving it will be expression, not idea. On the facts before it, the Third Circuit found that 'the idea of the Dentalab program was the efficient management of a dental laboratory . . . Because that idea could be accomplished in a number of different ways with a number of different structures, the structure of the Dentalab program is part of the program's expression, not its idea'.[196]

The Third Circuit's analysis in *Whelan Associates Inc v Jaslow Dental Laboratory Inc* has been widely criticized by academic writers.[197] A particular concern has been that the court's 'sweeping rule and broad language extend copyright protection too far' by moving towards a degree of monopoly protection previously only given to patent holders.[198] An indication of how widely the *Whelan* ruling could be applied came in *Broderbund Software Inc v Unison World Inc*,[199] where it was cited as 'stand[ing] for the proposition that copyright protection is not limited to the literal aspects of a computer program, but rather that it extends to the overall structure of a program, including its audiovisual displays'.[200] The last part of this statement is rather surprising, given that the *Whelan* case was about infringement of a copyright in program code (ie, a literary work), not infringement of copyright in screen displays (ie, audiovisual works). Moreover, in place of the structural analysis conducted by the *Whelan court*, the *Broderbund* court was more concerned with whether 'the infringing work captures the "total concept and feel" of the protected work'. Noting 'the eerie resemblance between the screens of the two programs', the court found that infringement had indeed occurred.[201]

An illustration of the flexibility of the 'total concept and feel' or 'look and feel' approach can be seen in the analysis of an Ohio District Court in *Worlds of Wonder Inc v Vector Intercontinental Inc*.[202] The case concerned allegations of infringement of copyright in a talking animated toy bear known as Teddy Ruxpin. The bear was designed to be used with cassette tapes containing a soundtrack together with software to control the bear's movements. The defendants, in competition with the claimant, produced various tapes containing stories and software for Teddy Ruxpin.

---

[195] Whelan Associates, 19.
[196] Ibid.
[197] eg, D Nimmer, RL Bernacchi, and GN Frischling, 'A Structured Approach to Analysing the Substantial Similarity of Computer Software in Copyright Infringement Cases' (1988) 20 Ariz St LJ 625.
[198] Ibid 630. See also, Ganz, 'Whelan and "work made for hire" threaten job mobility' (1988) 4 Computer Law Strategist 1.
[199] 648 F Supp 1127 (1986).
[200] Ibid 1133.
[201] Ibid 1137.
[202] (1986) unreported.

The court found infringement of copyright in the bear as an audiovisual work on the ground that:

> ... the general feel and concept of Teddy Ruxpin when telling a fairy tale is the same regard-less of whether a WOW or Vector tape is used; the visual effects are identical, and the voices are similar, and the difference in stories does not alter the aesthetic appeal ... At least, the work created by the Vector tapes is a derivative work, if not an exact copy.[203]

These and other look-and-feel cases set the scene for an action brought by Lotus against alleged infringers of copyright in the look and feel of the user interfaces of its enormously successful '1-2-3' spreadsheet product.

Before identifying the principal issues at stake in the *Lotus* case, however, consideration should be given to a move by a District Court in California to limit the breadth of the monopoly given to software copyright owners. In *NEC Corp v Intel Corp*,[204] the court confirmed that microcodes embodied in various Intel chips were protected by copyright as computer programs, yet ruled that the reverse engineering of those programs by NEC did not infringe the relevant copyrights.[205] The court found that 'overall, and particularly with respect to the microroutines, NEC's microcode is not substantially similar to Intel's; but some of the shorter, simpler microroutines resemble Intel's. None, however, are identical.' To resolve the issue of whether those of the shorter microroutines which were similar infringed Intel's copyrights, the court placed great emphasis on the possibility of a merger of idea and expression, not as a basis for denying copyrightability but as a justification for the production of substantially similar code:

> In determining an idea's range of expression, constraints are relevant factors to consider ...
> In this case, the expression of NEC's microcode was constrained by the use of the macroin-struction set and hardware of the 8086/88 ... Accordingly, it is the conclusion of this court that the expression of the ideas underlying the shorter, simpler microroutines (including those identified earlier as substantially similar) may be protected only against virtually identical copying, and that NEC properly used the underlying ideas, without virtually identically copying their limited expression.[206]

In *Lotus Development Corp v Paperback Software International*,[207] the District Court for the District of Massachusetts was called upon to decide whether the defendant's software package 'VP-Planner' infringed the copyright in Lotus's '1-2-3' package. Both products are electronic spreadsheets intended to facilitate accounting and other processes that involve the manipulation and display of

---

[203] Transcript at p 9.

[204] (1989) 1 CCH Computer Cases 46,020.

[205] In addition, the court ruled that Intel's failure to ensure that chips containing its microcode were properly marked with appropriate copyright notices had resulted in a forfeiture of its copyrights (1 CCH Computer Cases at 60,845).

[206] 1 CCH Computer Cases 60,853.

[207] 740 F Supp 37 (D Mass, 1990).

numerical data. District Judge Keeton identified three elements that appeared to him to be 'the principal factors relevant to a decision of copyrightability of a computer program such as Lotus 1-2-3'.[208] These were, first 'some conception or definition of the "idea"'—for the purpose of distinguishing between the idea and its expression'. Secondly, the court must determine 'whether an alleged expression of the idea is limited to elements essential to expression of *that* idea (or is one of only a few ways of expressing the idea) or instead includes identifiable elements of expression not essential to every expression of that idea'. Finally, 'having identified elements of expression not essential to every expression of the idea, the decision-maker must focus on whether those elements are a substantial part of the allegedly copyrightable "work"'.[209]

Interestingly, the District Court judge was fairly dismissive of the 'look–and-feel' concept. He did not find the concept 'significantly helpful' because it was a 'conclusion' rather than a means of reaching a conclusion. Instead, in applying his three-limb test, Judge Keeton looked at the 'user interface' of the two programs. He seemed to accept as a basis for analysis the claimant's description of the user interface as including such elements 'as the menus (and their structure and organisation), the long prompts, the screens on which they appear, the function key assignments [and] the macro commands language'.[210] Applying his three-stage test to these elements of the user interface, Judge Keeton found that neither the idea of developing an electronic spreadsheet nor the idea of a two-line moving cursor menu were copyrightable. Both elements thus failed to get beyond the first stage. The basic screen display of a 'rotated L' layout used in most spreadsheet packages to set out columns and rows failed to pass the second stage as 'there is a rather low limit, as a factual matter, on the number of ways of making a computer screen resemble a spreadsheet'. Similarly the use of a particular key to invoke the menu command system was found to be 'Another expressive element that merges with the idea of an electronic spreadsheet'.[211]

One element of the 1-2-3 package did, however, satisfy all three elements of the copyrightability test. The menu command system itself was capable of many types of expression and its precise 'structure, sequence and organisation' was 'distinctive'. Reaching the third element of his test, Judge Keeton found it to be 'incontrovertible' that the menu command system was a substantial part of the alleged copyrighted work:

The user interface of 1-2-3 is its most unique element, and is the aspect that has made 1-2-3 so popular. That defendants went to such trouble to copy that element is a testament to its

---

[208] *Lotus Development*, 61.
[209] Ibid 61.
[210] Ibid 63.
[211] Ibid 66.

substantiality. Accordingly, evaluation of the third element of the legal test weighs heavily in favour of Lotus.[212]

The court's conclusion was that it was 'indisputable that defendants have copied substantial copyrightable elements of plaintiff's [claimant's] copyrighted work . . . therefore . . . liability has been established'.[213]

However, subsequently, in *Brown Bag Software v Symantec Corp*,[214] the Ninth Circuit rejected the claimant's argument that the *Lotus* approach should be applied in deciding whether the graphical user interface of the defendant's outlining program infringed the claimant's copyright. Instead, the court held that it should engage in 'analytical dissection not for the purposes of comparing similarities and identifying infringement, but for the purposes of defining the scope of plaintiff's [claimant's] copyright'.[215] Thus, the court should first determine which elements are uncopyrightable, applying the idea–expression dichotomy and the merger doctrine to each element. Only then should it compare the protectable elements of expression to determine whether infringement may have occurred.

Many district and circuit judges have also been critical of the Third Circuit's approach in *Whelan Associates Inc v Jaslow Dental Laboratory Inc* to the separation of ideas, which may not be protected, from expressions which may be.[216] In *Plains Cotton Cooperative Association of Lubbock Texas v Goodpasture Computer Services Inc*,[217] the Court of Appeals for the Fifth Circuit 'declined to embrace' *Whelan*. Subsequently the Second Circuit, in *Computer Associates v Altai*[218] commented that the *Whelan* approach to separating idea and expression 'relies too heavily on metaphysical distinctions'. Instead, the *Altai* court suggested that district courts would be 'well advised' to adopt a three-step procedure for determining substantial similarity of non-literal elements of computer programs. First, the court should break down the allegedly infringed program into its constituent structural parts. Secondly, the court should examine each of these parts for such things as incorporated ideas, expression that is necessarily incidental to those ideas, and elements that are taken from the public domain, thus sifting out all non-protectable material. Thirdly, 'left with a kernel, or possibly kernels, of creative expression after following this process of elimination, the court's last step would be to compare this material with the structure of an allegedly infringing program'.[219] This has become known as the 'abstraction-filtration-comparison' analysis.

---

[212] *Lotus Development*, 68.
[213] Ibid 70.
[214] 960 F2d 146 (1992) 1465.
[215] Ibid 1475–6.
[216] See, eg, *Comprehensive Technologies Int'l v Software Artisans Inc*, Civil No 90-1143-A (ED Va, 2 June 1992).
[217] 807 F2d 1256 (1987).
[218] 982 F2d 693 (2nd Cir, 1992).
[219] Ibid 706.

The court concluded that 'we seek to ensure two things: (1) that programmers may receive appropriate copyright protection for innovative utilitarian works containing expression; and (2) that non-protectable technical expression remains in the public domain for others to use freely as building blocks in their own work'.[220] It is interesting to note that the court relied heavily on the Supreme Court's decision in *Feist Publications Inc v Rural Telephone Service Co Inc*,[221] noting that '*Feist* teaches that substantial effort alone cannot confer copyright status on an otherwise uncopyrightable work' and that 'despite the fact that significant labour and expense often goes into computer program flow-charting and debugging, that process does not always result in inherently protectable expression'.[222]

In subsequent cases, there was something of a shift away from the 'look–and-feel' approach towards *Altai*'s analytical three-step test. Indeed, in *Gates Rubber Co v Bando Chemical Industries Ltd*,[223] the Court of Appeals for the Tenth Circuit formulated a refined version of the *Altai* test. The court suggested that before beginning the abstraction-filtration-comparison process it would normally be helpful for the court to compare the programs as a whole, as 'an initial holistic comparison may reveal a pattern of copying that is not obvious when only certain components are examined'.[224] The abstraction-filtration-comparison test itself remained comparable to the *Altai* version:

First, in order to provide a framework for analysis, we conclude that a court should dissect the program according to its varying levels of generality as provided in the abstraction test. Second, poised with this framework, the court should examine each level of abstraction in order to filter out those elements of the program that are unprotectable. Filtration should eliminate from comparison the unprotectable elements of ideas, processes, facts, public domain information, merger material, *scénes à faire* material, and other unprotectable elements suggested by the particular facts of the program under examination. Third, the court should then compare the remaining protectable elements with the allegedly infringing program to determine whether the defendants have misappropriated substantial elements of the plaintiff's [claimant's] program.[225]

Applying this test the court found that certain mathematical constants in a computer program were not protectable because they represented scientific observations of relationships that existed and were not invented or created by the claimant.

In the case of *Kepner-Tregoe v Leadership Software Inc*,[226] concerning management training software, the Court of Appeals, Fifth Circuit, held that non-literal aspects of copyrighted works may be protected. This decision was applied in

---

[220] *Computer Associates*, 721.
[221] 499 US 340 (1991).
[222] *Computer Associates v Altai*, 982 F 2d 693 at 711 (2nd Cir, 1992).
[223] 9 F3d 823 (10th Cir, 1993).
[224] Ibid 841.
[225] Ibid 834.
[226] 12 F3d 527 (5th Cir, 1994).

Engineering Dynamics Inc v Structural Software Inc[227] to apply to non-literal aspects of a computer program, reversing a District Court's decision that input and output formats were uncopyrightable. The District Court, in coming to its conclusion, had thought *Lotus* was 'persuasive' but had declined to follow the decision. The Court of Appeals for the Fifth Circuit stated that the District Court had 'erred' and that the abstraction-filtration-comparison of *Gates Rubber* and *Altai* was appropriate on the facts albeit that:

Describing this approach as abstraction-filtration-comparison should not convey a deceptive air of certitude about the outcome of any particular computer copyright case. Protectable originality can manifest itself in many ways, so the analytic approach may need to be varied to accommodate each case's facts.[228]

Since *Engineering Dynamics, Altai*'s abstraction-filtration-comparison analysis has tended to be applied more or less as a matter of course to determine the scope of copyright protection in cases involving non-literal copying.[229]

7.5.6 Infringement by non-literal copying under UK law

As already noted, the extent to which ideas are excluded from protection under UK copyright law has perhaps tended to be exaggerated. Some commentators have suggested that there is, on the contrary, considerable scope for protection of ideas provided merely that they have been reduced to writing or some other material form. Laddie, Prescott, and Vitoria, for example, identify the 'pithy catch-phrase' that 'there is no copyright in ideas or information but only in the form in which they are expressed' and comment:

A moment's thought will reveal that the maxim is obscure, or in its broadest sense suspect. For example, in the case of a book the ideas it contains are necessarily expressed in words. Hence, if it were really true that the copyright is confined to the form of expression, one would expect to find that anyone was at liberty to borrow the contents of the book provided he took care not to employ the same or similar language. This is not so, of course. Thus, it is an infringement of the copyright to make a version of a novel in which the story or action is conveyed wholly by means of pictures; or to turn it into a play, although not a line of dialogue is similar to any sentence in the book. Again, a translation of a work into another language can be an infringement; yet, since the form of expression is necessarily different—indeed,

---

[227] 26 F3d 1335 (5th Cir, 1994).
[228] Ibid 1343.
[229] See, eg, *Cognotec Services Ltd v Morgan Guarantee Trust Co of New York*, 862 F Supp 45 at 49–51 (SDNY, 1994); *Mitek Holdings Inc v ARCE Engineering Co Inc*, 864 F Supp 1568 at 1577–8 (SD Fla, 1994); *Bateman v Mnemonics Inc*, 79 F 3d 1532 (11th Cir, 1996); and *Country Kids 'n Slicks Inc v Sheen*, 77 F 3d 1280 at 1288–9 (10th Cir, 1996).

if it is turned into a language such as Chinese the translation will consist of ideograms—the only connecting factor must be the detailed ideas and information.[230]

Laddie, Prescott, and Vitoria also note that most of the cases commonly cited in support of the exclusion of ideas from protection were decided prior to the 1956 Act, many indeed prior to the 1911 Act, and would probably be decided differently today.[231] Similar scepticism about the blanket exclusion of ideas from copyright has been expressed in judicial circles. In *LB (Plastics) Ltd v Swish Products Ltd*, Lord Hailsham of St Marylebone LC observed:

. . . it is trite law that there is no copyright in ideas . . . But, of course, as the late Professor Joad used to observe, it all depends on what you mean by 'ideas'. What the respondents in fact copied from the appellants was no mere general idea.[232]

Along similar lines, in *Plix Products Ltd v Frank M Winstone (Merchants)*,[233] a case concerning infringement of artistic copyright, Pritchard J of the High Court of New Zealand suggested that the so-called 'idea–expression dichotomy' can perhaps best be understood by distinguishing two different kinds, or levels, of 'ideas'. The first type of idea, 'the general idea or basic concept of the work', cannot be protected by copyright. Copyright can, however, subsist in the second type, namely 'the ideas which are applied in the exercise of giving expression to basic concepts'. As Pritchard J then observed:

The difficulty, of course, is to determine just where the general concept ends and the exercise of expressing the concept begins . . .The basic idea (or concept) is not necessarily simple—it may be complex. It may be something innovative; or it may be commonplace, utilitarian or banal. The way the author treats the subject, the forms he uses to express the basic concept, may range from the crude and simplistic to the ornate, complicated—and involving the collation and application of a great number of constructive ideas. It is in this area that the author expends the skill and industry which (even though they may be slight) give the work its originality and entitle him to copyright. Anyone is free to use the basic idea—unless, of course, it is a novel invention that is protected by the grant of a patent. But no one can appropriate the forms or shapes evolved by the author in the process of giving expression to the basic idea. So he who seeks to make a product of the same description as that in which another owns copyright must tread with care.[234]

This analysis has interesting implications for the debates relating to the development of compatible software by means of reverse engineering, and the emulation of the look and feel of the user interfaces of popular software packages.

---

[230] H Laddie, P Prescott, and M Vitoria, *The Modern Law of Copyright and Designs*, 4th edn (London: Butterworths, 2007) 3.76, footnotes omitted.

[231] Ibid 3.77–3.78.

[232] [1979] FSR 145 at 159.

[233] [1986] FSR 63.

[234] Ibid 93–4.

Since the mid-1990s there has been a growing body of case law indicating that UK courts are tending, like the High Court of New Zealand, to be concerned more with whether a significant amount of an author's labour and skill has been misappropriated, than with whether what has been taken is 'merely' an idea. The first full English trial for alleged infringement of copyright in software, however, served to muddy the waters somewhat before this trend emerged.

That case was *John Richardson Computers Ltd v Flanders* (*'Richardson'*).[235] The case concerned allegations of literal and semi-literal copying of the claimant's program as evidenced at the user interface level. The defendant had worked for the claimant when the claimant was developing his program and had later developed his own. The programs were for use by pharmacists and had a number of idiosyncratic user features and routines in common. Ferris J referred to US case law and commented:

> . . . at the stage at which the substantiality of any copying falls to be assessed in an English case the question which has to be answered, in relation to the originality of the plaintiff's [claimant's] program and the separation of an idea from its expression, is essentially the same question as the US court was addressing in Computer Associates v Altai. In my judgment it would be right to adopt a similar approach in England.[236]

In deciding the case he drew on the filtration and comparison parts of *Computer Associates v Altai*,[237] but rejected the abstraction test as inappropriate in the circumstances. The reliance he placed on US law, which is, after all, based on a statutory bar on the grant of copyright protection for ideas, was somewhat surprising. Such an approach might result in computer programs being treated differently from other kinds of work. This would be an undesirable outcome both in terms of the functioning of copyright law and for the computer industry in its production of multimedia products. Moreover, the *Richardson* case was evidentially somewhat unclear. Ferris J did not attempt to compare the codes of the two programs, relying entirely on visual evidence at the user interface level. Although understandable given the complexities of the case and the genuine difficulty of comparing code, this tended to obscure what the work in issue really was.

The following year in *Ibcos Computers Ltd v Barclays Mercantile Highland Finance Ltd* (*'Ibcos'*),[238] Jacob J took a markedly different approach. He rejected the notion that US precedents should be applied by the English courts, instead favouring a more traditional copyright analysis based on English legal principles. The facts were somewhat simpler than in *Richardson*, involving the literal or semi-literal copying of source code in an agricultural dealer system. Jacob J discussed at length not only the *Richardson* case, but also an earlier interlocutory judgment,

---

[235] [1993] FSR 497.
[236] Ibid.
[237] 982 F2d 693 (1992).
[238] [1994] FSR 275.

Total Information Processing Systems Ltd v Daman Ltd.[239] In that case Paul Baker QC, sitting as a deputy High Court judge, had not been prepared to find prima facie evidence of infringement notwithstanding admitted copying. He gave a preliminary ruling that there was no arguable case that the claimant had infringed copyright by copying various field and record specifications in the defendant's costing program. The defendant claimed, first, that the three-program package was a compilation, copyright in which was infringed when the claimant substituted its payroll program for the defendant's. Secondly, the defendant claimed that the copying of the specification of the files and records from the costing program infringed copyright in that program. The judge rejected the argument that the compilation was protected, partly because:

. . . to accord it copyright protection would lead to great inconvenience. It would mean that the copyright owners of one of the components could not interface with another similar program to that of the other components without the licence of the compiler.[240]

Regarding the specification that had been copied, he ruled that:

The part copied can be likened to a table of contents. It would be very unusual that that part of a book could be described as a substantial part of it. The specification in high-level language of fields and records in the data division tells one little or nothing about the costing program and so, in my judgment, cannot be regarded as a substantial part of it.[241]

Both of these conclusions are curious. Regarding the first, it has never been a criterion for copyright protection that the partial monopoly afforded by a copyright must not lead to 'great inconvenience'. In *Ibcos* Jacob J commented:

I cannot agree. Of course the owner of the copyright in an individual program could interface his program with that of another. What he could not do is to put his program into an original compilation of another without that other's licence. The same is true of any other copyright works, be they poems, songs or whatever.[242]

Regarding the second of Mr Baker's conclusions, it seems quite likely that a detailed table of contents for a book could constitute not only a substantial part of a work but might even be a work in its own right. Similarly, a program specification could qualify as either a substantial part of a work or as a discrete work. Jacob J commented:

Very often the working out of a reasonably detailed arrangement of topics, sub-topics and sub-sub-topics is the key to a successful work of non-fiction. I see no reason why the taking of that could not amount to an infringement. Likewise, there may be a considerable degree of skill involved in setting up the data division of a program. In practice, this is done with the

---

[239] [1992] FSR 171.
[240] Ibid 179.
[241] Ibid 180–1.
[242] [1994] FSR 275, 290.

operating division in mind and its construction may well involve enough skill, labour and, I add, judgment, for it to be considered a substantial part of the program as a whole.[243]

Paul Baker QC further stated that there could be no copyright in the expression of an idea if the expression has a function and there is only one or a limited number of ways of achieving it. Jacob J took the view that, unlike US law, English law does protect certain types of ideas. Rather:

The true position is that where an 'idea' is sufficiently general, then even if an original work embodies it, the mere taking of that idea will not infringe. But if the 'idea' is detailed, then there may be infringement. It is a question of degree. The same applies whether the work is fictional or not, and whether visual or literary.[244]

Paul Baker QC also suggested that copyright could not subsist in source code because the industry makes copious efforts to protect itself via confidentiality. Jacob J disagreed, saying:

I do not understand this observation . . . Because people keep confidential material which would be of considerable use to pirates is no reason for saying that copyright does not protect it . . . I unhesitatingly say that source code can be the subject of copyright.[245]

Moving on to discuss *Richardson*, Jacob J noted that Ferris J had supported the US approach of looking for the core of protectable expression and separating it from the unprotectable idea, leaving only 'expression' to be taken into account in determining substantiality. Jacob J found this method unhelpful. Instead, he returned to a more traditional English legal analysis, whereby ideas are not precluded from protection and the test is a question of degree, a 'good guide' being:

. . . the notion of overborrowing of the skill, labour and judgment which went into the copyright work. Going via the complication of the concept of a 'core of protectable expression' merely complicates the matter so far as our law is concerned. It is likely to lead to an overcitation of US authority based on a statute different from ours.[246]

Jacob J's straightforward approach towards finding substantiality and his rejection of some of Paul Baker's views in *Total Information Processing Systems Ltd v Daman Ltd* were well received in the industry.

Further light has been shed on the approach of the English courts to the scope for protection of ideas under copyright law in four recent cases, though the last of these has been referred to the Court of Justice of the European Union. These are *Baigent and Leigh v The Random House Group Ltd* ('*Baigent and Leigh*'),[247] *Navitaire Inc*

---

[243] *Ibcos*, 303.
[244] Ibid 291.
[245] Ibid 296.
[246] Ibid 302.
[247] [2006] EWHC 719.

v easyJet Airline Co and Bulletproof Technologies Inc ('Navitaire'),[248] *Nova Productions Ltd v Mazooma Games Ltd and Nova Productions Ltd v Bell Fruit Games Ltd ('Nova')*;[249] and *SAS Institute Inc v World Programming Ltd*.[250]

In *Baigent and Leigh*,[251] Mr Justice Peter Smith held that the *Da Vinci Code* ('DVC'), a popular and controversial novel by Dan Brown, did not infringe the copyright in the claimants' book, *The Holy Blood and The Holy Grail* ('HBHG'). At the heart of the case was an allegation that Dan Brown had taken one or more 'Central Themes', comprising at least 15 elements, of HBHG and that this constituted infringement of copyright by non-literal copying. Most of the old issues, and many of the prior cases, regarding protection of ideas under copyright law were rehearsed in the trial and the judgment. The court stressed that:

. . . ideas and facts of themselves cannot be protected but the architecture or structure or way in which they are presented can be. It is therefore not enough to point to ideas or facts that exist in the Central Themes that are to be found in HBHG and DVC. It must be shown that the architecture or structure is substantially copied.[252]

After analysing HBHG and DVC in considerable detail, and struggling to disguise his contempt for both books and for more than one of the witnesses, the judge rejected the action in sweeping terms. Regarding the Central Theme(s), he concluded that the claimants had in fact started with the plot of DVC and had worked backwards to try to find evidence of plagiarism, creating the Central Theme in HBHG to do so. It is important to note, however, that the case did not fail for want of protection for the structure of HBHG, or for the complex arrangement of the ideas in that earlier book. Rather, it failed because of a fundamental lack of evidence of actual copying. This was notwithstanding that the judge was satisfied that Dan Brown, and his wife Blythe who undertook most of the research for DVC, relied heavily on HBHG in writing DVC.

Navitaire[253] was an action for infringement of copyright in the software underlying an airline reservation system. The airline easyJet retained BulletProof, working closely with easyJet's IT department, to develop a system called 'eRes' which was intended to have a user interface which was 'substantially indistinguishable' from the claimant's system, 'OpenRes'. It was not alleged that the underlying source code was copied and it was accepted that the underlying software in the two systems was completely different, except that the inputs and outputs were very similar. The central allegation was that 'non-textual copying' occurred in three ways:

---

[248] [2004] EWHC 1725.
[249] [2006] EWHC 24, [2007] EWCA Civ 219.
[250] [2010] EWHC 1829 (Ch).
[251] [2006] EWHC 719.
[252] Ibid para 227.
[253] [2004] EWHC 1725.

The first was the adoption of the 'look and feel' of the running OpenRes software. The second . . . was a detailed copying of many of the individual commands entered by the user to achieve particular results. The third was the copying of certain of the results, in the form of screen displays and of 'reports' displayed on the screen in response to prescribed instructions.[254]

Pumfrey J dealt with the claims relating to protection of commands, screens, and reports, before turning to the database claims. As regards individual command names, he applied the *Exxon* case[255] and held that such basic command names lacked the necessary qualities of a literary work.[256] He then found that complex commands, such as instructions to check availability of seats on a particular route on a particular date, could not be protected either as they in fact constituted a computer language which only made any sense when used by a human operator. Although the CDPA 1988 does not explicitly exclude computer languages from copyright protection, one of the recitals to the Software Directive states that 'to the extent that logic, algorithms and programming languages comprise ideas and principles those ideas and principles are not protected under this Directive'. In this connection, Pumfrey J commented:

The Software Directive is a harmonising measure. I must construe any implementing provision in accordance with it: if the implementing provision means what it should, the Directive alone need be consulted: if it departs from the Directive, then the latter has been incorrectly transposed into UK law.[257]

This same presumed statutory bar on protection for programming languages was also a barrier to the claim for protection for the various commands as compilations. Alternatively, that claim failed because the collection of commands was ad hoc and there was insufficient evidence of skill and labour to demonstrate that there was a protected compilation. As for the screens, the judge found that the character-based screens were tables that were not protected. However, he held that the graphical user interface ('GUI') screens were protected as artistic works and had in fact been infringed.[258]

   One of the more interesting features of the *Navitaire* judgment is the discussion of whether there might be a sustainable claim for infringement of copyright in relation to 'something else'. This 'something else' was at various times in the trial called the 'business logic', 'non-technical copying', or the 'dynamic user interface'.[259] Having reviewed the principles of idea versus expression, and after getting limited assistance from either *Richardson* or *Ibcos*, Pumfrey J observed:

---

[254] *Navitaire*, para 3.

[255] *Exxon Corp v Exxon Insurance Consultants International Ltd* [1982] RPC 69.

[256] *Navitaire Inc v easyJet Airline Co and Bulletproof Technologies Inc* [2004] EWHC 1725, paras 78–9.

[257] Ibid para 88. In support of this approach to statutory interpretation he cited *Marleasing* [1990] ECR I-4135 and *Customs and Excise Commissioners v Century Life plc* [2001] STC 38.

[258] Ibid paras 90–9.

[259] Ibid paras 107–31.

. . . two completely different computer programs can produce an identical result: not a result identical at some level of abstraction but identical at any level of abstraction. This is so even if the author of one has no access at all to the other but only to its results. The analogy with a plot is for this reason a poor one. It is a poor one for other reasons as well. To say these programs possess a plot is precisely like saying that the book of instructions for a booking clerk acting manually has a plot: but a book of instructions has no theme, no events, and does not have a narrative flow. Nor does a computer program, particularly one whose behaviour depends upon the history of its inputs in any given transaction. It does not have a plot, merely a series of pre-defined operations intended to achieve the desired result in response to the requests of the customer.[260]

Starting from these assumptions it was perhaps not surprising that the court was unimpressed by Navitaire's arguments that it was entitled to copyright protection for the 'business logic' of its system. The court reached the following conclusion on the point:

Navitaire's computer program invites input in a manner excluded from copyright protection, outputs its results in a form excluded from copyright protection and creates a record of a reservation in the name of a particular passenger on a particular flight. What is left when the interface aspects of the case are disregarded is the business function of carrying out the transaction and creating the record, because none of the code was read or copied by the defendants . . . I do not come to this conclusion with any regret. If it is the policy of the Software Directive to exclude both computer languages and the underlying ideas of the interfaces from protection, then it should not be possible to circumvent these exclusions by seeking to identify some overall function or functions that it is the sole purpose of the interface to invoke and relying on those instead. As a matter of policy also, it seems to me that to permit the 'business logic' of a program to attract protection through the literary copyright afforded to the program itself is an unjustifiable extension of copyright protection into a field where I am far from satisfied that it is appropriate.[261]

From the perspective of software developers and rights owners this seems to be a highly unsympathetic stance compared to that adopted by, for example, courts in the USA. Many software products are in fact highly structured and are based on very detailed functional specifications. Needless to say, the stakes can be high in software litigation as investments in software development can be very substantial indeed. If, however, the approach of the High Court in *Navitaire* becomes established it appears that the scope for using copyright in the UK to protect against non-literal copying will be very limited.

Before turning to *Nova*, however, one further aspect of *Navitaire* should be mentioned. The court also considered certain complex issues in relation to the OpenRes database. Following a detailed discussion, Pumfrey J concluded that Navitaire had failed to prove infringement of copyright in the underlying structure, or 'schema' of

---

[260] *Navitaire*, para 125.
[261] Ibid para 130.

its database, principally because easyJet had no access to the source code. Copying did, however, occur during the course of data migration but this was permitted under section 50D of the CDPA 1988 which allows certain acts necessary for access to and use of a database, though only in certain respects.[262]

Nova concerned alleged infringement of artistic, literary, and dramatic copyrights in Nova's arcade video game called 'Pocket Money'. As regards subsistence of copyright, Kitchen J held that the bitmap files which created visual effects when the game was played were graphic works and were protected as artistic works. Similarly, the composite frames that were built up as a game was played were artistic works similar to the frames of a cartoon.[263] The program embodied in Pocket Money was a literary work and the design notes created by the programmer, Mr Jones, constituted preparatory design material for a computer program which were therefore also protected (as expressly provided for under s 3(1)(c) of the CDPA 1988).[264]

Nova also argued that the visual experience generated by Pocket Money was a dramatic work. The court rejected this for various reasons including that it was not intended to be performed in front of an audience and that the source code was a set of instructions which dictated the way the game must be played and what would appear on the screen and was not a record of any dramatic work.[265] A claim for infringement of film copyright was withdrawn at first instance but the allegation was formally reserved for argument on appeal, as discussed below. Nova conceded this point in the High Court on the basis that it was not alleging that the defendants had copied its game by photographic means as apparently required for an infringement of film copyright since *Norowzian v Arks (No 1)*.[266]

Having dealt with copyright subsistence issues, Kitchen J turned to questions of infringement. He stressed that the copied features must be a substantial part of the copied work but need not be a substantial part of the defendant's work. This meant that the overall appearance of the defendant's work might be very different while nevertheless infringing. While somewhat different from the three-step 'abstraction-filtration-comparison' test established in the US *Altai* case (see discussion in section 7.5.5 above), he proposed a series of principles to be respected in determining whether infringement has occurred. The first step is to identify the alleged similarities and differences, taking care to disregard those which are 'commonplace, unoriginal, or consist of general ideas'. The second step, assuming copying is established, is to determine whether what has been taken is all or a substantial part of the copyright work. A third principle he laid down is that copying should be assessed on

---

[262] *Navitaire*, paras 272–85. See, further, Chapter 8, section 8.5.3.
[263] *Nova Productions Ltd v Mazooma Games Ltd and Nova Productions Ltd v Bell Fruit Games Ltd* [2006] EWHC 24 (Ch), paras 98–106.
[264] Ibid paras 107–9.
[265] Ibid paras 110–19.
[266] [1998] FSR 394. *Nova*, para 120.

a holistic, not piecemeal, basis. Having said that, each separate copyright work in relation to which infringement is disputed should be assessed separately.[267]

As in *Navitaire*, the court in *Nova* had to assess whether indirect copying had occurred. In relation to one of the games in issue, Kitchen J made express reference to the approach taken by Pumfrey J in *Navitaire* and concluded:

Nothing has been taken in terms of program code or program architecture. Such similarities that exist in the outputs do not mean that there are any similarities in the software. Further, what has been taken is a combination of a limited number of generalised ideas which are reflected in the output of the program. They do not form a substantial part of the computer program itself. Consideration of Article 1(2) of the Software Directive confirms this position. Ideas and principles which underlie any element of a computer program are not protected by copyright under the Directive.[268]

On appeal,[269] Jacob LJ accepted that the individual frames stored in the computer memory were graphic works and therefore protected under section 4(1) of the CDPA 1988. However, Mazooma had not substantially reproduced the corresponding screen in Nova's game.[270] The judge also rejected, because it had no foundation, the claim that Mazooma copied the artistic work consisting in the dynamic re-posting created by the 'in-time' movement of the cue and the power meter.[271] Finally Jacob LJ rejected the argument that, notwithstanding *Navitaire*, copying the function of a program to achieve the same result is a misappropriation of the skill and labour in designing the original program.[272] The judge underlined the fact that design materials may be protected by copyright even when they consist of ideas and principles, but what is protected in relation to a computer program is the expression of the ideas and principles in a literary work (the program), not the ideas and principles themselves.[273]

There are currently three trends that might result, generally, in a weakening of copyright protection for software. One trend which, if developed, would significantly weaken the scope of copyright protection for software is reliance on the principle of non-derogation from grant as a basis for permitting what would otherwise be infringing acts. The limited 'repair right' recognized by the House of Lords in *British Leyland Motor Corp Ltd v Armstrong Patents Co Ltd*[274] was applied by the Official Referee's Court in *Saphena Computing Ltd v Allied Collection Agencies Ltd*[275] to permit acts necessary for software maintenance which would

---

[267] *Nova*, paras 121–8.
[268] Ibid para 248.
[269] *Nova Productions Ltd v Mazooma Games Ltd and Nova Productions Ltd v Bell Fruit Games Ltd* [2007] EWCA Civ 219 (14 March 2007).
[270] Ibid para 18.
[271] Ibid para 16.
[272] Ibid para 48.
[273] Ibid para 50.
[274] [1986] AC 577.
[275] [1995] FSR 616.

normally infringe copyright.[276] However, Jacob LJ considered a similar issue in the *Ibcos* case and held that the right to repair held to exist in *British Leyland* could not be relied upon by analogy to establish a right to copy file transfer utilities.[277]

A second basis for a weakening of the monopoly given by copyright would rest on a development of competition law principles. How would a UK court respond if asked to decide on the scope of copyright protection in circumstances where, for example, a single set of machine instructions was the only way to achieve a particular functional result, such as interfacing with a particular item of hardware or software? In such a case, it might be possible for the court to conclude that the subject matter in question is not protected by copyright due to lack of originality. However, a particular interface specification or procedure may be highly original and the result of considerable labour and skill. As has already been established, UK courts cannot invoke a 'merger doctrine' as a justification for excluding material from copyright on the ground that idea and expression have merged. In practice, however, a person who sought to use copyright as a basis for monopolizing a de facto industry standard might be vulnerable to challenge under UK or EU competition law.

A third, and related, consideration is the Software Directive.[278] Article 1(2) of the Software Directive requires all EU Member States to protect programs as literary works but to exclude from protection 'Ideas and principles which underlie any element of a computer program, including those which underlie its interfaces'. The Copyright (Computer Programs) Regulations 1992 contained no reference to the exclusion of ideas from copyright protection. This was presumably because the UK Government believed that ideas were already excluded from protection as a result of judicial pronouncements to that effect. More than a decade later, the Copyright and Related Rights Regulations 2003 introduced a new section 50BA into the CDPA 1988 which, while still not excluding explicitly from protection ideas and principles underlying programs, at least confirmed the legitimacy of observation, study, and testing of a program by a licensed user during normal use to ascertain the ideas and principles underlying the program. Moreover, this section renders void any attempt to prohibit such analysis by contract.[279]

---

[276] *British Leyland Motor Corp Ltd v Armstrong Patents Co Ltd* concerned the protection of the designs of functional objects, spare parts for cars, through artistic copyright in the underlying design drawings. This basis of claim has been severely restricted by the CDPA 1988. On appeal in *Saphena Computing Ltd v Allied Collection Agencies Ltd* [1995] FSR 616 the Court of Appeal did not comment on the official referee's finding. See also *Canon Kabushiki Kaisha v Green Cartridge Co (Hong Kong) Ltd* [1997] FSR 817.

[277] See also *Mars UK Ltd v Teknowledge Ltd (No 2) The Times*, 23 June 1999, where it was held that *British Leyland* had been decided under the Copyright Act 1956 and there was no longer room for such a common law exception because there was now a complete statutory code to cover any exceptions.

[278] Council Directive (EEC) 91/250.

[279] CDPA 1988, s 50BA(1) and (2).

In *SAS Institute Inc v World Programming Ltd*,[280] SAS alleged that World Programming had infringed the copyright in various manuals and quick reference guides and had thereby indirectly infringed the copyright in SAS's software. The court found that the copyright in the SAS manuals (but not the quick reference guides) was infringed by the creation of manuals by World Programming. However, as regards whether the software itself was infringing Arnold J elected to refer several issues of interpretation to the European Court of Justice. Although the precise questions have not yet been formulated, they will concern. the 'true' interpretation of Article 1(2) of the Software Directive[281] as to whether copyright in computer programs protects against:

(a) programming languages being copied;[282]

(b) interfaces being copied where this can be achieved without decompiling the object code;[283]

(c) the functions of the programs being copied.[284]

Moreover, the judge suggested that guidance from the ECJ is also required to determine whether the interpretation of Article 1(2) of the Software Directive also applies to Article 2(a) of the Information Society Directive; and the interpretation of Article 5(3) of the Software Directive.

However, Arnold J commented that without such a reference to the Court of Justice, he would have found there to be no infringement of copyright in the computer program due to copying of functionality and would have held that World Programming was protected by Article 5 of the Software Directive while studying the functioning of SAS's software in order to determine the ideas and principles underlying it.[285] Finally, Arnold J deemed the data file formats to be interfaces and therefore not protectable.

7.5.7 Decompilation of computer programs

During the Software Directive's turbulent passage through the EU legislative process, by far the most contentious issue concerned the new right to be given to users permitting them to decompile a program where necessary to achieve the interoperability of that program with another program. The complex compromise agreed by the principal protagonists, after many months of heated debate and lobbying, is now enshrined in Article 6 of the Directive. The wording of the Directive is altered

---

[280] [2010] EWHC 1829 (Ch).
[281] Ibid para 332.
[282] Ibid paras 211–18.
[283] Ibid paras 219–27.
[284] Ibid paras 228–38.
[285] Thus following *Navitaire Inc v easyJet Airline Co and Bulletproof Technologies Inc* [2004] EWHC 1725, and *Nova Productions Ltd v Mazooma Games Ltd and Nova Productions Ltd v Bell Fruit Games Ltd* [2006] EWHC 24, [2007] EWCA Civ 219. The two cases are discussed above.

somewhat in the Copyright (Computer Programs) Regulations 1992 but in effect, the provisions of Article 6(1) and (2) are implemented in full. The Regulations state that it is not an infringement of copyright for a 'lawful user' of a copy of a computer program which is 'expressed in a low level language' to convert it into a higher level language, so copying it, provided two conditions are met. These are that such decompilation is necessary 'to obtain the information necessary to create an independent program which can be operated with the program decompiled or with another program', which is defined as the 'permitted objective', and that 'the information so obtained is not used for any purpose other than the permitted objective'.

Exercise of the decompilation right is hedged about by four further restrictions. The Regulations state that the two conditions described above are not met if the lawful user has the information necessary to achieve the permitted objective readily available to him; does not confine decompilation to acts necessary to achieve the permitted objective; supplies information obtained by decompiling to a third party to whom it is not necessary to supply it to achieve the permitted objective; or uses the information to create a program which is substantially similar in its expression to the decompiled program or to do any act restricted by copyright.[286]

Consistent with Article 9(1) of the Directive, the Regulations render void any provisions which purport to prohibit or restrict the decompilation right.

7.5.8 Back-up copies of computer programs

Article 5(2) of the Software Directive provides that: 'The making of a back-up copy by a person having a right to use the computer program may not be prevented by contract insofar as it is necessary for that use.' The Copyright (Computer Programs) Regulations 1992 have implemented Article 5(2). Section 50A of the CDPA 1988 permits the making of an additional copy of a program by a lawful user 'which it is necessary for him to have for the purposes of his lawful use'. In practice, most PC software must be loaded on to the hard disk of a PC before it can be run. The loading process often entails the 'explosion' of compressed files and the installation of the package for a particular configuration of hardware and software. The making of a back-up copy, in the sense of a verbatim copy of the original media, may be unnecessary, as the original CD or other media will be available for back-up purposes. Thus, the back-up exemption may be of limited application.

7.5.9 Second-hand copies of works in electronic form

Section 56 of the CDPA 1988 contains a complex and somewhat convoluted statement of the rights to be enjoyed by a person taking a transfer from the original

---

[286] CDPA 1988, s 50B(3) inserted by the Copyright (Computer Programs) Regulations 1992 (SI 1992/3233), reg 8.

purchaser of a copy of a program or other work in electronic form. The provision is applicable where a copy of such a work 'has been purchased on terms which, expressly or impliedly or by virtue of any rule of law, allow the purchaser to copy the work, or to adapt it or make copies of an adaptation, in connection with his use of it'. Subject to any express terms to the contrary, where the copy is transferred to a third party, that person is entitled to do anything with the copy which the original purchaser was permitted to do. From the moment of transfer, however, any copy or adaptation retained by the original purchaser will be treated as an infringing copy. The same rules apply to any subsequent transfers made by the new owner and that person's successors in title.

Section 56 is not a model of clarity. Taking its application to computer programs, packaged software is typically distributed with a licence 'agreement' in which the software producer purports to retain title to part or all of the product. Where title to the physical copy of the program does not pass, it will make no sense to speak of the 'purchaser' of the copy. Moreover, the scope for inferring licences in this area is quite uncertain and thus the reference to terms which the purchaser has the benefit of 'impliedly or by virtue of any rule of law' is not particularly illuminating. In practice, quite apart from the theoretical question of whether or not there is a 'purchaser', it is likely to continue to be common for computer programs, and many other works published in electronic form, to be distributed with an express prohibition, or at least restriction, on transfers to third parties. In all such cases, the operation of section 56 will be completely pre-empted.

7.6 MORAL RIGHTS

7.6.1 The nature of moral rights

The Berne Union, of which the UK is a member, provides for its members to give authors various 'moral rights'. Such rights are to be personal to the author or creator of a work and are to be capable of exercise independently of the economic exploitation rights in the work. For the first time in the UK, the CDPA 1988 gave the author of a work or director of a film the right, in certain circumstances, to be identified as such (s 77). Relevant circumstances include commercial publication of the work or any adaptation of it. This right is otherwise known as the right of 'paternity'. Authors and directors also have the right to object to 'derogatory treatment' of their works (s 80(1)), which right is otherwise known as the right of 'integrity'. Treatment of a work will be deemed derogatory 'if it amounts to distortion or mutilation of the work or is otherwise prejudicial to the honour or reputation of the author or director' (s 80(2)). Two other moral rights give protection against false attribution of a work,[287] and the right to privacy of certain photographs and films (s 85). With the

---

[287] ie, the right not to have a work wrongly attributed to one (CDPA 1988, s 84).

exception of the false attribution right, which expires 20 years after a person's death, all of the moral rights continue to subsist for as long as copyright subsists in the work in question (s 86). The rest of the discussion here will be focused on the rights of paternity and integrity as they apply to literary, dramatic, musical, and artistic works.

7.6.2 Restrictions on scope

The right of paternity must be asserted in writing and will in most cases only bind third parties who have notice of it (s 78). In the case of works created in the course of employment, the right does not apply to anything done by, or with the authority of, the employer or any subsequent owner of copyright in the work (s 79(3)). The right of integrity is also severely cut back in relation to works created by employees, copyright in which originally vested in their employers (s 82(1)).[288] Neither right applies, in any event, in relation to computer programs and computer-generated works (ss 79(2) and 81(2)).

These exclusions appear, at first sight, to abrogate moral rights as they apply to works produced by the computer industry. Moral rights will, nevertheless, have significant implications for the computer and related industries and those who work in them. As already noted in this chapter, software packages, for example, are much more than computer programs for copyright purposes. While moral rights will not be available in respect of any programs and computer-generated works incorporated in a package nor any work owned automatically by an employer, moral rights will be available in respect of many other works produced on a commissioning basis. For example, a freelance technical author would be able to assert the right of paternity and object to unjust modification of published manuals or other documentation, and a freelance artist may make such claims with regard to published artwork. Moreover, moral rights will be applicable to many works that are included in databases and in that context it is difficult to see how the right of paternity could be exercised without becoming unduly cumbersome. Protection against false attribution applies to all categories of works but is less likely to cause problems in practice.

7.6.3 Consents and waivers

Although moral rights are 'inalienable' and thus cannot be assigned like the economic rights in a work,[289] a person entitled to moral rights can forgo the right to exercise the rights in part or completely. In general, it is not an infringement of

---

[288] The right will only apply if the author '(a) is identified at the time of the relevant act, or (b) has previously been identified in or on published copies of the work' (CDPA 1988, s 82(2)).

[289] Although they do form part of an author's estate on death and consequently can pass to third parties under a will or on intestacy (CDPA 1988, s 95).

moral rights to do anything to which the rightholder has consented. Moreover, any of the moral rights 'may be waived by instrument in writing signed by the person giving up the right'. Such waivers may relate to specific works or to works generally, may be conditional or unconditional, and may be made subject to revocation (s 87). Given the potential difficulties that were identified in section 7.6.2, it is not surprising that many organizations include express consents or waivers of moral rights in their standard terms of business for commissioned works.

7.6.4 Remedies

Infringements of moral rights are actionable as breaches of statutory duty owed to the person entitled to the right (s 103(1)). In relation to infringement of the right to object to derogatory treatment of a work, a court may grant an injunction requiring a disclaimer to be given, for example on publication, dissociating the author from the treatment of the work (s 103(2)). In relation to the right of paternity, a court must, in considering what remedy should be given for an infringement, take into account any delay in asserting the right (s 78(5)). Both of these qualifications on remedies have the effect of further limiting the potential commercial leverage which moral rights may confer on an author. Where, for example, a publisher has incurred considerable expense over a period of time in preparing a work for publication, instead of stopping publication because of derogatory treatment a court may merely order that a disclaimer be printed. Likewise, the author's right of paternity may effectively be undermined as a result of any delay in asserting the right.

7.7 CIVIL REMEDIES, CRIMINAL SANCTIONS, AND PROCEDURAL MATTERS

7.7.1 Civil remedies

Copyright is a property right, and where infringement has been proved, the copyright owner can, subject to certain special rules, benefit from 'all such relief . . . as is available in respect of the infringement of any other property right' (s 96). In practice, the principal remedies are injunctions to prevent further breaches of copyright, damages for breach of copyright, and orders for delivery up of infringing copies. Other remedies include accounts of profits (used relatively rarely because of the difficulty of proving the precise profits made) and orders for disposal of infringing copies which have been seized or delivered up to a claimant (see generally ss 96–106 and 113–15).

Various court orders can be obtained at the pre-trial stage, in some circumstances without the alleged infringer being given any warning or opportunity to make representations to the court. One such order that has been used with particular success against audio, video, and software pirates is the 'search order'.[290] Such an order can authorize a claimant to enter a defendant's premises, without prior warning, to seize evidentiary material which might otherwise be tampered with or disappear before trial. This is obviously a powerful remedy capable of abuse in the hands of overenthusiastic claimants and the courts now supervise its use quite strictly.[291]

Whilst a final injunction may be granted at trial, it is quite common in cases of alleged software copyright infringement for an 'interim' injunction to be granted in pre-trial proceedings. An injunction may be prohibitory, for example enjoining a defendant from copying or in any way dealing with the material that is the subject of the dispute.[292] Alternatively, or in addition, an injunction may be mandatory, for example requiring delivery up of source code pending trial.[293]

As a general rule, damages for copyright infringement are intended to compensate a claimant for actual loss incurred as a result of the infringement. This might typically be calculated on the basis of royalties which would have been payable to the claimant had the defendant, instead of infringing copyright, obtained a licence for the acts in question. The CDPA 1988 specifies one set of circumstances in which damages must not be awarded, and one in which they may be increased beyond the compensatory level. The former arises where it is shown that the defendant did not know and had no reason to believe that copyright subsisted in the work in question at the time of infringement. In such circumstances, 'the plaintiff [claimant] is not entitled to damages against him, but without prejudice to any other remedy' (s 97(1)). In other cases, however, the court may award 'such additional damages as the justice of the case may require' in all the circumstances, with particular reference to '(a) the flagrancy of the infringement, and (b) any benefit accruing to the defendant by reason of the infringement' (s 97(2)).[294]

---

[290] Formerly called an 'Anton Piller order' after the case in which it was first obtained, *Anton Piller KG v Manufacturing Processes Ltd* [1976] Ch 55. For an example of the grant of such an order in a case of alleged software piracy, see *Gates v Swift* [1981] FSR 57.

[291] In another software copyright case, *Systematica Ltd v London Computer Centre Ltd* [1983] FSR 313 at 316, Whitford J observed that: 'A situation is developing where I think rather too free a use is being made by plaintiffs [claimants] of the Anton Piller provision.' Subsequently, in *Columbia Picture Industries v Robinson* [1986] FSR 367 at 439, Scott J commented 'that the practice of the court has allowed the balance to swing too far in favour of the plaintiffs [claimants] and that Anton Piller orders have been too readily granted and with insufficient safeguards for respondents'. The court laid down a number of procedural safeguards which should be complied with to ensure minimum protection for defendants.

[292] eg, *Raindrop Data Systems Ltd v Systematics Ltd* [1988] FSR 354; *Leisure Data v Bell* [1988] FSR 367.

[293] eg, *Redwood Music Ltd v Chappell & Co Ltd* [1982] RPC 109.

[294] In *Nottinghamshire Healthcare NHS Trust v News Group Newspapers Ltd* (14 March 2002), a photograph of a patient was published by *The Sun* newspaper in breach of copyright. Under s 96 damages of £450 were awarded on the basis that this would have been the agency fee payable if the photograph had been published with consent. A further £10,000 was awarded under s 97 as additional damages. Factors taken into consideration in reaching this figure included the fact that the photograph was stolen; the conduct of the defendant (in particular destruction of evidence); and failure to apologize to the claimant.

7.7.2 Criminal sanctions

The CDPA 1988 sets out a number of categories of criminal copyright infringement which, in general, are intended to penalize those who deliberately infringe copyright with a view to commercial gain. Specifically, it is an offence, if done without a licence, to manufacture for sale or hire, import into the UK other than for private and domestic use, distribute in the course of business or otherwise 'to such an extent as to affect prejudicially' the rights of the copyright owner, an article which the offender knows to be, or has reason to believe to be, an infringing copy of a work (s 107(1)(a), (b), (d)(iv), and (e)). On summary conviction the penalties for such an offence are imprisonment for up to six months and a fine not exceeding the statutory maximum, or both (s 107(4)(a)).[295] On conviction on indictment the maximum penalties are imprisonment for up to ten years or a fine, or both.[296]

It is an offence, if done without a licence, to possess in the course of a business with a view to committing an infringing act, or in the course of business to sell or let for hire, to offer or expose for sale or hire, or exhibit in public, an article which the offender knows to be, or has reason to believe to be, an infringing copy of a work (s 107(1)(c), (d)(i), (ii), and (iii)). It is also an offence to make or possess 'an article specifically designed or adapted for making infringing copies of a particular copyright work' if the offender knows or has reason to believe that the article will be used to make infringing copies for sale or hire or use in the course of a business (s 107(2)).[297] These latter categories of offences are only triable summarily and the maximum penalties are imprisonment for up to six months or a fine not exceeding level 5 on the standard scale, or both (s 107(5)).[298]

Since 31 October 2003 it has been an offence to communicate a work to the public in the course of a business or otherwise to such an extent as to affect prejudicially the owner of the copyright knowing, or having reason to believe, that doing' so is an infringement (s 107(2A)). On summary conviction the penalties for such an offence are imprisonment for up to three months and a fine not exceeding the statutory maximum, or both (s 107(4A)(a)).[299] On conviction on indictment the maximum penalties are imprisonment for up to two years or a fine, or both.[300]

---

[295] As amended by s 42 of the Digital Economy Act 2010. At the time of writing, the statutory maximum was £50,000.

[296] s 107(4)(b). There is no statutory limit on the fine which may be imposed on conviction for one of these offences on indictment. In practice, however, the amount will be governed by the general principle that a fine should be within an offender's capacity to pay (*R v Churchill (No 2)* [1967] 1 QB 190).

[297] Interpretation of the equivalent civil infringement is discussed at section 7.4.2 above.

[298] As amended by s 42 of the Digital Economy Act 2010. At the time of writing, the statutory maximum was £50,000.

[299] As amended by s 42 of the Digital Economy Act 2010. At the time of writing, the statutory maximum was £50,000.

[300] CDPA 1988, s 107(4A)(b).

Where a person is charged with any of the criminal offences under the CDPA 1988, the court before which proceedings are brought may order delivery up of any infringing copy or article for making infringing copies (s 108). The CDPA 1988 also provides for a magistrate, if satisfied that one of the offences which are triable either way has been or is about to be committed and that relevant evidence is in specified premises, to 'issue a warrant authorising a constable to enter and search the premises, using such reasonable force as is necessary' (s 109). Moreover, where any of the offences is committed by a company 'with the consent or connivance of a director, manager, secretary or other similar officer . . . or a person purporting to act in any such capacity' that person is also guilty of the offence, and liable to be prosecuted and punished accordingly (s 110).

Taken as a whole, these criminal offences set high stakes for commercial copyright infringement and are intended to provide an effective deterrent against commercial infringement of copyright in software and other works. Moreover, a software pirate who fraudulently uses a trade mark may be convicted of a counterfeiting offence, the maximum penalty for which is ten years' imprisonment.[301]

7.7.3 Presumptions

A prerequisite to a successful action for copyright infringement, whether in civil or criminal proceedings, is proof of authorship and ownership of the relevant copyright(s). For practical and procedural reasons, proof of such facts can some-times constitute a substantial hurdle to a claimant or prosecutor, as the case may be. The CDPA 1988 provides that various presumptions will apply in proceedings relat-ing to various types of copyright work. These include a presumption that where a name purporting to be that of the author of a literary, dramatic, musical, or artistic work appears on published copies of the work, the named person shall, until the contrary is proved, be deemed to be the author. It is, moreover, presumed that the special rules as to first ownership of works created during the course of employment, etc were not applicable and thus that the named person was the first owner (s 104).

A special rule applies to copyright notices appearing on copies of computer programs. In litigation relating to program copyright, 'where copies of the program are issued to the public in electronic form bearing a statement—(a) that a named person was the owner of copyright in the program at the date of issue of the copies, or (b) that the program was first published in a specified country or that copies of it were first issued to the public in electronic form in a specified year, the statement shall be admissible as evidence of the facts stated and shall be presumed to be

---

[301] Trade Marks Act 1994, s 92(6). An offender convicted on indictment may also be liable to pay an unlimited fine. The penalty limits for summary conviction are six months' imprisonment and a fine not exceeding the statutory maximum.

correct until the contrary is proved' (s 105(3)). This special presumption is likely, on occasions at least, to be of major assistance to claimants in civil cases and the prosecution in criminal proceedings. As a result, program copyright owners should ensure that they affix appropriate copyright notices to all copies of a program they publish and that any licensees are obliged to do likewise.

8

DATABASE PROTECTION

Chris Reed

Information has always been of primary importance to human society, and all but the simplest societies require access to more information than can be stored in a single human brain. For example, the need for accurate accounting information is thought to have been one of the factors leading to the Sumerian development of writing around 4,000 years ago.[1]

The ability to record information is only one part of the story, however. If that information cannot be retrieved in a meaningful way it is, for practical purposes, quite useless. Techniques to structure stored information, such as indexes and filing systems, are one way of ensuring that at least some of the information required can be retrieved. More recently, information technology developments have enabled meaningful information to be extracted from semi-structured or even unstructured repositories.

Modern electronic databases have become an essential element of human existence. Without them employees would not be paid, airline travel would be impossible

---

[1] C Tyler, 'Clay Tablets Reveal Accounting Answers', *The Gazette* 10, no 36 (Library of Congress, 1 October 1999).

at its current scale and lawyers would need to spend more time in libraries, to pick just a few examples. The internet is in some respects a giant, freeform database, distributed worldwide and accessible in numerous ways via a variety of search tools.[2]

The main part of this chapter concerns the system of database protection introduced by Council Directive 96/9 on the legal protection of databases,[3] implemented in the UK by the Copyright and Rights in Databases Regulations 1997.[4] However, to understand the issues which that legislation aimed to address, and those which remain to be resolved, it is necessary first to analyse why databases might merit protection and the ways in which such protection might be offered.

8.1 ELECTRONIC DATABASES AND THE NEED FOR LEGAL PROTECTION

Until the second half of the twentieth century almost all recorded information had to be held in hard copy form. Clay tablets gave way to writing on papyrus, skins, and paper, printing made multiple copies easier to generate, and in the last century punched cards made a limited degree of automated searching possible.[5]

All of these hard copy technologies share two characteristics which vastly reduce the need for any special legal protection of a collection of information:

(a) To be usable, the collection has to be stored in a single physical location. Access to the information is therefore easily controllable by whoever has possession of the information records. These records are physical property, and so long-established legal theories of property law are available to the possessor of the collection to control unauthorized access to the information. These include trespass to land and burglary (for those who break into archives) and trespass to goods and theft (for those who take records away). A further protection derives from the law of contract, which can be used to restrict access and use of the information to particular persons and for specified purposes.

(b) Copying a physical collection of information is time-consuming and expensive, and in any event requires access to the collection and the cooperation of its possessor. Even though such copying is not theft[6] and may not infringe copyright in

---

[2] For a useful brief history of internet search tools, see <http://en.wikipedia.org/wiki/Web_search_engine> (accessed 9 August 2011).

[3] OJ L77/20, 27 March 1996.

[4] SI 1997/3032, implementing Council Directive 96/9 on the legal protection of databases, OJ L77/20, 27 March 1996.

[5] One of the earliest automated searching technologies was the Hollerith Tabulator, invented to process punched cards for the 1890 US census and which laid down the foundation of the IBM corporation—see <http://www.columbia.edu/cu/computinghistory/tabulator.html> (accessed 9 August 2011).

[6] *Oxford v Moss* (1978) 68 Cr App R 183.

many instances,[7] the legal mechanisms which control access enable the possessor of the collection to control copying in practice.

Neither of these two characteristics is exhibited to nearly the same extent, if at all, by electronic databases. Copying an electronic database is a comparatively cheap and quick process and the copy is identical to, and therefore equally as useful as, the original. Measures to prevent copying are technologically complex and often quite easy to circumvent using third party tools.[8]

In addition, electronic databases can only be exploited commercially by distributing copies or by making the database available online. In either case, the practical protection provided for physical information collections by limiting access is thereby weakened or destroyed. Additionally, the legal protections of property law fall away, so that if the information is not protected by copyright the only traditional legal regime available to the database owner is the law of contract. Once unauthorized copies of the database begin to circulate or are made available online, contract is of no use in controlling the use of those copies by others who have made no contract with the database owner.

For these reasons it has become necessary, over the last 20 years or so, for the law to examine what protections should be available to the database owner. As we shall see, this examination has produced a range of solutions, none of which yet appear to be optimal.

8.2 ELECTRONIC DATABASE CHARACTERISTICS

To understand the law as it has developed, we will find it useful to investigate those characteristics of electronic databases which have made it difficult to apply existing legal protections and to develop new forms of protection.

8.2.1 Identifying the database

The first of these characteristics is that it can be very difficult to determine precisely what constitutes a particular database. In the early days of computing a database would consist of a particular stack of punched cards or reel of punched tape, and the program which searched that database would be a separate set of cards or reel of tape. When disk storage became available, this distinction initially persisted so that it was possible to identify a single file which constituted the data.

---

[7] Such as public domain works and, most notably in relation to electronic databases, records of factual information. On the latter, see further section 8.4.2 below.

[8] A well-known example of copy-prevention circumvention tools is DeCSS, which removes the copy protection from commercial DVDs. A series of injunctions against distributing this tool have been granted by the US courts, beginning with *Universal City Studios, Inc v Reimerdes*, 82 F Supp 2d 211 (SDNY, 2000).

However, advances in computing technology have blurred this distinction almost to vanishing point. It is perfectly feasible to conduct database searches across multiple data files. These files do not need to be located on any particular computer, and may therefore be in different 'ownership'. Further, a particular data file might be a constituent of more than one such virtual database.

To make matters even more complicated, it is no longer essential that data should be in a particular structured form to be searched by software. The 'Search' function of Windows allows me to search the contents of all the files on my laptop, and so in that sense the contents of my hard disk constitute a database. I can install a software application which indexes all those files, enabling me to conduct more sophisticated searches, at which point my laptop contents look even more like a database.

At the most extreme, as has been suggested above, the entire internet can be considered to be a giant database, searchable via tools such as Google.[9] However, no one person could claim to be the creator of this database and thus seek legal protection for it as a whole.[10] More difficult is where someone makes accessible a subset of the internet for searching—an obvious example is Google Scholar[11] which limits searches to academic and related websites. Can it be said that Google thereby 'created' a new database?

8.2.2 What might be protected?

Assuming that we can identify the boundaries of the database in question, the second characteristic which creates legal difficulties is that databases have a number of different elements which the law might wish to protect. We have seen earlier that the protections which a database owner might require are protections against copying or other forms of unauthorized use of the database.

The first of these elements is the contents of the database. The most obvious distinction here is between facts (which generally receive no protection against copying per se) and works of intellectual creation (texts, images, sound recordings, video, etc), which will be protected by copyright unless they are in the public domain. It is important to note that if a particular content element is protected by copyright, that only grants protection to the copyright owner. The database creator need not be the author of a copyright work contained in the database, and we are examining the protections given to the creator.

The second element, related to content, is semantic information which gives meaning (or additional meaning) to that content. For example, a database consisting of 12,000 numbers is meaningless on its own. However, if those numbers represent ten years of monthly stock prices for FTSE 100 companies then the content has a

---

[9] <http://www.google.com> (accessed 9 August 2011).
[10] Although each individual website might well constitute a database for at least some purposes.
[11] <http://scholar.google.com> (accessed 9 August 2011).

high level of meaning. This semantic information might be contained in the data file itself, or in a separate configuration file.

The structure or arrangement of data can also enhance its meaning. For example, information about a person might be contained in the format:

Name, Address

or alternatively in the format:

Title, First name, Last name, House number, Street, Town, Country, Postal code The information in the data is the same in both cases, but the semantic content of the second format is clearly much greater.

Where the data element is a work of intellectual creation it will, of course, have semantic content per se. However, further semantic content can be added to a document by, for example, inserting XML tags,[12] which because they explain the nature of each part of that document (headings, abstract, footnote, etc) can be used to enhance the precision of searches.

Semantic information of these kinds might be described as meta-content (ie, information about the content, rather than the information contained in the content), and originate from a different source than the content itself. Because this meta-content adds substantial value to the database, it might be considered worthy of legal protection.

The third element of a database which might merit legal protection is the selection of information incorporated in the database. Some databases are only really useful if there is no selection—the share price database mentioned above would be of little value if 10 per cent of the data were missing. Others, however, may be more valuable precisely because they are a subset of the available information. An obvious example might be a database of worldwide case law on a particular legal topic, selected by a leading expert in that field. The selection embodies the expertise of the selector, and is thus perhaps a species of implicit meta-content which could merit protection against copying by third parties.

A fourth element of databases which might deserve legal protection is any innovative technique which enhances the usefulness of the database, such as techniques which increase the speed or effectiveness of searching. These techniques will normally be embodied in the database software itself, rather than the data content, and so are not considered in this chapter.[13] They will probably benefit from copyright protection (see Chapter 7) and may possibly be patentable (see Chapter 6[14]), and can also be protected as confidential information or know-how to the extent that they can be kept confidential.

---

[12] XML (Extensible Markup Language) is developed via recommendations from the World Wide Web Consortium, <http://www.w3.org>.

[13] Unless the techniques are for enhancing the meta-content of the database—see above.

[14] Although note that, in Europe at least, inventions which are at heart methods of presenting information are excluded from patentability—see in particular Chapter 6, section 6.2.2.

Finally, we should note that the output which results from a database search is likely to have value such that it should be protected by law. However, that output is distinct from the database itself, and protection will depend on whether the output qualifies as a copyright-protected work or is confidential information.

8.3 RATIONALES FOR PROTECTING DATABASES

Why should databases receive any legal protection at all? The answer to this question will assist us in deciding what form, if any, that protection should take.

There are two main arguments in favour of granting some level of legal protection. The first is that creativity merits protection against those who wish to use the results of that creativity. This is the rationale which underlies the law of copyright. However, the reasons why it is argued that the law should protect creativity are not uniform.

In the civil law tradition, protection of creativity is seen as an aspect of human rights.[15] The thing created was achieved by the workings of a human mind, and as such can be seen as an expression of the creator's personality. The test for whether a work is sufficiently original to attract copyright protection is that it is the maker's 'own intellectual creation'.[16]

By contrast, the common law tradition has based its copyright protection of creativity on the economic value of the created work. The Copyright Clause of the US Constitution, Article 1 Section 8 Clause 8, is the basis for Federal copyright law, and provides that Congress shall have the power:

To promote the Progress of Science and useful Arts, by securing for limited Times to Authors and Inventors the exclusive Right to their respective Writings and Discoveries.

The purpose of US copyright protection is to provide the economic incentive for the creation of such writings and discoveries. Similarly, UK courts have used an economic test in deciding whether parts of a creative work are protected from copying; the most commonly cited statement is that of Petersen J in *University of London Press Ltd v University Tutorial Press Ltd*[17]—'what is worth copying is prima facie worth protecting'.

The second argument in favour of protection is also primarily economic, and may be difficult to distinguish from the economic case for protecting creativity. This argument is that the labour, skill, and effort applied to making the database are

---

[15] See A Dietz, *Legal Principles of Moral Rights in Civil Law Countries* (Antwerp: ALAI, 1993).

[16] See, eg, Council Directive 91/250/EEC of 14 May 1991 on the legal protection of computer programs, OJ L122/42, 17 May 1991, Art 1(3). US copyright law has recently moved some way towards this position—see *Feist Publications Inc v Rural Telephone Service Co, Inc*, 499 US 340 (1990), discussed below at section 8.4.2.

[17] [1916] 2 Ch 601 at 610.

themselves worthy of some legal protection, even if the results are not creative in the intellectual sense.[18] The legal theory on which such protection is based is usually that of misappropriation or unfair competition, which prevents one business from misusing for its own benefit the reputation or work product of another business.[19] This rationale would not provide legal protection to databases created outside a business, but in practice the makers of such databases are unlikely to seek or require protection from the law.

We must also recognize that there is a powerful argument against providing too much protection for database contents. Where those contents are factual information, granting protection to the maker of the database has the potential also to grant a monopoly over the use of those facts in electronic form. US copyright law sets out a list of those matters which cannot be protected by copyright: 'any idea, procedure, process, system, method of operation, concept, principle, or discovery'[20] and the courts have consistently interpreted this to prohibit the granting of rights over facts per se.[21] Similarly, UK law requires a copyright work to exhibit a de minimis element of skill, judgement, and labour, although not necessarily any literary merit,[22] and the mere recording of a fact will not meet this test.

One of the theoretical justifications for refusing protection to facts is that they are discovered rather than created.[23] However, it is clear that substantial effort and cost might be expended in discovering facts and in transforming them into an appropriate format for use in a database. The question whether this economic expenditure confers some element of protection has recently received attention from the UK and EU courts—see sections 8.6.1 and 8.6.2 below.

---

[18] This is still a basis for granting copyright protection under UK law—*Ladbroke (Football) Ltd v William Hill (Football) Ltd* [1964] 1 WLR 273—but it no longer applies to databases. See further section 8.5.2 below.

[19] 'Unfair competition provides a means of countering the undesirable effects of misuse of another's exploits . . .', A Kamperman Sanders, *Unfair Competition Law* (Oxford: Clarendon Press, 1997) 22.

[20] 17 USC § 102(b).

[21] 'No author may copyright . . . the facts he narrates', *Harper & Row Publishers Inc v Nation Enterprises*, 471 US 539 at 556 (1985). For an examination of the problem of distinguishing non-copyrightable facts from the remainder of a database or compilation see JC Ginsburg, 'No "sweat"? Copyright and other protection of works of information after Feist v Rural Telephone' (1992) 92 Colum L Rev 338 at 348–53.

[22] *Ladbroke v William Hill* [1964] 1 WLR 273 (HL).

[23] '. . . the first person to find and report a particular fact has not created the fact; he or she has merely discovered its existence', *Feist Publications Inc v Rural Telephone Service Co, Inc*, 499 US 340 at para 15 (1990).

8.4 LEGAL STRUCTURES FOR PROTECTION

8.4.1 Contract

Contract provides a potentially excellent legal structure to protect online databases. If some form of access control is used, such as username and password, contractual terms can be imposed as a condition of receiving access. In addition to payment terms, the database contents will be protected by terms requiring the user not to allow others access, not to make copies of the contents except as authorized, and not to use copies except as authorized.

If, however, a database needs to be exploited by way of distributing copies, contract will rarely be adequate as the main method of protection. The contract with the authorized user might contain similar terms to a contract for online use, but those terms cannot bind an unauthorized user who obtains access to the database copy.[24] In these circumstances the database owner will need to identify a non-contractual claim against the unauthorized user.

When drafting a contract for the exploitation of a database it is important to be aware that there are some limitations on the owner's ability to restrict use of the database and impose liability on the other contracting party:

(a) the Copyright and Rights in Databases Regulations 1997[25] confer certain use rights on the lawful user, and terms which attempt to restrict those rights are void—see further sections 8.5.3 and 8.7.4 below;

(b) onerous terms in contracts with consumers, such a terms requiring an indemnity, may be unenforceable as unfair under the Unfair Terms in Consumer Contracts Regulations[26]; and

(c) use restrictions may need to be reviewed for compliance with competition law if the database owner meets the relevant market tests.[27]

8.4.2 Copyright

In addition to the obvious category of sole authored works, copyright systems also protect 'collected works'. These are works where the author of the collection is not the author of the individual elements which make up the collection—the simplest

---

[24] Although some indirect protection for the database contents can be secured by, eg, requiring the authorized user to indemnify the database owner against losses caused by the authorized user's failure to comply with the contract terms.

[25] SI 1997/3032, implementing Council Directive 96/9 on the legal protection of databases, OJ L77/20, 27 March 1996.

[26] SI 1999/2083.

[27] See generally R Whish, *Competition Law*, 6th edn (Oxford: Oxford University Press, 2008).

example is an anthology of poems—and in these cases a new copyright comes into existence to protect the collection against copying.

There is an international consensus about the minimum level of protection, set out in Article 2(5) of the Berne Convention for the Protection of Literary and Artistic Works:

Collections of literary or artistic works such as encyclopaedias and anthologies which, by reason of the selection and arrangement of their contents, constitute intellectual creations shall be protected as such, without prejudice to the copyright in each of the works forming part of such collections.

However, national laws may protect a wider range of collected works than this minimum:

(a) collections of non-works (ie materials or facts which do not attract copyright) may fall within the national law definition; and/or

(b) collections which are not intellectual creations may be protected on the basis of the work involved in making the collection.

For example, the Nordic catalogue rule[28] (the model for the Directive) grants protection for ten years post-publication or 15 years from creation, whichever is the lesser. Protection is based on the effort required to create the catalogue, and there is no originality requirement.

Prior to the Copyright and Rights in Databases Regulations 1997, UK copyright law took the widest possible approach to the protection of collected works. Section 3(1)(a) of the Copyright, Designs and Patents Act 1988 provided:

'literary work' means any work, other than a dramatic or musical work, which is written, spoken or sung, and accordingly includes . . . a table or compilation.

Case law had long established that compilations of facts or other non-copyright materials received protection as compilations. In *Ladbroke (Football) Ltd v William Hill (Football) Ltd*,[29] the court held that a football pool coupon which listed forthcoming football matches was protected by copyright, and similar decisions have been handed down with respect to directories,[30] listings of radio programmes,[31] lists of share prices[32] and railway stations,[33] etc. Although the point had not been raised in litigation, there was a clear consensus that databases would potentially be protected as compilations.[34]

---

[28] First implemented into Swedish law by Upphovsrättslagen 729/1960 §49.
[29] [1964] 1 WLR 273.
[30] *Kelly v Morris* (1866) LR 1 Eq 697.
[31] *BBC v Wireless League Gazette Publishing Co* [1936] Ch 433.
[32] *Exchange Telegraph Co Ltd v Gregory & Co* [1896] 1 QB 147.
[33] *Blacklock v Pearson* [1915] 2 Ch 376.
[34] 'On similar principles, a computer database, stored on tape, disk or by other electronic means, would also generally be a compilation and capable of protection as a literary work', *Copinger & Skone James on Copyright*, 13th edn (London: Sweet & Maxwell, 1991) chs 2–8.

In order to be protected a compilation needed to be original, and the test here was based on originality in the selection and arrangement of the compilation. UK law does not require intellectual creativity as a constituent of originality; it is enough if sufficient labour, skill, or judgement have been used to create the compilation.[35] Copyright protection for compilations is only refused if the effort involved in their creation is negligible.[36]

Databases no longer receive copyright protection as compilations,[37] but other compilations continue to be protected in this way.

Prior to 1990 US law appeared to protect collections of non-copyright materials on the basis of the effort involved in their creation (the so-called 'sweat of the brow' doctrine), and thus to protect databases as well. In that year, however, the Supreme Court handed down its decision in *Feist Publications Inc v Rural Telephone Service Company, Inc.*[38] In that case, Feist produced a consolidated white pages telephone directory for a particular area, integrating the directory entries from all the telephone companies with subscribers in that area. Rural refused to license its directory to Feist, who copied it anyway. The lower courts held that Feist had infringed Rural's copyright, and Feist appealed to the Supreme Court. The court held that compilations of facts could be protected by copyright, but that:

(a) the basis for protection was originality in the sense of being the intellectual creation of the maker of the compilation;

(b) originality could not reside in the facts themselves by definition, and so had to be found in the selection and arrangement of those facts. If this selection and arrangement showed sufficient, minimal creativity, the compilation would attract copyright protection. The other effort, or sweat of the brow, expended in making the compilation was immaterial; and

(c) the protection afforded by copyright could only extend to the original elements of the compilation, that is, its selection and arrangement. Others were free to copy the facts provided they did not also copy the protected expression in the form of selection and arrangement.

Although the level of creativity required was low, Rural's white pages directory did not meet that threshold. It consisted only of names, addresses, and telephone numbers arranged in alphabetical order. There was no selection, because to be useful the directory had to include all subscribers. The arrangement was not creative because

---

[35] *Ladbroke (Football) Ltd v William Hill (Football) Ltd* [1964] 1 WLR 273. A similar view is taken in many other common law jurisdictions—see, eg, *Desktop Marketing Systems Pty Ltd v Telstra Corp Ltd* [2002] FCAFC 112 (Federal Court of Australia).

[36] *GA Cramp & Sons Ltd v Frank Smythson Ltd* [1944] AC 329.

[37] Copyright, Designs and Patents Act 1988, s 3(1)(a) as amended by Copyright and Rights in Databases Regulations 1997 (SI 1997/3032), reg 5.

[38] 499 US 340 (1990).

alphabetical order was the only possible arrangement to make the directory useful. The directory was therefore not protected by copyright.

Later cases have established that the level of creativity required is sufficiently low that yellow pages directories are protected,[39] but the protection still does not extend to the contents of the directory. The effect of these decisions is that databases receive very little protection under US copyright law.[40] It might be thought that this lack of protection would create problems for the US database industry, but in practice this seems not to be the case—see section 8.4.4 below.

8.4.3 Unfair competition or misappropriation of work product

Copyright is not the only non-contractual mechanism through which databases might be protected. Unfair competition or misappropriation laws can provide a remedy, though usually this is limited to claims by one business against another. The UK does not have a general law of unfair competition—the tort of passing off is the closest equivalent and is clearly of no use to protect database contents against copying.

Probably the best-developed unfair competition law is that of Germany, extensively revised as the UWG in 2004.[41] Section 3 of the law sets out a general prohibition on unfair acts of competition which are likely to have more than an insubstantial impact on competition to the detriment of competitors, consumers, or other market participants. The general prohibition is expanded on in sections 4–7, which are a list of examples of acts of competition which are regarded as unfair under the law. Databases would potentially receive protection under section 4(9) of the UWG, which declares that exploitation or misappropriation of another's work or reputation is an act of unfair competition. Section 9 of the UWG gives those injured by an act of unfair competition a right to claim damages if the defendant undertook the act intentionally or negligently, and there are also criminal sanctions for breach of the law. Similar laws are found in some, but by no means all, other civil law jurisdictions.[42]

Unfair competition-type laws are also found in some common law countries; for example, many US states have a tort of unfair competition. Thus, in *Metropolitan Opera Association v Wagner-Nichols Recorder Corp*,[43] the defendant was held

---

[39] *BellSouth Advertising & Publishing Corp v Donnelly Information Publishing Inc*, 933 F 2d 952 (11th Cir, 1991).

[40] For a discussion of the application of *Feist* to databases see JF Hayden, 'Copyright Protection of Computer Databases after *Feist*' (1991) Harvard Journal of Law & Technology 215.

[41] *Gesetz gegen den unlauteren Wettbewerb* (UWG) of 3 July 2004 (BGBl I 2004 32/1414).

[42] See, eg, art 1365 Indonesian Civil Code which prohibits, inter alia, acts or omissions which are contrary to honest usage, good faith, and good conduct; art 2598 Italian Civil Code which prohibits directly or indirectly making use of means not in conformity with the principles of professional ethics and which are likely to damage the business of others.

[43] 101 NYS2d 483 (1950).

liable for unfair competition by misappropriating the intellectual product of the plaintiff when it made unauthorized recordings of broadcast performances of operas and released them as gramophone records. The basis of liability is using unfair business practices to profit from the labour, skill, and expenditure of another.

The difficulty with such laws is that they potentially overlap with copyright protection, and such overlap cannot be permitted under US Federal law. In *National Basketball Association v Motorola, Inc*,[44] a team of reporters employed by Motorola typed up information on the current state of play in basketball games from news reports and game broadcasts, and made these available to customers' pagers. The NBA brought a claim under New York State unfair competition law against Motorola on the ground that Motorola was misappropriating information generated by the NBA, and the case came to the Federal courts to decide whether that claim was pre-empted by Federal law. The court held that the information was not copyrightable under the Copyright Act 1976, and thus the state law claim would be pre-empted as it would have given protection to information declared non-copyrightable by Congress. However, a misappropriation claim could succeed if what was taken was 'hot news'. To establish this the NBA would need to establish five elements:

(a) the plaintiff generates or collects the information at some cost or expense;

(b) the value of the information is highly time-sensitive;

(c) the defendant's use of the information constitutes free-riding on the plaintiff's costly efforts to generate or collect it;

(d) the defendant's use of the information is in direct competition with a product or service offered by the plaintiff; and

(e) the ability of others to free-ride on the efforts of the plaintiff or others would so reduce the incentive to produce the product or service that its existence or quality would be substantially threatened.[45]

The NBA claim failed because it did not itself generate the information (although it did generate the sporting activity to which the information related), and the collection of the information was undertaken by the defendants, not the NBA.

8.4.4 *Sui generis* database right

It should be apparent from the foregoing that none of the legal structures discussed so far—contract, copyright, and unfair competition—provide an entirely appropriate scheme for protecting databases. The alternative to adapting an existing legal structure is to devise an entirely new, *sui generis* form of protection.

This is what Directive 96/9 on the legal protection of databases[46] ('the Directive') aims to achieve. Although it is closely based on the Nordic catalogue right

---

[44] 105 F3d 841 (2nd Cir, 1997).
[45] Ibid 852, citing *International News Service v Associated Press*, 248 US 215 (1918).
[46] OJ L77/20, 27 March 1996.

(see section 8.4.2 above), the Directive modifies that scheme of protection to attempt to strike a balance between the rights of database makers and users, and also attempts to identify the boundaries between those elements of a database which should be protected by copyright and those which receive the *sui generis* protection.

The basic scheme of the Directive is as follows:

(a) Databases[47] are protected by the *sui generis* right if 'there has been qualitatively and/or quantitatively a substantial investment in either the obtaining, verification or presentation of the contents' (Art 7(1)).

(b) The maker of such a database has the right 'to prevent extraction and/or re-utilization of the whole or of a substantial part evaluated qualitatively and/or quantitatively, of the contents of that database' (Art 7(1)) subject to the lawful user's rights (Art 8(1)).

(c) Protection under the *sui generis* right lasts for 15 years from first making the database available to the public or 15 years from its creation, whichever is the shorter (Art 10).

(d) Copyright protection is restricted to those databases which 'by reason of the selection or arrangement of their contents, constitute the author's own intellectual creation', but this protection does not extend to the database contents[48] (Art 3).

The detailed provisions of the Directive, as transposed into UK law, are explained in sections 8.5 to 8.7 below.

The US is the most significant producer of databases, but US-produced databases do not receive protection via the *sui generis* right.[49] This has led to calls[50] for the USA to adopt a protection model similar to that of the Directive. The US Congress has discussed this issue at length on a number of occasions since 1996,[51] and various Bills have been introduced. However, all have been rejected for one or more of the following reasons:

(a) a reluctance to grant monopolies over factual information, as such monopolies are prohibited by the Copyright Clause of the Constitution as interpreted by the courts;[52]

---

[47] '"Database" shall mean a collection of independent works, data or other materials arranged in a systematic or methodical way and capable of being individually accessed by electronic or other means', Directive 96/9 on the legal protection of databases, OJ L77/20, 27 March 1996, Art 1(2).

[48] Those contents will be protected separately by copyright if they meet the relevant national law requirements to constitute a copyright work.

[49] Directive 96/9 on the legal protection of databases, OJ L77/20, 27 March 1996, Art 11.

[50] See, eg, N Thakur, 'Database Protection in the European Union and the United States: The European Database Directive as an Optimum Global Model' [2001] IPQ 100.

[51] For a detailed analysis of the discussions, see J Band, 'The Database Debate in the 108th US Congress: The Saga Continues' (2005) 27(6) EIPR 205. Davison predicts that 'the prospects of any legislation being passed on the topic are small and diminishing further with the passage of time'— MJ Davison, 'Database Protection: Lessons from Europe, Congress, and WIPO' (2007) 57 CWRLR 829 at 850.

[52] *Feist Publications Inc v Rural Telephone Service Co, Inc*, 499 US 340 (1990).

(b) concerns that protecting databases might restrict free speech; and

(c) scepticism about the economic arguments that such protection is needed, given the continued strength of the US database industry and the fact that lack of copyright protection under US law for most databases does not seem to have inhibited the production of new databases.[53]

8.5 UK PROTECTION OF DATABASES THROUGH COPYRIGHT

Since the coming into force of the Copyright and Rights in Databases Regulations 1997 ('the Regulations') on 1 January 1998, new databases can no longer be protected by copyright as compilations.[54] However, under regulation 29 if a database was protected by copyright before 1 January 1998 it remains protected by copyright for the remainder of its copyright term.[55] The regulations do not describe how a pre-existing database which qualified for copyright prior to that date, but which has since been extended or updated, should be dealt with. The most likely solution is that the post-1997 additions will fall under the new copyright and database right regime, whilst the pre-1997 contents will retain their copyright protection.

'Database' is defined as:[56]

. . . a collection of independent works, data or other materials which—

(a) are arranged in a systematic or methodical way, and

(b) are individually accessible by electronic or other means.

This means that non-electronic collections, such as a filing cabinet of data or even a library, would qualify as a database. Where the individual items are not individually accessible, for example the chapters in this book, the existing law on compilations continues to apply. Thus even if this book were sold as a single .pdf file on a CD, it would not be a database. However, if each chapter were recorded as a separate .pdf file, individually accessible via an index page also recorded on the CD, then

---

[53] Band, n 51, 210.

[54] Databases are specifically excluded from the definition of compilation in Copyright, Designs and Patents Act 1988, s 3(1)(a) as amended by Copyright and Rights in Databases Regulations 1997 (SI 1997/3032), reg 5.

[55] 70 years after the death of the author, or 50 years after creation in the case of computer-generated databases—see Chapter 7, section 7.3.3.

[56] Copyright, Designs and Patents Act 1988, s 3A, inserted by Copyright and Rights in Databases Regulations 1997 (SI 1997/3032), reg 6.

the electronic version of the book might well[57] fall within this definition and be a database.[58]

The requirement that the contents of a database should be arranged in a systematic or methodical way has potentially interesting consequences. As explained in section 8.2.1 above, it is no longer technologically essential for data to be stored in a structured form to be searchable. In theory therefore, a database consisting of unstructured information together with a powerful search engine would fall outside the Act's definition of 'database'. In such a case it would be a compilation, and thus potentially benefit from the high level of copyright protection given to databases before the Directive and Regulations came into force. This may be a purely theoretical point for two reasons:

(a) To be useful, such a database would require some minimal structure. For example, a database of court decisions would be unwieldy if each decision was not recorded as a separate file, but instead as random chunks of text or as a single undifferentiated file. This minimal structure might be sufficient for a court to decide that the database was in fact arranged in a systematic or methodical way.

(b) Commercially exploitable databases require more functionality than is achievable by a search engine which accesses unstructured material—compare, for example, the results of a Google search with the far more targeted results achievable from a specialist database such as Westlaw or Lexis. Such enhanced functionality can only, at present, be achieved by structuring each database element so that searches can be run on only part of it, such as on headnotes in legal databases. That enhanced functionality can be achieved by marking up the data, for example using XML, but the act of marking it up gives sufficient structure to bring the database within the definition. If in the future, however, search software becomes so sophisticated that it can identify semantic content (such as titles) without the data being marked up, the Directive will need amendment to ensure that such databases remain within the harmonized EU regime of copyright and *sui generis* protection.

---

[57] This example assumes that each chapter is an 'independent' work, which might not be the case as the chapters were commissioned for this book. It is not clear precisely what the Directive (and consequently the Regulations) means by the requirement for the database contents to be independent. In a previous edition of this book Simon Chalton wrote:

> 'Independent works, data or other materials' is apparently intended to exclude from the definition works such as films, musical compositions and books which comprise distinct but related elements or materials (for example, frames, movements or chapters) and which, though separately accessible, are interrelated within the collection . . .
> It is suggested that independence in relation to items of content in a collection should be judged from the standpoint of those items as they appear in the compiled collection: it is not sufficient for an item to be capable of being read or used by itself if reading or use of other items in the collection, or the collection as a whole, is dependent on reading or use of that item.

(S Chalton, 'Property in Databases' in C Reed and J Angel (eds), *Computer Law*, 5th edn (Oxford: Oxford University Press, 2003) ch 6.4.)

[58] The editor hopes that in such circumstances, the selection and arrangement of the chapters is sufficiently creative to attract copyright—see section 8.5.2 below.

8.5.1 Copyright in the content of databases

The Regulations do not make any changes to the copyright protection of the individual contents of a database. The question whether a content element is itself a copyright-protected work is answered by the normal copyright law pertaining to that particular type of work. Thus, for example, in a database of law journal articles the copyright in each article would be owned by the author or his or her assignee, and in a database of photographs the copyright in each photograph would be owned by the photographer, etc.

8.5.2 Copyright in the database itself

Section 3(1)(d) of the Copyright, Designs and Patents Act 1988[59] now specifically includes databases within the category of literary works. However, such databases only attract copyright if they are *original* literary works. Section 3A(2) of the Act sets out a test of originality for databases which differs from the test for other literary works:

For the purposes of this Part a literary work consisting of a database is original if, and only if, by reason of the selection or arrangement of the contents of the database the database constitutes the author's own intellectual creation.

The requirement for an author's intellectual creation seems to imply that there can be no copyright in computer-generated databases.[60]

Litigation relating to the fixtures lists of the English and Scottish football leagues has raised an interesting question about Article 3 of the Directive, which section 3 implements. The *Fixtures Marketing* decisions of the ECJ (see section 8.6.2 below) had made it clear that no database right subsisted in these lists, so the English litigation asserted that they were protected by copyright under Article 3. At first instance the judge found that the creation of those lists was not a mere mechanical exercise but required substantial labour and a high degree of skill, and therefore held that they constituted a database protected by copyright.[61] The case went to the Court of Appeal under the name *Football Dataco Ltd v Yahoo*,[62] where the distinction made by the ECJ in the *British Horseracing Board* case between creation of underlying data and the database itself (see section 8.6.1 below) was explored. The argument put forward by the defendants was that although the creation of the fixtures list itself required labour and skill, its transformation into a database did not and thus could not amount to an intellectual creation within the meaning of Article 3. The Court of

---

[59] Inserted by Copyright and Rights in Databases Regulations 1997 (SI 1997/3032), reg 5(c).

[60] Other forms of computer-generated work attract copyright under Copyright, Designs and Patents Act 1988, ss 9(3) and 178.

[61] *Football Dataco v Brittens* [2010] EWHC 841 (Ch).

[62] [2010] EWCA Civ 1380.

Appeal has referred this question to the ECJ, together with the question of whether labour and skill alone are sufficient for an intellectual creation.

If, as in the author's opinion seems likely, the ECJ decides that the relevant act for Article 3 is the creation of the database, rather than its underlying data, this would mean that the fixtures list database is not protected by copyright work. However, the question whether the original list (before its transformation into a database) was itself a copyright-protected work would still remain (see section 8.4.2 above). It is unclear whether the Directive has removed the possibility that copyright can subsist in such works, and this is a further question which the Court of Appeal has referred to the ECJ.

The Regulations do not explain whether a database which attracts Article 3 copyright protection is infringed in the normal way, that is, by copying the whole or a substantial part of the contents, or whether copyright will only be infringed if the whole or a substantial part of the *selection or arrangement* is copied. The answer must be the latter, as the Regulations need to be interpreted by the UK courts so as to give effect to the Directive. The Directive makes it clear that copyright in databases only extends to the selection or arrangement, that is, those elements which are the intellectual creation of the author:

> . . . copyright as covered by this Directive applies only to the selection or arrangements of the contents of a database . . .[63]

Thus, it appears, so far as copyright is concerned, that the Directive produces almost identical results to the US Supreme Court decision in *Feist*.[64] Because under the Berne Convention nationals of a signatory state receive the same copyright protection under UK law as UK nationals, foreign-authored databases will also be protected by copyright.[65]

Database copyright will be infringed by any of the acts which would infringe copyright in other literary works, that is, the copying of a whole or a substantial part, distributing or communicating the database to the public, making an adaptation or communicating or displaying the results of an adaptation to the public.[66] However, as copyright protects only the selection or arrangement these acts will only infringe if done in relation to that selection or arrangement. Thus, copying the contents of a database will only infringe copyright if the effect is also to copy the selection or arrangement; similar principles will apply to adaptation and communication to the public. In practice, most of the activities to which a database maker might object

---

[63] Directive 96/9 on the legal protection of databases, OJ L77/20, 27 March 1996, recital 35; see also recitals 15, 27, and 39.

[64] *Feist Publications Inc v Rural Telephone Service Company, Inc*, 499 US 340 (1990).

[65] These foreign-made databases will, however, not benefit from database right unless made by a national or resident of an EU Member State or nationals or residents of those countries specified in a decision of the Council—Directive 96/9 on the legal protection of databases, OJ L77/20, 27 March 1996, Art 11.

[66] For a more detailed discussion of infringing acts, see Chapter 7, section 7.4.

will consist of copying or displaying the content, rather than the selection or arrangement, and will thus be pursued as infringements of database right. Verbatim copying of an entire database will, of course, infringe both the copyright (if any) and the database right in that database.

8.5.3 Permitted acts

In addition to the normal permitted acts under copyright law, the Regulations insert a new section 50D into the Copyright, Designs and Patents Act 1988 which provides that access to the contents of a database by a lawful user is not an infringement of the copyright in the database. Any term (eg, in a licence of the database) which purports to prohibit or restrict such access is void.[67]

8.6 DATABASE RIGHT

To be protected by database right a database must meet the definition in section 3A of the Copyright, Designs and Patents 1988,[68] and so must be 'a collection of independent works, data or other materials which—(a) are arranged in a systematic or methodical way, and (b) are individually accessible by electronic or other means'. This definition has been analysed in section 8.5 above. The maker of the database must be an EEA national or resident, or a company incorporated and established in the EEA.[69]

The first question we need to answer is what is required for a database to qualify for protection via database right. As we will see from the discussion in section 8.6.1 below, these requirements make it difficult for a 'single source' database to qualify for protection, and so single source databases are discussed further in section 8.6.2. The rights conferred on the creator of a protected database are then examined in section 8.7.

8.6.1 Qualifying for protection

The requirements which qualify a database for protection by database right are set out in regulation 13(1) of the Copyright and Rights in Databases Regulations 1997 ('the Regulations'):

---

[67] Copyright, Designs and Patents Act 1988, s 296B, inserted by Copyright and Rights in Databases Regulations 1997 (SI 1997/3032), reg 10.

[68] Copyright, Designs and Patents Act 1988, s 3A, inserted by Copyright and Rights in Databases Regulations 1997 (SI 1997/3032), reg 6.

[69] Reg 18.

A property right ('database right') subsists, in accordance with this Part, in a database if there has been a substantial investment in obtaining, verifying or presenting the contents of the database.

8.6.1.1 *Ownership*

The first owner of this right is the maker[70] of the database,[71] defined in regulation 14(1) as:

the person who takes the initiative in obtaining, verifying or presenting the contents of a database and assumes the risk of investing in that obtaining, verification or presentation.

Database right in a database created by an employee in the course of his employment belongs to the employer, subject to any agreement to the contrary,[72] and similar rules apply to databases made by officers or servants of the Crown or under the direction of Parliament.[73] However, if a database is created by an independent contractor then the right will belong to the contractor, not the person who commissioned its creation, unless there is a contractual term assigning database right to the commissioner.[74]

Identifying whether a database was made in the course of employment can be difficult because individuals commonly use their computing technologies in a converged manner, integrating home and work information. A particularly difficult issue is email and telephone contact information. In *PennWell Publishing v Orstein and Others*,[75] the High Court had to decide whether an Outlook contacts database belonged to the employee or the employer. The employee was a journalist who had imported his pre-employment contacts into Outlook on his work laptop, and then added further work and home contacts during the course of his employment. On leaving employment he made a copy of this database. The judge held that because the Outlook contacts database contained work-related contacts and was created using technology supplied by the employer, and backed up on the employer's computer systems, it was created during the course of employment and thus belonged to the employer.[76]

However, the judge also went on to recognize that this convergence of personal and work information in a single database meant that the question of ownership did not determine all the rights to use that information. The employee would have been entitled to delete his private contacts before leaving, and to take copies of (but not delete) those contacts which he had imported on starting work and those which

---

[70] Or the joint makers—reg 14(5).
[71] Reg 15.
[72] Reg 14(2).
[73] Reg 14(3) and (4).
[74] *Cureton v Mark Insulations Ltd* [2006] EWHC 2279 (QB).
[75] [2007] EWHC 1570 (QB).
[76] Ibid paras 109, 127–8.

formed part of his general employee knowledge under the principles in *Faccienda Chicken v Fowler*.[77] If, as in this case, he had taken a copy of the database away, he was obliged to return it but could similarly delete and/or copy that personal information on the basis of an implied term in his contract of employment.[78]

This case does not exhaust all the possibilities. If we imagine an employee who works primarily via a smartphone, entering work and home contact details on the phone and synchronizing it with both work and home computers, we are faced with three copies of an identical contacts database. On the analysis in *PennWell Publishing*, the work copy would belong to the employer, the home copy to the employee, and the ownership of the copy on the smartphone would depend on who owned the phone and/or paid the phone bills. What is clear, however, is that use rights would depend on the contract of employment and on the law of confidence, rather than ownership of the databases.

8.6.1.2 *Investment*

Both regulation 13(1) and regulation 14(1) make it clear that the crucial elements for determining the maker of a database, and whether it attracts database right, are the investment in obtaining, verifying, or presenting the contents. The third of these elements requires little discussion; it covers the investment of resources, primarily time and money,[79] required to transform the contents into a form suitable for use in the database.

However, the concepts of obtaining and verification are more complex. Where the contents pre-exist the making of the database, the maker of the database needs to obtain those contents from their creators. The cost of so doing will clearly be an investment in the making of the database. Similarly, the costs of checking the accuracy of the contents will also be unquestionably an investment.

The position is potentially different if the contents do not already exist, but are brought into existence by the maker of the database. To understand the issues involved it will help to take the example of a database of stock prices used earlier, and to proceed on the basis that the database is created by the stock exchange itself. There are two ways of looking at the process of database creation:

(a) In order to capture the information which will be incorporated in the database, the stock exchange will need to invest in technology which records and verifies the activities of the trading parties, including the prices at which trades were effected. It will also need to employ staff to operate the technology and undertake other activities. An identifiable proportion of the costs of doing so will be attributable to capturing the stock prices. These costs are the investment which the stock

---

[77] [1987] 1 Ch 117.

[78] [2007] EWHC 1570 (QB), para 131, and see also paras 136, 148.

[79] ' "investment" includes any investment, whether of financial, human or technical resources', reg 12(1).

exchange has made in obtaining and verifying the data, and as a result the database of stock exchange prices qualifies for database right protection.

(b) The alternative view is that there is a distinction between *creating* data and *obtaining* data which has already been created. On this view, the only investment which can be taken into account in deciding whether the database qualifies for database right is the investment *after* the creation of the data. In our example, that investment would be minimal. Almost all the costs of the exchange relate to making trades possible and capturing records of those trades, in other words in creating the data. Extracting the stock prices from those records using modern computing technology costs almost nothing—indeed, it is probable that these costs need to be incurred in any event for regulatory purposes or for reporting to traders. On this view, there will have been little or no investment in obtaining or verifying the database contents, and it will therefore not qualify for database right protection unless there has been a *subsequent* substantial investment in presenting the contents.

This issue came to the fore in *British Horseracing Board Ltd and Others v William Hill Organization Ltd.*[80] The British Horseracing Board ('BHB') maintains a comprehensive database relating to British horse racing, as explained in the first Court of Appeal judgment in 2001:[81]

4. . . . BHB is concerned with the creation of the fixture list for each year's racing, weight adding and handicapping, supervision of race programmes, producing various racing publications and stakesbooks and compiling data related to horseracing. In 2000 there were 1209 race meetings scheduled to be held at 59 racecourses on 327 days of the year with 7,800 races. That year there were 175,000 entries for races and 80,000 declarations to run and declarations of riders. At any one time there are 15,000 horses in training, 9,000 active owners and 1,000 trainers. Each owner must have registered unique racing colours in which his horses will run. In 1985 Weatherbys on behalf of the Jockey Club started to compile an electronic database of racing information comprising (amongst other things) details of registered horses, their owners and trainers, their handicap ratings, details of jockeys, information concerning fixture lists comprising venues, dates, times, race conditions and entries and runners. Since June 1993 the task of maintaining and developing the database has been carried out by Weatherbys on behalf of BHB in consequence of various assignments and agreements.

5. The database is constantly updated with the latest information, and the scale and complexity of the data kept by BHB have grown with time. The judge said that there was no substantial challenge to the pleaded assertions by BHB that the establishment of the database, at considerable cost, has involved, and its maintenance and development continue to involve, extensive work including the collection of raw data, the design of the database, the selection and verification of data for inclusion in the database and the insertion and arrangement of selected data in the database, the annual cost of continuing to obtain, verify and present its

---

[80] [2001] EWHC 516 (Pat) (High Court); [2001] EWCA Civ 1268 (CA); Case C-203/02, 9 November 2004 [2005] RPC 260 (ECJ); [2005] EWCA Civ 863 (CA).

[81] [2001] EWCA Civ 1268 (CA), paras 4–8.

contents being approximately £4,000,000 and involving approximately 80 employees and extensive computer software and hardware.

6. There is a huge amount of data accumulated over the years in the database, including details of over one million horses. The database contains pre-race information for each race, covering the place and date on which the meeting is to be held, the distance over which it is to be run, the criteria for eligibility to enter the race, the date by which entries are to be made, the entry fee payable, the initial name of the race and the like. Close to the day of a race, that information is expanded to include the time at which the race is provisionally scheduled to start, the final name of the race, the list of horses entered, the owners and trainers and the weight each horse has been allotted to carry. The final stage of the pre-race information contained in the database includes the list of declared runners, their jockeys, the weight each will carry (which may differ from the allotted weight for a number of reasons), its saddlecloth number, the stall from which it will start and the owner's racing colours. After the race, details of the outcome are recorded. An estimated total of 800,000 new records or changes to existing records are made each year.

7. A painstaking process of verification of the pre-race information is undertaken to ensure its complete accuracy and reliability. Thus in the case of declarations made by trainers by telephone, the conversations are tape-recorded and replayed and checked by an operator other than the one who took the call against an audit report produced by the computer.

8. The cost of running the database is a little over 25% of BHB's total annual expenditure of £15,000,000 . . .

The dispute arose when William Hill established an online betting service. The information displayed on the William Hill website about forthcoming races was derived via third party news feeds from the BHB database. William Hill took the view that this information was published in newspapers and was thus in the public domain, and therefore that it could be used freely. BHB argued that the information was extracted from the BHB database, which was protected by database right, and therefore that William Hill should pay licence fees for the right to use that data.

Initially, the case proceeded on the assumption that the BHB database was protected by database right,[82] and the High Court and first Court of Appeal proceedings concentrated on whether William Hill's use infringed that right. The Court of Appeal decided that various questions about the proper interpretation of the Database Directive should be referred to the European Court of Justice. Even at this stage it appears that the arguments were directed primarily to whether William Hill had infringed the database right which was presumed to exist, or whether what William Hill had used were only unprotected parts of the database. Nine of the eleven

---

[82] [2001] EWHC 516 (Pat), para 21.

questions referred to the ECJ[83] related to infringement, but two of them asked for a ruling on the proper interpretation of 'obtaining' and 'verification'.

In its judgment, the ECJ concentrated first on these two questions. It made the distinction noted above between *creating* and *obtaining* data and held that any investment in the creation of data should not be counted in deciding whether the investment in making a database was substantial:

30 Under the 9th, 10th and 12th recitals of the preamble to the directive, its purpose . . . is to promote and protect investment in data 'storage' and 'processing' systems which contribute to the development of an information market against a background of exponential growth in the amount of information generated and processed annually in all sectors of activity. It follows that the expression 'investment in . . . the obtaining, verification or presentation of the contents' of a database must be understood, generally, to refer to investment in the creation of that database as such.

31 Against that background, the expression 'investment in . . . the obtaining . . . of the contents' of a database must . . . be understood to refer to the resources used to seek out existing independent materials and collect them in the database, and not to the resources used for the creation as such of independent materials. The purpose of the protection by the *sui generis* right provided for by the directive is to promote the establishment of storage and processing systems for existing information and not the creation of materials capable of being collected subsequently in a database.

32 That interpretation is backed up by the 39th recital of the preamble to the directive, according to which the aim of the *sui generis* right is to safeguard the results of the financial and professional investment made in 'obtaining and collection of the contents' of a database. As the Advocate General notes in points 41 to 46 of her Opinion, despite slight variations in wording, all the language versions of the 39th recital support an interpretation which excludes the creation of the materials contained in a database from the definition of obtaining.

Similarly, the ECJ held investment in 'verification' should only be counted in relation to the cost of verifying already created materials, as opposed to the cost of verifying them in the course of creation.[84]

Thus, where the contents of a database are created by its maker, it is essential to separate the investment in creation from the investment in obtaining and/or verifying those contents post creation. Only if the latter investment is 'substantial' will the database qualify for protection by database right.[85]

8.6.2 Single source databases

The ECJ ruling suggests that many databases which consist of information which originates from the database maker ('single source databases') will not benefit from

---

[83] Set out at Case C-203/02, 9 November 2004, para 22.
[84] Ibid para 34.
[85] Ibid para 35.

database right protection. This was made very clear in the three *Fixtures Marketing* cases[86] which were decided by the ECJ at the same time as *British Horseracing Board Ltd and Others v William Hill Organization Ltd*. All three cases concerned claims by the distributor of British football fixtures lists against pools or betting organizations in Sweden, Finland, and Greece. Fixtures Marketing had the exclusive right to exploit these fixtures lists outside the UK under a contract with the English and Scottish football leagues. In each case the defendant had used the fixtures list in its betting activities without obtaining a licence from Fixtures Marketing. The ECJ decisions applied the same reasoning as in the *British Horseracing Board* judgment in almost identical language, and held that the investment in the creation of fixtures lists was not to be counted in deciding whether the database constituted by those lists attracted database right. However, the court went further, and also held that there was insufficient investment post the list creation to be substantial, so that the lists were completely unprotected by database right.[87]

44 Finding and collecting the data which make up a football fixture list do not require any particular effort on the part of the professional leagues. Those activities are indivisibly linked to the creation of those data, in which the leagues participate directly as those responsible for the organisation of football league fixtures. Obtaining the contents of a football fixture list thus does not require any investment independent of that required for the creation of the data contained in that list.

45 The professional football leagues do not need to put any particular effort into monitoring the accuracy of the data on league matches when the list is made up because those leagues are directly involved in the creation of those data. The verification of the accuracy of the contents of fixture lists during the season simply involves, according to the observations made by Fixtures, adapting certain data in those lists to take account of any postponement of a match or fixture date decided on by or in collaboration with the leagues. As Veikkaus submits, such verification cannot be regarded as requiring substantial investment.

46 The presentation of a football fixture list, too, is closely linked to the creation as such of the data which make up the list, as is confirmed by the absence of any mention in the order for reference of work or resources specifically invested in such presentation. It cannot therefore be considered to require investment independent of the investment in the creation of its constituent data.

47 It follows that neither the obtaining, nor the verification nor yet the presentation of the contents of a football fixture list attests to substantial investment which could justify protection by the *sui generis* right provided for by Article 7 of the directive.

---

[86] Case C-46/02 *Fixtures Marketing Ltd v Oy Veikkaus Ab*, 9 November 2004; Case C-338/02 *Fixtures Marketing Ltd v Svenska Spel Ab*, 9 November 2004; Case C-444/02 *Fixtures Marketing Ltd v Organismos prognostikon agonon podosfairou AE (OPAP)*, 9 November 2004.

[87] Case C-46/02 *Fixtures Marketing Ltd v Oy Veikkaus Ab*, 9 November 2004. The other two judgments contain wording which is identical in all material respects.

In *British Horseracing Board Ltd and Others v William Hill Organization Ltd*, the ECJ had noted that the process of transforming data, once created, into a database might amount to a substantial investment.[88] The case therefore returned to the Court of Appeal to determine this matter.

Before the Court of Appeal BHB argued that the ECJ had misunderstood the process involved in making the database. BHB suggested that it was not creating the contents per se—instead, it was gathering information from external sources (racehorse owners) and spending substantial time and money on verifying that information for inclusion in the database. Jacob LJ rejected this argument. The whole point of BHB's database was not to list the intentions of racehorse owners as to whether their horse would run in a particular race; rather, the database's purpose was to list those horses which were officially entered in the race. The effort on BHB's part was in determining which horses could be accepted for the race, according to the rules, and all the investment was devoted to this end. The definitive list was thus data *created* by BHB:

What marks that out from anything that has gone before is the BHB's stamp of authority on it. Only the BHB can provide such an *official* list. Only from that list can you know the accepted declared entries. Only the BHB can provide such a list. No one else could go through a similar process to produce the official list.[89]

For this reason the lists of entries were not protected by database right, so William Hill's appeal succeeded.

Applying these principles to other single source databases is not simple, but the following appears to represent the current state of the law:

(a) In deciding whether, and if so what parts of, a single source database are protected by database right it is essential to separate the investment in creating the data from any later investment in transforming that data into the database.

(b) If the process of creation results in data which are already in their final form, for example football fixtures lists or horserace entries lists, it is almost certain that the resulting database will not be protected.

(c) If, however, further work is required to transform the created data into the database, then the database will be protected by database right if that further work amounts to a substantial investment in creating the database.

In order to determine these matters it is necessary to know precisely *when* data were created. This can be a somewhat metaphysical question.[90] Jacob LJ in the Court of

---

[88] Case C-203/02, 9 November 2004, para 36, although on the facts as the ECJ understood them it appeared that no such substantial investment had been made—paras 38–41.

[89] [2005] EWCA Civ 863, para 29.

[90] See, eg, J Davison and B Hugenholz, 'Football Fixtures, Horseraces and Spin Offs: The ECJ Domesticates the Database Right' (2005) 27(3) EIPR 113 at 115, discussing whether recording meteorological data is a process of obtaining or of creation. See also DJG Visser, 'The Database Right and the

Appeal appears at one point to suggest that the moment of creation is when the data are published,[91] but this must surely be wrong. If correct, no single source database could ever be protected by database right because all investment takes place pre-publication, whereas the ECJ has clearly stated that such protection is possible.[92]

A better test, though less easy to apply, would be that data are created when they are in a form which achieves the purpose for which they were created. In case of a list of horserace entries, for example, this would be when sufficient checking had been completed so that the list *could* be published as definitive; similar reasoning would apply to a football fixtures list, whose creation would not be complete until the relevant football league had decided that no further changes would be made. In deciding whether the published version of that data attracted database right, the question would then be whether, after that time, further investment had been made to make the data available as a database, and if so whether that investment was substantial.

The immediately obvious way to avoid this issue is to separate the creation of the data from its incorporation in a database. In the case of the BHB, this might be achieved by separating between different legal entities the functions of accepting entries for a race and compiling the list of those horses which had been accepted. The first entity would undertake the checking and verification process for a particular horse, accept it for the race, and then pass that information to the second entity. The second entity would compile the information received into the list of runners and riders for each race and market the resulting database. The argument would be that the costs of operating the second entity, plus the licence fees paid to the first entity, amounted to a substantial investment.

This is, of course, a completely artificial structure; the first entity could just as easily compile the information and pass it complete to the second entity for marketing, as happened in *Fixtures Marketing*. If that occurred, however, the database would have been made before the second entity received it, so that the second entity's costs (except perhaps for any licence fee) would not count as an investment

---

Spin-Off Theory' in H Snijders and S Weatherill (eds), *E-commerce Law: National and Transnational Topics and Perspectives* (The Hague: Kluwer Law International, 2003) 105–10; E Derclaye, 'Databases Sui Generis Right: Should We Adopt the Spin-Off Theory?' [2004] EIPR 402–13.

[91] [2005] EWCA Civ 863, para 29. Masson suggests that the appropriate test for whether data has been created is to distinguish between 'material', which is still capable of modification by the creator because it has not yet been communicated to the 'information market', and 'data' which has been communicated and can no longer be modified because the creator has, by communicating it, crystallized it in its final form (A Masson, 'Creation of Database or Creation of Data: Crucial Choices in the Matter of Database Protection' (2006) 28(5) EIPR 261 at 266). 'Verification' would thus be the process of checking the accuracy of data already communicated (whether by the creator or a third party) to the information market (ibid, 267), which would provide a bright-line rule for distinguishing between investment in creation or verification. However, the justification for this approach is purely etymological, based on the Latin meaning of data as something given and the French term, *base de donnée*, which has an equivalent semantic origin (ibid 266), and no has no obvious legal basis.

[92] See n 85 above.

in obtaining the database contents. It seems likely that single sources of commercially valuable information will investigate structures of this type in an attempt to secure database right protection, and this will no doubt result in further litigation when third parties seek to use that data without payment.

If single source databases which qualify for database right protection can be created, then competition law questions will inevitably arise. It has already been determined that the proprietor of an intellectual property right can be abusing its dominant position if it refuses to licence that intellectual property to a third party in order to reserve a different market to the proprietor or to prevent that different market from emerging.[93] Thus, if the BHB database were in future to be protected by database right but BHB refused to license the data to online betting companies in order, for example, to preserve the market for its database among offline betting companies, Article 82 of the EC Treaty might apply to force BHB to grant licences.[94] It is important to note that the original compulsory licensing provisions in the first draft of the Database Directive[95] were abandoned in the final text, so that it is not possible for any person to insist on being granted a licence to use a single source database other than via the rules of competition law.

8.7 RIGHTS OF THE DATABASE OWNER

8.7.1 Extraction and re-utilization

The owner's rights are defined in regulation 16:[96]

(1) Subject to the provisions of this Part, a person infringes database right in a database if, without the consent of the owner of the right, he extracts or re-utilises all or a substantial part of the contents of the database.

(2) For the purposes of this Part, the repeated and systematic extraction or re-utilisation of insubstantial parts of the contents of a database may amount to the extraction or re-utilisation of a substantial part of those contents.

'Extraction' is 'the permanent or temporary transfer of all or a substantial part of the contents of a database to another medium by any means or in any form', and 're-utilisation' occurs by 'making those contents available to the public by any means'.[97]

---

[93] *RTE & ITP v EC Commission* [1995] 4 CMLR 718.

[94] See further Davison and Hugenholz, n 90, 115–16; G Westkamp, 'Balancing Database Sui Generis Right Protection with European Monopoly Control Under Article 82 EC' (2001) 22(1) ECLR 13.

[95] COM(92)24 final—SYN 383, 13 May 1992.

[96] Implementing Art 7(1) Database Directive.

[97] Reg 12(1).

Where the entirety of a database is copied or made available to the public, the right will clearly be infringed. However, where there is only partial extraction or re-utilization, or where the alleged infringement is the extraction or re-utilization of insubstantial parts which, taken together, amount to a substantial part, the position is less clear.

Article 7(1) of the Database Directive refers to 'a substantial part evaluated qualitatively and/or quantitatively'. At first sight this looks very like the test for infringement of copyright. However, the test is in fact subtly different as explained by the ECJ in *British Horseracing Board Ltd and Others v William Hill Organization Ltd*. There, BHB had extracted and re-utilized information from the BHB database for each race, and each of these was not of a substantial part of the database. Were they, taken together, a substantial part?

The quantitative test refers simply to the proportion of the database which is extracted or re-utilized.[98] In other words, the greater the percentage of the database involved, the more likely that part is to be substantial. However, the ECJ did not give any guidelines as to what percentage would suffice. It was clear that William Hill had taken only a small proportion of the BHB database, so on the quantitative test that could not be a substantial part.

The qualitative test applies where, merely as a percentage, the amount taken or re-used is not substantial. In that case, the test is whether the part taken corresponds to a substantial part of the *investment* in obtaining, verifying, or presenting the database contents. 'A quantitatively negligible part of the contents of a database may in fact represent, in terms of obtaining, verification or presentation, significant human, technical or financial investment.'[99]

BHB argued that weight should also be given to the importance of the data in question; in other words, even if all data elements required the same investment, some would be of more interest to users of the database and thus be qualitatively more substantial than other elements. This argument was rejected. Accepting it would, in effect, grant a right in individual content elements rather than the database as a whole, and this was not the purpose behind the Directive.[100] The correct test was whether the material taken by William Hill represented a substantial part of BHB's investment in the database as a whole, and on the facts what was taken was an insubstantial part.[101]

This ruling further weakens the protection offered by database right, and the larger the database the weaker the right becomes. A database can cost many millions of pounds to create, but in practice only a small percentage of its contents may be of interest to users. Copying that small percentage would give the copier almost all of the economic value of the database, but would be likely to amount to taking only a

---

[98] Case C-203/02, 9 November 2004, para 70.
[99] Ibid para 71.
[100] Ibid para 72.
[101] Ibid paras 78–80.

small proportion of the investment required to make the database, and thus not infringe.

In the opinion of the author the courts may seek to find a way of protecting, in part, database owners in these circumstances. Taking 1 per cent of the contents of a £100 million database will clearly not be substantial quantitatively, but still amounts to taking data representing £1 million of the investment. £1 million can be seen as a substantial sum, and thus a substantial part of the investment qualitatively. However, the language of the ECJ does not support this approach; it appears that the court had in mind the situation where obtaining, verifying, and presenting that 1 per cent required a far higher proportion of the investment than other parts of the database.

A more fruitful line of argument in such circumstances would be to rely on Article 7(5) of the Directive, which provides:

The repeated and systematic extraction and/or re-utilization of insubstantial parts of the contents of the database implying acts which conflict with a normal exploitation of that database or which unreasonably prejudice the legitimate interests of the maker of the database shall not be permitted.

It would seem clear that the extraction or re-utilization of an insubstantial part of a database, which nonetheless represented a major part of the database's economic value, contravenes this article. Unfortunately for UK database owners, the implementation of this provision in regulation 16(2) adopts different wording:

For the purposes of this Part, the repeated and systematic extraction or re-utilisation of insubstantial parts of the contents of a database may amount to the extraction or re-utilisation of a substantial part of those contents.

A database owner will only need to use this regulation if the repeated acts do not relate to a substantial part, as defined by the ECJ, as if they do amount to a substantial part the database right has clearly been infringed. If, however, the cumulation of parts taken do not amount to a substantial part regulation 16(2) does not apply, and unlike Article 7(5) the regulation gives the owner no rights in these circumstances. Thus, the provision will never be of assistance. It is to be hoped that the UK courts can interpret regulation 16 ingeniously so as to give effect to Article 7(5) in UK law. Article 8(2) imposes a more general obligation on lawful users which might also be of use in such circumstances—see section 8.7.5 below.

Two further points arising from the ECJ decision are worth noting here:

(a) First, infringement of database right requires extraction and/or re-utilization. Thus mere consultation of the database is not an infringement, and the database owner cannot use database right against those who do so.[102] If the owner wishes to control mere use of the database he will need to do so via contract, for example by

---

[102] Case C-203/02, para 74.

granting access on terms that the contractual user will not allow third parties to have access.

(b) William Hill had not taken their data directly from the BHB database, but had acquired it from data feeds and other sources which had obtained that data by direct consultation of the database. The ECJ held that the purpose of database right is to protect the investment in a database, and that this investment is equally prejudiced by both direct and indirect extraction or re-utilization. Thus infringement can occur if a person recreates a substantial part of the database by constructing it from publicly available sources which themselves derive from the database.[103]

Where databases are accessible online, the question arises as to where any acts of extraction or re-utilization take place. In *Football Dataco v Sportradar*,[104] Floyd J held, answering a preliminary question on jurisdiction, that in the case of a website which was alleged to be making available data taken from the claimant's Sports Live service, this occurred at the location of the server, in this case in Germany and Austria.[105] However, the action could proceed in the English courts on the basis of a claim that the defendants had authorized extraction and re-utilization by users situated in England. The Court of Appeal[106] agreed that the better interpretation of the law was that these acts occurred where the server was located, but because the authorities were uncertain on the point referred the question to the ECJ.

8.7.2 Exhaustion of rights

Where a copy of a database is distributed to the public, the database right is exhausted.[107] This means that the database owner cannot prevent the lawful owner of a copy from selling that copy by asserting that this act infringes the database right. However, online databases are made available to the public without distributing copies, and so that making available does not exhaust the database owner's right to prevent a lawful user making the database available to others.[108]

Rental of a copy of a database is specifically defined as an act of re-utilization[109] and therefore the right to control such rental is not exhausted by sale of a copy, with an exception for non-commercial public lending (eg, by libraries).[110]

---

[103] Case C-203/02, para 53.
[104] [2010] EWHC 2911 (Ch).
[105] Ibid para 74.
[106] [2011] EWCA Civ 330.
[107] Reg 12(5), Art 7(2) Database Directive.
[108] Recital 43 Database Directive.
[109] Art 7(2)(b) Database Directive—note that this is not stated expressly in the Regulations.
[110] Reg 12(2)–(4).

8.7.3 Duration of rights

8.7.3.1 *Initial term*

The initial term of protection is 15 years from 1 January following completion of the database, or from its first making available to the public, whichever is the later. If, however, the database is not made available to the public within 15 years from its making, database right expires and is not revived by subsequent publication.[111]

8.7.3.2 *Updating*

Databases are rarely static objects. In most cases, their economic value derives from the fact that they are regularly updated. To take account of this, regulation 17(3) provides:

> Any substantial change to the contents of a database, including a substantial change resulting from the accumulation of successive additions, deletions or alterations, which would result in the database being considered to be a substantial new investment shall qualify the database resulting from that investment for its own term of protection.

This wording is identical to Article 11 of the Directive.

For the example of a database which is published on CD-ROM and updated annually, this wording is simple to apply. We have merely to look at the investment made in the update and decide whether that investment was substantial. If so, the new CD-ROM acquires a fresh term of protection. If not, the preceding protected CD-ROM retains its term of protection. Copying the additional material from the new CD-ROM would then not infringe, but copying other material might still infringe database right in the preceding edition as an act of indirect extraction.[112]

In the case of an online database, however, the database is never made available to the public in a fixed form. Such databases are continuously updated, and this has raised the question as to when the contents of such a database fall outside protection. Are they protected for 15 years from the time they entered the database, or does a database with a fresh term of protection come into existence from time to time and if so when?

In the light of the ECJ decision in *British Horseracing Board Ltd and Others v William Hill Organization Ltd*,[113] it is clear that this is in fact a meaningless question. The contents never fall outside the protection of database right because the right does not protect the contents. Instead it protects the database *as a whole*. The relevant question is thus not when the content was added to the database, but whether taking that content amounts to taking a substantial part of the database *as it existed at the moment of the taking*.

---

[111] Reg 17(1)–(2).
[112] See section 8.7.1 above.
[113] Case C-203/02, 9 November 2004.

If this interpretation of the law is correct, it follows that continuously updated databases will never fall out of database protection provided that the cumulative effect of updating amounts to a substantial investment over successive 15-year periods.

8.7.4 Exceptions to the owner's rights

As with all intellectual property rights, there are a number of exceptions to the owner's rights.[114] Unfortunately the Directive permits Member States to choose which, if any, of these to implement, so the scheme of protection is not uniform throughout the EU. The most important exceptions enacted by the UK are:

(a) A lawful user is entitled to extract and re-utilize insubstantial parts of a database, and any contractual term to the contrary is void.[115] Article 8(1) of the Directive provides that if the lawful user is only authorized to access particular parts of the database then this exception applies only to those parts, but this is not reproduced in the UK Regulations.

(b) A lawful user is entitled to extract and re-utilize substantial parts of a database if that amounts to fair dealing for the purposes of illustration for teaching or research and not for any commercial purpose.[116]

(c) A number of exceptions relating to public security and administrative or judicial proceedings are set out in Schedule 1 to the Regulations.

8.7.5 Obligations of users

Unlike other intellectual property rights, lawful users of databases have positive obligations imposed on them by the Directive. These are set out in Article 8 which provides:

2. A lawful user of a database which is made available to the public in whatever manner may not perform acts which conflict with normal exploitation of the database or unreasonably prejudice the legitimate interests of the maker of the database.

3. A lawful user of a database which is made available to the public in any manner may not cause prejudice to the holder of a copyright or related right in respect of the works or subject matter contained in the database.

Article 8(3) seems merely to restate copyright law, but Article 8(2) would potentially be of use to assist a database owner in preventing those actions in respect of insubstantial parts of a database which are not infringements of database right but

---

[114] Art 9 Database Directive.
[115] Reg 19.
[116] Reg 20(1).

which are clearly prejudicial to the economic interests of the owner. This point was not raised in *British Horseracing Board Ltd and Others v William Hill Organization Ltd*, perhaps because the UK Regulations do not contain an equivalent provision, so it is unclear whether Article 8(2) will be of any real assistance in UK litigation.

8.8 FUTURE DEVELOPMENTS

As the discussion above has demonstrated, the state of legal protection for databases is far from satisfactory. The law is by no means clear, both in respect of which databases receive protection from database right and what constitutes an infringement of that right.

Owners of single source databases have a particular reason to feel aggrieved. Prior to the Database Directive it was clear that their databases received copyright protection in the UK under the 'sweat of the brow' doctrine,[117] and the quid pro quo for losing that protection for new databases was that they would be protected by the *sui generis* database right.[118] Since the decision in *British Horseracing Board Ltd and Others v William Hill Organization Ltd*,[119] it seems likely that they may now receive no protection at all.

Change may be on the way, though what form that change will take is still uncertain. In autumn 2005 DG Internal Market and Services carried out an assessment of the Database Directive.[120] This assessment made a number of important findings:

(a) The Directive has not achieved its purpose of encouraging the creation of new databases.[121]

(b) The distinction between creation and obtaining of data, made by the ECJ in *British Horseracing Board Ltd and Others v William Hill Organization Ltd*,[122] goes against the original intention of the European Commission that a wide range of databases, including single source databases, should be protected by the *sui generis* right, and as a consequence of the decision 36 per cent of database owners think they will suffer weaker legal protection.[123]

---

[117] See section 8.4.2 above.
[118] 'First evaluation of Directive 96/9/EC on the legal protection of databases', DG Internal Market and Services Working Paper (Brussels, 12 December 2005) p 8.
[119] Case C-203/02, 9 November 2004.
[120] 'First evaluation of Directive 96/9/EC', n 118.
[121] Ibid, pp 15–20, 22–3.
[122] See sections 8.6.1 and 8.6.2 above.
[123] 'First evaluation of Directive 96/9/EC', n 118, pp 13–14.

(c) There are concerns that the Directive has made access to information more difficult for non-commercial users, although this may be due mainly to the complexity of the law.[124]

However, the uniform legal regime is broadly welcomed by the database industry, compared to the differing national laws prior to the Directive.

DG Internal Market and Services identifies four options for the future:[125]

(a) To repeal the Directive and revert to the pre-existing national laws.

(b) To withdraw the *sui generis* database right but retain the harmonized copyright provisions. This would allow national legislatures to decide whether and to what extent they should grant protection to databases via their own individual *sui generis* rights.

(c) To amend the *sui generis* database right to clarify the law and reintroduce protection for those databases where the substantial investment lies in the creation of the data, rather than its obtaining and verification.

(d) No change.

Consultation on these four options closed in March 2006, and from the responses received there was little support for options (a) and (b). Opinion is evenly split between options (c) (amendment of the *sui generis* right) and (d) (no change).[126] As many of those who supported 'no change' appear to have done so on the basis that the current position was less bad for them than the changes they anticipated, and there are numerous comments that the current state of the law is unsatisfactory, it seems likely that the European Commission will at some point propose reforms to database right. However, at the time of writing (over five years after the consultation) there is no sign of activity on this matter.

---

[124] 'First evaluation of Directive 96/9/EC', n 118, pp 21–2.
[125] Ibid pp 25 ff.
[126] See <http://ec.europa.eu/internal_market/copyright/prot-databases/prot-databases_en.htm> (accessed 9 August 2011), which also links to the responses.

9

ONLINE USE OF TRADE MARKS AND DOMAIN NAMES

Ben Allgrove, Peter O'Byrne, and Mike Jury

9.1 INTRODUCTION

The commercialization of the internet has led to an increasing number of issues arising in respect of the use of trade marks online. Some are little different to those which arise in the offline world; others are unique to the internet. In this chapter we explore the particular legal and practical issues that arise from the exploitation of trade marks online, seeking to give the reader some strategies that can be employed to deal with them. Some of these issues are currently hotly contested in high-profile disputes. In recent years, a succession of references to the European Court of Justice ('ECJ') have provided some clarity for those operating in the EU, including in the UK. However, as at the date of publication, there remain several outstanding decisions awaited from the ECJ which are likely to be of central importance to the issues discussed below.

9.2 TRADE MARKS

This chapter is not a text on trade mark law. It deals with the particular issues that arise when trade marks are used online. Notwithstanding that, a basic understanding of the legal framework for the protection of trade marks is necessary in order to appreciate the particular issues that affect trade marks online.

9.2.1 Definition and functions of a trade mark

The functions of a trade mark have recently been described by the ECJ as extending beyond the so-called 'essential function' of guaranteeing origin in the following terms:

These functions include not only the essential function of the trade mark, which is to guarantee to consumers the origin of the goods or services, but also its other functions, in particular that of guaranteeing the quality of the goods or services in question and those of communication, investment or advertising.[1]

There is no definition of a trade mark in the Trade Marks Directive[2] or the Community Trade Mark Regulation[3] ('CTMR'). However, Article 2 of the Directive[4] sets out examples of signs which may constitute a trade mark and refers to the essential function they serve:

A trade mark may consist of any sign capable of being represented graphically, particularly words, including personal names, designs, letters, numerals, the shape of goods or of their packaging, provided that such signs are capable of distinguishing the goods or services of one undertaking from those of other undertakings.

The Trade Marks Act 1994 ('TMA') provides a definition along similar lines.[5] A trade mark must, therefore, have a 'distinctive character' before it will be protected at law.

---

[1] Case C-487/07 *L'Oréal v Bellure* [2009] ECR I-5185 at para 58. More broadly, 'brands' (as opposed to registered marks) are also increasingly developing a value in their own right, independent of their source-identifying function, as recognized recently in *Och-Ziff Management Europe Ltd and Another v Och Capital LLP and Others* [2010] EWHC 2599 (Ch). See also B Allgrove and P O'Byrne, 'Pre-Sale Misrepresentations In Passing Off: An Idea Whose Time Has Come Or Unfair Competition By The Back Door?' (2006) 1(6) Journal of Intellectual Property Law & Practice 413 and B Allgrove and P O'Byrne, 'Initial Interest Confusion Recognised by the English Courts' 6(3) Journal of Intellectual Property Law & Practice 147.

[2] First Council Directive 89/104/EEC to approximate the laws of the Member States relating to trade marks, OJ L40/1, 11 February 1989.

[3] Council Regulation 40/94/EEC on the Community trade mark, OJ L11/1, 14 January 1994.

[4] Art 4 of the CTMR, the corresponding provision to Art 2 of the Directive, contains the same wording, but in relation to Community Trade Marks.

[5] TMA, s 1.

This is not the only limitation on the protection of trade marks. Trade marks are not true monopoly rights. The protection the law affords them, both by statute and via the common law, is limited by various other threshold requirements. These include depending on the cause of action pursued, requirements for identity or similarity of goods or services, confusion, misrepresentation, fame, unfairness, and damage.

9.2.2 Obtaining registered trade mark protection in the UK

All countries in Europe, including the UK, operate a system of national trade mark registrations, and national laws across the EU relating to trade marks have been largely harmonized by the Trade Marks Directive. There are three routes by which one can obtain registered trade mark protection in the UK. The first is via a national trade mark registration in the UK, which gives its proprietor an exclusive right to use the registered mark in the UK in respect of the goods and services for which the trade mark is registered along with some ancillary rights. The second route is to obtain a Community Trade Mark ('CTM'). The CTM system was established on 1 April 1996 and is governed by the CTMR. A CTM is a unitary right which covers all countries of the European Union and will also extend to any Member States which join in the future. The CTM system is administered by the Office for Harmonization in the Internal Market. Thirdly, there is also a well-established international system of registration covering a number of countries which are party to the Madrid Agreement[6] and the Madrid Protocol.[7] An international registration is best described as a bundle of national trade mark rights. The marks are centrally filed, registered, and renewed but consist of individual national rights which can each be assigned, licensed, challenged, or cancelled separately. The marks are individually governed by the national laws in each designated country.

9.2.3 Infringement of registered trade marks in the UK

The rights conferred by a UK registered trade mark are set out in sections 9 and 10 of the TMA. Section 9(1) provides that:

The proprietor of a registered trade mark has exclusive rights in the trade mark which are infringed by use of the trade mark in the United Kingdom without his consent.

Section 10 specifies three distinct categories of infringement. Section 10(1) provides:

A person infringes a registered trade mark if he uses in the course of trade a sign which is identical with the trade mark in relation to goods or services which are identical with those for which it is registered.[8]

---

[6] Madrid Agreement Concerning the International Registration of Marks (1891).
[7] Protocol Relating to the Madrid Agreement (1989).
[8] TMA, s 10(1) implementing Art 5(1)(a) Trade Marks Directive. The corresponding provision in relation to infringement of a CTM is Art 9(1)(a) CTMR.

A sign will be identical with a registered mark where it reproduces, without any modification or addition, all the elements constituting the mark or where, viewed as a whole, it contains differences so insignificant they may go unnoticed by an average consumer.[9] Whether the mark and offending sign are in fact identical must be assessed from the perspective of an average consumer who is deemed to be reasonably well-informed, observant, and circumspect.[10] The identity of the goods or services is determined by reference to the specification of goods and services covered by the registered mark.

Section 10(2) provides:

A person infringes a registered trade mark if he uses in the course of trade a sign where because—

(a) the sign is identical with the trade mark and is used in relation to goods or services similar to those for which the trade mark is registered, or

(b) the sign is similar to the trade mark and is used in relation to goods or services identical with or similar to those for which the trade mark is registered,

there exists a likelihood of confusion on the part of the public, which includes the likelihood of association with the trade mark.[11]

Section 10(2) infringement requires a likelihood of confusion on the part of the public, resulting from the degree of identity or similarity between the mark and the offending sign and the goods/services. The likelihood of confusion is assessed globally, taking into account all factors relevant to the circumstances of the case.[12] The factors are interdependent, such that a lesser degree of similarity between the goods or services may be offset by a greater similarity between the marks, and vice versa.

Confusion as to origin is required. A mere likelihood of *association*, where the public upon seeing the offending sign are reminded of the registered mark, does not constitute confusion for the purposes of section 10(2).[13]

In order for there to be similarity between a mark and a sign, there must exist elements of visual, aural, and conceptual similarity between the two, based upon the overall impression given by the mark and sign, bearing in mind their distinctive and dominant components.[14] The more distinctive the mark, the greater the likelihood of confusion. In determining the similarity of the goods or services in question, all factors relating to the goods or services themselves must be taken into account, such

---

[9] Case C-291/00 *LTJ Diffusion v Sadas ('Arthur et Felicie')* [2003] FSR 34 at para 54.

[10] Ibid para 52.

[11] TMA, s 10(2) implementing Art 5(1)(b) Trade Marks Directive. The corresponding provision in relation to infringement of a CTM is Art 9(1)(b) CTMR.

[12] Case C-251/95 *Sabel v Puma* [1997] ECR I-6191 at para 22.

[13] Ibid para 16.

[14] Ibid para 23.

as their nature, end-users, method of use, and the extent to which they are in competition with each other.[15]

Recent case law has shown that initial interest confusion is sufficient to ground a trade mark infringement action.[16] That is, even if there is no confusion at the point of sale, if a trade mark is used to divert sales from the trade mark proprietor by grabbing the attention of customers, then that may suffice.

Section 10(3) provides:

A person infringes a registered trade mark if he uses in the course of trade, in relation to goods or services, a sign which is identical with or similar to the trade mark where the trade mark has a reputation in the United Kingdom and the use of the sign, being without due cause, takes unfair advantage of, or is detrimental to, the distinctive character or the repute of the trade mark.[17]

In order to establish infringement under section 10(3), the registered trade mark must have a reputation in the UK, which means that the mark is recognized by a significant part of the public concerned by the goods or services covered by the trade mark.[18] Reputation may exist independently of goodwill.[19] Infringement under section 10(3) does not require a likelihood of confusion.[20] The unfair advantage or detriment to the distinctive character or repute of the mark must be proved by evidence, and not be merely theoretical[21] (unlike the likelihood of confusion, in which actual confusion does not need to be shown).

Any one of the three heads of infringement will suffice under section 10(3):

(a) Detriment to distinctive character is caused 'when that mark's ability to identify the goods or services for which it is registered and used as coming from the proprietor of that mark is weakened, since use of the later mark leads to dispersion of the identity and hold upon the public mind of the earlier mark'.[22]

(b) Detriment to the repute of the mark is caused 'when the goods or services for which the identical or similar sign is used by the third party may be perceived by the public in such a way that the trade mark's power of attraction is reduced'.[23]

---

[15] *British Sugar v James Robertson* [1996] RPC 281 at 296–7.

[16] *Och-Ziff Management Europe Ltd and Another v Och Capital LLP and Others* [2010] EWHC 2599 (Ch).

[17] TMA, s 10(3) implementing Art 5(2) Trade Marks Directive. The corresponding provision in relation to infringement of a CTM is Art 9(1)(c) CTMR.

[18] *Kerly's Law of Trade Marks and Trade Names*, 14th edn (London: Sweet & Maxwell, 2005) para 9-103.

[19] Ibid para 9-102.

[20] Case C-102/07 *Marca Mode v Adidas* [2000] ECR I-4861 at para 36.

[21] *Intel Corp v Kirpla Singh Sihra* [2003] EWHC 17 at para 23. Also Case C-252/07 *Intel Corp v CPM United Kingdom* [2008] ECR I-8823 at paras 37–8 and 77.

[22] Case C-252/07 *Intel Corp v CPM United Kingdom* [2008] ECR I-8823 at para 29.

[23] Case C-487/07 *L'Oréal v Bellure* [2009] ECR I-5185 at para 40.

(c) Taking unfair advantage of the distinctive character or the repute of the trade mark concerns not detriment to the mark but the advantage taken by the third party through using an identical or similar sign. That advantage will be unfair 'where that party seeks by that use to ride on the coat-tails of the mark with a reputation in order to benefit from the power of attraction, the reputation and the prestige of that mark and to exploit, without paying any financial compensation, the marketing effort expended by the proprietor of the mark in order to create and maintain the mark's image'.[24]

9.2.4 Unregistered marks—passing off and unfair competition

The English common law also provides a level of protection for marks which are not registered. This protection comes via the tort of passing off. The classic example of passing off is where a trader causes damage to another trader by adopting for his own goods or business a name, mark, get-up, or other indicia which are deceptively similar to those of the claimant. The 'classic trinity' of elements underlying the tort are:

(a) goodwill or a reputation;

(b) a misrepresentation by the defendant leading or likely to lead the public to believe that the goods or services offered by him are the goods or services of the claimant; and

(c) damage caused by the defendant's misrepresentation.[25]

Although this statement of the law will cover most cases of passing off, the boundaries are not set in stone and the cause of action is continuing to develop over time to encompass a number of different situations, including, as in the case of trade mark infringement, actions based on initial interest confusion.[26] The key to obtaining protection for unregistered marks in the UK, therefore, is use of those marks so that the requisite reputation or goodwill is established.

While there is at present no recognized tort of unfair competition actionable in the UK,[27] unfair competition is a recognized cause of action in many other jurisdictions, including most European jurisdictions. Unfair competition may also present a way of protecting interests in unregistered rights outside the UK.

---

[24] Ibid para 50.

[25] Lord Oliver in *Reckitt & Colman v Borden* [1990] 1 All ER 873 at para 880.

[26] *Och-Ziff Management Europe Ltd and Another v Och Capital LLP and Others* [2010] EWHC 2599 (Ch).

[27] Lord Justice Jacob in *L'Oréal v Bellure* [2007] EWCA Civ 968 at paras 135–61.

9.3 INFRINGEMENT ONLINE

9.3.1 Use

Under section 10 of the TMA there must be 'use' before there can be infringement. Section 10(4) says that there is use of a sign if the defendant:

(a) affixes it to goods or the packaging thereof;

(b) offers or exposes goods for sale, puts them on the market or stocks them for those purposes under the sign, or offers or supplies services under the sign;

(c) imports or exports goods under the sign; or

(d) uses the sign on business papers or in advertising.

The use in question must be 'trade mark use', that is use to indicate origin[28] or use so as to create the impression that there is a material link in the course of trade between the goods or services in issue and the trade mark proprietor[29] or use such as to affect one of the other functions of a trade mark such as the advertising function.

Where the use of a sign online is visible use on a website, there should be little problem applying 'offline' infringement principles in the online environment. More difficult questions arise when the alleged infringement is in the domain name alone or, even more difficult, invisible.

9.3.2 Online marketing: metatags and keywords

Online marketing is advertising like any other and subject to relevant regulation concerning not deceiving consumers, etc.[30] However, in the online world particularly thorny issues have arisen around the liability for the use of registered trade marks in metatags and search engine keywords as a tool in marketing. Although an important element of liability is the potential deception of consumers, claims in this area are made by the proprietors of the trade marks, rather than regulators or deceived consumers.

9.3.2.1 *In the UK*
Metatags are markers written into the invisible computer code (usually HTML) that underlies a webpage. They serve to make indexing easier for search engines by summarizing the page's content; the more times a metatag appears in a website's HTML, the higher the page will appear in search results. In choosing metatags, website owners often use generic terms which describe the contents of their website, for

---

[28] Case C-245/02 *Anheuser-Busch v Budejovicky Budvar NP* [2005] ETMR 2 at para 59.
[29] *Kerly's Law of Trade Marks and Trade Names*, n 18, para 14-018.
[30] See further Chapter 2, sections 2.2.1.4 and 2.5.

example car, flight, etc. However, they may also choose to use registered trade marks belonging to a third party, with the result that their site is ranked amongst the search results when the third party trade mark is entered as a search term.

Search engines also sell keywords which, when entered in a search, generate sponsored links or banner advertisements. Sponsored links are used by businesses to drive traffic to their website. Businesses can purchase certain keywords from search engines. When an internet user searches against these keywords, the business's website is shown as the promoted or sponsored site. As with metatags, keywords can be either generic terms relating to the business or content of the website or they can be, and often are, registered trade marks.

So is the use of a trade mark in a metatag or as part of a keyword search an infringement? The English courts have not to date provided clear guidance and three completed or pending references to the ECJ are in the process of clarifying this difficult area.

The first English case to touch on the issue, albeit not conclusively, was *Reed Executive plc v Reed Business Information Ltd.*[31] The claimant, Reed Executive, was an employment agency which owned a UK trade mark registration for 'REED' in respect of employment agency services in Class 35. The defendant, Reed Business Information, advertised jobs online via its www.totaljobs.com website. The defendant used the words 'Reed Business Information' in the metatags for its site and used the word 'Reed' as a keyword for generating various forms of web advertising. The claimant sued for trade mark infringement and passing off.

Importantly, the case focused on the need for the claimant to establish a likelihood of confusion, which the Court of Appeal held it could not do on the facts. This was particularly because in all cases where a search under the phrase 'Reed jobs' was made, the www.totaljobs.com website was listed below the claimant's site in the search results. The Court of Appeal also found that the banner advertisements would not lead to confusion as internet users are used to web searches throwing up numerous banner advertisements and would not necessarily think there was a trade connection between the claimant and a 'totaljobs' banner making no reference to the word 'Reed'.

The Court of Appeal reserved its position on the threshold question as to whether there had been 'trade mark use' of the 'REED' mark, but did suggest that invisible use may not be sufficient to constitute 'trade mark use'. This was on the basis that use which is read only by computers does not convey 'a message' (representation) to anyone, and thus cannot be perceived by potential customers as a badge of origin.

In *Wilson v Yahoo! UK Ltd and Another,*[32] the High Court at summary judgment stage found against a claimant partially on the basis that neither the search engine

---

[31] *Reed Executive plc v Reed Business Information Ltd* [2004] EWCA Civ 159.
[32] *Wilson v Yahoo! UK Ltd and Another* [2008] EWHC 361 (Ch).

nor the purchaser of a keyword similar to the claimant's trade mark 'MR SPICY' was using the mark at all, or alternatively using it as a trade mark. This case should be treated with caution for a variety of reasons[33] and indeed has been distinguished in the following case which is set to provide more authoritative guidance from the English courts.

L'Oréal v eBay[34] concerned trade in products infringing L'Oréal's trade marks on eBay's UK website. As well as claiming infringement against the individual sellers, L'Oréal argued that eBay was directly liable for trade mark infringement in a variety of ways. One of these was that eBay purchased keywords consisting of L'Oréal marks which triggered sponsored links on third party search engines such as Google and Yahoo. A search on a search engine using one of the L'Oréal marks caused a sponsored link to www.ebay.co.uk to be displayed. If the user clicked on the sponsored link, he or she was taken to a display of search results on www.ebay.co.uk for L'Oréal products sold under the relevant L'Oréal mark, some of which were infringing.

The High Court considered many issues concerning eBay's use of L'Oréal's trade marks in sponsored links. It decided some and referred others to the ECJ which determined them in its recent judgment.[35] These can be summarized as follows:

Issue	High Court view re sponsored links/use on www.ebay.co.uk	ECJ conclusion
Is there a 'use' of the signs by eBay	Yes, display to users was use, but not acte clair.	On sponsored links—yes. On the website itself—no.
Is the use 'in relation to' all relevant goods listed on www.ebay.co.uk at the time the search is carried out, and is thus an infringement in relation to any infringing goods?	It is arguable that there is a sufficient nexus between the use and the infringing goods.	Not determined.
Is use in the course of trade?	Yes.	Yes.

---

[33] Particularly the fundamental claim was misconceived by a litigant in person, and the judgment was only at summary judgment stage and without the full issues (including the Reed decision) being argued before the court.

[34] *L'Oréal v eBay* [2009] EWHC 1094 (Ch).

[35] Case C-324/09 *L'Oréal v eBay*.

Issue	High Court view re sponsored links/use on www.ebay.co.uk	ECJ conclusion
Is use in the UK?	Yes, as listings are clearly targeted at UK consumers.	Yes, including non-EEA listings targeted to multiple regions including the EEA.
Must it be shown that the use necessarily entails putting items on the UK market?	No, infringement by advertisement, offer for sale and exposure for sale does not require placing on the market, but not acte clair.	No.

9.3.2.2 *ECJ decisions*

The important decision of *LVM v Google*[36] has clarified liability for keyword use by search engines and also the visible and invisible trade mark use debate. In this case, three sets of proceedings were brought against Google in France by different trade mark owners regarding its keywords programme where keywords corresponding to relevant trade marks were used without the consent of the claimants. When the respective trade marks were entered into the Google search engine, advertisements were displayed which linked to websites selling either counterfeit products (as was the case in the Louis Vuitton reference) or products which were identical or similar to those covered by the trade marks offered by competitors.

The ECJ concluded that Google is not liable for trade mark infringement in relation to its keywords programme, but that advertisers may be. Particularly:

(a) In the conduct of its keyword service in which advertisers may select registered trade marks of third parties, Google is not using those marks in the course of trade and therefore is not liable for trade mark infringement.

(b) Advertisers who sponsor registered trade marks as keywords are using the marks in the course of trade, even where the trade marks do not appear in the text of the advertisements. If such use triggers confusion of the reasonably attentive internet user about the source of the advertiser's products, or such a user is unable to determine the origin of the goods on the basis of the link and accompanying text, then the advertiser will be liable for infringement.[37]

---

[36] Joined Cases C-236/08, C-237/08 and C-238/08 *Google France v Louis Vuitton Malletier & Others* [2010] RPC 19. Also re-affirmed in the Banabay case, Case C-91/09 *Eis.de GmbH v BBY Vertreibsgesellschaft mbH*.

[37] This reasoning was also applied by the ECJ to whether eBay was liable for keyword advertising using L'Oréal trade marks in Case C-324/09 *L'Oréal v eBay*.

Similarly, the ECJ concluded in the case of *Portakabin v Primakabin*[38] that the re-sale of authentic but second-hand goods, using keywords corresponding to the registered trade mark of the original maker of the goods, cannot be prevented except where the advertising does not enable internet users to determine the source of the goods.

The ECJ in *LVM v Google* did not answer the question whether Google's service falls within the so-called 'hosting' exemption to liability available under the e-Commerce Directive, preferring to leave this for the national courts to decide. The ECJ also did not make any ruling on whether use by advertisers may take unfair advantage of the trade mark or cause dilution where there is no confusion.

The issues surrounding liability of advertisers which *LVM v Google* left open will likely be determined by the ECJ in the pending reference in the English High Court case of *Interflora v M&S*.[39] This case involves a trade mark infringement claim by Interflora for the use by M&S of Interflora's trade mark to trigger sponsored links on search engines for the flower service of M&S. The Advocate General Opinion was released on 24 March 2011, and judgment in this reference is expected before the end of 2011.[40]

9.3.2.3 *A provisional conclusion*

While this area is fast developing, some provisional guidance can be provided at the time of writing:

(a) While as a matter of principle, it may be hard to see how the invisible use of a mark or sign online can constitute 'trade mark use' for the purposes of establishing an action for trade mark infringement, in the *Google* decision the ECJ did not highlight this issue as important but rather focused on whether use of the sign was in the course of trade. So the invisible versus visible use issue would, at least in the context of search engines, appear to be less important than the Reed decision had indicated might be the case.

(b) Regardless, the use of a sign in metatags or keywords may well form part of the matrix of facts that leads one to the conclusion that there has been a misrepresentation and confusion sufficient to ground an action in passing off. Whether or not an invisible use of a sign alone is sufficient for passing off is something that is yet to be resolved.

(c) The *Google* case has made clear that search engine providers of keyword services will not be liable for trade mark infringement, although the extent of advertiser liability remains to be determined.

---

[38] Case C-558/08 *Portakabin v Primakabin* [2010] ETMR 52.
[39] *Interflora v Marks & Spencer* [2009] EWHC 1095 (Ch).
[40] Case C-323/09 *Interflora v Marks & Spencer*.

9.3.3 Online infringements: intermediary liability

The issue of when an intermediary should also be liable for infringing activity on its website has required the courts to apply the classic principles of joint tortfeasorship to the online world. In *CBS Songs v Amstrad*,[41] involving use of Amstrad double audio-cassette decks, the House of Lords defined joint infringers as being 'two or more persons who act in concert with one another pursuant to a common design'.[42] Further a defendant who 'procures a breach of copyright' is also a joint infringer.[43]

The various cases brought by brand owners against online auction sites such as eBay around the world are gradually providing clarity in this area. There is considerable variation across jurisdictions at the time of writing, with brand owners broadly being successful in France[44] and Germany,[45] but less so in Belgium[46] and the USA.[47] These cases have been brought and decided on a mix of trade mark infringement, unfair competition, and general civil liability laws applicable in the particular country.

In England the *L'Oréal v eBay*[48] case (discussed above in relation to keywords) is providing guidance on the extent to which online intermediaries can be liable for trade mark infringement on the internet Both the initial High Court judgment[49] and the ECJ decision[50] have now been handed down, although the High Court's application of the ECJ judgment is now keenly anticipated. As well as arguing that eBay was liable for its use of L'Oréal's trade marks as paid keywords on search engines, similar arguments were made for liability for eBay's use of L'Oréal marks to enable users to browse and search the eBay site by reference to those marks. These issues were referred to the ECJ which concluded that eBay was not infringing L'Oréal's trade marks by allowing users on the platform to browse and search the contents by reference to L'Oréal trade marks. The court ruled that the 'use' was actually by the traders on the marketplace and not by the marketplace operator itself. There could therefore be no infringement of those trade marks by eBay itself.

L'Oréal further argued that eBay was liable as a joint tortfeasor with the individual infringing sellers on its site. The High Court held that eBay was not jointly liable. This illustrates that the bar is set quite high for establishing joint liability in

---

[41] *CBS Songs v Amstrad* [1988] RPC 567.

[42] Ibid 607.

[43] In addition, 'authorization' of a restricted act is infringement of copyright pursuant to Copyright Designs and Patents Act 1988, s 16(2).

[44] *Hermès International v eBay* (Tribunal de grande instance, Troyes, 4 June 2008); *LVMH v eBay* (Tribunal de commerce, Paris, 30 June 2008); but the *L'Oréal v eBay* (Tribunal de grande instance, Paris, 13 May 2009) case is more equivocal.

[45] *Rolex v eBay* (19 April 2007) 1 ZR 35/04.

[46] *L'Oréal v eBay* (11 February 2009) [2010] ETMR 1.

[47] *Tiffany v eBay* (1 April 2010) (2nd Cir, 2010).

[48] *L'Oréal v eBay* [2009] EWHC 1094 (Ch).

[49] Ibid.

[50] Case C-324/09 *L'Oréal v eBay*.

England and Wales. L'Oréal had argued that eBay had participated in a common design with the individual sellers to secure the doing of acts which proved to be infringements. This was based particularly on the fact that eBay: (a) actively promotes listings; (b) exercises control over listings, seller behaviour, and the sale process both technically and legally; (c) profits from both the listing and sale of items; and (d) fails to take all reasonable measures to prevent the infringements. eBay had argued that: (a) it was under no obligation to prevent third parties infringing trade marks; (b) www.ebay.co.uk operates in a neutral and impartial manner; and (c) at worst, eBay had facilitated infringements with knowledge that infringements were likely to occur and this was not enough to be joint tortfeasorship.

An additional issue in cases involving intermediary liability is whether the intermediary has access to the 'hosting defence' in the e-Commerce Directive.[51] eBay have a potential defence under Article 14(1) of the e-Commerce Directive on the basis that it provides a service that consists of the storage of information provided by a recipient of the service and cannot be held liable unless:

(a) it had actual knowledge of illegal activity; or

(b) it was aware of facts and circumstances that make this illegal activity apparent; and

(c) it had not acted expeditiously to remove content once it had such knowledge or awareness.

Under Article 14(2) this defence will not apply when the recipient of the service is acting under the authority or the control of the provider. Further Article 14(3) also states that Article 14(1) shall not affect the ability of a court to require the service provider to terminate or prevent an infringement. Article 15 of the e-Commerce Directive states that no 'general obligation' can be imposed on providers to monitor information or activity when providing services. The High Court referred the issue of whether it applied to eBay to the ECJ.

As normal, the ECJ left the final determination of this matter on the facts to the English Court. However it held that the e-Commerce Directive defence applied to the operator of an online marketplace where that operator has not played an 'active role' allowing it to have knowledge or control of the data stored. The operator plays such an active role when it provides assistance which entails, in particular, optimizing the presentation of the offers for sale in question or promoting them. This was something the ECJ considered eBay did provide.

Further, where the operator of the online marketplace has not played an active role and therefore has access to the hosting defence, the operator cannot rely on the exemption from liability 'if it was aware of facts or circumstances on the basis of which a diligent economic operator should have realised that the offers for sale

---

[51] Council Directive 2000/31/EC on certain legal aspects of information society services, in particular electronic commerce, in the Internal Market, OJ L178/1, 8 June 2000. See Chapter 5, section 5.2.2.

in question were unlawful' and then did not act expeditiously to remove such offers for sale.

The forthcoming High Court judgment and subsequent cases will therefore need to interpret the meaning of when online intermediaries are 'actively involved' in trade on their systems such as to prevent the defence applying. Online marketplaces are now at risk of liability for traders' trade mark infringements where they promote such trade.

Finally, L'Oréal relied on Article 11 of the Enforcement Directive[52] as entitling it to an injunction against eBay to prevent future similar infringements by individual sellers even if eBay were not liable for trade mark infringement. The High Court then referred a question to the ECJ concerning the scope of the injunction which Article 11 requires to be available against intermediaries.

The court rejected the view of eBay that the injunction against it should be restricted to preventing specific and clearly identified infringements. The need for effective protection meant that the Enforcement Directive must allow for prevention of further infringements. That said, such an injunction needed to be limited in appropriate ways.

The ECJ concluded that EU national courts must be able to order the operator of an online marketplace to take measures which contribute, not only to bringing to an end infringements of those rights by users of that marketplace, but also to preventing further infringements of that kind. Those injunctions must be 'effective, proportionate, and dissuasive and must not create barriers to legitimate trade'. The court suggested that effective and proportionate measures may include suspending the infringing seller and clearly identifying marketplace sellers.

The full scope of what injunctive remedy is available to IP right holders under the Enforcement Directive will become clearer as national courts apply this judgment and rule on the meaning of what are 'proportionate' and 'effective' remedies. The scope of injunction available against intermediaries after this judgment now appears to go beyond the current industry practice for notice and take-down procedures by online marketplaces, such as eBay's VeRO programme. Trade mark owners' position is now stronger in agreeing the balance to be struck in how online IP infringements are policed on online marketplaces and other platforms.

9.3.4 Domain names

There are over 125 million domain names registered in the five most popular Top-Level Domains ('TLDs') on the internet.[53] This creates a myriad of opportunities for abuse, with potentially serious consequences for trade mark owners.

---

[52] Council Directive 2004/48/EC on the enforcement of intellectual property rights, OJ L157/1, 30 April 2004.
[53] <http://www.domaintools.com/internet-statistics/> (accessed 9 August 2011).

9.3.4.1 *What is a domain name?*

In order properly to understand domain names in their legal context, it is necessary to have at least a rudimentary understanding of what, from a technical perspective, a domain name actually is.[54] In simple terms, a domain name is like a street address or telephone number. More specifically, a domain name identifies a specific computer,[55] which is either sending or receiving packets of information over the internet. A domain name is shorthand for what is known as a particular computer's Internet Protocol (or 'IP') address. Rather than being in a domain name format, with which most people will be familiar, an IP address is a numeric identifier of a computer's location. IP addresses traditionally come in a 123.456.789.01 format.[56] IP addresses can be 'static' or 'dynamic'—that is, a particular computer can have the same IP address whenever it connects to the internet or it can have a different one each time.[57] In contrast, domain names are static.

The domain name system enables internet users to ignore these complex numeric IP addresses so instead of having to remember a long number a user only has to remember a single, word-based domain name which remains constant.[58] When an internet user requests a domain name, the user's computer sends a request to a computer known as a domain name server ('DNS'),[59] which sends the IP address associated with that domain back to the user's computer so that the user's computer can communicate directly with the computer at the IP address in question.

It is important to remember that a domain name is not the same thing as a website. Websites are hosted *at* domains.[60] It may seem like semantics, but the difference between www.computerlaw.com, which is a website address, and computerlaw. com, which is a domain name identifying the computerlaw 'domain', is potentially

---

[54] A useful explanation can be found at <http://searchwindevelopment.techtarget.com/definition/domain-name> (accessed 10 August 2011).

[55] The name used by a particular computer in a local area network (ie, its Ethernet address) may actually differ from its IP address. If that is the case, the network will have a system which maps the various local addresses to the IP addresses used for the purposes of the internet.

[56] New technology, such as Internet Protocol v6 also known IPng (Internet Protocol next generation) and Classless Inter-Domain Routing (or supernetting), is altering the precise format of IP addresses with a view to increasing the IP address pool, but, for present purposes, the basic concept remains the same—it identifies the source or destination of data travelling over the internet.

[57] Static IP addresses are most akin to physical street addresses—one IP address is associated with one computer. Dynamic IP addresses are allocated from a pool as needed—one IP address can be associated with multiple computers from time to time. Many larger networks economize on the number of IP addresses that they need by allocating them from a pool which they share amongst users. If you use dynamic IP addresses, the IP address of your computer will change each time that you connect to the internet.

[58] There are protocols and systems which work in the background to allow the domain name to be matched to the appropriate IP address.

[59] In practice a DNS may be spread across several computers and a request to a DNS may have to be rooted to multiple DNSs in order to find the authoritative DNS for the particular domain name in question.

[60] Also important is the concept of a 'URL' or 'uniform resource locator' which is the address of a specific file which is accessible via the internet and which is hosted at a domain and may be, but need not be, a page of a website.

important from a legal perspective. Strictly speaking, the alternative dispute resolution ('ADR') procedures discussed later in this chapter only relate to domain names, not websites.

Domain names are constructed hierarchically and should really be read from right to left. The full stops in a domain name separate the different components of the domain name. For example, in the computerlaw.com domain name, the .com component is what is known as the 'generic Top-Level Domain' or 'gTLD'.[61] The computerlaw component is the specific identifier for the computer in question; for lack of a better term, it is the 'name' of the computer or, more commonly, the domain. In addition to gTLDs, there are 'country code TLDs' or 'ccTLDs'. Examples of ccTLDs are .co.uk, reserved for the UK and .cn, reserved for the People's Republic of China.[62] Nearly all countries, and indeed some sub-sovereign political units, have been allocated a ccTLD.[63] In the case of .co.uk (and other ccTLDs), the .co component is sometimes known as a 'second-level domain'.

9.3.4.2 *Registrars*
It is all very well having an address, but it is useless if there is no street map. That is where the registrars of domain names come in. Each TLD has a registrar. Some have just one registrar. Others have multiple registrars.[64] These registrars provide a system of road maps, which include the DNSs, which identify which domain names map to which IP addresses. The registrar is also where one turns to identify who is registered as the owner of a particular domain name. Registrars provide what is known as a 'whois' search facility which enables the registration details of a domain name on their register to be retrieved.[65]

9.3.4.3 *Internationalized Domain Names and customized top-level domains*
The Internet Corporation for Assigned Names and Numbers ('ICANN') has invested significant resources in increasing the pool of available domain names as well as

---

[61] The most common gTLDs are .com, .net, .edu, .org, .gov, and .info. A full list of gTLDs can be found at <http://www.iana.org/domains/root/db/#> (accessed 10 August 2011).

[62] The Internet Assigned Numbers Authority ('IANA') appoints an appropriate trustee for a ccTLD in each ccTLD jurisdiction. The trustee is then responsible for the administration and control of the domain including registering subdomains. The trustees of the ccTLDs may implement varying requirements and fees for registering these subdomains.

[63] A full list of ccTLDs can be found at <http://www.iana.org/domains/root/db/#> (accessed 10 August 2011).

[64] A list of gTLD registrars can be found at <http://www.internic.net/alpha.html> (accessed 10 August 2011). The number of ccTLD registrars is now so great that no consolidated lists appear to be available.

[65] Unfortunately there is no central register where a whois search of all domain names can be performed. For .co.uk domain names, the whois search can be found at <http://www.nominet.org.uk> (accessed 10 August 2011). For .com domain names, there are multiple registrars, but a good place to start is <http://betterwhois.com> (accessed 10 August 2011) or <http://registrar.verisign-grs.com/whois> (accessed 10 August 2011). Registrars are required to provide a 'whois' search facility under the terms of the ICANN Accreditation Agreement which can be found at <http://www.icann.org/en/registrars/ra-agreement-21may09-en.htm> (accessed 10 August 2011).

facilitating internet use by the non-Latin character-using world and increasing options for those choosing to register domain names.

Internationalized Domain Names ('IDNs') contain characters from outside the standard ASCII character set (a–z, 0–9, and the hyphen). Most domain name registries now offer some level of IDN capability, and may cover character sets in, for example, Arabic, Cyrillic, Hebrew, or Han. ICANN is also in the process of implementing ccTLDs in non-Latin script. These IDN ccTLDs are top-level domains designated for use by a country or territory internet community expressed in letters other than those of the basic Latin alphabet so, for example, Chinese entities can register domain names written using Chinese symbols and ending with the two Chinese symbols for China appearing '中国' rather than '.cn'. ICANN is still finalizing some of the technical aspects of implementing IDN ccTLDs although the IDN ccTLD Fast Track Process is open with applications from countries proposing their ccTLDs already processed, meaning an increasing pool of IDNs are becoming available. The impact of this expansion as well as the difficulties for brand owners in policing objectionable registration and use of non-Latin character domain names is yet to be fully realized.

Following another of ICANN's proposals, the introduction of customized top-level domains is being finalized to facilitate the creation of new internet extensions, such as '.brand'. Under the new scheme an applicant will be able to apply to provide a registry service for the new TLD. For example, a brand owner applicant may seek to obtain their own internet extension relating to their brand and will effectively become the registry for that TLD, either selling or issuing second level domains or keeping the registry closed for their own use. The applicant will have to satisfy a number of criteria, such as general business diligence and a clean cybersquatting record, to obtain a TLD registration. Applications will be published, and comments from the public will be considered as part of the evaluation process. There are also processes to deal with formal objections to the application, which will most likely be made by third parties claiming legal rights in a mark similar to the extension applied for, and by governments. The process was approved by the ICANN board in June 2011 with the TLD application window opening for three months commencing 12 January 2012. This is not an inexpensive endeavour for potential applicants as the initial outlay is $185,000 for the ICANN evaluation fee before the running costs of operating a registry are even considered. However, there are commercial opportunities for applicants to exploit and the exact strategies to be adopted will become clearer once the process commences.[66]

---

[66] The process is set out in ICANN, *gTLD Applicant Guidebook* (May 2011), available from <http://www.icann.org/en/topics/new-gtlds/rfp-clean-30may11-en.pdf> (accessed 10 August 2011).

9.3.4.4 *The legal nature of a domain name*

Given this context, one can appreciate that it is questionable whether a domain name is a species of property.[67] Rather, a domain name should really be considered a contractual right as against a registrar to use the domain name and to have the domain name map to an IP address that the domain name owner specifies. This is expressly set out in the registration terms and conditions of most registrars.[68] It is also a proposition that has been considered in the courts, resulting in a strong indication in the UK at least that a domain name is not to be considered property.[69] This is no different to the position with telephone numbers or street addresses. The holders of those 'identifiers' have no property, as a matter of law, in the identifier. They simply have non-property rights which may, or may not, be enforceable in any given situation. Of course, the use of a particular domain name may become part of the holder's goodwill and thereby be enforceable as a property right via the law of passing off, but whether such goodwill exists can only be assessed on a case-by-case basis.

9.3.4.5 *How are domain names 'abused'?*

Most trade mark owners use their trade mark or a variant of their trade mark in the 'name' portion of their domain name. Offline, trade marks are principally concerned with identifying trade origin[70] so it is logical to extend that use onto the internet. However, the use of trade marks in domain names creates a problem. That is because domain names are, and must due to their technological function, be *unique* identifiers. To have a domain name is to have an absolute monopoly on the location that domain name resolves to. In contrast, trade marks by their nature only confer a limited monopoly on the trade mark owner. This is in contrast to phone numbers and street addresses. Apart from some limited examples, it is very rare that a person's street address or phone number becomes so associated with him or her that it functions as an identifier in and of itself.

The internet community has traditionally resolved the inevitable clash between the limited monopoly of a trade mark and the unique nature of a domain name on a 'first come, first served' basis, but this does not always lead to satisfactory results in practice. Effective dispute-resolution mechanisms are therefore important.

---

[67] This is also contrary to the position with trade marks. The TMA 1994, s 22 expressly states that trade marks are property.

[68] eg, see cl 10 of the Nominet terms and conditions of registration which can be found at <http://www.nominet.org.uk/registrants/aboutdomainnames/legal/terms/> (accessed 10 August 2011).

[69] The argument was raised in an application for permission to appeal in *Plant v Service Direct* [2006] EWCA Civ 1259, where Jacob LJ expressed doubt as to whether a domain name could constitute a 'good' and refused the application. In the USA, domain names have been held to be property albeit in some cases a *sui generis* property right of some kind—see *Kremen v Cohen*, 337 F3d 1024 (9th Cir, 2003) and *OnlinePartners.com, Inc v Atlanticnet Media Corp*, 2000 WL 101242 (ND Cal, 2000). However, conflicting case law also suggests implicitly that the right to use a domain name is in fact a *contractual* right subject to the terms between the registrar and registrant—see *Network Solutions, Inc v Umbro International*, 529 SE2d 80 (2000).

[70] See section 9.2.1 above.

There are four principal ways that trade marks can be 'abused' in a domain name context:[71]

(a) *Cybersquatting* Cybersquatting occurs where a person other than the trade mark owner registers a domain name containing a trade mark or something similar to it. This is generally done with the intention of either selling the domain name to the trade mark owner (or a competitor) for a profit, or 'blocking' the trade mark owner from securing the domain name. This is the 'original' form of domain name abuse. More sophisticated methods of abusing domains have now emerged, including using advertising to generate pay per click revenue from web users stumbling over 'parked' domains. This is often referred to as 'domaining'.

(b) *Typosquatting* Typosquatting is the practice of registering a domain name with a common misspelling of a trade mark. This is usually done with the intention of luring internet users looking for the trade mark holder to another site. Like cyber-squatting, it may also be done with the intention of selling the domain to the trade mark owner for a profit or generating pay per click revenue.

(c) *Gripe sites* Gripe sites are websites which *criticize* someone or something. Where the person or thing *criticized* is a trade mark owner, the publishers of gripe sites often use the trade mark of the person or thing *criticized* in the domain name for the site.

(d) *Foreign language variations* These are domain names which include the foreign language equivalent of a trade mark. Objectionable profiteering from foreign language variation domain names has become increasingly common over recent years. Often this takes the form of brand owners being approached by third parties offering to sell such domain names or register them on the brand owners behalf.[72]

Another practice that receives considerable press is the criminal act of 'phishing', which occurs where a website is designed to impersonate the website of another party in order to defraud users of that website. Spoof emails may be used in a phishing attack. This may also involve the use of a trade mark in the domain name for the copy site. 'Dropcatching'[73] and 'domain kiting'/'domain tasting'[74] are other forms of abuse that readers may hear about, but these pose more practical or

---

[71] When we use the term 'abused' in this context, it is important to note that we do not necessarily mean that the trade mark is wrongly used or that the trade mark owner will be able to stop its use. Rather, we mean that these are uses of trade marks by persons other than the trade mark owner or a licensee, to which the trade mark owner may object.

[72] See <http://www.chinalawblog.com/2009/11/china_domain_name_scams_just_m.html> (accessed 10 August 2011).

[73] Waiting for domains to expire and then registering them quickly before that appropriate registrant can do so.

[74] Taking advantage of the five-day refund period registrants get when they register a domain to seek to solicit third party interest in the domain, before cancelling it if there is no interest—see <http://en.wikipedia.org/wiki/Domain_Kiting> (accessed 10 August 2011).

systemic problems, rather than trade mark problems, so will not be specifically dealt with here.

9.3.4.6 *The courts' approach to domain names*

The English courts' approach to cybersquatting was established by the Court of Appeal in *British Telecommunications plc and Another v One in a Million.*[75] One in a Million registered a large number of domain names incorporating the names and trade marks of various very well-known UK companies, including marksandspencer.com and britishtelecom.co.uk. The domain names were not in active use, but all were either actually or potentially available for sale. The claimants brought proceedings for passing off and registered trade mark infringement.

The court drew a distinction between, on the one hand, the domain names including inherently distinctive names such as Marks and Spencer, which would denote the claimant company alone, and domain names including company names which might also be legitimately used by third parties with that name (eg, a person named J Sainsbury might wish to use J Sainsbury in a domain name). It held that the *mere registration* of a domain name incorporating Marks and Spencer constituted passing off, because the placing on the register of such a distinctive name makes a representation to persons who consult the register that the registrant is connected or associated with the name registered and thus the owner of the goodwill in the name. In addition, registration of the domain name also constitutes an erosion of the exclusive goodwill in the name, which damages or is likely to damage the rightsholder. The court further held that such domain names are 'instruments of fraud', as any realistic use of them as domain names would result in passing off.

The other domain names were not considered inherently deceptive, but the court still found them to be instruments of fraud in the circumstances, as a result of the defendant's motive in registering the domain names. Although the trade names might conceivably have been shared by third parties, they were also well-known household names. The defendants registered the domain names comprising these names without any distinguishing words precisely because of the goodwill attaching to those names, intending to use that goodwill to obtain money from the claimants by threatening to sell the domains to third parties, whose use of the domains would constitute passing off. The value of the domains therefore derived from the threat that they would be used in a fraudulent way. The court upheld the finding at first instance that there was infringement under section 10(3) of the TMA on similar reasoning.

The principle set down by the Court of Appeal in *One in a Million* has been applied in a number of subsequent cases. For example, in *Lifestyle Management Ltd v Frater,*[76] the High Court granted an interim injunction against a company which

---

[75] [1998] 4 All ER 476.
[76] [2010] EWHC 3258 (TCC).

had registered the domain names offshoreslm.net, offshoreslm.org, and offshoreslm. co.uk, holding that the registration resulted in the deceptive use of a company name used to damage the owner of that name. The facts of the case were slightly different to those in *One in a Million* but the case was applied by Mr Justice Edwards-Stuart as it was clear from the respondent's conduct that it intended to cybersquat and cause damage to the owners of the website www.offshoreslm.com. The claimant argued that the respondent's actions amounted to reverse passing off, in that potential clients would be deceived by the websites resolved to from the objectionable domain names and then exposed to information intended to damage or undermine the credibility of the claimant's business. Similarly, in *Global Projects Management Ltd v Citigroup Inc*,[77] the High Court granted summary judgment to Citigroup Inc on its passing off claim against a company which had registered the domain name citigroup.co.uk, holding that the registration was an instrument of fraud. As with the second category of domain names in *One in a Million*, the name 'citigroup' was not considered uniquely indicative of Citigroup Inc. However, it was clear from Global Projects' conduct that its object was to obtain a domain name which carried the potential threat of deception harmful to Citigroup. Global Projects had argued in its defence that it had not attempted to sell the domain name to a third party, but this was found to be irrelevant given that it was the registration and maintenance of the domain name that constituted the act of passing off, not any subsequent attempt to sell the domain.

It is therefore clear that under English law, the use of an unauthorized trade mark in a domain name is also potentially infringing, regardless of whether a website is actually put up at that domain and regardless of the content of any site that is put up. The courts would be expected to apply the same approach to typosquatting. The reasoning in *One in a Million* can be queried, especially in relation to 'trade mark use' but the reasoning has been applied since and can be taken as settled law.

Gripe sites will generally not come within the purview of trade mark infringement because the use will usually not be 'in the course of trade', which is a requirement for infringement. However, if goods or services were being offered from the gripe site, trade mark infringement may obviously arise. Notable is the recent dispute concerning the domain name ihateryanair.co.uk in which the Nominet Dispute Resolution Service Expert found that trade mark infringement had occurred due to the domain name owner profiting from sponsored weblinks from the www. ihateryanair.co.uk website.[78] Following the decision, the website has moved to the domain name ihateryanair.org. Of particular interest in this context would be the extent to which the gripe site could be said to dilute the trade mark. However, defamation may come into play in such cases. Foreign language variations are even

---

[77] [2005] EWHC 2663.
[78] *Ryanair Ltd v Robert Tyler*, DRS 08527.

more challenging, given the issue of whether the mark is even being used. Passing off may, of course, provide avenues of action where trade mark infringement is precluded and, in some jurisdictions, unfair competition should be considered.

9.4 DOMAIN NAME ALTERNATIVE DISPUTE RESOLUTION

9.4.1 The problem with pursuing 'abusers' offline

One way of pursuing cybersquatting, typosquatting, gripe sites, and foreign language variations would be to pursue those engaging in such activities through the courts in a traditional manner. Many, but not all, of the uses of trade marks set out above would be infringements under English (and other) trade mark or other intellectual property law. However, as the internet developed, it quickly became apparent that using the courts to combat domain name abuse was problematic. For one, there was often a jurisdiction problem (an issue we return to in section 9.5 below). Secondly, the barriers to abuse are low, with domain names being cheap to register. Thirdly, the cost of pursuing domain name abuse may often be disproportionate to the issue at hand, yet the damage to the trade mark owner can often be quite serious, especially over time. And finally, the traditional court process often takes too long to resolve disputes which may be very serious for a trade mark owner and which may, in an extreme case, prevent a trade mark owner from being able properly to commercialize its trade mark on the internet.

9.4.2 Alternative dispute-resolution procedures

In light of these problems, several ADR procedures were recommended for the resolution of domain name disputes. The intention was to create procedures which were (a) efficient, (b) fair, (c) cost effective, and (d) enforceable no matter where in the world an 'abuser' was located. For present purposes, three principal ADR procedures are of relevance—the UDRP, Nominet, and EURid procedures. Notwithstanding the benefits of using ADR to resolve domain name disputes, some ccTLDs, such as .ru (Russia) still have no dispute-resolution procedure, meaning that the victims of domain name abuse are compelled to resort to the courts for a remedy.

9.4.2.1 *The UDRP*
The Uniform Domain Name Dispute Resolution Policy ('UDRP') applies to all gTLDs. The registrars for ccTLDs can elect to adopt the UDRP and it currently applies to over 60 ccTLDs (eg, .fr in France, .ie in Ireland, and .nl in the Netherlands).

Under the UDRP, a complainant may file a complaint with an approved dispute-resolution service provider, of which there are four, the most popular being the

World Intellectual Property Organization ('WIPO'). There are three elements to a successful complaint:[79]

(a) the domain name must be identical or confusingly similar to a trade mark or service mark in which the complainant has rights;

(b) the respondent must have no rights or legitimate interests in respect of the domain name; and

(c) the respondent must have registered *and* be using the domain name in 'bad faith'.

The UDRP contains a non-exhaustive list of factors which provide evidence of bad faith registration and use.[80] This list includes:

(a) the respondent registered the domain name primarily for the purpose of selling it to the complainant or a competitor for more than the documented out-of-pocket expenses related to the domain name;

(b) the respondent registered the domain name in order to prevent the trade mark owner from using it, provided that the registrant has engaged in a pattern of such conduct;

(c) the respondent registered the domain name primarily for the purpose of disrupting the business of a competitor; or

(d) by using the domain name, the registrant has intentionally attempted to attract users for commercial gain by creating a likelihood of confusion as to source or affiliation.

Similarly, there is a non-exhaustive list of factors which demonstrate that the respondent has rights or legitimate interests in the domain name:[81]

(a) before any notice to the respondent of the dispute, the respondent has used or made preparations to use the domain name in connection with a bona fide offering of goods and services; or

(b) the respondent has been commonly known by the domain name; or

(c) the respondent is making a legitimate non-commercial or fair use of the domain name.

9.4.2.2 *The Nominet Dispute Resolution Service Policy*

Nominet, the registry for the .uk ccTLD, offers its own Dispute Resolution Service ('DRS') under its DRS Policy and Procedure. This differs from the UDRP in certain

---

[79] UDRP, para 4a. Available online at <http://www.icann.org/dndr/udrp/policy.htm> (accessed 10 August 2011).

[80] Ibid para 4b.

[81] Ibid para 4c.

respects, some of which are important. Two elements must be satisfied for a complainant to be successful under the Nominet DRS:[82]

(a) the complainant must have rights in respect of a name or mark which is identical or similar to the domain name in dispute. The DRS Policy defines 'rights' as including, but not being limited to, rights enforceable under English law; and

(b) the domain name, in the hands of the respondent, must be an 'abusive registration'.

An 'abusive registration' is a domain name which either (a) was registered or otherwise acquired in a manner which, at the time when the registration or acquisition took place, took unfair advantage of or was unfairly detrimental to the complainant's rights; or (b) has been used in a manner which took unfair advantage of or was unfairly detrimental to the complainant's rights.[83] This means that, unlike the 'bad faith' requirement under the UDRP, the *effect* of the registration rather than the intention of the respondent must be considered when deciding whether there is an 'abusive registration'.

The Nominet DRS Policy also includes a non-exhaustive list of factors which may be evidence that the domain name is an abusive registration.[84] These largely mirror the UDRP 'bad faith' factors. The Nominet DRS Policy further provides that there shall be a presumption of abusive registration if the complainant proves that the respondent has been found to have made an abusive registration in three or more DRS cases in the two years before the complaint was filed. It also explicitly states that failure on the respondent's part to use the domain name for the purposes of email or a website is not in itself evidence that the domain name is an abusive registration. This can be contrasted with the Court of Appeal's approach in *One in a Million*.

There is also a non-exhaustive list of factors which may show that the domain name is not an abusive registration and these follow the wording of the UDRP 'rights or legitimate interests' factors.[85]

After submission of a complaint, the respondent has the opportunity to submit a response[86] and the complainant may then file a reply to the respondent's response (if any) before the case enters a mediation phase.[87] Mediation is described by Nominet as 'one of the cornerstones' of the DRS and is a major difference between the DRS and the UDRP. According to Nominet's statistics, a settlement is traditionally

---

[82] DRS Policy, para 2(a). Available online at <http://www.nominet.org.uk/disputes/drs/?contentId=5239> (accessed 10 August 2011).

[83] DRS Policy, para 1.

[84] Ibid para 3.

[85] Ibid para 4.

[86] DRS Procedure, para 5. Available online at <http://www.nominet.org.uk/disputes/drs/?contentId=5240> (accessed 10 August 2011).

[87] DRS Procedure, para 6.

reached in over 50 per cent of cases which reach the mediation stage.[88] The mediation period lasts for ten working days. If it is not successful, Nominet will refer the case to an independent expert to make a decision.[89] The complainant has been successful in nearly 80 per cent of cases referred to an independent expert.

9.4.2.3 *The EURid Alternative Dispute Resolution Policy*

EURid operates the .eu ccTLD, which was first available for general registration on 7 April 2006. The .eu domain is interesting because it is one of the only domains which are governed by specific legislation: Council Regulation (EC) 733/2002,[90] which sets out the conditions for implementation of the domain, and Council Regulation (EC) 874/2004 ('.eu Regulation'),[91] which sets out a number of policy matters, including the principles governing registration. The .eu domain has gained in popularity since its launch and at time of writing there are over three million registrations.[92] Just two months after its general launch, it already had more registrations than 23 of the EU ccTLDs (leaving only .uk and .de in advance of it) and was the seventh most popular domain on the internet.[93] The Arbitration Court in the Czech Republic administers .eu ADR proceedings under the 'ADR Rules' which apply to disputes about .eu domain names.

Unlike the UDRP and Nominet DRS, the default remedy under the .eu ADR Rules is for the domain name to be cancelled, rather than transferred to the complainant.[94] However, a complainant can request the domain name be transferred to it, so in practice the significance of this difference is likely to be minimal for complainants who meet the .eu registration requirements (which is not everyone). In order for the domain name to be transferred to the complainant, the complainant must satisfy the criteria for ownership of .eu domain names, that is, it must be an undertaking having its registered office, central administration, or principal place of business within the Community, or a person resident within it.[95]

---

[88] At time of writing, Nominet is in the process of analysing its mediation and settlement statistics since Version 3 of its Policy and Procedure was implemented on 29 July 2008.

[89] DRS Procedure, para 7(e).

[90] Council Regulation (EC) 733/2002 on the implementation of the .eu Top Level Domain [2002] OJ L113/1, 30 April 2002.

[91] Council Regulation (EC) 874/2004 laying down public policy rules concerning the implementation and functions of the .eu Top Level Domain and the principles governing registration [2004] OJ L162/4, 30 April 2004.

[92] At the time of writing the total number of .eu domain name registrations is 3,370,599. The number of new .eu registrations declined in 2010 compared to that of 2009. Germany accounts for the vast majority of .eu TLD domain name registrations. (See <http://www.eurid.eu/files/Q3_2010.pdf> (accessed 10 August 2011).)

[93] The top ten TLDs during Q1 of 2010 were .com, .de, .net, .cn, uk, .org, .info, .nl, .eu, and .ru. (See <http://verisigninc.com/assets/domain-name-report-june10.pdf> (accessed 10 August 2011).)

[94] ADR Rules, para B11(b). Available online at <http://www.adreu.eurid.eu/adr/adr_rules/index.php> (accessed 10 August 2011).

[95] Regulation EC No 733/2002, para 4(2)(b).

A complainant under the ADR Rules must show:

(a) that the disputed domain name is identical or confusingly similar to the name in respect of which a right is recognized or established by national and/or Community law; and, either

(b) that the disputed domain name has been registered by its owner without rights or legitimate interests in respect of the disputed domain name; or

(c) that the domain name has been registered or is being used in 'bad faith'.[96]

The ADR Rules list a number of non-exhaustive factors which may indicate bad faith registration or use[97] and which may indicate that the respondent does have a right or legitimate interest in the domain name.[98] While these elements of a .eu complaint appear similar to the UDRP elements, they are in fact wider. Unlike the UDRP, the second and third elements that a complainant has to prove are alternative. Therefore, under the EURid ADR Rules, a registrant could lose a domain name registration even if there is no evidence of any bad faith. Furthermore, like the Nominet DRS Policy, the EURid ADR Rules provide for transfer or cancellation of a domain where it has been registered *or* used in bad faith; the UDRP requires there to be bad faith in both registration *and* use.[99] Note also that the EURid ADR Rules list an additional example of what might be evidence of bad faith. That example is where the domain name registered is a personal name for which no demonstrable link exists between the domain name home holder and the domain name registered.

9.4.3 Trends in domain name ADR decisions

The UDRP, the Nominet DRS, and the .eu ADR Rules are not administered by courts. The experts who make decisions under them are not bound by precedent and their decisions, save as provided for in the ADR procedures themselves, are not

---

[96] ADR Rules, para B11(d)(i).

[97] Ibid para B11(f).

[98] Ibid para B11(e). The UDRP, the list of approved dispute resolution service providers, and a searchable list of UDRP proceedings can be found on the ICANN website at <http://www.icann.org/udrp/udrp.htm> (accessed 10 August 2011). Nominet's website is located at <http://www.nic.uk> (accessed 10 August 2011). This features the Nominet DRS Policy, a list of all decided cases, and other helpful guidance. EURid's website is at <http://www.eurid.eu> (accessed 10 August 2011) and includes a link to the Arbitration Center for .eu disputes (<http://www.adreu.eurid.eu> (accessed 10 August 2011)) which sets out the ADR Rules.

[99] Although note that in the decision *LOT v Schubert* ADR 01959, the Panel stated that is was necessary to prove both the second and third elements of the complaint, in contrast to the approach seemingly required by the ADR Rules. Recent cases have also applied the Rules inconsistently: in *Titanium Metals Corp v Atak Teknoloji* (ADR 05792), as well as In *Československá obchodní banka, asv Martin Ladyr* (ADR 05757) the Panel stated the requirement to be either (a) the domain was registered without a legitimate right or interest in the name, or (b) the domain name has been registered or is being used in bad faith. In *Metro-Goldwyn-Mayer Studios Inc v Parrothouse, Ware, P* (ADR 05670), the Panel stated that it was necessary to prove both that the respondent had no legitimate interests in respect of the domain *and* that the domain name was registered or used in bad faith.

subject to appeal. As such, there is a certain risk in seeking to glean too much 'principle' from the decisions. Nevertheless, Jacob LJ of the English Court of Appeal described the jurisprudence arising out of these ADR procedures as a 'world common law',[100] which suggests it is valuable to assess whether any unifying and significant trends can be found in the decisions made to date.

9.4.3.1 Trends in UDRP decisions

Gripe sites The general view held by WIPO panellists is that a domain name consisting of a trade mark and a negative term is confusingly similar to the complainant's mark. For example, WIPO ordered the transfer of radioshacksucks.com to TRS Quality, Inc, the owner of the US trade marks for RADIO SHACK and of the domain name radioshack.com. The addition of the derogatory term 'sucks' to RADIO SHACK did not prevent the Panel from finding the domain name to be confusingly similar to the trade mark.[101] This view is consistent with the jurisprudence where the domain name does not contain a criticism in itself—the criticism being contained on the website alone. In the latter cases, most WIPO panellists are of the view that the right to criticize does not extend to registering a domain name that is identical or confusingly similar to the owner's registered trade mark or conveys an association with the mark. For example, in *Kirkland & Ellis LLP v DefaultData.com*,[102] the complainant was a well-known US law firm. The disputed domain name was kirklandandellis.com. The Panellist held that 'the right to express one's views is not the same as the right to identify oneself by another's name when expressing those views'. This approach was confirmed in subsequent decisions such as *MLP Finanzdienstleistungen AG v WhoisGuard Protected.*[103]

On the other hand, in the *Synagis* case,[104] the respondent registered the domain names synagisisbadforyou.com and synagisisnotsafe.com. The Panel decided that the pejorative phrases 'isbadforyou' and 'isnotsafe' indicated criticism of SYNAGIS and the complaint failed because the complainant could not show a likelihood of confusion with the derogatory domain names.

Bad faith The National Arbitration Forum ('NAF') decision in the morganstanleyplatinum.com[105] case provides an interesting insight into the 'bad faith' requirement under the UDRP. The respondent was a business consultant and said he used the disputed domain name in seminars as 'an example of a large company's negligence and ineptitude in the registration of domain names pertinent

---

[100] Speech given by Jacob LJ at a Society for Computers and Law presentation on 12 January 2006.
[101] *TRS Quality, Inc v Gu Bei*, D2009-1077.
[102] D2004-0136.
[103] D2008-0987.
[104] *MedImmune Inc v Jason Tate*, D2006-0159.
[105] *Morgan Stanley v Michael Woods*, Claim Number FA0512000604103.

to its business'. The NAF Panel therefore took the view that the respondent had made a legitimate, non-commercial fair use of the domain name, without intent for commercial gain misleadingly to divert customers or to tarnish the trade mark in issue. He had therefore shown that he had rights and a legitimate interest in the morganstanleyplatinum.com domain name and so there was no bad faith.

Website content Due to the possibility of trade mark owners suffering from 'initial interest confusion', website content is *not* considered relevant when deciding whether a domain name is confusingly similar to the complainant's mark.[106] However, from a practical perspective, use of the complainant's trade mark on the website would obviously assist a complainant's case.

No pre-registration trade mark rights If the complainant does not have relevant trade mark rights at the date of registration of the domain name, it will inevitably be much harder for the complainant to show that the domain name was registered in bad faith. However, a domain name can still have been registered in bad faith even if trade mark rights arose *after* the registration of the domain name. One example given in *ExecuJet Holdings Ltd v Air Alpha America, Inc*[107] is where a registrant speculated on an impending merger between companies that would create a new name combining in whole or in part the names of the merger partners.

Fan sites   As with gripe sites, there are two opposing views of fan sites which emerge from the UDRP jurisprudence. The first is that a registrant may have rights and legitimate interests in the domain name that includes the complainant's trade mark. Following this reasoning, the complainant in *White Castle Way, Inc v Glyn O Jacobs*,[108] a commercial entity representing Pat Benatar, failed in its attempt to obtain the transfer of the domain name patbenatar.com. The respondent's website provided a wide range of information about the recording artist, there were clear disclaimers to the effect that it was not endorsed by or an official website of Pat Benatar and there was no evidence that the respondent gained any commercial benefit from the website. The combination of these and other factors led the Panellist to decide that the respondent was engaged in legitimate, non-commercial use of the disputed domain name. The second approach finds bad faith registration and use where there is evidence of commercial use, or at least plans to make commercial use, of the domain name in issue.[109]

Passive holding of domain names The UDRP requires the domain name to be used in bad faith. What if there is no active use of the domain name in issue, for example

---

[106] *AT&T Corp v Amjad Kausar*, D2003-0327.
[107] D2002-0669.
[108] D2004-0001.
[109] See, eg, *Galatasaray v Maksimum Iletisim, AS* D2002-0726.

what if the related website is blank? Although this does makes it more difficult to show bad faith use, *Telstra Corp Ltd v Nuclear Marshmallows*[110] identified five factors which could establish bad faith on the part of the registrant: (a) the complainant's trade mark had a strong reputation and was widely known; (b) the respondent provided no evidence of any actual or contemplated good faith use by it of the domain name; (c) the respondent took active steps to conceal its true identity; (d) the respondent actively provided, and failed to correct, false contact details, in breach of its registration agreement; and (e) it was not possible to conceive of any plausible actual or contemplated active use of the domain name by the respondent that would not be illegitimate. This decision is consistent with the reasoning in *One in a Million*.

Disclaimers A disclaimer to the effect that the website is not connected with the trade mark owner does not cure bad faith. Indeed, it may do the respondent a disservice by providing evidence that he knew of the complainant's earlier trade mark rights.

9.4.3.2 Trends in Nominet DRS decisions

Through the jurisprudence of Nominet's Dispute Resolution Service certain principles have become more settled including the registration of generic names,[111] the combining of words and marks,[112] and initial interest confusion.[113]

The 'rights' test The requirement to demonstrate 'rights' under the DRS 'is not a particularly high threshold'.[114] The Panel needs to be persuaded on the balance of probabilities that relevant rights exist but will not expect the same volume of evidence as might be required by a court to establish goodwill or reputation. The less straightforward the claim, the more evidence the better.

Rights at the date of registration It is sufficient for the complainant's rights to exist as at the date of the complaint for the complainant to have standing to make the complaint. However, as the Appeal Panel pointed out in *Verbatim Ltd v Michael Toth*,[115] 'the Complainant must satisfy the Panel . . . that the respondent was aware of the existence of the Complainant or its brand at the date of registration of the

---

[110] D2000-0003.

[111] See *Maestro International, Inc v Mark Adams*, DRS 04884 regarding maestro.co.uk in which the Appeal Panel stated: 'Where a domain name is a single ordinary English word, the meaning of which has not been displaced by an overwhelming secondary meaning, the evidence of abuse will have to be very persuasive, if it is to be held to be an Abusive Registration.'

[112] See, eg, the DRS appeal decisions in *RuggedCom Inc v LANstore Inc*, DRS 02802 and *EPSON Europe BV v Cypercorp Enterprises*, DRS 03027.

[113] *Goldmoney Network Ltd v Mr Peter Cosgrove*, DRS 08581.

[114] *Seiko UK Ltd v Designer Time/Wanderweb*, DRS 00248.

[115] DRS 04331.

Domain Name or at commencement of an objectionable use of the Domain Name'. It should be noted that mass sales of domain names involving automated bulk transfers are increasingly commonplace, and some Nominet Experts consider that while the *Verbatim* decision suggests that actual knowledge is required for a finding of abusive registration, a respondent who acquired the name via such a bulk transfer will usually be found to have the requisite knowledge of the complainant and/or its rights at the time the transfer was negotiated.

Taking unfair advantage of a trade mark The Nominet Appeal Panel answered this question in *Seiko UK Ltd v Designer Time/Wanderweb*,[116] which involved the seikoshop.co.uk and spoonwatchshop.co.uk domain names. The complainant argued that the respondent had gone further than representing 'we are a shop selling Seiko/ Spoon watches' and was instead representing 'we are The Seiko/Spoon watch shop'. The Panel found that the complainant had provided evidence (ie, letters from customers showing that they were confused) that the domain names in issue made, or were liable to be perceived as making, the latter representation. This was held to constitute unfair advantage taken by the respondent and unfair detriment caused to the complainant.

Tribute sites The Appeal Panel held in relation to the scoobydoo.co.uk domain name[117] that

in the context of a tribute site, the vice is in selecting a domain name, which is not one's own name, but which to one's knowledge is identical to the name of another, which one has selected precisely because it is the name of that other and for a purpose which is directly related to that other. For a tribute or criticism site, it is not necessary to select the precise name of the person to whom one wishes to pay tribute or criticise. In this case, the domain name could have been ilovescoobydoo.co.uk, for example.

The Panel therefore held that the respondent's 'honest intentions' were not enough and that the domain name had been used in a manner which took unfair advantage of or was unfairly detrimental to the complainant's rights. Indeed, the Appeal Panel decision relating to rayden-engineering.co.uk[118] confirmed the view that the nature of the domain name chosen for a tribute or criticism website is crucial. Including 'ihate' or 'ilove', for example, indicates clearly what the visitor is likely to find at the site, rather than indicating a domain name of or authorized by the complainant. However, the Panel in this case did not rule that use of an identical name would always and automatically be unfair, but concluded that it was only in exceptional circumstances that such use could be fair.

---

[116] *Seiko UK Ltd v Designer Time/Wanderweb*, DRS 00248.
[117] *Hanna-Barbera Productions, Inc v Graeme Hay*, DRS 00389.
[118] *Rayden Engineering Ltd v Dianne Charlton*, DRS 06284.

It should be noted that the commercial activity associated with the website at www.scoobydoo.co.uk was also highlighted as being detrimental to the owner's position. The owner's steps to benefit commercially from the domain name were also a strong factor leading to transfer of ihateryanair.co.uk.[119]

Generic/descriptive domain and fair use Paragraph 4(a)(ii) of the DRS Policy states that if the disputed domain name is generic or descriptive and the respondent is making fair use of it, this may be evidence that the registration is not abusive. The Appeal Panel in *Consorzio del Prosciutto di Parma v Vital Domains Ltd*[120] concluded that the respondent genuinely and reasonably believed that the parmaham.co.uk and parma-ham.co.uk domain names were generic or descriptive when it registered them. In fact, the complainant owned UK and Community trade marks for PROSCIUTTO DI PARMA and PARMA. Nevertheless, the Appeal Panel held that the complainant had not satisfied the test that, on the balance of probabilities, the respondent's continuing to offer the domain names for sale to the public, in knowledge of the complainant's trade marks, constituted unfair use. This was because of the nature of the domain names (ie, they were not that distinctive) and the conclusion that the respondent had acquired them fairly. Therefore the domain names were not registered or used in a manner that took unfair advantage of or was unfairly detrimental to the complainant's rights. The use made of a generic or descriptive domain name was also considered in *MySpace, Inc v Total Web Solutions Ltd*.[121] In this case, myspace.co.uk was registered prior to the complainant's rights in the MySpace name being established. The complainant took issue with, among other things, the owner earning revenue from a 'parking page' operated by Sedo at www.myspace. co.uk. A Nominet Appeal Panel confirmed the view that in such cases problems only arise for the registrant if he actively does something to take unfair advantage of his position in holding such a domain name and, as there was insufficient evidence to support that the owner had done more than passively earning from a parking page, the domain name was not transferred.

9.4.3.3 *Trends in EURid ADR decisions*

Following its first published decision in April 2006,[122] EURid now deals with approximately 25 .eu ccTLD cases per quarter initiated through its dispute-resolution procedure. As the .eu registration process was tiered, with two initial 'Sunrise' phases, allowing public bodies and those with existing rights (national or Community trade marks) to register domain names first, followed by a Land Rush phase open to all, the bulk of early disputes related to the validity of public

---

[119] *Ryanair Ltd v Robert Tyler*, DRS 08527.
[120] DRS 00359.
[121] *MySpace, Inc v Total Web Solutions Ltd*, DRS 04962.
[122] *Leonie Vestering v EURid*, Case No 35, 18 April 2006. See <http://www.adreu.eurid.eu/adr/decisions/decision.php?dispute_id=35> (accessed 10 August 2011).

body registrations[123] and issues surrounding the procedure for filing applications during the Sunrise period.[124]

However, while the .eu registry can still be considered a newcomer, there are now over three million .eu domain names registered[125] and, following these early disputes, EURid ADR commenced ruling on more substantial complaints under paragraph 11(d) of the ADR Rules. The interaction between national, European, and international law combined with the consideration of UDRP and EURid ADR decisions by Panelists means that, perhaps more so than with other providers, EURid's ADR is constantly evolving.[126] The EURid decisions database[127] is not as sophisticated as some other more established ADR regimes, and as such the ability to search custom strings is not available which makes a comprehensive review of particular trends in EURid decisions over the years quite difficult to ascertain.

Gripe sites At the time of writing, only one English language translation of a dispute relating to domain names consisting of a trade mark and a pejorative term can be found on the EURid database of decisions. EURid ordered the transfer of airfrancesucks.eu and airfrance-jp.eu to Société Air France, the owner of numerous trade marks worldwide for AIR FRANCE and of the domain name airfrance.com.[128] In this decision, the Panel found that additional element 'sucks' was not sufficient to put aside a risk of confusion with the complainant's company name. This view is consistent with the general view held by WIPO panellists. However, it is interesting to note that the Panel in this decision made clear that it was not bound by previous decisions in ADR or UDRP cases, as in their opinion these types of cases are based upon very specific facts.

Bad faith The decision of the Panel in the *myhome.eu* case[129] provides an insight into the 'bad faith' requirement under the ADR Rules and the .eu Regulation. The complainant was a company incorporated in Ireland trading under the name Myhome Ltd. Its business consisted of an internet-based property service using the domain name myhome.ie and a number of other related websites such as www.myhome-shop.ie. The respondent was a company incorporated in Luxembourg with the name Myhome SA, which provided short-term business support services and apartments

---

[123] See *Marstall v EURid*, ADR 00168 and *BOC v EURid*, ADR 00139.

[124] Notably, EURid ADR refused to overturn a registration by a Belgian diamond company, Eurostar Diamond Traders NV ('EDT'), in the domain eurostar.eu, despite a complaint by the cross-channel train operator Eurostar UK Ltd. EDT held a legitimate trade mark incorporating the word 'Eurostar' and under the rules governing registration during the Sunrise period, it had properly submitted its application ahead of Eurostar UK Ltd. (See *Eurostar (UK) Ltd v EURid*, ADR 00012.)

[125] See <http://www.eurid.eu/> (accessed 10 August 2011).

[126] For a full list of decisions, see <http://eu.adr.eu/adr/decisions/index.php> (accessed 15 August 2011).

[127] Accessed at <http://eu.adr.eu/adr/decisions/index.php> (accessed 10 August 2011).

[128] Case 04141, 10 January 2007.

[129] Case 04560, 11 June 2007.

for rent. The correspondence between the parties evidenced a willingness to sell the domain name by the respondent, but the respondent had asserted that when the domain name was originally applied for it was not with the intention of selling it on, and as such there was no registration of the domain name in bad faith. The respondent also denied using the domain name in bad faith, as it did not offer any services in Ireland or target the real estate portal market and was not responsible for the Irish property-related content on the temporary parking page which was displayed when users accessed the domain.

The Panel took the view that on the facts of the case only two of the examples listed in Article 21 of the .eu Regulation required examination; that the domain was registered or acquired primarily for the purpose of selling, and the domain name was intentionally used to attract internet users for commercial gain. In relation to the registration of the domain name, the Panel found that the respondent had entertained the complainant's offer to purchase the domain and evinced further interest in selling in the future and that this established at least a prima facie case that the domain name was registered primarily for the purpose of selling. The Panel considered the reasoning in a number of WIPO cases[130] and found that the relevant bad faith must be specific to the complainant, or at least 'had the complainant in mind' when he registered the domain name. On this basis the Panel found that the primary intention of the respondent was not to sell the disputed domain name to the complainant and as such no bad faith under this head was found. In relation to the respondent's intention to attract internet users for commercial gain, the Panel found that there was a prima facie case established on this ground of bad faith, as the website resolved to the disputed domain was a parking page (ie, a page which is put in place to host a domain that is not otherwise put to use) linked to websites which competed with the business of the complainant. The links were deemed to be created automatically and outside the respondent's control and, as the Panel noted that intention, actual or apparent, was required for bad faith under this head, bad faith in this respect was not made out on the facts.

Good faith Perhaps a good example of a respondent 'trying it on' is found in the *prague.eu* case.[131] The Panel discussed what constitutes the use of a domain name in good faith in this case, stating that where a respondent claimed a prior right as the basis for registration, the use of the domain name in good faith would mean the respondent used the domain name to offer the goods to which their prior right referred, or made actual preparation to do so. However, here the respondent's prior right was an expedited Benelux trade mark registration for PR & AGUE under class 6 for base metals, and the respondent did not use the domain name to advertise base metals but merely offered completely unrelated services—information on the city of

---

[130] D2005-1033, D2000-1786, D2004-0748.
[131] Case 04681, 27 November 2007.

Prague—which claim the Panel disbelieved and so refused to consider a good faith element to the use of the domain name.

Generic domains Certain inconsistencies are highlighted in the Panel's decisions over the years relating to disputes regarding generic domain names. The Panel decided that a complainant's 'device' mark GAME (registered as a stylized version of the word 'game' with some very slight, device elements, rather than merely the word 'game') was identical or confusingly similar to the disputed domain name game.eu,[132] as the word GAME could clearly be distinguished in and was integral to the image and it was *undeniable* that the mark was identical to the disputed domain name. On the other hand, in the *Euroairport.eu* case[133] the Panel held that a claimant's device mark incorporating the term EUROAIRPORT was not identical with the disputed domain. The Panel followed prevailing case law of former UDRP decisions[134] and considered a former .eu ADR decision[135] stating that a word/device trade mark can never be identically reproduced in a domain name. Further, the Panel held that the device mark and the disputed domain were not confusingly similar either. The Panel stated that even when ignoring the graphical elements of the device mark, the word elements of the mark were not distinctive and as such, merely descriptive word elements of a word/device mark cannot give rise to a confusing similarity. This analysis can be contrasted somewhat with the view of the Panel in the *bookings.eu* case.[136] In this case the complainant held a number of trade mark registrations for BOOKINGS. The respondent argued that the term BOOKINGS is generic, and as such any assertion of prior rights in the term must fail. The Panel rejected this view, and stated that the Panel merely decides whether a trade mark right is recognized in the European Union, 'without placing itself on the chair of the examination division of the Trademark Office' and further, whether or not an application for the trade mark BOOKINGS would be refused today was not part of the assessment of the Panel.

9.4.4 Are decisions of ADR providers judicially reviewable?

An interesting question that arises in light of the rise and rise of domain name ADR decisions is whether such decisions are judicially reviewable. To date there has been no English court decision which deals with this issue. A claim for judicial review was launched by the registrant of the itunes.co.uk domain after a Nominet expert had decided that the domain name should be transferred to Apple Computer Inc.[137]

---

[132] Case 04014, 11 December 2006.
[133] Case 05309, 13 December 2008.
[134] D2003-0614.
[135] Case 04261, 17 January 2008.
[136] Case 04090, 28 December 2006.
[137] *The Queen (on the application of Cyberbritain Group Ltd) v Nominet UK Ltd and Apple Computer Inc* (CO/3860/05).

This claim was resisted by Nominet on the grounds, amongst others, that the power of Nominet to determine the dispute was entirely contractual and that the function it was exercising was not relevantly public. The claim was settled before trial so we are still left without judicial guidance on this point.[138] It remains an issue worth bearing in mind for those disappointed by a domain name ADR decision. The importance of the internet to the global economy and governance and the incredibly powerful position of domain name registrars like Nominet suggests that domain name ADR decisions *should* potentially be judicially reviewable.

9.5 JURISDICTION

The online use of trade marks throws up one other issue which cannot be ignored—the issue of jurisdiction. This chapter cannot deal with this issue in the depth that it warrants, but the following is a basic introduction to the ways in which jurisdiction affects both the use and enforcement of trade marks online.

9.5.1 Basic principles under English law

As an EU Member State, the exercise of jurisdiction by the courts of the UK is governed by Council Regulation (EC) 44/2001 of 22 December 2000 on jurisdiction and the recognition and enforcement of judgments in civil and commercial matters ('the Brussels Regulation')[139] with the exception that the exercise of jurisdiction in matters concerning CTMs is governed by the CTMR. Therefore, whenever considering whether the English courts have jurisdiction in a trade mark infringement or passing off matter, the starting point is always to consider either the Brussels Regulation[140] or the CTMR.

For both the Brussels Regulation and the CTMR the applicable rules will vary depending upon whether the defendant is domiciled in an EU Member State.

Under the Brussels Regulation a defendant domiciled within an EU Member State[141] may be sued under the general jurisdiction provisions[142] in the jurisdiction of his domicile or, under the special jurisdiction provisions applicable to tort,[143]

---

[138] Nominet's position remains that it does not fall into the category of bodies which are judicially reviewable. (See <http://www.nominet.org.uk/disputes/courtcases/itunes/> (accessed 10 August 2011).)

[139] Council Regulation 44/2001/EC on jurisdiction and the recognition and enforcement of judgments in civil and commercial matters, OJ L12/1, 16 January 2001.

[140] A detailed analysis of the rules of jurisdiction contained within the Brussels Regulation is outside the scope of this chapter. For more detailed guidance see Briggs, *Civil Jurisdiction and Judgments*, 4th edn (London: Informa, 2005).

[141] Jurisdiction over defendants domiciled in either Denmark or an EFTA Member State (Iceland, Liechtenstein, Norway, and Switzerland) is governed by either the Brussels Convention or Lugano Convention, whose provisions are substantially the same as those of the Brussels Regulation.

[142] Brussels Regulation, Art 2.

[143] Brussels Regulation, Art 5(3).

in the place where the harmful event occurred (or may occur). This has been held to mean either where the harmful event itself occurred or where the damage was sustained.[144] In relation to defendants not domiciled within an EU Member State,[145] the Brussels Regulation provides that jurisdiction is determined by national rules.[146] Under English common law jurisdiction rules, jurisdiction depends upon service of process: a defendant may be sued in the English courts if he is served within the jurisdiction or court permission is granted to serve him outside the jurisdiction. In relation to claims of registered UK trade mark infringement or passing off, the English rules provide that a defendant may be served outside the jurisdiction where damage was sustained within England or the damage sustained resulted from an act committed in England.[147]

Under the CTMR the courts of the EU Member State in which the defendant is domiciled, or where the defendant is not domiciled in any EU Member State, established, will have jurisdiction.[148] Where the defendant is neither domiciled nor established in an EU Member State then the proceedings can be brought in the EU Member State in which the claimant is domiciled or established.[149] Alternatively, in the event that neither the defendant nor the claimant is domiciled or established within an EU Member State then the action can be brought in the Spanish courts, as the courts of the EU Member State in which the Office for Harmonization in the Internal Market is located.[150] Similarly to the provisions relating to jurisdiction in tortious matters under the Brussels Regulation, the CTMR also allows a claimant to bring an action in the courts of the EU Member State in which the act of infringement has been committed or threatened.[151]

It can be seen that the criteria for establishing jurisdiction in the English courts over an overseas defendant for a claim in trade mark infringement/passing off do not differ significantly under the Brussels Regulation, the English common law rules, and the CTMR. Under all three regimes it is necessary to determine where the harmful event, or the damage arising from the harmful event, occurred.

This is where the unique nature of the internet causes a jurisdictional headache. The internet is free of national territorial boundaries and, subject to geo-blocking or other technical blocks, is accessible anywhere in the world. Therefore, if trade mark infringement and/or passing off is committed online, we must ask where the harmful event has occurred. Is it where the website owner is located, where the server is based, or where the website containing the infringing use is accessed? If the latter, jurisdiction might potentially be founded in any country in the world.

---

[144] *Shevill v Press Alliance SA* [1995] ECR I-415 at para 20.
[145] Or defendants not domiciled in Denmark or an EFTA Member State.
[146] Brussels Regulation, Art 4.
[147] Civil Procedure Rules and Practice Direction 6B.3.1(9), rule 6.36.
[148] CTMR, Art 93(1).
[149] CTMR, Art 93(2).
[150] CTMR, Art 93(3).
[151] CTMR, Art 93(5).

Many countries have approached this dilemma by applying a threshold based upon the extent of the connection between the website and the country. For example, both the US courts and the Australian courts have adopted a 'targeting approach' whereby the ability to access a website from a jurisdiction will by itself not be a sufficient basis upon which to found jurisdiction. The US courts, which have to deal with inter-state jurisdictional issues, exercise extraterritorial jurisdiction ('long-arm jurisdiction') in two ways: general jurisdiction and specific jurisdiction. General jurisdiction is established where a defendant has 'continuous and systematic' contacts with the forum state.[152] Once 'continuous and systematic' contacts have been established, a non-resident defendant can be subject to litigation in the forum in relation to any matter, including those not arising from activities within the forum. Specific jurisdiction is established where the litigation arises out of or relates to the defendant's actions within the forum, and therefore arises where the defendant has 'purposely availed' himself of the privilege of conducting activities within the forum and the claim arises out of these activities. The standard for establishing general jurisdiction is very high (a defendant's contacts with the state must be such as to approximate physical presence) and, as a result, cases concerning internet jurisdiction have generally focused on establishing specific jurisdiction. In contrast, the French courts were previously known for their readiness to establish jurisdiction over non-resident defendants and had on more than one occasion found jurisdiction solely on the basis of the ability to access a website from France rather than by seeking to establish a connection between the website and the French public.[153] However, in recent years the French courts' approach has changed. The French courts now look to see whether the website targets the French public[154] and will consider the following factors: (a) the language of the website (ie, whether it is French); (b) whether the website offers delivery to France; and (c) whether the website has a .fr domain name.

So far, English law has also followed the 'targeting approach' taken by the US, Australian, and now French courts although case law on this issue still remains scarce. In *1-800-Flowers v Phonenames*,[155] the Court of Appeal held that the mere existence of a website overseas which was clearly not aimed at UK internet users did not establish use of a trade mark in the UK. Similarly, in the case of *Euromarket Designs v Peters*,[156] the High Court held that the website www.crateandbarrel.ie promoting a store in Dublin did not infringe the UK registered trade mark for 'Crate and Barrel' as the website was clearly not directed at customers in England.

---

[152] eg, he is incorporated or licensed to do business in the forum state, he has offices, property, employees, or bank accounts there, or advertises, solicits business, or makes sales in that state.

[153] eg, as in the *Yahoo!* case, *La Ligue Contre Le Racisme Et l'Antisemitisme v Yahoo! Inc*, TGI de Paris, 22 May 2000 and 22 November 2000 and also the case of *SA Castellblanch v SA Champagne Louis Roederer*, Cour de Cassation, 1ere Chambre Civile, 9 December 2003.

[154] eg, as in *Axa v Google Inc*, Cour de cassation, Chambre commerciale, 23 November 2010.

[155] *1-800 Flowers Inc v Phonenames Ltd* [2002] FSR 12.

[156] *Euromarket Designs v Peters* [2001] FSR 20.

By contrast, in *V & S Vin Spirit v Absolut Beach*,[157] the High Court held that where the defendant circulated a brochure in the UK in response to orders received on its Australian website, this would be enough to found jurisdiction for a claim brought in relation to infringing material appearing on the website. A similar targeting approach has also been adopted by the Scottish Court of Session in the case of *Bonnier Media*,[158] in which it assumed jurisdiction over defendants based in Greece and Mauritius who had registered domain names with the intention of passing themselves off as the claimant, who was located in Scotland. The court found that the acts were clearly aimed at the claimant's business in Scotland and stated that, in determining whether a website was of 'significant interest' in a particular country it was necessary to look at the content of the website and the commercial context in which it operated.

The issue was most recently considered by the High Court in *L'Oréal v eBay*,[159] where the court confirmed the principle that a site must be aimed or targeted at consumers within the UK for courts to be able to exercise jurisdiction. In this case the court considered whether allegedly infringing eBay listings posted by non-UK sellers were targeted at consumers in the UK. The court found that where listings were revealed as the result of a European or worldwide search they would still be considered to be targeted at UK consumers because such listings would only be returned by the search if the seller had indicated that they were prepared to deliver to the UK. The fact that prices were shown in sterling in italics (indicating that they had been converted from a foreign currency) did not prevent the site from clearly targeting UK customers.

In the recent ECJ judgment in this case,[160] the court adopted a similar approach and ruled that unauthorised offers of genuine goods targeted towards EU consumers could be prevented by owners of EU Member State trade marks. 'Targeting' must involve more than a website simply being accessible, but is assessed by reference to matters such as where the seller is offering to dispatch the product. eBay had argued that offers to the world including the EEA could not be infringing, as the goods would not *necessarily* be sold to the EEA. The ECJ rejected this as it would effectively eliminate the force of the law against parallel imports from outside the EEA.

It is hoped further clarity may be given at a European-wide level as a result of the pending reference to the ECJ by the Austrian courts in *Wintersteiger v Products 4U*.[161] The decision is expected in the second half of 2012. The reference relates to whether the Austrian courts can exercise jurisdiction over a defendant domiciled in Germany where the defendant has infringed the claimant's national Austrian trade

---

[157] *V & S Vin Spirit Aktiebolag AB v Absolut Beach Pty Ltd* [2002] IP & T 2003 (Ch D).
[158] *Bonnier Media Ltd v Greg Lloyd Smith and Kestrel Trading Corp* [2002] ScotCS 347.
[159] *L'Oréal v eBay* [2009] EWHC 1094.
[160] Case C-324/09 *L'Oréal v eBay*.
[161] Case C-523/10 *Wintersteiger AG v Products 4U Sondermaschinenbau GmbH*.

marks through use of an identical mark as a keyword on the German website www. google.de. While this reference refers to jurisdiction under the Brussels Regulation, the issue of where a harmful event occurs will be relevant to jurisdiction under the CTMR as well. The Austrian courts have asked whether:

(a) jurisdiction is established if the top-level domain of a website is that of the EU Member State of the court seised;

(b) jurisdiction is established if the website concerned can be accessed in the EU Member State of the court seised; or

(c) if jurisdiction is dependent on the satisfaction of other requirements additional to the accessibility of the website?

9.5.2 Conclusion

When attempting to establish jurisdiction in England against an overseas defendant in relation to online trade mark infringement, the offending website must target the jurisdiction to a certain degree. No exact threshold has been laid down by the courts, but as a guide, the mere accessibility of the website in the UK will not suffice to found jurisdiction. Advertising directed to the UK may prove sufficient, but the strongest case would be where the website is clearly targeted at the UK market, for example where the website offers products for sale which can be delivered to the UK, or as demonstrated by the language and currency used (where sales are an issue).

Part IV

ELECTRONIC PRIVACY AND ACCESS TO INFORMATION

10

PRIVACY AND DATA PROTECTION

Ian Walden

10.1 INTRODUCTION

Intangible information has become a basic asset, the fuel driving the 'Information Economy'; and personal data comprises a substantial share of such information assets. During the dot.com boom, much of the value ascribed by stock markets to companies, such as eBay and lastminute.com, was based on the personal data they held: millions of registered users (*read* future customers), rather than the products and services they had sold. Indeed, we are currently experiencing this phenomenon again, with companies like Facebook and Twitter. However, personal data reveals our lives to others and, as such, its use and abuse engages and impinges on our right to privacy. As information increases in value, so the appropriateness of the legal regime protecting personal data becomes increasingly important, balancing the needs of individuals, commerce, and society as a whole.

Personal data may be protected under a range of different regimes including intellectual property,[1] trespass to persons,[2] and the interception of communications;[3]

---

[1] eg, *Ashdown v Telegraph Group* [2001] EWCA Civ 1142.
[2] eg, *Morris v Beardmore* [1981] AC 447.
[3] eg, Regulation of Investigatory Powers Act 2000, s 1.

all of which are beyond the scope of this chapter. We are concerned here with data protection laws and the regulatory schemes operating under them.

Data protection law as a distinct legislative field is predominantly a European phenomenon. Currently such laws exist in all European countries, and of these, many have already revised or amended their original legislation, sometimes more than once. Outside Europe other industrialized nations have adopted data protection laws, such as Australia, Japan, and Canada, however they are in the minority of trading nations and their laws tend to be less all-embracing than the European approach.

European data protection law is primarily about controlling the automated processing of personal data.[4] A more expansive definition of data protection has been suggested by some less-developed countries, encompassing the protection of information pertaining to states. Resolutions at Latin American and African conferences have proposed that 'information and knowledge affecting national sovereignty, security, economic well-being and socio-cultural interests should be brought within the ambit of data protection'.[5] Indeed, some European countries, such as Denmark, Austria, and Italy, extend the protection afforded under data protection laws to legal persons, such as companies and trade unions, as well as individuals. In some non-European countries, such as Australia and Japan, data protection laws are limited to public sector data processing activities, and do not apply to the private sector.[6]

Within Europe, the 1981 Council of Europe Convention on data protection has been the foundation upon which national legislation and the 1995 EU Directive has been constructed.[7] Two distinct motives underpin the 1981 Convention: the threat to individual privacy posed by computerization; and the desire to maintain a free flow of information between trading nations. The Convention therefore attempts to reconcile the Article 8 right of privacy under the European Convention for the Protection of Human Rights and Fundamental Freedoms ('ECHR') with the principle of the free flow of information, viewed as an element of the right to freedom of expression under Article 10 of the ECHR.[8]

Throughout this chapter the reader will be introduced to elements which go towards an understanding of data protection law. The first section will give consideration to the nature of the subject itself, primarily from a European perspective;

---

[4] Convention for the Protection of Individuals with regard to Automatic Processing of Personal Data, Strasbourg, 28 January 1981 (European Treaty Series No 108) (Cmnd 8341, 1981), Explanatory Report, 5.

[5] Intergovernmental Bureau for Informatics, TDF 270, 55. See also A Murray, 'Should States Have a Right to Informational Privacy?' in A Murray and M Klang (eds), *Human Rights in the Digital Age* (London: Glasshouse Press, 2005) ch 15.

[6] In 2000, the Australian federal Privacy Act was amended to extend its provisions to most of the private sector.

[7] See, further, section 10.2.1.

[8] See Council of Europe Recommendation No R(91)10, 'Communication to third parties of personal data held by public bodies', Explanatory Memorandum, at para 10.

as well as reviewing international instruments addressing data protection issues. The second section will focus on UK law, specifically the Data Protection Act 1998 ('DPA 1998').

10.1.1 With privacy

Since the Warren and Brandeis formulation of privacy as the 'right to be let alone',[9] considerable effort has been devoted to establishing an exhaustive definition of the constituent components of a right to privacy.[10] The United Nations Universal Declaration of Human Rights at Article 12 states that every individual has a right to privacy, yet fails to define the term. However, what does seem to be agreed upon in the literature is the extent to which the meaning of 'privacy' is dependent on a nation's culture. The classic contrast to the British attitude to privacy being Sweden, where their long tradition of open government means much information considered private in Britain, such as the amount of tax a person pays, is readily accessible to a Swedish citizen. For some, the privacy threat is perceived to lie primarily with governments and their multifarious administrative organs. For others, the private sector is seen as an equal or even greater threat, as customer data has become an increasingly valuable asset.

However, to what extent does data protection legislation differ from privacy law? Data protection and privacy are clearly substantially overlapping concepts, although certain distinctions have been drawn. In the 1978 Lindop Report on Data Protection, for example, the following distinction was made:

a data protection law should be different from that of a law on privacy: rather than establishing rights, it should provide a framework for finding a balance between the interests of the individual, the data user and the community at large.[11]

Such a balancing act can be recognized in the two motives that underpin the Council of Europe Convention. The Report also gave the example of the use of inaccurate or incomplete information when decision-making. While within the proper scope of data protection, in terms of good information practices, such issues do not necessarily raise privacy issues.[12]

Data protection laws do not map neatly onto a privacy framework, but rather represent a range of differing interests. Bygrave makes a broad distinction between 'interests that relate to the quality of (personal) information and information systems', such as accessibility and reliability, and 'interests pertaining to the condition

---

[9] See SD Warren and LD Brandeis, 'The Right to Privacy' (1890) IV(5) Harvard Law Review 193–220.

[10] See, eg, A Westin, *Privacy and Freedom* (London: Bodley Head, 1975) and R Wacks, *Personal Information: Privacy and the Law* (Oxford: Clarendon Press, 1993).

[11] Report of the Committee on Data Protection, (Chairman: Sir Norman Lindop) (Cmnd 7341, 1978) xix. See further section 10.3.1.

[12] Ibid para 2.03.

of persons as data subjects and to the quality of society generally', such as privacy, autonomy, and democracy.[13]

Despite differences between the concepts, data protection jurisprudence has inevitably extended to wider questions regarding an individual's 'right to privacy'. In Germany, for example, a Constitutional Court decision declared unconstitutional an act that had authorized the government to undertake a comprehensive population census. The court declared that each data subject has a right to 'determine in general the release and use of his or her personal data'; therefore establishing a constitutional right of individual 'informational self-determination'.[14] The decision led to a fundamental revision of the German Data Protection Act. It should also been noted that judicial opinion within the European Commission of Human Rights has referred to the Council of Europe Convention on data protection to enliven and strengthen Article 8 of the ECHR.[15]

In the UK, prior to 1998, any concept of a right of privacy resided primarily within the equitable action for breach of confidence, however inadequately, rather than the statutory framework established under the Data Protection Act 1984 ('DPA 1984').[16] However, two legal developments in the UK have driven data protection and privacy ever closer together. First, the European Directive, upon which the DPA 1998 was based, expressly recognizes its origins in the right of privacy as expressed in Article 8 of the ECHR.[17] Secondly, the Convention itself was incorporated into UK law by the Human Rights Act 1998, which imposed an obligation upon the courts, as public authorities, not 'to act in a way which is incompatible with a Convention right' (s 6(1)). As a consequence, the English courts have increasingly been called upon to interpret questions of data protection and confidentiality law in privacy-related terms.[18]

As a result of the latter development, the English courts have developed a new cause of action, referred to as a tort for the misuse of private information.[19] Under the action, a claimant must first establish a 'reasonable expectation of privacy' in relation to the information that is threatened with disclosure.[20] If found, taking the perspective of 'a reasonable person of ordinary sensibilities',[21] then the next question is whether there is a public interest justification for the disclosure and whether

---

[13] See L Bygrave, *Data Protection Law: Approaching its Rationale, Logic and Limits* (Alphen aan den Rijn: Kluwer, 2002).

[14] Judgment of 15 December 1983, Bundesverfassungsgericht [BVerfG], 65 Entscheidungen des Bundesverfassungsgericht [BVerfGE] 1 at 43.

[15] See, eg, *Amann v Switzerland* (2000) 30 EHRR 843 at para 65; *Rotaru v Romania* (2000) 8 BHRC 449 at para 43; *S v Marper* (2009) 48 EHRR 50 at paras 41 et seq.

[16] See *Kaye v Robertson* [1991] FSR 62.

[17] See Council Directive (EC) 95/46 on the protection of individuals with regard to the processing of personal data and on the free movement of such data [1995] OJ L281 at recital 10 and Art 1.

[18] See *Douglas v Hello! Ltd* [2001] QB 967.

[19] Lord Nicholls in *Campbell v MGN Ltd* [2004] UKHL 22 at para 14.

[20] *Murray v Express Newspapers* [2008] EWCA Civ 446.

[21] Lord Hope in *Campbell*, n 19 above, at para 99.

an injunction against disclosure would be both necessary and proportionate.[22] The new action illustrates a distinction between data protection and privacy law. Under the former, *ex ante* controls are placed on the processing of personal data, whether the information is private or not,[23] while privacy as a tort of misuse is only engaged *ex post*, once an abuse has arisen or is anticipated.[24]

As well as certain substantive distinctions between data protection and privacy laws, a procedural distinction can also be seen, particularly within Europe. An assertion of privacy is generally made by an individual before a court, which then exercises its discretion often through a process of balancing between the conflicting rights present. By contrast, data protection law, whilst granting individuals specific rights, is primarily enforced through the intervention of a regulatory authority, with an ongoing supervisory remit over the actions of those that process personal data, and generally concerned with pursuing a compliance strategy. This has led, arguably, to the profile of concerns of the authority, whether as an individual or as a collective body, becoming a surrogate for the interests of individuals.

10.1.2 With freedom of information

One area of law that has developed an intricate relationship with data protection and privacy laws is that concerning freedom of information ('FOI') or access to official information. The potential conflict between these areas of law is obvious: data protection and privacy laws are primarily concerned with restricting the disclosure of information, while freedom of information laws are designed to facilitate access to information. Generally, privacy is one of a number of recognized exemptions under FOI regimes.[25]

Historically, data protection and FOI have been subject to distinct legal regimes. The primary exception to this has been Canada, where a number of provinces within the Federation have enacted statutes that embrace both freedom of information and data protection laws.[26] However, as has been noted, there are potential disadvantages of addressing these areas separately:

. . . the coexistence of access to official information legislation and data protection legislation may come into conflict especially where they are administered separately by different organs and under different criteria . . .[27]

---

[22] *LNS (John Terry) v Persons Unknown* [2010] EWHC 119 (QB) at para 56.
[23] See, further, section 10.3.1 below.
[24] eg, where injunctive relief is sought.
[25] eg, in the USA, 5 USC § 552(b)(6), (7).
[26] eg, Quebec (1982), Ontario (1988), Saskatchewan (1991), British Columbia (1992), and Alberta (1994).
[27] Council of Europe Assembly Recommendation 1037 (1986) on data protection and freedom of information at para 10.

Recognizing the synergies between data protection and freedom of information laws, when the UK Government put forward legislation which eventually became the Freedom of Information Act 2000 ('FOIA 2000'), it was decided to place the regulatory functions created under the Act with the existing Office of the Data Protection Commissioner: in a new entity known as the Office of the Information Commissioner (s 18).[28]

In addition, a specific exemption from the right of access was granted for 'personal information' under the FOIA regime.[29] Section 40 distinguishes between two distinct scenarios. First, where the applicant is requesting personal data about themselves, as data subject.[30] In this situation the information is subject to an absolute exemption from disclosure, as the applicant should request the information using his rights under the data protection regime. Where the applicant is not the data subject then it may still be exempt from disclosure where one of a number of conditions is present, such as where the disclosure would result in a breach of the data protection principles or disclosure is likely to cause damage or distress.[31]

10.2 INTERNATIONAL DEVELOPMENTS

The nature of the global economy inevitably means that large amounts of personal data cross national borders every day, either over communication networks, such as the internet, or through the manual transfer of media, such as hard disks in notebook computers and personal digital assistants. Such transfers will predominantly occur in the absence of any form of effective control or supervision by any regulatory authority. However, such transfers could obviously pose a threat to individual privacy, not least because national data protection laws may be circumvented by transferring data to so-called 'data havens' that lack such protections.

In order to discourage organizations from avoiding data protection controls and to guarantee a free flow of information, intergovernmental organizations have been active in attempting to achieve harmonization for data protection legislation; including the Council of Europe, the OECD, the United Nations, and the European Union.

10.2.1 Council of Europe

The Council of Europe has been the major international force in the field of data protection since the 1981 Convention for the Protection of Individuals with regard

---

[28] See section 10.3.4 below.
[29] See also the Environmental Information Regulations 2004 (SI 2004/3391), at reg 13 'Personal data'.
[30] s 40(1).
[31] s 40(2)–(4). See generally Chapter 11.

to Automatic Processing of Personal Data.[32] Of the 47 members of the Council of Europe, some 43 members have signed and ratified the Convention, therefore incorporating the Convention's data protection principles into national law. The Convention came into force on 1 October 1985 when five countries had ratified it: Sweden, Norway, France, the Federal Republic of Germany, and Spain.

The Council of Europe has been involved in the field since 1968, when the Parliamentary Assembly passed Recommendation 509 (68), asking the Council of Ministers to look at the ECHR to see if domestic laws gave adequate protection for personal privacy in the light of modern scientific and technical developments. The Council of Ministers asked the Committee of Experts on Human Rights to study the issue, and they reported that insufficient protection existed.

A specialist Committee of Experts on the Protection of Privacy was subsequently asked to draft appropriate resolutions for the Committee of Ministers to adopt: Resolution 22 (1973) covered the 'ground rules' for data protection in the private sector; while Resolution 29 (1974) focused on the public sector. In 1976, a new Committee of Experts on Data Protection was established. Its primary task was to prepare a convention on the protection of privacy in relation to data processing abroad and transfrontier data processing. The text of this Convention was finalized in April 1980, and opened for signature on 28 January 1981.

The Convention is based around a number of basic principles of data protection, upon which each country is expected to draft appropriate legislation. Such legislative provision will provide for a minimum degree of harmonization between signatories, and should therefore prevent restrictions on transborder data flows for reasons of 'privacy' protection.

Since 1981, the Committee of Experts on Data Protection has been primarily involved in the drafting of sectoral rules on data protection. These form part of an ongoing series of recommendations issued by the Committee of Ministers designed to supplement the provisions of the Convention.[33] In addition, the Convention was amended in 1999, to enable the European Communities to accede,[34] and an additional protocol was adopted in 2001 on 'Supervisory Authorities and Transborder Data Flows'.[35] A process of modernization of the 1981 Convention has recently been commenced, with the intention of adopting a revised text in 2012.[36]

---

[32] n 4, above.

[33] Some 14 Recommendations have been published, including the use of personal data in 'automated medical data banks' (R(81) 1); 'scientific research and statistics' (R(83) 10); 'employment records' (R(89) 2), and 'payment' (R(90) 19); 'the communication to third parties of personal data held by public bodies' (R(91) 10); 'telecommunication services' (R(95) 4), 'protection of privacy on the internet' (R(99) 5), and 'in the context of profiling' (R(2010) 13).

[34] See text accompanying n 50 below.

[35] European Treaty Series No 181, opened for signature on 8 November 2001.

[36] See <http://www.coe.int/t/dghl/standardsetting/dataprotection/Modernisation_en.asp> (accessed 10 August 2011).

The major weakness of the Convention is its lack of enforceability against countries that fail to uphold the basic principles. No enforcement machinery was created under the Convention, and therefore any disputes have to be resolved at the diplomatic level. However, to date, no such disputes have been reported.

10.2.2 OECD

The Organisation for Economic Co-operation and Development (OECD) was established in 1961, and currently comprises 30 of the leading industrial nations. The nature of the organization has meant that interest in data protection has centred primarily on the promotion of trade and economic advancement of Member States, rather than 'privacy' concerns per se.

In 1963, a Computer Utilization Group was set up by the third Ministerial Meeting and aspects of the Group's work concerned with privacy went to a subgroup, the Data Bank Panel. This body issued a set of principles in 1977. In the same year, the Working Party on Information Computers and Communications Policy ('ICCP'), was created out of the Computer Utilization and Scientific and Technical policy groups. Within this body, the Data Bank Panel became the 'Group of Government Experts on Transborder Data Barriers and the Protection of Privacy', with a remit 'to develop guidelines on basic rules governing the transborder flow and the protection of personal data and privacy, in order to facilitate the harmonization of national legislation'.

The OECD Guidelines were drafted by 1979, adopted September 1980, and endorsed by the UK Government in 1981.[37]

The Guidelines are based, as with Council of Europe Convention, upon eight, self-explanatory, principles of good data protection practice. The Guidelines are simply a recommendation to countries to adopt good data protection practices in order to prevent unnecessary restrictions on transborder data flows; they have no formal authority. However, some companies and trade associations, particularly in the USA and Canada, have publicly adhered to the Guidelines. In addition, the OECD has published further policy guidance addressing various aspects of privacy, such as information security, the online challenges, and Radio Frequency Identification systems.[38]

10.2.3 United Nations

While its historic Universal Declaration of Human Rights of 1948 was one of the first instruments of public international law to recognize a right to privacy,[39]

---

[37] OECD, 'Guidelines on the Protection of Privacy and Transborder Flows of Personal Data' (Paris: OECD, 1980).
[38] See <http://www.oecd.org/sti/security-privacy> (accessed 10 August 2011).
[39] Art 12.

the United Nations only comparatively recently focused on the human rights aspects of the use of computer technology. In 1989, the General Assembly adopted a set of draft 'Guidelines for the regulation of computerized personal data files'.[40] These draft guidelines were subsequently referred to the Commission on Human Right's Special Rapporteur, Mr Louis Joinet, for redrafting based on the comments and suggestions received from member governments and other interested international organizations. A revised version of the 'Guidelines' was presented and adopted in 1990.[41]

The Guidelines are divided into two sections. The first section covers 'Principles concerning the minimum guarantees that should be provided in national legislations'. These 'principles' echo those put forward by both the Council of Europe Convention and the OECD Guidelines, except for three additional terms:

(a) principle of non-discrimination—sensitive data, such as racial or ethnic origin, should not be compiled at all;

(b) power to make exceptions—justified only for reasons of national security, public order, public health, or morality; and

(c) supervision and sanctions—the data protection authority 'shall offer guarantees of impartiality, independence via-à-vis persons or agencies responsible for processing . . . and technical competence'.

The second section considers the 'Application of the guidelines to personal data files kept by governmental international organizations'. This requires that international organizations designate a particular supervisory authority to oversee their compliance. In addition, it includes a 'humanitarian clause', which states that:

. . . a derogation from these principles may be specifically provided for when the purpose of the file is the protection of human rights and fundamental freedoms of the individual concerned or humanitarian assistance.

Such a clause is intended to cover organizations such as Amnesty International, which holds large amounts of personal data, but would be wary of sending information out to a data subject on the basis of an access request made while the person was still imprisoned.

10.2.4 European Union

Despite an interest and involvement in data protection and privacy issues for nearly two decades, from both the European Parliament and the Commission, the emergence of a binding legal instrument in the area only occurred in 1990.

---

[40] Resolution 44/132, on 15 December 1989.
[41] Adopted by the Commission on Human Rights, Resolution 1990/42 (6 March 1990); subsequently by the UN Economic and Social Council, Resolution 1990/38, 14th Plenary Session (25 May 1990), and finally by the UN General Assembly, Resolution 45/95, 68th Plenary Session (14 December 1990).

The European Parliament's involvement in data protection issues has primarily been through its Legal Affairs Committee, although the issue has been subject to parliamentary questions and debates over previous years. In 1976, the European Parliament adopted a resolution calling for a directive to ensure that 'Community citizens enjoy maximum protection against abuses or failures of data processing' as well as 'to avoid the development of conflicting legislation'.[42]

In 1977, the Legal Affairs Committee established the Sub-Committee on Data Processing and the Rights of the Individual. The Sub-Committee produced the 'Bayerl Report' in May 1979.[43] The resultant debate in the European Parliament led to recommendations being made to the Commission and the Council of Ministers concerning the principles that should form the basis of the Community's attitude to data protection.[44] These recommendations called on the European Commission to draft a directive to complement a common communications system; to harmonize the data protection laws and to secure the privacy of information on individuals in computer files.

In July 1981, the European Commission recommended that all members sign the Council of Europe Convention and seek to ratify it by the end of 1982.[45]

A second parliamentary report, the 'Sieglerschidt' Report, was published in 1982.[46] The report noted 'that data transmission in general should be placed on a legal footing and not be determined merely by technical reasons'.[47] It recommended the establishment of a 'European Zone', of members in the EEC and Council of Europe, within which authorization prior to the export of data would not be needed. It also indicated that initiatives, such as a directive, were still necessary. Following the report, a resolution was adopted by the European Parliament, on 9 March 1982, calling for a directive if the Convention proved inadequate.[48]

In July 1990, the European Commission finally published a proposal for a directive on data protection,[49] as part of a package of proposals which included:

(a) A recommendation that the European Community adheres to the Council of Europe Convention on data protection.[50]

---

[42] Resolution on the protection of the rights of individuals in connection with data processing [1976] OJ C100/27, 3 May 1976.

[43] Named after the rapporteur. Report on the Protection of the Individual in the face of the technical developments in data processing (1979–80 EurParlDoc (No 100) 13 (1979)).

[44] [1979] OJ C140/34, 5 June 1979.

[45] Commission Recommendation (EEC) 81/679 relating to the Council of Europe Convention for the protection of individuals with regard to automatic processing of personal data [1979] OJ L246/31, 29 August 1979.

[46] Second Report on the Protection of the Rights of the Individual in the Face of Technical Developments in Data Processing (EPDoc1-548/81, 12 October 1981).

[47] Ibid p 7.

[48] OJ C87/39, 5 April 1982.

[49] OJ C277, 5 November 1990.

[50] In 1996, however, the ECJ held that the Community cannot adhere to the ECHR: *Opinion No 2/94* [1996] 2 CMLR 265. The Convention has subsequently been amended to enable adherence: 'Amendments

(b) A declaration applying data protection principles to Community institutions.[51] This was subsequently embodied within the European Community Treaty, Article 286, and a supervisory authority, the 'European Data Protection Supervisor', was subsequently established.[52]

(c) A draft directive addressing data protection issues in the telecommunications sector.[53]

(d) A draft Council decision to adopt a two-year plan in the area of security for information systems.[54]

After considerable controversy and political debate at all stages of the legislative process, the general framework directive on data protection was finally adopted by the European Parliament and Council on 24 October 1995.[55] Member States had to implement the Directive by 24 October 1998, although only five managed to adopt legislation by that date.[56] The provisions of the Directive shall be considered below in the context of the UK's implementing statute: the DPA 1998.

The justification for Commission action was as part of the Single Market programme, under Article 95 of the then European Community Treaty;[57] as well as to protect the rights of individual data subjects, 'and in particular their right to privacy' (Art 1(1)). In 1990, only eight of the (then) 12 Member States had passed data protection legislation. Even between these eight considerable divergence existed in terms of the scope of protection; the nature of the obligations imposed on data users and restrictions on the use and export of data. Such differences were seen as a potential obstacle to the development of an integrated European Information Market.

After some 20 years, the Commission has recently embarked on a process of reforming the 1995 Directive to ensure that the principles and rules continue to remain valid in our rapidly changing technological environment.[58] The coming into force of the Lisbon Treaty, in December 2009, has also changed the legal landscape

---

to the Convention for the protection of individuals with regard to automatic processing of personal data (ETS No 108) allowing the European Communities to accede', adopted by the Committee of Ministers, Strasbourg, 15 June 1999.

[51] Commission Declaration on the application to the institutions and other bodies of the European Communities of the principles contained in the Council Directive concerning the protection of individuals in relation to the processing of personal data (COM(90)314 final) OJ C277/74, 5 November 1990.

[52] See Regulation (EC) 45/2001 of the European Parliament and of the Council of 18 December 2000 on the protection of individuals with regard to the processing of personal data by the Community institutions and bodies and on the free movement of such data [2001] OJ L8/1, 12 January 2001.

[53] See section 10.4 below.

[54] Adopted as Council Decision (EEC) 92/242 in the field of information security [1992] OJ L123, 8 May 1992.

[55] Council Directive (EC) 95/46 on the protection of individuals with regard to the processing of personal data and on the free movement of such data [1995] OJ L281/31, 23 November 1995.

[56] ie, Greece, Italy, Portugal, Sweden, and the UK, although the UK Act had not entered into force.

[57] See Case C-465/00 *Rechnungshof v Österreichischer Rundfunk and Others* [2003] 3 CMLR 10.

[58] Communication from the Commission, 'A comprehensive approach on personal data protection in the European Union', COM(2010)609 final, 4 November 2010 ('2010 Communication').

for data protection in Europe. First, the Charter of Fundamental Right of the European Union[59] now has full legal effect.[60] Reflecting our earlier discussion, the Charter recognizes a 'right to the protection of personal data' (Art 8), which is distinct from a right of privacy (Art 7). Secondly, the 1995 Directive was limited to those areas within the scope of Community law, which excluded such areas as 'police and judicial co-operation in police matters' (Art 3(2)). With the integration of this 'third pillar' into Community law, the limitation of scope is no longer necessary. Taken together, we are likely to see a significant strengthening of European data protection law, including enhanced rights for individuals, greater legal certainty and harmonization, as well as a simplified regulatory burden.

10.3 DATA PROTECTION ACT 1998

While privacy and data protection are distinct legal concepts under English law, an examination of the history of the statutory regime for data protection illustrates that policymakers and legislators have often viewed them as a single issue. As long ago as 1961, a private member's bill on privacy was introduced by Lord Mancroft which can be seen to mark the beginning of a 23-year history that finally led to the successful passage of the DPA 1984. This first private member's bill was followed by four others until the government finally decided to establish a formal committee of inquiry into the area.

In May 1970, a Committee on Privacy was appointed under the Chairmanship of Kenneth Younger (the Younger Report).[61] The Committee's purview was limited to the private sector, despite the Committee's request that it be extended to encompass the public sector as well. During its establishment, the Committee set up a special Working Party on Computers. The Working Party concluded that:

Put quite simply, the computer problem as it affects privacy in Great Britain is one of apprehensions and fears and not so far one of facts and figures. (para 580)

Indeed, their report went on to note that the most credible anxieties were those held about computers in the *public* sector, an area outside the Committee's scope. The Committee noted that the main areas of concern were with universities, bank records, and credit agencies. The Committee recommended that an independent body composed of computer experts and lay persons should be established to monitor growth in the processing of personal information by computer, as well as the use of new technologies and practices.

While the sentiment in 1970 was one of 'wait and see', the special attention given to computerization can be seen as the beginnings of the divergence between the

---

[59] The 'Charter'; OJ C303/1, 14 January 2007.
[60] Treaty on European Union, Art 6(1) (OJ C83/13, 30 March 2010).
[61] Report of the Committee on Privacy (Cmnd 5012, 1972).

issue of privacy and that of data protection under English law, and their subsequent different treatment. The history of data protection law in the UK has been intimately tied up with the spread of computerization and concerns arising out of such developments.

In response to the Younger Report, the government promised a White Paper. However, it was three years before 'Computers and Privacy' was presented to Parliament.[62] In it, the government accepted the need for legislation to protect computer-based information. Despite the concerns expressed in the Younger Report with regard to manual records, the government felt that computers posed a special threat to individual privacy:

6. The speed of computers, their capacity to store, combine, retrieve and transfer data, their flexibility, and the low unit cost of the work which they can do have the following practical implications for privacy:

(1) they facilitate the maintenance of extensive record systems and the retention of data on those systems;

(2) they can make data easily and quickly accessible from many distant points;

(3) they make it possible for data to be transferred quickly from one information system to another;

(4) they make it possible for data to be combined in ways which might not otherwise be practicable;

(5) because the data are stored, processed and often transmitted in a form which is not directly intelligible, few people may know what is in the records, or what is happening to them.[63]

The government also issued a second White Paper, 'Computers: Safeguards for Privacy',[64] which agreed with the comments made by the Younger Report with regard to the concerns generated by public sector information.

Rather than establish a standing commission to monitor the use of personal data, the White Paper proposed legislation to cover both public and private sector information systems. The creation of a Data Protection Authority was also proposed, to supervize the legislation and ensure that appropriate safeguards for individual privacy were implemented. In order to provide a detailed structure for the proposed data protection authority, the government established a Data Protection Committee, under the chairmanship of Sir Norman Lindop, which reported in 1978.[65]

The Lindop Report proposed that a number of data protection principles should form the core of the legislation, with the Data Protection Authority being responsible for ensuring compliance with those principles. In particular, the Authority would be required to draft codes of practice for various sectors, which would then become law

---

[62] White Paper, 'Computers and Privacy' (Cmnd 6353, 1975).
[63] Ibid 6.
[64] Cmnd 6354.
[65] See n 11.

through statutory instruments. Failure to comply with a code would lead to criminal sanctions. Overall, the Lindop Report was concerned to produce a flexible solution which would not hold back the growing use of computers within both the public and private sector.

After the fall of the Labour Government in 1979, legislation on data protection was further delayed. However, finally in 1982, spurred on in part by its obligations under the 1981 Convention, the government issued a White Paper, 'Data Protection: The Government's Proposals for Legislation'.[66] The approach put forward in the White Paper was much less comprehensive than that proposed in the Lindop Report. The DPA 1984 received the Royal Assent on 12 July 1984. In terms of scope, the Act was limited to data defined as 'information recorded in a form in which it can be processed by equipment operating automatically in response to instructions given for that purpose',[67] reflecting the perceived threat of computerization, which is also present in the 1981 Convention.

With the adoption of Council Directive (EC) 95/46 ('the 1995 Directive'), the government had an obligation to transpose it into national law by 24 October 1998. The government chose to enact new primary legislation and repeal the DPA 1984, rather than amend it through secondary legislation. The DPA 1998 received Royal Assent on 16 July 1998. While it repealed the DPA 1984, transitional provisions effectively meant that processing carried out prior to 24 October 1998 continued to be subject to a 1984-style regime until October 2001 and the DPA 1998 did not enter into force until 1 March 2000, when the necessary ministerial orders had been passed.

To date, the DPA 1998 has not met with universal approval being variously described as 'fiendishly complicated'[68] and 'almost incomprehensible',[69] the latter sentiment being expressed by Lord Falconer, the government minister at the then Department for Constitutional Affairs, the department responsible for the Act! One issue that has driven the desire for reform has been problems concerning data sharing between government departments, seen as a key tool for improving efficiency within the public sector and achieving 'joined-up' government.[70] In addition, however, calls for reform have come on the back of a series of high-profile cases involving data protection issues. In the case of the Soham murders, a police authority was severely criticized for erasing records about the perpetrator's past based, in part, on a misapplication of the DPA 1998.[71] In another widely reported case, two elderly people were found dead in their home after British Gas had cut off their supply while failing to notify the local social services department of the couple's plight.

---

[66] Cmnd 8539.

[67] s 1(2).

[68] J Rozenberg, *Privacy and the Press* (Oxford: Oxford University Press, 2004).

[69] P Wintour, 'Fees pledge on information act', *The Guardian*, 18 October 2004.

[70] See Department for Constitutional Affairs report, 'Public Sector Data Sharing: Guidance on the Law', November 2003.

[71] The Bichard Inquiry Report (HMSO, HC653, 2004).

British Gas claimed that the DPA 1998 prohibited such disclosure.[72] While such cases have created significant public disquiet about the DPA 1998, the reality is that the Act often serves 'as a handy whipping-boy for organizations whose data protection policies fail'.[73]

A series of amendments were made to the 1998 Act in 2008, via the Criminal Justice and Immigration Act, and again in 2009, by the Coroners and Justice Act. Both contained measures to strengthen the enforcement powers of the Information Commissioner;[74] although amendments in the latter instrument at Bill stage, designed to facilitate data sharing between public authorities, were withdrawn following widespread criticism.

Parallel to these legislative developments, parliamentarians have continued to debate the need for privacy legislation. In 1990, the Calcutt Committee 'Report on Privacy and Related Matters'[75] stopped short of calling for a privacy law, recommending instead the establishment of a self-regulatory scheme in the form of the Press Complaints Commission and its Code.[76] However, Calcutt's subsequent review in 1993 was critical of this approach and recommended a statutory system for complaints and a new tort of invasion of privacy.[77] The then Conservative Government rejected any such statutory approach.[78] In June 2003, the House of Commons Select Committee on Culture, Media and Sport published a report, which included in its recommendations that 'the Government reconsider its position and bring forward legislative proposals to clarify the protection that individuals can expect from unwarranted intrusion . . . into their private lives'.[79] However, yet again, the Labour administration declined to accept this recommendation, believing that existing legal provisions, including the DPA 1998 and the Human Rights Act 1998, as well as self-regulatory mechanisms, provide sufficient protection.[80] Recent renewed calls for a 'privacy' law have been driven, in part, by concerns that the courts have been creating such a law in the absence of parliamentary action.

---

[72] See 'Data Act "not to blame" for deaths', BBC, 23 December 2003, available at <http://news.bbc. co.uk/1/hi/england/london/3342977.stm> (accessed 10 August 2011). See also Statement by the Information Commissioner, 22 December 2003.

[73] J Lettice, 'Government FOI Act chief trails Data Act "reform"', *The Register*, 18 October 2004.

[74] See further section 10.3.9 below.

[75] Report of the Committee on Privacy and Related Matters (Chairman David Calcutt QC) (Cmnd 1102, 1990).

[76] The PCC Code (April 2011) includes specific reference to individual privacy (Art 3).

[77] Department of National Heritage, D Calcutt, *Review of Press Self Regulation* (Cm 2135, 1993).

[78] Department of National Heritage, *Privacy and Media Intrusion* (Cm 2918, 1995).

[79] <http://www.parliament.the-stationery-office.co.uk/pa/cm200203/cmselect/cmcumeds/458/458. pdf> (accessed 10 August 2011).

[80] 'The Government's Response to the Fifth Report of the Culture, Media and Sport Select Committee on "Privacy and Media Intrusion"' (HC 458, Session 2002–2003) <http://webarchive.nationalarchives. gov.uk/+/http://www.culture.gov.uk/images/publications/895260Cm5985PRIVACY710.pdf> (accessed 10 August 2011).

10.3.1 Terminology

Under data protection law, the protection offered to an individual data subject is on the basis of 'personal data', defined in the following terms:

data which relate to a living individual who can be identified—

(a) from those data, or

(b) from those data and other information which is in the possession of, or is likely to come into the possession of, the data controller,

and includes any expression of opinion about the individual and any indication of the intentions of the data controller or any other person in respect of the individual.[81]

Until recently, this definition was considered to involve an objective question of fact in each particular case. However, in *Durant v Financial Services Authority*,[82] the Court of Appeal re-evaluated the concept of 'personal data' under the DPA 1998 more narrowly, such that the mere mention of an individual within a document or, by implication, in any collection of data does not render it 'personal data' as defined by the Act.

In *Durant*, there was no question that the data identified an individual, instead however the court focused on the meaning of 'relates to' in the definition, stating that data that relates to a person 'is information that affects [a person's] privacy, whether in his personal or family life, business or professional capacity' (para 28). To assist, Auld LJ suggested two criteria for assessment. First, whether the data is biographical in nature, that is, the more concerned it is with the person's private life and, secondly, its focus, whether on the person or someone or something else.[83] In taking this stance, Auld LJ has introduced a subjective privacy-style filter over the objective statutory definition. As a result of the *Durant* decision, the UK Government has been involved in infraction correspondence with the European Commission.[84] Both the Information Commissioner and the Article 29 Working Party have subsequently issued guidance and an opinion on the concept of 'personal data'.[85] The Commissioner's guidance attempts to advise the reader, using a flowchart of questions, as to the application of the 'relates to' concept. The first criterion is whether the data is 'obviously about' an individual. Second, whether the data is 'linked' to an individual. Third, the purpose of the processing is examined, whether it is being used to inform or influence actions or decision affecting an individual.

---

[81] s 1(1).

[82] [2003] EWCA Civ 1746.

[83] See Information Commissioner guidance, 'The "Durant" Case and its impact on the interpretation of the Data Protection Act 1998', 4 October 2004. The approach taken in *Durant* has been followed in *Johnson v Medical Defence Union* [2004] EWHC 347 (Ch) and *Smith v Lloyds TSB Bank* [2005] EWHC 246 (Ch).

[84] See D Thomas, 'UK to respond to EU data demands', *Computing*, 20 October 2004.

[85] Art 29 WP Opinion 136 (4/2007) and ICO Guidance (August 2007).

Fourthly, the *Durant* concept of 'biographical significance' is used, although the Commissioner is at pains to point out that it is only relevant where the other criteria have not resolved the issue; similarly with the fifth criterion, that of 'focus'. The sixth criterion is to ask whether processing the data will, or could, have an impact on the individual.

Interestingly, the court in *Durant* seemingly returns to the concept of 'personal data' provided under the DPA 1984, where data was considered 'personal' only where it was processed 'by reference to the data subject'.[86] This concept was restated by the Data Protection Tribunal in the *Equifax* case to mean where 'the object of the exercise is to learn something about individuals',[87] which is not dissimilar from the view taken by the court in *Durant*. The Information Tribunal has also opined that the notions of biographical significance and focus have been 'given more significance than we believe that Auld LJ intended' and that the key consideration is where the data lies on a 'continuum of relevance and proximity to the data subject'.[88]

A second issue of interpretation that has come before the courts has been the question: when does 'personal data' cease to be personal through manipulation to render it anonymous? In *Common Services Agency v Scottish Information Commissioner*,[89] the House of Lords considered the meaning of the phrase 'and other information', in the section 1(1) definition, when evaluating whether data continued to be 'personal'. The data in question concerned medical data about incidences of leukaemia. The data had been 'barnardized', which is a statistical technique designed to anonymize the data. However, to the extent that the data controller continued to possess 'other information' that could enable the process of anonymization to be reversed, it meant that the barnardized data continued to be personal data under the 1998 Act.

While data protection law objectifies personal information through the criterion of being able to 'identify' a person, either directly or indirectly (subject to the stance taken in *Durant*), the scheme of the DPA 1998 clearly indicates that data subjects have no property interest in the 'personal data' processed by a data controller. First, the data protection regime fails to grant a data subject a general right to prevent a data controller from processing personal data about him, contrary to popular perceptions. Under the DPA 1998, provided the data controller legitimately processes the data in compliance with the data protection principles, a data subject can only prevent the processing of his personal data in two specific circumstances: where the processing is likely to cause damage or distress and where the purpose of the processing is for direct marketing.[90] Secondly, the remedies available

---

[86] s 1(7).
[87] *Equifax Europe Ltd v The Data Protection Registrar* (1991) Case DA/90 25/49/7 at para 50.
[88] *Kelway v ICO* (Information Tribunal, 14 April 2009).
[89] [2008] UKHL 47.
[90] The rights granted data subjects are examined in section 10.3.6 below.

against the unlawful obtaining of personal data from a data subject are only civil or administrative; while such unlawful obtaining from a data controller is subject to criminal sanction,[91] analogous to property-based crimes such as theft or fraud.[92]

As noted above, UK data protection has its roots in concerns about the impact of computerization on our lives. Hence, the DPA 1984 was solely concerned with automatically processed personal data. In contrast, the 1995 Directive and the DPA 1998 extend the scope of protection to manual records as well as computer records, provided they comprise a 'relevant filing system'. To constitute a 'relevant filing system', the set of information must be 'structured, either by reference to individuals or by reference to criteria relating to individuals, in such a way that specific information relating to a particular individual is readily available' (s 1).

The DPA 1998 extends the scope of coverage even further in respect of personal data held in manual form by public authorities. At the time of adoption, the Act defined protectable 'data' to include 'accessible records',[93] which included certain health records, educational records, and certain other specified public records.[94] The term 'accessible records' was incorporated into the DPA 1998 in order that the government could comply with the European Court of Human Rights' decision in *Gaskin v UK*.[95] In this case, the court held that certain records relate to 'private and family life' in such a way that the issue of access falls within the ambit of Article 8(1) of the ECHR.

The FOIA 2000 has subsequently further amended the definition of 'data' under the DPA 1998 by adding another category of the term: information recorded by a 'public authority', which does not fall within any of the other categories, that is, unstructured manual records.[96] Data subject access to such 'unstructured personal data', under section 7, is qualified by the need for the request to contain a description of the data being sought, and where the estimated cost of compliance exceeds a prescribed amount,[97] the data need not be supplied.[98] Such records are also exempt from many of the DPA 1998's provisions,[99] including six of the eight data protection principles.

UK data protection law has therefore, in respect of public sector data, broken from its obsession with computer-based 'personal data'. However, the concept of a 'relevant filing system' has been subject to a restrictive interpretation in the

---

[91] See, further, section 10.3.9 below.
[92] See Chapter 12, section 12.2.2.
[93] s 1(1)(d).
[94] s 68, Schs 11 and 12.
[95] (1990) 12 EHRR 36.
[96] FOIA 2000, s 68.
[97] The Freedom of Information and Data Protection (Appropriate Limit and Fees) Regulations 2004 (SI 2004/3244).
[98] FOIA 2000, s 69(2), inserting a new s 9A into DPA 1998.
[99] FOIA 2000, s 70, inserting a new s 33A into DPA 1998.

Durant case. The judge noted that 'it is only to the extent that manual filing systems are broadly equivalent to computerized systems in ready accessibility to relevant information capable of constituting "personal" data that they are within the system of data protection' (para 47), which severely limits the range of manual files held by the private sector to which the Act applies.

The concept of 'processing' is defined in terms which reflects the all-encompassing definition in Council Directive (EC) 95/46:

. . . any operation or set of operations which is performed upon personal data, whether or not by automatic means, such as collection, recording, organization, storage, adaptation or alteration, retrieval, consultation, use, disclosure by transmission, dissemination or otherwise making available, alignment or combination, blocking, erasure or destruction. (Art 2(b))

While this definition seemingly extends to all forms of processing, both manual and automatic, the concept of 'data' is more narrowly drawn to cover only 'automatically' processed data, data held in a 'relevant filing system' and the manual data held by public authorities, noted above. The breadth of the concept has been examined by the Court of Appeal in *Johnson v Medical Defence Union*,[100] where it was argued that a person's selection of material for insertion into a computer fell within the definition of 'processing', as a stage of 'obtaining'. The court was divided on the issue, the majority holding that such an interpretation would be an inappropriate extension of the scope of the 1998 Act, overturning previous dicta on the issue.[101]

The DPA 1998 is primarily concerned with three categories of persons:

(a) 'Data subjects': the individual who is the subject of the personal data.

(b) 'Data controllers': a person who, whether alone, jointly, or in common with others, 'determines the purposes for which and the manner in which' the data are processed.[102]

(c) 'Data processor': a third party simply processes personal data on behalf of a data controller without controlling the contents or use of the data.

The obligations under the Act reside upon the data controller. While the definition is based on two criteria, whether the entity determines the purpose and the means of processing, determination of purpose is generally viewed as paramount, since means

---

[100] [2007] EWHC Civ 262.
[101] See *Campbell v MGN Ltd* [2003] QB 633 at paras 101 et seq. Also *Johnson v MDU* [2006] EWHC 321 at paras 86 et seq.
[102] In *Data Protection Registrar v Francis Joseph Griffin, The Times*, 5 March 1993, the court held that limitations imposed on an individual's use of personal data for his own purposes, either contractual or professional, does not necessarily prevent him from being a separate registrable 'data user' under the DPA 1984.

is seen as an inherent element of the purpose.[103] In a Commission report on the transposition of Council Directive (EC) 95/46, it noted that Member States have adopted various textual divergences from the Directive's definitions, but with a focus on determination of purpose or use as the key definitional criteria.[104] An entity may be both data controller and data processor in respect of different collections of personal data. So, for example, within a group of companies, an establishment may process data on its own behalf, such as payroll and accounts; while also hosting facilities on which databases controlled and used by another company in the group reside.

10.3.2 Sensitive data

Under European data protection law, greater legal protections are granted to 'special categories of data', those 'which are capable by their nature of infringing funda-mental freedoms or privacy'.[105] These protections include requirements for data controllers to obtain explicit rather than implied consent, enhance the security meas-ures implemented, and/or further limit the types of processing that may be carried out.[106] Such enhanced protection is deemed necessary because discriminatory use of the data is considered more likely substantially to infringe an individual's privacy than other categories of personal information.

Provisions concerning so-called 'sensitive data' were contained in the DPA 1984, but were never brought into operation by the Secretary of State.[107] Under the DPA 1998, the following categories of information are considered 'sensitive personal data', transposing Article 8 of the 1995 Directive:

(a) the racial or ethnic origin of the data subject,

(b) his political opinions,

(c) his religious beliefs or other beliefs of a similar nature,

(d) whether he is a member of a trade union (within the meaning of the Trade Union and Labour Relations (Consolidation) Act 1992),

(e) his physical or mental health or condition,

(f) his sexual life,

(g) the commission or alleged commission by him of any offence, or

---

[103] See 'Data Controller—Definition', Guidance issued by the Information Commissioner, January 2001.
[104] Report from the Commission—First report on the implementation of the Data Protection Directive (95/46/EC) (COM(2003)265 final). See also Article 29 Working Party Opinion 1/2010 'on the concepts of "controller" and "processor"' (WP 169).
[105] Council Directive (EC) 95/46, recital 33.
[106] Ibid Art 8.
[107] DPA 1984, s 2(3). Based on the 1981 Convention, Art 6.

(h) any proceedings for any offence committed or alleged to have been committed by him, the disposal of such proceedings, or the sentence of any court in such proceedings.[108]

Neither the Directive nor the DPA 1998 make express provision for this list to be amended over time, which seems unnecessarily rigid considering the evolving nature of privacy concerns in society. The Commission has proposed, however, that the list be reconsidered as part of the current reform process.[109]

The Directive provides for the possibility of 'prior checking' of 'processing operations likely to present specific risks to the rights and freedoms of data subjects',[110] which has been transposed into the DPA 1998 through a procedure for preliminary assessment by the Information Commissioner. To become operable, however, the provision requires the Secretary of State to issue an order specifying those types of processing activities that are considered by him to be likely to cause 'substantial damage or distress to the data subject' or 'significantly prejudice the rights and freedoms of data subjects' (s 22). To date, no such order has been issued, although in a consultation paper in August 1998 three possible categories were identified: data matching, the processing of genetic data, and processing by private investigators.[111]

Although there is no process to amend what is defined as 'sensitive data' at either an EU or domestic level, there have been subsequent regulatory instruments imposing additional controls on the processing of certain categories of personal data in particular contexts. Two examples originating in EU law are data relating to a person's use of telecommunication services (eg, number called, call duration), referred to as 'traffic' and 'billing' data, which can only be processed for limited purposes,[112] and limitations placed on a 'certification service provider' involved in the provision of electronic signature services.[113] At a domestic level, the Identity Cards Act 2006, until repealed, included provisions restricting the use made of data held under the scheme;[114] while the Protection of Freedoms Bill, currently before Parliament, contains proposed rules for processing certain types of biometric data.[115] Such de facto but piecemeal extensions of the concept of 'sensitive data' may undermine the

---

[108] s 2. See also Sch 3 and the Data Protection (Processing of Sensitive Personal Data) Order 2000 (SI 2000/417).

[109] 2010 Communication, n 58 above, at 2.1.6.

[110] Art 20(1).

[111] Home Office, 'Data Protection Act 1998: Consultation on Subordinate Legislation', para 22. This list was initially proposed in a government White Paper, 'Data Protection: The Government's Proposals' (Cm 3725, 1997).

[112] See section 10.3.4 below.

[113] The Electronic Signatures Regulations 2002 (SI 2002/318), reg 5. These Regulations transpose Council Directive (EC) 1999/93 on a community framework for electronic signatures [2000] OJ L13/12, 19 January 2000.

[114] eg, ss 17–21: 'Other purposes for which registered information can be provided'.

[115] eg, fingerprints and DNA.

coherence of national data protection regimes and harmonization between Member States.

10.3.3 Data protection principles

The Data Protection Act 1984 was built around certain data protection principles, an approach that the DPA 1998 reiterates. These principles are intended to be good practices that data controllers should comply with in order to protect the data they hold, reflecting both their interests and those of data subjects. The DPA 1998 contains a limited redraft and renumbering of the 1984 principles, and data controllers have a duty to comply with the principles, except where an exemption exists.[116]

1. Personal data shall be processed fairly and lawfully and, in particular, shall not be processed unless—

(a) at least one of the conditions in Schedule 2 is met, and

(b) in the case of sensitive personal data, at least one of the conditions in Schedule 3 is also met.

2. Personal data shall be obtained only for one or more specified and lawful purposes, and shall not be further processed in any manner incompatible with that purpose or those purposes.

3. Personal data shall be adequate, relevant and not excessive in relation to the purpose or purposes for which they are processed.

4. Personal data shall be accurate and, where necessary, kept up to date.

5. Personal data processed for any purpose or purposes shall not be kept for longer than is necessary for that purpose or those purposes.

6. Personal data shall be processed in accordance with the rights of data subjects under this Act.

7. Appropriate technical and organizational measures shall be taken against unauthorized or unlawful processing of personal data and against accidental loss or destruction of, or damage to, personal data.

8. Personal data shall not be transferred to a country or territory outside the European Economic Area unless that country or territory ensures an adequate level of protection for the rights and freedoms of data subjects in relation to the processing of personal data.

The first and key principle requires that personal data be processed fairly and lawfully. The principle is qualified by the requirement that one of the conditions in Schedule 2 is present, and Schedule 3 where sensitive data is processed.[117] These conditions primarily relate to the issue of lawful processing. Schedules 2 and 3

---

[116] s 4(4) and Sch 1.
[117] Implementing Arts 7 and 8 of Council Directive (EC) 95/46.

substantially amend the concept of 'lawful' processing, which represents a significant modification in focus from an English law perspective.

The traditional common law approach to the concept of 'lawfulness' is that processing must not be carried out in breach of any legal obligation, such as contractual or equitable obligation of confidence.[118] By requiring that one of the Schedule 2 and 3 conditions is applicable in order to legitimize the processing, the regime becomes akin to a civil law approach, whereby all processing is unlawful unless one or more of the conditions applies. In reality, from a compliance perspective, a UK data controller needs to ensure lawfulness both in terms of not breaching any legal obligation, as well as meeting one of the specified criteria. A public authority, for example, would first need to ensure that it had the necessary vires to carry out the intended processing activity, under administrative law principles. Secondly, that the intended processing was not subject to any statutory, contractual, equitable, or other restriction, such as the need to comply with the Human Rights Act 1998.[119] Finally, compliance with Schedule 2 and, if relevant, 3 would then be the issue.

One condition legitimizing processing is having the data subject's consent. The 1995 Directive defines 'data subject's consent' as being freely given, specific, and informed (Art 2(h)). However, the concept is further supplemented in the body of the Directive when reference is made to consent being 'unambiguously' given (Arts 7(1) and 26(1)(a)). Such terminology would seem to provide little opportunity for a data controller to rely on the implied consent of a data subject; where, for example, a data subject has not ticked an 'opt-out' box on an application form. Significantly, however, the DPA 1998 does not include any definition of 'consent'. In justification of this position, the government stated:

The Government are content for the issue of whether consent has been validly given to be determined by the courts in the normal way . . . It is better for the courts to decide according to ordinary principles of law than for the Act to contain specific consent provisions.[120]

This absence provides data controllers with greater flexibility with regard to claiming the consent of the data subject through implication, although the courts would have to consider the terminology used in the Directive when interpreting the application of the DPA 1998.

Consent would seem to be the key mechanism by which an individual can exercise control over the processing of their personal data. It is broadly accepted by

---

[118] See eg, the Data Protection Tribunal decision in *British Gas Trading Ltd v The Data Protection Registrar* (24 March 1998).

[119] eg, *Peck v UK* (2003) 36 EHRR 41, where an authority was found to be in breach of Art 8(1), on the ground of proportionality.

[120] Comments made by Mr Hoon (Parliamentary Secretary, Lord Chancellor's Department), 12th sitting of Standing Committee D, 4 June 1998 (morning).

academic commentators[121] and the English courts that control is a central element of the concept of privacy; as noted by Lord Hoffmann, privacy comprises 'the right to control the dissemination of information about one's private life'.[122] However, data subject control through consent is not necessarily viewed as central to the UK data protection regime. While Schedules 2 and 3 list consent first, the Act gives no greater weight to consent as a ground for legitimate processing as the other conditions. This is position is confirmed in the Information Commissioner's guidance to the Act, which notes:

. . . consent is not particularly easy to achieve and data controllers should consider other conditions . . . before looking at consent. No condition carries greater weight than any other. All the conditions provide an equally valid basis for processing. Merely because consent is the first condition to appear . . . does not mean that data controllers should consider consent first.[123]

As such, recognition should be given to the 'fallacy of necessity', that is, where there is no consent, there must be a wrong; and the 'fallacy of sufficiency', that is, where there is consent, there cannot be a wrong.[124]

Where the data controller does not have the consent of the data subject, the processing of personal data must be 'necessary' for one of the specified purposes, either detailed in the Schedules themselves, such as 'the performance of a contract to which the data subject is a party' (para 2) or 'the exercise of any functions conferred on any person by or under any enactment' (para 5(b)), or in related secondary legislation.[125] The phrase 'necessary' has been construed as matters 'reasonably required or legally ancillary to' the specified purpose, rather than 'absolutely essential' to the purpose.[126]

For non-sensitive personal data, the final criterion is:

The processing is necessary for the purposes of legitimate interests pursued by the data controller or by the third party or parties to whom the data are disclosed, except where the processing is unwarranted in any particular case by reason of prejudice to the rights and freedoms or legitimate interests of the data subject.[127]

Compared to the other criteria, this could clearly be a potential fall-back justification to a controller. How is such a provision intended to operate? Guidance from the Office of the Information Commissioner has stated that where a data subject is

---

[121] eg, G Phillipson, 'Transforming Breach of Confidence? Towards a Common Law Right of Privacy under the Human Rights Act' (2003) 66 Modern Law Review 726 at 732.

[122] *Campbell*, n 19 above, para 51.

[123] Data Protection Act 1998: Legal Guidance, version 1 at s 3.1.5.

[124] See D Beyleveld and R Brownsword, *Consent in the Law* (Oxford: Hart, 2007).

[125] See Data Protection (Processing of Sensitive Personal Data) Order 2000 (SI 2000/417).

[126] DCA Report, n 70, at para 6.11, based on AG Walker 3 Ex 242, per Pollock CB, cited in *Stroud's Judicial Dictionary* (London: Sweet & Maxwell, 2000) 1660.

[127] Sch 2, para 6(1).

provided with an opportunity to object to the processing of his data—the so-called 'opt-out' option—but fails to take it, then while the data controller is not able to imply consent, it may provide the basis for reliance on the 'legitimate interests' criteria.[128]

The 'legitimate interests' criterion has also been subject to judicial examination. In *Douglas v Hello!*,[129] the defendant claimed that freedom of expression through the publication of pictures of the claimants was the legitimate interest that overrode the privacy interests of the claimants. However, Justice Lindsay stated that:

> The provision is not, it seems, one that requires some general balance between freedom of expression and rights to privacy or confidence . . . Paragraph 6 does not provide, as it so easily could have done, how serious has to be the prejudice before the processing becomes unwarranted and in point of language any prejudice beyond the trivial would seem to suffice.

Justice Lindsay suggests, therefore, that the provision should not be viewed as a balancing exercise, simply whether the data subject has an identifiable interest that will be prejudiced.

A potentially contrasting view has been expressed by the European Court of Justice in a reference for a preliminary ruling from the English High Court: *R v Minister of Agriculture, Fisheries and Food, ex p Trevor Robert Fisher and Penny Fisher*.[130] Here the claimant wanted disclosure of personal data concerning a previous land owner in respect of the receipt of certain agricultural subsidies. In relation to the application of Article 7(f) of Council Directive (EC) 95/46, on which the paragraph 6 provision is based, the Court briefly considered the relevant interests of the parties and concluded that the data could be disclosed 'after balancing the respective interests of the persons concerned' (para 39). In support of the court's interpretation, the European Commission, in its first report on the implementation of Council Directive (EC) 95/46, commences the relevant paragraph in the following manner: 'The "balance" criterion, Art. 7(f) . . .'.[131] Subsequent paragraphs also refer to the 'balance' test in relation to Article 7(f).

Whether through consent or necessity under the other conditions, the burden will be upon the data controller to evidence that his processing operations are 'lawful'. In terms of what constitutes 'fair' processing, the Data Protection Tribunal held, in a decision under the DPA 1984, *Innovation (Mail Order) Ltd v Data Protection Registrar*,[132] that 'fair obtaining' means that at the time that information is collected, the data user needs to inform the data subject of certain matters that will enable the individual to decide whether or not to provide the information. This requirement for

---

[128] Guidance, at s 3.1.5.
[129] [2003] EWHC 786 (Ch).
[130] C-369/98 [2000] ECR I-06751.
[131] Commission Report, 'Technical Analysis of the Transposition in the Member States', p 10, May 2003.
[132] Judgment delivered 29 September 1993, Case DA/92 31/49/1.

informed choice was adopted in the 1995 Directive, both through the concept of 'data subject's consent' and the requirement for a data controller to provide certain information to the data subject, either when the data are collected from the data subject or where the data were not obtained from the data subject.[133]

The data controller obligations have been incorporated into the DPA 1998 within the concept of 'fair' processing, as part of the interpretation provisions.[134] While the Directive refers only to the data controller providing such information to the data subject, 'except where he already has it'; the DPA 1998 also enables the data controller to comply with the obligation by making the information 'readily available' to the data subject. The manner in which this phrase is interpreted may have important implications for a controller in terms of the procedural mechanisms it establishes, such as the use of intranet-based techniques to disseminate information to employees. Where the data controller has not obtained the data from the data subject themselves, the controller is exempt from the requirement to provide information where it would involve either 'disproportionate effort', or the recording or disclosure is required under a non-contractual legal obligation.[135]

The second data principle is concerned with the use made of personal information. Data controllers must obtain data 'only for one or more specified and lawful purposes, and shall not be further processed in any manner *incompatible* with that purpose or those purposes'.[136] Thus, the 'use' made of personal data is a related but distinct point of regulatory control from that provided for under the first data protection principle. In similar fashion, the third limb of an action for breach of confidence requires that the person with the obligation does not use the information in contravention of the limited purpose for which the information was or became disclosed.[137]

The second part of the second principle envisages the possibility that further processing of data may occur for purposes other than those specified and lawful, provided that such other purposes are not 'incompatible', which would seem to imply only that the secondary purpose should not have negative consequence vis-à-vis the primary purpose. However, the UK's Information Commissioner has posed a more restrictive interpretation of the principle:

The effect of the principle is to reinforce the First principle and also to limit the range of cases where data may be processed for purposes of which the data subject was not informed to one which are *compatible* with those for which data were originally obtained.[138]

---

[133] Arts 10 and 11.

[134] Sch 1, Pt II, paras 1–3.

[135] See the Data Protection (Conditions under Paragraph 3 of Part II of Schedule 1) Order 2000 (SI 2000/185).

[136] Sch 1, Pt I, para 2. This transposes Art 6(1)(b) of the 1995 Directive.

[137] See *R v Department of Health, ex p Source Informatics* (2000) 1 All ER 786.

[138] Office of the Information Commissioner ('OIC') Guidance, 'Use and Disclosure of Health Data', May 2002.

This suggests the need to show a positive relationship between the primary and secondary purpose, which is clearly more supportive of privacy concerns than a strict language-based interpretation that is more favourable to data controller interests.

Building on the second principle, the third, fourth, and fifth principles address usage-related matters, potentially supportive of both data subject and data controller interests.[139] The sixth principle asserts data subject rights under the Act, as distinct from a general right to privacy. The seventh principle concerns data security issues, although UK law only criminalizes 'unauthorized and unlawful processing' in qualified circumstances primarily reflecting the interests of data controllers.[140] The final eighth principle encompasses all the other principles by ensuring that protections are not lost through the transfer of personal information outside the European Economic Area, and is discussed further below.

10.3.4 Information Commissioner

European data protection law requires the establishment of a supervisory authority capable of acting with 'complete independence' (Art 28(1));[141] a principle also enshrined in the Charter (Art 8(3)). The 1998 Act renamed the UK supervisory authority the 'Data Protection Commissioner', which has subsequently been renamed the 'Information Commissioner'.[142] The Commissioner has a number of duties and enforcement powers under the Act. Under the DPA 1984, the Data Protection Registrar had a duty to promote observance of the data protection principles. This has been significantly broadened to a general duty to promote 'good practice', defined as:

. . . 'good practice' means such practice in the processing of personal data as appears to the Commissioner to be desirable having regard to the interests of data subjects and others, and includes (but is not limited to) compliance with the requirements of this Act. (s 51(9))

One mechanism for such promotion is the development of codes of practice. Under the DPA 1998, the Commissioner can draft such codes rather than merely encourage trade associations to do so (s 51(3)(b)). However, to date, only three such codes have been issued, addressing CCTV, employment practices, and telecommunications

---

[139] Although see the Information Tribunal decision in *The Chief Constables of West Yorkshire, South Yorkshire and North Wales Police v The Information Commissioner* (12 October 2005) for an examination of the difficulties when reconciling individual and societal interests.

[140] ie, the DPA 1998, s 55 and the Computer Misuse Act 1990.

[141] See *Commission v Germany* [2010] 3 CMLR 3, in which Germany was held to have failed to fulfil its obligations in this respect by subjecting the data protection authorities in the Länder to state scrutiny.

[142] The first Registrar was Eric Howe. He was replaced by Elizabeth France in August 1994. A new Information Commissioner, Richard Thomas, was appointed from 2 December 2002. The current Information Commissioner is Christopher Graham.

directory information.[143] Such paucity is perhaps surprising, although there are numerous codes drafted by industry associations and other bodies, which address data protection issues in whole or part.[144] The Commissioner also has the power to carry out 'good practice'-based assessments, with the consent of the data controller (s 51(7)).

The Commissioner has the power to pursue administrative remedies, in the form of notices issued against data controllers and/or criminal remedies for the commission of offences under the Act (see section 10.3.9 below). In terms of investigating compliance with the Act, the Commissioner can issue an 'information notice' against a data controller requiring the provision of specific information (s 43). Where necessary, the Commissioner can apply to a court for a warrant to access, search, and seize material held by an individual or organization (Sch 9). The Commissioner can instigate a prosecution for an offence under the Act; however, he is not able to commence civil proceedings against a data controller where a data subject's statutory rights have been breached, so complete surrogacy is not provided for under the Act.

The Act also provides the Commissioner with the ability to serve an 'enforcement notice' against a data controller that has failed to observe any of the data protection principles (s 40). The notice specifies the nature of the breach that has occurred and outlines the measures that will need to be taken in order to correct the breach. If the data controller fails to comply with the notice, then an offence is committed (s 47).

Any person who is, or believes himself to be, directly affect by any processing of personal data may require the Commissioner to carry out an 'assessment' of whether the Act is being complied with (s 42). If provided with sufficient information to identify the relevant processing, the Commissioner has a duty to make such an assessment. Further powers for the Information Commissioner to issue 'assessment notices' against public authorities have recently been adopted.[145]

In 2008, the Information Commissioner was granted new powers to impose monetary penalties on a data controller, where there has been a 'serious contravention' of the data protection principles; of a kind likely to cause substantial damage or distress, and the contravention was either deliberate or the data controller knew or should have known of the risks and failed to take reasonable steps to prevent such a contravention.[146] These powers came into force in April 2010, with the possibility of a fine of up to £500,000 being imposed.

Under the DPA 1984, a Data Protection Tribunal was established to hear appeals by data controllers against any notice issued against them by the Registrar. Data subjects had no such right of appeal. This position is broadly maintained under the

---

[143] Available at <http://www.informationcommissioner.gov.uk> (accessed 10 August 2011).

[144] eg, Direct Marketing Association, *Direct Marketing Code of Practice*, 3rd edn. See generally the *Encyclopedia of Data Protection* (London: Sweet & Maxwell, 1999 (updated)).

[145] s 41A, inserted by the Coroners and Justice Act 2009, Pt 8, s 173.

[146] Criminal Justice and Immigration Act 2008, s 144; inserting new ss 55A–E into the 1998 Act.

DPA 1998, although data subjects will now have the right to appeal to the First-tier Tribunal (Information Rights), previously known as the Information Tribunal[147] where they are 'directly affected' by the issuance of a certificate exempting data from the Act's provisions for reasons of national security (s 28(4)–(5)).[148]

10.3.5 Data controller notification

Under the DPA 1984, the Registrar was required to establish a public register of all data users and computer bureaux. The principal functions of the register were to identify systems and facilitate supervision and compliance with standards; as well as generating income to pay for the regulatory oversight. The Office of the Data Protection Registrar initially estimated the number of registrations to be around 300,000; however, just over half that number were received. Much criticism was levelled at the registration process from both data users, as a bureaucratic burden, and data subjects, for being impenetrable!

Under the DPA 1998, data controllers are required to continue to notify the Information Commissioner in a similar fashion to the previous registration system, although, as noted by the Home Office, 'notification will be an element of the main regime rather than triggering application of that regime'.[149] The Act prohibits processing without notification (s 17), except for:

(a) manual data processed as part of a 'relevant filing system' or an 'accessible record';

(b) where the Secretary of State has, in 'notification regulations', exempted categories of processing from the notification obligation as 'unlikely to prejudice' data subject rights and freedoms;[150] or

(c) the processing is for the *sole* purpose of maintaining a public register.

Such notification shall include 'the registrable particulars' (eg, name, address, and description of purposes for which the data are being processed: s 16(1)) and 'a general description of measures to be taken for the purpose of complying with the seventh data protection principle'. Controllers also have a duty to notify the Commissioner of any changes relating to such matters. The Commissioner

---

[147] See <http://www.informationtribunal.gov.uk> (accessed 10 August 2011).

[148] There is a separate National Security Appeals Panel of the Tribunal, which hears appeals under the Data Protection Acts, s 28 and the FOIA 2000, ss 23–4. It reviews the issuance of the certificate under judicial review principles. See *Norman Baker MP v Secretary of State for the Home Department* (2001) UKHRR 1275, where a certificate was overturned by the Tribunal; although a further appeal is under way.

[149] See 'Consultation Paper on Notification Regs', Home Office, August 1998, para 8.

[150] See the Data Protection (Notification and Notification Fees) Regulations 2000 (SI 2000/188), reg 3 and Sch, paras 2–5. The Data Protection (Notification and Notification Fees) (Amendment) Regulations 2009 (SI 2009/1677), introduced a two-tier system, based on size of data controller. It also provided for a notification exemption for judges.

shall maintain a register of notifications which shall be made available to the public for inspection,[151] although this only includes the 'registrable particulars', not the information relating to data security measures (s 19(2)). Considerable controversy has surrounded the need to supply a description of security measures. Data controllers are obviously concerned to limit the amount of information disclosed; whilst the Commissioner needs to obtain sufficient detail to make the process meaningful.

One innovation under the Directive, imported from German data protection law,[152] is the possibility that a controller may be exempted from the notification obligation through the appointment of a 'personal data protection official' to act as an internal supervisory authority. However, the government found little private sector enthusiasm for the idea and, therefore, the Act simply grants the Secretary of State the power to issue an order at some point in the future.[153]

Exemption from notification does not take the relevant processing outside the terms of the Act, since data controllers will still be required to comply with the data protection principles. In addition, even where a data controller is exempt from notification, for example by processing only manual data (s 17(2)) or under the Notification Regulations, the data controller may be required to provide details of its 'registrable particulars' to any person who submits a request in writing (s 24(1)). Such information is to be provided free of charge, within 21 days. The potential burden involved in meeting this obligation may have convinced many data controllers voluntarily to notify the Commissioner of their details (s 18).[154]

10.3.6 Data subject's rights

The DPA 1998 extends and amends those rights given to data subjects under the DPA 1984 and provides data subjects with additional rights, in line with the Directive.

10.3.6.1 *Subject access*
A data subject is entitled to be informed by any data controller whether processing of his personal data is being carried out and to be given copies, 'in an intelligible form', of any such data (s 7). However, the requirement to provide information to the data subject is significantly enhanced over that required under the DPA 1984 regime. Under the DPA 1998, the following information must be supplied:

(a) the personal data being processed;

---

[151] See <http://www.ico.gov.uk> (accessed 10 August 2011).
[152] Gesetz zur Fortentwicklung der Datenverarbeitung und des Datenschutzes (Bundesgesetzblatt 1990 I, p 2954), at s 28.
[153] Government White Paper, 'Data Protection: The Government's Proposals' (Cm 3725, July 1997) para 5.11.
[154] Ibid, para 5.10.

(b) the purpose(s) for which data are being processed;

(c) the recipients or classes of recipients to whom data may be disclosed;

(d) and, where relevant, the logic involved in any automated decision-taking.

In the event that the data subject then requests a copy of such information, the data controller must also provide the data subject with 'any information available to the data controller as to the source of those data' (s 7(1)(c)(ii)).

Such metadata adds significantly to the value of the access right. Under the DPA 1984, such contextual information was only indirectly and imperfectly made available to the data subject through the data user's registration entry. The onus was placed on the data subject to figure out the likely source of their personal data, how it is used, and to whom it may be disclosed. The DPA 1998's provisions require the direct provision of specific information on a per request basis. This will require significant additional processing overhead for data controllers responding to subject access requests.

The information must be supplied in 'permanent form' unless this is either impossible or would involve a disproportionate effort, or the data subject agrees otherwise (s 8(2)). Any terms that are not intelligible without an explanation must be accompanied with an appropriate explanatory note. The only amendments that may be made to the information held by the data controller once an access request has been received and before it is supplied are: those that would have occurred in the normal course of events (s 8(6)); those required to respect third party personal data (see below); or information subject to an exemption from access (see section 10.3.7 below).

A data controller is not required to supply such information unless he has received a request in writing and any prescribed fee (s 7(2)). The Act provides the Secretary of State with the ability to prescribe different levels of fees, which have been laid down in the Data Protection (Subject Access) (Fees and Miscellaneous Provisions) Regulations 2000:[155]

(a) the general maximum fee is £10;

(b) for requests concerning an individual's financial standing from a credit reference agency the fee is £2;

(c) for requests in respect of educational records, a sliding scale is detailed in the Schedule, with a maximum of £50;[156] and

(d) for health records the maximum fee is £50, although no fee may be charged in certain circumstances.[157]

---

[155] DPA 1998, s 7(11) and SI 2000/191.

[156] See Commissioner compliance advice on 'Subject Access—Education Records in England' (November 2001).

[157] Under the initial regs, the £50 maximum applied only to requests made before 24 October 2001 (s 6(1)(c)). However, transitional provision was subsequently deleted, leaving £50 as the maximum

As well as submitting a request in writing and paying any required fee, the data subject can be required to provide any information the data controller may 'reasonably require' in order to satisfy himself of the identity of the requesting party (s 7(3)). Such an authentication process is clearly required in order to prevent unauthorized disclosures; however, it could also be abused in order to frustrate access requests.

In addition, the data subject must provide information that indicates the potential location of their personal data (s 7(3)). So, for example, a requesting data subject would be expected to notify the data controller of his relationship to the data controller, for example as a customer or ex-employee. Such information could also extend to an indication of methods of communication used in any interaction with the data controller, such as email.[158]

The data controller has an obligation to provide the requested information within a prescribed period (s 7(8)). The scope of the data controller's obligation to search for potentially discloseable information was considered in *Ezsias v Welsh Ministers*,[159] where the court held that a data controller only has to engage in a 'reasonable and proportionate' search for data. The standard period is 40 days, although different periods are prescribed for requests from credit reference agencies (ie, seven working days) and educational records (ie, 15 school days).[160]

Concerns about the operation of the subject access provisions, particularly the exemptions from subject access, have been raised in a consultation paper published by the Lord Chancellor's Department, the government department responsible for data protection policy.[161] The process is designed to uncover whether 'any "running" adjustments are needed to take account of legal and technological changes' (para 5). However, respondents seemed to consider that the system was working generally satisfactorily.[162]

An important new protection for data subjects, not originating in the Directive, is the issue of enforced subject access. This is the practice whereby potential employees ask individuals to supply them with a copy of their criminal record, obtained through the exercise of the individual's subject access right to the Police National Computer. The Commissioner has indicated disapproval of such practices, but was unable to prevent them under the DPA 1984.[163] The government's White Paper

---

permitted fee: see Data Protection (Subject Access) (Fees and Miscellaneous Provisions) (Amendment) Regulations 2002 (SI 2002/223). See also Commissioner compliance advice on 'Subject Access and Health Records' (version 2.1, 13 November 2001).

[158] See the Commissioner's compliance advice on 'Subject Access and Emails' (version 1, 14 June 2000).

[159] High Court, QBD, Cardiff, 23 November 2007, unreported.

[160] Data Protection (Subject Access) (Fees and Miscellaneous Provisions) Regulations 2000 (SI 2000/191), paras 4(1)(b) and 5(4) respectively.

[161] 'Data Protection Act 1998: Subject Access', October 2002.

[162] DCA, Response to the Consultation Paper, July 2003.

[163] See DPR Guidance Note 21, 'The use of the subject access provisions of the Data Protection Act to check the criminal records of applicants for jobs or licences', GN21-JB-3/89; see also The Tenth Report of the Data Protection Registrar (June 1994), Appendix 2.

announced its intention to prohibit such practices and the Act creates an offence where the requirement relates to criminal records, prison records, and DSS records (s 56[164]). Where 'health records' are concerned any contractual term requiring the provision of such information is rendered void (s 57). The offence contains the following features:

(a) the data subject has to have been required to provide the information, rather than such information being requested;

(b) it applies in only certain types of situations: employment, placing of contracts, and the provision of goods, facilities, or services to the public;

(c) defences exist where the requirement was authorized by law, or was in the public interest.[165]

However, the offence only came into force when the Criminal Records Bureau ('CRB'), an executive agency of the Home Office, became operational; established under Part V of the Police Act 1997. The CRB provides a 'disclosure service' to organizations to assist in recruitment decisions.[166] These 'CRB Checks' provide an alternative mechanism for obtaining criminal conviction data.

10.3.6.2 *Third party personal data*

The subject access provisions also address the issue of the provision of requested information that includes personal data relating to another individual. Coverage of the issue is in considerably greater detail than under the DPA 1984, reflecting the problems experienced by data controllers in the past.

In determining whether 'information relating to another individual who can be identified from that information' will be disclosed through the subject access request, the data controller must take into account 'any other information which, in the reasonable belief of the data controller, is likely to be in, or come into, the possession of the data subject making the request' (s 8(7)). This is likely to prove difficult for data controllers to apply, and it may require them to demand further information from the data subject prior to responding to their access request. A data controller is obliged to provide such information to the data subject as he can without 'disclosing the identity of the individual concerned'.

The DPA 1984 only permitted disclosure of third party identifying information where the data user was 'satisfied that the other individual has consented'. This is extended under the Act to include situations where 'it is reasonable in all the circumstances to comply with the request without the consent of the other individual'.

---

[164] This section is not yet force. It will come into force when the Criminal Records Bureau enables individuals to request copies of their own information.

[165] The public interest defence does not include the prevention or detection of crime, due to the Police Act 1997 (DPA 1998, s 56(4)).

[166] See <http://www.crb.homeoffice.gov.uk> (accessed 10 August 2011). The scheme is likely to undergo significant reform under proposals in the Protection of Freedoms Bill.

The Act elaborates a non-exhaustive list of factors that may be relevant to such a determination, such as any duty of confidentiality owed to the other individual (s 7(6)).

A data controller will need to establish appropriate internal procedures to handle subject access requests for information which contain data on third parties, in order to evidence the appropriateness of any decision to disclose or withhold data. The Commissioner has issued guidance to data controllers, advising them to follow a three-step process:

(a) Does the request require the disclosure of information which identifies a third party individual?

(b) Has the third party consented?

(c) Would it be reasonable in all the circumstances to disclose without consent?[167]

It must also be borne in mind that a person could request the third party information through a request made under the FOIA 2000. The FOIA 2000 only exempts access to personal information where it is either: the personal data of the requester, that is, when the request can be made under the DPA 1998; it contravenes the data protection principles; causes damage or distress (see section 10.3.6.3 below); or is exempt from access under Part IV of the DPA 1998 (see section 10.3.7 below).[168]

10.3.6.3 *Right to prevent and restrict processing*

One common misperception about the data protection regime is that it grants a data subject a general right to prevent a data controller from processing his personal data. Neither the 1984 nor the 1998 Act grant such a broad right. Provided that a data controller legitimately processes the data in compliance with the data protection principles, particularly the first principle concerning fair and lawful processing, a data subject can only prevent the processing of his personal data in two specific circumstances: where the processing is likely to cause damage or distress and where the purpose of the processing is for direct marketing.

Under Article 14(a) of the Directive, a data subject has the right to object to the processing of his data 'on compelling legitimate grounds' and, if the complaint is 'justified', the data controller is obliged to stop such processing. The Act has specified the scope of such legitimate grounds as causing, or is likely to cause (a) 'substantial damage or substantial distress to him [the data subject] or to another' and (b) such damage is 'unwarranted' (s 10(1)). Where such circumstances arise, the data subject may give notice to the data controller in writing and, in the

---

[167] See OIC Technical guidance note: 'Dealing with subject access requests involving other people's information' (July 2006).
[168] FOIA 2000, s 40.

event of dispute, apply for a court order requiring the data controller to stop such processing (s 10(4)).

Article 14(b) of the Directive grants data subjects a specific right to object to processing for the purpose of direct marketing, 'or to be informed before personal data are disclosed for the first time to third parties or used on their behalf for the purposes of direct marketing'. The Act clearly implements the first part of this provision, by granting the data subject a right to require the data controller to cease processing for the purposes of direct marketing (s 11(1)). However, the further element (in quotations) is not present in the Act, which would appear to be a significant limitation of the rights being granted to the data subject.

Data subjects have a new right in respect of automated decision-taking, such as credit reference scoring and the use of psychometric testing for screening applicants (s 12). The Act gives data subjects an entitlement to notify a data controller not to take decisions which 'significantly affect' the data subject and are based 'solely' on automated processing. In the absence of notification, a data controller must proactively notify the individual, 'as soon as reasonably practicable', where such a decision *was* taken and give them the opportunity to require the data controller to 'reconsider the decision or to take a new decision otherwise than on that basis'. However, this right of notification does not apply where the Secretary of State has exempted particular circumstances, or the following conditions are met:

(a) the decision is an aspect of entering into, or performing, a contract with the data subject (s 12(6)(a)); or

(b) the automated decision-making is required under an enactment (s 12(6)(b)); and

(c) the decision grants the request of the data subject (s 12(7)(a)); or

(d) steps have been taken to protect the data subject's interests, for example there is a procedure for appeal (s 12(7)(b)).

The operation of these provisions seem unnecessarily complex, which creates compliance uncertainties and procedural overheads for data controllers whilst offering minimal effective protection for data subjects.

10.3.6.4 *Compensation*
The DPA 1998 extends the grounds upon which a data subject may recover compensation. Under the DPA 1984, compensation was only available in situations of inaccuracy, loss, destruction, or unauthorized disclosure or access.[169] The DPA 1998 substantially broadens this right to compensation for 'damage by reason of *any* contravention by a data controller of *any* of the requirements of this Act' (s 13(1)). Compensation can extend to any 'distress' suffered by the individual,

---

[169] ss 22–23. See further *Lord Ashcroft v Attorney-General and Department for International Development* [2002] EWHC 1122 (QB).

although only as a supplement to damage (s 13(2)(a)). Compensation may be for distress alone only where the contravention relates to processing for the 'special purposes' (s 13(2)(b)).

The Information Commissioner has noted that the concept of 'damage' includes 'financial loss or physical injury'.[170] The courts were obliged to considered the scope of the compensation provisions in *Campbell v Mirror Group Newspapers Ltd*,[171] where a concurrent claim for damages arose under section 13 of the DPA 1998 and for breach of confidence. The court noted that the concept of 'damage' under section 13 'means special or financial damages in contra-distinction to distress in the shape of injury to feelings' (para 123). The court in *Campbell* also found that the plaintiff had suffered both primary and aggravated damage, that is, 'increased distress and injury', suffered as a result of the defendant's conduct subsequent to the breach giving rise to the action, although the level of award was minimal.[172] The nature of the compensation provisions were again examined in *Johnson v MDU*,[173] where the judge held, *obiter*, that the damages available under section 13(1) only extended to pecuniary damages; while distress was the only general head of damages, under section 13(2)(a), and no claim could be made out in respect of general harm caused to a person's reputation (para 219).

The European Court of Human Rights also examined the compensation provisions when deciding on the admissibility of an application made by Janette Martin against the UK for breach of her privacy rights under Article 8.[174] The UK argued that the claim was inadmissible due to her failure to exhaust the possibility of domestic remedies. In examining such remedies, the court held that recourse under section 13 was neither practical nor effective and the respondent had failed 'to demonstrate that it was reasonably arguable that the matters that the applicant has described, including her allegation that she was distressed to such an extent that she became depressed', were sufficient to constitute 'damage' as opposed to distress, under domestic law.

It has been suggested that this provision may not comply with the Directive because the concept of 'damage', under Article 23(1), has been interpreted too narrowly. The European Commission's Article 29 Working Party on data protection has stated:

It should be borne in mind that 'damage' in the sense of the data protection directive includes not only physical damage and financial loss, but also any psychological or moral harm caused (known as 'distress' under UK and US law).[175]

---

[170] See Commissioner's publication: 'Data Protection Act 1998—Legal Guidance', s 4.5.
[171] [2002] HRLR 28.
[172] This was subsequently overturned on appeal: [2002] EWCA Civ 1373.
[173] [2006] EWHC 31.
[174] Application No 63608/00, 27 March 2003, [2004] ECHR 82.
[175] Working Document, 'Judging industry self-regulation: When does it make a meaningful contribution to the level of data protection in a third country?', adopted by the Working Party on 14 January 1998.

Whether the government's interpretation is non-compliant, or whether such issues of relief are beyond the competence of EU law, may have to be resolved before the European Court of Justice. It should also be noted that a data subject may have a right to bring the government before a national court for a failure to protect an individual's rights under the Directive, and this could give rise to a compensatory award.[176]

Where the data controller is a 'public authority', a concurrent claim could be brought before the UK courts under the Human Rights Act 1998. Section 6(1) of the Human Rights Act states that it is 'unlawful for a public authority to act in a way that is incompatible with a Convention right'. In *R (Robertson) v Wakefield Metropolitan DC*,[177] for example, the authority was found to be acting in breach of the Directive and the DPA 1998, as well as an individual's right to respect for private life under Article 8(1) of the ECHR, by selling the electoral register to commercial concerns 'for direct marketing purposes' without an individual right to object. However, in a subsequent decision, *R (on the application of Brian Robertson) v The Secretary of State & (1) Experian Ltd (2) Equifax plc*,[178] it was held that the sale of the complete electoral register to credit reference agencies for the 'facilitation of credit and the control of fraud' was considered legitimate.

Section 8 of the Human Rights Act 1998 provides that a court may grant 'such relief or remedy, or make such order, within its powers as it considers just and appropriate', including an award of damages.[179] A court could therefore make an award of damages that reflects non-pecuniary injury such as distress, without making an award in respect of pecuniary damage. Indeed, such a situation arose in the *Gaskin* case, where the European Court of Human Rights awarded £5,000 as compensation for non-pecuniary injury in respect of emotional distress and anxiety, even though the claim for pecuniary damage was rejected (at paras 57–8). Therefore, the remedy available under the Human Rights Act, whilst coexisting with the remedy provided for under section 13 of the DPA 1998, is considerably wider.[180]

10.3.6.5 *Rectification, erasure, destruction, and blocking*
The DPA 1998 provides data subjects with the right to apply to the courts for an order requiring a data controller to rectify, erase, destroy, or block incomplete and inaccurate data (s 14).

---

[176] eg, Joined Cases C-6 & 9/90 *Francovich and Others v Italy* [1991] ECR 1-5357. See also *Wakefield* at para 19.

[177] [2002] 2 WLR 889.

[178] [2003] EWHC 1760 (Admin), para 15.

[179] Subject to a general limitation that the principles applied by the European Court of Human Rights must be taken into account (s 8(4)).

[180] The issue was recognized by the court in *Wakefield*, at para 44, as raising 'some difficult questions', but was left for further submissions, the outcome of which is unreported.

The Directive also requires that data subjects be given the right to 'obtain from' data controllers notification to third parties, to whom data have been disclosed, of any rectification erasure and blocking, unless this is impossible or involves a 'disproportionate effort' (Art 12(c)). However, the Act has qualified this provision. Imposition upon a data controller of an obligation to notify third parties lies within either the discretion of the court, or an enforcement notice issued by the Commissioner, but not with the data subject. This would seem to be potentially non-compliant with the Directive.

10.3.7 Exemptions

Three broad categories of exemption are provided for in the DPA 1998:

(a) General exemptions from the majority of the Act's provisions, for example processing of personal data for reasons of national security (s 28).

(b) Exemptions from the 'subject information provisions', under section 7 and the information obligations under the first data protection principle, for example for the prevention and detection of crime (s 29).[181]

(c) Exemptions from the 'non-disclosure provisions', for example data made public under enactment (s 34)[182] or required by law or in connection with legal proceedings (s 35).[183]

This section reviews some of the key areas where exemptions are applicable.

10.3.7.1 'Special purposes'

One of the most significant exemptions relates to personal data processed for the 'special purposes', defined under section 3 of the Act as the purposes of journalism, artistic purposes, and literary purposes. This exemption arises from Article 9 of the Directive, which stresses the need to balance the right of privacy against the need to protect freedom of expression.[184] However, it also reflects wider government policy, which places a high priority upon the protection of freedom of expression and a clear intention not to allow data protection laws to risk such freedom. This exemption is also affected by the Human Rights Act 1998 and Article 10 of the ECHR.

Data processed for a 'special purpose' will be exempt from compliance with certain of the Act's requirements, including the data protection principles; the

---

[181] See also Data Protection (Miscellaneous Subject Access Exemptions) Order 2000 (SI 2000/419).

[182] However, note that the FOIA 2000, s 40(2), provides that personal data is exempt from access if such access would contravene the data protection principles or where the data subject has exercised his rights under DPA 1998, s 10.

[183] See further *Totalise plc v Motley Fool Ltd & Interactive Investor* (2002) 1 WLR 1233.

[184] See also Recommendation 1/97, 'Data protection law and the media', of the Article 29 Working Party.

subject access right, and the right of rectification, blocking, erasure, and destruction. However, this exemption will only be activated where all of the following conditions apply:

(a) the processing is *only* for one or more of the 'special purposes';

(b) the processing is 'with a view to publication';

(c) the data controller 'reasonably believes' that publication is in the public interest, 'having regard in particular to the special importance of freedom of expression';[185] and

(d) the data controller 'reasonably believes' that compliance with the exempted provisions would be incompatible with the 'special purposes' (s 32(1)).

The scope of this provision was extensively examined in *Campbell v Mirror Group Newspapers Ltd.*[186] At first instance, the judge held that the phrase 'with a view to publication' limited the scope of the exemption to journalistic activities prior to publication, preventing the use of 'gagging injunctions' and related actions, but did not provide protection against a breach of the Act once publication had occurred (Mr Justice Morland, at para 95). On appeal, the court rejected this interpretation on the basis that 'giving the provisions of the sub-sections [(1)–(3)] their natural meaning and the only meaning that makes sense of them, they apply both before and after publication' (Lord Phillips, at para 121).

Where a data subject commences civil proceedings against a data controller, the controller can raise a defence based on this exemption. In such an event, the court would be obliged to stay the proceedings pending a determination by the Commissioner whether the processing is only for the special purposes or with a view to publication (s 32(5)). The Information Commissioner has strongly criticized the complexity of the mechanism by which this exemption will operate, since it shifts the burden of proof between the various parties and could provide the data controller with a legitimate mechanism to delay proceedings for an unnecessary period of time.

10.3.7.2 *Research*

Research data may be exempt from the subject access provisions. The research exemption includes data held for 'statistical and historical purposes'. As with the 'special purpose' exemption, certain conditions must exist:

(a) the data are not to be processed 'to support measures or decisions with respect to particular individuals'; and

---

[185] An assessment of whether such a belief was reasonable will take into account any relevant, or designated, code of practice (s 32(3)), eg, Press Complaints Commission Code of Practice, see Data Protection (Designated Codes of Practice) (No 2) Order 2000 (SI 2000/1864).

[186] See n 171 and accompanying text.

(b) 'substantial' damage or distress must not be, or be likely to be, caused (collectively referred to as the 'relevant conditions'); and

(c) the research results 'are not made available in a form which identifies data subjects'.

These conditions should encourage the use of techniques that render data anonymous. The second condition has been viewed as potentially problematic in the sense that such data may be used for research purposes on which the data subject may have strong moral or religious opinions, such as research into abortion.[187] However, compliance with the information requirement under the 'fairness' principle would seem to extend only to the purpose of the processing, that is, anonymization, not any subsequent use made of the anonymized data set, to which the DPA 1998 does not apply.

10.3.7.3 Domestic purposes

Under the Directive, the processing of data for 'a purely personal or household activity' is considered outside of the scope of its application (Art 3(2)). The DPA 1998 provides that data controllers processing personal data 'only for the purposes of that individual's personal, family or household affairs (including recreational purposes)' are exempt from the data protection principles, the rights of data subjects or the notification obligations (s 36). However, such processing may be subject to an 'information notice' or 'special information notice' issued by the Commissioner.

While such an exemption makes sense from an enforcement perspective, it may also raise difficult issues in respect of drawing a clear line between regulated and non-regulated personal data. In an internet environment, for example, a person may post photographs of his family members or a list of his local five-a-side football team on his website. At what point does a personal activity enter the public sphere?

The issue was examined by the European Court of Justice in *Lindqvist v Åklagarkammaren i Jönköping*.[188] The defendant had established a website from home containing information about her colleagues in the local Swedish parish. She was prosecuted under Swedish data protection law for failing to notify the authority, processing sensitive data, and transferring data to a third country. It was argued that her activities were exempt by virtue of the domestic purpose exemption at Article 3(2). However, the court held that this was 'not the case with the processing of personal [data] consisting in publication on the internet so that those data are made accessible to an indefinite number of people'. This implies that the boundary

---

[187] See D Beyleveld and E Histed, 'Case Commentary—Anonymisation Is Not Exoneration' (1999) 4 *Medical Law International* 69–80.
[188] Case C-101/01 [2004] QB 1014, 6 November 2003.

between 'personal' and public activities is to be objectively determined, based on considerations of accessibility.

10.3.7.4 *Commercial purposes*
For data controllers, there are some important exemptions designed to reflect the needs of commerce:

(a) 'confidential references' given or to be given for the purposes of either (i) the education, training, or employment, or prospective education, training, or employment of the data subject, (ii) the appointment or prospective employment of the data subject to an office, or (iii) the provision or prospective provision of a service by the data subject;[189]

(b) processing for the 'purposes of management forecasting or management planning';

(c) processing relating to the provision of a 'corporate finance service'; or

(d) processing 'of records of the intentions of the data controller in relation to any negotiations with the data subject' (Sch 7).

Management forecasting and planning is not defined, which leaves data controllers with a potentially broad, although uncertain, scope to withhold information. However, under both the management and negotiation exemptions, the data controller will have the burden to show that providing subject access 'would be likely to prejudice' the activities in question.[190]

10.3.8 Transborder data flows

Despite the harmonization initiatives outlined above, many important trading nations still lack comprehensive data protection laws, extending in particular to private sector use of personal data, such as the USA and Japan. Where countries do not have legislation or, indeed, where the level of protection is of a different nature (eg, extending only to public sector data), an issue arises as to whether transfers of personal data should be permitted to jurisdictions that do not have 'equivalent' or 'adequate' protection,[191] since such transfers could enable national data protection regimes to be avoided. Indeed, under the DPA 1998, data controllers have an express obligation to consider such issues under the eighth data protection principle:

Personal data shall not be transferred to a country or territory outside the European Economic Area unless that country or territory ensures an adequate level of protection for

---

[189] The recipient of the reference would be subject to s 7(4), regarding 'information relating to another individual', eg, references given in confidence could not be disclosed.

[190] Note similar 'likely to prejudice' exemptions exist under the FOIA 2000. See further Chapter 11.

[191] The Convention uses the term 'equivalent' (Art 12(3)(a)); while the Directive uses the term 'adequate' (Art 25(1)).

the rights and freedoms of data subjects in relation to the processing of personal data.

The principle is accompanied by an interpretation section (Sch 1, Part II, paras 13–15) and by Schedule 4, which details situations where the principle is not applicable.

Data controllers are also required to notify the Commissioner of those countries outside the EEA to which they transfer, or intend to transfer, personal data. This will enable him to take proactive steps against transfers to countries perceived as providing inadequate protection. The eighth principle will require a data controller to make an assessment of 'adequacy' on a country-by-country basis.

In procedural terms, where a data controller intends to transfer personal data, the first issue that will need to be addressed is whether the transfer falls within one of the criteria specified in Schedule 4. If it does, then the eighth principle would not be applicable.

Schedule 4 substantially echoes the derogations provided for under Article 26(1) of the Directive, that is, either where the data subject has given consent, or where the transfer is necessary for a particular reason (eg, to perform a contract with the data subject). These conditions are similar to those that render processing 'lawful', as discussed above. Article 26(2) provides an additional circumstance arising where a Member State, through the offices of the Information Commissioner, authorizes 'a transfer or a set of transfers of personal data to a third country which does not ensure an adequate level of protection'. Such authorizations will only arise where the data controller 'adduces adequate safeguards'. The initiative is clearly upon the individual data controller to seek such authorization before making a transfer.

Under the Act, the Directive's Article 26(2) has been implemented through two distinct procedural situations:

(a) the transfer 'is made on terms of a kind approved by the Commissioner'; or

(b) the transfer 'has been authorized by the Commissioner'.

The former is addressed to the possibility that the Commissioner could approve the use of certain contractual terms, which would then be considered suitable to cover a 'set of transfers' carried out by the data controller over a period of time. The latter procedure seems to presume some form of case-by-case prior authorization process.

The Commissioner is required to notify the European Commission and the other Member States of all approvals and authorizations granted. Objections may be lodged against such decisions and the European Commission, through its Committee procedure (under Art 31(2)), may make a determination prohibiting such an authorization. Therefore, any approval or authorization a data controller obtains from the Commissioner must be viewed as qualified, subject to this consultation process.

The Commissioner is also obliged to notify data controllers of any Community finding in respect of non-EEA countries that are considered to either have 'adequate' protection or not (s 51(6)). To date, findings of adequacy have been made for a number of countries: Switzerland, Argentina, Guernsey, Faeroe Islands, Israel, Isle of Man, Andorra, Jersey, and Canada; while favourable opinions have been adopted by the Article 29 Working Party in respect of Uruguay and New Zealand. The Commission has also made a finding of 'adequacy' in respect of the US 'Safe Harbor' scheme.[192] Under the scheme, US-based organizations can voluntarily sign-up to the 'Safe Harbor' Agreement, where they agree to abide with certain data protection principles, based on the provisions of the Directive; as well as make themselves subject to an enforcement regime operated by the Federal Trade Commission.[193]

Where a transfer *does* fall within the scope of the eighth principle, then a data controller will need to assess whether the 'country or territory' to which the transfer is to be made ensures an adequate level of protection. The interpretation provision, Part II of Schedule 1, provides a non-exclusive list of criteria relevant to making such an assessment, echoing the terminology of Article 25(2). Where it can be shown that other forms of protection exist in the recipient country, such as constitutional or sectoral legal provisions and/or that the real risk to personal data is low, due to one or a combination of alternative forms of control, such as industry self-regulatory codes of practice, data security measures, or contractual protection, then the transfer should be compliant.

Of particular interest is paragraph 13(g), which states:

. . . any relevant codes of conduct or other rules which are enforceable in that country or territory (whether generally or by arrangement in particular cases).

This is phrased in broad enough terms to include contractual mechanisms, as rules may be 'enforceable' through contractual agreement. Such an interpretation suggests that contractual mechanisms can be a factor in cases where the eighth principle is applicable, as well as those where it does not apply because a derogation is sought. The procedural advantage of complying with the eighth principle is the avoidance of

---

[192] eg, Commission Decision (EC) 2000/250 of 26 July 2000 pursuant to Directive 95/46/EC of the European Parliament and of the Council on the adequacy of the protection provided by the Safe Harbor privacy principles and related frequently asked questions issued by the US Department of Commerce [2000] OJ L215/7, 25 August 2000.

[193] The basis for such enforcement is under the Federal Trade Commission Act (15 USC § 45), which empowers the FTC to obtain injunctive relief against unfair or deceptive practices (s 5), which would include non-compliance with the principles. Similar jurisdiction has been provided for under European law, Directive 2005/29/EC (OJ L149/39, 11 June 2005), Art 6(2)(b): 'non-compliance by the trader with commitments contained in codes of conduct by which the trader has undertaken to be bound, where: (i) the commitment is not aspirational but is firm and is capable of being verified, and (ii) the trader indicates in a commercial practice that he is bound by the code.' This has been transposed into UK law by the Consumer Protection for Unfair Trading Regulations 2008 (SI 2008/1277), reg 5(3)(b).

the need for the Information Commissioner to notify the European Commission and the other Member States.[194]

Since the Council of Europe Convention, particular interest has been shown in the use of contractual terms between the sender and recipient of personal data as a mechanism for achieving 'equivalent' protection. In 1992, the Council of Europe's Committee of Experts on data protection published a set of model contractual provisions which were designed to replicate, as far as possible, the principles of the Convention on data protection in a set of enforceable contractual provisions.[195] The clauses are primarily intended for situations where a contracting party, in a jurisdiction bound by the Council of Europe Convention, wishes to export personal data to a party based in a jurisdiction that has not legislated for data protection. Subsequently, other organizations have issued similar model terms, designed specifically to achieve 'adequate' protection.[196]

However, the role of contracts in protecting the transborder flows of personal data has been extended significantly under the Directive. The Directive states that safeguards enabling a data controller to derogate from the requirement for 'adequate' protection 'may in particular result from appropriate contractual clauses' (Art 26(2)). In addition, the Commission had the right to decide that certain terms offered sufficient protection (Art 26(4)); and subsequently the Commission has adopted two decisions concerning such model contractual clauses.[197] In 2004, the 2001 decision was amended to give official recognition to an ICC-led model.[198] However, use of the term 'model' is somewhat misleading in the sense that a data exporter intending to utilize the clauses is not allowed to amend these sets or totally or partially merge them in any manner';[199] a more appropriate word would be 'standard'.

The major issue when looking to rely on contractual safeguards is whether such provisions can be sufficiently enforceable by, or on behalf of, the data subject whom they are intended to protect. The data user exporting the data is unlikely to suffer damage from any breach of such contractual terms, and therefore has little incentive either to police the agreement or to sue for any breach. In addition, until recently, the primary obstacle under English law to a third party, such as a data subject, acting

---

[194] See generally, Guidance note: 'The Eighth Data Protection Principle and International Data Transfers' (June 2006).

[195] Council of Europe, 'Model Contract to ensure equivalent data protection in the context of transborder data flows' (T-PD (92) 7, October 1992).

[196] eg, International Chamber of Commerce ('ICC'), Model clauses for use in contracts involving transborder data flows (1999) <http://www.icc.org> (accessed 10 August 2011).

[197] Commission Decision (EC) 2001/497 on standard contractual clauses for the transfer of personal data to third countries, under Directive 95/46/EC [2001] OJ L181/19, 4 July 2001, and Commission Decision (EC) 2002/16 on standard contractual clauses for the transfer of personal data to processors established in third countries [2002] OJ L6/52, 10 January 2002.

[198] Commission Decision 2004/915/EC 'amending Decision 2001/497/EC as regards the introduction of an alternative set of standard contractual clauses for the transfer of personal data to third countries' OJ L 385/74, 29 December 2004. The ICC led a coalition of business associations, which included the CBI and FEDMA.

[199] Decision 2004/915/EC, recital 3.

against the importing data user has been the 'privity of contract' rule, whereby only the parties to a contract can enforce its obligations.[200]

Under the Commission's 2001 decision, liability was addressed on the basis of 'joint and several' liability between the data exporter and data importer, which has proved unpopular with businesses operating at arm's length. By contrast, the ICC model, accepted under the 2004 decision, imposes liability upon each party for any breach of their respective obligations to the data subject, as well as liability upon the data exporter for a failure to exercise due diligence and use its reasonable efforts to ensure that the data importer is capable of meetings its obligations under the agreement.[201] The beneficiary data subject is also able to request assistance from the data exporter in the event that the data importer is non-compliant or enforce against the data importer by bringing an action before a court within the European Union.[202]

The use of contractual terms to achieve harmonized protection for personal data between jurisdictions is a solution strongly promoted by industry; as well as schemes for 'binding corporate rules', which are designed to govern transfers between entities within a multinational corporate structure.[203] Thirteen National Regulatory Authorities have established a coordinated approval regime.[204] Companies perceive contractual terms as a practical means of extending data protection rights and obligations to jurisdictions where the adoption of comprehensive data protection laws appears unlikely. The widespread adoption of such terms depends, in part, on the attitude of the appropriate national data protection authorities.[205]

10.3.9 Enforcement

The Commissioner can instigate criminal proceedings for offences under the DPA 1998.[206] The Act establishes five categories of offence: notification-related;[207] failure to comply with a notice (s 47); unlawful obtaining or procurement of data;[208] requiring the provision of certain records (s 56); and obstructing or failing to assist

---

[200] The Contracts (Rights of Third Parties) Act 1999 has removed this obstacle.

[201] Decision 2004/915/EC, at Annex, cl III(b).

[202] Ibid. The accepted jurisdiction is that where the data exporter is established.

[203] eg, Article 29 Data Protection Working Party, 'Working Document Establishing a Model Checklist Application for Approval of Binding Corporate Rules' (WP108, April 2005).

[204] See ICO Press Release, 'Hyatt to transfer personal information outside Europe based on binding corporate rules', 23 September 2009.

[205] See Article 29 Working Party report, 'Transfers of personal data to third countries: Applying arts 25 and 26 of the EU data protection directive' (WP12, 24 July 1998). See, generally, <http://ec.europa.eu/justice/dataprotection/index_en.htm>.

[206] s 60. Alternatively, an individual could institute private proceedings, but only with the consent of the Director of Public Prosecutions, which is an unlikely scenario.

[207] ie, processing without notification (s 21(1)) and the obligation to supply accurate notification information (s 21(2)).

[208] s 55. See *Attorney General's Reference (No 140 of 2004)* [2004] EWCA Crim 3525, which concerned the disclosure, by a person working at the Driver and Vehicle Licensing Agency, of names and addresses of persons that had visited an animal breeding site.

a person in the execution of a warrant (Sch 9, para 12). These offences can be further divided into offences of strict or absolute liability; and those that require the data user to have acted 'knowingly or recklessly'.[209]

As well as a data controller being prosecuted for an offence, a 'director, manager, secretary or similar officer' can also be found personally liable, where the offence was committed with 'the consent or connivance of or to be attributable to any neglect on the part' of any such individual (s 61). However, government departments are exempt from prosecution (s 63(5)).

It is an offence to 'knowingly or recklessly' obtain or disclose, or procure the disclosure of, personal data or information contained in personal data without the consent of the data controller (s 55(1)). The offence was designed to address the growth of private investigation agencies in the mid-1990s offering services based on the acquisition of such personal information. It is also an offence to advertise that such information may be for sale (s 55(4)–(6)). The penalty is not custodial in nature, but a potential unlimited fine.[210] However, of 22 prosecutions brought between November 2002 and January 2006, only two resulted in a fine over £5,000.[211] The paucity of such penalties in the face of a rapidly expanding market in obtaining personal data prompted the Information Commissioner to call upon government to increase the level of penalty to a maximum of two years' imprisonment.[212] The government accepted this proposal and the amendment was introduced by the Criminal Justice and Immigration Act 2008.[213] However, in the face of intense lobbying from the newspaper industry, concerned that such rules could operate as a chilling effect on investigative journalism, the provision was amended to grant the Secretary of State the power to issue an order raising the tariff at some point in the future.[214] Such an order has not yet been forthcoming, despite a consultation process.[215] The Information Commissioner, Christopher Graham, has noted, when giving evidence to the Commons media select committee, as part of its inquiry into press standards, privacy, and libel, that he felt that

. . . we were let down by the courts, who didn't seem to be interested in levying even the pathetic fines they had at their disposal; we were rather let down by parliament in the end,

---

[209] See, further, *Data Protection Registrar v Amnesty International (British Section), The Times,* 23 November 1994 and *Information Commissioner v Islington London BC* [2002] EWHC 1036 (Admin).

[210] DPA 1998, s 60(2). Maximum fine of £5,000 in a magistrates' court and unlimited in the Crown Court.

[211] Information Commissioner, *What Price Privacy? The unlawful trade in confidential personal information,* 10 May 2006. Presented to Parliament pursuant to the DPA, s 52(2).

[212] Ibid.

[213] s 77.

[214] Criminal Justice and Immigration Act 2008, s 77. Before issuing such an order, the Secretary of State has an obligation to consult, including with 'media organizations'.

[215] Ministry of Justice, *The knowing or reckless misuse of personal data: Introducing custodial sentences,* CP22/09, 15 October 2009.

with no legislation; and we were let down by the newspaper groups, which didn't take it seriously.[216]

There are a number of defences that may be argued in a section 55 prosecution, including that the obtaining or disclosure was for the purpose of preventing or detecting a crime, or that the act was in the public interest.[217] A new statutory defence was inserted by the Criminal Justice and Immigration Act 2008:

(ca) that he acted—

(i) for the special purposes,

(ii) with a view to the publication by any person of any journalistic, literary or artistic material, and

(iii) in the reasonable belief that in the particular circumstances the obtaining, disclosing or procuring was justified as being in the public interest,[218]

One can suggest that this addition was unnecessary, given the existing public interest defence, but again shows the power of the media.

Although these defences are specific to the offence, one wonders whether they could not also be argued in respect of a prosecution under an alternative offence, to the extent that the defence is couched in terms of a breach of individual rights. So, for example, in a prosecution for unlawful interception, could it be argued that in order to protect the right of an individual's freedom of expression, under Article 10(1), there should be an excuse based on the reasoning and balancing test that underpins the statutory defence under section 55? If this not acceptable as an excuse or defence, then the alternative would be for the court to make a declaration that the Regulation of Investigatory Powers Act 2000 is incompatible[219] with the ECHR, which would then give the defendant, who has been found guilty, the basis on which to bring an action against the government before the ECtHR.

As noted above, the Information Commissioner has been given the power to impose monetary penalties upon data controllers. The extent of the penalty is determined by the Commissioner, although subject to the upper limit of £500,000 prescribed by the government. To safeguard a data controller, any notice will be preceded by the serving of a notice of intent by the Commissioner,[220] enabling written representations to be made. The Commissioner was also required to publish guidance about his exercise of these powers,[221] which was approved by the

---

[216] *The Guardian*, 'Information Commissioner's Office "let down" over illegal snooping', 2 September 2009.

[217] s 55(2). See, eg, *Rooney* [2006] EWCA Crim 1841.

[218] Criminal Justice and Immigration Act 2008, s 78.

[219] Human Rights Act 1998, s 4.

[220] Ibid s 55B.

[221] Ibid s 55C. See ICO, 'Guidance about the issue of monetary penalties prepared and issued under section 55C(1) of the Data Protection Act 1998'.

Secretary of State and laid before the Houses of Parliament.[222] The penalties are recoverable through civil proceedings.[223] The first such notices were issued in November 2010, against Hertfordshire County Council (£100,000), for allowing highly sensitive data to be faxed to the wrong recipients, and A4e (£60,000), after the loss of a unencrypted laptop containing the personal details of 24,000 people.[224]

Under the DPA 1984, data users took a number of appeals against 'enforcement notices' to the Data Protection Tribunal; under the DPA 1998, such appeals go to the Information Tribunal.[225] The most interesting decisions under the DPA 1984 were concerned with the credit reference and utility industries, and continue to be applicable precedents.

The former Registrar was in a long-running dispute with the four UK credit reference agencies concerning the definition of what information it is 'fair' for the agencies to consider when assessing a person's eligibility for credit. In particular, the Registrar was concerned with the use of information relating to past residents of a person's accommodation. In *CCN Systems Ltd v Data Protection Registrar*,[226] the Registrar had issued an enforcement notice to the appellants, requiring them to cease to provide information relating to applicants for credit that was based purely on their address. The practice of CCN and other credit reference agencies was to provide not only details of the applicant's credit record, but also details of others (whether they bear the same name or not) who formerly or subsequently resided at the applicant's current or previous address. CCN appealed against this notice on the ground that the processing they undertook was not unfair.

The case was concerned primarily with the issue of what is 'fair processing'. The question was whether the processing undertaken by the appellants extracted data which were *relevant* to the decision whether to grant credit. CCN argued that such data were relevant to the credit decision because, on the statistical evidence present, adverse information against third parties at the same address increased the likelihood *in the aggregate* that applicants in that category would default on the loan. On the other hand, the Registrar argued that the proper test was whether the information was relevant *to the particular applicant*, and it was clear that for any individual case such third party information did not generally increase the risk of default. In coming to its judgment on this point, the Tribunal held:

In our view, in deciding whether the processing . . . is fair *we must give first and paramount consideration to the interests of the applicant for credit—the 'data subject' in the Act's terms.*

[222] Human Rights Act 1998, s 55C(5) and (6) respectively.

[223] Ibid s 55D.

[224] ICO Press Release, 'First monetary penalties served for serious data protection breaches', 24 November 2010.

[225] The Information Tribunal's structure has altered as a result of the Tribunal, Courts and Enforcement Act 2007, which creates a two-tier structure, First-tier and the Upper Tribunal. Copies of all the Tribunal's data protection decisions are available at <http://www.informationtribunal.gov.uk/Public/search/aspx> (accessed 15 August 2011).

[226] Judgment delivered 25 February 1991, Case DA/90 25/49/9.

We are not ignoring the consequences for the credit industry of a finding of unfairness, and we sympathise with their problems, but we believe that they will accept that they must carry on their activities in accordance with the principles laid down in the Act of Parliament. (Emphasis added)

The Tribunal therefore held that CCN's processing was unfair in this respect, and disallowed the appeal on that point. It was particularly influenced by the fact that in some cases the inquirer never saw the raw data, and thus had no opportunity to make a separate assessment of their relevance, because CCN offered a number of credit scoring systems which gave the inquirer only a credit score, based in part on this third party information.

However, the Tribunal did hold that the enforcement notice had been too wide, as certain types of third party information would be relevant and thus fairly extracted if there was a clear connection with the applicant for credit. The enforcement notice was therefore amended so as to permit the extraction of certain types of third party information, such as individuals that have the same surname.

The most important principle to be extracted from this judgment is that 'fairness' must always be assessed in relation to the data subject. The mere fact that such processing is to the advantage of the data user is not a relevant consideration.

Enforcement notices have also been issued against companies in the gas and electricity industries. In the *British Gas* case,[227] the Registrar took action against the gas supplier over the use of its customer data for marketing purposes. The Data Protection Tribunal was required to consider whether such processing was both unlawful and unfair, in breach of the first principle.

On the issue of lawfulness, the Registrar had previously stated that processing requires that 'a data user must comply with all relevant rules of law, whether derived from statute or common law'.[228] The Tribunal was therefore asked to consider whether such processing could be considered unlawful by virtue of: (a) a statutory limitation on use of the data rendering the processing *ultra vires*; (b) breach of an implied contractual provision; or (c) breach of an equitable obligation of confidence between British Gas and its customers. The Tribunal held that none of these obligations were present and, therefore, the processing was not unlawful.

On the issue of fair processing, two key issues arose. First, with respect to whether customers had been appropriately informed that their data would be used for marketing purposes. The Tribunal held that it was not unfair to process customer data for marketing gas and gas-related products, including electricity, since it may be considered 'reasonably obvious' to customers that their personal data may be used in that way. However, disclosure of such data to third parties for marketing

---

[227] *British Gas Trading Ltd v The Data Protection Registrar* (24 March 1998). See also *Midlands Electricity plc v The Data Protection Registrar* (7 May 1999): See <http://www.informationtribunal. gov.uk> (accessed 10 August 2011).

[228] See DPR Guideline 4, 'The Data Protection Principles' (3rd Series, November 1994) para 1.18.

purposes would not be fair. Secondly, British Gas provided customers with the opportunity to 'opt-out' of having their data used for marketing purposes, through the use of a separate form sent with customers' bills. On this issue the Tribunal held that it would be unfair for British Gas to imply consent from a customer's failure to return this opt-out form, since customers would have to positively send the form back to British Gas even though they may pay their bill through another mechanism (eg, their bank) which does not require communication with British Gas. As subsequently stated by the Registrar:

> The fact that the data subject must 'signify' their agreement means that there must be some active communication between the parties. Data controllers cannot infer consent from non-response to a communication, for example from a customer's failure to return or respond to a leaflet.[229]

Although the concepts of fair and lawful processing are significantly more specific under the DPA 1998, the issues raised by these Tribunal decisions continue to be relevant and applicable.

10.4 DATA PROTECTION AND TELECOMMUNICATIONS

As noted in section 10.2.4 above, when the European Commission published its first proposal for a Directive in the field of data protection in 1990, it also published a proposal for a sectoral Directive addressing the use of personal data within the telecommunications sector. The Commission was of the opinion that the general data protection Directive would not be sufficient to address concerns about the use of personal data made within particular areas. It was envisaged, therefore, that the general Directive would be supplemented by a series of sectoral Directives, similar to that proposed for the telecommunications sector. Such proposals have not been forthcoming, although the proposal for the telecommunications sector was eventually adopted in 1997.[230] However, concerns that the measure did not adequately address the evolving communications market led to the measure being replaced in 2002: Council Directive (EC) 02/58 of the European Parliament and of the Council concerning the processing of personal data and the protection of privacy in the electronic communications sector ('Communications Privacy Directive').[231]

---

[229] Data Protection Registrar, *An Introduction to the Data Protection Act 1998* (October 1998) ch 3, s 1.6.

[230] Council Directive (EC) 97/66 of the European Parliament and of the Council concerning the processing of personal data and the protection of privacy in the telecommunications sector [1998] OJ L24/1, 30 January 1998.

[231] OJ L201/37, 31 July 2002.

The Communications Privacy Directive was transposed into UK law primarily under the Privacy and Electronic Communications (EC Directive) Regulations 2003 (SI 2003/2426), although protections against the unauthorized interception of communications were implemented by the Regulation of Investigatory Powers Act 2000.[232] The Regulations contain provisions supplementing the general Directive, imposing additional obligations upon data controllers in the communications sector to those already contained within the general Directive. It is beyond the scope of this chapter to detail all the provisions of the Directive,[233] however the key themes are outlined.

Though sectoral in nature, the Communications Privacy Directive is broad in application, addressing four distinct privacy relationships within a communications environment:

(a) between a provider of 'publicly available electronic communication services'[234] and his customer or 'subscriber';

(b) between a subscriber and the actual user of a service;

(c) between users, for example the called and calling party; and

(d) between a user and the state.

First, the use of communication services generates significant amounts of personal data about the attributes of a communication session (eg, the number of the person called, time of call, and duration), as well as the content of the communication itself, which could be of significant value to the service provider. Under the Communications Privacy Directive, a communications service provider ('CSP') is restricted in its ability to process such communication attributes (referred to as 'traffic data') to a much greater degree than that provided for under the general obligation to process data fairly and lawfully. In addition, the definition of a 'subscriber' extends protection to legal persons (eg, a corporation) as well as individuals.

'Traffic data' must be erased or rendered anonymous upon termination of the call and may only be retained for billing purposes, until 'the end of the period during which the bill may lawfully be challenged or payment may be pursued' (Art 6(2)); marketing purposes or the provision of so-called 'value added services'.[235]

One form of communications attribute addressed in detail in the Directive is the processing of 'location data', that is, data which identifies the geographical location of a user. With the growth of mobile telephony, concerns have been raised about the

---

[232] Part 1, Ch I. See, further, Chapter 12, section 12.7.1.

[233] See further C Millard, 'Communications Privacy' in I Walden (ed), *Telecommunications Law and Regulation*, 3rd edn (Oxford: Oxford University Press, 2009).

[234] This term is used in Directive 02/58/EC, at Art 3(1), although it is based on the definitions in Directive 02/21/EC, at Art 2.

[235] '"value added service" means any service which requires the processing of traffic data or location data other than traffic data beyond what is necessary for the transmission of a communication or the billing thereof' (Art 2(g)).

potential abuse of location data to infringe privacy. Processing restrictions are therefore imposed on service providers, including the obligation to provide users with the ability to block the disclosure of such data (Art 9).

The second privacy relationship is that between the 'subscriber' and 'users' of the service. Clearly a user of a telephone may have legitimate reasons why he may not wish data relating to its use to be disclosed to the subscriber, such as a child calling a counselling helpline. The Communications Privacy Directive requires that Member States ensure that users have alternative means for making calls and paying for such calls, which would include, for example, certain numbers not appearing on itemized bills (Art 7(2)).

A third category of privacy relationship is that between users of a communications service, that is, the called and the calling party. Modern digital telephony enables data to be displayed to the recipient of a call concerning the number from which the call was made: generally referred to as 'caller line identification' ('CLI'). However, a calling party may have a legitimate reason to want to prevent the disclosure of such information. As a consequence, the Directive requires that users be given, 'via a simple means, free of charge', the ability to prevent the display of such CLI data.[236] Conversely, the privacy rights of the called party must also be maintained; therefore the called party must have the ability to (a) reject calls which fail to display the calling party's CLI, and (b) prevent disclosure of the CLI data related to the equipment they are using for receipt of the call.

Another aspect of the privacy relationship between users that has become of increasing concern among the general public over recent years is that of unsolicited contact. Forms of unsolicited contact, including 'cold calling', faxing, and emails (generally referred to as 'spam') are primarily used as a direct marketing technique. As such, the problem has been addressed in a number of consumer protection measures at an EU level, including the Communications Privacy Directive.[237] The Directive generally restricts the use of such unsolicited communication techniques without the prior consent of the subscriber (Art 13).[238]

The final privacy relationship addressed in the Communication Privacy Directive is that between the state and users. This primarily relates to issues of the confidentiality of communications, that is, the content and related traffic data, and restricts any form of interception (Art 5(1)). Member States may provide for lawful interception by the state where necessary to protect national security, the prevention and detection of crime, and related circumstances (Art 15(1)); as well as by data

---

[236] In the UK, this can generally be achieved through inputting certain numbers into the handset.

[237] See Council Directive (EC) 1997/7on the protection of consumers in respect of distance contracts [1997] OJ L144/19, 4 June 1997) Art 9; and Council Directive (EC) 2000/31 on certain legal aspects of information society services, in particular electronic commerce, in the Internal Market [2000] OJ L178/1, 17 July 2000) Art 7.

[238] See, eg, *Scottish National Party v The Information Commissioner* (Appeal No EA/2005/0021), 15 May 2006, concerning the use of an automated calling system in breach of reg 19 of the 2003 Regulations.

controllers in the course of a 'lawful business practice' (Art 5(2)). In the wake of the Madrid train bombings in March 2004 and the terrorist attacks in London in July 2005, the Communications Privacy Directive was amended in 2006 to enable Member States to impose requirements on service providers to engage in the wholesale retention of traffic data and related subscriber information for between six and 24 months.[239] The personal data generated by our use of communications technologies has become pan increasingly valuable source of forensic data in the fight against terrorism and organized crime; privacy protections have therefore diminished in the face of such security concerns.

In November 2009, the Communications Privacy Directive was further revised,[240] including the imposition of an obligation upon CSPs to notify end-users when they suffer a breach of security that results in personal data being lost or compromised. The Commission stated that due to the 'special responsibility' of communication providers as 'gatekeepers' to the online world, they should be obliged to notify their customers of any security breach concerning their personal data, as well as the national regulatory authority, which may decide to make the breach public if considered in the public interest.[241] Such an approach was first adopted in the USA, in the State of California,[242] which obliges private businesses and public agencies to report if they have suffered 'a breach of the security'[243] of a system that contains personal information, including financial data.[244]

10.5 CONCLUDING REMARKS

Data protection law became a high-profile political issue during the late 1970s and early 1980s, as European countries began to adopt legislation and companies voiced fears that the spread of such laws would act as an obstacle to the international flow of data, even as a deterrent to the adoption of computer systems altogether. Reality, particularly in the age of the internet, would suggest that such fears were unfounded. However, the adoption and implementation of the EU Data Protection Directive

---

[239] Council Directive (EC) 2006/24 on the retention of data generated or processed in connection with the provision of publicly available electronic communications services or of public communications networks and amending Directive 2002/58/EC, OJ L105/54, 13 April 2006 ('Retention Directive').

[240] By Directive 2009/136/EC ('Citizen's Rights'), OJ L 337/11, 18 December 2009, which needs to be transposed into national law by 25 May 2011.

[241] Communication from the Commission 'on the review of the EU regulatory framework for electronic communications networks and services', COM(2006)334 final, 28 June 2006, at s 7.2.

[242] California Civil Code §§ 1798.29 and 1798.82. The original Senate Bill 1386, available at: <http://info.sen.ca.gov/pub/01-02/bill/sen/sb_1351-1400/sb_1386_bill_20020926_chaptered.pdf> (accessed 10 August 2011). Some 33 states have since enacted similar legislation.

[243] Ibid § 1798.82(d): 'means unauthorized acquisition of computerized data that compromises the security, confidentiality, or integrity or personal information'.

[244] The obligation to notify may be delayed if a law enforcement agency determines that it would impede a criminal investigation (ibid § 1798.82(c)).

has given new life to the debate. A full-scale trade row nearly arose between the EU and the USA over the extent to which US companies could avoid potential restrictions on international data flows by agreeing to abide by a set of self-regulatory principles.

When the first national data protection law was passed in Sweden, in 1973, the major privacy fears were generated through the use of large mainframe computers. Currently developments such as the internet, CCTV, and the use of genetic data are some of the current areas of concern. Such rapid technological change renders data protection laws vulnerable to an accusation of obsolescence. However, the promotion of general principles of good information practice, together with an independent supervisory regime, should enable the law to maintain sufficient flexibility to achieve an appropriate balance between the need to protect the rights of individuals to control how data about them is used, and the needs of an increasingly networked economy.

11

ACCESS TO ELECTRONIC INFORMATION[1]

Timothy Pitt-Payne

11.1 INTRODUCTION

The law about information has developed rapidly over the last 25 years or so. The UK now has an Information Commissioner, and a specialist tribunal dealing with information rights[2] ('the Tribunal'). Major organizations in both the public and private sector increasingly regard the information that they hold as being a valuable asset; yet it can also be a source of acute legal difficulty, as for instance in cases where it impacts on the privacy of individuals. The accidental loss of personal

---

[1] This chapter includes a revised and updated version of material that previously appeared in D Goldberg, G Sutter, and I Walden (eds), *Media Law* (Oxford: Oxford University Press, 2009) ch 7.

[2] The Tribunal's full name is the First-tier Tribunal (General Regulatory Chamber) (Information Rights). With effect from 18 January 2010 it acquired the jurisdiction formerly exercised by the Information Tribunal which was constituted under the Data Protection Act 1998. This change was part of the tribunal reform process under the Tribunals, Courts and Enforcement Act 2007.

information can lead both to acute political or commercial embarrassment[3] and to substantial financial penalties.[4]

To a great extent, developments in this area of law have been driven by the advance of computer technology. It is now possible for large organizations to store and manipulate very substantial bodies of data with ease; at the same time, the internet and the rapid expansion of the use of email have dramatically increased the volume of information and the speed of communication available to ordinary private individuals. The pace of change continues unabated, with the emergence of cloud computing and the explosive growth of participation in social networking sites. There is an extensive literature discussing the political, economic, and cultural implications of all these developments.[5]

Traditionally the law about information has served two major purposes. One is to protect commercial interests. Intellectual property law has long recognized particular types of information as being a valuable commercial asset, and has developed various tools to protect it: patents, copyright, and so on. A second purpose has been to protect the confidentiality of certain sorts of relationship within which private information is readily disclosed: thus, for instance, there is a long-standing concern to protect the confidentiality of the relationship between doctors and their patients.

The scope of information law has however expanded very considerably over the last 25 years or so, beginning with the passage of the Data Protection Act 1984. As well as the technological developments referred to above, there have been at least three other influences of importance. One is an increased concern about the protection of individual privacy. This has been prompted in part by the passage of the Human Rights Act 1998, and the resulting increase in the importance of the rights conferred by the European Convention on Human Rights ('ECHR') (in particular the right to privacy under Article 8 of the Convention). A second influence has been a policy both at UK and European level of promoting rights of access to information held by the public sector. Thirdly, there is the increasing legislative concern for the

---

[3] See eg HMRC's loss of millions of child benefit records, discussed at length in Kieran Poynter's June 2008 report: <http://webarchive.nationalarchives.gov.uk/+/http://www.hm-treasury.gov.uk/media/0/1/poynter_review250608.pdf> (accessed 10 August 2011).

[4] The Information Commissioner has power to issue financial penalties under ss 55A and 55B of the Data Protection Act 1998. For guidance on the exercise of these powers, see <http://www.ico.gov.uk/upload/documents/library/data_protection/detailed_specialist_guides/ico_guidance_monetary_penalties.pdf> (accessed 10 August 2011).

[5] For a broadly optimistic approach, see C Shirky, *Here Comes Everybody: The Power of Organizing without Organizations* (Harlow: Penguin, 2008); and *Cognitive Surplus: Creativity and Generosity in a Connected Age* (Harlow: Penguin, 2010). For a more equivocal view, see J Lanier, *You are Not a Gadget* (Harlow: Penguin, 2011). R Susskind has written extensively about the implications of modern information technology for the legal profession: see, eg, *The End of Lawyers? Rethinking the Nature of Legal Services* (Oxford: Oxford University Press, 2010).

protection of 'whistle-blowers', that is, those who disclose information about wrongdoing in the organizations for which they work.[6]

This chapter does not attempt to cover the whole field of information law. It deals specifically with rights of access to information. The focus is on electronic information, although most of the access rights with which the chapter is concerned are framed by reference to information generally, not simply electronic information. The following areas are discussed.

(a) The subject access right under the Data Protection Act 1998 ('DPA 1998').

(b) Rights of access to information under the Freedom of Information Act 2000 ('FOIA 2000').

(c) Rights of access to environmental information.

(d) Rights of access to local authority information.

(e) Access to information in relation to consumer law and ecommerce.

(f) Specific rights of access in relation to medical records and reports.

(g) Access to information and human rights.

Much of the law in this area is not about the application of clear-cut rules; instead it involves striking a balance between competing considerations. One recurring and important tension is that between concerns about openness and transparency (tending to favour the wider disclosure of information) and concerns about the protection of individual privacy (tending to favour restricted dissemination of information). The principal focus in this chapter is on the freedom of information legislation (including rights of access to environmental information); the other areas mentioned above are covered more briefly.

11.2 DATA PROTECTION ACT 1998[7]

The DPA 1998 is covered in detail elsewhere in this book.[8] This chapter considers, in outline only, one aspect of the Act, namely the right of subject access conferred by section 7. This right is of relevance for present purposes because of the way in which it interacts with the right of access to information held by public authorities under the FOIA 2000.

---

[6] See the Public Interest Disclosure Act 1998, inserting new provisions into the Employment Rights Act 1996; and compare the whistle-blowing provisions in US Federal legislation under the Sarbanes-Oxley Act 2002.

[7] This Act replaced the DPA 1984 referred to above. It gives effect in the UK to Directive 95/46/EC. The Directive, as its preamble makes clear, is itself intended to give further effect in the EU to the privacy right under Art 8 of the ECHR, while at the same time facilitating the free movement of data within EU Member States.

[8] See Chapter 10.

Under section 7 of the DPA 1998, an individual is entitled to be informed by a data controller upon written request whether personal data of which that individual is the data subject are being processed by or on behalf of that data controller. If so, the data subject has the right to have communicated to him the information constituting any personal data of which he is the data subject.[9] The information must be provided in permanent form, unless that is not possible or would involve disproportionate effort, or unless the data subject agrees otherwise.[10] The information must be provided promptly, and in any event within 40 days.[11] In general the data controller may charge a fee of up to £10; however, credit reference agencies may charge no more than £2 for personal data relevant to an individual's financial standing, while the fee for access to educational records is on a sliding scale between £1 and £50.[12] According to the Court of Appeal in *Durant v Financial Services Authority*,[13] the purpose of the right of subject access is to enable an individual to check whether data processing unlawfully infringes his privacy, and if so to take steps to remedy the infringement.

The right of subject access is limited by the meaning of various fundamental concepts in the DPA 1998. It does not apply to information generally, but only to *data* as defined in the DPA 1998, section 1. This term is discussed elsewhere in this book.[14] Data includes information which is being processed by means of equipment operating automatically in response to instructions given for that purpose, and information recorded with the intention that it should be processed by means of such equipment. This wide definition would cover information held on computer, as well as other automatic systems (eg, CCTV images). Health and educational records and certain other specified public records are also data under the Act. Other paper-based files will not be covered unless they are broadly equivalent to computerized systems in providing ready access to information capable of constituting personal data.[15] In relation to public authorities the concept of data has an extended meaning for certain purposes: this is discussed later in this section.

The right of access does not apply in relation to all data, but only in relation to *personal data* of the person seeking access. Personal data are data which relate to a living individual who can be identified from those data, or from those data in conjunction with other data in the possession of the data controller: see the definition in the DPA 1988, section 1(1). The term 'personal data' has been considered by the

---

[9] DPA 1998, s 7(2).

[10] DPA 1998, s 8(2).

[11] The maximum period for the provision of information about financial standing by credit reference agencies is seven days; and the maximum for educational records is 15 schools days. See the Data Protection (Subject Access) (Fees and Miscellaneous Provisions) Regulations 2000 (SI 2000/191).

[12] These fees are set by the Data Protection (Subject Access) (Fees and Miscellaneous Provisions) Regulations 2000 (SI 2000/191).

[13] [2003] EWCA Civ 1746.

[14] Chapter 10, section 10.3.1.

[15] *Durant v Financial Services Authority* [2003] EWCA 1746 at para 47.

Court of Appeal in the *Durant* case; in general whether information is personal data depends on its impact on individual privacy, and this will depend on whether the information is biographically significant in respect of a particular individual and has that individual as its focus. The right of access may be exercised against a *data controller*, defined in section 1 as being a person who (whether alone or jointly with others) determines the purposes for and the manner in which personal data are to be processed.

There are various important points to note about the scope of the subject access right. One is that the right is conferred on individuals, not on organizations. Only individuals can make subject access requests; and such requests can only relate to *personal* data. So the right of subject access does not permit companies or other organizations to find out what information is held about them. Even where a company is the commercial vehicle for an individual, information which is focused on the company rather than the individual will not be personal data.[16] Another limitation is that the right of subject access relates only to *living* individuals; thus it does not give surviving relatives any right of access to information about the deceased.[17] A third and final point to note is that there are a number of exemptions to the right of subject access.[18]

The right of subject access can be exercised against both public sector and private sector data controllers, but there is an important difference in its scope. Where the data controller is a public authority then for the purpose of the subject access right under section 7 the term 'data' has an extended meaning, and covers all recorded information held by the public authority. The practical effect is that where an individual is seeking access to information about themselves that is held by a public authority, the request will usually be dealt with under the DPA 1998 (as a subject access request) and not under the FOIA 2000. Many requests for information to public authorities cover both personal data about the requester, and other information: in which case, both the DPA 1998 and the FOIA 2000 will be relevant in handling the request, and the interaction between the two provisions can give rise to considerable practical difficulties.

If the data controller fails to provide information, in breach of the right of subject access under section 7, then the remedies available to the individual are limited. There is a right to request an assessment from the Information Commissioner as to

---

[16] See *Smith v Lloyds TSB Bank plc* [2005] EWHC 246.

[17] For an unsuccessful attempt to use Art 8 of the ECHR as the foundation for such a right of access, see *R (on the application of Addinell) v Sheffield CC*, CO/3284/2000. For an attempt to obtain access to such information under the FOIA see *Bluck v Information Commissioner and Another*, EA/2006/0090. The latter case discusses a wide range of issues relating to information about the deceased, including whether a duty of confidence can survive the death of the person to whom it is owed.

[18] See Part IV of the DPA 1998. The exemptions are considered in detail at Chapter 10, section 10.3.7.

whether personal data are being processed in compliance with the DPA 1988.[19] If, however, the Information Commissioner takes no action then the data subject has no right to complain to the Tribunal.[20] There is a right to make an application to court for disclosure of the information, under section 7(9) of the Act.[21] The disadvantage from an individual point of view is that those who do not qualify for legal aid are likely to face a serious costs risk in taking the case to the High Court or a county court: even if they can find cheap (or indeed free) legal representation, they will be at risk of having to pay the other side's costs if their claim fails. As will be apparent from the discussion below, the remedies available to an individual who makes an unsuccessful subject access request are rather less extensive than those available to an unsuccessful applicant for information under the FOIA 2000. There is an interesting policy question about whether the respective treatment of these different types of individual right of access to information is justified.

At one stage it was common to see wide-ranging subject access requests used in litigation as, in substance, a means for obtaining early or additional disclosure of information. The decision of the Court of Appeal in *Durant* has discouraged this use of the DPA 1988, by indicating that it considers that the court has an untrammelled discretion to refuse to make an order under section 7(9) even where there is an apparent breach of the section 7 right. It is now often argued that subject access requests made for a collateral purpose (eg, obtaining disclosure of information to assist in litigation) rather than for the purpose of protecting privacy ought not to be enforced by a court order under section 7(9).[22]

11.3 FREEDOM OF INFORMATION ACT 2000

The FOIA 2000 came fully into force on 1 January 2005. Section 1 confers a general right of access to information held by public authorities, subject to exemptions. Both the scope of the right and the nature of the exemptions are discussed in detail below. The initial decision as to whether a request under the Act should be granted is taken by the public authority itself, but a dissatisfied requester can complain to the Information Commissioner. Either the requester or the public authority can then appeal to the Tribunal against the Commissioner's decision, and there are further rights of appeal thereafter, on a point of law. These decision-making processes are

---

[19] See DPA 1998, s 42.

[20] For the Tribunal, see n 2 above. See section 11.3.2 below for a general discussion of the Information Commissioner and the Tribunal.

[21] Both *Durant* and *Smith v Lloyds Bank TSB plc*, n 16 above, are examples of unsuccessful applications under s 7(9).

[22] See, eg, *Smith v Lloyds TSB Bank plc*, n 16 above, where the argument was raised but the court did not find it necessary to rule on it.

complex and can be time-consuming.[23] They do, however, provide individuals with a relatively accessible and inexpensive means of enforcing their rights of access.

The Act also makes provision for publication schemes (s 19), whereby public authorities specify the information that they will routinely make available to the public without requiring a specific request. All public authorities are required to adopt publication schemes, which must be approved by the Information Commissioner. Discussion of the FOIA 2000 usually focuses on the right of access to information under section 1, rather than on publication schemes. However, the approach adopted by the coalition government formed after the May 2010 General Election is placing an increasing emphasis on the regular and routine disclosure of information by public authorities.[24]

11.3.1 Background to the FOIA 2000

Unlike the DPA 1998, and unlike the Environmental Information Regulations (discussed in section 11.4 below), the FOIA 2000 does not implement an EC Directive. The EU or EC does not have any institutional competence in relation to the law on access to official information in the various Member States. Article 15 of the Treaty on the Functioning of the European Union (formerly Art 255 of the EC Treaty) confers a general right of access to European Parliament, Council, and Commission documents, and is the legal basis for Regulation (EC) No 1049/2001, but these provisions relate to the European institutions themselves rather than to the Member States. That said, there is freedom of information legislation in force in most Member States, the longest established being the Swedish Freedom of the Press Act (introduced in 1766).[25] Other notable freedom of information provisions include the US FOIA 1966, the Commonwealth of Australia FOIA 1982, the New Zealand Official Information Act 1982, and the Canadian Access to Information Act 1982. In theory these various enactments are a potential source of comparative material when interpreting the UK legislation, though in practice the case law under the FOIA 2000 has so far shown little evidence of this.

The FOIA 2000 is the product of a long gestation period. There is a lengthy history of piecemeal legislation about access to local government information: see, for instance, the right of access to information about the audit of local authority bodies, under the Audit Commission Act 1998, which can be traced back to the

---

[23] *Cabinet Office v Information Commissioner*, EA/2010/0031 is an extreme example. The requester sought disclosure of Cabinet minutes from 1986 relating to the 'Westland Affair'. The request was made in February 2005. The Tribunal decision, upholding the Commissioner's Decision Notice requiring disclosure, was promulgated in September 2010.

[24] See the 'Transparency' section of the Cabinet Office website: <http://www.cabinetoffice.gov.uk/transparency> (accessed 10 August 2011).

[25] This is often regarded as the world's first freedom of information statute, although it appears that the legislation was in turn inspired by certain features of Chinese Government under the Tang Dynasty (AD 618–907); see Lamble in *Freedom of Information Review* No 97, February 2002.

Poor Law Act of 1844.[26] Access to information held by central government bodies has developed more slowly. A 1979 Green Paper on Open Government[27] was followed shortly after publication by the defeat of the Labour Government at the 1979 General Election, and was quickly forgotten. In 1994 the Conservative Government under John Major introduced a non-statutory Code of Practice on Access to Government Information. Following the 1997 General Election, the newly elected Labour Government published a White Paper in December 1997.[28] A Freedom of Information Bill was introduced in 1999, and the FOIA became law in 2000, but the right of access under the Act to information held by public authorities did not actually come into force until 1 January 2005.

The FOIA 2000 applies to England, Wales, and Northern Ireland. There is a separate Scottish Act, the Freedom of Information (Scotland) Act 2002 ('FOISA 2002'). This applies to the public authorities listed in Schedule 1 to that Act (which operate solely in or in relation to Scotland); UK-wide public authorities, even in relation to their activities in Scotland, are covered by the FOIA 2000. The discussion in this chapter concentrates on the FOIA 2000 rather than on the Scottish Act.

The FOIA 2000 has now been fully in force for over six years. There have undoubtedly been a number of high-profile disclosures under the Act. Successive decisions of the Tribunal[29] (one of which was unsuccessfully appealed to the High Court) have required greater openness in relation to MPs expenses. During the 2005–10 Parliament the deficiencies of the MPs' expenses system became notorious, and the FOIA made a significant contribution to this. Policy-related information has been disclosed in relation to matters such as the ID cards scheme[30] and education funding.[31] A decision of the Information Commissioner requiring disclosure of Cabinet minutes relating to the Iraq war was upheld by the Tribunal,[32] but subsequently overturned by ministerial veto.[33]

In the light of developments such as these, the initial suggestions by some commentators that the Act would have no real impact have not been borne out by events.[34] Indeed, there have been suggestions from within the public sector that the Act has led to a wider range of disclosure than had been anticipated, particularly

---

[26] For discussion of the history, see *R (ota HTV Ltd) v Bristol CC* [2004] EWHC 1219.

[27] *Open Government* (Cmnd 7520, 1979).

[28] *Your Right to Know—the Government's Proposals for a FOIA* (Cm 3818, 1997).

[29] See *Corporate officer of the House of Commons v Information Commissioner and Norman Baker MP*, EA/2006/0015 and 0016; *Corporate Officer of the House of Commons v Information Commissioner*, EA/2006/0074 (and others); *Corporate Officer of the House of Commons v Information Commissioner, Ben Leapman, Heather Brooke and Michael Thomas*, EA/2007/0060 (and others) [2008] EWHC 1084 (Admin).

[30] *OGC v Information Commissioner* [2008] EWHC 737 (Admin), EA/2006/0068 and 0080.

[31] *DfES v Information Commissioner and Evening Standard*, EA/2006/0006.

[32] *Cabinet Office v Information Commissioner and Christopher Lamb*, EA/2008/0024 and 0029.

[33] The veto is discussed further in section 11.3.2 below.

[34] See, eg, T Cornford, 'The Freedom of Information Act 2000: Genuine or Sham?' [2001] 3 Web JCLI, suggesting that the Act was closer to being a sham than to being genuine.

as to policy-related information, with adverse effects on the policy-making process.[35]

11.3.2 Decision-making under the FOIA 2000

The institutional architecture of freedom of information in the UK is complex. Public authorities, the Information Commissioner, the Tribunal, and the courts all have a role to play. It is important to understand the interaction of these different bodies for two reasons. First, the practical significance of rights of access to freedom of information very much depends on who makes decisions about disclosure, and how those decisions are made. Secondly, it is the decisions of the Commissioner, the Tribunal, and the courts that provide guidance on the interpretation of the Act. For these reasons the decision-making process under the FOIA 2000 is discussed in this section, before going on in the following sections to a detailed consideration of the right of access under the Act and the various exemptions to disclosure.

Applications for information under the FOIA 2000 are made directly to the public authority that holds the information. In the first instance it is for the public authority to make a decision as to whether the information must be disclosed under the Act. There is no statutory duty to consult with third parties that have an interest in whether the information should be disclosed, although such consultation is good practice and is recommended in the Code of Practice made by the Secretary of State under section 45 of the Act.[36] Nor is there any statutory duty on public authorities to operate an internal complaints procedure for dissatisfied requesters, although again the section 45 Code recommends this.

A dissatisfied requester can apply to the Information Commissioner under section 50 of the Act for a decision as to whether the public authority has dealt with his request in accordance with the Act. The Commissioner is a statutory office-holder with various regulatory functions under both the DPA 1998 and the FOIA 2000;[37] the UK is unusual in having a single regulator who deals both with data protection and with rights of access to public information. It is important to note that the only person who can complain to the Commissioner under section 50 is the person who made the relevant request for information. So if a request is made and the public authority agrees to provide the information requested then a third party who is affected by the disclosure cannot complain to the Commissioner. For instance, if

---

[35] For detailed discussion of the Act's impact on policy-making, and the critical views of some politicians and civil servants, see R Hazell and D Busfield-Birch, 'Opening the Cabinet Door: Freedom of Information and Government Policy Making' [2011] Public Law 260.

[36] <http://www.dca.gov.uk/foi/codesprac.htm>.

[37] The office was created under the DPA 1984 and was then known as the Data Protection Registrar; the title changed to the Data Protection Commissioner (under the DPA 1998) and then to the Information Commissioner (under the FOIA 2000). Section 6 of and Sch 5 to the DPA 1998 make provision for the continued existence of the office.

a local authority agrees to disclose information under the FOIA 2000 about the companies that tendered for a contract to operate its IT system, then the companies themselves cannot go the Commissioner and ask him to rule that the information should be withheld. The most likely route for a legal challenge would be for them to seek judicial review of the public authority's decision to disclose.

There are various grounds under section 50 on which the Commissioner may refuse to make a decision—for instance, that the complainant has not exhausted any internal complaints procedure provided by the public authority: otherwise, the Commissioner must determine the complaint.[38] Where the Commissioner makes a decision he may order the public authority to disclose information, and if so he must set a time within which this must be done. The Commissioner's decision notices are published on his website.[39] It is important not to regard them as a series of binding precedents; each case must turn on its own facts, and neither the Tribunal nor the courts are in any way bound by the Commissioner's interpretation of the legislation. That said, the decision notices are a very important source of information about the practical application of the FOIA 2000, and about the sorts of requests for information that are being made.

Either the public authority or the complainant may appeal to the Tribunal against the Commissioner's decision. Note that these are the only parties who can appeal: in the example given above about the IT tendering exercise, if the local authority refused disclosure but the Commissioner ordered it to disclose then although the local authority could appeal the companies themselves could not do so. As in the case where they wished to challenge the public authority's decision to disclose, any remedy would probably have to be by way of judicial review.

The arrangements for appealing against the Information Commissioner's decisions changed in January 2010. Previously, appeals went to the Information Tribunal (a specialist tribunal originally established under the DPA 1984). The Tribunals, Courts and Enforcement Act 2007 introduced extensive reforms to tribunals generally, creating a unified system with a First-tier Tribunal and an Upper Tribunal each divided into various chambers. The jurisdiction of various specialist tribunals has now been transferred to the new tribunal structure. On 18 January 2010 the jurisdiction of the Information Tribunal was transferred to the General Regulatory Chamber of the First-tier Tribunal. So what was previously the Information Tribunal is now the First-tier Tribunal (General Regulatory Chamber) (Information Rights). I shall continue to refer to this simply as 'the Tribunal'.

---

[38] In practice many complaints are resolved informally, eg because the public authority agrees to disclose further information and the requester does not pursue his complaint any further. In these cases no formal Decision Notice is issued by the Commissioner.

[39] <http://www.ico.gov.uk> (accessed 10 August 2011).

The procedural rules for the General Regulatory Chamber apply to the Tribunal.[40] Information about the Tribunal, including guidance for those wishing to appeal, procedural forms, and previous decisions, is available online.[41]

In formal terms the Tribunal is hearing an appeal against the Decision Notice issued by the Commissioner, though in practice the underlying dispute is likely to be between the person seeking information and the public authority from which it is sought. The Commissioner's position is an unusual one; in considering a complaint under section 50 he is an adjudicator, but then when his decision is appealed to the Tribunal he becomes a litigant, defending the decision that he reached. Where an appeal is brought by a person seeking information then the public authority may be joined as a party, and vice versa; and other interested parties may also be joined; but in every case it is the Information Commission who will be the respondent to the appeal.

Is there any justification for the Commissioner's role in defending his own decisions on appeal? In cases where the Commissioner has ruled in favour of the public authority, and the requester appeals to the Tribunal, the Commissioner may well have little to contribute. However, the situation is very different where the Commissioner has ordered disclosure, and it is the public authority that brings the appeal. Here the Commissioner has the advantage of having seen the disputed information (ie, the information sought by the requester and withheld by the public authority) and so his legal representatives can make submissions by reference to its actual content. Usually this is done in closed session (ie, with the exclusion of members of the public and the requester), to ensure that the disputed information is not made public prior to the completion of the appeal process.

The Tribunal considers whether the Commissioner's Decision Notice was not in accordance with the law, or whether the Commissioner ought to have exercised any relevant discretion differently.[42] It has the power to review any finding of fact on which the Decision Notice was based.[43] Appeals are considered either on paper or at an oral hearing. Where there is an oral hearing there will often be witness evidence: the requester may well give evidence or call witnesses, and the public authority will usually do so; sometimes the Information Commissioner will also call evidence, although this is unusual. The Tribunal can make its own findings of fact and substitute them for the Commissioner's findings; it is not confined to considering whether there was material capable of supporting the Commissioner's findings.[44]

---

[40] See the Tribunal Procedure (First-tier Tribunal) (General Regulatory Chamber) Rules 2009 (SI 2009/1976). The rules have been repeatedly amended: a version updated to 1 April 2011 is available at <http://www.justice.gov.uk/downloads/guidance/courts-and-tribunals/tribunals/tribunals-rules-2009-at010411.pdf> (accessed 10 August 2011).

[41] See <http://www.justice.gov.uk/guidance/courts-and-tribunals/tribunals/information-rights/index.htm> (accessed 10 August 2011).

[42] FOIA 2000, s 58(1).

[43] FOIA 2000, s 58(2).

[44] See *Hemsley v Information Commissioner* [2006] UKITEA 2005 0026, EA/2005/0026.

The Tribunal may allow an appeal (in which case the Decision Notice issued by the Commissioner no longer stands) or it may substitute another Decision Notice for the Commissioner's decision.

There is provision for an appeal against the Tribunal's decisions, on a point of law only.[45] Formerly the appeal was to the High Court; following the changes made by the Tribunals, Courts and Enforcement Act 2007, the appeal now goes to the Upper Tribunal (Administrative Appeals Chamber). Permission to appeal must be sought from the Tribunal: if refused, the application for permission can be renewed in the Upper Tribunal. Appeals to the Upper Tribunal are governed by the Tribunal Procedure (Upper Tribunal) Rules 2008.[46]

Given that there is a right to complain to the Commissioner under section 50 of the FOIA 2000, and then a further right to appeal to the Tribunal under section 57, it is most unlikely that the court will grant permission for judicial review of a refusal by a public authority to disclose information under the FOIA 2000.[47]

Finally, mention should be made of section 53 of the Act, which gives the government of the day power to overrule the Commissioner and the Tribunal on the question of whether particular information should be disclosed.

Section 53 applies to a decision notice or enforcement notice of the Information Commissioner which is served on a government department, the National Assembly for Wales, or any public authority designated by Order for the purposes of this section, and which relates to a failure to comply with the duty to confirm or deny or with the duty to disclose. Any such decision notice or enforcement notice shall fail to have effect if the 'accountable person' in relation to that authority certifies to the Commissioner that he has formed the opinion on reasonable grounds that there was no failure to comply with the duty to confirm or deny or with the duty to disclose. Such a certificate may be issued after the Commissioner's decision notice or enforcement notice was issued, or after an appeal to the Information Tribunal has been determined. An 'accountable person' would be a Cabinet Minister, the Attorney General, the Advocate General for Scotland, or the Attorney General for Northern Ireland.[48] The certificate must be laid before Parliament,[49] and the

---

[45] See FOIA, s 59.

[46] SI 2698/2008. The rules have been repeatedly amended. An up-to-date version (as at 1 April 2008) is available at <http://www.justice.gov.uk/downloads/guidance/courts-and-tribunals/tribunals/general/consolidated_TP_UTRules2008asat010411.pdf> (accessed 10 August 2011).

[47] R (on the application of Carruthers) v South Norfolk DC and Others [2006] EWHC 478 (Admin).

[48] See s 53(8). In relation to a Northern Ireland department or any other Northern Ireland public authority the term 'accountable person' means the First Minister and Deputy First Minister in Northern Ireland acting jointly. In relation to the National Assembly for Wales the term 'accountable person' means the Assembly First Secretary.

[49] s 53(3). In certain cases involving Northern Ireland the certificate would instead be laid before the Northern Ireland Assembly, and in certain cases involving Wales the certificate would be laid before the National Assembly for Wales.

accountable person must inform the applicant of his reasons for issuing the certificate.[50]

In simple terms, a certificate under section 53 can effectively overrule either the Commissioner or the Tribunal on the question whether information should be disclosed. There is no provision in the Act for any appeal against such a certificate. The only means of challenge would appear to be by a claim for judicial review.[51] Potentially the issue of a certificate under section 53 is a very serious incursion into the decision-making functions of the Commissioner and the Tribunal.

It is extremely important to note, however, that when issuing a certificate under section 53 the 'accountable person' is in effect overruling the Commissioner and/or the Tribunal on the question whether *the Act* requires compliance with the duty to confirm or deny or with the duty to disclose. A certificate under section 53 is not simply an assertion that the information in the view of the accountable person ought not to be disclosed. Hence in deciding whether to issue a certificate under the section the accountable person must properly address the requirements of the Act and must identify a basis within the Act itself on which the duty to confirm or deny and/or the duty to disclose is excluded. A failure to do so will render the certificate liable to be quashed following a claim for judicial review. The applicant would no doubt have standing to apply for judicial review, but, it is suggested, so would the Commissioner, at any rate in a case where it was a decision notice or enforcement notice of the Commissioner that was overturned by the certificate.[52]

So far the power of veto under section 53 has only been used twice. The first occasion was on 23 February 2009, overruling the decision of the Tribunal[53] requiring the disclosure of Cabinet minutes relating to the decision to go to war in Iraq.[54] The second occasion was on 10 December 2009: this time the disputed information consisted of Cabinet committee minutes relating to devolution.[55]

---

[50] See s 53(6). The provision in fact refers to 'the complainant' rather than 'the applicant', because a certificate will only be issued after the applicant has made a complaint to the Commissioner under s 50 about the way in which the public authority has dealt with his request for information.

[51] This would be governed by Pt 54 of the Civil Procedure Rules.

[52] There might be a case where the Commissioner did not order disclosure, but the Tribunal varied his decision on appeal so as to order disclosure, and then a certificate was issued under s 53 in effect to overturn the Tribunal's decision. It is arguable that the Commissioner would not have standing to challenge the certificate, which would in effect restore the Commissioner's decision.

[53] See *Cabinet Office v Information Commissioner and Another*, EA/2008/0024 and 0029.

[54] The exercise of the veto was the subject of a report to Parliament by the Information Commissioner: see <http://www.official-documents.gov.uk/document/hc0809/hc06/0622/0622.pdf> (accessed 10 August 2011).

[55] See the Information Commissioner's report to Parliament: <http://www.ico.gov.uk/upload/documents/library/freedom_of_information/research_and_reports/ic_report_to_parliament_hc218.pdf> (accessed 10 August 2011).

11.3.3 The right of access to information: essential features

The above discussion is about the process whereby decisions are made under the FOIA 2000: but what about the substance of the right of access to information, and its limitations?

Section 1 is the fundamental provision that confers the right of access with which the Act is concerned. It states that a person making a request for information to a public authority is entitled to two things. He is entitled to be informed in writing by the public authority whether it holds information of the specified description; and if that is the case he is entitled to have that information communicated to him. The public authority's duty to say whether it holds the information as sought is referred to in the Act as the 'duty to confirm or deny'. The duty to provide the information sought can be conveniently referred to as the 'duty to disclose', although this term is not used in the Act itself. The scheme of the Act is that it sets out in general terms in section 1 the public authority's duty to confirm or deny and duty to disclose, but then goes on to introduce various qualifications to those rights. Part I of the Act is considered in this section; the next section considers Part II, which contains a number of exemptions to section 1.

The duty to disclose is in practice much the more significant of the two duties, and much the more onerous from the point of view of the public authority. The duty to confirm or deny simply requires the public authority to state whether it holds information of the relevant description; it does not require the authority to list that information, as would be required for the purpose of disclosure in civil litigation. So compliance with the duty to confirm or deny will not in itself usually be of any great benefit to the applicant: though there are a limited number of cases (eg, involving information that is security sensitive) where confirmation or denial that information is held will be of real significance. By contrast, the duty to disclose will require public authorities to locate information and to communicate it to applicants.

The Act imposes duties on *public authorities*. The public/private distinction is notoriously elusive: the Act seeks to deal with this difficulty by setting out in Schedule 1 to the Act a list of bodies or types of body that are public authorities for the purpose of the Act. Further bodies may be added to Schedule 1 by order, provided that they satisfy certain specified conditions (see s 4). Other bodies that appear to the Secretary of State to exercise functions of a public nature, or that are providing under a contract made with a public authority any service whose provision is a function of that authority, may be designated as public authorities by an order made under section 5 of the Act. Publicly owned companies (as defined by s 6) are also public authorities under the Act.

The purpose of the elaborate provisions in sections 3–6 and in Schedule 1 is to avoid the difficulties that have arisen in other areas of law where the courts are left to determine on a case-by-case basis whether particular bodies are public in nature. For instance, the Human Rights Act 1998 defines the term 'public authority' in general terms (see s 6(3)), and the courts have to determine whether particular bodies fall within that definition.[56] It is extremely important to remember that the term 'public authority' has a special definition for the purposes of the FOIA 2000. So a body that is public for the purpose of that Act will not necessarily be treated for all legal purposes as being public in nature.

The Act confers rights in relation to *information* that is *held* by a public authority. Information is defined in section 84 as being 'information that is recorded in any form'. The definition is therefore unhelpfully circular: the FOIA 2000, like the DPA 1998, assumes that information is something that we can recognize when we see it. The definition will include information that is recorded on computer or other electronic form, but will also cover information recorded on paper. Information is *held* by a public authority if it is held by the authority itself (other than on behalf of another person) or if it is held by another person on behalf of the authority.[57] The duty to confirm or deny and the duty to disclose apply to information that is held by the public authority at the time that the request is received, although account may be taken of any amendment or deletion made between the receipt of the request and the statutory deadline for responding to the request, provided that the amendment or deletion would have been made regardless of the receipt of the request.[58]

Sometimes a request for information will require a public authority to collate information from a variety of different sources. This may give rise to an issue as to whether the request is truly for information that is held by the authority, or whether instead it is a request for the authority to create new information that it does not currently hold. The House of Lords considered a similar issue arising under the FOISA 2002, in *Common Services Agency v Scottish Information Commissioner*.[59] The Scottish Commissioner had required disclosure of information about childhood leukaemia in a particular locality, in 'barnardized' form. Barnardization is a technique for the random modification of small numbers, intended to allow health statistics to be disclosed while minimizing the risk that there will be any resulting disclosure of individual identities. It was argued that the Scottish Commissioner had gone beyond the requirements of the FOISA 2002[60] by requiring the public authority to create new information that it did not hold at the time of the request. The House of Lords rejected this: barnardization did not involve the creation of new information, but was similar to a process of redaction.[61]

---

[56] See, eg, the decision of the House of Lords in *Wallbank v Parochial Church Council of Aston Cantlow* [2003] UKHL 37, [2004] 1 AC 546.

[57] FOIA 2000, s 3(2).

[58] FOIA 2000, s 1(4).

[59] [2008] UKHL 47, [2008] 1 WLR 1550.

[60] For the purposes of this issue there is no material difference between the FOIA 2000 and the FOISA 2002.

[61] See [2008] UKHL 47 at paras 14–16 (Lord Hope).

In *Johnson v Information Commissioner and Ministry of Justice*,[62] the Information Tribunal considered a request for information about decisions by High Court Masters to strike out claims. In order to answer the request the Ministry of Justice would have had to collate information manually from a large number of individual paper files. The Tribunal considered that the requested information was 'held' by the Ministry; collating it manually from the paper files, although time-consuming, would have been a mechanical process involving minimal skill and judgement. However, the Ministry was not required to answer the request, because the cost of doing so would exceed the appropriate limit in section 12 of the FOIA 2000 (discussed below).

There are various specific difficulties in applying these concepts to electronic information. One problem is in dealing with computer data that was deleted prior to the receipt of the request. Is such data still 'held' by the public authority when the request is received? Detailed guidance was given by the Information Tribunal in the important case of *Harper v Information Commissioner*.[63] The Tribunal explained some of the technical means by which deleted data can be recovered. It considered that where information has been deleted but can still be recovered by technical means then the question whether it is still 'held' will be one of fact and degree, depending on the technical difficulty involved in recovery. If recovery would be expensive then, even if the information is still properly to be regarded as being held by the public authority, the public authority may nevertheless be entitled to refuse disclosure on the basis that the 'appropriate limit' under section 12 would be exceeded.

Another interesting issue relates to the statistics associated with word-processing documents. These can be of significance in establishing when a document was created, and hence for instance in clarifying whether or not it is a contemporaneous note of a particular meeting.[64] It is suggested that this information can be obtained by a properly worded request under the Act: even if the statistics as such are not displayed until a specific request is made to display them, the underlying data will be recorded on the computer and hence it seems that they will be 'held' by the public authority in recorded form at the time that the request is received.

A request for information under the FOIA 2000 may be informal and does not need specifically to mention the Act. The request must be in writing (see s 8(1)), but email will suffice (see s 8(2)), and indeed requests are commonly made and answered by email. It is, however, advisable for an applicant to give as much detail as he can about the information that is being sought: this is likely to help the public authority locate the information promptly. A public authority is not entitled to refuse to

---

[62] EA/2006/0085.

[63] [2005] UKITEA 2005 0001, EA/2005/0001. This had the distinction of being the first appeal received by the Tribunal under the FOIA 2000.

[64] For an interesting example of the significance that disclosure of such information can have in ordinary civil litigation, see *Comfort v Lord Chancellor's Department* [2004] EWCA Civ 349.

consider a request merely because it regards the language of the request as tendentious: see the Tribunal's decision in *Barber v Information Commissioner*.[65] The request must give the applicant's name and address, and so requests cannot be made anonymously;[66] there is, however, some anecdotal evidence of requests being made via third parties so as to conceal the identity of the person who actually wishes to obtain the information, and there is nothing in the Act to prevent this.[67]

The Act recognizes that applicants have the difficulty that they may not know what information a public authority holds, or how it is stored. This difficulty is likely to be particularly acute when dealing with computer records. Under section 16 public authorities have a duty to provide applicants with reasonable advice and assistance: and any authority which conforms with the section 45 Code in this regard will be taken to have complied with its statutory duty. The Code states that the provision of advice and assistance might include providing access to detailed catalogues and indexes of information held (see para 9 of the Code). Where the information is held on computer, it might be appropriate to provide a list of files, or an explanation of the structure under which information is organized. The Tribunal has indicated that in considering complaints under section 50 the Commissioner should be willing to ask himself whether the public authority has complied with its section 16 duty, even if the point is not specifically raised in the complaint: see *Barber v Information Commissioner*, above.

Public authorities must answer requests promptly and in any event within 20 working days: see section 10(1). If a public authority is relying on a exemption then within that same period it must give the applicant a notice which specifies the exemption in question, states (if not otherwise apparent) why it applies, and give various other specified information: see section 17. If a public authority is relying on a qualified exemption under Part II of the Act then it is entitled to reasonable further time in order to consider whether the balance of public interest is in favour of maintaining the exemption.[68] It must, however, inform the applicant of the exemption on which it relies, within the primary time limit (ie, 20 working days). If the public authority's decision is that the balance of public interest is in favour of maintaining the exemption then it must inform the applicant of the reasons for this conclusion, either within 20 working days or within such time as is reasonable in the circumstances.[69]

---

[65] [2005] UKITEA 2005 0004, EQ/2005/0004.

[66] The Information Commissioner has given guidance about dealing with anonymous requests. See <http://www.ico.gov.uk/upload/documents/library/freedom_of_information/detailed_specialist_guides/name_of_applicant_fop083_v1.pdf> (accessed 10 August 2011).

[67] The true identity of the person interested in obtaining the information might be relevant to the question whether the request was vexatious under s 14.

[68] See FOIA 2000, s 10(3). Qualified exemptions, and the balance of public interest, are discussed in the next section.

[69] FOIA 2000, s 17(3).

There are numerous decision notices where the Commissioner has recorded a breach of these time limits, but has taken no action in respect of the breach; but this does not mean that the time limits can simply be disregarded. If a public authority consistently or systematically breached time limits then the Commissioner could issue an enforcement notice under section 52 of the Act requiring compliance in the future; and under section 54 of the Act failure to comply with an enforcement notice can be certified to the court by the Information Commissioner and dealt with as if it were a contempt of court.[70] In April 2011 the Information Commissioner announced that regulatory action was being considered for various public bodies that had a consistent record of delay.[71]

Under section 11 of the Act, it is open for an applicant to ask for the information to be provided in one of three ways: (a) by means of a copy in permanent form; (b) by means of a reasonable opportunity to inspect a record containing the information; and (c) in the form of a digest or summary. The public authority must give effect to the applicant's preference so far as reasonably practicable. In the case of records held on computer it is suggested that a reasonable opportunity to inspect the record might involve giving the applicant an opportunity himself to interrogate the relevant computer system. Care would of course have to be taken that the applicant would not be able to view information falling outside the scope of the request. In practice, applicants usually prefer to receive a copy of information in permanent form.

Although the main provisions about exemptions are in Part II of the Act, Part I contains two important general exemptions (not related to the specific subject matter of the request). Under section 12 there is an exception if the authority estimates that the cost of compliance exceeds the 'appropriate limit'. Under section 14, public authorities are not obliged to respond to vexatious or repeated requests.

The provision in section 12 is designed to limit the amount of work that public authorities are required to do in answering requests under the Act. The appropriate limit is currently £600 for central government and Parliament, and £450 for other public authorities.[72] In calculating whether this figure has been exceeded the public authority can attribute £25 an hour to the cost of time spent in complying with the request.[73] In practice the limit means that a public authority can refuse to comply with a request if it would take more than 24 hours' work (for central government and Parliament) or 18 hours' work (for other public authorities). However, only certain kinds of work can be taken into account in applying the costs

---

[70] See *Harper v Information Commissioner* [2005] UKITEA 2005 0001, EA/2005/0001 above, for discussion of the various steps open to the Commissioner where a public authority persistently or deliberately breaches the time limits in the Act.

[71] See <http://www.ico.gov.uk/~/media/documents/pressreleases/2011/foi_monitoring_news_release_20110412.ashx> (accessed 10 August 2011).

[72] See the Freedom of Information and Data Protection (Appropriate Limit and Fees) Regulations 2004 (SI 2004/3244).

[73] This figure is set by reg 4(4) of SI 2004/3244, above.

limit, namely: determining whether the public authority holds the information; locating the information or a document which may contain it; retrieving the information; and extracting the information from a document containing it.[74] This means that the public authority cannot take into account costs incurred (or time spent) in considering whether information is exempt, in applying the public interest test, or in redacting information prior to disclosure so as to exclude any exempt material.[75]

Section 14 of the FOIA 2000 deals with vexatious or repeated requests. Under section 14(1), a public authority is not obliged to comply with a request if it is vexatious. By section 14(2), if a public authority has previously complied with a request for information then it is not obliged to comply with a subsequent identical or substantially similar request from that person, unless a reasonable interval has elapsed between compliance with the previous request and the making of the current request.

The Information Commissioner has given detailed guidance on the operation of section 14(1).[76] This identifies five questions:

(a) Can the request fairly be seen as obsessive?

(b) Is the request harassing the authority or causing distress to staff?

(c) Would complying with the request impose a significant burden?

(d) Is the request designed to cause disruption or annoyance?

(e) Does the request lack any serious purpose or value?

According to the Information Commissioner, a public authority should generally be able to make out a reasonably strong case under at least two of these headings, if it is to reject a request as vexatious. The Tribunal has indicated that the guidance is helpful, although it should not lead to an overly structured approach to section 14(1).[77]

A public authority is entitled to charge a fee under the FOIA 2000 (see ss 9 and 13). Where the appropriate limit is not exceeded then the public authority may only charge a very limited fee, and may not take account of staff time.[78] If the appropriate limit is exceeded then the public authority may nevertheless be willing to provide the information for a fee, in which case the fee charged may include an element for staff time, again at £25 per hour.[79]

---

[74] See SI 2004/3244, reg 4(3).

[75] See, eg, *APG v Information Commissioner and Ministry of Defence* [2011] UKUT 153 (AAC), para 27.

[76] See   <http://www.ico.gov.uk/upload/documents/library/freedom_of_information/detailed_specialist_guides/awareness_guidance_22_vexatious_and_repeated_requests_final.pdf> (accessed 10 August 2011).

[77] See *Rigby v Information Commissioner and Blackpool, Flyde and Wyre Hospitals NHS Trust*, EA/2009/0103.

[78] See SI 2004/3244, above.

[79] See SI 2004/3244, above.

11.3.4 Exemptions under Part II: general considerations

As was explained in the previous section, the Act imposes two wide-ranging general duties on public authorities—the duty to confirm or deny, and the duty to disclose—and then sets out a number of exemptions from those duties. Most of these are in Part II of the Act.[80] The application of the exemptions gives rise to some of the most difficult issues that arise under the Act, particularly where the 'qualified exemptions' are at stake and an assessment of competing heads of public interest is required.

11.3.4.1 *The exemptions in outline*

The exemptions fall into two main groups. Some are absolute: if information falls within the exemption then there will be no duty to disclose it. So in relation to these provisions there is only one question to consider, that is, whether the information sought comes within the description specified in the exemption. Some exemptions are qualified: if the public interest in maintaining the exemption outweighs the public interest in disclosure then the information need not be disclosed, but otherwise the duty of disclosure still applies. Here there are two separate questions to consider (though in practice the questions are closely linked). The first is whether the information comes within the scope of the exemption, or, as it is sometimes put, whether the exemption is 'engaged'.[81] The second is whether the balance of public interest is in favour of maintaining the exemption or not. To put the point another way, in the case of the absolute exemptions the legislation itself makes a value judgement that the interests protected by the exemption are more important than the public interest in open government.[82] In the case of the qualified exemptions the legislation leaves that value judgement to be made on a case-by-case basis, depending on all the circumstances of the individual case.

A different distinction can also be made, between those exemptions that are prejudice or harm-based, and those that are class-based (ie, they apply to particular classes of information).[83] Many of the absolute exemptions are class-based, as are some of the qualified exemptions. Other qualified exemptions are prejudice or harm-based. This means that the exemption is not engaged except where there

---

[80] The other exemptions, eg for cases where the cost of compliance exceeds the appropriate limit, are in Part I of the Act, and were discussed in the previous section of this chapter.

[81] The Act itself does not use this term. However, when discussing qualified human rights under the ECHR—eg the privacy right under Art 8—lawyers often distinguish between the question whether the right is 'engaged', that is to say whether there is some prima facie interference with the substance of the right, and whether the interference can be justified.

[82] This statement needs to be qualified in relation to the exemptions under ss 40 and 41: as explained below, a balance between competing interests is built into the question of whether information falls within the scope of these exemptions.

[83] Not all exemptions can be categorized in this way: FOIA 2000, ss 40 and 41 do not fit comfortably into either category.

is prejudice or harm to a specific interest (eg, to the prevention or detection of crime).

A further complication is that whenever an exemption is relevant one must consider separately whether it excludes: (a) the duty to confirm or deny, and (b) the duty to disclose. In practice in most cases the real issue is whether the duty to disclose is excluded, that is, whether the requested information is exempt from disclosure under the Act. Hence the discussion in this chapter focuses on this issue.

The following provisions create an *absolute* exemption from disclosure (note that the description below is a summary of the nature of each provision, and is not a precise reflection of the statutory language).

(a) section 21: information that is reasonably accessible to applicant by other means;

(b) section 23: information supplied by, or relating to, one of certain specified bodies dealing with security matters;

(c) section 32: information held in certain court records;

(d) section 34: information the disclosure of which would infringe parliamentary privilege;

(e) section 36: information the disclosure of which would prejudice the effective conduct of public affairs, but only in relation to information held by either House of Parliament;

(f) section 37: information relating to communications with Her Majesty, the conferring of honours, and related matters (note however that some information falling within this section is subject to a qualified exemption);

(g) section 40: personal information—(i) in cases where the information sought is personal information about the applicant, and (ii) in cases where the information sought is personal information about a third party, and disclosure would breach one of the data protection principles;

(h) section 41: information obtained by the public authority from another person, if disclosure would constitute a breach of confidence actionable by that or any other person;

(i) section 44: information the disclosure of which is prohibited by or under any enactment, is incompatible with any Community obligation, or would be a contempt of court.

The following provisions create a *qualified* exemption from disclosure.

(a) section 22: information intended for future publication;

(b) section 24: information that is required to be exempt for the purposes of safeguarding national security (note however that if the information falls within s 23 then the exemption is absolute);

(c) section 26: information the disclosure of which would or would be likely to prejudice certain defence interests;

(d) section 27: information the disclosure of which would or would be likely to prejudice certain aspects of international relations;

(e) section 28: information the disclosure of which would or would be likely to prejudice relations between any of 'UK administrations', that is to say, the UK Government, and the devolved governments operating in Scotland, Wales, and Northern Ireland;

(f) section 29: information the disclosure of which would or would be likely to prejudice certain economic interests;

(g) section 30: information that has at any time been held for the purpose of certain investigations and proceedings conducted by public authorities;

(h) section 31: information the disclosure of which would or would be likely to prejudice the prevention or detection of crime or certain other interests related to law enforcement;

(i) section 33: information the disclosure of which would or would be likely to prejudice the exercise of certain public sector audit functions;

(j) section 35: information relating to the formulation of government policy, ministerial communications, and other similar matters;

(k) section 36: information the disclosure of which would or would be likely to prejudice the effective conduct of public affairs (except in the case of information held by the House of Commons or the House of Lords, where this exemption is absolute not qualified);

(l) section 37: information relating to communications with Her Majesty, the conferring of honours, and related matters (note however that some information falling within this section is subject to an absolute exemption);

(m) section 38: information the disclosure of which would or would be likely to endanger physical or mental health or safety;

(n) section 39: environmental information—the purpose of this exemption is so that disclosure of this information can be considered instead under the Environmental Information Regulations 2004 (discussed below);

(o) section 40: personal information, in circumstances where the information is about a third party not about the applicant, and where disclosure would contravene section 10 of the DPA 1998 (the right to prevent processing likely to cause damage or distress); or in cases where the information is about a third party, and is exempt from the third party's own right of subject access by virtue of any provision of Part IV of the DPA 1998;

(p) section 42: information that is subject to legal professional privilege;

(q) section 43: trade secrets, and information the disclosure of which would or would be likely to damage certain commercial interests.

The following provisions specifically require consideration of the harm or prejudice that would result from disclosure of the information in question:[84]

(a) section 26: defence;

(b) section 27: international relations;

(c) section 28: relations within the UK;

(d) section 29: the economy;

(e) section 31: law enforcement;

(f) section 33: audit functions;

(g) section 36: prejudice to effective conduct of public affairs (except information held by the House of Commons or the House of Lords);

(h) section 38: health and safety;

(i) section 43: commercial interests.

Apart from these various provisions, there is another route by which certain information is taken outside the scope of the FOIA 2000. The Act only applies to information held by public authorities, and as was explained above there is a specific and very detailed definition of which bodies are public authorities for the purpose of the Act. So if a body is not defined as a public body then any information that it holds will fall outside the Act altogether and there is no need to consider whether any relevant exemptions apply. The most conspicuous example is that the three main security bodies (the Security Service, the Secret Intelligence Service, and the Government Communication Headquarters) are not public authorities under the Act. Any request under the Act directed to any of these bodies can therefore be immediately refused. Another interesting case is the BBC, which is a public authority under the Act in respect of information held for purposes other than those of journalism, art, or literature.[85]

A detailed discussion of each exemption would make this chapter unfeasibly lengthy. Instead, the following sections discuss some general issues about the exemptions, and then consider two particular issues: the treatment of personal data under the FOIA 2000; and the right of access to policy-related information.

11.3.4.2 *How 'absolute' are the absolute exemptions?*
The 'absolute' exemptions are, in fact, not always as 'absolute' as they might appear. Some of them involve an assessment of reasonableness, or a consideration of the balance between competing interests. Thus for instance section 21 requires a consideration as to whether information is *reasonably* accessible to the applicant.

---

[84] It is also arguable that s 24 of the Act (in relation to national security) should be regarded as a harm-based exemption.

[85] The operation of this derogation has given rise to extensive litigation. See *Sugar v BBC and Another* [2009] UKHL 9, [2010] EWCA Civ 715.

Section 40, relating to personal information, is complex and creates a number of different exemptions, both absolute and qualified. At first sight it is surprising that there is an absolute exemption where the applicant is applying for personal information about himself. The explanation is that this exemption is a procedural device to ensure that applications for access to one's own personal information are dealt with as subject access requests under the DPA 1998 and not as requests for information under the FOIA 2000, whether the application is made to a public authority or to a private body. In order to avoid an awkward split between those requests for information about oneself that are dealt with under the DPA 1998 and those that are dealt with under the FOIA 2000, in relation to public authorities the right of access to 'personal data' under the DPA 1998 extends to personal information recorded in any form.[86] Of course when requests for access to one's own personal data are dealt with as subject access requests under the DPA 1998 then, far from there being an exemption from disclosure, the general rule is that there is an entitlement to obtain such information.[87]

Where the applicant is seeking personal information about a third party then there is an absolute exemption from disclosure under section 40 in cases where disclosure would breach any of the data protection principles. At first sight this suggests a rather striking policy choice by the legislature that privacy interests (protected by the DPA 1998) are more important than the interest in open government. That would, however, be an unduly simplistic reading of section 40. The data protection principles themselves are not expressed in absolute terms, and very often require a balance between competing interests. For instance, in deciding whether processing is *necessary* for a particular purpose, so as to give rise to a lawful basis for processing under Schedule 2 and/or Schedule 3 to the DPA 1998, the courts will assess the legitimacy of any interference with personal privacy by reference to a proportionality test.[88]

Another absolute exemption which does in fact incorporate a balance between competing interests is the exemption in section 41 in relation to actionable breach of confidence. The action for breach of confidence is itself subject to a defence that the public interest is in favour of disclosure of the information.[89] So here there is a balancing exercise comparable to the exercise that must be carried out in respect of

---

[86] See the new limb (e) inserted into the definition of 'data' in the DPA 1998, s 1(1), by s 68(1) and (2)(a) of the FOIA 2000. For further discussion see section 11.2 of this chapter, and see also Chapter 10, section 10.3.1.

[87] This is of course subject to the various specific exemptions in the DPA 1998 itself: see Chapter 10, section 10.3.7. It should also be noted that the direct enforcement route for subject access under the DPA 1998 is by way of the ordinary courts, which is likely to take longer and to be more costly.

[88] See, eg, *R (Stone) v South East Coast SHA and Others* [2006] EWHC 1668 (Admin); *Corporate Officer of the House of Commons v Information Commissioner and Others* [2008] EWHC 1084 (Admin), para 43.

[89] See, eg, *London Regional Transport v Mayor of London* [2003] EWCA Civ 1491: public interest in disclosure of criticism of a proposed public-private partnership relating to the London Underground outweighed the preservation of confidentiality in a report prepared by a firm of accountants.

the qualified exemptions under the FOIA 2000. The balance is, however, subtly different in each case: in relation to the qualified exemptions, the balance is between competing heads of *public interest*; under section 41 the balance is between a *private interest* in maintaining confidentiality, and a *public interest* that may give rise to a defence to any action for breach of confidence.

Finally, the exemption in section 44 is on its face absolute, but will in each case require consideration as to whether a relevant statutory prohibition is in fact in operation. The statutory prohibition may itself include exceptions, and these may require to be considered by reference to the specific facts of the individual case.[90] If the disclosure of information would breach a Convention right (eg, the privacy right under Art 8) then such disclosure would be likely to fall within section 44, on the basis that disclosure would infringe section 6(1) of the Human Rights Act 1998 prohibiting a public authority from acting in breach of a Convention right.[91] In order to assess whether a Convention right had been breached there would in many cases need to be an assessment of whether any inference pursued a legitimate aim and was necessary and proportionate.

The assumption behind the FOIA 2000, it is suggested, is that there is a general public interest in the disclosure on request of information held by public authorities. That public interest may, however, need to give way in certain cases to competing, more compelling interests. The legislative choice to create an absolute exemption appears at first sight to be a determination that in an entire class of cases the public interest in the disclosure of information is outweighed, or 'trumped', by some other consideration. In practice however, as illustrated above, even the absolute exemptions will often in practice require the making of difficult and case-sensitive judgements. And when it comes to the qualified exemptions, in particular those that are prejudice-based or harm-based, such judgements lie at the very heart of the Act.

11.3.4.3 *Interpreting the harm or prejudice-based exemptions*
As already indicated a number of the qualified exemptions are prejudice-based or harm-based. In these cases the first question is whether the qualified exemption is engaged at all, and this must be resolved before one goes on to consider the balance of competing public interests.

The prejudice-based exemptions are all phrased in similar terms: the question is whether the disclosure under the Act of the information sought would, or would be

---

For discussion of the public interest defence in the context of the FOIA 2000, s 41, see *Derry CC v Information Commissioner*, EA/2006/0014.

[90] For an illustration, see *Slann v Information Commissioner* [2006] UKITEA 2005 0019, EA/2005/0019. Disclosure was sought from the Financial Services Authority; the relevant prohibitions were contained in s 348 of the Financial Services and Markets Act 2000.

[91] Compare, however, *Bluck v Information Commissioner and Another*, EA/2006/0090, where the Tribunal considered that s 44 was not intended to cover cases where disclosure would breach a Convention right.

likely to, prejudice some specified matter. For instance, section 33 creates an exemption for information the disclosure of which would or would be likely to prejudice the exercise of certain public sector audit functions by a public authority which has such functions. One variation on this theme is section 38, using the language of endangering rather than of prejudice: information is exempt under that section if its disclosure under the Act would or would be likely to endanger the physical or mental health, or safety, of any individual. There is another variation in section 36(2)(b): the question under that provision is whether disclosure would or would be likely to *inhibit* the free and frank provision of advice or the free and frank exchange of views for the purposes of deliberation. It might also be suggested that section 24 is a prejudice-based or harm-based exemption. Section 24 applies where exemption is required for the purpose of safeguarding national security, and one could regard 'safeguarding' national security as being equivalent to 'avoiding harm to' or 'avoiding prejudice to' national security.

The first question in applying these exemptions is what is meant by 'prejudice'. The Information Commissioner's general guidance about the application of the prejudice-based exemptions suggests that the term is equivalent to 'harm', and it is suggested that this is the correct approach.[92] The Commissioner's guidance also indicates that although prejudice need not be substantial he would expect it to be more than trivial. The Tribunal has upheld this approach in *Hogan and Oxford City Council v Information Commissioner*.[93]

In applying these exemptions it is necessary to consider whether disclosure *under the Act* would prejudice the particular matter with which the exemption is concerned, and so the specific characteristics of disclosure under the Act (as opposed to other sorts of disclosure, eg in civil litigation) must be taken into account. Disclosure of information under the Act will in the first instance be made to the specific individual who has requested the information. That individual will, however, be free to disseminate the information further if he so chooses.[94] Disclosing information under the FOIA 2000 thus amounts to putting the information in the public domain. Where there is a duty to disclose information under the FOIA 2000, there is nothing in the Act that permits the disclosure to be made subject to a restriction that the applicant must treat the information disclosed as confidential, or that he may only use it for particular purposes. On the other hand, if there is no duty to disclose under the FOIA it may nevertheless be open to the public authority to make a voluntary disclosure of the information to the requester only, and on confidential terms. For example, there may be cases where disclosure of information to

---

[92] See FOIA Awareness Guidance No 20, 'Prejudice and Adverse Affect'. This is available on the Commissioner's website at <http://www.ico.gov.uk> (accessed 10 August 2011). The guidance also deals with the corresponding provision in the Environmental Information Regulations 2004.

[93] EA/2005/0026 and 0030.

[94] Note, however, that a document disclosed in response to a request under the FOIA 2000 may still be protected by copyright, thus restricting the applicant's freedom to copy and disseminate the document itself.

the applicant alone would not be likely to prejudice the prevention or detection of crime, but wider disclosure would be likely to do so: in that case, it is suggested, the prejudice-based exemption in section 31 of the Act would be engaged, and (depending on the application of the public interest test) the information might very well be exempt from disclosure. However, if the public authority considered that it could safely be disclosed to the applicant alone, there would be nothing to stop the authority from voluntarily disclosing it to the applicant on a confidential basis.

The formula used repeatedly in the Act is whether disclosure under the Act *would* or *would be likely* to prejudice the specified interest. Disclosure *would* prejudice the specified interest, if prejudice is more probable than not.[95] There has been a considerable amount of discussion in the Tribunal case law as to the standard to apply in deciding whether disclosure *would be likely* to prejudice the specified interest. In a number of decisions, the Tribunal has stated that what is required is a significant and weighty chance of prejudice,[96] albeit that this may fall short of establishing that prejudice is more probable than not.[97]

11.3.4.4 *Qualified exemptions and the public interest test*
If a qualified exemption is engaged then the duty to disclose does not apply if:

in all the circumstances of the case, the public interest in maintaining the exemption outweighs the public interest in disclosing the information.[98]

The application of this test is one of the most difficult aspects of the FOIA 2000. It is necessary to identify the respects in which there is a public interest in maintaining the exemption, and in disclosing the information sought; and it is then necessary to assess the respective weight of those public interests. The exercise must be carried out having regard to *all the circumstances of the case*. The test will need to be applied by the public authority itself (both when the request is first considered, and in carrying out any internal review); by the Information Commissioner (in considering a complaint under s 50 of the Act); and by the Tribunal (in determining an appeal against the Commissioner's Decision Notice, under s 57).[99]

Is this exercise to be carried out on the basis that there is any presumption in favour of disclosure? Or does the exercise begin with the scales equally balanced between the competing public interests?

---

[95] See *Hogan*, n 93 above, para 35.

[96] See *John Connor v Information Commissioner*, EA/2005/005; *Guardian Newspapers and Brooke v Information Commissioner and the BBC*, EA/2006/0011 and 0013; and *Hogan and Oxford CC v Information Commissioner*, EA/2005/0026 and 0020. This approach draws on decision of Munby J in relation to the construction of similar language in the DPA 1998, in *R (Lord) v Home Secretary* [2003] EWHC 2073 (Admin) at paras 99–100.

[97] See, eg, *Office for Government Commerce v Information Commissioner*, Decision promulgated 19 February 2009, on remission from the High Court: EA/2006/0068 and 0080, paras 120–36.

[98] FOIA 2000, s 2(2)(b).

[99] See section 11.3.2 for a discussion of the respective roles played by these bodies.

The FOIA 2000 does not include any general provision that there is a presumption in favour of the disclosure of information held by public authorities. In that respect it is different from the Environmental Information Regulations 2004, discussed below.[100] Nor does the FOIA 2000 include any purpose clause to assist in determining the respective weight of the competing public interests.[101]

On the other hand, in one important respect the FOIA 2000 does contain a presumption in favour of disclosure. The duty to communicate is displaced by a qualified exemption only if the public interest in maintaining the exemption *outweighs* the public interest in disclosure of the information sought. So if the competing interests are equally balanced, then the public authority must communicate the information sought.

There is also a wider point. In *Office of Government Commerce v Information Commissioner and Another*,[102] Stanley Burnton J (as he then was) approved of the following statement from the Information Tribunal decision in *Secretary of State for Work and Pensions v The Information Commissioner*:[103]

It can be said, however, that there is an assumption built into FOIA that the disclosure of information by public authorities on request is in itself of value and in the public interest, in order to promote transparency and accountability in relation to the activities of public authorities. What this means is that there is always likely to be some public interest in favour of the disclosure of information under the Act. The strength of that interest, and the strength of the competing interest in maintaining any relevant exemption, must be assessed on a case by case basis: section 2(2)(b) requires the balance to be considered 'in all the circumstances of the case'.

What this passage recognizes is that in applying the public interest test it is necessary to have regard to the purpose of the Act. The whole premise behind the Act is that it is in the public interest for public authorities to be transparent and accountable. Of course, the extent to which a particular disclosure will contribute to these objectives, and the weight of any competing public interest considerations in favour of maintaining an exemption, will need to be assessed on a case-sensitive basis. What ought not to happen, however, is that the application of the public interest test turns into what is in substance a debate about whether the FOIA ought to have been introduced in the first place.

Public interest in the disclosure of information The Commissioner's guidance about the public interest test[104] refers to five general public interest factors that may favour the disclosure of information:

---

[100] See reg 12(2) of the Regulations.
[101] As is found, eg, in s 4 of New Zealand's Official Information Act 1982.
[102] [2008] EWHC 737 (Admin) at para 71.
[103] EA/2006/0040.
[104] Available at <http://www.ico.gov.uk/upload/documents/library/freedom_of_information/detailed_specialist_guides/awareness_guidance_3_public_interest_test.pdf> (accessed 10 August 2011).

(a) furthering understanding of and participation in public debate about issues of the day;

(b) promoting accountability and transparency in respect of decisions taken by public authorities;

(c) promoting accountability and transparency in the spending of public money;

(d) allowing individuals and companies to understand decisions made by public authorities that affect their lives; and

(e) bringing to light information affecting public health and public safety.

These considerations are not exhaustive. The Guidance itself suggests some additional factors that may be relevant: for instance, the disclosure may contribute to scientific advancements, ensure the better operation of financial and currency markets, or assist in access to justice and other fundamental rights.

The mere fact that a substantial section of the public is interested in a subject does not, of itself, mean that disclosure of information about that subject is in the public interest.[105] For example, there may be widespread and prurient interest among members of the public in the private life of a celebrity; this does not of itself mean that disclosure of relevant information would be in the public interest. Essentially, to say that disclosure of information is in the public interest is equivalent to saying that disclosure is for the public benefit, or that it serves the common good.[106]

What is relevant is the *public* interest in disclosure, as opposed to any private interest. So, for example, the fact that disclosure of a piece of information would be to the financial benefit of an individual or organization is not, in itself, a public interest factor in favour of disclosure. On the other hand, sometimes interests that appear at first sight to be private may turn out to have a public element. Take a case where a public authority is investigating an individual on the grounds of suspected misconduct, but has not disclosed the reasons for its investigation. The individual seeks disclosure of information that would reveal those reasons. It might be argued that the individual's interest in disclosure of the information, so as to be able to answer the allegations against him, is a purely private one. However, if disclosure of the information would enhance the fairness of the investigation, then it is suggested that this is a matter of public, not merely private, interest.

In *Scotland Office v Information Commissioner*,[107] the Tribunal recognized that similar arguments (based on transparency, accountability, etc) were likely to be put forward in favour of disclosure in very many FOIA cases. This did not in any way diminish their importance, although the weight to be attached to these

---

[105] See, eg, *Lion Laboratories Ltd v Evans* [1985] QB 526 at 537.
[106] See *DTI v Information Commissioner*, EA/2006/0007, para 50.
[107] EA/2007/0128: see at paras 57–60.

considerations would vary depending on the circumstances of the case. The question to be considered is in what way will disclosure of this information, at this specific point in time, foster the desired objectives such as accountability or transparency.[108]

Articulating the public interest in favour of disclosure can often be a challenging task. For example, explaining how disclosure of particular information would contribute to informed public debate on a particular subject may require both a knowledge of the subject matter concerned, and an understanding of how much information about that subject is already in the public domain. However, there is a practical problem that affects all requesters (however well resourced and well informed), which is that they are seeking to identify the public interest in disclosure of information of which (inevitably) they do not know the actual content. This is where the role of the Information Commissioner is crucial,[109] not merely as a decision-maker in complaints under the Act, but also as a party to proceedings in the Information Tribunal or the courts. The Commissioner has the advantage that he is likely to have seen the actual content of the disputed information, and that he can articulate the public interest in disclosure by reference to that content.

Public interest in maintaining the exemption The first point to note is that the statute refers to the public interest *in maintaining the exemption*, not *in withholding the information*. It is suggested that this means the focus should be on the public interest as it is reflected in the particular exemption. The question is not: would harm flow from the disclosure of the information? The question, rather, is whether disclosure would lead to the sort of harm that comes within the scope of the FOIA 2000 exemption on which the public authority seeks to rely.

Where the exemption is a harm-based or prejudice-based exemption, then the same considerations are likely to be relevant both to determining whether the exemption is engaged and to identifying the public interest in maintaining the exemption. At both stages of the analysis, the focus will be on identifying any harmful consequences of disclosure, and assessing their weight.

When considering the class-based qualified exemptions there is a somewhat different approach. Here the exemption will be engaged merely because the information is of a particular description. At the first stage of the analysis, when considering whether or not the exemption is engaged, there will be no need to consider the consequences of disclosure. However, when considering the public interest in maintaining the exemption then the consequences of disclosure will be highly relevant. Take the case of a public authority that is claiming an exemption

---

[108] See *OGC v Information Commissioner*, EA/2006/0068 and 0080 (19 February 2009, on remission from High Court) at para 149.

[109] See section 11.3.2 for more detailed discussion of the role of the Commissioner in enforcing the Act.

on the basis of section 30(1), on the basis that the information is held for the purpose of a criminal investigation that the authority has a duty to conduct. At the first stage of the analysis, in deciding whether or not the exemption is engaged, the only issues will be whether the public authority has the duty to conduct such investigations, and if so whether the information is held for that purpose. Usually these questions will not be difficult to resolve. Moving on to the balance of public interests, the public interest in maintaining the exemption requires a consideration of whether disclosure will damage the public authority's ability to carry out this particular investigation, or other similar future investigations. It might be suggested by the authority, for instance, that disclosure of the information sought would enable the person under investigation to conceal or destroy relevant documents, or that disclosure would make it harder for the authority to secure cooperation from potential witnesses in the future.

The public interest in maintaining an exemption is to be assessed 'in all the circumstances of the case'. This means that, whether the exemption is class-based or prejudice-based, the public authority is not permitted to maintain a blanket refusal to disclose all information of a particular type or nature. The question is not, is the balance of public interest in favour of maintaining the exemption in relation to this type of information? The question is, is the balance of public interest in favour of maintaining the exemption in relation to *this* information, and in the circumstances of *this* case?[110] The public authority may well have a general policy that the public interest is likely to be in favour of maintaining the exemption in respect of a specific type of information, but such a policy must not be inflexibly applied and the authority must always be willing to consider whether the circumstances of the case justify a departure from the policy.[111] The issue is whether there is a public interest in maintaining the exemption, and so any private interests in maintaining the exemption should be disregarded. For instance, it is not relevant that the disclosure of the information would embarrass particular individuals.

11.3.5 Personal data under the FOIA 2000

Requests under the FOIA 2000 will often be for the disclosure of personal data about identifiable individuals. For instance, there may be requests for information about the salaries of individual public sector employees,[112] their job titles and position

---

[110] See, eg, *DfES v Information Commissioner*, EA/2006/0006, para 75(i); *ECGD v Friends of the Earth and Information Commissioner* [2008] EWHC 638 (Admin), paras 25–8 (this is a case under the EIR 2004, but also relevant to the construction of FOIA 2000).

[111] In relation to policies or guidelines about FOIA disclosure, see *OGC v Information Commissioner*, EA/2006/0068 and 0080 (19 February 2009, on remission from High Court) at paras 165–9 (relevance of 'working assumption' about the disclosure of Office of Government Commerce Gateway Reviews).

[112] See Decision Notice FS50062124, Corby Borough Council (request for information about payments made to local authority's Temporary Finance Officer).

within their organization,[113] or the circumstances in which their employment came to an end.[114]

There is a complex exemption under section 40 of the FOIA 2000 in relation to requests for personal information. This exemption cross-refers to the DPA 1998; and where section 40 refers to 'personal data', the term bears the same meaning as in the DPA 1998.[115]

There is an absolute exemption under the FOIA 2000 where the requested information is for personal data of which the applicant is the data subject: section 40(1). As already explained, the purpose of this provision is to ensure that requests by individuals for their own personal data are dealt with as subject access requests under the DPA 1998, section 7 rather than as requests under the FOIA 2000, section 1. Hence this provision is a piece of legal traffic flow management; it is not intended to prevent individuals from obtaining their own personal data from public authorities.

There are also three exemptions in relation to requests for third party personal data (ie, personal data of individuals other than the requester):

(a) there is an absolute exemption where disclosure to a member of the public otherwise than under the FOIA 2000 would contravene any of the data protection principles.[116] For this purpose all data held by public authorities[117] are treated as being covered by the data protection principles;[118]

(b) there is a qualified exemption where disclosure of the information to a member of the public otherwise than under the FOIA 2000 would contravene section 10 of the DPA 1998 (right to prevent processing likely to cause damage or distress);[119]

(c) there is a qualified exemption where the information is exempt from the data subject's own right of subject access.[120]

So far, most of the Tribunal case law under section 40 has been about the exemption relating to breach of the data protection principles. The Tribunal's approach to the data protection principles in the context of section 40 is illustrated by a series of three cases involving the disclosure of information about MPs' expenses, the third of which was the subject of an unsuccessful appeal to the High Court by the House

---

[113] See, eg, *Ministry of Defence v Information Commissioner and Rob Evans*, EA/2006/0027 (request by Guardian journalist for disclosure of internal directory of Defence Export Services Organisation).

[114] Cf *Salmon v Information Commissioner and King's College Cambridge*, EA/2007/0135 (request for information about circumstances in relation to resignation of Provost of a Cambridge college).

[115] See FOIA 2000, s 40(7).

[116] FOIA 2000, s 40(2), read with ss 40(3)(a)(i) and 40(3)(b).

[117] Including data falling within limb (e) of the definition of data in the DPA 1998, s 1(1), which are in fact exempt from most of the data protection principles; see s 33A of the DPA 1998.

[118] See s 40(3)(b), which provides that the exemptions in s 33A of the DPA 1998 are to be disregarded for this purpose.

[119] FOIA 2000, s 40(2), read with s 40(3)(a)(ii).

[120] FOIA 2000, s 40(2), read with s 40(4).

of Commons.[121] In all these cases the Tribunal required disclosure of information (and in the third case, it required wider disclosure than the Information Commissioner had done).

The first case in the series[122] ('the *Baker* case') arose out of requests made by the Liberal Democrat MP, Norman Baker, and a *Sunday Times* journalist, for information about MPs' travel expenses. These expenses were already published in aggregate form (showing how much was claimed by each MP, in total, each year); the request was for the annual figure for each MP, broken down by mode of transport. The Information Commissioner ordered the information to be disclosed, and the Information Tribunal upheld his decision on appeal.

The House of Commons argued that the information was exempt from disclosure under section 40. Disclosure would breach the first data protection principle (it would be unfair to individual MPs, and would not satisfy any of the conditions in Sch 2 to the Act); it would also breach the second data protection principle. Individual MPs had an expectation that disclosure would not go beyond the terms of the publication scheme adopted by the House of Commons (under the FOIA 2000, s 19), which envisaged that travel expenses would be disclosed annually on an aggregate basis.

The Tribunal accepted that the requested information was personal data. However, in assessing fairness for the purpose of the first data protection principle, the interests of the individuals MPs were important but were not the first and paramount consideration, given that the allowances were paid from public money and related to the performance of public duties.[123] On this basis, disclosure would not be unfair to MPs. The Tribunal's approach, therefore, indicates that personal data in relation to an individual's public life carry a lower expectation of privacy than would data in relation to domestic or private matters. Clearly, this approach is of general importance in applying the section 40 exemption.

As to whether any of the conditions in Schedule 2 to the DPA 1998 were satisfied, the Tribunal considered the application of condition 6. This is satisfied if:

The processing is necessary for the purposes of legitimate interests pursued by the data controller or by the third party or parties to whom the data are disclosed, except where the processing is unwarranted in any particular case by reason of prejudice to the rights and freedoms or legitimate interests of the data subject.

---

[121] The House of Commons is a public authority under the FOIA 2000: Sch 1 Pt 1 para 5. Individual MPs are not themselves public authorities under the Act.

[122] *Corporate Officer of the House of Commons v Information Commissioner and Norman Baker MP,* EA/2006/0015 and 0016.

[123] The Tribunal therefore distinguished *CCN Systems Ltd v The Data Protection Registrar* (DA/90 25/49/8) and *Infolink Ltd v The Data Protection Registrar* (DA/90 25/49/6), earlier Tribunal decisions under the DPA 1984 to the effect that the interests of the data subject were the first and paramount consideration in assessing fairness.

The Tribunal considered[124] that the application of this paragraph involved a balance between competing interests, broadly comparable, but not identical, to the balance that applies under the public interest test for qualified exemptions under the FOIA 2000. Paragraph 6 required a consideration of the balance between: (a) the legitimate interests of those to whom the data would be disclosed, which in this context were members of the public; and (b) prejudice to the rights, freedoms, and legitimate interests of the data subjects (in this case, MPs). However, because the processing must be 'necessary' for the legitimate interests of members of the public to apply, the Tribunal considered that only where (a) outweighs or is greater than (b) should the personal data be disclosed. Applying this approach, the Tribunal considered that the legitimate interests of the public in receiving this information outweighed any prejudice to MPs. Finally, the Tribunal considered that the publication of this information did not amount to its use for a purpose incompatible with the purpose for which it had been obtained; so there was no breach of the second data protection principle.

The approach taken in the *Baker* case was followed in the second case in the series[125] ('the *Moffat* case'), which related to the travel expenses of Anne Moffat MP. A number of requests for information were made, seeking more detailed disclosure than had been ordered in the *Baker* case. The Information Commissioner required the information to be disclosed, and again the Tribunal upheld the decision. It appears that the reason why this particular MP was targeted was that she was in the highest 5 per cent of travel expenders among MPs, and for one year she made the highest claim for travel expenses of any MP; there were however good reasons for this, as she was in a largely rural constituency a long way from Westminster.[126] The only issue considered by the Tribunal was the application of Schedule 2 paragraph 6 (applying a similar approach as in the *Baker* case), and the Tribunal considered that the balance came down in favour of disclosure.

The third case in the series ('the *Brooke* case'[127]), unlike the *Baker* and *Moffat* cases, was not concerned with travel expenses. This case arose out of requests for information about the claims made by various MPs under the Additional Costs Allowance ('ACA'). This is intended to defray the costs incurred by MPs representing constituencies outside Inner London, in residing in two different places (ie, in Westminster and in their constituencies). Three journalists sought full details of the ACA claims made by various MPs. The Information Commissioner did not uphold the requests in full. He required disclosure to be made of the total sum

---

[124] See at para 90 of the decision.

[125] *Corporate Officer of the House of Commons v Information Commissioner*, EA/2006/0074 (and others).

[126] See para 19 of the Tribunal's decision. The constituency in question was West Lothian.

[127] *Corporate Officer of the House of Commons v Information Commissioner, Leapman, Brooke and Thomas*, EA/2007/0060 (and others).

claimed under the ACA by each MP in each year, broken down into a number of different headings.

The Tribunal upheld an appeal by the requesters, and dismissed an appeal by the House of Commons. It required disclosure (with very limited exceptions) of all of the documentation submitted by these MPs in respect of their claims for ACA. The Tribunal applied the same principles as in the *Baker* case, and was clearly heavily influenced by its view that the ACA system was highly unsatisfactory, being both unclear in its rules and lax in its controls.[128] The *Brooke* case received a considerable amount of media attention, not least because it brought into the public domain the existence of the so-called 'John Lewis list', setting out the maximum permissible claim by way of ACA for various standard domestic items.

On appeal, the Divisional Court of the High Court upheld the Tribunal's decision.[129] The main ground of appeal was that the Tribunal had failed to give adequate weight to the expectations of MPs (derived from the publication scheme) as to how much information about the ACA would be made public. The court considered that the Tribunal had taken this argument into account and rejected it, and that there was no error of law. In any event, the court could not discern any basis for an expectation by MPs that the requested information would not enter the public arena.

The MPs expenses cases are a good illustration of the sorts of issues that arise when applying the data protection principles in the context of the FOIA 2000, section 40. Although there are eight data protection principles in all, the main focus is on the first principle: and within that context the discussion centres on whether disclosure is fair, and whether it meets a Schedule 2 condition. Within Schedule 2 the focus is on condition 6 (set out above).

The question of how section 40 applies to the disclosure of statistical information, or other information that does not identify individuals by name, has caused considerable difficulty. The problem has been in interpreting and applying the decision of the House of Lords in *Common Services Agency v Scottish Information Commissioner*.[130] This was a case under the FOISA 2002, section 38, but there is no material difference between that provision and the FOIA 2000, section 40.

The *Common Services Agency* case involved a request for disclosure of statistics about childhood leukaemia, in an area of extensive military and civilian nuclear activity. The request was for statistics for very small geographical areas. The Scottish Information Commissioner refused to order disclosure of the raw statistics, as he was concerned that—because of the low numbers involved, coupled with the small geographical areas—it would be possible for the individuals concerned to

---

[128] See decision at para 33.
[129] *Corporate Officer of the House of Commons v Information Commissioner, Brooke, Leapman and Thomas* [2008] EWHC 1084 (Admin).
[130] [2008] UKHL 47, [2008] 1 WLR 1550.

be identified. In his view the raw statistics would constitute personal data, and their disclosure would contravene the data protection principles. However, he ordered that the statistics should be disclosed in 'barnardized' form.[131]

In the House of Lords the question was whether the Scottish Information Commissioner was entitled to order the disclosure of barnardized information. One issue was whether, even in barnardized form, the statistics would constitute personal data. If so, given that the information related to health, would it be 'sensitive personal data' as defined in the DPA 1998, section 2? If the information was sensitive personal data then it would be necessary to consider both Schedule 2 and Schedule 3 to the DPA 1998: in order for the information to be disclosed, a condition under each Schedule would need to be satisfied, and if this was not possible then the information would be exempt from disclosure.[132]

The House of Lords accepted—as was common ground—that the public authority held both the raw statistics, and information enabling it to identify the individuals to whom the raw statistics related. Section 1(1) of the DPA 1998 provides that information is personal data if it relates to individuals who can be identified from those data and other information in the possession of the data controller. Nevertheless, the House of Lords considered that it was possible that the barnardized statistics would not constitute personal data. Whether or not the barnardized statistics would be personal data was remitted to the Scottish Information Commissioner for further consideration. If the barnardized statistics were personal data then in the view of the House of Lords they would be sensitive personal data, and so both Schedule 2 and Schedule 3 to the DPA 1998 would need to be considered in order to decide whether they were exempt from disclosure under the FOIA 2000, section 40.

The Tribunal was faced with having to interpret and apply the *Common Services Agency* case in *Department of Health v Information Commissioner*.[133] The issue in that case was whether certain abortion statistics had to be disclosed under the FOIA 2000, relating to the medical condition for which so-called 'Ground E' abortions had taken place (ie, abortions on the ground that there was a substantial risk that if the child were born it would be seriously disabled). The requested information consisted of national level statistics, but broken down in such a way that for some items there would be a very low figure indeed, which might include a figure of 1 or 0.

The Information Commissioner argued that the requested information was not personal data at all. Notwithstanding the low numbers involved, because the

---

[131] Barnardization is a technique for the random modification of statistical information involving low numbers, intended to enable useful statistical information to be made public without the risk of disclosure of individual identities.

[132] In the MPs expenses cases, discussed above, only Sch 2 was relevant, since the information sought was not sensitive personal data.

[133] EA/2008/0074.

statistics were at national level the risk that they would allow any individual to be identified was negligible.

The Tribunal agreed that there was a negligible risk of identification. However, it held that the information was still personal data in the hands of the Department of Health. This is because the Department held other information—consisting of forms provided to it in relation to each abortion—that would enable it, in each case, to identify the individuals to whom the statistics related. Because the Department, as data controller, would be able to perform this identification, the requested information was personal data. The Tribunal went on to conclude that disclosure of the information would not contravene the data protection principles: hence the requested information was not exempt under the FOIA 2000, section 40, and had to be disclosed.

The obvious objection to the Tribunal's analysis was that in *Common Services Agency* the public authority was able to identify the individuals to whom the statistical information related. If this was sufficient to render the statistical information personal data then the House of Lords would have concluded that the barnardized statistics would be personal data: it would not have needed to remit the issue to the Scottish Information Commissioner. The Tribunal dealt with this point by saying that the issue in the *Common Services Agency* case was whether, after barnardization, even the public authority itself would be unable to link the barnardized statistics to particular individuals. That, in the Tribunal's view, was the issue that was remitted to the Scottish Information Commissioner for further consideration. In the *Department of Health* case, it was common ground that the Department would be able (using the abortion forms) to identify the individuals to whom the statistical information related: on that basis, the Tribunal held that the statistics were personal data.

On appeal the High Court held that the Tribunal was wrong on this issue, and that the statistics did not constitute personal data.[134] On a proper interpretation of the *Common Services Agency* case, the right question to ask was whether the statistical information allowed members of the public to identify individual women who had undergone abortions. On the Tribunal's findings the answer to that question was no; hence disclosure of the statistics did not involve the processing of personal data, and the FOIA 2000, section 40 did not apply. The Upper Tribunal reached a similar conclusion—by a different process of reasoning—in *APG v Information Commissioner and Ministry of Defence*.[135] However, the divergent views about the

---

[134] See *Department of Health v Information Commissioner* [2011] EWHC 1430 (Admin) at paras 49–55 per Cranston J.

[135] [2011] UKUT 153 (AAC). The difference is that in the *APG* case the Upper Tribunal followed the reasoning of Baroness Hale in the *Common Services Agency* case. In *Department of Health* the High Court treated Lord Hope's speech in *Common Services Agency* as being the leading speech, but held that the Tribunal had misinterpreted Lord Hope's reasoning.

proper application of the *Common Services Agency* case will not be definitively resolved until the Court of Appeal has had the opportunity to consider the issue.

11.3.6 Policy-related information under the FOIA 2000

When the FOIA 2000 first came into force, there was considerable interest in how it would apply to policy-related information. How far, if at all, would it alter established understandings about the confidentiality of civil service advice? Would it bring documents that were at the heart of the policy-making process into the public domain?

The framework within which the FOIA 2000 deals with policy-related information is set by sections 35 and 36.

Section 35 provides as follows:

(1) Information held by a government department or by the National Assembly of Wales is exempt information if it relates to—

   (a) the formulation or development of government policy,
   (b) Ministerial communications
   (c) the provision of advice by any of the Law Officers or any request for the provision of such advice, or
   (d) the operation of any Ministerial office.

(2) Once a decision as to government policy has been taken, any statistical information used to provide an informed background to the taking of the decision is not to be regarded—

   (a) for the purposes of subsection 1(a), as relating to the formulation or development of government policy, or
   (b) for the purposes of subsection (1)(b), as relating to Ministerial communications.

Section 35(4) provides that in assessing the public interest regard is to be had to the particular public interest in the disclosure of factual information which has been used to provide an informed background to decision-taking.

The leading Tribunal case on section 35 is *Department for Education and Skills v Information Commissioner and the Evening Standard*,[136] where the Tribunal required disclosure of information contained in the minutes of the DfES Board (the most senior committee in the DfES) and the Schools Directorate Management Group (the next most senior committee). The Tribunal heard evidence from senior civil servants about the implications of disclosing policy-related information, including from Lord Turnbull (the former Cabinet Secretary) and Paul Britton (Director General of the Domestic Policy Group in the Cabinet Office). That evidence included material about the indirect implications for future policy-making

---

[136] EA/2006/006.

if the requested information were disclosed: it was argued that disclosure would inhibit the frankness and candour of policy advice by civil servants, and would interfere with the 'safe space' needed by government in order to develop policy without the pressure of publicity. The case for the government was essentially that any disclosure of policy-related information, even if the information itself appeared innocuous, was inherently damaging and a threat to good government.[137]

The Tribunal accepted that all of the requested information came within section 35(1)(a) as relating to the formulation or development of government policy. In relation to the public interest test, the Tribunal accepted that it was relevant to consider the indirect consequences of disclosure.[138] However, when it came to assessing what those consequences would be the Tribunal was not bound to accept the evidence of the witnesses called, however eminent, but was entitled and indeed bound to reach its own conclusions. The Tribunal set out[139] some guiding principles in relation to the disclosure of policy-related information. These included the following points.

(a) Every decision was specific to the actual content of the particular information in question. Whether there might be significant indirect or wider consequences from disclosure had to be considered case by case.

(b) No information was exempt from disclosure simply by virtue of its status (eg by being classified as advice to a minister).

(c) The purpose of confidentiality was to protect civil servants, not ministers, from compromise or unjust public opprobrium.

(d) The timing of a request was of paramount importance. Disclosure of discussion of policy options while policy was in the process of formulation was unlikely to be in the public interest unless, for example, it would expose wrongdoing. Disclosure after policy formulation had been completed was, however, a different matter.

(e) Whether formulation or development of a particular policy was complete was a question of fact. The Act itself (see ss 35(2) and 35(4)) assumed that policy was formulated, announced, and in due course superseded; policy-making was not a 'seamless web'. However, this did not mean that any public interest in maintaining the exemption disappeared immediately the policy had been announced; everything would depend on the particular facts of the case.

---

[137] See para 48 of the Tribunal decision.
[138] See para 70 of the decision.
[139] See para 75 of the decision.

(f) In judging the likely consequences of disclosure the Tribunal was entitled to expect of civil servants 'the courage and independence that has been the hallmark of our civil service since the Northcote-Trevelyan reforms'.

The Tribunal has endorsed and applied these principles in a number of cases, while recognizing that they are guidelines only and not a binding statement as to the law.[140] In *OGC v Information Commissioner*, a High Court appeal from the Information Tribunal, Stanley Burnton J (as he then was) discussed these principles without disapproval.[141]

The case-sensitive approach set out in the *DfES* case has been applied in a number of subsequent cases. For instance, the Tribunal has required disclosure of two Office of Government Commerce Gateway Reports regarding the ID cards scheme.[142] On the other hand, the Tribunal refused to order disclosure of information about the decision as to which sporting events should be protected under the Broadcasting Act 1996 from having television rights sold for exclusive viewing by subscription or pay-per-view.[143] The Tribunal considered that the value of the requested information in informing public debate was very limited, and that any public interest in disclosure was outweighed by generalized 'good government' considerations in favour of maintaining the confidentiality of advice given by civil servants. The High Court has emphasized (in a case about the comparable exemption in regulation 12(4)(e) of the Environmental Information Regulations 2004 ('EIR 2004')) that the considerations in favour of maintaining the confidentiality of advice within and between government departments are likely to be material in every case when assessing the public interest, albeit that the weight to be given to those considerations will vary from case to case.[144]

If the submissions made for the Government in the *DfES* case had been accepted in their entirety then the practical effect could well have been to turn section 35 into a quasi-absolute exemption, with policy-related information being disclosed only where an exceptionally strong public interest case could be made out. The case law has not taken this course. It is clear that any adverse consequences of disclosure, both in relation to the particular policy-making exercise concerned and in respect of policy formation in general, must be taken into account in applying the public interest test. However, the content of the information sought and the timing of the request are both highly material in determining how much weight to give those considerations in any individual case.

---

[140] See, eg, *Secretary of State for Work and Pensions v Information Commissioner*, EA/2006/0040 at para 110; *Scotland Office v Information Commissioner* (EA/2007/0128) at paras 49–53.

[141] [2008] EWHC 774 (Admin), paras 68–102.

[142] *OGC v Information Commissioner*, EA/2006/0068 and 0080 (19 February 2009, on remission from the High Court).

[143] *DCMS v Information Commissioner*, EA/2007/0090.

[144] *Export Credit Guarantee Department v Friends of the Earth and the Information Commissioner* [2008] EWHC 638 (Admin) at para 38.

Section 35 only applies in relation to information held by a government department or the National Assembly of Wales. Other public authorities wishing to resist disclosure of policy-related information are likely to rely on the qualified exemption[145] in section 36.[146] This applies where in the reasonable opinion of a qualified person[147] disclosure of the information under the Act would or would be likely (among other matters) to inhibit the free and frank provision of advice[148] or the free and frank exchange of views for the purpose of deliberation,[149] or would otherwise prejudice or be likely otherwise to prejudice the effective conduct of public affairs.[150]

The leading Tribunal case on this section is *Guardian Newspapers & Brooke v Information Commissioner and BBC*,[151] where the Tribunal required the BBC to disclose the minutes of a BBC Governors' meeting at which it considered the Hutton Report into the death of Dr David Kelly. The Director-General of the BBC, Greg Dyke, had resigned on the day following the meeting.

The Tribunal considered that in order for the exemption to be engaged the relevant opinion of the qualified person (ie, his opinion that the specified adverse consequences would or would be likely to occur) must be both reasonable in substance and reasonably arrived at.[152] If the exemption was engaged, then the public interest test fell to be applied. In relation to that test, the opinion of the qualified person was an important piece of evidence, but the person applying the test needed to form his own view on the severity, extent, and frequency with which the specified adverse consequences would occur.[153]

11.3.7 Amendments to the FOIA: the Protection of Freedoms Bill

The Protection of Freedoms Bill was introduced into Parliament in February 2011. The most important change made by the Bill to the FOIA 2000 is the introduction of special provisions relating to the disclosure of datasets by public authorities under the Act.[154]

---

[145] The s 36 exemption is absolute so far as relating to information held by the House of Commons or the House of Lords, but is otherwise qualified: FOIA 2000, s 2(3)(e).

[146] This section also applies to information held by a government department or the National Assembly of Wales which is not exempt information under s 35.

[147] s 36(5) makes provision as to who is the appropriate 'qualified person' in respect of various public authorities.

[148] s 36(2)(b)(i).

[149] s 36(2)(b)(ii).

[150] s 36(2)(c).

[151] EA/2006/0011 and 0013.

[152] See at para 64 of the decision.

[153] See at para 92 of the decision.

[154] The Bill also amends FOIA 2000, s 6 to widen the definition of 'publicly-owned company', and makes further provision about the appointment, tenure, and powers of the Information Commissioner.

Datasets are to be defined by a new subsection 11(5) of the FOIA 2000. A dataset is a collection of information held in electronic form, where all or most of the information meets the following criteria:

(a) the information has been obtained or recorded by a public authority for the purpose of providing the authority with information in connection with the provision of a service or carrying out of a function by that authority;

(b) the information is factual in nature, is not the product of interpretation or analysis other than calculation, and is not an official statistic within the meaning of the Statistics and Registration Service Act 2007;

(c) the information within datasets has not been materially altered since it was obtained or recorded by the public authority.

Hence a dataset is not a new category of information available under the FOIA 2000: it is a subset of the 'information' that is currently available under the FOIA 2000. The Bill does not affect the question of *whether* a dataset, as defined, can be obtained under the FOIA 2000: the answer will depend on the application of the existing exemptions.

However, the important point about the Bill is that it affects the form in which disclosure of datasets must be made, in cases where they are required to be disclosed. New subsection 11(1A) of the FOIA 2000 will require that, where the request is for a dataset (or part of a dataset), and the requester asks for disclosure in electronic form, then the information must so far as reasonably practicable be provided to the requester in a re-usable format. A new section 11A will require the public authority to make the dataset available to the requester for re-use in accordance with the terms of a specified licence, provided that the public authority is the sole owner of any copyright in the dataset.

The purpose of these provisions is to facilitate the re-use of information that is held in electronic form by public authorities and that consists of 'raw' or 'source' data. The provisions do not seem to be aimed at information representing the product of analysis or judgement.

The explanatory notes to the Bill give examples of datasets (at para 333), including: combinations of letters and numbers used to identify property or locations, such as postcodes and references; datasets comprising numbers and information related to numbers, such as expenditure data; and datasets comprising text or words, such as information about job roles in a local authority.

11.4 ENVIRONMENTAL INFORMATION

The EIR 2004 came into force at the same time as the FOIA 2000. In many respects the two pieces of legislation can be considered side by side, as part of a single package. There is, however, an important difference between them at the outset.

The FOIA 2000 does not implement an EU obligation; it is an entirely domestic piece of legislation. The EIR 2004 gives effect in UK law to Council Directive 2003/4/EC on public access to environmental information. The language of the EIR 2004 in many respects reflects the language of the Directive.

The EIR 2004 applies to 'public authorities'. The term does not bear exactly the same meaning as in the FOIA 2000. Under regulation 2(2), a public authority means a government department, or a public authority as defined in section 3(1) of the FOIA 2000, disregarding the exceptions in paragraph 6[155] of Schedule 1 to the Act. However, any body or office-holder listed in Schedule 1 to the FOIA 2000 only in relation to information of a specified description is not a 'public authority' under the EIR 2004;[156] nor is any person designated by Order under section 5 of the Act. In two respects the definition of public authority under the EIR 2004 is wider than under the Act. First, the EIR 2004 applies to any body or person that carries out functions of public administration.[157] Secondly, the EIR 2004 also applies to any body or person that carries out various environmental functions and that is under the control of another body that is itself a public authority within the EIR 2004.[158]

The Act applies to 'environmental information', which has the same meaning as in Article 2(1) of Directive 2003/4/EC: see regulation 2(1). It covers any information in written, visual, aural, *electronic* (emphasis added) or any other material form on a number of matters, including the state of the elements of the environment, and factors likely to affect the elements of the environment. The definition is complex and requires to be considered in full when applying it to the facts of any case.

The core of the EIR 2004 is regulation 5(1), which creates a general duty on a public authority that holds environmental information to make that information available 'on request'. A request under the EIR 2004 does not even have to be in writing. The information is to be made available within 20 working days (reg 5(2)), although where the public authority reasonably believes that the complexity and volume of the information make it impracticable to comply within that period then it can extend the period to 40 working days: see regulation 7(1). There is no separate provision in the EIR 2004 for a duty to confirm or deny: the only duty is to make available on request the information that is requested.

It appears that the intention of the FOIA 2000 was that requests for environmental information should in general be dealt with under the EIR 2004 not under the FOIA 2000: see section 39 of the FOIA 2000,[159] and see also section 21 (the exemption from the FOIA 2000 in respect of information that is reasonably accessible other than under s 1).

---

[155] Sch 1 para 6 excludes certain aspects of the armed forces from the scope of the FOIA 2000.
[156] Thus, the BBC is not a public authority within the EIR 2004.
[157] See reg 2(2)(c).
[158] See reg 2(2)(d).
[159] It is questionable whether s 39 does in fact apply to the EIR 2004. The section applies to information that is covered by regulations made under s 74 of the FOIA 2000 to implement the Aarhus Convention. But the EIR 2004 was made under s 2(2) of the European Communities Act 1972.

Under regulation 12(4) and (5), there are a number of exceptions to the right of access conferred by regulation 5(1). These are all qualified exemptions: disclosure may only be refused if in all the circumstances of the case the public interest in maintaining the exceptions outweighs the public interest in disclosing the information. Moreover, regulation 12(2) specifically provides that a public authority is to apply a presumption in favour of disclosure.

The exceptions in regulation 12(4) apply in the following circumstances:

(a) where the public authority does not hold the information in question when the applicant's request is received (reg 12(4)(a));

(b) where the request for information is manifestly unreasonable (reg 12(4)(b));

(c) where the request for information is formulated in too general a manner and the public authority has provided advice and assistance[160] (reg 12(4)(c));

(d) where the request relates to material still in the course of completion, to unfinished documents or to incomplete data (reg 12(4)(d)); or

(e) where the request involves the disclosure of internal communications (reg 12(4)(e)).

The exceptions in regulation 12(5) are all based on the concept of 'adverse effect'. A public authority may refuse to disclose information to the extent that its disclosure would adversely affect:

(a) international relations, defence, national security, or public safety (reg 12(5)(a));

(b) the course of justice, the ability of a person to receive a fair trial, or the ability of a public authority to conduct a criminal or disciplinary enquiry (reg 12(5)(b));

(c) intellectual property rights (reg 12(5)(c));

(d) the confidentiality of the proceedings of any public authority (not limited to the authority that received the request (reg 12(5)(d)));

(e) the confidentiality of commercial or industrial information where such confidentiality is provided by law to protect a legitimate economic interest (reg 12(5)(e));

(f) the interests of a person who provided the information, where that person did not and could not have had a legal obligation to disclose it, did not supply it in circumstances such that any public authority is entitled to disclose it apart from the Regulations, and has not consented to its disclosure (reg 12(5)(f)): or

(g) the protection of the environment to which the information relates (reg 12(5)(g)).

---

[160] As it is required to do by reg 9.

It is interesting to note the relative simplicity of the drafting of regulation 12. There is a distinct contrast with the elaborate exemptions in Part II of the FOIA 2000. Regulation 12(5) covers similar ground to Part II of the FOIA 2000, but there are interesting contrasts. One is that there is no equivalent to the provision in section 40, whereby requests for access to the claimant's own personal data are treated as subject access requests under the DPA 1998 rather than as requests under the FOIA 2000. So it would appear that where personal data of the applicant is also environmental information then the request would constitute both a subject access request under the DPA 1998, section 7 and a request for environmental information under regulation 5. The advantage for the applicant of relying on the EIR 2004 as opposed to the DPA 1998 is that the applicant would be able to make use of the enforcement mechanisms under the EIR 2004, which are essentially the same as under the FOIA 2000 (see below), rather than having to go to court to enforce his subject access right.

Regulation 13 deals with requests under the EIR 2004 for personal data of third parties; it does not apply to personal data of which the applicant is the data subject. Disclosure is prohibited in any of the following cases:

(a) disclosure would contravene any of the data protection principles (see regs 13(2)(a)(i) and 13(2)(b));

(b) disclosure would contravene section 10 of the DPA 1998, *and* in all the circumstances of the case the public interest in not disclosing the information outweighs the public interest in disclosing it (reg 13(2)(a)(ii)); or

(c) the information is exempt from the data subject's own subject access right under the DPA 1998 section 7, *and* in all the circumstances of the case the public interest in not disclosing the information outweighs the public interest in disclosing it (reg 13(3)).

Regulation 13 is thus in very similar terms to the DPA 1998, section 40 (so far as that section relates to personal data of third parties rather than of the applicant himself). As will be apparent, some parts of regulation 13 create absolute rather than qualified exemptions to the general duty of disclosure under regulation 5.

The EIR 2004 uses the same enforcement mechanisms as does the Act.[161] A dissatisfied applicant may make representations to a public authority seeking a reconsideration of its decision, if it appears to him that the authority has failed to comply with a requirement of the EIR 2004 in relation to his request: see regulation 11(1). Thereafter the applicant may apply to the Commissioner for a decision as to whether the public authority has complied with the EIR 2004 in relation to his request; and either the public authority or the applicant may appeal to the Information

---

[161] See reg 18 of the EIR 2004, extending those enforcement mechanisms but with certain minor modifications.

Tribunal against the Commissioner's decision. There is no equivalent in the EIR 2004 to the power of executive override under section 53 of the FOIA 2000.

There is a power to charge for making environmental information available under the EIR 2004: see regulation 8(1). By regulation 8(3), the charge:

shall not exceed an amount which the public authority is satisfied is a reasonable amount.

The Tribunal considered this provision in *Markinson v Information Commissioner*.[162] It took the view that in general a guide price for providing photocopied information was 10 pence per sheet, and a public authority that wished to charge a higher figure would need to show specific justification.

An issue that has arisen in the case law is whether the public interest should be considered separately in respect of each exception that is engaged, or whether the public interest should be aggregated as between all relevant exceptions. Take the case where two exceptions are engaged. One approach would be to ask separately, for each exception, whether the public interest in maintaining that exception outweighs the public interest in disclosure. If for each exception the answer is no, then the information must be disclosed. An alternative approach would be to aggregate the public interest as between all relevant exceptions, and to ask whether the aggregated public interest in maintaining those exceptions outweighs the public interest in disclosure. On the latter approach, even if no individual exception viewed in isolation would justify withholding the information, the relevant exceptions considered collectively might have that effect.

In *Ofcom v Information Commissioner*,[163] the Supreme Court made a reference to the European Court of Justice, asking which of these two approaches was a correct application of the Directive. In March 2011 the Advocate General gave her opinion in the case,[164] supporting the aggregation approach. The judgment of the European Court of Justice is awaited.

11.5 CONSUMER INFORMATION AND E-COMMERCE

The EU has undertaken extensive regulation of distance selling to consumers, primarily via the Distance Selling Directive,[165] and has also regulated aspects of electronic commerce via the e-Commerce Directive.[166] Both contain provisions which are relevant to information access. They are discussed in detail in Chapters 2 and 4 and so are not considered further here.

---

[162] EA/2005/0014.

[163] [2010] UKSC 3.

[164] 10 March 2011, opinion of Advocate General Kokott in Case C-71/10.

[165] Directive 97/7/EC of the European Parliament and of the Council of 20 May 1997 on the protection of consumers in respect of distance contracts, OJ L144/19, 4 July 1997.

[166] Directive 2000/31/EC on electronic commerce, OJ L178/1, 17 July 2000.

11.6 LOCAL AUTHORITY RECORDS AND REPORTS

Local authorities are public authorities under the FOIA 2000 and so are subject to the duty to confirm or deny and the duty to disclose, under section 1 of that Act. In addition there are a number of statutory provisions that create rights of access specifically relating to information held by public authorities. Two types of provision are discussed here: (a) provisions relating to access to local government meetings and to the accompanying documentation; and (b) provisions relating to the audit of local authority accounts.

As far as the first group of provisions is concerned, the position is made more confusing as a result of the changes to local authority governance introduced by the Local Government Act 2000 ('LGA 2000'). There are now two regimes existing side by side; and the two may well be relevant to different meetings of the same local authority. The provisions are complex, and the account given below is a brief summary.

One of the two parallel regimes is set out in Part VA of the Local Government Act 1972 ('LGA 1972'). The LGA 1972, Part VA governs full council meetings, and meetings of committees of the council. Under section 100A(1) of the LGA 1972, these meetings must in general be held in public. However, the public *must* be excluded if 'confidential information' is likely to be disclosed in the discussion. For these purposes 'confidential information' means information furnished to the council by a government department upon terms forbidding its disclosure to the public, and information the disclosure of which to the public is prohibited by enactment or court order.[167] The public *may* be excluded by resolution under section 100A(4) in circumstances where 'exempt information' is likely to be disclosed by the discussion. 'Exempt information' is defined in Part I of Schedule 12A to the LGA 1972.

Members of the public have a right of access in advance to copies of agenda and of reports prepared for the meetings,[168] but these papers may be excluded from publication if they relate to items that are not likely to be open to the public.[169] After a meeting has been held there is an entitlement, for a period of six years beginning with the date of the meeting, to have access to the agenda, minutes, and reports,[170] but again there is no entitlement in relation to documents that would disclose exempt information.

---

[167] LGA 1972, s 11A(3)(a).
[168] LGA 1972, s 100B.
[169] LGA 1972, s 100B(2).
[170] LGA 1972, s 100C.

The second regime, in the LGA 2000 and regulations made under that Act,[171] applies to meetings of the executive of a local authority, and committees of the executive. In certain circumstances these meetings must be held in public,[172] including when the meeting is likely to make a 'key decision'.[173] Where a meeting will be held in public then in general the agenda and reports for that meeting must be available for public inspection in advance of the meeting: however, confidential and exempt information[174] and the advice of political advisers or assistants need not be disclosed.[175] There are additional requirements for advance publicity in respect of key decisions.[176] Executive decisions made after a private or public meeting of a decision-making body must be recorded, and the record open to public inspection along with any relevant report and background papers.[177] The same applies to executive decisions made by individual council members, and key decisions made by officers.[178] However, again there is no requirement to disclose confidential or exempt information or the advice of a political adviser or assistant.[179]

These various rights of access are less important now than they were before the right of access under the FOIA 2000 came into force. There are two general issues as to the relationship between these provisions and the FOIA 2000. One arises out of section 21 of the FOIA 2000: information that is available under any of these local government provisions may be exempt from disclosure under the FOIA 2000, section 21 on the ground that it is reasonably accessible to the applicant other than under the FOIA 2000, section 1. The second issue is whether any of the provisions in the local government legislation amounts to a prohibition on disclosure giving rise to an absolute exemption under the FOIA 2000, section 44. Here, it is very important to distinguish between: (a) provisions that *prohibit* disclosure; and (b) provisions that merely set a limit to a duty of disclosure. It is only the first sort of provision that can be a prohibition for the purposes of section 44. Thus, for instance, the mere fact that information comes within Schedule 12A of the LGA 2000 does not mean that it is exempt from disclosure under section 44 of the FOIA 2000: although most information in Schedule 12A is likely to come within one or more of the other exemptions in the FOIA 2000.

As to information relating to the audit of local authorities, this is governed by the Audit Commission Act 1998. Under this Act, a local government elector for the area

---

[171] The Local Authorities (Executive Arrangements) (Access to Information) (England) Regulations 2000 (SI 2000/3272): 'the Access Regulations 2000'.

[172] Access Regulations 2000, reg 7.

[173] As defined by Access Regulations 2000, reg 8. Key decisions are defined by reference to their financial significance or their impact on communities living or working in the local authority's area.

[174] These terms are defined as in the LGA 1972, above.

[175] See regs 11 and 21 of the Access Regulations 2000.

[176] See regs 12–16 of the Access Regulations 2000.

[177] See regs 3 and 5 of the Access Regulations 2000.

[178] See regs 4 and 5 of the Access Regulations 2000.

[179] Access Regulations 2000, reg 21.

of a body subject to audit by the Audit Commission is entitled to inspect and make a copy of any statutory statement of accounts prepared by the body under the Act.[180] At each audit under the Act a 'person interested'[181] may inspect and copy the accounts to be audited, and all books, deeds, contracts, bills, vouchers, and receipts relating to them.[182] There is an exception in relation to personal information regarding local authority staff or other identifiable individuals.[183] The Act gives rise to considerable practical difficulties in modern conditions, when the supporting documentation that is relevant to the audit—the 'books, deeds, contracts', and so forth mentioned in section 15—may be held on computer, and at a wide variety of different sites.

In *Veolia ES Nottinghamshire Ltd v Nottinghamshire CC*,[184] the Court of Appeal considered whether confidential commercial information could be withheld from inspection under section 15. There was no specific exemption in the 1998 Act to protect such information. Nevertheless the court held that section 15 had to be 'read down' so as not to confer a right to inspect or copy confidential commercial information in cases where this would involve a breach of the right to peaceful enjoyment of possessions under Article 1 Protocol 1 of the ECHR.

11.7 MEDICAL RECORDS AND INFORMATION

Medical information may of course fall within the DPA 1998, in which case it will be covered by the right of subject access under section 7 of that Act. Medical records held in computerized form will be accessible under section 7, as will medical records held by a public authority in any recorded form. In addition, the DPA 1998 specifically defines certain 'health records' as being 'data' for the purpose of the Act.[185] A health record for this purpose means any record which consists of information relating to the physical or mental health or condition of an individual, and has been made by or behalf of a health professional in connection with that individual's care: see the DPA 1998, section 68.

The right of access to health records under the Access to Health Records Act 1990 was largely repealed by the DPA 1998, which conferred rights of access on most of the information covered by the earlier Act. However, the 1990 Act remains in force in relation to access to health records by the personal representative of a deceased patient, or by someone who might have a claim arising out of the patient's death: see section 3(1)(f) of the 1990 Act.

---

[180] See Audit Commission Act 1998, s 14.
[181] See *R (on the application of HTV Ltd) v Bristol City Council* [2004] EWHC 1219 (Admin) for a discussion of what is meant by this.
[182] See s 15 of the Act.
[183] See s 15(3) and (3A) of the Act.
[184] [2010] EWCA Civ 1214.
[185] See s 1(1) of the DPA 1998, read in conjunction with s 68 of the Act.

The Access to Medical Reports Act 1988 confers on an individual a right of access to any medical report relating to him and supplied by a medical practitioner for the purposes of employment or insurance.

11.8 ACCESS TO INFORMATION AS A HUMAN RIGHT?

This chapter has referred from time to time to Article 8 of the ECHR as the human rights foundation for a right to privacy, given further effect by the DPA 1998. That raises the question whether there is a comparable human rights foundation for the FOIA 2000 and the other access rights discussed in this chapter. In other words, can access to information be regarded in any sense as being a human right?

Article 10 of the ECHR confers a right to freedom of expression, including:

freedom to hold opinions and to receive and impart information and ideas without interference by public authority.

This applies in the case where one person wishes to communicate information to another, who wishes to receive that information. A well-known example is *Open Door Counselling v Ireland*:[186] an injunction preventing communication between abortion clinics and pregnant women was a breach of the Article 10 rights of both parties.

However, the Strasbourg case law generally does not treat Article 10 as extending to the case where one party wishes to obtain information from another, but that other does not wish to provide the information sought. Thus, in *Leander v Sweden*,[187] where an individual sought to obtain confidential government information in the context of a claim arising out of an unsuccessful job application, the European Court of Human Rights held that Article 10 did not confer any right of access to that information. A similar approach was taken in *Gaskin v UK*:[188] there was no right of access under Article 10 to information about the applicant's childhood.

Decided cases in the UK have taken a similar approach to Article 10. See, for instance, *Persey and Others v Secretary of State for the Environment, Food and Rural Affairs and Others*:[189] the decision that public inquiries into the foot and mouth disease outbreak should be closed, not open, did not give rise to any issues under Article 10. See also *Howard and Another v Secretary of State for Health*,[190] where it was held that Article 10 was not engaged by a decision not to hold public inquiries in relation to allegations about the conduct of two doctors, and

---

[186] (1992) 15 EHRR 244.
[187] (1987) 9 EHRR 433.
[188] (1989) 12 EHRR 36.
[189] [2002] EWHC 371 (Admin).
[190] [2002] EWHC 396 (Admin).

Decision on Application by CNN,[191] where Dame Janet Smith decided that no Article 10 issue was raised by CNN's application to be allowed to film the Shipman inquiry.

Until recently, the only UK case that took a different approach was *R (on the application of Wagstaff) v Secretary of State for Health*,[192] where the court accepted that Article 10 was engaged by the decision that the Shipman inquiry should be held in private. The *Wagstaff* case is disapproved in *Howard* and it is suggested that UK courts are unlikely to follow it.

The Court of Appeal's decision in *Kennedy v Information Commissioner and Charity Commission*[193] may however require the relationship between Article 10 and the FOIA to be reconsidered. The case was about a request under the FOIA by a journalist, seeking disclosure of information relating to a Charity Commission inquiry. The court considered the construction of the absolute exemption in section 32(2), relating to inquiries and arbitrations. One argument made on behalf of the requester was that section 32(2) should be read down in order to be consistent with Article 10. The Court of Appeal remitted the case to the Tribunal for further evidence and argument relating to this point, following which the case was to be restored to the Court of Appeal for further hearing in the light of the Tribunal's report. The case is therefore likely to involve further detailed argument about the extent to which Article 10 confers a positive right to obtain information from a public authority.

On occasion the Strasbourg Court has also held that the right to privacy under Article 8 extends to a positive right to receive information from public authorities that has a bearing on one's private or family life. In *Gaskin*, referred to above, the court considered that Article 8 conferred a right of access to highly personal information about the applicant's early life. In *Guerra v Italy*,[194] the court held that respect for private and family life carried with it a right of access to information that would enable the applicants to assess the risks inherent in continuing to live near a particular factory. Of course, any right of access to information under Article 8 will cover only a small fraction of information held by public authorities, since it is only a limited category of information where a right of access will be ancillary to the applicant's privacy rights.

Regardless of whether the right of access to information held by public authorities falls within the human rights framework, it is undoubtedly an important right. Modern computer technology continuously enhances the ability of public authorities to store, communicate, and manipulate information of all kinds: against this technological background the right of access to public sector information is likely to be of increasing importance.

---

[191] Unreported, 25 October 2001.
[192] [2001] 1 WLR 292.
[193] [2011] EWCA Civ 367.
[194] (1998) 26 EHRR 357.

Part V

ELECTRONIC INFORMATION MISUSE

12

COMPUTER CRIME AND INFORMATION MISUSE

Ian Walden

12.1 INTRODUCTION

The proliferation and integration of computers into every aspect of economic activity and society has inevitably resulted in a growth of criminality involving computers. The computer may constitute the instrument of the crime, such as in murder and fraud; the object of the crime, such as the theft of processor chips; or the subject of the crime, such as hacking and distributing viruses. However, the internet is the environment that currently dominates any discussion of computers and their usage and, as the 'network of networks', facilitates connectivity between computers across the world. As such, computers per se are not the sole object of concern, rather computers connected to other computers, 'cybercrime'. This chapter is concerned with how the criminal law has adapted and been amended to address some of the issues that have emerged from the rise of computers and cybercrime.

The first half of the chapter considers some of the offences under English law that are relevant to crimes involving the use of computers. Such offences can generally be distinguished into three categories. The first category is traditional types of criminal offence that may be committed using computers as the instrument of the crime, referred to as 'computer-related crime', such as fraud. The second category concerns 'content-related crimes', where computers and networks are the instrument, but the content itself is illegal, such as infringing intellectual property and certain forms of pornography. The third category is offences that have been established specifically to address activities that attack the integrity, confidentiality, and availability of computer and communications systems, such as viruses and other malware; 'computer integrity crimes'. It is this final category that is most often considered as computer crime in the public's mind, and will be the primary focus of this chapter.[1]

The second half of the chapter will examine issues relating to the prosecution of perpetrators of computer crime. To date, few cases have been brought before the courts, relative to the estimated incidence of such crime. Such paucity is generally seen as being due to a range of factors. First, there is a lack of reporting by victims, as commercial organizations avoid adverse publicity. Secondly, there continues to be a shortage of resource, expertise, and experience among law enforcement and prosecuting authorities in dealing with such criminality. Thirdly, the transnational nature of computer crime and the associated jurisdictional problems contribute to the complexity of investigating and prosecuting offenders. Finally, networked computers create significant forensic challenges to law enforcement agencies ('LEAs') when obtaining evidence and subsequently presenting it before the courts.

12.2 COMPUTER-RELATED OFFENCES

It is obvious that computers may play a part in the commission of nearly every form of criminal activity, from fraud to murder. This section will not review the broad range of English criminal law, but will focus on those areas of existing law that have given rise to particular problems where computers are involved, either because the legislation was drafted in an era before such technology was envisaged, or because statutory drafting has failed to be robust enough to appropriately address computer and communications technology.

12.2.1 Fraud

The range of fraudulent activity is not substantially altered by the use of computers, although they may facilitate certain forms, such as securities fraud. Computers may be involved in any aspect of the fraudulent process, from altering information being

---

[1] For a more detailed treatment of the topics addressed in this chapter, see I Walden, *Computer Crimes and Digital Investigations* (Oxford: Oxford University Press, 2007).

input into a system, manipulating the operation of programs processing the information, to altering the output. The computer is simply a modern tool by which the defendant's actions have been carried out.

In the majority of cases involving computer-related fraud, existing legislation has been an adequate instrument under which to prosecute. However, as with other areas of legislation, traditional statutory terminology can give rise to problems of application not anticipated before computers appeared. In certain jurisdictions, for example, it is a requirement to show that a 'person has been deceived' for a fraud to be deemed to have occurred.

Under English law, section 15 of the Theft Act 1968 stated:

A person who by any deception dishonestly obtains property belonging to another, with the intention of permanently depriving the other of it . . .

(4) For purposes of this section 'deception' means any deception (whether deliberate or reckless) by words or conduct as to fact or as to law, including a deception as to the present intentions of the person using the deception or any other person.

Case law further interpreted 'deception' to mean 'to induce a man to believe a thing which is false, and which the person practising the deceit knows or believes to be false'.[2] If an innocent person was involved at some moment in a fraud, such as the processing of computer output, there did not appear to be any problem with a prosecution under section 15,[3] but where the process was completely automated, the courts indicated that an offence may not be deemed to have taken place.[4] Where a machine has been deceived to obtain property, then the offence of theft was also generally applicable.[5] However, where a service was obtained from a machine, such as the use of false credit card details during an online registration process, the absence of 'deception' proved fatal to the founding of a criminal prosecution.

To address this lacuna, the Law Commission recommended that a new offence related to theft should be established, rather than extend the concept of 'deception' to include machines.[6] This was implemented through the Fraud Act 2006, which repeals the 'deception' offences under the 1968 Act and replaces them with three new fraud offences:

(a) fraud by false representation;

(b) fraud by failing to disclose information; and

(c) fraud by abuse of position (ss 2–4).

---

[2] In the words of Buckley J in *Re London and Globe Finance Corp Ltd* [1903] 1 Ch 728 at 732.
[3] eg, *Thompson* [1984] 3 All ER 565.
[4] See *Clayman*, Times Law Reports, 1 July 1972. See also *R v Moritz*, unreported 17–19 June 1981, Acton Crown Court.
[5] Theft Act 1978, s 1.
[6] Report No 276, *Fraud* (Cm 5569, 2002) at Part VIII.

In each case, both dishonesty[7] and intention to make gain or cause loss must be present, although an actual gain or loss does not need to be shown. For the offence of fraud by misrepresentation, such misrepresentation could be made to a machine as well as a person:

a representation may be regarded as made if it (or anything implying it) is submitted in any form to any system or device designed to receive, convey or respond to communications (with or without human intervention). (s 2(5))

The need to obtain property 'belonging to another' in the commission of a fraud also gave rise to a lacuna in English law in the House of Lords decision in *Preddy*.[8] The court acquitted the defendants of mortgage fraud on the basis that the process of altering the accounting data recorded in the accounts of the lending institution and the mortgagor, by the amount representing the loan, did not constitute the obtaining of property 'belonging to another'. Instead, the court characterized the process as one where property, as a chose in action, is extinguished in one place and a different chose in action is created in another place. This decision required the government to push through emergency legislation creating an appropriate offence; although subsequently replaced by the Fraud Act 2006. However, *Preddy* illustrates the types of problem raised when trying to apply traditional criminal concepts to acts involving intangible computer data.

While, prior to the Fraud Act 2006, the offence of fraud faced problems when computers were involved, the process of reform did not involve the inclusion of any express provisions referring to such technologies. The current law of fraud can therefore be seen as technology neutral, remedying the previous regime, which discriminated against computer-based fraud. By contrast, international legal instruments in the field of computer and cybercrime have chosen to recommend specific fraud offences in respect of computers. The Council of Europe Convention on Cybercrime, for example, has formulated an offence of computer-related fraud in the following terms:

Each Party shall adopt such legislative and other measures as may be necessary to establish as criminal offences under its domestic law, when committed intentionally and without right, the causing of a loss of property to another by:

a. any input, alteration, deletion or suppression of computer data,

b. any interference with the functioning of a computer system,

with fraudulent or dishonest intent of procuring, without right, an economic benefit for oneself or for another.[9]

---

[7] As defined in *Ghosh* [1982] QB 1053.
[8] [1996] 3 All ER 481.
[9] European Treaty Series No 185, 8. See further, section 12.5.1 below.

As with the Fraud Act 2006, this formulation focuses on the intent of the perpetrator rather than the mind of the victim, as required under the concept of 'deception'. In (a) it attempts to detail the different means by which data may be manipulated. The possibilities of hardware manipulations are covered by (b).[10] Jurisdictions may have differing conceptions of 'property', although it was conceived as a 'broad notion', including 'intangibles with an economic value'.[11] However, English law remains somewhat hostile to the treatment of information as property.

One aspect of fraud which has received considerable publicity over recent years has been the phenomenon of so-called 'identity theft', where a person's identification[12] details are obtained through various surreptitious methods, from rifling through the contents of household dustbins to 'phishing', where emails are sent to individuals falsely claiming to originate from their financial institutions and asking them to re-register their account details at a replica website, or contain a virus which surreptitiously obtains and discloses an individual's confidential details. However achieved, the objective is to obtain details about a person in order to enable a fraudulent operation to be carried out, either using the person's existing privileges or creating new privileges under that person's identity. Identity theft can therefore be viewed as a form of preliminary conduct in the course of committing fraud; although obviously other criminal acts may be the ultimate objective.

The vulnerability of personal information in an internet environment and the growth of 'identity theft', has led to calls for specific legislative measures to be adopted. In the USA, for example, the Identity Theft and Assumption Deterrence Act of 1998[13] establishes a range of offences related to the abuse of identification documents. Under current English criminal law, there are a range of potentially applicable offences being committed depending on the form of 'identity theft' carried out. The term 'identity theft' is generally a misnomer, since information itself is not capable of being stolen.[14] Theft would only be applicable where the identification details are contained in some tangible property, such as a payment card, which is also taken. Forgery may be applicable, where the identification is incorporated into some form of 'instrument'.[15] The new offences under the Fraud Act 2006 should also be applicable in most circumstances, especially fraud by false representation.

---

[10] Explanatory Report at para 87.

[11] Ibid para 88.

[12] The details involved may not always identify a person (ie, who you are); rather they may authenti-cate (ie, are you genuine) or authorize (ie, what you can do) a person without necessarily identifying a specific individual.

[13] 18 USC § 1028.

[14] See section 12.2.2 below.

[15] See section 12.2.3 below.

12.2.2 Theft of information

Industrial espionage is a feature of modern business, as processes and know-how have become increasingly valuable assets. Today, such activities will virtually always involve the use of computers, whether as a means of accessing information, through hacking or electronic eavesdropping,[16] or as a tool for removing the appropriated information, such as a USB memory stick. Espionage may be carried out by competitors or at a state level. It may be achieved with the complicity of someone within the victim organization, with rights to possess the information; or by external persons acting illegally either directly for themselves, or as a commercial service for others.

An example of cyber-industrial espionage is that concerning Mr and Mrs Haephrati, Israeli and German citizens operating out of the UK. In May 2005, in a coordinated operation, the Haephratis and a large number of major businessmen in Israel were arrested on charges of industrial espionage, carried out against competing Israeli businesses.[17] The Haephratis were accused of developing and deploying a 'Trojan Horse' virus designed to penetrate the computer systems of the victim company and provide covert access to the systems for private investigators hired to investigate business rivals. The virus was deployed either as an attachment to an email or on a disk sent to the victim that appeared to contain a legitimate business proposal.[18] The illicitly obtained documents were stored on FTP servers located in Israel and the USA. The Haephratis were subsequently extradited to Israel, entered into plea-bargain agreements with the authorities, and received reduced custodial sentences in return for providing evidence against the private investigators.[19]

Under English law, the primary means for protecting trade secrets is under the equitable remedy for breach of confidence. English criminal law is hostile to the treatment of information per se as 'property'. In the leading case, *Oxford v Moss*,[20] a student took a forthcoming examination paper from a lecturer's desk drawer, photocopied it, and returned the original. The High Court when considering the appeal addressed two questions: first, was the confidential information a form of 'intangible property', as defined under the Theft Act 1968, section 4(1):

'Property' includes money and all other property real or personal, including things in action and other intangible property.

Secondly, if the information was property, had the owner been permanently deprived of it? The court held that the offence of theft had not been committed because the

---

[16] Where emissions from computer VDU screen are surreptitiously received and reconstituted for viewing on external equipment.

[17] 'Israel's biggest industrial espionage case', *The Guardian*, 31 May 2005.

[18] 'Court remands top Israeli execs in industrial espionage affair', Financial Cryptography, 31 May 2005, available at <http://financialcryptography.com> (accessed 10 August 2011).

[19] 'Israel jails spyware-for-hire couple', *The Register*, 27 March 2006.

[20] [1979] 68 Cr App R 183.

information did not constitute 'property' under the Theft Act 1968.[21] This decision has not been subsequently re-examined, although it has since been held that export quotas[22] and an electronic funds transfer[23] were forms of 'intangible property', which suggests that *Oxford v Moss* should not be applied too broadly. Although the court was not required to decide the second question, Justice Wein noted *obiter* that the victim had not been permanently deprived of the asset, a copy had simply been taken. However, in a subsequent English court decision, it has been held that a person can be 'permanently deprived' of something where the value of an object has been significantly affected.[24]

The issue of granting commercial information the protection of the criminal law has been the subject of a Law Commission consultation paper, which proposed the establishment of an offence of the unauthorized use or disclosure of a trade secret.[25] To commit an offence, a person would have to use or disclose the trade secret, knowing both that the information is a trade secret belonging to another; and that he does not have the consent of the owner to use or disclose it.[26] Such an offence would place the UK in a similar position to that existing in other industrialized countries. However, to date, the Law Commission's initiative has not progressed.

12.2.3 Forgery

We use a broad range of documentation in our daily lives, from £20 notes to driving licences and insurance certificates. Creating forged versions of these documents is an obvious area of crime that has benefited from developments in computer technology. Most genuine documents are now created using computers, therefore computers provide the opportunity to amend them in an often-undetectable manner. Current software-based digital manipulation products provide a powerful tool for even the most amateur of forgers.[27]

In a cyberspace environment, a perpetrator is either going to create new privileges, on the basis of false credentials, or exploit existing privileges, through the use of information obtained from a range of sources. Such information may come from the victim themselves, through the use of 'social engineering' techniques, which rely on human interaction to trick people into disclosing information that helps to overcome data security mechanisms and procedures. Alternatively, a person may hack into the customer database of an electronic commerce website to obtain

---

[21] See generally RG Hammond, 'Theft of Information' (1984) 100 LQR 252–64.

[22] *Attorney-General of Hong Kong v Nai-Keung* (1988) 86 Cr App R 174.

[23] *Crick, The Times*, 18 August 1993.

[24] *Lloyd* (1985) 2 All ER 661.

[25] Law Commission, *Legislating the Criminal Code: Misuse of Trade Secrets* (Law Com No 150, 1997).

[26] Consultation Paper, at paras 5.3 and 5.8.

[27] eg, Adobe® Photoshop® .

credit card details and other identity data. Both acts may constitute an offence of forgery under the Forgery and Counterfeiting Act 1981.

Under the Forgery and Counterfeiting Act 1981, section 1 states:

A person is guilty of forgery if he makes a false instrument with the intention that he or another shall use it to induce somebody to accept it as genuine.

As relatively recent legislation, one could expect the Act to avoid the interpretative issues raised by the use of computer technology in respect of fraud. However, the leading English case concerning the use of computers to commit forgery, *R v Gold, Schifreen*,[28] illustrates the problems faced by the statutory draftsman.

In *Gold*, the defendants gained unauthorized access to BT's Prestel service and discovered the password codes of various private email accounts, including the Duke of Edinburgh's. The defendants were prosecuted under the 1981 Act for creating a 'false instrument', by entering customer authorization codes to access the system. The Act defines an 'instrument' seemingly broadly to include 'any disc, tape, sound track or other device on or in which information is recorded or stored by mechanical, electronic or other means' (s 8(1)(d)). In addition, the meaning of 'induce' expressly avoids the need for a real person, as required in respect of 'deception':

. . . references to inducing somebody to accept a false instrument as genuine . . . include references to inducing a machine to respond. (s 10(3))

However, the House of Lords held that the electronic signals that comprised the identification codes could not be considered tangible in the sense that a disk or tape were. It also held that the signals were present in the system for such a fleeting moment, that they could not be considered to have been 'recorded or stored':

The words 'recorded' and 'stored' are words in common use which should be given their ordinary and natural meaning. In my opinion both words . . . connote the preservation of the thing which is the subject matter of them for an appreciable time with the object of subsequent retrieval and recovery.[29]

In respect of the issue of whether someone had been 'induced', the Court of Appeal in *Gold* had recognized that the prosecution's case could be rendered absurd because the machine being induced was also claimed to be the false instrument.[30]

The Court of Appeal was also highly critical of the application of the Act to such a set of circumstances:

---

[28] [1988] 2 All ER 186.
[29] Lord Brandon at 192c.
[30] [1997] 3 WLR 803, Lord Lane CJ at 809G. This question was not considered by the House of Lords.

The Procrustean attempt to force these facts into the language of an Act not designed to fit them produced difficulties for both judge and jury which we would not wish to see repeated.[31]

Such explicit recognition by the judiciary of the need to draft new legislation, rather than try to extend traditional terminology to fit computer technology, lent significant pressure to the calls for reform of the criminal law.

12.3 CONTENT-RELATED OFFENCES

Classifying certain types of subject matter as criminally illegal can be a highly contentious matter, raising complex definitional issues, questions of causation, and human rights concerns, specifically rights to privacy and freedom of expression. Content-related crimes also raise difficult enforcement issues, in terms of the technical issues of managing content and the foreign sourcing of such material. Yet despite the complexities surrounding content regulation, in recent years we have witnessed substantial policy and legislative activity in the area, both in terms of expanding the subject matter considered illegal,[32] and raising the tariff applicable to such offences.[33]

If any topic is unequivocally associated in the minds of politicians, the media, and the public with the 'dark side' of the internet, it is that of child pornography or child abuse images. The internet has facilitated the supply of this form of illegal content to such an extent that it is now considered a multi-billion dollar industry.[34] While at the same time, cyberspace engenders broader child protection concerns about the harms children can suffer from the content and contact available over the internet.[35] As a consequence, child protection is currently at the forefront of government policy on cybercrime.

12.3.1 Child pornography

The two principal statutory provisions under UK law in respect of child porno-graphic images are in relation to the supply of such images, under the Protection of Children Act 1978 ('POCA 1978'), and the possession of such images, under the

---

[31] Ibid 809H. Such sentiment was echoed by Lord Brandon in the House of Lords: [1988] 2 All ER 186 at 192d.

[32] eg, Terrorism Act 2006, s 1, 'Encouragement of terrorism'.

[33] eg, Trade Marks (Offences and Enforcement) Act 2002 raised the tariff for criminal copyright infringement from two to ten years.

[34] National Center for Missing and Exploited Children, Press Release: 'Financial and Internet Industries to combat Internet child pornography', 15 March 2006, available at <http://www.missingkids. com> (accessed 10 August 2011).

[35] See, generally, A Millwood Hargrave and S Livingstone, *Harm and Offence in Media Content* (Kirkland, WA: Intellect, 2006).

Criminal Justice Act 1988, section 160. As with computer-related offences, English law has sometimes struggled adequately to address computer-based activities and the unique features of computer-generated pornography. As a result, these laws have required on-going amendment or supplementation in an attempt to address the changing nature of activities engaged in by paedophiles. In 1994, the concept of photographic images was extended to include 'pseudo-photographs', created through the use of digital images;[36] in 2008, the concept of 'tracing' photographs or pseudo-photographs was included;[37] while in 2009, a new offence relating to non-photographic images was adopted, designed to capture certain types of computer-generated images, including cartoons.[38]

In addition, the courts have been required to consider to what extent the types of activities that occur across networks, such as the internet, are adequately covered by existing legislation. In *R v Fellows and Arnold*,[39] the court considered whether the legislation would enable computer data to be considered a 'copy of an indecent photograph' and whether making images available for downloading from a website constituted material being 'distributed or shown'. The court held that the statutory wording was drafted in sufficiently wide terms to encompass the use of computer technology.

While the *actus reus* of the offences of supplying and possessing child abuse images are clearly specified, the *mens rea* component was not. In *Atkins & Goodland v Director of Public Prosecutions*,[40] the court was required to address a situation where the offending images, upon which the prosecution was based, were contained in the cache memory of the defendant's machine. Such copies are generally created and stored automatically by the browser software, used to access the internet, for reasons of efficiency. Expert evidence was submitted which indicated that most computer users are unaware of the operation of the cache memory feature on their machines.

Two issues for the court, therefore, were whether the cache copies could be said to have been 'made' under the POCA 1978, section 1(1)(a) or 'possessed' under the Criminal Justice Act 1988, section 160(1). The prosecution could not prove that the defendant was aware of the cache copies and therefore liability for 'making' or 'possession' could only be found if the offences were construed as imposing strict liability. The court held that knowledge was required and the appeal succeeded on this point. If the prosecution could have proved that the defendant was aware of the cache memory, perhaps by showing that the individual had altered the default settings for the caching function, then the conviction may have been upheld.

---

[36] POCA 1978, s 1(1), amended by Criminal Justice and Public Order Act 1994, s 84.
[37] POCA 1978, s 4(4), inserted by the Criminal Justice and Immigration Act 2008, s 69.
[38] Coroners and Justice Act 2009, ss 62–68.
[39] [1997] 2 All ER 548.
[40] [2000] 2 All ER 425.

While in *Atkins* the courts accepted that subjective knowledge was required for the offence of 'possession' to be made out, in *Warwick*,[41] the appeal court was required to further consider what comprises 'possession' in a computer environment. The defendant had been charged with two counts of possession in respect of some 3,000 still images and 40 movie files. However, for the period in respect of which the charge related, it was agreed that the images and files had been either placed in the operating system's 'recycle bin' and the bin emptied; were viewable only in thumbnail format;[42] or were only present in the computer cache. The court held that 'if a person cannot retrieve or gain access to an image, in our view he no longer has custody or control of it', and therefore cannot be said to be in possession for the purposes of the section 160 offence (at para 21). Whether in a particular set of circumstances a defendant could be found to remain in control of deleted files, due to his level of technical skill and ability, will be a matter for the jury to decide in each case.

In *Westgarth Smith and Jayson*,[43] a similar argument to *Atkins* was advanced in respect of the receipt of an email with an attachment containing a pornographic image. Here Smith's counsel argued that the 'making' involved in the receipt of an unsolicited email was similar to that of the cache copy in *Atkins*. The court accepted this assertion in general terms, but held that this was not the situation before the court. In *Jayson*, the prosecution was able to prove that the defendant was aware of the caching function within his browser software. However, the court also held that the mere 'act of voluntarily downloading an indecent image from a web page on to a computer screen is an act of making',[44] whether or not there was an intention to store the images for subsequent retrieval.

While *Jayson* addressed in part the *Atkins* problem of reliance on technical ignorance as a defence, it did so at the cost of treating the most basic electronic act in a cyberspace environment, downloading information, as a form of 'making'. The POCA 1978 offences are addressed at those that supply child pornography, criminalizing the taking, making, distribution, showing, or publishing of an advertisement. By contrast, the Criminal Justice Act is concerned with the demand for such material, criminalizing mere possession. While the two are clearly interrelated, demand creates supply, Parliament has perceived the latter, possession, to be of a lesser seriousness, attracting a substantially lower tariff. However, under *Jayson*, the process of obtaining possession is itself being viewed as an act of supply. Prosecutors have also charged those involved with purchasing such material with incitement to supply, again blurring the line between supply and possession.[45]

---

[41] [2006] EWCA Crim 560.
[42] Comprising a subset of the image, not the full image itself; this would be stored as a separate file elsewhere, but had been deleted.
[43] [2002] EWCA Crim 683.
[44] Ibid, comment by Dyson LJ at para 33.
[45] eg, *Goldman* [2001] EWCA Crim 1684.

To address the drift from possession to production represented by *Jayson*, in May 2002 the Sentencing Advisory Panel issued sentencing guidelines in respect of child pornography.[46] In the guidelines, it stated:

23 ... the downloading of indecent images onto a computer for personal use should be treated, for sentencing purposes, as equivalent to possession ... Our reason for this was that 'making' in the sense of making or taking an original indecent film or photograph of a child is clearly a more serious matter than downloading an image from the internet, which is more akin to buying a pornographic magazine from a shop or mail order service.

However, as it currently stands, the intention of Parliament to distinguish between production and possession is being subverted through judicial interpretation and prosecution charging policy. However abhorrent such material is, it would seem more appropriate to address such issues through legislative amendment, rather than through sentencing policy and the discretion of the judiciary.

12.4 COMPUTER INTEGRITY OFFENCES

When considering computer crime, most people think in terms of 'hacking' into systems and the distribution of 'viruses'. Such activities target the computers themselves, rather than use them as a tool to facilitate other crimes. With the spread of computerization and our consequential dependency, the adequacy of criminal law to deter such activities has had to be addressed by policymakers and legislators. In most jurisdictions, the application of traditional criminal law is often uncertain or completely inappropriate. As such, *sui generis* legislation has been adopted to tackle the threat to the security of computer systems, their integrity, confidentiality, and availability.

In the UK, the Computer Misuse Act 1990 became law on 29 August 1990. The direct origins of the Act are found in the Law Commission report on 'Computer Misuse',[47] published in October 1989; additionally, the Scottish and English Law Commission had published previous reports and working papers,[48] and a Private Member's Bill on the topic had been introduced during the previous parliamentary session. In December 1989, Michael Colvin MP introduced a Private Member's Bill, with the tacit support of the government, closely following the English Law Commission's recommendations.

The 1990 Act introduced three new categories of offence: unauthorized access to computer material, unauthorized access with intent to commit a further offence, and

---

[46] <http://www.scribd.com/doc/34316014/Advice-Child-Pornography> (accessed 10 August 2011).
[47] Law Commission, *Computer Misuse* (Law Com No 186, Cm 819, 1989).
[48] Scottish Law Commission, *Report on Computer Crime* (Cm 174, 1987) and Law Commission, *Computer Misuse* (Law Com No 186, Cm 819, 1988) ('Report 186').

unauthorized modification. The Act has subsequently been amended, most recently and substantially, by the Police and Justice Act 2006.

12.4.1 Unauthorized access

The section 1 offence of unauthorized access is the basic 'hacking' or 'cracking' offence. Commission of the offence requires the *actus reus* of causing 'a computer to perform any function'. Some form of interaction with the computer is required, but actual access does not need to be achieved. This broad formulation means that simply turning on a computer could constitute the necessary act.[49]

The Act also does not define a 'computer', therefore potentially extending its scope to everyday domestic appliances and cars that incorporate computer technology. The Law Commission found general support for the view that to attempt such a definition would be 'so complex, in an endeavour to be all-embracing, that they are likely to produce extensive argument'.[50] This position exists in other jurisdictions, such as France and Germany; but in the USA the following definition is used:

. . . an electronic, magnetic, optical, electrochemical, or other high speed data processing device performing logical, arithmetic, or storage functions, and includes any data storage facility or communications facility directly related to or operating in conjunction with such device.[51]

The *mens rea* of the section 1 offence comprises two elements. First, there must be 'intent to secure access to any program or data held in any computer'. This was amended in 2006 also to encompass acts which 'enable any such access';[52] which criminalizes those that go beyond the mere provision of 'hacking' tools to others, an offence under the new section 3A, and interfere, directly or indirectly, with the target computer, such as disabling an access control mechanism without then attempting to penetrate the system to access programs or data, but leaving it for other persons, or for entry at some later date.[53] Secondly, the person must know at the time that he commits the *actus reus* that the access he intends to secure is unauthorized. The intent does not have to be directed at any particular program, data, or computer (s 1(2)).

The first prosecution under the new Act addressed the nature of the *actus reus* under section 1. In *R v Sean Cropp*,[54] the defendant returned to the premises of his former employer to purchase certain equipment. At some point when the sales

---

[49] s 17(1) broadly defines 'function' to include alterations or erasure, copying or moving data, using it or producing output from the computer.
[50] Report 186, para 3.39.
[51] 18 USC § 1030(e)(1).
[52] Inserted by the Police and Justice Act 2006, s 35(2).
[53] See statement of Lord Bassam, Home Officer Minister, Hansard, HL col 604 (11 July 2006).
[54] Snaresbrook Crown Court, 4 July 1991.

assistant was not looking, the defendant was alleged to have keyed in certain commands to the computerized till granting himself a substantial discount. During the trial, the judge accepted the submission of defence counsel that section 1(1)(a) required 'that a second computer must be involved'. He believed that if Parliament had intended the offence to extend to situations where unauthorized access took place on a single machine, then section 1(1)(a) would have been drafted as 'causing a computer to perform any function with intent to secure access to any program or data held in *that or any other computer'*.

Such an interpretation would have seriously limited the scope of the Act, especially since a large proportion of instances of hacking are those carried out by persons within the victim organization.[55] The critical nature of this distinction led the Attorney General to take the rarely invoked procedure of referring the decision to the Court of Appeal. The Court of Appeal subsequently rejected the lower court's interpretation, stating that the 'plain and natural meaning is clear'.[56] It is interesting to note, however, that the Council of Europe Convention offence of 'illegal access' does permit Member States to limit the offence to 'exclude the situation where a person physically accesses a stand-alone computer without any use of another computer system'.[57]

The section 1 offence was originally only punishable on summary conviction by a fine of up to £2,000 or six months in jail; however, the tariff has since been revised and on indictment attracts a maximum two-year prison term (s 1(3)(c)).[58] A person can be found guilty of the basic section 1 offence where a jury could not find him guilty of an indictment under section 2 or section 3 (s 12). In addition, a person who 'aids, abets, counsels or procures' the commission of the offence may attract secondary liability,[59] such as those who distribute passwords and other authorization codes via bulletin boards.[60]

In May 1993, the first classic 'hackers' were given six-month jail sentences for conspiracy to commit offences under section 1 and section 3 of the Computer Misuse Act 1990.[61] The defendants' activities were said to have caused damage, valued at £123,000, to computer systems ranging from the Polytechnic of Central London to NASA. In passing sentence the judge said:

There may be people out there who consider hacking to be harmless, but hacking is not harmless. Computers now form a central role in our lives, containing personal details . . . It is

---

[55] See Audit Commission survey, 'ICT fraud and abuse 2004', available at <http://www.auditcommission.gov.uk> (accessed 10 August 2011).

[56] *Attorney-General's Reference (No 1 of 1991)* [1992] 3 WLR 432 at 437F.

[57] Explanatory Report to the Convention, para 50.

[58] Amended by the Police and Justice Act 2006, s 40.

[59] Accessories and Abettors Act 1861, s 8 (for indictable offences) and the Magistrates' Courts Act 1980, s 44(1) (for summary offences).

[60] See also section 12.4.3 below.

[61] *R v Strickland, R v Woods* (Southwark Crown Court, March 1993).

essential that the integrity of those systems should be protected and hacking puts that integrity in jeopardy.

Such judicial sentiment is critical if the Act is to have a significant deterrent effect.

However, the jury acquitted one of the co-defendants in the same case, Bedworth, because defence counsel successfully argued that the necessary *mens rea* for a charge of conspiracy was absent because the defendant was an 'obsessive' hacker. This case was widely publicized and was seen by many as a potential 'hacker's charter'.[62] However, the decision seems to have arisen from a mistaken choice by the prosecuting authorities to pursue an action for conspiracy, rather than a charge under the Computer Misuse Act.

The issue of prosecution for the inchoate offence of incitement with others to commit an offence[63] arose in respect of the publication of the 'Hackers Handbook', a popular guide to current developments in this area. Following the 1990 Act coming into force, the publishers apparently decided to withdraw the book from circulation to avoid potential legal action.[64]

12.4.1.1 *Intent to commit a further offence*

The section 2 offence involves the commission of a section 1 offence together with the intent to commit, or facilitate the commission, of a further offence. A relevant further offence is one for which the sentence is fixed by law, for example life imprisonment for murder, or where imprisonment may be for a term of five years or more, for example a computer fraud.[65] The access and the further offence do not have to be intended to be carried out at the same time (s 2(3)), and it also does not matter if the further offence was in fact impossible (s 2(4)). Upon conviction, a person could be sentenced to imprisonment for up to a five-year term (s 2(5)).

The following cases illustrate a range of situations that have arisen under the section 2 offence:

(a) In *Pearlstone*,[66] an ex-employee used his former company's telephone account and another subscriber's account to defraud the computer-administered telephone system and place calls to the USA.

(b) In *Borg*,[67] an investment company analyst was accused of setting-up dummy accounts within a 'live' fund management system. The alleged 'further offence' was expected to be fraudulent transfers into the dummy accounts.

---

[62] See, eg, 'Bedworth case puts law on trial', *Computing*, 25 March 1993, 7.

[63] Criminal Law Act 1977, s 1.

[64] See E Dumbill, 'Computer Misuse Act 1990—Recent Developments' (1992) 8(4) Computer Law and Practice 107. See also *R v Maxwell-King*, Times Law Reports (2 January 2001).

[65] ie, for a first offender at 21 or over.

[66] Bow Street Magistrates' Court, April 1991.

[67] Snaresbrook Crown Court, March 1993.

(c) In *Farquharson*,[68] the defendant was prosecuted for obtaining mobile telephone numbers and codes necessary to produce cloned telephones. The computer system containing this information was actually accessed by his co-defendant, Ms Pearce, an employee of the mobile telephone company, who was charged with a section 1 offence. Farquharson was found to have committed the 'unauthorized access' required for the section 2 offence even though he never touched the computer himself, but had simply asked Pearce to access the information.

(d) In *Grey*,[69] the defendant exploited a weakness in electronic commerce sites using Microsoft's Internet Information Server application to access customer databases and obtain the credit card and other personal details of at least 5,400 customers, which were then published on the internet; as well as purchasing various goods and services.

Prosecutions under section 2 are likely to be relatively infrequent, since in many cases prosecutors will pursue a prosecution for the further offence rather than the unauthorized access, even though the individual may be initially charged with the section 2 offence. In addition, the perpetrator's act of unauthorized access may be sufficient to found a prosecution for an attempt to commit the further offence.[70]

12.4.1.2 *Intent and authorization*
During passage of the Computer Misuse Bill, an attempt was made to add a provision whereby hackers would be able to offer a defence if computer users had not implemented security measures.[71] A similar approach has been adopted in other jurisdictions, where the presence of security measures is a necessary element of the offence[72] and, indeed, the Convention on Cybercrime states that a party 'may require that the offence be committed by infringing security measures' (Art 2). Whilst the Bill amendment was rejected, the issue of the existence of security measures does arise in the context of establishing whether access was 'unauthorized'.

Under the Act, access is considered to be unauthorized access if:

(a) he is not himself entitled to control access of the kind in question to the program or data; and

---

[68] Croydon Magistrates' Court, 9 December 1993.

[69] Swansea Crown Court, 6 July 2001.

[70] See Criminal Attempts Act 1981, s 1: 'If, with intent to commit an offence to which this s applies, a person does an act which is more than merely preparatory to the commission of the offence, he is guilty of attempting to commit the offence'. This provision was amended by the Computer Misuse Act 1990, s 7(3).

[71] See Standing Committee C, 14 March 1990. The following amendment was proposed by Harry Cohen MP: 'For the purposes of this section, it shall be a defence to prove that such care as is in all the circumstances, was reasonably required to prevent the access or intended access in question was not taken'.

[72] eg, Norwegian Penal Code, s 145, refers to persons 'breaking security measures to gain access to data/programs'.

(b) he does not have consent to access by him of the kind in question to the program or data from any person who is so entitled. (s 17(5))

Where the accused is external to the victim's organization, showing knowledge of an absence of entitlement or consent is not generally an issue. However, where the accused is an employee of the organization, the burden is upon the prosecution to show that the accused knew that 'access of the kind in question' was unauthorized, rather than a misuse of express or implied rights of access, for example an accounts clerk entering false expenses claims. As noted by the Law Commission:

An employee should only be guilty of an offence if his employer has clearly defined the limits of the employee's authority to access a program or data.[73]

The interpretation of section 17(5) was first considered in detail in *DPP v Bignell*.[74] The case concerned two serving police officers who had accessed the Police National Computer ('PNC'), via an operator, for personal purposes. They were charged with offences under section 1 of the Computer Misuse Act and convicted in the magistrates' court. They successfully appealed to the Crown Court against their conviction, and this decision was the subject of a further appeal before the Divisional Court, which was dismissed.

The central issue addressed to the court was whether a person authorized to access a computer system for a particular purpose (eg, policing) can commit a section 1 offence by using such authorized access for an unauthorized purpose (eg, personal). The Crown Court asserted that the Computer Misuse Act was primarily concerned 'to protect the integrity of computer systems rather than the integrity of the information stored on the computers', therefore such unauthorized usage was not caught by the Act. The Divisional Court upheld this view. First, Justice Astill stated that the phrase in section 17(5)(a), 'access of the kind in question', was referring to the types of access detailed in section 17(2): alteration, erasure, copying, moving, using, and obtaining output. Secondly, the phrase 'control access' was referring to the authority granted to the police officers to access the PNC. He concluded that this did not create a lacuna in the law as the Data Protection Act 1984 ('DPA 1984') contained appropriate offences in relation to the use of personal data for unauthorized purposes.[75]

The decision attracted significant criticism and, as with *Sean Cropp*, was seen as significantly limiting the scope of the Act.[76] However, aspects of the decision were re-examined by the House of Lords in *R v Bow Street Magistrates' Court and Allison (AP), ex p US Government*.[77] The case concerned an extradition request by

---

[73] Report 186, para 3.37.
[74] [1998] 1 Cr App R 1.
[75] DPA 1984, s 5(6).
[76] eg, D Bainbridge, 'Cannot Employees Also Be Hackers?' (1987) 13(5) Computer Law and Security Report 352–4
[77] [1999] 3 WLR 620, [1999] 4 All ER 1.

the US Government of an individual accused in a fraud involving an employee of American Express who was able to use her access to the computer system to obtain personal identification numbers to encode forged credit cards. As in *Bignell*, defence counsel argued that a section 1 offence had not been committed since the employee was authorized to access the relevant computer system. The House of Lords, whilst agreeing with the decision in *Bignell*, rejected the subsequent interpretation of section 17(5) made by Justice Astill.[78]

On the first issue, 'access of the kind in question', Lord Hobhouse stated that this phrase simply meant that the authority granted under section 17(5) may be limited to certain types of programs or data, and is not referring to the kinds of access detailed in section 17(2). Evidence showed that the employee at American Express accessed data in accounts for which she was not authorized, therefore the access she obtained was 'unauthorized access'. Secondly, 'control access' did not refer to the individual authorized to access the system, but the organizational authority granting authority to the individual. In the *Bignell* case, it was the Police Commissioner who exercised such control and, through employee manuals, specified that access was for police purposes only.

Whilst the decision in *Allison* clarifies the interpretation of 'control' under section 17(5), the court's acceptance of *Bignell* would seem to perpetuate the uncertain jurisprudence under the 1990 Act. First, Lord Hobhouse stresses the point that in *Bignell* 'the computer operator did not exceed his authority' and therefore did not commit an offence (at 627G). This would seem irrelevant to the question of whether the Bignells were committing a section 1 offence, since the operator is simply an innocent agent.[79] Secondly, Lord Hobhouse recognizes that the concept of authorization needs to be refined, as 'authority to secure access of the kind in question', and the example given is where access 'to view data may not extend to authority to copy or alter that data' (at 626F–G). On this reasoning, it seems incongruous that the court should hold, by implication, that authority to view the data may not also be limited to particular circumstances. The Bignells knew that they were only authorized to access the PNC for policing purposes and knowingly misrepresented the purpose for their request.

12.4.2 Unauthorized acts

Obtaining access to a computer system clearly threatens the confidentiality of any information residing in it. However, the greater concern is often that such access enables a perpetrator to affect the integrity and availability of the information being processed by the system. The consequences of unauthorized modifications can range

---

[78] This interpretation had been followed by the Divisional Court from which the appeal had been made: see *R v Bow Street Magistrates' Court, ex p Allison* [1999] QB 847.

[79] eg, *R v Manley* (1844) 1 Cox 104.

from simply inconvenience to life-threatening incidents, such as *Rymer*,[80] where a hospital nurse altered patient prescriptions and treatment records.

12.4.2.1 *Criminal damage*

The offence of criminal damage may obviously be relevant in many situations where a computer is the subject of the crime. The value of a computer system normally resides in the information it contains, software and data, rather than the physical hardware.[81] However, as with the concept of theft, to what extent does the unauthorized deletion or modification of computer-based information constitute 'damage' to property, as required under the Criminal Damage Act 1971?[82]

The question was first examined in *Cox v Riley*,[83] where an employee deleted computer programs from a plastic circuit card that was required to operate a computerized saw. The court stated that the property (ie, the plastic circuit card) had been damaged by the erasure of the programs to the extent that the action impaired 'the value or usefulness' of the card and necessitated 'time and labour and money to be expended' to make the card operable again.

This interpretation was upheld in *R v Whiteley*,[84] where the defendant was convicted of causing damage through gaining unauthorized access into the Joint Academic Network, used by UK universities, and deleting and amending substantial numbers of files. It was argued, on his behalf, that the defendant's activities only affected the information contained on a computer disk, not the disk itself. However, the court stated:

What the Act [Criminal Damage Act 1971] requires to be proved is that tangible property has been damaged, not necessarily that the damage itself should be tangible. (at 28)

The alteration of the magnetic particles contained on a disk, whilst imperceptible, did impair the value and usefulness of the disk and therefore constituted damage. However, if the disk had been blank, any alteration would not necessarily be 'damage'.

Despite these successful prosecutions, the Law Commission considered that uncertainty continued to exist when prosecuting computer misuse under the Criminal Damage Act and, therefore, proposed the creation of a new offence under the Computer Misuse Act 1990. One concern was the possibility of situations where it would be difficult to identify the tangible 'property' that had been damaged when altering data, for example deleting information being sent across the public telephone network. A second major concern was that police and prosecuting authorities

---

[80] A Liverpool Crown Court, 1993.

[81] Although the theft of computers for their processor chips has been significant during periods where market demand has exceeded supply.

[82] Criminal Damage Act 1971, s 1(1). Under s 10(1), 'Property' means property of a tangible nature, whether real or personal.

[83] (1986) 83 Cr App R 54.

[84] (1991) 93 Cr App R 25.

were experiencing practical difficulties 'explaining to judges, magistrates and juries how the facts fit in with the present law of criminal damage'.[85]

12.4.2.2 *Section 3*

The third substantive offence under the Computer Misuse Act was that of 'unauthorized modification of computer material'. The offence was principally promoted by the spate of publicity and fear surrounding the use of computer viruses and other malware, as well as concerns about what hackers do once they obtain access to a machine. The provision was amended in 2006 and retitled 'unauthorized acts with intent to impair, or with recklessness as to impairing, operation of computer, etc.':

(1) A person is guilty of an offence if—

    (a)   he does any unauthorized act in relation to a computer;

    (b)   at the time when he does the act he knows that it is unauthorized; and

    (c)   either subsection (2) or subsection (3) below applies.

(2) This subsection applies if the person intends by doing the act—

    (a)   to impair the operation of any computer;

    (b)   to prevent or hinder access to any program or data held in any computer;

    (c)   to impair the operation of any such program or the reliability of any such data; or

    (d)   to enable any of the things mentioned in paragraphs (a) to (c) above to be done.

(3) This subsection applies if the person is reckless as to whether the act will do any of the things mentioned in paragraphs (a) to (d) of subsection (2) above.

As discussed below, the amendment arose primarily in response to concerns about the original provision's suitability to address denial-of-service attacks. However, while the scope of the provision has been widened, much of the original wording has been retained.

The concept of damage in the Criminal Damage Act 1971 is amended by section 3 to the extent that 'a modification of the contents of the computer' shall not be regarded as damage, and therefore an offence under the 1971 Act, if it does not impair the 'physical condition' of the computer or computer storage medium.[86] In the case of removable data media, such as a computer disk or CD-ROM, deletion of data would only be an offence under section 3 if the storage medium were in the computer (s 17(6)). Once removed, any subsequent damage would be subject to the terms of the 1971 Act.

The original offence created a substantial discrepancy with the situation prior to the 1990 Act, since conviction under the Criminal Damage Act could be punishable by imprisonment for up to ten years (s 4), twice that available for an offence under

---

[85] Report 186, para 2.31.

[86] Criminal Damage Act 1971, s 10(5), as amended by the Police and Justice Act 2006, Sch 15 Pt 1.

section 3 (s 3(7)(b)). In addition, liability for criminal damage could arise through the defendant 'being reckless as to whether any such property would be destroyed' (s 1(1)), without a requirement for the prosecution to show intent. Such reckless damage is often a feature of 'hacking' cases, where a hacker inadvertently deletes or alters files and data during the course of his activities, causing the victim substantial loss.[87] However, the Law Commission considered that the section 3 offence should be limited to those engaged in intentional acts of sabotage and noted that those causing inadvertent damage would already be guilty of the section 1 offence, which should be a sufficient deterrent. However, reflecting government concerns about the role of computer integrity offences in organized crime and terrorism, amendments introduced under the Police and Justice Act 2006 have raised the maximum tariff for the section 3 offence to ten years and recklessness has been inserted into the amended offence.

The offence comprises *mens rea* of intent or recklessness, as well as knowledge that the act was unauthorized. The conduct element is broadly defined to include the causing of an act and a series of acts (s 3(5)). In respect of the former, a person would still have committed the act where the actual keystrokes were executed by an innocent agent, such as a system operator inadvertently triggering a virus. As with the other Computer Misuse Act offences, the issue of authorization is further defined:

An act done in relation to a computer is unauthorized if the person doing the act (or causing it to be done)—

(a) is not himself a person who has responsibility for the computer and is entitled to determine whether the act may be done; and

(b) does not have consent to the act from any such person. (s 17(8))

This differs from the original provision by the inclusion of the concept of 'responsibility' in addition to that of entitlement. It is unclear what the purpose of the phrase is, except perhaps to address perceived uncertainties about the nature of authorization. However, to the extent that distinctions can be argued between the concept of responsibility and entitlement, further uncertainty may result.

The nature of any 'modification' may be permanent or temporary (s 3(5)(c)). Also, as with the section 1 offence, the intent or recklessness need not be directed at any particular program, data, or computer (s 3(4)). Knowledge only relates to the issue of authorization, not the act being committed. This was illustrated in the first prosecution of a virus writer, Christopher Pile, aka the 'Black Baron', in 1995.[88] In *Pile*,[89] the defendant was found guilty of the offence even though he had no

---

[87] Report 186, para 3.62.

[88] See R Battcock, 'Prosecutions under the Computer Misuse Act 1990' (1996) 6 Computers and Law (February/March) 22.

[89] Plymouth Crown Court, 1995.

knowledge of which computers were affected by his virus, one of which was called 'Pathogen', and had not targeted any specific computer.

Under the original provision, there was a requirement for the presence of dual intention, in respect of causing a modification and of causing impairment:

the requisite intent is an intent to cause a modification of the contents of any computer and by so doing—

(a) to impair the operation of any computer . . .

This was illustrated in the *Sean Cropp* case. In the Crown Court, the judge had agreed with the defence counsel's argument that the defendant's actions more appropriately fell under the unauthorized modification offence rather than that of unauthorized access. However, in the Court of Appeal, Lord Taylor put forward the opinion that the only form of modification that could be applicable to the defendant's actions was with respect to the impairment of the reliability of the data, and went on to note:

That would involve giving the word 'reliability' the meaning of achieving the result in the printout which was intended by the owner of the computer. It may not necessarily impair the reliability of data in a computer that you feed in something which will produce a result more favourable to a customer than the store holder intended.[90]

This statement clearly recognizes the requirement for dual intention and also seems to support the Law Commission's stance that 'the offence should not punish unauthorized modifications which improve, or are neutral in their effect'.[91]

However, the meaning of the term 'reliability' was subsequently revisited in *Yarimaka v Governor of HM Prison Brixton; Zezev v Government of the United States of America*.[92] The case concerned the hacking into the systems of the financial information company Bloomberg, and the subsequent attempt to blackmail the founder Michael Bloomberg. In the course of extradition proceedings, defence counsel for Zezev challenged the validity of the section 3 charge. It was submitted that the purpose of section 3 was confined to acts which 'damage the computer so that it does not record the information which is fed into it' (para 14). In this case, the defendant fed false information into the system concerning the source of certain information and as such he did not alter or erase the data, the apparent mischief against which the section was directed.

A clear similarity could be drawn between this situation and the position in *Sean Cropp*. In the former, false information was also input into the computer to benefit the perpetrator, and yet Lord Taylor was of the opinion that this does not 'necessarily impair the reliability of the data in a computer'. In *Yarimaka*, Lord Woolf did not

---

[90] *Attorney-General's Reference (No1 of 1991)* [1992] 3 WLR 432 at 438A.
[91] Report 186, para 3.72.
[92] [2002] EWHC 589 (Admin).

feel inclined to make a distinction between an intention to modify and an intention to impair, stating '[i]f a computer is caused to record information which shows that it came from one person, when it in fact came from someone else, that manifestly affects its reliability' (para 18). Such an approach, whilst chiming with common sense, potentially generated uncertainty regarding the scope of the original section 3 offence. Under the new section, the dual intention would seem to have disappeared, the act simply being a question of fact.

The first major prosecution brought under section 3 was *Goulden*.[93] In this case, Goulden installed a security package on an Apple workstation for a printing company, Ampersand. The package included a facility to prevent access without use of a password. Goulden made use of this facility as part of his claim for fees totalling £2,275. Due to the computerized nature of their printing operations, Ampersand were unable to function for a period of a few days. They claimed £36,000 lost business as a result of Goulden's actions, including £1,000 for a specialist to override the access protection. The court imposed a two-year conditional discharge on Goulden and a £1,650 fine. The judge also commented that Goulden's actions were 'at the lowest end of seriousness'!

In *Whitaker*,[94] the courts were required to consider the extent to which the unauthorized modification offence could be applied against an owner of intellectual property. The case concerned a software developer and his client, and arose when the developer initiated a logic bomb designed to prevent use of the software following a dispute over payment. The defendant programmer argued that since under the contract he had retained all intellectual property rights in the software (title transferred upon payment), he had the requisite right to modify the software. The court held that, despite the existence of copyright in the software, the nature of the development contract constituted a limitation on the exercise of the developer's rights. The court did recognize, however, that such an action would have been permitted if it had been explicitly provided for in the contract, that is, the licensee was made aware of the consequences of a failure to pay. He was therefore found guilty of an offence under section 3. This was an important decision, since the software industry has sometimes resorted to such techniques as a means of ensuring payment for their services.

12.4.2.3 *Denial-of-service attacks*

One issue that arose concerning the unauthorized modification offence was its applicability to the carrying out of so-called 'denial-of-service' ('DOS') attacks launched against commercial websites, such as eBay and Amazon. Such attacks are designed to disrupt the operation of the site by deliberately flooding the host server with multiple requests for information. Sometimes the DOS attacks succeed by

---

[93] *The Times*, 10 June 1992.
[94] Scunthorpe Magistrates' Court, 1993.

causing congestion in the communications links, rather than the target machine; which was the case in October 2002 when the 13 DNS root name servers were subjected to an attack.[95] Whether the attack impacts on connection capacity or bandwidth, DOS attacks primarily concentrate on the availability of an online resource, rather than its confidentiality or integrity. Motivations range from extortion attempts, such as against gambling sites, to political protest, such as anti-globalization activists against the WTO site.

To achieve the necessary volumes and to conceal the location of the perpetrator, 'distributed denial-of-service' ('DDOS') attacks are increasingly the normal mode of attack. To mobilize the multiple computers required, the perpetrator will generally surreptitiously seize control of what are known as 'zombie' computers, or 'botnets'—computers acting under the control of the perpetrator without the owner's knowledge. Figures have been published that suggest that a surprising number of computers are operating as zombies at any one time;[96] and that the UK has one of the highest proportions of 'bot-infected' computers, due to the rapid take-up of broadband connectivity.[97] Indeed, there is even a black market in 'botnets', where computers, in sets of hundreds, thousands, or even hundreds of thousands, can be hired for criminal activities.[98]

Because of the different means of carrying out a DOS attack, there had been concern that the original section 3 offence may be unable to address all such activities. With direct attacks, the nature of the communications sent to the target machine will often fall within a class of transmission which the target machine was designed to receive. As such, while there may be the necessary intent to cause a modification and impairment, the modification itself may not be considered unauthorized. Such an argument was accepted in a written judgment in *Lennon*[99] given by District Judge Grant at Wimbledon Magistrates' Court in November 2005, a case involving a teenage boy. The defence had been argued after the teenager had admitted to carrying out a DOS attack against his former employer using a specialist email-bomber program, called Avalanche. On the issue of authorization, Judge Grant stated:

. . . the individual e-mails caused to be sent each caused a modification which was in each case an 'authorized' modification. Although they were sent in bulk resulting in the overwhelming of the server, the effect on the server is not a modification addressed by section 3 [of the Computer Misuse Act 1990].

---

[95] P Vixie, G Sneeringer, and M Schleifer, 'Events of 21-Oct-2002', available at <http://www.isc.org/f-root-denial-of-service-21-oct-2002> (accessed 10 August 2011).

[96] Press release, 'CipherTrust Tracks a Record 250,000 Zombies Per Day', 5 December 2005, available at <http://www.itbsecurity.com/pr/3929> (accessed 15 August 2011).

[97] See Symantec Internet Security Threat Report, *Trends for July 05-December 05* (vol IX, March 2006), available at <http://www.symantec.com> (accessed 10 August 2011).

[98] See DOJ Press Release, 'Computer virus broker arrested for selling armies of infected computers to hackers and spammers', 3 November 2005, available at <http://www.justice.gov/usao/cac/pressroom/pr2005/149.html> (accessed 15 August 2011).

[99] [2005] ECLR 5(5).

In this decision, the court adopted a limited perspective on the perpetrator's activities. If it is clear that the defendant caused the modification and had the 'requisite intent', to treat each message in isolation when addressing the issue of authorization, rather than as a totality, seems to be unnecessarily literal. If each message is treated as separate, it is inevitably difficult to argue logically that at a certain increment all the messages, those already received and those to be received, become unauthorized. However, if the perpetrator's initial act is viewed as triggering the sending of a sum x of messages that are designed to overwhelm the recipient system, then a lack of authorization could be found by implication. Such an approach was indeed taken on appeal and found favour with the Divisional Court:

The owner of a computer able to receive emails would ordinarily be taken to have consented to the sending of emails to the computer. However, such implied consent was not without limits, and it plainly did not cover emails that had been sent not for the purpose of communication with the owner but for the purpose of interrupting his system.[100]

With DDOS attacks, an offence is likely to have occurred against the 'zombie' computers, even if uncertainty exists about the nature of what is carried out against the target computer. Where an attack effectively disables the communication links to the target computer, rather than the target itself, the original section 3 offence would only have been appropriate in respect of those computers that form part of the network, such as routers; although the question of authorization arises here as well.

In July 2003, the government announced its intention to review the 1990 Act, in part to address the potential lacuna in respect of DOS activities, as well as to comply with its international commitments under the Cybercrime Convention and EU Framework Decision. Provisions to amend the Computer Misuse Act were contained in the Criminal Justice Act 2006. Rather than establishing a supplementary offence, the amendment replaced the section 3 offence. The new provision shifts the locus of the crime from the 'contents of the computer', to potentially any point in a network which is held to be 'in relation to' the target computer, a phrase not further defined.

12.4.3 Unlawful devices

Under Article 6 of the Cybercrime Convention, Member States are obliged to criminalize the supply and possession of a 'device', computer password, access code, or similar data. This would include, for example, information about a known weakness or vulnerability in a software application, such as the Windows operating system, generally referred to as 'exploits' and which are commonly used to introduce 'malware' into another person's system. The provision is designed to

---

[100] *DPP v Lennon* [2006] All ER (D) 147 (May).

criminalize the market for 'hacker tools', referred to as the 'malicious marketplace',[101] which has become an inevitable feature of cybercrime.

The Computer Misuse Act 1990 did not originally contain provisions in relation to 'devices', however to meet its commitment under the Cybercrime Convention, the government introduced such a provision into the Act, through the Police and Justice Act 2006:

3A Making, supplying or obtaining articles for use in offence under section 1 or section 3

(1) A person is guilty of an offence if he makes, adapts, supplies or offers to supply any article—

(a) intending it to be used to commit, or to assist in the commission of, an offence under section 1 or 3; or

(b) believing that it is likely to be so used.

The provision establishes three separate offences. The second offence, of 'believing', was designed to address the growth of the 'malicious marketplace', with persons creating tools for sale to others, but with no specific intention concerning their use. However, it has been criticized for potentially criminalizing researchers in the security field, who may create such tools in the course of their study or work. The third offence is the obtaining of such an article, but only with a view to it being supplied (s 3A(2)). The offences are subject to a maximum tariff of two years (s 3A(4)).

12.5 INTERNATIONAL HARMONIZATION

Computer crime has an obvious international dimension and governments have recognized the need to ensure that legal protection is harmonized among nations. Attempts have been made within various international organizations and forums, such as the G8 Member States, to achieve a harmonized approach to legislating against computer crime and thereby try to prevent the appearance of 'computer crime havens'. The first major attempt was under the auspices of the Organisation for Economic Co-operation and Development, when it published a report in 1986 listing five categories of offence that it believed should constitute a common approach to computer crime.[102] However, the most significant institution in the field

---

[101] See comments by Roger Cummings, Director of the UK National Infrastructure Security Co-ordination Centre ('NISCC') in 'Foreign powers are main cyberthreat, UK says', CNET News.com.

[102] 'Computer-Related Criminality: Analysis of Legal Policy in the OECD Area' (Report DSTI-ICCP 84.22, 18 April 1986).

has been the Council of Europe, although the European Union has also recently become active.

12.5.1 Council of Europe

In 1985, a select committee of experts, the European Committee on Crime Problems, was established under the auspices of the Council of Europe to consider the legal issues raised by computer crime. The final report was published in September 1989.[103] As part of the Committee's work, it produced guidelines for national legislatures on a 'Minimum List of Offences Necessary for a Uniform Criminal Policy'.[104] These eight offences were seen by all Member States to be the critical areas of computer misuse that required provisions in criminal law. In addition, the Report put forward an 'optional list' of four offences that failed to achieve consensus among members, but was thought to be worthy of consideration.[105] The Report was published with a Council of Ministers Recommendation urging governments to take account of the Report when reviewing and initiating legislation in this field.[106]

Following the Recommendation, the Council of Europe shifted its attention to the issue of prosecution of computer crime and the particular problems faced by LEAs. In 1995, it adopted a Recommendation addressing issues of search and seizure, the admissibility of evidence, and international mutual assistance.[107]

Despite these various initiatives, Council of Europe Recommendations are not binding legal instruments on Member States and inevitably, therefore, such harmonizing measures have had limited effect. However, the growth of the internet as a transnational environment for the commission of crime has refocused the attention of policymakers on the need for harmonized criminal laws in the area. As a consequence, in April 1997, the Council of Europe embarked on the adoption of a Convention in the area, which Member States would have an obligation to implement.

In November 2001, the Council of Ministers adopted the Convention on Cybercrime, which was opened for signature in Budapest on 23 November 2001, and has since been signed by 43 of the 47 members of the Council of Europe.[108]

---

[103] 'Computer-related crime', Report by the European Committee on Crime Problems (Strasbourg, 1990).

[104] The list of offences: computer fraud; computer forgery; damage to computer data or computer programs; computer sabotage; unauthorized access; unauthorized interception; unauthorized reproduction of a computer program; unauthorized reproduction of a topography.

[105] ie, alteration of computer data or computer programs; computer espionage; unauthorized use of a computer, and unauthorized use of a protected computer program.

[106] Recommendation No R(89) 9, 13 September 1999.

[107] Recommendation No R(95) 13, 'concerning problems of procedural law connected with information technology'.

[108] Convention on Cybercrime (Budapest, 23 November 2001; TS 185 (2004)) and Explanatory Report (available at <http://www.coe.int>). Number of signatories as at 18 April 2011.

However, of particular significance to the status of the Convention, four non-members were involved in the drafting process, the USA, Japan, South Africa, and Canada, and became signatories. The Convention also contains a mechanism whereby other non-members can sign and ratify the Convention. It entered into force once five states ratified the Convention, which occurred on 1 July 2004.

The Convention addresses issues of substantive and procedural criminal law, which Member States are obliged to take measures to implement in national law, as well as issues of international cooperation.

In terms of offences, section 1 distinguishes four categories of offence:

(a) 'Offences against the confidentiality, integrity and availability of computer data and systems': illegal access, illegal interception, data interference, systems interference and misuse of devices (Arts 2–6).[109]

(b) 'Computer-related offences': forgery and fraud (Arts 7 and 8).

(c) 'Content-related offences': that is, child pornography (Art 9).

(d) 'Offences related to and infringements of copyright and related rights' (Art 10).

Relevant aspects of these provisions have been examined in earlier sections of this chapter. In addition, the Convention addresses related liability issues in relation to attempts and aiding or abetting (Art 11) and corporate liability (Art 12).

Section 2 of the Convention addresses procedural provisions that Member States are obliged to implement in national law. These include measures to enable the 'expedited preservation of stored computer data' (Art 16); 'expedited preservation and partial disclosure of traffic data' (Art 17); the production and search and seizure of computer data (Arts 18 and 19); the 'real-time collection of traffic data' (Art 20); and the interception of content data (Art 21). Section 3 addresses the issue of jurisdiction (Art 22).

In terms of international cooperation, the Convention addresses issues of extradition (Art 24), mutual legal assistance between national LEAs (Arts 25–34), and the establishment of a 24/7 network of points of contact to support such assistance (Art 35).

The comprehensive nature of the Convention, as well as the geographical spread of its signatories, means it is likely to remain the most significant international legal instrument in the field for the foreseeable future. The success of the Cybercrime Convention as a spur to harmonization can be measured not only on the basis of the number of signatories, including non-European countries, but also as the basis for other harmonization initiatives, such as the Commonwealth 'Model Computer and

---

[109] Devices, including passwords, being produced or used with the intent to commit one of the offences within the category.

Computer-related Crimes Bill' (October 2002),[110] addressing the needs of some 53 developed and developing nations.

However, criticism has also been directed at the Cybercrime Convention, from different quarters. First, the lack of transparency in the drafting process has been a source of frustration. Secondly, criticism has come from human rights and civil society groups for alleged incursions on individual rights and the absence of sufficient safeguards against state abuse. Thirdly, providers of communication services have complained about the burdens placed upon them to assist LEAs.

After the adoption of the Convention in 2001, an additional protocol to the Convention was agreed by Member States, 'concerning the criminalisation of acts of a racist and xenophobic nature committed through computer systems', in January 2003.[111] Such issues were considered during the drafting of the main instrument, but consensus could not be reached, therefore the approach of drafting a separate instrument was agreed.[112] The Protocol entered into force in March 2006, with the fifth ratification, and 32 Member States have since signed the Protocol, as well as Canada and South Africa.[113]

The Protocol requires the establishment of a range of substantive offences concerning 'racist or xenophobic material', defined in the following terms:

> . . . any written material, any image or any other representation of ideas or theories, which advocates, promotes or incites hatred, discrimination or violence, against any individual or group of individuals, based on race, colour, descent or national or ethnic origin, as well as religion if used as a pretext for any of these factors.[114]

The offences include the dissemination of such material (Art 3); threats and insults motivated by racism or xenophobia (Arts 4 and 5), and the denial of genocide and crimes against humanity (Art 6).

In terms of existing English law, the Public Order Act 1986 criminalizes acts intending to stir up racial and religious hatred, which includes threatening and insulting words, as well as displays.[115] These provisions would therefore seem generally to cover the offences detailed in Articles 3–5. Indeed, the offence in relation to religious hatred goes beyond that required under the Protocol, which is only concerned with religion to the extent that it is used as an alibi or substitute for the racism.[116] The Article 6 offence has no equivalence under English law; although

---

[110] <http://www.thecommonwealth.org/shared_asp_files/uploadedfiles/{DA109CD2-5204-4FAB-AA77-86970A639B05}_Computer%20Crime.pdf> (accessed 10 August 2011).

[111] Additional Protocol to the Convention on cybercrime, concerning the criminalisation of acts of a racist and xenophobic nature committed through computer systems (Strasbourg, 23 January 2003; TS 189) ('Additional Protocol').

[112] Explanatory Report, para 4. Available at <http://conventions.coe.int/Treaty/en/Reports/Html/189.htm> (accessed 10 August 2011).

[113] As of 18 April 2011.

[114] Additional Protocol, Art 2(1).

[115] Public Order Act 1986, ss 18–23 and 29B–F respectively.

[116] Explanatory Report, para 21.

prosecutions of ISPs under such laws in France and Germany were cause célèbre in terms of internet regulation.[117] The Terrorism Act 2006 criminalizes the glorification of the commission of terrorist acts,[118] which clearly has similarities with the 'approval' of crimes against humanity. The UK Government has not yet signed the Protocol, however, and has made no announcement that it intends to do so.

12.5.2 European Union

The role of the European Union in criminal policy and law has evolved and widened significantly over the past 20 years, from the introduction of the 'third pillar' on Justice and Home Affairs ('JHA') in 1992, to its integration under Title V, 'Area of Freedom, Security and Justice', of the Treaty on the Functioning of the European Union, which came into force in December 2009. During this period, measures addressing both substantive and procedural law aspects of computer crime have been adopted.

At a special meeting of the European Council in October 1999, Member State governments agreed that efforts should be made to reach common positions with respect to definitions of criminal offences and appropriate sanctions for particular areas of crime, including computer crime.[119] Subsequently, the Commission adopted a Communication on computer crime that included proposals for legislative measures in the area.[120]

In May 1997, the Justice and Home Affairs Council requested that the Commission fund a study on computer crime, which was presented to the Council in April 1998.[121] On the basis of this study, the Commission adopted a Communication on network security and computer crime that included proposals for legislative measures in the area addressing both substantive and procedural issues.[122] While recognizing the work being carried out by the Council of Europe, including the adoption of a common position during the negotiations on the Convention, the perceived advantages for the Commission of legislative activity at an EU level are the ability to 'go further' than the approximation achieved by the Convention; as well as to adopt a binding instrument within a shorter period of time, with the added force of EU enforcement mechanisms.[123]

---

[117] *League Against Racism and Antisemitism (LICRA), French Union of Jewish Students, v Yahoo! Inc (USA), Yahoo France*, TGI de Paris, 20 November 2000; EBLR (2001).

[118] Terrorism Act 2006, s 1(3).

[119] Press Release C/99/0002, Presidency conclusions, Tampere European Council 'on the creation of an area of freedom, security and justice in the European Union', 15–16 October 1999.

[120] Communication from the European Commission to the Council and the European Parliament, 'Creating a Safer Information Society by Improving the Security of Information Infrastructures and Combating Computer-related Crime', COM(2000)890 final ('2000 Communication') at s 7.1.

[121] The 'COMCRIME' study, available at <http://www.edc.uoc.gr/~panas/PATRA/sieber.pdf> (accessed 15 August 2011).

[122] 2000 Communication, s 7.1.

[123] Ibid p 17.

The EU has adopted a range of harmonization measures covering activities within the three categories of offences discussed above, computer-related, content-related, and computer integrity, including:

(a) Council Framework Decision on 'combating fraud and counterfeiting of non-cash means of payment';[124]

(b) Council Framework Decision 'on combating the sexual exploitation of children and child pornography';[125]

(c) Council Framework Decision 'on attacks against information systems'.[126]

In terms of procedural measures, both the European Arrest Warrant[127] and the European Evidence Warrant[128] expressly extend to computer crime offences.

The 2005 Decision criminalizes three distinct acts: illegal access, illegal system interference, and illegal data interference (Arts 2–4). In respect of illegal access, the 2005 Decision mandates the optional position taken under the Convention that for the offence to be committed either the 'information system' is subject to 'specific protection measures' or there is intent to cause damage or obtain an economic benefit (Art 3).

The most significant innovation of the 2005 Decision over that of the Convention is in respect of the harmonization of penalties. The Convention simply requires Member States to implement 'effective, proportional and dissuasive criminal sanctions';[129] while the 2005 Decision imposes a minimum tariff in respect of illegal system and data interference, of between one and three years, and a higher tariff, of between two and five years, where there are 'aggravating circumstances'.[130] Member States are obliged to impose the higher tariff where the activity was committed within the framework of a criminal organization. Member States may also impose the higher tariff where the conduct has caused 'serious damage or has affected essential interests'.[131]

In September 2010, the Commission issued a proposal for a Directive to replace the 2005 Decision.[132] As well as retaining the existing offences, the proposal will introduce new offences in respect of illegal interception and the use of 'tools' for the commission of offences. As such, it will more closely resemble the relevant provisions of the Convention on Cybercrime. The proposal would also raise the minimum

---

[124] 2001/413/JHA of 28 May 2001, OJ L149/1, 2 June 2001.

[125] 2004/68/JHA of 22 December 2003, OJ L13/44, 20 January 2004.

[126] 2005/222/JHA of 24 February, OJ L69/67, 16 March 2005 ('2005 Decision').

[127] Council Framework Decision (2002/584/JHA) of 13 June 2002 on the European arrest warrant and the surrender procedures between Member States, OJ L190/1, 18 July 2002.

[128] Council Framework Decision 2008/978/JHA of 18 December 2008 on the European evidence warrant for the purpose of obtaining objects, documents and data for use in proceedings in criminal matters, OJ L350/72, 30 December 2008.

[129] Convention, Art 13.

[130] 2005 Decision, Arts 6(2) and 7(1) respectively.

[131] 2005 Decision, Art 7(2).

[132] Memo/10/463, 30 September 2010.

tariff to two years' imprisonment and extend the scope of what constitutes 'aggravating circumstances'. Measures designed to improve cooperation are also included in the proposal, such as mandating an eight-hour response time for urgent requests received via the 24/7 contact points.

12.6 JURISDICTIONAL ISSUES

Computer crime inevitably often has an extraterritorial aspect to it that can give rise to complex jurisdictional issues; that is, it involves persons present and acts being carried out in a number of different countries. Such issues are either addressed explicitly in the governing legislation, or are left to general principles of international criminal law.

The general principle of international criminal law is that a crime committed within a state's territory may be tried there. Although the territoriality of criminal law does not coincide with territorial sovereignty, it derives from such sovereign powers.[133] Under English common law, the general principle for determining jurisdiction has recently been stated by the courts to be when 'the last act took place in England or a substantial part of the crime was committed here'.[134] Previously, the general principle was drawn more narrowly, as being where the *actus reus* is completed,[135] also referred to as 'result crimes' or the 'terminatory theory'. The 'last act' rule echoes the civil law principle *lex loci delicti commissi*, whereby torts are governed by the law of the place where the act was committed.

In terms of statutory provision, under the Computer Misuse Act 1990, the offences may be committed by any person, British citizenship being immaterial to a person's guilt (s 9). Jurisdiction in transnational activities is asserted through the concept of a 'significant link' being present in the 'home country', that is, England and Wales, Scotland, or Northern Ireland (s 4(6)). Where an unauthorized access offence has been committed, the following are considered a 'significant link':

(a) that the accused was in the home country concerned at the time when he did the act which caused the computer to perform the function; or

(b) that any computer containing any program or data to which the accused by doing that act secured or intended to secure unauthorized access, or enabled or intended to enable unauthorized access to be secured, was in the home country concerned at that time. (s 5(2))

Where a section 2 offence is involved, the Act addresses two potential scenarios. First, the need for a 'significant link' is dispensed with in respect of the unauthorized

---

[133] A Cassese, *International Criminal Law* (Oxford: Oxford University Press, 2003) 277.
[134] *Smith (Wallace Duncan) (No 4)* [2004] QB 1418 at 57.
[135] *Manning* (1998) 2 Cr App R 461.

element of the action, as long as the further offence is triable under English law (s 4(3)). If the further offence is extraterritorial in nature, then an offence may be committed which requires no connection with England and Wales at all.[136] Secondly, in the alternate, if a 'significant link' does exist, and what was intended to be committed would involve the commission of an offence under the law of the country where the act was intended to take place, whether under the laws of England and Wales or elsewhere, then the domestic courts can still seize jurisdiction.[137] In the case of an unauthorized act, under section 3, the 'significant link' is either the presence of the accused or that the acts occurred in the UK (s 5(3)).

In the USA, the US Patriot Act of 2001 amended the Computer Fraud and Abuse Act to extend the concept of a 'protected computer' to include 'a computer located outside the US that is used in a manner that affects interstate or foreign commerce or communication of the US' (s 1030(e)(2)(B)). This effectively extends the territorial scope of the domestic offence, when the attacked computer is in another jurisdiction.

Both the Convention on Cybercrime and the EU draft decision address the question of establishing jurisdiction. The Convention states that jurisdiction should exist when committed:

a. in its territory; or

b. on board a ship flying the flag of that Party; or

c. on board an aircraft registered under the laws of that Party; or

d. by one of its nationals, if the offence is punishable under criminal law where it was committed or if the offence is committed outside the territorial jurisdiction of any State. (Art 22)

The fourth scenario, based on the nationality of the offender, is generally referred to as the 'active personality' extraterritorial principle, and is often applicable in civil law jurisdictions.[138] The Decision also adopts the territorial and 'active personality principle' (Art 11). Both instruments, however, also permit states not to implement such a principle;[139] an option upon which the UK Government has decided to rely. In addition, both the Convention and the Decision require a Member State to establish jurisdiction over its own nationals and to prosecute them where, as a matter of national law, such persons may not be extradited to a requesting state where the crime was committed.

The Citibank fraud is illustrative of some of the issues that can arise when prosecuting transnational criminal activities. In 1994 Citibank suffered a significant breach of security in its cash management system, resulting in funds being

---

[136] M Hirst, *Jurisdiction and the Ambit of the Criminal Law* (Oxford: Oxford University Press, 2003) 194.
[137] ss 4(4) and 8(1).
[138] Explanatory Report, para 236.
[139] Convention, Art 22(2); Framework Decision, Art 10(5).

transferred from customer accounts into the accounts of the perpetrator and his accomplices.[140] The eventual sum involved was $12m, although the vast majority, $11.6m, was transferred subsequent to the discovery of the breach as part of the efforts to locate the perpetrators. After significant international cooperation between national LEAs, an individual was identified. Vladimer Levin was arrested in the UK and, after appeals, was subsequently extradited to the USA.[141]

In an action for extradition the applicant is required to show that the actions of the accused constitute a criminal offence exceeding a minimum level of seriousness in both jurisdictions, that is, the country from which the accused is to be extradited and the country to which the extradition will be made; sometimes referred to as the 'double criminality' principle. Under the Extradition Act 2003, the 'double criminality' is no longer required for offences which are part of the European Arrest Warrant regime.[142] Both the Convention and Decision provide that Member States should establish jurisdiction over offenders that they refuse to extradite.[143]

In *Levin*, the defendant was accused of committing wire and bank fraud in the USA. No direct equivalent exists in English law, and therefore Levin was charged with 66 related offences, including unauthorized access and unauthorized modification under the Computer Misuse Act. However, as discussed previously in this chapter, even where similar offences exist, a particular computer-related activity may not be deemed to fall within the terminology of existing criminal law. Levin's counsel argued, for example, that one of the offences cited by the extradition applicant, under the Forgery and Counterfeiting Act 1981, had not been committed based on an earlier decision by the English courts in *Gold*.[144]

A second jurisdictional issue in *Levin* revolved around the question of *where* the offences were held to have taken place. Defendant's counsel claimed that the criminal act occurred in St Petersburg at the moment when Levin pressed particular keys on the keyboard instigating fraudulent Citibank transfers, and therefore Russian law applied. Counsel for the extradition applicant claimed that the place where the changes to the data occurred, the Citibank computer in Parsipenny (USA), constituted the place where the offence took place. The judge decided in favour of the applicant on the basis that the real-time nature of the communication link between Levin and the Citibank computer meant that Levin's keystrokes were actually occurring on the Citibank computer.[145] With the decision in *Smith*

---

[140] The system, called the 'Financial Institutions Citibank Cash Manager' ('FICCM'), provided large institutional customers with dial-in access from any geographic location to the online service, based on a system in Parsipenny, NJ. Once accessed, customers could carry out a range of financial transactions, including the execution of credit transfers between accounts.

[141] *R v Governor of Brixton Prison and Another, ex p Levin* [1996] 4 All ER 350.

[142] Council Framework Decision (JHA) 2002/584 on the European arrest warrant and the surrender procedures between Member States [2002] OJ L190/1, 18 July 2002.

[143] Convention, Art 22(3) and 2005 Decision, Art 11(4).

[144] See also the *Levin* case at 360e–361e.

[145] Ibid 363a.

(Wallace Duncan) (No 4)[146] and other subsequent statutory developments, such
an issue would be unlikely to arise again; although the nature of computer and
communications technologies can create legal uncertainty about where an act
occurs, which is likely to be a common ground for challenge by defendants.

12.7 FORENSIC ISSUES

The investigation of computer crimes and the gathering of appropriate evidence
for a criminal prosecution can be an extremely difficult and complex issue, due
primarily to the intangible and often transient nature of data, especially in a
networked environment. The technology renders the process of investigation
and recording of evidence extremely vulnerable to defence claims of errors,
technical malfunction, prejudicial interference, or fabrication. Such claims may lead
to a ruling from the court against the admissibility of such evidence.[147] A lack
of adequate training of law enforcement officers will often exacerbate these
difficulties.

Law enforcement investigative techniques are generally subdivided into coercive
and covert techniques; the former involving powers of search and seizure, while the
latter involving interception and surveillance. In contrast to other forms of crime, the
investigation of cybercrimes will more frequently involve the deployment of
techniques falling into both categories of activity. Covert techniques are generally
used at an earlier stage in the investigative process, for the gathering of intelligence
as much as evidence; while coercive techniques are used primarily to gather
evidence once the relevant ICT resources have been identified.

In terms of obtaining evidence, relevant data may be resident on the computer
system of the victim, the suspect, and/or some third party, such as the perpetrator's
ISP. Alternatively, evidence may be obtained in the process of its transmission
between computer systems. While specific procedural rules address access to these
forms of evidence, the following considers two key sources: data obtained from a
communications service provider ('CSP') and material that is seized.

12.7.1 Interception and communications data

During the course of an investigation, a substantial amount of evidence may be
obtained from the intermediaries providing the communication services, CSPs. Such
evidence may comprise the content of a communication ('content data'), such as a
list of passwords; or the attributes of a communication session, such as the duration
of a call or the location of the caller ('communications data'). Some such data may

---

[146] [2004] QB 1418.
[147] Police and Criminal Evidence Act, s 78.

be considered as being 'at rest', in the sense that it is stored by the CSP in the course of the provision of its services; other data will be available 'in transmission' across or through the communication networks, through a process referred to as interception.

Interception of content data and access to communications data is governed in the UK under the Regulation of Investigatory Powers Act 2000 ('RIPA 2000'). The Act makes it an offence to intercept a communication being transmitted over a public telecommunications system without a warrant issued by the Secretary of State; or over a private telecommunication system without the consent of the system controller (s 1). The first prosecution under this provision arose when Cliff Stanford, founder of Demon, had intercepted the emails of three staff members at Redbus Interhouse plc, where he had previously worked, including the company Chairman. He had induced an employee at the company to obtain access to the email system by using the user name and password given to him by a senior employee. A program was then installed on the system that automatically copied emails to a Hotmail account operated by a private investigator.[148]

An interception is lawful, however, where both the sender and recipient have consented to the interception (s 3(1)); or it is carried out by a CSP 'for purposes connected with the provision or operation of that service or with the enforcement . . . of any enactment relating to the use of . . . telecommunications services' (s 3(3)). This latter provision renders lawful an interception carried out by a telecommunications operator to prevent fraudulent use of a telecommunication service or its improper use, under the Communications Act 2003, sections 125 and 126.

The RIPA 2000 regime is not primarily designed to tackle the activities of those intercepting communications in the furtherance of their criminal activities; rather its purpose is to control the interception practices of law enforcement agents and the use of intercepted material as evidence. On a number of occasions, the European Court of Human Rights has found UK law to be in breach of the Convention in respect of protecting the right of privacy of those who have been subject to interception.[149]

An interception warrant should only be issued by the Secretary of State on the grounds of national security, 'serious crime',[150] or the 'economic well-being of the UK' (s 5); and must identity a particular subject or a set of premises (s 8(1)).

---

[148] *Stanford* [2006] Times Law Reports, 7 February 2006.
[149] See *Malone v United Kingdom* [1984] 7 EHRR 14 and *Halford v United Kingdom* (1997) IRLR 471.
[150] ie:

(a) . . . an offence for which a person who has attained the age of twenty-one and has no previous convictions could reasonably be expected to be sentenced to imprisonment for a term of three years or more; (b) that the conduct involves the use of violence, results in substantial financial gain or is conduct by a large number of persons in pursuit of a common purpose. (s 81(3))

A procedure for scrutiny exists through the office of the Interception Commissioner, and a right of appeal to an Interception Tribunal.

One feature of the UK interception regime is that it does not generally permit information obtained through an interception to be adduced as evidence in legal proceedings (s 17).[151] Such evidence is for the purpose of an investigation, not for any subsequent prosecution. The reasoning behind such a provision is to protect from disclosure information about the investigative activities of LEAs. Such activities would enter the public domain if intercept evidence was used in court and became subject to challenge by a defendant's counsel. Conversely, interception evidence is not inadmissible where a service provider carries out the interception under the Communications Act 2003,[152] or if the evidence comes from an interception carried out in another country,[153] since neither would reveal anything about the activities of UK law enforcement.

Access to communications data held by a communications service provider is governed by a new regime under RIPA 2000. 'Communications data' encompasses three categories of data: (a) 'traffic data', which would include the number or address of the sender and recipient of a communication; (b) usage data, such as time and date of log-in to a service; and (c) subscriber data, which would include data such as the subscriber's billing address. Under Part I, Chapter II of RIPA 2000, the police and law enforcement persons can, under an appropriate authorization, give a notice to a CSP requiring access to specified communications data.[154] Such a notice shall only be issued where it is considered necessary for any of the public interest grounds set out in the Act, including the prevention or detection of crime and public health and safety (s 22(2)).

Communications data will only be available to be accessed by investigators, however, if the architecture of the communications system generates such data. Also, if the service provider has either preserved the data in response to a specific request, or such data has been routinely retained by the provider. Generally, such data is retained for relatively short periods, due both to the cost to the provider as well as compliance with data protection rules.

With heightened concerns about the threat of terrorism, the issue of the potential unavailability of evidence led to calls for obligatory data retention to be imposed on CSPs. In the UK, a voluntary scheme was initially established under Part 11 of the Anti-terrorism, Crime and Security Act 2001. However, a mandatory measure has subsequently been adopted at a European level, harmonizing data retention rules

---

[151] However, it may be retained for certain 'authorized purposes' (s 15(4)), eg, 'it is necessary to ensure that a person conducting a criminal prosecution has the information he needs to determine what is required of him by his duty to secure the fairness of the prosecution', and may be subsequently disclosed to the prosecutor or trial judge (s 18(7)).

[152] eg, *Morgans v DPP* [1999] 2 Cr App R 99.

[153] See *R v P & Others* (2001) 2 All ER 58.

[154] The Regulation of Investigatory Powers (Communications Data) Order 2003 (SI 2003/3172), as amended by SI 2005/1083.

among the Member States.[155] The Retention Directive imposes a mandatory retention requirement of between six months and 24 months in respect of communications data relating to the use of fixed telephony, mobile telephony and internet access, email and telephony services. The measure was fully transposed into UK law in 2009, with the government opting for a 12-month retention period.[156] The Retention Directive continues to be highly controversial, with claims that its non-discriminatory scope represents a disproportionate interference in the privacy of all citizens.

12.7.2 Search and seizure

When carrying out a search and seizure operation, the objective is to obtain any data that may be relevant to the investigation, subject to any rules protecting certain categories of material, such as legally privileged; and to obtain it in a manner that does not enable any material subsequently adduced as evidence to be successfully challenged. Such data may be contained in various forms of digital media and/or may comprise physical source documents, such as photographs, or printouts from the media. Where the digital media form part of, or are connected to, a computing resource, then the process of seizure will vary considerably according to whether the system is in operation at the time, and whether it is connected to a network; since the process of closing down a system and disconnecting it from a network may have serious forensic implications.

Generally, powers to enter and search premises will either be granted by a magistrate,[157] which then confers a general power of seizure;[158] or arise in the course of an arrest, which confers certain powers of search and seizure.[159] The statutory framework governing seizure expressly includes 'any information stored in any electronic form'[160] and 'any computer disk or other electronic storage device'.[161]

While an investigating officer has the power to seize material, he also has the option of arranging for such material to be imaged or copied;[162] which may be considered the most appropriate course of action to minimize the intrusion and

---

[155] Directive 2006/24/EC of the European Parliament and of the Council of 15 March 2006 on the retention of data generated or processed in connection with the provision of publicly available electronic communications services or of public communications networks and amending Directive 2002/58/EC, OJ L105/54, 13 April 2006 ('Retention Directive'). See also Chapter 10, section 10.4.

[156] The Data Retention (EC Directive) Regulations 2009 (SI 2009/859).

[157] Under the Police and Criminal Evidence Act 1984, ss 8 and 19–20.

[158] Police and Criminal Evidence Act 1984, s 19.

[159] Ibid s 32.

[160] Ibid s 20.

[161] Serious Organised Crime and Police Act 2005, s 66(3)(c).

[162] Police and Criminal Evidence Act 1984, Code B, at 7.5.

disturbance caused by a search, which an investigating officer is under a duty to do.[163]

A search and seizure warrant can give rise to problems where the relevant material is held on a computer system being used at the time of the search, since any attempt to seize the material for further examination may result in either the loss or alteration of the evidence. Other problems for law enforcement are the geographical scope of a warrant, where the seized computer is connected to a network; and the volume of data that is generally subject to seizure, especially as the cost of data storage has fallen and capacity increased dramatically in recent years. The time and expense involved in sifting and scrutinizing seized data can be a serious impediment to a process of investigation.

In a networked environment, what is the geographical scope of such warrants? Under the Police and Criminal Evidence Act 1984, a constable may require 'any information which is stored in any electronic form and is accessible from the premises to be produced in a form in which it can be taken away'.[164] On the face of it, this provision would appear to enable law enforcement officers to obtain information held on remote systems, since information in electronic form will be accessible from a networked computer on the searched premises.

Accessing remote data became problematic for UK LEAs during the early 1990s, as a consequence of the Computer Misuse Act 1990. Certain electronic bulletin boards, containing illegal material such as virus code, began placing messages at the point of access to the site stating that 'law enforcement officials are not permitted to enter the system'. Such a warning was considered to be an effective technique in restricting the police from monitoring the use made of such bulletin boards.[165] As a consequence, in 1994 the Computer Misuse Act was amended to prevent LEAs committing a section 1 offence of unauthorized access:

. . . nothing designed to indicate a withholding of consent to access to any program or data from persons as enforcement officers shall have effect to make access unauthorized for the purposes of the said section 1(1).

In this section 'enforcement officer' means a constable or other person charged with the duty of investigating offences; and withholding consent from a person 'as' an enforcement officer of any description includes the operation, by the person entitled to control access, of rules whereby enforcement officers of that description are, as such, disqualified from membership of a class or persons who are authorized to have access.[166]

---

[163] Ibid, 6.10. See, eg, *R (on the application of Paul Da Costa & Co) v Thames Magistrates' Court* [2002] EWHC 40, where images were taken of the two hard disks on the firm's server.

[164] s 19(4), as amended by the Criminal Justice and Police Act 2001, Sch 2 Pt 2 para 13(2)(a). See also s 20, which extends this provision to powers of seizure conferred under other enactments, such as the Computer Misuse Act, s 14.

[165] See Home Affairs Committee Report No 126, 'Computer Pornography', p xii, para 31–2 (HMSO, February 1994).

[166] The Criminal Justice and Public Order Act 1994, s 162, amending s 10 of the Computer Misuse Act 1990.

While this provides protection against LEAs engaging in criminal conduct in a domestic context, law enforcement officers could still be in breach of unauthorized access offences in other jurisdictions.

In terms of police powers, a distinction can be made between the exercise of specific coercive powers, such as powers of search or surveillance, and general investigative activities. As with any public body, all police actions must have appropriate *vires*, otherwise they may be subject to control by the courts by way of judicial review and considered unlawful.[167] In all cases, the exercise of police powers are subject to the jurisdictional limitation placed on the police under the Police Act 1996: a member of a police force shall have all the powers and privileges of a constable throughout England and Wales and the adjacent UK waters.[168]

As a consequence of the jurisdictional limitation, investigators are obliged to give mind to the legality of any extraterritorial activity, since evidence obtained unlawfully from a foreign state may be excluded by a court, either as an abuse of process[169] or through the exercise of statutory discretion.[170] However, prior to such a decision, the court would first need to determine whether to characterize police access as a territorial or extraterritorial exercise of power; then whether the activity is unlawful, under domestic or foreign law, either through breach of specific provisions, such as unauthorized access, or based on general principles of breach of national sovereignty and the comity of nations implied into the operation of such principles.

An example of this arose in *United States v Gorshkov*.[171] In 2000, as part of an investigation into the activities of two Russian hackers, Vasiliy Gorshkov and Alexey Ivanov, the FBI in the USA accessed computers in Russia via the internet, using surreptitiously obtained passwords to download data from computers operated by the accused already under arrest in the USA. At an evidentiary hearing, Gorshkov first sought to have the evidence suppressed on the grounds that it was obtained in violation of the Fourth Amendment. Of critical relevance to our discussion, the court in *Gorshkov* also held that the FBI's act of copying data was not a 'seizure' under the Fourth Amendment 'because it did not interfere with Defendant's or anyone else's possessory interest in the data'.[172] While this may be true at a technical level,

---

[167] See, eg, *R v Robin Edward Hounsham* [2005] EWCA Crim 1366.

[168] s 30(1), 'Jurisdiction of constables'.

[169] See *R v Loosely (Attorney General's Reference No 3 of 2000)* [2001] UKHL 53, (2001) 4 All ER 897.

[170] Police and Criminal Evidence Act 1984, s 78(1):

> In any proceedings the court may refuse to allow evidence on which the prosecution proposes to rely to be given if it appears to the court that, having regard to all the circumstances in which the evidence was obtained, the admission of the evidence would have such an adverse effect on the fairness of the proceedings that the court ought not to admit it.

[171] 2001 WL 1024026 (WD Wash, 2001).

[172] Ibid 3.

that is, a copied document does not interfere with the source document,[173] one has to question whether it is appropriate as a matter of legal principle to rely on such a distinction.

A second argument raised by the defence in *Gorshkov* was that the actions of the FBI agents were in breach of Russian law. On this, the court held that Russian law was not applicable and even if it were, the agents had complied sufficiently.[174] However, in retaliation for this breach of sovereignty, the Russian authorities charged the FBI agent responsible for the intrusion with hacking, not with any anticipation of success, but as a 'matter of principle'.[175]

In an attempt to minimize the inevitable conflicts of law arising from 'direct penetration', efforts have been made at an intergovernmental level to address extraterritorial searches under public international law. The first significant movement in the area was within the G8 forum. At a meeting of Justice and Interior Ministers in Moscow in October 1999, a document entitled 'Principles on Transborder Access to Stored Computer Data' was adopted.[176] Within the Council of Europe, the negotiators on the Cybercrime Convention agreed two sets of provisions that addressed obtaining access to data stored in another jurisdiction, without requiring authorization of the state in which the data resides. First, a person in the territory of the Member State may be subject to a production order that extends to data that is in that person's 'possession or control', which would clearly include data held in another jurisdiction.[177] The second situation is where law enforcement needs to obtain direct access to the transborder-stored data. In this situation, the two circumstances where such access may be obtained are virtually identical to those contained in the G8 document.[178] The former circumstance would be applicable where information was contained on a public website. The latter would extend, for example, to a person's email stored in another country by a service provider, such as Hotmail.

A procedural issue raised by the volume of data stored on a computer subject to seizure is whether the scope of the warrant extends to all material contained on the disk. In *R v Chesterfield Justices and Others, ex p Bramley*,[179] the potential vulnerability of the police was exposed when the court held that the Police and Criminal Evidence Act 1984 did not contain a defence to an action for trespass to goods in respect of items subject to legal privilege being seized during the execution

---

[173] This is true in terms of the document's content, but not in respect of the metadata concerning the document's attributes or properties, which may record the fact that the original document was accessed at the time and date of copying.

[174] *United States v Gorshkov*, 2001 WL 1024026 (WD Wash, 2001) at 4, n 4.

[175] N Seitz, 'Transborder Search: A New Perspective in Law Enforcement?' (Fall 2004–05) Yale Journal of Law and Technology 32.

[176] 'Principles on Transborder Access to Stored Computer Data', adopted in Moscow in October 1999: available at <http://www.usdoj.gov/ag/events/g82004/99TransborderAccessPrinciples.pdf> (accessed 10 August 2011).

[177] Convention, Art 18.

[178] Ibid Art 32.

[179] (2000) 2 WLR 409.

of a search warrant. The decision placed law enforcement in an invidious position: searching and shifting the data at the premises of the suspect was not feasible, but removal for subsequent examination could give rise to liability. Subsequently, it was held that *Bramley* only extends to situations involving legal privilege material, not any situation where irrelevant material is seized in the course of taking a computer as evidence.[180]

To address the potential liability established by *Bramley*, the government added provisions to the Criminal Justice and Police Act 2001. The Act grants LEAs the right to remove material, including material potentially outside the scope of a warrant, where it is 'not reasonably practicable' to separate it.[181] An exhaustive list of relevant factors is provided for determining whether it is 'reasonably practicable', including 'the apparatus or equipment that it would be necessary or appropriate to use for the carrying out of the determination or separation',[182] which would presumably encompass the various software tools used in computer forensics.

12.7.3 Protected data

Even when data has been lawfully obtained, the next problem that investigators increasingly face is that the seized data, or device on which the data reside, may be protected by some form of security measure, such as a password or cryptographic mechanism, which renders the data inaccessible, unintelligible, or, indeed, undiscovered by investigators.[183] In the USA, for example, when the notorious hacker Kevin Mitnick was finally arrested, many of the files found on his computers were encrypted and investigators were never able to access them.[184] Indeed, protected data is likely to become a standard feature of computing applications in the future and access to such protected data is therefore seen by many as one of the biggest future challenges for computer forensics in the twenty-first century.[185]

In the context of criminal procedure, access issues are not simply binary, the data being attainable or not; LEAs are also subject to temporal constraints, such as custody and prosecution time limits, which may be missed if the data cannot be accessed within a reasonable period of time.

Protection measures applied to data may be implemented at an individual user level, by an organization with whom the individual is associated or in which he resides, by the provider of the communications service, or at any combination of these or other points within the processing life cycle of data.

---

[180] *H v Commissioners of Inland Revenue* [2002] EWHC 2164 (Admin).
[181] Criminal Justice and Police Act 2001, s 50(1)(c).
[182] Ibid s 50(3)(d).
[183] Home Affairs Committee Report No 126, 'Computer Pornography', para 58 (HMSO, February 1994).
[184] See US DOJ Press Release, 9 August 1999, available at <http://www.usdoj.gov/criminal/cybercrime/mitnick.htm>.
[185] See N Barrett, *Traces of Guilt* (London: Bantam Press, 2004) 373.

The nature of data security technologies means that investigating authorities have essentially three options in respect of gaining access to, or conversion of, such protected data:

(a) require the person from whom the data has been obtained to access, or convert, the data into an intelligible plain-text format;

(b) require the person to disclose the necessary information and/or tools, or provide assistance to enable the authorities to access, or convert, the data into an intelligible format themselves; or

(c) utilize technologies and techniques that enable the data to be accessed, or converted, without the active involvement of the person from whom the data was obtained.

As coercive investigative techniques, the first two options require lawful authority, and UK law contains provisions addressing both situations. In the latter case, the issue is primarily one of having the necessary technical resource that can be applied to the task within the relevant timescales. Part III of RIPA 2000 contains provisions designed to address the first two options outlined above. The provisions did not enter into force until 2007, with the adoption of a code of practice.[186]

In respect of the first approach, RIPA 2000 provides that a notice may be served on a person in possession of protected information requiring that they disclose the 'protected information' in an 'intelligible form'.[187] 'Protected information' means:

. . . any electronic data which, without the key to the data—

(a) cannot, or cannot readily, be accessed, or

(b) cannot, or cannot readily, be put into an intelligible form. (s 56(1))

A 'key' comprises

. . . any key, code, password, algorithm or other data the use of which (with or without other keys):

(a) allows access to the electronic data, or (b) facilitates the putting of the data into an intelligible form. (s 56(1))

The notice provision was necessary because the Police and Criminal Evidence Act 1984 only requires that information be provided in a 'visible and legible form'.[188] This would potentially enable a suspect to deliver-up a printout of ciphertext that is visible and legible to investigators, but unintelligible.

---

[186] The Regulation of Investigatory Powers Act 2000 (Commencement No 4) Order 2007 (SI 2007/2196) and Home Office Code of Practice: 'Investigation of Protected Electronic Information', 2007.

[187] RIPA 2000, s 49(2)(d).

[188] Police and Criminal Evidence Act 1984, s 19.

Under the second approach, RIPA 2000 states that, where necessary and proportionate, a person may be required by notice to disclose the 'key' that would enable investigators to render the information intelligible themselves.[189] The Act recognizes that such a requirement should only arise when 'special circumstances' are present.[190] However, when the Act progressed through Parliament, there was substantial criticism directed at this part of the Bill from both civil society organizations and industry. The former were concerned that the obligation breached the principle against self-incrimination; although the courts have subsequently held that this does occur.[191] The latter were concerned that a disclosure requirement could undermine the deployment and reliance on the use of cryptographic techniques as a security technology; as well as damage the UK economy by placing it in a unfavourable position vis-à-vis its trading partners.[192]

The third approach is for investigators to break the protection mechanism. The totality of seized material either provides the possibility of shortcut attacks, such as keys or passwords being recovered from disk space or memory sticks, or via back-doors built into the technology; or investigators have to engage in brute force attacks, involving heavy computational processing. The viability of the latter course of action, converting the data into an intelligible form through utilizing available techniques, would seem to depend on a number of factors, including the strength of the security technology employed,[193] the multiplicity of protection systems employed, and the period within which the data realistically needs to be converted. In 2001, the government established a National Technical Assistance Centre ('NTAC') which is designed to provide the necessary technical expertise to LEAs, on a 24-hour basis, to try and access protected data without the involvement of the suspect.

12.8 EVIDENTIAL ISSUES

Having carried out the investigations and obtained what appears to be sufficient evidence, the next stage in the criminal justice process is the prosecution of the cybercriminal; a process of presenting evidence to a court or tribunal of fact. Prosecuting counsel will present evidence with the objective of showing to the requisite criminal standard, of 'beyond reasonable doubt', that the defendant is guilty of committing all, or some, of the offences for which he has been charged. On the other hand, defence counsel will be concerned, unless a guilty plea is submitted, to tender evidence that either challenges or contradicts the version of events indicated by the prosecution or offers an alternative version, with the objective of raising

---

[189] RIPA 2000, ss 50(3)(c) and 51.
[190] Ibid s 52(4)(b), (5).
[191] S and A [2008] EWCA Crim 2177.
[192] See, eg, Leader 'RIP, R.I.P', *Financial Times*, 14 July 2000.
[193] eg, the key length, such as over 128 bits.

sufficient doubt in the minds of the court for the defendant to be acquitted. The process is governed by a complex set of rules and procedures designed, primarily, to safeguard the rights of the defendant. Computer-derived evidence, whether obtained from the victim, accused, third parties, or generated by the investigators themselves, may present a range of issues that need to be addressed, whether by the prosecution, defence, or court.

The nature of the evidence being presented to court will be determined by a range of factors. First, the nature of the offences with which the perpetrator has been charged will dictate what issues will have to be proved in a court of law. In a case of phishing, for example, if the defendant was charged with fraud, under the Theft Act 1968, then evidence would have to be adduced that the victim was deceived. However if, instead, the defendant was charged with money laundering offences, then evidence is required to show that the person acquired, used, or possessed 'criminal property'.[194]

The choice of charge will also have resource implications that, as for all areas of public administration, may be a determinant factor. Thirdly, the availability of evidence obtained through the forensic process will often dictate the charges laid against the perpetrator. Seized data may be encrypted, for example such that the prosecution has to proceed merely on the basis of the evidence not so protected. Fourthly, a conspiracy may involve international elements in jurisdictions with which no suitable mutual legal assistance procedure exists, which can render evidence gathering effectively impossible.

Until recently, English law had special rules governing the admissibility of computer records in criminal proceedings. These rules presented an increasing obstacle to the prosecution of computer-based crime and led to their eventual repeal. However, while the challenge of admissibility has broadly disappeared, many of the issues raised in relation to this 'old' admissibility requirement continue to be relevant in respect of questions concerning the exclusion of hearsay evidence[195] and the probative value of computer-derived evidence, especially in relation to issues of data integrity.

Under the Police and Criminal Evidence Act 1984, all computer evidence had to comply with section 69:

(1) In any proceedings, a statement in a document produced by a computer shall not be admissible as evidence of any fact stated therein unless it is shown—

(a) that there are no reasonable grounds for believing that the statement is inaccurate because of improper use of the computer;

(b) that at all material times the computer was operating properly, or if not, that any respect in which it was not operating properly or was out of operation was not such as to affect the production of the document or the accuracy of its contents . . .

---

[194] Proceeds of Crime Act 2002, s 329.
[195] eg, Criminal Justice Act 2003, s 126(1).

To satisfy a court that the section 69(1) conditions had been met, it was necessary to obtain either a signed statement or oral testimony from a person who occupies 'a responsible position' in relation to the operation of the computer system.[196]

The broad nature of the language used in section 69(1) presented obvious opportunities for a party to challenge computer-derived evidence. The conditions were therefore the subject of significant consideration by the courts.

In a networked environment, one issue that arose is the extent to which section 69(1) was to be complied with in respect of each and every machine involved in the processing of the evidential information. In *R v Cochrane*,[197] the court upheld an appeal concerning a prosecution for theft of moneys from a building society's cash machines because the Crown were unable to adduce evidence about the operation of the company's mainframe computer as well as the cash machine itself. However, identifying all the relevant computers could be problematic in an open networked environment such as the internet. In *R v Waddon*,[198] the court held that the computers involved in the transmission of an image across the internet were not involved in its 'production' when printed from the investigator's computer and therefore did not require certification under section 69. Network-derived evidence does, however, raise the possibility of challenge both in respect of the provenance of any data and the nature of any intermediate processing that may have occurred.

In terms of the system 'operating properly', two broad categories of argument would be pursued by defence counsel. First, the system had faults, errors, or other malfunctions that impacted on the reliability of the data produced from the system. Secondly, that the criminal conduct itself had generated such faults, errors, or malfunctions in the computer system and/or its data content.

With respect to the first argument, the House of Lords was asked to consider the issue in *DPP v McKeown and Jones*.[199] Here an intoximeter used to analyze the amount of alcohol in a person's breath was found to have an inaccurate clock. In the Divisional Court, the defendants successfully argued that the clock's inaccuracy rendered the statement detailing the level of alcohol present in the defendant inadmissible on the grounds that section 69(1)(b) could not be complied with. This was subsequently overturned in the House of Lords, with Lord Hoffmann stating:

A malfunction is relevant if it affects the way in which the computer processes, stores or retrieves the information used to generate the statement tendered in evidence. Other malfunctions do not matter. (at 302)

---

[196] Police and Criminal Evidence Act 1984, Sch 3 Pt II paras 8 and 9.
[197] [1993] Crim LR 48.
[198] [2000] All ER (D) 502.
[199] [1997] 1 WLR 295.

Expert testimony would still be required, however, as to the source and impact of any discernable malfunction within a computer on its various data processing functions.

As an example of the second argument, in *Governor of Brixton Prison and another, ex p Levin*,[200] defence counsel challenged certain evidence presented by Citibank on the grounds that since the accused had improperly used the computer system operated by Citibank, the requirements of section 69(1)(a) could not be satisfied. The court rejected this argument noting that 'unauthorised use of the computer is not of itself a ground for believing that the statements recorded by it were inaccurate' (at 359c). Clearly, were there more extensive evidence of deliberate or unintended modification to data held on the system, the value of such computer-derived evidence could be open to challenge on such grounds.

Section 69(1)(b) also required that a computer must have been 'operating properly' at the 'material time'. In *Connolly v Lancashire CC*,[201] audit records were submitted with respect to the correct operation of a computerized weighing bridge. However, the records related to an examination of the weighbridge system carried out nearly three months prior to the date of the alleged offence. The records were not accepted by the courts as evidence that the system was operating properly at the 'material time'. A party may therefore need to be able to show that any system from which evidence is derived was functioning appropriately at the time the evidence was generated, for example through audit records.

Despite the generally favourable attitude of the courts to the admission of computer-derived evidence, considerable disquiet had been voiced against the section 69 conditions. In response, the Law Commission proposed reform of the rules to reintroduce the pre-1984 maxim *omnia praesumuntur rite esse acta*, a common law presumption that things have been done properly.[202] It justified this change of position on five grounds, although the fifth was subsequently resolved by the House of Lords decision in *McKeown*:

(a) that the majority of inaccuracies were due to errors in data entry and were obvious (the 'garbage in, garbage out' adage again);

(b) developments in the complexity of ICTs rendered compliance with section 69 increasingly impracticable;

(c) a relying party may not be in a position to comply with the conditions, since they are simply a recipient of the computer-derived document, which may have been produced by a computer located in another jurisdiction;

(d) the conditions were only applicable to tendered evidence, not to processes external to the trial, such as the forensic analysis carried out by an expert.[203]

---

[200] [1996] 4 All ER 350.
[201] (1994) RTR 79.
[202] See Law Commission, *Evidence in criminal proceedings: Hearsay and related topics* (Law Com No 245, Cm 3670, 1997) Pt XIII and recommendation 50.
[203] Ibid 13.6–13.11.

The presumption effectively shifts the burden of proof with respect to the reliability of computer evidence from the party submitting the evidence to the party against whom the evidence is being adduced; therefore considerably reducing the likelihood of a challenge being raised. A similar reform was adopted with respect to the admissibility of computer evidence in civil proceedings by the Civil Evidence Act 1995, repealing the special provisions for computer evidence under section 5 of the Civil Evidence Act 1968. The repeal of section 69 came into force in April 2000.[204]

12.9 CONCLUDING REMARKS

Public perception of computer crime contrasts sharply with reality. The news and entertainment media have promoted the image of the 'hacker' as an almost 'Robin Hood'-like figure attacking the computers of Big Brother organizations. The reality of computer crime is that such activities encompass a broad range of perpetrators: organized crime exploiting the power of a new tool; disgruntled employees utilizing their inside knowledge; the curious and thrill-seekers treating the medium as a challenge; and those engaged in industrial espionage and information warfare.

Nation states have generally needed to react to the phenomenon of computer crime by updating their criminal law, whether through amendments to existing statutes or the adoption of sui generis offences. However, prosecutors, the judiciary, and juries continue to struggle to comprehend the nature of computer-related crime and computer-derived evidence. Over recent years, policymakers have shifted their focus from the need for appropriate offences to the needs of LEAs in a networked environment.

From a commercial perspective, computer misuse legislation is a final resort to which companies are generally reluctant to turn. The impact that such a prosecution may have on a company can be substantial, often affecting the systems upon which the company is reliant, consuming considerable management time and effort, and generating adverse publicity.

Perpetrators of computer crime usually exploit weaknesses in the systems either being used or attacked. Inadequate security procedures—physical, organizational, and logical—continue to be a central feature in the vast majority of examples of computer crime. The growth of the internet, with the prospect of 'always-on' connectivity for large segments of population, presents very significant new and enhanced security threats to individuals, and society as a whole, as well as challenges to LEAs.

---

[204] Youth Justice and Criminal Evidence Act 1999, s 60.

Index

Computer Law

Seventh Edition

EDITED BY

Chris Reed

OXFORD

UNIVERSITY PRESS

Great Clarendon Street, Oxford ox2 6DP

Oxford University Press is a department of the University of Oxford.
It furthers the University's objective of excellence in research, scholarship,
and education by publishing worldwide in

Oxford New York

Auckland Cape Town Dar es Salaam Hong Kong Karachi
Kuala Lumpur Madrid Melbourne Mexico City Nairobi
New Delhi Shanghai Taipei Toronto

With offices in

Argentina Austria Brazil Chile Czech Republic France Greece
Guatemala Hungary Italy Japan Poland Portugal Singapore
South Korea Switzerland Thailand Turkey Ukraine Vietnam

Oxford is a registered trademark of Oxford University Press
in the UK and in certain other countries

Published in the United States
by Oxford University Press Inc., New York

First published 1990
Seventh edition published 2011

British Library Cataloguing in Publication Data

Data available

Library of Congress Cataloging in Publication Data

Library of Congress Control Number: 2011939852

Typeset by Cenveo Publisher Services
Printed in Great Britain
on acid-free paper by
Clays Ltd, St Ives plc

ISBN 978–0–19–969646–8

1 3 5 7 9 10 8 6 4 2